BUSINESS LAW AND THE LEGAL ENVIRONMENT

COMPREHENSIVE VOLUME • SEVENTEENTH EDITION

Ronald A. Anderson

Professor Emeritus
Drexel University
Member of the Pennsylvania and Philadelphia Bars

Ivan Fox

Professor of Law
Pace University
Member of the New York Bar

David P. Twomey

Professor of Law, Carroll School of Management
Boston College
Member of the Massachusetts and Florida Bars

Marianne M. Jennings

Professor of Legal and Ethical Studies in Business
Arizona State University
Director, Lincoln Center for Applied Ethics
Member of the Arizona Bar

with

Peter S. Smith

Judge of the Superior Court of California (Retired)

WEST **West Educational Publishing Company**
an International Thomson Publishing company I(T)P®

Cincinnati • Albany • Boston • Detroit • Johannesburg • London • Madrid • Melbourne • Mexico City
New York • Pacific Grove • San Francisco • Scottsdale • Singapore • Tokyo • Toronto

Team Director: Jack W. Calhoun
Senior Acquisitions Editor: Rob Dewey
Acquisitions Editor: Scott Person
Developmental Editor: Mignon D. Worman,
    member of California and Ohio Bars
Production Editor: Sharon L. Smith
Production House: Navta Associates, Inc.
Technology Coordinator: Kurt Gerdenich
Designer: Craig LaGesse Ramsdell
Cover Designer: Kim Torbeck, Imbue Design
Manufacturing Coordinator: Georgina Calderon
Team Assistant: Kristen Meere
Marketing Manager: Michael W. Worls

Library of Congress Cataloging-in-Publication Data

Business law and the legal environment / Ronald A. Anderson . . . [et al.].
    — Comprehensive vol., 17th ed.
        p.   cm.
        Rev. ed. of: Business law and the legal environment / Ronald A.
    Anderson, Ivan Fox, David P. Twomey. Comprehensive vol., 15th ed. c1993.
        Includes bibliographical references and index.
        ISBN 0–538–88244–1 (alk. paper). — ISBN 0–538–88245–X (alk. paper)
        1. Commercial law—United States.   2. Business law—United States.
    I. Anderson, Ronald Aberdeen.   II. Anderson, Ronald Aberdeen, Business
    law and the legal environment.
    KF888.A44   1998b
    346.7307— dc21   98–6847
                                                                              CIP

ISBN: 0-538-88244-1

1 2 3 4 5 6 WCBS 3 2 1 0 9 8

Printed in the United States of America

I(T)P®

International Thomson Publishing
West Educational Publishing is an ITP Company.
The ITP trademark is used under license.

P R E F A C E

LAW MEANS BUSINESS

One need only glance at the business page of the newspaper to recognize how tightly interwoven business and law have become. For better or worse, entrepreneurial start-ups, billion dollar mergers, marketing campaigns, technological breakthroughs, and almost all other business events are likely to be touched in some way by legal regulations or actions. No business or manager can hope to succeed without an understanding of the legal environment, what it is for, and how it can be utilized for both protection and advantage.

So now, more than ever, the business law instructor prepares students for the real world of business. This text, in turn, provides the business law instructor with all of the tools needed to make the teaching process successful. The seventeenth edition responds strongly to the ever increasing connections between the worlds of business and law. We have expanded coverage of those topics most relevant to today's business challenges, and added features that make it easier for future businesspeople to understand and analyze legal situations and to respond with appropriate decisions. *Business Law and The Legal Environment* continues to set the pace as the comprehensive leader in the discipline.

We also would like to welcome a new member to the author team, Professor Marianne Jennings of Arizona State University. An acclaimed expert in the field of ethics, public policy, real estate and business law, her ability to present complex issues through examples and language that students understand is evident in her many contributions to this edition. The authors would also like to thank the Honorable Peter S. Smith, Superior Court of California (Ret.), for his contributions to the coverage of alternative dispute resolution.

Note that this text is also available in the Standard Version, which includes the first seven parts of this Comprehensive Volume.

CASES AT THE CORE

In keeping with its unrivaled reputation in this area, *Business Law and The Legal Environment* continues to feature the strongest and most relevant selection of cases in the field. These cases represent not only classic landmark decisions, but also important new appellate decisions that will shape the business environment in coming years, and cases of special relevance to preparation for the CPA examination.

AUTHORITATIVE COVERAGE OF THE UCC

Selected provisions of the Code have been reprinted in the appendix. Each topic has been fully updated to reflect the majority adoptions of the Code sections. In addition, the first footnote of the UCC lists the states that have adopted the code sections.

PREPARATION FOR THE CPA EXAM

As in the sixteenth edition, material pertinent to the CPA exam is identified by a margin icon. Below is a chapter outline of each topic covered by the business law section of the exam entitled "Business Law and Social Responsibility." New to this edition are end-of-chapter questions that cover common CPA exam topics. These questions and answers (answers to odd-numbered questions are provided at the end of the text) are drawn from previous tests administered by the AICPA, and provide very realistic preparation for students planning to take the CPA exam.

Content Specification Outline

Text Chapter

I. Professional Responsibilities (15 percent)
A. Code of Conduct and Other Responsibilities
   1. Code of Professional Conduct
   2. Proficiency, Independence, and Due Care
   3. Responsibilities in Consulting Services
   4. Responsibilities in Tax Practice

Chapter 21

B. The CPA and the Law
   1. Common Law Liability to Clients and Third Parties
   2. Federal Statutory Liability
   3. Working Papers, Privileged Communication, and Confidentiality
II. Business Organizations (20 percent)

Chapters 39–40

A. Agency
   1. Formation and Termination
   2. Principal's Liabilities
   3. Disclosed and Undisclosed Principals
   4. Agent's Authority and Liability

Chapters 43–45

B. Partnerships and Joint Ventures
   1. Formation and Existence
   2. Liabilities and Authority of Partners and Joint Owners
   3. Allocation of Profit or Loss
   4. Transfer of Interest
   5. Termination and Dissolution

Chapters 46, 47, 49

C. Corporations
   1. Formation, Purposes, and Powers
   2. Stockholders, Directors, and Officers
   3. Financial Structure, Capital, and Distribution
   4. Merger, Consolidation, and Dissolution

Chapter 53

D. Estates and Trusts
   1. Formation and Purposes
   2. Allocation Between Principal and Income
   3. Fiduciary Responsibilities
   4. Distributions and Terminations

Chapters 11–20

III. Contracts (10 percent)
A. Formation
B. Performance
C. Third-Party Assignments
D. Discharge, Breach, and Remedies

Chapters 35–37

IV. Debtor-Creditor Relationships (10 percent)
A. Rights and Duties—Debtors and Creditors
   1. Liabilities and Defenses
   2. Release of Parties
   3. Remedies of Parties
B. Rights and Duties—Guarantors
   1. Liabilities and Defenses
   2. Release of Parties
   3. Remedies of Parties
C. Bankruptcy
   1. Voluntary and Involuntary Bankruptcy
   2. Effects of Bankruptcy on Debtors and Creditors
   3. Reorganizations
V. Government Regulation of Business (15 percent)

Chapters 41–42

A. Regulation of Employment
   1. Payroll Taxes
   2. Employee Safety

ETHICAL FOCUS

Chapter 3, *Business Ethics, Social Forces and the Law,* brings new relevance and currency to the discussion of ethics in this text. The straightforward approach of this new chapter will help students understand their own responsibility for ethical behavior and decision making. Ethics are also reinforced with a new feature called "Ethics and the Law" which appears in all chapters. These vignettes and accompanying questions describe ethical issues drawn from current events and culture that will be familiar and meaningful to students.

THE WORLD WE LIVE IN: UPDATES TO THIS EDITION

All of the changes incorporated in this edition not only continue the straightforward, black letter law approach of this text but also mirror the latest changes in the business-legal environment. For instance, our new chapter 10, *Intellectual Property Rights,* addresses current issues such as trade secrets, privacy, and software protection. We have expanded to two chapters, chapters 1 and 2, coverage of litigation and alternative dispute resolution as it becomes a more prevalent and often more desirable tool than litigation. Chapter 7: *The Legal Environment of International Trade* has been thoroughly updated to reflect changes in the global economy and the rules that shape it. Chapter 45 features expanded and timely coverage of limited liability companies. All of these topics and the many others that have been enhanced in this edition provide students with solid background where they are likely to need it most.

While we have always been careful to define and present legal concepts in ordinary language rather than stilted jargon, we have also taken several important steps in the new edition to explicitly tie legal principles to real world-based events, trends and challenges. Each chapter now features examples drawn from or based upon current events and business to illustrate chapter concepts; students will find these examples extremely relevant and readable.

New *"What's Behind the Law?"* vignettes trace the evolution of legal principles in the context of social and historical forces and help students understand not only laws, but why they exist in their current forms.

WHAT'S BEHIND THE LAW?

The Internet and the Law

While we cannot yet begin to understand the full impact that the Internet will have on business in the new millennium, we must help students to use it to their greatest advantage. The new *Business Law and the Legal Environment* Home Page, provides the optimal starting point for finding and using powerful on-line resources related to law and business. Go to http://anderson.westbuslaw.com to access these learning resources. In addition, at the end of each "What's Behind the Law?" feature, Internet sites are referenced to encourage the student to use the Internet as a resource for learning and ultimately for use in their business careers. Alternatively, the instructor may assign these sites for independent research projects for students, if desired.

West Educational's Business Law Discipline Page services the everchanging needs of the business law professor. Click to http://www.westbuslaw.com to find the most recent case updates of selected state and federal courts, updated bi-monthly, in order to give your students the most current business law developments.

AACSB Curriculum Requirements

This edition continues to fulfill the requirements mandated by the AACSB by its case selection, inclusion of social and historical policy in the "What's Behind the Law?" feature and business ethics considerations in chapter 3. The intersection of ethics and the business world is creatively addressed in each chapter. "Ethics and the Law" features current , student-friendly business situations drawn from the media such as Pearl Jam, *Friends, Melrose Place,* plus many others. The global context of business is thoroughly covered in the newly updated chapter 7, *The Legal Environment of International Trade.* Critical thinking requirements are addressed with case problems at the end of each chapter, questions which follow each "Ethics and the Law" scenario, Comprehensive Case Analyses and examples which reinforce the legal concepts discussed in each chapter. Instructors who desire to test students' critical thinking skills during class discussion are provided with in-class discussion questions tied to the "What's Behind the Law?" and "Ethics and the Law" in the Instructor's Resource Manual.

Suggested Legal and Regulatory Environment Outline

An introductory course that emphasizes societal or public law may include the chapters below and other appropriate chapters selected for the course. An introductory course emphasizing private law may cover selected chapters from Part I, *The Legal and Social Environment of Business,* and chapters on contracts, personal property, or agency. The instructor may choose to cover additional topics in this introductory course, depending on the ability level of the students and the time allotted to the course at the institution. The remainder of the book may be covered in advance courses. Suggested outline:

TOTAL LEARNING SOLUTIONS

West Educational Publishing is committed to providing you, our educational partners, with the finest educational resources available including the full suite of West resources. Because we prepare our instructor resources with a variety of teaching environments in mind, it is likely that you will need only a portion of these for your course. Before you request an item, we ask that you please read thoroughly the description of each resource. If you still need more information about resources, we urge you to contact your local West sales representative or visit our web site at www.westbuslaw.com. Many teaching and learning resources can be downloaded directly from this site. The resources that are available may vary significantly between products and adoptions.

New! Instructor's Resource Guide includes instructor insights, lecture outlines, and teaching strategies for each chapter. Chapter overviews and transparency integration notes ease lecture preparation. In-class discussion notes are provided for "What's Behind the Law?" and "Ethics and The Law" vignettes. Also included are a chapter transition guide for competitive texts, restructured case briefs, and numerous references for CPA exam preparation. Prepared by Marianne Jennings, Arizona State University (ISBN 0-538-88557-2)

New! Study Guide features include AICPA questions drawn from past exams in order to prepare students for the CPA exams, Internet Research problems, and chapter checklists. The Quicken *Business Law Partner*™3.0 CD-ROM accompanies each manual with exercises for each chapter which familiarize students with common legal documents. The study guide is prepared by Ronald L. Taylor, Metropolitan State College of Denver. (ISBN 0-538-88246-8)

"The Legal Tutor in Contracts" and "The Legal Tutor on Sales," are interactive software programs that reinforce and practice the concepts in contracts and sales. Developed by Ronald L. Taylor, Metropolitan State College of Denver. (Contracts: ISBN 0-538-81476-4; Sales: ISBN 0-538-81478-0).

Study Guide Key offers solutions to exercises and problems that appear in the study guide. (ISBN 0-538-88247-6)

Test Bank allows reliable test preparation, including all features of previous editions. (ISBN 0-538-88556-4)

Thomson World Class Testing Tools™ provides nearly 3000 questions on diskette for fast, comprehensive test preparation. (ISBN 0-538-88560-2)

New! PowerPoint™ **Presentations** speed lecture preparation and help students follow lectures. (ISBN 0-538-88558-0)

80 Transparency Acetates provide instructors with additional in-classroom aids. (ISBN 0-538-88559-9)

Unique! Ten Free Hours of WestLaw. West's computerized legal research gives qualified instructors and students access to U.S. Code, federal regulations, and numerous specialized libraries.

COURT TV Trial Stories. Court TV's Trial Story series features highly relevant cases condensed into one-hour programs. Each Trial Story captures the whole story of a trial, including news footage, courtroom testimony and interviews with defendants, plaintiffs, witnesses, lawyers, jurors and judges. Each Trial Story video is a real drama that engages students while presenting important legal concepts.

CNN Legal Issues update video brings the latest legal issues into the classroom, generating lively class discussion. This video is produced by Turner Learning, Inc. using the resources of CNN, the world's first 24-hour, all-news network.

Complimentary Web Page is available, for a limited time, to instructors who adopt this text. This page will be professionally designed and maintained within the West Legal Studies Resource Center. Contact your West representative for eligibility requirements.

South-Western's Business Law Video Series, a set of situational videos, covers a range of topics for the full business law course including the UCC, employment law, and the business law portion of the CPA exam

Business Law and Legal Environment Video Library includes seven different types of professionally produced legal videos: *Drama of the Law I & Drama of the Law II, The Making of a Case, Law and Literature, Ethics in America, American Bar Association* and other mock trial videos, *Equal Justice* Series, and *West's Business Profiles.*

U.S. Supreme Court Audiocassette Library. These audiotapes feature 10 unedited arguments made before the Supreme Court.

Contracts and UCC Article 2, Sales. Two Interactive Software Cases. Students learn by doing with this interactive software and receive immediate feedback on their reasoning and decisions. (ISBN 0-314-08348-0)

You Be the Judge Software. This easy-to-use program presents students with new cases and directs them to resolve the relevant issues. (ISBN 0-314-08713-3)

ACKNOWLEDGMENTS

The development and revision of a textbook represents teamwork in its highest form. West Educational Publishing is the only business law publisher which counts a lawyer on its development team. Mignon Worman, a member of the California and Ohio Bars, as senior development editor, helped to maintain the high standards in accuracy and authority.

The authors wish to thank the innumerable instructors, students, attorneys, and managers who have added to the quality of this textbook through its many editions. Deserving special recognition are the entire staff at West Educational Publishing, Rob Dewey, Scott Person, Mike Worls, Sharon Smith, Kristen Meere, Lorenzo Valdez, and the following reviewers who provided their honest and valuable commentary to the revision process for the seventeenth edition:

Dean Alexander, Miami-Dade Community College
Robert Boeke, Delta College
Greg Cermigiano, Widener University
Anne Cohen, University of Massachusetts
Adam Epstein, University of Tennessee
Phillip Evans, Kutztown University of Pennsylvania
Darrel Ford, University of Central Oklahoma
David Grigg, Pfeiffer University
Ronald Groeber, Ball State University
Florence Elliot Howard, Stephen F. Austin University
Richard Hurley, Francis Marion University
Claire La Roche, Longwood College
Steven Murray, Community College of Rhode Island
Francis Polk, Ocean County College
Robert Prentice, University of Texas at Austin
Linda Reppert, Marymount University
Gary Sambol, Rutgers University School of Business
Lester Smith, Eastern New Mexico University
Michael Sugameli, Oakland University
Bob Vicars, Bluefield State University
James Welch, Kentucky Wesleyan College

WRITE THE AUTHORS

Any teacher may write to any of the authors regarding any questions as to teaching methodology or specific rules of law. We represent in the aggregate over a century of teaching and will be happy to respond to your questions:

Ronald A. Anderson
252 S. Van Pelt Street
Philadelphia, PA 19103

Ivan Fox
Business Law Department
Pace University
Pace Plaza
New York, NY 10038

David P. Twomey
Carroll School of Management
Boston College
Fulton Hall
Chestnut, MA 02167

Marianne Jennings
Lincoln Center for Applied Ethics
Arizona State University
P.O. Box 874806
Tempe, AZ 85287-4806
marianne.jennings@asu.edu

BRIEF CONTENTS

CONTENTS

ABOUT THE AUTHORS

Ronald A. Anderson, Professor of Law and Government, Drexel University, taught the subjects covered by this book for 40 years. He is the internationally renowned author of the definitive, 20-volume treatise, *Anderson on the Uniform Commercial Code,* published by Clark Boardman Callaghan. He has written many other well-respected professional works.

Professor Anderson was graduated from the University of Pennsylvania and also earned his Juris Doctor from that school. He is a member of the American Bar Association and is an active member of the legal community.

Ivan Fox, Professor of Law at Pace University, is widely known for his work with the Fox-Gearty CPA Review Course. He has lectured extensively to professional and banking groups on various business law topics.

Professor Fox was graduated from Pace University, earned his Juris Doctor from New York Law School, and received his LL.M. from New York University. He is a member of the New York Bar and the New York State Bar Association.

David P. Twomey is Professor of Law at Boston College Carroll School of Management. He has a special interest in curriculum development, having served three terms as chairman of his school's Educational Policy Committee. He is chairman of the Business Law Department at Boston College.

Professor Twomey was graduated from Boston College and earned his MBA at the University of Massachusetts at Amherst. After two years of business experience, he entered Boston College Law School and earned his Juris Doctor. He is a member of the Massachusetts, Florida, and Federal Bars. Professor Twomey is a nationally known labor arbitrator and was elected to membership in the National Academy of Arbitrators. His service includes appointment by Presidents Reagan, Bush, and Clinton to Presidential Emergency Boards formed to recommend resolutions to nationwide railway disputes. He has written a great number of books and articles on labor and employment law and other business law topics.

Professor Marianne Jennings is a member of the Department of Business Administration in the College of Business at Arizona State University, a professor of legal and ethical studies in business and director of the Joan and David Lincoln Center for Applied Ethics. Jennings has consulted with law firms, businesses and professional groups, including the Dial Corporation, Motorola, Southern California Edison, and Bell Helicopter, plus many others. Currently Jennings has six texts in circulation and has authored more than 130 articles in academic and professional trade journals. She contributes columns to the *Arizona Republic* (syndicated) and contributes to the *Wall Street Journal,* the *Chicago Tribune,* and other newspapers around the country. She is also a commentator on business issues for *All Things Considered* for National Public Radio. Professor Jennings is a member of twelve professional organizations, including the State Bar of Arizona, and has served on four boards of directors.

PART 1

The Legal and Social Environment of Business

The Nature and Sources of Law

CHAPTER 1

A. NATURE OF LAW AND LEGAL RIGHTS

1. Legal Rights
2. Individual Rights
3. The Right of Privacy
4. Privacy and Technology

B. SOURCES OF LAW

C. UNIFORM STATE LAWS

D. CLASSIFICATIONS OF LAW

OBJECTIVES

After studying this chapter, you should be able to

1. *Discuss the nature of law;*
2. *Define legal rights and give examples;*
3. *Explain how rights and duties relate;*
4. *Discuss the right to privacy and the protections it provides;*
5. *List the sources of law and give examples from each level;*
6. *Describe uniform laws and their purposes; and*
7. *Give the classifications of law.*

Why have law? If you have ever been stuck in a traffic jam or jostled in a crowd leaving a stadium, you have observed the need for order to keep those involved moving in an efficient and safe manner. What is true on a small scale for traffic jams and crowds is true on a large scale for society in general. The order or pattern of rules that society uses to govern the conduct of individuals and their relationships is called **law**. Law keeps society running smoothly and efficiently.

A. NATURE OF LAW AND LEGAL RIGHTS

Law consists of the body of principles that govern conduct and that can be enforced in courts or by administrative agencies. The law could also be described as a multitude of rights.

1. Legal Rights

A right is a legal capacity to require another person to perform or refrain from performing an act.

Duty is an obligation of law imposed on a person to perform or refrain from performing a certain act.

A **right** is a legal capacity to require another person to perform or refrain from performing an act. Our rights flow from the U.S. Constitution, state constitutions, federal and state statutes, and ordinances at the local levels, including cities, counties, and boroughs. Within these same sources of rights are **duties**. A duty is an obligation of law imposed on a person to perform or refrain from performing a certain act.

Duties and rights coexist. No right can rest on one person without a corresponding duty resting on some other person or persons. For example, if the terms of a lease provide that the premises will remain in a condition of good repair so that the tenant can live there comfortably, it is the duty of the landlord to provide a dwelling that has hot and cold running water.

2. Individual Rights

Based on the documents that created the government for the United States, individuals were given certain rights. Those rights include the right to freedom of speech, the right to due process or the right to have a hearing before any freedom is taken away, and the right to vote. There are also duties that accompany individual rights, such as the duty to speak in a way that does not cause harm to others. For example, individuals are free to express their opinions about the government or its officials, but they would not be permitted to yell "Fire!" in a crowded theater and cause unnecessary harm to others. The rights given in the U.S. Constitution are rights that cannot be taken away or violated by any statutes, ordinances, or court decisions. These rights provide a framework for the structure of government and other laws.

3. The Right of Privacy

A right of privacy is the right to be free from unreasonable searches and intrusion by others.

One very important individual legal right is the **right of privacy**. There are two aspects to the right of privacy. The first is the right to be secure against unreasonable searches and seizures by the government. This aspect of the right of privacy is guaranteed by the Fourth Amendment of the U.S. Constitution. For example, a police officer may not search your home unless he or she has a reasonable suspicion (which is generally established through a warrant) that your home contains evidence of a crime, such as illegal drugs. If your home or business is searched unlawfully, any items obtained during that unlawful search will not be admitted as evidence in a criminal trial under the protection of the Fourth Amendment's exclusionary rule. ◆ *For example*, in the murder trial of O.J. Simpson, Judge Lance Ito excluded some of the evidence the police had obtained from inside Mr. Simpson's Ford Bronco, which was parked on the street outside his home. Judge Ito ruled that the officers should have first obtained a warrant for the locked vehicle, which was not going to be taken anywhere because Mr. Simpson was out of town at that time. ◆

A second aspect of the right of privacy protects individuals against intrusions by others. Your private life is not subject to public scrutiny when you are a private citizen. This right is articulated in many state constitutions and was found through interpretation at the federal level in the landmark case of *Roe v Wade*,[1] in which the U.S. Supreme Court established a right of privacy that gives women the right to choose whether to have an abortion.

There are many interpretations of these two aspects of the right to privacy. These interpretations are often found in statutes that afford privacy rights with respect to certain types of conduct. ◆ *For example*, a federal statute provides a right of privacy to bank customers that prevents their banks from giving out information about their accounts except to law enforcement agencies conducting investigations. There are laws that protect the rights of students. For example, the Family Educational Rights and Privacy Act (FERPA or the Buckley Amendment) prevents colleges and universities from disclosing students' grades to third parties without their permission. ◆

ETHICS & THE LAW

On January 21, 1998, a *Newsweek* story leaked to the media alleged that President Bill Clinton had engaged in sexual conduct with a White House intern. Many citizens voiced concern about the media coverage of the president's personal life. Some noted that his private life is irrelevant in governing the country. Is it possible to maintain a right of privacy when an individual holds national office? Should there be more privacy? What about employers who require employees to submit to drug tests on a regular or random basis? Is such a test an invasion of privacy? Are there ever times when the right of privacy is less important than duty or risk? Is drug testing for pilots different from drug testing for a grocery store clerk?

4. Privacy and Technology

Technology creates new situations that may require the application of new rules of law. As technology changes the way we interact with each other, new rules of law develop to protect our rights when the old laws are not suited to the new methods of interaction. Today, business is conducted by computers, wire transfers of funds, E-mail, EDI (electronic data interchange) order placements, and the Internet. When we exchange faxes and E-mails, we still have an expectation that our words are private. However, technology also affords others the ability to eavesdrop on conversations and intercept electronic messages. The right of privacy still exists even in these technologically nonprivate circumstances, and there are new laws that make it a crime and a breach of privacy to engage in such interceptions of communications.

---

[1] 410 U.S. 113 (1973).

WHAT'S BEHIND THE LAW?

Employers, E-mail, and Privacy

Courts have taken the position that E-mail accounts of employees that are created through their employer are not private and that any messages or information in the employees' E-mail is the property of the employer and can be reviewed. Courts also permit, during the course of litigation, discovery of employee E-mail messages when the employer is named in a lawsuit. All the E-mail messages can be retrieved and read for information relevant to the litigation. A recent survey revealed that 22 percent of executive-level managers review their employees' E-mail. Two Nissan Motor Corporation employees were fired after their managers warned them not to use company E-mail for personal messages. The managers were monitoring all of their employees' E-mails. Should employees have any workplace protections for their E-mail? What problems would be created if the employer were denied the right to review employees' E-mail? What problems arise when managers are given access to employee E-mail?

CASE SUMMARY

Neighbors, Eavesdropping, and Marijuana Arrests

Facts: Wayne C. Fields eavesdropped on his neighbors' telephone conversations 24 hours a day, 7 days a week over several months. Fields's neighbors—Robert Faford, Lisa Faford, Bryan Caskey, and Gale Faford—used a cordless telephone, and Fields was able to use a police scanner, purchased specifically for that purpose, to listen to conversations. Fields reported the substance of those conversations to the police because the conversations indicated they were running a marijuana-growing operation out of their home. Fields also noted the neighbors going in and out of a shed at the back of their house carrying white nursery bags. Fields made his calls to law enforcement agencies anonymously, explaining his scanner was the source of his information. After a few weeks, the neighbors apparently noticed Fields observing their activities in the shed and moved a trailer so that the view from Fields's property was blocked.

Based on Fields's information, including his revealing the address of the property, the police went to the Faford house and with their consent searched the shed and removed the marijuana. The case was referred for prosecution, and Robert, Bryan, and Lisa were charged with cultivating marijuana and conspiracy to cultivate marijuana. At trial, the Fafords and Caskey objected to the admission of the evidence from the shed on the grounds that the police had obtained information about the shed from Fields's violation of their privacy. The trial court admitted the evidence, they were convicted, and they appealed.

Decision: The evidence was inadmissible because it had been obtained as a result of Fields's violation of their privacy. Washington's Privacy Act specifically prohibits the interception of telephone conversations. Any information obtained in violation of the law cannot be used against defendants in a criminal case. The court reversed the conviction. [State v Faford (Wash) 910 P2d 447 (1996)]

B. SOURCES OF LAW

Statutory law is legislative acts declaring, commanding, or prohibiting certain conduct.

The expression "a law" is ordinarily used to indicate a statute enacted by a state legislature or by the Congress of the United States. **Statutory law** includes these legislative acts declaring, commanding, or prohibiting conduct. An act of the federal Congress to provide leave for employee medical needs is an example of a statutory law. In addition to the state legislatures and the U.S. Congress, every city, county, or other subdivision has some power to adopt ordinances that, within their sphere of operation, have the same binding effect as legislative acts. However, the statutes and ordinances enacted by these bodies are not the only source of law.

Constitutional law is the branch of law that is based on the constitution for a particular level of government. A **constitution** is a body of principles that establishes the structure of a government and the relationship of that government to the people who are governed. A constitution is generally a combination of the written document and the practices and customs that develop with the passage of time and the emergence of new problems. In each state, two constitutions are in force: the state constitution and the federal Constitution.

Administrative regulations are rules promulgated by state and federal administrative agencies, such as the Securities and Exchange Commission and the National Labor Relations Board. These regulations generally have the force of statutes.

Law also includes principles that are expressed for the first time in court decisions. This form of law is called **case law**. For example, when a court decides a new question or problem, its decision becomes a **precedent**, which stands as the law in future cases that involve that particular problem.

Using precedent and following in similar cases is the doctrine of *stare decisis*.

However, the rule of stare decisis is not cast in stone. Judges enjoy some flexibility. When a court finds that its earlier decision was incorrectly decided, it will overrule that decision. ◆ *For example,* in 1954 the U.S. Supreme Court departed from the rule of stare decisis in *Brown v Board of Education*.[2] In that case, it decided that the court was incorrect in 1896 when it held in *Plessy v Ferguson*[3] that separate facilities for blacks were equal to facilities for whites. ◆

Court decisions do not always deal with new problems or make new rules. In many cases, courts apply rules as they have been for many years, even centuries. These time-honored rules of the community are called the **common law**. Statutes will sometimes repeal or redeclare the common law rules. Many statutes depend on the common law for definitions of the terms in the statutes.

Law also includes treaties made by the United States and proclamations and orders of the president of the United States or of other public officials.

C. UNIFORM STATE LAWS

To secure uniformity as far as possible, the National Conference of Commissioners on Uniform State Law, composed of representatives from every state, has drafted statutes on various subjects for adoption by the states. The best example of such laws is the Uniform Commercial Code (UCC).[4] The UCC regulates the sale and leasing of goods; commercial paper, such as checks; funds transfers; secured transactions in personal property; bulk transfers; and particular aspects of banking, letters of credit, warehouse receipts, bills of lading, and investment securities.

---

[2] 349 U.S. 294 (1954).
[3] 163 U.S. 537 (1895).
[4] The UCC has been adopted in every state, except that Louisiana has not accepted Article 2, Sales. It has also been adopted for Guam, the Virgin Islands, and the District of Columbia. The National Conference of Commissioners on Uniform State Law has adopted amendments to Article 8, Investment Securities (1977 and 1994), and Article 9, Secured Transactions (1972). It has also adopted new articles: 2A, Leases; 4A, Funds Transfers; and 6, Bulk Sales. Revisions of Article 3, Commercial Paper (now called Negotiable Instruments), and Article 4, Bank Deposits and Collections, were adopted in 1990. A revision of Article 5, Letters of Credit, was adopted in 1995. The states that have adopted these later articles are listed in Appendix 3 of this book. Uniformity has also reached international scope. The United Nations Convention on Contracts for the International Sale of Goods (CISG) applies to contracts between parties in the United States and those in the other nations that have approved the convention. The provisions of this convention, or international agreement, have been strongly influenced by Article 2 of the UCC.

Sidebar notes:

A constitution is a body of principles that establishes the structure of a government and the relationship of that government to its people.

Administrative regulations are rules made by state and federal administrative agencies.

Case law is law expressed for the first time in a court decision.

Precedent is a decision that stands as the rule of law for future cases.

Stare decisis is the principle that requires a court to examine past case decisions in reaching a conclusion in a similar present matter.

Common law is time-honored rules of law followed by courts that are not necessarily statutes.

D. CLASSIFICATIONS OF LAW

Substantive law is law that creates, defines, and regulates rights and liabilities.

Procedural law is law that specifies the steps to be followed in enforcing the rights and liabilities given under law.

Equity is principles or rules that provide special relief in the event the usual remedies at law are not sufficient.

Law is classified in many ways. For example, **substantive law**, which creates, defines, and regulates rights and liabilities, is contrasted with **procedural law**, which specifies the steps that must be followed in enforcing those rights and liabilities. Law may also be classified in terms of its origin from Roman (or civil) law, from English common law based on customs and usages of the community,[5] or from the law merchant. Law may be classified according to subject matter, such as the law of contracts, the law of real estate, or the law of wills.

Law is at times classified in terms of principles of law and principles of equity. The early English courts were very limited as to the kinds of cases they could handle. Persons who could not obtain relief in those courts would petition the king to grant them special relief according to principles of **equity** and justice. In the course of time, these special cases developed certain rules that are called principles of equity. In general, they require that the plaintiff be in a situation in which the law courts cannot grant relief in the form of money damages. Equitable relief is denied unless the plaintiff has suffered or will suffer a loss that cannot be compensated by the payment of damages. At one time in the United States, there were separate law courts and equity courts. Except in a few states, these courts have been combined, so that one court applies principles of both law and equity. Even though administered by the same court, the two systems of principles remain distinct. That is, a party may ask for what historically would be equitable relief when the case is governed by equitable principles. If the plaintiff brings what historically would have been an action at law, the action is governed by law principles rather than equitable principles.[6] *For example,* suppose a homeowner contracts to sell his home to a buyer. If the homeowner then refuses to go through with the contract, the rules of law will permit the buyer to sue the owner for damages. The rules of equity will go further and compel the owner to actually transfer the ownership of the house to the buyer. This equitable remedy is called *specific performance.*

SUMMARY

Law consists of the pattern of rules established by society to govern conduct and relationships. These rules can be expressed as constitutional provisions, statutes, administrative regulations, and case decisions. Law can be classified as substantive or procedural, and it can be described in terms of its historical origins, by the subject to which it relates, or in terms of law or equity.

Law provides rights and imposes duties. One such right is the right of privacy, which affords protection against unreasonable searches of our property and intrusion into or disclosure of our private affairs.

The sources of law include constitutions, federal and state statutes, administrative regulations, ordinances, and uniform laws generally codified by the states in their statutes. The courts are also a source of law through their adherence to case precedent under the doctrine of *stare decisis* and through their development of time-honored principles called the common law.

---

[5] *Samsel v Wheeler Transport Services* (Kan) 789 P2d 541 (1990).
[6] *Gibbons v Stillwell,* 149 Ill App 3d 411, 102 Ill Dec 864, 500 NE2d 965 (1986).

QUESTIONS AND CASE PROBLEMS

1. What social forces affect the strength and subject areas of law? For example, how and why are there laws that establish speed limits?
2. How do you account for the rise of both remedies in law and remedies in equity?
3. List the sources of law.
4. What is the difference between common law and statutory law?
5. Classify the following laws as substantive or procedural:
   a. A law that requires public schools to hold a hearing before a student is expelled.
   b. A law that establishes a maximum interest rate for credit transactions of 24 percent.
   c. A law that provides employee leave for the birth or adoption of a child for up to 12 weeks.
   d. A law that requires the county assessor to send four notices of taxes due and owing before a lien can be filed (attached) to the property.
6. What do uniform laws accomplish? Why do states adopt them? Give an example of a uniform law.
7. Cindy Nathan is a student at West University. While she was at her 9:00 A.M. anthropology class, campus security entered her dorm room and searched all areas, including her closet and drawers. When Cindy returned to her room and discovered what had happened, she complained to the dorm's senior resident. The senior resident said that this was the university's property and that Cindy had no right of privacy. Do you agree with the resident's statement? Is there a right of privacy in a dorm room?
8. Professor Lucas Phelps sent the following E-mail to Professor Marlin Jones: "I recently read the opinion piece you wrote for the *Sacramento Bee* on affirmative action. Your opinion is incorrect, your reasoning and analysis are poor, and I am embarrassed that you are a member of the faculty here at Cal State Yolinda." Professor Jones forwarded the note from Professor Phelps to the provost of the university and asked that Professor Phelps be disciplined for using the university E-mail system for harassment purposes. Professor Phelps objected when the provost contacted him: "He had no right to send that E-mail to you. That was private correspondence. And you have no right of access to my E-mail. I have privacy rights." Do you agree with Professor Phelps? Was there a breach of privacy?
9. Under what circumstances would a court disregard precedent?
10. Who develops the common law?
11. Can a statutory right conflict with a constitutional right?
12. Describe the relationship between rights and duties, and give an example that shows their correlation.
13. What is the principle of *stare decisis*?
14. What are administrative regulations, and where do they originate?
15. Give examples of governmental bodies that enact statutory law.

The Court System and Dispute Resolution

CHAPTER 2

OBJECTIVES

After studying this chapter, you should be able to

1. *Explain the federal and state court systems;*
2. *Define the types of jurisdiction courts can have and how these are different;*
3. *Give the names of the parties and persons involved in a lawsuit;*
4. *List the initial steps in a lawsuit and explain how pleadings are used;*
5. *Describe the actual steps in a trial;*
6. *Explain how a party who prevails in court collects the judgment; and*
7. *List the forms of alternative dispute resolution and distinguish among them.*

Despite carefully negotiated and well-written contracts and high safety standards in the workplace or in product design and production, businesses can still encounter disputes that may result in a lawsuit. ◆ *For example*, one could hire the brightest and most expensive lawyer in town to prepare a contract with another party, and the agreement could be considered "bulletproof." However, such a contract will not guarantee performance by the other party, and a lawsuit for damages may be necessary. ◆

Parties in a dispute either go to court or resolve the situation through alternative means. This chapter covers the structure of the court system and the litigation process but also covers the forms of alternative dispute resolution used to resolve disputes outside the court system.

A.   THE COURT SYSTEM

A court is a tribunal established by government to hear and decide matters brought before it, provide remedies when there has been a wrong committed, and prevent possible wrongs from happening. ◆ *For example*, a court could award a business money damages for a breach of contract following a trial, but it could also issue an order or injunction to prevent a copyright infringement, such as when the release of a movie is stopped until authorship of the script can be determined and the rights to the movie proceeds determined. ◆

1.   The Types of Courts

Jurisdiction is the power to hear and decide particular classes of cases.

Original jurisdiction is a court with authority to hear the initial proceedings in a case.

General jurisdiction is the power to hear a wide range of civil and criminal matters.

Limited or special jurisdiction is the power to hear only disputes involving specific subject matter or limited amounts of damages.

Every type of court is given the authority to decide certain types or classes of cases. The power to hear cases is called **jurisdiction**. One form of jurisdiction covers the type of proceedings that the court holds. A court with **original jurisdiction** is the trial court or the court with the authority to conduct the first proceedings in the case. ◆ *For example*, a court of original jurisdiction would be one where the witnesses appear to testify, the documents are admitted into evidence, and the jury, in the case of a jury trial, is present to hear all of the evidence and make a decision. ◆

There are other types of jurisdiction applicable to courts. A court with **general jurisdiction** has the authority to hear a large number of cases, for its authority is over general civil and criminal cases. A court with **limited** or **special jurisdiction** has the authority to hear only particular kinds of cases. ◆ *For example*, many states have courts that can hear only disputes in which the damages are $10,000 or less. ◆ There are many types of courts with specialized jurisdiction, including equity courts, juvenile courts, probate courts, and domestic relations courts. States vary in the names they give these courts, but all are courts of special or limited jurisdiction because there is a very narrow scope for their jurisdiction.

There are additional classifications of courts based on the nature of their cases. A court may have criminal jurisdiction with the authority to try criminal cases. A court with civil jurisdiction has the authority to hear civil disputes, such as breach of contract cases and disputes about leases between landlords and tenants.

Appellate jurisdiction is the power to review the work of a lower court, such as a trial court or court of original jurisdiction.

A court with **appellate jurisdiction** reviews the work of a lower court. ◆ *For example*, a trial court may issue a judgment that a defendant sued for breach of contract should pay $5,000 in damages. That defendant could appeal the decision to an appellate court and seek review of the decision itself or even the amount of the damages. ◆ An appeal is a review of the trial and decision of the lower court.

An appellate court does not hear witnesses or take testimony. An appellate court, usually a panel of three judges, simply reviews the transcript and evidence from the lower court and determines whether there has been **reversible error**. For example, a reversible error would be a mistake in applying the law or a mistake in admitting evidence that affected the outcome of the case. An appellate court can **reverse** a lower court decision or **remand** that decision for another trial or additional hearings.

2.   The Federal Court System

The federal court system consists of three levels of courts.

(a) Federal District Courts. The **federal district courts** are the general trial courts of the federal system. They are courts of original jurisdiction that hear both civil and criminal matters. Criminal cases in federal district court are those in which the defendant is charged with a violation of federal law (the U.S. Code). The types of civil cases that can be brought in federal district courts are (1) civil suits in which the United States is a party, (2) cases between citizens of different states that involve damages of $50,000 or more, and (3) cases that arise under the U.S. Constitution or federal laws and treaties.

Federal district courts are organized by and within the states. Each state has at least one federal district, and judges and courtrooms are assigned according to the caseload in that particular geographic area of the state. Some states, such as New York and California, have several federal districts because of the population base and the resulting caseload.

There are additional trial courts in the federal system that have limited jurisdiction, as opposed to the general jurisdiction of the federal district courts. These courts are, for example, the federal bankruptcy court, Indian tribal courts, Tax Court, U.S. Claims Court, Court of Military Appeals, and the U.S. Court of International Trade.

(b) U.S. Courts of Appeals. The final decision in a federal district court is not necessarily the end of a case because it is a court of original jurisdiction and its decisions can be appealed to a court with appellate jurisdiction. In the federal court system, the federal districts are grouped together geographically into 12 judicial circuits, with an additional circuit for overload cases. Each circuit has an appellate court called the U.S. court of appeals, and the judges for these courts review the decisions of the federal district courts. Generally, a panel of three judges will review the cases.

(c) U.S. Supreme Court. The final court in the federal system is the U.S. Supreme Court. The U.S. Supreme Court has appellate jurisdiction over cases that are appealed from the federal courts of appeals as well as from state supreme courts when there is a constitutional issue involved in the case or a state court has reversed a federal court ruling. Not all cases from the federal courts of appeals are heard by the U.S. Supreme Court. The U.S. Supreme Court has a process called granting a **writ of certiorari**, which is a preliminary review of those cases appealed to decide whether a case will be heard or allowed to stand as ruled on by the lower courts.

The U.S. Supreme Court is the only court expressly created in the U.S. Constitution. All other courts in the federal system were created by Congress pur-

---

Reversible error is a mistake made in the trial of the case that is serious enough to have affected the outcome and requires a reversal or a remand for new hearings or a new trial.

Reverse means the appellate court sets aside the verdict or judgment of a lower court.

Remand means appellate court sends a case back to the trial court for more hearings or a new trial.

Federal district court is a general trial court of the federal system.

Writ of certiorari is an order by the U.S. Supreme Court granting a right of review by the court of a lower court decision.

suant to the Constitution's language allowing such a system if Congress found it necessary. The Constitution also makes the U.S. Supreme Court a court of original jurisdiction. The U.S. Supreme Court serves as the trial court for cases involving ambassadors, public ministers, or consuls and for cases in which two states are involved in a lawsuit. For example, the U.S. Supreme Court has served for a number of years as the trial court for a Colorado water rights case in which California, Nevada, and Arizona are parties.

3. State Court Systems

(a) General Trial Court. Most states have trial courts of general jurisdiction that may be called superior courts, circuit courts, or county courts. These courts of general and original jurisdiction usually hear both criminal and civil cases. Cases that do not meet the jurisdictional requirements for the federal district courts would be tried in these courts.

(b) Specialty Courts. Most states also have courts with limited jurisdiction, also referred to as specialty courts. *For example*, most states have juvenile courts, or courts with limited jurisdiction over criminal matters that involve defendants who are under the age of 18. Other specialty courts or lesser courts in state systems are probate and family law courts.

Cities and counties may also have lesser courts with limited jurisdiction, and they may be referred to as municipal courts or justice courts. These courts generally handle civil matters in which the claim made in the suit is an amount below a certain level, such as $5,000 or $10,000. These courts may also handle misdemeanor types of offenses and the trials for them, such as traffic violations or violations of noise ordinances.

Most states will also have small claims courts at the county or city level. These are courts of limited jurisdiction where parties with small amounts in dispute may come to have a third party, such as a justice of the peace or city judge, review their disputes and determine how they should be resolved. A true small claims court is one in which the parties are not permitted to be represented by counsel. Rather, the parties present their cases to the judge in an informal manner without the strict procedural rules that apply in courts of general jurisdiction. Small claims courts provide a faster and an inexpensive means for resolving a dispute that does not involve a great deal of claimed damages.

(c) State Appellate Courts. Most states also have intermediate-level courts similar to the federal courts of appeals. These are courts with appellate jurisdiction that review the decisions of lower courts in that state. Decisions of the general trial courts in a state would be appealed to these courts.

(d) State Supreme Court. The highest court in most states is known as the state supreme court. Generally, the name is "supreme court," but a few states, such as New York, may call their highest court the court of appeals. State supreme courts primarily have appellate jurisdiction, but some states' courts do have original jurisdiction, such as in Arizona, where counties in litigation will have their trial at the supreme court level. Most state supreme courts do not hear all cases appealed. These courts also have a screening process. There are some cases they are required to hear, such as those criminal cases where the defendant has received the death penalty. A decision of a state supreme court is final except in those circumstances in which a federal law or treaty or the U.S. Constitution is involved. Those cases with federal subject matter can then be appealed to the U.S. Supreme Court.

B.   COURT PROCEDURE

Once a party decides to use the court system for resolution of a dispute, he or she enters a world with specific rules, procedures, and terms that must be used in order to have a case proceed.

4.   Participants in the Court System

A plaintiff is the party who initiates a lawsuit in a court of original jurisdiction.

A prosecutor is the party who originates a criminal proceeding.

A defendant is the party who is charged with a violation of civil or criminal law in a proceeding brought in a court of original jurisdiction.

A judge is the primary officer of the court who presides over cases before the court.

A jury is the body of citizens sworn by a court to determine the verdict in a case presented to them.

A complaint is the document that commences a lawsuit.

The **plaintiff** is the party who initiates the proceedings in a court of original jurisdiction. In a criminal case in which charges are brought, the party initiating the proceedings would be called the **prosecutor**. The party against whom the civil or criminal proceedings are brought is the **defendant**. A **judge** is the primary officer of the court and is either an elected or an appointed official who presides over the matters brought before the court. Attorneys or lawyers are trained individuals selected by the plaintiff and the defendant as their representatives in the matter for purposes of presenting their cases.

A **jury** is a body of citizens sworn by a court to reach a verdict on the basis of the case presented to them. Jurors are chosen for service based on lists compiled from voter registration and driver's license lists.

5.   Initial Steps in a Lawsuit

The following steps in a lawsuit will generally apply in cases brought in courts of original jurisdiction. Not every step will apply in every case, but the terminology and process are still important to understand.

(a) Commencement of a Lawsuit. A lawsuit begins with the filing of a **complaint**. The complaint generally contains a description of the conduct complained of by the plaintiff and a request for damages, such as a monetary amount. *For example,* a plaintiff in a contract suit would describe the contract, when it was entered into, and when the defendant stopped performance on the contract. A copy of the contract would be attached to the complaint.

Process is the notice to a defendant that a lawsuit has begun.

An answer is the defendant's response to the allegations in the plaintiff's complaint.

A motion to dismiss is the defendant's request that a court dismiss a lawsuit for the failure of the plaintiff to state a claim.

(b) Service of Process. Once the plaintiff has filed the complaint with the clerk of the court that has jurisdiction over the case, the plaintiff has the responsibility of notifying the defendant that the lawsuit has been filed. The defendant must be served with **process**. Process, often called a *writ, notice,* or *summons* is delivered to the defendant and includes a copy of the complaint and notification that the defendant must appear and respond to the allegations in the complaint.

(c) The Defendant's Response and the Pleadings. After the defendant is served with process in the case, the defendant is required to make some response or **answer** the complaint within the time provided under the court's rules. In answering the plaintiff's complaint, the defendant has several options. The defendant could make a **motion to dismiss**, which is a request to the court to

A demurrer is another name for a motion to dismiss.

A counterclaim is a claim by a defendant in a lawsuit for damages against the plaintiff.

Pleadings are the complaint, answer, counterclaim, and other filings in the initial stage of the case that provide a statement of the facts and the grounds for relief if all facts are established at trial.

dismiss the lawsuit on the grounds that even if everything the plaintiff said in the complaint were true, there is no right of recovery. A motion to dismiss is also called a **demurrer**.

A defendant could also respond and deny the allegations. ◆ *For example,* in a contract lawsuit, the defendant could say he did not breach the contract but stopped shipment of the goods because the plaintiff did not pay for the goods in advance as the contract required. ◆ A defendant could also **counterclaim** in the answer, which is asking the court for his damages as a result of the underlying dispute. ◆ *For example,* the defendant in the contract lawsuit might ask for damages for the plaintiff's failure to pay as the contract required. ◆

All of the documents filed in this initial phase of the case are referred to as the **pleadings**. The pleadings, when accepted following the defendant's objections and the plaintiff's corrections, are a statement of the case and the basis for recovery if all the facts alleged can be proved.

Discovery is the process of uncovering the evidence in a case through depositions, document production, and so on.

Deposition is sworn testimony of a witness taken outside the courtroom.

To impeach means using prior inconsistent evidence to challenge the credibility of a witness.

Interrogatories are written questions, used as a discovery tool, that must be answered under oath.

Request for production of documents is a discovery tool for uncovering paper evidence in a case.

A motion for summary judgment is a request that the court decide the case on the basis of the law only because there are no issues of material fact disputed by the parties.

An expert witness is a witness, such as an economist, named by a party to give testimony on technical matters in the case within the witness's field of expertise.

(d) Discovery. The Federal Rules of Civil Procedure and similar rules in a large number of states permit one party to inquire of the adverse party and all witnesses about anything relating to the action. This includes asking the adverse party the names of witnesses; asking the adverse party and the witnesses what they know about the case; examining, inspecting, and photographing books, records, buildings, and machines; and examining the physical or mental condition of a party when it has a bearing on the action. These procedures are known as **discovery**. The scope of discovery is extremely broad because the rules permit any questions that are likely to lead to admissible evidence.

(1) Deposition. A **deposition** is the testimony of a witness taken under oath outside the courtroom. Each party is permitted to question the witness. The deposition is transcribed by a court reporter. If a party or a witness gives testimony at the trial that is inconsistent with his or her deposition testimony, the prior inconsistent testimony can be used to **impeach** the witness's credibility at trial.

Depositions can be taken either for discovery purposes or to perpetuate the testimony of a witness who will not be available during the trial. Some states now permit the videotaping of depositions. A videotape is a more effective way of presenting deposition testimony than reading that testimony at trial from a reporter's transcript.

(2) Other Forms of Discovery. Others forms of discovery include written **interrogatories** (questions) and written **requests for production of documents**. These discovery requests can be very time-consuming to the answering party and very often lead to pretrial legal disputes between the parties and their attorneys due to the legal expenses involved.

(e) Motion for Summary Judgment. If there is no triable issue of material fact in the case, either party can file a **motion for summary judgment**. Using affidavits or deposition testimony obtained in discovery, the party can establish that there are no factual issues and that the case can be decided as an issue of law by a judge.

(f) Designation of Expert Witnesses. If a case will go on to trial, the parties may want to designate an **expert witness**. An expert witness is a witness who has some special expertise, such as an economist who will give expert opinion on the value of future lost income. Expert witnesses have been utilized in greater numbers in recent years. There are rules for naming expert witnesses.

6.   The Trial

(a) Selecting a Jury. Jurors drawn for service are questioned by the judge and lawyers for purposes of determining possible bias in the case or any pre-formed judgments about the parties in the case. Jury selection is called **voir dire examination.** *For example,* in the trial of Timothy McVeigh, the man convicted of bombing the Oklahoma City Federal Building, jury selection took a great deal of time as the lawyers questioned the potential jurors' prior knowledge about the case because of the nationwide attention and media coverage it had received.

Lawyers have the opportunity to remove jurors who know parties in the case or who indicate they have already formed opinions about guilt or innocence. The attorneys question the potential jurors to determine if a juror should be **challenged for cause** (e.g., when the prospective juror states he is employed by plaintiff's company). Challenges for cause are unlimited, but each side can exercise six to eight **peremptory challenges**. A peremptory challenge is an arbitrary challenge that may be used for any reason except racial reasons.

> Voir dire examination is the questioning of potential jurors by the attorneys and the judge to determine bias.

> Challenge for cause is a removal of a juror because of a connection with parties in the case.

> A peremptory challenge is a challenge to a juror that need not be explained; a limited number are available in each case.

ETHICS & THE LAW

Jimmy Elem was convicted of second-degree robbery in a Missouri court. During jury selection for his trial, the prosecutor used his two peremptory challenges to strike two black men from the jury panel.

Mr. Elem, who is also black, appealed his conviction on the grounds that the prosecutor struck the two black men from the jury panel on the basis of race. The prosecutor supplied the following statement about his peremptory challenges:

> *I struck [juror] number twenty-two because of his long hair. He had long curly hair. He had the longest hair of anybody on the panel by far. He appeared to not be a good juror for that fact, the fact that he had long hair hanging down shoulder length, curly, unkempt hair. Also, he had a mustache and a goatee-type beard. And juror number twenty-four also has a mustache and goatee-type beard. Those are the only two people on the jury . . . with facial hair. . . . And I don't like the way they looked, with the way the hair is cut, both of them. And the mustaches and the beards look suspicious to me.*

The prosecutor also said that juror number twenty-four had a sawed-off shotgun pointed at him during a supermarket robbery. Mr. Elem had not used a gun in his robbery.

Mr. Elem's appeal said the prosecutor's reason was a guise for a race-based decision. Is it fair to have peremptory challenges? Do you think the prosecutor's reason is valid? Do you think facial hair is a legitimate basis for a peremptory challenge? What effect do these challenges have on jury composition and verdicts? *Purkett v Elem*, 115 S. Ct. 2407 (1995).

> An opening statement is the statement by a lawyer to the jury of what he or she intends to prove in the case.

(b) Opening Statements. After the jury is called, the opposing attorneys make their **opening statements** to the jury of what they intend to prove.

Admissibility is the quality of evidence in a case that allows it to be presented to the jury.

A direct examination is the questioning of one's own witness at trial.

A cross-examination is the questioning of the other side's witnesses at trial.

A redirect examination is the questioning of ones' own witness following cross-examination by the other side.

A recross-examination is the questioning the other side's witness following redirect examination.

Directed verdict is a verdict entered by the court following the presentation of the plaintiff's case when the plaintiff fails to prove all the elements required for recovery; sometimes allowed to be made by the plaintiff following the defendant's case.

A summation is the closing argument by a lawyer in a case.

A mistrial is a judge's ruling to end the case and start over because of misconduct that prejudices one of the parties.

Instructions are a summary of the law given to jurors by the judge before they begin deliberation.

A judgment n.o.v. is a judgment made "notwithstanding the verdict"; a reversal of a jury verdict by the trial judge because the verdict was contrary to law.

(c) The Presentation of Evidence. The plaintiff then begins to present his case with witnesses and other evidence. A judge rules on the **admissibility** of evidence. Evidence can consist of documents and testimony.

In the case of testimony, the attorney for the plaintiff conducts **direct examination** during his or her case, and the defense attorney then **cross-examines** the witness. The plaintiff's attorney can then ask questions again in what is called **redirect examination**. Finally, the defendant may question again in **recross-examination**.

This procedure is followed with all of the plaintiff's remaining witnesses—and with all of the defendant's witnesses.

(d) Motion for a Directed Verdict. After the presentation of all the evidence at trial, either party may request the court to direct the jury to return a verdict in favor of the requesting party. When the plaintiff would not be entitled to recover, even if all of the testimony in the plaintiff's favor were believed, the defendant is entitled to have the court direct the jury to return a verdict for the defendant. The plaintiff is entitled to a **directed verdict** when, even if all the evidence on behalf of the defendant were believed, the jury would still be required to find for the plaintiff. In some states, the defendant may make a motion for a directed verdict at the close of the plaintiff's proof.

(e) Summation. After the witnesses of both parties have been examined and all the evidence has been presented, each attorney makes another address to the jury. This is called a **summation** or closing argument, and it sums up the case and suggests that a particular verdict be returned by the jury.

(f) Motion for Mistrial. During the course of trial, when necessary to avoid great injustice, the trial court may declare that there has been a **mistrial**. This terminates the trial and postpones it to a later date. A mistrial can be declared for jury misconduct or attorney misconduct. As a practical matter, except for juror misconduct, a motion for mistrial is rarely granted because the court has the discretion to grant a new trial after the aggrieved party receives an adverse verdict.

(g) Jury Instructions. After the summation by the attorneys, the court gives the jurors **instructions** on the appropriate law to apply to the facts they find to be true or untrue. The jury then deliberates and renders its verdict. After the jury renders a verdict, the court enters a judgment conforming to the verdict. If the jury is deadlocked and unable to reach a verdict, the case is reset for a new trial at some future date.

(h) Motion for New Trial; Motion for Judgment N.O.V. A court may grant a new trial for a variety of reasons, but the most common reasons are that the judge finds that the evidence is insufficient to support the verdict or that the damages awarded to the plaintiff are either excessive or too low.

A court may grant a **judgment n.o.v.** (notwithstanding the verdict) if the verdict is clearly wrong as a matter of law. The court can set aside the verdict and enter a judgment in favor of the other party. Perhaps one of the most famous judgments n.o.v. occurred in Boston in 1997 when a judge reversed the murder conviction of nanny Louise Woodward.

7. Post-trial Procedures

(a) Recovery of Costs/ Attorneys Fees. Generally, the prevailing party will be awarded costs. Costs include filing fees, service of process fees, witness fees, deposition transcript costs, and jury fees. Costs do not include compensation spent by a party for preparing the case or being present at trial, including the time lost from work because of the case and the fee paid to the attorney.

Attorney fees may be recovered by a party who prevails if a statute permits the recovery of attorney fees or if the complaint involves a claim for breach of contract and the contract contains a clause for attorney fees. As a general rule, the costs that a party recovers represent only a small part of the total expense incurred in the litigation.

(b) Execution of Judgment. After a judgment has been entered or after an appeal has been decided, the losing party generally complies with the judgment of the court. If not, the winning party may then take steps to execute, or carry out, the judgment. The **execution** is accomplished by the seizure and sale of the losing party's assets by the sheriff pursuant to a writ of execution or a writ of possession.

Garnishment is a common method of satisfying a judgment. Where the judgment debtor is an employee, the sheriff garnishes (by written notice to the employer) a portion of the employee's wages. The employer writes a check to the sheriff.

> Execution is the process of collecting a judgment awarded following a verdict.

> A garnishment is the process of taking wages or other funds to satisfy a judgment.

C. ALTERNATIVE DISPUTE RESOLUTION

There are others means besides litigation that can be used to resolve disagreements or disputes. The discussion of the details of litigation shows its time and money costs and should encourage those with disputes to pursue alternative methods for resolving them. Those methods include arbitration, mediation, and several other forms of resolution that are enjoying increasing popularity. Figure 2-1 provides an overall view of dispute resolution.

8. Arbitration

In **arbitration**, a dispute is settled by one or more arbitrators (disinterested persons selected by the parties to the dispute). Arbitration first reached extensive use in the field of commercial contracts. This procedure is encouraged as a means of avoiding expensive litigation and easing the workload of courts.[1] Arbitration enables the parties to present the facts before trained experts familiar with the practices that form the background of the dispute.

> An arbitration is the settlement of a dispute through the use of one or more arbitrators.

---

[1] *Lancaster v West* (Ark) 891 SW2d 357 (1995).

FIGURE 2-1
*Dispute Resolution
Procedures*

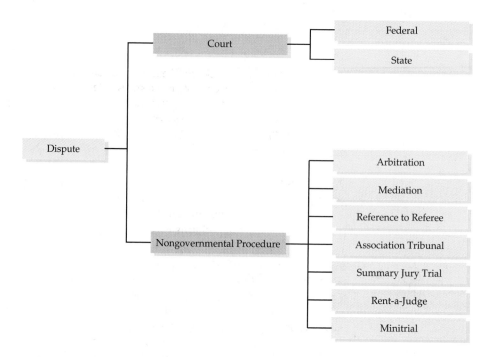

A Uniform Arbitration Act has been adopted in a number of states.[2] Under this act and similar statutes, the parties to a contract may agree in advance that all disputes arising under it will be submitted to arbitration. In some instances, the contract will name the arbitrators for the duration of the contract. The uniform act requires a written agreement to arbitrate.[3]

The Federal Arbitration Act[4] declares that an arbitration clause in a contract relating to an interstate transaction is valid, irrevocable, and enforceable. When a contract subject to the Federal Arbitration Act provides for the arbitration of disputes, the parties are bound to arbitrate in accordance with the federal statute even if the agreement to arbitrate would not be binding under state law.

CASE SUMMARY

The Feds vs. Contract Arbitration

Facts: A Missouri landowner made a contract with a Missouri builder to construct an office building in Missouri. The materials for the construction of the building were supplied by 29 enterprises located in other states. The contract expressly provided that disputes were to be submitted to arbitration. By Missouri law, this arbitration clause was not binding because it did not contain the clause required by Missouri law: "THIS CONTRACT CONTAINS A BINDING ARBITRATION PROVISION WHICH MAY BE ENFORCED BY THE PARTIES." When a dispute arose under the contract, the contractor insisted that it be submitted to arbitration. The owner opposed arbitration on the ground that the arbitration clause was not binding because it did not satisfy Missouri law. The contractor claimed that the Federal Arbitration Act overrode the

---

[2] The 1955 version of the Uniform Arbitration Act has been adopted in Alaska, Arizona, Arkansas, Colorado, Delaware, Florida, Idaho, Illinois, Indiana, Iowa, Kansas, Kentucky, Maine, Maryland, Massachusetts, Michigan, Minnesota, Missouri, Montana, Nebraska, Nevada, New Mexico, North Carolina, North Dakota, Oklahoma, Pennsylvania, South Carolina, South Dakota, Tennessee, Texas, Utah, Vermont, Virginia, Wyoming, and the District of Columbia. The 1925 version of the Act is in force in Wisconsin.

[3] *Anderson v Federated Mutual Ins. Co.* (Minn App) 465 NW2d 68 (1991).

[4] 9 USC §§ 114 et seq.

Missouri requirement and because the federal law did not require a notice clause, the agreement to arbitrate was binding. The lower court denied arbitration, and the contractor appealed.

Decision: The court reversed the lower court and held that the parties must submit to arbitration. The federal law on arbitration controls state laws when the parties are involved in interstate commerce. Under federal law, the arbitration clause, even without the Missouri warning, was valid and enforceable. [*McCarney v Nearing, Staats, Prelogar and Jones (Mo App) 866 SW2d 881 (1993)*]

(a) Mandatory Arbitration. In contrast with statutes that merely regulate arbitration when selected voluntarily by the parties, some statutes require that certain kinds of disputes be submitted to arbitration. In some states, by rule or statute, the arbitration of small claims is required.

(b) Scope of Arbitration. When arbitration is required by statute, the terms of the statute will define the scope of the arbitration. When the parties have voluntarily agreed to arbitrate, their agreement will control the scope of the dispute. In such a case, questions may arise as to what disputes are covered. As arbitration is now favored, any doubt as to its scope should be decided in favor of arbitration.[5]

(c) Finality of Arbitration. When arbitration is based on the agreement of the parties, it is generally agreed that the decision of the arbitrator shall be final. This is so even if the decision is wrong unless there is clear proof of fraud, arbitrary conduct, or a significant procedural error.

In contrast, when arbitration is mandatory under statute or rule, it is generally provided that the losing party may appeal from such arbitration to a court.[6] The appeal will proceed just as though there never had been any prior arbitration. This is called a **trial *de novo*** and is required to preserve the constitutional right to a jury trial. As a practical matter, however, relatively few appeals are taken from arbitration decisions.

Trial de novo is a trial that starts the full process over following an unsuccessful arbitration.

9. Mediation

A mediation is the settlement of a dispute through the use of a messenger who carries to each side of the dispute the issues and offers in the case.

In mediation, a neutral person acts as a messenger between opposing sides of a dispute, carrying to each side the latest settlement offer made by the other. The mediator has no authority to make a decision, although in some cases the mediator may make suggestions that might ultimately be accepted by the disputing parties.

The use of mediation has the advantage of keeping discussions going when the disputing parties have developed such fixed attitudes or personal animosity that direct discussion between them has become impossible.

10. Reference to a Third Person

Reference to a third person is settlement by allowing a non-party to resolve the dispute.

Many types of transactions provide for a third person or a committee to make an out-of-court determination of the rights of persons. Thus, employees and an employer may have agreed as a term of the employment contract that claims of

---

5 *South Carolina Public Service Authority v Great Western Coal Inc.* (SC) 437 SE2d 22 (1993).
6 *Porreco v Red Top RV Center,* 216 Cal App 3d 113, 264 Cal Rptr 609 (1989).

employees under retirement plans shall be decided by a designated board or committee. The seller and buyer may have selected a third person to determine the price to be paid for goods. Construction contracts often include as a term of the contract that any dispute shall be referred to the architect in charge of the construction and that the architect's decision shall be final.

Ordinarily the parties agree that the decision of such a third person or board shall be final and that no appeal or review may be had in any court. In most cases, referral to a third person is used in situations that involve the determination of a particular fact. In contrast, arbitration seeks to end a dispute.

◆ *For example*, fire insurance policies commonly provide that if the parties cannot agree on the amount of the loss, each will appoint an appraiser, the two appraisers will appoint a third appraiser, and the three will determine the amount of the loss the insurer is required to pay. ◆ These appraisers must be independent and impartial.

CASE SUMMARY

The Disinterested Appraiser with a Percentage of the Take

Facts: The Central Life Insurance Co. insured its building against fire with the Aetna Casualty & Surety Co. When a fire loss occurred, both Central and Aetna agreed to submit the matter to appraisers to determine the extent of the loss. The appraiser selected by Aetna was paid a flat fee. Central agreed to pay its appraiser a percentage of the amount recovered by it. The assessment made by the Central appraiser was about three times the assessment made be the Aetna appraiser. Aetna applied to the court to set aside the assessment made by the appraisers. From a judgment for Central, Aetna appealed.

Decision: The percentage fee arrangement violated the role of the appraiser as a quasi-judicial decision maker, and the appraisal of Central's appraiser should have been set aside. [*Central Life Ins. Co. v Aetna Cas. & Surety Co.* (Iowa) 466 NW2d 257 (1991)]

---

11. Association Tribunals

Association tribunal is a court created by a trade association or group, for example, the National Association of Home Builders, for the resolution of disputes among its members.

Many disputes never reach the courts because both parties to a dispute belong to a group or an association, and the tribunal created by the group or association disposes of the matter. Thus, a dispute between members of a labor union, a stockbrokers' exchange, or a church may be heard by some board or committee within the association or group. Courts will review the action of such tribunals to determine that a fair and proper procedure was followed, but generally the courts will not go any further. Courts will not examine the facts of the case to see if the association tribunal reached the same conclusion that the court could have reached.

Trade associations commonly require their members to employ out-of-court methods of dispute settlement. ◆ *For example*, the National Association of Home Builders requires its member builders to employ arbitration. The National Automobile Dealers Association provides for panels to determine warranty claims of customers. ◆ The decision of such a panel is final as to the dealer, but the consumer is allowed to bring a regular lawsuit after losing before the panel.

Members of an association must make use of an association tribunal. This means that they cannot ignore the association tribunal and go directly to a law court.[7]

---

[7] *Canady v Meharry Medical College* (Tenn App) 811 SW2d 902 (1991).

12. Summary Jury Trial

Summary jury trial is a mock or dry-run trial, in which the parties get a feel for how their cases will play to a jury.

A **summary jury trial** is in effect a dry run or mock trial in which the lawyers present their claims before a jury of six persons. The object is to get the reaction of a sample jury. No evidence is presented before this jury, and it bases its opinion solely on what the lawyers state. The determination of the jury has no binding effect, but it has value in that it gives the lawyers some idea of what a jury might think if there were an actual trial. This has special value when the heart of a case is whether something is reasonable under all the circumstances. When the lawyers see how the sample jury reacts, they may moderate their positions and reach a settlement.

13. Rent-a-Judge

Rent-a-judge is a dispute resolution through private courts with judges paid to be referees for the cases.

Under the **rent-a-judge** plan, the parties hire a judge to hear the case. In many states, the parties voluntarily choose the judge as a "referee," and the judge acts under a statute authorizing the appointment of referees. Under such a statute, the referee hears all the evidence just as though there were a regular trial, and the referee's determination is binding on the parties unless reversed on appeal if such an appeal (like a court trial) is permitted under the parties' agreement. In some jurisdictions, special provision is made for the parties to agree that the decision of the judge selected as referee shall be final.

14. Minitrial

When only part of a case is disputed, the parties may stay within the framework of a lawsuit but agree that only the disputed issues will be submitted to a jury. For example, when there is no real dispute over the liability of the defendant but the parties disagree as to the damages, the issue of damages alone may be submitted to the jury.

Minitrial is a trial held on portions of the case or certain issues in the case.

In some states, instead of submitting the matter to a regular jury, attorneys will agree to hold a **minitrial**. Under this system, the parties agree that a particular person, frequently a retired judge, should listen to the evidence on the disputed issues and decide the case. The agreement of the parties for the minitrial may specify whether this decision is binding on the parties. As a practical matter, the evaluation of the case by a neutral person will often bring the opposing parties together to reach a settlement.

15. Contract Provisions

The parties' contract may pave the way for the settlement of future disputes by containing clauses requiring the parties to make use of one of the procedures described above. In addition, contracts may provide that no action may be taken until after the expiration of a specified cooling-off period. Contracts may also specify that the parties shall continue in the performance of their contract even though there is a dispute between them.

16. Disposition of Complaints and Ombudsmen

In contrast with the traditional and alternative procedures for resolving disputes are the procedures aimed at removing the grounds for complaint before it develops into a dispute that requires resolution. For example, the complaint department in a department store will often be able to iron out a difficulty before the customer and the store are locked in an adversarial position that could end in a lawsuit. Grievance committee procedures will often be effective in bringing about an adjustment or a removal of the grounds for complaint. A statute may designate a government official to examine complaints. Such an official is often called an **ombudsman**.[8] The few federal statutes that have required such an officer have not given the ombudsman any judicial power. Typically, the ombudsman is limited to receiving complaints, supervising the administration of the system, and making recommendations for improvements. Two federal statutes expressly declare that the creation of the office of ombudsman does not impair any right existing by law.[9] In addition, when a complaint involves a right that would require a jury trial at common law, the Seventh Amendment to the U.S. Constitution guarantees that right. An ombudsman could not be given the power to decide such a matter. Moreover, the trend in America is to create special tribunals or administrative agencies, rather than to give an ombudsman greater power.

> Ombudsman is a Swedish term for commissioner, which refers to an official charged by a company or government with the resolution of disputes among employees or customers or among citizens.

WHAT'S BEHIND THE LAW?

How Much Do We Need Lawyers to Remind Us of Our Rights? Constraints on Advertising and Solicitation by Lawyers

Following a ValuJet airplane crash in the Florida Everglades and the crash of TWA Flight 800 just outside New York City in the 1990s, lawyers solicited grieving family members for representation in suits against these airlines.

Under the American Bar Association's Model Rules of Professional Conduct, direct solicitation of clients is prohibited. Advertising of legal services and firms is, however, permitted. The West Virginia Supreme Court of Appeals stated the following when discussing the propriety of lawyer contact with potential clients:

> The rationale for [the rule on solicitations] is that there is potential for abuse when in-person or telephone solicitations are made. Such contacts can be especially upsetting when made shortly after a loved one has been killed or injured, and personal contact with the recipient means the situation is "fraught with the possibility of undue influence, intimidation and overreaching." And personal contacts can't be monitored by disciplinary authorities, . . . unlike solicitations by mail, which leave a written record.

Are restrictions on solicitations necessary to protect the public? Why is advertising being treated differently from solicitations? For more on advertising issues and law, see advertising law at http://www.law.emory.edu/FOCAL/ad.html

---

[8] This Swedish name means *commissioner*.
[9] For example, see the Solid Waste Disposal Act of November 8, 1984, PL 98-616, § 703(a), 98 Stat 3225, 42 USC § 6917; and the Panama Canal Commission Act of September 17, 1979, PL 96-70, § 1113, 93 Stat 460, 22 USC § 3623.

SUMMARY

Courts have been created to hear and resolve legal disputes. A court's specific power is defined by its jurisdiction. Courts of original jurisdiction are trial courts, and courts that review the decisions of trial courts are appellate courts. Trial courts may have general jurisdiction to hear a wide range of civil and criminal matters, or they may be courts of limited jurisdiction, with the subject matter of their cases restricted to certain areas, such as a probate court or the Tax Court.

The courts in the United States are organized into two different systems: the state and federal court systems. There are three levels of courts, for the most part, in each system, with trial courts, appellate courts, and a supreme court in each. The federal courts are called federal district courts, federal Courts of Appeals, and the U.S. Supreme Court. In the states there may be specialized courts, such as municipal, justice, and small claims courts.

Within the courts of original jurisdiction, there are rules for procedures in all matters brought before them. A civil case begins with the filing of a complaint by a plaintiff, which is then answered by a defendant. The parties may be represented by their attorneys. Discovery is the pretrial process used by the parties to find out the evidence in the case. The parties can use depositions, interrogatories, and document requests in order to uncover relevant information.

The case is managed by a judge and may be tried to a jury selected through the process of *voir dire,* with the parties permitted to challenge jurors on the basis of cause or through the use of their peremptory challenges. The trial begins following discovery and will involve opening statements and the presentation of evidence, including the direct and cross-examination of witnesses. Once a judgment is entered, the party who has won can collect the judgment through garnishment and a writ of execution.

There are alternatives to litigation for dispute resolution, and they include arbitration, mediation, reference to a third party, association tribunals, summary jury trials, rent-a-judge plans, minitrials, and the use of ombudsmen.

QUESTIONS AND CASE PROBLEMS

1. Carlton and Ricardo had a dispute over building construction costs. They submitted the matter to a summary jury trial. The jury decided that Ricardo owed Carlton $60,000. Ricardo did not pay Carlton. After 60 days, Carlton directed the sheriff to seize and sell property of Ricardo's in order to raise money to pay the debt of $60,000. Ricardo objected to this. Decide.

2. Jerry Lewinsky was called for jury duty. When *voir dire* began, Jerry realized that the case involved his supervisor at work. Can Jerry remain as a juror on the case? Why?

3. Carolyn, Elwood, and Isabella are involved in a real estate development. The development is a failure, and Carolyn, Elwood, and Isabella want to have their rights determined. They could bring a lawsuit, but they are afraid that the case is so complicated that a judge and jury not familiar with the problems of real estate development would not reach a proper result. What can they do?

4. List the steps in a lawsuit. Begin with the filing of the complaint, and explain the points at which there can be a final determination of the parties' rights in the case.

5. Distinguish between mandatory and voluntary arbitration.

6. What is the difference between mediation and arbitration?

7. John Reese has brought suit against the board of directors of Ace, Inc., a company in which he owns stock. John has information that the directors voted on issues affecting the company when they stood to benefit from positive votes. How could John find out how the directors voted and what contracts were entered into as a result? What steps in the litigation process will allow him to find out this information?

8. Esmeralda sued Adolphus. She lost the lawsuit because the judge made a wrong decision. What can Esmeralda do now? Explain her options.

9. Indicate whether the following courts are courts of original, general, limited, or appellate jurisdiction:

   small claims court
   federal bankruptcy court
   federal district court
   ✓ U.S. Supreme Court
   municipal court
   probate court
   federal court of appeals

10. The right to trial by jury is a fundamental procedure that must always be used whenever any issue of fact is to be determined. Appraise this statement.

11. Mostek Corp., a Texas corporation, made a contract to sell computer-related products to North American Foreign Trading Corp., a New York corporation.

North American used its own purchase order form, on which appeared the statement that any dispute arising out of an order shall be submitted to arbitration, as provided in the terms set forth on the back of the order. Acting on the purchase order, Mostek delivered almost all of the goods but failed to deliver the final installment. North American then demanded that the matter be arbitrated. Mostek refused to do so. Was it required to arbitrate? [Application of *Mostek Corp.,* 120 App Div 2d 383, 502 NYS2d 181]

12. The parties to a contract agreed to submit disputes to arbitration by a specified date but no later. The arbitration deadline expired, but one party sued the other to compel arbitration. Should the court order arbitration? [*Platt Pacific, Inc. v Andelson,* ____ Cal ____, 24 Cal Rptr 597, 862 P2d 158]

13. Fabricator Corp., a California company, purchased component parts from various suppliers in Europe, Asia, and the United States, which it assembled into systems for producing electricity. Fabricator entered into a contract with SLM, a German manufacturer, for the purchase of a generator for $25 million. The terms of the contract were discussed in detail by the attorneys and executive officers of Fabricator and SLM, who met in both California and Germany over a period of several months. The contract finally agreed to by them specified that any lawsuit under the contract would be brought in a German court and would be subject to German law. SLM did not deliver the generator, and Fabricator brought suit against it in New York. SLM claimed that suit could be brought only in Germany. Fabricator asserted that the requirement of suit in Germany was not binding, because it imposed an unreasonable burden on it. Decide and explain your decision.

14. What is the difference between the role of a trial court and the role of an appellate court? What functions do they perform, and how do they perform them?

15. A young man purchased heavy farm equipment on credit. The sales contract specified that any dispute that might arise under the contract would be submitted to arbitration. In order to boost the buyer's credit rating so that the sale could be made, the buyer's father wrote the seller that the father would stand behind the buyer's contract. Difficulties appeared in the machinery, a dispute between the buyer and the seller arose, and the buyer stopped making payments. The seller insisted that the buyer and his father arbitrate the dispute with the seller. Was the seller correct?

Business Ethics, Social Forces, and the Law

CHAPTER 3

OBJECTIVES

After studying this chapter, you should be able to

1. *Describe the role of ethics in business and law;*
2. *List the methods for recognizing ethical dilemmas; and*
3. *Explain the questions to address in resolving ethical dilemmas.*

Each day business people work together on contracts and projects. Their completion of the work is partially the result of the laws that protect contract rights. Much of what business people do, however, is simply a matter of their word. Executives arrive at a 9:00 A.M. meeting because they promised they would be there. An employee meets a deadline for an ad display board because she said she would. Business transactions are completed through a combination of the values of the parties and the laws that reflect those values and the importance of one's word in business. Over time, the rules that govern business, from written laws to unwritten expressions of value, have evolved to provide a framework of operation that ensures good faith in our dealings with each other.

This chapter takes you behind the rules of law to examine the objectives in establishing rules for business conduct. Both social forces and business needs contribute to the standards that govern businesses and their operations.

A. WHAT IS BUSINESS ETHICS?

Ethics is the branch of philosophy that deals with values that relate to the nature of human conduct.

Business ethics balance the goal of profits with the values of individuals and society.

Some people have said that the term *business ethics* is an oxymoron, that the word *business* and the word *ethics* contradict each other. **Ethics** is a branch of philosophy dealing with values that relate to the nature of human conduct. Conduct and values within the context of business operations become more complex because individuals are working together to maximize profit. Balancing the goal of profits with the values of individuals and society is the focus of **business ethics.** Some economists make the point that insider trading on the stock market is an efficient way to run that market. To an economist, inside information allows those with the best information to make the most money. This quantitative view ignores the issues of fairness: What about those who trade stock who do not have access to that information? Is this view fair to them? What will happen to the stock market if investors perceive there is not a level playing field? In the U.S. Supreme Court decision *United States v O'Hagan*[1] on insider trading, Justice Ginsburg noted, "Investors likely wouldn't invest in a market where trading based on misappropriated nonpublic information is unchecked." The field of business ethics seeks to balance the values of society with the need for businesses to remain profitable.

1. The Law as the Standard for Business Ethics

Moral standards are the rules for conduct dictated by law, society, or religion.

Positive law is codified laws and regulations used as the measuring standard for ethical behavior.

Moral standards come from different sources, and philosophers debate the origin of moral standards and which ones are appropriate for application. One set of moral standards is simply what codified or **positive law** requires. Business people often use the question "Is it legal?" as their moral standard for business. Codified law is used as the standard for ethical behavior. Absent illegality, all behavior is ethical under this simple standard. For example, the phrase "as is," when written conspicuously on a contract (see chapter 28 for further discussion), means, by law, that there are no warranties for the goods being sold. ◆ *For example,* If a buyer purchases a used car and the phrase "as is" is in the contract, the seller has no legal obligation, in most states, if the transmission falls apart the day after the buyer's purchase. Following a positive law standard, the seller who

---

[1] 117 S. Ct 2199 (1997).

refuses to repair the transmission has acted ethically. However, the issue of fairness still arises. There was no legal obligation to fix the transmission, but was it fair to have a useless car just the day after it was purchased?

2.   The Notion of Universal Standards for Business Ethics

In philosophy, another view of ethics holds that standards exist universally and cannot be changed or modified by law. Proponents of this **natural law** theory maintain that higher standards of behavior than those required by law must be followed even if those higher standards run contrary to the law. In the early nineteenth century when slavery was legally permissible in the United States, a positive law standard would sanction such ownership as legal. However, such deprivation of a person's rights violated the natural law principle of individual freedom and would be unethical. Accordingly, civil disobedience occurs when natural law proponents violate positive law.

Supreme Court Justice Sandra Day O'Connor, who was second in her class at Stanford Law School (Chief Justice William Rehnquist was first), was unable to secure employment as an attorney. She found a job as a receptionist for a law firm instead. At that time, no law prohibited discrimination against women, so the law firms' hiring practices, using only a positive law standard, were ethical. However, if the natural law standard of equality is applied, the refusal to hire Sandra Day O'Connor as a lawyer, a position for which she was qualified, was discriminatory conduct and unethical.

> Natural law is the set of behavioral standards developed through universally accepted principles or religious beliefs that take priority in controlling conduct; it has priority even over codified laws.

3.   The Standard of Situational Business Ethics or Moral Relativism

Situational ethics or **moral relativism** is a flexible standard of ethics that permits an examination of circumstances and motivation before attaching the label of *right* or *wrong* to conduct. The classic example of moral relativism: Would it be unethical to steal a loaf of bread to feed a starving child? More recently, the question a Florida court faced was whether to go forward with the prosecution for arson of a man who set fire to an abandoned property in his neighborhood that was used as a crack-cocaine house. In both cases, the law has been broken. The first crime is theft, and the second crime is arson. Neither person denied committing the crime. The issue in both cases is not whether the crime was committed but whether the motivation and circumstances excuse the actions and eliminate the punishment. An employee embezzles money from his employer because he is a single parent trying to make ends meet. Was his conduct unethical? The conduct is illegal, but moral relativism would consider the employee's personal circumstances in determining whether it is ethical.

Businesses use moral relativism standards frequently in their international operations. Bribery is illegal in the United States, but, as many businesses argue, it is an accepted method of doing business in other countries.[2] The standard of moral relativism is used to allow behavior in international business transactions that would be a violation of the law in the United States.

> Situational ethics are the standards and values dictated by circumstances.
>
> Moral relativism takes into account motivation and circumstances to determine whether an act was ethical. There are no universal standards, only situational standards.

---

[2] Twenty-nine countries, including the United States, Mexico, Korea, and most of the European Union nations, have signed a resolution denouncing bribery as a legally or culturally accepted practice in their countries.

4. The Business Stakeholder Standard of Behavior

Stakeholder theory requires a business to examine the impact of business behavior on all those who have an interest in the business (employees, customers, shareholders, community) before making a decision.

Shareholders are owners of a business who have contributed capital.

Businesses have different constituencies, referred to as **stakeholders**, often with conflicting goals for the business. Shareholders, for example, may share economists' view that earnings, and hence dividends, should be maximized. Members of the community where a business is located are also stakeholders in the business and have an interest in preserving jobs. The employees of the business itself are stakeholders and certainly wish to retain their jobs. A downsizing, or reduction in workforce, would offer the shareholders of the company a boost in earnings and share price. But that same reduction would impact the local economy and community in a negative way. Balancing the interests of these various stakeholders is a standard used in resolving ethical dilemmas in business. Figure 3-1 lists the areas of concern that should be examined as businesses analyze ethical dilemmas.

As Figure 3-1 indicates, stakeholder analysis requires the decision maker to view a problem from different perspectives in the light of day. Stakeholder analysis requires measurement of the impact of a decision on various groups but also requires that public disclosure of that decision be defensible. The questions help the employee who is about to leave the office for half a day without taking vacation time: Could I tell my family or my supervisor that I have done this? These questions also help a company faced with the temptation of price fixing: Could I describe before a congressional committee what I am about to do?

In other situations, a business is not facing questions of dishonesty or unfair competition. In many ethical dilemmas, a business faces the question of taking voluntary action or simply complying with the law. Some experts maintain that the shareholders' interest is paramount in resolving these conflicts among stakeholders. Others maintain that a business must assume some responsibility for social issues and their resolution. Economist Milton Friedman, a Nobel Prize winner in economics, expresses his views on resolving the conflicts among stakeholders as follows:

FIGURE 3-1
Guidelines for Analyzing a Contemplated Action

> *A corporate executive's responsibility is to make as much money for the shareholders as possible, as long as he operates within the rules of the game. When an executive decides to take action for reasons of social responsibility, he is taking money from someone else—from the stockholders, in the form of lower dividends; from the employees, in*

1. Define the problem from the decision maker's point of view.
2. Identify who could be injured by the contemplated action.
3. Define the problem from the opposing point of view.
4. Would you (as the decision maker) be willing to tell your family, your supervisor, your CEO, and the board of directors about the planned action?
5. Would you be willing to go before a community meeting, a congressional hearing, or a public forum to describe the action?
6. With full consideration of the facts and alternatives, reach a decision about whether the contemplated action should be taken.

the form of lower wages; or from the consumer, in the form of higher prices. The responsibility of the corporate executive is to fulfill the terms of his contract. If he can't do that in good conscience, then he should quit his job and find another way to do good. He has the right to promote what he regards as desirable moral objectives only with his own money.

Social responsibility is the extension of voluntary conduct, beyond legal mandates, to business.

In direct opposition to the Friedman view is the **social responsibility** view of Anita Roddick, the CEO of the Body Shop International, a personal care company founded in England with stores throughout the United States. She has stated that she does not care about earning money because the sole reason for a business to exist is to solve social problems. In between these two views are compromise positions in which businesses exist primarily to benefit the shareholders but do take opportunities to solve social problems. Many businesses today have created flex time, job sharing, and telecommuting as work options for their employees to accommodate family needs. These options are a response to larger societal issues surrounding children and their care but may also serve as a way to retain a quality workforce that is more productive without the worry of poor child-care arrangements. The law currently does not require businesses to furnish such options, but the businesses offer the programs voluntarily as a means of addressing a social issue and creating a better atmosphere for productivity.

In between the Friedman and Roddick views on business ethics and social responsibility are businesses that respond to all those who are affected by the activity of a business, or its stakeholders. Stakeholders include not just shareholders but also employees and communities who can be affected by the decisions a business makes. These businesses remain profitable but are also involved in their communities through employees' volunteer work and companies' charitable donations. In 1997, the average amount for corporate charitable giving was 1 percent of pretax income.

ETHICS & THE LAW

ETHICS AND SOCIAL RESPONSIBIITY

Ben & Jerry's Homemade, Inc., is a Vermont-based ice cream company founded by Ben Cohen and Jerry Greenfield, who began the company with the goal of social contribution. A portion of all proceeds from the sale of their ice cream is donated to charity. The company issues strong position statements on social issues. Following some slowing in market growth and reduction in profits, Cohen and Greenfield retired as officers of the company (although they remain majority shareholders and therefore in control of the board) and have since had two outside CEOs.

After Robert Holland had been Ben & Jerry's first outside CEO for a year, a Japanese supplier approached him and offered to distribute Ben & Jerry's ice cream in Japan. Holland turned down the offer because the Japanese company had no history of involvement in social issues, explaining that the only clear reason to take the opportunity was to make money. Do you agree with Holland's decision? What approach do Ben & Jerry's and Holland take with respect to their stakeholders? Is it troublesome that the company had not turned around financially when the offer was declined? Holland added that the only growth opportunities are in international markets. Is Ben & Jerry's passing up business? Is this a good or bad practice for a company? In 1997, Holland resigned as CEO of Ben & Jerry's.

B. WHY IS BUSINESS ETHICS IMPORTANT?

Regardless of a firm's views on social responsibility issues, the notions of compliance with the law and fairness in business transactions and operations are universal concerns. Values are an important part of business success. Business ethics is important for more than the simple justification that it is the right thing to do. This section covers the significance of ethics in business success.

5. The Importance of Trust

Capitalism succeeds because of trust. Investors provide capital for a business because they believe the business will use it and return it with earnings. Customers are willing to purchase products and services from businesses because they believe the businesses will honor their commitments to deliver quality and then stand behind their products or services. Businesses are willing to purchase equipment and hire employees on the assumption that investors will continue to honor their commitment to furnish the necessary funds and will not withdraw their promises or funds. Business investment, growth, and sales are a circle of trust. While courts provide remedies for breaches of agreements, no economy could grow if it were based solely on positive law and court-mandated performance. It is the reliance on promises, not the reliance on litigation, that produces good business relationships. In economics, the concept of rational expectations of investors and consumers plays a role in economic growth and performance. The assumption every investor makes is that his or her initial investment will earn a return. An assumption that employees make is, absent problems with their performance, their employment will continue. Those assumptions encourage investment by investors and spending by employees. Their assumptions demonstrate trust in the relationship and in the underlying economic system.

As economists have had the opportunity to watch nations with new forms of government enter the international markets, they have documented distinctions in growth rates. In those countries where government officials control market access through individual payments to them personally, the business climate is stalled, and growth lags behind free-market nations.

ETHICS & THE LAW

Michael Irvin, a professional football player with the Dallas Cowboys, was hired as a spokesman for Toyota dealers in the Dallas area. Irvin was given a $50,000 Toyota Landcruiser and fees for promotional activities as part of his contract. Shortly after entering into the contract, he entered a no-contest plea to drug possession charges, was given a deferred prosecution, and was sentenced to 800 hours of community service. The Toyota dealers brought suit against Irvin, seeking the return of the Landcruiser and damages of $1.4 million for the loss of sales and cost of the abandoned campaign. The dealers said that they assumed their contract was with a moral person. The dealers explained that Irvin's activities made him a questionable spokesperson and that they had assumed his personal life did not involve illegal or immoral activities. Did the dealers have trust in Irvin? Do you think that moral behavior is a condition for acting as a product's spokesperson?

6. Business Ethics and Financial Performance

Studies centering around a business's commitment to values and its financial performance suggest that those with the strongest value systems survive and do so successfully. The book *Built to Last,* by James C. Collins and Jerry I. Porras (Harper Business, 1994), an in-depth look at companies with long-term growth and profits, produced a common thread. That common thread was the companies' commitment to values. All the firms studied had focused on high standards for product quality, employee welfare, and customer service.

A study by the Lincoln Center for Applied Ethics of companies that had paid dividends for 100 years without interruption revealed the same pattern of values. Companies that had survived two world wars and a depression without missing a dividend remained committed to their customers and employees with standards of fairness and honesty.

An examination of companies involved in an ethical breach demonstrates the impact of poor value choices on financial performance. A recent study of firms that had violations of federal law, from environmental fines and penalties to labor violations, showed that for five years after their violations, these firms experienced declines in sales, earnings, and return on investment.[3] ◆ *For example,* after Salomon Brothers illegally controlled the bond market, its Wall Street rank in terms of earnings and asset base slipped dramatically. Salomon's earnings dropped $29 million in one quarter. The firm paid $122 million in fines and was required to establish a $100 million fund to compensate the victims of its bond market activity. After the scandal at Kidder, Peabody in which falsification of trades and income was uncovered, the firm had to be sold at a $600 million loss. Kidder, Peabody was eventually liquidated. ◆

Asbestos liability bankrupted Johns-Manville because documentation showed that, despite knowledge of the company's executives about the health effects of asbestos on the lungs, no action was taken to warn buyers and users of the product. Bausch & Lomb, Leslie Fay, and Phar-Mor are all financial victims of accounting improprieties carried out by company officers assisted by many employees. Often bankruptcy and large drops in the worth of a company's shares are the fates that await firms that make the types of poor ethical choices these examples have illustrated.

7. The Importance of a Good Reputation

Richard Teerlink, the former CEO of Harley-Davidson, once said, "A reputation, good or bad, is tough to shake."[4] A breach of ethics is costly to a firm not only in the financial sense of drops in earnings and possible fines. A breach of ethics often carries with it a lasting memory that impacts the business and its sales for years to come. ◆ *For example,* following Sears, Roebuck's settlement with the California Consumer Affairs Department of fraud charges involving the operation of its auto centers, Montgomery Ward Auto Centers enjoyed an increase in business. Customers were concerned about taking their cars to Sears because of the scandal surrounding the nationally reported charges of unnecessary repairs.

3 Baucus and Baucus, "Paying the Piper: An Empirical Examination of Longer-term Financial Consequences of Illegal Corporate Behavior," 40 *Academy of Management Journal* 129 (1997).
4 David K. Wright, *The Harley-Davidson Motor Co.: An Official Ninety-Year History* (Motorbook, Int'l, 1993).

Because business declined, Sears was forced to close some of its auto centers. Sears is now facing repayment of credit card payments solicited and received from customers who were already in bankruptcy. Sears' payments placed it ahead in priority, but that position was unfair to other creditors who played by the rules of bankruptcy, which require that they honor the court's stay against collection (see chapter 37 for more information on bankruptcy). ◆

When an ethical breach occurs, businesses lose that component of trust important to customers' decisions to buy and invest. ◆ *For example,* Beech-Nut, the baby food company, has an outstanding product line and offers quality at a good price. Yet it has not regained its former market share as a result of the federal charges it faced in 1986. Its apple juice tasted good, but it was a chemical concoction containing no apple juice, despite advertising claims to the contrary. Even though no one was harmed, the customers' view of Beech-Nut changed. Trust disappeared, and so did a good portion of the company's market share. A decade later the company continued to struggle to overcome that one-time breach in ethics. ◆

Recent evidence in the Dow Corning silicone implant litigation indicates that the extent of health problems resulting from the implants that was originally reported by the media may not have been accurate. Nonetheless, Dow Corning is in bankruptcy, unable to defend itself against national class-action lawsuits. Dow Corning was forced into bankruptcy just from reports of problems that later proved inaccurate. An examination of the files from Dow Corning reveals that the issue could have been avoided if Dow Corning had just included additional disclosures and warnings with its products so that patients could have made their decisions with full information. Dow Corning's initial ethical issue was one of fairness. The consequence of nondisclosure was the destruction of the business and its owners' investment.

8.   Business Ethics and Business Regulation: Public Policy, Law, and Ethics

When business behavior results in complaints from employees, investors, or customers, laws or regulations are often used to change the behavior. ◆ *For example,* the bankruptcy of Orange County and the large losses experienced by Procter & Gamble and Gibson Greetings resulting from their heavy investments in high-risk financial instruments motivated the Securities and Exchange Commission (SEC) (see chapter 48) to promulgate regulations about disclosures in financial statements on high-risk investments known as *derivatives.* ◆

The Federal Reserve stepped in to regulate virtually all aspects of credit transactions, focusing on the disclosure of the actual costs of credit to ensure full information for borrowers. Confusion among consumers about car leasing and its true costs and the fees applicable at the end of the lease terms caused the Federal Reserve to expand its credit regulation to car leases.

The tobacco industry's proposed settlement with state attorneys general will result in the elimination of billboard advertisements for cigarettes and the demise of Joe Camel and the Marlboro man. While the use of billboards and colorful characters to sell tobacco products was certainly legal, there was public concern about their impact on children and teenagers. There was a time when the companies could have made the value choice to curb the advertising. Potentially the settlement with government agencies has regulated tobacco advertising completely with a ban on all billboards.

Figure 3-2 depicts the relationship among ethics, the social forces of customers and investors, and the laws that are passed to remedy the problems raised as part of the social forces movement.

From the nutrition facts that appear on food packages to the type of pump at the gas station, government regulation of business activity is evident. Congress begins its legislative role and administrative agencies begin their process of regulation (see chapter 6) when congressional hearings and studies reveal abuses and problems within an industry or throughout business. Legislation and regulation are responses to activities of businesses that are perfectly legal but that raise questions of fairness that cause customer and investor protests.

Antidiscrimination laws were passed when evidence established that many companies had policies that required, for example, pregnant employees to stop working. Hotels at one time had policies that permitted minorities to work in kitchens and perform housekeeping tasks but did not permit them to hold "guest-contact" positions. These policies did not violate any laws at the time. However, employees justifiably raised concerns about the fairness or the ethics of such policies. Because, in large part, of the unwillingness of business to change its practices, legislation was passed to remedy employees' concerns.

Businesses that act voluntarily on the basis of value choices often avoid the costs and sometimes arbitrariness of legislation and regulation. Voluntary change by businesses is less costly and considered less intrusive. Regulation costs are substantial, and regulation is extensive.

ETHICS & THE LAW

ETHICS AND GOVERNMENT REGULATION

Rowena Fullinwider is the founder of Rowena's, Inc., which makes Rowena Fullinwider's Wonderful Almond Pound Cake and other products, such as lemon curd and carrot jam. The specialty gourmet food manufacturer specializes in high-calorie and, often, high-fat treats. When the Nutrition Labeling and Education Act requiring disclosure of food products' nutrients and contents went into effect in 1995, compliance with the new federal mandates for Rowena's 30 products cost $100,000 for the redesign of labels, the

FIGURE 3-2
The Endless Cycle of Societal Interaction

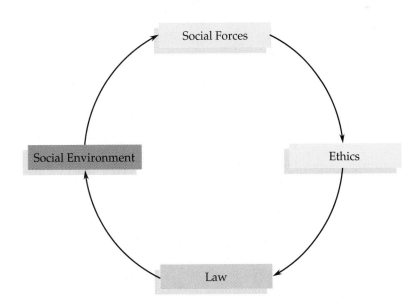

testing of the products for verification of ingredients, and printing and production.

Rowena's, like many other specialty food manufacturers, has very narrow profit margins ranging from 0.5 to 5 percent. It employs 16 people and has $1 million in annual sales. At the top end of its profit margin, Rowena's has a net profit of $50,000.

Fullinwider expresses her concerns with the labeling act as follows: "I am not going to put new products out. In the gourmet industry, we are always improving our recipes. I want to make improvements, but I can't afford to if I'm all bound up by regulations."

Why do you believe the federal food labeling act was necessary? Do you think Rowena's was guilty of deception in the sale of its products? Should food manufacturers have disclosed voluntarily the content of their products? Why would they resist? Is it possible that the label requirements will put some companies out of business? Is it desirable to have regulations that eliminate businesses?

Businesses that respond to the public's concerns and the resulting movements of the cycle gain a competitive advantage. Businesses that act irresponsibly and disregard society's views and desire for change will speed the transition from value choice to enforceable law. Businesses should watch the cycle of social forces and follow trends there to understand the values attached to certain activities and responses. These values motivate change in the form of either voluntary business activity or legislation. All values that precipitate change have one of several basic underlying goals. These underlying goals offer signals about the pattern of social change.

(a) Protection of the State. A number of laws exist today because of the underlying goal or value of protection of the state. Laws that condemn treason are examples of laws passed to preserve the government of the state. Other, less dramatic laws that offer protection to the state are the tax codes, which provide authority for collecting taxes for the operation of government facilities and enforcement agencies. The armed forces and draft registration are also examples of government programs and regulations created with protection and security of the state as the goals.

(b) Protection of the Person. A second social force is protection of the person. From the earliest times, laws were developed to protect the individual from being injured or killed. Criminal laws are devoted to protection of individuals and their property. In addition, civil suits permit private remedies for wrongful acts toward people and their property. Over time, the protection of personal rights has expanded to include the rights of privacy and the protection of individuals from defamation. Contract rights are protected from interference by others. Laws continue to evolve to protect the reputations, privacy, and mental and physical well-being of individuals.

Individual rights have been the values at the core of legislation and regulation relating to governmental assistance programs, public schools, service on a jury, and access to public facilities. The antidiscrimination laws that affect nearly all businesses are grounded in the value of protection of the individual. Labor laws and regulations exist to protect the individual rights of workers.

(c) Protection of Public Health, Safety, and Morals. The food-labeling regulations discussed earlier are an example of laws grounded in the value of protecting the safety and health of individuals. Food and restaurant inspections, mandatory inoculation, speed limits on roadways, mandatory smoke detectors and sprinkler systems in hotels, and prohibitions on the sale of alcohol to minors are all examples of laws based on the value of safety for the public. Zoning laws that prohibit the operation of adult bookstores and movie theaters near schools and churches are examples of laws based on moral values.

(d) Protection of Property: Its Use and Title. Someone who steals another's automobile is a thief and is punished by law with fines and/or imprisonment. A zoning law that prohibits the operation of a steel mill in a residential area also provides protection for property. A civil suit brought to recover royalties lost because of another's infringement of one's copyrighted materials is based on federal laws that afford protection for property rights in intangible or intellectual property (see chapter 10). Laws afford protection of title for all forms of property. The deed that is recorded in the land record is the legal mechanism for protecting the owner's title. The copyright on a software program or a song protects the creator's rights in that intellectual property. The title document issued by a department of motor vehicles affords protection of title for the owner of a car.

Those who have title to property are free to use the property in any manner they see fit. However, even ownership has restrictions imposed by law. A landowner cannot engage in activities on his property that damage another's land or interfere with another's use of land. A business may operate a factory on its real property, but if the factory creates a great deal of noise, adjoining landowners may successfully establish it a nuisance (see chapter 51) that interferes with their use and enjoyment of their land. The law provides remedies for those who are suffering because of a nuisance. Those remedies could include an injunction, or court order, limiting the hours of the factory's operation so that neighbors have the opportunity to sleep.

If that factory releases chemicals into the river flowing nearby, others' rights and use of their land are affected. Environmental laws (see chapter 51) have been passed that regulate the use of property. Those environmental laws evolved through social activism after landowners and residents located near factories and other operations with harmful emissions became concerned about the impact on the value of their properties as well as the impact on their health and safety. Environmental laws thus emerged as regulation of land use in response to concerns about legal, but harmful, emissions by companies.

(e) Protection of Personal Rights. The desire for individual freedom to practice religion and freedom from political domination gave rise to the colonization of the United States and eventually the American Revolution. The desire for freedom from economic domination resulted in the free enterprise philosophy that exists in the United States today. Individual freedoms and personal rights continue as a focus of values discussions, followed by legislation if those individual rights are violated.

Economic freedoms and the free enterprise system were in jeopardy at the end of the nineteenth century as large conglomerates began to dominate certain markets and inhibit the ability of individuals to compete. Repressive activities in the marketplace by some companies led to federal regulation in the form of antitrust laws. These laws were passed in response to social concerns about economic freedom and individual opportunities within the economy (see chapter 5).

(f) Enforcement of Individual Intent. When someone has voluntarily entered into a transaction, there is a responsibility to carry forward the promises made. Principles of honesty and honoring commitments are the ethical values at the heart of the parties' conduct in carrying out contracts. If, however, the parties do not keep their promises, the law does enforce transactions through sets of rules governing requirements for them. ◆ *For example*, if a person provides by will for the distribution of property at death, the law will generally allow the property to pass to the persons intended by the deceased owner. ◆ The law will also carry out the intentions of the parties to a business transaction.

Laws exist to honor the intent of parties because not all commitments are fulfilled voluntarily. The law may impose requirements that a transaction or an agreement be in writing to ensure that the intent of the parties is documented adequately and fulfilled (see chapter 16). The law may also place restrictions on honoring intentions. A contract to commit a murder may be evidenced by intent and fully documented in writing. However, the intent of parties will not be honored because laws provide for the protection of individuals and individuals' rights and safety.

(g) Protection from Exploitation, Fraud, and Oppression. Many laws have evolved because businesses took advantage of another group. Some groups or individuals have been given protection by the law because of excesses by businesses in dealing with them. Minors, or persons under legal age (see chapter 13), are given special protections under contract laws that permit them to disaffirm their contracts so they are not disadvantaged by excessive commitments without the benefit of the wisdom of age and with the oppressive presence of an adult party.

The federal laws on disclosure with respect to the sales of securities and shareholder relations (see chapter 48) were developed following the 1929 stock market crash, when many investors lost all they had because of the lack of candor and information by the businesses in which they were investing.

Food manufacturers have exclusive control over the canning and processing of their products. The opportunity for taking advantage of customers who do not generally have access to the factories and plants is great. The contents of canned products are not visible to consumers before they make their purchases. Because of excesses and exploitations by food processors, there is both federal and state regulation of food processing and food labeling. Adulteration or poisoning of food products carries criminal penalties. Misrepresenting the contents in food packages may constitute a federal felony.

(h) Furtherance of Trade. Some laws are the result of social forces seeking to simplify business and trade. Installment sales and credit transactions, and their accompanying laws and regulations, have made additional capital available for businesses and provided consumers with alternatives to cash purchases. The laws on checks, drafts, and notes have created instruments used to facilitate trade. The Federal Reserve System's Board of Governors and its oversight of federal banks and interest rates have minimized the harmful effects of alternating economic periods of depression and inflation.

(i) Protection of Creditors and Rehabilitation of Debtors. Society seeks to protect the rights of creditors and to protect them from dishonest or fraudulent acts of debtors. Initially creditors are protected by the laws that make contracts binding and enforceable. Creditors are also protected by statutes that make it a fraud for a debtor to conceal property from a creditor. To meet the social demands for facilitation of trade, credit transactions were authorized. But with that authorization came the demand for the creditor's assurance of repayment by the debtor. Mortgages, security interests, and surety relationships (see chapters 35, 36, and 50) are mechanisms created by law to provide creditors with mechanisms for collecting their obligations.

When collection techniques became excessive and exploitative, new laws on debtors' rights were enacted. Debtors' prisons were abolished. Disclosure requirements for credit contracts were mandated by Congress. Collection techniques were limited through the Fair Debt Collections Practices Act (see chapter 30). The remedy of bankruptcy was afforded debtors under federal law to provide them with an opportunity to begin a new economic life when their existing debts reached an excessive level and could no longer be paid in a timely fashion (see chapter 37).

(j) Stability and Flexibility. Stability is particularly important in business transactions. When you buy a house, for example, you not only want to know the exact meaning of the transaction under today's law but also want the transaction to have the same meaning in the future.

Because of the desire for stability, courts will ordinarily follow former decisions unless there is a strong reason to depart from them. Similarly, when no former case bears on the point involved, a court will try to reach a decision that is a logical extension of some former decision or that follows a former decision by analogy, rather than striking out on a new path to reach a decision unrelated to the past.

If stability were always required, however, the cause of justice would often be defeated. The reason that originally existed for a rule of law may have ceased to exist. Also, a rule may later appear unjust because it reflects a concept of justice that is outmoded or obsolete. The policies surrounding adoption of children and the rights of natural versus adoptive parents have continued to evolve because of changing attitudes about the relationships of the parties and new technology that permits laboratory creation and insemination.

The typical modern statute, particularly in the area of business regulation, often contains an escape clause, by which a person can "escape" from the operation of the statute under certain circumstances. *For example*, a rent control law may impose a rent ceiling, that is, a maximum rent a landlord can charge a tenant. The same law may also authorize a greater charge when special circumstances make it just to allow such an exception. For example, the landlord may have made expensive repairs to the property, or the taxes on the property may have increased substantially.

Protection of the person is frequently the controlling factor in determining whether a court should adhere to the common law, thereby furthering stability, or whether it should change the law, thereby furthering flexibility.

In the following case, the court was faced with a question of whether it should extend protection under product liability to bystanders.

The Case of the Innocent and Injured Suzuki Bystander

Facts: James M. McCoy saw a Suzuki Samurai swerve across the freeway and roll after hitting a patch of black ice. At the time of the accident, questions had been raised about the safety of the Suzuki Samurai, especially whether its design and high profile made it prone to rollovers. Mr. McCoy stopped to help the occupants of the Samurai. Mr. McCoy then helped a Washington state trooper by placing flares along the highway. Mr. McCoy was then injured by a hit-and-run vehicle while returning to his car some two hours later. Mr. McCoy and his wife, Donna, sued the driver and passenger of the Samurai and also sued American Suzuki Motor Corporation and its parent company, Suzuki Motor Company, Ltd., for product liability. Suzuki moved for summary judgment on the ground that being struck by a hit-and-run driver was too remote a circumstance and not a foreseeable consequence of a defective design in the Suzuki Samurai.

Decision: Suzuki is not entitled to a summary judgment because there are issues of fact as to whether the design defect and resulting product liability for the Samurai were the cause of Mr. McCoy's injuries. Danger invites rescue, and if a manufacturer has created a product that results in accidents, then it is foreseeable that others will come to help and might be injured in the process. Whether being hit by another driver was caused by Suzuki's defective product is a question a jury should decide. However, the possibility of third parties recovering for product liability when the product itself is not the cause of the injury is not eliminated. Resulting injuries from defective products may be recovered once a jury finds a causal connection. [*McCoy v American Suzuki Motor Corp.* (Wash App) 936 P2d 31 (1997)]

The law works to bring resolution in situations where values conflict. In the *McCoy* case, the product manufacturer's position was one based on the notion of liability for injury from the product itself. A pedestrian injured because a defect in a car causes its driver to lose control and strike him would be protected. But extending the liability of the manufacturer to those rendering assistance was a new step for the law and an expansion of product liability. Traditionally the view of courts was that policy considerations required careful limitations on liability for consequences. In the two-to-one decision in the McCoy case, the judges struggled with previous standards and Mr. McCoy's misfortune. With these conflicting values, the court molded and applied the law to balance those conflicting interests.

C. HOW TO RECOGNIZE AND RESOLVE ETHICAL DILEMMAS

Business managers find themselves in circumstances in which they are unclear about right and wrong and are confused about how to resolve the dilemmas they face. A recent survey showed that 98 percent of all Fortune 500 companies have codes of ethics designed to help their employees recognize and resolve ethical dilemmas. Nearly 60 percent of those firms provide their employees with some form of training in ethics. These codes of ethics provide employees with categories of behavior that constitute ethical breaches. Regardless of the industry, the type of business, or the size of the company, certain universal categories can help managers recognize ethical dilemmas. Figure 3-3 provides a list of those categories.

FIGURE 3-3
Categories of
Ethical Behavior

1. Integrity and truthfulness
2. Promise-keeping
3. Loyalty—avoiding conflicts of interest
4. Fairness
5. Doing no harm
6. Maintaining confidentiality

9. Categories of Ethical Behavior

(a) Integrity and Truthfulness. Mark Twain once wrote, "Always tell the truth. That way you don't have to remember anything." As discussed earlier, trust is a key component of business relationships and of the free enterprise system. Trust begins with the belief that honesty is at the heart of relationships. Many contract remedies in law are based on the failure of the parties to be truthful with each other. If you purchase a home that has been certified as termite-free and you then discover termites in the home shortly after you move in, someone has not been truthful. If you discover there were two termite inspections conducted and the first one, which revealed there were termites, was concealed from you, then your trust in sellers and exterminators is diminished. An assurance that a seller has the expertise to handle your project is important in building that relationship. If you discover later that the seller lacks the expertise, you will be harmed by the delay and possible poor work that has been done.

When the prospectus for a stock offering fails to provide full information about the company's obsolete inventory, investors are not given the full truth and are harmed when they invest without complete disclosure. Investors become skeptical when offerings do not carry with them a very basic level of honesty in their disclosures. Honesty is necessary for the wheels of commerce to turn.

Integrity is keeping one's values and principles despite the costs and consequences. ◆ *For example,* an executive contracted with a variety of companies to sell his hard-to-find computer components. When he was approached by one of his largest customers to break a contract with a small customer, the executive refused. The customer assured the executive it would be his last order with the company if he did not get more components. Despite facing the threat of losing a multimillion-dollar customer, the executive fulfilled his promises to the small purchasers. The executive kept his word on all of his contracts and demonstrated integrity. ◆

ETHICS & THE LAW

ETHICS AND LYING TO GET AHEAD
A study by an executive search firm revealed that 20 percent of all the resumes they review contain inaccurate information about the individual's educational background or past employment. The types of inaccuracies include listing attendance at a university as having received a degree and misrepresenting responsibilities at previous jobs (as when a sales manager refers to himself as "director of marketing" on his resume).

Another study by Dartmouth University concluded, based on surveys conducted of students, that 75 percent of all students in MBA programs lied or cheated to get into their graduate programs. Examples of their listed misconduct included cheating in undergraduate school, falsifying letters of reference, and having someone else take the GMAT for them.

A recent study by ethics officers revealed that 48 percent of all employees have engaged in unethical conduct, with the most frequent breach being sacrificing quality in the products sold to their customers and the second most frequent breach being covering up a mistake.

Why do people lie about their backgrounds and qualifications? Is anyone really hurt by this individual misconduct? Why is it important that the information on resumes and applications for graduate school be accurate? Why must employees be honest with customers and about their work?

(b) Promise-keeping. If we examine the types of things we do in a day, most are based on promises. We promise to deliver goods either with or without a contract. We promise to pay the dentist for our dental work. We promise to provide someone with a ride. Keeping those promises, regardless of whether there is a legal obligation, is a key component of an ethical person and an ethical business. Keeping promises is also evidence of integrity.

The issue of employee downsizing is debated, with the underlying question being whether the "downsized" employees had a promise from their company of continued employment. As stakeholder analysis is reviewed, the ethical issue surrounding the question is whether there are promises to others who are at risk. Weren't shareholders promised a return on their investment? Weren't suppliers promised payment? In many circumstances, the question is not whether a promise will be kept but rather which promise will be kept. The strategic issue is whether businesses should make commitments and promises in circumstances that create a very thin margin of profit and perhaps an even thinner margin for error. Over the long term, the importance of keeping its promises to all stakeholders translates into the reputation of the business.

ETHICS & THE LAW

ETHICS AND DOWNSIZING

Aaron Feuerstein is the owner of Malden Mills, a textile plant in Methuen, Massachusetts. The company was founded by Feuerstein's grandfather in 1906 as a swimsuit and sweater manufacturer. Feuerstein changed the direction of traditional garment manufacturing when he switched the factory to Polartec production. Polartec, a revolutionary fabric made from recycled plastic bottles, is used in skiing and hiking clothing because of its unique qualities of being very warm, very lightweight, and easy to dry and dye. L.L. Bean, Patagonia, and Eddie Bauer are all on Malden Mills' customer list, which has generated $425 million in sales each year.

On December 11, 1995, the Malden Mills factory was nearly completely destroyed by a fire started by a boiler that exploded. Feuerstein held a meeting with his employees several days later and guaranteed their pay for 30 days and their health benefits for 90 days. Malden Mills has 3,000 employees and an annual payroll of $65 million.

Feuerstein gave all of his employees three months of pay and had all but 20 percent working full-time again by March 1996. By midsummer 1996, Malden Mills was back at full production. One employee said, "Another person would have taken the insurance money and walked away. I might have done that."

Feuerstein describes his role as follows: "The fundamental difference is that I consider our workers an asset, not an expense. I have a responsibility to the worker, both blue-collar and white-collar. I have an equal responsibility to the community. It would have been unconscionable to put 3,000 people on the streets and deliver a death blow to the cities of Lawrence and Methuen. Maybe on paper our company is worth less to Wall Street, but I can tell you it's worth more. We're doing fine."[5]

Was it right for Feuerstein to keep his promise to employees? Did he really have a promise to keep? Does it matter that Malden Mills is not a publicly held company?

(c) Loyalty—Avoiding Conflicts of Interest. An employee who works for a company owes his or her allegiance to that company. Conduct that compromises that loyalty is a conflict of interest. For example, suppose that your sister operates her own catering business. Your company is seeking a caterer for its monthly management meetings. You are responsible for these meetings and could hire your sister to handle the lunches furnished at the meetings. Your sister would have a substantial contract, and your problems with meal logistics would be solved. Nearly all companies have a provision in their codes of ethics covering this situation. An employee cannot hire a relative, friend, or even his own company without special permission because it is a conflict of interest. Your loyalty to your sister conflicts with the loyalty to your employer, which requires you to make the best decision at the best price.

A conflict of interest arises when a purchasing agent accepts gifts from suppliers, vendors, or manufacturers' representatives. The purchasing agent has introduced into the buy/sell relationship an element of quid pro quo, or the supplier's expectation that the gift will enjoy a return from the agent in the form of a contract. Some companies have a zero tolerance for conflicts, with a complete prohibition on any gifts from suppliers and manufacturers. ◆ *For example*, Wal-Mart buyers are not permitted to accept even a cup of coffee from potential merchandise suppliers. Amgen's purchasing staff can accept invitations to meals only if Amgen pays for the meal. ◆

ETHICS & THE LAW

ETHICS AND CONFLICTS OF INTEREST

ABC news correspondent and *20/20* anchorwoman Barbara Walters did a profile piece for *20/20* on composer Andrew Lloyd Webber. After the piece, which was very flattering to Webber, ran on network television, a *New York Daily News* article revealed that Walters had invested $100,000 in Webber's Broadway production of *Sunset Boulevard*. Further, ABC's parent company, Walt Disney Co., produced Webber's *Evita* and has an interest

---

[5] Steve Wulf, "The Glow from a Fire," *Time*, p. 49 (Jan. 8, 1996).

in a number of Webber's other musicals. Disney's relationship with Webber was disclosed in the piece, but Walters's investment was not. Should the information about Walters's investment have been disclosed? Should she have done the story on Webber?

(d) Fairness. In business transactions in which the buyer was not told about the crack in the engine block or the dry well on the property, a typical response is "That's not fair. I wouldn't have bought it if I'd known." A question often posed to the buyer in response is "Wouldn't you have done the same thing?" It feels different when we are the victims of unfairness than when we hold the superior knowledge in the transaction. The ethical standard of fairness requires both sides to ask these questions: "How would I want to be treated? Would this information make a difference to me?" Imposing our own standards and expectations on our own behavior in business transactions produces fairness in business.

ETHICS & THE LAW

ETHICS AND FAIRNESS

Dateline NBC, a TV news-magazine program that airs several nights a week, presented a segment on General Motors (GM) and the safety of GM's trucks with side-saddle gas tanks. *Dateline* producers staged and taped an accident with a GM truck that showed a gas tank explosion and subsequent fire that engulfed the pickup truck. The tape was shown on *Dateline.* Through disclosures of several crew members, it was later revealed that explosive devices had been used to create the scene for the cameras. The use of those devices was not disclosed during the *Dateline* piece. Was it fair to use the explosive devices? Was it fair to use the explosive devices and not disclose that to the audience? Was it fair to GM?

NOTE: *Dateline* later read an on-air apology for the tape.

(e) Doing No Harm. Imagine selling a product that your company's internal research shows presents significant health dangers to its users. Selling the product without disclosure of the information is unfair. But there is the additional ethical breach of physical harm to your customers and users. *For example,* Ford designed and sold its Pinto with a fundamental flaw in the placement of the car's gas tank. Rear-end collisions in which a Pinto was involved resulted, even at very low speeds, in fires that engulfed the car so quickly that occupants could not always escape from it. An internal memo from engineers at Ford revealed that an analysis of the risk of the tanks versus the cost of redesign was considered and put in memo form, but the changes in design were never made so that the risk of injury would be reduced. Peter Drucker's advice on ethics for businesses is *primum non nocere,* or above all do no harm.

(f) Maintain Confidentiality. Often the success of a business depends on information or technology that it holds. If the competitive edge that comes from the business's peculiar niche or knowledge is lost through disclosure, so also are profits. Not only do employees owe a duty of loyalty to their employers but also they owe an obligation of confidentiality. Information that employees obtain through their employer's work or research should not be used by the employees either personally or through a competitor. Providing customer lists or leads is a breach of that confidentiality.

ETHICS & THE LAW

ETHICS AND COMPETITION

In a long-running case that involves international competition, General Motors and Volkswagen AG have battled in court and in newspapers over the departure of several GM employees for Volkswagen and their alleged taking of GM proprietary information. The information GM alleges was taken related to GM's future plans as well as its unique supply chain management plans for its European operations. This case resulted in the passage of the Economic Espionage Act (EEA) in the United States. The EEA is a federal law that makes it a felony to copy, download, transmit, or in any other way communicate trade secrets of a company to another. While the Volkswagen/GM battle continues, employers remain concerned about employees departing and taking trade secrets with them. Why is it a problem for employees to take what is in their minds with them to a new job? What risks do you see in hiring someone who has offered to bring you proprietary information?

In addition to an ethical obligation to employers about proprietary information, managers have responsibilities regarding their employees' privacy. Performance evaluations of individual employees are private and should never be disclosed or revealed even in one-on-one conversations outside the lines of authority and the workplace.

10. Resolving Ethical Dilemmas

Recognizing an ethical dilemma is perhaps the easiest part of business ethics. Resolution of that dilemma is more difficult. The earlier section on stakeholders offers one model for resolution of ethical dilemmas (see Figure 3-1). Other models have been developed to provide managers with methods of analysis for resolving dilemmas in a timely fashion.

(a) Blanchard and Peale Three-Part Test. Dr. Kenneth Blanchard, author of *The One-Minute Manager,* and the late Dr. Norman Vincent Peale, author of *The Power of Positive Thinking,* developed a model for evaluating ethical breaches that is widely used among Fortune 500 companies. The following three questions should be asked: Is it legal? Is it balanced? How does it make me feel?

In answering the questions on legality, a manager should look to positive law both within and outside the company. If the proposed conduct would be a violation of antitrust laws, then the manager's analysis can stop there. If the proposed conduct would violate company policy, then the manager's analysis can stop. In the field of business ethics, there is little room for civil disobedience. Compliance with the law is a critical component of a successful ethics policy in any company.

The question on balance forces the manager to examine the ethical value of fairness. Perhaps the decision to downsize must be made, but couldn't the company offer the employees a severance package and outplacement assistance to ease the transition? *For example,* Levi Strauss announced a downsizing that would eliminate 6,395 employees, but the employees would be paid for eight months and would be given three weeks additional pay for every year they had been with the company. Levi Strauss would spend a total of $200 million or an average of $31,274 as a compensation package on each employee who is downsized. Another aspect of balance forces an employee to examine his conduct from his perspective and perhaps ask how he would feel if someone treated him in the same fashion as he treats others?

The final question of the Blanchard/Peale model is conscience based. While some managers may employ any tactics to maximize profits, this final question forces a manager to examine the physical impact of a decision: Does it cause sleeplessness or appetite changes? Personalizing business choices often helps managers to see the potential harm that comes from poor ethical choices.

(b) The Front-Page-of-the-Newspaper Test. This simple, but effective, model for ethical evaluation helps a manager to visualize the public disclosure of proposed conduct. When he took over Salomon Brothers after its bond-trading controversy, Warren Buffet described the newspaper test as follows:

> *Contemplating any business act, an employee should ask himself whether he would be willing to see it immediately described by an informed and critical reporter on the front page of his local paper, there to be read by his spouse, children, and friends. At Salomon, we simply want no part of any activities that pass legal tests but that we, as citizens, would find offensive.*[6]

ETHICS & THE LAW — ETHICS AND THE GLARE OF PUBLIC DISCLOSURE

Edwin Garrity, the assistant fire chief, retired from the Phoenix Fire Department after an internal audit revealed he had issued holiday pay for employees who had actually never worked. The audit also revealed that Garrity and his family owned a company that sold T-shirts and other fire department souvenirs.

What categories of ethical breaches occurred here? Could any of the ethical models have helped Garrity avoid the pitfalls that forced his retirement?

(c) Laura Nash Model. In her work, business ethicist Laura Nash has developed a series of questions to help business people reach the right decision in ethical dilemmas. Grouped together, her questions are: Have you defined the problem accurately? How would you define the problem if you stood on the other side of the fence? How did this situation occur in the first place? What is your intention in making this decision? How does the intention compare with the probable results? Whom could your decision or action injure? Can you discuss your decision with the affected parties? Are you confident that your position will be as valid over a long period of time as it seems now? Could you discuss your decision with your supervisor, co-workers, officers, board, friends, and family?

The Nash model requires an examination of the dilemma from all perspectives. Defining the problem and how the problem arose provides the business with assistance in avoiding the dilemma again. For example, suppose that a supervisor is asked to provide a reference for a friend who works for her. The supervisor is hes-

[6] Janet Lowe, *Warren Buffett Speaks: Wit and Wisdom from the World's Greatest Investor* (Wiley, 1997).

itant because the friend has not been a very good employee. The ethical dilemma the manager believes she faces is whether to lie or tell the truth about the employee. The real ethical dilemma is why the supervisor never provided evaluation or feedback indicating the friend's poor performance. Avoiding the problem in the future is possible through candid evaluations. Resolving the problem requires that the supervisor talk to her friend now about the issue of performance and the problem with serving as a reference.

One final aspect of the Nash model that business people find helpful is the question that asks for a perspective on an issue from family and friends. The problem of group think in business situations is very real. As business people sit together in a room and discuss an ethical dilemma, they can persuade each other to think the same way. The power of consensus overwhelms each person's concerns and values. There is a certain fear in bringing up a different point of view in a business meeting. Proper perspective is often lost as the discussion centers around numbers, but bringing in views of an outsider is often helpful. For example, when McNeil, the manufacturer of Tylenol, was faced with the cyanide poisonings in the Chicago area, the decision about existing inventory had to be made. It was clear to both insiders and outsiders that the poisonings had not occurred at McNeil but, rather, after delivery to the stores. Despite the huge numbers involved in the recall and destruction of inventory, the McNeil managers made the decision easily because they viewed the risk to their own families, that is, from the outside. From this standpoint, it became a question of life and not a question of numbers.

ETHICS & THE LAW

ETHICS WHEN NO ONE KNOWS

While making a sales call using a company car, you hit another vehicle in a customer's parking lot. You are positive no one has seen you. You cannot locate the owner of the vehicle. Would you leave a note with full information and ask the owner to contact you? Use all of the models discussed to reach a decision.

SUMMARY

Business ethics is the application of values and standards to business conduct and decisions. These values originate in various sources from positive (codified) law to natural law to stakeholder values. Business ethics is important because trust is a critical component of good business relationships and free enterprise. A business with values will enjoy the additional competitive advantage of a good reputation and, over the long term, better earnings. When businesses make decisions that violate basic ethical standards, social forces are set into motion, and the area of abuse is regulated, with resulting additional costs and restrictions for business. Voluntary value choices by busi-

nesses position them for a competitive advantage.

The categories of ethical values in business are truthfulness and integrity, promise-keeping, loyalty and avoiding conflicts of interest, fairness, doing no harm, and maintaining confidentiality.

Resolution of ethical dilemmas is possible through the use of various models that require a businessperson to examine the impact of a decision before it is made. The models include stakeholder analysis, Blanchard/Peale, the front-page-of-the-newspaper test, and the Laura Nash model.

QUESTIONS AND CASE PROBLEMS

1. What is the relationship between ethics and law? How does one affect the other? How do social forces connect the two?

2. Ann Elkin, who works for Brill Co., has been sent out to conduct two customer evaluations, which went much more quickly than Ann anticipated. Her supervisor does not expect Ann back until after lunch. It is now 10:30 A.M., and Ann would like to run some personal errands and then go to lunch before returning to work at 1:00 P.M. Should Ann take the time? Would you? Why or why not? Be sure to consider the categories of ethical values and apply one or two models before reaching your conclusion.

3. Fred Sanguine is a New York City produce broker. Ned Santini is a 19-year-old college student who works for Sanguine from 4:00 A.M. until 7:00 A.M. each weekday before he attends classes at Pace University. Fred has instructed Ned on the proper packing of produce as follows: "Look, put the bad and small cherries at the bottom. Do the same with the strawberries and blueberries. Put the best fruit on top and hide the bad stuff at the bottom. This way I get top dollar on all that I sell." Ned is uncomfortable about the instructions but as he explains to his roommate, "It's not me doing it. I'm just following orders. Besides, I need the job." Should Ned just follow instructions? Is the manner in which the fruit is packed unethical? Would you do it? Why or why not? Is anyone really harmed by the practice?

4. Alan Gellen is the facilities manager for the city of Milwaukee and makes all final decisions on purchasing items such as chairs and lights as well as other supplies and materials. Alan also makes the final decisions for the award of contracts to food vendors at event sites. Grand Beef Franks has submitted a bid to be one of the city's vendors. Alan went to school with Grand Beef's owner, Steve Grand, who phones Alan and explains that Grand Beef owns a condominium in Maui that Alan could use. "All it would cost you for a vacation is your airfare. The condo is fully stocked with food. Just let me know," was Steve's offer to Alan. Should Alan take the offer? Would you? Be sure to determine which category of ethical values this situation involves and apply several models as you resolve the question of whether Alan should accept the invitation.

5. Anna Bowen, who works in corporate relations for Deli Corp., was hired in 1994 shortly after her graduation from college. Anna has noticed that several of the people in her department are rarely in the office. Corporate relations necessarily involves a great deal of time outside the office, and Anna has never mentioned the problem to the vice president who supervises the area. One afternoon, as Anna was answering the phone, the spouse of a co-worker called in and asked to talk with him. Anna responded, "Well, he's not here right now. Could I take a message?" Anna was puzzled because the co-worker had called in sick early that morning. Anna then wondered why she had lied to the spouse. Then she worried about whether she should tell the vice president. Would you say anything? Would you have covered for the co-worker with his spouse? Is it best for Anna to just do her job and ignore the habits of her co-workers? Are there ethical violations here? On whose part?

6. Adam Smith wrote the following in *The Theory of Moral Sentiments:*

   > In the practice of the other virtues, our conduct should rather be directed by a certain idea of propriety, by a certain taste for a particular tenor of conduct, than by any regard to a precise maxim or rule; and we should consider the end and foundation of the rule, more than the rule itself.[7]

   Do you think Adam Smith adhered to positive law as his ethical standard? Is he a moral relativist? Does his quote match stakeholder analysis? What would the ethical posture be on violating the law?

7. If you were asked by your new employer to reveal your salary at your previous job, would you include your bonus as part of your salary and not reveal the bonus? Why or why not?

8. Marv Albert, the longtime NBC sportscaster famous for his "Yes!" commentary, was charged with violations of several Virginia statutes, including criminal assault, battery, and sodomy, for his alleged conduct with a woman in a hotel room. Initially Mr. Albert went to trial on the case and denied that the charges were true. During the trial, another woman testified that Mr. Albert had engaged in similar behavior with her. Following plea negotiations, Mr. Albert entered a guilty plea the next day. He was then fired by NBC under a provision in his contract that prohibited

---

[7] Adam Smith, *The Theory of Moral Sentiments* (Arlington House, 1969; Originally published in 1769).

employees from making false statements. Mr. Albert had assured his superiors at NBC that the charges were baseless. Do you agree with NBC's decision to fire Mr. Albert? Is his personal behavior relevant for his job performance? Do you agree that lying to your employer should result in automatic termination? How do you compare Michael Irvin's conduct with Mr. Albert's?

9. In 1997, the Federal Trade Commission (FTC) issued a "cease and desist" order against Toys "R" Us. The order requires Toys "R" Us to stop what the FTC calls its "blacklisting" practices. The FTC ruled that Toys "R" Us had forced the large toy manufacturers, such as Mattel and Hasbro, to withhold their products from the discount warehouse stores such as Sam's Club and Costco. Toys "R" Us allegedly threatened not to carry these companies' products if they were also sold at the discount warehouse chains. Mattel's Barbie doll is one example of a toy Toys "R" Us carried that the discount warehouses were not permitted to carry. Costco's CEO, James Sinegal, said, "You could fill Madison Square Garden with the people who don't want to sell to us." Are these types of sales agreements ethical? Is it fair for Toys "R" Us to insist on these arrangements? What do you think these arrangements do to price?

10. The president and athletic director at UCLA fired the school's basketball coach because an expense form he had submitted for reimbursement had the names of two students he said had joined him for a recruiting dinner. The students had not been to the dinner. The coach was stunned because he had been there eight years and had established a winning program. He said, "And to throw it all away on a meal?" Do you agree with the coach's assessment? Was it too harsh to fire him for one inaccurate expense form? Did the coach commit an ethical breach?

The Constitution as the Foundation of the Legal Environment

CHAPTER 4

OBJECTIVES

After studying this chapter, you should be able to

1. *Describe the governmental system created by the U.S. Constitution;*
2. *List the branches and levels of government and describe their relationship to each other;*
3. *Explain how the U.S. Constitution adapts to change;*
4. *List and describe three significant federal powers; and*
5. *List and describe two significant constitutional limitations on governmental power.*

This chapter introduces you to the powers of government and to the protection that you have for your rights. The Constitution of the United States sets forth not only the structure and powers of government but also the limitations on those powers. This Constitution, together with the constitutions of each of the states, forms the foundation of our legal environment.

A. THE FEDERAL SYSTEM

Our government is a federal system.

By establishing a central government to coexist with the governments of the individual states, the U.S. Constitution created a federal system. In a **federal system** a central government is given power to administer to national concerns, while the individual states retain the power to administer to local concerns.

1. What a Constitution Is

A constitution sets the structure of government and the relation of people to it.

The term *constitution* refers to either the structure of the government and its relation to the people within its sphere of power or the written document setting forth that structure. When capitalized, the word refers to the written document that specifies the structure and powers of the U.S. national government and its relation to the people within the territory of the United States.

In speaking of the Constitution, it is often necessary to distinguish between the written Constitution and the living Constitution. This is required because the Constitution has grown and changed, as described in section 7 of this chapter.

2. The Branches of Government

American governments are tripartite.

The written Constitution establishes a **tripartite** (three-part) government: a **legislative branch** (Congress) to make the laws, an **executive branch** (the president) to execute the laws, and a **judicial branch** (courts) to interpret the laws. The national legislature or Congress is a **bicameral** (two-house) body consisting of a Senate and a House of Representatives. Members of the Senate are popularly elected for a term of six years. Members of the House of Representatives are popularly elected for a term of two years. The president is elected by an electoral college whose membership is popularly elected. The president serves for a term of four years and is eligible for reelection for a second term. Judges of the United States are appointed by the president with the approval of the Senate and serve for life, subject to removal only by impeachment because of misconduct.

B. THE STATES AND THE CONSTITUTION

The effect of the adoption of the Constitution was to take certain powers away from the states and give them to the national government.

3. Delegated and Shared Powers

The national government possesses only the powers given by the states. These powers are set forth in the U.S. Constitution.

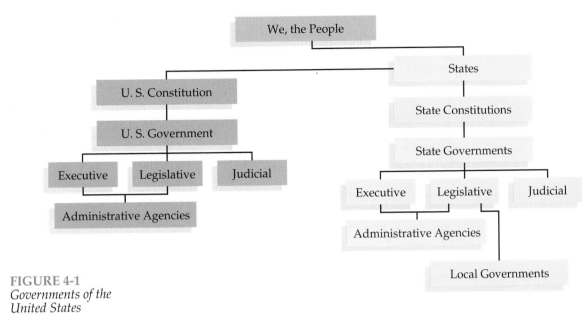

FIGURE 4-1
Governments of the United States

(a) Delegated Powers. The powers given by the states to the national government are described as **delegated powers**. Some of these delegated powers are given exclusively to the national government. Thus, the national government alone may declare war or establish a currency.

(b) Shared Powers. Some of the powers delegated to the national government may still be exercised by the states. ◆ *For example,* the grant of power to the national government to impose taxes did not destroy the state power to tax. Some of the shared powers may be exercised by the states only as long as there is no federal exercise. Thus, a state appliance safety law may apply until a federal law on the subject is adopted by Congress. In other cases a state may provide regulation along with, but subject to the supremacy of, federal law. Regulation of navigation on navigable waterways within a state is an example. ◆

ETHICS & THE LAW

American Airlines provides frequent flyer benefits through its AAdvantage program. Members of AAdvantage receive points each time they fly American, and when they reach certain point levels, they can use these points to upgrade coach tickets to first class or, with enough points, obtain free flights.

In 1988 American placed qualifications on AAdvantage members' benefits—it limited the number of seats per flight that could be used on free flights and "blacked out" dates so that the AAdvantage free flight benefits could not be used.

Several AAdvantage club members objected because their materials for membership did not say American could change the terms of the program. Several members in Illinois filed suit against American, alleging that the changes and cutbacks violated the Illinois Consumer Fraud and Deceptive Business Practices Act.

American Airlines defended the suit on the ground that the federal government has exclusive jurisdiction over airlines. The Airline Deregulation Act includes the following clause: "No State . . . shall enact or enforce any law, rule, regulation, standard, or other provision having the force and effect of law relating to rates, routes, or services of an air carrier. . . . "

Do you think the Illinois law is preempted by the federal government's exclusive jurisdiction? Do you think it was fair or honest of American Airlines to change the AAdvantage program's terms? What would you recommend American Airlines put in its AAdvantage membership materials to prevent this problem in the future?

States have a welfare or police power.

(c) State Police Power. The states possess the power to adopt laws to protect the general welfare, health, safety, and morals of the people. This is called the **police power.** Thus, a state may require that an out-of-state business make a security deposit with a state official in order to protect persons dealing with the business from loss. The exercise of the police power is subject to the limitation that it may not unreasonably interfere with federal powers.

Some powers are prohibited to all governments.

(d) Prohibited Powers. The Constitution prohibits states from doing certain acts even though the federal government is similarly prohibited. Thus, neither states nor the national government may adopt **ex post facto** laws. Ex post facto laws make criminal an act already committed that was not criminal when committed. Laws that increase the penalty for an act already committed above the penalty in force at the time the act was committed are also ex post facto laws.

4. Federal Supremacy

Federal law will bar conflicting state action when there is a federal law regulating the particular subject. Federal law will also bar state action when the silence of Congress is seen as showing the congressional intent that there should be no regulation by anyone.

CASE SUMMARY

Who's the Boss?

Facts: The parents of Charles McSorley, Jr., an infant, sued Philip Morris, Inc., on his behalf for the serious birth defects (blindness, deafness, and mental retardation) they claim he suffered as the result of his mother's smoking cigarettes made by that company. They claimed that the company was liable because it did not give the consumer adequate warning of health dangers. The company proved that its packages carried the warning required by the Federal Cigarette Labeling and Advertising Act. The parents claimed that state law required a fuller warning.

Decision: There was a conflict between the state and federal requirements, and therefore the federal supremacy concept displaced the state law. The warning given by the corporation satisfied the federal law. Therefore, liability could not be based on the theory that the warning was not adequate. [*McSorley v Philip Morris, Inc.*, 170 App Div 2d 440, 565 NYS2d 537 (1991)]

(a) **Express Federal Regulation.** The Constitution and statutes properly adopted by Congress are the supreme law of the land. They cancel out any conflicting state law.

> A valid federal law overrides a state statute.

This **federal supremacy** is expressly declared by the Constitution.[1] When there is a direct conflict between federal and state statutes, the decision as to which prevails is thus easy to make.

In some cases there is no obvious conflict because the federal statute covers only part of the subject matter. In such cases the question arises whether a state law can regulate the areas not regulated by Congress or whether the partial regulation made by Congress preempts, or takes over, the field so as to prohibit state legislation.

> The silence of Congress may bar state action.

(b) **Silence of Congress.** In some situations the silence of Congress in failing to cover a particular phase of a subject, or in failing to have any law on the subject at all, is held to indicate that Congress does not want any law on the matter. Therefore, no state law will be allowed to regulate the matter. When national uniformity is essential, it is generally held that the silence of Congress means that the subject has been preempted by Congress and that no state law on the subject may be adopted.

(c) **Effect of Federal Deregulation.** The fact that the federal government removes the regulations from a regulated industry does not automatically give the states the power to regulate that industry. If under the silence-of-Congress doctrine the states cannot regulate, they are still barred from regulating after deregulation. That is, deregulation is not to be considered as authorization to the states to regulate.[2]

(d) **Silence of Administrative Agency.** In contrast with the silence of Congress, the fact that a federal agency does not regulate a particular matter does not automatically preempt the field. That is, the failure of the federal agency to act is not a declaration of "hands off."[3]

C.   INTERPRETING AND AMENDING THE CONSTITUTION

The Constitution as it is interpreted today has changed greatly from the Constitution as originally written. The change has been brought about by interpretation, amendment, and practice.

5. Conflicting Theories

> Bedrock and living document are rival views on interpreting the Constitution.

Shortly after the Constitution was adopted, conflict arose over whether the Constitution was to be interpreted strictly, so as to give the federal government the least power possible, or broadly, so as to give the federal government the greatest power that the words would permit. These two views may be called the bedrock view and the living-document view, respectively.

---

[1] US Const, Art VI, C1 2. *Michigan Canners and Freezers Ass'n, Inc. v Agricultural Marketing and Bargaining Board*, 467 US 461 (1984).
[2] *New York v Trans World Airlines*, 556 NYS2d 803 (1990).
[3] *Freightliner v Myrick*, ____ US ____, 115 S Ct 1483 (1995).

In the **bedrock view** the purpose of a constitution is to state certain fundamental principles for all time. In the **living-document view** a constitution is merely a statement of goals and objectives and is intended to grow and change with time.

Whether the Constitution is to be liberally interpreted under the living-document view or narrowly interpreted under the bedrock view has a direct effect on the Constitution. For the last century the Supreme Court has followed the living-document view. This has resulted in strengthening the power of the federal government, permitting the rise of administrative agencies, and expanding the protection of human rights. The living-document view has given us the living Constitution described in section 7 of this chapter.

Can we decide that we should adopt the bedrock view or the living-document view? We cannot select one to the exclusion of the other for the simple reason that we want both. Contradictory as this sounds, it is obvious that we want our Constitution to be durable. We do not want a set of New Year's resolutions that will soon be forgotten. At the same time we know that the world changes, and therefore we do not want a constitution that will hold us tied in a straitjacket of the past.

In terms of social forces that make the law, we are torn between our desire for stability and our desire for flexibility. We want a constitution that is stable. At the same time we want one that is flexible. That is why we have conflict.

If we do not see the conflict, we do not see the Constitution as it really is today. Even more important, we lack the understanding needed to meet the problems of tomorrow.

6. Amending the Constitution

The U.S. Constitution has been amended in three ways: (1) expressly, (2) by interpretation, and (3) by practice.

The Constitution has been amended according to its provisions.

(a) Constitutional Method of Amending. Article V of the Constitution sets forth the procedure to be followed for amending the Constitution. Relatively few changes have been made to the Constitution by this formal process, although thousands of proposals have been made.

The Constitution has been amended by court decisions.

(b) Amendment by Judicial Interpretation. The greatest change to the written Constitution has been made by the U.S. Supreme Court in interpreting the Constitution. Generally, interpretation is used to apply the Constitution to a new situation that could not have been foreseen when the written Constitution was adopted.

The Constitution has been amended by practice.

(c) Amendment by Practice. In practice the letter of the Constitution is not always followed. Departure from the written Constitution began as early as 1793, when George Washington refused to make treaties, as required by the Constitution, by and with the consent of the Senate. Washington began the practice of the president's negotiating a treaty with a foreign country and then submitting it to the Senate for approval. This practice has been followed since that time. Similarly, the electoral college was originally intended to exercise independent judgment in selecting the president, but it now automatically elects the official candidate of the party that elected the majority of the members of the electoral college.

Other practices have added to the Constitution "provisions" that are not there.

* **Article V of the U.S. Constitution specifies the procedure for adopting amendments.**

FIGURE 4-2
Amending the U.S Constitution

As written, the Constitution contemplates that Congress will originate and adopt laws. With the rise of the party system, which was not anticipated by the framers of the Constitution, the president has become the leader of the legislative program. This position of leadership has been strengthened greatly by the modern media, beginning with Franklin D. Roosevelt's radio fireside chats of the 1930s and broadening into presidential television appearances in later years.

7.   The Living Constitution

The living Constitution has departed from the written version.

The Constitution that has developed in the manner described in the preceding section is radically different from the Constitution that was written on paper. The living Constitution has the following characteristics.

(a) Strong Government. One of the characteristics of the new Constitution is strong government. Business enterprises can now be regulated and the economy controlled.

(b) Strong President. Instead of being merely an officer who carries out the laws, the president has become the political leader of a party, exerting a strong influence on the lawmaking process. If the president's political party is in control of both houses of Congress, the president acts as the leader of the lawmaking process.

(c) Eclipse of the States. Under the new Constitution all governments have powers that they never possessed before, but the center of gravity has shifted from the states to the nation. When the Constitution was adopted in 1789, the federal government was to have only the very limited powers specified in Article I, Section 8, of the Constitution. Whatever regulation of business was permissible was to be imposed by the states. Today, the great bulk of the regulation of business is adopted by the federal government through Congress or its administrative agencies. As the American economy moved from the local community stage to the nationwide stage, the individual states were unable to provide effective regulation of business. It was inevitable that regulation would be drawn to the central government. Consequently, when we speak of governmental regulation of business, we ordinarily mean the national government, not state or local governments.

(d) Administrative Agencies. These were virtually unheard of in 1789, and no mention is made of them in the Constitution of 1789. The vast powers of the new Constitution are exercised to a very large degree by administrative agencies. They are in effect a fourth branch of the government, not provided for in the written Constitution. More important, it is the administrative agencies that come in contact with the majority of businesspersons and citizens. The agencies are the government for most people.

In other words the vast power of government to regulate business is not exercised directly by the legislatures, the courts, or the executive officers. Rather, this power is exercised by agencies. The members of the agencies or the boards, commissions, or persons heading the agencies are not elected by the voters. The decisions of agencies are to a large degree not subject to effective review or reversal by the courts.

(e) Human Rights. The scope of human rights protected from governments has dramatically broadened. These rights are protected from invasion not only by the federal government but also by any government. Most significant of all, unwritten rights are protected, although they are not guaranteed by any express constitutional provision.

D.   FEDERAL POWERS

The federal government possesses powers necessary to administer matters of national concern.

8. The Power to Regulate Commerce

The United States can regulate interstate commerce.

The desire to protect commerce from restrictions and barriers set up by the individual states was a prime factor leading to the adoption of the Constitution of 1789. To protect commerce, Congress was given, by Article I, Section 8, Clause 3, the power "[t]o regulate commerce with foreign nations, and among the several states, and with the Indian tribes."

Until 1937 the Supreme Court held that this provision gave Congress the power to control or regulate only that commerce crossing a state line, such as an interstate railway train or an interstate telegraph message.

The United States commerce power is now a general welfare power.

(a) The Commerce Power Becomes a General Welfare Power. In 1937 the Supreme Court began expanding the concept of interstate commerce. By 1946 the power to regulate interstate commerce had become very broad. By that year the power had expanded to the point that it gave authority to Congress to adopt regulatory laws that were "as broad as the economic needs of the nation."[4] By virtue of this broad interpretation, Congress can regulate manufacturing, agriculture, mining, stock exchanges, insurance, loan sharking, monopolies, and conspiracies in restraint of trade. If desired, Congress can set standards, quotas, and priorities for industries. The far reach of the interstate commerce power is seen in the Freedom of Access to Clinic Entrances Act[5] that prohibits obstruction of entrances to clinics.[6]

The case that was the starting point in this transition of the Commerce Clause was *Jones & Laughlin Steel.*

---

[4] *American Power & Light Co. v Securities and Exchange Commission,* 329 US 90 (1946). The wide scope of this view is seen in such statutes as the Food, Agriculture, Conservation, and Trade Act of 1990. Act of November 28, 1990, PL 101-624, 104 Stat 3359. The provisions of this statute are allocated to numerous sections of Titles 7 and 16 of USC.
[5] 18 USC § 248.
[6] The act is constitutional. *United States v Wilson* CA 7 73 F3d 675 (1995).

CASE SUMMARY

Here It Comes!

Facts: The Jones & Laughlin Steel Company was the fourth largest producer of steel in the United States and distributed its products nationwide. It was an integrated company, owning ore and coal mines in Michigan and Minnesota as well as the means of transporting those materials to its mills in Pennsylvania. It employed over 533,000 people. In 1935 the company was brought before the National Labor Relations Board and found to be in violation of the National Labor Relations Act for engaging in unfair labor practices. The company was found to have discriminated against union members with regard to hire and tenure of employment, and of coercing and intimidating employees so as to interfere with their self-organization. Additionally, its discharge of 10 employees for being active union leaders was discriminatory and coercive in violation of the Act. Congress created The National Labor Relations Act of 1935 under its constitutional power to regulate interstate commerce.

Decision: The Constitution does not give Congress the power to regulate labor or production, but it does give Congress the power to regulate interstate commerce. The power to regulate includes the power to protect. Strikes and labor disputes in major industries slow down or stop the interstate flow of goods. This is a harm to interstate commerce, and therefore Congress can adopt a law to prevent such a harm. This was accomplished by the National Labor Relations Act, and that act was therefore constitutional. [*NLRB v Jones & Laughlin Steel Corp., 301 US 1 (1937)*]

The United States commerce power limits state action.

(b) The Commerce Power as a Limitation on States. The federal power to regulate commerce not only gives Congress the power to act but also prevents states from acting in any way that interferes with federal regulation or burdens interstate commerce. *For example*, if the federal government establishes safety device regulations for interstate carriers, a state cannot require different devices.

Because modern commerce is typically interstate in character, the fact that Congress does not impose any regulation is generally interpreted as excluding state action over interstate commerce.

States may not use their tax power for the purpose of discriminating against interstate commerce because such commerce is within the protection of the national government. *For example*, a state cannot impose a higher tax on goods imported from another state than it imposes on the same kind of goods produced in its own territory. Likewise, when goods are on their way to being exported, a state cannot impose a property tax on them even though they are temporarily stopped within the state.[7]

The fact that a local law may have some effect on out-of-state markets does not mean that the local law is unconstitutional as a burden on interstate commerce.

CASE SUMMARY

We Still Have States

Facts: Gerald Dunn took cocaine into Mexico and was arrested at a border inspection station when he brought 1.8 grams of the controlled substance back. The federal attorney declined prosecution of Dunn. Dunn was subsequently convicted under the state's importation of a controlled substance statute. He claimed that the state statute was unconstitutional because the federal statute had preempted the field.

---

[7] *Virginia Indonesia Co. v Harris County Appraisal District* (Tex) 910 SW2d 905 (1995).

> **Decision:** The statute was constitutional. Neither the letter nor the purpose of the federal statute required that there be no state laws on the subject. There was accordingly no federal preemption. The state statute did not conflict directly with the federal statute and therefore no question of overriding federal supremacy existed. *[Arizona v Dunn (App) _____ Ariz _____, 803 P2d 917 (1990)]*

State regulations designed to advance local interests may come into conflict with the Commerce Clause. In that case they are invalid. Thus, a state cannot refuse to allow an interstate waste collector to conduct business within the state on the ground that the state already has enough waste collectors.

9.   The Financial Powers

The financial powers of the federal government include the powers to tax and to borrow, spend, and coin money.

The United States can tax.

(a) The Taxing Power. The federal Constitution provides that "Congress shall have power [t]o lay and collect taxes, duties, imposts and excises, to pay the debts and provide for the common defence and general welfare of the United States."[8] Subject to the express and implied limitations arising from the Constitution, the states may impose such taxes as they desire and as their own individual constitutions and statutes permit. In addition to express constitutional limitations, both national and local taxes are subject to the unwritten limitation that they be imposed for a public purpose.

The federal government is subject to certain limitations on the form of the taxes it imposes. Capitation or poll taxes and all direct taxes must be apportioned among the states according to their census-determined population.[9] Direct taxes include taxes on real estate or personal property and taxes imposed on persons because of their ownership of property. Income taxes, to the extent that they tax income from property, are direct, although because of the Sixteenth Amendment, their apportionment is no longer required.

All other taxes imposed by the federal government are regarded as indirect taxes. These include customs duties, taxes on consumption (such as gasoline and cigarette taxes), taxes on the exercise of a privilege (such as an amusement tax), taxes on the transmission of property at death (such as estate taxes), taxes on the privilege of making a gift, and taxes on the privilege of employing workers (such as the employer's Social Security tax). In the case of a federal tax on the exercise of a privilege, it is immaterial whether the privilege arises by virtue of a state or a federal law.

The only restriction on the form of indirect federal taxes is that they must be uniform throughout the continental United States and the incorporated territories. This requirement of uniformity does not prohibit a progressively graduated tax in which the greater the monetary value of the tax base, the greater the rate of tax. The requirement of uniformity also is not violated by a provision allowing credits against the federal tax for taxes paid to a state even though the amount of

---

[8] US Const, Art 1, § 8, Cl 1.
[9] US Const, Art 1, § 8, Cl 4.

the federal tax paid will vary from state to state, depending on the existence of a state tax for which credit is allowable.

The federal taxing power is subject to the implied limitation that state and municipal governments may not be directly taxed. In earlier years this concept was interpreted to exempt from federal income tax any money received from state or local governments by private persons. This immunity of private persons has been destroyed by decisions of the Supreme Court. Now the federal income tax reaches income received by private persons working for or dealing with state and municipal governments. If Congress wishes, it may subject income from state and municipal bonds to the general federal income tax.[10]

The United States can borrow.

(b) The Borrowing Power. Congress is authorized to borrow money on the credit of the United States.[11] No limitation is imposed on the purposes for which the United States can borrow.

Obligations of the United States issued to those lending money to the United States are binding. Congress cannot attempt to repudiate these obligations or make them repayable in a less valuable currency than called for by the obligations without violating the legal rights of the holders.

The states have an inherent power to borrow money. State constitutions and statutes may impose a limit on the amount that can be borrowed. Frequently, these limitations can be evaded by the creation of independent authorities or districts that borrow money by issuing bonds. The bonded indebtedness of such independent authorities and districts is not regarded as a debt of the state and therefore is not subject to the limitations applicable to state borrowing.

The United States can spend.

(c) The Spending Power. The federal government may use tax money and borrowed money "to pay the debts and provide for the common defence and general welfare of the United States."[12]

Congress may reduce federal funds that would otherwise be distributed to a state if that state has a drinking age lower than 21. The objective of Congress is to eliminate the hazard of persons under 21 driving to lower-drinking-age states, becoming drunk, and then becoming involved in highway accidents.[13]

The United States can establish currencies.

(d) The Currency Power. The Constitution authorizes Congress "[t]o coin money, regulate the value thereof," and "provide for the punishment of counterfeiting the securities and . . . coin of the United States."[14] This federal power is made exclusive by prohibiting the states from coining money, emitting bills of credit, or making anything but gold and silver coins legal tender in payment of debts.[15]

The national government can determine what shall be legal tender and is not restricted to the use of metallic money but may issue paper money.[16] Congress can establish whatever base it desires for paper currency and may change the base of existing currency.

---

[10] *South Carolina v Baker,* 485 US 505 (1988).
[11] US Const, Art 1, § 8, Cl 2.
[12] US Const, Art 1, § 8, Cl 1.
[13] *South Dakota v Dole,* 483 US 203 (1987).
[14] US Const, Art 1, § 8, Cls 5, 6.
[15] US Const, Art 1, § 10.
[16] *Julliard v Greenman,* 110 US 421 (1884); *Schickler v Santa Fe Southern Pacific Corp.,* ___ Ill App 2d ___, ___ Ill Dec ___, 953 NE2d 961 (1992).

(e) The Banking Power. The federal Constitution is liberally interpreted to authorize the U.S. government to create banks and to regulate banks created under state laws. This is generally done though the Federal Reserve system. Interstate branch banking is now subject to federal regulation.[17]

10. The Power to Own Businesses

In a sense governmental ownership of what would ordinarily be deemed private business represents the ultimate in the regulation of private business.

Governments can own businesses.

(a) Constitutionality of Governmental Ownership. Speaking generally, there is no constitutional barrier against state or federal governmental ownership and operation of businesses. It had formerly been assumed there were certain purposes that were not public or for the general welfare as distinguished from those that were. It is impossible today to draw such a line between public and private and to prohibit a government from entering into any particular business on the ground that to do so is not in furtherance of a public purpose or does not advance the general welfare. Cities and states, for example, may own cable TV systems and may issue bonds to finance such activity.[18]

Governments can sell products of their businesses.

(b) Sale and Distribution of Governmental Production. A government may sell or otherwise dispose of the products that a government-owned business manufactures. The power of a government to dispose of its property permits the government to compete with private enterprises and to dispose of its products at any price it chooses without regard to whether the price is below cost. No constitutional privilege of private businesses is violated by being underpriced by national, state, or local government's.[19]

E.   CONSTITUTIONAL LIMITATIONS ON GOVERNMENT

The limitations discussed in the following sections are those most important to persons and businesses.

11. Due Process

Governments are limited by due process guarantees.

The most important limitation on the power of government is that found in the Fifth and Fourteenth Amendments to the Constitution. Those amendments respectively prohibit the national government and state governments from depriving any person of life, liberty, or property without due process of law.

The scope of due process has expanded.

(a) Expansion of Due Process. As a result of liberal interpretation of the Constitution, the **Due Process Clause** is now held to be a guarantee of protection from unreasonable procedures and unreasonable laws. It is also held to be a guarantee of equal protection of the law and a guarantee of protection of significant interests. The Supreme Court has extended the Due Process Clause to protect the record or standing of a student.

---

[17] Riegle-Neal Interstate Banking and Branching Efficiency Act of 1994, PL 103-328.
[18] *Paragould Cablevision, Inc. v City of Paragould,* ____ Ark____, 809 SW2d 688 (1991).
[19] *Puget Sound Power & Light Co. v Seattle,* 291 US 619 (1934).

Through judicial construction due process of law affords the individual a wide protection. However, the guarantee affords no protection when a matter is reasonably debatable. Therefore, due process of law does not bar the regulation of business because any regulation that would have sufficient support to pass a legislature or Congress would have sufficient claim to validity to be debatable. The fact that many persons would deem a law unsound, unwise, hazardous, or un-American does not in itself make the law invalid under the Due Process Clause.

Because the due process concept is a limitation on governmental action, it does not apply to transactions between private persons or to private employment or other nonpublic situations. In some cases, however, such statutes as the federal Civil Rights Act and those addressing consumer protection apply due process concepts to private transactions.

Shortcut procedures must not deprive one of due process.

(b) Shortcut Procedures. The delays of the law have often been a source of criticism. Shortcut procedures are inspired by the legitimate desire to speed up litigation and give everyone easy access to a day in court. However, procedures must not be so streamlined that they deprive defendants of reasonable notice and an opportunity to be heard. In an era in which a defendant may be a resident or a business of a foreign state, statutes have generally been adopted to allow a plaintiff to sue a foreign defendant in the state where the plaintiff lives. These state statutes are subject to the limitation that they can be applied only when the defendant has such a relationship—for example, by carrying on business—within the plaintiff's state that it is reasonable to require the defendant to defend an action in the courts of the plaintiff's state. Conversely, if the defendant does not have such a reasonable relationship to the plaintiff's state, it is a denial of due process to require the defendant to go to that state.

12. Equal Protection of the Law

Governments are limited by the equal protection guarantee.

The Constitution prohibits states and the national government from denying any person the equal protection of the law.[20] This guarantee prohibits a government from treating one person differently from another when there is no reasonable ground for classifying them differently.

In harmony with this concept of equality, it has been held that a wife may be held responsible for necessaries furnished to her husband.[21] This parallels the common law liability of the husband for necessaries furnished to the wife.

Reasonable classification is permitted.

(a) Reasonable Classification. The Equal Protection Clause does not require that all persons be protected or treated equally, and a law is valid even though it does not apply to everyone or everything. Whether a classification is reasonable depends on whether the nature of the classification bears a reasonable relation to the evil to be remedied or to the object to be attained by the law. In determining this, the courts have been guided generally by considerations of historical treatment and by the logic of the situation. The trend is to permit the classification to stand as long as there is a rational basis for the distinction made.[22] This means

---

[20] US Const, Fourteenth Amendment as to the states; modern interpretation of Due Process Clause of the Fifth Amendment as to national government. Congress adopted the Civil Rights Act to implement the concept of equal protection. *Newport News Shipbuilding and Dry Dock Co. v EEOC*, 212 US 669 (1983).

[21] *Webb v Hillsborough County Hospital Authority* (Fla App) 521 So 2d 199 (1988).

[22] *Urton v Hudson*, 101 Or App 147, 790 P2d 12 (1990).

that a statute will be sustained unless it is clear that the lawmaking body has been arbitrary or capricious.

(b) Improper Classification. Laws that make distinctions in the regulation of business, the right to work, and the right to use or enjoy property on the basis of race, alienage, or religion are invalid. Also invalid are laws that impose restrictions on some, but not all, persons without any justification for the distinction.[23] A law prohibiting the ownership of land by aliens has been traditionally regarded as an exception to this rule. Large alien holdings of land are considered such a social evil that it justifies legislation directly prohibiting this. However, it appears that in the course of time this discrimination may be declared invalid.[24] A state statute taxing out-of-state insurance companies at a higher rate than in-state insurance companies violates the Equal Protection Clause.[25]

Lawmakers may not discriminate on the basis of moral standards and cultural patterns. People cannot be deprived of the same treatment afforded others just because they do not have the same moral standards or cultural patterns as the lawmakers, nor can lawmakers penalize people because they do not live, think, and dress the same as the lawmakers.

CASE SUMMARY

What If You Don't Like Me?

Facts: The Federal Food Stamp Act provided for the distribution of food stamps to needy households. In 1971 section 3(e) of the statute was amended to define households as limited to groups whose members were all related to each other. This was done because of congressional dislike for the lifestyles of unrelated hippies who were living together in hippie communes. Moreno and others applied for food stamps but were refused them because the relationship requirement was not satisfied. An action was brought to have the relationship requirement declared unconstitutional.

Decision: The relationship requirement did not bear any reasonable relationship to the object of the statute. The statute was designed to assist those in need. Persons without food were in need without regard to their relationship to other persons. The relationship requirement was therefore unconstitutional as a denial of equal protection. *[United States Department of Agriculture v Moreno, 413 US 528 (1973)]*

---

13. Privileges and Immunities

States are limited by the privileges and immunities guarantee.

The federal Constitution declares that "[t]he citizens of each state shall be entitled to all privileges and immunities of citizens in the several states."[26] This means that a person going into another state is entitled to make contracts, own property, and engage in business to the same extent as the citizens of that state. *For example,* a state cannot bar a traveler from another state from engaging in local business or from obtaining a hunting or fishing license merely because the traveler is not a resident. Likewise, a law that requires an attorney to be a resident of the state in order to practice is unconstitutional as a violation of this provision.[27]

---

[23] *Associated Industries of Missouri v Lohman,* 511 US 641 (1994).
[24] The alien land laws have been declared unconstitutional by the supreme courts of California, Montana, and Oregon, as being in violation of the Fourteenth Amendment of the U.S. Constitution.
[25] *Metropolitan Life Ins. Co. v Ward,* 470 US 869 (1985).
[26] US Const, Art IV, § 2, Cl 1.
[27] *Barnard v Thorstenn,* 489 US 546 (1989).

14. Protection of the Person

The Constitution does not contain any express provision protecting "persons" from governmental action. Persons are expressly protected by the Constitution with respect to particular matters, such as freedom of speech, ownership of property, right to a jury trial, and so on. There is, however, no general provision declaring that the government shall not impair rights of persons. There is not a word in the Constitution about the inalienable rights that were so important on July 4, 1776.[28]

CASE SUMMARY

The Street Is My Soapbox

Facts: A trial involving police brutality led to a number of public demonstrations and protests. In order to protect the public from violence, the city officials prohibited all demonstrations in the public streets.

Decision: The prohibition was unconstitutional. People have the right to demonstrate in public streets even though their speech stirs passions, resentment, or anger. This is protected free speech and can be limited only when the speech is directed to inciting or producing illegal action or is likely to have that result. This requires a case-by-case determination. A blanket prohibition is unconstitutional. [*Collins v Jordan CA 9 110 F3d 1363 (1996)*]

The Supreme Court has found constitutional protection for personal rights not expressly protected by the Constitution.

(a) Rise of Constitutional Protection of the Person. During the last six decades the Supreme Court has been finding constitutional protection for a wide array of rights of the person that are not expressly protected by the Constitution. Examples are the right of privacy, the right to marry the person one chooses,[29] protection from unreasonable zoning, protection of parental control, protection from durational residency requirements, protection from discrimination because of poverty, and protection from gender discrimination.[30]

(b) Who Is a Living Person? Only living persons are protected by the Constitution. But when is a person living? When is a person dead? At common law the test of being alive was as simple as whether the person was breathing and had a heartbeat. This is known as the cardiopulmonary test. With modern advances in medicine it is possible in many cases to keep a person breathing and the heart beating by drugs or mechanical equipment, such as respirators. Is a person whose breath and heartbeat depend on external assistance alive? The question becomes important in determining cases involving organ donations, abortions, and the mercy killing of hopelessly handicapped infants or the old or sick. In some states

---

28 The term *inalienable right* is employed in preference to *natural right, fundamental right,* or *basic right.* Apart from the question of scope of coverage, the adjective *inalienable* emphasizes the fact that the people still possess the right, rather than having surrendered or subordinated it to the will of society. The word *alien* is the term of the old common law for transferring title or ownership. Today, we would say *transfer* and, instead of saying inalienable rights, would say *nontransferable rights.* Inalienable rights of the people were therefore rights that the people not only possessed, but also could not give up even if they wanted to. Thus, these rights are still owned by everyone.

29 *Akron v Akron Center for Reproductive Health, Inc.,* 462 US 416 (1983).

30 In some cases the courts have given the Due Process and Equal Protection Clauses a liberal interpretation in order to find a protection of the person, thereby making up for the fact that there is no express constitutional guarantee of protection of the person. *Davis v Passman,* 442 US 228 (1979) (due process); *Orr v Orr,* 440 US 268 (1979) (equal protection).

the problem has been met by statutes declaring persons dead when the brain ceases to function: the human vegetable case.[31] In a number of states, statutes authorize competent persons to adopt a living will that directs they be permitted to die if terminally ill. Is a newly born child who is certain to die a living person?

CASE SUMMARY

When Do You Come Alive?

Facts: In the eighth month of a woman's pregnancy, she and her husband petitioned the court to declare that their unborn child, T.A.C.P., was legally dead. This was requested because the mother was informed that the child would be born anencephalic. This meant that the child would have much of the brain and part of the skull missing and that the child would die shortly after birth. The parents filed the petition to enable taking the child's organs for transplant immediately upon the child's birth. Speed of removal was essential to the value of the organs, and the parents hoped that others could find life in those organs.

Decision: The newly born child is a living person even though death is certain. The common law applies the cardiopulmonary test to tell if a person is living: Is the person breathing? Is the heart beating? The Florida legislature had not changed this definition, and a court would not change it by decision unless it was clear that a social need existed for the change. In the case of anencephalics it was not clear whether there was any value in obtaining their organs, and the constitutional, legal, and ethical questions were confusing with no clear indication of what was good for the general welfare. Petition denied. [Re T.A.C.P. (Fla) 609 So 2d 588 (1992)]

---

15. Limitation of Protection of Freedom of Action

The fact that freedom of action of the person is protected does not give any person an uncontrolled right to do anything. In the exercise of freedom a person cannot violate the freedom of another person. Likewise, the need to protect the government and society in general may in a particular case outweigh the right to freedom of action of the person.

CASE SUMMARY

New Technology and an Old Constitution

Facts: The cable television industry is comprised of operators who own the physical assets and franchises to transmit the signals of proprietary programming to its subscribers. Because the cables must be laid in public rights-of-way, cable operators are franchised by localities and are thus a natural monopoly within the areas they serve. In response to the industry's explosive growth and potential for abuse, the Federal Cable Television Consumer Protection and Competition Act was made law in 1984. The Act requires that cable operators make between 4 and 7 percent of their cable capacity available for non-commercial educational programs. The industry challenged the Act claiming it was an unconstitutional interference with freedom of speech.

---

[31] A Uniform Determination of Death Act has been adopted in Arkansas, California, Colorado, Delaware, Georgia, Idaho, Indiana, Kansas, Maine, Maryland, Michigan, Minnesota, Mississippi, Missouri, Montana, Nebraska, Nevada, New Hampshire, New Mexico, North Dakota, Ohio, Oklahoma, Oregon, Pennsylvania, Rhode Island, South Carolina, South Dakota, Utah, Vermont, West Virginia, and Wyoming. It has also been adopted for the District of Columbia and the Virgin Islands. The uniform act adds brain death to the common law test of death.

> **Decision:** The statute is constitutional. The furthering of public information is an important objective of government and is essential to the protection of the common welfare. As the statute did not regulate the content of the noncommercial educational programs, there was no interference with the right of free speech of cable operators. [*Time Warner Entertainment Co. v FCC, 93 F3d 957 (Cir 1996)*]

16. Democracy and Protection of the Person

Because the goal of a democracy is to promote the well-being and development of each individual, the concept of protecting a person and the goal of democracy would appear to be moving toward the same objective. This is ordinarily true, but there may be a conflict between the democratic system of government and the protection of the person. We think of a democratic society as one in which the majority of the people govern. But is being governed by the majority sufficient for those who cherish the American ideal?

If we look closely at our individual and national desires, we see that the American way of life is not a society run by the will of the majority. Instead, we find that the American way divides life into two zones. In one zone, the democratic concept is that the majority rules. In the other zone—that of the person—not even the majority can interfere. To illustrate, the majority can declare by statute that before you marry, you must have a health certificate. This is perfectly reasonable for the protection of the general health and welfare. But no one, not the majority or even the unanimous action of everyone in the United States, can command you to marry or not marry or choose your mate for you.

Most amazing is the fact that a relatively short time ago the second zone was unheard of and everything was thought to be in the zone that was controlled by the majority unless there was an express prohibition of such action by the Constitution. Even more startling, the emergence of the second zone has taken place for the most part within the lifetime of your parents and your lifetime. The expansion of the second zone will have a profound effect on the rest of your life.

WHAT'S BEHIND THE LAW?

Corporate Political Speech and Corporate Political Contributions

The Lippo Group, an Indonesian conglomerate, contributed over $1 million to U.S. political campaigns from 1993 to 1996. Mochtar Riady, the head of the Lippo Group, has written letters to elected officials in the United States that outline his views and recommendations on trade policy. For example, one letter he sent to President Clinton recommended normalization of trade relations with Vietnam. The letter was written in March 1993, and trade relations with Vietnam were normalized in February 1994. John Huang, the Department of Commerce official assigned to Vietnam trade issues, helped obtain the political contributions from the Lippo Group and then left the federal government to solicit international campaign contributions.

Should there be restrictions on foreign corporate political contributions? Is giving money a form of speech? What public policy issues arise from the presence of foreign funds in U.S. political campaigns? For more on First Amendment rights, visit constitutional law at http://www.law.emory.edu/FOCAL/const.html

SUMMARY

The U.S. Constitution created the structure of our national government and gave it certain powers. It also placed limitations on those powers. It created a federal system with a tripartite division of government and a bicameral national legislature.

Some governmental powers are possessed exclusively by the national government, while other powers are shared by both the states and the federal government. In areas of conflict federal law is supreme.

The U.S. Constitution is not a detailed document. It takes its meaning from the way it is interpreted. In recent years liberal interpretation has expanded the powers of the federal government. Among the powers of the federal government that directly affect business are the power to regulate commerce; the power to tax and to borrow, spend,

and coin money; and the power to own and operate businesses. Among the limitations on government that are most important to business are the requirement of due process and the requirement of equal protection of the law.

The due process requirement stipulates that no person shall be deprived of life, liberty, or property without due process of law. This requirement applies to both the federal government and the state governments but does not apply to private transactions.

The equal protection concept of the U.S. Constitution prohibits both the federal government and the state governments from treating one person differently from another unless there is a legitimate reason for doing so and unless the basis of classification is reasonable.

QUESTIONS AND CASE PROBLEMS

1. What are the characteristics of the Constitution as it is today?
2. Would a constitutional amendment that deleted the present Article V and in its place provided that an amendment could be adopted by a majority of those voting in a presidential election be valid?
3. Does equal protection prevent classification? If not, when is classification proper?
4. The federal interstate commerce power goes no further than to give the federal government power to regulate goods and vehicles crossing state lines. Appraise the statement.
5. The Crafts' home was supplied with gas by the city gas company. Because of some misunderstanding the gas company believed that the Crafts were delinquent in paying their gas bill. The gas company had an informal complaint procedure for discussing such matters, but the Crafts had never been informed that such a procedure was available. The gas company notified the Crafts that they were delinquent and that the company was shutting off the gas. The Crafts brought an action to enjoin the gas company from doing so on the theory that a termination without any hearing was a denial of due process. The lower courts held that the interest of the Crafts in receiving gas was not a property interest protected by the Due Process Clause and the procedures that the gas company followed satisfied the requirements of due process. The Crafts appealed. Were they correct in contending that they had been denied due process of law? Why or why not? [*Memphis Light, Gas and Water Division v Craft*, 436 US 1]
6. The New York Civil Service law provided that only U.S. citizens could hold permanent civil service positions. Dougall was an alien who had lawfully entered and was lawfully residing in the United States. He held a job with the city of New York but was fired because of the state statute. He claimed that the statute was unconstitutional. Was he correct? Why or why not?
7. Montana imposed a severance tax on every ton of coal mined within the state. The tax varied depending on the value of the coal and the cost of production. It could be as high as 30 percent of the price at which the coal was sold. Montana mine operators and some of the out-of-state customers claimed that this tax was unconstitutional as an improper burden on interstate commerce. Decide. [*Commonwealth Edison Co. v Montana*, 452 US 609]
8. What social force guided the court in deciding the *Commonwealth Edison* case in Case Problem 7?
9. Heald was the executor of the estate of a deceased person who had lived in Washington, D.C. Heald refused to pay federal tax owed by the estate on the ground that the tax had been imposed by an act of Congress, but because residents of the District of Columbia had no vote in Congress, the tax law was necessarily adopted without their representation. Not only did District residents have no voice in the adoption of the tax laws, but also the proceeds from taxes collected in the District were paid into the general treasury of the United States and were not maintained as a separate District of Columbia fund. Heald objected that the tax law was void as contrary to the

Constitution because it amounted to taxation without representation. Decide. [*Heald v District of Columbia*, 259 US 114]

10. Ellis was employed by the city of Lakewood. By the terms of his contract he could be discharged only for cause. After working for six years, he was told that he was going to be discharged because of his inability to generate safety and self-insurance programs, because of his failure to win the confidence of employees, and because of his poor attendance. He was not informed of the facts in support of these conclusions and was given the option to resign. He claimed that he was entitled to a hearing. Decide. [*Ellis v City of Lakewood*, (Colo App) 789 P2d 449]

11. Because of misconduct Lopez and other public high school students were suspended for periods of up to ten days. A state statute authorized the principal of a public school to suspend a student for periods of up to ten days without any hearing. A suit was brought by Lopez and others. They claimed that the statute was unconstitutional because it deprived them of due process by not giving them notice and a hearing to determine whether a suspension was justified. Was the state statute constitutional? Why or why not? [*Goss v Lopez*, 419 US 565]

12. New Hampshire adopted a tax law that in effect taxed the income only of nonresidents working in New Hampshire. Austin, a nonresident who worked in New Hampshire, claimed that the tax law was invalid. Was he correct? Explain. [*Austin v New Hampshire*, 420 US 656]

13. Arkansas is primarily a rural state, and in many areas there it is not feasible to employ cable television. Arkansas imposes a tax on sales and services, and cable television service was added to the list of taxed enterprises. No tax, however, was imposed on satellite television service. The cable companies claimed there was a denial of equal protection by taxing them but not satellite transmission of television. Decide. [*Medlock v Leathers*, ___ Ark ___, 842 SW2d 428]

14. In view of the fact that written constitutions constantly change, it can be said that there is no value in having a written constitution. Appraise this statement.

15. The Michigan Constitution provides a special procedure for amending the constitution. In addition, it gives voters the right to adopt laws by public vote. Under this plan, called the "initiative," a specified percentage of voters may require that a particular law be placed on the ballot of the next state general election. If the proposal is then approved by a majority of the voters, it is a law just as though it had been adopted by the state legislature. A public welfare law was adopted by such an initiative procedure. The law was challenged as violating the Michigan Constitution. The defense was made that because the law had been adopted by the people, it was not subject to the limitations of the state constitution. Was this correct? [*Doe v Director of Department of Social Services*, ___ Mich App ___, 468 NW2d 862]

Government Regulation of Competition and Prices

CHAPTER 5

OBJECTIVES

After studying this chapter, you should be able to

1. *State the extent to which government can regulate business;*
2. *State what Congress has done to protect free enterprise from unfair competition and from unfair restraints;*
3. *State when price discrimination is prohibited and when it is allowed;*
4. *List statutory and judicial exceptions to the Sherman Antitrust Act; and*
5. *Describe the constitutional limitations on state regulation of business.*

Constitutionally, the government *can* regulate business and much of our lives. Whether government *should* exercise this power comes down to a question of policy—whether we, the people, want government to do so. Although there is some movement toward deregulation, the overwhelming pattern continues to be regulation of business by government. It may come as a shock that in a country that believes in free enterprise, so much is in fact regulated by government.

A. POWER TO REGULATE BUSINESS

By virtue of their police power, states may regulate all aspects of business so long as they do not impose an unreasonable burden on interstate commerce or any activity of the federal government. Local governments may also exercise this power to the extent each state permits. The federal government may impose on any phase of business any regulation that is required by the nation's economic needs.[1]

1. Regulation, Free Enterprise, and Deregulation

Regulation of enterprise is dominant.

The regulation of business is flatly opposed to the concept of free enterprise. Under a true free enterprise system, there would not be any regulation of airline safety, safety of food and drugs for human consumption, prices, and so on.

Recent years have seen some movement toward deregulation of industry. For many years, for example, the banking and savings industry was heavily regulated, but, beginning in 1978, various acts were adopted to deregulate this industry.[2] These acts did not produce the desired results, however, so Congress adopted several bank-regulating laws toward the end of the 1980s. The broadest regulation was the Financial Institutions Reform, Recovery, and Enforcement Act of 1989 (FIRREA),[3] which regulates savings and loan associations and similar organizations to ensure their financial stability.

FIGURE 5-1
Government Regulation of American Life

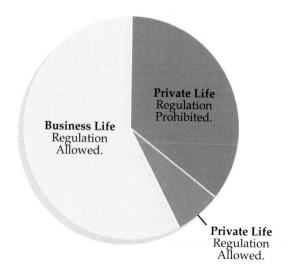

---

[1] *American Power & Light Co. v SEC,* 329 US 90 (1946).

[2] See, for example, the Depository Institutions Deregulation and Monetary Control Act of 1980, 12 USC § 1735. *Grunbeck v Dime Savings Bank of New York* (CA1 NH) 74 F3d 331 (1996).

[3] Act of October 9, 1989, PL 101-73, 103 Stat 183, codified at various sections of Titles 12 and 15 of USC.

The regulation of rates of plane and truck transport, on the other hand, has been removed, and it seems unlikely that the move to deregulate will go much beyond removing restrictions on rates.[4]

The Telecommunications Act of 1996 is designed to reduce regulation and to secure better service at lower prices for users of telephones.[5] However, it imposes a wide range of regulations governing ownership, service, and cable systems.

2. Regulation of Production, Distribution, and Financing

Production, distribution, and financing are regulated.

To protect the public from harm, government may prohibit false advertising and labeling, and government may establish health and purity standards for cosmetics, foods, and drugs. Licenses may be required of persons dealing in certain goods, and these licenses may be revoked for improper dealings.[6] Without regard to the nature of the product, government may regulate business with respect to what materials may be used, the quantity of a product that may be produced or grown, and the price at which the finished product may be sold. Government may also engage in competition with private enterprises or own and operate an industry.

Regulation of production may take the form of providing encouragement or assistance for enterprises that would otherwise not prove attractive to private investors.[7]

Under its commerce power, the federal government may regulate all methods of interstate transportation. A similar power is exercised by each state over its intrastate traffic.

The financing of business is directly affected by the national government, which creates a national currency and maintains the Federal Reserve banking system. State and other national laws may also affect financing by regulating financing contracts and documents, such as bills of lading and commercial paper. Some regulation is directed at a particular phase of the economy, such as the Farm Credit Reform Act of 1996.[8]

The federal power to regulate interstate commerce gives the national government the power to regulate interstate communication without regard to the type of communication.

The federal government may establish standards for weights and measures. The Metric Conversion Act of 1975 declares that it is the policy of the United States to convert to the metric system, and various agencies have adopted regulations to carry out this policy.

3. Regulation of Competition

Competition is regulated to prevent unfairness.

The states in varying degrees and the federal government prohibit unfair methods of competition. Frequently, a commission is established to determine whether a given practice comes within the general class of unfair methods of competition. In other instances, statutes specifically define condemned practices.

---

4 Airline Deregulation Act of Oct. 24, 1978, PL 95-504, 92 Stat 1705, 49 USC §§ 1301 et seq.; Bus Regulatory Reform Act of Sept. 20, 1982, PL 97-261, 96 Stat 1102, 49 USC §§ 10101 et seq.
5 PL 104-104.
6 *Evans Packing Co. v Department of Agriculture and Consumer Services* (Fla App) 550 So 2d 112.
7 Orphan Drug Act of January 4, 1983, PL 97-44, 96 Stat 2049, 21 USC §§ 301, 306 (encouraging development of drugs to fight diseases so rare that there is no commercial interest in developing drugs to prevent or treat them).
8 PL 104-105.

Congress has enacted the Federal Trade Commission Act, which declared unlawful all unfair methods of competition and created a Federal Trade Commission (FTC) to administer the act. The FTC has condemned using harassing tactics, coercing by refusing to sell, boycotting, discriminating, disparaging competitors' products, and wrongfully enforcing payment. The FTC has also condemned cutting off or restricting the market, securing and using confidential information, spying on competitors, and inducing breach of customer contracts. The law prohibits misrepresentation by appropriating business names, simulating trade or corporate names, appropriating trademarks, simulating the appearance of a competitor's goods, simulating a competitor's advertising, using deceptive brands or labels, and using false and misleading advertising. When packaged foods are sold with false statements on the packages about the nutritional content of the food, the seller is guilty of an unfair method of competition.[9]

CASE SUMMARY

No Phony Promotion Allowed

Facts: Bonnie Moore had a degree in accounting but was not a licensed CPA. She was president of a company called the "Accounting Center." This company provided small businesses with routine accounting services and installed basic accounting systems but did not conduct audits or certify financial statements. The California State Board of Accountancy ordered her to stop using the terms "accounting" and "accountant" in referring to herself or her firm. Moore sought injunctive protection from the court on grounds that the Board could not constitutionally prohibit the use of generic terms such as "accounting" and "accountant." The California Attorney General's office commissioned an independent poll which showed that most people thought that an "accountant" was someone licensed by the state.

Decision: To protect the public from being misled, the use of the word *accountant* or *accounting* would be enjoined unless accompanied by words showing that the persons did not have a license. [*Moore v California State Board of Accountancy, 230 Cal App 3d 877, 272 Cal Rptr 108 (1990)*]

A shift of emphasis is currently taking place in appraising methods of doing business. Instead of harm to competitors being the sole consideration, the effect on consumers is being given increasing recognition. Many practices that were condemned earlier only because they would harm competitors by diverting customers are now condemned because they prevent customers from getting full value for money spent. ◆ *For example,* a seller violates federal law when a drug is advertised as producing a particular result even though the consensus of medical opinion is that it *may* have such an effect in some cases.[10] ◆

4. Regulation of Prices

Prices are regulated to prevent unfair competition or to protect consumers.

Governments, both national and state, may regulate prices. This may be done directly by the lawmaker (the Congress or the state legislature), or the power to do so may be delegated to an administrative officer or agency. This power extends to prices in any form. It includes not only what a buyer pays for goods purchased from a store but also what a borrower pays as interest on a loan and what a tenant pays for rent.

---

[9] In many states, such a seller would also be guilty of committing a deceptive trade practice or violating a consumer protection statute.

[10] *FTC v Pantron 1 Corp.* (CA9 Cal) 33 F3d 1088 (1994).

Price discrimination
is prohibited.

(a) Prohibited Price Discrimination.

The Clayton Act of 1914 applies to interstate and foreign commerce.[11] This act prohibits price discrimination between different buyers of like commodities where the effect of this discrimination may be to substantially lessen competition or create a monopoly in any line of commerce.

This federal law prohibits the furnishing of advertising or other services that, when rendered to one purchaser but not another, will have the effect of granting one purchaser a price advantage or lower rate. It is illegal for a seller to accept any fee or commission in connection with a sale except for services actually rendered or unless the services are equally available to all on the same terms. The Clayton Act makes both the giving and the receiving of any illegal price discrimination a crime.

State statutes frequently prohibit favoring one competitor by giving a secret discount when the effect is to harm the competition.[12]

A state may prohibit selling below cost to harm competitors or selling to one customer at a secret price that is lower than the price charged other customers when there is no economic justification for the lower price. A statute permitting a seller to set prices that will meet competition gives only the power to equal competitive prices, not the right to undercut a competitor's prices.[13]

Legitimate price
differences are lawful.

(b) Permitted Price Discrimination.

Price discrimination is expressly permitted when it can be justified on the basis of (1) a difference in grade, quality, or quantity; (2) the cost of transportation involved in performing the contract; (3) a good-faith effort to meet competition; (4) differences in methods or quantities; (5) deterioration of goods; or (6) a close-out sale of a particular line of goods. The Robinson-Patman Act of 1936 reaffirms the right of a seller to select customers and refuse to deal with anyone. The refusal, however, must be in good faith and not for the purpose of restraining trade.

When a supplier offers to sell to anyone at a reduced price if certain conditions are met, the fact that every buyer cannot meet the conditions does not condemn the supplier's pricing plan as discriminatory.

ETHICS & THE LAW

James Owen was the general manager of Obron Atlantic Corp., a manufacturer of powdered brass. Powdered brass is finely flaked metal used in metallic paints, brakes, and explosives. Trained as a chemist, Owen earned his MBA at night school while he worked in Obron's labs during the day. In 1985 he was promoted from the lab to management.

During a business trip in 1986, Owen was told by a fellow executive from Obron's German operations, Bruno Dachlauer, that a price increase for the company's products would be coming in the fall. Dachlauer added that details of the price increase would have to be worked out with Obron's two main competitors based in the United States. Owen reminded Dachlauer that such an agreement about price was against the law in the United States, to which Dachlauer allegedly responded, "There are laws against speeding, too."

Owen complied with the fall price increases but admitted he began "cheating" by lowering those prices to win customers, and he was then threatened by

---

[11] 15 USC §§ 1, 2, 3, 7, 8.
[12] *Diesel Electric Sales and Service, Inc. v Marco Marine San Diego, Inc.,* ____ Cal App 3d ____, 20 Cal Rptr 2d 62 (1993).
[13] *McGuire Oil Co. v Mapco, Inc.* (Ala) 612 So 2d 417 (1992).

competitors. Following the threats, Owen went to the Antitrust Division of the Justice Department and explained his situation. The FBI wired Owen for his meetings. One taped conversation between him and his supervisor, Carl Eckart, (which will be used in a price-fixing case filed in Ohio) is as follows:

Owen: Carl, can we go over this one more time?

Eckart: You . . . (expletive) dummy. One more time. On fine powders, 30 cents. Coarse powders, 15 cents.

Owen: Are you sure Rink will go along with it?

Eckart: Of course.

In the course of a year, Owen taped over 100 conversations involving internal and external meetings for the FBI and the Justice Department. Owen's activities were not revealed until Obron was served with a subpoena from the Justice Department for its sales records. Officers and directors of Obron and its competitors have been indicted, and some have entered guilty pleas.

Owen, whose marriage of 32 years ended in 1993, says that his undercover work took a tremendous toll on him and his family. Owen said of his conduct, "I could see people being hurt, customers being cheated. My concern shifted to protecting the customer. Maybe that's not the fiduciary role of the general manager."

Was what Owen did in recording the conversations ethical? Was it honest? What do you think of Owen's view of focusing on the customers' rights? Is his duty to his company even when the conduct is illegal?

5.   Prevention of Monopolies and Combinations

To protect competitors and the public from monopolies and combinations in restraint of trade, the federal government and almost all of the states have enacted antitrust statutes.

> The Sherman Antitrust Act prohibits monopolies and combinations that restrain trade.

(a) The Federal Antitrust Act. The federal antitrust act, known as the Sherman Antitrust Act, is applicable to both sellers and buyers.[14] It provides: "[§ 1] Every contract, combination in the form of trust or otherwise, or conspiracy, in restraint of trade or commerce among the several states, or with foreign nations, is declared to be illegal. [§ 2] Every person who shall monopolize or attempt to monopolize, or combine or conspire with any other person or persons to monopolize any part of the trade or commerce among the several states, or with foreign nations, shall be deemed guilty of a felony."[15]

(b) Prohibited Conduct. Section 1 of the Sherman Act applies only when two or more persons in different corporations agree or conspire to restrain trade. The act is not violated when there is an agreement between a corporation and its own employees or officers only.

Under section 2, one person or corporation may violate the act by monopolizing or attempting to monopolize interstate commerce.

---

[14] This act has been amended by the Clayton Act, the Federal Trade Commission Act, the Shipping Act, and other legislation.

[15] 15 USC, ch. 1, §§ 1, 2. Free competition has been advanced by the Omnibus Trade and Competitiveness Act of August 23, 1988, as amended, PL 106-418, 102 Stat 1107, 19 USC §§ 2901 et seq. *Gray v Marshall County Board of Education* (W Va) 367 SE2d 751 (1988).

The Sherman Act applies not only to buying and selling activities generally associated with trade and commerce but also to manufacturing and production activities without regard to whether consumers, brokers, or manufacturers are involved.

CASE SUMMARY

Power Breeds Power

Facts: American Crystal Sugar Co. was one of several refiners of beet sugar in northern California and distributed its product in interstate commerce. American Crystal and the other refiners had a monopoly on the seed supply and were the only practical market for the beets. In 1939 all of the refiners began using identical form contracts which computed the price paid to the sugar beet growers using a "factor" common to all the refiners. As a result, all refiners paid the same price for beets of the same quality. Though there was no hard evidence of an illegal agreement, the growers brought suit under the Sherman Act against the refiners alleging that they conspired to fix a single uniform price amongst themselves so as to hold down the cost of the beets. The growers sued for the treble damages available under Sherman.

Decision: The combination of refiners was a conspiracy in interstate commerce. While their acts were committed locally, the consequences of those acts would be seen in the prices charged in distant markets in other states. This made their acts "in interstate commerce." [*Mandeville Island Farms v American Crystal Sugar Co. 334 US 219 (1948)*]

It is a violation of the federal statute to force "tying" sales on buyers; this refers to a situation in which a buyer wants to purchase one product and the seller makes him buy an additional product that he doesn't want.

The essential characteristic of a tying arrangement that violates section 1 of the Sherman Act is the use of control over the tying product within the relevant market to compel the buyer to purchase the tied article that either is not wanted or could be purchased elsewhere on better terms.[16]

The Sherman Act also prohibits professional persons, such as doctors, from using a peer review proceeding to pressure another professional who competes with them in private practice and refuses to become a member of a clinic formed by them.

Permitted conduct. A manufacturer does not violate the Sherman Act by virtue of the natural monopoly it holds over its own product. Likewise, no violation occurs when a seller dominates a market as the result of a superior product or business judgment.[17]

The Sherman Act does not deprive a city of the power to impose rent ceilings, because such a regulation does not involve concerted action.

The fact that a manufacturer sells only through a particular distributor and refuses to sell through anyone else does not in itself constitute an illegal restraint of trade.

(c) Bigness. The Sherman Antitrust Act does not prohibit bigness. However, section 7 of the Clayton Act, as amended in 1950, provides that "no corporation . . . shall acquire the whole or any part of the assets of another corporation . . . where in any line of commerce in any section of the country, the effect of such acquisition may be substantially to lessen competition, or to tend to create a monopoly."

Bigness is unlawful when based on asset acquisition of a competitor.

---

16 *Eastman Kodak Co. v Image Technical Services, Inc.* 504 US 451 (1992).
17 *McCluney v Zap Professional Photography, Inc.* (Ala) 663 So 2d 922 (1995).

If the Clayton Act is violated through ownership or control of competing enterprises, a court may order the violating defendant to dispose of such interests by issuing a decree called a **divestiture order.**[18]

Notice is required of an intended merger.

(1) Premerger Notification. When large-size enterprises plan to merge, they must give written notice to the FTC and to the attorney in charge of the Antitrust Division of the Department of Justice. This gives the department the opportunity to block the merger and thus avoid the loss that would occur if the enterprises merged and were then required to separate.[19]

Corporate takeovers are regulated to prevent abuse.

(2) Takeover Laws. Antitrust laws are usually concerned with whether the combination or agreement is fair to society or to a particular class, such as consumers. Some legislation is aimed at protecting the various parties directly involved in the combining of different enterprises. Concern arises that one enterprise may in effect be raiding another enterprise. **Takeover laws,** which seek to guard against unfairness in such situations, have been adopted by Congress and four-fifths of the states. State laws are limited in effect because they can operate only within the area over which a state has control.

Price fixing is illegal.

(d) Price Fixing. Agreements fixing prices, whether horizontally or vertically, violate the federal antitrust law. Thus, manufacturers must not agree among themselves on the price at which they will sell (**horizontal price fixing**). Likewise, a wholesaler must not require a dealer to agree not to resell below a stated price (**vertical price fixing**).[20]

(e) Exceptions to the Antitrust Law. By statute or decision, associations of exporters, marine insurance associations, farmers' cooperatives, and labor unions are exempt from the Sherman Antitrust Act with respect to agreements between their members. Certain pooling and revenue-dividing agreements between carriers are exempt from the antitrust law when approved by the appropriate federal agency. The Newspaper Preservation Act of 1970 grants an antitrust exemption to operating agreements entered into by newspapers to prevent financial collapse. The Soft Drink Interbrand Competition Act[21] grants the soft drink industry an exemption when it is shown that, in fact, there is substantial competition in spite of the agreements.

The general approach of the Supreme Court of the United States to the trust problem has been that an agreement should not be automatically or per se condemned as a restraint of interstate commerce merely because it creates the power to or the potential to monopolize interstate commerce. It is only when the restraint imposed is unreasonable that the practice is unlawful.

---

[18] *California v American Stores Co.,* 495 US 1301 (1989).

[19] Antitrust Improvement Act of 1976, PL 94-435, § 201, PL 94-435, 90 Stat 1383, 15 USC §§ 1311 et seq.

[20] Vertical price-maintenance agreements were authorized by statutes in varying degrees from 1931 to 1975, but the Consumer Goods Pricing Act of 1975, PL 94-145, 89 Stat 801, abolished the immunity from the federal antitrust law that had been given to such agreements. Although states may permit such agreements so long as interstate commerce is not involved, the area of intrastate commerce is so slight that for all practical purposes such agreements are now illegal.

[21] Act of July 9, 1980, PL 96-308, 94 Stat 939, 15 USC §§ 3501 et seq.

(f) Punishment and Civil Remedy. A violation of either of the Sherman Act provisions stated in section 5(a) of this chapter is punishable by fine or imprisonment or both at the discretion of the court. The maximum fine for a corporation is $1 million. A natural person can be fined a maximum of $100,000 or imprisoned for a maximum term of three years or both. In addition to these criminal penalties, the law provides for an injunction to stop the unlawful practices and permits suing the wrongdoers for damages.

(1) *Individual Damage Suit.* Any person or enterprise harmed may bring a separate action for **treble damages** (three times the damages actually sustained).

(2) *Class Action Damage Suit by State Attorney General.* When the effect of an antitrust violation is to raise prices, the attorney general of a state may bring a class action to recover damages on behalf of those who have paid the higher prices. This action is called a *parens patriae* **action** on the theory that the state is suing as the parent of its people.

6. Right of Person to Sue

When a statute imposes a regulation but does not state whether a private person can sue for noncompliance, courts differ in their approaches to the problem. Some courts follow the *legislative intent approach*. This can also be called the *strict approach*. By this view, if the legislature did not expressly give the right to sue, no such right exists. By the Restatement (Second) of Torts, section 874A, the court may go beyond the express terms of the statute and recognize a private right to sue if the court is of the opinion that such a right to sue is "appropriate" and "needed."

The Electronic Communications Privacy Act of 1986[22] gives the person whose privacy was improperly invaded the right to sue the person or government committing such act.[23]

CASE SUMMARY

Strictly by the Book

Facts: Crusader Insurance Company sued Scottsdale Insurance on grounds that it violated California's insurance code. The regulatory statute requires a broker such as Scottsdale to conduct a "diligent search" for an insurance carrier (e.g., Allstate) "admitted" to conduct business in California before placing a policy with a "non-admitted" carrier. Under the regulation, the state's Insurance Commissioner is given the task of enforcing the statute. The statute is silent as to whether anyone could sue an insurance company for violating the law.

Decision: The court applied the strict or legislative intent approach and held that there is no right to sue for breach of the government regulation. *[Crusader Ins. Co. v Scottsdale Ins. Co. (Ct App) 62 Cal Rptr 620 (1997)]*

---

[22] 18 USC §§ 2701 et seq.
[23] *Tucker v Waddell* (CA4 NC) 83 F3d 688 (1996).

B. LIMITATIONS ON STATE POWER TO REGULATE

By virtue of their police power, the states may regulate business to prevent the sale of harmful products, prevent fraud, and so on. The power of the states, however, is subject to important limitations.

7. Constitutional Limitations

State regulation is limited by the U.S. Constitution.

A state law, although made under the police power, cannot impose an unreasonable burden on or discriminate against interstate commerce or invade a right that is protected by the federal Constitution.

The fact that a city deprives plaintiffs of their constitutional rights does not give the plaintiffs the right to recover damages for the violation unless such a right is authorized by statute.[24]

8. Federal Supremacy

Federal regulation overrides state law.

A state law cannot conflict with a federal law or regulation covering the same subject matter. Moreover, when the federal government regulates a particular activity, state regulation is generally excluded, even regarding matters not covered by the federal regulation. In other words, the federal government occupies or preempts the entire field even though every detail is not regulated.

The federal authority that overrides state action may be a federal administrative agency regulation as contrasted with an act of Congress. Thus, the Federal Communications Commission (FCC) may prohibit states and cities from imposing stricter standards on cable television companies than those imposed by the FCC.[25]

9. State and Local Governments as Market Participants

State and local governments may act as market participants instead of as governments.

When a state or local government, such as a city or county, enters the marketplace to buy or sell goods, whether produced by itself or others, it is not acting as a government. It is a market participant as contrasted with a government regulating the conduct of others. When state governments are market participants, they are not subject to the limitations imposed on state governments by the U.S. Constitution. When local governments are market participants, their actions are not a regulation of interstate commerce.[26]

When a state or local government is a market participant, it is subject to all laws applicable to ordinary persons. *For example*, when a city owns and operates a mass transit system, it is in the position of a private employer and therefore is subject to the federal minimum wage law.

---

[24] *Hunter v City of Eugene*, 309 Or 298, 787 P2d 881 (1990).
[25] *City of New York v FCC*, 486 US 57 (1988).
[26] *USA Recycling, Inc. v Town of Babylon* (CA2 NY) 66 F3d 1272 (1995).

WHAT'S BEHIND THE LAW?

Cost-Benefit Analysis and Federal Regulation

Following a Supreme Court decision on the issue in 1983, the Department of Transportation (DOT) promulgated auto safety regulations that required automobile manufacturers to equip all vehicles with some form of passive restraint. The most popular was the air bag. The DOT had attempted to hold off on regulation until further information could be obtained about the efficacy and risks of air bags. General Motors warned in 1979 that if an air bag were inflated while a child was sitting in the front passenger side of the vehicle, the effect would be severe injury or death. In 1984 Lee Iacocca, then CEO of Chrysler, wrote: "Air bags are one of those areas where the solution may actually be worse than the problem." Insurers and consumer groups dismissed the claims as reflecting self-interest because of the costs mandatory passive restraints would impose on automobile manufacturers.

In 1996 the DOT revealed 23 people had been killed by air bags; 22 were children between the ages of one week and nine years. A mother of one of those killed by an air bag said, "It's wrong for it to be in cars."

Did the regulation move too quickly? What was the purpose of the regulation? Should more studies have been done? Is cost-benefit analysis a good approach to making decisions on rules? For more on federal regulatory agencies, visit the Code of Federal Regulations at http://www.access.gpo.gov/nara/cfr/cfr-table-search.html

SUMMARY

Regulation by government has occurred primarily to protect one group from the improper conduct of another group. Until the middle third of this century, regulation of business was primarily directed at protecting competitors from misconduct of other competitors. Beginning with the middle third of this century, regulation expanded in the interest of protecting consumers.

In the last 100 years, the federal government has regulated advertising and food, drugs, and cosmetics. This protects consumers from false claims and from untested and possibly unsafe drugs. Unfair methods of competition are prohibited.

Prices have been regulated both by the setting of the exact price or a maximum price and by prohibiting discrimination as to prices. Price discrimination between buyers is prohibited when the effect of such discrimination could tend to create a monopoly or lessen competition. Certain exceptions are made where the circumstances are such that the price discrimination does not have the purpose or result of harming someone else.

The Sherman Antitrust Act prohibits conspiracies in restraint of trade and the monopolization of trade. The Clayton Act prohibits mergers or the acquisition of the assets of another corporation when this conduct would tend to lessen competition or give rise to a monopoly. Violation of these statutes subjects the wrongdoer to criminal prosecution and suit by persons harmed for treble damages. The application of these laws is modified to some extent by express exceptions and by the Supreme Court's approach to antitrust cases.

Many of the regulations imposed by the federal government are paralleled or duplicated by state laws similarly regulating local matters. State action is restricted by the limitations arising from the Constitution and by the doctrine of the supremacy of federal law.

QUESTIONS AND CASE PROBLEMS

1. What social forces are involved in each of the following rules of law? (a) Horizontal price fixing is illegal under the federal law without regard to whether the price fixed is fair and reasonable. (b) Farmers' and dairy farmers' cooperatives are exempt by statute from the operation of the Sherman Antitrust Act.

2. A Wisconsin statute prohibits "the secret payment or allowance of rebates, refunds, commissions, or unearned discounts" to some customers without allowing them to all on the same conditions when such practices injure or tend to injure competition or a competitor. Kolbe generally gave dealers a 50 percent discount, but it gave Stock Lumber Co. a discount of 54 percent. Other dealers were not informed of this or of the conditions that had to be satisfied in order to obtain the same discount. Kolbe gave Jauquet, anoth-

er lumber dealer, only a 50 percent discount and, when asked, expressly stated that it did not give any other dealer a greater discount. When Jauquet learned of the greater discount given to Stock, it brought suit against Kolbe for violation of the Wisconsin statute. Did Kolbe violate the statute? [*Jauquet Lumber Co., Inc. v Kolbe & Kolbe Millwork, Inc.* (Wis App) 476 NW2d 305]

3. Chrysler owns a factory, but she refuses to obey the state's safety laws on the ground there is no constitutional provision that grants the state the power to make such laws. Does this justify Chrysler's refusal to obey the state law? Explain.

4. The mayor of Boston issued an executive order that on all construction work done by the city of Boston, at least one-half of the workforce had to be bona fide residents of Boston. An employer organization claimed that this requirement was a violation of the Commerce Clause of the U.S. Constitution. Decide. [*White v Massachusetts Council of Construction Employers, Inc.* 460 US 204]

5. Hines Cosmetic Co. sold beauty preparations nationally to beauty shops at a standard or fixed-price schedule. Some of the shops were also supplied with a free demonstrator and free advertising materials. The shops that were not supplied with these claimed that the giving of the free services and materials constituted unlawful price discrimination. Hines replied that there was no price discrimination because it charged everyone the same. What it was giving free was merely a promotional campaign that was not intended to discriminate against those who were not given anything free. Was Hines guilty of unlawful price discrimination? Explain.

6. Moore ran a bakery in Santa Rosa, New Mexico. His business was wholly intrastate. Meads Fine Bread Co., his competitor, engaged in an interstate business. Mead cut the price of bread in half in Santa Rosa but made no price cut in any other place in New Mexico or in any other state. As a result of this price cutting, Moore was driven out of business. Moore then sued Mead for damages for violation of the Clayton and Robinson-Patman Acts. Mead claimed that the price cutting was purely intrastate and therefore did not constitute a violation of federal statutes. Was Mead correct? Why or why not? [*Moore v Meads Fine Bread Co.* 348 US 115]

7. The federal Cable Television Consumer Protection and Competition Act regulates cable telecasting. Among other things, cable television operators are required to carry the TV signals of certain commercial and certain noncommercial educational stations. These "must-carry" provisions were challenged as impairing the freedom of speech of the stations that were required to carry the signals of other stations. Was this provision constitutional? [*Turner Broadcasting System, Inc. v FCC* (DC Dist Col) 819 F Supp 32]

8. Some time after Copperweld Corp. purchased Regal Tube Co., Independence Tube Corp. sued Copperweld and Regal for damages for conspiring in violation of the Sherman Antitrust Act. They denied liability for conspiring because Regal was the wholly owned subsidiary of Copperweld. Were they liable? Explain. [*Copperweld Corp. v Independence Tube Corp.* 467 US 752]

9. What is a decree of divestiture?

10. John Kircos purchased raw pork from the Holiday Food Center, but he failed to cook it sufficiently and became infected from the trichinae in the pork. He sued Holiday Food for damages on the ground that it had failed to place a warning label on the pork packages instructing the public to cook it to 140° Fahrenheit to destroy trichinae. The Federal Meat Inspection Act specified that any statement required by state law to be in a label that went beyond the statements required by the federal law was void. The federal law did not require any warning about cooking to be on the raw pork labels. Kircos claimed that failure to include such a warning on the labels is negligence and he could therefore sue for damages for the harm he sustained. Was he entitled to recover? [*Kircos v Holiday Food Center, Inc.* (Mich App) 477 NW2d 130]

11. Favorite Foods Corp. sold its food to stores and distributors. It established a quantity discount scale that was publicly published and made available to all buyers. The top of the scale gave the greatest discount to buyers purchasing more than 100 freight cars of food in a calendar year. Only two buyers, both national food chains, purchased in such quantities, and therefore they alone received the greatest discount. Favorite Foods was prosecuted for price discrimination in violation of the Clayton Act. Was it guilty?

Administrative Agencies

CHAPTER 6

OBJECTIVES

After studying this chapter, you should be able to

1. *List and illustrate the functions that may be exercised by an administrative agency;*
2. *State the constitutional limitations on the power of an administrative agency to require the production of papers;*
3. *Describe the typical pattern of administrative procedure;*
4. *State the extent to which an administrative agency's decision may be reviewed and reversed by a court; and*
5. *Define and state the purpose of the* Federal Register.

Late in the last century, a new type of governmental structure began to develop to meet the highly specialized needs of government regulation of business: the administrative agency.

The administrative agency is now typically the instrument through which government makes and carries out its regulation of your life.

A. NATURE OF THE ADMINISTRATIVE AGENCY

An **administrative agency** is a government body charged with administering and implementing legislation. An agency may be a department, independent establishment, commission, administration, authority, board, or bureau. Agencies exist on the federal and state levels. One example of a federal agency is the Federal Trade Commission (FTC), whose structure is shown in Figure 6-1.

1. Importance of the Administrative Agency

Government regulations are administered by agencies.

Large areas of the American economy are governed by federal administrative agencies created to carry out general policies specified by Congress. The law governing these agencies is known as **administrative law.**

State administrative agencies may also affect business and the citizen. State agencies may have jurisdiction over fair employment practices, workers' compensation claims, and the renting of homes and apartments.

2. Uniqueness of Administrative Agencies

Administrative agencies are unique in combining functions of government.

The federal government and state governments alike are divided into three branches—executive, legislative, and judicial. Many offices in these branches are filled by persons who are elected. In contrast, members of administrative agencies are ordinarily appointed (in the case of federal agencies by the president of the United States with the consent of the Senate).

In the tripartite structure, the judicial branch acts as a superguardian to prevent the executive and legislative branches from exceeding the proper spheres of their

FIGURE 6-1
Federal Trade Commission

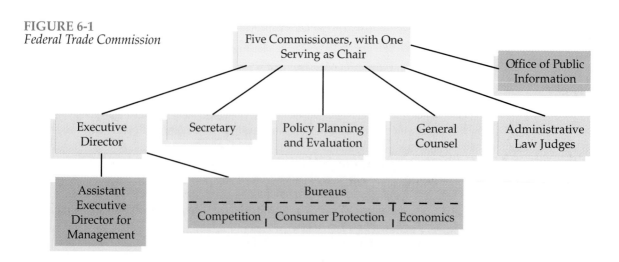

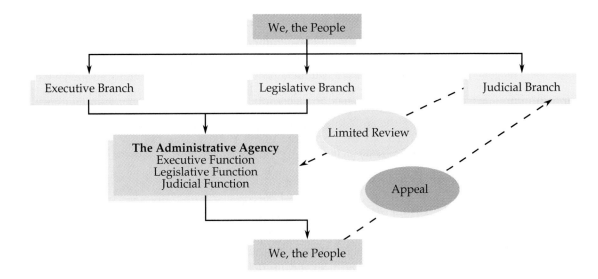

FIGURE 6-2
*The Administrative
Chain of Command*

power. However, the major agencies combine legislative, executive, and judicial powers. These agencies may make the rules, police the community to see that the rules are obeyed, and sit in judgment to determine whether there have been violations of their rules.

CASE SUMMARY

Private Eye and Trial Court in One

Facts: Duane Larkin was a physician licensed to practice medicine in Wisconsin. The state medical licensing board, of which Withrow was a member, conducted an investigation of Larkin's activities and concluded that it should hold a hearing to determine whether Larkin's license should be suspended. Larkin was charged with practicing medicine under an assumed name, permitting an unlicensed physician to perform abortions at his clinic, and fee-splitting. The Board held its hearing and decided to suspend Larkin's license. Larkin sought to enjoin the Board from enforcing its decision to suspend his license on grounds that the same board that had investigated his case acted as judge to determine whether his license should be suspended. He claimed that his procedural due process rights were denied him because the board could not have been an impartial decision maker.

Decision: Injunction refused. There was no evidence that the board was prejudiced against Larkin as the result of its investigation, nor was there any evidence that the board members would not judge the case fairly. The fact that the investigation and trial would not be conducted by separate bodies was therefore reasonable. There is no requirement in the Constitution that administrative powers be separated. [*Withrow v Larkin*, 421 US 35 (1975)]

To meet the objection that the exercise of executive, legislative, and judicial powers by the same body is a potential threat to impartiality, steps have been taken toward decentralizing the administrative functions of some agencies. Thus, the prosecution power of the National Labor Relations Board (NLRB) was withdrawn from the board and entrusted to an independent general counsel by the Labor-Management Relations Act of 1947. In a number of agencies, such as the FTC, the judicial function is assigned to administrative law judges.

3. Right to Know

To avoid the evils of secret government, provision is made for public knowledge of the activity of administrative agencies. This is done through (1) open records, (2) open meetings, and (3) public announcement of agency guidelines. More recently adopted statutes creating new agencies usually contain provisions regulating these matters. For most federal agencies not otherwise regulated, these matters are controlled by the Administrative Procedure Act (APA). Many states have adopted statutes that copy the provisions of the APA. By definition, these statutes relate only to government records and thus do not, for example, allow a business to examine the records of a competitor.[1]

(a) Open Records. The Freedom of Information Act[2] provides that information contained in records of federal administrative agencies shall be made available upon proper request. The primary purpose of this statute is "to ensure that government activities be opened to the sharp eye of public scrutiny."[3] Numerous exceptions to this right of public scrutiny are made to prevent persons from obtaining information that is not necessary to their legitimate interests.[4] State statutes typically exempt from disclosure information that would constitute an invasion of the privacy of others. However, freedom of information acts are broadly construed, and, unless an exemption of particular papers is clearly given, the papers in question are subject to public inspection. Moreover, the person claiming that there is an exemption that prohibits disclosure has the burden of proving that there is an exemption and that the facts of the case come within the scope of the exemption. Commercial or financial information of such nature not ordinarily made public by the person supplying the information is generally exempt from disclosure under a freedom of information act.[5]

The Privacy Act[6] provides that, when an agency maintains records as to persons, any person so included has the opportunity to examine the record to determine when there is a wrong statement and to obtain the correction of any errors.[7]

CASE SUMMARY

Don't Ask So Many Questions

Facts: The Tacoma-Pierce County Health Department conducted an investigation into the quality of care provided by ambulance service providers in its jurisdiction. On the basis of that investigation, the Department issued a set of temporary rules and regulations that set minimum requirements for equipment, drugs, and service availability for ambulance service providers in Pierce County. The *Tacoma News* wanted to publish an article on the matter and sought discovery of everything that had led to the adoption of the regulations, including all of the details of the investigation made by the Health Department. The Health Department objected to disclosing the names of the persons who had volunteered information on which the department had based its action and the names of the ambulance companies.

---

[1] *KMEG Television, Inc. v Iowa State Board of Regents* (Iowa) 440 NW2d 382 (1989).
[2] Added to the APA by Act of December 31, 1974, PL 93-579, 88 Stat 1897, as amended, 5 USC §§ 552 et seq.
[3] *Detroit Free Press, Inc. v Department of Justice* CA 6 73 F3d 93 (1996).
[4] Additional protection is provided by the Privacy Act of 1974, 5 USC § 552a(b); *Pilon v U.S. Department of Justice* (CA Dist Col) 73 F3d 1111 (1996).
[5] *Critical Mass Energy Project v Nuclear Regulatory Comm'n* (CA Dist Col) 975 F2d 871 (1992).
[6] 5 USC § 552.
[7] *Henke v U.S. Department of Commerce* (CA Dist Col) 83 F3d 1453 (1996).

> **Decision**: The disclosure of the identity of persons volunteering information could not be required. This would be invading the privacy of such volunteers and would have a chilling effect on future investigations by discouraging future volunteering. This would be contrary to the public interest because it would hamper the Health Department in the performance of its duties. The names of the ambulance companies could be required, since this would not interfere with such future enforcement of the law. [*Tacoma News, Inc. v Tacoma-Pierce County Health Department*, 55 Wash App 515, 778 P2d 1066 (1989)]

The primary purpose of the Freedom of Information Act is to subject agency action to public scrutiny. Therefore, its provisions are to be liberally interpreted, and agencies must make good-faith efforts to comply with its terms.

The Electronic Freedom of Information Act Amendments of 1996 extend the public availability of information to electronically stored data.[8]

(b) Open Meetings. By means of the Sunshine Act of 1976, the federal government requires most meetings of major administrative agencies to be open to the public. The object of this statute is to enable the public to know what is being done and to prevent administrative misconduct by making an agency aware that the public is watching. Many states also have enacted sunshine laws.

The right to be present at a hearing does not give the right to begin the proceedings that require the hearing.[9]

(c) Public Announcement of Agency Guidelines. To inform the public of the way administrative agencies operate, the APA, with certain exceptions, requires that each federal agency publish the rules, principles, and procedures followed by the agency.[10]

B.   LEGISLATIVE POWER OF THE AGENCY

An administrative agency has the power to make laws that regulate a particular segment of life or industry.

4.   Agency's Regulations as Law

An agency regulation is law.

An agency may adopt regulations within the scope of its authority. The power of an agency to carry out a Congressional program "necessarily requires the formulation of policy and the making of rules to fill any gap left by Congress."[11] If the regulation is not authorized by the law creating the agency, the regulation is invalid. Until proven invalid, however, a rule adopted by an administrative agency is deemed valid.

---

[8] PL 104-231.
[9] *Williams v Department of Insurance and Finance*, ____ Or App ____, 806 P2d 1161 (1991).
[10] APA codified at 5 USC § 552, Act of September 13, 1976, PL 94-409, 90 Stat 1247. See section 6 of this chapter for a description of the *Federal Register*, the publication in which these agency rules, principles, and procedures are printed.
[11] *Virginia v Browner* (CA4 Va) 80 F3d 869 (1996).

Regulations adopted by an agency may be intended to interpret or clarify the law. In deciding to accept the agency's judgment in adopting regulations, a court is influenced by such factors as the circumstances of their promulgation, the consistency with which the agency has followed the position established by the regulations, the consideration that has gone into their formulation, and the nature of the agency's expertise.[12]

In the early days of administrative regulation, the legislative character of administrative rules was not clearly perceived. An agency's sphere of power was so narrow that the agency was in effect merely a thermostat—that is, the lawmaker told the agency when to do what, and all the agency did was act in the manner specified by such direction. For example, the cattle inspector was told to take certain steps when it was determined that cattle had hoof-and-mouth disease. Here it was clear that the lawmaker had set the standard, and the agency authority merely swung into action when the specified situation existed.

The next step in the growth of administrative power in our example was authorization of the cattle inspector to act when discovering a contagious cattle disease. Thus, the inspector had to formulate a rule or guide as to which diseases were contagious. Here again, the discretionary and the legislative aspects of the agency's conduct were obscured by the belief that the field of science would define *contagious*, leaving no area of discretionary decision to the agency.

Today's health commission, an agency, is authorized to make such rules and regulations for the protection or improvement of the common health as it deems desirable. Its rules thus make up the health law.

Gradually, many courts have come to recognize the authority of an agency even though the lawmaker creating the agency did nothing more than state the goal or objective to be attained by the agency. The modern approach is to regard the administrative agency as possessing all powers necessary to effectively perform the duties entrusted to it. When the agency establishes a rational basis for its rule, the court will accept that rule. The court will not substitute its own policy as to what the rule should be.[13] This liberal approach tends to be taken in particular when the work of the agency involves protection of public health and welfare.

It has been sufficient for a legislature to authorize an agency to grant licenses "as public interest, convenience, or necessity requires"; "to prohibit unfair methods of competition"; to regulate prices so that they, "in [the agency's] judgment, will be generally fair and equitable"; to prevent "profiteering"; "to prevent the existence of intercorporate holdings, which unduly or unnecessarily complicate the structure [or] unfairly or inequitably distribute voting power among security holders"; and to renegotiate government contracts to prevent "excessive profits."

Expanding on the Statute

Facts: The practice developed for owners of trucks who drove their loaded trucks from one point to another to hire themselves and their trucks out to a common carrier so that the return trip would not be made with empty trucks. The Interstate Commerce Commission concluded that these one-trip rentals made it possible for the carriers to operate in part without satisfying the requirements otherwise applicable to them. To stop this practice, the commission

[12] *Rowinsky v Bryan Independent School District* (CA5 Tex) 80 F3d 1006 (1996).
[13] *Reytblatt v U.S. Nuclear Regulatory Commission* (CA Dist Col) 103 F3d 715 (1997).

adopted a set of rules that provided that trucks could not be rented by a carrier for less than 30 days. A number of suits were brought to prevent the enforcement of these rules on the ground that they were not authorized by the Interstate Commerce Act and their enforcement would cause financial loss and hardship.

Decision: The one-trip rental regulations were authorized. The fact that Congress had not authorized the commission to adopt such regulations did not mean that the commission did not have the power to do so. The commission had the responsibility to make regulations to promote the transportation system of the country. If it deemed that the one-trip rental regulation was desirable to achieve this goal, the commission could impose such regulation. Since the commission had the power to act, it was immaterial what the economic consequences would be. These would not be considered by the Court. The Court did not have the responsibility or power to consider the economic wisdom or effect of administrative regulations. [American Trucking Associations v United States, 344 US 298 (1953)]

In state courts, greater emphasis is placed on establishing "standards" to prevent the administrative agency from being arbitrary or capricious. In any case, an administrative regulation that goes beyond the power granted the agency is invalid. ◆ *For example,* an insurance commissioner is authorized to regulate the forms of insurance policies and to prevent discrimination. However, this authority does not give the commissioner power to adopt a regulation prohibiting insurers from considering whether an applicant for health insurance has human immunodeficiency virus (HIV). Such a condition clearly affects the health of an applicant and is properly considered by an insurer in deciding whether to accept an application.[14] ◆

An administrative agency cannot act beyond the scope of the statute that created it.[15] However, the authority of an agency is not limited to the technology existing when the agency was created. On the contrary, the sphere in which an agency may act expands with new scientific developments.[16]

When the matter is a question of policy not specifically addressed by statute, the agency given the discretion to administer the statute may establish new policies covering such issues. This power is granted whether the lawmaker had intentionally left such matters to the discretion of the agency or had merely never foreseen the problem. In either case, the matter is one to be determined within the discretion of the agency, and a court will not review an agency's policy decision.[17]

5. Public Participation in Adoption of Regulations

In some instances, nongovernmental bodies or persons play a part in furnishing information or opinions that may ultimately affect the adoption of a rule by an agency. This pattern of public participation can be illustrated by the FTC practice,

14 *Health Insurance Ass'n v Corcoran,* ____ App Div 2d ____, 551 NYS2d 615 (1990).
15 *Home Depot U.S.A. v Contractors' State License Board,* ____ Cal App 3d ____, 49 Cal Rptr 302 (1996).
16 *United States v Midwest Video Corp.,* 406 US 649 (1972) (sustaining a commission regulation that provided that "no CATV system having 3,500 or more subscribers shall carry the signal of any television broadcast station unless the system also operates to a significant extent as a local outlet by cablecasting and has available facilities for local production and presentation of programs other than automated services").
17 *Chevron, U.S.A., Inc. v National Resources Defense Council, Inc.,* 467 US 837 (1984).

Public participation may be invited or required for formulation of agency regulations.

begun in 1919, of calling together members of each significant industry so that the members can discuss which trade practices are fair and which are not. The conclusions of these conferences are not automatically binding on the FTC. They do, however, serve as a valuable means of bringing to the commission detailed information regarding the conduct of the particular industry or business in question. Under the FTC practice, the rules of fair practice agreed to at a trade conference may be approved or disapproved by the commission. When the rules are approved, a further distinction is made between those rules that are "affirmatively approved" by the commission and those that are merely "accepted as expressions of the trade." In the case of the former, the commission will enforce compliance by the members of the industry. In the case of the latter, the commission will accept the practices as fair trade practices but will not enforce compliance by persons not willing to comply. This technique of industry participation has recently been followed by several other major federal administrative agencies. In addition, the APA, with certain exceptions, requires that a federal agency planning to adopt a new regulation give public notice of such intent. The agency must then hold a public hearing.[18]

ETHICS & THE LAW

The Food and Drug Administration (FDA) has proposed rules that would restrict cigarette advertisements. The FDA declared that tobacco was a drug and therefore under its jurisdiction. Convenience stores, cigarette companies, and others have filed suit, challenging the proposed rules on two grounds. The first is that the regulations are a violation of the First Amendment. The second basis is that Congress assumed jurisdiction over cigarette ads through the Federal Cigarette Labeling and Advertising Act of 1965. Congressional intent to retain control has been clear from its refusal to grant the FDA jurisdiction.

The ads the FDA has targeted are the "Joe Camel" ads that have attracted the attention of children and teenagers. One study showed that children recognized Joe Camel as easily as they recognized Mickey Mouse. A Canadian study showed that since the time of the introduction of Joe Camel as a marketing tool, cigarette use among teenagers had increased.

Do you agree with the companies' position that the FDA is exceeding its authority? Even if the FDA does not have the authority to regulate advertising, should the companies undertake voluntary restrictions? Why or why not? What are the implications of continuing the ads? Should magazines, newspapers, and billboard companies refuse the cigarette ads?

6. Public Knowledge of Regulations

Federal agency regulations are published in the *Federal Register*.

When an agency adopts a regulation, a practical problem arises about how to inform the public of its existence. Some regulations will have already attracted enough public attention that the news media will provide the desired publicity. The great mass of regulations, however, does not attract such attention. To provide publicity

---

[18] APA codified at 5 USC §§ 553, 556, by Act of September 6, 1966, PL 89-554, 80 Stat 383, as amended. The Negotiated Rulemaking Act of 1990, Act of November 15, 1990, PL 101-552, 104 Stat 2736, ___ USC ____, encourages federal agencies to formulate their regulations with the cooperation of those affected.

for all regulations, the Federal Register Act provides that an administrative regulation is not binding until it is printed in the *Federal Register*. This is a government publication, published five days a week, that lists all administrative regulations, all presidential proclamations and executive orders, and other documents and classes of documents that the president or Congress directs to be published.

The Federal Register Act provides that the printing of an administrative regulation in the *Federal Register* is sufficient to give notice of the contents of the regulation to any person subject to it or affected by it. This means that no one can claim as an excuse ignorance of the published regulation. This is so even though the person in fact did not know that the regulation had been published in the *Register*. A regulation is effective 30 days after publication.

C. EXECUTIVE POWER OF THE AGENCY

The modern administrative agency has the power to execute the law and to bring proceedings against violators.

7. Execution of the Law

The power of an agency to execute the law is, of course, confined to matters within an agency's jurisdiction. Within that sphere, an agency typically has the power to investigate, to require persons to appear as witnesses, to require witnesses to produce relevant papers and records, and to bring proceedings against violators of the law. In this connection, the phrase *the law* embraces regulations adopted by an agency as well as statutes and court decisions. Increasingly, agencies are required to file opinions and reports or to give explanations for their actions.

CASE SUMMARY

That's Going Too Far!

Facts: The Reserve Mining Company obtained a permit from the Minnesota Pollution Control Agency to dump wastewater into the nearby Beaver River. The permit specified that no more than 1 million fibers per liter may be discharged in the company's wastewater. The agency did not make or file any explanation as to how or why that maximum was selected. Normally the wastewater generated by the company was kept in a tailings dam with a discharge in the river necessary only in an emergency. Because of a sudden economic downturn, the company foresaw the need to dispose of wastewater in the river and discovered that the discharge it would have to make would likely be between 10 to 15 times the amount of fiber allowed by the permit. Reserve Mining appealed the maximum limitation imposed by the agency.

Decision: The agency had acted arbitrarily and capriciously in setting the maximum without any explanation or justification as to how or why it selected that particular specified maximum. Because of the importance of waste pollution control, reasonable action by an agency required it to explain and justify its action. Only in this way would the parties and an appellate court have the advantage of the expertise of the agency. Without this explanation, no one could know why the limitation was imposed or whether in fact it was a good limitation. Because the action of the agency had been arbitrary and capricious, the matter was sent back to the agency to do its job properly. [*Reserve Mining Co. v Minnesota Pollution Control Agency (Minn App) 364 NW2d 411 (1985)*]

An agency may investigate to determine if there is any violation of the law or of its rules generally. An agency may also investigate to determine whether additional rules need to be adopted, to ascertain the facts with respect to a particular suspected or alleged violation, and to see if the defendant in a proceeding before it is complying with its final order.

The federal Antitrust Civil Process Act is an example of the extent to which administrative investigation is authorized. The act authorizes the attorney general or the assistant attorney general in charge of the Antitrust Division of the Department of Justice to make a civil investigative demand (CID) on any person believed to have knowledge relevant to any civil antitrust investigation. This might be in connection with an investigation before bringing a suit to enjoin a monopolistic practice or an investigation made on receiving a premerger notification. The person so notified can be compelled to produce relevant documents, furnish written answers to written questions, or appear in person and give oral testimony.[19] Similar power to require the production of papers is possessed by the Federal Trade Commission, the Federal Maritime Commission, the National Science Foundation, the Treasury Department, the Department of Agriculture, the Department of the Army, the Department of Labor, and the Veterans Administration.

CASE SUMMARY

I Ain't Accusing—Just Snooping

Facts: Wilson Corp. was served with a CID issued under state law. It refused to give the requested information on the ground that there was no evidence that a crime had been committed.

Decision: Wilson's objection was not valid. A CID is not a search warrant that may be issued only when there is probable cause that a crime has been committed. In contrast, a CID is an investigative device that may be used to see if there is any violation of the law. This purpose would be defeated if the CID could not be used until it was shown that a crime had been committed. [*Wilson Corp. v New Mexico (NM) 916 P2d 1344 (1996)*]

An agency may issue subpoenas to obtain information reasonably required by its investigation.[20]

8.   Constitutional Limitations on Administrative Investigation

The Constitution does not impose any significant limitations on the power of an agency to conduct an investigation.

(a) Inspection of Premises. In general, a person has the same protection against unreasonable search and seizure by an administrative officer as by a police officer.

In contrast, when the danger of concealment is great, a warrantless search can be made of the premises of a highly regulated business, such as one selling liquor or firearms. Likewise, when violation of the law is dangerous to health and safety, the law may authorize inspection of the workplace without advance notice or a search warrant when such a requirement could defeat the purpose of the inspection.

---

[19] Antitrust Civil Process Act of 1962, as amended by the Antitrust Improvement Act of 1976, §§ 101, 102, PL 94-435, 90 Stat 1383, 15 USC §§ 1311 et seq.

[20] *United States v Construction Products Research, Inc.* (CA2 Conn) 73 F3d 464 (1996).

(b) Aerial Inspection. A search warrant is never required when the subject matter can be seen from a public place. ◆ *For example,* when a police officer walking on the public pavement can look through an open window and see illegal weapons, a search warrant is not required to enter the premises and seize the weapons. Using airplanes and helicopters, law enforcement officers can see from the air. Can an agency gather information in this manner? It has been held that a police officer may do so,[21] and there is no reason to believe an agency does not possess the same power. ◆

(c) Production of Papers. For the most part, the constitutional guarantee against unreasonable search and seizure does not afford much protection with regard to papers and records being investigated by an agency. That guarantee does not apply if there is not an actual seizure. ◆ *For example,* a subpoena to testify or to produce records cannot be opposed on the ground that it is a search and seizure. The constitutional protection is limited to cases of actual physical search and seizure rather than the obtaining of information by compulsion. ◆

The protection afforded by the guarantee against self-incrimination is likewise narrow. It cannot be invoked when a corporate employee or officer in control of corporate records is compelled to produce those records even though he or she would be incriminated by them.[22] It cannot be invoked if records that by law must be kept by the person subject to the administrative investigation are involved.

(d) Fair Return on Regulated Business. When governments regulate the rates of a public utility or an insurance company, the business regulated is constitutionally entitled to a rate that will produce a fair return on assets used in the business.[23]

D.   JUDICIAL POWER OF THE AGENCY

The modern administrative agency possesses judicial powers.

9.   The Agency as a Specialized Court

An agency can function as a court.

An agency may be given power to sit as a court and to determine whether there have been any violations of the law or of agency regulations. Thus, the NLRB determines whether a prohibited labor practice has been committed. The FTC acts as a court to determine whether unfair competition exists.

Although an administrative agency may be given judicial power, it is not a court.[24]

At first glance, the conferring of any judicial power on an administrative agency seems contrary to American tradition. When an administrative agency sits as judge to determine whether one of its regulations has been violated, there is

---

[21] *California v Ciraolo,* 476 US 207 (1986).
[22] *Braswell v United States,* 487 US 99 (1988).
[23] *California Automobile Assigned Risk Plan v Gillespie,* ____ Cal App 3d ____, 280 Cal Rptr 217 (1991).
[24] *Beyer v Employees Retirement System of Texas* (Tex App) 808 SW2d 622 (1991).

some question whether the agency is impartial. The agency is trying the accused for violating agency law rather than "the law." There is also the objection that an agency is determining important rights without a jury. This seems inconsistent with the long-established emphasis of our history on the sanctity of trial by jury. In spite of these objections to an agency's exercise of judicial power, such exercise is now firmly established.

An agency cannot make a decision without first deciding that the matter comes within its scope of authority.

10. Pattern of Administrative Procedure

Agency procedure may begin with a complaint or an investigation leading to pleading and trial similar to a lawsuit but much simplified.

At the beginning of the era of modern regulation of business, the power of agencies to adjudicate rested, to a large extent, on minor executives or police officers charged with the responsibility of enforcing laws applicable to limited fact situations. The example of the health officer empowered to condemn and destroy diseased cattle was typical. In view of the need for prompt action, and because of the relative simplicity of the fact determination to be made, it was customary for such a person to exercise summary powers. On finding cattle believed to be diseased, the officer would destroy the animals immediately. There would be no delay to find their true owner or to hold a formal hearing to determine whether the animals were in fact diseased.

Today, the exercise of summary powers is the exceptional case. Concepts of due process generally require that some notice be given those who will be adversely affected and that some form of hearing be held at which they may present their case.

(a) Preliminary Steps. It is commonly provided that either a private individual aggrieved by the conduct of another or an agency may file a written complaint. This complaint is then served on the alleged wrongdoer, who is given the opportunity to file an answer. There may be other phases of pleading between the parties and the agency, but eventually the matter comes before the agency to be heard. After a hearing, the agency makes a decision and enters an order either dismissing the complaint or directing the adverse party to carry out or refrain from certain acts.

The complaint filing and prehearing stage of the procedure may be more detailed. In many modern administrative statutes, provision is made for an examination of the informal complaint by some branch of the agency to determine whether the case comes within the scope of the agency's authority. It is also commonly provided that an investigation be made by the agency to determine whether the facts are such as to warrant a hearing of the complaint. If it is decided that the complaint is within the jurisdiction of the agency and that the facts appear to justify it, a formal complaint is issued and served on the adverse party.

An answer is then filed as stated above.

With the increasing complexity of the subjects regulated by administrative agencies, the trend is to require greater preliminary examination on the basis of an informal complaint.

(b) The Administrative Hearing. To satisfy the requirements of due process, it is generally necessary for an agency to give notice and hold a hearing at which all

An administrative hearing does not require a jury trial and is not subject to the rules of evidence.

persons affected may be present. A person indirectly affected by administrative action cannot take part in the administrative hearing. An existing enterprise has no standing to challenge the granting of a license to a new business that will be a competitor.[25]

A significant difference between an agency hearing and a court hearing is that there is no right of trial by jury before an agency. ◆ *For example,* a workers' compensation board may decide a claim without any jury. ◆ Similarly, there is no right to a jury trial in an action for violation of the Age Discrimination in Employment Act.[26] The absence of a jury does not constitute a denial of due process.

CASE SUMMARY

What! No Jury?

Facts: Johnny Boseman, a temporary employee of Atlas Roofing, was killed when he fell through the unfinished warehouse roof which Atlas was under contract to construct. The death initiated an inspection by the Department of Labor and Atlas was fined $600 for its "serious" violation of workplace safety standards pursuant to the Occupational Safety and Health Act of 1970. Atlas chose to contest the penalty claiming that it had been denied a jury trial as guaranteed by the Seventh Amendment of the Constitution: "In suits at common law, where the value in controversy shall exceed twenty dollars, the right of trial by jury shall be preserved . . . ."

Decision: Judgment against Atlas Roofing. The constitutional provision means only that where a jury was required at common law, it must now be provided. The constitutional provision has no application to new duties and liabilities created by statute that were unknown to the common law. Such new duties and liabilities may therefore be determined without a jury. *[Atlas Roofing Company, Inc. v Occupational Safety and Health Review Commission, 430 US 442 (1977)]*

An agency is ordinarily not subject to the rules of evidence. Another significant difference between an administrative hearing and a judicial determination is that an agency may be authorized to make an initial determination without holding a hearing. If an agency's conclusion is challenged, the agency will then hold a hearing. A court, on the other hand, must have a trial before it makes a judgment. This has important practical consequences in that when a hearing is sought after an agency has acted, the objecting party has the burden of proof and the cost of going forward. The result is that fewer persons go to the trouble of seeking such a hearing. This, in turn, reduces the number of hearings and the amount of litigation in which an agency becomes involved. Thus, from the government's standpoint, money and time are saved.

When an administrative action concerns only the individuals directly affected rather than a class of persons or the community in general, it is necessary to have some form of hearing before an agency may make a judicial decision. Thus, it has been held by the Supreme Court that, because a civil service employee may be removed only for cause, it is a denial of due process for a statute to authorize an agency to remove the employee without a hearing.[27] It is not sufficient that the

---

[25] *Pie Mut. Ins. Co. v Kentucky Medical Ins. Co.* (Ky App) 782 SW2d 51 (1990).
[26] 29 USC 621 et seq.
[27] *Cleveland Board of Education v Loudermill,* 470 US 532 (1985).

employee is given the right to appeal such action. Because the employee has a significant interest in continued employment, there must be some preremoval hearing to determine that there is no basic error in the administrative action.

With mutual consent, agency steps may be skipped or the matter referred to an alternative means of dispute resolution.

(c) Streamlined Procedure. Informal settlement and consent decrees are practical devices to cut across the procedures outlined above. In many instances, the alleged wrongdoer is willing to change when informally notified that a complaint has been made. It is therefore sound public relations, as well as expeditious handling of the matter, for an agency to inform an alleged wrongdoer of the charge before the filing of any formal complaint. A matter that has already gone into the formal hearing stage may also be terminated by agreement, and a stipulation or consent decree may be filed, setting forth the terms of the agreement.

Streamlining procedure is encouraged by the Administrative Dispute Resolution Act of 1990, which authorizes federal agencies to use alternative means of dispute resolution.

(d) Rehearing and Correction of Administrative Action. Under some statutes, an agency is given power to rehear or correct a decision within a certain time.

(e) Form of Administrative Decision. When an administrative agency makes a judicial decision, it should file an opinion setting forth the facts and reasons on which the decision is based. In some instances, a statute will expressly require this, but an agency should always file an opinion so that the parties and the court to which an appeal is taken will understand the agency's action and reasons.[28]

11. Punishment and Enforcement Powers of Agencies

Agencies have punishment and enforcement powers.

Originally, agencies could not impose punishment or enforce decisions. If the person regulated did not voluntarily comply with an agency's decision, the agency could only petition a court to order that person to obey.

Within the last few decades, agencies have been increasingly given the power to impose a penalty and to issue orders that are binding on the regulated person unless an appeal is taken to a court and the administrative decision reversed. As an illustration of the power to impose penalties, the Occupational Safety and Health Act of 1970 provides for the assessment of civil penalties against employers failing to put an end to dangerous working conditions when ordered to do so by the administrative agency created by that statute.[29] Likewise, environmental protection statutes adopted by states commonly give the state agency the power to assess a penalty for a violation of the environmental protection regulations. As an illustration of the issuance of binding orders, the FTC can issue a **cease and desist order** to stop a practice that it decides is improper. This order to stop is binding unless reversed on an appeal.

---

[28] *Ballas v Town of Weaverville* (NC App) 465 SE2d 324 (1996).
[29] 29 USC 651 et seq.

CASE SUMMARY

Punishment Power Limited

Facts: Linda Olander filed a complaint with the California Fair Employment and Housing Commission, claiming that her employer, Dyna-Med, Inc., had discriminated against her on the basis of gender in denying her a promotion. Olander had worked as an editor for Dyna-Med for several years, receiving favorable performance evaluations and promotions during that time. She made it known that she wanted to be considered for the open publications manager position of another magazine which Dyna-Med produced. Dyna-Med's president instead hired a far less qualified man for the position. Five hours after agreeing in a settlement agreement not to engage in any retaliatory action against Olander for filing the complaint, Dyna-Med fired Olander. Olander filed another complaint and the commission found that Dyna-Med had further discriminated against Olander. The commission entered judgment in her favor for lost wages and $7,500 in punitive damages to punish the employer for its wanton behavior. The statute creating the commission gave it the power to "take such action . . . including . . . reinstatement . . . with or without back pay . . . as in the judgment of the Commission will effectuate the purposes" of the antidiscrimination statute. Dyna-Med claimed that the commission could not impose a judgment for punitive damages.

Decision: The statute gave the commission the power to take remedial and corrective measures. It was not expressly granted the power to impose punitive damages, and such a power does not exist unless expressly granted. The part of the commission's decision that granted Olander punitive damages was therefore improper and was set aside. [*Dyna-Med, Inc. v Fair Employment and Housing Commission, 43 Cal 3d 1379, 241 Cal Rptr 67, 743 P2d 1323 (1987)*]

(a) Compliance Verification. To assure itself that a particular person or business is obeying the law, including the agency's regulations and orders, an administrative agency may require proof of compliance. At times the question of compliance may be directly determined by an agency investigation, involving an examination either of a building or plant or of witnesses and documents. An agency may require the regulated person or enterprise to file reports in a specified form.[30] An agency may also hold a hearing or an audit on the question of compliance and may require the filing of a detailed statement or plan of operation showing that the regulated person or enterprise is acting properly.

An agency may have power to require a wrongdoer to compensate the victim of misconduct for loss inflicted.

(b) Complainant Indemnification. When the administrative decision is that the defendant has caused a loss to or harmed a particular person, can the administrative agency compensate or indemnify the harmed person for the loss? Until the 1930s, the answer to this question was that the administrative agency could stop further wrong but could not undo or compensate for past wrong. Beginning with the New Deal legislation of the 1930s, administrative agencies have been given the power in some cases to provide indemnity to the party harmed by the defendant's wrong. Such power is not unlimited: Its boundaries are defined by the statute creating the agency.

---

[30] *United States v Morton Salt Co.* 338 US 632 (1950).

12. Exhaustion of Administrative Remedy

A court will not review agency action until the remedy before the agency has been exhausted.

When the law creates an agency, all parties must follow the procedure specified by the law. An appeal may be taken to a court, but it cannot be taken until the agency has acted. The principle is that, as a matter of policy, parties are required to exhaust the administrative remedy before they may go into court or take an appeal.[31]

As long as an agency is acting within the scope of its authority or jurisdiction, a party cannot appeal before the agency has made a final decision. The fact that the complaining party does not want the agency to decide the matter, or is afraid that the agency will reach a wrong decision, is not grounds for bypassing the agency by going to court before the agency has acted.

Exceptions to exhaustion-of-remedy requirement. Exhaustion of administrative remedies is not required when (1) available remedies provide no genuine opportunity for adequate relief, (2) irreparable injury may occur if immediate judicial relief is not provided, (3) an appeal to the administrative agency would be useless, or (4) the plaintiff has raised a substantial constitutional question.

CASE SUMMARY

No Wild Goose Chase

Facts: Hardin Oldsmobile claimed that American Honda and the New Motor Vehicle Board were guilty of fraudulent practices. When Hardin brought suit, Honda claimed that Hardin was required to present his claim to the New Motor Vehicle Board and could not sue until that remedy had been exhausted.

Decision: Honda is wrong. The exhaustion rule applies only to matters within the jurisdiction of the agency. The agency had no authority to hear claims as to fraudulent practices. Therefore, Hardin was not required to assert such claims before the agency before being allowed to sue Honda in court. [*Hardin Oldsmobile v New Motor Vehicle Board, Cal App 3d, 60 Cal Rptr 583 (1997)*]

---

13. Appeal from Administrative Action

Persons aggrieved by agency action may generally appeal to a court.

The statute creating the modern administrative agency generally provides for the taking of an appeal from the administrative decision to a particular court. The statute may state that a party in interest or any person aggrieved by the administrative action may appeal. This requires the appellant to have a legally recognized right or interest that is harmed by the administrative action. The fact that a person or persons do not like the action of the agency does not entitle them to appeal.

14. Finality of Administrative Determination

A court will reverse the agency action if a clear error of law was made by the agency. It will not do so if the agency had discretion to act as it did or if there was substantial evidence to support the agency decision.

Basic to Anglo-American legal theory is the belief that no one, not even a branch of the government, is above the law. Thus, the growth of powers of the administrative agency was frequently accepted or tolerated on the theory that if the agency went too far, the courts would review the administrative action. The typical modern statute provides that an appeal may be taken from the administrative action.

---

[31] *Gezendorf v Washburn,* ____ Ill App 3d ____, ____ Ill Dec ____, 565 NE2d 1054 (1991).

If the procedure that an agency is to follow is specified by law, a decision of the agency that was made without following that procedure will be set aside and the matter sent back to the agency to proceed according to the required law.[32]

When the question that an agency decides is a question of law, the court on appeal will reverse the agency if the court disagrees with the decision.[33] This concept is being eroded to some extent by modern technology. Thus, a court held that it would accept an agency's interpretation of a statute when the statute relates to a technical matter. Here the court tended to accept the agency's interpretation so long as it was reasonable, even though it was not the only interpretation that could have been made.

In contrast with an agency's decision on matters of law, a controversy may turn on a question of fact or a mixed question of law and fact. In such cases, a court will accept the conclusion of an agency if it is supported by substantial evidence. This means that the court must examine the entire record of the proceedings before the administrative agency to determine if there was substantial evidence to support the administrative findings. So long as reasonable minds could have reached the same conclusion as the agency after considering all the evidence as a whole, the court must sustain the fact findings of the agency.[34]

A court will not reverse an agency's decision merely because the court would have made a different decision on the same facts.[35] Because most disputes before an agency are based on questions of fact, the net result is that the decision of the agency will be final in most cases.

Courts must give administrative agencies the freedom to do the work delegated to them and should not intervene unless the agency action is clearly unreasonable and arbitrary. The agency action is presumed proper, and a person seeking reversal of the agency action has the burden of proving a basis therefor.[36]

When the question is whether an administrative action is in harmony with the policy of the statute creating the agency, an appellate court will sustain the administrative action if it is supported by substantial evidence.

When an agency changes its prior course of decision, it must set forth its reasons for so doing. In the absence of such an explanation, a reviewing court cannot tell whether the agency changed its interpretation of the law for a valid reason or has made a mistake. The absence of an explanation condemns the agency action as arbitrary and requiring reversal.[37]

The greatest limitation on court review of administrative action is the rule that a decision involving discretion will not be reversed in the absence of an error of law or a clear abuse of, or the arbitrary or capricious exercise of, discretion. The courts reason that because agency members were appointed on the basis of expert ability, it would be absurd for the court, which is unqualified technically to make a decision in the matter, to step in and determine whether the agency made the proper choice. Courts will not do so unless the agency has clearly acted wrongly, arbitrarily, or capriciously. As a practical matter, the action of an agency is rarely found to be arbitrary or capricious. As long as an agency has followed proper

---

[32] *Tingler v State Board of Cosmetology* (Mo App) 814 SW2d 683 (1991)

[33] *Re* Minnesota Joint Underwriting Ass'n (Minn App) 408 NW2d 599 (1987).

[34] *Wilmer-Hutchins Independent School District v Brown* (Tex App) 912 SW2d 848 (1995).

[35] *In re* Corman, Wyo 909 P2d 966 (1996). An appellate court cannot review the evidence to determine the credibility of witnesses who testified before the administrative agency. *Hammann v City of Omaha,* ____ Neb ____, 417 NW2d 323 (1987).

[36] *Holloday v Louisiana State Board of Medical Examiners* (La App) 689 So 2d 718 (1997).

[37] *Richardson v Commissioner of New York City Department of Social Services,* 88NY 2d 35, 643 NYS2d 19, ____ NE2d ____, (1996).

procedure, the fact that the court disagrees with the conclusion reached by the agency does not make that conclusion arbitrary or capricious. In areas in which economic or technical matters are involved, it is generally sufficient that the agency had a reasonable basis for its decision. A court will not attempt to second-guess the agency about complex criteria with which an administrative agency is intimately familiar. The judicial attitude is that, for protection from laws and regulations that are unwise, improvident, or out of harmony with a particular school of thought, the people must resort to the ballot box, not to the court.

The fact that other agencies or trade associations disagree with the view of an agency does not make the latter's decision improper. ◆ *For example,* the decision of a state Board of Accounting was not arbitrary, capricious, or an abuse of discretion because it disagreed with the view of the Federal Trade Commission, the American Institute of Certified Public Accountants, and the National Association of State Boards of Accounting.[38] ◆

Because of limited funding and staff, an agency must exercise discretion in deciding which cases should be handled. Ordinarily, the decision of an agency to do nothing about a particular complaint will not be reversed by a court.[39] That is, the courts will not override an agency's decision to do nothing. Exceptions are made, however, when it is obvious that the agency is refusing to act; then the court may override the decision.

15. Liability of the Agency

An agency is ordinarily not liable for the economic loss caused by its action.

The decision of an agency may cause substantial loss to a business by increasing its operating costs or by making a decision that later is shown to be harmful to the economy. An agency is not liable for such loss when it has acted in good faith in the exercise of discretionary powers. An administrator who wrongly denies a person the benefit of a government program is not personally liable to that person even though that person's constitutional rights have been violated.[40]

SUMMARY

The administrative agency is unique because it combines the three functions that are kept separate under our traditional governmental system: legislative, executive, and judicial. By virtue of legislative power, an agency adopts regulations that have the force of law, although the members of the agency were not elected by those subject to the regulations. By virtue of the executive power, an agency carries out and enforces the regulations, makes investigations, and requires the production of documents. By virtue of the judicial power, an agency acts as a court to determine whether there has been a violation of any regulation. To some extent, an agency is restricted by constitutional limitations in inspecting premises and requiring the production of papers. These limitations, however, have a very

narrow application. The protection against unreasonable search and seizure and the protection against self-incrimination have been so narrowed by judicial construction as to have little protective value. When an agency acts as a judge, a jury trial is not required, nor must ordinary courtroom procedures be followed. Typically, an agency will give notice to the person claimed to be acting improperly, and a hearing will then be held before the agency. When the agency has determined that there has been a violation, it may order that the violation stop. Under some statutes, the agency may go further and impose a penalty on the violator.

An appeal to a court may be taken from any decision of the agency by a person harmed by the decision. Only a

---

[38] *Earles v Board of Certified Public Accountants* (La App) 665 So 2d 1288 (1995).
[39] *Heckler v Chaney,* 470 US 821 (1985).
[40] *Schweiker v Chilicky,* 487 US 412 (1988).

person with a legally recognized interest can appeal from the agency ruling. No appeal can be taken until every step available before the agency has been taken; that is, the administrative remedy must first be exhausted.

As a practical matter, an appeal from administrative action will ordinarily have little value. When a controversy turns on a determination of facts, a court will not reverse the decision of an agency because it disagrees with the conclusion that the agency drew from those facts. When an agency is given discretion to act, a court will never reverse the agency just because it disagrees with the choice the agency made. In contrast, if an agency makes a wrong decision on a question of law, a court will generally reverse the agency if the court disagrees with the decision. In the absence of an error of law, an agency's decision will be reversed only if the court decides that the administrative action was arbitrary and capricious.

Protection from secret government is provided by the right to know what most administrative agency records contain, by the requirement that most agency meetings be open to the public, by the invitation to the public to take part in rule making, and by publicity given, through publication in the *Federal Register,* to the guidelines followed by the agency and the regulations it has adopted.

QUESTIONS AND CASE PROBLEMS

1. What social forces are affected by the principle that the same administrative agency may conduct an investigation to determine if there is reason to believe there has been a violation and then hold a hearing to determine whether in fact there was a violation?

2. Congress adopted a law to provide insurance to protect wheat farmers. The agency in charge of the program adopted regulations to govern applications for this insurance. These regulations were published in the *Federal Register.* Merrill applied for insurance, but his application did not comply with the regulations. He claimed that he was not bound by the regulations because he never knew they had been adopted. Is he bound by the regulations? *[Federal Crop Ins. Corp. v Merrill, 332 US 380]*

3. The federal Department of Housing and Urban Development (HUD) decides to hold a conference of leading building contractors to decide patterns of urban development that should be encouraged by HUD. Culpepper wants to attend the meeting but is denied admission because she is neither a government official nor a building contractor. Is she entitled to attend the meeting?

4. Adams is appointed the state's price control administrator. By virtue of this position, he requires all sellers of goods and suppliers of services to keep records of the prices they charge. He suspects that Ace Overhead Garage Door Corp. is charging more than the prices permitted by law. To determine this, he notifies the company to produce the records that it was required to keep. It refuses to do so on the ground that Adams does not have the authority to require the production of papers. Is this a valid defense?

5. Bell was employed by Sinclair Radio Corp. She was fired from her job and filed a complaint with the National Labor Relations Board that she was fired because she belonged to a union. The examiner of the board held a hearing, at which Bell produced evidence of an antiunion attitude of the employer. The employer produced evidence that Bell had been fired because she was chronically late and did poor work. The examiner and the Labor Relations Board concluded that Bell was fired because of her union membership. Sinclair appealed. The court reached the conclusion that, if the court had been the board, it would have held that the discharge of Bell was justified because it would not have believed the testimony of Bell's witnesses. Will the court reverse the decision of the National Labor Relations Board?

6. Santa Monica adopted a rent control ordinance authorizing the Rent Control Board to set the amount of rents that could be charged. At a hearing before the board, the board determined that McHugh was charging his tenants a rent greater than the maximum allowed. McHugh claimed that the action of the board was improper because there was no jury trial. Decide. *[McHugh v Santa Monica Rent Control Board, 49 Cal 3d 348, 261 Cal Rptr 318, 777 P2d 91]*

7. New York City's charter authorized the New York City Board of Health to adopt a health code that it declared to have the force and effect of law. The board adopted a code that provided for the fluoridation of the public water supply. A suit was brought to enjoin the carrying out of this program on the grounds that it was unconstitutional and that money could not be spent to carry out such a program in the absence of a statute authorizing the expenditure. It was also claimed that the fluoridation program was unconstitutional because there were other means of reducing tooth decay; fluoridation was discriminatory by benefiting only children; it unlawfully imposed medication on children without their consent; and fluoridation was or may be dangerous to health. Was the code's provision valid? *[Paduano v City of New York, 257 NYS2d 531]*

8. The Federal Trade Commission directs Essex Manufacturing Co. to install safety devices in its factory. Essex claims that the order of the commission can be ignored because the members of the commission were not elected by the voters and therefore the commission cannot make an order that has the force of law. Is this defense valid?

9. By training and work experience, Templeton was a plumbing and heating maintenance worker. He sustained an injury that left his right arm useless. Because of this, he quit his regular employment and took a half-time job with Black Hills State College to run a program of preventive equipment maintenance. The job required a knowledge of computer programming and data processing. Templeton resigned after a while because he could not live on the half-time pay, and he filed a claim for disability benefits under the state's retirement system. The retirement statute defined disability as "any medically determinable physical or mental impairment which prevents a member from performing his usual duties for his employer, or the duties of a position of comparable level for which he is qualified by education, training, and experience . . . ." The retirement board denied his application because he could work for the state college. Templeton took an appeal. Decide. [In re Templeton (SD) 403 NW2d 398]

10. The Occupational Safety and Health Act of 1970 authorizes the secretary of labor to adopt job safety standards to protect workers from harmful substances. The secretary is directed by the statute to adopt the standard that most adequately assures, to the extent feasible on the basis of the best available evidence, that no employee will suffer material impairment of health. Acting under this authorization, the secretary adopted a cotton dust standard to protect workers exposed to cotton dust. This dust causes serious lung disease that disables about 1 out of 12 cotton factory workers. The cotton industry attacked the validity of the standard on the ground that the secretary, in adopting the standard, had not considered the cost to the cotton industry of complying with it (a cost of $656.5 million). Was the cotton dust standard valid? [American Textile Manufacturers Institute, Inc. v Donovan, 452 US 490]

11. The Macon County Landfill Corporation applied for permission to expand the boundaries of its landfill. This was opposed by Tate and others. After a number of hearings, the appropriate agency granted the requested permission to expand. Tate appealed and claimed that the agency had made a wrong decision on the basis of the evidence presented. Will the court determine if the correct decision was made? [Tate v

Illinois Pollution Control Board, 188 Ill App 3d 994, 136 Ill Dec 401, 544 NE2d 1176]

12. The planning commissioner and a real estate developer planned to meet to discuss rezoning certain land that would permit the real estate developer to construct certain buildings not allowed under the then-existing zoning law. A homeowners association claimed it had the right to be present at the meeting. This claim was objected to on the theory that the state's Open Meetings Act applied only to meetings of specified government units and did not extend to a meeting between one of them and an outsider. Was this objection valid?

13. The Michigan Freedom of Information Act declares that it is the state's policy to give all persons full information about the actions of the government and that "the people shall be informed so that they may participate in the democratic process." The union of clerical workers at Michigan State University requested the trustees of the university to give them the names and addresses of persons making monetary donations to the university. Objection was made that the disclosure of addresses could not be required and was a violation of the right of privacy. Decide. [Clerical-Technical Union of Michigan State University v Board of Trustees of Michigan State University, ___Mich App___, 475 NW2d 373]

14. The Jones Corp. wanted to build an additional plant. By state law, it was required to obtain the approval of the state environmental protection agency. Jones made an application for such approval. Nothing happened. Jones Corp. complained about the delay. The state agency explained that it was studying the environmental pollution problems of similar factories in other states and this was taking time. Jones was afraid that the delay would cause it to lose investors. Jones filed a petition in court to obtain approval of its expansion plan. What decision should the court make?

15. A state law authorized the state's insurance commissioner to impose a fine and suspend the license of any insurance agent selling "unnecessary or excessive" insurance. The insurance commissioner fined Eloise, a licensed agent, $600 and suspended her license for three months for selling "unnecessary and excessive" insurance. She objected to this action on the ground that the statute under which the commissioner had acted was unconstitutional in that "unnecessary" and "excessive" were too vague and indefinite to have any meaning and therefore it was unconstitutional to penalize her for violating such a standard. Decide.

The Legal Environment of International Trade

CHAPTER 7

A. GENERAL PRINCIPLES

1. The Legal Background
2. International Trade Organizations, Conferences, and Treaties
3. Forms of Business Organizations

B. GOVERNMENTAL REGULATION

4. Export Regulations
5. Protection of Intellectual Property Rights
6. Antitrust
7. Securities Regulation in an International Environment
8. Barriers to Trade
9. Relief Mechanisms for Economic Injury Caused by Foreign Trade
10. Expropriation
11. Government-Assisted Export Programs
12. The Foreign Corrupt Practices Act

OBJECTIVES

After studying this chapter, you should be able to

1. *Identify seven major international organizations, conferences, and treaties;*
2. *Describe the forms of business organizations that exist for doing business abroad;*
3. *Identify conduct outside of the United States to which the U.S. antitrust laws will apply;*
4. *Differentiate between secrecy laws and blocking laws in regard to SEC enforcement of U.S. securities laws;*
5. *List and explain the laws that provide protection against unfair competition from foreign goods;*
6. *List and explain the laws that provide economic relief for those adversely affected by import competition; and*
7. *List and explain the laws enacted to increase the foreign sales of U.S. firms.*

The success or failure of the American firms doing business in foreign countries may well depend on accurate information about the laws and customs of the host countries. In their domestic operations, American business firms compete against imports from other nations. Such imported goods include Japanese automobiles, German steel, French wine, Taiwanese textiles, and Chilean copper. To compete effectively, American firms should learn about the business practices of foreign firms. They should be alert to unfair trade practices that will put American firms at a disadvantage. Such practices may include the violation of American antitrust and antidumping laws or violation of international trade agreements. Individuals from all over the world participate in the U.S. securities markets. Special problems exist in the regulation and enforcement of American securities laws involving financial institutions of countries with secrecy laws.

A.   GENERAL PRINCIPLES

Nations enter into treaties and conferences to further international trade. The business world has developed certain forms of organizations for conducting that trade.

1.   The Legal Background

The parties often resolve the question of which country's law applies in a choice of law clause in their sales contract.

Because of the complexity and ever-changing character of the legal environment of international trade, this section will focus on certain underlying elements.

(a) What Law Applies. When there is a sale of goods within the United States, there is typically one law that applies to the transaction. Some variation may be introduced when the transaction is between parties in different states, but for the most part, the law governing the transaction is the American law of contracts and the Uniform Commercial Code. In contrast, when an international sale is made, it is necessary to determine whether it is the law of the exporter's state or the law of the importer's state that will govern. The parties to an international contract often resolve that question themselves as part of their contract, setting forth which state's law will govern should a dispute arise. Such a provision is called a **choice of law clause**.

A number of treaties have been entered into by the major trading countries of the world. When their citizens deal with each other and their respective rights are not controlled in their contract, their rights and liabilities are determined by looking at the treaty. These treaties are discussed in section 2 of this chapter.

(b) The Arbitration Alternative. Traditional litigation may be considered too time consuming, expensive, and divisive to the relationships of the parties to an international venture. The parties may therefore agree to arbitrate any contractual disputes that may arise according to dispute resolution procedures set forth in the contract.

Pitfalls exist for U.S. companies arbitrating disputes in foreign lands. *For example*, were an American company to agree to arbitrate a contractual dispute with a Chinese organization in China, it would find that the arbitrator must be Chinese. Also, under Chinese law only Chinese lawyers can present an arbitration case, even if one party is an American company. Because of situations like this, it is common for parties to international ventures to agree to arbitrate their disputes in neutral countries.

An arbitration agreement gives the parties greater control over the decision-making process. The parties can require that the arbitrator have the technical, language, and legal qualifications to best understand their dispute. While procedures exist for the prearbitration exchange of documents, full "discovery" is ordinarily not allowed. The decision of the arbitrator is final and binding on the parties, with very limited judicial review possible.

(c) Conflicting Ideologies. Law, for all people and at all times, is the result of the desire of the lawmaker to achieve certain goals. These are the social forces that make the law. In the eyes of the lawmaker, the attainment of these goals is proper and therefore ethical. This does not mean that we all can agree on what the international law should be because different people have different ideas as to what is right. This affects our views as to ownership, trade, and dealings with foreign merchants. For example, a very large part of the world does not share the American dislike of trusts. Other countries do not have our antitrust laws; therefore, their merchants can form a trust to create greater bargaining power in dealing with American and other foreign merchants.

(d) Financing International Trade. There is no international currency. This creates problems as to what currency to use and how to make payment in international transactions. Centuries ago, buyers used precious metals, jewels, or furs in payment. Today, the parties to an international transaction agree in their sales contract on the currency to be used to pay for the goods. They commonly require that the buyer furnish the seller a **letter of credit**, which is a commercial device used to guarantee payment to a seller in an international transaction. By this, an issuer, typically a bank, agrees to pay the drafts drawn against the buyer for the purchase price. In trading with merchants in some countries, the foreign country itself will promise that the seller will be paid.

2.   International Trade Organizations, Conferences, and Treaties

A large number of organizations exist that affect the multinational markets for goods, services, and investments. A survey of major international organizations, conferences, and treaties follows.

> The **GATT** seeks to promote nondiscriminatory trade.

(a) GATT 1994 and WTO. The General Agreement on Tariffs and Trade 1994 (GATT 1994) is a multilateral treaty subscribed to by 125 member governments, including the United States but excluding China and Russia. It consists of the original 1947 GATT, numerous multilateral agreements negotiated since 1947, the Uruguay Round Agreements, and the agreement establishing the **World Trade Organization** (WTO). On January 1, 1995, the WTO took over responsibility for the policing of the objectives of the former GATT organization. Since 1947 and the end of the World War II era, the goal of the GATT has been to liberalize world trade and make it secure for furthering economic growth and human development.

The GATT is based on the fundamental principles of (1) trade without discrimination and (2) protection through tariffs. The principle of trade without discrimination is embodied in its **most favored nation clause**. In treaties between countries, a most favored nation clause is one whereby any privilege subsequently granted to a third country in relation to a given treaty subject is extended to the other party to the treaty. In the application and administration of import and export duties and charges under the GATT most favored nation clause, all member countries grant each other equal treatment. Thus, no country gives special trading advantages to another. All member countries are equal and share the benefits of any moves toward lower trade barriers. Exceptions to this basic rule are allowed in certain special circumstances involving regional trading arrangements, such as the European Union and the North American Free Trade Agreement (NAFTA). Special preferences are also granted to developing countries. The second basic principle is protection for domestic industry, which should be extended essentially through a tariff, not through other commercial measures. The aim of this rule is to make the extent of protection clear and to make competition possible.

The new WTO provides a **Dispute Settlement Body** (DSB) to enable member countries to resolve trade disputes, rather than engage in unilateral trade sanctions or a trade war. The DSB appoints panels to hear disputes concerning allegations of GATT agreement violations, and it adopts (or rejects) the panel's decisions. If a GATT agreement violation is found and not removed by the offending country, trade sanctions authorized by a panel may be imposed on that country in an amount equal to the economic injury caused by the violation.

(b) CISG. The **United Nations Convention on Contracts for the International Sale of Goods** (CISG)[1] sets forth uniform rules to govern international sales contracts. The CISG became effective on January 1, 1988, between the United States and the other nations that had approved it.[2] The provisions of the CISG have been strongly influenced by Article 2 of the Uniform Commercial Code.

(c) UNCTAD. The **United Nations Conference on Trade and Development** (UNCTAD) represents the interests of the less developed countries. Its prime objective is the achievement of an international redistribution of income through trade. Through UNCTAD pressure, the developed countries agreed to a system of preferences, with quota limits, for manufactured imports from the developing countries.

(d) EU. The **European Economic Community** (EEC) was established in 1958 by the Treaty of Rome in order to remove trade and economic barriers between member countries and to unify their economic policies. It changed its name and became the **European Union** (EU) after the Treaty of Maastricht was ratified on November 1, 1993. The Treaty of Rome contained the governing principles of this regional trading group. The treaty was signed by the original six nations of Belgium, France, West Germany, Italy, Luxembourg, and the Netherlands. Membership expanded by the entry of Denmark, Ireland, and Great Britain in 1973; Greece in 1981; Spain and Portugal in 1986; and Austria, Sweden, and Finland in 1995.

Four main institutions make up the formal structure of the EU. The first, the European Council, consists of the heads of state of the member countries. The council sets broad policy guidelines for the EU. The second, the European Commission, implements decisions of the council and initiates actions against individuals, companies, or member states that violate EU law. The third, the European

---

[1] 52 Fed Reg 6262 (1987).

[2] As of January 1998, the contracting nations were Argentina, Australia, Austria, Belgium, Bosnia and Herzegovina, Bulgaria, Byelorussian Republic, Canada, Chile, China, Cuba, Czech Republic, Denmark, Ecuador, Egypt, Estonia, Finland, France, Georgia, Germany, Greece, Guinea, Hungary, Iraq, Italy, Latvia, Lesotho, Lithuania, Luxembourg, Mexico, Mongolia, the Netherlands, New Zealand, Norway, Poland, Romania, Russian Federation, Singapore, Slovakia, Slovenia, Spain, Sweden, Switzerland, Syria, Uganda, Ukraine, United States, Uzbekistan, Venezuela, Yugoslavia, and Zambia. Ratification proceedings are presently under way in other countries.

Parliament, has an advisory legislative role with limited veto powers. The fourth, the European Court of Justice (ECJ), is the judicial arm of the EU. The courts of member states may refer cases involving questions on the EU treaty to the ECJ.

CASE SUMMARY

From a Member State Court to the ECJ—a Brewing Controversy

Facts: A contractual arrangement between Henninger Brau AG, a Frankfurt brewery, and Stergios Delimitis, a bar owner in Frankfurt, Germany, required that Delimitis purchase a minimum quantity of beer from Henninger. In the event that the minimum contractual quantity was not met, the bar owner was obligated to pay damages as set forth in the contract. The contract allowed the bar owner to sell other beers produced in other member states. Delimitis did not buy the minimum quantity, and Henninger deducted damages from a security deposit held by Henninger. The contractual arrangement between Henninger and Delimitis was one of a group of similar contracts in effect throughout Germany. Delimitis brought suit in a German court to recover the money deducted by the brewery. The German court submitted the case to the ECJ. A decision was sought on whether the common contractual arrangements between breweries and German bar owners had the effect of blocking access to the German market in violation of European Community Competition Rules.

Decision: Judgment for Henninger. Under the contractual arrangement, bar owners were authorized to purchase beer produced in other member states and foreign countries. The cumulative effect of the contractual arrangements between German breweries and beer retailers did not have the effect of blocking national and foreign competitors' access to the German market. Article 85 (a) of the Treaty was not violated. *[Delimitis v Henninger Brau AG, European Law Reports C-23489 of Rome (February 28, 1991)]*

The Single European Act eliminated internal barriers to the free movement of goods, persons, services, and capital between EU countries. The Treaty on European Union, signed in Maastricht, Netherlands (the Maastricht Treaty), amended the Treaty of Rome with a focus on monetary and political union. It set goals for the EU of (1) single monetary and fiscal policies, (2) common foreign and security policies, and (3) cooperation in justice and home affairs.

(e) NAFTA. The **North American Free Trade Agreement** (NAFTA) is an agreement among Mexico, Canada, and the United States, effective January 1, 1994, that included Mexico in the arrangements previously initiated under the U.S.-Canada Free Trade Agreement of 1989. NAFTA eliminates all tariffs among the three countries over a 15-year period. Side agreements exist to prevent the exploitation of Mexico's lower environmental and labor standards.

Products are qualified for NAFTA tariff preferences only if they originate in one or more of the three member countries. Documentation is required in a *NAFTA Certificate of Origin*, except for certain "low value" items for which the statement of North American origin is recorded on an invoice. NAFTA ensures nondiscriminatory and open markets for a wide range of services;[3] and lowers barriers to U.S. investments in both Canada and Mexico.[4] While NAFTA does not create a common labor market, as in the European Union, the agreement provides temporary access for business persons across borders.

---

[3] NAFTA art. 1202.
[4] NAFTA art. 1102.

(f) Regional Trading Groups of Developing Countries. In recent years, numerous trading arrangements between groups of developing countries have been established.

(g) IMF–World Bank. The **International Monetary Fund** (IMF) was created after World War II by a group of nations meeting in Bretton Woods, New Hampshire. The Articles of Agreement of the IMF state that the purpose is "to facilitate the expansion and balanced growth of international trade" and to "shorten the duration and lessen the disequilibrium in the international balance of payments of members." The IMF helps to achieve such purposes by administering a complex lending system. A country can borrow money from other IMF members or from the IMF by means of **special drawing rights** (SDRs) sufficient to permit that country to maintain the stability of its currency's relationship to other world currencies. The Bretton Woods conference also set up the **International Bank for Reconstruction and Development** (World Bank) to facilitate the lending of money by capital surplus countries—such as the United States—to countries needing economic help and wanting foreign investments after World War II.

(h) OPEC. The **Organization of Petroleum Exporting Countries** (OPEC) is a producer cartel or combination. One of its main goals was to raise the taxes and royalties earned from crude oil production. Another major goal was to take control over production and exploration from the major oil companies. Its early success in attaining these goals led other nations that export raw materials to form similar cartels. ◆ *For example,* copper- and bauxite-producing nations have formed cartels. ◆

3. Forms of Business Organizations

Forms of doing business abroad include
- export sales,
- agencies,
- distributorships,
- licensing, and
- subsidiaries.

The decision to participate in international business transactions and the extent of that participation depend on the financial position of the individual firm, production and marketing factors, and tax and legal considerations. There are a number of forms of business organizations for doing business abroad.

(a) Export Sales. A direct sale to customers in a foreign country is an **export sale**. An American firm engaged in export selling is not present in the foreign country in such an arrangement. The export is subject to a tariff by the foreign country, but the exporting firm is not subject to local taxation by the importing country.

(b) Agency Requirements. A U.S. manufacturer may decide to make a limited entry into international business by appointing an agent to represent it in a foreign market. An agent is a person or firm with authority to make contracts on behalf of another—the **principal**. The agent will receive commission income for sales made on behalf of the U.S. principal. The appointment of a foreign agent commonly constitutes "doing business" in that country and subjects the U.S. firm to local taxation.

(c) Foreign Distributorships. A **distributor** takes title to goods and bears the financial and commercial risks for the subsequent sale of the goods. To avoid making a major financial investment, a U.S. firm may decide to appoint a foreign distributor. A U.S. firm may also appoint a foreign distributor to avoid managing a foreign operation with its complicated local business, legal, and labor conditions. Care is required in designing an exclusive distributorship for an EU country lest it violates EU antitrust laws.

(d) Licensing. American firms may select licensing as a means of doing business in other countries. **Licensing** involves the transfer of technology rights in a product so that it may be produced by a different business organization in a foreign country in exchange for royalties and other payments as agreed. The technology being licensed may fall within the internationally recognized categories of patents, trademarks, and "know-how" (trade secrets and unpatented manufacturing processes outside the public domain). These intellectual property rights, which are legally protectable, may be licensed separately or incorporated into a single, comprehensive licensing contract. **Franchising**, which involves granting permission to use a trademark, trade name, or copyright under specified conditions, is a form of licensing that is now very common in international business.

(e) Wholly Owned Subsidiaries. A firm seeking to maintain control over its own operations, including the protection of its own technological expertise, may choose to do business abroad through a wholly owned subsidiary. In Europe the most common choice of foreign business organization, similar to the U.S. corporate form of business organization, is called the *société anonyme* (S.A.). In German-speaking countries, this form is called *Aktiengesellschaft* (A.G.). Small and medium-sized companies in Europe now utilize a newly created form of business organization called the limited liability company (*Gesellschaft mit beschränkter Haftung* or "GmbH" in Germany; *Società a responsabilità limitata* or "S.r.l." in Spain). It is less complicated to form but is restrictive for accessing public capital markets.

A corporation doing business in more than one country poses many taxation problems for the governments in those countries where the firm does business. The United States has established tax treaties with many countries granting corporations relief from double taxation. Credit is normally given by the United States to U.S. corporations for taxes paid to foreign governments.

There is a potential for tax evasion by U.S. corporations from their selling goods to their overseas subsidiaries. Corporations could sell goods at less than the fair market value to avoid a U.S. tax on the full profit for such sales. By allowing the foreign subsidiaries located in countries with lower tax rates to make higher profits, a company as a whole would minimize its taxes. Section 482 of the Internal Revenue Code (IRC), however, allows the IRS to reallocate the income between the parent and its foreign subsidiary. The parent corporation is insulated from such a reallocation if it can show, based on independent transactions with unrelated parties, that its charges were at arm's length.[5]

---

[5] *Bausch & Lomb Inc. v Commissioner*, 933 F2d 1084 (2d Cir 1991).

A Taxing Case

Facts: E.I. Du Pont de Nemours created a wholly owned Swiss marketing and sales subsidiary: Du Pont International S.A. (DISA). Most of the Du Pont chemical products marketed abroad were first sold to DISA, which then arranged for resale to the ultimate consumer through independent distributors. Du Pont's tax strategy was to sell the goods to DISA at prices below fair market value so that the greater part of the total corporate profit would be realized by DISA upon resale. DISA's profits would be taxed at a much lower level by Switzerland than Du Pont would be taxed in the United States. The IRS, however, under section 482 of the IRC, reallocated a substantial part of DISA's income to Du Pont, increasing Du Pont's taxes by a considerable amount. Du Pont contended that the prices it charged DISA were valid under the IRC.

Decision: Judgment for the IRS. The reallocation of DISA's income to Du Pont was proper. Du Pont's prices to DISA were set wholly without regard to the factors that normally enter into the setting of intercorporate prices on an arm's length basis. For example, there was no correlation of prices to cost. Du Pont set prices for the two years in question based solely on estimates of the greatest amount of profits that could be shifted without causing IRS intervention. [*E.I. Du Pont de Nemours & Company v United States, 608 F2d 445 (Ct Cl 1979)*]

(f) Joint Ventures. A U.S. manufacturer and a foreign entity may form a joint venture, whereby the two firms agree to perform different functions for a common result. The responsibilities and liabilities of such operations are governed by contract. ◆ *For example,* Hughes Aircraft Co. formed a joint venture with two Japanese firms, C. Itoh & Co. and Mitsui, and successfully bid on a telecommunications space satellite system for the Japanese government. ◆

B. GOVERNMENTAL REGULATION

Nations regulate trade to protect the economic interests of their citizens or to protect themselves in international relations and transactions.

4. Export Regulations

Exports require either a general or a validated license.

For reasons of national security, foreign policy, or short supply of certain domestic products, the United States controls the export of goods and technology. The Export Administration Act[6] imposes export controls on goods and technical data from the United States. The Bureau of Export Administration of the Department of Commerce issues Export Administration Regulations to enforce export controls.

In April 1996, new Export Administration Regulations took effect that simplify the process and enhance export trade by U.S. citizens.[7] The new regulations eliminate the former system of general and validated licenses under which every export required a license. Under the 1996 **Simplification Regulations**, no license is required unless the regulations affirmatively require a license.

---

[6] The Export Administration Act of 1979 expired in August 1994 and was extended by Executive Order 12924, signed on August 19, 1994.

[7] Simplification of Export Regulations, 61 Fed Reg 12,714 (1996).

(a) Determining If a License Is Needed. In order to determine whether a product requires an export license, the exporter should review the Commerce Control List (CCL) to see if the product to be exported is listed. Listed products have Export Control Classification Numbers (ECCNs) that conform to those used by the EU. If a product is on the list, the ECCN code will provide the reason for control, such as national security, missile technology, nuclear nonproliferation, chemical and/or biological weapons, antiterrorism, crime control, short supply, or UN sanctions.[8] The exporter should then consult the Commerce Country Chart to determine if a license is needed to send the product to its proposed destination. Domestic crude petroleum products and western red cedar are on the Commerce Control List because of the "short supply" of these products. As a result, they are controlled to all destinations, and no reference to the Commerce Country Chart is necessary.

(b) Criminal Sanctions. Export licenses are required for the export of certain high-technology and military products. *For example*, a company intending to ship "maraging 350 steel" to a user in Pakistan would find by checking the CCL and the ECCN code for the product that such steel is used in making high-technology products and also has nuclear applications. Thus, an export license would be required. Because Pakistan is a nonsignatory nation of the Nuclear Non-Proliferation Treaty, the Department of Commerce would be expected to deny a license application for the use of this steel in a nuclear plant. However, a license to export this steel for the manufacture of high-speed turbines or compressors might be approved. The prospective purchaser must complete a "Statement of Ultimate Consignee and Purchaser" form with the application for an export license. The prospective purchaser must identify the "end use" for the steel and indicate where the purchaser is located and the location in Pakistan where a U.S. embassy official can make an on-site inspection of the product's use. Falsification of the information in the license application process is a criminal offense. Thus, if the exporter of maraging 350 steel asserted that it was to be used in manufacturing high-speed turbines when in fact the exporter knew it was being purchased for use in a nuclear facility, the exporter would be guilty of a criminal offense.[9]

(c) Expert Assistance. The Department of Commerce's Exporter Assistance Staff provides assistance to exporters needing help in determining if an export license is needed.[10] Licensed foreign-freight forwarders are in the business of handling the exporting of goods to foreign destinations. They are experts on U.S. Department of Commerce export license requirements. Licensed foreign-freight forwarders can attend to all of the essential arrangements required to transport a shipment of goods from the exporter's warehouse to the overseas buyer's specified port and inland destination. They are well versed in all aspects of ocean, air, and inland transportation as well as banking, marine insurance, and other services relating to exporting.

---

[8] *Id.*

[9] See *U.S. v Perez*, 871 F2d 310 (3d Cir 1989), on the criminal application of the Export Administration Regulations to an individual who stated a false end use for maraging 350 steel on his export application to ship this steel to Pakistan. See also *U.S. v Bozarov*, 974 F2d 1037 (9th Cir 1992).

[10] Exporter Assistance Staff, U.S. Department of Commerce, Washington, DC 20230.

5. Protection of Intellectual Property Rights

United States laws protect **intellectual property rights**, which consist of trademarks, copyrights, and patents.

(a) Counterfeit Goods. The importation into the United States of counterfeit compact discs, tapes, computer software, and movies violates U.S. copyright laws. Importing goods such as athletic shoes, jeans, or watches bearing counterfeits of U.S. companies' registered trademarks violates the Lanham Act. Importing machines or devices that infringe on U.S. patents violates U.S. patent laws. A full range of remedies is available to American firms under U.S. laws. Possible remedies include injunctive relief, seizure and destruction of counterfeit goods that are found in the United States, damages, and attorney fees. American firms injured by counterfeit trademarks may recover triple damages from the counterfeiters.[11]

Intellectual property rights are also protected by international treaties, such as the Berne Convention, which protects copyrights; the Patent Cooperation Treaty; and the Vienna Trademark Registration Treaty.

(b) Gray Market Goods. A U.S. trademark holder may license a foreign business to use its trademark overseas. If a third party imports these foreign-made goods into the United States to compete against the U.S. manufacturer's goods, the foreign-made goods are called **gray market goods**. The Tariff Act of 1930 prevents importation of foreign-made goods bearing a U.S. registered trademark owned by a U.S. firm unless the U.S. trademark owner gives written consent.[12] The Lanham Act may also be used to exclude gray market goods.

CASE SUMMARY

Barring Imported Soap!

Facts: Lever Brothers (Lever-U.S.) manufactures a soap product under the trademark "Shield" and a dishwashing liquid under the trademark "Sunlight" for sale in the United States. A British affiliate, Lever-U.K., also makes products using the marks "Shield" and "Sunlight." Due to different tastes of American and British consumers, the products have physical differences. Third parties imported these British products into the United States. The Lanham Act prohibits "copying or simulating a trademark." The U.S. Customs Service refused to bar these foreign products because a markholder cannot "copy or simulate" its own trademark. That is, Lever-U.K. could not copy the marks of its affiliated company, Lever-U.S. Lever-U.S. sought an injunction against the U.S. Customs Service, requiring it to bar these foreign products.

Decision: Judgment for Lever-U.S. American consumers desiring to purchase "Shield" and "Sunlight" may end up with different products not suited to their tastes and needs if the British products continued to be allowed into the United States. Because of the confusion and dissatisfaction, the importation of foreign goods that bear trademarks identical to valid U.S. trademarks but that are physically different, regardless of the affiliation of markholders, are prohibited from import under Section 42 of the Lanham Act. [*Lever Brothers Co. v United States, 796 F Supp 1 (DDC 1992)*]

---

[11] 15 USC § 1117(b); *Nintendo of America v NTDEC*, 822 F Supp 1462 (D Ariz 1993).

[12] 19 USC § 1526(1). The copyright Act of 1976 may also apply to gray market goods. One provision of this act gives the copyright holder exclusive right to distribute copies of the copyrighted work. Still another section states that once a copyright owner sells an authorized copy of the work, subsequent owners may do what they like with it. The grey market issue occurs when American manufacturers sell their products overseas at deep discounts, and other firms reimport the products back to the U.S. for resale. The Supreme Court held that a copyrighted label on the products would not protect an American manufacturer's claim of unauthorized importation because the copyright owner's rights cease upon the original sale to the overseas buyer. *Quality King v L'Anza Research*, 66 LW 4189 (Mar. 10 1998).

A gray market situation also arises where foreign products made by affiliates of U.S. companies have trademarks identical to U.S. trademarks but the foreign products are physically different from the U.S. products.

6. Antitrust

Antitrust laws exist in the United States to protect the American consumer by assuring the benefits of competitive products from foreign competitors as well as domestic competitors. Competitors' agreements designed to raise the price of imports or to exclude imports from our domestic markets in exchange for not competing in other countries are restraints of trade in violation of our antitrust laws.

The antitrust laws also exist to protect American export and investment opportunities against privately imposed restrictions whereby a group of competitors seeks to exclude another competitor from a particular foreign market. Antitrust laws exist in other countries where American firms compete. These laws are usually directed not at breaking up cartels to further competition but rather at regulating the cartels in the national interest.

(a) Jurisdiction. In U.S. courts, the U.S. antitrust laws have a broad extraterritorial reach. Our antitrust laws must be reconciled with the rights of other interested countries as embodied in international law.

(1) *The Effects Doctrine.* Judge Learned Hand's decision in *United States v Alcoa*[13] established the **effects doctrine**. Under this doctrine, U.S. courts will assume jurisdiction and will apply the antitrust laws to conduct outside of the United States where the activity of the business firms outside the United States has a direct and substantial effect on U.S. commerce. This basic rule has been modified to require that the effect on U.S. commerce also be foreseeable.

(2) *The Jurisdictional Rule of Reason.* The jurisdictional rule of reason applies when conduct taking place outside of the United States affects U.S. commerce but a foreign state also has a significant interest in regulating the conduct in question. The **jurisdictional rule of reason** balances the vital interests, including laws and policies, of the United States with those of the foreign country involved. This rule of reason is based on the principle of comity. **Comity** is a principle of international law that the laws of all nations deserve the respect legitimately demanded by equal participants in international affairs.

(b) Defenses. Three defenses are commonly raised to the extraterritorial application of U.S. antitrust laws. These defenses are also commonly raised to attack jurisdiction in other legal actions involving international law.

(1) *Act of State Doctrine.* By the **act of state doctrine** every sovereign state is bound to respect the independence of every other sovereign state, and the courts of one country will not sit in judgment of another government's acts done within its own territory.[14]

The act of state doctrine is based on the judiciary's concern over its possible interference with the conduct of foreign relations. Such matters are considered to be political, not judicial, questions.

---

[13] 148 F2d 416 (2d Cir 1945).
[14] *Underhill v Hernandez,* 108 US 250, 252 (1897).

T-i-m-b-e-r! The Act of State Doctrine Does Not Apply

Facts: The Timberlane Lumber Company, an Oregon partnership, brought an antitrust suit alleging violations of sections 1 and 2 of the Sherman Act against the Bank of America and others. Timberlane alleged that the defendants conspired to prevent Timberlane, through Honduran subsidiaries, from milling lumber in Honduras and exporting it to the United States. Thus, control of the Honduran lumber business was kept in the hands of individuals financed and controlled by the bank. The defendants contended that the action must be dismissed in conformance with the act of state doctrine because a Honduran court approved certain of the challenged activities.

Decision: Judgment for Timberlane. The act of state doctrine did not require dismissal of this action. The allegedly sovereign acts of Honduras consisted of judicial proceedings that were initiated by a private party, rather than by the Honduran government. Timberlane's action under the Sherman Act did not seek to name Honduras or any Honduran officer as defendant. Timberlane did not challenge Honduran policy or sovereignty or threaten relations between Honduras and the United States. [*Timberlane Lumber Co. v Bank of America, 549 F2d 597 (9th Cir 1976)*]

(2) The Sovereign Compliance Doctrine. The sovereign compliance doctrine allows a defendant to raise as an affirmative defense to an antitrust action the fact that the defendant's actions were compelled by a foreign state. To establish this defense, compulsion by the foreign government is required. The Japanese government uses informal and formal contacts within an industry to establish a consensus on a desired course of action. Such governmental action is not a defense for a U.S. firm, however, because the activity in question is not compulsory.

(3) The Sovereign Immunity Doctrine. This doctrine states that a foreign sovereign generally cannot be sued unless an exception to the Foreign Sovereign Immunities Act of 1976 applies.[15] The most important exception covers the commercial conduct of a foreign state.

(c) Legislation. In response to business uncertainty as to when the antitrust laws apply to international transactions, Congress passed the Foreign Trade Antitrust Improvements Act of 1982. This act, in essence, codified the effects doctrine. The act requires a direct, substantial, and reasonably foreseeable effect on U.S. domestic commerce or exports by U.S. residents before business conduct abroad may come within the purview of U.S. antitrust laws.[16]

(d) Foreign Antitrust Laws. Attitudes in different countries vary toward cartels and business combinations. Because of this, antitrust laws vary in content and application. Japan, for example, has stressed consumer protection against such practices as price fixing and false advertising. However, with regard to mergers, stock ownership, and agreements among companies to control production, Japanese law is much less restrictive than American law.

Europe is a major market for American products, services, and investments. American firms doing business in Europe are subject to the competition laws of the EU. The Treaty of Rome uses the term *competition*, rather than *antitrust*. Articles 85

---

[15] See *Verlinden B.V. v Central Bank of Nigeria*, 461 US 574 (1983).
[16] PL 97-290, 96 Stat 1233, 15 USC § 6(a).

and 86 of the Treaty of Rome set forth the basic regulation on business behavior in the EU.[17]

Article 85(1) expressly prohibits agreements and concerted practices that

1. even indirectly fix prices of purchases or sales or fix any other trading conditions;
2. limit or control production, markets, technical development, or investment;
3. share markets or sources of supply;
4. apply unequal terms to parties furnishing equivalent considerations, thereby placing one at a competitive disadvantage; or
5. make a contract's formation depend on the acceptance of certain additional obligations that, according to commercial usage, have no connection with the subject of such contracts.

Article 85(3) allows for an individual exemption if the agreement meets certain conditions, such as improving the production or distribution of goods, promoting technical or economic progress, and reserving to consumers a fair share of the resulting economic benefits.

Article 86 provides that it is unlawful for one or more enterprises having a dominant market position within at least a substantial part of the European Union to take improper advantage of such a position if trade between the member states may be affected.

CASE SUMMARY

EU Won't Tolerate Abuse of Dominant Positions

Facts: Magill TV Guide, an Irish publisher, started a comprehensive weekly television guide in Ireland that listed all weekly television programming of Irish station Radio Telefis Eireann (RTE) and Britain's BBC and ITV. These three companies sold their own individual weekly program guides, while making daily listings available to newspapers. The three companies obtained a court injunction from an Irish court preventing Magill TV Guide from listing the three stations' weekly programs on the ground that Magill was violating the three stations' copyrights. Magill brought the matter before the European Commission, which found that the three companies had violated article 86. The matter was referred to the ECJ.

Decision: Judgment for Magill TV Guide. By reserving the exclusive right to publish their weekly television program listings, the three television companies were preventing the emergence of a new product on the market that would compete against their own television program magazines. The anticompetitive effect of the television companies' obtaining a court injunction based on their copyrights was an abuse of their dominant position within the meaning of article 86 of the Treaty of Rome. [*Radio Telefis Eireann v European Commission, 1995 All ERptr 416*]

---

7.   Securities Regulation in an International Environment

Illegal conduct in the U.S. securities markets, whether this conduct is initiated in the United States or abroad, threatens the vital economic interests of the United States. Investigation and litigation concerning possible violations of the U.S. securities laws often have an extraterritorial effect. Conflicts with the laws of foreign countries may occur.

---

[17] See *Osakeyhtio v EEC Commission*, 1988 Common Mkt Rep (CCH) ¶ 14,491 for discussion of the extraterritorial reach of the European Commission.

(a) Jurisdiction. United States district courts have jurisdiction over violations of the antifraud provisions of the Securities Exchange Act of 1934 where losses occur from sales to Americans living in the United States.[18] This is true whether or not the actions occurred in this country. United States district courts also have jurisdiction where losses occur to Americans living abroad if the acts occurred in the United States. The antifraud provisions do not apply, however, to losses from sales of securities to foreigners outside the United States unless acts within the United States caused the losses.

(b) Impact of Foreign Secrecy Laws in SEC Enforcement. Secrecy laws are confidentiality laws applied to home-country banks. These laws prohibit the disclosure of business records or the identity of bank customers. **Blocking laws** prohibit the disclosure, copying, inspection, or removal of documents located in the enacting country in compliance with orders from foreign authorities. These laws impede, and sometimes foreclose, the SEC's ability to police its securities markets properly.

CASE SUMMARY

The Long Reach of the SEC

Facts: Banca Della Suizzera Italiana (BSI), a Swiss bank with an office in the United States, purchased certain call options and common stock of St. Joe Minerals Corporation (St. Joe), a New York corporation, immediately prior to the announcement on March 11, 1981, of a cash tender offer by Joseph Seagram & Sons Inc. for all St. Joe common stock at $45 per share. On March 11, 1981, when BSI acted, the stock moved sharply higher in price. BSI instructed its broker to close out the purchases of the options and sell most of the shares of stock, resulting in an overnight profit of $2 million. The SEC noticed the undue activity in the options market and initiated suit against BSI. The SEC, through the Departments of State and Justice, and the Swiss government sought without success to learn the identity of BSI's customers involved in the transactions. The SEC believed that the customers had used inside information in violation of the Securities Exchange Act of 1934. The SEC brought a motion to compel disclosure. BSI objected on the ground that it might be subject to criminal liability under Swiss penal and banking laws if it disclosed the requested information.

Decision: Judgment for the SEC. BSI made deliberate use of Swiss nondisclosure law to evade the strictures of American securities law against insider trading. Whether acting solely as an agent or also as a principal (something that can only be clarified through disclosure of the requested information), BSI voluntarily engaged in transactions in American securities markets and profited in some measure thereby. It cannot rely on Swiss nondisclosure law to shield this activity. [SEC v Banca Della Suizzera Italiana, 92 FRD 111 (DC SDNY 1981)]

The SEC is not limited to litigation when a securities law enforcement investigation runs into secrecy or blocking laws. For example, the SEC may rely on the 1977 Treaty of Mutual Assistance in Criminal Matters between the United States and Switzerland.[19] Although this treaty has served to deter the use of Swiss secrecy laws to conceal fraud in the United States, its benefits for securities enforcement have been limited. It applies only where there is a dual criminality—that is, the

---

[18] *SEC v Eurobon Exchange Ltd.*, 13 F2d 1334 (9th Cir 1994).
[19] 27 UST 2021.

conduct involved constitutes a criminal offense under the laws of both the United States and Switzerland.

8.   Barriers to Trade

The most common barrier to the free movement of goods across borders is a tariff. A wide range of nontariff barriers also restricts the free movement of goods, services, and investments. Government export controls used as elements of foreign policy have proven to be a major barrier to trade with certain countries.

(a) Tariff Barriers. A **tariff** is an import or export duty or tax placed on goods as they move into or out of a country. It is the most common method used by countries to restrict foreign imports. The tariff raises the total cost and thus the price of an imported product in the domestic market. Thus, the price of a domestically produced product not subject to the tariff, is more advantageous.

The U.S. Customs Service imposes tariffs on imported goods at the port of entry. The merchandise is classified under a tariff schedule, which lists each type of merchandise and the corresponding duty rate (or percentage). The Customs Service also determines the "computed value" of the imported goods under very precise statutory formulas.[20] The total amount of the duty is calculated by applying the duty percentage to the computed value figure.

> **CASE SUMMARY**
>
> ## In the Soup
>
> **Facts:** The Campbell Soup Co. imports tomato paste from a wholly owned Mexican subsidiary, Sinalopasta S.A. de C.V. It deducted $416,324 from the computed value of goods shipped to the United States, which amount was the cost of transportation of the finished tomato paste from Sinalopasta's loading dock in Mexico to the U.S. border. The deduction thus lowered the computed value of the goods and the amount of duty to be paid the U.S. government by Campbell Soup Co. United States Customs questioned this treatment of freight costs. Tariff Act § 1401a(e)(1)(B) requires that profits and general expenses be included in calculating the competed value of goods, which factors in part quantify the value of the merchandise in the country of production. From a judgment for U.S. Customs, Campbell Soup appealed.
>
> **Decision:** Judgment for the U.S. government. Transportation costs solely within the foreign country are not excluded from the computed value of goods under the Tariff Act. This treatment of this expense was similar to that of other producers and consistent with generally accepted accounting principles in Mexico. The court thus rejected Campbell's attempt to recharacterize the cost. [*Campbell Soup Co. Inc. v United States, 107 F3d 1556 (Fed Cir 1997)*]

(b) Nontariff Barriers. Nontariff barriers consist of a wide range of restrictions that inhibit the free movement of goods between countries. An import quota, such as a limitation on the number of automobiles that can be imported into one country from another, is such a barrier. More subtle nontariff barriers exist in all countries. ◆ *For example*, Japan's complex customs procedures resulted in the restriction of the sale of U.S.-made aluminum baseball bats in Japan. The customs

Barriers to trade include
• tariffs,
• import quotas,
• government subsidies, and
• foreign policy restrictions.

---

20 See Tariff Act of 1930, as amended, 19 USC § 1401a(e).

procedures required the individual uncrating and "destruction testing" of bats at the ports of entry. Government subsidies are also nontariff barriers to trade. ◆

One U.S. law—the Turtle Law—prohibits the importation of shrimp from countries that allow the harvesting of shrimp with commercial fishing technology that could adversely affect endangered sea turtles. Two U.S. importers sought an exemption from the embargo, representing that their Brazilian supply of shrimp was caught in the wild by vessels using turtle excluder devices (TEDs). Because Brazil had failed to comply with the U.S. Turtle Law by requiring TEDs on its commercial shrimp fleet, even though it had seven years to do so, the exemption was not granted.[21]

(c) Export Controls as Instruments of Foreign Policy. United States export controls have been used as instruments of foreign policy in recent years. For example, the United States has sought to deny goods and technology of strategic or military importance to unfriendly nations. The United States has also denied goods such as grain, technology, and machine parts to certain countries to protest or to punish activities considered violative of human rights or world peace.

9. Relief Mechanisms for Economic Injury Caused by Foreign Trade

United States laws provide some relief for certain industries, workers, and communities adversely affected by foreign competition.

Certain U.S. industries may suffer severe economic injury because of foreign competition. American law provides protection against unfair competition from foreigners' goods and provides economic relief for U.S. industries, communities, firms, and workers adversely affected by import competition. American law also provides certain indirect relief for American exporters and producers who encounter unfair foreign import restrictions.

(a) Antidumping Laws and Export Subsidies. Selling goods in another country at less than their fair value is called dumping. The dumping of foreign goods in the United States is prohibited under the Trade Agreement Act of 1979.[22] Proceedings in antidumping cases are conducted by two federal agencies, which separately examine two distinct components. The International Trade Administration (ITA) of the Department of Commerce investigates whether specified foreign goods are being sold in the United States at less than fair value (LTFV). The International Trade Commission (ITC) conducts proceedings to determine if there is an injury to a domestic industry as a result of such sales. Findings of both LTFV sales and injury must be present before remedial action is taken. Remedial action might include the addition of duties to reflect the difference between the fair value of the goods and the price being charged in the United States. ITA and ITC decisions may be appealed to the Court of International Trade. Figure 7-1 illustrates an antidumping proceeding.

A settlement of the matter may be reached through a suspension agreement, whereby prices are revised to eliminate any LTFV sales and other corrective measures are taken.

---

[21] *Earth Island Institute v Christopher,* 948 F Supp 1062 (Ct Int'l Trade 1996).
[22] PL 96-39, 1062, 93 Stat 193, 19 USC § 160.

Phase 1: International Trade Administration	
Date	**Event**
December 28, 1992	Complaint by U.S. manufacturers to the ITA, alleging dumping of small business telephones on the U.S. market by named Asian manufacturers.
January–July 1993	ITA investigates whether these foreign-made goods are being sold in the United States at less than fair value (LTFV). Investigation includes questionnaires on costs and pricing from all parties.
July 27, 1993	Preliminary finding by the ITA that Japanese and Taiwanese firms are dumping business phones on the U.S. market.
October 11, 1993	Final determination by the ITA that the named firms are dumping phones on the U.S. market.
October 11, 1993	U.S. Customs Service commences requirement of cash deposit or bond on imports equal to the difference between the fair value of the goods as determined by the ITA and the prices being charged for the goods in the United States.

Phase 2: International Trade Commission	
Date	**Event**
October 31, 1993	Hearing before the ITC to determine whether there is an injury to the domestic phone manufacturing industry as a result of the LTFV sales by the named Asian firms.
November 20, 1993	Decision of the ITC that U.S. manufacturers of small business telephone systems are suffering injury because of the dumped exports.
November 20, 1993	U.S. Customs Service commences the actual collection of anti-dumping duties.

FIGURE 7-1
*Antidumping
Proceedings*

CASE SUMMARY

No Dumping

Facts: In 1971, to protect the U.S. television industry from injury by sales of television receivers from Japan at less than fair value (LTFV), an antidumping duty order was issued by the ITC. In 1981, Matsushita Electric Ltd. (Panasonic) and other Japanese television receiver manufacturers petitioned the ITC to review the antidumping duty order, contending that the revocation of the order would not be injurious to the U.S. television industry. American manufacturers opposed the petition. The ITC sent out questionnaires to domestic producers, importers, and purchasers and held two days of hearings. It determined that LTFV sales would resume or continue upon revocation of the antidumping order. Its decision not to revoke the order was reversed by the Court of International Trade. The matter was appealed to the U.S. court of appeals.

Decision: Judgment for the American manufacturers. The ITC used an appropriate standard for conducting a review investigation, and its determination is supported by substantial evidence. While contrary evidence existed, the evidence relied on by the ITC indicated that excess tube production capacity in Japan and lower U.S. duty rates on complete sets would lead to increased exports from Japan to the attractive U.S. market. *[Matsushita Electric Ltd v United States, 750 F2d 927 (Fed Cir 1984)].*

The 1979 act also applies to subsidy practices by foreign countries. If subsidized goods are sold in the United States at less than their fair value, the goods may be subject to a countervailing duty.

(b) Relief from Import Injuries. Title II of the Trade Act of 1974[23] provides relief for U.S. industries, communities, firms, and workers when any one or more of them are substantially adversely affected by import competition. The Department of Commerce, the secretary of labor, and the president have roles in determining eligibility. The relief provided may be temporary import relief through the imposition of a duty or quota on the foreign goods. Workers, if eligible, may obtain readjustment allowances, job training, job search allowances, or unemployment compensation.

(c) Retaliation and Relief against Foreign Unfair Trade Restrictions. American exporters of agricultural or manufactured goods or of services may encounter unreasonable, unjustifiable, or discriminatory foreign import restrictions. At the same time, producers from the foreign country involved may be benefiting from trade agreement concessions that allow producers from that country access to U.S. markets. Prior trade acts and the Omnibus Trade and Competitiveness Act of 1988[24] contain broad authority to retaliate against "unreasonable," "unjustifiable," or "discriminatory" acts by a foreign country. The authority to retaliate is commonly referred to as "section 301 authority." The fear or actuality of the economic sting of section 301 retaliation often leads offending foreign countries to open their markets to imports. Thus, indirect relief is provided to domestic producers and exporters adversely affected by foreign unfair trade practices.

Enforcement of the act is entrusted to the U.S. trade representative (USTR), who is appointed by the president. Under the 1988 act, mandatory retaliatory action is required if the USTR determines that (1) rights of the United States under a trade agreement are being denied or (2) actions or policies of a foreign country are unjustifiable and burden or restrict U.S. commerce. The overall thrust of the trade provisions of the 1988 act is to open markets and liberalize trade.

10. Expropriation

A major concern of U.S. businesses that do business abroad is the risk of expropriation of assets by a host government. Firms involved in the extraction of natural resources, banking, communications, or defense-related industries are particularly susceptible to nationalization. Multinational corporations commonly have a staff of full-time political scientists and former Foreign Service officers studying the countries relevant to their operations to monitor and calculate risks of expropriation. Takeovers of American-owned businesses by foreign countries may be motivated by a short-term domestic political advantage or by the desire to demonstrate political clout in world politics. Takeovers may also be motivated by long-term considerations associated with planned development of the country's economy.

Treaty commitments, or provisions in other international agreements between the United States and the host country, may serve to narrow expropriation uncertainties. Treaties commonly contain provisions whereby property will not be

---

[23] PL 93-618, 88 Stat 1978, 19 USC §§ 2251, 2298.
[24] PL 100-418, 102 Stat 1346, 15 USC 4727.

expropriated except for public benefit and with the prompt payment of just compensation.

One practical way to mitigate the risk of investment loss due to foreign expropriation is to purchase insurance through private companies, such as Lloyds of London. Commercial insurance is also available against such risks as host governments' arbitrary recall of letters of credit and commercial losses due to embargoes.

The Overseas Private Investment Corporation (OPIC) is a U.S. agency under the policy control of the secretary of state. OPIC supports private investments in less developed, friendly countries. OPIC offers asset protection insurance against risk of loss to plant and equipment as well as loss of deposits in overseas bank accounts to companies that qualify on the basis of the involvement of a "substantial U.S. interest."

11. Government-Assisted Export Programs

The U.S. government has taken legislative action to increase the foreign sales of U.S. firms.

United States laws assist U.S. export companies by providing
- limited protection from antitrust liability,
- export tax incentives to foreign sales corporations, and
- Eximbank loan credits to foreign imports, with payments made directly to U.S. exporters.

(a) Export Trading Company Act. The Export Trading Company Act of 1982 (ETCA)[25] is designed to stimulate and promote additional U.S. exports. The ETCA promotes the formation of U.S.-based export trading companies and allows banks to invest in these export trading companies. The ETCA also clarifies applicable antitrust restrictions and provides a limited exception from antitrust liability.

Trading companies exist in many European and East Asian countries. They are primary competitors of U.S. exporters. Japan's export trading companies, or *sogo shosha*, provide comprehensive export services and may serve as models for U.S. trading companies created under the 1982 act. *For example*, a *sogo shosha* may participate in the purchase transaction of goods for export. It may then handle the paperwork and documents related to the export transaction. It may obtain insurance coverage and provide warehousing and transportation services. Through access to or ownership of banks, the *sogo shosha* may extend credit or make loans or loan guarantees to buyers, sellers, and suppliers. It has expertise in marketing research relative to target export markets and expertise in foreign exchange and tariff requirements. By encouraging exporters to form trading companies with banking institutions (banks have been prohibited by law from engaging in commercial as opposed to banking activities) and specifically allowing and encouraging the bank-related firms to perform comprehensive export services, Congress believes that increased export activity will be generated.

(b) Foreign Sales Corporations. The Foreign Sales Corporation Act of 1984, title VIII of the Tax Reform Act of 1984,[26] provides export incentives for U.S. firms that form foreign sales corporations (FSCs). To qualify for the tax incentives provided under the 1984 act, an FSC subsidiary of an American firm must be organized under the laws of a U.S. possession (such as the Virgin Islands or Guam, but not Puerto Rico) or under the laws of a foreign country with an income tax treaty with

---

25 PL 97-290, 96 Stat 1233, 15 USC 4001.
26 Title VIII of the Tax Reform Act of 1984, PL 98-369, 98 Stat 678. See IRC §§ 921–927.

the United States containing an exchange-of-information program. The FSC must satisfy certain other organizational requirements in order to be eligible for the tax incentives provided by the law.

(c) United States Export–Import Bank (EXIMBANK). Eximbank is wholly owned by the U.S. government. Its primary purpose is to facilitate U.S. exports by making direct loans in the form of dollar credits to foreign importers for the purchase of U.S. goods and services. Payments are then made directly to the U.S. exporter of goods and services. Such loans are made when private financial sources are unwilling to assume the political and economic risks that exist in the country in question. Loans are also made by Eximbank to enable U.S. suppliers of goods and services to compete for major foreign contracts with foreign firms that have government-subsidized export financing.

(d) Other Programs. As stated previously, OPIC provides expropriation insurance for U.S. private investments in friendly, less developed countries. The Commodity Credit Corporation (CCC) provides financing for agricultural exports. In addition, the Small Business Administration has an export loan program.

12. The Foreign Corrupt Practices Act

There are restrictions on U.S. firms doing business abroad that disallow payments to foreign government officials for getting business from their governments. The Foreign Corrupt Practices Act of 1977 requires strict accounting standards and internal control procedures to prevent the hiding of improper payments to foreign officials. The act prohibits any offers, payments, or gifts to foreign officials, or third parties who might have influence with foreign officials, to influence a decision on behalf of the firm making the payment. It provides for sanctions of up to $1 million against the company and fines and imprisonment for the employees involved. Moreover, the individuals involved may be responsible for damages as a result of civil actions brought by competitors under federal and state antiracketeering acts.[27]

CASE SUMMARY

You Just Can't Do That!

Facts: Harry Carpenter, CEO of Kirkpatrick Co., agreed to pay Nigerian government officials a "commission" equal to 20 percent of the contract price if Kirkpatrick obtained the contract to build an aeromedical center in Nigeria. Kirkpatrick was awarded the contract, and the "commission" was paid to the Nigerian officials. A competitor for the project, ETC, International (ETC), learned of the "20 percent commission" and informed U.S. officials. Kirkpatrick and Carpenter pleaded guilty to violations of the Foreign Corrupt Practices Act by paying bribes to get the Nigerian contract. ETC then brought this civil action against Kirkpatrick, Carpenter, and others for damages under the Racketeer Influenced and Corrupt Organizations Act (RICO) and the New Jersey Antiracketeering Act. The district court ruled the suit was barred by the act of state doctrine, the court of appeals reversed, and the U.S. Supreme Court granted certiorari.

Decision: Judgment for ETC. The act of state doctrine does not establish an exception for cases that may embarrass foreign governments. The doctrine merely requires that, in the process

---

[27] PL 95-213, 94 Stat 1494, 15 USC 78a nt.

of deciding cases, the acts of foreign governments, taken in their own jurisdictions, shall be deemed valid. The doctrine has no application to the present case: The validity of a foreign sovereign act is not at issue because the payment and receipt of bribes are prohibited by Nigerian law. *[Kirkpatrick v ETC, International, 493 US 400 (1990)]*

The act does not apply to payments made to low-level officials for expediting the performance of routine government services.

ETHICS & THE LAW

Clothing made of cashmere, the wool of goats, brings much higher prices and returns to manufacturers than clothing made with ordinary wool. As one goat breeder phrased it, "Goats turn weeds into profits." China's Inner Mongolia goat herds provide the world's chief supply of soft down. The Chinese goats produce an abundant yield of the most desirable fine, soft down. European manufacturers purchase the down from the Chinese and process the wool into highly marketable clothing products.

The Chinese, however, wish to do more than just sell the crude wool and are trying to import the technology for processing the down, thereby adding value to their product and increasing sales dollars. Arabs followed a similar pattern of trade realignment when, rather than simply selling crude oil, they pressed to obtain the technology for refinement and increased sales dollars. Crude oil was not sold to those who were unwilling to provide expertise, equipment, and information about processing. The result of the Chinese effort is that cashmere prices and sales in Europe are now controlled by Chinese sellers.

European clothing manufacturers have responded by funding projects for raising goats in the Tuscan mountains of Italy. The projects are expensive because getting the herds to a point of providing adequate supplies will take years. The Chinese, on the other hand, continue to struggle to introduce cashmere processing and train their workers. Some clothing manufacturers have begun to invest directly in Chinese plants in an effort to secure their supplies.

Are these market realignments just a function of international competition? Are the necessary impacts of international business the demise of certain industries in some countries? Is it economically efficient for Europeans to develop their own goat herds? Evaluate the ethics of forcing the transfer of a lucrative part of a business in exchange for raw materials. Will this realignment give the Chinese a monopoly?

SUMMARY

The General Agreement on Tariffs and Trade, a multilateral treaty subscribed to by the United States and most of the industrialized countries of the world, is based on the principle of trade without discrimination. The United Nations Convention on Contracts for the International Sale of Goods provides uniform rules for international sales contracts between parties in contracting nations. The European Union is a regional trading group that includes most of Western Europe. The North American Free Trade Agreement is among Mexico, Canada, and the United States and eliminates all tariffs between the three countries over a 15-year period.

American firms may choose to do business abroad by making export sales or contracting with a foreign distributor to take title to their goods and sell them abroad. American firms may also license their technology or trademarks for foreign use. An agency arrangement or the organization of a foreign subsidiary may be required to participate effectively in foreign markets. This results in subjecting the U.S. firm to taxation in the host country.

However, tax treaties commonly eliminate double taxation.

The Export Administration Act is the principal statute imposing export controls on goods and technical data.

In choosing the form for doing business abroad, U.S. firms must be careful not to violate the antitrust laws of host countries. Anticompetitive foreign transactions may have an adverse impact on competition in U.S. domestic markets. United States antitrust laws have a broad extraterritorial reach. United States courts apply a "jurisdictional rule of reason," weighing the interests of the United States against the interests of the foreign country involved in making a decision on whether to hear a case. Illegal conduct may occur in U.S. securities markets. United States enforcement efforts sometimes run into foreign countries' secrecy and blocking laws that hinder effective enforcement.

Antidumping laws offer relief for domestic firms threatened by unfair foreign competition. In addition, economic programs exist to assist industries, communities, and workers injured by import competition. Programs also exist to increase the foreign sales of U.S. firms.

QUESTIONS AND CASE PROBLEMS

1. What social forces are affected by the extraterritorial application of U.S. antitrust laws?

2. How does the most favored nation clause of the GATT work to foster the principle of trade without discrimination?

3. How does the selling of subsidized foreign goods in the United States adversely affect free trade?

4. Ronald Sadler, a California resident, owned a helicopter distribution company in West Germany called Delta Avia. This company distributed American-made Hughes civilian helicopters in Western Europe. Sadler's West German firm purchased 85 helicopters from Hughes Aircraft Co. After export licenses were obtained in reliance on the purchaser's written assurance that the goods would not be disposed of contrary to the export license, the helicopters were exported to West Germany for resale in Western Europe. Thereafter, Delta Avia exported them to North Korea, which was a country subject to a trade embargo by the United States. The helicopters were converted to military use. Sadler was charged with violating the Export Administration Regulations. In Sadler's defense, it was contended that the U.S. regulations have no effect on what occurs in the resale of civilian helicopters in another sovereign country. Decide.

5. Mirage Investments Corp. (MIC) planned a tender offer for the shares of Gulf States International Corp. (GSIC). Archer, an officer of MIC, placed purchase orders for GSIC stock through the New York office of the Bahamian Bank (BB) prior to the announcement of the tender offer, making a $300,000 profit when the tender offer was made public. The Bahamas is a secrecy jurisdiction. The bank informed the SEC that under its law it could not disclose the name of the person for whom it purchased the stock. What, if anything, may the SEC do to discover whether the federal securities laws have been violated?

6. United Overseas Ltd. (UOL) is a United Kingdom firm that purchases and sells manufacturers' closeouts in Europe and the Middle East. UOL's representative, Jay Knox, used stationery listing a UOL office in New York to solicit business from Revlon Inc. in New York. On April 1, 1992, UOL faxed a purchase order from its headquarters in England to Revlon's New York offices for the purchase of $4 million worth of shampoo. The purchase order on its face listed six conditions, none of which referred to a forum selection clause. When Revlon was not paid for the shampoo it shipped, it sued UOL in New York for breach of contract. UOL moved to dismiss the complaint because of a forum selection clause, which it stated was on the reverse side of the purchase order and provided that "the parties hereby agree to submit to the jurisdiction of the English Courts disputes arising out of the contract." The evidence did not show that the reverse side of the purchase order had been faxed with the April 1992 order. Should the court dismiss the complaint based on the "forum selection clause"? Read chapter 36 on letters of credit and advise Revlon how to avoid similar litigation in the future. [*Revlon Inc. v United Overseas Ltd.*, 1994 WL 9657 (SDNY)]

7. Reebok manufactures and sells fashionable athletic shoes in America and abroad. It owns the federally registered REEBOK trademark and has registered this trademark in Mexico as well. Nathan Betech is a Mexican citizen residing in San Diego, California, with business offices there. Reebok believed that Betech was in the business of selling counterfeit Reebok shoes in Mexican border towns, such as Tijuana, Mexico. It sought an injunction in a federal district court in California ordering Betech to cease his counterfeiting activity and to refrain from destroying certain documents. It also asked the court to freeze Betech's assets pending the outcome of a Lanham Act lawsuit. Betech contended that a U.S. district court has no jurisdiction or authority to enter the injunction for

the activities allegedly occurring in Mexico. Decide. [*Reebok Int'l, Ltd v Marnatech Enterprises, Inc.*, 970 F2d 552 (9th Cir)]

8. Assume that before the formation of the European Union the lowest-cost source of supply for a certain product consumed in France was producers from the United States. Explain the basis by which, after the EU was formed, higher-cost German producers could have replaced the U.S. producers as the source of supply.

9. A complaint was filed with the U.S. Commerce Department's ITA by U.S. telephone manufacturers AT&T, Comidial Corp., and Eagle Telephones, Inc., alleging that 12 Asian manufacturers of small business telephones, including the Japanese firms Hitachi, NEC, and Toshiba and the Taiwanese firm Sun Moon Star Corp., were dumping their small business phones in the U.S. market at prices that were from 6 to 283 percent less than those in their home markets. The U.S. manufacturers showed that the domestic industry's market share had dropped from 54 percent in 1985 to 33 percent in 1989. They asserted that it was doubtful if the domestic industry could survive the dumping. Later, in a hearing before the ITC, the Japanese and Taiwanese respondents contended that their domestic industry was basically sound and that the U.S. firms simply had to become more efficient to meet worldwide competition. They contended that the United States was using the procedures before the ITA and ITC as a nontariff barrier to imports. How should the ITC decide the case? [*American Telephone and Telegraph Co. v Hitachi*, 6 ITC 1511]

10. Timken Roller Bearing Co. of Ohio (American Timken) owns 30 percent of the outstanding shares of British Timken, a foreign competitor. In 1928, American Timken and British Timken organized French Timken, and since that time they have together owned all the stock of the French company. Since 1928, American Timken, British Timken, and French Timken have continuously kept operative "business agreements" regulating the manufacture and sale of antifriction bearings by the three companies and provided for the use by the British and French corporations of the trademark TIMKEN. Under these agreements, the contracting parties have (1) allocated trade territories among themselves, (2) fixed prices on products of one of the parties sold in the territories of the others, and (3) cooperated to protect each other's markets and to eliminate outside competition. The U.S. Department of Justice contended that American Timken violated the Sherman Act, but American Timken contended that its actions were legal because it was entitled to enter a joint venture with British Timken to form French Timken and was legally entitled to license the trademark TIMKEN to the British and French companies. Decide. [*Timken Roller Bearing Co. v United States*, 341 US 593]

11. Roland Staemphfli was employed as the chief financial officer of Honeywell Bull S.A. (HB), a Swiss computer company operating exclusively in Switzerland. Staemphfli purportedly arranged financing for HB in Switzerland through the issuance of promissory notes. He had the assistance of Fidenas, a Bahamian company dealing in commercial paper. Unknown to Fidenas, the HB notes were fraudulent. The notes were prepared and forged by Staemphfli, who lost all of the proceeds in a speculative investment and was convicted of criminal fraud. HB denied responsibility for the fraudulently issued notes when they came due. Fidenas's business deteriorated because of its involvement with the HB notes. It sued HB and others in the United States for violations of U.S. securities laws. HB defended, arguing that the U.S. court did not have jurisdiction over the transactions in question. Decide. [*Fidenas v Honeywell Bull, S.A.*, 606 F2d 5 (2d Cir)]

12. Marc Rich & Co., A.G., a Swiss commodities trading corporation, refused to comply with a grand jury subpoena requesting certain business records maintained in Switzerland and relating to crude oil transactions and possible violations of U.S. income tax laws. Marc Rich contended that a U.S. court has no authority to require a foreign corporation to deliver to a U.S. court documents located abroad. The court disagreed and imposed fines, froze assets, and threatened to close a Marc Rich wholly owned subsidiary that did business in the state of New York. The fines amounted to $50,000 for each day the company failed to comply with the court's order. Marc Rich appealed. Decide. [*Marc Rich v United States*, 707 F2d 633 (2d Cir)]

13. The U.S. Steel Corp. formed Orinoco Mining Co., a wholly owned corporation, to mine large deposits of iron ore that U.S. Steel had discovered in Venezuela. Orinoco, which was incorporated in Delaware, was subject to Venezuela's maximum tax of 50 percent on net income. Orinoco was also subject to U.S. income tax, but the U.S. foreign tax credit offset this amount. U.S. Steel purchased the ore from Orinoco in Venezuela. U.S. Steel formed Navios, Inc., a wholly owned subsidiary, to transport the ore. Navios, a Liberian corporation, was subject to a 2.5 percent Venezuelan excise tax and was exempt from U.S. income tax. Although U.S. Steel was Navios's primary customer, it charged other customers the same price it charged U.S. Steel. U.S. Steel's investment in Navios was $50,000. In seven years Navios accumulated

nearly $80 million in cash but had not paid any dividends to U.S. Steel. The IRS used IRC § 482 to allocate $52 million of Navios's income to U.S. Steel. U.S. Steel challenged this action, contending Navios's charges to U.S. Steel were at arm's length and the same it charged other customers. Decide. [*United States Steel Corp. v Commissioner,* 617 F2d 942 (2d Cir)]

14. National Computers, Inc., a U.S. firm, entered into a joint venture with a Chinese computer manufacturing organization, TEC. A dispute arose over payments due the U.S. firm under the joint venture agreement with TEC. The agreement called for disputes to be arbitrated in China, with the arbitrator being chosen from a panel of arbitrators maintained by the Beijing arbitration institution, Cietac. What advantages and disadvantages exist for the U.S. firm under this arbitration arrangement? Advise the American firm on negotiating future arbitration agreements with Chinese businesses.

15. Sensor, a Netherlands business organization wholly owned by Geosource, Inc., of Houston, Texas, made a contract with C.E.P. to deliver 2,400 strings of geophones to Rotterdam by September 20, 1982. The ultimate destination was identified as the U.S.S.R. Thereafter, in June 1982, the president of the United States prohibited shipment to the U.S.S.R. of equipment manufactured in foreign countries under license from U.S. firms. The president had a foreign policy objective of retaliating for the imposition of martial law in Poland, and he was acting under regulations issued under the Export Administration Act of 1979. Sensor, in July and August of 1982, notified C.E.P. that as a subsidiary of an American corporation it had to respect the president's embargo. C.E.P. filed suit in a district court of the Netherlands asking that Sensor be ordered to deliver the geophones. Decide. [*Compagnie Européenne des Pétroles v Sensor Nederland,* 22 ILM 66]

Crimes

CHAPTER 8

After studying this chapter, you should be able to

1. *Discuss the nature and classification of crimes;*
2. *Describe the basis of criminal liability;*
3. *Identify who is responsible for criminal acts;*
4. *Explain the penalties for crimes and sentencing for corporate crimes;*
5. *List examples of white-collar crimes and their elements;*
6. *Discuss crimes related to computers; and*
7. *Describe the rights of businesses charged with crimes and the constitutional protections afforded them.*

Society sets certain standards of conduct and punishes a breach of those standards as a crime. This chapter introduces the means by which government protects people and businesses from prohibited conduct.

A.   GENERAL PRINCIPLES

Crimes are defined and their punishment specified by detailed criminal codes and statutes. These vary from state to state but still show the imprint of a common law background.

1.   Nature and Classification of Crimes

A crime is conduct that violates statutorily established standards of society.

A **crime** is conduct that is prohibited and punished by a government.

Crimes are classified as common law or statutory according to their origin. Some offenses are punishable by less than one year in prison and are called misdemeanors, while more serious crimes are called felonies. **Felonies** include serious business crimes such as bribery and embezzlement, which are punishable by confinement in prison for more than one year. **Misdemeanors** include weighing goods with uninspected scales or operating without a sales tax license. An act may be a felony in one state and a misdemeanor in another.[1]

Felonies are crimes with sentences greater than one year or punishable by death.

Misdemeanors are crimes with sentences of less than one year.

CASE SUMMARY

Customers Can't Sue for Bribery

Facts: H.J. Inc. and other customers of Northwestern Bell Corporation alleged that Northwestern Bell had furnished cash and tickets for air travel, plays, and sporting events and had offered employment to members of the Minnesota Public Utilities Commission in exchange for favorable treatment in rate cases before the commission. A Minnesota statute makes it a felony to bribe public officials. H.J. and other customers brought suit against Northwestern for the violation of the criminal bribery statute.

Decision: The case was dismissed because even if bribery of the members of the commission had occurred, it is up to the state of Minnesota to prosecute. There is no right under a criminal statute for private citizens to bring suit in order to obtain a conviction. Bribery is a crime and can be punished only by criminal prosecution brought by the state government against Northwestern. [*H.J. Inc. v Northwestern Bell Corp.* (Minn App) 420 NW2d 673 (1988)]

---

[1] Some states make a further subdivision in terms of seriousness by defining different degrees of a crime, as first-degree murder, second-degree murder, and so on. Misdemeanors may be differentiated by giving special names to minor misdemeanors.

2. Basis of Criminal Liability

A crime generally consists of two elements: (1) a mental state and (2) an act or omission. Harm may occur as a result of a crime, but harm is not an essential element of a crime.

(a) Mental State. Mental state does not require an awareness or knowledge of guilt. In most crimes, it is sufficient that the defendant voluntarily did the act that is criminal, regardless of motive or intent. The lawmaker may make an act a crime even though the actor has no knowledge that a law is being broken.

CASE SUMMARY

Brokering Is a Crime When There's No License

Facts: Bernard Flinn operated a business known as Harvey Investment Co. Inc./High Risk Loans. Flinn worked as a loan broker, matching those who came to him with lenders willing to loan them money given the amount and credit history. From 1982 through 1985 Flinn found loans for five people. Indiana requires that persons engaged in the business of brokering loans obtain a license from the state. Flinn was prosecuted for brokering loans without having a license. He raised the defense that he did not know that a license was required and that accordingly he lacked the criminal intent to broker loans without having a license.

Decision: This defense was invalid. It was not necessary that Flinn intended to violate the law. It was sufficient that he voluntarily intended to do an act that was prohibited by law. [Flinn v Indiana (Ind) 563 NE2d 536 (1990)]

Actions that are in themselves crimes are not made innocent by the claim that the defendant was exercising a constitutional right. For example, freedom of speech does not give the right to send threatening letters.

(b) Act or Omission. The conduct that, when coupled with sufficient mental state, constitutes a crime is defined by specific statutes. For example, writing a check knowing you do not have the funds available is conduct that is a crime.

3. Responsibility for Criminal Acts

In some cases, persons who did not necessarily commit the criminal act itself are still held criminally responsible for acts committed by others.

CASE SUMMARY

Common Sense versus the Letter of the Law

Facts: Grabert ran an amusement center in Louisiana called Beck's. He held a license for video gambling machines. Louisiana makes it illegal to allow a minor to play a video gambling machine. A mother came into Grabert's center carrying her 23-month-old baby in her arms. She sat at the video poker machine with her child on her lap and proceeded to play. State troopers witnessed the baby pushing the buttons on the machine at least three times. The Department of Public Safety and Corrections then sought to revoke Grabert's videogaming license because a minor had been allowed to play the machines.

> **Decision:** While the statute literally applied, as the baby was under 18 years of age, such a construction was absurd. Because the baby was merely pushing buttons as directed by the mother, it was the mother who was playing the machine. The statute was obviously aimed at the conduct of young adults and would therefore be construed to exclude the present case. *[Grabert v Department of Public Safety and Corrections (La App) 680 So 2d 764 (1996)]*

(a) Corporate Liability. Corporations are held responsible for the acts of their employees. A corporation may also be held liable for crimes based on the failure of its employees to act. Thus, a corporation may be held criminally responsible when an employee is killed because of the failure to install safety devices required by law.

(b) Officers and Agents of Corporations. One of the main differences between nonbusiness and business crimes is that more people in a company can be convicted for the same business crime. For nonbusiness crimes, only those who are actually involved in the act itself can be convicted of the crime. For business crimes, however, managers of firms whose employees commit criminal acts can be held liable if the managers authorized the conduct of the employees or knew about the conduct of the employees and did nothing or failed to act reasonably in their supervisory positions in order to prevent the employees from engaging in criminal conduct.

CASE SUMMARY

Rats in the Warehouse and a CEO with a Fine

Facts: The federal Food and Drug Administration (FDA) had inspected the Philadelphia warehouses of Acme Markets, Inc., a food retailer with 36,000 employees, in 1970, 1971, and 1972 and had found the same problem with rodent infestation. The FDA, frustrated with the lack of response by warehouse employees, sent a letter to John Park, the president of Acme detailing the problems in the warehouse.

We note with much concern that the old and new warehouse areas used for food storage were actively and extensively inhabited by live rodents. Of even more concern was the observation that such reprehensible conditions obviously existed for a prolonged period of time without any detection, and were completely ignored.

We trust this letter will serve to direct your attention to the seriousness of the problem and formally advise you of the urgent need to initiate whatever measures are necessary to prevent recurrence and ensure compliance with the law.

Park asked his vice president to take care of the problem. Two months after the letter was sent, the FDA inspected the warehouse again and still found rodent infestation. Acme and Park were charged with violations of the federal pure food laws. Acme pleaded guilty, and Park was found guilty and fined $500. Park appealed his conviction because he was not responsible for the warehouse.

Decision: The court affirmed Park's conviction on the grounds that he was told of a serious situation at one of his facilities that constituted a violation of federal law and that after two months he had failed to get the situation corrected. His knowledge of the problem and his inaction were sufficient to hold him criminally liable. *[United States v Park, 421 U.S. 658 (1975)]*

Figure 8-1 is a summary of the federal laws under which individuals within a company can be held liable for criminal violations.

Agency	May complaint name individual?	Maximum individual penalty	Maximum corporate penalty
Internal Revenue Service	Yes	Willful failure to pay, $10,000/five years; willful failure to file, $25,000/one year; fraud, $100,000/three years	Willful failure to pay, $10,000, 50% assessment, prosecution costs; willful failure to file, $100,000; fraud, $500,000
Antitrust Division of the Justice Department	Yes	$100,000, three years, or both	$1 million, injunction, divestiture
Food and Drug Administration	Yes	$1,000, one year, or both for first offense; $10,000, three years, or both thereafter; illegal drug importation, $250,000/ten years	$1,000 for first offense, $10,000 thereafter; seizure of condemned products; illegal drug importation, $250,000
Federal Trade Commission	Yes	Restitution, injunction	Restitution, injunction, divestiture, $10,000 per day for violation of rules, orders
Securities and Exchange Commission	Yes	$10,000, five years, or both (1933); $100,000, five years, or both (1934)	$2,000,000
Equal Employment Opportunity Commission	No	Injunction (some state liability possible)	Injunction, back pay award, reinstatement
Office of Federal Contract Compliance Programs	No		Suspension, cancellation of contract
Environmental Protection Agency	Yes	Medical waste, $50,000/two years; solid waste, $250,000/two years; $50,000 per day of violation penalty	Medical waste, $1,000,000; solid waste, $1,000,000; $50,000 per day of violation penalty
Occupational Safety and Health Administration	No	Willful, maximum of $70,000 per violation; minimum of $5,000 per violation; death, $10,000 and/or six months; false reports, $10,000 and/or six months; advance notice of inspection, $1,000 and/or six months	$70,000
Consumer Product Safety Commission	Yes	$50,000, one year, or both	$500,000 (civil)
Fair Labor Standards Act Department	Yes	$10,000 per employee, six months, or both	$100,000, reimbursement of wages

FIGURE 8-1
Penalties for Business Crime under Federal Law

(c) Penalty for Crime: Forfeiture. When a defendant is convicted of a crime, the court may also declare that the defendant's rights in any instrument of that crime are forfeited. When the forfeited property can be used only for a criminal purpose, as in the case of engraved plates used for making counterfeit money, there is no question of the right of the government to confiscate the property. This confiscation is allowable even though it in effect increases the penalty imposed on the defendant.

Forfeiture is not limited to property that can be used only for crime. Thus, an automobile that is used to carry illegal merchandise may itself be seized by the government even though it is obvious that the automobile could also be put to a lawful use.

(d) Reforming Penalties for Crimes. Some regulators and legislators worry that most criminal penalties were created with "natural" persons in mind, as opposed to "artificial" corporate persons. Fines may be significant to individuals, but a $10,000 fine to a corporation with $3 billion is assets and hundreds of millions in income is viewed as simply a cost of doing business.

One recommendation for reforming criminal penalties is to compute the fine in terms of net earnings. *For example*, a bad decision on a product line would cost a company 10 to 20 percent of its earnings. A criminal penalty could be imposed in the same fashion with the idea that the company simply made a bad legal decision that should be reflected in earnings.

Another recommendation that has been implemented to a certain extent is mandatory prison sentences for officers and directors who are convicted of crimes. The human element of the corporation is then punished for the crimes committed for the business. The U.S. Sentencing Commission, established by Congress in 1984, has developed both federal sentencing guidelines and a carrot-and-stick approach to fighting business crime. If the managers of the company are involved and working to prevent criminal misconduct in a company and a crime occurs, the guidelines permit sentence reductions for the managers' efforts. If the managers are not adequately supervising conduct and encouraging compliance with the law, then the guidelines require judges to impose harsher sentences and fines.

> Federal sentencing guidelines are the federal standards used by judges in determining mandatory sentence terms for those convicted of federal crimes.

The guidelines, referred to as the **federal sentencing guidelines**, apply to securities, antitrust, bribery, money laundering, employment, and contract laws at the federal level. The sentencing guidelines permit a judge to place a guilty company on probation for a period of up to five years if the offense occurred during a time when there were no crime prevention programs in place in the company. The guidelines take into account the seriousness of the offense, the company's history of violations, its cooperation in the investigation, the effectiveness of its compliance program (often called an ethics program), and the role of senior management in the wrongdoing. Corporate managers found to have masterminded any criminal activity must be sentenced to prison time.

4.   Indemnification of Crime Victims

Typically the victim of a crime does not benefit from the criminal prosecution and conviction of the wrongdoer. Any fine that is imposed on the defendant is paid to the government and is not received in any way by the victim.

(a) **Statutory Assistance.** Several states have adopted statutes providing a limited degree of indemnification to victims of crime in order to compensate them for the harm or loss sustained.[2] Under some criminal victim indemnification statutes, dependents of a deceased victim are entitled to recover the amount of support they were deprived of by the victim's death. The Victims of Crime Act of 1984 creates a federal Crime Victims Fund. This fund receives the fines paid into the federal courts and other moneys. From this fund grants are made to the states to assist them in financing programs to provide indemnity to and assistance for victims of crime.[3] The Victim and Witness Protection Act of 1982 authorizes the sentencing judge in a federal district court to order, in certain cases, that the defendant make restitution (restoration) to the victim or pay the victim the amount of medical expenses or loss of income caused by the crime.[4] When a court enters a restitution order against a defendant, the order becomes a lien on all property owned by the defendant at that time.[5]

(b) **Action for Damages.** Although criminal prosecution of a wrongdoer does not financially benefit the victim of the crime, the victim is typically entitled to bring a civil action for damages against the wrongdoer for the harm sustained. The modern pattern of statutes creating business crimes is to give the victim the right to sue for damages. For example, the wrongdoer violating the federal antitrust act is liable to the victim for three times the damages actually sustained.

(c) **Indemnification of Unjustly Convicted.** If an innocent person is convicted of a crime, the state legislature typically pays the person indemnity to compensate for the wrong that has been done. In some states this right to indemnity is expressly established by statute, as in the case of the New York Unjust Conviction and Imprisonment Act. The fact that a person has been imprisoned while awaiting trial and is then acquitted does not entitle that person to compensation under such a statute because an acquittal does not mean that the person was found innocent. It means only that the government was not able to prove guilt beyond a reasonable doubt.[6]

B.   WHITE COLLAR CRIMES

Those crimes that do not use, or threaten to use, force or violence or do not cause injury to persons or physical damage to property are called **white collar crimes**. A particular defendant may be guilty of both a white-collar crime and a traditional crime of the kind described in part C of this chapter.

---

[2] A 1973 Uniform Crime Victims Reparations Act has been adopted in Kansas, Louisiana, Montana, North Dakota, Ohio, and Utah. This act has been superseded by the Uniform Victims of Crime Act of 1992.
[3] Act of October 12, 1984, PL 98-473, 98 Stat 2170, 18 USC §§ 1401 et seq.
[4] Act of October 12, 1982, PL 97-291, 96 Stat 1253, 18 USC § 3579, as amended by Act of November 15, 1990, PL 101-581, 104 Stat 2865, 18 USC § 18. 18 USC § 3579; *Hughey v United States*, 495 US 411 (1990). Some states likewise provide for payment into a special fund. *Ex parte* Lewis (Ala) 556 So 2d 370 (1989).
[5] *United States v Mills*, 991 F2d 609 (9th Cir 1993).
[6] *Reed v New York*, 78 NY2d 1, 574 NE2d 433 (1991).

5. Conspiracies

Prior to the commission of an intended crime, a person may engage in conduct that is itself a crime, such as a conspiracy.

A **conspiracy** is an agreement between two or more persons to commit an unlawful act or to use unlawful means to achieve an otherwise lawful result. The crime is the agreement, and generally it is immaterial that nothing is done to carry out the agreement. Some statutes, however, require that some act be done to carry out the agreement before the crime of conspiracy is considered committed.

6. Crimes Related to Production, Competition, and Marketing

A person or enterprise in business may be guilty of various crimes relating to labor and employment practices, conspiracies, combinations in restraint of trade, price discrimination, and environmental pollution.

(a) Improper Use of Interstate Commerce. The shipment of improper goods or the transmission of improper information in interstate commerce constitutes a crime under various federal statutes. Thus, it is a federal crime to use interstate commerce to send a statement as part of a scheme to defraud; to send a blackmail or extortion threat; to ship adulterated or mislabeled foods, drugs, or cosmetics; or to ship into a state child-labor-made or convict-labor-made goods or intoxicating liquor when the sale of such goods is prohibited by the destination state.

The Communications Act of 1934, as amended,[7] makes it a crime to manufacture or sell devices knowing their primary use is to unscramble satellite telecasts without having paid for the right to do so.[8]

(b) Securities Crimes. To protect the investing public, both state and federal laws have regulated the issuance and public sale of stocks and bonds. Between 1933 and 1940, seven such regulatory statutes were adopted by Congress. These statutes and the crimes associated with sales of securities are covered in chapter 48.

7. Money Laundering

The federal government has adopted a Money Laundering Control Act.[9] The act prohibits the knowing and willful participation in any type of financial transaction involving unlawful proceeds when the transaction is designed to conceal or disguise the source of the funds.

8. Racketeering

The Racketeer Influenced and Corrupt Organizations Act (RICO)[10] was enacted by Congress in 1970 as part of the Organized Crime Control Act. The law was designed primarily to prevent individuals involved in organized crime from investing money obtained through racketeering in legitimate businesses. However,

---

[7] Section 705(d)(1), (e)(4), 47 USC § 605 (d)(1), (e)(4).
[8] *United States v Harrell*, 983 F2d 36 (5th Cir 1993).
[9] Act of October 28, 1992, PL 102-550, 106 Stat 3672, 42 USC § 5301. *Walls v First State Bank*, 900 SW2d 117 (Tex App 1995).
[10] 18 USC §§ 1961-1968.

the broad language of the act, coupled with a provision that allows individuals and businesses to sue for treble damages, has resulted in an increasing number of lawsuits against ordinary businesspersons not associated with organized crime.

(a) Criminal and Civil Applications. RICO authorizes criminal and civil actions against persons who use any income derived from racketeering activity to invest in, control, or conduct an enterprise through a pattern of racketeering activity.[11] Under RICO, *racketeering activity* is defined to include some twenty-six types of federal crimes and some nine types of state felonies, including extortion, fraud, and obtaining money under false pretenses. The essential aspect of a RICO case regarding state crimes is not that state law has been violated, but that conduct illegal under state law, when combined with its impact on interstate commerce, constitutes a violation of federal law.[12]

In criminal and civil actions under RICO, a pattern of racketeering activity must be established by proving that at least two acts of racketeering activity—so-called predicate acts—have been committed within ten years. Conviction under RICO's criminal provisions may result in a $25,000 fine and up to 20 years' imprisonment as well as forfeiture of the property involved. A successful civil plaintiff may recover three times the actual damages suffered and attorney fees.

CASE SUMMARY

Shedding Light on RICO and Price Fixing

Facts: Marvin Rosenthal, Mark Rosenthal, and Eduardo Mariani distributed electrical supplies from their business, Broadway Electrical Supply Inc. Starting in 1988 they fraudulently obtained discounted prices on large quantities of light bulbs from GTE Products Corp. by creating a sham business known as Glomar, Inc. They obtained "end-user" discounts from GTE by using phony records, including order forms, checks, and receipts, all of which purported to show that Glomar had actually purchased the light bulbs from Broadway. Instead, Broadway sold the light bulbs to another distributor, who, in turn, resold them to the general public at prices substantially lower than those offered by other GTE distributors. GTE discovered the ruse in 1991 and sued the three individuals for the difference in price between its regular wholesale price and the lower end-user discounted price related to Glomar, which amounted to $312,394. From a judgment for $937,182 on GTE's civil RICO claim, the defendants appealed, claiming that there were not two or more predicate crimes, as needed for a civil RICO claim.

Decision: Judgment for GTE. The individual claims submitted to GTE for end-user discounts under the Glomar scheme may be seen primarily as discrete episodes of fraud that were perpetrated over a lengthy period of time until they were caught. It was a string of individual fraudulent acts akin to a larceny spree. Thus, there were far more than the two predicate crimes needed for a civil RICO claim [*GTE Products Corporation v Broadway Electric Supply Co. Inc. (Mass App) 676 NE2d 1151 (1997)*]

(b) Expanding Usage. Civil RICO suits have been successfully brought against business entities, such as accounting firms, labor unions, insurance companies, commercial banks, stock brokerage firms, and a wide range of businesses. Antiabortion protesters are also subject to civil RICO suit, even though the protesters did not act out of an economic motive, because while the racketeering activities

---

[11] 18 USC § 1962(a)-(d).
[12] *Williams v Stone* 109 F3d 890 (3rd Cir 1997).

A predicate act is a qualifying underlying offense for RICO liability.

of the protesters may not benefit them financially, they may still drain money from the economy by harming businesses, such as health clinics.[13] However, under the Private Securities Litigation Reform Act of 1995, securities fraud is eliminated as a *predicate act*, or a qualifying underlying offense, for private RICO actions, absent a prior criminal conviction.[14]

9. Bribery

Bribery is the act of giving money, property, or any benefit to a particular person to influence that person's judgment in favor of the giver.

Bribery is the act of giving money, property, or any benefit to a particular person to influence that person's judgment in favor of the giver. At common law, the crime was limited to doing such acts to influence a public official. In this century the common law concept has expanded to include *commercial bribery*. For example, it is now a crime to pay a competitor's employee money to obtain secret information about the competitor.

The giving and the receiving of a bribe constitute separate crimes. In addition, the act of trying to obtain a bribe may be a crime of solicitation of bribery; in some states in fact bribery is broadly defined to include solicitation of bribes.

10. Extortion and Blackmail

Extortion and blackmail are crimes in which the wrongdoer seeks to force the victim to do some act—typically paying money—that the victim would not otherwise desire to do.

Extortion is an illegal demand by a public officer, acting with apparent authority.

(a) Extortion. When a public officer, acting under the apparent authority of the office, makes an illegal demand, the officer has committed the crime of **extortion**. For example, if a health inspector threatens to close down a restaurant on a false charge of violation of the sanitation laws unless the restaurant pays the inspector a sum of money, the inspector has committed extortion. (If the restaurant voluntarily offers the inspector the money to prevent the restaurant from being shut down because of actual violations of the sanitation laws, the crime committed would be bribery.)

Modern statutes tend to ignore the public officer aspect of the common law and expand extortion to include obtaining anything of value by threat. This might be in connection with loan-sharking or labor racketeering. In a number of states, statutes extend the extortion concept to include the making of terroristic threats.[15]

Blackmail is extortion by a nonpublic official.

(b) Blackmail. In jurisdictions where extortion is limited to the conduct of public officials, a nonofficial commits **blackmail** by making demands that would be extortion if made by a public official. Ordinarily blackmail is the act of threatening someone with publicity about a matter that would damage the victim's personal or business reputation.

11. Corrupt Influence

In harmony with changing concepts of right and wrong, society has increasingly outlawed certain practices on the ground that they exert a corrupting influence on business transactions.

---

[13] *National Organization for Women v Scheidler*, 510 U.S. 249 (1994).
[14] 15 USC § 78a, n-t.
[15] *Pennsylvania v Bunting*, 284 Pa Super 444, 426 A2d 130 (1981).

(a) Improper Political Influence. To protect from the improper influencing of political or governmental action, various acts have been classified as crimes. For example, it is a crime for the holder of a government office to be financially interested in or to receive money from an enterprise that is seeking to do business with the government. Such conflict of interests is likely to produce a result that is harmful to the public. Likewise, lobbyists and foreign agents must register in Washington, D.C.,[16] and must adhere to statutes regulating the giving and receiving of contributions for political campaigns. Violation of these regulatory statutes is a crime.

Foreign Corrupt Practices Act (FCPA) is a federal law that prohibits bribery by U.S.-based companies in their international operations.

(b) Foreign Corrupt Practices Act. The **Foreign Corrupt Practices Act (FCPA)** is a federal criminal statute that applies to businesses with their principal offices in the United States and is an antibribery and anticorruption statute covering these companies' international operations. The FCPA prohibits making, authorizing, or promising payments or gifts of money or anything of value with the intent to corrupt. This prohibition applies to payments or gifts designed to influence official acts of foreign officials, parties, party officials, candidates for office, or any other person who will transmit the gift or money to this type of person.

Grease (facilitation) payments are legal payments to speed up or ensure performance of normal governmental duties.

The FCPA does not prohibit **grease** or **facilitation payments**. These are payments made only to get officials to perform their normal duties or to perform them in a timely manner. Facilitation payments are those made to (1) secure a permit or a license; (2) obtain paper processing; (3) secure police protection; (4) provide phone, water, or power services; or (5) obtain any other similar action.

WHAT'S BEHIND THE LAW?

Why Regulate Bribes?

The Foreign Corrupt Practices Act makes payment of bribes to government officials illegal. However, the use of grease payments to facilitate, but not influence, government conduct is not prohibited. The terms *guanxi* in China and *mordida* in Mexico are associated with the facilitation of business. Regardless of the term, the effect is the same: Something beyond the consideration under a contract itself is given in exchange for the award of the contract. Most people, however, are surprised to learn there is no country in the world that permits commercial bribery. Despite U.S. views about the nature of international business, quid pro quo is not legally acknowledged anywhere in the world. Nations that seek to develop their economic base understand that under-the-counter payments breed corruption in government and introduce inefficiencies into a country's markets. To protect free markets, bribes are prohibited regardless of the name given them.

To check the laws of other countries, visit law by country at
http://www.law.emory.edu/LAW/refdesk/country/foreign

---

12. Counterfeiting

Counterfeiting is the manufacturing, with fraudulent intent, of a document or coin that appears genuine.

Counterfeiting is the making, with fraudulent intent, of a document or coin that appears to be genuine but is not because the person making it did not have the authority to make it. It is a federal crime to make or to possess with intent to pass or to pass counterfeit coins, bank notes, or obligations or other securities of the United States. Legislation has also been adopted prohibiting the passing of counterfeit foreign securities or notes of foreign banks.

---

[16] Foreign Agents Registration Act, Act of June 8, 1938, 52 Stat 631, 22 USC §§ 611 et seq., as amended.

Various states also have statutes prohibiting the making and passing of counterfeit coins and bank notes. These statutes often provide, as does the federal statute, a punishment for the mutilation of bank notes or the lightening (of the weight) or mutilation of coins.

13. Forgery

Forgery consists of the fraudulent making or material altering of an instrument, such as a check, that apparently creates or changes a legal liability of another person.[17] The instrument must have some apparent legal efficacy in order to constitute forgery.

Ordinarily forgery consists of signing another's name with intent to defraud, but it may also consist of making an entire instrument or altering an existing one. It may result from signing a fictitious name or the offender's own name with the intent to defraud. When the nonowner of a credit card signs the owner's name on a credit card invoice without the owner's permission, this act is a forgery.

The issuing or delivery of a forged instrument to another person constitutes the crime of *uttering* a forged instrument. The elements of the crime are (1) the offering of a forged instrument with a representation by words or acts that it is true and genuine; (2) the knowledge that it is false, forged, or counterfeit; and (3) the intent to defraud.[18] Any sending of a forged check through the channels of commerce or of bank collection constitutes an uttering of a forged instrument. Thus, the act of depositing a forged check into the forger's bank account by depositing it in an automatic teller machine constitutes uttering within the meaning of a forgery statute.[19]

14. Perjury

Perjury consists of knowingly giving false testimony in a judicial proceeding after having been sworn or having affirmed to tell the truth. By statute, knowingly making false answers on any form filed with a government is typically made perjury or is subjected to the same punishment as perjury. In some jurisdictions, the out-of-court offense is called *false swearing*.

15. False Claims and Pretenses

Many statutes declare it a crime to make false claims or to obtain goods by false pretenses.

(a) False Claims. A statute may expressly declare that the making of a false claim to an insurance company, a government office, or a relief agency is a crime. The federal false statement statute makes it a crime to knowingly and willfully make a false material statement about any matter within the jurisdiction of any department or agency of the United States. Thus, it is a crime for a contractor to make a

---

[17] A bank withdrawal slip may be a forged written instrument. *Washington v Aitken* (Wash App) 905 P2d 1235 (1995).
[18] *Nebraska v Ward* (Neb App) 510 NW2d 320 (1993).
[19] *Wisconsin v Tolliver* (Wis App) 440 NW2d 571 (1989).

false claim against the United States for payment for work that was never performed. Other statutes indirectly regulate the matter by declaring that signing a false written claim constitutes perjury or is subject to the same punishment as perjury.[20]

(b) Obtaining Goods by False Pretenses. Almost all states have statutes that forbid obtaining money or goods under false pretenses.[21] These statutes vary in detail and scope. Sometimes they are directed against a particular form of deception, such as using a bad check. In some states the false pretense crime has been expanded to include obtaining any thing or service of value by false pretenses. In any case, an intent to defraud is an essential element of obtaining property by false pretenses.

The Trademark Counterfeiting Act of 1984[22] makes it a federal crime to deal in goods and services under a counterfeit mark.

A false pretense statute is violated when a person delivers a check and assures the person to whom it is delivered that there is sufficient money in the bank to cover the check but in fact there is not and this is known to the speaker.[23]

False representations as to future profits or the identity of the defendant are other common forms of false pretenses.

The fact that a contract is broken does not establish a false pretense crime unless it is also shown that the contract had been entered into with the intent of not performing it.[24]

(c) False Information Submitted to Government. Within recent decades the concept of false claims and pretenses has been expanded to protect government agencies that are reorganizing or liquidating failed banks and savings institutions.

It is also a crime for a landowner to put a false value on land transferred to a bank as security for a loan.[25]

(d) Unauthorized Use of Automated Teller Machine. Obtaining money from an automated teller machine (ATM) by the unauthorized use of the depositor's ATM card is a federal crime.[26]

(e) False Information Submitted to Banks. Knowingly making false statements in a loan application to a federally insured bank is a federal crime.[27]

16. Bad Checks

The use of a bad check is commonly made a crime by a statute directly aimed at the use of bad checks. In the absence of a bad check statute, the use of a bad check could generally be prosecuted under a false pretenses statute.

Under a bad check statute, it is a crime to use or pass a check with intent to defraud with knowledge that there will not be sufficient funds in the bank to pay

---

[20] The Federal False Claims Act is violated only when the false claim is submitted with knowledge of its falsity. *Hagood v Sonoma County Water Agency,* 81 F3d 1465 (9th Cir 1996).
[21] *North Carolina v Lang* (NC App) 417 SE2d 808 (1992).
[22] Act of October 12, 1984, § 1502, PL 98-473, 98 Stat 2178, 18 USC § 113.
[23] *Utah v LeFevre* (Utah App) 825 P2d 681 (1992).
[24] *Baker v Alabama* (Ala App) 588 So 2d 945 (1991).
[25] *United States v Faulkner,* 17 F3d 745 (5th Cir 1994).
[26] *United States v Miller,* 70 F3d 1353 (DC Cir 1995).
[27] 18 USC § 1014. *United States v Key,* 76 F3d 350 (11th Cir 1996).

the check when it is presented for payment. Knowledge that the bad check will not be paid when presented to the bank is an essential element of the crime. The bad check statutes typically provide that if the check is not made good within a specified number of days after payment by the bank is refused, it is presumed that the defendant had acted with the intent to defraud.[28] For more information on checks see chapter 34.

17. Cheats and Swindles

Various statutes are designed to protect the public from being deceived.

(a) False Weights, Measures, and Labels. Cheating, defrauding, or misleading the public by use of false, improper, or inadequate weights, measures, and labels is a crime. The federal government and state governments, too, have adopted many statutes on this subject.

> A swindle or confidence game is obtaining money or property by trick, deception, or fraud.

(b) Swindles and Confidence Games. The act of a person who, intending to cheat and defraud, obtains money or property by trick, deception, or fraud is known as a **swindle** or **confidence game**. Bad stock and spurious works of art are frequently employed in swindling operations.

The essential elements of a confidence game crime are (1) an intent to defraud; (2) the swindler's gaining the victim's confidence; (3) intentional false statements about past or existing facts; and (4) in some states the victim's sustaining a loss of more than a stated amount, such as $50.

Federal and state statutes prohibit obtaining money by any chain letter or pyramid plan. Under the prohibited plans, persons solicited are persuaded that they can get their money back or win a prize by inducing others to write similar letters.[29]

18. Credit Card Crimes

It is a crime to steal a credit card and, in some states, to possess the credit card of another person without that person's consent. Using a credit card without the permission of the rightful cardholder constitutes the crime of obtaining goods or services by false pretenses or with the intent to defraud. Likewise, a person continuing to use a credit card with knowledge that it has been canceled is guilty of the crime of obtaining goods by false pretenses.

When, without permission, the wrongdoer signs the name of the rightful cardholder on the slip for the credit card transaction, the wrongdoer commits the crime of forgery. The district attorney has the discretion to choose the particular crime for which to prosecute the wrongdoer.

The Credit Card Fraud Act of 1984[30] makes it a federal crime to obtain anything of value in excess of $1,000 in a year by means of a counterfeit credit card, to make or traffic in such cards, or to possess more than 15 counterfeit cards at one time.

---

[28] *United States v Williams*, 81 F3d 1321 (4th Cir 1996).
[29] *Sheehan v Bowden* (Ala) 572 So 2d 1211 (1990).
[30] Act of October 12, 1984, § 1029, PL 98-473, 98 Stat 2183, 18 USC § 1029.

19. Use of the Mails or Wires to Defraud

Congress has made it a crime to use the mails or wires to further any scheme or artifice to defraud. To constitute this offense, there must be (1) a contemplated or organized scheme to defraud or to obtain money or property by false pretenses and (2) the mailing or the causing of another to mail a letter, writing, or pamphlet for the purpose of executing or attempting to execute such a scheme or artifice.[31]

Illustrations of schemes that come within the statute are false statements to secure credit, circulars announcing false cures, false statements to induce the sale of a corporation's stock, and false statements about the origin of a fire and the value of destroyed goods for securing indemnity from an insurance company. Federal law also makes it a crime to use a telegram or a telephone to defraud.

20. Embezzlement

Embezzlement is the fraudulent conversion of another's property or money by a person to whom it has been entrusted.

Embezzlement is the fraudulent conversion of another's property or money by a person to whom it has been entrusted.[32] An example would be an employee's taking his employer's money for personal use. Embezzlement is a statutory crime designed to cover the case of unlawful takings that are not larceny because the wrongdoer did not take the property from the possession of another and not robbery because there is neither a taking from the possession of another nor the use of force or fear.

It is immaterial whether the defendant received the money or property from the victim or from a third person who wanted the money or property delivered to the victim. Thus, an agent commits embezzlement when the agent receives and keeps payments from third persons—payments the agent should have turned over to the principal. Likewise, when an insured gives money to an insurance agent to pay the insurance company but the insurance agent uses the money to pay premiums on the policies of other persons, the agent is guilty of embezzlement.

Generally, the fact that the defendant intends to return the property or money embezzled, or does in fact do so, is no defense.

Today, every jurisdiction has not only a general embezzlement statute but also various statutes applicable to particular situations. For example, statutes cover embezzlement by government officials, employees, trustees, and bailees.

ETHICS & THE LAW

Patricia Rue had worked at a Bucks County, Pennsylvania, Kmart for 12 years. After she was fired by her supervisor for allegedly eating a bag of the store's potato chips, the supervisor told Rue's co-workers that she had been fired for stealing a bag of potato chips.

Do you believe firing someone for stealing a bag of potato chips is appropriate punishment? Should employees with longer service histories be treated more leniently? Would you have fired Rue?

Rue did file suit against Kmart for defamation and won $1.4 million in punitive damages and $90,000 in compensatory damages because a jury found that disclosing the potato chip incident to other employees was "outrageous." Was her supervisor fair to her? Is it important that an employer discloses to other employees the nature of one employee's conduct and the disciplinary action taken?

---

[31] *Cesnik v Edgewood Baptist Church* 88 F3d 902 (11th Cir. 1996).
[32] *North Carolina v Speckman* (NC) 391 SE2d 165 (1990).

C. CRIMINAL LAW AND THE COMPUTER

In some situations the ordinary law of crimes fits the computer crime situation. In other situations new law is required.

21. What Is a Computer Crime?

Computer crimes are various wrongs committed using a computer or with knowledge of computers.

The term *computer crime* is frequently used even though it has no established definition. Generally, the phrase is used to refer to a crime that can be committed only by a person having some knowledge of the operation of a computer. Just as stealing an automobile requires knowledge of how to operate and drive a car, so the typical computer crime requires knowledge of how the computer works. This concept of a computer crime is satisfactory for the purpose of setting the stage, but it fails to tell us what law will be applied: the law of crimes or a new law relating to computers.

Some crimes may involve a computer without making direct use of one. In this case, the ordinary law of crimes will apply. For example, a person using the mail to falsely advertise a service as computerized is guilty of committing the federal crime of using the mails to defraud.

Because the more serious and costly wrongs relating to computers do not fit into the ordinary definitions of crime, a definite trend of adopting statutes to declare new computer crimes is apparent. These statutes are strictly construed: Only that conduct covered by the statute can be punished as the crime.

A criminal law statute must be sufficiently clear to be understood by ordinary persons of ordinary intelligence. In some cases, statutes covering computer crimes have been held unconstitutional as too vague.

22. The Computer as Victim

A traditional crime may be committed by stealing or intentionally damaging the computer.

(a) Theft of Hardware. When the computer itself is stolen, the ordinary law relating to theft crimes should apply. No reason can be found why the theft of a computer should not be subject to the same law as the theft of a typewriter or a desk. Whatever the crime would be by statute in the case of these other objects, the same crime is committed when a computer is the subject matter of the theft.

(b) Theft of Software. When a thief takes software, whether in the form of a program written on paper or a program on a disk or tape, a situation arises that does not fit into the common law definition of larceny. Larceny at common law was confined to the taking of tangible property. At common law the value of stolen software would be determined by the value of the tangible substance on which the program was recorded. Thus, under a traditional concept of property, which would ignore the value of the intangible program, the theft would be only petty larceny. Now, however, virtually every state has amended its definition of larceny or theft so that the stealing of software is a crime. In some states the unauthorized taking of information may constitute a crime under a trade secrets protection statute.

(c) Intentional Damage. The computer may be the "victim" of a crime when it is intentionally destroyed or harmed. In the most elementary form of damage, the computer could be harmed if smashed with an ax or destroyed in an explosion or a fire. In such cases the wrongdoer may be seeking to do more than merely destroy or harm the computer. The intent may be to cause the computer's owner the financial loss of the computer and the destruction of the information that is stored in it.

When the wrongdoer's purpose is to destroy software or the stored information, the wrongdoer might gain access to the computer and then erase or alter the data. The wrongdoer might also achieve the desired purpose by interfering with the air-conditioning required by the computer, thus causing it to malfunction. Or the wrongdoer may intentionally plant a "bug" or "virus" in the software, causing the program to malfunction or to give incorrect output. Such damage may be the work of an angry employee or ex-employee, or it may be the work of a competitor.

In earlier years the criminal was probably guilty only of the crime of malicious destruction of or damage to property.[33] Again, lawmakers have filled the gap between the technological environment and the law. Statutes adopted in many states now make it a crime to damage software or computer-stored information.

23. Unauthorized Use of Computers

In contrast with conduct intended to harm a computer or its rightful user or to acquire secret information, the least serious of the computer crimes is the unlawful use of someone else's computer. In some states, however, the unlawful use of a computer is not a crime. Although the user is stealing the time of the computer, the wrongdoer is not regarded as committing the crime of larceny because the wrongdoer has no intent to deprive the owner permanently of the computer.[34] This computer crime has been widely regulated by recent statutes.

24. Computer Raiding

A serious computer crime involves taking information from a computer without the consent of the owner of the information. Whether this is done by instructing the computer to make a printout of stored information or by tapping into the data bank of the computer by some electronic means is not important. In many instances taking information from the computer constitutes the crime of stealing trade secrets. In some states taking information is known as the crime of "computer trespass."[35]

Both Congress and state legislatures have adopted statutes that declare it a crime to make any unauthorized use of a computer or to gain unauthorized access to a computer or the information stored in its data base in order to cause harm to the computer or its rightful user.[36]

---

[33] The crime of maliciously damaging or destroying property is ordinarily a misdemeanor and, as such, is subject only to a relatively small fine or short imprisonment.

[34] The court in *Indiana v McGraw* (Ind) 480 NE2d 552 (1985) followed this approach.

[35] *Washington v Riley*, 846 P2d 1365 (Wash 1993).

[36] The Counterfeit Access Device and Computer Fraud Act of October 12, 1984, § 2102, PL 98-473, 98 Stat 2190, 18 USC §§ 1030 et seq.; Computer Fraud and Abuse Act of 1986, Act of October 16, 1986, PL 99-474, 100 Stat 1213, 18 USC § 1001, as amended; Electronic Communications Privacy Act of 1986, Act of October 21, 1986, PL 99-508, 100 Stat 1848, 18 USC § 2510; Computer Fraud Act of 1987, Act of January 8, 1988, PL 100-235, 101 Stat 1724, 15 USC §§ 272, 278, 40 USC § 759. Provision is made for training small businesses in the use and security of computers by the Small Business and Computer Security and Education Act of July 16, 1984, PL 98-362, 98 Stat 431, 15 USC §§ 633 et seq.

25. Diverted Delivery by Computer

In many industries deliveries are controlled by a computer. The person in charge of that computer or a criminal unlawfully gaining access to that computer may cause the computer to direct delivery to an improper place. That is, instead of shipping goods to the customers to whom they should go, the wrongdoer diverts the goods to a different place, where they will be received by the wrongdoer or a confederate.

In precomputer days written orders were sent from the sales department to the shipping department. The shipping department would then send the ordered goods to the proper places. If the person in the sales department or the person in the shipping department was dishonest, either one could divert the goods from the proper destination. Today, this fraudulent diversion of goods may be effected by instructing the computer to give false directions. Basically the crime has not changed. The computer is merely the new instrument by which the old crime is committed. This old crime has taken on a new social significance because of the amazingly large dollar value of the theft accomplished by means of it. In one case several hundred loaded freight cars were made to disappear. In another case a loaded oil tanker was diverted to unload into a fleet of tank trucks operated by an accomplice of the computer operator.

The crime of diverted delivery is not limited to goods. It has embraced transferring money from a proper account to a wrong account. Here millions of dollars have been involved in a single crime.

The case of diverted delivery by computer does not require any new law because the appropriation of goods or money improperly delivered comes within the larceny-theft-embezzlement spectrum of crime. However, when a diverted delivery crime is effected by means of a computer, future statutes may classify the crime as aggravated larceny or the like in order to impose the more severe penalty that society feels is called for because of the huge dollar values involved.

26. Economic Espionage by Computer

The Economic Espionage Act (EEA) is a federal law[37] passed in response to several cases in which high-level executives were downloading information from their computers before transferring to other companies. These executives were able to take proprietary information with them. In one case an executive was accused of taking General Motors' full plan for supply chain management in Europe. The EEA makes it a felony to steal, appropriate, or take a trade secret but also makes it a felony to copy, duplicate, sketch, draw, photograph, download, upload, alter, destroy, replicate, transmit, deliver, send, mail, or communicate a trade secret. The penalties extend up to $500,000 and 15 years in prison for individuals and $10 million for organizations.

When employees take new positions with another company, their former employers are permitted to check the former employee's computer E-mails and hard drives in order to determine whether the employee has engaged in computer espionage.

---

[37] 18 USC § 1831.

27. Electronic Fund Transfer Crimes

Electronic Fund Transfers Act (EFTA) is a federal law that prohibits the use of a counterfeit, stolen, or fraudulently obtained card, code, or other device to obtain money or goods in excess of a specified amount through an electronic transfer system.

The Electronic Fund Transfers Act (EFTA)[38] makes it a crime to use any counterfeit, stolen, or fraudulently obtained card, code, or other device to obtain money or goods in excess of a specified amount through an electronic fund transfer system. The EFTA also makes it a crime to ship in interstate commerce devices or goods so obtained or to knowingly to receive goods that have been obtained by means of the fraudulent use of the transfer system.

D.   CRIMINAL PROCEDURE RIGHTS FOR BUSINESSES

Business criminals are treated the same procedurally as other criminals. They have the same rights under the criminal justice system. The U.S. Constitution guarantees the protection of individual rights within the criminal justice system.

28. Fourth Amendment Rights for Businesses

The Fourth Amendment is a constitutional protection against unreasonable searches and seizure.

A search warrant is a judicial authorization for a search of property where there is an expectation of privacy.

(a) Search and Seizure: Warrants. The **Fourth Amendment** to the U.S. Constitution provides that "the right of the people to be secure in their persons, houses, papers, and effects, against unreasonable searches and seizures, shall not be violated." This amendment protects individual privacy by preventing unreasonable searches and seizures. Before a government agency can seize the property of individuals or businesses, there must be a valid **search warrant**—or an applicable exception to warrant requirement—which must be issued by a judge or magistrate and must be based on probable cause. In other words there must be good reason to believe that instruments or evidence of a crime is present at the business location to be searched. The Fourth Amendment applies equally to individuals and corporations. In an unauthorized search a corporation's property is given the same protection. If an improper search is conducted, then any evidence obtained during the course of that search will be inadmissible in the criminal proceedings for the resulting criminal charges.

(b) Exceptions to the Warrant Requirement. Exceptions to the warrant requirement are emergencies, such as a burning building, and the "plain view" exception, which allows law enforcement officials to take any property that anyone can see, for no privacy rights are violated when items and property are left in the open for members of the public to see. ◆ *For example,* you have an expectation of privacy in the garbage in your garbage can when it is in your house. However, once you move that garbage can onto the public sidewalk for pickup, you no longer have an expectation of privacy because you have left your garbage out in plain view of the public. ◆

---

[38] Act of November 10, 1978, § 916(n), PL 95-630, 92 Stat 3738, 15 USC § 1693(n).

CASE SUMMARY

Low-Flying Searches

Facts: Dow Chemical's 2,000-acre-plant at Midland, Michigan, was visible from the air, but Dow took precautions to preclude low-flying aircraft over the plant for fear of industrial espio .ge. However, no part of the plant was covered or concealed. The Environmental Protection Agency (EPA) hired a commercial aerial photographer to fly over the plant and take photos of Dow's facilities from 12,000, 3,000, and 1,200 feet. The EPA did not have a warrant, but the photos were all taken from what is considered navigable air space above the plant. Dow brought suit for violation of its Fourth Amendment rights.

Decision: Dow had no right of privacy in aerial views of its plant, for the entire plant was visible by anyone from an airplane in public and navigable space. The EPA did nothing different from what any member of the public could do and as such was not required to have a warrant. For Dow to claim privacy, it would have to take steps to cover its plant with some type of tent or roofing. [*Dow Chemical Co. v United States, 476 U.S. 1819 (1986)*]

(c) Business Records and Searches. In many business crimes the records used to prosecute the defendant are not in the possession of that defendant. Accountants, attorneys, and other third parties may have the business records in their possession. In addition to the Fourth Amendment issues involved in seizing these records (a warrant is still required), there may be protections for the business defendants. All states recognize an attorney/client privilege, which means that an individual's conversations with his or her lawyer and the notes of those conversations are not subject to seizure. Some states recognize an accountant/client privilege, and there are other privileges, such as those between priest and parishioner.

29. Fifth Amendment Self-Incrimination Rights for Businesses

The Fifth Amendment is a constitutional protection against self-incrimination, and also guarantees due process.

(a) Self-Incrimination. The words "I take the Fifth" are used to invoke the constitutional protections against self-incrimination provided under the **Fifth Amendment**. Under the Fifth Amendment no one can be compelled to be a witness against himself. ● *For example,* Charles Keating, a former CEO of a California savings and loan who was tried for fraud and other business crimes, invoked the Fifth Amendment 80 times in his testimony before Congress on the failure of his Lincoln Savings and Loan. ● The Fifth Amendment protection applies only to individuals; corporations are not given Fifth Amendment protection. A corporation cannot prevent the disclosure of its books and records on the grounds of self-incrimination. Only the officers and employees of a corporation can assert the Fifth Amendment, but the records of the corporation belong to the corporation and not to them, so they cannot use the Fifth Amendment to prevent their disclosure.

Miranda warnings are the warnings required to prevent self-incrimination in a criminal matter.

(b) *Miranda* Rights. The famous *Miranda* warnings come from a case interpreting the extent of Fifth Amendment rights. In *Miranda v Arizona*,[39] the U.S. Supreme Court ruled that certain warnings must be given to those who are in custody for purposes of possible criminal proceedings. Custody is liberally defined and can

[39] 384 US 436 (1996).

include something as simple as retaining someone for questioning. The warnings consist of an explanation to individuals that they have the right to remain silent; that anything said, if they do speak, can be used against them; that they have the right to have an attorney present; and that if they cannot afford an attorney, one will be obtained for them. Failure to give the *Miranda* warnings means that any statements, including a confession, obtained while the individual is in custody cannot be used as evidence against him or her. The prosecution will have to rely on evidence other than the statements made in violation of *Miranda*, if such evidence exists.

30. Due Process Rights for Businesses

Due process is the constitutional right to be heard, question witnesses, and present evidence.

Also included in the Fifth Amendment is the language of **due process**. Due process is the right to be heard, question witnesses, and present evidence before any criminal conviction can occur. Due process in criminal cases consists of an initial appearance at which the charges and the defendant's rights are outlined, a preliminary hearing or grand jury proceeding in which the evidence is determined to be sufficient to warrant a trial, an arraignment for entering a plea and setting a trial date when the defendant pleads innocent, a period of discovery for obtaining evidence, and a trial at which witnesses for the prosecution can be cross-examined and evidence presented to refute the charges. In addition to these procedural steps, the Sixth Amendment guarantees that the entire process will be completed in a timely fashion because this amendment guarantees a speedy trial.

SUMMARY

When a person does not live up to the standards set by law, society may regard this person's conduct as so dangerous to the government, to other people, or to property that society will prosecute the person for the misconduct. This punishable conduct, called crime, may be common law or statutory in origin. Crimes are classified as felonies and misdemeanors. A felony is a crime that is punishable by imprisonment or death.

Minors, the insane, and the intoxicated are held criminally responsible to a limited extent. This means that in some cases they will not be held responsible for a crime that a normal, adult person would be. Employers and corporations may be criminally responsible for their acts and the acts of their employees.

The federal sentencing guidelines impose mandatory sentences for federal crimes and allow judges to consider whether the fact that a business promotes compliance with the law is a reason for reducing a sentence.

White collar crimes include those relating to illegal methods of production, competition, and marketing, such as the illegal use of interstate transportation and communication. Other white collar crimes include bribery, extortion, blackmail, and corrupt influence in politics and in business. Also included as white collar crimes are coun-

terfeiting, forgery, perjury, the making of false claims against the government, and the obtaining of goods or money by false pretenses. Also included are the use of bad checks, swindles and confidence games, credit card fraud, the use of the mails to defraud, and embezzlement.

Statutes have expanded the area of criminal law to meet situations in which computers are involved. The unauthorized taking of information from a computer is made a crime under both federal and state statutes. The diversion of deliveries of goods and the transfer of funds, the theft of software, and computer raiding are made crimes to some extent by the federal Computer Access Device and Computer Fraud and Abuse Act of 1984 and the Electronic Fund Transfers Act of 1978.

There is no uniform law of crimes. Each state and the federal government define and punish crimes as they choose. Although the tendency is to follow a common pattern, many variations exist between the law of different states and federal law.

Criminal procedure is dictated by the Fourth, Fifth, and Sixth Amendments. The Fourth Amendment protects against unreasonable searches, the Fifth Amendment protects against self-incrimination and provides due process, and the Sixth Amendment guarantees a speedy trial.

1. What are the social forces advanced by holding an officer of a company criminally liable for the company's conduct?

2. Hunter, who was employed by Watson Corp., was killed at work by an explosion caused by the gross negligence of the corporation. When the corporation was prosecuted for manslaughter, it raised the defense that only people could commit manslaughter and that it was therefore not guilty. Was this defense valid?

3. Baker and others entered a Wal-Mart store shortly after 3 A.M. They entered by cutting through the metal door with an acetylene torch. Some of the merchandise in the store was moved to the rear door, but the police arrived before the merchandise could be taken from the store. Baker was prosecuted for larceny. He raised the defense that he was not guilty of larceny: There had not been any taking of the merchandise because it had never left the store. Is there enough intent and action for a crime? [*Tennessee v Baker* (Tenn App) 751 SW2d 154]

4. Gail drove her automobile after having had dinner and several drinks. She fell asleep at the wheel and ran over and killed a pedestrian. Prosecuted for manslaughter, she raised the defense that she did not intend to hurt anyone and because of the drinks did not know what she was doing. Was this a valid defense?

5. A state law made it a crime to use a "device to assist . . . in analyzing the probability of the occurrence of an event relating to the game." The defendant took part in a card game played for money. Unknown to the other players, he had a microcomputer that he used to show the probabilities of cards appearing in the game. When this was discovered, he was prosecuted under the law quoted above. He raised the defense that a microcomputer was not a "device." Was he guilty of violating the statute? Why did the statute state "device" rather than listing the specific devices that were to be outlawed? [*Sheriff, Clark County, Nevada v Anderson*, 103 Nev Adv 119, 746 P2d 643]

6. Buckley took a credit card from the coat of its owner with the intent never to return it. He then purchased some goods at a department store and paid for them by presenting the credit card to the sales clerk and signing the credit card slip with the name of the credit card's owner. What crimes, if any, did Buckley commit? [*Buckley v Indiana*, 163 Ind App 113, 322 NE2d 113]

7. Berman organized Greatway Travel, Ltd. Greatway sold travel consultant franchises and promised that franchisees would receive various discounts and assistance. None of these promises was ever kept because Greatway lost all its money through mismanagement. Berman was prosecuted for obtaining money by false pretenses. Was he guilty? [*Berman v Maryland*, 35 Md App 193, 370 A2d 580]

8. Hysell took a bank card belonging to someone else and made an unauthorized withdrawal with it from a bank's 24-hour automatic teller machine. The machine was mounted inside the bank, but the card entry slot was flush with the exterior wall of the bank. When Hysell was prosecuted for burglary, he argued that the Florida burglary statute declares there is no burglary if "the premises are at the time open to the public or the defendant is licensed or invited to remain." Was Hysell guilty of burglary? [*Florida v Hysell* (Fla App) 569 So 2d 866]

9. Skelton attempted to rob a general store. He used a small wooden pistol. The attempt failed, and he was arrested. He was prosecuted for attempted armed robbery. Was he guilty? [*Illinois v Skelton*, 83 Ill 2d 58, 46 Ill Dec 571, 414 NE2d 455]

10. Jennings operated a courier service to collect and deliver money. The contract with his customers allowed Jennings a day or so to deliver the money that had been collected. Instead of holding collections until delivered, Jennings made short-term investments with the money. He always made deliveries to the customers on time, but because he kept the profit from the investments for himself, Jennings was prosecuted for embezzlement. Was he guilty? [*New York v Jennings*, 69 NY2d 103, 512 NYS2d 652, 504 NE2d 1079]

11. Chaussee sold franchises to a number of persons authorizing them to sell a product that did not exist. He was prosecuted under the Colorado Organized Crime Control Act on the ground that he was guilty of a pattern of racketeering. His defense was that there was no pattern because there was only one scheme. Was he guilty?

12. Awan was prosecuted for money laundering. He contended that the federal Money Laundering Control Act was unconstitutional because it was too vague. As a matter of constitutional law, if a criminal law statute is too vague to be reasonably understood, it violates the Due Process Clause and cannot be enforced. The Money Laundering Control Act condemns money laundering knowing the property involved in a financial transaction represents proceeds from some form of unlawful activity. Was the act unconstitutionally vague? [*United States v Awan* (CA11) 966 F2d 1415]

13. The Banco Central administered a humanitarian plan for the government of Ecuador. Fernando Banderas and his wife presented false claims that were paid by the bank. After the fraud was discovered, the bank sued Banderas and his wife for damages for fraud and treble damages under the Florida version of RICO. Defendants asserted that they were not liable for RICO damages because there was no proof that they were related to organized crime and because the wrong committed by them was merely ordinary fraud. They had not used any racketeering methods. Is involvement with organized crime a requirement for liability under RICO? [*Banderas v Banco Central del Ecuador* (Fla App) 461 So 2d 265]

14. Kravitz owned 100 percent of the stock of American Health Programs, Inc. (AHP). In order to obtain the Philadelphia Fraternal Order of Police as a customer for AHP, Kravitz paid money bribes to persons who he thought were officers of that organization, but who in fact were federal undercover agents. He was prosecuted for violating RICO. He was convicted, and the court ordered the forfeiture of all of the shares of AHP stock owned by Kravitz. Can a forfeiture be ordered? [*United States v Kravitz*, (CA3) 738 F2d 102 (1984)]

15. Howell made long-distance telephone calls through the telephone company's computer-controlled switching system in order to solicit funding for a nonexistent business enterprise. What crimes did Howell commit? *New Mexico v Howell* (NM App) 895 P2d 232]

Torts

OBJECTIVES

After studying this chapter, you should be able to

1. *Define torts and distinguish them from crimes;*
2. *List the types of torts;*
3. *Provide examples of intentional torts and the elements of each;*
4. *Discuss the elements of negligence;*
5. *Explain the defenses to negligence liability; and*
6. *Explain concerns about levels of tort liability and possible reforms.*

The law of torts permits individuals and companies to recover from other individuals and companies for wrongs committed against them. Tort law provides rights and remedies for conduct that meets the elements required to establish that a wrong has occurred.

A. GENERAL PRINCIPLES

Civil, or noncriminal, wrongs that are not breaches of contract are governed by tort law. This chapter covers the types of civil wrongs that constitute torts and the remedies available for those wrongs.

1. What Is a Tort?

A tort is a civil wrong that interferes with someone's person or property.

Tort comes from the Latin term *tortus*, which means "crooked, dubious, twisted." Torts are actions that are not straight, but crooked, or civil wrongs. A tort is an interference with someone's person or property. *For example*, entering someone's house without his or her permission is an interference and constitutes the tort of trespass. Causing someone's character to be questioned is a wrong against the person and is the tort of defamation. The law provides protection against these harms in the form of remedies awarded after the wrongs are committed. These remedies are civil remedies for the acts of interference by others.

2. Tort and Crime Distinguished

A crime is a wrong arising from a violation of a public duty, whereas a tort is a wrong arising from a violation of a private duty. A crime is a wrong of such a serious nature that the appropriate level of government steps in to prosecute and punish the wrongdoer in order to deter others from engaging in the same type of conduct. However, whenever the act that is committed as a crime causes harm to an identifiable person, that person may sue the wrongdoer for monetary damages to compensate for the harm. For the person who experiences the direct harm, the act is called a tort, and for the government, the same act is called a crime.

When the same act is both a crime and a tort, the government may prosecute the wrongdoer for a violation of criminal law, and the individual who experiences the direct harm may bring suit for recovery of damages. *For example*, O.J. Simpson was charged by the state of California with the murder of his ex-wife, Nicole Brown Simpson, and her friend Ron Goldman. A criminal trial was held in which Mr. Simpson was acquitted. Had he been convicted, his sentence would have been either death or life in prison. Mr. Simpson was also sued civilly by the families of Mrs. Simpson and Mr. Brown for wrongful death, which is the tort equivalent of the crime of murder. The jury in the civil case did find Mr. Simpson civilly liable and required him to pay large judgments to both families for the loss of their family members.

Other types of acts may not rise to the level of criminal conduct that the government would prosecute, but do constitute wrongs that entitle the person harmed to recover for his or her damages. ◆ *For example,* someone who issues false statements about you or your business would harm you by perhaps causing you to lose current and potential customers for your product. However, the government would not prosecute the individual for those statements. You could bring a civil suit to recover for the tort of defamation. ◆

3. The Types of Torts

An intentional tort is a civil wrong that results from intentional conduct.

There are three types of torts: intentional torts, negligence, and strict liability. **Intentional torts** are those that occur when wrongdoers engage in intentional conduct. ◆ *For example,* striking another person in a fight is an intentional act and would be the tort of battery, and possibly also the crime of battery. Your arm striking another person's nose in a fast-moving crowd of people at a rock concert is not a tort or crime because your arm was pushed unintentionally by the force of the crowd. ◆ If you stretched out your arms in that crowd or began to swing your arms about, you would be behaving carelessly in a crowd of people, and although you may not have committed an intentional tort, it is possible that your careless conduct constitutes the tort of **negligence**. Careless actions, or actions taken without thinking through their consequences, constitute negligence. The harm to the other person's nose may not have been intended, but there is liability for these accidental harms under negligence. ◆ *For example,* if you run a red light, hit another car, and injure its driver, you did not intend the result. However, your careless behavior of disregarding a traffic signal resulted in the injury, and you would have liability for your negligence to that driver. ◆

Negligence is a civil wrong that results from careless behavior.

Strict liability is a civil wrong for which there is absolute liability because of the inherent danger in the underlying activity, for example, the use of explosives.

Strict liability is another aspect of tort law that imposes liability without regard to whether there was any intention to harm or any negligence. Strict liability is imposed without regard to fault. Strict or absolute liability is imposed because the activity involved is so dangerous that there must be full accountability. Nonetheless, the activity is necessary and cannot be prohibited. The compromise is to allow the activity but ensure that its dangers and resulting damages are fully covered through the imposition of full liability for all injuries that result. ◆ *For example,* contractors often need to use dynamite to take a roadway through a mountainside or demolish a building that has become a hazard. When the dynamite is used, noise, debris, and possibly dangerous pieces of earth and building will descend on others' land and possibly on people. In most states contractors are held strictly liable for the resulting damage from the use of dynamite. The activity is necessary and not illegal, but those who use dynamite must be prepared to compensate those who are injured as a result. ◆

Other areas in which there is strict liability for activity include the storage of flammable materials and crop dusting. The federal government and the states have pure food laws that impose absolute liability on manufacturers who fail to meet the statutory standards for their products.

Another area of strict liability is **products liability**, which is covered in chapter 28.

Figure 9-1 provides a statistical look at the types of torts by their percentages of court actions brought to recover damages.

FIGURE 9-1
*Type of Torts for which
Suit Is Brought*

Auto	60.1%
Premises liability	17.3%
Other negligence	5.9%
Medical malpractice	4.9%
Products liability	3.4%
Intentional injury	2.9%
Nonmedical malpractice	1.8%
Toxic substance	1.6%
Unknown tort	1.2%
Slander/libel	0.8%

Source: Wall Street Journal, August 21, 1995, © Dow Jones & Company

B. INTENTIONAL TORTS

4. False Imprisonment

False imprisonment is
the intentional detention
of a person without his or
her permission; the shop-
keeper's tort when
shoplifters are unlawfully
detained.

Shopkeeper's privilege is
the right of a store owner
to detain a suspected
shoplifter based on rea-
sonable cause and for a
reasonable time without
resulting liability for false
imprisonment.

False imprisonment is the intentional detention of a person without that person's consent.[1] The detention need not be for any specified period of time, for any detention against one's will is false imprisonment. False imprisonment is often called the shopkeeper's tort because there has been so much liability imposed on store owners for their unreasonable detention of customers for suspicion of shoplifting. Requiring a customer to sit in the manager's office or not allowing a customer to leave the store can constitute the tort of false imprisonment. Shop owners do, however, need the opportunity to investigate possible thefts in their stores. As a result, all states have some form of privilege or protection for store owners called a **shopkeeper's privilege**.

The shopkeeper's privilege permits the store owner to detain a suspected shoplifter based on reasonable suspicion for a reasonable time without resulting liability for false imprisonment to the accused customer.[2] The privilege applies even if the store owner was wrong about the customer being a shoplifter, so long as the store owner acted based on reasonable suspicions and treated the accused shoplifter in a reasonable manner. These privilege statutes do not protect the store owner from liability for unnecessary physical force or for invasion of privacy. ◆ *For example,* if a store owner used the store's public address system to describe a customer and ask her to stop and remain for questioning, the store owner has behaved in an unreasonable fashion and would not enjoy the protection of immunity from the privilege statutes. ◆ Store owners must investigate shoplifting in a private fashion and act as quickly as possible under the circumstances.

---

[1] *Roddell v Town of Flora* (Ind App) 580 NE2d 255 (1991).
[2] *Limited Stores, Inc. v Wilson-Robinson* (Ark) 876 SW2d 248 (1994).

You Have to Know When to Hold Them and When to Let Them Go

Facts: On November 16, 1986, Joseph Canto, 11, and his sister, Samantha Canto, 16, were shopping at the Ivey department store in Gainesville, Florida. The children stopped at the counter for metallic chain-link belts. The security camera's videotape shows them looking at the belts, talking, laughing, and looking around. The videotape also shows Samantha hand something to Joseph, which he then puts in his pocket. After observing the children at the belt counter, a store security officer, Jo Ann Williams, stopped them at the door of Ivey's as they were preparing to leave. Ms. Williams told the children she had reason to believe they had stolen something, and she asked them to accompany her to the store security office.

Ms. Williams called the police, but the police did not arrive for an hour. The children were detained for another hour of questioning after the arrival of the police. They were released after two hours, but they were not permitted to use the bathroom or call their parents during that time. The employees in the security office referred to them as "shoplifters" and "delinquents" during the time they were detained. Ivey's concluded that the two had not shoplifted and released them. The children required psychological counseling, and their parents filed suit for false imprisonment.

Decision: Florida's shopkeeper statute provides: "A merchant, merchant's employee, or farmer who takes a person into custody . . . shall not be criminally or civilly liable for false arrest or false imprisonment when the merchant, merchant's employee, or farmer has probable cause to believe that the person committed retail or farm theft." The videotape gave Ms. Williams probable cause to detain the children, and their detention was not unreasonable. There was no ill will on the part of the store and no harm was done to the children during their detention. The privilege protects Ivey's and Williams from any liability. *[Canto v J.B. Ivey and Co. (Fla) 595 So 2d 1025 (1982)]*

5.   Intentional Infliction of Emotional Distress

Intentional infliction of emotional distress is a tort that produces mental anguish caused by conduct that exceeds all bounds of decency.

The **intentional infliction of emotional distress** is a tort that involves conduct that goes beyond all bounds of decency and produces mental anguish in the harmed individual. This tort requires proof of outrageous conduct and resulting emotional distress in the victim. The types of conduct for which this tort is used for recovery include outrageous collection methods employed by debt collection agencies. *For example,* if a collection agent called a debtor while he was hospitalized following heart surgery, such conduct would rise to the level of outrageous beyond all standards of decency. Such a collection effort would constitute the tort of intentional infliction of emotional distress.

6.   Invasion of Privacy

Invasion of privacy is the tort of intentional intrusion into the private affairs of another.

The right of privacy is the right to be free of unreasonable intrusion into one's private affairs. The tort of **invasion of privacy** actually consists of three different torts: (1) intrusion into the plaintiff's private affairs (for example, planting a microphone in an office or home); (2) public disclosure of private facts (for example, disclosing private financial information, as when a business posts returned checks from customers near its cash register in a public display); and (3) appropriation of another's name, likeness, or image for commercial advantage (for example, using David Letterman's picture on refrigerator magnets without his permission). This third type of invasion of privacy is often called, in lay terms, commercial exploitation and can be as simple as using a photo without permission as a product indorsement.

CASE SUMMARY

Bette Midler Doesn't Want to Dance with Ford

Facts: In 1985 Ford Motor Company asked its advertising agency, Young & Rubicam, Inc., to launch a campaign for Ford-Lincoln-Mercury with a series of 30- or 60-second television ads referred to as the "Yuppie Campaign." The ads were designed to appeal to the baby boomer generation with music from their college days. The agency was instructed to use "original people," the artists who had made the original recordings of the songs.

While preparing the campaign, Young & Rubicam approached Ms. Bette Midler to perform her song "Do You Want to Dance?" from her 1973 album *The Divine Miss M.* Craig Hazen of Young & Rubicam contacted Jerry Edelstein, Ms. Midler's agent, and Mr. Edelstein responded with Ms. Midler's standard refusal because she does not do commercial endorsements. Young & Rubicam then hired Ula Hedwig, one of Ms. Midler's back-up singers for ten years, to perform the song. Ms. Hedwig was told to "sound as much as possible like the Bette Midler record."

When the commercial ran on television, Ms. Midler was complimented by many people who thought she had done the ad. Ms. Midler filed suit for appropriation. The district court entered judgment for Ford and Young & Rubicam, and Ms. Midler appealed.

Decision: A voice is as distinctive and personal as a face and is entitled to the same protection of privacy. When a distinctive voice, such as Ms. Midler's, is deliberately imitated for commercial purposes, there is appropriation of part of Ms. Midler's identity without her permission. The court held Ford and Young & Rubicam liable. *[Midler v Ford Motor Co., 849 F2d 460 (9th Cir 1988)]*

7. Defamation

Defamation is an untrue statement by one party about another to a third party.

Slander is oral or spoken defamation.

Libel is written (sometimes broadcast) defamation.

Defamation is an untrue statement by one party about another to a third party. **Slander** is oral or spoken defamation, and **libel** is written (and in some cases broadcast) defamation. The elements for defamation are (1) a statement about a person's reputation, honesty, or integrity that is untrue; (2) publication (which is accomplished when a third party hears or reads the defamatory statement); (3) a statement that is directed at a particular person; and (4) damages that result from the statement. ◆ *For example*, a false statement by the owner of a business that the former manager was fired for stealing when he was not would be defamation, and the former manager's damages could be his inability to find another position because of the statement's impact on his reputation. ◆

In cases in which the victim is a public figure, such as a celebrity from Hollywood or a professional sports player, another element is required, the element of malice, which means that what was said or written was done with the knowledge that the information was false or with reckless disregard for whether it was true or false.[3]

The defenses to defamation include the truth. If the statement is true, even if it is harmful to the victim, it is not the tort of defamation. ◆ *For example*, a news story could report that the new CEO of a company had taken LSD while he was in college in 1968. The story could be damaging to the CEO, but its truth is a complete defense to defamation. ◆

An absolute privilege is a complete defense against the tort of defamation, as in the speech of members of Congress on the floor and witnesses in a trial.

Some statements are privileged, and this privilege provides a full or partial defense to the tort of defamation. ◆ *For example*, members of Congress enjoy an absolute privilege when they are speaking on the floor of the Senate or the House because public policy requires a free dialogue on the issues pending in a legislative

---

[3] *Gray v HEB Food Store #4* (Tex App) 941 SW2d 327 (1997).

body. The same absolute privilege applies to witnesses in court proceedings in order to encourage witnesses with information to come forward and testify. ◆

The media enjoy a **qualified privilege** for stories that turn out to be false. Their qualified privilege is a defense to defamation, so long as the information was released without malice and a retraction or correction is made when the matter is brought to their attention.

A new statutory privilege has been evolving over the past few years with respect to letters of recommendation and references given by employers for employees who are applying for jobs at other companies. Most companies, because of concerns about liability for defamation, will only confirm that a former employee did work at their firm and will provide the time period during which he or she was employed. However, many employees who had histories that should have been revealed for safety reasons have been hired because no negative information was released. About one-third of the states now have statutes that provide employers a qualified privilege with respect to references and recommendations. So long as the employer acts in good faith in providing information, there is no liability for defamation to the former employee as a result of the information provided. With this privilege employers now have an obligation to provide complete and accurate information about former employees.

> Qualified privilege is a media privilege to print inaccurate information without liability for defamation, so long as a retraction or correction is printed and there was no malice.

CASE SUMMARY

Putting in an Exaggerated Good Word

Facts: Robert Gadams was formerly employed by the Muroc School District as an administrative employee. The school district provided a letter of recommendation with unreserved and unconditional praise for Gadams when he was in the process of applying for other positions through the Fresno Pacific College placement center. The letter failed to mention that Gadams had in his file several complaints of sexual misconduct with students and that allegations against him of "sexual touching" of female students had induced Muroc to force Gadams to resign. The letter described Gadams as "an upbeat, enthusiastic administrator who relates well to students" and who was "in large part" responsible for making the campus at Muroc "a safe, orderly and clean environment for students and staff." The letter recommended Gadams "for an assistant principalship or equivalent position without reservation." Gadams was hired by another school district, and there he molested Randi, a young student. Randi sued Muroc School District for its inaccurate letter of reference.

Decision: The court found for Randi and held that a former employer owes a duty to prospective employers and third persons to speak the truth about a former employee. The former employer is liable to third persons who are injured as a result of its misrepresentations when the harm to those third persons is foreseeable. In light of Gadams's employment history, it was foreseeable that other students could be harmed. Muroc was held liable for the injuries to Randi. [*Randi v Muroc Joint Unified School District*, 60 Cal Rptr 263, 929 P2d 582 (1997)]

ETHICS & THE LAW

Deidre Thompson, a manager at the First Bank credit card processing facility in Phoenix, Arizona, supervises 152 employees who perform a wide range of credit functions, from payment processing through bill inquiries to collection. Herb Kelman had been an employee at First Bank for 12 years, most of which he had spent working in payment processing.

On June 9, 1997, Thompson, along with First Bank's outside auditors, detected some irregularities in several accounts that Kelman managed. Thompson and the auditors talked with Kelman about the accounts, and he responded, "Other people have access to those accounts." The auditors continued their work for several more weeks.

Shortly after the meeting with the auditors, Kelman told Thompson that he had taken another job at Second Bank's credit-processing facility and he would be leaving in two weeks. That same day Thompson received a call from the head of human resources at Second Bank, seeking verification of Kelman's employment. Thompson verified that he had been employed there for 12 years but said nothing further.

Approximately nine months later Kelman was charged with embezzlement from Second Bank. Second Bank had learned through the criminal investigation of Kelman about First Bank's audit and the irregularities that were uncovered but never resolved with Kelman. Second Bank's head of human resources called Thompson again and asked, "Why didn't you mention the problems with the audit? That wasn't fair to us. We're out a lot of money on this one. Can't we at least be honest with each other on these employee verifications?"

What do you think of Thompson's conduct? Did she have legal constraints? Would you have said something about the audits? Is withholding information here ethical? Is withholding information here legal? Does the law require Thompson to be dishonest in this case?

8. Product Disparagement

Product disparagement is false statements about a product or service that cause damage to the seller or provider.

Trade libel is written defamation about a product or service.

Slander of title is oral defamation about a product or service.

While the comparison of products and services is healthy for competition, false statements about another's products constitute a form of slander called **slander of title** or libel called **trade libel**; collectively these are known as **product disparagement**. Product disparagement occurs when someone makes false statements about another business, its products, or its abilities.[4] The elements of product disparagement are (1) a false statement about a particular business product or about its service in terms of honesty, reputation, ability, or integrity; (2) communication of the statement to a third party; and (3) damages. ◆ *For example*, Oprah Winfrey's statements on her television show about mad cow disease and beef ("It has just stopped me cold from eating another burger. I'm stopped.") resulted in a trade libel suit brought by a rancher. The rancher alleged that her remarks had an impact on consumers and their beef purchases and that his damages were reduced sales of beef. ◆ Many states now have specific statutes, often referred to as veggie libel laws, that provide protection for producers of generic products, such as beef, broccoli and eggs.

9. Wrongful Interference with Contracts

Contract interference is a tort in which a third party interferes with others' freedom to contract.

Tortious interference or tortious interference with contracts is the same as contract interference.

The tort of **contract interference** or **tortious interference with contracts** or **tortious interference** occurs when parties are not allowed the freedom to contract without interference from third parties. While the elements required to establish the tort of contract interference are complex, a basic definition is that the law affords a remedy when a third party intentionally persuades another to break a contract already

---

[4] *Sannerud v Brantz* (Wyo) 879 P2d 341 (1994).

in existence.[5] The following example is given in the book *Tortious Interference* by Bryan A. Garner: "Say you had a contract with Joe Blow, and I for some reason tried to get you to break that contract. Or say that Pepsi has an exclusive contract with a hotel chain to carry Pepsi products, and Coke tries to get the hotel to carry Coke despite that contract. That's interference."

CASE SUMMARY

If You Step In and Stop the Train, That's Contract Interference

Facts: The board of directors of Getty Oil had agreed to sell a substantial portion of its oil reserves to Pennzoil. While Getty and Pennzoil were in the process of drafting their agreement, Texaco stepped in and made a competing bid to Getty. The Getty board then accepted the Texaco offer. Pennzoil filed suit for tortious interference of contract.

Decision: The trial court found there was tortious interference of contract by Texaco and awarded Pennzoil $7.53 billion in actual damages and $3 billion in punitive damages. The appellate court did reduce the damages to $2 billion but upheld the finding of contract interference, noting that Pennzoil and Getty already had an oral agreement and Texaco, in effect, stepped in and "stopped the train." [*Texaco, Inc. v Pennzoil (Tex) 729 SW2d 768 (1987)*]

---

10. Trespass

Trespass is an unauthorized action with respect to person or property.

A **trespass** is an unauthorized action with respect to a person or property. A trespass to the person is any contact with a person for which consent was not given.

A trespass to land is any unpermitted entry below, on, across, or above the land of another. *For example,* using another's land for a short-cut on a walk is a trespass.

A trespass to personal property is the invasion of personal property without the permission of the owner. *For example,* the use of someone's car without their permission is a trespass to personal property.

11. Computer Torts

There are specific applications of the torts just covered with respect to computers and their unique technology and applications.

(a) Trespass to personal property and computers. Damage to hardware, including its destruction, will impose tort liability under the same principles of law that would apply if a typewriter, a car, a desk, or any other tangible property were damaged or destroyed. The fact that the damage to the computer may cause a shutdown of the activities of the computer owner is significant in determining the extent of damages awarded. Punitive damages or damages imposed to punish or make an example of the defendant are often awarded in cases where there is a shutdown.

With regard to computer software, a defendant may have damaged the software, for example, by erasing a part of the computer's memory. Many recently adopted statutes expressly impose tort liability for such misconduct.

---

[5] *Idaho First National Bank v Bliss Valley Foods, Inc.* (Idaho) 824 P2d 841 (1991).

When an insurance policy does not expressly state that it covers computer property, a question may arise over whether hardware, software, and a data base are protected by the policy.

One case has held that a computer tape and the data stored on the tape are protected by an insurance policy covering damage to tangible property.[6]

(b) Computers and Privacy. The law relating to the protection of privacy applies whether or not a computer is involved. That is, there is no change made or needed in the law of privacy because a computer was used to invade the privacy in question. Statutes have been adopted to protect against such invasion of computer-stored data.[7]

(1) Why Is There Concern over Protection of Privacy? There is much public concern over protection of privacy because of the efficiency of the computer. Consider the number of places that have some information about you. Every school you ever attended has some of your personal history. If you have applied for any kind of license, purchased goods on credit, obtained insurance, applied for a job, been treated by a doctor, or been admitted to a hospital, more of your life story is on paper. But this has never bothered you because, assuming that you had thought about it, you would have recognized that it would be practically impossible for anyone to assemble all the information about you from all the places where it is kept. Even assuming that the prying stranger would know where to inquire, the cost of going back into old files to dig up information would be prohibitive.

In the computer age, by connecting separate computers into a network, it is possible to print out the story of your life within a matter of seconds.

To this danger of efficiency we add the ability of an outsider to invade a computer by raiding and acquire its information even without anyone knowing this has been done. We then have a terrifying product of *A* (efficiency of the computer) times *B* (availability of information to unauthorized outsiders).

(2) Who Is Liable for Computer Invasion of Privacy? The person making public the information stored in the computer may be an authorized user of the computer. The person may be an outsider without authority who invades the computer and then makes public the private information obtained from it. In either case, such a person is liable for tort damages for invasion of privacy. If the wrongdoer is an employee, it is possible that management will be liable for the employee's misconduct on the theory that management had not properly screened job applicants, was negligent in supervising employees, or is liable for employee misconduct under the circumstances. If the wrongdoer is an outsider, management can be held liable for the invasion of privacy if management could have prevented the invasion of privacy by maintaining a better security system over the computer.

(c) Defamation by Computer. A person's credit standing or reputation may be damaged because a computer contains erroneous information that is supplied to

---

6 *Retail Systems, Inc. v CNA Ins. Cos.* (Minn App) 469 NW2d 735 (1991).
7 The federal Electronic Communications Privacy Act of October 21, 1986, PL 99-508, 100 Stat 1848, 18 USC § 2510 note. Protection from the invasion of privacy by the improper release of data stored in the federal government computers is made by the Computer Security Act of 1987, Act of January 8, 1988. PL 100-235, 101 Stat 899, 15 USC §§ 272, 278, 40 USC § 159 , and the Computer Matching and Privacy Protection Act of October 18, 1988, PL 100-503, 102 Stat 2507, 5 USC § 552a note.

third persons. Will the data bank operator or service company be held liable to the person who is harmed? If the operator or the company had exercised reasonable care to prevent errors and to correct errors, it is probable there will not be liability on either the employee operating the equipment or the management providing the computer service.

The supplier of wrong information is liable for the damages caused by it when the error was caused by its negligence. Because the supplier is furnishing information to a limited group of subscribers, it is not protected by the guarantee of free speech.[8]

When negligence or an intent to harm is shown, the wrongdoer could be held liable for what may be called *defamation by computer*. It is likely that liability could be avoided by supplying the person to whom the information relates with a copy of any printout of information that the data bank supplies the third person. This would tend to show good faith and due care on the part of the management of the data bank operation and a reasonable effort to keep the information accurate. There are also federal statutes that provide protection against false credit information. See chapter 30.

C. NEGLIGENCE AND STRICT LIABILITY

The widest range of tort liability today arises in the field of negligence. Negligence exists whenever someone acts with less care than would be used by a reasonable person in the same circumstances. All of us are subject to a duty of using a minimum standard of care in certain circumstances, such as in our driving, in our work, and in the care and upkeep of our property. Negligence imposes liability when we do not live up to the minimum standard of care, which is the care a reasonable person would exercise in those circumstances.

12. Elements of Negligence

The first element of negligence is a duty. There is a general duty imposed to act as an ordinary and reasonably prudent person would in similar circumstances. When we do not live up to the standard of the ordinary and reasonably prudent person, we are negligent. Compliance with applicable laws is a beginning for reasonable behavior, but it is not always enough. *For example,* suppose that you were driving on a curvy highway late at night during a rainstorm. The posted speed limit, or the law, allows you to go 45 mph. However, the ordinary and reasonably prudent person would not drive that fast in those circumstances because the weather creates additional dangers. To drive the speed limit in those circumstances would be negligent.

Malpractice is negligence by a professional in performing his or her skill.

Professionals have a duty to perform their jobs at the level of a reasonable professional. For a professional, such as an accountant, doctor, lawyer, dentist, or architect, to avoid liability for **malpractice**, the professional must perform his or her skill in the same manner as and at the level of other professionals in the same field.

---

8 *Dunn and Bradstreet, Inc. v Greenmoss Builders,* 472 U.S. 749 (1985).

Those who own real property have a duty to keep their property in a condition that does not create hazards for guests. Businesses have a duty to inspect and repair their property so that their customers are not injured by hazards, such as spills on the floor or uneven walking areas. Where customer safety is a concern, businesses have a duty to provide adequate security, such as when there are security patrols in mall parking lots.

CASE SUMMARY

To Catch a Thief: Don't Let Your Guests Be the Bait

Facts: The Charlotte, North Carolina, area was being victimized by a group of thieves who had been dubbed the "Motel Bandits." These thieves preyed on out-of-town visitors who were staying at Charlotte area motels and hotels. The sheriff's office contacted motel managers to let them know about the thieves and advised the managers to increase the security at their motels. Brian McRorie, the manager of the Holiday Inn–Concord received a call about the problem and asked a security expert to come and evaluate his motel for any security lapses. The expert said no additional security was needed but added that he had added security officers to the parking lot of the motel he owned in the area. Mr. McRorie told employees to be alert, and he continued to use a discount program to encourage local law enforcement officials to frequent the Holiday Inn restaurant next to the hotel.

Sarah and James Crinkley checked into the Holiday Inn–Concord and were attacked by the Motel Bandits as they were moving their luggage from their car to their room. Mr. Crinkley was beaten severely, their property was taken, and both were bound and gagged. Mrs. Crinkley suffered a heart attack after the robbery. The Crinkleys sued Holiday Inn for negligence.

Decision: Sarah Crinkley was awarded $400,000, and James Crinkley was awarded $100,000. Holiday Inn–Concord knew of the Motel Bandits and their presence in the area. It knew that other motels had added security. The thieves managed to attack the Crinkleys in the parking lot and take a good deal of time as they robbed them without any employee of the Holiday Inn noticing a problem or coming to their assistance. Additional security in the parking lot could have prevented the attack, and a reasonable person would have retained such security when law enforcement agencies provided advance warning of heightened criminal activity. The motel had a duty in these circumstances to provide additional security. [*Crinkley v Holiday Inns, Inc.*, 844 F2d 156 (4th Cir 1988)]

The second element of negligence is the breach of a duty imposed by law or by the reasonable person standard. ◆ *For example,* a reasonable person places a sign to warn customers of a slippery floor. The failure to post such a sign when the floor of a grocery store is wet is a breach of the duty of ordinary care of a grocer. An accountant who completes tax returns but does not know the changes in the tax law has breached the standard of care for a reasonable accountant. ◆ Determining whether a duty has been breached requires courts to examine whether the defendant's action satisfied the standard of reasonable care in those circumstances. The exact answer to the question of whether a duty has been breached is often unknown until a lawsuit is over. There are many borderline cases in negligence, in which the standards for the duty and the resulting breach vary. However, this flexibility is important in allowing courts to consider variables in cases, such as the extent and gravity of the harm, the ease with which precautions can be taken, and the impact of liability on industries, communities, and businesses.[9]

CASE SUMMARY

Highway Robbery: The ATM Alongside the Road

Facts: JoKatherine Page and her 14-year-old son, Jason, were robbed at their bank's ATM at 9:30 P.M. one evening by a group of four thugs. The thieves took $300, struck Mrs. Page in the face with a gun, and ran. Mrs. Page and her son filed suit against the bank for its failure to provide adequate security. The jury awarded Mrs. Page $125,000 and Jason $10,000, and the bank appealed.

Decision: The bank is not liable for the sudden, intentional, and criminal acts of unidentified third persons. No amount of care could prevent such third-party criminal activity from occurring. To impose such a duty would prevent businesses from locating in areas where crime occurs. [Page v American National Bank & Trust Co. (Tenn) 850 SW2d 133 (1991)]

A third element of negligence is causation. Causation is the element that connects the duty and the breach of duty to the injuries to the plaintiff. Did the grocer's failure to post a "Wet Floor" sign cause the shopper's broken leg? The duty of maintenance and upkeep of the grocer's premises was breached by his failure to follow the standard industry practice of placing warning signs. The lack of a sign caused the shopper to walk at a normal pace on a slippery floor, which caused her to fall and break her leg. Often courts will use the "but for" test for causation. *But for* the fact that no "Wet Floor" sign was posted, the shopper would not have been injured. Another question asked in determining causation focuses on foreseeability. Is it foreseeable that someone will be injured if a "Wet Floor" sign is not posted?

CASE SUMMARY

Negligence in the Air in Train Stations

Facts: Helen Palsgraf was standing on the platform at the railroad station for the Long Island Railway as she waited for her train to Rockaway Beach. Two men at the other end of the platform where Mrs. Palsgraf was standing ran to catch another train that was already moving. One man, with the help of a railroad employee who was on the train, made it safely onto the moving train, but the second man, who was carrying a package, fell and dropped the package. The package, full of fireworks, exploded, and the resulting vibrations of the platform caused the scales standing near Mrs. Palsgraf to fall and strike and injure her. Mrs. Palsgraf sued the railroad for negligence.

Decision: The railroad was held not liable for Mrs. Palsgraf's injuries. While the railroad could foresee injury to those the employee helped onto the train and even those passengers in the same car, it could not foresee injury to Mrs. Palsgraf, who was not in the immediate zone of danger created by the unreasonable conduct of the employee. While there was negligence in the air, it was not sufficiently close or tied to Mrs. Palsgraf to permit her to recover. [Palsgraf v Long Island Ry. Co. 162 NE 99 (NY 1928)]

---

[9] Because the law is stated in terms of reasonableness, it is necessary to make a value judgment in which the extent of harm is measured against the cost and burden of taking precaution to prevent the harm. That is, when the product of the possibility of harm multiplied times the gravity of the harm, if it happens, exceeds the burden of precautions, the failure to take those precautions is negligence. *Levi v Southwest Louisiana Electric Membership Cooperative* (La) 542 So 2d 1081 (1989).

Punitive damages are a civil penalty that the defendant is required to pay the plaintiff in negligence cases where the carelessness was particularly high.

The final element of negligence is damages. To recover damages, the plaintiff must be able to show that his or her injuries were the result of the breach of duty by the defendant. Damages could include medical bills, lost wages, property damage, and pain and suffering. In some cases where the breach of duty was shocking, plaintiffs are awarded **punitive damages**. Punitive damages, sometimes called "smart money," are a form of a civil penalty paid to plaintiffs because of a high level of carelessness on the defendant's part.

13. Defenses to Negligence

Contributory negligence is a defense to negligence that is a bar to recovery if negligence on the part of the plaintiff is at least a partial cause of the accident and the plaintiff's resulting damages.

(a) Contributory Negligence. In some cases an accident results from the combined negligence of two or more people. A plaintiff who is also negligent gives the defendant the opportunity to raise the defense of **contributory negligence**. Contributory negligence is simply negligence on the part of the plaintiff that is at least a partial cause of the accident and the plaintiff's resulting damages. *For example*, suppose that a boat owner is operating his boat at a high speed late at night on a choppy lake. One of the owner's friends who is aboard is sitting at the bow of the boat trying to put her hands and feet into the water as they travel. Both have been drinking. The friend is tossed into the lake and then run over by the boat. The issue of causation is complicated because both parties were engaged in behaviors that reasonable people would not do. The boat owner should not have been drinking and operating his boat in dangerous conditions. But reasonable people do not sit on the bow of a boat traveling at high speeds and try to reach into the water.

At common law, and under true contributory negligence, the friend would be barred from recovering anything for her injuries because contributory negligence is a complete defense to negligence. If it is determined that both parties caused the accident, then there is contributory negligence and no recovery.

Comparative negligence is a defense to negligence that allows the plaintiff to recover a reduced amount of damages based on his or her level of fault or causation for the accident.

(b) Comparative Negligence. Because contributory negligence produced harsh outcomes, many states have adopted the defense of **comparative negligence**. Comparative negligence is a defense that permits the determination of levels of fault for an accident and permits negligent plaintiffs to recover for their damages, but only a portion determined according to degree of fault. *For example*, in the boating accident a jury might determine that the boat owner was 60 percent at fault and the friend 40 percent at fault. The friend, under the comparative negligence defense, could still recover, but she would recover only 60 percent of her damages.

In some states the comparative negligence concept is modified by ignoring the negligence of the plaintiff if it is slight and the negligence of the defendant is great or gross. At the other extreme, some states refuse to allow the plaintiff to recover anything if the negligence on the part of the plaintiff was more than 50 percent of the cause of the harm.[10]

---

[10] *Davenport v Cotton Hope Plantation Horizontal Property Regime* (SC App) 482 SE2d 569 (1997).

Concrete Defenses and Head-On Collisions

Facts: James Lee Boyter, a cement truck driver for Concrete Specialties of America, collided head-on with Robin Langley as she drove on a curved portion of a two-lane road. Ms. Langley testified that Mr. Boyter hit her head-on as he came around the curve because he was in her lane and hence driving on the wrong side of the road. A witness testified that Ms. Langley was driving at an excessive rate of speed before Mr. Boyter's truck struck her car between the left front fender and the door. Ms. Langley filed suit against Mr. Boyter and Concrete Specialities. They defended on the grounds that Ms. Langley was contributorily negligent.

Decision: Langley's negligence merely reduced her recovery. The court would no longer follow the common law rule that any negligence of the plaintiff barred recovery. Instead, the plaintiff would recover as long as the defendant's negligence was greater than the plaintiff's. In this case Mr. Boyter's truck was well into Ms. Langley's lane prior to the collision, and her speed was a minor cause of the accident. [Langley v Boyter (SC App) 325 SE2d 550 (1984)]

Assumption of risk is a defense to negligence that requires proof that the plaintiff knew of the risks involved in an activity and went forward with it anyway.

(c) Assumption of Risk. The **assumption of risk** defense requires the defendant to prove that the plaintiff knew there was a risk of injury in the conduct he or she undertook but decided to go forward with it anyway. ◆ *For example,* there are inherent risks in skiing, in-line skating, and sky diving, and you assume those inherent risks when you engage in those activities. ◆ When you ski, you assume the natural risks of speed, mountain and snow conditions, and your lack of skill. To assume risk, you must be completely aware of the dangers involved in the activity and agree to go forward with that activity voluntarily. For many of these high-risk activities, the operators will require that you sign a release so that they have written documentation regarding your assumption of risk.

I Got Hooked, But I Assumed So When I Went Fishing

Facts: Joseph Mosca, a sport fisherman, went on a fishing expedition off San Clemente Island with other fishermen aboard a chartered boat. Another fisherman, David Lichtenwalter, got his line from his fishing pole entangled in kelp and could not get it loose. A deckhand from the charter fishing expedition company approached Lichtenwalter to help him, but as he did, Lichtenwalter backed up and handed his pole to the deckhand. The line "sling-shotted" back over the rail toward Mosca, who was struck in the eye with the sinker, causing a partial vision loss. Mosca filed suit against Lichtenwalter and the fishing expedition company. Lichtenwalter raised the defense of assumption of risk.

Decision: Mosca had assumed the risks inherent in sport fishing. Assumption of risk is not applicable just to active sports. While Mosca may not have known of the specific dangers of recoiling lines, he did know that catching fish involves skill, hooks, and unknown dangers in the sea. There was nothing the boat owner and operator did that increased Mosca's risk. Mosca assumed the risks inherent in deep sea fishing, and injuries from recoiling lines were part of that risk. [Mosca v Lichtenwalter, 58 Cal App 4th 551, 68 Cal Rptr 2d 58 (1997)]

---

14. Liability for Negligence

Basically every person who commits a tort is liable for damages for the harm caused by that tort.

Age Is Not a Defense

Facts: Boughner was 17. He drove a semitrailer. It overturned and killed Osner, who was a passenger in the truck. Suit was brought against Boughner by Osner's estate. He raised the defense that because he was a minor, he was required to observe only a minor's standard of care.

Decision: Driving a semitrailer is an adult activity, and a 17-year-old so driving must be held to the standard of care required of an adult. *[Osner v Boughner, 180 Mich App 248, 446 NW2d 873 (1989)]*

Immunity is not being subject to liability ordinarily imposed by law.

(a) Immunity. There are, however, certain persons and entities that are not subject to tort liability. This is called **immunity** from liability.

Governments are generally immune from tort liability.[11] This rule has been eroded by decisions and in some instances by statutes, such as the Federal Tort Claims Act. Subject to certain exceptions, this act permits the recovery of damages from the United States for property damage, personal injury, or death action claims arising from the negligent act or omission of any employee of the United States under such circumstances that the United States, if a private person, would be liable to the claimant in accordance with the law of the place where the act or omission occurred. A fast-growing number of states have abolished governmental immunity, although many still recognize it.

Up until the early 1900s charities were immune from tort liability, and children and parents and spouses could not sue each other. These immunities are fast disappearing. *For example,* if a father's negligent driving of his car caused injuries to his minor child passenger, the child can sue the father for his injuries.[12]

(b) Liability for Negligently Caused Mental Distress. In many jurisdictions the concept of liability for distress has been expanded to impose liability for negligently caused mental distress. For example, when an undertaker through negligence buried a decedent the day before the burial was scheduled, the survivors could recover damages for the mental distress they sustained.[13] There is some indication that courts will impose wider liability for emotional distress when the circumstances are such as to exclude false claims even though the defendant did not intentionally cause the distress. Thus, it has been held that when a mining company removed coal by burrowing under a graveyard, the company was liable for the subsidence and cracking of the graveyard caused by failure to leave sufficient supporting pillars of coal and earth underneath the graveyard.[14]

(c) Bystander Recovery. When a bystander is a spectator to the negligent conduct of the defendant and witnessing such conduct causes serious and reasonably foreseeable emotional distress, some courts hold that the bystander may recover damages for such harm from the wrongdoer. Most of these courts limit this liability to spectators who are closely related to the person directly endangered by the

---

[11] *Kirby v Macon County* (Tenn) 892 SW2d 403 (1994).
[12] *Cates v Cates* 588 NE 2d 330 (Ill App 1992).
[13] *Holsen v Heritage Mutual Ins. Co.* (Wis App) 478 NW 2d 59 (1991).
[14] *Benett v 3C Coal Co.* 379 SE2d 388 (W Va 1989).

defendant's conduct. Thus, one court held that an employee could not recover for spectator shock upon seeing a fellow worker killed while at work.

A few courts have eliminated the requirement that the bystander actually see the event that causes shock. Thus, a relative arriving shortly after an event's actual occurrence may recover damages for the emotional distress caused by the negligence of the defendant. Likewise, two young teenagers were allowed to recover for the emotional distress caused by the negligent injuring of their mother even though they did not witness the collision of her car. They first learned of it while in a neighbor's home and then went to the hospital, where they were told that their mother would probably die.[15]

CASE SUMMARY

Shock, Impact, and Recovery

Facts: A truck of the Barberton Glass Co. was transporting large sheets of glass down the highway. Elliot Schultz was driving his automobile some distance behind the truck. Because of the negligent way that the sheets of glass were fastened in the truck, a large sheet fell off the truck, shattered upon hitting the highway, and then bounced up and broke the windshield of Shultz's car. He was not injured but suffered great emotional shock. He sued Barberton to recover damages for this shock. Barberton denied liability on the ground that Schultz had not sustained any physical injury at the time or as the result of the shock.

Decision: The absence of any physical injury or impact or contact with the body of the plaintiff does not bar recovery for emotional distress caused by the negligence of the defendant. The argument in favor of the impact rule requiring such contact was that without an impact there was the danger of fraudulent claims being made. This argument was shown to be invalid by the fact that those states that had already abolished the impact rule had not been confronted with fraudulent claims. [*Schultz v Barberton Glass Co.* 4 Ohio 3d 131, 447 NE2d 109 (1983)]

Similarly, when a three-year-old girl was killed by the falling of a storage cabinet in a house that the parents were planning to buy, the parents and the brother of the girl could recover bystander distress damages when they knew the girl was in the house, heard the crash of the falling cabinet, and saw the fallen cabinet a few seconds later.[16]

15. Tort Reform

The United States permits greater recovery for torts while requiring less in terms of proof than other nations. Over the past decade a number of reforms have been proposed, particularly with respect to tort litigation, to limit recovery or place other limitations on the amount of increasing tort litigation. These limitations may be general limitations on damage awards or limitations like the Canadian system of $200,000 for pain and suffering. Although nearly all states have adopted some form of limitations in tort recovery, these reforms are a maze of laws differing from state to state, have been subject to judicial challenges (in many cases successful), and have provided little hope for insurers as they try to forecast their risks in insuring businesses and their properties and agents. Proposals for reform continue and in many cases are ballot propositions that permit voters to decide the kinds and types of limits for tort recovery.

---

15 *Hickman v McKoin* (NC App) 428 SE2d 251 (1993).
16 *Chen v Superior Court* 62 Cal Rptr 526 (1997).

The $4 Million BMW Paint Job

Facts: Dr. Ira Gore, Jr., purchased a black BMW sports sedan for $40,750.88 from an authorized BMW dealer in Birmingham, Alabama. After driving the car for nine months, without noticing any flaws in its appearance, Dr. Gore took the car to "Slick Finish," an auto detailer, to make the car look "snazzier than it normally would appear." Mr. Slick, the owner, told Dr. Gore that his BMW had been repainted. The car had experienced acid rain damage to its paint on its journey from Germany to the United States. Dr. Gore, convinced that he had been cheated, filed suit against BMW of North America. The jury awarded Dr. Gore the cost of repainting the BMW ($601.37), plus the reduced value of a BMW that has been repainted ($4,000), plus $4 million in punitive damages for BMW's failure to disclose to its buyers of new vehicles that they had been repainted. BMW appealed the damage award as excessive.

Decision: The damage award was excessive. The factors to be examined in determining if a damage award is excessive include the relationship between the actual damages and the punitive damages, the reprehensibility of the conduct, and the sanctions for comparable misconduct in the past. The case was sent back for a redetermination of the damages. [BMW of North America, Inc. v Gore, 116 S Ct 1589 (1996)]

WHAT'S BEHIND THE LAW?

Torts and Public Policy

When a jury awarded $3 million to a woman who was burned after she spilled a cup of McDonald's coffee in her lap, a juror was quoted in the New York Times as saying, "We wanted to send a strong message that fast food restaurant coffee is too hot!"

Tort remedies have evolved because of public policy incentives for the prevention and protection of individuals from mental, physical, and economic damage. Tort remedies provide economic motivation for conduct that does not harm others. But the question of how much should be paid is more important in order to strike a balance between economic incentive and economic destruction.

The amount of the compensation and the circumstances in which compensation for torts should be paid are issues that courts, juries, and legislatures review. Many legislatures have examined and continue to review the standards for tort liability and damages. Referred to as tort reform, these changes shift the burdens of proof on tort liability or limit the damages recoverable. These changes often involve reviewing the balance between individual rights and the need for business stability. A message on hot coffee in restaurants perhaps should not cost $3 million to deliver. Tort reform focuses on cases like this one and on striking the right balance in advancing the public policies involved.

To examine the scope of tort liability and the highly organized class actions visit the Consumer Law Page at http://consumerlawpage.com

SUMMARY

A tort is a civil wrong that affords recovery for damages that result. The three forms of torts are intentional torts, negligence, and strict liability. A tort differs from a crime in the nature of its remedy. Fines and imprisonment result from criminal violations, whereas money damages are paid to those who are damaged by conduct that constitutes a tort. An action may be both a crime and a tort, but the tort remedy is civil in nature.

The intentional torts consist of false imprisonment, defamation, product disparagement, contract interference or tortious interference, trespass, and the computer torts. False imprisonment is the detention of another without his or her permission. Because false imprisonment is often called the shopkeeper's tort, as store owners detain suspected shoplifters, many states provide a privilege to store owners if they detain shoplifting suspects based on reasonable cause and in a reasonable manner. Defamation is slander (oral) or libel (written) and consists of false statements about another that damage his or her reputation or integrity. Truth is an absolute defense to defamation, and there are some privileges that protect against defamation, such as those for witnesses at trial and for members of

Congress during debates on the floor. There is a developing privilege for employers when they give references for former employees. Invasion of privacy is intrusion into private affairs; public disclosure of private facts; or appropriation of someone's name, image, or likeness for commercial purposes.

Computer torts are simply specialized applications of torts, as in privacy and trespass to property.

To establish the tort of negligence, one must show that there has been a breach of duty in the form of a violation of a statute or professional competency standards or of behavior that does not rise to the level of that of a reasonable person. That breach of duty must have caused the injuries to the plaintiff, and the plaintiff must be able to quantify the damages that resulted. Possible defenses to negligence include contributory negligence, comparative negligence, and assumption of risk.

Liability for torts has been expanding in terms of the amounts awarded and the persons who can be held liable. Currently there are numerous statutes, decisions, and ballot propositions designed to reduce tort liability.

QUESTIONS AND CASE PROBLEMS

1. What are the social forces advanced by liability for harm without regard to whether there was any negligence or intention to cause harm?

2. Coleman Construction Co. was building a highway. It was necessary to blast rock with dynamite. The company's employees did this with the greatest of care, but in spite of their precautions, some flying fragments of rock damaged a neighboring house. The owner of the house sued the company for damages. The company raised the defense that the owner was suing for tort damages and that such damages could not be imposed because the company had been free from fault. Was this defense valid?

3. Burnstein drove a car on a country road at 35 miles an hour. The maximum speed limit was 45 miles an hour. He struck and killed a cow that was crossing the road. The owner of the cow sued Burnstein for the value of the cow. Burnstein argued that because he was not driving above the speed limit, there could be no liability for negligence. Was this defense valid?

4. Mallinckrodt produces nuclear and radioactive medical pharmaceuticals and supplies. Maryland Heights Leasing, an adjoining business owner, claimed that low-level radiation emissions from Mallinckrodt damaged its property and caused a loss in earnings. What

remedy should Maryland Heights have? What torts are involved here? [*Maryland Heights Leasing, Inc. v Mallinckrodt, Inc.* (Mo App) 706 SW2d 218]

5. An owner abandoned his van in an alley in Chicago. In spite of repeated complaints to the police, the van was allowed to remain in the alley. After several months it was stripped of most of the parts that could be removed. Jamin Ortiz, aged 11, was walking down the alley when the van's gas tank exploded. The flames from the explosion set fire to Jamin's clothing, and he was severely burned. Suit was brought against the city of Chicago to recover damages for his injuries. Decide. [*Ortiz v Chicago* (Ill App) 398 NE2d 1007]

6. Henry Neiderman was walking with his small son when an automobile driven by Brodsky went out of control, ran up on the sidewalk, and struck a fire hydrant, a litter pole and basket, a newsstand, and Neiderman's son. The car did not touch Neiderman, but the shock and fright caused damage to his heart. He sued Brodsky for the harm he sustained as the result of Brodsky's negligence. Brodsky defended on the ground that he was not liable because he had not touched Neiderman. Was this a valid defense? [*Neiderman v Brodsky* (Pa) 261 A2d 84]

7. Carrigan, a district manager of Simples Time Recorder Co., was investigating complaints of mismanagement of the company's Jackson office. He called at the home of Hooks, the secretary of that office, who expressed the opinion that part of the trouble was caused by the theft of parts and equipment by McCall, another employee. McCall was later discharged and sued Hooks for slander. Was she liable? [*Hooks v McCall* (Miss) 272 So 2d 925]

8. Defendant no. 1 parked his truck in the street near the bottom of a ditch on a dark, foggy night. Iron pipes carried in the truck projected beyond the truck nine feet in back. Neither the truck nor the pipes carried any warning light or flag, thus violating both a city ordinance and a state statute. Defendant no. 2 was a taxicab owner whose taxicab was negligently driven at an excessive speed. Defendant no. 2 ran into the pipes, thereby killing the passenger in the taxicab. The plaintiff brought an action for the passenger's death against both defendants. Defendant no. 1 claimed he was not liable because it was the negligent act of defendant no. 2 that had caused the harm. Was this defense valid? [*Bumbardner v Allison* (NC) 78 SE2d 752]

9. A statute required that air vent shafts on hotel roofs have parapets at least 30 inches high. Edgar Hotel had parapets only 27 inches high. Nunneley, who was visiting a registered guest at the Edgar Hotel, placed a mattress on top of a parapet. When she sat on the mattress, the parapet collapsed, and she fell into the air shaft and was injured. She sued the hotel, claiming that its breach of the statute regulating the height of the parapets constituted negligence. Decide. [*Nunneley v Edgar Hotel* (Cal) 225 P2d 497]

10. A customer was shopping at the handbag counter of the defendant's store. She did not make any purchase and left the store. When she was a few feet away from the store, a store employee tapped her lightly on the shoulder to attract her attention and asked her if she had made any purchase. When she inquired why, he asked, "What about that bag in your hand?" The customer said that it belonged to her, and she opened it to show by its contents that it was not a new bag. The employee gave the customer a "real dirty look" and went back into the store without saying a word. The customer then sued the store for false imprisonment. Was the store liable? [*Abner v W.T. Grant Co.,* (Ga App) 408 (Ga App) 139 SE2d]

11. Hegyes was driving her car when it was negligently struck by a Unjian Enterprises truck. She was injured, and an implant was placed in her body to counteract the injuries. She sued Unjian, and the case was settled. Two years later Hegyes became pregnant. The growing fetus pressed against the implant, making it necessary for her doctor to deliver the child 51 days prematurely by Cesarean section. Because of its premature birth, the child had a breathing handicap. Suit was brought against Unjian Enterprises for the harm sustained by the child. Was the defendant liable? [*Hegyes v Unjian Enterprises, Inc.* (Cal App) 286 Cal Rptr 85]

12. A farmer sued five factories that were located several miles from his farm. He proved that industrial fumes from the factories had seriously damaged his crops. Has any tort been committed? Why or why not?

13. Kendra Knight took part in a friendly game of touch football. She had played before and was familiar with football. Michael Jewett was on her team. In the course of play, Michael bumped into Kendra and knocked her to the ground. He stepped on her hand, causing injury to a little finger that later required its amputation. She sued Michael for damages. He defended on the ground that she had assumed the risk. Kendra claimed that assumption of risk could not be raised as a defense because the state legislature had adopted the standard of comparative negligence. Decide.

14. An eight-year-old boy with curable cancer was receiving x-ray treatment at a hospital. He was negligently given overdoses of x-ray, which produced deadly radiation poisoning that resulted in a grotesque alteration in his appearance. His parents could see the alteration as well as his pain and suffering up to the time of his death within the following year. They sued the hospital for the emotional distress they suffered because of the negligence of the hospital. The hospital claimed that the parents had not seen the negligent acts that caused the harm and therefore could not recover as bystanders. Decide. [*Golstein v San Francisco Superior Court* (Cal App) 273 Cal Rptr 270]

15. Blaylock was a voluntary psychiatric outpatient treated by Dr. Burglass, who became aware that Blaylock was violence-prone. Blaylock told Dr. Burglass that he intended to do serious harm to Wayne Boynton, Jr., and shortly thereafter he killed Wayne. Wayne's parents then sued Dr. Burglass on grounds that he was liable for the death of their son because he failed to give warning or to notify the police of Blaylock's threat and nature. Decide. [*Boynton v Burglass* (Fla App) 590 So 2d 446]

Intellectual Property Rights

CHAPTER 10

After studying this chapter, you should be able to

1. *Explain how to obtain a copyright, a patent, and a trademark;*
2. *Identify the rights obtained by owners of copyrights, patents, and trademarks;*
3. *State the duration of the protection afforded owners of copyrights, trademarks, and patents;*
4. *Set forth the remedies available to owners for infringement of intellectual property rights; and*
5. *List and explain the extent of protection provided by federal laws for owners of software and mask works.*

Intellectual property comes in many forms: the writings of an author, the new product or process developed by an inventor, the company name Microsoft, and the secret formula used to make Coca-Cola. Federal law provides rights to owners of these works, products, company names, and processes called copyrights, patents, trademarks, and trade secrets. State laws provide protection for trade secrets. Federal laws and trade secrecy laws protect the special category of intellectual property rights relating to computer software development and use. This chapter discusses the federal and state laws governing these areas of intellectual property.

A.   TRADEMARKS AND SERVICE MARKS

The Lanham Act, a federal law, grants a producer the exclusive right to register a trademark and prevent competitors from using that mark. This law helps assure a producer that it, and not an imitating competitor, will reap the financial, reputation-related rewards of a desirable product.

1. Introduction

A mark is any combination of words and symbols used by businesses or professionals to identify their products or services.

A **mark** is any word, name, symbol, device, or combination of these used to identify a product or service.[1] If the mark identifies a product, such as an automobile or soap, it is called a **trademark**. If it identifies a service, such as a restaurant or dry cleaner, it is called a **service mark**.

The owner of a mark may obtain protection from others using it by registering the mark in accordance with federal law.[2] To be registered, a mark must distinguish the goods or service of the applicant from those of others. Under the federal statute, a register, called the Principal Register, is maintained for recording such marks. Inclusion on the Principal Register grants the registrant the exclusive right to use the mark. Challenges may be made to the registrant's right within five years of registration, but after five years the right of the registrant is incontestable.

An advance registration of a mark may be made not more than three years before its actual use by filing an application certifying a bona fide "intent-to-use." Fees must be paid at six-month intervals from the filing of the application until actual use begins.[3]

---

[1] 15 USC § 1127.
[2] Lanham Act, 15 USC §§ 1050–1127.
[3] PL 100-667, 15 USC § 1051 (1988); effective November 16, 1989.

2. Registrable Marks

Marks that are coined, completely fanciful, or arbitrary are capable of registration on the Principal Register. The mark Exxon, for example, was coined by the owner. The name Kodak is also a creation of the owner of this trademark and has no other meaning in English, but it serves to distinguish the goods of its owner from all others.

A suggestive term may also be registered. Such a term suggests rather than describes some characteristics of the goods to which it applies and requires the consumer to exercise some imagination to reach a conclusion about the nature of the goods. For example, as a trademark for refrigerators, Penguin would be suggestive of the product's superior cooling and freezing features. As a trademark for paperback books, however, Penguin is arbitrary and fanciful.

Ordinarily, descriptive terms, surnames, and geographic terms are not registrable on the Principal Register.[4] A descriptive term identifies a characteristic or quality of an article or service, such as color, odor, function, or use. Thus, Arthriticare was held not to be registrable on the Principal Register because it was merely descriptive of a product used to treat symptoms of arthritis. Boston Beer was denied trademark protection because it was a geographic term.[5]

An exception is made, however, when a descriptive or geographic term or a surname has acquired a *secondary meaning*; such a mark is registrable. A term or terms that have a primary meaning of their own acquire a secondary meaning when, through long use in connection with a particular product, they have come to be known by the public as identifying the particular product and its origin. ◆ *For example*, the geographic Philadelphia has acquired a secondary meaning when applied to cream cheese. It is widely accepted by the public as denoting a particular brand rather than any cream cheese made in Philadelphia. ◆ Factors considered by a court in determining whether a trademark has acquired secondary meaning are the amount and manner of advertising, volume of sales, length and manner of use, direct consumer testimony, and consumer surveys.

With a limited number of colors available for use by competitors, along with possible shade confusion, courts had held for some 90 years that color alone could not function as a trademark. This legal rule has been overturned by the U.S. Supreme Court, and now, if a color serves as a symbol that distinguishes a firm's goods and identifies their source without serving any other significant function, it may, sometimes at least, meet the basic legal requirements for use as a trademark.[6] ◆ *For example*, Owens-Corning Fiberglass Corp. has been allowed to register the color pink as a trademark for its fiberglass insulation products. ◆

Generic terms—that is, terms that designate a kind or class of goods, such as *cola* or *rosé wine*—are never registrable.

3. Trade Dress Protection

Firms invest significant resources to develop and promote the appearance of their products and the packages in which these products are sold so that they are clearly recognizable by consumers. **Trade dress** involves a product's total image and, in

---

4 A Supplemental Register exists for recording such marks. This recording does not give the registrant any protection, but it provides a source to which other persons designing a mark can go to make sure they are not duplicating an existing mark. See *Cushman v Mutton Hollow Land, Inc.* (Mo App) 782 SW2d 150 (1990).

5 *Boston Beer Co. v Slesar Bros. Brewing Co.*, 9 F3d 125 (1st Cir 1994).

6 *Qualitex Co. v Jacobson Products Co., Inc.*, 514 US 159 (1995).

the case of consumer goods, includes the overall packaging look in which each product is sold.

Keeping the Toilet Bank Flush with Cash

Facts: Fun-Damental Too, Ltd, developed a toy called the Toilet Bank, a toy coin bank closely resembling a white tank toilet, which emits a flushing sound when its handle is depressed. It took two years to develop, and, since 1994, it has sold over 860,000 at a retail price of $15 to $20 each. In May 1995, Kay-Bee, a major toy retailer, expressed interest in buying the banks for resale but later decided against it. Also in May 1995, Gemmy Industries Corp. sent a toilet bank to its Chinese manufacturer and asked it to design a similar product. A product called the Currency Can was designed and manufactured for Gemmy, with dimensions identical to those of the Toilet Bank. It was packaged in a box identical in its configuration and dimensions to Fun-Damental's box, including the various tabs, and Gemmy's overall color schemes, particularly the bright yellow tiles on the royal blue background, were very similar to Fun-Damental's use of royal blue with yellow lettering. When Fun-Damental discovered the Currency Can being sold at Kay-Bee for $9.99, it filed a complaint against Gemmy and Kay-Bee, alleging trade dress infringement in violation of section 43(a) of the Lanham Act; it also sought a preliminary injunction. Gemmy contended that intentionally copying a product is not a relevant legal consideration in a trade dress infringement claim.

Decision: Judgment for Fun-Damental. Fun-Damental's packaging was distinctive and nonfunctional. Alternative packaging options existed for Gemmy, yet it chose a package identical to Fun-Damental's. Gemmy's overall color schemes were very similar to Fun-Damental's. While Gemmy is correct that the intentionally copying of a product by itself is not relevant in a trade dress infringement claim, the combined effect of placing an identical product in copied packaging supports the inference that the copying competitor was acting with intent to create confusion of source. [*Fun-Damental Too, Ltd v Gemmy Industries Corp., 111 F3d 993 (2d Cir 1997)*]

Trade dress (the overall appearance of a product) is protected under the Lanham Act.

When a competitor adopts a confusingly similar trade dress, it dilutes the first user's investment and goodwill and deceives consumers, hindering their ability to distinguish between competing brands. The law of trade dress protection has been settled by the U.S. Supreme Court,[7] and courts have subsequently become more receptive to claims of trade dress infringement under section 43(a) of the Lanham Act. In order to prevail, a plaintiff must prove its trade dress is distinctive and nonfunctional and the defendant's trade dress is confusingly similar to the plaintiff's.[8] Thus, a competitor who copied the Marlboro cigarettes package for its Gunsmoke brand of cigarettes was found to have infringed the trade dress of the Marlboro brand.[9] Trade dress protection under the Lanham Act is the same as that provided a qualified unregistered trademark and does not provide all of the protection available to the holder of a registered trademark.

4. Injunction against Improper Use of Mark

A person who has the right to use a mark may obtain a court order prohibiting a competitor from imitating or duplicating the mark. The basic question in such litigation is whether the general public is likely to be confused by the mark of the

---

[7] *Two Pesos, Inc. v Taco Cabana, Inc.,* 505 US 763 (1992).
[8] *Paddington v Attiki Importers and Distributors Inc.,* 996 F2d 577, 582 (2d Cir 1993).
[9] *Philip Morris Inc. v Star Tobacco Corp.,* 879 F Supp 379 (SDNY 1995).

defendant and to believe wrongly that it identifies the plaintiff. If there is this danger of confusion, the court will enjoin the defendant from using the particular mark.

CASE SUMMARY

Confusion on the Web

Facts: Digital Equipment Corporation owns an Internet and World Wide Web "search engine" service known as Alta Vista. Digital purchased ATI's rights in ATI's trademark *Alta Vista* and then licensed back to ATI the limited right to use *Alta Vista* in certain defined ways as part of ATI's corporate name and with ATI's Uniform Resource Locator. The license precluded ATI from using *Alta Vista* as "the name of a product or service offering." ATI's Web site in October 1996 was designed to look, feel, and function very much like Digital's Alta Vista Web site. Visitors to ATI's site could easily have the impression that they were actually at Digital's Alta Vista site. A *Wall Street Journal* article reported on October 18, 1996, that "Every day hundreds of thousands of Web users looking for Digital's Alta Vista accidentally call upon the home page for Jack Marshall's Alta Vista," and the article reported that some of ATI's advertisers thought they were buying space on Digital's site, which boasts some 20 million "hits" each day. Digital brought suit against ATI, seeking a preliminary injunction, claiming ATI's Web site breaches the licensing agreement and infringes on Digital's trademark rights in *Alta Vista*. ATI asserts that it has the right to use the mark to exploit the name *Alta Vista*.

Decision: Judgment for Digital. Digital has acquired the right to control the use of the Alta Vista trademark, and nothing in its license with ATI allows ATI to capitalize on Digital's investment in creating one of the most recognized marks in use on the Web. There is a strong likelihood of confusion between ATI's Web site and Digital's. ATI's Web site is a service that sells advertising space and software, and its use is unauthorized under the licensing agreement. ATI's use may cause tremendous confusion among Web users, both consumers and advertisers alike. ATI is therefore enjoined from using the *Alta Vista* mark other than as authorized in the licensing agreement and must prominently display on each Web page that it "is not affiliated with" Digital's Alta Vista Internet Software Inc., as an Internet search service. [*Digital Equipment Corp. v ATI, 960 F Supp 456 (D Mass 1997)*]

In some cases, the fact that the products of the plaintiff and the defendant did not compete in the same market was held to entitle the defendant to use a mark that would have been prohibited as confusingly similar if the defendant manufactured the same product as the plaintiff. ◆ *For example*, it has been held that Cadillac as applied to boats is not confusingly similar to Cadillac as applied to automobiles; therefore, its use cannot be enjoined.[10] ◆

5. Abandonment of Exclusive Right to Mark

If the owner of a mark passively allows others to use the mark, the owner may lose the right to its exclusive use.

An owner who has an exclusive right to use a mark may lose that right. If other persons are permitted to use the mark, it loses its exclusive character and is said to pass into the English language and become generic. Examples of formerly enforceable marks that have made this transition into the general language are *aspirin, thermos, cellophane,* and *shredded wheat.*

---

[10] *General Motors Corp. v Cadillac Marine and Boat Co.,* 140 USPQ (BNA) 447 (1964). See also *Amstar Corp. v Domino's Pizza Inc.,* 615 F2d 252 (5th Cir 1980), where the mark Domino as applied to pizza was held not to be confusingly similar to Domino as applied to sugar.

6. Prevention of Dilution of Famous Marks

The Federal Trademark Dilution Act of 1995[11] provides a cause of action against the "commercial use" of another's famous mark or trade name when it results in a "dilution of the distinctive quality of the mark." The act protects against discordant uses, such as Du Pont shoes, Buick aspirin, and Kodak pianos. Unlike an ordinary trademark infringement action, a dilution action applies in the absence of competition and likelihood of confusion. The act exempts "fair use" of a mark in comparative advertising as well as uses in news reporting and commentary.

The Federal Trademark Dilution Act has been used against *cybersquatters*, who register and set up domain names on the Internet for resale to the famous users of the names in question. For example, Toeppen registered the domain name "panavision.com" with Network Solutions Inc., which registers Internet domain names on a first come, first served basis. Toeppen demanded $13,000 from Panavision to discontinue use, and Panavasion sued Toeppen under the Federal Trademark Dilution Act. The court held that Toeppen diluted Panavision's famous mark by preventing it from identifying and distinguishing its goods on the Internet.[12]

B.   COPYRIGHTS

A **copyright** is the exclusive right given by federal statute to the creator of a literary or an artistic work to use, reproduce, and display the work. Under the international treaty called the Berne Convention, copyright of the works of all U.S. authors is protected automatically in all Berne Convention nations, who have agreed under the treaty to treat nationals of other member countries like their own nationals.

A copyright prevents not the copying of an idea but only the copying of the way the idea is expressed. That is, the copyright is violated when there is a duplicating of the words, pictures, or other form of expression of the creator but not when there is just use of the idea those words, pictures, or other formats express.

7. Duration of Copyright

Article 1, section 8 of the U.S. Constitution empowered Congress to "promote the Progress of Science and useful Arts, by securing for limited times to Authors and Inventors the exclusive Right to their respective Writings and Discoveries." The first U.S. copyright statute was enacted soon after in 1790 and provided protection for any "book, map or chart" for 14 years, with a privilege to renew for an additional 14 years. In 1831, the initial 14-year term was extended to 28 years, with a privilege for an additional 14 years. Under the 1909 Copyright Act, the protection period was for 28 years, with a right of renewal for an additional 28 years.

Under the presently applicable copyright law, enacted in 1976, the duration of a copyright is the life of the creator of the work plus 50 years. The Copyright Act of 1976 brought the duration aspect of U.S. copyright law into harmony with that of most comparable nations. Also under present law, if a work is a "work made for hire,"—that is, a business pays an individual to create the work—the

---

[11] PL 104-98, 109 Stat 985, 15 USC § 1125(c)(1).
[12] *Panavision v Toeppen*, 945 F Supp 1296 (CD Cal 1996).

business employing the creator registers the copyright. This copyright runs for 100 years from creation or 75 years from publication of the work, whichever period is shorter. After a copyright has expired, the work is in the public domain and may be used by anyone without cost.

8.   Copyright Notice

Prior to March 1, 1989, the author of an original work secured a copyright by placing a copyright notice on the work, consisting of the word *copyright* or the symbol ©, the year of first publication, and the name or pseudonym of the author. The author also was required to register the copyright with the Copyright Office. Under the Berne Convention Implementation Act of 1988,[13] a law that adjusts U.S. copyright law to conform to the Berne Convention, it is no longer mandatory that works published after March 1, 1989, contain a notice of copyright. However, placing a notice of copyright on published works is strongly recommended. This notice prevents an infringer from claiming innocent infringement of the work, which would reduce the amount of damages owed. In order to bring a copyright infringement suit for a work of U.S. origin, the owner must have submitted two copies of the work to the Copyright Office in Washington, D.C., for registration.

9.   What Is Copyrightable

Copyrights protect literary, musical, dramatic, and artistic work. Protected are books and periodicals; musical and dramatic compositions; choreographic works; maps; works of art, such as paintings, sculptures, and photographs; motion pictures and other audiovisual works; sound recordings; and computer programs.

10.   Rights of Copyright Holders

A copyright holder has the exclusive right to (1) reproduce the work; (2) prepare derivative works, such as a script from the original work; (3) distribute copies of recordings of the work; (4) publicly perform the work, in the case of plays and motion pictures; and (5) publicly display the work, in the case of paintings, sculptures, and photographs.

The copyright owner may assign or license some of the rights listed above and will receive royalty payments as part of the agreement. The copyright law also assures royalty payments.   *For example,* Jessie Riviera is a songwriter whose songs are sung at public performances and are also recorded by performers on records, tapes, and CDs. Jessie is entitled to royalties from the public performance of her works. Such royalties are collected by two performing right societies, the American Society of Composers, Authors and Publishers (ASCAP) and Broadcast Music Inc. (BMI), who act on behalf of the copyright holders. Jessie is also entitled to so-called mechanical royalties that refer to the royalty stream derived from "mechanically" reproduced records, tapes, and CDs.   The principal payers of mechanical royalties are record companies, and the rate is set by the Copyright Royalty Tribunal. The statutory rate is based on the greater of a flat fee or a per-minute, per-song, or per-record fee.[14]

---

13 PL 100-568, 102 Stat 2854, 17 USC §§ 101 et seq.
14 The rate as of January 1, 1997, is the greater of 6.6¢ per song or 1.25¢ per minute and is shared by the songwriter and a publishing company, if there is one.

In addition to rights under the copyright law and international treaties, federal and state laws prohibit record and tape piracy.

11. Limitation on Exclusive Character of Copyright

"Fair use" allows the limited use of copyrighted material for teaching, research, and news reporting.

A limitation on the exclusive rights of copyright owners exists under the principle of *fair use*, which allows limited use of copyrighted material in connection with criticism, parody, news reporting, teaching, and research. Four important factors to consider when judging whether the use made in a particular case is fair use include

1. the purpose and character of the use, including whether such use is of a commercial nature or is for nonprofit educational purposes;[15]
2. the nature of the copyrighted work;
3. the amount and substantiality of the portion used in relation to the copyrighted work as a whole; and
4. the effect of the use on the potential market for or value of the copyrighted work.

CASE SUMMARY

Fair Use or Not Fair Use——That Is the Question

Facts: The American Geophysical Union and 82 other publishers of scientific and technical journals brought a class-action lawsuit against Texaco, claiming that Texaco's unauthorized photocopying of articles from their journals constituted a copyright infringement. Texaco's defense was that the copying was fair use under section 107 of the Copyright Act of 1976. To avoid extensive discovery, the parties agreed to focus on one randomly selected Texaco scientist, Dr. Donald Chickering, who had photocopies of eight articles from the *Journal of Catalysis* in his files. The trial court judge held that the copying of the eight articles did not constitute fair use, and Texaco appealed.

Decision: Judgment for the publishers. Applying the four statutory standards to determine whether Texaco's photocopying of the scientific journal articles was fair use, three of the four factors favor the publishers. The first factor, purpose and character of use, favors the publishers because the purpose of Texaco's use was to multiply the number of copies for the benefit of its scientists, which is the same purpose for which additional subscriptions are normally sold. The second factor, the nature of the copyrighted work, which in this case is scientific articles, favors Texaco. The third factor, the amount and substantiality of the portion used, favors the publishers because Texaco copied the entire works. The fourth factor, effect on the potential market or value of the work, favors the publishers because they have shown substantial harm due to lost licensing revenue and lost subscription revenue. The aggregate assessment is that the photocopying was not fair use. [*American Geophysical Union v Texaco Inc., 60 F3d 913 (2d Cir 1995)*]

---

[15] In *Princeton University Press v Michigan Document Services, Inc.*, 99 F3d 1381 (6th Cir 1996), a commercial copyshop reproduced "coursepacks" and sold them to students attending the University of Michigan. The court refused to consider the "use" as one for nonprofit educational purposes because the use challenged was that of the copyshop, a for-profit corporation that had decided to duplicate copyrighted material for sale, to maximize its profits, and give itself a competitive edge over other copyshops, by declining to pay the royalties requested by the holders of the copyrights.

C.   PATENTS

Under Article 1, section 8, of the U.S. Constitution, the founding fathers of our country empowered Congress to promote the progress of science by securing for limited times to inventors the exclusive rights to their discoveries. Federal patent laws established under Article 1, section 8, protect inventors just as authors are protected under copyright law authorized by the same section of the U.S. Constitution.

12. Types, Duration, and Notice

There are three types of patents, the rights to which may be obtained by proper filing with the Patent and Trademark Office (PTO) in Washington, D.C. The types and duration of patents are as follows.

(a) Utility Patents. *Utility* or *functional patents* grant inventors of any new and useful process, machine, manufacture, or composition of matter or any new and useful improvement of such devices the right to obtain a patent.[16] Prior to 1995, these utility patents had a life of 17 years from the date of grant. Under the Uruguay Round Trade Agreement Act, effective June 8, 1995, the duration of U.S. utility patents was changed from 17 years from the date of grant to 20 years from the date of filing to be consistent with the patent law of General Agreement on Tariffs and Trade (GATT) member states.

> The duration of utility and plant patents is 20 years from the date of filing. Design patents have a life of 14 years from the date of filing.

(b) Design Patents. A second kind of patent exists under U.S. patent law that protects new and nonobvious ornamental features that appear in connection with an article of manufacture.[17] These patents are called *design patents* and have a duration of 14 years. Design patents have limited applicability, for not only must they be new and have nonobvious ornamental features but they must be nonfunctional as well. Thus, when the "pillow shape" design of Nabisco Shredded Wheat was found to be functional, the design patent was held invalid as the cereal's shape was not capable of design patent protection.[18]

(c) Plant Patents. A third type of patent, called *plant patents*, protects the developers of asexual reproduction of new plants. The duration is 20 years from the date of filing, the same as applied to utility patents.

(d) Notice. The owner of a patent is required to mark the patented item or device using the word *patent* and must list the patent number on the device in order to recover damages from an infringer of the patent.

13. Patentability and Exclusive Rights

> An invention must be new and not obvious to a person of ordinary skill and knowledge in the field in question in order to be patentable.

To be patentable, an invention must be something that is new and not obvious to a person of ordinary skill and knowledge in the art or technology to which the invention is related. Whether an invention is new and not obvious in its field may lead to highly technical proceedings before a patent examiner, the PTO's Board of

---

[16] 35 USC § 101.
[17] 35 USC § 173.
[18] *Kellogg Co. v National Biscuit Co.*, 305 U.S. 111 (1938).

Patent Appeals, or the U.S. Court of Appeals for the Federal Circuit (CAFC). ◆ *For example,* Thomas Devel's application for a patent on complementary DNA (cDNA) molecules encoding proteins that stimulated cell division was rejected by a patent examiner as "obvious" and affirmed by the PTO's Board of Patent Appeals. However, after a full hearing before the CAFC, which focused on the state of research in the field as applied to the patent application, Devel's patent claims were determined to be "not invalid because of obviousness."[19] ◆

The invention itself is what is patented. Thus, new and useful ideas and scientific principles by themselves cannot be patented. There must be an actual physical implementation of the idea or principle in the form of a process, machine, composition of matter, or device.

CASE SUMMARY

Crude Life Forms Can Be Patented

Facts: Chakrabarty was a microbiologist. He found a way of creating a bacterium that would break down crude oil. This could not be done by any bacteria that exist naturally. His discovery had a great potential for cleaning up oil spills. When he applied for a patent for this process, the commissioner of patents refused to grant it because what he had done was not a "manufacture" or "composition of matter" within the meaning of the federal statute and because a patent could not be obtained on something that was living. Chakrabarty appealed.

Decision: Judgment for Chakrabarty. Discovering a way to produce a living organism that is not found in nature is within the protection of the patent laws. The fact that this kind of invention was not known when the patent laws were first adopted has no effect on the decision. The patent laws are to be interpreted according to the facts existing when an application for a patent is made. [*Diamond v Chakrabarty, 447 US 303 (1980)*]

Under the Supreme Court's "doctrine of equivalents," infringers may not avoid liability for patent infringement by substituting insubstantial differences for some of the elements of the patented product or process. The test for infringement requires an essential inquiry: Does the accused product or process contain elements identical or equivalent to each claimed element of the patented invention?[20]

The patent owner has the exclusive right to make, use, sell, or import into the United States the product or process that uses the patented invention. It is a violation of U.S. patent law to make, use, sell, offer to sell, or import any patented invention within the United States without authority from the patent owner.

D. SECRET BUSINESS INFORMATION

A business may have developed information that is not generally known but that cannot be protected under federal law. Or a business may want to avoid the disclosure required to obtain a patent or copyright protection of computer software. As long as such information is kept secret, it will be protected under state law relating to trade secrets.[21]

---

[19] *In re* Devel, 51 F3d 1552 (Fed Cir 1995).
[20] *Warner-Jenkinson Co. v Hilton-Davis Chemical Co.*, 117 S Ct 1040 (1997).
[21] The Uniform Trade Secrets Act was officially amended in 1985. It is now in force in Alabama, Alaska, Arizona, Arkansas, California, Colorado, Connecticut, Delaware, Florida, Hawaii, Idaho, Illinois, Indiana, Iowa, Kansas, Kentucky, Louisiana, Maine, Minnesota, Mississippi, Montana, Nebraska, Nevada, New Hampshire, New Mexico, North Dakota, Oklahoma, Oregon, Rhode Island, South Carolina, South Dakota, Utah, Virginia, Washington, West Virginia, and Wisconsin. Trade secrets are protected in all states either under the uniform act or common law and under both criminal and civil statutes.

14. Trade Secrets

Trade secrets are protected under state law for an unlimited period of time, as long as the secrets are not made public.

A **trade secret** may consist of any formula, device, or compilation of information that is used in one's business and is of such a nature that it provides an advantage over competitors who do not have the information. It may be a formula for a chemical compound; a process of manufacturing, treating, or preserving materials; or, to a limited extent, certain confidential customer lists.[22]

Courts will not protect customer lists if customer identities are readily ascertainable from industry or public sources or if products or services are sold to a wide group of purchasers based on their individual needs.[23]

15. Loss of Protection

When secret business information is made public, it loses the protection it had while secret. This loss of protection occurs when the information is made known without any restrictions. In contrast, there is no loss of protection when secret information is shared or communicated for a special purpose and the person receiving the information knows that it is not to be made known to others.

Competitors may, through reverse engineering, discover the secret behind unpatented goods sold to the public.

When a product or process is unprotected by a patent or a copyright and is sold in significant numbers to the public, whose members are free to resell to whomever they choose, competitors are free to reverse engineer (start with the known product and work backwards to discover the process) or copy the article. *For example*, Crosby Yacht Co., a boatbuilder on Cape Cod, developed a hull design that is not patented. Maine Boatbuilders Inc. (MBI) purchased one of Crosby's boats and copied the hull by creating a mold from the boat it purchased. MBI is free to build and sell boats utilizing the copied hull.

16. Defensive Measures

Employers seek to avoid the expense of trade secret litigation by limiting disclosure of trade secrets to employees with a "need to know." Employers also have employees sign nondisclosure agreements, and they conduct exit interviews when employees with confidential information leave, reminding the employees of the employer's intent to enforce the nondisclosure agreement. In addition, employers have adopted industrial security plans to protect their unique knowledge from "outsiders," who may engage in theft, trespass, wiretapping, or other forms of commercial espionage.

17. Criminal Sanctions

Owners who take reasonable and proper measures to protect their trade secrets can rely on the criminal and civil protections provided in the Industrial Espionage Act.

Under the Industrial Espionage Act of 1996,[24] knowingly stealing, soliciting, or obtaining trade secrets by copying, downloading, or uploading via electronic means or otherwise with the intention that it will benefit a foreign government or agent is a crime. This act also applies to the stealing or purchasing of trade secrets by American companies or individuals who intend to convert trade secrets to the economic benefit of anyone other than the owner. The definition of trade secret is

---

[22] Restatement (Second) of Torts § 757 cmt b. See also *Avnet, Inc. v Wyle Labs, Inc.* (Ga) 437 SE2d 302 (1993).
[23] *Xpert Automation Systems Corp. v Vibromatic Co.* (Ind App) 569 NE2d 351 (1990).
[24] PL 104-294, 18 USC §§ 1831 et seq. (1996).

closely modeled on the Uniform Trade Secrets Act and includes all forms and types of financial, business, scientific, technical, economic, and engineering information. The law requires the owner to have taken "reasonable and proper" measures to keep the information secret. Offenders are subject to fines of up to $500,000 or twice the value of the proprietary information involved, whichever is greater, and imprisonment for up to fifteen years. Corporations may be fined up to $10,000,000 or twice the value of the secret involved, whichever is greater. In addition, the offender's property is subject to forfeiture to the U.S. government, and import-export sanctions may be imposed.

E. PROTECTION OF COMPUTER SOFTWARE AND MASK WORKS

Computer programs, chip designs, and mask works are protected from infringement with varying degrees of success by federal statutes, restrictive licensing, and trade secrecy.

18. Copyright Protection of Computer Programs

Under the Computer Software Copyright Act of 1980,[25] a written program is given the same protection as any other copyrighted material regardless of whether the program is written in source code (ordinary language) or object code (machine language). *For example,* Franklin Computer Corp. copied certain operating-system computer programs that had been copyrighted by Apple Computer, Inc. When Apple sued Franklin for copyright infringement, Franklin argued that the object code on which its programs had relied was an uncopyrightable "method of operation." The Third Circuit held that computer programs, whether in source code or in object code embedded on ROM chips, are protected under the act.[26]

In determining whether there is a copyright violation under the Computer Software Copyright Act, courts will examine the two programs in question to compare their structure, flow, sequence, and organization. Moreover, the courts in their infringement analysis look to see whether the most *significant* steps of the program are similar, rather than whether most of the program's steps are similar. To illustrate a copyright violation, substantial similarity in the structure of two computer programs for dental laboratory recordkeeping was found even though the programs were dissimilar in a number of respects because five particularly important subroutines within both programs performed almost identically.[27]

The protection afforded software by the copyright law is not entirely satisfactory to software developers because of the distinction made by the copyright law of protecting expressions but not ideas. Also, section 102(b) of the Computer Software Copyright Act does not provide protection for "methods of operation." A court has allowed a competitor to copy the identical menu tree of a copyrighted spreadsheet program because it was a noncopyrightable method of operation.[28] A move is now under way to enact broad new legislation that balances the need to protect the interests of software developers in their products with the need, after a reasonable time, to provide accessibility to other developers so they may build on

[25] Act of December 12, 1980, PL 96-517, 94 Stat 3015, 17 USC §§ 101, 117.
[26] *Apple Computer Inc. v Franklin Computer Corp.,* 714 F2d 1240 (3d Cir 1983).
[27] *Whelan Associates v Jaslow Dental Laboratory,* 797 F2d 1222 (3d Cir 1986).
[28] *Lotus Development Corp. v Borland International, Inc.,* 49 F3d 807 (1st Cir 1995), aff'd, 116 S Ct 804 (1996).

the technology for the public good. It has been suggested that the life of copyrighted software should be widely protected but drastically shortened from its present 75-year life.

19. Patent Protection of Programs

Patents have been granted for computer programs; for example, a method of using a computer to carry out translations from one language to another has been held patentable.

Patenting a program has the disadvantage that the program is placed in the public records and may thus be examined by anyone. This practice poses a potential danger that the program will be copied. To detect patent violators and bring legal action is difficult and costly.[29]

20. Trade Secrets

Software can be protected by trade secrecy.

While primary protection for computer software is found in the Computer Software Copyright Act, industry also uses trade secret law to protect computer programs. When software containing trade secrets is unlawfully appropriated by a former employee, the employee is guilty of trade secret theft.[30]

21. Restrictive Licensing

Software can be protected by restrictive licensing.

To retain greater control over proprietary software, it is common for the creator of the software to license its use to others, rather than selling it to them. Such licensing agreements typically include restrictions on the use of the software by the licensee and give the licensor greater protection than that provided by copyright law. These restrictions commonly prohibit the licensee from providing, in any manner whatsoever, the software to third persons or subjecting the software to reverse engineering.[31]

CASE SUMMARY

Playing Hardball over Software

Facts: Data General (DG) developed a sophisticated computer program called ADEX to diagnose problems in its most advanced computer hardware—its MV series of computers. DG had 90 percent of the "aftermarket" for service to its computers. A group of third-party maintainers (TPMs) earned 7 percent of the available service revenue, and defendant Grumman was the leading TPM, with 3 percent of the service business. In the mid-1980s, DG altered its policy of liberally selling or licensing software diagnostics to TPMs, and it severely restricted the licensing of ADEX. It would not license ADEX to TPMs. Grumman found ways to skirt DG's ADEX restrictions, including using copies of ADEX that some former DG employees, in violation of their employment contracts, brought when they joined Grumman and obtaining copies from former service customers in violation of licensing agreements. DG brought suit, alleging copyright infringement and misappropriation of trade secrets. Grumman counterclaimed, alleging antitrust violations. The jury awarded DG $27,417,000 in damages, and Grumman appealed.

---

[29] The PTO has adopted guidelines for the examination of computer-related inventions. 61 CFR § 7478-02.
[30] As of the date of publication of this book, a new Article 2B of the Uniform Commercial Code is being prepared to regulate software transactions and licensing.
[31] See *Fonar Corp. v Domenick,* 105 F3d 99 (2d Cir 1997).

Decision: Judgment for DG. DG had properly registered each of the ADEX copyrights. Grumman used copyrighted ADEX diagnostic concepts software obtained from former DG employees, without authority from DG. DG was therefore entitled to appropriate damages for this infringement under the Computer Software Copyright Act. The act does not prevent the states from imposing additional liability for misappropriating trade secrets by the knowing participation in the breach of a confidentiality agreement. Grumman acquired ADEX by participating in the breach of confidentiality agreements binding on former employees and former customers and was therefore properly subject to a trade secrets violation claim. The antitrust laws were not violated, as a copyright holder may refrain from licensing a copyrighted work to a competitor. [*Data General Corp. v Grumman Systems Support Corp. 36 F3d 1147 (1st Cir 1994)*]

22. Semiconductor Chip Protection

> The SCPA gives copyright protection to mask works but limited protection from reverse engineering.

The Semiconductor Chip Protection Act of 1984 (SCPA).[32] created a new form of industrial intellectual property by protecting "mask works" and the semiconductor chip products in which they are embodied against chip piracy. **Mask work** refers to the specific form of expression embodied in chip design, including the stencils used in manufacturing semiconductor chip products. A **semiconductor chip** product is a product placed on a piece of semiconductor material in accordance with a predetermined pattern that is intended to perform electronic circuitry functions. This definition includes such products as analog chips, logic function chips like microprocessors, and memory chips like RAMs and ROMs.

(a) Duration and Qualifications for Protection. The SCPA provides the owner of a mask work fixed in a semiconductor chip product the exclusive right for ten years to reproduce and distribute the products in the United States and to import them into the United States. These rights fully apply to works first commercially exploited after November 8, 1984, the date of the law's enactment. However, the protection of the act applies only to those works that, when considered as a whole, are not commonplace, staple, or familiar in the semiconductor industry.

(b) Application Procedure. The owner of a mask work subject to protection under the SCPA must file an application for a certificate of registration with the Register of Copyrights within two years of the date of the work's first commercial exploitation. Failure to do so within this period will result in forfeiture of all rights under the act. Questions concerning the validity of the works are to be resolved through litigation or arbitration.

(c) Limitation on Exclusive Rights. Under the SCPA's reverse engineering exemption, competitors may not only study mask works but also use the results of that study to design their own semiconductor chip products embodying their own original masks even if the masks are substantially similar (but not substantially identical) so long as their products are the result of substantial study and analysis and not merely the result of plagiarism.

Innocent infringers are not liable for infringements occurring before notice of protection is given them and are liable for reasonable royalties on each unit distributed after notice has been given them. However, the continued purchasing of infringing semiconductors after notice has been given can result in penalties of up to $250,000.

---

[32] PL 98-620, 98 Stat 3347, 17 USC § 901.

Type of Intellectual Property	Trademarks	Copyrights	Patents	Trade Secrets
Protection	Words, names, symbols, or devices used to identify a product or service	Original creative works of authorship, such as writings, movies, records, and computer software	Utility, design, and plant patents	Advantageous formulas, devices, or compilation of information
Applicable Standard	Identifies and distinguishes a product or service	Original creative works in writing or in another format	New and nonobvious advances in the art	Not readily ascertainable, not disclosed to the public
Where to Apply	Patent and Trademark Office	Register of Copyrights	Patent and Trademark Office	No public registration necessary
Duration	Indefinite so long as it continues to be used	Life of author plus 50 years, or 75 years from publication for "works for hire"	Utility and plant patents, 20 years from date of application; design patents, 14 years	Indefinite so long as secret is not disclosed to public

FIGURE 10-1
Summary Comparison of Intellectual Property Rights

(d) Remedies. The SCPA provides that an infringer will be liable for actual damages and will forfeit its profits to the owner. As an alternative, the owner may elect to receive statutory damages of up to $250,000 as determined by a court. The court may also order destruction or other disposition of the products and equipment used to make the products.

ETHICS & THE LAW

In the summer of 1996, the dance song "Macarena" hit the pop music scene and charts in the United States. The line-type dance inspired by the song is called the Macarena. At camps around the country, the song was played, and children were taught the dance.

The American Society of Composers, Authors and Publishers (ASCAP) is the organization that serves as a clearinghouse for fee payments for use of copyrighted materials belonging to its members. ASCAP sent a letter to the directors of camps and nonprofit organizations sponsoring camps (Girl Scouts, Boy Scouts, Camp Fire Girls, American Cancer Association, and so forth) that warned them that licensed songs should not be used without paying ASCAP the licensing fees and that violators would be pursued. ASCAP's prices for songs are, for example, $591 for the camp season for "Edelweiss" (from *The Sound of Music*) or "This Land Is Your Land."

Some of the nonprofit-sponsored camps charge only $44 per week per camper. The directors could not afford the fees, and the camps eliminated their oldies dances and dance classes. ASCAP declined to offer discounted licensing fees for the camps.

Why did ASCAP work so diligently to protect its rights? What ethical and social responsibility issues do you see with respect to the nonprofit camps? Some of these camps are summer retreats for children who suffer from cancer, AIDS, and other terminal illnesses. Does this information change your feelings about ASCAP's fees? What would you do if you were an ASCAP member and owned the rights to a song a camp wished to use?

SUMMARY

Property rights in trademarks, copyrights, and patents are acquired as provided primarily in federal statutes. A trademark or service mark is any word, symbol, design, or combination of these used to identify a product (in the case of a trademark) or a service (in the case of a service mark). Terms will fall into one of four categories: (1) generic, (2) descriptive, (3) suggestive, or (4) arbitrary or fanciful. Generic terms are never registrable. However, if a descriptive term has acquired a secondary meaning, it is registrable. Suggestive and arbitrary marks are registrable as well. If there is likelihood of confusion, a court will enjoin the second user from using a particular registered mark.

A copyright is the exclusive right given by federal statute to the creator of a literary or an artistic work to use, reproduce, or display the work for the life of the creator and 50 years after the creator's death.

A patent gives the inventor an exclusive right for 20 years from the date of application to make, use, and sell an invention that is new and useful but not obvious to those in the business to which the invention is related. Trade secrets that give an owner an advantage over competitors are protected under state law for an unlimited period so long as they are not made public.

Protection of computer programs and the design of computer chips and mask works is commonly obtained, subject to certain limitations, by complying with federal statutes, by using the law of trade secrets, and by requiring restrictive licensing agreements. Many software developers pursue all of these means to protect their proprietary interests in their programs.

QUESTIONS AND CASE PROBLEMS

1. What qualities must an invention possess to be patentable?

2. Compare the protection afforded by a patent and the protection afforded by a trademark registration.

3. Banion manufacturers semiconductor chips. He wants to obtain protection for his mask works under federal law, particularly so that competitors will be prohibited from reverse engineering these works. Advise Banion of his legal options, if any, to accomplish his objective.

4. Jim and Eric work for Audio Visual Services (AVS) at Cramer University in Casper, Wyoming. For "expenses" of $5 and the provision of a blank tape, Jim and Eric used AVS facilities after hours to make tapes of Pearl Jam's CD *Vitology* for 25 friends or friends of friends from school. When Mrs. Mullen, who is in charge of AVS, discovered this and confronted them, Jim, a classics major, defended their actions, telling her, "It's de minimus . . . I mean, who cares?" Explain to Jim and Eric the legal and ethical ramifications of their actions.

5. Sullivan sold T-shirts with the name *Boston Marathon* and the year of the race imprinted on them. The Boston Athletic Association (BAA) sponsors and administers the Boston Marathon and has used the name *Boston Marathon* since 1917. The BAA registered the name *Boston Marathon* on the Principal Register. In 1986, the BAA entered into an exclusive license with Image, Inc., to use its service mark on shirts and other apparel. Thereafter, when Sullivan continued to sell shirts imprinted with the name *Boston Marathon*, the BAA sought an injunction. Sullivan's defense was that the general public was not being misled into thinking that his shirts were officially sponsored by the BAA. Without this confusion of source, he contended, no injunction should be issued. Decide. [*Boston Athletic Ass'n v Sullivan*, 867 F2d 22 (1st Cir)]

6. *Bambi*, written by Austrian citizen Felix Salten, was first published in Germany in the German language in 1923 without a copyright notice. A second edition was published in Germany in 1926 with a U.S. copyright notice and was timely registered in the United States in early 1927. In 1936, Salten assigned rights to the book to Sidney Franklin, who assigned his rights to Walt Disney Co. Disney released the *Bambi* motion picture in 1942, which had a derivative copyright

from the *Bambi* book. Salten died in 1945, and the copyright in the *Bambi* book was renewed in 1954 by his daughter Anna Wyler. She executed agreements with Disney concerning derivative works from the *Bambi* book. Anna died in 1977, and her husband and two children assigned their rights to Twin Books Corp. in 1993. Twin Books sought profits from the rereleased Disney motion picture through the derivative copyrights emanating from the *Bambi* book. Disney contended that the book fell into the public domain in 1951, when Anna Wyler failed to timely renew the copyright at the end of its first 28-year period after first publication in 1923. Twin Books responded that it was renewed in 1954, within 28 years after the initial copyright was secured, which was 1926. Decide.

Even if the *Bambi* book copyright was timely renewed, how did Twin Books have standing to sue Disney for profits on the rereleased animated *Bambi* motion picture when the copyright on the *Bambi* book ended 56 years after 1926, in 1982? [*Twin Books Corp. v Walt Disney Co.*, 1996 Copyright Rep (CCH) ¶ 27,518 (9th Cir)]

7. Twentieth Century Fox (Fox) owned and distributed the successful motion picture *The Commitments*. The film tells the story of a group of young Irish men and women who form a soul music band. In the film, the leader of the band, Jimmy, tries to teach the band members what it takes to be successful soul music performers. Toward that end, Jimmy shows the band members a videotape of James Brown's energetic performance of the song "Please, Please, Please." This performance came from Brown's appearance in 1965 on a TV program called the *TAMI Show*. Portions of the 1965 performance are shown in *The Commitments* in seven separate "cuts" for a total of 27 seconds. Sometimes the cuts are in the background of a scene, and sometimes they occupy the entire screen. Brown's name is not mentioned at all during these relatively brief cuts. His name is mentioned only once later in the film, when Jimmy urges the band members to abandon their current musical interests and tune in to the great soul performers, including James Brown: "Listen, from now on I don't want you listening to Guns & Roses and The Soup Dragons. I want you on a strict diet of soul. James Brown for the growls, Otis Redding for the moans, Smokey Robinson for the whines, and Aretha for the whole lot put together." Would it be fair use under U.S. copyright law for Fox to use just 27 seconds of James Brown cuts in the film without formally obtaining permission to use the cuts? Advise Fox as to what, if anything, would be necessary to protect it from a lawsuit. [See *Brown v*

Twentieth Century Fox Film Corp., 799 F Supp 166 (DDC)]

8. Sony Corp. manufactures video cassette recorders (VCRs) to tape television shows for later home viewing (time-shifting). Sony sold them under the trade name Betamax through retail establishments throughout the country. Universal City Studios and Walt Disney Productions owned the copyrights on some of the television programs that were broadcast on public airwaves. Universal and Disney brought an action against Sony and certain large retailers, contending that VCR consumers had recorded some of their copyrighted works that had been shown on commercially sponsored television and thereby infringed the copyrights. These plaintiffs sought damages and an injunction against the manufacture and marketing of VCRs. Sony contended that the noncommercial, home-use recording of material broadcast over public airwaves for later viewing was a fair use of copyrighted works. Decide. [*Sony Corp. v Universal Studios*, 464 US 417]

9. The menu commands on the Lotus 1-2-3 spreadsheet program enable users to perform accounting functions by using such commands as "Copy," "Print," and "Quit." Borland International, Inc., released its Quattro spreadsheet, a program superior to Lotus-1-2-3 that did, however, use an identical copy of the entire Lotus 1-2-3 menu tree but did not copy any of Lotus's computer code. Lotus believed that its copyright in Lotus 1-2-3 had been violated. Borland insisted that the Lotus menu command was not copyrightable because it is a method of operation foreclosed from protection under section 102(b) of the Copyright Act of 1976. Decide. [*Lotus Development Corp. v Borland International, Inc.*, 49 F3d 807, (aff'd, 1st Cir) 116 S Ct 904]

10. Diehr devised a computerized process for curing rubber that was based on a well-known mathematical formula related to the cure time, and he devised numerous other steps in his synthetic rubber-curing process. The patent examiner determined that because abstract ideas, the laws of nature, and mathematical formulas are not patentable subject matter, the process in this case (based on a known mathematical formula) was also not patentable. Diehr contended that all of the steps in his rubber-curing process were new and not obvious to the art of rubber curing. He contended also that he did not seek an exclusive patent on the mathematical formula, except for its use in the rubber-curing process. Decide. [*Diamond v Diehr*, 450 US 175]

11. Aries Information Systems, Inc., develops and markets computer software specifically designed to meet the financial accounting and reporting requirements of such public bodies as school districts and county

governments. One of Aries's principal products is the POBAS III accounting program. Pacific Management Systems Corp. was organized by Scott Dahmer, John Laugan, and Roman Rowan for marketing a financial accounting and budgeting system known as FAMIS. Dahmer, Laugan, and Rowan were Aries employees before, during, and shortly after they organized Pacific. As employees, they each gained access to Aries's software materials (including the POBAS III system) and had information about Aries's existing and prospective clients. Proprietary notices appeared on every client contract, source code list, and magnetic tape. Dahmer, Laugan, and Rowan signed an Employee Confidential Information Agreement after beginning employment with Aries. While still employees of Aries, they submitted a bid on behalf of Pacific to Rock County and were awarded the contract. Pacific's FAMIS software system is substantially identical to Aries's proprietary POBAS III system. Aries sued Pacific to recover damages for misappropriation of its trade secrets. Pacific's defense was that no "secrets" were misappropriated because many employees knew the information in question. Decide. [*Aries Information Systems, Inc. v Pacific Management Systems Corp.* (Minn App) 366 NW2d 366]

12. The plaintiff, Herbert Rosenthal Jewelry Corp., and the defendant, Kalpakian, manufactured jewelry. The plaintiff obtained a copyright registration of a jeweled pin in the shape of a bee. Kalpakian made a similar pin. Rosenthal sued Kalpakian for infringement of copyright registration. Kalpakian raised the defense that he was only copying the idea, not the way the idea was expressed. Was he liable for infringement of the plaintiff's copyright? [*Herbert Rosenthal Jewelry Corp. v Kalpakian*, 446 F2d 738 (9th Cir)]

13. Mineral Deposits Ltd. (MD Ltd.), an Australian company, manufactures the Reichert Spiral, a device used for recovering gold particles from sand and gravel. The spiral was patented in Australia, and MD Ltd. had applied for a patent in the United States. Theodore Zigan contacted MD Ltd., stating he was interested in purchasing up to 200 devices for use in his gravel pit. MD Ltd. agreed to lend Zigan a spiral for testing its efficiency. Zigan made molds of the spiral's components and proceeded to manufacture 170 copies of the device. When MD Ltd. found out that copies were being made, it demanded the return of the spiral. MD Ltd. also sought lost profits for the 170 spirals manufactured by Zigan. Recovery was sought on a theory of misappropriation of trade secrets. Zigan offered to pay for the spiral lent him by MD Ltd. He argued that trade secret protection was lost by the public sale of the spiral. What ethical values are involved? Was Zigan's conduct a violation of trade secret law? [*Mineral Deposits Ltd. v Zigan* (Colo App) 773 P2d 609]

14. From October 1965 through July 1967, Union Carbide Corp. sold certain bulbs for high-intensity reading lamps under its Eveready trademark. Carbide's sales of electrical products under the Eveready mark exceeded $100 million for every year after 1963; from 1963 to 1967, Carbide spent $50 million in advertising these products. In 1969, the defendant, Ever-Ready, Inc., imported miniature lamp bulbs for high-intensity lamps with *Ever-Ready* stamped on their base. In two surveys conducted by Carbide, 50 percent of those interviewed associated Carbide products with the marks used by Ever-Ready, Inc. Carbide sought an injunction against Ever-Ready's use of the name *Ever-Ready* on or in connection with the sale of electrical products. No monetary damages were sought. Ever-Ready, Inc., contended that Carbide's trademark Eveready was descriptive and therefore the registration of the mark was improper and invalid. Carbide raised the defense that its mark had acquired secondary meaning. Decide. [*Union Carbide Corp. v Ever-Ready, Inc.*, 531 F2d 366 (7th Cir)]

15. Anheuser-Busch made an application for registration of the trademark LA and began marketing low-alcohol beer under the LA label. Following Anheuser-Busch's introduction of its product, the Stroh Brewery Co. introduced Schaefer LA, also a low-alcohol beer. An action to enjoin Stroh's use of LA followed. Anheuser-Busch contended that the term *LA* was suggestive in that it required some imagination to connect it with the product and, accordingly, was a protectable trademark. Stroh argued that LA was generic or descriptive in nature because the term is comprised of the initials of the phrase *low alcohol*. Decide. [*Anheuser-Busch Inc. v Stroh Brewery Co.*, 750 F2d 631 (8th Cir)]

Analysis of a Court Opinion

COMPONENTS OF A COURT OPINION

The information for a case is presented in three parts: (1) the heading, (2) the facts of the case, and (3) the opinion. In this explanation, the case *Hegyes v Unjian Enterprises, Inc.*, will be used as an example.

1. HEADING
The heading of the case consists of the title and the source.

(a) Title. The title of the case usually consists of the names of the parties to the action. In the illustrative case, *Hegyes*, as plaintiff, sued *Unjian Enterprises, Inc.*, as defendant.

The title of an appealed case may not reveal who the plaintiff was or who the defendant was in the original or lower court. When the action is begun in the lower court, the first party named is the plaintiff, and the second is the defendant. When the case is appealed, the name of the party who takes the appeal may appear first on the records of the higher court, so that if the defendant takes the appeal, the original order of the names of the parties is reversed.

(b) Source. The second part of the heading gives the source of the opinion. *Hegyes v Unjian Enterprises, Inc.*, was decided by a California intermediate appellate court and is found or reported in two places. It is set forth or reported in 234 Cal App 3d 1103 and in 286 Cal Rptr 85. This means that it is found in the 234th volume of the Third series of the California Appellate Reports, beginning at page 1103. It is also found in the 286th volume of another reporter of California cases, called the California Reporter, beginning at page 85.

2. FACTS
The paragraph in smaller type following the heading is a summary of the facts of the case. This summary, written by the authors of the textbook, provides a background for an understanding and analysis of the opinion. Read the statement of facts. Keep in mind the principles of law that you studied in the chapters. Then read the opinion carefully to see how the court made its decision, what it decided, and whether it agrees with what you thought would be decided.

3. OPINION
The opinion of the court includes the name of the judge, excerpts from the reasoning of the court, and the judgment.

(a) Judge. At the beginning of the opinion is the name of the judge who wrote it. The opinion in the *Hegyes* case was written by Judge Woods.

The letter or letters following the name of the judge

indicate the judge's rank or title. *J.* stands for Judge or Justice. (*JJ.* is the plural form.) Other abbreviations include *C.J.* for Chief Justice or Circuit Judge, *D.J.* for District Judge, *P.J.* for Presiding Judge or President Judge, and *C.* for Chancellor or Commissioner.

When a case is perfectly clear and obvious, the opinion will frequently be filed without naming the writing judge and will then have a heading of "memorandum" or "per curiam."

(b) Body of the Opinion. The material following the judge's name is quoted from the opinion of the court. Words enclosed in brackets [ ] did not appear in the original opinion but have been added to explain a legal term, to identify a party, or to clarify a statement. Ellipses (three or four periods) are used to indicate that something has been omitted that is not pertinent to the point of law with which we are concerned at this time.

Decisions vary in length from less than a page to more than a hundred pages, and opinions frequently involve several points of law. The cases provided in this book has been carefully edited.

Opinions do not follow a standard pattern of organization, but usually the well-written opinion will carefully examine the arguments presented by all parties and then explain why the court accepts or rejects those arguments in whole or in part. In this process, the opinion may discuss the opinion of the lower court, the decisions in similar cases in other courts, and material from other sources.[1]

(c) Judgment. The case is concluded with a statement of the court's decision. If the case has been appealed and if the court agrees with the lower court, the decision may simply be "Judgment affirmed" or a similar expression. If the appellate court disagrees, the decision may be expressed as "Judgment reversed." "Case remanded" means that the case is returned to the lower court to proceed further in harmony with the appellate court's decision. In lower court cases when the judgment is on a narrow issue, the judgment of the court may be limited to "Objection sustained" or "Objection dismissed."

A judge of the court who disagrees with the majority may file a dissenting opinion. Such an opinion was filed in the *Hegyes* case by Judge Johnson. Dissenting opinions play an important role in the development of the law. While they are not the law today, they often begin a chain of thought that changes the law. Thus, the dissent of today often becomes the majority rule of tomorrow.

1 *See Appendix, "How to Find the Law."*

CHECKLIST FOR CASE STUDY

The questions in the following checklist will serve as a guide for the analysis of a case. It should be understood, however, that not every case will provide answers to all these questions.

1. *Court.* In what court was the action brought originally, and which court filed the opinion being studied?
2. *Parties.* Who were the parties to the action? Were they the parties to the original transaction, or were they strangers, such as creditors?
3. *Purpose of the Action.* What was the relief or remedy sought in the action?
4. *Action Appealed From.* What was done in the lower court that the appellant deemed wrong and from which the appeal was taken?
5. *Arguments of the Parties.* What were the arguments made by the respective parties?
6. *Decision of the Court.* What did the court decide?
7. *Basis for Decision.* On what authority or ground did the court base its decision? Was it common law, decision, statute, Restatement of the Law, text, logic, or the personal belief of the court?
8. *Appraisal of the Decision.* What social objectives are advanced by the decision? What social objectives are hindered or defeated by the decision? What ethical principles are involved in the case? Is the decision socially desirable? Is it practical in application? Does it give rise to any dangers?

Selected Ethical Principles or Issues to Discuss in Relation to Cases	Elementary Guidelines for an Ethical Analysis of Contemplated Action
1. Integrity and truthfulness.	1. Identify the ethical principle(s) involved in the case.
2. Promise-keeping.	2. Define the problem from the decision maker's point of view.
3. Loyalty.	3. Identify who could be injured by the contemplated action.
4. Fairness.	4. Define the problem from the opposing point of view.
5. Doing no harm.	5. Would you (as the decision maker) be willing to tell your family, your supervisor, your CEO, and the board of directors about the planned action?
6. Maintaining confidentiality.	
7. Avoiding conflict of interest.	
8. Whistleblowing.	6. Would you be willing to go before a community meeting, a congressional hearing, or a public forum to describe the action?
9. Efficiency and effectiveness (create new jobs and the products necessary for a humane life).	7. With moral common sense and full consideration of the facts and alternatives, reach a decision about whether the contemplated action should be taken.
10. Innovation.	

FIGURE 1
Guidelines to Business Ethics

Hegyes v Unjian Enterprises, Inc.

234 Cal App 3d 1103, 286
Cap Rptr 85 (1991)

Mrs. Hegyes was driving her car when it was negligently struck by a truck of Unjian Enterprises. She was injured, and an implant was placed in her body to counteract the injuries. She sued Unjian, and the case was settled. Two years later Mrs. Hegyes became pregnant. The growing fetus pressed against the implant, making it necessary to deliver the child 51 days prematurely by means of a Caesarean birth. Because of this premature birth, the child, named Cassondra, had a breathing handicap. Suit was brought against Unjian Enterprises for the harm sustained by Cassondra. The trial court dismissed the case, and an appeal was taken on behalf of Cassondra.

WOODS, A.J. . . . The trial court correctly held that no legal duty of care existed. Plaintiff urges this court to recognize a novel approach to the tort of negligence, which abandons the concept of duty and works backwards from causation. . . . The existence or nonexistence of "duty" is the initial obstacle which must be mastered before any liability for negligence is legally permissible. . . .

In a preconception tort case, as in any negligence case, there is an overwhelming need to keep liability within reasonable bounds and to limit the areas of actionable causation by applying the concept of duty. In a nonmedical preconception negligence case where there is no alleged "special relationship," it becomes more difficult to find a legal duty owed to the minor child and, hence, liability on the part of defendant. It cannot be said that, under the facts presented, defendant motorist owed a legal duty to plaintiff. . . .

. . . A claim for preconception negligence will fail, unless it satisfies all elements of an ordinary negligence cause of action. . . .

. . . A special relationship between physician and patient may, in certain circumstances where the conduct is directly related to the resulting pregnancy and birth, give rise to a duty to the subsequently conceived child. . . .

On the other hand, there is no "special relationship" between motorists. The ordinary principles of negligence apply. Those principles cannot be validly extended to encompass a duty owed to a child conceived several years after her mother was involved in an automobile accident. If plaintiff has more children who sustain injuries as a result of plaintiff's alleged condition, shall defendant once again be hailed into court? The implications associated with finding a duty under the present facts are indeed staggering, and the trial court properly refused to find one.

California precedent absolutely requires a preliminary finding of duty in order for this case to proceed. "Duty " encompasses the question of whether a defendant is under any obligation to the plaintiff to avoid negligent conduct. Here, there was no relationship between this defendant and this plaintiff which gave rise to any legal obligation on defendant's part for the benefit of plaintiff. The trial court's dismissal of plaintiff's claim for want of a legal duty was proper. In examining precedents on this issue on a national level, we conclude that an initial finding of duty is likewise a requirement . . . .

. . . The law does not countenance recovery for all injuries caused by allegedly negligent conduct. . . . On occasion, the law cannot provide a remedy. The courts must draw requisite boundaries. . . .

No legal duty is violated where the plaintiff's injury is not reasonably foreseeable. While the question of whether one owes a duty to another must be decided on a case by case basis, every case is governed by the rule of general application that persons are required to use ordinary care for the protection of those to whom harm can be reasonably foreseen. . . . This rule not only establishes, but limits, the principle of negligence liability. The court's task in determining duty is to evaluate "whether the category of negligent conduct at issue is sufficiently likely to result in the kind of harm experienced" such that liability may appropriately be imposed upon the negligent party. . . .

Defendant's conduct was not "likely to result" in plaintiff's conception or birth, let alone her alleged injuries nearly three years after the car accident. Unlike a medical professional's conduct which is directly and intentionally related to whether a child is conceived or born, such conception or birth is not a reasonably foreseeable result of the operation of a car. . . .

In determining to whom a legal duty is owed, foreseeability is the prime element by which courts are guided. However, the existence of a legal duty is not to be bottomed on the factor of foreseeability alone. The [California] Supreme Court in *Rowland v Christian*, 69 Cal.2d 108, 112, 70 Cal.Rptr. 97, 443 P.2d, 561, advanced the following considerations in evaluating whether a duty of care was owed: "The foreseeability of harm to the plaintiff, the degree of certainty that the plaintiff suffered injury, the closeness of the connection between the defendant's conduct and the injury suffered, the moral blame attached to the defendant's conduct, the policy of preventing future harm, the extent of the burden to the defendant and consequences to the community of imposing a duty to exercise care with resulting liability for breach, and the availability, cost, and prevalence of insurance for the risk involved."

The Supreme Court, however, to ensure recognition that the law does not champion legal redress for *all* foreseeable harm, stated in *Dillon v Legg* (1968) 68 Cal.2d 728, 729, 69 Cal.Rptr. 72, 441 P.2d 912: "In order to limit the otherwise potentially infinite liability which would follow every negligent act, the law of torts holds defendant amenable only for injuries to others which to defendant *at the time were reasonably foreseeable.*". . .

The court in *Dillon* sought to confine the potential reach of foreseeability by limiting it to "those risks or hazards whose likelihood made the conduct unreasonably dangerous" and, then, by evaluating the nature of the injury and its causal relation to the conduct which caused it. . . .

Soon thereafter . . . the court . . . adopted the rationale of cases which forthrightly acknowledged that *Dillon*'s limitations on duty are formed by more than lack of foreseeability. . . . Nevertheless our decision must take into account considerations in addition to logical symmetry and sympathetic appeal. . . . Not every loss can be made compensable in money damages, and legal causation must terminate somewhere. In delineating the extent of a tortfeasor's responsibility for damages under the general rule of tort liability . . . courts must locate the line between liability and nonliability at some point, a decision which is essentially political. . . .

Thus, despite the broad maxim that for every wrong there is a remedy, the courts and legislature of this state have decided that *not* all injuries are compensable at law. . . .

Even accepting, arguendo, that it is foreseeable that a woman of child bearing years may some day have a child, there are areas of foreseeable harm where legal obligation still does not arise. It must be admitted that there existed the bare *possibility* that the injury complained of in this case could result from the acts of defendant. However, the creation of a legal duty requires more than a mere possibility of occurrence since, through hindsight, everything is foreseeable.

Judicial discretion is an integral part of the duty concept in evaluating foreseeability of harm. That sentiment is best evidenced by the following comment by Dean Prosser: "In the end the court will decide whether there is a duty on the basis of the mores of the community, 'always keeping in mind the fact that we endeavor to make a rule in each case that will be practical and in keeping with the general understanding of mankind.'" (Prosser, Palsgraf Revisited (1953) 52 Mich.L.Rev. 1, 15.)

Thus, the concept of legal duty necessarily includes and expresses considerations of social policy. . . .

. . . The law requires more than a mere failure to exercise care and resulting injury. There must be a legal duty owed to the person injured. It is the breach of that duty that must be the proximate cause of the resulting injury. The determination that a duty of care exists is an essential prerequisite to liability founded on negligence. . . . In fact, since it is the breach of that duty which must be the causal factor in the injury alleged, duty must be found before causation or injury can even be considered.

. . . Plaintiff's position is that actual causation substitutes for duty, and the existence of damage obviates the necessity of a finding that duty was violated. In other words, causation and damage would become the sole elements of a cause of action for negligence, jettisoning the traditionally included elements of duty and violation of duty.

. . . In *Renslow v Mennonite Hospital*, . . . 67 Ill.2d 348, 10 Ill.Dec 484, 367 N.E.2d 1250 . . . the court *refused* to focus on the aspect of causation in rendering its opinion. Indeed, the court discounted the value of causation analysis in determining whether a child who sustains injury as a result of preconception conduct should be afforded a cause of action. The court instructed: "It has been aptly observed, however, that 'causation cannot be the answer, in a very real sense the consequences of an act go forward to eternity. . . . Any attempt to impose responsibility on such a basis would result in infinite liability for all wrongful acts, which would "set society on edge and fill the courts with endless litigation.'" Thus, policy lines, to some extent arbitrary, must be drawn to narrow an area of actionable causation. We see no inherent advantage to discarding the policy lines, defined traditionally as 'duty,' in favor of new policy lines which would be necessary to circumscribe actionable causation. *We reaffirm the utility of the concept of duty as a means by which to direct and control the course of common law.*". . .

The *Renslow* court correctly resolved that causation alone does not impute liability in a negligence context absent a preliminary finding of duty and reasonable foreseeability. California courts agree that in order to establish liabilities, there must be more than a mere failure to exercise care for a resulting injury. . . . There must be a legal duty owed to the person injured to exercise care under the circumstances, and a breach of that duty must be the proximate cause of the resulting injury. . . . The determination that a duty exists is therefore an essential precondition to liability founded on negligence.

We refuse to be persuaded by appellant's notion that causation and injury are the sole determinants of liability. . . .

[Judgment Affirmed]

Johnson, A.J., Dissenting. . . . Tortfeasors in general, including negligent automobile operators, owe a duty to post-conceived children for damages these infants later sustain as a result of injuries the tortfeasor inflicted on their mothers. . . .

. . . In *Rowland v Christian*, (1968) 69 Cal.2d 108, 70 Cal.Rptr. 97, 443 P2d 561, the California Supreme Court adopted, as a general principle, the concept contained in section 1714 of the California Civil Code which reads in part: "Everyone is responsible . . . for an injury occasioned to another by his want of ordinary care or skill in the management of his property or person.". . .

To aid in the determination of when public policy might demand a departure from this principle, the *Rowland* court set out a number of factors to be balanced. These factors are: the foreseeability of harm to the plaintiff, the degree of certainty that the plaintiff suffered injury, the closeness of the connection between the defendant's conduct and the injury suffered, the moral blame attached to the defendant's conduct, the policy of preventing future harm, the extent of the burden to the defendant and consequences to the community of imposing a duty to exercise care, and the availability, cost and prevalence of insurance for the risk involved. . . .

Applying these principles to our analysis of the present case, we must ask whether negligent operation of a motor vehicle is sufficiently likely to cause injury to an infant resulting from its premature birth. . . .

This is the appropriate question to ask, since the "category of negligent conduct" at issue is an alleged lack of reasonable care in the operation of a motor vehicle, and the "kind of harm experienced" was the respiratory condition suffered by appellant. The fact that Cassondra Hegyes was not yet born at the time of the tortious conduct is outside the scope of the court's analysis; if the condition she suffers from was sufficiently likely to result from negligent driving, a duty exists, and an inquiry questioning whether *this* plaintiff would have been foreseeably injured by *this* defendant must be determined by the jury as an element of proximate cause.

"The great majority of respiratory infections [in children] occur" in premature infants. (5 *Lawyer's Medical Cyclopedia of Personal Injuries and Allied Specialties* (3d ed. 1986) § 37.24b, p. 106.) Moreover, there is a ten-fold increase in the death rate in premature infants as compared to full-term infants, and there is a corresponding increase in the rate of serious complications in such infants who survive premature birth; "they are prone especially to pulmonary infections and brain hemorrhage.". . . Thus, it is reasonably foreseeable that premature birth would give rise to a serious injury similar to the one suffered by the appellant in the present case.

Also, it is reasonably foreseeable that a pregnant woman would be a driver, passenger, or pedestrian who could be affected by an automobile operator's failure to drive with reasonable care. Since this is the case, under California law any injury to the woman's unborn infant would give rise to a valid cause of action on behalf of the infant for personal injuries sustained prior to birth. . . .

Having established that premature birth is reasonably likely to give rise to the "kind of harm experienced" by the appellant in this case, and that it is foreseeable that the class of persons to whom the plaintiff belongs would be affected by a negligent driver, the last question must be: is it reasonably foreseeable that a woman would suffer injuries in an automobile accident which would result in the premature birth of her child?

. . . I find that it is sufficiently likely the negligent operation of a motor vehicle would give rise to the "kind of injuries experienced" by the appellant in the case. . . .

. . . There is no question that Cassondra Hegyes was injured. While premature birth in itself is no injury, attendant respiratory conditions in premature infants are potentially life-threatening. . . . Moreover, such injuries are often permanent or may require lengthy treatment or surgery to remedy. Hence, there can be no doubt that Cassondra has in fact suffered a very real injury. . . .

A motor vehicle is a powerful engine of destruction unless handled with great care and responsibility. For this reason, the law regards operating a motor vehicle to be a privilege. A driver's license is required especially so the only persons allowed to drive a car on public streets are those who have demonstrated they can operate an automobile safely and with reasonable care. The purpose of this requirement is an attempt to ensure the public safety and prevent injury to the driver and others. Thus, one who fails to observe the standards necessary to accomplish this goal is putting his own and innocent lives at risk. Significant moral blame must inevitably attach to one who operates something so dangerous to life and limb in a careless manner.

Assuming the truth of appellant's allegations the respondent failed to exercise ordinary care in the operation of a motor vehicle, and this failure resulted in appellant's injuries, an additional measure of moral blame attaches to respondent's conduct. . . . There is a right to be born free from prenatal injuries foreseeably caused by a breach of duty to the child's mother. . . . A person who interferes with this right wrongfully deprives the infant of the opportunity to begin life free of injuries which would not have existed but for the actor's tortious conduct. Cassondra's premature birth and resulting respiratory problems must be taken to have constituted serious injury to one who had no choice but to incur the one, and who may never experience life without the other. Thus, at least as much moral blame attaches to respondent's conduct in this case as in that of any other automobile negligence case which seriously injures someone.

There is, of course, nothing lost and everything to be gained from encouraging motorists to exercise reasonable care while driving. There already exists a strong public policy in favor of preventing injury due to negligent operation of a motor vehicle. To the extent a finding of liability in this case would encourage automobile operators to act with even greater care, the policy of preventing future harm to victims of automobile accidents, including post-conceived children, would be advanced by such a finding. . . .

Automobile drivers already have a duty to exercise ordinary care under the circumstances towards other drivers, passengers and pedestrians they may encounter. Yet our streets and highways still witness far too many deaths and injuries. Any extra burden placed on drivers by making them responsible to post-conceived children—and it seems unlikely to be a significant burden—would only serve to increase the degree of care drivers must exercise. I seriously doubt many would contend the present burden is so heavy and drivers already are so careful we should not increase the burden or enhance the degree of care any further than we already have. As for the community at large, the consequences, at worst and at best, would be fewer automobile accidents and thus fewer deaths and injuries. This would be a welcome—not an unfortunate—consequence.

Realistically, however, recognizing drivers have a duty toward post-conceived children is unlikely to impose a significant new burden on the driving population nor achieve a significant improvement in the standard of care exhibited on our streets and highways. Compared to the millions of people toward whom drivers already owe a duty of care, the handful of post-conceived children whose injuries they might proximately cause represent an infinitesimal increment—like a single sliver of straw dropped on a haystack. . . .

Upon balancing these factors I find the facts of the instant case do not warrant an exception to the general rule stated in *Rowland* . . . I find the kind of injury alleged by appellant in this case is a reasonably foreseeable result of the respondent's alleged negligent driving. . . .

Respondent's alleged activity carries a heavy measure of moral blame. The public policy of preventing injury due to automobile accidents is furthered by imposition of a duty of care on drivers to prevent injury to post-conceived children. . . . Since the standard of care which drivers must exercise to prevent such injury is the standard which already exists towards other motorists and pedestrians, neither the respondent nor the public is burdened by the finding of such a duty. Indeed, to the extent the burden is increased so is the incentive to drive safely which would represent a benefit not a burden for the public. Finally, insuring drivers against harm caused by automobile accidents is one of the main functions of insurance in our society today and [insurance] is required to be purchased by every California driver. There is no reason to believe the cost of automobile insurance would rise appreciably—if at all—were we to recognize drivers owed a duty toward post-conceived children.

. . . I conclude tortfeasors—including automobile drivers—owe a duty of care which extends to post-conceived children whose injuries are the proximate result of the tortfeasor's act. . . . I would remand for further proceedings which might or might not establish the requisite causal connection.

Questions

1. In paragraph 2 of the portion of the majority opinion printed here, the court states that "there is an overwhelming need to keep liability within reasonable bounds and to limit the areas of actionable causation by applying the concept of duty." Appraise this statement in terms of logic, ethics, and the social forces that make the law.
2. What does the first paragraph of the opinion printed here mean when the court says that it will not "work backwards from causation"?
3. Does the foreseeability test require that the harm be probable?
4. In the 13th paragraph of the portion of the majority opinion printed here, it is stated that the "courts must locate the line between liability and nonliability at some point, a decision which is essentially political." Does this mean that the people vote on the matter?
5. Which opinion, the majority opinion or the dissent, do you think produces the better result? Explain.

PART 2

Contracts

Nature and Classes of Contracts

OBJECTIVES

After studying this chapter, you should be able to

1. *List the essential elements of a contract;*
2. *Describe the way in which a contract arises;*
3. *State how contracts are classified;*
4. *Differentiate contracts from agreements that are not contracts;*
5. *Differentiate formal contracts from simple contracts;*
6. *Differentiate express contracts from implied contracts; and*
7. *Differentiate contractual liability from quasi-contractual liability.*

Practically every business transaction affecting anyone involves a contract.

A. NATURE OF CONTRACTS

This introductory chapter will familiarize you with the terminology needed to work with contract law. In addition, the chapter introduces quasi contracts, which are not true contracts but rather obligations imposed by law.

1. Definition of a Contract

A contract is a binding agreement.

A **contract** is a legally binding agreement.[1] By one definition, "a contract is a promise or a set of promises for the breach of which the law gives a remedy, or the performance of which the law in some way recognizes as a duty."[2] Contracts arise out of agreements, so a contract may be defined as an agreement creating an obligation.

The substance of the definition of a contract is that by mutual agreement or assent the parties create enforceable duties or obligations. That is, each party is legally bound to do or to refrain from doing certain acts.

2. Elements of a Contract

Supported By consideration means?

The elements of a contract are (1) an agreement (2) between competent parties (3) based on the genuine assent of the parties that is (4) supported by consideration, (5) made for a lawful objective, and (6) in the form required by law, if any. These elements will be considered in the chapters that follow.

3. Subject Matter of Contracts

A contract can involve any lawful transaction.

The subject matter of a contract may relate to the performance of personal services, such as contracts of employment to work on an assembly line, to work as a secretary, to sing on television, or to build a house. A contract may provide for the transfer of ownership of property, such as a house (real property) or an automobile (personal property), from one person to another. A contract may also call for a combination of these things. *For example*, a builder may contract to supply materials and do the work involved in installing the materials, or a person may contract to build a house and then transfer the house and the land to the buyer.

4. Parties to a Contract

Parties to a contract may be decribed generally as promisor or obligor and promisee or obligee.

privity is what?

The person who makes a promise is the **promisor**, and the person to whom the promise is made is the **promisee**. If the promise is binding, it imposes on the promisor a duty or obligation, and the promisor may be called the **obligor**. The promisee who can claim the benefit of the obligation is called the **obligee**. The parties to a contract are said to stand in privity with each other, and the relationship between them is termed *privity of contract*.

---

[1] The Uniform Commercial Code defines *contract* as "the total legal obligation which results from the parties' agreement as affected by [the UCC] and any other applicable rules of law." UCC § 1–201(11).
[2] Restatement (Second) of Contracts § 1.

In written contracts, parties may be referred to by name. More often, however, they are given special names that serve to better identify each party. For example, consider a contract by which one person agrees that another may occupy a house upon the payment of money. The parties to this contract are called landlord and tenant, or lessor and lessee, and the contract between them is known as a lease. Parties to other types of contracts also have distinctive names, such as vendor and vendee for the parties to a sales contract, shipper and carrier for the parties to a transportation contract, and insurer and insured for the parties to an insurance policy.

It takes two parties to make a contract. Consequently, when the board of directors of a bank voted in favor of merging with another enterprise, the vote did not constitute a contract between the bank and that enterprise to merge.[3]

A party to a contract may be an individual, a partnership, a corporation, or a government. A party to a contract may be an agent acting on behalf of another person.

CASE SUMMARY

Watch Your Step; Watch Your Signature

Facts: High Country Ceramics, Inc., sought to get a loan from New Mexico National Bank. As a condition to getting the loan, the company's president and vice-president would have to sign a guarantee making them both personally liable for the debt should High Country default on repayment. Richard Moore, the company's vice-president, signed the guarantee "Richard Moore" without reference to his position as a corporate officer of High Country. Shortly after the loan was made the bank became insolvent and the FDIC assumed its remaining assets. High Country later defaulted on the loan and the FDIC sued Moore for the amount of the loan under the guarantee agreement.

Decision: Judgment against Moore. He signed his own name. There is nothing to show that he was signing as vice president on behalf of the corporation. Accordingly, it was his contract, and he was personally liable. [*FDIC v Moore (NM) 879 P2d 78 (1994)*]

One or more persons may be on each side of a contract. Some contracts are three-sided, as in a credit card transaction, which involves the company issuing the card, the holder of the card, and the business furnishing goods and services on the basis of the credit card.

If a contract is written, the persons who are the parties and who are bound by it will ordinarily be determined by reading what the paper says and seeing how it is signed. A contract binds only the parties to the contract. It cannot impose a duty on a person who is not a party to it.[4] Ordinarily, only a party to a contract has any rights against another party to the contract.[5] In some cases, third persons have rights on a contract as third-party beneficiaries or assignees. But a person cannot be bound by the terms of a contract to which that person is not a party.[6]

---

3 *Standard Federal Bank v Bisys Group* (DC Mich) 920 F Supp 751 (1995).
4 *Continental Casualty Co. v Campbell Design Group, Inc.* (Mo App) 914 SW2d 43 (1996).
5 *Hooper v Yakima County* (Wash App) 904 P2d 1193 (1995).
6 *Walsh v Telesector Resources Group, Inc.*, 40 Mass App 227, 662 NE2d 1043 (1996).

A contract is created when an offer is accepted.

5. How a Contract Arises

A contract is based on an agreement. An agreement arises when one person, the **offeror,** makes an offer and the person to whom the offer is made, the **offeree,** accepts. There must be both an offer and an acceptance. If either is lacking, there is no contract.[7]

> **CASE SUMMARY**
>
> ## Wishing You Had a Contract Isn't Enough
>
> **Facts:** Boise Cascade gave its employees a handbook that stated that it was the policy of the company to retain employees. The handbook clearly stated that it was not a contract between Boise Cascade and its employees. Raedlin took a job with Boise Cascade. He was later fired. He claimed that this was improper because it violated provisions of the employees' handbook.
>
> **Decision:** Judgment for Boise Cascade. The handbook made it clear that its terms did not constitute a contract with its employees. Consequently, an employee could not sue Boise Cascade for a "breach" of the handbook. [Raedlin v Boise Cascade Corp. (Idaho) 931 P2d 621 (1996)]

6. Intent to Make a Binding Agreement

The parties must intend that their agreement be binding.

Because a contract is based on the consent of the parties and is a legally binding agreement, it follows that the parties must have an intent to enter into an agreement that is binding. Sometimes the parties are in agreement, but their agreement does not produce a contract. Sometimes there is merely a preliminary agreement, but the parties never actually make a contract, or there is merely an agreement as to future plans or intentions without any contractual obligation to carry out those plans or intentions.

7. Freedom of Contract

In the absence of some ground for declaring a contract void or voidable, parties may make such contracts as they choose. The law does not require parties to be fair, or kind, or reasonable, or to share gains or losses equitably.

B. CLASSES OF CONTRACTS

Contracts are classified according to their form, the way in which they were created, their binding character, and the extent to which they have been performed.

8. Formal and Informal Contracts

Contracts can be classified as formal or informal contracts.

Sealed contracts, contracts of record, and negotiable instruments are formal contracts.

(a) Formal Contracts. Formal contracts are enforced because the formality with which they are executed is considered sufficient to signify that the parties intend to be bound by their terms. Formal contracts include (1) contracts under seal, (2) contracts of record, and (3) negotiable instruments.

---

[7] *Orcutt v S&L Paint Contractors, Ltd* (NM App) 791 P2d 71 (1990).

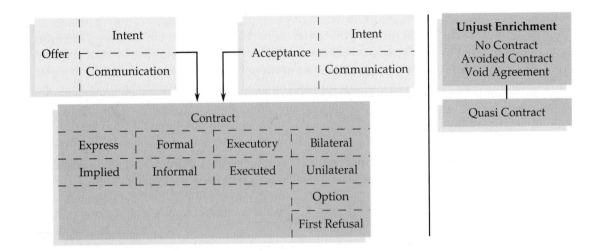

FIGURE 11-1
*Contractual
Liability*

C
P
A

(1) Contracts under Seal. A contract under seal is executed by affixing a seal or making an impression on the paper or on some adhering substance, such as wax, attached to the document. Although at common law an impression was necessary, the courts now treat various signs or marks to be the equivalent of a seal. Most states hold that there is a seal if a person's signature or a corporation's name is followed by a scroll or scrawl, the word *seal,* or the letters *L.S.*[8] In some jurisdictions, the body of the contract must recite that the parties are sealing the contract in addition to their making a seal following their signatures.[9]

A contract under seal was binding at common law solely because of its formality. In many states, this has been changed by statute. The Uniform Commercial Code makes the law of seals inapplicable to the sale of goods. In some states the law of seals has been abolished generally without regard to the nature of the transaction involved.

Unless expressly required by statute or administrative regulation, a seal is not needed to make a binding contract. The parties have the freedom of choice to use or do without a seal.

(2) Contracts of Record. A **contract of record** is an agreement or obligation that has been recorded by a court. One form of contract of record arises when one acknowledges before a proper court the obligation to pay a certain sum unless a specified condition is met. For example, a party who has been arrested may be released on a promise to appear in court and may agree to pay a certain sum on failing to do so. An obligation of this kind is known as a **recognizance.**

Similarly, an agreement made with an administrative agency is binding because it has been so made. ◆ *For example,* when a business agrees with the Federal Trade Commission that the enterprise will stop a particular practice that the commission regards as unlawful, the business is bound by its agreement and cannot thereafter reject it. ◆

---

[8] Some authorities explain L.S. as an abbreviation for *Locus Sigilium* (place for the seal).
[9] *Dunes South Homeowners Ass'n, Inc. v First Flight Builders, Inc.* (NC App) 451 SE2d 636 (1994) (corporate seal).

All contracts
other than formal
contracts are
informal or simple.

(b) Informal Contracts. All contracts other than formal contracts are called **informal** (or **simple**) **contracts** without regard to whether they are oral or written. These contracts are enforceable, not because of the form of the transaction, but because they represent agreement of the parties.

9. Express and Implied Contracts

Simple contracts may be classified as express contracts or implied contracts according to the way they are created.

Contracts may be
expressed by words or
implied from conduct.

(a) Express Contracts. An **express contract** is one in which the agreement of the parties is manifested by their words, whether spoken or written.

(b) Implied Contracts. An **implied contract** (or, as sometimes stated, a contract implied in fact) is one in which the agreement is shown not by words, written or spoken, but by the acts and conduct of the parties. *For example,* such a contract arises when one person renders services under circumstances indicating that payment for them is expected and the other person, knowing such circumstances, accepts the benefit of those services.[10] Similarly, when an owner requests a professional roofer to make repairs to the roof of a building, an obligation arises to pay the reasonable value of such services, although no agreement has been made about compensation.

In terms of effect, there is no difference between an implied contract and an express contract. The difference relates solely to the manner of proving the existence of the contract. However, in the case of an implied contract, the plaintiff has the burden of proving the value of the services performed or property sold.[11]

An implied contract cannot arise when there is an existing express contract on the same subject. However, the existence of a written contract does not bar recovery on an implied contract for extra work that was not covered by the contract.[12]

No contract is implied when the relationship of the parties is such that, by a reasonable interpretation, the performance of services or the supplying of goods was intended as a gift. The fact that the services are rendered by a neighbor does not show that the services were rendered as a gift.[13]

10. Valid and Voidable Contracts and Void Agreements

Contracts may be classified in terms of enforceability or validity.

A binding agreement
is a valid contract.
If set aside, it is
voidable.

(a) Valid Contracts. A **valid contract** is an agreement that is binding and enforceable.

(b) Voidable Contracts. A voidable contract is an agreement that is otherwise binding and enforceable, but because of the circumstances surrounding its execution or the lack of capacity of one of the parties, it may be rejected at the option of one of the parties. For example, a person who has been forced to sign an agreement that that person would not have voluntarily signed may, in some instances, avoid the contract.

---

[10] *Vortt Exploration Co. v Chevron U.S.A., Inc.* (Tex) 787 SW2d 942 (1990).
[11] *Gioffre v Simakis* (Ohio App) 594 NE2d 1013 (1991).
[12] *Jensen Construction Co. v Dallas County* (Tex App) 920 SW2d 761 (1996).
[13] *Estate of Holtmeyer v Piontek* (Mo App) 913 SW2d 352 (1996).

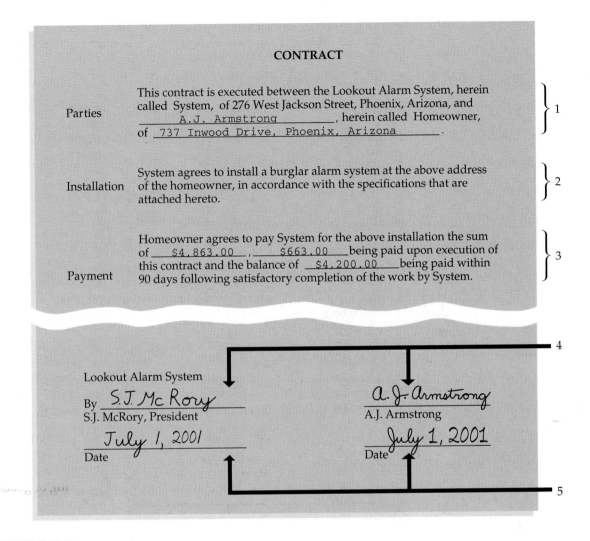

FIGURE 11-2
Contract

something may be unlawful in this type of

An agreement that
cannot be enforced
is void.

(c) Void Agreements. A **void agreement** is without legal effect. An agreement that contemplates the performance of an act prohibited by law is usually incapable of enforcement; hence it is void. Likewise, it cannot be made binding by later approval or ratification.[14]

agreement?

11. Executed and Executory Contracts

Contracts may be classified as executed contracts and executory contracts according to the extent to which they have been performed.

---

[14] Although the distinction between a void agreement and a voidable contract is clear in theory, there is frequently confusion. Some courts describe a given transaction as void, while others regard it as merely voidable.

A contract is executed when it is fully performed. It is executory if anything is yet to be done.

(a) Executed Contracts. An **executed contract** is one that has been completely performed. In other words, an executed contract is one under which nothing remains to be done by either party.[15] A contract may be executed at once, as in the case of a cash sale, or it may be executed or performed in the future.

(b) Executory Contracts. In an **executory contract,** something remains to be done by one or both parties. For example, if a utility company agrees to furnish electricity to a customer for a specified period of time at a stipulated price, the contract is executory. If the entire price is paid in advance, the contract is still deemed executory, although, strictly speaking, it is executed on one side and executory on the other.

12. Bilateral and Unilateral Contracts

In making an offer, the offeror is in effect extending a promise to do something, such as pay a sum of money, if the offeree will do what the offeror requests. Contracts are classified as bilateral or unilateral. Some bilateral contracts look ahead to the making of a later contract. Depending on their terms, these are called option contracts or first-refusal contracts.

A bilateral contract is formed by the exchange of promises.

(a) Bilateral Contract. If the offeror extends a promise and asks for a promise in return and if the offeree accepts the offer by making the promise, the contract is called a **bilateral contract.** One promise is given in exchange for another, and each party is bound by the obligation. For example, when the house painter offers to paint the owner's house for $2,700 and the owner promises to pay $2,700 for the job, there is an exchange of promises, and the agreement gives rise to a bilateral contract.

A unilateral contract is formed by doing the act called for by the offer.

I promise for act in Exchange for promise of Reward

(b) Unilateral Contract. In contrast with a bilateral contract, the offeror may offer to do something only when something is done by the offeree. ~~Because only one party is obligated to perform after the contract has been made~~, this kind of contract is called a **unilateral contract.**[16] This is illustrated by the case of the reward for the return of lost property. The offeror does not wish to have promises by members of the public that they will try to return the property. The offeror wants the property and promises to pay anyone who returns the property. The offer of a unilateral contract calls for an act; a promise to do the act does not give rise to a contract.

An option gives the holder an absolute right to make a described contract. A right of first refusal does not give the holder any right until the other party chooses to make an offer.

(c) Option and First-Refusal Contracts. The parties may make a contract that gives a right to one of them to enter into a second contract at a later date. If one party has an absolute right to enter into the later contract, the initial contract is called an **option contract.** Thus, a bilateral contract may be made today giving one of the parties the right to buy the other party's house for a specified amount. This is an option contract because the party with the privilege has the freedom of choice, or option, to buy or not buy. If the option is exercised, the other party to the contract must follow the terms of the option and enter into the second contract. If the option is never exercised, no second contract ever arises, and the offer protected by the option contract merely expires.

---

[15] *Marsh v Rheinecker,* ____ Ill App 3d ____, ____ Ill Dec ____, 641 NE2d 1256 (1994).
[16] *Anderson v Douglas & Lomason Co.* (Iowa) 540 NW2d 277 (1995).

In contrast with an option contract, a contract may merely give a **right of first refusal.** This imposes only the duty to make the first offer to the party having the right of first refusal. For example, the homeowner could make a contract providing that, should the owner desire to sell at some future time, the other party to the contract could buy either at a fixed price or at a price matching a good-faith bid by a third person. Here the homeowner cannot be required to sell, but if the owner attempts to sell, an option immediately comes into existence by which the other party can buy or not buy.[17]

Sometimes a question may arise over whether there is a contract to sell, an option to buy, or a right of first refusal. In all cases, the answer is determined by the intent of the parties. In any case, the nonparty seeking to obtain the benefit of the contract must show there has been compliance with a time limitation or other restrictions specified by the contract.

13. Quasi Contracts

> Quasi contracts are obligations imposed by law.

In some cases, a court will impose an obligation even though there is no contract. Such an obligation is called a **quasi contract,** which is an obligation imposed by law.[18] A quasi contract is a contract that is implied in law as distinguished from a contract implied in fact (discussed in section 9 (b) of this chapter). A contract that is implied in law is not a contract at all. It is merely a fictitious promise that the law assumes in order to do justice by enforcing a duty or righting a wrong.[19]

> Quasi contracts are implied to prevent unjust enrichment when there is no contract between the parties, the contract has been avoided, or the agreement of the parties is void.

(a) Prevention of Unjust Enrichment. Quasi contracts are recognized in a limited number of situations to attain an equitable or just result. Recovery in these cases is not based on any fault of the defendant but merely on the fact that the defendant has been unjustly enriched by having received a benefit to which he or she was not entitled. Conversely, a party who is free from fault and is merely receiving the benefit provided by the contract is not unjustly enriched.[20]

CASE SUMMARY

No Free Rides

Facts: PIC Realty leased farmland to Southfield Farms. After Southfield harvested its crop, it cultivated the land in preparation for the planting of the following year. However, its lease expired, so that it did not plant that crop. It then sued PIC for reimbursement for the reasonable value of the services and materials used in preparing the land, as this was a benefit to PIC. There was evidence that it was customary for landlords to compensate tenants for such work.

Decision: Southfield was entitled to recover the reasonable value of the benefit conferred upon PIC. This was necessary in order to prevent the unjust enrichment of PIC. [*PIC Realty Corp. v Southfield Farms, Inc. (Tex App) 832 SW2d 610 (1992)*]

---

17 *Bidache, Inc. v Martin* (Wyo) 889 P2d 872 (1995).
18 *Dana, Larson, Roubal and Associates v Board of Commissioners of Canyon County* (Idaho App) 864 P2d 632 (1993).
19 *Hercules Inc. v United States,* 116 S Ct 981, 134 L Ed 2d 47 (1996).
20 *Guaranty National Ins. Co. v Denver Roller, Inc.,* ____ Ala ____, 854 SW2d 312 (Ark 1993).

(1) No Contract. In some cases, the hoped-for contract is never formed. The parties expect a contract, but something happens that prevents their reaching a final agreement. Meanwhile, one or more of the parties may have acted prematurely and begun performing as though there were a contract. When it is finally clear that there is no contract, a party who had rendered some performance will seek to be paid for what was done. The claim will be made that if payment is not made, the other party will be unjustly enriched.

The no-contract case may arise in a situation where there is a mistake regarding the subject matter of the contract. For example, a painter may begin painting Adam's house because of a mistake about the address of the building. Adam sees the work going on and realizes the painter is making a mistake but does not stop the painter. When the painter finishes the work and presents a bill, Adam refuses to pay because there was never a contract: Adam never expressly agreed to the painting. Likewise, Adam's conduct never caused the painter as a reasonable person to believe that Adam was entering into a contract. (There was no contract implied in fact.) The painter just assumed that everything was all right. In such a case, however, the law deems it inequitable that Adam should have remained silent and then reaped the benefits of the painter's mistake. Adam will therefore be required to pay the painter the reasonable value of the painting. This liability is described as **quasi-contractual.**

The mistake that benefits the defendant may be the mistake of a third person.

CASE SUMMARY

Who Pays the Piper?

Facts: When improvements or buildings are added to real estate, the real estate tax assessment is usually increased to reflect the increased value of the property. Frank Partipilo and Elmer Hallman owned neighboring tracts of land. In 1977 Hallman made improvements to his land, constructing a new building and driveway on the tract. The tax assessor made a mistake concerning the location of the boundary line between Partipilo's and Hallman's land and thought the improvements were made on Partipilo's property. Instead of increasing the taxes on Hallman's land, the assessor wrongly increased the taxes on Partipilo's land. Partipilo paid the increased taxes for three years. When he learned why his taxes had been increased, he sued Hallman for the amount of the increase that Partipilo had been paying. Hallman raised the defense that he had not done anything wrong and that the mistake had been the fault of the tax assessor.

Decision: Judgment for Partipilo. Since the improvements were made to Hallman's land, Hallman should be the one to pay the tax increase. When it was paid by Partipilo, Hallman received a benefit to which he was not entitled. This was an unjust enrichment. Therefore, Partipilo could recover the amount of the increased taxes without regard to the fact that Hallman was free of any fault and that the only fault in the case was the fault of the tax assessor. [*Partipilo v Hallman,* 156 Ill App 3d 806, 109 Ill Dec 387, 510 NE2d 8 (1987)]

When there is no contract because essential terms are missing, but the plaintiff performs the services called for by the contemplated contract, the defendant receiving those services must pay their reasonable value to avoid unjust enrichment—that is, getting services without paying for them.[21]

---

[21] *Professional Recruiters, Inc. v Oliver,* ____ Neb ____, 456 NW2d 1 (1990).

Professor Arthur Bernstein was asked by the Association of Oil and Gas Executives (AOGE) to conduct a session on business ethics at the group's annual meeting in Houston, Texas. Professor Bernstein, a member of the faculty at UCLA, agreed to conduct the session for an honorarium of $1,200 plus travel expenses. The agreement between Professor Bernstein and AOGE was an oral one completed over the phone.

The professor took an early-morning flight from Los Angeles to Houston to conduct his 3:30 P.M. session for AOGE. Because Houston was experiencing severe thunderstorms and the Dallas airport was under fog, Professor Bernstein's flight could not land in either Houston or Dallas until 8 P.M. Professor Bernstein called the AOGE offices and left word about the difficulties. The plane was low on fuel and was routed to San Antonio for refueling.

At 3:30 P.M. (Houston time), the pilot offered anyone on board the opportunity to deplane and catch flights out of San Antonio. Professor Bernstein deplaned and caught a 4:30 flight back to Los Angeles because he would not be able to get to Houston on time.

When he returned, Professor Bernstein submitted a bill to AOGE for his airfare of $598. AOGE refused to pay and wrote in a letter, "Frankly, we're a bit surprised that you would submit a bill. We received absolutely no benefit from you. We were left without a presentation."

Professor Bernstein responded, "Frankly, I'm surprised that you can't compromise on the airfare. I put in a great deal of time preparing for my presentation, and I spent an entire day on an airplane trying to get there. I certainly had no benefit. And we had an understanding on travel expenses."

After you review the legal standing of these parties, consider the ethical issues. Is the weather anyone's fault? Did Professor Bernstein act in good faith? Is there unjust enrichment on the part of AOGE? Is AOGE's refusal to pay the airfare an ethical position? What would you do?

(2) The Avoided Contract. In some situations, one party to the contract may be able to avoid it or set it aside. The contract of a minor, for example, can be avoided. If the contract was for something necessary received by the minor, the minor must pay the reasonable value of what was received. The minor is not required to pay the contract price but only the reasonable value of the benefit received. As the liability enforced against the minor is not based on the contract, it is called quasi-contractual.

Likewise, when the parties rescind or set aside their contract, a party who has already conferred a benefit on the other party before the contract was rescinded may recover in a quasi contract for the value of the benefit. Thus, a contractor may recover for the value of an irrigation system installed on the defendant's land before the construction contract was set aside.[22]

(3) The Void Agreement. In some instances, the parties make a contract, and one of them receives the contract's benefit but then seeks to avoid paying on the ground that the contract was void because of illegality. An example might involve

---

[22] *Murdock-Bryant Construction Inc. v Pearson* (Ariz) 703 P2d 1197 (1985).

a government unit, such as a city, which must generally advertise for the lowest responsible bidder when a contract is to be made to obtain supplies or construct buildings. City officials might improperly skip advertising either because they have a corrupt purpose or because they honestly, but wrongly, believe a particular contract came within an exception to the advertising requirement. Whatever the reason, the officials may enter into a contract with a contractor without following statutory procedures. When the contractor requests payment after fully performing the contract, the city officials refuse to live up to the contract on the ground that it violated statutory requirements and was therefore illegal and void. In such a case a court may hold that, although the contract is void, the city must pay the reasonable value of what has been done. In this way, the contractor gets paid for what he or she really did, and the city is not required to pay for more than it actually received. The danger of the city's paying inflated prices, which was the evil that the advertising statute sought to avoid, does not arise because the court in this example did require the city to pay not the contract price but only the reasonable value of the benefit conferred on the city.

(b) When Quasi-Contractual Liability Does Not Exist. While the objective of the quasi contract is to do justice, one must not jump to the conclusion that a quasi contract arises every time there is an injustice. The mere fact that someone has benefited someone else without being paid will not necessarily give rise to a quasi contract.

> A quasi contract is not implied because there are unexpected costs, when there is an existing contract, when there is no unjust enrichment, or when the benefit was intended as a gift.

(1) Unexpected Cost. The fact that performance of a contract proves more difficult or more expensive than had been expected does not entitle a party to extra compensation when there was no misrepresentation of the conditions that would be encountered or the events that would occur. Courts are particularly unwilling to allow extra compensation when the complaining party is experienced with the particular type of contract and the problems that are likely to be encountered. In other words, the contractor is not entitled to quasi-contractual recovery for extra expense on the theory that the extra work had conferred a greater benefit than had been contemplated.

(2) Existing Contract. A plaintiff cannot sue in *quantum meruit,* or for reasonable value, when there is an express contract fixing the amount due.[23] In other words, a person cannot recover for the reasonable value of goods or services when an existing contract obligates the obligor to pay a set price for the goods or services rendered.

A subcontractor doing work that benefits a homeowner can sue only the contractor on the contract between the subcontractor and the contractor. The subcontractor cannot sue the owner merely because the owner was benefited by the work done by the subcontractor. Likewise, when a distributor of tires is not paid by a dealer, the distributor cannot sue the customer who bought the tires from the dealer for the bill that the dealer should have paid the distributor.

---

[23] *Threadgill v Farmers Ins. Exchange* (Tex App) 912 SW2d 264 (1995).

One Contract's Enough

Facts: La-Man made a contract with the city of Corpus Christi to build a recreation center. He purchased iron beams required for the construction from Heldenfels Brothers. He did not pay them for the beams. They then sued the city, claiming that the city would be unjustly enriched if they were not paid for the beams.

Decision: The Brothers had a contract claim against the contractor. It therefore could not sue the city on the theory that the city had been unjustly enriched. [*City of Corpus Christi v Heldenfels Brothers, Inc. (Tex App) 802 SW2d 35 (1990)*]

(3) No Unjust Enrichment. To recover in quasi contract, the plaintiff must prove that the defendant was enriched, the extent or dollar value of such enrichment, and that such enrichment was unjust. If the plaintiff cannot prove all these elements, there can be no recovery in quasi contract. A creditor receiving the money that is owed is not thereby unjustly enriched.

(4) Gift Benefit. There can be no recovery for unjust enrichment when the circumstances are such that it is reasonable to conclude that goods or services were furnished to the benefited party with the intent to make a gift and not in the expectation of being compensated.[24]

(5) Conferring of Unwanted Benefit. When a person confers a benefit that is not wanted, there can be no quasi-contractual recovery for the value of that benefit. Consequently, when a contractor begins building on a lot without the owner's consent and continues to build after the owner notifies the contractor to stop, the contractor cannot recover in quasi contract for the benefit conferred by the improvements made to the lot.[25]

> Quasi-contractual recovery is limited to the reasonable value of the benefit conferred.

(c) Extent of Recovery. When recovery is allowed in quasi contract, the plaintiff recovers the reasonable value of the benefit conferred on the defendant.[26] The fact that the plaintiff may have sustained greater damages, or have been put to greater expense, is ignored. Thus, the plaintiff cannot recover lost profits or other kinds of damages that would be recovered in a suit for breach of a contract.

SUMMARY

A contract is a binding agreement between two or more parties. A contract arises when an offer is accepted with contractual intent (the intent to make a binding agreement).

Contracts may be classified in a number of ways according to form, the way in which they were created, validity, and obligations. With respect to form, a contract may be either informal or formal, such as those under seal or those appearing on the records of courts or administrative agencies. Contracts may be classified by the way they were created as those that are expressed by words—written or oral—and those that are implied or deduced from conduct. The question of validity requires distinguishing between contracts that are valid; those that are voidable; and those that are not contracts at all but are merely void agreements. Contracts can be distinguished

---

24 As noted in section 9(b) of this chapter, no implied contract arises in this situation.
25 *Smith Development, Inc. v Flood,* ____ Ga App ____, 403 SE2d 249 (1991).
26 *Ramsey v Ellis* (Wis) 484 NW2d 331 (1992).

on the basis of the obligations created as executed contracts, in which everything has been performed, and executory contracts, in which something remains to be done. The bilateral contract is formed by exchanging a promise for a promise, so each party has the obligation of thereafter rendering the promised performance. In the unilateral contract, which is the doing of an act in exchange for a promise, no further performance is required of the offeree who performed the act. The only obligation is that of the promisor.

In certain situations, the law regards it as unjust for a person to receive a benefit and not pay for it. In such a case, the law of quasi contracts allows the performing person to recover the reasonable value of the benefit conferred on the benefited person even though no contract between them requires any payment. Unjust enrichment, which a quasi contract is designed to prevent, sometimes arises when there was never any contract between the persons involved or when there was a contract, but for some reason it was avoided or held to be merely a void agreement. Quasi-contractual recovery is not allowed merely because someone loses money.

QUESTIONS AND CASE PROBLEMS

1. What social forces that shape the law (from the list in chapter 3, section 8) are illustrated by the following quotation: "A person shall not be allowed to enrich himself unjustly at the expense of another." *Note*: As you study the various rules of law in this chapter and the chapters that follow, consider each rule in relationship to its social, economic, and ethical background. Try to determine the particular objective(s) of each important rule. To the extent that you are able to analyze law as the product of society's striving for justice, you will have greater insight into the law itself, the world in which you live, the field of business, and the human mind.

2. What is a contract?

3. Karl sent letters to names randomly selected from the phone book. Each letter stated: "It is agreed that we will paint your house for a price based on the cost of our labor and paint plus an additional 10 percent for profit." Maria received such a letter. Is there a contract between Karl and Maria? *no Because it has to accepted by maria*

4. Henry made a written contract to paint Betty's house for $500. The reasonable value of this work was $1,000. Henry made the price low in the hope that Betty's neighbors would have him paint their houses. He painted Betty's house but did not get work from the neighbors. He then sent Betty a bill for $1,000 on the ground that an implied contract existed to pay him the reasonable value of his services. Was he entitled to recover $1,000? *no Because he signed a contract*

5. Stephen said to Hilda, "I want to buy your old car." She replied, "It's yours for $400." Stephen replied, "I'll take it." Later Stephen changed his mind and refused to take or pay for the car. When Hilda sued him for damages, he contended that he had never made a contract with her because they had never expressly stated, "We hereby make a contract for the sale of the car." Stephen claimed that, in the absence of such an express declaration showing that they intended to make a contract, there could not be a binding agreement to purchase the car. Was he correct? *no*

6. Beck was the general manager of Chilkoot Lumber Co. Haines sold fuel to the company. To persuade Haines to sell on credit, Beck signed a paper by which he promised to pay any debt of the lumber company owed Haines. He signed this paper with his name followed by "general manager." Haines later sued Beck on this promise, and Beck raised the defense that the addition of "general manager" showed that Beck was signing on behalf of Chilkoot, was not personally liable, and did not intend to be bound by the paper. Was Beck liable on the paper? [*Beck v Haines Terminal and Highway Co.* (Alaska) 843 P2d 1229]

7. *A* made a contract to construct a house for *B*. Subsequently, *B* sued *A* for breach of contract. *A* raised the defense that the contract was not binding because it was not sealed. Is this a valid defense? [*Cooper v G.E. Construction Co.*, _____ *GA App* _____, 158 SE2d 305]

8. While Clara Novak was sick, her daughter Janie helped her in many ways. Clara died, and Janie then claimed that she was entitled to be paid for the services she had rendered her mother. This claim was opposed by three brothers and sisters who also rendered services to the mother. They claimed that Janie was barred because of the presumption that services rendered between family members are gratuitous. Janie claimed that this presumption was not applicable because she had not lived with her mother but had her own house. Was Janie correct? [*In re* Estate of Novak (Minn App) 398 NW2d 653]

9. Dozier and his wife, daughter, and grandson lived in the house Dozier owned. At the request of the daughter and grandson, Paschall made some improvements to the house. Dozier did not authorize these, but he

knew that the improvements were being made and did not object to them. Paschall sued Dozier for the reasonable value of the improvements. Dozier argued that he had not made any contract for such improvements. Was he obligated to pay for such improvements?

10. When Harriet went away for the summer, Landry, a house painter, painted her house. He had a contract to paint a neighbor's house but painted Harriet's house by mistake. When Harriet returned from vacation, Landry billed her for $1,200, which was what the painting was worth. She refused to pay. Landry claimed that she had a quasi-contractual liability for that amount. Was he correct?

11. Margrethe and Charles Pyeatte, a married couple, agreed that she would work so that he could go to law school and that when he finished, she would go back to school for her master's degree. After Charles was admitted to the bar and before Margrethe went back to school, the two were divorced. She sued Charles for breaking their contract. The court held there was no contract because the agreement between them was too vague to be enforced. Margrethe then claimed that she was entitled to quasi-contractual recovery of the money that she had paid for Charles' support and law school tuition. He denied liability. Was she entitled to recover for the money she spent for Charles' maintenance and law school tuition? [*Pyeatte v Pyeatte* (Ariz App) 661 P2d 196]

12. Carriage Way was a real estate development of approximately 80 houses and 132 apartments. The property owners were members of the Carriage Way Property Owners Association. Each year the association would take care of certain open neighboring areas that were used by the property owners, including a nearby lake. The board of directors of the association would make an assessment or charge against the property owners to cover the cost of this work. The property owners paid these assessments for a number of years and then refused to pay any more. In spite of this refusal, the association continued to take care of the areas in question. The association then sued the property owners and claimed that they were liable for the benefit that had been conferred on them. Were the owners liable? [*Board of Directors of Carriage Way Property Owners Ass'n v Western National Bank*, ____ Ill App 3d ____, ____ Ill Dec ____, 487 NE2d 974]

13. Lombard insured his car, and when it was damaged, the insurer took the car to General Auto Service for repairs. The insurance company did not pay the repair bill. General Auto Service then sued Lombard for the bill because he had benefited from the repair work. Was he liable?

14. When a junior college student complained about a particular course, the vice president of the college asked the teacher to prepare a detailed report about the course. The teacher did and then demanded additional compensation for the time spent in preparing the report. He claimed that the college was liable to provide compensation on an implied contract. Was he correct? [*Zadrozny v City Colleges of Chicago*, ____ Ill App 3d ____, ____ Ill Dec ____, 581 NE2d 44]

15. Smith made a contract to sell automatic rifles to a foreign country. Because the sale of such weapons to that country was illegal under an act of Congress, Smith was prosecuted by the U.S. government for making the contract. He raised the defense that because the contract was illegal, it was void and there is no binding obligation when a contract is void; therefore, no contract for which he could be prosecuted existed. Was he correct?

CPA QUESTION

1. Kay, an art collector, promised Hammer, an art student, that if Hammer could obtain certain rare artifacts within two weeks, Kay would pay for Hammer's post-graduate education. At considerable effort and expense, Hammer obtained the specified artifacts within the two-week period. When Hammer requested payment, Kay refused. Kay claimed that there was no consideration for the promise. Hammer would prevail against Kay based on
   a. Unilateral contract.
   b. Unjust enrichment.
   c. Public policy.
   d. Quasi contract.

The Agreement

OBJECTIVES

After studying this chapter, you should be able to

1. *Decide whether a statement is an offer or an invitation to negotiate;*
2. *Decide whether an agreement is too indefinite to be enforced;*
3. *Describe the exceptions that the law makes to the requirement of definiteness;*
4. *List all the ways an offer is terminated;*
5. *Compare offers, firm offers, and option contracts; and*
6. *Define what constitutes the acceptance of an offer.*

A contract consists of enforceable obligations that have been voluntarily assumed. Thus, one of the essential elements of a contract is an agreement. This chapter explains how the basic agreement arises, when there is a contract, and how there can be merely unsuccessful negotiations without a resulting contract.

A. REQUIREMENTS OF AN OFFER

An **offer** expresses the willingness of the offeror to enter into a contractual agreement regarding a particular subject. It is a promise that is conditional upon an act, a forbearance (a refraining from doing something one has a legal right to do), or a return promise.

1. Contractual Intention

An offer must manifest an intent to make a contract.

To make an offer, the offeror must appear to intend to create a binding obligation. Whether this intent exists is determined by objective standards.[1] This intent may be shown by conduct. For example, when one party signs a written contract and sends it to the other party, such action is an offer to enter into a contract on the terms of the writing.

There is no contract when a social invitation is made or when an offer is made in jest or excitement. A reasonable person would not regard such an offer as indicating a willingness to enter into a binding agreement.

An invitation to negotiate is not an offer but seeks an offer.

(a) Invitation to Negotiate. The first statement made by one of two persons is not necessarily an offer. In many instances, there may be a preliminary discussion or an invitation by one party to the other to negotiate or to make an offer. Thus, an inquiry by a school as to whether a teacher wished to continue the following year was merely a survey or invitation to negotiate and was not an offer that could be accepted. Therefore, the teacher's affirmative response did not create a contract.

Ordinarily, a seller sending out circulars or catalogs listing prices is not regarded as making an offer to sell at those prices. The seller is merely indicating a willingness to consider an offer made by a buyer on those terms. The reason for this rule is, in part, the practical consideration that because a seller does not have an unlimited supply of any commodity, the seller cannot possibly intend to make a contract with everyone who sees the circular. The same principle is applied to merchandise that is displayed with price tags in stores or store windows and to most advertisements. A "For Sale" advertisement in a newspaper is merely an invitation to negotiate and is not an offer that can be accepted by a reader of the paper.[2]

ETHICS & THE LAW   PepsiCo ran an ad and promotional campaign in 1996 called the "Drink Pepsi Get Stuff" campaign. The enormously successful campaign allowed customers to claim prizes in exchange for points on PepsiCo beverage containers, and the points could be combined with cash payments to obtain the prizes. The campaign was so successful that the second round of ads and promotions was not run because the prizes were nearly exhausted.

---

[1] *Glass Service Co. v State Farm Mutual Automobile Ins. Co.* (Minn App) 530 NW2d 867 (1995).
[2] *Ford Motor Credit Co. v Russell* (Minn App) 519 NW2d 460 (1994).

In one television ad, PepsiCo pictured a Harrier jet as a satirical spoof on the prizes available under the campaign. The jet was offered in the ad for 7 million beverage points. Harrier jets are made only for the Marine Corps and are not sold in the open market. They cost $33.8 million each and can be produced at a rate of only one dozen at a time.

John Leonard, a 21-year-old business student, called PepsiCo and was told he would need to drink 16.8 million cans of Pepsi in order to obtain the required points. He was also told that he had the option of buying PepsiCo points for 10¢ each. Leonard developed a pool of investors (Pepsi drinkers) and delivered 15 PepsiCo points and a check for $700,008.50 for the remaining 6,999,985 points plus shipping and handling.

PepsiCo refused to provide Leonard with a Harrier jet because it said the ad was not an offer but a joke. Leonard filed suit on August 6, 1996, but PepsiCo had already filed a preemptive suit on July 18, asking that Leonard's suit be dismissed and declared frivolous and that PepsiCo be reimbursed for its legal expenses.

Did PepsiCo make an offer? Did Leonard accept? What is the significance of Leonard's phone call and the verification of the PepsiCo points needed? Is there a contract? If you were a PepsiCo executive, what would you do? If there is a misunderstanding about the ad, is there an ethical obligation on the part of PepsiCo? Was Leonard taken advantage of, or is he taking advantage of PepsiCo?

Quotations of prices, even when sent on request, are likewise not offers unless there have been previous dealings between the parties or unless a trade custom exists that would give the recipient of the quotation reason to believe that an offer was being made. Whether a price quotation is to be treated as an offer or merely an invitation to negotiate is a question of the intent of the party giving the quotation. Although sellers are not bound by quotations and price tags, they will, as a matter of goodwill, ordinarily make every effort to deliver the merchandise at those prices.[3]

In some instances, it is apparent that an invitation to negotiate rather than an offer has been made. When construction work is done for the national government, for a state government, or for a political subdivision, statutes require that a printed statement of the work to be done be published and circulated. Contractors are invited to submit bids on the work, and the statute generally requires that the bid of the lowest responsible bidder be accepted. Such an invitation for bids is clearly an invitation to negotiate, both from its nature and from the fact that it does not specify the price to be paid for the work. The bid of each contractor is an offer, and there is no contract until the government accepts one of these bids. This procedure of advertising for bids is also commonly employed by private persons when a large construction project is involved.

In some cases, the fact that important terms are missing indicates that the parties are merely negotiating and that an oral contract has not been made. When a letter or printed promotional matter of a party leaves many significant details to be worked out later, the letter or printed matter is merely an invitation to negotiate. It is not an offer that may be accepted and a contract thereby formed.[4]

---

[3] Statutes prohibiting false or misleading advertising may also require adherence to advertised prices.
[4] *Lynx Exploration and Production Co. v 4-Sight Operating Co.* (Tex App) 891 SW2d 785 (1995).

would the tenant Be obligated to pay for the remaining out devorder lease?

(b) Statement of Intention. In some instances, a person may make a statement of intention but not intend to be bound by a contract. For example, a certain lease does not expressly allow the tenant to terminate the lease in case of a job transfer. The landlord states that should the tenant be required to leave for that reason, the landlord would try to find a new tenant to take over the lease. This declaration of intention does not give rise to a binding contract. The landlord cannot be held liable for breach of contract if the landlord should fail to obtain a new tenant or not even attempt to obtain a new tenant.

(c) Agreement to Make a Contract at a Future Date. No contract arises when the parties merely agree that at a future date they will consider making a contract or will make a contract on terms to be agreed on at that time.[5] In such a case, neither party is under any obligation until the future contract is made. Similarly, there is no contract between the parties if essential terms are left open for future negotiation.[6] Thus, a promise to pay a bonus or compensation to be decided on after three months of business operation is not binding. Likewise, no binding contract to renew a contract when it expires was created by a provision in the original contract that, when it expires, the parties intend to "negotiate in good faith to renew this agreement for an additional year upon terms and conditions to be negotiated." When the parties have prepared a draft agreement but it is clear that such agreement is not regarded by them as final, the draft is merely a step in negotiations and is not a contract.

The fact that all material terms have not been agreed on is significant in concluding that there is no contract. Thus, an agreement to construct a house was not binding when the size and shape of the house were not specified.[7]

FIGURE 12-1
Offer and Acceptance

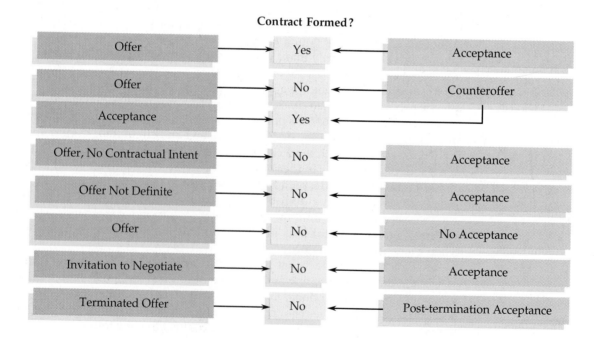

Contract Formed?

Offer	→ Yes ←	Acceptance
Offer	→ No ←	Counteroffer
Acceptance	→ Yes ←	
Offer, No Contractual Intent	→ No ←	Acceptance
Offer Not Definite	→ No ←	Acceptance
Offer	→ No ←	No Acceptance
Invitation to Negotiate	→ No ←	Acceptance
Terminated Offer	→ No ←	Post-termination Acceptance

---

5 *Ellis v Taylor* (SC) 49 SE2d 487 (1994).
6 *Hansen v Phillips Beverage Co.* (Minn App) 487 NW2d 925 (1992).
7 *Manley v Athan* (Mo App) 915 SW2d 792 (1996).

Just Talk

Facts: A cable television company, T.V. Transmission, Inc., made a contract to use the utility poles of the Lincoln Electric System, a utility owned by the city of Lincoln. The contract was to expire on a specified date but could be extended on such terms as would be agreed to by the parties. A lawsuit was brought to determine the effect of the contract after the specified expiration date.

Decision: There was no contract after the expiration date. There was merely an agreement to agree, which by itself is not a contract. In the absence of making a new contract, the contract would expire on the specified date. [*T.V. Transmission, Inc. v City of Lincoln, 220 Neb 887, 374 NW2d 49 (1985)*]

2. Definiteness

An offer, and the resulting contract, must be definite and certain. If an offer is indefinite or vague or if an essential provision is lacking,[8] no contract arises from an attempt to accept it. The reason is that courts cannot tell what the parties are to do. Thus, an offer to conduct a business for as long as it is profitable is too vague to be a valid offer. The acceptance of such an offer does not result in a contract that can be enforced. Likewise, a promise to give an injured employee "suitable" employment that the employee is "able to do" is too vague to be a binding contract. A statement by a landlord to the tenant that "some day it [the rented land] will be your own" is too indefinite to be an offer, and no contract for the sale of the land arises when the tenant agrees to the statement. Similarly, statements by a bank that it was "with" the debtors and would "support" them in their proposed business venture were too vague to be regarded as a promise by the bank to make necessary loans to the debtors. ◆ *For example*, Hernandes wrote a letter stating that he would sell his house to McIntosh Realty Co. The company wrote back an acceptance, but there was no contract because material terms, particularly the price, had not been agreed on. ◆

Offers and contracts must be definite so that it can be determined what should be done.

Now You Drew a Blank

Facts: The president and vice-president of Belle State Bank met Mr. Chapman for lunch and agreed to lend Chapman Toyota "up to $100,000" provided that he submit a financing form to the bank. Chapman submitted the forms but, before receiving an approval from the bank, wrote out checks on the line of credit which later bounced. Chapman sued the bank for breach of contract asserting that the bank's officers broke an oral agreement that they would lend him the money. The bank asserted that there was no agreement between the parties to open a line of credit since the exact amount of the credit, the length of time the credit would be held open, the rate of interest, and the repayment terms were not discussed.

Decision: Judgment for Belle State Bank. The absence of the missing terms made the agreement so indefinite that it was not capable of being enforced. The agreement was therefore not binding and was not a contract. [*Dennis Chapman Toyota, Inc. v Belle State Bank (Mo App) 759 SW2d 30 (1988)*]

---

[8] *T.O. Stanley Boot Co. v Bank of El Paso* (Tex) 847 SW2d 218 (1993).

The fact that minor details are left for future determination does not make an agreement too vague to be a contract.[9]

The law does not favor the destruction of contracts because that would go against the social force of carrying out the intent of the parties.[10] Consequently, when it is claimed that a contract is too indefinite to be enforced, a court will do its best to find the intent of the parties and thereby reach the conclusion that the contract is not too indefinite. However, a court may not rewrite the agreement of the parties in order to make it definite.

CASE SUMMARY

And It Seemed So Promising

Facts: Martin obtained a divorce from his wife, Shirley. He promised that he would "always take care of her." He made a number of monthly payments to her and then stopped.

Decision: Martin was not bound by a contract to make payments to Shirley. His promise to take care of her was too vague to be given effect. He was therefore not liable for stopping the payments. [*Yedvarb v Yedvarb* (App Div) 665 NYS2d 84 (1997)]

Lack of definiteness may be cured by incorporating another document by reference.

(a) Definite by Incorporation. An offer and the resulting contract that by themselves may appear "too indefinite" may be made definite by reference to another writing. For example, a lease agreement that was too vague by itself was made definite because the parties agreed that the lease should follow the standard form with which both were familiar. An agreement may also be made definite by reference to the prior dealings of the parties and to trade practices.

In some cases of indefiniteness, the law will cure the defect by implying terms not stated.

(b) Implied Terms. Although an offer must be definite and certain, not all of its terms need to be expressed. Some omitted terms may be implied by law. For example, an offer "to pay $50 for a watch" does not state the terms of payment. A court, however, would not condemn this provision as too vague but would hold that it required that cash be paid and that the payment be made on delivery of the watch. Likewise, terms may be implied from conduct. As an illustration, where borrowed money was given to the borrower by a check on which the word loan was written, the act of the borrower in indorsing the check constituted an agreement to repay the amount of the check.

(c) Precision Not Required. The fact that a contract's term is not precise does not mean that it is not sufficiently definite. Thus, a provision that an employee would be discharged only for "good cause" is not too vague to be binding.[11]

At times, a contract is divisible, and the definite part can be separated from the balance and enforced separately.

(d) Divisible Contracts. When the agreement consists of two or more parts and calls for corresponding performances of each part by the parties, the agreement is a **divisible contract.** Thus, in a promise to buy several separate articles at different prices at the same time, the agreement may be regarded as separate or divisible promises for the articles. When a contract contains a number of provisions or

---

[9] *Hsu v Vet-A-Mix, Inc.* (Iowa App) 479 NW2d 336 (1991).
[10] *Mears v Nationwide Mut. Ins. Co.* (CA8 Ark) 91 F3d 1118 (1996).
[11] *Scott v Pacific Gas & Electric Co.,* ____ Cal App 3d ____, 46 Cal Rptr 2d 427 (1995).

performances to be rendered, the question arises as to whether the parties intended merely a group of separate, divisible contracts or whether it was to be a package deal so that complete performance by each party was essential.

CASE SUMMARY

Just Throw the Bad Part Away

Facts: Kazem Moini's company, West Candies, Inc., manufactured candy which it sold to Maureen Hewes's candy store. Hewes made a contract with Moini in which he agreed (1) to purchase all his candy from Moini, (2) to keep his showcase adequately stocked at all times, and (3) to maintain an inventory equal to or greater than that specified in Exhibit A. In fact, there never was an Exhibit A. Hewes did not pay for candy delivered to him. He was sued by Moini and then claimed that the contract was not binding because it was too indefinite, since there was no Exhibit A defining the required inventory amount.

Decision: Judgment for Moini. The promise to maintain inventory or stock as specified in Exhibit A was too indefinite to be binding because there was no Exhibit A. That, however, did not establish that there was no contract, because the two other promises made by Hewes could be enforced. They were sufficiently definite in themselves and were not in any way related to the promise regarding inventory maintenance. There was nothing in the contract manifesting any intent that it was necessary that all three promises be binding before any of them could be binding. The contract was therefore divisible. As a result, it failed only as to the inventory promise but was binding as to the other promises. Therefore, Hewes was required to pay at the contract rate for the candy received. *[Moini v Hewes, 93 Or App 596, 763 P2d 414 (1988)]*

Unimportant vague terms may be ignored.

(e) Unimportant Vague Details Ignored. If a term that is too vague is not important, it may sometimes be ignored. If the balance of the agreement is definite, there can then be a binding contract. ◆ *For example,* where the parties agreed that one of them would manage a motel that was being constructed for the other, and where it was agreed that the contract would start to run before the completion of the construction, the management contract did not fail because it did not specify any date on which it was to begin. It was apparent that the exact date was not essential and could not be determined at the time when the contract was made. ◆

Definiteness is not required where precision is impossible and the parties rely on mutual good faith.

(f) Exceptions to Definiteness. The law has come to recognize certain situations in which the practical necessity of doing business makes it desirable to have a contract, yet the situation is such that it is either impossible or undesirable to adopt definite terms in advance. In these cases, the indefinite term is often tied to the concept of good-faith performance or to some independent factor that will be definitely ascertainable at some time in the future. For example, the indefinite term might be tied to market price, cost to complete, or production requirements. Thus, the law recognizes binding contracts in the case of a **requirements contract,** a contract to buy all requirements of the buyer from the seller. The law also recognizes as binding an **output contract,** the contract of a producer to sell the entire production or output to a given buyer. These are binding contracts even though they do not state the exact quantity of goods that are to be bought or sold. Contracts are also binding even though they run for an indefinite period of time, require a buyer to pay the costs plus a percentage of costs as profit, or require one person to supply professional services as needed.

If the Parties Are Happy, Why Complain?

Facts: Heat Incorporated made an agreement with Griswold, an accountant, by which it agreed to pay him $200 a month for rendering such accounting services "as he, in sole discretion, may render." Griswold had done the accounting work of the corporation for the preceding six years, and it was desired that he should continue to render the services as in the past. When the corporation refused to pay on the ground that the agreement was so indefinite that it was not binding, Griswold sued for damages.

Decision: Judgment for Griswold. The parties to the contract had six years of experience with the rendering of service by Griswold. It was their intention that such pattern of rendering service should continue in the future. Because of uncertainties of the future and possible changes in the law, it was obvious that the parties could not specify in precise detail the services that were to be rendered. The law should therefore allow them to make a vague contract if they so desire. The duty to perform contracts in good faith would be a sufficient protection for the corporation. [*Griswold v Heat Inc.*, 108 NH 119, 229 A2d 183 (1967)]

3. Communication of Offer to Offeree

An offer must be communicated to the offeree.

An offer must be communicated to the offeree. Otherwise, the offeree cannot accept even though knowledge of the offer has been indirectly acquired. Internal management communications of an enterprise that are not intended for outsiders or employees do not constitute offers and cannot be accepted by them. Sometimes, particularly in the case of unilateral contracts, the offeree performs the act called for by the offeror without knowing of the offer's existence. Such performance does not constitute an acceptance. Thus, without knowing that a reward is offered for the arrest of a particular criminal, a person may arrest the criminal. In most states, if that person subsequently learns that a reward has been offered for the arrest, the reward cannot be recovered.[12]

Not only must the offer be communicated, but also it must be communicated by the offeror or at the offeror's direction.

B. TERMINATION OF OFFER

An offeree cannot accept a terminated offer. Offers may be terminated by revocation, counteroffer, rejection, lapse of time, death or disability of a party, or subsequent illegality.

4. Revocation of Offer by Offeror

An offer can be revoked by the offeror before it is accepted.

Ordinarily, an offeror can revoke the offer before it is accepted. If this is done, the offeree cannot create a contract by accepting the revoked offer. Thus, the bidder at an auction sale may withdraw (revoke) a bid (offer) before it is accepted, and the auctioneer cannot accept that bid later.

---

[12] With respect to the offeror, it should not make any difference, as a practical matter, whether the services were rendered with or without knowledge of the existence of the offer. Only a small number of states have adopted this view, however.

An ordinary offer may be revoked at any time before it is accepted even though the offeror has expressly promised that the offer will be good for a stated period and that period has not yet expired. It may also be revoked even though the offeror has expressly promised to the offeree that the offer would not be revoked before a specified later date.

The fact that the offeror expressly promised to keep the offer open has no effect when no consideration was given for that promise.[13]

(a) What Constitutes a Revocation. No particular form or words are required to constitute a revocation. Any words indicating the offeror's termination of the offer are sufficient. A notice sent to the offeree that the property that is the subject of the offer has been sold to a third person is a revocation of the offer. A customer's order for goods, which is an offer to purchase at certain prices, is revoked by a notice to the seller of the cancellation of the order provided such notice is communicated before the order is accepted.

> **Any words or conduct manifesting intent to revoke an offer have that effect.**

(b) Communication of Revocation. A revocation of an offer is ordinarily effective only when it is made known to the offeree. Until it is communicated to the offeree, directly or indirectly, the offeree has reason to believe that there is still an offer that may be accepted, and the offeree may rely on this belief. Except in a few states, a letter or telegram revoking an offer made to a particular offeree is not effective until received by the offeree. It is not a revocation at the time it is written by the offeror or even when it is mailed or dispatched. A written revocation is effective, however, when it is delivered to the offeree's agent or to the offeree's residence or place of business under such circumstances that the offeree may be reasonably expected to be aware of its receipt.

> **A revocation is not effective until communicated in some way.**

It is ordinarily held that there is a sufficient communication of the revocation when the offeree learns indirectly of the offeror's revocation. This is particularly true in a land sale when the seller-offeror, after making an offer to sell the land to the offeree, sells the land to a third person and the offeree indirectly learns of such sale. The offeree necessarily realizes that the seller cannot perform the original offer and therefore must be considered to have revoked it.

If the offeree accepts an offer before it is effectively revoked, a valid contract is created. Thus, there may be a contract when the offeree mails or telegraphs an acceptance without knowing that a letter of revocation has already been mailed.

(c) Option Contracts. An **option contract** is a binding promise to keep an offer open for a stated period of time or until a specified date. An option contract requires that the promisor receive consideration—that is, something, such as a sum of money, as the price for the promise to keep the offer open. In other words, the option is a contract to refrain from revoking an offer.

> **An option contract is a contract to keep an offer open.**

When an option contract recites the giving of a specified consideration but such consideration in fact was never paid, the option contract is merely an offer. It may be revoked at any time prior to acceptance.

The holder of an option has full freedom to exercise the option or to refrain from doing so.[14]

---

[13] *Prenger v Baumhoer* (Mo App) 914 SW2d 413 (1996).
[14] *Ponder v Lincoln National Sales Corp.* (Ala) 612 So 2d 1169 (1992).

> By statute, a party making a firm offer may be barred from revoking it.

(d) Firm Offers. As another exception to the rule that an offer can be revoked at any time before acceptance, statutes in some states provide that an offeror cannot revoke an offer prior to its expiration when the offeror makes a firm offer. A firm offer is an offer that states that it is to be irrevocable, or irrevocable for a stated period of time. Under the Uniform Commercial Code, this doctrine of firm offers applies to a merchant's signed, written offer to buy or sell goods but with a maximum of three months on its period of irrevocability.[15]

> When the offeree relies on the continued existence of an offer, some courts hold that the offer cannot be revoked.

(e) Detrimental Reliance. There is growing authority that when the offeror foresees that the offeree will rely on the offer's remaining open, the offeror is obligated to keep the offer open for a reasonable time. The concept of detrimental reliance can thus prevent the revocation of an offer.[16]

CASE SUMMARY

Business Environment Bends the Law

Facts: Arango Construction Company wanted to do certain construction work for the U.S. government. In preparing its bid, Arango phoned Success Roofing to see what it would charge for doing the roofing work involved. Success offered to do the work for a specified price. Arango then made a bid to the government. Its bid was accepted. Success later notified Arango that it was withdrawing its bid to do the roofing work because it had made a significant mistake in its calculations. Arango claimed it could not do this because Arango had used the bid in making its own bid to the United States. Arango sued Success for damages caused by the revocation of its bid.

Decision: Success knew that Arango would be relying on its subcontract bid in making the general bid to the United States. Success could thus foresee that if it revoked the subcontract bid, Arango would be harmed financially. To prevent the infliction of such loss on Arango, the court departed from the general rule as to the revocability of offers and declared that Success was barred or estopped from revoking its subcontract offer after the general contractor had submitted its general bid. [*Arango Construction Co. v Success Roofing, Inc.*, 46 Wash App 314, 730 P2d 720 (1986)]

---

5. Counteroffer by Offeree

> An offer is rejected when the offeree makes a counteroffer.

The offeree rejects the offer when he ignores the original offer and replies with a different offer.[17] If the offeree purports to accept an offer but in so doing makes any change to the terms of the offer, such action is a counteroffer that rejects the original offer. An "acceptance" that changes the terms of the offer or adds new terms is a rejection of the original offer and constitutes a counteroffer.[18]

Ordinarily, if *A* makes an offer, such as to sell a used automobile to *B* for $1,000, and *B* in reply makes an offer to buy at $750, the original offer is terminated. *B* is in effect indicating refusal of the original offer and in its place making a different offer. Such an offer by the offeree is known as a **counteroffer.** No contract arises unless the original offeror accepts the counteroffer. Likewise, when a prospective buyer submits a written contract form that puts a ceiling on interest payments

---

[15] UCC § 2-205.
[16] *Branco Enterprises, Inc. v Delta Roofing, Inc.* (Mo App) 886 SW2d 157 (1994).
[17] *Bourque v FDIC* (CA1 RI) 42 F3d 704 (1994).
[18] *L.B. v State Committee of Psychologists* (Mo App) 912 SW2d 611 (1995).

and the prospective seller substitutes a provision stating that interest is not to exceed the prevailing rate, no contract is formed when the buyer never consents to such counteroffer.[19]

Counteroffers are not limited to offers that directly contradict the original offers. Any departure from, or addition to, the original offer is a counteroffer even though the original offer was silent on the point added by the counteroffer. For example, when the offeree stated that the offer was accepted and added that time was of the essence, the acceptance was a counteroffer because the original offer had been silent on that point. A conditional acceptance is a counteroffer.[20]

If the original offeror accepts the counteroffer before it is revoked, there is a binding contract on the basis of the counteroffer.[21]

6.   Rejection of Offer by Offeree

An offer is terminated when expressly rejected by the offeree.

If the offeree rejects the offer and communicates this rejection to the offeror, the offer is terminated. Communication of a rejection terminates an offer even though the period for which the offeror agreed to keep the offer open has not yet expired. It may be that the offeror is willing to renew the offer, but unless this is done, there is no longer any offer for the offeree to accept.

7.   Lapse of Time

An offer is terminated by the lapse of the time specified or of a reasonable time.

When the offer states that it is open until a particular date, the offer terminates on that date if it has not yet been accepted. This is particularly so where the offeror declares that the offer shall be void after the expiration of the specified time. Such limitations are strictly construed.

If the offer contains a time limitation for acceptance, an attempted acceptance after the expiration of that time has no effect and does not give rise to a contract.[22] When a specified time limitation is imposed on an option, the option cannot be exercised after the expiration of that time, regardless of whether the option was exercised within what would have been held a reasonable time if no time period had been specified. It has been held that the buyer's attempt to exercise an option one day late had no effect.

If the offer does not specify a time, it will terminate after the lapse of a reasonable time. What constitutes a reasonable time depends on the circumstances of each case—that is, on the nature of the subject matter, the nature of the market in which it is sold, the time of year, and other factors of supply and demand. If a commodity is perishable or fluctuates greatly in value, the reasonable time will be much shorter than if the subject matter is a stable article. An offer to sell a harvested crop of tomatoes would expire within a very short time. When a seller purports to accept an offer after it has lapsed by the expiration of time, the seller's acceptance is merely a counteroffer and does not create a contract unless that counteroffer is accepted by the buyer.

19 *Press v Jordan* (Fla App) 670 So 2d 1016 (1996).
20 *Anand v Marple*, ____ Ill App 3d ____, ____ Ill Dec ____, 522 NE2d 281 (1988).
21 *Cal Wadsworth Construction v City of St. George* (Utah) 898 P2d 1372 (1995).
22 *Century 21 Pinetree Properties, Inc. v Cason*, 220 Ga App 355, 469 SE2d 458 (1996).

CASE SUMMARY

Nothing Lasts Forever

Facts: Wilkins and Butler had a dispute arising from an automobile collision. Wilkins offered to settle the matter for $4,500. There was no reply from Butler. One year later she stated that she accepted the offer. Wilkins claimed that the offer had lapsed and could not be accepted. Butler claimed that she could accept the offer because it had never been withdrawn.

Decision: Judgment for Wilkins. When no time is stated for the duration of an offer, it lapses after a reasonable time. The fact that the offeror had not withdrawn the offer was immaterial. Ordinarily, it would be a question of fact whether the time was reasonable, but when there was as much as a one-year delay, a court could declare as a matter of law that a reasonable time had expired and that the offer had lapsed. Consequently, the acceptance that was made one year later had no effect. [*Wilkins v Butler*, 187 Ga App 84, 369 SE2d 267 (1988)]

8. Death or Disability of Either Party

If either the offeror or the offeree dies or becomes insane before the offer is accepted, the offer is automatically terminated. *For example*, Johann offers to sell his ranch to Interport, Inc. Five days later Johann dies in a plane crash. Interport writes to his son, Mateo, that his father's offer is accepted. This cannot be done, as the offer made by Johann died with him.

9. Subsequent Illegality

Subsequent illegality terminates an offer.

If the performance of the contract becomes illegal after the offer is made, the offer is terminated. Thus, if an offer is made to sell alcoholic liquors but a law prohibiting such sales is enacted before the offer is accepted, the offer is terminated.

C. ACCEPTANCE OF OFFER

An acceptance is the assent of the offeree to the terms of the offer. Whether there has been an agreement of the parties is determined by objective standards. The uncommunicated subjective intent of either party has no effect.[23]

10. What Constitutes an Acceptance

No particular form of words or mode of expression is required, but there must be a clear expression that the offeree agrees to be bound by the terms of the offer.

If the offeree reserves the right to reject the offer, such action is not an acceptance.[24]

11. Privilege of Offeree

An offeree has the choice to accept or reject.

Ordinarily, the offeree may refuse to accept an offer. If there is no acceptance, by definition there is no contract. The fact that there had been a series of contracts between the parties and that one party's offer had always been accepted before

---

[23] *McDaniel v Park Place Care Center, Inc.* (Mo App) 918 SW2d 820 (1996).
[24] *Pantano v McGowan*, ____ Neb ____, 530 NW2d 912 (1995).

by the other does not create any legal obligation to continue to accept subsequent offers.

Certain partial exceptions exist to the offeree's privilege of refusing to accept an offer.

(a) Places of Public Accommodation and Public Utilities. Places of public accommodation and public utilities are under a duty to serve any person. They cannot refuse to serve a person because of a disability.[25] When a person offers to register at a hotel, the hotel has the obligation to accept the offer and to enter into a contract for the renting of the room. However, there is no duty on the part of the hotel to accept unless the person is properly attired and is behaving properly and the hotel has space available.

Freedom of the offeree may be limited by antidiscrimination and consumer protection laws.

(b) Antidiscrimination. When offers are solicited from members of the general public, an offer generally may not be rejected because of the race, nationality, religion, or color of the offeror. If the solicitor of the offer is willing to enter into a contract to rent, sell, or employ, antidiscrimination laws compel the solicitor to accept an offer from any person.

(c) Consumer Protection. Statutes and regulations designed to protect consumers from false advertising may require a seller to accept an offer from a customer to purchase advertised goods and may impose a penalty for an unjustified refusal.

12. Effect of Acceptance

An acceptance of an offer creates a contract and binds both parties.

When an offer has been accepted, a binding agreement or contract is created,[26] assuming that all of the other elements of a contract are present. Neither party can subsequently withdraw from or cancel the contract without the consent of the other party (or the existence of facts that under the law justify such unilateral action).

When an enterprise conducts a prize contest, its offer to conduct the contest according to stated rules is accepted when an entrant sends in the entry form. The enterprise must then conduct the contest according to the announced contest rules because it is bound by a contract. Likewise, when Richard mailed Blount Co. a letter accepting an offer made by Blount, Richard then realized that he had been reckless and phoned Blount that he would be able to pay only one-half of the offer price. Richard is bound by contract to pay the amount stated in the offer, as that offer had been accepted by him when he mailed the letter of acceptance.

13. Nature of Acceptance

Any manifestation of intent to accept an offer of a binding agreement is an acceptance.

An acceptance is the offeree's manifestation of intent to enter into a binding agreement on the terms stated in the offer. Whether there is an acceptance depends on whether the offeree has manifested an intent to accept. It is the objective or outward appearance that is controlling rather than the subjective or unexpressed intent of the offeree.[27]

---

25 Americans with Disabilities Act of 1990, Act of July 26, 1990, PL 101-336, 104 Stat 327, 42 USC §§ 12101 et seq.
26 *Ochoa v Ford* (Ind App) 641 NE2d 1042 (1994).
27 *Cowan v Mervin Mewes, Inc.* (SD) 546 NW2d 104 (1996).

OPA

In the absence of a contrary requirement in the offer, an acceptance may be indicated by an informal "okay," by a mere affirmative nod of the head, or, in the case of an offer of a unilateral contract, by performance of the act called for. However, while the acceptance of an offer may be shown by conduct, it must be very clear that the offeree intended to accept the offer.

The acceptance must be absolute and unconditional. It must accept just what is offered. If the offeree changes any terms of the offer or adds any new term, there is no acceptance because the offeree does not agree to what was offered.

Where the offeree does not accept the offer exactly as made, the addition of any qualification converts the "acceptance" into a counteroffer, and no contract arises unless such a counteroffer is accepted by the original offeror.[28]

CASE SUMMARY

There's No Turning Back

Facts: As a lease was about to expire, the landlord, CRA Development, wrote the tenant, Keryakos Textiles, setting forth the square footage and the rate terms on which the lease would be renewed. Keryakos sent a reply stating that it was willing to pay the proposed rate but wanted different cancellation and option terms in the renewal contract. CRA rejected Keryakos' terms and upon learning this, Keryakos notified CRA that it accepted the terms of its original letter. Nonetheless, CRA threatened to evict Keryakos from the property claiming that no lease contract existed between it and Keryakos.

Decision: The lease contract is governed by ordinary contract law. When the tenant offered other terms in place of those made by the landlord's offer, the tenant made a counteroffer. This had the effect of rejecting or terminating the landlord's offer. The tenant could not then accept the rejected offer after the tenant's counteroffer was rejected. Therefore, there was no contract. *[Keryakos Textiles, Inc. v CRA Development, Inc., 167 App Div 2d 738, 563 NYS2d 308 (1990)]*

OPA

The addition of new terms in the acceptance, however, does not always mean that the attempted acceptance fails. The acceptance is still unqualified if the new terms are merely those that (1) would be implied by law as part of the offer, (2) constitute a mere request, or (3) relate to a mere clerical detail.

14. Who May Accept

Only the offeree can accept.

An offer may be accepted only by the person to whom it is directed. If anyone else attempts to accept it, no agreement or contract with that person arises.

If the offer is directed to a particular class rather than a specified individual, it may be accepted by anyone within that class. If the offer is made to the public at large, it may be accepted by any member of the public at large having knowledge of the existence of the offer.

When a person to whom an offer was not made attempts to accept it, the attempted acceptance has the effect of an offer. If the original offeror is willing to accept this offer, a binding contract arises. If the original offeror does not accept the new offer, there is no contract.

---

[28] *Logan Ranch, Karg Partnership v Farm Credit Bank of Omaha,* ____ Neb ____, 472 NW2d 704 (1991).

C
P
A

15. Manner of Acceptance

The offeror may specify the manner for accepting the offer. When the offeror specifies that there must be a written acceptance, no contract arises when the offeree makes an oral acceptance. If the offeror calls for acceptance by a specified date, a late acceptance has no effect. When an acceptance is required by return mail, it is usually held that the letter of acceptance must be mailed the same day that the offer was received by the offeree. If the offer specifies that the acceptance be made by the performance of an act by the offeree, the latter cannot accept by making a promise to do the act but must actually perform it.

When the offer calls for the performance of an act or of certain conduct, the performance thereof is an acceptance of the offer and creates a unilateral contract.

When a person accepts services offered by another and it reasonably appears that compensation was expected, the acceptance of the services without any protest constitutes an acceptance of the offer. As a result, a contract exists for payment for the services.

Acceptance must be made as specified by the offer or, if no way is specified, by any reasonable means.

When the offeror has specified a particular manner of acceptance, the offeree cannot accept in any other way.[29] However, acceptance in some other way is effective (1) if the manner of acceptance specified was merely a suggested alternative and was not clearly the exclusive method of acceptance, or (2) if the offeror has proceeded on the basis that there had been an effective acceptance.

CASE SUMMARY

When Do You Have a Deal?

Facts: Joseph Papa applied to the New York Telephone Company to have an advertisement for his business placed in the yellow pages directory. The application form stated: "*Publication of any unit in any issue of the directory specified shall constitute acceptance of this order....The omission of a unit from any issue shall constitute a rejection by the Company of the order for such unit with respect to such issue...*" The application form stated that he had read the terms of the application. Among those terms, it was stated that the printing of Papa's material in the telephone directory constituted an acceptance of Papa's offer and that not printing it constituted a rejection of his offer. For some unknown reason, Papa was not included in the yellow pages, and he sued the phone company for damages for breach of contract.

Decision: Judgment for the phone company. There was no contract. Papa's application was merely an offer. If he had been included in the yellow pages, there would have been an acceptance of his offer, but the failure to include him, as was expressly stated in the application, constituted a rejection of his offer. Consequently, no contract ever arose. As a result, Papa could not sue for breach of contract. *[Papa v New York Telephone Company, 72 NY2d 879, 532 NYS2d 359, 528 NE2d 512 (1988)]*

Ordinarily, silence cannot be an acceptance.

C
P
A

(a) Silence as Acceptance. In most cases, the offeree's silence and failure to act cannot be regarded as an acceptance. Ordinarily, the offeror is not permitted to frame an offer in such a way as to make the silence and inaction of the offeree operate as an acceptance.

In the case of prior dealings between the parties, as in a record or book club, the offeree may have a duty to reject an offer expressly, and the offeree's silence may be regarded as an acceptance.

---

[29] *Hreha v Nemecek,* 119 Or App 65, 849 P2d 1131 (1993).

Keeping unordered
mailed goods and tickets
is not an acceptance.

(b) Unordered Goods and Tickets. Sometimes a seller writes to a person with whom the seller has not had any prior dealings, stating that, unless notified to the contrary, the seller will send specified merchandise and the recipient is obligated to pay for it at stated prices. There is no acceptance if the recipient of the letter ignores the offer and does nothing. The silence of the person receiving the letter is not an acceptance, and the sender, as a reasonable person, should recognize that none was intended.

This rule applies to all kinds of goods, books, magazines, and tickets sent through the mail when they have not been ordered. The fact that the items are not returned does not mean that they have been accepted; that is, the offeree is required neither to pay for nor to return the items. If desired, the recipient of the unordered goods may write "Return to Sender" on the unopened package and put the package back into the mail without any additional postage. The Postal Reorganization Act of 1970 provides that the person who receives unordered mailed merchandise from a commercial (noncharitable) sender has the right "to retain, use, discard, or dispose of it in any manner the recipient sees fit without any obligation whatsoever to the sender."[30] It provides further that any unordered merchandise that is mailed must have attached to it a clear and conspicuous statement of the recipient's right to treat the goods in this manner.

16. Communication of Acceptance

If the offeree accepts the offer, must the offeror be notified? The answer depends on the nature of the offer.

Communication of
acceptance is not
required for a unilateral
contract.

(a) Unilateral Contract. If the offeror makes an offer of a unilateral contract, communication of acceptance is ordinarily not necessary. In such a case, the offeror calls for a completed or accomplished act. If that act is performed by the offeree with knowledge of the offer, the offer is accepted without any further action by way of notifying the offeror. As a practical matter, there will eventually be some notice to the offeror because the offeree who has performed the act will ask the offeror to pay for the performance that has been rendered.

When the offer of a unilateral contract calls for a performance that requires some time to complete, there is authority that there is an acceptance when the offeree commences the performance.[31]

Communication of
acceptance is vital for
a bilateral contract.

(b) Bilateral Contract. If the offer pertains to a bilateral contract, an acceptance is not effective unless communicated. The acceptance must be communicated directly to the offeror or the offeror's agent.

---

[30] Federal Postal Reorganization Act § 3009.
[31] *Strata Production Co. v Mercury Exploration Co.* (NM) 916 P2d 822 (1996).

CASE SUMMARY

So You Won't Talk?

Facts: Behee made an offer to purchase land from the Smiths. They accepted the offer and gave their acceptance to their agent. Before the acceptance was communicated by the agent to Behee, he notified the agent that he was revoking the offer. The Smiths claimed that there was a binding contract because they had accepted Behee's offer.

Decision: There was no contract. The Smiths' acceptance was not effective because it was not communicated to Behee. Delivery of the acceptance to their own agent was not a communication to Behee. Consequently, there was no acceptance prior to the time that Behee revoked his offer, and he therefore had the right to revoke if he chose. [Hendricks v Behee (Mo App) 786 SW2d 610 (1990)]

17. Acceptance by Mail or Telegraph

When the offeree sends an acceptance by mail, questions may arise as to the right to use such means of communication and the time the acceptance is effective.

(a) Right to Use Mail. Express directions of the offeror, prior dealings between the parties, or custom of the trade may make it clear that only one method of acceptance is proper. For example, in negotiations with respect to property of rapidly fluctuating value, such as wheat or corporation stocks, an acceptance sent by mail may be too slow. When there is no indication that mail is not a proper method, an acceptance may be made by this means regardless of how the offer was made. The trend of modern decisions supports the following provision of the Uniform Commercial Code relating to sales of personal property: "Unless otherwise unambiguously indicated by the language or circumstances, an offer to make a [sales] contract shall be construed as inviting acceptance in any manner and by any medium reasonable in the circumstances."[32]

Use of mail or telegraph depends on the offer terms and circumstances.

Just Be Reasonable

Facts: Maria Cantu was a special education teacher under a one-year contract with the San Benito School District for the 1990-91 school year. On Saturday, August 18, just weeks before fall term classes were to begin, she hand-delivered a letter of resignation to her supervisor. Late Monday afternoon the superintendent put in the mail a properly stamped and addressed letter to Cantu accepting her offer of resignation. The next morning at 8:00 and before the superintendent's letter reaches her, Cantu hand-delivers a letter withdrawing her resignation. The Superintendent refused to recognize the attempted rescission of the resignation.

Decision: She was wrong. The resignation became binding when the acceptance of the resignation was mailed. The fact that the offer to resign had been delivered by hand did not require that the offer be accepted by a hand-delivery of the acceptance. The use of mail was reasonable under the circumstances, and therefore the mailing of the acceptance made it effective. [Cantu v Central Education Agency (Tex App) 884 SW2d 563 (1994)]

---

[32] UCC § 2-206 (1)(a).

Acceptance is
effective when
mailed or
telegraphed.

(b) When Acceptance by Mail Is Effective. If the offeror does not specify otherwise, a mailed acceptance takes effect when the acceptance is properly mailed. This is called the "mailbox rule." If the offeror specifies that an acceptance shall not be effective until received, there is no acceptance until the acceptance is received. Likewise, the mailbox rule does not apply when the offeror requires receipt of a payment to accompany an acceptance.

The handing of an acceptance letter by the offeree to the offeree's mail clerk does not constitute mailing within the above mailbox rule.

The letter must be properly addressed to the offeror, and any other precaution that is ordinarily observed to ensure safe transmission must be taken. If it is not mailed in this manner, the acceptance does not take effect when mailed, but only when received by the offeror.

The rule that a properly mailed acceptance takes effect at the time it is mailed is applied strictly. The rule applies even if the acceptance letter never reaches the offeror.

Acceptance by
mail or telegraph
requires proof of
fact.

(c) Proof of Acceptance by Mail. How can the time of mailing be established, or even the fact of mailing in the case of a destroyed or lost letter? The problem is not one of law but one of fact: a question of proving the case to the jury. The offeror may testify in court that an acceptance was never received or that an acceptance was sent after the offer had been revoked. The offeree may then testify that the acceptance letter was mailed at a particular time and place. The offeree's case will be strengthened if postal receipts for the mailing and delivery of a letter sent to the offeror can be produced, although these, of course, do not establish the contents of the letter. Ultimately, the case goes to the jury (or to the judge, if a jury trial has been waived) to determine whether the acceptance was made at a certain time and place as claimed by the offeree.

(d) Revocation and Acceptance Crossing in Mail. The offeree may mail an acceptance without knowing that the offeror has mailed a revocation of the offer. As the revocation of the offer is not effective until received, the mailbox rule still applies to the acceptance mailed by the offeree, and thus there is a contract.[33]

> **When the Mailbox Bangs Shut**
>
> **Facts:** The Thoelkes owned land. The Morrisons mailed an offer to the Thoelkes to buy their land. The Thoelkes agreed to this offer and mailed back a contract signed by them. While this letter was in transit, the Thoelkes notified the Morrisons that their acceptance was revoked. Were the Thoelkes bound by a contract?
>
> **Decision:** The acceptance was effective when mailed, and the subsequent revocation of the acceptance had no effect. [Morrison v Thoelke (Fla App) 155 So 2d 889 (1963)]

18. Acceptance by Telephone

Ordinarily, acceptance of an offer may be made by telephone unless the circumstances are such that, by the intent of the parties or the law of the state, no acceptance can be made or contract arise in the absence of a writing.

---

[33] *Buchbinder Tunick & Co. v Manhattan National Life Ins. Co.,* ___ App Div 2d ___, 631 NYS2d 148 (1995).

A telephoned acceptance is effective when and where the acceptance is spoken into the phone. Consequently, when a person who lived in Kansas applied for a job in Missouri and the employer telephoned from Missouri to Kansas accepting the application, the employment contract was a Missouri contract. Thus, the Kansas workers' compensation statute did not apply when the employee was subsequently injured.

19. Electronic Acceptance by E-mail or Fax

Much of modern business communicates electronically by E-mail or facsimile transmission (fax). The law governing acceptance by these devices has not yet been established. It is to be expected that courts will apply the law that had developed covering mailed, telephoned, or telegraphed acceptances in determining questions arising in the context of electronic transmission.

The fact that an offer is made by E-mail or fax will be a factor indicating that a speedy reply is required and that a mailed acceptance would be too slow. Other circumstances of a case might cancel out this inference, such as when the subject matter made it obvious that speedy action was not required.

On the basis of the extension of the prior law to electronic transmission, it is expected courts will hold that an acceptance may be sent by electronic transmission when it is reasonable under the circumstances to do so. It is also to be expected that the acceptance so made will be held effective at the point where and at the time when the acceptance was dispatched or its transmission initiated.

It is probable that the above statement will be applied to an acceptance sent by fax without regard to whether the transmitting machine is owned by the offeree or by an independent contractor.

20. Auction Sales

At an auction sale, the statements made by the auctioneer to draw forth bids are merely invitations to negotiate. Each bid is an offer, which is not accepted until the auctioneer indicates that a particular offer or bid is accepted. Usually this is done by the fall of the auctioneer's hammer, indicating that the highest bid made has been accepted.[34] Since a bid is merely an offer, the bidder may withdraw the bid at any time before it is accepted by the auctioneer.

Ordinarily, the auctioneer may withdraw any article or all of the property from the sale if not satisfied with the amounts of the bids that are being made. Once a bid is accepted, however, the auctioneer cannot cancel the sale. In addition, if it had been announced that the sale was to be made "without reserve," the property must be sold to the person making the highest bid regardless of how low that bid may be.

In an auction "with reserve," bids are taken by the auctioneer as agent for the seller with the understanding that no contract is formed until the seller accepts the transaction.[35]

---

[34] *Dry Creek Cattle Co. v Harriet Bros. Limited Partnership* (Wyo) 908 P2d 399 (1995).
[35] *Marten v Staab*, ____ Neb ____, 543 NW2d 436 (1996).

SUMMARY

Because a contract arises when an offer is accepted, it is necessary to find that there was an offer and that it was accepted. If either element is missing, there is no contract.

An offer does not exist unless the offeror has contractual intent. This intent is lacking if the statement of the person is merely an invitation to negotiate, a statement of intention, or an agreement to agree at a later date. Newspaper ads, price quotations, and catalog prices are ordinarily merely invitations to negotiate and cannot be accepted.

An offer must be definite. If an offer is indefinite, its acceptance will not create a contract because it will be held that the resulting agreement is too vague to enforce. In some cases, an offer that is by itself too indefinite is made definite because some writing or standard is incorporated by reference and made part of the offer. In some cases, the offer is made definite by implying terms that were not stated. In other cases, the indefinite part of the offer is ignored when that part can be divided or separated from the balance of the offer. In other cases, the requirement of definiteness is ignored either because the matter that is not definite is unimportant or because there is an exception to the rule requiring definiteness.

Assuming that there is in fact an offer that is made with contractual intent and that it is sufficiently definite, it still does not have the legal effect of an offer unless it is communicated to the offeree by or at the direction of the offeror.

In some cases, no contract arises because there is no offer that satisfies the requirements just stated. In other cases, there was an offer, but it was terminated before it was accepted. By definition, an attempted acceptance made after the offer has been terminated has no effect. The ordinary offer may be revoked at any time by the offeror. All that is required is the showing of intent to revoke and the communication of that intent to the offeree. The offeror's power to revoke is barred by the existence of an option contract under common law or a firm offer under the Uniform Commercial Code or local non-Code statute and by the application of the doctrine of detrimental reliance by the offeree. An offer is also terminated by the express rejection of the offer or by the making of a counteroffer; by the lapse of the time stated in the offer or of a reasonable time when none is stated; by the death or disability of either party; or by a change of law that makes illegal a contract based on the particular offer.

When the offer is accepted, a contract arises. Only the offeree can accept an offer, and the acceptance must be of the offer exactly as made without any qualification or change. Ordinarily, the offeree may accept or reject as the offeree chooses. Limitations on this freedom of action have been imposed by antidiscrimination and consumer protection laws.

The acceptance is any manifestation of intent to agree to the terms of the offer. Ordinarily, silence or failure to act does not constitute acceptance. The recipient of unordered goods and tickets may dispose of the goods or use the goods without such action constituting an acceptance. An acceptance does not exist until the words or conduct demonstrating assent to the offer is communicated to the offeror. Acceptance by mail takes effect at the time and place when and where the letter is mailed or the fax is transmitted. A telephoned acceptance is effective when and where spoken into the phone.

In an auction sale, the auctioneer asking for bids makes an invitation to negotiate. A person making a bid is making an offer, and the acceptance of the highest bid by the auctioneer is an acceptance of that offer and gives rise to a contract. When the auction sale is without reserve, the auctioneer must accept the highest bid. If the auction is not expressly without reserve, the auctioneer may refuse to accept any of the bids.

QUESTIONS AND CASE PROBLEMS

1. City Paint Co. made an offer to paint the Jones factory for $50,000. The board of directors of Jones held a meeting and unanimously voted to accept City Paint's offer. A Jones Co. secretary was a friend of a secretary at City Paint and relayed the information through her that Jones had accepted the City Paint offer. The next day Jones' board of directors decided they had been too reckless in accepting the offer and voted to reject it. When Jones sent City Paint a rejection of City Paint's offer, City Paint sued Jones for breach of contract. Decide.

2. Brown made an offer to purchase Overman's house on a standard printed form. Underneath Brown's signature was the statement: "ACCEPTANCE ON REVERSE SIDE." Overman did not sign the offer on the back but sent Brown a letter accepting the offer. Later

Brown refused to perform the contract, and Overman sued him for breach of contract. Brown claimed there was no contract because the offer had not been accepted in the manner specified by the offer. Decide. [*Overman v Brown*, ____ Neb ____, 372 NW2d 102]

3. Katherine mailed Paul an offer stating that it was good for 10 days. Two days later she mailed Paul another letter stating that the original offer was revoked. That evening Paul phoned Katherine to say he accepted the offer. She said that he couldn't because she had mailed him a letter of revocation that he would undoubtedly receive in the next morning's mail. Was the offer revoked by Katherine?

4. Nelson wanted to sell his home. Baker sent him a written offer to purchase the home. Nelson made some changes to Baker's offer and wrote him that he, Nelson, was accepting the offer as amended. Baker notified Nelson that he was dropping out of the transaction. Nelson sued Baker for breach of contract. Decide. What social forces and ethical values are involved? [*Nelson v Baker* (Mo App) 776 SW2d 52]

5. Lessack Auctioneers advertised an auction sale that was open to the public and was to be conducted with reserve. Gordon attended the auction and bid $100 for a work of art that was worth much more. No higher bid, however, was made. Lessack refused to sell the item for $100 and withdrew the item from the sale. Gordon claimed that because he was the highest bidder, Lessack was required to sell the item to him. Was he correct?

6. Willis Music Co. advertised a television set at $22.50 in the Sunday newspaper. Ehrlich ordered a set, but the company refused to deliver it on the ground that the price in the newspaper ad was a mistake. Ehrlich sued the company. Was it liable? Why or why not? [*Ehrlich v Willis Music Co.*, ____ Ohio App ____, 113 NE2d 252]

7. When a movement was organized to build a Charles City College, Hauser and others signed pledges to contribute to the college. At the time of signing, Hauser inquired what would happen if he should die or be unable to pay. The representative of the college stated that the pledge would then not be binding and that it was merely a statement of intent. The college failed financially, and Pappas was appointed receiver to collect and liquidate the assets of the college corporation. He sued Hauser for the amount due on his pledge. Hauser raised the defense that the pledge was not a binding contract. Decide. What ethical values are involved? [*Pappas v Hauser* (Iowa) 197 NW2d 607]

8. *A* signed a contract agreeing to sell land he owned but reserved the right to take the hay from the land until the following October. He gave the contract form to *B*, a broker. *C*, a prospective buyer, agreed to buy the land and signed the contract but crossed out the provision regarding the hay crop. Was there a binding contract between *A* and *C*?

9. A. H. Zehmer discussed selling a farm to Lucy. After a 40-minute discussion of the first draft of a contract, Zehmer and his wife, Ida, signed a second draft stating: "We hereby agree to sell to W. O. Lucy the Ferguson farm complete for $50,000 title satisfactory to buyer." Lucy agreed to purchase the farm on these terms. Thereafter, the Zehmers refused to transfer title to Lucy and claimed they had made the contract for sale as a joke. Lucy brought an action to compel performance of the contract. The Zehmers claimed there was no contract. Were they correct? [*Lucy v Zehmer*, (Va App) 84 SE2d 516]

10. Wheeler operated an automobile service station, which he leased from W. C. Cornitius, Inc. The lease ran for three years. Although the lease did not contain any provision for renewal, it was in fact renewed six times for successive three-year terms. The landlord refused to renew the lease for a seventh time. Wheeler brought suit to compel the landlord to accept his offer to renew the lease. Decide. [*William C. Cornitius, Inc. v Wheeler*, ____ Or ____, 556 P2d 666]

11. Cogdill made an offer to the Bank of Benton. The proper officer stated that he would start the paperwork. Did Cogdill have a contract with the Bank of Benton? [*Bank of Benton v Cogdill*, ____ Ill App 3d ____, ____ Ill Dec ____, 454 NE2d 1120]

12. Jake Fries had an option to purchase at $223 an acre a 160-acre farm owned by Mary Fries. He transferred this option to his seven children and died from cancer a few months later. Six of the seven children then claimed six-sevenths of the land by virtue of the option, but one, Mary, refused to recognize a fractional exercise of the option. Could she do this? [*Fries v Fries* (ND) 470 NW2d 232]

13. An agreement was made between *C* Corporation and *S*, a shareholder of *C*, that *S* would sell his stock to *C*. The agreement did not specify any price but stated that the price should be determined by Lenox, a certified public accountant. The agreement also specified that the computations would be made on the basis of the value of corporate assets as shown by the corporate books. Lenox determined the value of the stock on that basis. *S* then refused to carry out the terms of the agreement. He claimed (1) there was no contract because the agreement failed for lack of definiteness by not stating the price to be paid, and (2) he was not bound by the price determined by Lenox because inflation and other factors made the corporate assets worth much more than appeared from the corporate books. *S* also claimed that the formula specified in the

agreement was not in accord with good accounting practices. Was S required to sell his stock to C at the price determined by Lenox?

14. Sanchis owned a building. He agreed to rent it to Rosell for commercial purposes for three years at $50,000 a year. The agreement provided that at the end of that time Rosell had the option to extend the lease for another three years at a rent to be determined then. The first three years expired, and the parties could not agree to the rent to be paid for the next three years. Rosell insisted that Sanchis was required to lease the building for another three years at the same rent as for the first three years. Was he correct?

CPA QUESTIONS

1. Able Sofa Inc. sent Noll a letter offering to sell Noll a custom-made sofa for $5,000. Noll immediately sent a telegram to Able purporting to accept the offer. However, the telegraph company erroneously delivered the telegram to Abel Soda Inc. Three days later, Able mailed a letter of revocation to Noll which was received by Noll. Able refused to sell Noll the sofa. Noll sued Able for breach of contract. Able
   a. Would have been liable under the deposited acceptance rule only if Noll had accepted by mail.
   b. Will avoid liability since it revoked its offer prior to receiving Noll's acceptance.
   c. Will be liable for breach of contract.
   d. Will avoid liability due to the telegraph company's error.

   (5/86, Law, #2, 9911)

2. On September 27, Summers sent Fox a letter offering to sell Fox a vacation home for $150,000. On October 2, Fox replied by mail agreeing to buy the home for $145,000. Summers did not reply to Fox. Do Fox and Summers have a binding contract?
   a. No, because Fox failed to sign and return Summers' letter.
   b. No, because Fox's letter was a counteroffer.
   c. Yes, because Summers' offer was validly accepted.
   d. Yes, because Summers' silence is an implied acceptance of Fox's letter.

   (5/90, Law, #2, 0462)

3. On June 15, Peters orally offered to sell a used lawn mower to Mason for $125. Peters specified that Mason had until June 20 to accept the offer. On June 16, Peters received an offer to purchase the lawn mower for $150 from Bronson, Mason's neighbor. Peters accepted Bronson's offer. On June 17, Mason saw Bronson using the lawn mower and was told the mower had been sold to Bronson. Mason immediately wrote to Peters to accept the June 15 offer. Which of the following statements is correct?
   a. Mason's acceptance would be effective when received by Peters.
   b. Mason's acceptance would be effective when mailed.
   c. Peters' offer had been revoked and Mason's acceptance was ineffective.
   d. Peters was obligated to keep the June 15 offer open until June 20.

   (11/92, Law, #13, 3095)

Capacity and Genuine Assent

OBJECTIVES

After studying this chapter, you should be able to

1. *Define contractual capacity;*
2. *State the extent and effect of avoidance of a contract by a minor;*
3. *Classify unilateral and bilateral mistakes;*
4. *Distinguish between innocent misrepresentation, fraud, and nondisclosure;*
5. *List those classes of persons who lack contractual capacity; and*
6. *Distinguish between undue influence and duress.*

A contract is a binding agreement. This agreement must be made between parties who have the capacity to do so. They must also truly agree so that all parties have really consented to the contract. This chapter explores the elements of contractual capacity of the parties and the genuineness of their assent.

A. CONTRACTUAL CAPACITY

Parties to a contract must have capacity.

Some persons lack contractual capacity, a lack that embraces both those who have a status incapacity, such as minors, and those who have a factual incapacity, such as insane persons.

1. Contractual Capacity Defined

Contractual capacity requires the ability to understand that a contract is made and its general meaning.

Contractual capacity is the ability to understand that a contract is being made and to understand its general meaning. However, the fact that a person does not understand the full legal meaning of a contract does not mean that contractual capacity is lacking. Everyone is presumed to have capacity unless it is proven that capacity is lacking, or unless there is status incapacity.[1] *For example,* Jacqueline, aged 22, entered into a contract with Sunrise Storage Co. but later claimed it was not binding because she did not understand several clauses in the printed contract. The contract was binding. No evidence supported her claim that she lacked capacity to contract or to understand its subject. Contractual capacity can exist even though a party doesn't understand every provision of the contract.

Some persons lack capacity because they belong to a particular class.

(a) Status Incapacity. Over the centuries, the law has declared that some classes of persons lack contractual capacity. The purpose is to protect these classes by giving them the power to get out of unwise contracts. Of these classes, the most important today is the class identified as minors.

Until recent times, some other classes were held to lack contractual capacity in order to discriminate against them. Examples are married women and aliens. Still other classes, such as persons convicted of and sentenced for a felony, were held to lack contractual capacity in order to punish them. Today, these discriminatory and punitive incapacities have largely disappeared. Married women generally have the same contractual capacity as unmarried persons.[2]

CASE SUMMARY

We Really Mean Equal Rights

Facts: An Alabama statute provided that a married woman could not sell her land without the consent of her husband. Montgomery made a contract to sell land she owned to Peddy. Montgomery's husband did not consent to the sale. Montgomery did not perform the contract and was sued by Peddy. The defense was raised that the contract was void and could not be enforced because of the statute. Peddy claimed that the statute was unconstitutional.

---

1 *Re* Adoption of Smith (La App) 578 So 2d 988 (1991).
2 A few states have a limitation that a married woman cannot make a binding contract to pay the debt of her husband if he fails to.

> **Decision:** The statute was unconstitutional. Constitutions, both federal and state, guarantee all persons the equal protection of the law. Married women are denied this equal protection when they are treated differently than married men and unmarried females. The fact that such unequal treatment had once been regarded as proper does not justify its modern continuation. [*Peddy v Montgomery* (Ala) 345 So 2d 631 (1977)]

By virtue of international treaties, the discrimination against aliens has been removed. The destruction of contractual capacity as a punishment for crime still exists in some states, but recent cases regard it as unconstitutional, so it is likely that it will soon disappear.

(b) Factual Incapacity. A factual incapacity contrasts with incapacity imposed because of the class or group to which a person belongs. A factual incapacity may exist when, because of mental or physical condition caused by shock, medication, drugs, alcohol, illness, or age, a person does not understand that a contract is being made or understand its general nature. If the factual incapacity later disappears, the party affected can ordinarily avoid the contract. In some extreme cases, the contract made while the incapacity existed is void.

Some persons lack capacity because of their mental or physical condition.

2.   Minors

Minors may make contracts.[3] To protect them, however, the law has always treated minors as a class lacking contractual capacity.

Generally a minor is under 18.

(a) Who Is a Minor? At common law, any person, male or female, under 21 years of age was a minor (or an infant). At common law, minority ended the day before the 21st birthday. The "day before the birthday" rule is still followed, but the age of majority has been reduced from 21 years to 18 years in most states and to 19 in a few.

Generally a minor can avoid contracts.

(b) Minor's Power to Avoid Contracts. With exceptions that will be noted later, a contract made by a minor is voidable at the election of the minor. The minor may affirm or ratify the contract on attaining majority by performing the contract, by expressly approving the contract, or by allowing a reasonable time to lapse without avoiding the contract. Once the contract is affirmed, it can no longer be avoided.

In some states, a statute declares that certain kinds of contracts made by minors are void and not merely voidable. When such a statute is applicable, a minor does not need to declare that the contract is not binding because there is nothing for the minor to avoid.[4]

(1) What Constitutes Avoidance. A minor may avoid or disaffirm a contract by any expression of an intention to repudiate the contract. Any act inconsistent with the continuing validity of the contract is also an avoidance.

Thus, when a minor sold property to Martin and later, on reaching majority, made a sale of the same property to Gomez, the second sale was an avoidance of the first.

---

3 *Buffington v State Automobile Mutual Ins. Co.*, ____ Ga App ____, 384 SE2d 873 (1989).
4 *Moran v Williston Cooperative Credit Union* (ND) 420 NW2d 353 (1988).

(2) Time for Avoidance. A minor can avoid a contract only during minority and for a reasonable time after attaining majority. After the lapse of a reasonable time, the contract is deemed ratified and cannot be avoided by the minor.

(3) Minor's Misrepresentation of Age. Generally, the fact that the minor has misrepresented his or her age does not affect the minor's power to avoid the contract. Some states hold that such fraud of a minor bars contract avoidance. Some states permit the minor to avoid the contract in such a case but require the minor to pay for any damage to the property received under the contract.

In any case, the other party to the contract may avoid it because of the minor's fraud.

An avoiding minor must restore whatever remains from a contract.

(c) Restitution by Minor after Avoidance. When a minor avoids a contract, the question arises as to what must be returned by the minor to the other contracting party.

(1) Original Consideration Intact. When a minor still has what was received from the other party, the minor, on avoiding the contract, must return it to the other party or offer to do so. That is, the minor must put things back to the original position or, as it is called, restore the **status quo ante**.

(2) Original Consideration Damaged or Destroyed. What happens if the minor cannot return what has been received because it has been spent, used, damaged, or destroyed? The minor's right to avoid the contract is not affected. The minor can still avoid the contract and is required to return only what remains. The fact that nothing remains or that what remains is damaged does not bar the right to avoid the contract. In states that follow the common law rule, minors can thus refuse to pay for what has been received under a contract or can get back what had been paid or given even though they do not have anything to return or return property in a damaged condition. There is, however, a trend to limit this rule.

A minor on avoiding a contract can recover money or property given unless it was acquired by a good-faith purchaser.

(d) Recovery of Property by Minor on Avoidance. When a minor avoids a contract, the other contracting party must return the money received. Any property received from the minor must also be returned. If the property has been sold to a third person who did not know of the original seller's minority, the minor cannot get the property back. In such cases, however, the minor is entitled to recover the property's monetary value or the money received by the other contracting party.

A minor avoiding a contract for necessaries must pay for reasonable benefit received.

(e) Contracts for Necessaries. A minor can avoid a contract for necessaries but must pay the reasonable value for furnished necessaries. This duty of the minor is a quasi-contractual liability. It is a duty that the law imposes on the minor rather than a duty created by contract.

The definition of necessaries has expanded to include property appropriate to the social status of the minor and property needed to earn a living.

(1) What Constitutes Necessaries. Originally, **necessaries** were limited to those things absolutely necessary for the sustenance and shelter of the minor. Thus limited, the term would extend only to the simplest food, clothing, and lodging. In the course of time, the rule was relaxed to extend generally to things relating to the health, education, and comfort of the minor. Thus, the rental of a house used by a married minor is a necessary. Services reasonably necessary to obtaining employment by a minor have been held to be necessaries.

The rule has also been relaxed to hold that whether an item is a necessary in a particular case depends on the financial and social status, or station in life, of the minor. The more recent decisions hold that property used by a minor to earn a living is a necessary. Thus, it has been held that a tractor and farm equipment were necessaries for a married minor who supported a family by farming.

Expansion of the definition of necessaries has come about because, in this century, minors have taken a greater part in the business and working world. In many cases, minors have left the parental home to lead independent lives.

(2) Contract with Parent or Guardian. When a third person supplies the parents or guardian of a minor with goods or services that the minor needs, the minor is not liable for these necessaries because the third person's contract is with the parent or guardian, not with the minor.

(f) Ratification of Former Minor's Voidable Contract. A former minor cannot avoid a contract that has been ratified after reaching majority.[5]

(1) What Constitutes Ratification. Ratification consists of any words or conduct of the former minor manifesting an intent to be bound by the terms of a contract made while a minor.

Making payments after attaining majority may constitute a ratification. Many courts, however, refuse to recognize payment as ratification in the absence of further evidence of an intent to ratify, an express statement of ratification, or an appreciation that such payment might constitute a ratification.

An acknowledgment that a contract had been made during minority without an intent to be bound by it is not a ratification.

(2) Form of Ratification. Generally, no special form is required for ratification of a minor's voidable contract, although in some states a written ratification or declaration of intention is required.

(3) Time for Ratification. A person can avoid a contract any time during minority and for a reasonable time after that but, of necessity, can ratify only a contract after attaining majority. The minor must have attained majority, or the ratification would itself be regarded as voidable.

(g) Contracts That Minors Cannot Avoid. Statutes in many states deprive a minor of the right to avoid an educational loan;[6] a contract for medical care; a contract made while running a business; a contract approved by a court; a contract made in performance of a legal duty; or a contract relating to bank accounts, insurance policies, or corporate stock. In most states, the contract of a veteran, although a minor, is binding, particularly a contract for the purchase of a home. In some states, by court decision a minor who is nearly an adult, or who appears to be an adult, cannot avoid a contract, particularly when it is made in connection with a business or employment.

On attaining majority, a minor's contract can be ratified and ceases to be voidable. Any indication of intent to approve the contract is a ratification.

Some contracts of minors cannot be avoided.

---

[5] *Fletcher v Marshall,* ____ Ill App 3d ____, ____ Ill Dec ___, 632 NE2d 1105 (1994).
[6] A Model Student Capacity to Borrow Act makes educational loans binding on minors in Arizona, Mississippi, New Mexico, North Dakota, Oklahoma, and Washington. This act was reclassified from a uniform act to a model act by the Commissioners on Uniform State Law, indicating that uniformity was viewed as unimportant and that the matter was primarily local in character.

Some courts take an intermediate position with respect to employment contracts. These courts allow minors to avoid a contract but prohibit them from using any secret information obtained in the course of employment or from competing with the former employer when the avoided contract contained a noncompetition clause. It has also been held that when a minor has settled a claim and received the amount specified in a release, the release is binding and cannot be set aside when the minor attains majority.

(h) Liability of Third Person for a Minor's Contract. The question arises whether parents are bound by the contract of their minor child. The question also arises whether a person cosigning a minor's contract is bound if the contract is avoided.

A parent is ordinarily not liable for a minor's contract.

(1) Liability of Parent. Ordinarily, a parent is not liable on a contract made by a minor child. The parent may be liable, however, if the child is acting as the agent of the parent in making the contract. For example, when a mother sends her daughter to the store to buy a coat for the daughter and have it charged on the mother's account, the daughter is acting as agent for her mother, and the contract is the contract of the mother and not the daughter. Also, the parent is liable to a seller for the reasonable value of necessaries supplied by the seller to the child if the parent had deserted the child.

A cosigner is not affected by a minor's avoidance.

(2) Liability of Cosigner. When the minor makes a contract, another person, such as a parent or a friend, may sign along with the minor to make the contract more attractive to the third person.

With respect to the other contracting party, the cosigner is bound independently of the minor. Consequently, if the minor avoids the contract, the cosigner remains bound by it. When the debt to the creditor is actually paid, the obligation of the cosigner is discharged.

If the minor avoids a sales contract but does not return the goods, the cosigner remains liable for the purchase price.

3.   Incompetents

A contract of an incompetent may generally be avoided.

A person who is mentally deficient is generally called an **incompetent** and lacks capacity to make a contract. The cause of the incapacity is immaterial. It may be the result of insanity, senile dementia, imbecility, excessive use of drugs or alcohol, or a stroke. If the person is so mentally incompetent as to be unable to understand that a contract is being made or the general nature of the contract, the person lacks contractual capacity. The fact that a person is mentally retarded does not in itself constitute incapacity if the person understands the nature of the transaction and that a contract is being made.

An incompetent may have lucid intervals. If a contract is made during such an interval and is not affected by any delusion, the contract is valid and binding.

The modern trend bars avoidance of an incompetent's contract when terms are reasonable, incompetence was unknown, and restoration is not possible.

(a) Effect of Incompetency. An incompetent person may ordinarily avoid a contract in the same manner as a minor. Upon the removal of the disability (that is, upon becoming competent), the formerly incompetent person can either ratify or disaffirm the contract.

A current trend in the law is to treat the incompetent's contract as fully binding when its terms and the surrounding circumstances are reasonable and the incompetent person is unable to restore the other contracting party to the status quo ante.

CASE SUMMARY

Protecting the Good-Faith Party

Facts: Cora Haith obtained a loan from the Home Savings and Loan Association to refinance an existing mortgage on her home and to remodel the home. Some time later she was declared incompetent, and Hedgepeth was appointed her guardian. The guardian sued Home Savings to set aside the loan transaction on the ground that it was void because of Haith's incompetence. Home Savings defended on the ground that it had no reason to know of Haith's incompetence, the loan transaction did not take advantage of Haith, and Haith was not able to return to Home Savings what she had received.

Decision: Assuming that Haith was incompetent when the contract with Home Savings was made, that contract was merely voidable and not void, since she had not yet been adjudicated incompetent. However, the contract could not be avoided where, as here, the other contracting party did not know or have reason to know or inquire as to Haith's incompetence, the transaction did not take advantage of the incompetent, and the incompetent was not able to return what had been received under the contract. [*Hedgepeth v Home Savings and Loan Ass'n, 87 NC App 610, 361 SE2d 888 (1987)*]

As in the case of minors, the other party to the contract has no right to disaffirm the contract merely because the incompetent has the right to do so.

An incompetent's contract is void if the incompetent has a guardian.

(b) Appointment of Guardian. If a court appoints a guardian for the incompetent person, a contract made by that person before the appointment may be ratified or, in some cases, disaffirmed by the guardian. If the incompetent person makes a contract after a guardian has been appointed, the contract is void and not merely voidable.

4. Intoxicated Persons

The capacity of a party to contract and the validity of the contract are not affected by the party's being drunk at the time of making the contract so long as the party knew that a contract was being made.

If the degree of intoxication is such that a person does not know that a contract is being made, the contract is voidable by that person. The situation is the same as though the person were insane at the time and did not know what was being done. On becoming sober, the person may avoid or rescind the contract. However, an unreasonable delay in taking steps to set aside a known contract entered into while intoxicated may bar the intoxicated person from asserting this right.[7] *For example,* Edward made a contract while intoxicated. When he sobered up, he immediately avoided the contract for lack of capacity as the result of his intoxication. The other contracting party claimed that voluntary intoxication cannot void a contract, but Edward could avoid the contract because he lacked the legal capacity to enter a contract.

---

[7] *Diedrich v Diedrich* (Minn App) 424 NW2d 580 (1988).

FIGURE 13-1
Avoidance of Contract

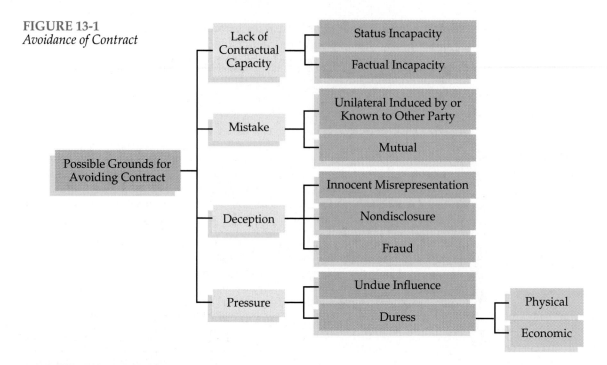

Globe Life Insurance Co. has undertaken a new sales program that targets neighborhoods in Los Angeles where drive-by shootings are a nightly occurrence. Over the past two months, two such shootings occurred in which children were killed as they sat in their living rooms. Another child was paralyzed by a bullet from a drive-by shooting three months ago.

Globe salespeople are instructed to "hit" the houses surrounding those where children were victims. They are also told to contact the parents of those children to sell policies for their other children.

Tom Raskin, an experienced Globe salesman, read of a drive-by shooting last night at Nancy Leonard's home, in which Leonard's five-year-old son was killed. The *Los Angeles Times* reported that Leonard was a single parent with four other children.

Raskin traveled to Leonard's home and described the benefits of a Globe policy for her other children. He offered her the $10,000 term life policy for each of the children for a total cost of $21 per month. Leonard was in the process of making funeral arrangements for her son, and Raskin noted, "See how much it costs for a funeral."

Leonard had been given several tranquilizers the night before by a physician at the hospital's emergency room. The physician had also given her 15 more tranquilizers to help her through the following week. She had taken one additional tranquilizer an hour before Raskin arrived, using a Coors Lite beer to take the pill.

Leonard signed the contract for the policy. After her son's funeral, she received the first month's bill for it and exclaimed, "I didn't buy any life insurance! Where did this come from?"

After you discuss Leonard's legal standing, discuss the ethical issues involved in Globe's sales program. Discuss the legal issues involved in Raskin's decision to target Leonard the day after her son's death.

B.   MISTAKE

The validity of a contract may be affected by the fact that one or both of the parties made a mistake. In some cases the mistake may be caused by the misconduct of one of the parties.

5.   Unilateral Mistake

A unilateral mistake generally does not affect a contract.

A unilateral mistake—that is, a mistake by only one of the parties—as to a fact does not affect the contract when the mistake is unknown to the other contracting party.[8] When a contract is made on the basis of a quoted price, the validity of the contract is not affected by the fact that the party furnishing the quotation had made a mathematical mistake in computing the price if there was no reason for the other party to recognize that there was a mistake.[9]

For example, Office Supply Outlet, which sold office supplies at retail, ordered a large quantity of computers from Compuware, Inc. The sales contract did not permit a reduction in the quantity ordered, but, because of a clerical error, Office Supply ordered about five times what it would need for the coming year. When Office Supply realized the mistake, it wrote Compuware to reduce the quantity. Because Office Supply's mistake was unilateral, the contract for the original quantity was enforceable.

An agreement has no effect if it states that it shall be void if the fact is not as believed. The party making the mistake may also avoid the contract if the mistake is known, or should be known or recognized, by the other contracting party.

A unilateral mistake as to expectations or the law does not have any effect on the contract.[10] Thus, the fact that a signer of a contract would not have signed if the signer had understood the legal effect of the contract is not a defense.

CASE SUMMARY

You Can't Pass the Buck

Facts: Sanif, Inc., made a contract to obtain burglar alarm system protection for its place of business. In spite of the system, the place of business was burglarized. Sanif sued for damages on the theory that there was negligent failure of the alarm system. The defendant raised the defense that the contract expressly limited its liability in case of failure. The officer of the plaintiff claimed that this limitation was not binding because it had not been explained to him when the contract was signed.

Decision: The limitation was binding. The officer of the plaintiff had voluntarily signed the contract on behalf of the corporation. There was no evidence that the other contracting party had committed any fraud. Therefore, the failure to have explained the limitation clause did not affect the validity of the limitation clause. *[Sanif, Inc. v Iannotti, 119 App Div 2d 654, 500 NWS2d 798 (1986)]*

A minority of states recognize unilateral mistake as a defense unless (1) the mistake is the result of inexcusable lack of due care or (2) the other party has so changed position in reliance on the contract that rescission would be unconscionable.

---

[8] *Oh v Wilson ,____ Nev ____, 210 P2d 276 (1996).*
[9] *Procan Construction Co. v Oceanside Development Corp., ____ App Div 2d ____, 539 NYS2d 437 (1989).*
[10] *Hedging Concepts, Inc. v First Alliance Mortgage Co., ____ Cal App 4th ____, 49 Cal Rptr 191 (1996).*

(a) Mistake as to Nature of Document. When a party makes a negligent mistake as to the nature of a document, the party is bound according to its terms. For example, when the printed form for a corporation's loan application contained a guarantee of the corporate debt by the president of the corporation, the president signing the application without reading it was bound by this guarantee. This is true even though the president did not know that it was in the application and the application was headed merely "Application for Credit."

The educated person who signs a promissory note without reading it is bound by it even though the lender had falsely stated to the signer that the note was merely a character reference.[11]

(b) Mistake as to Terms of Document. A person who has the ability and the opportunity to read a document before signing is bound by its terms even though the person signed without reading it.[12] Such a signer cannot avoid liability on the ground there had not been any explanation given of the terms of the writing.

CASE SUMMARY

Sign Now, Read Later——If You're Nuts!

Facts: An automobile driven by Sofio and a truck driven by Hughes collided. A settlement of claims was agreed to, and Sofio signed a contract entitled "Release of All Claims." The release clearly covered both personal injuries and property damage claims. It contained the warning "Read Carefully Before Signing." The title and the warning were in boldface type. Later Sofio claimed that the release did not bar him from suing for personal injuries because he had signed the release without reading it and wrongly believed that it covered only property damages.

Decision: The release was binding. It clearly covered all kinds of claims. Sofio could not avoid the release on the ground that he had made a mistake as to what it covered. Because he had signed the release without reading it, he was bound by its terms, without regard to his subjective belief or opinion as to what it covered. [Sofio v Hughes, 162 App Div 2d 518, 556 NYS2d 717 (1990)]

In contrast to a person who is mistaken about the terms of a document from carelessness in reading it, a person may be unable to read or to understand the terms of a document. Such a person is bound by signing the document without obtaining an explanation of it unless the other contracting party knows, or has reason to know, of the signer's disability or educational limitation.

Courts differ as to the effect of unknown claims on a release of claims.

(c) Mistake as to Release. An insurance claimant is bound by a release given to the insurance company when there is a unilateral mistake about its meaning resulting from carelessness in reading the release. When a release is given and accepted in good faith, it is immaterial that the releasor or both parties were mistaken about the seriousness or possible future consequences of a known injury or condition. If the release covers all claims known or unknown, courts following the common law hold the releasor bound even though there were other injuries of which the releasor was unaware because the effects of the unknown injuries had not yet appeared. Some courts depart from this and hold the release effective only with

---

[11] *DeHart v Dodge City of Spartanburg, Inc.* (SC App) 427 SE2d 720 (1993).
[12] *Huber v Hovey* (Iowa) 501 NW2d 53 (1993).

respect to the conditions or consequences that were known at the time the release was given. By this view, it is held that general release language releasing "any and all claims whether or not now known" does not bar the releasing party from later asserting a claim that was unknown when the release was executed.[13]

6.   Mutual Mistake

An agreement is void if there is mutual mistake of fact.

When both parties make the same mistake of fact, the agreement is void. Thus, the agreement is not binding when both contracting parties bargained on the basis that certain property was junk when in fact it was valuable art.[14]

A contract is not affected by a mutual mistake as to expectations.

(a) Mistake as to Expectations. A mutual mistake with respect to expectations ordinarily has no effect on the contract unless the realization of those expectations is made an express condition of the contract. For example, certain parties bought and sold a little country highway store in the belief that the United States would build an army base about a mile away. The contract remained binding and was not affected by the fact that the army did not build the base, with the result that the expectations of a thriving business at the store were never realized. This means that the mistake has no effect unless the contract says it shall be void if the matter is not as believed.

A contract is ordinarily not affected by a mutual mistake of law.

(b) Mistake of Law. When the mutual or bilateral mistake is one of law, the contract generally is binding. Thus, even if both parties to a lease mistakenly believe that the leased premises can be used for boarding animals because they are unaware of a zoning regulation that prohibits such a use of the property, the tenant does not have a right to rescind the lease for mutual mistake of law. In the eyes of the law, the parties should have known what the zoning regulations allowed. A few courts have refused to follow this rule. In several states, statutes provide that a mutual mistake of law shall have the same effect as a mutual mistake of fact.

(c) Mistake as to Collateral Matter. A mutual mistake as to collateral matter does not affect the binding character of a contract. Consequently, the fact that the seller and the buyer of equipment were mistaken about the adequacy of the buyer's power supply did not avoid the sales contract, as it was a matter that was collateral to the contract and did not relate to performance by the seller. To justify rescission for mutual mistake, the mistake must be fundamental in order to defeat the intent of both parties in entering the contract.[15]

C.   DECEPTION

Deception may make a contract voidable.

One of the parties to a contract may have been misled by an innocent misrepresentation, a failure to disclose information, or a fraudulent statement.

---

13 *Farrin v Norfolk & Western Rwy Co.*, 106 Ohio App 3d 401, 666 NE2d 291 (1995) (cancer from asbestos exposure later discovered).
14 *Monet v Pera* (Tex App) 877 SW2d 552 (1994).
15 *South v Transportation Ins. Co.*, ____Mont ____, 913 P2d 233 (1996).

7. Innocent Misrepresentation

Suppose one party to a contract makes a statement of fact that is false but is innocently made without intending to deceive the other party. Can the other party set aside the contract on the ground of being misled by the statement?

Equity will permit the rescission of the contract when the innocent misstatement of a material fact induces another to make the contract. If the deceived person is a defendant in an action at law for breach of contract, it is generally held that such innocent deception by the plaintiff cannot be asserted as a defense. There is a tendency, however, for courts to adopt the rule of equity. For example, it may be possible for an insurance company to avoid its policy because of an innocent misstatement of a material fact by the applicant. Contracts between persons standing in confidential relationships, such as guardian and ward or parent and child, can be set aside for the same reason. Some courts go beyond this and permit recovery of damages because of misrepresentation.

Modern law is increasingly concerned with the plight of the plaintiff and less concerned with whether the defendant was at fault. Courts that take this approach see no difference between an intentional fraudulent statement and innocent misrepresentation—the plaintiff is misled and harmed in either case.

In some states, statutes have defined fraud to include innocent misrepresentation. Under such a statute, a wrong statement of the model year of an automobile imposes liability on the seller even though the misrepresentation was a mistake and no common law fraud or bad faith was present.

8. Nondisclosure

Under certain circumstances, nondisclosure will serve to make a contract voidable, especially when the nondisclosure consists of active concealment.

(a) General Rule of Nonliability. Ordinarily, a party to a contract has no duty to volunteer information to the other party. For example, if Fox does not ask Tehan any questions, Tehan is not under any duty to make a full statement of material facts. Consequently, the nondisclosure of information that is not asked for does not impose fraud liability or impair the validity of a contract. A number of states have adopted laws to protect the seller of a house from liability for failing to volunteer that there had been a murder or suicide in the house or that an occupant had certain diseases.[16]

CASE SUMMARY

Welcome to the Seesaw: Buyer versus Seller

Facts: Dalarna Management Corp. owned a building constructed on a pier on a lake. There were repeated difficulties with rainwater leaking into the building, and water damage was visible in the interior of the building. Dalarna made a contract to sell the building to Curran. Curran made several inspections of the building and had the building inspected two times by a licensed engineer. The engineer reported that there were signs of water leaks. Curran assigned his contract to Puget Sound Service Corp., which then purchased the building from Dalarna. Puget Sound spent approximately $118,000 attempting to stop the leaks. Puget Sound then sued Dalarna for damages, claiming that Dalarna's failure to disclose the extent of the water leakage problem constituted fraud.

---

[16] See, for example, South Carolina, Act of May 14, 1990, Act No. 481.

> **Decision:** Judgment for Dalarna. Curran was aware that there was a water leakage problem, and therefore the burden was on the buyer to ask questions to determine the extent of the problem. There was no duty on the seller to volunteer the extent of the water damage merely because it had been a continuing problem that was more than just a simple leak. This conclusion was reached by the court because the law "balances the harshness of the former rule of caveat emptor [let the buyer beware] with the equally undesirable alternative of courts standing in loco parentis [in the place of a parent] to parties transacting business." *[Puget Sound Service Corp. v Dalarna Management Corp., 51 Wash App 209, 752 P2d 1353 (1988)]*

When a house is sold "as is," the seller has no duty to disclose any latent defects. However, the seller is liable for fraud if defects are actively concealed or misrepresented.

(b) Exceptions. Some statutes require the seller of a house to report murders committed in the house. Other exceptions have been created by other courts. In all such cases, failure to disclose information that was not requested is regarded as fraudulent, and the party to whom the information was not disclosed has the same remedies as if a known false statement were intentionally made.

> *There may be nondisclosure liability where a hidden defect exists that the other party would not discover or inquire about.*

(1) Unknown Defect or Condition. A duty is developing in the law for one party who knows of a defect or condition to disclose that information to the other party where the defect or condition is obviously unknown to the other person and is of such a nature that it is unlikely that the other person would discover the truth or inquire about it. However, a defendant who had no knowledge of the defect cannot be held liable for failure to disclose it.[17]

CASE SUMMARY

When Silence Is Not Golden

Facts: Wire purchased a house. The sale was transacted by him with Jackson, the real estate agent acting for the owner. Jackson knew that the house was infested with termites. Wire was not informed of the termites. Later Wire learned of the termite condition and sued Jackson.

Decision: Jackson had the duty to volunteer the information about the termites. *[Wire v Jackson (La App) 576 So 2d 1198 (1991)]*

Manufacturers and distributors of asbestos were guilty of fraud when they sold asbestos products without disclosing the information they possessed showing a relationship between cancer and asbestos products.[18] An automobile dealer who sells a used car without informing the buyer that the odometer had been set back is liable for fraud.[19]

---

[17] *Nesbitt v Dunn* (La App) 672 So 2d 226 (1996).
[18] *Board of Education of City of Chicago v A,C & S, Inc.,* ____ Ill App 3d ____, ____Ill Dec ____, 525 NE2d 950 (1988).
[19] *Pelster v Ray* (CA8 Mo) 987 F2d 514 (1993).

There is nondisclosure liability where a confidential relationship imposed the duty to disclose.

(2) Confidential Relationship. If parties stand in a confidential relationship, failure to disclose information may be regarded as fraudulent. For example, in an attorney-client relationship,[20] the attorney has a duty to reveal anything that is material to the client's interest when dealing with the client. The attorney's silence has the same legal consequence as a knowingly made false statement that there was no material fact to be told to the client.

The relationship between the buyer of a house and a financial institution lending the money to finance the purchase is not a confidential relationship. Therefore, the lender is not under any duty to disclose information it possesses.

Fine print may show fraud or violate other law.

(3) Fine Print. An intent to conceal may be present when a printed contract or document contains certain clauses in such fine print that it is reasonable to believe the other contracting party will neither take the time nor even be able to read such provisions.

In some instances, legislatures have outlawed certain fine-print contracts. Statutes commonly declare that insurance policies may not be printed in type of smaller size than designated by statute. Consumer protection statutes frequently require that particular clauses be set in large type. When a merchant selling goods under a written contract disclaims the obligation that goods be fit for their normal use, the Uniform Commercial Code requires the waiver to be set forth in "conspicuous" writing. Conspicuous is defined as "a term or clause . . . so written that a reasonable person against whom it is to operate ought to have noticed it. A printed heading in capitals . . . is conspicuous. Language in the body of a form is 'conspicuous' if it is in larger or other contrasting type or color . . . ."[21]

There is a growing trend to treat a fine-print clause as not binding on the party who would be harmed by it without considering whether fraud was involved. A provision freeing the other contracting party from liability is not binding when it is printed in type that is so small that a person with normal vision would have difficulty reading it.

Nondisclosure constituting concealment is fraud.

(4) Active Concealment. Nondisclosure may be more than the passive failure to volunteer information. It may consist of a positive act of hiding information from the other party by physical concealment, or it may consist of knowingly or recklessly furnishing the wrong information. Such conduct constitutes fraud.

◆ *For example*, when Nigel wanted to sell his house, he covered the wooden cellar beams with plywood to hide extensive termite damage. He sold the house to Kuehne, who sued Nigel for damages on later discovering the termite damage. Nigel claimed he had no duty to volunteer information about the termites, but by covering the damage with plywood, he committed active fraud as if he had made a false statement that there were no termites. ◆

9. Fraud

Knowledge of falsity or reckless indifference to truth is essential to fraud.

Fraud is making a false statement of fact with (1) knowledge of its falsity or reckless indifference to its truth; (2) the intent that the listener rely on it; (3) the result that the listener does so rely; and (4) the consequence that the listener is harmed.[22]

---

[20] *Re* Boss Trust (Minn App) 487 NW2d 256 (1992).
[21] UCC § 1-201(10).
[22] *Maack v Resource Design & Construction, Inc.* (Utah) 875 P2d 570 (1994).

CASE SUMMARY

Don't Bluff When You Don't Know

Facts: Karan purchased a used truck from a dealer, Bob Post, Inc. In selecting his purchase, he asked whether the odometer reading of 27,000 miles was correct. The salesman did not know whether it was or not but assured Karan that it was correct and also stated that certain parts of the truck were still covered by the manufacturer's 50,000-mile warranty. The actual mileage of the truck was over 48,000 miles, and the truck was not eligible for any warranty protection. After taking possession of the truck, Karan discovered its poor condition and then learned that the statements of the salesman had been false. Karan sued the dealer for fraud. The defense was made that the salesman had not known that his statements were false and did not have any reason to know that they were false, and therefore he could not have been guilty of fraud.

Decision: The salesman was guilty of fraud even though he did not actually know that his statements were false. He knew that he did not have definite knowledge that what he said was true, but he made his statements as being true. He therefore took the risk that they might be false, and if they were false, his statements constituted fraud. [Karan v Bob Post, Inc. (Colo App) 521 P2d 1276 (1974)]

An automobile salesman committed fraud by presenting a car as a new demonstrator when in fact the car had been damaged and repaired three times. A used-car seller commits fraud by failing to disclose that an automobile is the front half of one model welded to the rear half of a model from a different year.[23]

CASE SUMMARY

The Silent Lie

Facts: Roy Cadek took his funny car, "Risky Asset," to the Great Lakes Dragway to do some racing on the park's track. During a run, Cadek's car veered to the left and collided with Cadek's support van which was parked on the side of the track. The collision was minor, but leaking fuel ignited and fire engulfed the two vehicles. Great Lakes had a fire truck parked on the track, but it was unmanned and its fire extinguishers empty. Both of Cadek's vehicles were a total loss with combined damages of $45,000. Cadek sued Great Lakes. Great Lakes knew that the fire truck wasn't operable and defended on grounds that it had not made a representation to Cadek as to the fire truck's fire fighting capacity.

Decision: Judgment for Cadek. While no words had been said, the placing of the fire truck by the side of the race track was a statement by conduct that there was the capacity to extinguish fires. As Great Lakes knew that the truck would not work, such action was fraudulent, and Great Lakes was liable. [Cadek v Great Lakes Dragway, Inc. (CA7 Ill) 58 F3d 1209 (1995)]

Reliance on a false statement is essential to impose fraud liability.

(a) Reliance on Statement. A fraudulent statement made by one party has no importance unless the other party relies on the statement's truth. Consequently, fraud is not present when the victim has the same knowledge of the true facts as the alleged wrongdoer or should have known these facts. When false statements are made after a contract has been signed, it is obvious that the making of the contract was not induced by the statements and that the other party to the contract had not relied on them. ◆ *For example,* after making thorough tests of the Nagel Co.'s pump, Beatrice ordered 100 pumps. She later sued Nagel on the ground that advertising statements made about the pumps were false. Beatrice cannot impose fraud liability on Nagel for the advertisements, even if they were false, because she

---

[23] *Clark v McDaniel* (Iowa) 546 NW2d 590 (1996).

had not relied on them in making her purchase but had acted on the basis of the tests she had conducted. ◆

If the alleged victim of the fraud knew that the statements were false because the truth was commonly known, the victim cannot rely on the false statements. When the statements of a seller are so "indefinite and extravagant" that reasonable persons would not rely thereon, the statements cannot be the basis of a claim for fraud.[24]

If the victim of the false statement could have easily determined that it was false, a court may hold there is no fraud liability.[25] However, a person is ordinarily entitled to rely on the honesty of the person making a representation and is not required to conduct an independent investigation to determine whether it is true. The modern American economy depends on a fast turnover of goods, and this is possible only when there is reliance by buyers on statements of sellers. Thus, the buyer of a used car is entitled to rely on the statement of the seller that the car had never been in a wreck and that it had nothing wrong with it. This is true even though, if the buyer had the car raised on a lift, the buyer could have seen the wreck-caused damage to the car and thus learned that the statements of the seller were false.

(b) Statement of Intention or Promise. A statement of intention or promise can constitute fraud when made by a person who does not intend to keep it.[26] To illustrate, a customer purchases goods from a merchant on credit and agrees to pay for them in 60 days. If the customer does not intend to pay for the goods and does not do so, the customer is guilty of fraud by misrepresenting intention.

Statement of intention or a promise as to the future is generally not fraud.

The mere fact that the defendant has not performed a promise does not in itself establish that the defendant was guilty of fraud. It must be shown that the person made the promise with the intention of not keeping it.[27]

It is necessary to distinguish between a mere statement of intention or promise and a statement that involves a past or existing fact. A statement based on construction plans to construct a double traffic lane is a statement of promise. No liability for fraud would be found if the double traffic lane could not be constructed as the result of zoning restrictions. However, if a single traffic lane existed and representations indicated the existence of a double traffic lane, liability could be imposed for misrepresentation of fact (i.e., fraud).[28]

(c) Statement of Opinion or Value. Ordinarily, a misstatement of opinion or value is not regarded as fraudulent. Thus, statements that a building was "very good," it "required only normal maintenance," and the "deal was excellent" were merely matters of opinion. Therefore, a court considered the sophistication and expertise of the parties and the commercial setting of the transaction and enforced the contract "as is." The theory is that the person hearing the statement recognizes or should recognize that it is merely the speaker's personal view and not a statement of fact. A statement that is mere sales talk cannot be the basis of fraud liability. Hence, fraud liability does not arise when an automobile salesman tells the purchaser that the automobile is "smooth riding" and "top of the line."

Statement of opinion or value is generally not fraud.

---

[24] *Eckert v Flair Agency, Inc.* (Okla App) 909 P2d 1201 (1995) (seller's statement that house would never be flooded again).
[25] *Burman v Richmond Homes* (Colo App) 821 P2d 913 (1991).
[26] *Lazar v Superior Court*, 49 Cal Rptr 2d 377, 909 P2d 981 (1996).
[27] *Peco Construction Co. v Guajardo* (Tex App) 919 SW2d 736 (1996).
[28] *R.R.S. II Enterprises, Inc. v Regency Associates* (Ind App) 646 NE2d 56 (1995).

However, if the defendant, in making a statement about future expectations, had knowledge not available to the plaintiff that showed such expectations could not be realized, the statement can be held fraudulent. Thus, a statement that a business would make a stated profit in the future is actionable when the speaker knew that, on the basis of past events, such a prediction was false. Likewise, a statement of opinion may be fraudulent when the speaker knows of past or present facts that make the opinion false.

CASE SUMMARY

When the Prophet Is a Liar

Facts: Master Abrasives Corp. sold a dealership to Williams. He purchased the dealership because the manager of Abrasives told him that there was the potential of earning $30,000 to $40,000 a year. Actually the existing dealership had net earnings of $6,000 to $9,000. When Williams learned the truth, he claimed the right to avoid the sale to him on the ground of fraud.

Decision: The contract could be avoided for fraud. The statements as to future potential earnings by themselves would not be fraud, but when these statements were combined with the manager's knowledge of past events it was clear that the manager knew that the forecast goals were impossible to attain. Thus his forecast constituted fraud that was material to the contract and the contract could be rescinded. [*Master Abrasives Corp. v Williams (Ind App) 469 NE2d 1196 (1984)*]

"It is not always an easy matter to determine whether a given statement is one of fact or opinion. The relative expertise of the parties, their intentions, and the surrounding circumstances, gathered from the evidence, affect the court's determination of whether the representations were fact or opinion."[29] When the underlying facts are not known equally to both parties, a statement of opinion by the person with superior knowledge of the facts may have the effect of an assertion that no fact exists that would contradict the opinion. In such case, if the opinion is intentionally made with knowledge that there are such contradictory facts, fraud liability will be imposed for such false opinion.[30]

(d) Statement of Law. A misstatement of law is treated in the same manner as an opinion or misstatement of value. Ordinarily, the listener is regarded as having an opportunity equal to that of the speaker of knowing what the law is, so that the listener is not entitled to rely on what the speaker says. Thus, a claim of fraud cannot be based on a landlord's assurance that a tenant "should have no trouble" in obtaining a desired license.[31] When the speaker has expert knowledge of the law or claims to have such knowledge, however, the misstatement of law can be the basis for fraud liability.

Statement of law is generally not fraud.

(e) Unconscionability and Consumer Protection. In many states, greater protection than is allowed under the common law doctrine of fraud is granted by applying the concept of unconscionability or the specific provisions of a consumer protection statute. That is, relief is at times given the victim in deception and hardship cases even though some of the elements required to impose fraud liability are not present.

---

[29] *Mortarino v Consultant Engineering Services, Inc.,* ____ Va ____, 467 SW3d 778 (1996).
[30] *Sperau v Ford Motor Co.* (Ala) 674 So 2d 24 (1995).
[31] *Watkins v Gross* (Mo App) 772 SW2d 22 (1989).

D.   PRESSURE

What appears to be an agreement may not in fact be voluntary because one of the parties entered into it as the result of undue influence or physical or economic duress.

10. Undue Influence

An aged parent may entrust all business affairs to a trusted child; an invalid may rely on a nurse; a client may follow implicitly whatever an attorney recommends. The relationship may be such that for practical purposes one person is helpless in the hands of the other. When such a confidential relationship exists, it is apparent that the parent, the invalid, or the client is not exercising free will in making a contract suggested by the child, nurse, or attorney but is merely following the will of the other person. Because of the great possibility of unfair advantage, the law presumes that the dominating person exerts undue influence on the other person whenever the dominating person obtains any benefit from a contract made with the dominated person. The contract is then voidable. It may be set aside by the dominated person unless the dominating person can prove that, at the time the contract was made, no unfair advantage had been taken.

The class of confidential relationships is not well defined. It ordinarily includes the relationships of parent and child, guardian and ward, physician and patient, and attorney and client and any other relationship of trust and confidence in which one party exercises a control or influence over another.

> **Undue influence makes a contract voidable. Undue influence is likely where a confidential relationship exists.**

CASE SUMMARY

When Does Fiduciary Begin?

Facts: Studley and Bentson made a contract by which Bentson agreed to transfer to Studley certain property in consideration of the promise of Studley to provide a home and take care of Bentson for life. The contract was prepared by a third person, and its effect was explained to Bentson by the president of the bank where he deposited his money. Bentson died, and the administratrix of his estate sued to set aside the contract, claiming undue influence.

Decision: Judgment for Studley. The fact that Studley and Bentson had been friends and that the latter had confidence in the former did not make the relationship a confidential relationship. Therefore, Studley did not have the burden of sustaining the validity of the contract. [*Johnson v Studley, 80 Cal App 538, 252 P 638 (1926)*]

Whether undue influence exists is a difficult question for courts (ordinarily juries) to determine. The law does not regard every influence as undue. Thus, nagging may drive a person to make a contract, but that is not ordinarily regarded as undue influence. Persuasion and argument are not in themselves undue influence.

An essential element of undue influence is that the person making the contract does not exercise free will. In the absence of a recognized type of confidential relationship, such as that between parent and child, courts are likely to take the attitude that the person who claims to have been dominated was merely persuaded and there was therefore no undue influence.

11. Duress

A party may enter into a contract to avoid a threatened danger. The danger threatened may be a physical harm to person or property, called **physical duress,** or it may be a threat of financial loss, called **economic duress.**

The threat of violence to person or property is physical duress and makes a contract voidable.

(a) Physical Duress. A person makes a contract under duress when there is such violence or threat of violence that the person is deprived of free will and makes the contract to avoid harm. The threatened harm may be directed either at a near relative of the contracting party or against the contracting party. A contract is executed under duress when it is executed by parents under threat that their child will be prosecuted for a crime if they do not make the contract. If a contract is made under duress, the resulting agreement is voidable at the victim's election.

Whether duress existed in a particular case is a question of fact to be determined on the basis of all the circumstances of the case, including the age, sex, and capacity of the party claiming duress.[32]

Agreements made to bring an end to mass disorder or violence are ordinarily not binding contracts because they were obtained by duress.

(b) Economic Duress. The economic pressure on a contracting party may be so great that it will be held to constitute duress. Economic duress occurs when the victim is threatened with irreparable loss for which adequate recovery could not be obtained by suing the wrongdoer.

Generally, a threat of economic loss or pressure caused by economic conditions does not constitute duress that makes a contract voidable. The fact that the plaintiff drove a hard bargain does not give rise to the defense of economic duress. It is not economic duress to take advantage of another's financial difficulties. When money is in fact owed a creditor, a threat by the creditor to sue the debtor to collect the amount owed does not constitute unlawful duress. It is merely a statement of what the law entitles the creditor to do. A seller's threat to forfeit a buyer's down payment if the buyer did not comply with contractual terms does not constitute duress.[33] *For example*, when Lum's car was totaled in a collision, he bought a used car from Smiling Sam, a used-car dealer. Lum knew he was paying too much but bought the car to be able to get to work. Later he located a reasonably priced used car and sued Smiling Sam to set aside the contract on the ground of economic duress. Lum cannot avoid the contract. Although he entered into the contract because of economic pressure, it was the pressure created by Lum's need for transportation to his job, not Smiling Sam's sales techniques.

12. Adhesion Contracts

Unconscionability and consumer protection laws replace the concept of "adhesion" contracts.

Pressure on a contracting party may not be as extreme as physical duress or economic duress. It may still be sufficient to justify the conclusion that there was no genuine assent freely given and that, accordingly, the basic element of a voluntary agreement was lacking. Because of this, what appears to be a contract is merely a voidable transaction. Such a situation may involve a **contract of adhesion.** A contract of adhesion is one that is offered by a dominant party to a party with infe-

---

[32] *Willms Trucking Co. v JW Construction Co.* (SC App) 442 SE2d 197 (1994).
[33] *Anziano v Appalachee Enterprises, Inc.,* ____Ga App ____, 432 SE2d 117 (1993).

rior bargaining power on a take-it-or-leave-it basis. The weaker person cannot go elsewhere to obtain the goods or services desired and therefore must deal on the terms dictated by the superior party or do without.

With the rise of the concept of unconscionability and the adoption of consumer protection laws, the need to apply the concept of the adhesion contract has diminished greatly. In most cases, it is held that the concept is not applicable either because there is not a gross inequality of bargaining power or because the goods or services could be obtained elsewhere.[34] The fact that the contract places a risk of loss on one party does not in itself establish that there was any improper pressure. Freedom of contract means that the parties can place any risk of loss where they choose. ◆ *For example,* Connie made a contract for parking her car on a monthly basis with Center City Garage. The contract was a printed form that Center City used for all its customers. Connie later claimed that a provision limiting liability for loss constituted adhesion. Adhesion does not exist in this case because it did not arise to the level of unconscionability. ◆

E. REMEDIES

When a genuine agreement of the parties is lacking, the remedy may be a rescission of the contract, an action for damages, or an action for reformation of the contract. Mistake, fraud, undue influence, and duress may make the agreement voidable or, in some instances, void. The following remedies are available.

13. Rescission

A voidable contract may be rescinded.

If the contract is voidable, it can be rescinded, or set aside, by the party who has been injured or of whom advantage has been taken. In no case can the wrongdoer set aside the contract. The object of rescission is to restore the status quo ante.

If not avoided, the contract that had been voidable is valid and binding. If the

> **CASE SUMMARY**
>
> ### Saved from the Trap
>
> **Facts:** Hart purchased the business of Steel Products, Inc., on the basis of tax returns that showed that the business was profitable. Hart was not shown amended tax returns that showed that the business ran at a loss. When Hart learned of that fact, he claimed the right to rescind the contract.
>
> **Decision:** The court held that Hart was entitled to rescind. The concealment of the fact that the business was losing money and the use of the tax returns that showed that it was a profitable business constituted fraud in the inducement. This made the contract voidable, and Hart, as the victim of the fraud, could rescind the contract. [*Hart v Steel Products, Inc. (Ind App) 666 NE2d 1270 (1996)*]

agreement is void, neither party can enforce it, and no act of avoidance is required by either party to set the contract aside. The power to avoid a contract because of mistake or misrepresentation is lost if, with knowledge or reason to know of the

---

[34] *Larned v First Chicago Corp.,* ____ Ill App ____, ____ Ill Dec ____, 636 NE2d 1004 (1994).

mistake or misrepresentation, the aggrieved party delays an unreasonable time, affirms the transaction, or does any act inconsistent with avoiding the transaction.

14. Damages

A deceived party may recover damages.

Some states allow the person harmed by an innocent misrepresentation to recover compensatory damages. Because such a misrepresentation is, by definition, neither intentional nor reckless, punitive damages cannot be recovered.[35] If the other party was guilty of a wrong, such as fraud, the injured party may sue for damages caused by the wrong. In the case of the sale of goods, the aggrieved party may both rescind the contract and recover damages, but in other contracts the victim must choose one of these two remedies.[36] For example, Guido purchased a used car from Oliver Auto Center, which represented that the car had never been in a wreck even though it knew that this was false. The car had sustained serious collision damage, but expert repairs had hidden the damage. When Guido learned the truth, he sued Oliver for damages. He recovered not only compensatory damages but also punitive damages because of the willful and wanton nature of Oliver's misrepresentation.

15. Reformation of Contract by a Court

Either party may obtain correction of writing.

At times, a written contract does not correctly state the agreement already made by the parties. When this occurs, either party can have the court reform or correct the writing to state the agreement actually made. A court action for reformation may be necessary because a change of circumstances or the occurrence of certain events may cause the other party to refuse to change the written contract voluntarily. For example, suppose Lauer obtains a collision insurance policy on an automobile, but through a mistake the policy describes the wrong car. Lauer can obtain a decree of court declaring that the policy covers the car that Lauer and the insurance company intended to insure rather than the car wrongly identified in the policy. The insurance company would gladly have made the correction prior to any loss being sustained, but if the car Lauer intended to insure has been damaged, court reformation would probably be necessary.

CASE SUMMARY

Oops! We Made a Mistake

Facts: Bramsem rented a warehouse in Arizona from Mastroni and Kuhse in 1975 for $4,150 per month on a twenty-year lease. The lease provided that the rent amount would be recomputed every five years using the consumer price index for Phoenix, Arizona, published by the U.S. Department of Labor. Because of a mistake by the attorney preparing the lease, the index was identified as being prepared by the U.S. Department of Labor for the city of Phoenix. There was no such index, and the lessee brought a suit to rescind the lease on the ground that there was no such cost-of-living index. The lessor counterclaimed, seeking a reformation of the lease. The lower court reformed the lease to refer to the Phoenix cost-of-living index prepared by the Bureau of Business and Economic Research at Arizona State University.

---

35 *Christopher v Heimlich* (Ala Civ App) 523 So 2d 466 (1988).
36 *Eklund v Koenig & Associates, Inc.* (Wis App) 451 NW2d 150 (1989).

> **Decision:** The lower court was correct in granting reformation. It was clear that the parties intended that the rent should escalate according to a cost-of-living index for Phoenix. Through the mistake of the person preparing the lease, a nonexistent index was named. Both parties to the lease mistakenly believed that the index named in the lease did exist. There was thus a mutual mistake of fact because of which the written lease did not carry out the intent of the agreement of the parties. The lease was therefore properly reformed to substitute the name of the applicable cost-of-living index. This would carry out the intent of the parties. *[Phil Bramsen Distributor, Inc. v Mastroni and Kuhse (Ct App) 151 Ariz 194, 726 P2d 610 (1986)]*

In order to reform a written contract, it is necessary to establish the exact agreement to which the writing is to conform.[37]

A party seeking reformation of a contract must clearly prove both the grounds for reformation and what the agreement actually was. This burden is particularly great when the contract to be reformed is written. This is so because the general rule is that parties are presumed to read their written contracts and therefore intended to be bound thereby when they signed them.[38]

16. Loss of Remedy

When the absence of genuine consent merely makes the contract voidable, the right to assert a remedy is lost if the aggrieved person delays unreasonably in acting or ratifies the contract either by express declaration or by accepting benefits under it.

SUMMARY

An agreement that otherwise appears to be a contract may not be binding because one of the parties lacks contractual capacity. In such a case, the contract is ordinarily voidable at the election of that party who lacks contractual capacity. In some cases, the contract is void. Ordinarily, contractual incapacity is the inability, for mental or physical reasons, to understand that a contract is being made and to understand its general terms and nature. This is typically the case when it is claimed that incapacity exists because of insanity or intoxication. The incapacity of minors arises because society is discriminating in favor of that class to protect them from unwise contracts.

In most states today, the age of majority is 18. Minors can avoid most contracts. If a minor received anything from the other party, the minor, on avoiding the contract, must return what had been received from the other party if the minor still has it.

When a minor avoids a contract for a necessary, the minor must pay the reasonable value of any benefit received. The concept of a necessary has expanded.

Only minors are liable for their contracts. Parents of a minor are not liable on the minor's contracts merely because they are the parents. Frequently, an adult will enter into the contract as a co-party of the minor and is then liable without regard to whether the minor has avoided the contract.

The contract of an insane person is voidable to much the same extent as the contract of a minor. An important distinction is that if a guardian has been appointed for the insane person, a contract made by the insane person is void and not merely voidable.

An intoxicated person lacks contractual capacity to make a contract if the intoxication is such that the person does not understand that a contract is being made.

The consent of a party to an agreement is not genuine or voluntary in certain cases of mistake, deception, or

---

[37] *Smith v Royal Automotive Group, Inc.* (Fla App) 675 So 2d 144 (1996).
[38] *Ballard v Chavez* (NM) 868 P2d 646 (1994). Reformation requires the plaintiff to show that the writing does not express the true intent of the signers.

pressure. When this occurs, what appears to be a contract can be avoided by the victim of such circumstances or conduct.

As to mistake, it is necessary to distinguish between unilateral mistakes that are unknown to the other contracting party and those that are known. Mistakes that are unknown to the other party usually do not affect the binding character of the agreement. A unilateral mistake of which the other contracting party has knowledge or has reason to know makes the contract avoidable by the victim of the mistake.

The deception situation may be one of innocent misrepresentation, nondisclosure, or fraud. Innocent misrepresentation generally has no effect on the binding quality of an agreement, although there is a trend to recognize it as a ground for avoiding the contract. A few courts allow recovery of damages. When one party to the contract knows of a fact that has a bearing on the transaction, the failure to volunteer information about that fact to the other contracting party is called nondisclosure. The law ordinarily does not attach any significance to nondisclosure. Contrary to this rule, there is a duty to volunteer information when a confidential relationship exists between the possessor of the knowledge and the other contracting party. A strong modern trend in the law imposes a duty to disclose or volunteer information relating to matters that are not likely to be inquired about by the other contracting party.

When concealment goes beyond mere silence and consists of actively taking steps to hide the truth, the conduct may be classified as fraud rather than nondisclosure. There is a growing trend to hold fine-print clauses not binding on the theory that they are designed to hide the truth from the other contracting party. Consumer protection statutes often outlaw fine-print clauses by requiring particular contracts or particular clauses in contracts to be printed in type of a specified size. A statement of opinion, value, or law cannot ordinarily be the basis for fraud liability, although it can be when the maker of the false statement claims to be an expert on the particular subject matter and is making the statement as an expert.

The free will of a person, essential to the voluntary character of a contract, may be lacking because the agreement had been obtained by pressure. This may range from undue influence through the array of threats of extreme economic loss (called economic duress) to the threat of physical force that would cause serious personal injury or damage to property (called physical duress). The mere fact that one party to the contract has great bargaining power and offers the other party a printed contract on a take-it-or-leave-it basis (an adhesion contract) does not prove that the agreement was not voluntary. However, some courts have held that in such cases the agreement is not voluntary if the weaker party cannot obtain the desired goods or services elsewhere.

When the voluntary character of an agreement has been destroyed by mistake, deception, or pressure, the victim may avoid or rescind the contract or may ratify the contract and obtain money damages from the wrongdoer. When the mistake consists of an error in putting an oral contract in writing, either party may ask the court to reform the writing so that it states the parties' actual agreement.

QUESTIONS AND CASE PROBLEMS

1. Lester purchased a used automobile from MacKintosh Motors. He asked the seller if the car had ever been in a wreck. The MacKintosh salesperson had never seen the car before that morning and knew nothing of its history but quickly answered Lester's question by stating: "No. It has never been in a wreck." In fact, the auto had been seriously damaged in a wreck and, although repaired, was worth much less than the value it would have had if there had been no wreck. When Lester learned the truth, he sued MacKintosh Motors and the salesperson for damages for fraud. They raised the defense that the salesperson did not know the statement was false and had not intended to deceive Lester. Did the conduct of the salesperson constitute fraud?

2. Helen, aged 17, wanted to buy a motorcycle. She didn't have the money to pay cash but persuaded the dealer to sell a cycle to her on credit. The dealer did so partly because Helen said that she was 22 and showed the dealer an identification card that falsely stated her age as 22. Helen drove the motorcycle away. A few days later, she damaged it and then returned it to the dealer and stated that she avoided the contract because she was a minor. The dealer said that she couldn't because (1) she had misrepresented her age and (2) the motorcycle was damaged. Can she avoid the contract?

3. Yang and Richard make a contract for the sale of an automobile. They orally agree that the price Richard is to pay is $2,000, but when the written contract is typed, the amount is wrongly stated as $3,000. This contract is signed before anyone notices the mistake. Yang then claims that the written contract is binding and that Richard is required to pay $3,000. Richard

claims that he is required to pay only the originally agreed-on amount of $2,000. Is he correct?

4. High-Tech Collieries borrowed money from Holland. High-Tech later refused to be bound by the loan contract, claiming the contract was not binding because it had been obtained by duress. The evidence showed that the offer to make the loan was made on a take-it-or-leave-it basis. Was the defense of duress valid? [*Holland v High-Tech Collieries, Inc.* (DC WA) 911 F Supp 1021]

5. Thomas Bell, a minor, went to work in the Pittsburgh beauty parlor of Sam Pankas and agreed that when he left the employment, he would not work in or run a beauty parlor business within a 10-mile radius of downtown Pittsburgh for a period of two years. Contrary to this provision, Bell and another employee of Pankas' opened a beauty shop three blocks from Pankas' shop and advertised themselves as Pankas's former employees. Pankas sued Bell to stop the breach of the noncompetition, or restrictive, covenant. Bell claimed that he was not bound because he was a minor when he had agreed to the covenant. Was he bound by the covenant? [*Pankas v Bell*, ____ Pa ____, 198 A2d 312] No

6. Aldrich and Co. sold goods to Donovan on credit. The amount owed grew steadily, and finally Aldrich refused to sell any more to Donovan unless Donovan signed a promissory note for the amount due. Donovan did not want to but signed the note because he had no money and needed more goods. When Aldrich brought an action to enforce the note, Donovan claimed that the note was not binding because it had been obtained by economic duress. Was he correct? [*Aldrich & Co. v Donovan*, ____ Mont ____, 778 P2d 397]

7. Adams claimed that Boyd owed him money but was under the impression that Boyd didn't have much money. On the basis of this impression, Adams made a settlement agreement with Boyd for a nominal amount. When Adams later learned that Boyd was in fact reasonably wealthy, Adams sought to set the agreement aside. Was Adams entitled to do so?

8. An agent of Thor Food Service Corp. was seeking to sell Makofske a combination refrigerator-freezer and food purchase plan. Makofske was married and had three children. After being informed of the eating habits of Makofske and his family, the agent stated that the cost of the freezer and food would be about $95 to $100 a month. Makofske carefully examined the agent's itemized estimate and made some changes to it. Makofske then signed the contract and purchased the refrigerator-freezer. The cost proved to be greater than the estimated $95 to $100 a month, and Makofske

claimed that the contract had been obtained by fraud. Decide. [*Thor Food Service Corp. v Makofske*, 28 Misc 2d 872, 218 NYS2d 93]

9. Blubaugh was a district manager of Schlumberger Well Services. Turner was an executive employee of Schlumberger. Blubaugh was told that he would be fired unless he chose to resign. He was also told that if he would resign and release the company and its employees from all claims for wrongful discharge, he would receive about $5,000 in addition to his regular severance pay of approximately $25,000 and would be given job-relocation counseling. He resigned, signed the release, and received about $40,000 and job counseling. Some time thereafter, he brought an action claiming that he had been wrongfully discharged. He claimed that the release did not protect the defendants because the release had been obtained by economic duress. Were the defendants protected by the release? [*Blubaugh v Turner* (Wyo) 842 P2d 1072]

10. Sippy was thinking of buying Christich's house. He noticed watermarks on the ceiling, but the agent showing the house stated that the roof had been repaired and was in good condition. Sippy was not told that the roof still leaked and that the repairs had not been able to stop the leaking. Sippy bought the house. Some time later, heavy rains caused water to leak into the house, and Sippy claimed that Christich was guilty of fraud. Was he correct? [*Sippy v Christich* (Kan App) 609 P2d 204]

11. Pileggi owed Young money. Young threatened to bring suit against Pileggi for the amount due. Pileggi feared the embarrassment of being sued and the possibility that he might be thrown into bankruptcy. To avoid being sued, Pileggi executed a promissory note to pay Young the amount due. He later asserted that the note was not binding because he had executed it under duress. Is this defense valid? [*Young v Pileggi*, ____ Pa Super ____, 455 A2d 1228]

12. Scott was employed by Litigation Reprographics and Support Services, Inc. The contract of employment was "at will," which gave the employer the right to fire Scott at any time for any reason or for no reason. Reprographics told Scott that if he wanted to keep his job, he would have to sign a contract stating that he would not compete with Reprographics when he was no longer employed by it. He signed the contract but later claimed he was not bound by it because it had been obtained by economic duress, as he had to have the job. Decide.

13. C&J Publishing Co. told a computer salesman that it wanted a computer system that would operate its printing presses. C&J specified that it wanted only new equipment and no used equipment would be

acceptable. The seller delivered a system to C&J that was a combination of new and secondhand parts because it did not have sufficient new parts to fill the order. When the buyer later learned what had happened, it sued the seller for fraud. The seller contended that no statement or warranty had been made that all parts of the system were new and that it would not therefore be liable for fraud. Decide.

14. The city of Salinas entered into a contract with Souza & McCue Construction Co. to construct a sewer. City officials knew unusual subsoil conditions (including extensive quicksand) existed that would make performance of the contract unusually difficult. This information was not disclosed when city officials advertised for bids. The advertisement for bids directed bidders to examine carefully the site of the work and declared that the submission of a bid would constitute evidence that the bidder had made an examination. Souza & McCue was awarded the contract, but because of the subsoil conditions, it could not complete on time and was sued by Salinas for breach of contract. Souza & McCue counterclaimed on the basis that the city had not revealed its information on the subsoil conditions and was thus liable for the loss. Was the city liable? [*City of Salinas v Souza & McCue Construction Co.*, ____Cal App 3d ___, 424 P2d 921]

CPA QUESTIONS

1. A building subcontractor submitted a bid for construction of a portion of a high-rise office building. The bid contained material computational errors. The general contractor accepted the bid with knowledge of the errors. Which of the following statements best represents the subcontractor's liability?
   a. Not liable, because the contractor knew of the errors.
   b. Not liable, because the errors were a result of gross negligence.
   c. Liable, because the errors were unilateral.
   d. Liable, because the errors were material.

   (5/95, Law, #17, 5351)

2. Egan, a minor, contracted with Baker to purchase Baker's used computer for $400. The computer was purchased for Egan's personal use. The agreement provided that Egan would pay $200 down on delivery and $200 thirty days later. Egan took delivery and paid the $200 down payment. Twenty days later, the computer was damaged seriously as a result of Egan's negligence. Five days after the damage occurred and one day after Egan reached the age of majority, Egan attempted to disaffirm the contract with Baker. Egan will
   a. Be able to disaffirm despite the fact that Egan was **not** a minor at the time of disaffirmance.
   b. Be able to disaffirm only if Egan does so in writing.
   c. Not be able to disaffirm because Egan had failed to pay the balance of the purchase price.
   d. Not be able to disaffirm because the computer was damaged as a result of Egan's negligence.

   (11/93, Law, #21, 4318)

Consideration

CHAPTER 14

OBJECTIVES

After studying this chapter, you should be able to

1. *Define what constitutes consideration;*
2. *State the effect of the absence of consideration;*
3. *Identify promises that can serve as consideration;*
4. *Distinguish between present consideration and past consideration;*
5. *State when forbearance can be consideration;*
6. *Recognize situations in which adequacy of consideration has significance; and*
7. *List the exceptions to the requirement of consideration.*

Will the law enforce every promise? Generally, a promise will not be enforced unless something is given or received for the promise.

A. GENERAL PRINCIPLES

As a general rule, one of the elements needed to make an agreement binding is consideration.

1. Definition

Consideration is the price of a promise.

Consideration is what a promisor demands and receives as the price for the promise.[1] Consideration is something to which the promisor is not otherwise entitled and which the promisor specifies as the price for the promise.

CASE SUMMARY

The Unrequired Benefit

Facts: The Life Insurance Company of Arkansas issued a group life insurance policy. It later desired to add a limitation to the policy and would have canceled the policy if the limitation was not agreed to. However, the company did not inform anyone of this intention. The limitation was agreed to although no threat of cancellation was made. Thereafter, David Davis, a person protected by the group policy, was killed in an accident. When suit was brought on the group policy, the insurer claimed that it was protected by the limitation that had been added to the policy. The plaintiff claimed that the limitation was not binding because there was no consideration for adding the limitation.

Decision: Judgment for plaintiff. The forbearance of the company by refraining from canceling the policy was not consideration because there had not been any agreement that if the insureds agreed to the limitation, the company would forbear from canceling the policy. Consequently, the forbearance was not the price of the promise to accept the limitation. The limitation was therefore not a binding term of the contract and could not be asserted as a defense to suit on the policy. [*Wold v Life Ins. Co. of Arkansas* 24 Ark App 113, 749 SW2d 346 (1988)]

It is not necessary that the promisor expressly use the word consideration.

Because consideration is the price paid for the promise, it is unimportant who pays that price as long as it has been agreed that it should be paid in that way. For example, consideration may be the extending of credit to a third person, such as extending credit to the corporation of which the promisor is a stockholder. Likewise, when a bank lends money to a third person, such lending is consideration for the promise of its customer to repay the loan to the bank if it will loan the money to the third person.

When the creditor releases a third person in consideration of the promise of another person to pay the debt of the released person, the fact that the promisor did not receive a direct benefit is immaterial. The obtaining of the release of the third person as desired was consideration for the promise to pay the debt.[2]

---

[1] *Roark v Stallworth Oil and Gas, Inc.* (Tex) 813 SW2d 492 (1991).
[2] *First Union National Bank of Georgia v Gurley,* ___ Ga App ___, 431 SE2d 379 (1993).

Consideration for a unilateral contract is doing the requested act.

Consideration for a bilateral contract is making a return promise.

Consideration is an agreed exchange.

(a) Nature of Contract. In a unilateral contract, the consideration for the promise is the doing of the act called for. The doing of the act in such case is also the acceptance of the offer of the promisor.

In a bilateral contract, which is an exchange of promises, each promise is the consideration for the other promise. When a lawsuit is brought for breaking a promise, it is the consideration for the broken promise to which attention is directed.

(b) Agreed Exchange. Consideration is what is agreed to in return for the promise. In most cases, this will directly benefit the promisor and will be some burden or detriment to the promisee. For example, an employer who promises to pay wages sustains detriment by promising to pay the wages in exchange for the benefit of receiving the employee's promise to work. The important thing, however, is that what is received is what was asked for as the price of the promise.

For example, Rodney, a retailer, ordered goods from Daniel, a distributor. With his order Rodney sent a check for payment in full. In a later dispute, Rodney claimed that Daniel had promised to take back unsold goods and that the consideration for this promise was the check for the goods ordered. Rodney is wrong. Daniel had not specified that if Rodney would pay at the time he ordered, Daniel would allow him to return unsold goods. Although the payment for the goods at the time of ordering was a benefit to Daniel, it did not constitute consideration.

As long as someone gives what was asked for by the promisor, the promisor's obligation is supported by consideration even though the economic benefit of the promise is not received by the person giving the consideration. Thus, when a third person comes to the financial aid of a debtor by making some promise to the creditor in exchange for some promise from the creditor, consideration exists. The contract is binding even though the creditor's promise benefits the debtor rather than the third person. A promise guaranteeing repayment of a loan to a corporation is binding although all the money loaned was received by the corporation and nothing was received by the promisor, even though the promisor is not a shareholder of the corporation.

CASE SUMMARY

He Got What He Wanted——That's Consideration

Facts: Joy Manufacturing Co. sold goods on credit to Marrick Co. Joy was not paid for the goods. In order to induce Joy to continue to sell on credit, an agreement was made by which Kennedy, a shareholder and vice president of Marrick, would pay Joy if Marrick did not. Kennedy later claimed he was not bound by his promise because he had not received consideration for his promise, as it was Marrick that received the benefit.

Decision: Kennedy was wrong. Joy's promise to continue selling on credit to Marrick was consideration for the promise of Kennedy to pay if Marrick did not. The fact that Marrick received the direct benefit from Joy's promise did not mean that it was not consideration for the promise of Kennedy. Joy's promise was the price that Kennedy asked for his promise. Joy's promise was therefore consideration for Kennedy's promise, and Kennedy's promise was binding. *[Kennedy v Joy Manufacturing Co. (Ky App) 707 SW2d 362 (1994)]*

(c) Unspecified Benefit. The fact that the promisor receives a benefit does not show that there was consideration for the promise. The benefit received must have been the price demanded for the making of the promise. Consequently, the fact that a creditor does not enforce a debt is not consideration for the promise of a third person to pay the debt when there was no agreement that the guarantor would pay the debt if the creditor would not enforce it.

(d) Modification of Terminable Contract. A contract may be terminated by either party. If one party proposes a modification of a contract's terms and the other party continues to perform under the contract, such continued performance is consideration for the proposed modification. Consequently, when an at-will employee continues to work after the employer announces a proposed change in employment terms, such continuation of working constitutes consideration, and the modification is binding.[3]

2.   Effect of Absence of Consideration

A promise is not binding without consideration.

The absence of consideration makes a promise not binding.[4] Thus, a person sued for breaking a promise will not be held liable when no consideration was received for the promise. For example, an employee may promise to refrain from competing with the employer when the employment relationship ends. If the promise is not supported by consideration, the promise is not binding, and the former employee may compete with the former employer.

Moral obligation is not consideration.

(a) Moral Obligation. The fact that the promisor feels morally obligated to make the promise does not make the promise binding when there is no consideration for it.[5]

For example, when Jimmy learned that his younger brother Bendigo was unemployed and owed his landlord rent, Jimmy promised the landlord to pay the rent Bendigo owed. Jimmy later reneged and claimed that his promise was not binding because it lacked consideration. Jimmy is correct. The promise was nothing more than a moral obligation to pay rent to aid members of his family in need. Moral obligations do not constitute consideration.

A promise is not illegal because consideration is lacking.

(b) Legality Distinguished. While the absence of consideration ordinarily prevents enforcing a promise, the absence of consideration has no greater effect; that is, the agreement is not illegal because there was no consideration. Consequently, when a person keeps the promise, the performance rendered cannot later be revoked on the ground that there was no consideration. To illustrate, a promise to make a gift cannot be enforced because there is no consideration for the promise. However, once the gift is made, the donor cannot take the gift back because there was no consideration.

---

[3] *Habeck v MacDonald* (ND) 520 NW2d 808 (1994).
[4] *Rothell v Continental Casualty Co.,* ___ Ga App ___, 402 SE2d 283 (1991).
[5] *Production Credit Ass'n of Mandan v Rub* (ND) 475 NW2d 532 (1991). As to the Louisiana rule of moral consideration, see *Thomas v Bryant* (La App) 596 So 2d 1065 (1992).

3. Legality of Consideration

Consideration must be lawful.

The law will not permit persons to make contracts that violate the law. Accordingly, a promise to do something that the law prohibits or a promise to refrain from doing something that the law requires is not valid consideration, and the contract is illegal.

◆ *For example,* Sandrovar, a security guard for Apex Co., promised to obtain the secret access code to the company's computer system and deliver it to Tancred Co., a competitor of Apex, for $1 million. Sandrovar's promise is not consideration because it involves the commission of an illegal act—revealing trade secrets. An illegal act is not a valid form of consideration. ◆

4. Failure of Consideration

When a promise is given as consideration, the question arises whether the promisor will perform the promise.

(a) Nonperformance of Promise. If the promise is not performed, the law describes the default as a failure of consideration. This is a breach of the contract because what was required by the contract has not been performed.

Failure of consideration is nonperformance and is a breach of contract.

When the promise of the agent to pay the face value of bonds was made on the basis that valid redeemable bonds would be delivered, there is a failure of consideration when the bonds delivered are worthless and cannot be redeemed.[6]

(b) Bad Bargain Distinguished. When the promisor performs the promise, there is never a failure of consideration. The fact that the consideration turns out to be disappointing does not mean there has been a failure of consideration. In other words, the fact that the contract proves to be a bad bargain for the promisor does not constitute a failure of consideration, nor does it affect the binding character of the contract. Thus, the fact that a business purchased by a group of buyers proves unprofitable does not constitute a failure of consideration that releases the buyers from their obligation to the seller.[7]

A bad bargain is not a failure of consideration.

CASE SUMMARY

Expectations Versus Consideration

Facts: The Aqua Drilling Company made a contract to drill a well for the Atlas Construction Company. It was expected that this would supply water for a home being constructed by Atlas. Aqua did not make any guarantee or warranty that water would be produced. Aqua drilled the well exactly as required by the contract, but no water was produced. Atlas refused to pay. It asserted that the contract was not binding on the theory that there had been a failure of consideration because the well did not produce water.

Decision: The contract was binding. Atlas obtained the exact performance required by the contract. While Atlas had expected that water would be obtained, Aqua did not make any guarantee or warranty that this would be so. Hence there was no failure of consideration. *[Atlas Construction Co., Inc. v Aqua Drilling Co. (Wyo) 559 P2d 39 (1977)]*

---

[6] *Hoffman v Bankers Trust Co.* (DC Pa) 925 F Supp 315 (1995).
[7] *Commerce Bank of Joplin v Shallenburger* (Mo App) 766 SW2d 764 (1989).

B. WHAT CONSTITUTES CONSIDERATION

The sections that follow analyze certain common situations in which a lawsuit turned on whether the promisor received consideration for the promise sued on.

5. A Promise as Consideration

In a bilateral contract, each party makes a promise to the other. The promise that one party makes is consideration for the promise made by the other.

The fact that parties appear to be in agreement does not mean that there is a promise. Thus, a statement that a proposed loan would be no problem does not constitute a promise to make a loan.

A promise may be consideration.

A promise is not consideration unless it is binding.

(a) Binding Character of Promise. To constitute consideration, a promise must be binding; that is, it must impose a liability or create a duty. An unenforceable promise cannot be consideration. Suppose that a coal company promises to sell to a factory at a specific price all the coal that it orders, and that the factory agrees to pay that price for any coal that it orders from the coal company. The promise of the factory is not consideration because it does not obligate the factory to buy any coal from the coal company.

A promise that in fact does not impose any obligation on the promisor is often called an illusory promise because, although it looks like a binding promise, it is not.

A promise may be consideration although it is conditional.

(b) Conditional Promise. Can a conditional promise be consideration? Assume that an agreement states that buyer promises to buy, provided buyer can obtain financing. Is such a promise consideration for the seller's promise to sell, or is the buyer's promise not consideration because it does not impose any obligation on the buyer at the time that the promise is made?

The fact that a promise is conditional does not prevent it from being consideration, even when, as a practical matter, it is unlikely that the condition would ever be satisfied.[8] Thus, the promise of a fire insurance company to pay the homeowner in case of fire is consideration for the payment of premiums by the homeowner even though it is probable that there will never be a fire.

A promise may be binding and therefore consideration although the contract may be canceled.

(c) Cancellation Provision. Although a promise must impose a binding obligation, it may authorize one or either party to terminate or cancel the agreement under certain circumstances or upon giving notice to the other party. The fact that the contract may be terminated in this manner does not make the contract any less binding prior to such termination.

For example, Stu obtained an automobile insurance policy from Coverall Insurance Co. stating that either party could cancel the policy on five days' notice. Later, Coverall claimed it was not bound by the policy because Stu could cancel it. Coverall is wrong. While theoretically the ability to cancel violates the requirement that promises be binding in order to be consideration, the law accepts that a power to cancel does not destroy the obligation of the contract. Until there is a cancellation, there is a binding contract. Therefore, if a loss is sustained before the insurance company cancels the policy, the insurance company is bound to pay even though it could have canceled the policy before the loss was sustained.

---

[8] *Charles Hester Enterprises, Inc. v Illinois Founders Ins. Co.,* 114 Ill 2d 278, 102 Ill Dec 306, 499 NE2d 1319 (1986).

A promise to perform
an existing obligation
is not consideration.

C
P
A

6. Promise to Perform Existing Obligation

Ordinarily, doing or promising to do what one is already under a legal obligation to do is not consideration.[9] Similarly, a promise to refrain from doing what one has no legal right to do is not consideration. This preexisting duty or legal obligation can be based on statute, on general principles of law, on responsibilities of an office held by the promisor, or on a preexisting contract.

CASE SUMMARY

You're Already Under Contract

Facts: Crookham & Vessels had a contract to build an extension of a railroad for the Little Rock Port Authority. They made a contract with Larry Moyer Trucking to dig drainage ditches. The ditch walls collapsed because water would not drain off. This required that the ditches be dug over again. Larry Moyer refused to do this unless extra money was paid. Crookham & Vessels agreed to pay the additional compensation, but after the work was done, they refused to pay it. Larry Moyer sued for the extra compensation promised.

Decision: Judgment against Moyer. Moyer was bound by its contract to dig the drainage ditches. Its promise to perform that obligation was not consideration for the promise of Crookham & Vessels to pay additional compensation. Performance of an obligation is not consideration for a promise by a party entitled to that performance. The fact that performance of the contract proved more difficult or costly than originally contemplated does not justify making an exception to this rule. [*Crookham & Vessels, Inc. v Larry Moyer Trucking, Inc.* 16 Ark App 214, 699 SW2d 414 (1985)]

(a) Completion of Contract. Suppose that a contractor refuses to complete a building unless the owner promises a payment or bonus in addition to the sum specified in the original contract, and the owner promises to make that payment. The question then arises whether the owner's promise is binding. Most courts hold that the second promise of the owner is without consideration.

If the promise of the contractor is to do something that is neither expressed nor implied as part of the first contract, then the promise of the other party is binding. For example, if a bonus of $1,000 is promised in return for the promise of a contractor to complete the building at a date earlier than that specified in the original agreement, the promise to pay the bonus is binding.

(1) Good-faith Adjustment. A recent trend is to enforce a second promise to pay a contractor a greater amount for the performance of the original contract when there are extraordinary circumstances caused by unforeseeable difficulties and when the additional amount promised the contractor is reasonable under the circumstances.

When parties to a contract, in a good-faith effort to meet the business realities of a situation, agree to a reduction of contract terms, there is some authority that the promise of the one party to accept the lesser performance of the other is binding. These cases have held that the promise is binding even though technically the promise to render the lesser performance is not consideration because the obligor was already obligated to render the greater performance. Thus, a landlord's promise to reduce the rent was binding when the tenant could not pay the original rent and the landlord preferred to have the building occupied even though receiving a smaller rental.

The modern trend holds that a promise to perform an existing contract is consideration when made in a good-faith adjustment to an unexpected situation.

---

[9] *Waide v Tractor and Equipment Co.* (Ala) 545 So 2d 1327 (1989).

(2) Contract for Sale of Goods. When the contract is for the sale of goods, any modification made in good faith by the parties to the contract is binding without regard to the existence of consideration for the modification.

A contract for the sale of goods may be modified without consideration.

(b) Compromise and Release of Claims. The rule that doing or promising to do what one is bound to do is not consideration applies to a part payment made in satisfaction of an admitted debt. Thus, a promise to pay part of an amount that is admittedly owed is not consideration for a promise to discharge the balance. It will not prevent the creditor from demanding the remainder later.

Payment of part of an admitted debt is not consideration. Payment of part of a disputed debt may be consideration.

If the debtor pays before the debt is due, there is consideration because, on the day when the payment was made, the creditor was not entitled to demand any payment. Likewise, if the creditor accepts some article (even of slight value) in addition to the part payment, consideration exists, and the agreement is held to be binding.

A debtor and creditor may have a bona fide dispute over the amount owed or whether any amount is owed. In such a case, payment by the debtor of less than the amount claimed by the creditor is consideration for the latter's agreement to release or settle the claim. It is generally regarded as sufficient if the claimant believes in the merit of the claim.[10] Conversely, if the claimant knows that the claim does not have any merit and is merely pressing the claim to force the other party to make some payment to buy peace from the annoyance of a lawsuit, the settlement agreement based on the part payment is not binding.

(c) Part-Payment Checks. The acceptance and cashing of a check for part of a debt releases the entire debt when the check bears a notation that it is intended as final or full payment and the total amount due is disputed or unliquidated. It probably has this same effect even though the debt is not disputed or is liquidated.[11] In some jurisdictions, this principle is applied without regard to the form of payment or whether the claim is disputed. Section 1541 of the California Civil Code provides: "An obligation is extinguished by a release therefrom given to the debtor by the creditor upon a new consideration, or in writing, with or without new consideration."

Acceptance and cashing of a part-payment check releases the entire debt, at least when the amount is disputed.

(d) Composition of Creditors. In a **composition of creditors,** the various creditors of one debtor mutually agree to accept a fractional part of their claims in full satisfaction of the claims. Such agreements are binding and are supported by consideration. When creditors agree to extend the due date of their debts, the promise of each creditor to forbear is likewise consideration for the promise of other creditors to forbear.

Composition of creditors is binding although each creditor gets less than the amount claimed.

7. Present Consideration versus Past Benefits

If consideration is what the promisor states must be received in return for the promise, then consideration must be given when or after the promisor states what is demanded.

---

[10] *F. H. Prince & Co. v Towers Financial Corp.,* ___ Ill App 3d ___, ___ Ill Dec ___, 656 NE2d 142 (1995).
[11] *Hearst Corp. v Lauerer, Martin & Gibbs, Inc.,* ___ Ohio App ___, 524 NE2d 193 (1987).

Past benefit cannot ordinarily be consideration.

C.P.A

(a) Past Consideration. Past benefits already received by the promisor cannot be consideration for a later promise.

> **CASE SUMMARY**
>
> ## What's Done Is Done
>
> **Facts:** Warner & Co. procured a purchaser for Brua's house and submitted to Brua sales papers to be signed. The papers contained a promise to pay Warner & Co. commissions for finding a purchaser. Brua signed the papers but later refused to pay Warner & Co. Thereafter Warner & Co. brought a suit to recover the commissions from Brua, who contended that there was no consideration for his promise.
>
> **Decision:** There was no consideration for the owner's promise to pay the broker. The broker's services that the owner promised to compensate had been performed and were therefore past consideration. A promise given because of past consideration is not binding. [*Warner & Co. v Brua 33 Ohio App 84, 168 NE 571 (1929)*]

why

Past benefit may be consideration if part of a present complex transaction.

(b) Complex Transactions. In applying the rule that past benefits cannot be consideration, care must be taken to distinguish between the situation in which the consideration is in fact past and the situation in which the earlier consideration and subsequent promises were all part of one complex transaction. In such cases, the earlier consideration is not regarded as past and supports the later promises.[12]

8. Forbearance as Consideration

Forbearance may be consideration.

In most cases, consideration consists of the performance of an act or the making of a promise to act.[13] Consideration may also consist of forbearance, which is refraining from doing an act, or a promise of forbearance. In other words, the promisor may desire to buy the inaction or a promise of inaction of the other party.

The waiving or giving up of any right can be consideration for the promise of another. Thus, the relinquishment of a right in property or of a right to sue for damages will support a promise given in return for it.

> **CASE SUMMARY**
>
> ## Nail Down the Promise's Price
>
> **Facts:** The owner of an apartment building, Wood Realty Trust, claimed that contamination on Storonske's land was contaminating the water supply of the apartment building. Storonske promised to supply the tenants with bottled water. This was done for awhile, during which time Wood Realty did not sue Storonske. Storonske stopped supplying the water. Wood Realty sued Storonske for breach of the promise to supply water.
>
> **Decision:** The promise was not binding. While the apartment owner did not sue the neighbor, there was no agreement that there would be such forbearance in return for providing the bottled water. The forbearance did not constitute consideration for the water supply promise, as it was not the price of that promise. Thus, there was no consideration for the promise, and it was not binding. [*Wood Realty Trust v N. Storonske Cooperage Co., Inc. App Div 2d 646 NYS2d 410 (1996)*]

---

[12] Such a complex transaction is called "contemporaneous" in some states. *Soukop v Snyder* (Haw App) 709 P2d 109 (1985).
[13] *Kapoor v Robins,* ___ Ill App 3d ___, ___ Ill Dec ___, 573 NE2d 292 (1991).

The promise of a creditor to forbear collecting the debt is consideration for a promise by the debtor to modify the terms of the transaction.

◆ *For example,* Rex was the major stockholder of Wyndham Corp., which owed a large bill to Natural Gas Co. Rex asked Natural to "go easy" and stated that he would pay the bill if necessary. Natural delayed taking any action for a month and then demanded payment from Rex. Rex is not bound by his promise to pay the Wyndham debt owed to Natural because there was no consideration for it. The voluntary forbearance of Natural was not consideration because it was not the price of Rex's promise; the promise was made without any commitment to forbear, and there was nothing to show that the parties regarded the promise as the price for the forbearance. ◆

The right that is surrendered in return for a promise may be a right against a third person as well as against the promisor. Consequently, when a creditor has a claim against a corporation, the creditor's promise to forbear his legal right can be consideration for the guarantee of the debt by the corporation's president.[14]

As under the rule governing compromises, forbearance to assert a claim is consideration when the claim has been asserted in good faith even if it is without merit. In the absence of a good-faith belief, forbearance with respect to a worthless claim is not consideration.

(a) What Constitutes Consideration. The consideration for forbearance is anything that constitutes consideration under the general rules discussed in this chapter. Usually, it is a payment of money to the promisor or a third person to guarantee the debt of another. The extending of the date for payment of a debt is consideration for the promise of a third person that the debt will be paid.[15]

(b) Consideration in Employment Contracts. In employment contracts, an employee may promise not to compete with the employer after leaving the employment. What is the consideration for this promise? When the promise is made at the time of the making of the contract of employment, the promise of the employer to employ and to pay compensation is consideration for the employee's promise to refrain from competing after leaving the employment. If the employee's promise is made after the contract of employment has been made, it is necessary to see whether the contract (1) is for an indefinite duration with no job security provision or (2) is for a definite period of time, such as five years, or contains job security provisions that prevent the employer from discharging the employee at will.

If the employment contract is for a definite period or is covered by job security provisions, the employee's promise not to compete when made after the contract of employment has been made is not binding on the employee unless the employer gives some consideration for the promise not to compete. In the case of the indefinite-duration contract that has no job security provision, the employer can ordinarily terminate the contract at will. Therefore, according to some courts, the employer's continuing to employ the person after the employee's making of the promise not to compete is consideration for that promise even though the parties did not express these thoughts in words. Other courts, however, do not make a distinction based on the type of employment contract. These courts follow the common law rule that a restrictive covenant agreed to by an employee already

Forbearance in employment contracts may be continuation of a contract when there is no definite duration.

---

[14] *Gooch v American Sling Co.* (Tex App) 902 SW2d 181 (1995).

under a contract of employment is not binding because it is not supported by consideration.

(c) Obligation to Forbear Distinguished. Forbearance as consideration for a promise is distinct from an obligation to forbear. When the latter arises, it is necessary to find consideration to forbear; without consideration, the ordinary rule is followed. There is accordingly no obligation to forbear when consideration is lacking.[16]

9.   Adequacy of Consideration

Generally, adequacy of consideration is ignored.

Ordinarily, courts do not consider the adequacy of the consideration given for a promise. The fact that the consideration supplied by one party is slight when compared with the burden undertaken by the other party is immaterial. It is a matter for the parties to decide when they make their contract whether each is getting a fair return. In the absence of fraud or other misconduct, courts usually will not interfere to make sure that each side is getting a fair return.

Because the adequacy of consideration is ignored, it is immaterial that consideration is so slight that the transaction is in part a "gift."

CASE SUMMARY

Who's to Say?

Facts: On the death of their aunt, a brother and sister became the owners of shares of stock of several corporations. They made an agreement to divide these shares equally between them, although the sister's shares had a value approximately seven times those of the brother. The brother died before the shares were divided. The sister then claimed that the agreement to divide was not binding because the consideration for her promise was not adequate.

Decision: The value of stock cannot be determined precisely. It may change with time. In addition, the value that one person may see may be different than that seen by another. The court therefore will not make a comparison of the value that each party was to receive under the agreement. It was sufficient that a promise was exchanged for a promise. The adequacy of the consideration would not be examined. This sister was therefore bound by her promise to divide the shares. [*Emberson v Hartley, 52 Wash App 597, 762 P2d 364 (1988)*]

ETHICS & THE LAW

Alan Fulkins, who owns a construction company that specializes in single-family residences, is constructing a small subdivision with 23 homes. Tretorn Plumbing, owned by Jason Tretorn, was awarded the contract for the plumbing work on the homes at a price of $4,300 per home.

Plumbing contractors complete their residential projects in three phases. Phase one consists of digging the lines for the plumbing and installing the pipes that are placed in the foundation of the house. Phase two consists of the pipes within the walls of the home, and phase three is the surface plumbing, such as sinks and tubs. However, industry practice dictates that the plumbing contractor receive one-half of the contract amount after completion of phase one.

---

15 *Hope Petty Motors of Columbia Inc. v Hyatt* (SC App) 425 SE2d 786 (1992).
16 *GECC Financial Corp. v Jaffarian* (Haw App) 904 P2d 530 (1995).

Tretorn completed the digs of phase one for Fulkins and received payment of $2,150. Tretorn then went to Fulkins and demanded an additional $600 per house for completion of the work. Fulkins said, "But you already have a contract for $4,300!" Tretorn responded, "I know, but the costs are killing me. I need the additional $600."

Fulkins explained the hardship of the demand, "Look, I've already paid you half. If I hire someone else, I'll have to pay them two-thirds for the work not done. It'll cost me $5,000 per house." Tretorn responded, "Exactly. I'm a bargain because the additional $600 I want only puts you at $4,900. If you don't pay it, I'll just lien the houses and then you'll be stuck without a way to close the sales. I've got the contract all drawn up. Just sign it and everything goes smoothly."

Should Fulkins sign the agreement? Does Tretorn have the right to the additional $600? Was it ethical for Tretorn to demand the $600? Is there any legal advice you can offer Fulkins?

C.   EXCEPTIONS TO THE LAW OF CONSIDERATION

The ever-changing character of law clearly appears in the area of consideration because the rules stated earlier in this chapter are slowly eroding.

10. Exceptions to Adequacy of Consideration Rule

Inadequacy of consideration may be evidence of fraud or undue influence.

The insufficiency or inadequacy of the consideration may lead a court to the conclusion that a contract is not binding because it is unconscionable.[17] Inadequate consideration may also indicate that fraud was practiced on the promisor.

The inadequacy of the consideration may be evidence of the exercise of undue influence or the taking advantage of the condition of the other contracting party. Several factors may combine to challenge the validity of the contract.

For the enforcement of an unconscionable contract, some courts may consider the adequacy of consideration. For example, "if the sum total of the provisions of a contract drive too hard a bargain, a court of conscience will not assist its enforcement."[18]

11. Exceptions to Requirement of Consideration

By statute or decision, consideration is no longer required in a number of situations.

Consideration is not required for charitable subscriptions.

(a) Charitable Subscriptions. When charitable enterprises are financed by voluntary subscriptions of a number of persons, the promise of each is generally enforceable. For example, when a number of people make pledges or subscriptions for the construction of a church, for a charitable institution, or for a college, the subscriptions are binding. Some states require proof that the charity has relied on the subscription.[19]

---

[17] *Mimica v Area Interstate Trucking, Inc.,* ___ Ill App 3d ___, ___ Ill Dec ___, 620 NE2d 1328 (1993).
[18] *Waters v Min Ltd,* ___ Mass ___, 587 NE2d 231 (1992).
[19] *King v Trustees of Boston University,* ___ Mass ___, 647 NE2d 1196 (1995).

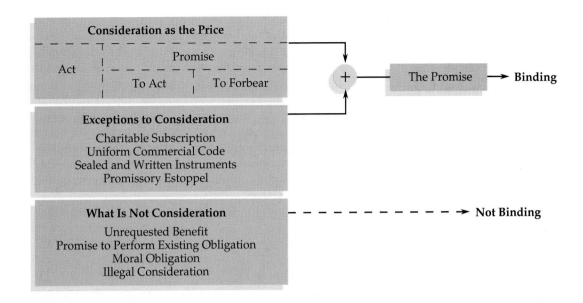

FIGURE 14-1
Consideration and Promises

You Can't Back Out Now

Facts: Salsbury was attempting to establish a new college, Charles City College. Salsbury obtained a pledge from the Northwestern Bell Telephone Company to contribute to the college. When the company did not pay, Salsbury sued the company. The company raised the defense that there was no consideration for its promise and that nothing had been done by the college in reliance on the promise.

Decision: Judgment for Salsbury. As a matter of public policy, a promise of a charitable contribution is binding even though there is no consideration for the promise and without regard for whether the charity had done any acts in reliance on the promise. The company was therefore liable on its promise to contribute. *[Salsbury v Northwestern Bell Telephone Co. (Iowa) 221 NW2d 609 (1974)]*

The theories for sustaining such promises vary. Consideration is lacking according to the technical standards applied in ordinary contract cases. Nevertheless, the courts enforce such promises as a matter of public policy.

UCC makes exceptions to the need for consideration.

(b) Uniform Commercial Code. In a number of situations, the Uniform Commercial Code abolishes the requirement of consideration. For example, under the Code, consideration is not required for (1) a merchant's written, firm offer for goods stated to be irrevocable; (2) a written discharge of a claim for an alleged breach of a commercial contract; or (3) an agreement to modify a contract for the sale of goods.[20]

Some states do not require consideration if a contract is sealed or written, or they presume consideration in such cases unless the contrary is shown.

(c) Sealed and Written Instruments. At common law, consideration was not necessary to support a promise under seal. In a state that gives the seal its original common law effect, the gratuitous promise or a promise to make a gift is enforceable when it is set forth in a sealed instrument.

---

[20] UCC § 2-209(1).

In some states, a promise under seal must be supported by consideration, just as though it did not have a seal. Other states take a middle position and hold that the presence of a seal is prima facie proof that there is consideration to support the promise. This means that if nothing more than the existence of the sealed promise is shown, it is deemed supported by consideration. The party making the promise, however, may prove that there was no consideration. In that case, the promise is not binding.

In some states, a rebuttable presumption arises whenever a contract is in writing that the promises of the parties are supported by consideration.[21]

When a sealed instrument calls also for consideration, the instrument cannot be enforced if there is a failure of consideration despite the fact that an ordinary sealed instrument would be enforced even without consideration.[22]

12. Promissory Estoppel

Consideration is not required when promissory estoppel is applied.

A promise that is not supported by consideration may still be binding if the doctrine of promissory estoppel can be applied. A person may make a promise to another under circumstances that the promisor should reasonably foresee will induce the promisee to rely on it and will cause the promisee to sustain substantial loss if the promise is not kept. Under the doctrine of **promissory estoppel,** such a promise is binding even though there is no consideration for it. In applying the doctrine of promissory estoppel, courts are ignoring the requirement of consideration in order to attain a just result.

When there is an express contract between the parties, the concept of promissory estoppel is not applicable.[23]

CASE SUMMARY

The Old Law Has Just Gotta Go!

Facts: Hoffman wanted to acquire a franchise for a Red Owl grocery store. (Red Owl was a corporation that maintained a system of chain stores.) An agent of Red Owl informed Hoffman and his wife that if they would sell their bakery in Wautoma, acquire a certain tract of land in Chilton (another city), and put up $6,000, they would be given a franchise. In reliance on the agent's promises, Hoffman sold his business and acquired the land in Chilton, but he was never granted a franchise. He and his wife sued Red Owl. Red Owl raised the defense that there had been only an assurance that Hoffman would receive a franchise, but since there was no promise supported by consideration, there was no binding contract to give him a franchise.

Decision: Judgment for the Hoffmans. Injustice would result under the circumstances of the case if the Hoffmans were not granted relief. The plaintiffs had acted in reliance on a promise made by Red Owl's authorized agent. They would be harmed substantially if the promise were not held binding. [*Hoffman v Red Owl Stores, Inc.* 26 Wis 2d 683, 133 NW2d 267 (1967)]

---

21 *Hammons v Ehney* (Mo) 924 SW2d 843 (1996).
22 *Thomas v Webster Spring Co.,* ___ Mass App ___, 638 NE2d 51 (1994).
23 *Tiberi v Cigna Corp.* (CA10 NM) 89 F3d 1423 (1996).

(a) Promissory Estoppel Distinguished from Consideration. Promissory estoppel differs from consideration in that with promissory estoppel the reliance of the promisee is not the bargained-for price or response sought by the promisor. Under promissory estoppel it is sufficient that the promisor foresees that there will be such reliance. The doctrine of promissory estoppel applies only when (1) the promisor has reason to foresee the detrimental reliance by the promisee, and (2) the promisee in fact would sustain a substantial loss because of such reliance if the promise were not performed.

Promissory estoppel cannot be applied unless the promise is sufficiently definite for the court to determine what the promisor is required to do.

(b) Promise Essential. The making of an express promise is essential to applying the concept of promissory estoppel. Thus the fact that one party has certain hopes or expectations is in itself not sufficient. There must be a promise by the other party to produce the hoped-for result before promissory estoppel can be applied. Vague statements are not sufficient. Thus a statement by the creditor bank that it was "with" the debtors and would "support" them in their proposed venture was too vague to constitute a promise to make loans to the debtors. Likewise, a promissory estoppel cannot be based on a statement that "good employees are taken care of."[24]

Detrimental reliance is essential to promissory estoppel.

(c) Detrimental Reliance Essential. Promissory estoppel cannot be applied merely because the promisor has not performed the promise. In the absence of the promisee's detrimental reliance on the promise, the doctrine of promissory estoppel is not applicable. Thus a promise made to the debtor by the creditor that the creditor would collect only $20 a month on the debt of approximately $12,000 was not binding because there was no proof that the debtor relied in any manner on that promise.[25]

What constitutes detrimental reliance sufficient to satisfy the promissory estoppel rule has been diluted in recent years. In the early promissory estoppel cases, it was necessary to show that if the defendant did not perform the promise, the plaintiff would suffer a substantial loss—of a nature that could not be compensated for by the payment of money. Many courts are now willing to accept any financial loss as sufficient to show detrimental reliance. Thus, it has been held that when the plaintiff quit a job in reliance on the defendant's promise to employ the plaintiff, there was sufficient detrimental reliance to make the defendant's promise binding.

---

[24] *Ruud v Great Plains Supply, Inc.* (Minn) 526 NW2d 369 (1995).
[25] *Lawrence v Board of Education,* ___ Ill App 3d ___, ___ Ill Dec ___, 503 NE2d 1201 (1987). Some courts hold the promisor liable for tort damages when the promisee has sustained harm because the promisee relied on the promise but the promise was never kept. *ITT Terryphone Corp. v Tri-State Steel Drum, Inc.,* ___ Ga App ___, 344 SE2d 686 (1986). The explanation for these differing views is that those courts do not believe it is just for the promisor to break a promise on which the promisee had detrimentally relied, but, at the same time, they do not feel that they can flatly state that consideration is not required to make the broken promise binding on the defendant.

SUMMARY

A promise is not binding if there is no consideration for the promise. Consideration is what the promisor requires as the price for the promise. That price may be doing an act, refraining from the doing of an act, or merely promising to do or to refrain. In a bilateral contract, it is necessary to find that the promise of each party is supported by consideration. If either promise is not so supported, it is not binding, and the agreement of the parties is not a contract. Consequently, the agreement cannot be enforced. When a promise is the consideration, it must be a binding promise. The binding character of a promise is not affected by the circumstance that there is a condition precedent to the performance promised. Likewise, the binding character of the promise and of the contract is not affected by a provision in the contract for its cancellation by either one or both of the parties. A promise to do what one is already obligated to do is not consideration, although some exceptions are made. Such exceptions include the rendering of a partial performance or a modified performance accepted as a good-faith adjustment to a changed situation, a compromise and release of claims, a part-payment check, and a compromise of creditors. Because consideration is the price that is given to obtain the promise, past benefits conferred on the promisor cannot be consideration. In the case of a complex transaction, however, the past benefit and the subsequent transaction relating to the promise may in fact have been intended by the parties as one transaction. In such a case, the earlier benefit is not past consideration but is the consideration contemplated by the promisor as the price for the promise subsequently made.

A promise to refrain from doing an act can be consideration. A promise to refrain from suing or asserting a particular claim can be consideration. Generally, the promise to forbear must be for a specified time as distinguished from agreeing to forbear at will. When consideration is forbearance to assert a claim, it is immaterial whether the claim is valid as long as the claim has been asserted in good faith in the belief that it was valid.

When the promisor obtains the consideration specified for the promise, the law is not ordinarily concerned with the value or adequacy of that consideration. Exceptions are sometimes made in the case of fraud or unconscionability and under consumer protection statutes.

There is a current trend to abandon the requirement of consideration, with promissory estoppel the most extensive repudiation of that requirement.

All transactions must be lawful; therefore, consideration for a promise must be legal. If it is not, there is no consideration, and the promise is not binding.

When the promisor does not actually receive the price promised for the promise, there is a failure of consideration, which constitutes a breach of the contract.

Although consideration is required to make a promise binding, the promise that is not supported by consideration is not unlawful or illegal. If the promisor voluntarily performs the promise, the promisor cannot undo the performance and restore matters to their position prior to the making of the agreement. The parties are free to perform their agreement, but the courts will not help either of them because there is no contract.

QUESTIONS AND CASE PROBLEMS

1. Sarah's house caught on fire. Through the prompt assistance of her neighbor Odessa, the fire was quickly extinguished. In gratitude, Sarah promised to pay Odessa $1,000. Can Odessa enforce this promise if Sarah does not pay the money?

2. Clifton agreed to work for Acrylics Inc. for $400 a month. He later claimed there was no contract because the consideration for the services to be rendered was inadequate. Is there a binding contract?

3. Dale Dyer, who was employed by National By-Products, Inc., was seriously injured at work as the result of a job-related accident. He agreed to give up his right to sue the employer for damages in consideration of the employer's giving him a lifetime job. The employer later claimed that this agreement was not binding because Dyer's promise not to sue could not be consideration for the promise to employ on the ground that Dyer in fact had no right to sue. Dyer's only remedy was to make a claim under workers' compensation. Was the agreement binding? [*Dyer v National By-Products, Inc.* (Iowa) 380 NW2d 732]

4. Galloway induced Marian to sell her house to Galloway by false statements that a factory was going to be built on the vacant lot adjoining Marian's house.

No factory was ever built, and Marian then sued Galloway for damages for fraud. Marian offered to prove that Galloway had paid her only a fraction of the true value of her house. Galloway claimed that this evidence of value could not be admitted because it was immaterial whether the consideration paid Marian was adequate. Is Galloway correct?

5. Koedding hired West Roofers to put a roof on her house. She later claimed that the roofing job was defective, and she threatened to sue West. Both parties discussed the matter in good faith. Finally, West guaranteed that the roof would be free from leaks for 20 years in return for the guarantee by Koedding not to sue West for damages. The roof leaked the next year, and Koedding sued West on the guarantee. West claimed that the guarantee was not binding because there was no consideration for it. According to West, Koedding's promise not to sue had no value because Koedding in fact did not have any valid claim against West; therefore, she was not entitled to sue. Was this defense valid?

6. Fedun rented a building to Gomer, who did business under the name of Mike's Cafe. Later, Gomer was about to sell out the business to Brown and requested Fedun to release him from his liability under the lease. Fedun agreed to do so. Brown sold out shortly thereafter. The balance of the rent due by Gomer under the original lease agreement was not paid, and Fedun sued Gomer on the rent claim. Could he collect after having released Gomer? [*Fedun v Mike's Cafe,* ___ Pa Super ___, 204 A2d 776]

7. Alexander Proudfoot Co. was in the business of devising efficiency systems for industry. It told Sanitary Linen Service Co. that it could provide an improved system for Sanitary Linen that would save Sanitary Linen money. It made a contract with Sanitary Linen to provide a money-saving system. The system was put into operation, and Proudfoot was paid the amount due under the contract. The system failed to work and did not save money. Sanitary Linen sued to get the money back. Was it entitled to do so? [*Sanitary Linen Service Co. v Alexander Proudfoot Co.* (CA5 Fla) 435 F2d 292]

8. Sears, Roebuck and Co. promised to give Forrer permanent employment. Forrer sold his farm at a loss to take the job. Shortly after beginning work, he was discharged by Sears, which claimed that the contract could be terminated at will. Forrer claimed that promissory estoppel prevented Sears from terminating the contract. Was he correct? [*Forrer v Sears, Roebuck & Co.* (Wis) 153 NW2d 587]

9. Kemp leased a gas filling station from Baehr. Kemp, who was heavily indebted to Penn-O-Tex Oil Corp., transferred to it his right to receive payments on all claims. When Baehr complained that the rent was not paid, he was assured by the corporation that the rent would be paid to him. Baehr did not sue Kemp for the overdue rent but later sued the corporation. The defense was raised that there was no consideration for the promise of the corporation. Decide. [*Baehr v Penn-O-Tex Corp.* (Minn) 104 NW2d 661]

10. Bogart owed several debts to Security Bank & Trust Co. and applied to the bank for a loan to pay the debts. The bank's employee stated that he would take the application for the loan to the loan committee and "within two or three days, we ought to have something here, ready for you to go with." The loan was not made. The bank sued Bogart for his debts. He filed a counterclaim on the theory that the bank had broken its contract to make a loan to him and that promissory estoppel prevented the bank from going back on what the employee had said. Was this counterclaim valid?

11. Kelsoe worked for International Wood Products, Inc., for a number of years. One day Hernandez, a director and major stockholder of the company, promised Kelsoe that the corporation would give her 5 percent of the company's stock. This promise was never kept, and Kelsoe sued International for breach of contract. Had the company broken its contract? [*Kelsoe v International Wood Products, Inc.* (Ala) 588 So 2d 877]

12. Norma Elmore was in a Wal-Mart store when she slipped and fell on an open package of mints on the floor. She asked the store representative who came to her aid if the store would pay her medical expenses. The representative assured her that the store would pay. The store failed to do so, and Norma sued for medical expenses. Was the store liable?

13. On the death of their mother, the children of Jane Smith gave their interests in their mother's estate to their father in consideration of his payment of $1 to each of them and his promise to leave them the property on his death. The father died without leaving them the property. The children sued their father's second wife to obtain the property in accordance with the agreement. The second wife claimed that the agreement was not a binding contract because the amount of $1 and future gifts given for the children's interests were so trivial and uncertain. Decide.

14. Radio Station KSCS broadcast a popular music program. It announced that it would pay $25,000 to any listener who detected that it did not play three consecutive songs. Steve Jennings listened to and heard a program in which two songs were followed by a commercial program. He claimed the $25,000. The station refused to pay on the ground that there was no consideration for its promise to pay that amount. Was the station liable? [*Jennings v Radio Station KSCS* (Tex App) 708 SW2d 60]

Legality and Public Policy

OBJECTIVES

After studying this chapter, you should be able to

1. *State the effect of illegality on a contract;*
2. *Compare illegality and unconscionability;*
3. *Distinguish between illegality in performing a legal contract and the illegality of a contract;*
4. *Recognize when a contract is invalid because it obstructs legal processes;*
5. *State the elements of a lottery; and*
6. *State the extent to which agreements not to compete are lawful.*

A court will not enforce a contract if it is illegal, contrary to public policy, or unconscionable.

A. GENERAL PRINCIPLES

An agreement is illegal either when its formation or performance is a crime or a tort or when it is contrary to public policy or unconscionable.

1. Effect of Illegality

Illegal contracts are void and courts will not aid any of the parties.

Ordinarily, an illegal agreement is void. When an agreement is illegal, the parties are usually not entitled to the aid of the courts. If the illegal agreement has not been performed, neither party can sue the other to obtain performance or damages. Likewise, the party who relied on the validity of the illegal contract cannot obtain its enforcement on the theory of promissory estoppel.[1] If the agreement has been performed, neither party can sue the other to obtain damages or to set the agreement aside.

> **CASE SUMMARY**
>
> ## Bad Boys Can't Win
>
> **Facts:** Celia Henry was promoting an illegal pyramid scheme where a person, upon making an investment, is granted a license to recruit similar "licensees." David Ford gave Henry $1,500 in order to obtain a piece of the action. He later sued Henry to get the money back.
>
> **Decision:** Judgment for Henry. The pyramid scheme was illegal. By investing money in the scheme, Ford was *in pari delicto* with Henry. He therefore could not recover from Henry any of the money that he had paid him. [*Ford v Henry,* App Div 2d, 598 NYS2d 660 (1993)]

When a promissory note is given as part of an illegal transaction, the note cannot be enforced by the promisee.[2]

2. Exceptions to Effect of Illegality

Exceptions are made to the illegality rule.

To avoid hardship, exceptions are made to the rules stated in section 1.

(a) Protection of One Party. When the law that the agreement violates is intended for the protection of one of the parties, that party may seek relief. For example, when, in order to protect the public, the law forbids the issuance of securities by certain classes of corporations, a person who has purchased them may recover the money paid.

(b) Unequal Guilt. When the parties are not *in pari delicto*—not equally guilty—the least guilty party is granted relief when public interest is advanced by so doing. For example, when a statute is adopted to protect one of the parties to a transaction, such as a usury law adopted to protect borrowers, the person to be protected will not be deemed to be *in pari delicto* with the wrongdoer when entering into a transaction that is prohibited by the statute.

---

[1] *Weese v Davis County Comm'n* (Utah) 834 P2d 1 (1992).
[2] *Minor v McDaniel,* ___ Ga App ___, 435 SE2d 508 (1993).

(c) Knowledge of Illegal Purpose of Other Contracting Party. A contract that is in itself lawful is not made unlawful by the fact that one of the parties intends to make unlawful use of the subject matter of the contract, even though this intention is known to the other contracting party.

(d) Criminal Law Distinguished. The rules of law discussed in this chapter relate only to the effect of a contract as between the parties to the contract. The rules have no application to the criminal liability of the parties to the contract for any crime committed pursuant to the illegal contract. Thus it is no defense to a forger that the forged check that he gave to the other contracting party was given to make an illegal purchase of cocaine. He can be prosecuted for the forgery even though he could not be sued by the cocaine dealer for breach of contract.[3]

3. Partial Illegality

Legal parts of a partially illegal contract will be enforced if they can be separated.

An agreement may involve the performance of several promises, some of which are illegal and some legal. The legal parts of the agreement may be enforced provided that they can be separated from the parts that are illegal.

When the illegal provision of a contract may be ignored without defeating the basic purpose of the contract, a court will merely ignore the illegal provision and enforce the balance of the contract. Consequently, when a provision for the payment of an attorney's fee in a car rental agreement was illegal because prohibited by a local statute, the court would merely ignore the fee provision and enforce the balance of the contract.[4]

If a contract is susceptible to two interpretations, one legal and the other illegal, the court will assume that the legal meaning was intended unless the contrary is clearly indicated.

4. Crimes and Civil Wrongs

An agreement to commit a crime or a civil wrong is illegal.

An agreement is illegal, and therefore void, when it calls for the commission of any act that constitutes a crime. To illustrate, one cannot enforce an agreement by which the other party is to commit an assault, steal property, burn a house, or kill a person. A contract to obtain equipment for committing a crime is illegal and cannot be enforced. Thus a contract to manufacture and sell illegal slot machines is void.

An agreement that calls for the commission of a civil wrong is also illegal and void. Examples are agreements to slander a third person; defraud another; infringe another's patent, trademark, or copyright; or fix prices.

5. Good Faith and Fairness

There is a trend in law to require good faith and fairness.

The law is evolving toward requiring that contracts be fair and made in good faith. The law is becoming increasingly concerned with whether one party has utilized a superior bargaining power or superior knowledge to obtain better terms from the other party than would otherwise have been obtained.

---

[3] *Burks v Texas* (Tex App) 795 SW2d 913 (1990).
[4] *Harbour v Arelco, Inc.* (Ind) 678 NE2d 381 (1997).

In the case of goods, the seller must act in good faith. In regard to merchant sellers, *good faith* is defined as honesty in fact and the observance of reasonable commercial standards of fair dealing in the trade.[5] ◆ *For example,* Delta made a contract to purchase Shirley's house. The contract stated that it would be void if Delta was not able to get a bank loan to finance the sale. Delta changed her mind about buying the house and made no effort to get a loan. When Shirley sued Delta for breach of contract, Delta claimed that the contract was void because no loan had been obtained. But Delta remained bound by the contract as she was under the duty to make reasonable efforts to obtain a bank loan. By not making any effort to obtain a loan, Delta did not act in good faith to carry out the contract. ◆

6. Unconscionable and Oppressive Contracts

Unconscionable and oppressive clauses or contracts are not valid.

Ordinarily, a court will not consider whether a contract is fair or unfair, is wise or foolish, or operates unequally between the parties. However, in a number of instances the law holds that contracts or contract clauses will not be enforced because they are too harsh or oppressive to one of the parties. This principle is most commonly applied to invalidate a clause providing for the payment by one party of a large penalty upon breaking the contract or a provision declaring that a party shall not be liable for the consequences of negligence. This principle is extended in connection with the sale of goods to provide that "if the court . . . finds the contract or any clause of the contract to have been unconscionable at the time it was made, the court may refuse to enforce the contract, or it may enforce the remainder of the contract without the unconscionable clause, or it may so limit the application of any unconscionable clause as to avoid any unconscionable result."[6]

(a) What Constitutes Unconscionability? A provision that gives what the court believes is too much of an advantage over a buyer is likely to be held void as **unconscionable**. To bring the unconscionability provision into operation, it is not necessary to prove that fraud was practiced. When there is a grossly disproportionate bargaining power between the parties so that the weaker or inexperienced party cannot afford to risk confrontation with the stronger party but just signs on the dotted line, courts will hold that grossly unfair terms obtained by the stronger party are void as unconscionable.

A provision is unconscionable when grossly unfair to a weaker party who has no freedom of choice.

Under the Uniform Consumer Credit Code, a particular clause or an entire agreement relating to a consumer credit sale, a consumer lease, or a consumer loan is void when such provision or agreement is unconscionable.[7]

Authority can be found that when the buyer has no meaningful choice of buy-

---

[5] UCC § 2-103(1)(b). Higher standards than those imposed on sellers in general are imposed on merchant sellers by other provisions of the UCC. See § 2-314, as to warranties, and § 2-509(3), as to the transfer of risk of loss. The provisions of the UCC noted above do not apply to contracts generally. However, there is a growing trend of courts to extend Article 2 of the UCC, which relates only to the sale of goods, to contract situations generally. This extension is based on the theory that the UCC represents the latest restatement of the law of contracts made by expert scholars and the legislators of the land. In other articles of the UCC, *good faith* means merely honesty in fact in the conduct or transaction concerned. UCC § 1-201(19). With respect to checks and other commercial paper, this definition has been expanded by the 1990 Revision of Article 3 to honesty in fact and the observance of reasonable commercial standards of fair dealing. UCC § 3-103(a)(4) [1990 Revision]. With respect to investment securities, such as stocks and bonds, the same expansion of good faith has been made by Article 8, UCC § 8-102(10).
[6] UCC § 2-302(1).
[7] UCC § 5-108.

ing elsewhere, a contract is unconscionable when the prices charged the buyer are excessively high.[8] However, the fact that a contract is a bad bargain does not make it unconscionable.

CASE SUMMARY

No Escape From Your Mistakes

Facts: Everette Marshall borrowed over $5,000 from the Mercury Finance Company to buy an automobile and agreed to pay 29.48 percent interest. Marshall was a college graduate with a degree in business management and admitted that he understood the loan papers when he signed them. Some time later, he tried to avoid the loan on the ground that it was unconscionable.

Decision: The contract was not unconscionable. While the interest rate was high, Marshall knew what he was doing and had the freedom of choice to reject the loan on the terms offered and go elsewhere. [*Marshall v Mercury Finance Co.* (Ala Civ App) 550 So 2d 1026 (1989).

Unconscionability is determined as a question of fact in light of circumstances when the contract was made.

(b) Determination of Unconscionability. Unconscionability is to be determined in the light of the circumstances existing at the time the contract was made. The fact that later events make the contract unwise or undesirable does not make the contract unconscionable. Hence, the fact that there is a sharp rise in the market price of goods after the contract has been made does not make the contract unconscionable. The decision that a provision or a contract is unconscionable can be made by a court only after holding a hearing to determine the real effect of the contract when viewed in its commercial setting. In a particular state, the concept of unconscionability may be based on the Uniform Commercial Code, the Uniform Consumer Credit Code, local nonuniform code statutes, or general principles of equity absorbed by the common law. The concept of unconscionability is given the same interpretation by the courts regardless of the source of the concept.

CASE SUMMARY

Did You Have a Real Choice?

Facts: The Walker-Thomas Furniture Co. sold furniture on credit under contracts that contained a provision that a customer did not own the purchase as long as any balance on any purchase remained due. It sold goods to Ora Lee Williams. At the time when the balance of her account was $164, Walker-Thomas Furniture Co. sold her a $514 stereo set with knowledge that she was supporting herself and seven children on a government relief check of $218 a month. From 1957 to 1962, Williams had purchased $1,800 worth of goods and made payments of $1,200. When she stopped making payments in 1962, Walker-Thomas sought to take back everything she had purchased since 1957. Williams defended on the ground that the contract was unconscionable and could not be enforced. Walker-Thomas insisted that the contract could be enforced according to its terms.

Decision: Judgment against Walker-Thomas. A contract will not be enforced according to its terms if those terms are unconscionable. This means that because of the inferior bargaining power of one of the parties, that party had no "meaningful choice" in agreeing to the contract terms and those terms unreasonably favored the other party. The terms of the contract with

---

8 *Rite Color Chemical Co. v Velvet Textile Co.* (NC App) 411 SE2d 645 (1992).

> Walker-Thomas were very favorable to the seller. Therefore, it was necessary to hold a hearing to determine whether Williams in fact had made a meaningful choice. The terms of the contract would not be enforced unless the court found that she had made such a choice. *[Williams v Walker-Thomas Furniture Co. (CA Dist Col) 350 F2d 445 (1965)]*

7. Social Consequences of Contracts

Modern law gives greater importance to social consequences of a contract.

The social consequences of a contract are an important element today in determining the contract's validity and the power of government to regulate it.

(a) The Private Contract in Society. The law of contracts was originally oriented to private relations between private individuals. Now it is moving from the field of bilateral private law to multiparty societal considerations. The Supreme Court has held that private contracts lose their private, do-not-touch character when they become such a common part of our way of life that society deems it necessary to regulate them.

(b) The *n* Factor. The number of times (*n*) that the given contract is used in the modern business world becomes increasingly significant in determining the validity of the contract as between the parties. Courts are considering a contract as a legal relationship only between *A* and *B* less and less often. The modern court is increasingly influenced in its decision by the recognition of the fact that the contract before the court is not one *in* a million but is one *of* a million. For example, an insurer makes a contract with Kelley that is of the same nature as one that the insurer makes with Fanta. Also, these contracts are the same as the one that a different insurance company makes with Vidas and so on. A similar industrywide pattern is seen in the case of the bank loan made by one bank to a borrower, by a second bank to a different borrower, and so on.

B. AGREEMENTS AFFECTING PUBLIC WELFARE

Agreements that may harm the public welfare are condemned as contrary to public policy and are not binding. Agreements that interfere with public service or the duties of public officials, obstruct legal process, or discriminate against members of minority groups are considered detrimental to public welfare and, as such, are not enforceable.

8. Agreements Contrary to Public Policy

Agreements are void if contrary to public policy.

A given agreement may not violate any statute but may still be so offensive to society that the courts feel that enforcing the contract would be contrary to public policy.

No Sneaking Around the Law

Facts: Robert Bovard contracted to sell American Horse Enterprises, Inc., to James Ralph. When Ralph did not make payments when due, Bovard brought suit against him. The trial judge raised the question as to whether the contract was void for illegality. American Horse Enterprises was predominantly engaged in manufacturing devices for smoking marijuana and tobacco, and to a lesser degree in manufacturing jewelry. When the contract was made, there was no statute prohibiting the manufacture of any of these items, but there was a statute making it illegal to possess, use, or transfer marijuana.

Decision: Although the question of illegality had not been raised by the parties, the trial judge had the duty to question the validity of the contract when it appeared that the contract might be illegal. Although there was no statute expressly making the contract illegal, the statute prohibiting the possession and sale of marijuana manifested a public policy against anything that would further the use of marijuana. It was therefore against public policy to make the devices used in smoking marijuana or to sell a business that engaged in such manufacture. The sales contract was therefore contrary to public policy and void and could not be enforced. *[Bovard v American Horse Enterprises, Inc. and Ralph, 201 Cal App 3d 832, 247 Cal Rptr 340 (1988)]*

(a) The Concept of Public Policy. *Public policy* cannot be defined precisely but is loosely described as protection from that which tends to be injurious to the public or contrary to the public good, or which violates any established interest of society. Contracts condemned as contrary to public policy frequently relate to the protection of the public welfare, health, or safety; to the protection of the person; and to the protection of recognized social institutions. For example, a contract that prohibits marriage under all circumstances or that encourages divorce is generally held invalid as contrary to public policy. Courts are reluctant to declare a contract contrary to public policy because of the strong policy in favor of freedom of contract.[9] They are slow and cautious in invalidating a contract on the ground that it is contrary to public policy because courts recognize that, on the one hand, they are applying a very vague standard and, on the other hand, they are restricting the freedom of the contracting parties to contract freely as they choose.[10]

FIGURE 15-1
*Illegal Agreements
Affecting Public Welfare*

Agreements Contrary to Public Policy

Agreements Evading Statutes

Agreements Injuring Public Service

Agreements Involving Conflicts of Interest

Agreements Obstructing Legal Process

Agreements Involving Illegal Discrimination

Wagers and Private Lotteries

---

[9] *Braye v Archer-Daniels-Midland Co.* 175 Ill 2d 201, 676 NE2d 1295 (1997).
[10] *Beacon Hill Civic Ass'n v Ristorante Toscano, Inc.,* ___ Mass ___, 662 NE2d 1015 (1996).

No Gravy Train Allowed Here!

Facts: Terry Upton wanted to construct an apartment complex. He made a contract with James Rome that if Rome could get the city council to finance the construction, he would pay Rome a commission of 1.25 percent of the public funds obtained. The city council authorized the payment of $8.5 million for the project. Upton refused to pay Rome. Rome sued him for breach of contract.

Decision: Judgment for Upton. Because Rome would be paid only if public funds were spent and because the more public funds were spent the more he would be paid, there was the danger of ignoring what was good for the public welfare in order to get more money for Rome. Hence the contract was contrary to public policy and could not be enforced. *[Rome v Upton, ___ Ill App 3d ___, ___ Ill Dec ___, 648 NE2d 1085 (1995)]*

(b) Agreements Evading Statutory Protection. Statutes frequently confer benefits or provide protection. If an agreement is made that deprives a person of such a statutory benefit, it is generally held that the agreement is invalid because it is contrary to the public policy declared by the statute. For example, a state law provides that automobile insurance policies should cover certain persons. A policy provision excluding persons covered by the statutory provision is not valid because it is contrary to the public policy declared in the statute.

The waiver of statutory provisions designed to protect debtors, creditors, or consumers may be held void as contrary to public policy.

(c) Fee Splitting. It is against public policy for a licensed professional to split fees with a person who is not a licensed professional.

9. Agreements Injuring Public Service

An agreement interfering with or corrupting government personnel is contrary to public policy.

An agreement that tends to interfere with the proper performance of the duties of a public officer—whether legislative, administrative, or judicial—is contrary to public policy and void. Thus, an agreement to procure the award of a public contract by corrupt means is not enforceable. Other examples are agreements to sell public offices, to procure pardons by corrupt means, and to pay a public officer more or less than legal fees or salary. Campaign promises to give a job to a particular person are contrary to public policy and cannot be enforced.[11]

One of the most common agreements within the class is the **illegal lobbying agreement.** This term is used to describe an agreement to use unlawful means to procure or prevent the adoption of legislation by a lawmaking body, such as Congress or a state legislature. Such agreements are clearly contrary to the public interest because they interfere with the democratic process. They are accordingly illegal and void.

Some courts hold illegal all agreements to influence legislation regardless of the means contemplated or employed. Other courts adopt the rule that such agreements are valid in the absence of the use of improper influence or the contemplation of using such influence.

---

[11] *Harris v Johnson,* ___ Ill App 3d ___, ___ Ill Dec ___, 578 NE2d 1326 (1991).

10. Agreements Involving Conflicts of Interest

A contract made by a government officer with conflicting interests is contrary to public policy.

Various statutes prohibit government officials from being personally interested, directly or indirectly, in any transaction entered into by such officials on behalf of the government. When there is a prohibited conflict of interest, a contract is invalid without regard to whether its terms are fair or advantageous to the public. *For example,* Charital, a procurement officer of a government department, was required to purchase large numbers of motor vehicles for various departments. He made the purchases from the Lafite Paramount Motor Co. Unknown to anyone in the government, Charital was the sole stockholder of the company. Any contract between Lafite and the government was void because undisclosed self-dealing presents a conflict of the public servant's duty to put the government's fiscal interests above personal interests.

11. Agreements Obstructing Legal Processes

An agreement to interfere with or corrupt courts is contrary to public policy.

Any agreement intended to obstruct or pervert legal processes is contrary to public interest and therefore void. Agreements that promise to pay money in return for the abandonment of the prosecution of a criminal case, for the suppression of evidence in any legal proceeding, for initiating litigation, or for the perpetration of any fraud on the court are therefore void.

CASE SUMMARY

Buying Off the Victim Is Bad

Facts: Alfred Coats embezzled $54,000 from Jim Jones, his employer at Auto Mart. To induce Jones to drop criminal charges, Coats, his stepfather and his mother, William and Diane Adams, signed papers promising to repay Jones the embezzled money. They later sued to set aside these papers.

Decision: Judgment for Adams. The papers were void. They were against public policy because their object was to prevent prosecution for a crime that had been committed. They were accordingly void and could not be enforced. *[Adams v Jones (NC App) 441 SE2d 699 (1994)]*

An agreement to pay an ordinary witness more than the regular witness fee allowed by law, or a promise to pay a greater amount if the promisor wins the lawsuit, is void. The danger here is that the witness will lie in order to help win the case.

12. Illegal Discrimination Contracts

An agreement that makes a prohibited discrimination is contrary to public policy.

A contract specifying that a homeowner will not sell to a member of a particular race cannot be enforced because it violates the Fourteenth Amendment of the Constitution.[12] Hotels and restaurants may not deal with their customers on terms that discriminate due to race, religion, color, or national origin.[13]

---

12 *Shelley v Kraemer* 334 US 1 (1948).
13 Federal Civil Rights Act of 1964, 42 USC §§ 2000a et seq.

13. Gambling, Wagers, and Lotteries

Gambling contracts are illegal.[14] Largely as a result of the adoption of antigambling statutes, wagers or bets are generally illegal. Private lotteries involving the three elements of prize, chance, and consideration (or similar affairs of chance) are also generally held illegal. In many states, public lotteries (lotteries run by a state government) have been legalized by statute. Raffles are usually regarded as lotteries. In some states, bingo games, lotteries, and raffles are legalized by statute when the funds raised are used for a charitable purpose.

Sales promotion schemes calling for the distribution of property according to chance among the purchasers of goods are held illegal as lotteries without regard to whether the scheme is called a guessing contest, a raffle, or a gift.

CASE SUMMARY

When a Good Purpose Is No Defense

Facts: The Economic Opportunity Commission of Nassau County was a charitable organization. It ran a raffle to raise money for its scholarship fund. The prize was an automobile. Harris purchased the ticket that won, but the organization refused to deliver the car because the raffle was an illegal lottery.

Decision: The raffle was an illegal lottery because a payment had to be made for a chance to win a prize. The fact that the raffle was run by a charity for a charitable purpose did not change the character of the raffle as being an illegal lottery. [*Harris v Economic Opportunity Commission of Nassau County, Inc. 542 NYS2d 913 (1989)*]

Giveaway plans and games are lawful so long as it is not necessary to buy anything or give anything of value to participate. If participation is free, the element of consideration is lacking, and there is no lottery.

An activity is not gambling when the result is solely or predominantly a matter of skill. In contrast, it is gambling when the result is solely a matter of luck. Rarely is any activity 100 percent skill or 100 percent luck.

C. REGULATION OF BUSINESS

Local, state, and national laws regulate a wide variety of business activities and practices.

14. Effect of Violation

Whether an agreement made in connection with business conducted in violation of the law is binding or void depends on how strongly opposed the public policy is to the prohibited act. Some courts take the view that the agreement is not void unless the statute expressly specifies this. In some instances, a statute expressly preserves the validity of the contract. For example, if someone fails to register a fictitious name under which a business is conducted, the violator, after registering the name as required by statute, is permitted to sue on a contract made while illegally conducting business.

---

[14] *Hertz Commercial Leasing Division v Morrison* (Miss) 567 So 2d 832 (1990).

15. Statutory Regulation of Contracts

To establish uniformity or to protect one of the parties to a contract, statutes frequently provide that contracts of a given class must follow a statutory model or must contain specified provisions. For example, statutes commonly specify that particular clauses must be included in insurance policies to protect the persons insured and their beneficiaries. Other statutes require that contracts executed in connection with credit buying and loans contain particular provisions designed to protect the debtor.

Consumer protection legislation gives the consumer the right to rescind the contract in certain situations. Laws relating to truth in lending, installment sales, and home improvement contracts commonly require that an installment-sale contract specify the cash price, the down payment, the trade-in value (if any), the cash balance, the insurance costs, and the interest and finance charges.

When a statute imposes a fine or imprisonment for violation, a court should not hold the contract void because that would increase the penalty the legislature had imposed. If a statute prohibits making certain kinds of contracts or imposes limitations on contracts that can be made, the attorney general or other government official is generally able to obtain an injunction, or court order, to stop the parties from entering into a prohibited contract.

16. Licensed Callings or Dealings

Statutes frequently require that a person obtain a license, certificate, or diploma before practicing certain professions, such as law and medicine. A license may also be required before carrying on a particular business or trade, such as that of a real estate broker, peddler, stockbroker, hotel keeper, or pawnbroker.

(a) Protective License. If a license is required to protect the public from unqualified persons, a contract made by an unlicensed person is void.[15] For example, it has been held that when a statute required that contractors be licensed and an unlicensed contractor made a contract to make repairs, the contractor could not recover from the owner either the price agreed to in their contract or the reasonable value of the services actually performed. A corporation that does not hold a required real estate broker's license cannot sue to recover fees for services as a

> *An unlicensed person cannot enforce or recover on a contract when a license is required for public protection.*

CASE SUMMARY

No License—No Suit

Facts: Jose Sangles was an unlicensed building contractor. A Florida statute stated that a contract with an unlicensed contractor was "unenforceable." Juan Castro made a contract with Sangles to build a duplex. In order to obtain a building permit for the construction, Castro falsely stated to the licensing department that he was building the house on his land without using a contractor. By this means, Castro obtained a license to build. However, he had Sangles do the building. The construction was not satisfactory, and Castro sued Sangles.

Decision: Judgment for Sangles. The contract on which Castro sued could not be enforced because Sangles was not a licensed contractor. In addition, the fraudulent conduct of Castro in obtaining a building permit showed that he was *in pari delicto* as to the particular contract. Accordingly he could not enforce the contract. [*Castro v Sangles (Fla App) 637 So 2d 989 (1994)*

---

15 *Portable Embryonics, Inc. v J.P. Genetics, Inc.*, ___ Mont ___, 810 P2d 1197 (1991).

FIGURE 15-2
Illegal Agreements
Affecting Business

> Contracts with Unlicensed Persons in
> Licensed Callings or Dealings
>
> Fraudulent Sales
>
> Agreements Restraining Trade
>
> Agreements Not to Compete
>
> Usurious Agreements

The illegality of contracts often comes into the picture when parties seek to set up some arrangement to evade government regulations or prohibitions of the criminal law or to avoid paying taxes.

An unlicensed insurance broker who cannot recover a fee because of the absence of a license cannot evade the statutory requirement by having a friend who is a licensed broker bill for the services and collect the payment for him.[16]

> **An unlicensed person may recover on a contract if a license is required to raise revenue.**

(b) Revenue-Raising License. In contrast with the protective license, a license may be required solely as a revenue measure by requiring payment of a fee for the license. In that event, an agreement made in violation of the statute by one not licensed is generally held valid. The contract may also sometimes be held valid when it is shown that no harm has resulted from the failure to obtain a permit to do the work contemplated by the particular contract.

17. Fraudulent Sales

> **Contracts to evade statutes prohibiting fraudulent sales are void.**

Statutes commonly regulate the sale of certain commodities. Scales and measures of grocers and other vendors must be checked periodically, and they must be approved and sealed by the proper official. Certain articles must be inspected before they are sold. Other articles must be labeled in a particular way to show their contents and to warn the public of the presence of any dangerous or poisonous substance. Because these laws regulating sales are generally designed for the protection of the public, transactions in violation of such laws are void.

18. Administrative Agency Regulation

> **A valid administrative agency regulation is law that a contract may not violate.**

Large segments of the American economy are governed by federal administrative agencies created to carry out the general policies specified by Congress. A contract must be in harmony with public policy, not only as declared by Congress and the courts, but also as applied by the appropriate administrative agency. For example, a particular contract to market goods might not be prohibited by any statute or court decision but may still be condemned by the Federal Trade Commission as an unfair method of competition. When the proper commission has made its determination, a contract not in harmony with the determination, such as a contract of a railroad charging a higher or a lower rate than that approved by the Interstate Commerce Commission, is illegal.

---

[16] *Gutfreund v DeMian* (App Div) 642 NYS2d 294 (1996).

19. Contracts in Restraint of Trade

A contract in restraint of trade is illegal.

An agreement that unreasonably restrains trade is illegal and void on the ground that it is contrary to public policy. Such agreements take many forms, such as a combination to create a monopoly or to obtain a corner on the market, or an association of merchants to increase prices. In addition to the illegality of the agreement based on general principles of law, statutes frequently declare monopolies illegal and subject the parties to various civil and criminal penalties.[17]

20. Agreements Not to Compete

Agreements not to compete are illegal unless incidental to a sale of a business or an employment contract.

In the absence of a valid restrictive covenant, the seller of a business may compete with the buyer, or an ex-employee may solicit customers of the former employer. If there is no sale of a business or the making of an employment contract, an agreement not to compete is illegal as a restraint of trade and a violation of the antitrust law. The agreement is therefore void

A noncompetition covenant may be held invalid because of vagueness concerning the duration and geographic area of the restriction.[18]

(a) Sale of Business. When a going business is sold, it is commonly stated in the contract that the seller shall not go into the same or a similar business again within a certain geographic area, or for a certain period of time, or both. In early times, such agreements were held void because they deprived the public of the service of the person who agreed not to compete, impaired the latter's means of earning a livelihood, reduced competition, and exposed the public to monopoly. To modern courts the question is whether, under the circumstances, the restriction imposed on one party is reasonably necessary to protect the other party. If the restriction is reasonable, it is valid.

On the ground of reasonableness, a restriction has been sustained by which a restaurant owner selling out to a new owner agreed not to reopen a restaurant within a five-mile radius for five years.[19]

An employment noncompetition clause is valid to the extent needed to give an employer reasonable protection.

(b) Employment Contract. Restrictions to prevent competition by a former employee are held valid when reasonable and necessary to protect the interest of the former employer. For example, the following provision is reasonable and will be enforced: A doctor employed by a medical clinic is not to practice medicine within a 50-mile radius of the city in which the clinic is located for one year after leaving the employ of the clinic. Likewise, a provision is valid that prohibited for two years an employee from calling on any customer of the employer called on by the employee during the last six months of employment.

Public policy requires that noncompetition covenants be strictly construed in favor of freedom of action of the employee.[20] A restrictive covenant is not binding when it places a restriction on the employee that is broader than reasonably necessary to protect the employer. The employer cannot prohibit competition by a former employee for all time or for the entire world merely because some

---

17 Sherman Antitrust Act, 15 USC §§ 1-7; Clayton Act, 15 USC §§ 12-27; Federal Trade Commission Act, 15 USC §§ 41-58.
18 *Gomez v Zamor* (Tex App) 814 SW2d 114 (1991).
19 *Cafe Associates v Gemgross* (SC) 406 SE2d 162 (1991).
20 *Dixie Parking Service, Inc. v Hargrove* (La App) 691 So 2d 1316 (1997).

customer might follow the former employee. In determining the validity of a restrictive covenant binding an employee, the court balances the aim of protecting the legitimate interests of the employer with the right of the employee to follow gainful employment and provide services required by the public and other employers.[21]

Restricting the Restrictive Covenant

Facts: Fred Gore, under the name of M.R.B., was engaged in developing and marketing computer software for controlling feeding programs for dairy cattle. Marvin Marshall went to work for M.R.B. under a contract that provided that, after termination of the employment, Marshall would not engage for two years in the business of developing or marketing computer software or in any business that competed with M.R.B. Marshall left the employment with M.R.B. M.R.B. then sued for an injunction to enforce the noncompetition provision.

Decision: An injunction was granted only as to the part of the provision preventing Marshall from competing with M.R.B. in the development and marketing of computer software for dairy feeding programs. No injunction would be granted to prevent Marshall from developing and marketing computer software for other purposes. M.R.B. had no legitimate interest to protect with respect to such software. Therefore, the restrictive covenant was too broad and was illegal and not binding to the extent that it went beyond software for dairy feeding programs. [Marshall v Gore (Fla App) 506 So 2d 91 (1987)]

(c) Effect of Invalidity. When a restriction of competition agreed to by the parties is invalid because its scope as to time or geographic area is too great, how does this affect the contract? Some courts trim the restrictive covenant down to a scope they deem reasonable and require the parties to abide by that revision.[22] This rule is nicknamed the "blue pencil rule." By applying this rule, one court has held that a covenant not to compete for three years was void because excessive but that it would be enforced for one year.[23]

Other courts refuse to apply the blue pencil rule and hold that the restrictive covenant is void[24] or that the entire contract is void. There is also authority that a court should refuse to apply the blue pencil rule when the restrictive covenant is manifestly unfair and would virtually keep the employee from earning a living.

> Courts differ on whether an excessive noncompetition clause should be held invalid or reduced by the blue pencil rule.

21. Usurious Agreements

Usury is committed when money is loaned at a greater rate of interest than is allowed by law. Most states prohibit by statute the taking of more than a stated amount of interest. These statutes provide a maximum contract rate of interest that is the highest annual rate that can be exacted or demanded under the law of a given state. This maximum is often stated as a flat percentage rate, although there is a trend to tie the usury ceilings to current market rates. Intentionally charging greater interest on a loan than allowed by law constitutes usury. It is not necessary to prove that the defendant knew that there was a violation of the usury law.

> An agreement violating usury law is void.

[21] *Chambers-Dobson, Inc. v Squier*, ___ Neb ___, 472 NW2d 391 (1991).
[22] *Smart Corp. v Grider* (Ind App) 650 NE2d 80 (1995).
[23] *Hopper v All Pet Animal Clinic, Inc.* (Wyo) 861 P2d 531 (1993).
[24] *A.L. Williams & Associates v Stelk* (CR11 Ga) 960 F2d 942 (1992).

In many states, the usury law does not apply to loans made to corporations.

When a lender incurs expenses in the making of a loan, such as the cost of appraising property or making a credit investigation of the borrower, the lender will require the borrower to pay the amount of such expenses. Lenders may attempt to obtain more than the expenses from the borrowers. Any fee charged by a lender that goes beyond the reasonable expense of making the loan constitutes "interest" for the purpose of determining whether the transaction is usurious.[25]

When the lender requires the borrower to assume the debt of a third person in addition to the loan made to the buyer, such third-party debt is included in determining whether the transaction is usurious.[26]

22. Credit Sale Contracts

Credit sale contracts generally are not subject to usury law.

Sales of goods and services on credit are not technically within the scope of the usury laws because the seller does not make an express "loan" to the buyer. When the sale is made on credit, the price that the seller charges is ordinarily not controlled by the usury law unless the court finds that the transaction was actually a disguised loan.

A time-price differential generally is not subject to usury law.

(a) Credit Sale Price. A seller may charge one price for cash sales and a higher price for credit or installment sales. The difference between these two prices is called the **time-price differential**. Because the usury law is not applicable, the time-price differential may be greater than the maximum amount of interest that could be charged on a loan equal to the cash price.[27]

A few states, however, hold that the time-price differential is subject to the usury law or have amended their usury laws or have adopted statutes to regulate the differential between cash and time prices charged by the seller. Such statutes are sometimes limited to sales by retailers to consumers or apply only to sales under a stated dollar maximum.

Many states have adopted retail and installment-sale laws that apply whenever the sale price is to be paid in installments and the seller retains a security interest in the goods. These laws frequently fix a maximum for the time-price differential, thereby remedying the situation created by the fact that the differential is not subject to the usury laws.

Service charges in revolving charge accounts generally are not subject to usury law.

(b) Revolving Charge Accounts. When a merchant sells on credit, puts the bill on a charge account, and then adds a charge to the unpaid balance due by the customer, most courts hold that the amount of such a charge is not controlled by the usury law.

---

25 *First American Bank & Trust v Windjammer Time Sharing Resort, Inc.* (Fla App) 483 So 2d 732 (1986).
26 *Lentino v Cullen Center Bank and Trust Co.* (Tex App) 919 SW2d 743 (1996).
27 *O'Connor v Televideo System, Inc.,* ___ Cal App 3d ___, 267 Cal Rptr 237 (1990).

Usury and Credit Selling

Facts: Sears, Roebuck and Co. issued credit cards by which the holder of a card could buy on credit and would be billed monthly for purchases. If payment of the balance shown on a monthly statement was made within 30 days, no service charge was added. If not so paid, a service charge of 1.5 percent a month on the balance but not less than fifty cents was added. On an annual basis, this amounted to 18 percent. Karl Overbeck made purchases on a Sears credit card and paid the monthly service charges. Thereafter he brought suit claiming that the 18 percent rate was usurious, since the maximum legal rate was 6 percent. He sought to recover the "excess" interest on behalf of himself and all other credit card holders.

Decision: Judgment for Sears. The credit card system did not make loans to the customers of Sears, and therefore the usury law did not apply. The practical effect of the credit card charges was that a person buying on such credit cards paid a higher price than a person purchasing for cash. Since a time-price differential does not violate the usury law, a credit card charge that amounts to a time-price differential likewise does not violate the usury law. [*Overbeck v Sears, Roebuck and Co.* 169 Ind App 501, 349 NE2d 286 (1976)]

ETHICS & THE LAW

William Stern and his wife were unable to have children because the wife suffered from multiple sclerosis, and pregnancy posed a substantial health risk. Stern's family had been killed in the Holocaust, and he had a strong desire to continue his bloodline.

The Sterns entered into a surrogacy contract with Mary Beth Whitehead through the Infertility Center of New York (ICNY). William Stern and the Whiteheads (husband and wife) signed a contract for Mary Beth to be artificially inseminated and carry Stern's child to term for which Stern was to pay Mary Beth $10,000 and ICNY $7,500.

Mary Beth was artificially inseminated successfully in 1985, and Baby M was born on March 27, 1986. To avoid publicity, the parents of Baby M were listed as "Mr. and Mrs. Whitehead," and the baby was called Sara Elizabeth Whitehead. On March 30, 1986, Mary Beth turned Baby M over to the Sterns at their home. They renamed the little girl Melissa.

Mary Beth became emotionally distraught and was unable to eat or sleep. The Sterns were so frightened by her behavior that they allowed her to take Baby M for one week to help her adjust. The Whiteheads took the baby and traveled throughout the East, staying in 20 different hotels and motels. Florida authorities found Baby M with Mary Beth's parents and returned her to the Sterns.

Mary Beth said the contract was one to buy a baby and was against public policy and therefore void. She also argued that the contract violated state laws on adoption and the severance of parental rights. The Sterns brought an action to have the contract declared valid and custody awarded to them. Should the contract be valid or void? What types of behavior would be encouraged if the contract were declared valid? Is it ethical to "rent a womb"? Is it ethical to sell a child? See *Re* Baby M, ____ NJ____, 537 A2d 15 (1988)

WHAT'S BEHIND THE LAW?

Legality and Public Policy

Karl Llewellyn, the principal drafter of the law that governs nearly all sales of goods in the United States—the Uniform Commercial Code (UCC)—once wrote, "Covert tools are never reliable tools." He was referring to unfairness in a contract or between the contracting parties.

The original intent of declaring certain types of contracts void because of issues of imbalance was based in equity. Courts stepped in to help parties who found themselves bound under agreements that were not fair and open in both their written terms and the communications between the parties. One contracts scholar wrote that the original intent could be described as courts stepping in to help "presumptive sillies like sailors and heirs and farmers and women" and others who, if not crazy, are "pretty peculiar."

However, as the sophistication of contracts and commercial transactions increased, the importance of accuracy, honesty, and fairness increased. Unconscionability is a contract defense that permits courts to intervene where contracts, if enforced, would "affront the sense of decency." *Unconscionability* is a term of ethics or moral philosophy used by courts to prevent exploitation and fraud.

For more on the UCC and current issues, visit commercial law at http://www.law.emory.edu/FOCAL/comm.html

SUMMARY

When an agreement is illegal, it is ordinarily void, and no contract arises from it. Courts will not allow one party to an illegal agreement to bring suit against the other party. There are some exceptions to this, such as when the parties are not equally guilty or when the law's purpose in making the agreement illegal is to protect the person who is bringing suit. When possible, an agreement will be interpreted as being lawful. Even when a particular provision is held unlawful, the balance of the agreement will generally be saved, so that the net result is a contract minus the clause that was held illegal.

The term illegality embraces situations in which a statute declares that certain conduct is unlawful or a crime; contracts requiring the commission of a tort; contracts that are contrary to public policy; contracts that are unconscionable; and, to some extent, contracts that are oppressive, unfair, or made in bad faith. The question of the legality of an agreement is not considered in the abstract, but the effect of the decision on the rest of society is considered. Increasingly, a given contract is not considered to be in a class by itself but is the same as thousands and even millions of other contracts.

Whether a contract is contrary to public policy may be difficult to determine because public policy is not precisely defined. That which is harmful to the public welfare or general good is contrary to public policy. Contracts condemned as contrary to public policy include those designed to deprive the weaker party of a benefit that the lawmaker desired to provide; agreements injuring public service, such as an agreement to buy a government job for an applicant; agreements involving conflicts of interest, such as when the purchasing officer of a government buys from a company that the officer privately owns; agreements obstructing legal process, such as an agreement with a witness to disappear; illegal discrimination contracts; and wagers and private lotteries. Statutes commonly make the wager illegal, as a form of gambling. The lottery is any plan under which, for a consideration, a person has a chance to win a prize.

Illegality may consist of the violation of a statute or administrative regulation adopted to regulate business. Statutes may make it illegal to do business unless a particular form of contract is used or unless the party promoting the transaction is licensed. The protection of buyers from fraud by sellers may make it unlawful to sell under certain circumstances or without making certain disclosures. Contracts in restraint of trade are generally illegal as violating federal or state antitrust laws. An agreement not to compete is illegal as a restraint of trade except when reasonable in its terms and when it is incidental to the sale of a business or to a contract of employment.

The charging by a lender of a higher rate of interest than allowed by law is usury. Courts must examine transactions carefully to see if there is a usurious loan disguised as a legitimate transaction.

When sellers of goods offer their buyers one price for a cash sale and another, higher price for a credit sale, the higher price is lawful. The credit price is not usurious even though the difference between the cash price and the credit price is greater than the amount that could be charged as interest on a loan equal to the cash price. This concept is called the time-price differential. A minority of states reject or abolish it or limit the increase of the credit price over the cash price to a specified percentage or to the maximum amount that could be charged on a loan equal to the cash price. Most states do not apply the usury law to a revolving charge account. A minority do so, with the result that the charges imposed on the account must not exceed the amount that could be charged as interest on a loan of the amount due on the account.

QUESTIONS AND CASE PROBLEMS

1. What social forces are affected by the rule that a credit sale price is not usurious, although the difference between the credit price and the cash price is greater than the interest that could be charged on a loan in the amount of the cash price?

2. When are the parties to an illegal agreement *in pari delicto?*

3. Alman made a contract to purchase an automobile from Crockett Motors on credit but failed to make payments on time. When Crockett sued to enforce the contract, Alman raised the defense that the price of the car had been increased because she was buying on credit and this increase was unconscionable. Crockett proved that the automobile was exactly what it was represented to be and that no fraud had been committed in selling the car to Alman. Does Crockett's evidence constitute a defense to Alman's claim of unconscionability?

4. The Civic Association of Plaineville raffled an automobile to raise funds to build a hospital. Lyons won the automobile, but the association refused to deliver it to her. She sued the association for the automobile. Can Lyons enforce the contract?

5. Ewing was employed by Presto-X-Co., a pest exterminator. His contract of employment specified that he would not solicit or attempt to solicit customers of Presto-X for two years after the termination of his employment. After working several years, his employment was terminated. Ewing then sent a letter to customers of Presto-X stating that he no longer worked for Presto-X and that he was still certified by the state. Ewing then set forth his home address and phone number, which the customers did not previously have. The letter then ended with the statement "I thank you for your business throughout the past years." Presto-X brought an action to enjoin Ewing from sending such letters. He raised the defense that he was only prohibited from soliciting and there was nothing in the letters that constituted a seeking of customers. Decide. What ethical values are involved? [*Presto-X-Co. v Ewing* (Iowa) 442 NW2d 85]

6. The Minnesota adoption statute requires that any agency placing a child for adoption make a thorough investigation and not give a child to an applicant unless such placement is in the best interests of the child. Tibbetts applied to Crossroads, Inc., a private adoption agency, for a child to adopt. He later sued the agency for breach of contract, claiming that the agency was obligated by contract to supply a child for adoption. The agency claimed that it was required only to use its best efforts to locate a child and was not required to supply a child to Tibbetts unless it found him to be a suitable parent. Decide. [*Tibbetts v Crossroads, Inc.* (Minn App) 411 NW2d 535]

7. Siddle purchased a quantity of fireworks from Red Devil Fireworks Co. The sale was illegal, however, because Siddle did not have a license to make the purchase, which the seller knew because it had been so informed by the attorney general of the state. Siddle did not pay for the fireworks, and Red Devil sued him. He defended on the ground that the contract could not be enforced because it was illegal. Was the defense valid? [*Red Devil Fireworks Co. v Siddle,* ____ Wash App ____, 648 P2d 468]

8. Onderdonk entered a retirement home operated by Presbyterian Homes. The contract between Onderdonk and the home required Onderdonk to make a specified monthly payment that could be increased by the home as the cost of operations increased. The contract and the payment plan were thoroughly explained to Onderdonk. As the cost of operations rose, the monthly payments were continually raised by the home to cover these costs. Onderdonk objected to the increases on the ground that the increases were far more than had been anticipated and that the contract was therefore unconscionable. Was his objection valid?

9. Smith was employed as a salesman for Borden, Inc., which sold food products in 63 counties in Arkansas, 2 counties in Missouri, 2 counties in Oklahoma, and 1 county in Texas. Smith's employment contract prohibited him from competing with Borden after leaving

its employ. Smith left Borden and went to work for a competitor, Lady Baltimore Foods. Working for this second employer, Smith sold in three counties of Arkansas. He had sold in two of these counties while he worked for Borden. Borden brought an injunction action against Smith and Lady Baltimore to enforce the anticompetitive covenant in Smith's former contract. Was Borden entitled to the injunction? [*Borden, Inc. v Smith* (Ark) 478 SW2d 744]

10. Central Water Works Supply, a corporation, had a contract with its shareholders that they would not compete with it. There were only four shareholders, of whom William Fisher was one, but he was not an employee of the corporation. When he sold his shares in the corporation and began to compete with it, the corporation went to court to obtain an injunction to stop such competition. Fisher claimed that the corporation was not entitled to an injunction because he had not obtained any confidential information or made customer contacts. The corporation claimed that such matters were relevant only when an employee had agreed not to compete, but were not applicable when there was a noncompetitive covenant in the sale of a business, and that the sale-of-a-business rule should be applied to a shareholder. Who was correct?

11. Vodra was employed as a salesperson and contracting agent for American Security Services. As part of his contract of employment, Vodra signed an agreement that for three years after leaving this employment, he would not solicit any customer of American. Vodra had no experience in the security field when he went to work for American. To the extent that he became known to American's customers, it was because of being American's representative rather than because of his own reputation in the security field. After some years, Vodra left American and organized a competing company that solicited American's customers. American sued him to enforce the restrictive covenant. Vodra claimed that the restrictive covenant was illegal and not binding. Was he correct? [*American Security Services, Inc. v Vodra*, ____ Neb ____, 385 NW2d 73]

12. Potomac Leasing Co. leased an automatic telephone system to Vitality Centers. Claudene Cato signed the lease as guarantor of payments. When the rental was not paid, Potomac Leasing brought suit against Vitality and Cato. They raised the defense that the rented equipment was to be used for an illegal purpose—namely, the random sales solicitation by means of an automatic telephone in violation of state statute; that this purpose was known to Potomac Leasing; and that Potomac Leasing could therefore not enforce the lease. Was this defense valid? [*Potomac Leasing Co. v Vitality Centers, Inc.* (Ark) 718 SW2d 928]

13. The English publisher of a book called *Cambridge* gave a New York publisher permission to sell that book any place in the world except in England. The New York publisher made several bulk sales of the book to buyers who sold the book throughout the world, including England. The English publisher sued the New York publisher and its customers for breach of the restriction prohibiting sales in England. Decide.

14. A state law required builders of homes to be licensed and declared that an unlicensed contractor could not recover compensation under a contract made for the construction of a residence. Although Annex Construction, Inc., did not have a license, it built a home for French. When he failed to pay what was owed, Annex sued him. He raised the defense that the unlicensed contractor could not recover for the contract price. Annex claimed that the lack of a license was not a bar because the president of the corporation was a licensed builder and the only shareholder of the corporation, and the construction had in fact been properly performed. Was Annex entitled to recover?

15. Carlos was campaigning to be elected the next governor of the state. Helena was a rival candidate. Carlos promised Helena that if she would withdraw as a candidate and support him for governor, he would appoint her the next attorney general for the state. She did so, and her support gave Carlos the necessary additional votes that he needed to be elected. Carlos, however, appointed Rodrigo as the attorney general. Helena sued Carlos for breach of contract. At the trial it was conceded that Helena was highly qualified for the position and no one even suggested that she was not the best possible candidate for attorney general. Was Carlos liable for breach of contract?

CPA QUESTIONS

1. West, an Indiana real estate broker, misrepresented to Zimmer that West was licensed in Kansas under the Kansas statute that regulates real estate brokers and requires all brokers to be licensed. Zimmer signed a contract agreeing to pay West a 5% commission for selling Zimmer's home in Kansas. West did not sign the contract. West sold Zimmer's home. If West sued Zimmer for nonpayment of commission, Zimmer would be

   a. Liable to West only for the value of services rendered.

   b. Liable to West for the full commission.

   c. Not liable to West for any amount because West did **not** sign the contract.

   d. Not liable to West for any amount because West violated the Kansas licensing requirements.

   (5/92, Law, #25)

2. Blue purchased a travel agency business from Drye. The purchase price included payment for Drye's goodwill. The agreement contained a covenant prohibiting Drye from competing with Blue in the travel agency business. Which of the following statements regarding the covenant is **not** correct.

   a. The restraint must be **no** more extensive than is reasonably necessary to protect the goodwill purchased by Blue.

   b. The geographic area to which it applies must be reasonable.

   c. The time period for which it is to be effective must be reasonable.

   d. The value to be assigned to it is the excess of the price paid over the seller's cost of all tangible assets.

   (11/87, Law, #2)

Form of Contract

CHAPTER 16

OBJECTIVES

After studying this chapter, you should be able to

1. *State when a contract must be evidenced by a writing;*
2. *List the requirements of a writing that evidence a contract;*
3. *State the effects of the absence of a sufficient writing when a contract must be evidenced by a writing;*
4. *List the exceptions that have been made by the courts to the laws requiring written evidence of contracts;*
5. *Compare statute of frauds requirements with the parol evidence rule; and*
6. *List exceptions to the parol evidence rule.*

When must a contract be written? What is the effect of a written contract? These questions lead to the statute of frauds and the parol evidence rule.

A.   STATUTE OF FRAUDS

A contract is a legally binding agreement. Must the agreement be evidenced by a writing?

1.   Validity of Oral Contracts

Generally, a contract is valid whether it is written or oral. By statute, however, some contracts must be evidenced by a writing.[1] Statutes requiring a writing do not apply when an oral agreement has been voluntarily performed by both parties. When the parties so intend, an oral contract is binding even though the parties also intend to execute a written contract that would cover details not stated in the oral contract.

The failure to sign and return a written contract does not establish that there is no contract because there may have been an earlier oral contract. Whether such a prior oral contract exists is to be determined from all the circumstances. The test is what intent was manifested by the parties.[2]

Although oral agreements are ordinarily binding and are therefore contracts, an exception will arise when it is the intent of the parties that there is no binding agreement until a written contract is prepared and signed. If, in fact, the parties intend not to be bound until a written contract is executed, their preliminary oral agreement does not constitute a contract. Such a preliminary agreement cannot be enforced when a written contract is not thereafter executed.

> Oral contracts are binding unless a statute requires writing or the parties intended no contract until there was a written contract.

2.   Contracts That Must Be Evidenced by a Writing

Ordinarily, a contract, whether oral or written, is binding if the existence and terms of the contract can be established to the satisfaction of the trier of fact—usually the jury. In some instances a statute, commonly called a statute of frauds,[3] requires that certain kinds of contracts be evidenced by a writing or else they cannot be enforced. This means that either the contract itself must be in writing and signed by both parties or there must be a sufficient written memorandum of the oral contract signed by the person being sued for breach of contract.

---

[1] *Putt v City of Corinth* (Miss) 579 So 2d 534 (1991).
[2] *Consarc Corp. v Marine Midland Bank* (CA2 NY) 996 F2d 568 (1993).
[3] The name is derived from the original English Statute of Frauds and Perjuries, which was adopted in 1677 and became the pattern for similar legislation in America. The seventeenth section of that statute governed the sale of goods, and its modern counterpart is § 2-201 of the UCC. The fourth section of the English statute provided the pattern for American legislation with respect to contracts other than for the sale of goods described in this section of the chapter. The English statute was repealed in 1954, except as to land sale and guarantee contracts. The American statutes remain in force, but the liberalization by UCC § 2-201 of the pre-Code requirements with respect to contracts for the sale of goods may be regarded as a step in the direction of the abandonment of the statute of frauds concept. Additional movement away from the writing requirement is seen in the 1994 Revision of Article 8, Securities, which abolishes the statute of frauds provision of the original UCC § 8-319 and goes beyond by declaring that the one-year performance provision of the statute of frauds is not applicable to contracts for securities. UCC § 8-113 [1994 Revision].

FIGURE 16-1
*Hurdles in the Path of a
Contract*

Writing Required	
Statute of Frauds	**Exceptions**
More than One Year to perform Sale of Land Answer for Another s Debt or Default Personal Representative to Pay Debt of Decedent Promise in Consideration of Marriage Sale of Goods for $500 or More Miscellaneous	Part Performance Promisor Benefit Detrimental Reliance
Parol Evidence Rule	**Exceptions**
Every Complete, Final Written Contract	Incomplete Contract Ambiguous Terms Fraud, Accident, or Mistake To Prove Existence or Nonbinding Character of Contract Modification of Contract Illegality

The statute of frauds requires writing if a contract cannot be performed within one year.

C P A

(a) Agreement That Cannot Be Performed within One Year after the Contract Is Made. A writing is required when the contract, by its terms or subject matter, cannot be performed within one year after the date of the agreement. An oral agreement to supply a line of credit for two years cannot be enforced because of the statute of frauds.[4] Likewise, a joint venture agreement to construct a condominium complex was subject to the one-year provision of the statute of frauds where the contract could not reasonably have been performed within one year. This was due to the complex nature of the project. The plans of the parties projected a development over the course of three years.

CASE SUMMARY

Too Long For Spoken Words

Facts: Jensen claimed that it had been orally agreed that he could have a taco restaurant franchise for five years. When the other party refused to recognize the franchise, he brought suit.

Decision: The five-year contract obviously could not be performed within one year. Therefore, the statute of frauds barred enforcing the oral contract, and the franchisor was not liable. [*Jensen v. Taco John's International, Inc. (CA8 Minn) 110 F3d 525 (1997)*]

---

[4] *ZBS Industries, Inc. v Anthony Cocca Videoland, Inc.*, ____ Ohio App ____, 637 NE2d 956 (1994).

O
P
A

The year runs from the time the oral contract is made rather than from the date when performance is to begin. In computing the year, the day on which the contract was made is excluded. The year begins with the following day and ends at the close of the first anniversary of the day on which the agreement was made.

When no time for performance is specified by the oral contract and complete performance could "conceivably occur" within one year, the statute of frauds is not applicable to the oral contract.[5] The statute of frauds does not apply if it is possible under the terms of the agreement to perform the contract within one year. Thus, a writing is not required when no time for performance is specified and the performance will not necessarily take more than a year. In this case, the statute is inapplicable without regard to the time when performance is actually begun or completed. Likewise, a writing is not required for a contract to employ for life, until retirement, or the employee voluntarily leaves, or the employer goes out of business, as the terminating event could occur within one year.[6] The fact that the parties anticipate a longer life for the contract does not alter this conclusion.

When a contract may be terminated at will by either party, the statute of frauds is not applicable because the contract may be terminated within a year.

O
P
A

(1) Oral Extension of Contract. An oral extension of a written contract must satisfy the statute of frauds if the extension cannot be performed within one year. Thus a two-year oral extension of a written employment contract cannot be enforced because of the statute of frauds.[7]

O
P
A

(b) Agreement to Sell or a Sale of Any Interest in Real Property. All contracts to sell—as well as sales of—land, buildings, or interests in land, such as mortgages, must be evidenced by a writing. The statute applies only to the agreement between the owner and purchaser or between their agents. It does not apply to agreements to pay for an examination or search of the title of the property or to agreements between the buyer and an attorney. The statute ordinarily does not apply to a contract between a real estate agent and one of the parties to the sales contract employing the agent. An agreement giving an option to buy real estate must also satisfy the statute of frauds.

An agreement to cancel or set aside a contract for the sale of land must also satisfy the statute of frauds by being evidenced by a writing.

O
P
A

(c) Promise to Answer for the Debt or Default of Another. If you promise C to pay D's debt to C if D does not do so, you are promising to answer for the debt of another. Such a promise must usually be evidenced by a writing to be enforceable.

If your promise is made directly to the debtor that you will pay the creditor what is owed, the statute of frauds is not applicable.[8] In contrast, if you make the promise to the creditor, it comes within the category of a promise made for the benefit of another. It must therefore be evidenced by a writing that satisfies the statute of frauds.

By definition, the provision of the statute of frauds considered here does not apply when the debt owed is the debt of the promisor and not the debt of a third person.

Writing is required where there is a sale of any interest in real property.

Writing is required where promise to answer for the debt of another exists.

---

5 *El Paso Healthcare System v Piping Rock Corp.* (Tex App) 939 SW2d 695 (1997).
6 *Pickell v Arizona Components Co.* (Colo App) 902 P2d 392 (1994).
7 *Chevron USA Inc. v Schirmer,* (CA9 Ariz) 11 F3d 1473 (1993).
8 *Magrann v Epes* (Fla App) 646 So 2d 760 (1994).

C O P A

Writing is required for promise of a personal representative to pay with own money.

(1) Self-benefit as Main Purpose of Promise. When the main or primary purpose of the promisor's promising to pay the debt of another is to benefit the promisor, the statute of frauds is not applicable and the oral promise to pay the debt is binding. For example, when an owner has hired a contractor to repair a building and the company supplying materials to the contractor is unwilling to sell to the contractor on credit, an oral promise by the owner to pay the contractor's debt is binding. The promise was made for the benefit of the owner, not the contractor, to ensure continuation of the construction work. Some states do not recognize this main purpose exception to the statute of frauds.[9]

CASE SUMMARY

Whose Debt Is It Anyway?

Facts: Dillard's was having difficulty with its computers. It orally promised some of its employees to pay each of them $25 for repairing each of the 1000 computers that required repair. In reliance on such oral promise, the employees made the repairs. Meanwhile the computer manufacturer paid Dillard's a lump sum to compensate for the computer problems and it was agreed that Dillard's would make payment from that sum to the employees who had made the repairs. When Dillard's failed to do so, Kenneth Strom and other employees sued Dillard's. It raised the defense that the promise to pay for the repair work could not be enforced because it was an oral promise to pay the debt of another, the computer manufacturer.

Decision: The statute of frauds was not applicable. The computer manufacturer did not owe any debt to the Dillard's employees. Its obligation ran to the computer buyer: Dillard's. The manufacturer had discharged that obligation by its lump sum payment to Dillard's. The only obligation to pay the Dillard's employees for the repair work was the obligation of Dillard's. The statute of frauds therefore did not require a writing for the promise of Dillard's. [*Dillard's Department Stores, Inc. v Strom (Tex App) 869 SW2d 654 (1994)*]

Writing is required for promise made in consideration of marriage.

(d) Promise by the Executor or Administrator of a Decedent's Estate to Pay a Claim against the Estate from Personal Funds. The personal representative (executor or administrator) has the duty of handling the affairs of a deceased person, paying the debts from the proceeds of the estate, and distributing any balance remaining. The executor or administrator is not personally liable for the claims against the estate of the decedent. If the personal representative promises to pay the decedent's debts with his or her own money, the promise cannot be enforced unless it is evidenced by a writing.

If the personal representative makes a contract on behalf of the estate in the course of administering the estate, a writing is not required. The representative is then contracting on behalf of the estate. Thus, if the personal representative employs an attorney to settle the estate or makes a burial contract with an undertaker, no writing is required.

Writing is required for sale of goods for $500 or more.

(e) Promise Made in Consideration of Marriage. If a person makes a promise to pay a sum of money or to give property to another in consideration of marriage or a promise to marry, the agreement must be evidenced by a writing in order to be enforceable. This provision of the statute of frauds is not applicable to ordinary

---

[9] *Warlock Paving Corp. v Camperlino,* ____ App Div 2d ____, 617 NYS2d 87 (1994).

mutual promises to marry. It is not affected by the statutes in some states that prohibit the bringing of any action for breach of promise of marriage.

(f) Sale of Goods. When the contract price for goods is $500 or more, the contract must ordinarily be evidenced by a writing.

(g) Miscellaneous Statutes of Frauds. In a number of states, special statutes require other agreements to be in writing or evidenced by a writing. Thus, a statute may provide that an agreement to name a person as beneficiary in an insurance policy must be evidenced by a writing.

The Uniform Commercial Code contains three statutes of frauds relating to sales of personal property. These deal with (1) goods; (2) securities, such as stocks and bonds; and (3) personal property other than goods and securities.

In some states, contracts with brokers relating to the sale of land are also subject to the statute of frauds. Some statutes require that a contract for medical care comply with the statute of frauds. In some states, agreements to extend credit must be in writing. The Illinois Credit Agreements Act requires a writing for all agreements relating to the extension of credit.[10]

> *Special statutes of frauds are applicable to certain contracts.*

ETHICS & THE LAW

Stephanie Martin, a recent graduate with a degree in fine arts, interviewed for a position with a fast-growing business involved in international transactions. During her interview with the CEO, she asked about the possibility of studying two nights each week in order to obtain her MBA. The CEO assured her that travel would not be a problem until the degree was completed and he would have the company pay her tuition each semester.

Stephanie was hired and returned to complete the necessary paperwork for her job. When she was signing her employment contract, she noticed a paragraph on mandatory travel. She also noticed no provisions were in the agreement for tuition reimbursement. Stephanie asked the vice president for human resources about her agreement with the CEO. The CEO was out of the country and the vice president could not obtain confirmation. Stephanie went ahead and signed the agreement so that she could begin work.

The CEO returned from his trip with the bad news that the company had lost a major contractor, and immediate budget reductions were initiated. Stephanie had already begun her first semester in a night MBA program and her tuition was due. When the request for tuition reimbursement was made, the CEO responded, "Show me where she has that in her contract. It's not there. No tuition."

Is the CEO correct from a legal perspective? Is Stephanie out of luck on tuition reimbursement? Ethically, is the CEO on solid ground? Would you pay Stephanie's tuition? Why or why not?

---

[10] *Nordstrom v Wauconda National Bank,* ____ Ill App____, ____ Ill Dec ____, 668 NE2d 586 (1996).

3.   E-mail, Facsimile Transmissions, and the Statutes of Frauds

The existing statutes of fraud in the United States were adopted many years before the invention of electronic mail (E-mail) and facsimile transmission (fax). How do the statutes of fraud apply to these forms of communication? Many states are amending their existing statutes of fraud to address these new electronic transmissions. As of today, however, an E-mail will not satisfy the statute of frauds, but a fax transmission can satisfy existing statutes. In some states the requirement that the statute of frauds writing be "subscribed" requires that the signature appear at the end of the fax transmission.

4.   Note or Memorandum

C·P·A

The statute of frauds requires a writing to evidence those contracts that come within its scope. This writing may be a note or memorandum as distinguished from a contract.[11] It may be in any form because its only purpose is to serve as evidence of the contract. The statutory requirement is, of course, satisfied if there is a complete written contract signed by both parties.

(a) Signing. The note or memorandum must be signed by the party sought to be bound by the contract.[12] A letter from an employer setting forth the details of an oral contract of employment satisfies the statute of frauds in a suit brought by the employee against the employer. The writing was signed by the party "sought to be charged." If the employer had sued the employee in such case, the employer's letter would not satisfy the statute of frauds, since it would not be signed by the employee.

Some states require that the authorization of an agent to execute a contract coming within the statute of frauds must also be in writing.[13] In the case of an auction, it is the usual practice for the auctioneer to be the agent of both parties for the purpose of signing the memorandum.

Ordinarily, the signature may be made at any place on the writing. In some states, it is expressly required that the signature appear at the end of the writing. The name of the sender appearing at the top of a fax transmission does not satisfy the statute of frauds. In order to comply, the sender must sign the fax.[14]

The signature may be an ordinary one or any symbol that is adopted by the party as a signature. It may consist of initials, figures, or a mark. When a signature consists of a mark made by a person who is illiterate or physically incapacitated, the name of the person is commonly required to be placed on the writing by someone else, who may be required to sign the instrument as a witness. A person signing a trade or assumed name is liable to the same extent as though the contract had been signed with the signer's name. In the absence of a local statute that provides otherwise, a signature may be made by pencil, pen, typewriter, print, or stamp.

> Writing must be signed by or on behalf of person against whom enforcement is sought.

---

[11] *Busler v D&H Manufacturing, Inc.,* ____ Ohio App ____, 611 NE2d 352 (1992).
[12] *Blackmon v Berry* (Ark App) 939 SW2d 863 (1997).
[13] *Re* W. H. Shipman, Ltd. (Haw App) 934 P2d 1 (1997).
[14] *Parma Tile Mosaic & Marble Co. v Estate of Shot,* ____ NY ____, 663 NE2d 633 (1996).

Except in the case of sale of goods, writing must contain all material terms.

O
P
A

(b) Content.

Except in the case of a sale of goods, the note or memorandum must contain all the material terms of the contract so the court can determine just what was agreed. If any material term is missing, the writing is not sufficient. The missing term cannot be supplied by parol evidence. A writing evidencing a sale of land that does not describe the land or identify the buyer does not satisfy the statute of frauds. Likewise, a writing is insufficient if the contract is partly oral and partly written. The subject matter must be identified either within the writing itself or in other writings to which it refers. A writing is not sufficient if it does not identify the subject of the contract. A deposit check given by the buyer to the seller does not take an oral land sales contract out of the statute of frauds. This is because the check does not set forth the terms of the sale.

CASE SUMMARY

All Material Terms or It Doesn't Count

Facts: Saul Simon had an option to rent part of a building for his men's clothing business. The writing giving the option did not state the duration of the lease that could be obtained by the option. Harold Simon, Saul's brother, granted the option and claimed that it was not binding because of this omission. Saul offered evidence that an oral agreement was reached regarding what duration had been intended.

Decision: The option was not binding. The writing did not satisfy the statute of frauds because it did not state the duration of the lease. This was a material term that had to be stated in the writing. The writing therefore did not satisfy the statute of frauds. This omission from the writing could not be corrected by producing parol evidence as to the missing term. Accordingly the statute of frauds barred enforcement of the option. [*Simon v Simon*, 35 Mass App 705, 625

O
P
A

A written contract is enforceable even though it omits a term that can be implied by law. Although the contract did not state the date of closing and currency of a home's purchase price, the contract is still enforceable. The law would imply that the currency was legal tender, and the closing of the sale would occur upon delivery of the deed to the buyer.[15]

The note or memorandum may consist of one writing or of separate papers, such as letters or telegrams, or of a combination of such papers. The writing that satisfies the statute of frauds may be a letter written by a party's attorney.

Separate writings cannot be considered together unless they are linked. Linkage may be by express reference in each writing to the other or by the fact that each writing clearly deals with the same subject matter.

The time of making writing is immaterial.

(c) Time of Writing.

The memorandum may be made at the time of the original transaction or at a later date. It must, however, ordinarily exist at the time a court action is brought upon the agreement.

---

[15] *160 Chambers Street Realty Corp. v Register of New York*, ____ App Div 2d ____, 641 NYS2d 351 (1996).

Existence of a Writing Is All That Counts

Facts: Harry Rice, as executor of an estate, auctioned off land that had been owned by the late Amelia Peabody. The land was sold to Robert Hunt, and a contract of sale was executed by Rice. The contract was not delivered to Hunt because Rice later received better bids for the property. Hunt brought an action against Rice to enforce the contract. Rice raised the defense that there was no writing that satisfied the statute of frauds because the sales contract had not been delivered to Hunt.

Decision: Judgment for Hunt. The undelivered sales contract was a writing sufficient to satisfy the statute of frauds even though that writing had not been delivered to the plaintiff. Once the existence of the writing was established by evidence, the statute of frauds was satisfied. [*Hunt v Rice, 25 Mass App 622, 521 NE2d 751 (1988)*]

5. Effect of Noncompliance

An oral contract cannot be enforced if necessary writing is missing.

The majority of states hold that a contract that does not comply with the statute of frauds is voidable.[16] A small minority of states hold that such an agreement is void. Under either view, if an action is brought to enforce the contract, the defendant can raise the objection that it is not evidenced by a writing. However, when it is held that the oral contract is not void but merely voidable, it can be enforced if the defendant does not raise the statute of frauds defense. That is, the court will not refuse to enforce the contract when it notices that it is oral unless the opposing party objects to it. No one other than the defendant can make the objection.

When an oral contract cannot be enforced, any value conferred may be recovered.

(a) Recovery of Value Conferred. In most instances, a person who is prevented from enforcing a contract because of the statute of frauds is nevertheless entitled to recover from the other party the value of any services or property furnished or money given under the oral contract. Recovery is not based on the terms of the contract but on a quasi-contractual obligation. The other party is to restore to the plaintiff what was received in order to prevent unjust enrichment at the plaintiff's expense. For example, when an oral contract for services cannot be enforced because of the statute of frauds, the person performing the work may recover the reasonable value of the services rendered.

Limited Effect of Oral Contract under Statute of Frauds

Facts: Richard Golden orally agreed to sell his land to Earl Golden, who paid a deposit of $3,000. The transaction was never completed, and Earl sued for the return of his deposit. Richard claimed that the statute of frauds prevented Earl from proving that there ever was an oral contract under which a deposit of money had been paid.

Decision: Judgment for Earl. The statute of frauds bars enforcement of an oral contract for the sale of land. It does not prevent proof of the contract for the purpose of showing that the seller has received a benefit that would unjustly enrich him if retained by him. Earl could therefore prove the existence of the unperformed oral contract to show that Richard had received a deposit that should be returned. [*Golden v Golden, 273 Or 506, 541 P2d 1397 (1975)*]

---

[16] The UCC creates several statutes of frauds of limited applicability in which it uses the phrase "not enforceable": § 1-206 (sale of intangible personal property); § 2-201 (sale of goods); and § 8-319 (sale of securities). The Official Code Comment, point 4, to § 2-201 describes "not enforceable" as meaning what would ordinarily be called "voidable." Note that the 1994 Revision of Article 8 abolishes the statute of frauds with respect to securities. UCC § 8-113 [1994 Revision].

The statue of frauds does not bar proof that an oral contract was fraudulently induced.

(b) Proof of Fraud. The statute of frauds does not bar proof that the promisor had no intention to pay the debt of the third person but had made such promise fraudulently to induce the promisee to supply goods or that the defendant bank had fraudulently substituted documents that were signed by the plaintiff borrower.[17]

(c) Who May Raise the Defense of Noncompliance. Only a party to the oral contract can raise a defense that it is not binding because there is no writing that satisfies the statute of frauds. Third persons, such as an insurance company or the Internal Revenue Service, cannot claim that a contract is void because the statute of frauds was not satisfied.[18]

6. Judicial Relief from Statute of Frauds

To prevent hardship, the courts have created certain exceptions to the statute of frauds.

The statute of frauds may be evaded by oral contract that is partly performed.

(a) Part Performance of Contract. In spite of the statute of frauds, an oral contract for the sale of an interest in land will be enforced if the buyer has taken possession of the land and has made substantial valuable improvements to the land, and the value of such improvements cannot be easily measured in dollars.

The performance of services will not make the oral contract enforceable when the value of services is too speculative to calculate.[19]

In some states, the concept of part performance has been expanded to bar the defense of the statute of frauds when the plaintiff has fully performed the obligations under the oral contract. To illustrate, the president of a corporation orally promised the insurer to pay the premiums on insurance to be furnished by the corporation. The insurer, after having furnished the corporation with the specified insurance in reliance on the promise of the president, could enforce that promise. Enforcement could be obtained even though there was no writing to satisfy the statute of frauds.

A buyer who has made part performance of an oral land sale contract cannot sue the seller for damages for breach of the oral contract by proving part performance.[20] The part performance doctrine is only applied when the buyer seeks to get the land.

In order to constitute part performance that takes an oral contract out of the statute of frauds, inconsistent performance of duties not specified in the contract constitutes part performance, and the statute of frauds no longer applies.[21]

CASE SUMMARY

It Don't Mean A Thing

Facts: Jim Wilson claimed that Beatrice Dolphin had orally agreed to sell her land to him. He claimed that he had made improvements to the land that took the oral contract out of the statute of frauds. He claimed that he had improved the property by mowing the land and keeping down the weeds. He also had bulldozed the land to remove the remains of a fire-destroyed building.

---

[17] *Hanson v American National Bank & Trust Co.* (Ky) 865 SW2d 302 (1993).
[18] *O'Daniels' Estate v United States* (CA5 Tex) 6 F3d 321 (1993).
[19] *Davis v Davis* (Wyo) 855 P2d 342 (1993).
[20] *Haughland v Parsons* (Mo App) 863 SW2d 609 (1992).
[21] *Wachter Development v Gomke* (ND) 544 NW2d 127 (1996).

> **Decision:** There was nothing in what was done that constituted an "improvement" as distinct from merely ordinary maintenance of the land. Moreover, nothing was clearly referable to the existance of an oral contract. There was no part performance that satisfied the statute of frauds. [*Dolphin v. Wilson, 328 Ark 1, 942 SW2d 815 (1997)*]

(b) Promisor Benefited by Promise to Pay Debt of Another. If a person orally promises a creditor to pay the debt owed to that creditor by a debtor, the promise is ordinarily not binding because of the statute of frauds. If the promise is made primarily to benefit the promisor, however, the courts refuse to apply the statute of frauds.[22] In this case, the promise to pay the debt of the third person is binding even though it is oral and benefits the debtor by discharging the debt that was due. For example, when the purpose of a majority stockholder's promise to pay the debt of the corporation is to benefit that stockholder, the statute of frauds is not applicable to that promise.

The statue of frauds may be evaded by oral promise to pay debt of another if promisor primarily benefits.

CASE SUMMARY

No Escape for the Selfish Promisor

Facts: Boyd-Scarp Enterprises (BSE) was building a house for James Rathmann. Al Booth's, Inc., sold appliances to BSE for installation in the house. Al Booth's was concerned about getting paid and asked Rathmann to guarantee that BSE would pay the bill. Rathmann orally promised to pay the bill if BSE did not. The appliances were then delivered to BSE. The bill was not paid and Al Booth's sued both BSE and Rathmann. Rathmann raised the defense that his oral promise to pay the debt of BSE could not be enforced because of the statute of frauds.

Decision: Judgment for Al Booth's. The primary purpose of Rathmann in promising to pay the debt was to benefit himself rather than to benefit or assist BSE. Accordingly, the statute of frauds did not apply and the oral promise of Rathmann could be enforced even though its enforcement would have the effect of paying the debt of BSE. [*Al Booth's, Inc. v Boyd-Scarp Enterprises, Inc. (Fla App) 518 So 2d 422 (1988)*]

(c) Detrimental Reliance on Oral Contract. The extent to which judicial relief from the statute of frauds will be granted in cases other than land sales and debt guarantees is not clear. The same forces that gave rise to the doctrine of promissory estoppel in connection with the law of consideration are to some extent causing courts to recognize detrimental reliance as excusing noncompliance with the statute of frauds. However, the mere fact that an employee changed employers in reliance on an oral promise of employment until retirement does not make the oral promise binding on the second employer.

The statute of frauds may be evaded by oral contract when there was detrimental reliance.

---

[22] *Smith, Seckman, Reid, Inc. v Metro National Corp.* (Tex App) 836 SW2d 817 (1992).

Will Harm to the Promisee Trump the Statute of Frauds?

Facts: John Lucas sued the Whittaker Corporation for breaking its oral contract to employ him for two years. Whittaker raised the statute of frauds as a defense. Lucas showed that he had given up his job in Missouri and moved to Colorado to take the job with Whittaker. In so doing, he gave up his former job after nine years of employment, thereby losing its fringe benefits, including college tuition for eligible dependents; sold his custom-built house in which he and his family had lived for only eight months; and gave up all business and social contacts.

Decision: Judgment for Lucas. Equitable principles bar applying the statute of frauds when an "unconscionable injury" will be inflicted if the oral contract is not enforced. Lucas had suffered greater detriment than was involved in the ordinary change of job situation. Whittaker was therefore barred from raising the defense of the statute of frauds. [*Lucas v Whittaker Corp.* (CA10 Colo) 470 F2d 326 (1972)]

There is a conflict of authority as to whether detrimental reliance excuses non-compliance with the statute of frauds. Some courts refuse to apply the doctrine of detrimental reliance to avoid the defense of the statute of frauds because that would defeat the purpose of the statute.[23]

The mere fact that the promisee relies on an oral promise is generally not sufficient to entitle the promisee to enforce the oral promise. The promisee must show that (1) because of the reliance on the promise, substantial or unconscionable injury would be sustained by the promisee, or (2) the promisor would be unjustly enriched if the oral promise were not enforced.

(d) Promise to Execute Writing. Some courts enforce an oral contract in spite of the statute of frauds when the defendant promised to execute a writing that would satisfy the statute but failed to do so.[24]

B. PAROL EVIDENCE RULE

When the contract is evidenced by a writing, may the contract terms be changed by the testimony of witnesses?

The parol evidence rule bars contradiction of a written contract by oral agreement made before or when the contract was written.

C P A

7. Exclusion of Parol Evidence Rule

The general rule is that spoken words, that is, **parol evidence,** will not be allowed to modify or contradict the terms of a written contract that is complete on its face. This rule is not followed if there is clear proof that because of fraud, accident, or a mistake, the writing is not in fact the contract or the complete or true contract. This is called the **parol evidence rule.** It excludes words spoken before or at the time the contract was made.

---

[23] *Meinhold v Huang* (Mo App) 687 SW2d 596 (1985). Courts commonly refer to this doctrine as "promissory estoppel." The term detrimental reliance is used in the text because the promissory estoppel applied in connection with the question of consideration requires greater detriment than is required by those courts recognizing reliance as avoiding the statute of frauds.

[24] *Magcobar North American v Grasso Oilfield Services, Inc.* (Tex App) 736 SW2d 787 (1987).

The parol evidence rule prevents a party from avoiding liability on a written contract by providing evidence that the writing does not mean what it says. For example, when a lender sues to recover the loan set forth in a written contract, the defendant cannot claim that before the contract was signed, the creditor had agreed to extend the time for repayment of the loan. The parol evidence rule also excludes proof of a prior oral agreement that is inconsistent with the later written agreement.[25]

CASE SUMMARY

Closing the Door on Different Terms

Facts: Airline Construction, Inc., made a contract to build a hotel for William Barr within 240 calendar days. He completed the work 57 days late. The other party sued for damages for delay, and the contractor raised the defense that he had been induced to enter into the contract because it had been agreed that he would have additional time in which to complete the work. The plaintiff objected to the admission of evidence of this agreement.

Decision: Parol evidence could not be admitted to show that there was a prior oral agreement that was inconsistent with the terms of the written contract. It was immaterial that the contractor had been "induced" to make the contract because of the alleged agreement. The fact remained that the written contract signed by him specified the time for performance and the parol evidence rule barred proof of any prior inconsistent oral agreement. [*Airline Construction, Inc. v Barr* (Tenn App) 807 SW2d 247 (1990)]

The parol evidence rule furthers stability by excluding agreements that were never made or that were abandoned.

(a) Reason for the Parol Evidence Rule. The parol evidence rule is based on the theory that either there never was an oral agreement, or, if there was, the parties purposely abandoned it when they executed their written contract. The social objective of the parol evidence rule is to give stability to contracts and to prevent the fraudulent assertion of oral terms that never actually existed. Some courts apply the parol evidence rule strictly.

For example, to illustrate the parol evidence rule, assume that *L*, the landlord who is the owner of several new stores in the same vicinity, discusses leasing one of them to *T* (tenant). *L* agrees to give to *T* the exclusive right to sell soft drinks. *L* agrees to stipulate in the leases with the tenants of other stores that they cannot do so. *L* and *T* then execute a detailed written lease for the store. The lease with *T* makes no provision with respect to an exclusive right of *T* to sell soft drinks. Thereafter, *L* leases the other stores to three other tenants without restricting their selling drinks. They begin to sell soft drinks, causing *T* to lose money. *T* sues *L*, claiming that the latter has broken the contract by which *T* was to have the exclusive right to sell soft drinks. *L* defends on the ground that there was no prior oral agreement to that effect. Will the court permit *T* to prove that there was such an oral agreement?

On the facts as stated, if nothing more is shown, the court will not permit such parol evidence to be presented. The operation of this principle can be understood more easily if the actual courtroom procedure is followed. When *T* sues *L*, the first step will be to prove that there is a lease between them. Accordingly, *T* will offer in evidence the written lease between *T* and *L*. *T* will then take the witness stand

---

[25] *Valley Bank v Christensen* (Idaho) 808 P2d 415 (1991).

and begin to testify about an oral agreement giving an exclusive right. At this point, *L*'s attorney will object to the admission of the oral testimony by *T* because it would modify the terms of the written lease. The court will then examine the lease to see if it appears to be complete. If the court decides that it is, the court will refuse to allow *T* to offer evidence of an oral agreement. The only evidence before the court then will be the written lease. *T* will lose because nothing is in the written lease about an exclusive right to sell soft drinks.

While a statement in the contract that it is the entire contract of the parties is important in reaching the conclusion that the writing is the final and complete contract, the fact that such a clause is missing does not bar the court from deciding that the contract as written is complete and final.[26]

If a written contract appears to be complete, the parol evidence rule prohibits its alteration not only by oral testimony but also by proof of other writings or memorandums made before or at the time the written contract was executed. An exception is made when the written contract refers to and identifies other writings or memorandums and states that they are to be regarded as part of the written contract. In such a case, it is said that the other writings are integrated or incorporated by reference.

A written contract prevails over a prior oral contract.

(b) Conflict between Oral and Written Contracts. Initially, when there is a conflict between the prior oral contract and the later written contract, the variation is to be regarded as (1) a mistake, which can be corrected by reformation, or (2) an additional term that is not binding because it was not part of the written agreement.

8. Liberalization of Parol Evidence

There is a trend to liberalize the parol evidence rule.

The strictness of the parol evidence rule has been relaxed in a number of jurisdictions. A trend is beginning to appear that permits the use of parol evidence as to the intention of the parties when the claimed intention is plausible from the face of the contract even though there is no ambiguity.

There is likewise authority that parol evidence is admissible as to matters occurring before the execution of the contract to give a better understanding of what the parties meant by their written contract.[27]

CASE SUMMARY

The Dictionary of the Parties

Facts: Olsen Media was an advertising agency. Energy Sciences, Inc., made a contract with Olsen Media to develop a brochure for a pistol it distributed. The contract stated a monthly compensation to be paid to Olsen and stated further that after six months this amount was "negotiable." The written contract also stated that it contained the entire contract of the parties. In a suit on the contract, evidence was offered to show that "negotiable" meant only "negotiable upwards" and that the compensation could not be lower than the amount stated in the contract.

---

[26] *Moore v Pennsylvania Castle Energy Corp.* (CA11 Ala) 89 F3d 791 (1996).
[27] *Plateau Mining Co. v Utah Division of State Lands and Forestry* (Utah) 802 P2d 720 (1990).

[handwritten margin note: OK to do this because you are explain the what was Gov meant meaning]

> **Decision:** Parol evidence is admissible to show what the parties meant by the words they used. The fact that the written contract stated that it contained all the terms of the contract did not prevent the admission of parol evidence for this purpose. Parol evidence was therefore admissible to show what was meant by "negotiable." *[Olsen Media v Energy Sciences, Inc. 32 Wash App 2d 579, 648 P2d 493 (1982)]*

The liberalization approach is not followed by all courts; some apply the **four corners rule.** Under this rule, the court must look for the contract within the four corners of the writing. The court may not look beyond the paper in the absence of an exception to the parol evidence rule.

9.   When the Parol Evidence Rule Does Not Apply

The parol evidence rule may not apply in certain cases. The most common of these are discussed in the following paragraphs.

Parol evidence is admissible when a written contract is incomplete.

(a) Incomplete Contract. The parol evidence rule necessarily requires that the written contract sum up or integrate the entire contract. If the written contract is on its face or admittedly not a complete summation, the parties naturally did not intend to abandon the points on which they agreed but that were not noted in the contract, and parol evidence is admissible to show the actual agreement of the parties.

A contract may appear on its face to be complete and yet not include everything the parties agreed on. It must be remembered there is no official standard by which to determine when a contract is complete. All that a court can do is consider whether all essential terms of the contract are present. That is, the court can determine whether the contract is sufficiently definite to be enforceable and whether it contains all provisions that would ordinarily be included in a contract of that nature.

The fact that a contract is silent about a particular matter does not mean that it is incomplete, for the law may attach a particular legal result (called implying a term) when the contract is silent. In such a case, parol evidence that is inconsistent with the term that would be implied cannot be shown. For example, when the contract is silent as to the time of payment, the obligation of making payment concurrently with performance by the other party is implied, and parol evidence is not admissible to show there was an oral agreement to make a payment at a different time.

Parol evidence is admissible when a written contract is ambiguous.

(b) Ambiguity. If a written contract may have two different meanings, parol evidence may generally be admitted to clarify the meaning.[28]

It has also been held that UCC § 1-205 permits proof of trade usage and course of performance with respect to non-Code contracts even though there is no

---

[28] *Berg v Hudesman,* ____ Wash ____ , 801 P2d 222 (1990). This is also the view followed by UCC § 2-202(a), which permits terms in a contract for the sale of goods to be "explained or supplemented by a course of dealing or usage of trade . . . or by course of performance." Such evidence is admissible not because there is an ambiguity, but "in order that the true understanding of the parties as to the agreement may be reached." Official Code Comment to § 2-202.

ambiguity. This is particularly true when the contract contains contradictory measurements or descriptions, or when the contract uses symbols or abbreviations that have no general meaning known to the court.

Parol evidence may also be admitted to show that a word used in a contract has a special trade meaning or a meaning in the particular locality that differs from the common meaning of that word.

The fact that the parties disagree about the meaning of the contract does not mean that it is ambiguous.[29]

Parol evidence is admissible to prove fraud, accident, or mistake.

(c) Fraud, Accident, or Mistake. A contract apparently complete on its face may have omitted a provision that should have been included. Parol evidence may be admitted to show that a provision was omitted as the result of fraud, accident, or mistake, and to further show what that provision stated.

Parol evidence is admissible to show that a provision of the written contract was a mistake even though the written provision is unambiguous.[30]

When one party claims to have been fraudulently induced by the other to enter into a contract, the parol evidence rule does not bar proof that there was fraud. For example, the parol evidence rule does not bar proof that the seller of land negligently misrepresented that the land was zoned to permit use as an industrial park. Such evidence does not contradict the terms of the contract but shows that there never was a binding agreement.[31]

Parol evidence is admissible to show whether a contract was ever made.

(d) Existence of Contract. Parol evidence is admissible to identify the writing of the parties. When several documents are executed as part of one transaction, parol evidence is admissible to show the relationship of the documents as forming one transaction.

Parol evidence is admissible to show whether a particular writing was in fact the final and complete agreement of the parties.[32]

When it is claimed that there is in fact no contract because of a mutual mistake, parol evidence is admissible to show the existence of such a mistake.

The parol evidence rule does not bar proof that the written contract is in fact not a binding agreement. Thus, it can be shown that there was no consideration for the contract, that the contract was void because it was illegal, or that the contract was voidable because of the incapacity of a party or because of fraud. Likewise, parol evidence may be used to show in a lawsuit between the original parties that a promissory note signed by the defendant was never to be enforced and that it was merely a note intended to create a paper loss for tax purposes.

Parol evidence is admissible to show whether a written contract was modified.

(e) Modification of Contract. The parol evidence rule prohibits only the contradiction of a complete written contract. It does not prohibit proof that the contract was thereafter modified or terminated.

Written contracts commonly declare that they can be modified only by a writing. In the case of construction contracts, there is ordinarily a statement that no payment will be made for extra work unless there is a written order from the owner or architect calling for such extra work. If the parties proceed in disregard of a clause requiring written modification, parol evidence may show that they have done so, and the contract will be modified accordingly.

---

[29] *Baker's Supermarkets, Inc. v Feldman*, ____ Neb ____, 502 NW2d 428 (1993).
[30] *CMI Food Service, Inc. v Hatridge Leasing* (Mo App) 890 SW2d 420 (1995).
[31] *Edwards v Centex Real Estate Corp.*, ____ Cal App 4th ____, 61 Cal Rptr 518 (1997).
[32] *National City Bank v Donaldson*, ____ Ohio App____, 642 NE2d 58 (1994).

What Comes After

Facts: Muther-Ballenger, a partnership of doctors, purchased an electronic spinal scanner from Griffin Electronic Consultants. They were dissatisfied with its performance. Griffin made certain oral warranties that the scanner would be adjusted or fixed so that it would meet the doctor's needs to persuade the doctors to keep the scanner. The scanner did not perform as warranted and the doctors sued Griffin for breach of the written contract and the oral warranties. Griffin claimed that the parol evidence rule barred the doctors from proving that any oral warranties were made.

Decision: The parol evidence rule does not bar proof of the modifying of a written contract subsequent to the making of the contract. It prohibits only parol evidence of contradictory agreements made before or at the time the written contract was executed. *[Muther-Ballenger v Griffin Electronic Consultants (NC App) 397 SE2d 247 (1990)]*

Parol evidence is admissible to show illegality.

(f) Illegality. The parol evidence rule does not bar proof of conduct that violates the law. It does not bar the defense that the defendant's signature was a forgery.[33]

No Shield for Bad Guys

Facts: Honeywell installed a heating and cooling system in the Imperial Condominium. When it did not work properly, Imperial sued Honeywell for damages under the state deceptive trade practices act. In order to prove a violation of that act, Imperial offered in evidence the advertising statements made by Honeywell. Honeywell claimed that it had made a written contract with Imperial so the parol evidence rule prevented admission of any advertising statements that had been made before the contract was executed.

Decision: The advertising statements were admissible. It was not a question of whether the written contract was being contradicted by parol evidence of statements made before the contract was signed. It was a question of whether the conduct of Honeywell before the signing of the contract violated the law. Parol evidence was properly admitted to determine if there was a violation of the law. The parol evidence rule did not bar proof of the advertising that had been made. *[Honeywell, Inc. v Imperial Condominium Ass'n (Tex App) 716 SW2d 75 (1986)]*

WHAT'S BEHIND THE LAW?

The Statute of Frauds and Public Policy

It was 1677 when England's Parliament enacted the first law governing the types of contracts that were required to be in writing. The name of that first law, an Act for the Prevention of Frauds and Perjuries, provides some insights into the policy reasons for its enactment. The history of English law shows that when oral promises were enforceable, perjury became quite commonplace. The 1677 statute addressed the 25 areas in which perjury was most prevalent. Those 25 areas remain today, with all states covering land conveyances, estates, and debt sureties in statutes that require written agreements.

There are other public policy reasons today for statutes of frauds. A lawyer once wrote, "False testimony stems from faulty recollection as well as from faulty morals." The requirement that a contract be written requires the parties to think through and formalize their commitments. A writing is some proof that the parties reached an agreement and there was intent to enter into a binding relationship.

---

[33] *Pathway Financial v Miami International Realty Co.* (Fla App) 588 So 2d 1000 (1991).

Statutes of frauds were a response to the need for stability in commercial transactions. The requirement that certain contracts be in writing to be enforceable has helped promote commerce while protecting the individual parties involved in those contracts.

To find more information on specific states and their statutes of frauds, visit hyperlinks to state legislation: http://lawlib.wuacc.edu/washlaw/uslaw/statelaw.html

SUMMARY

An oral agreement can be a contract unless it is the intention of the parties that they should not be bound by the agreement unless a writing is executed by them. If the parties intend to be bound by the oral agreement, it is a contract. As an exception to this statement, certain contracts must be evidenced by a writing, or else they cannot be enforced. The statutes that declare this exception are called statutes of frauds. Statutes of frauds commonly require that a contract be evidenced by writing in the case of (1) an agreement that cannot be performed within one year after the contract is made, (2) an agreement to sell or a sale of any interest in real property, (3) a promise to answer for the debt or default of another, (4) a promise by the executor or administrator of a decedent's estate to pay a claim against the estate from personal funds, (5) a promise made in consideration of marriage, and (6) a contract for the sale of goods for a purchase price of $500 or more. Local statutes may expand the above list to include other types of contracts, such as a contract between a landowner and a real estate agent employed to sell the land.

In order to evidence a contract to satisfy a statute of frauds, there must be a writing of all material terms. This must be signed by the defendant against whom suit is brought for enforcement of the contract or damages for its breach. The signing may be made by printing, stamping, typewriting, or any other means that is intended to identify the particular party. Two or more writings can be combined to form a writing sufficient to satisfy the statute of frauds, provided there is an express internal reference in the writings that ties them together.

If the applicable statute of frauds is not satisfied, the oral contract cannot be enforced. To avoid unjust enrichment, a plaintiff barred from enforcing an oral contract may recover from the other contracting party the reasonable value of the benefits conferred by the plaintiff on the defendant. To prevent the statute of frauds from being used to defraud a party to an oral contract, the courts by decision have made certain exceptions to the statute of frauds.

When there is a written contract, the question arises whether that writing is the exclusive statement of the parties' agreement. If the writing is the complete and final statement of the contract, parol evidence as to matters agreed to before or at the time the writing was signed is not admissible to contradict the writing. This is called the parol evidence rule. Some courts have liberalized the rule so that parol evidence is admitted when it will aid in interpreting the writing. In any case, the parol evidence rule does not bar parol evidence when (1) the writing is incomplete; (2) the writing is ambiguous; (3) the writing is not a true statement of the agreement of the parties because of fraud, accident, or mistake; or (4) the existence, modification, or illegality of a contract is in controversy. The fact that the parties disagree about the meaning of a contract or that a court decision is required to settle the point does not make the writing ambiguous. Parol evidence may be used to prove that there is in fact no contract because there is a mutual mistake or the writing that has been executed does not correctly set forth the terms of the contract.

QUESTIONS AND CASE PROBLEMS

1. What social forces are affected by the following rule of law? "Parol evidence is not admissible for the purpose of modifying a written contract when that evidence relates to an agreement made before or at the time that the written contract was executed."
2. In a telephone conversation, Roderick agreed to buy Dexter's house. All the details of the transaction were agreed to in the conversation. The next day Dexter wrote Roderick a letter stating: "This confirms the agreement we made last night that I should sell you my home." Later, Dexter refused to go through with the transaction. Roderick sued Dexter. Will Roderick recover?
3. Kelly made a written contract to sell certain land to

Brown and gave Brown a deed to the land. Thereafter, Kelly sued Brown to get back a 20-foot strip of the land. Kelly claimed that before making the written contract it was agreed that Kelly would sell all of his land to Brown to make it easier for Brown to get a building permit, but that after that was done, the 20-foot strip would be reconveyed to Kelly. Was Kelly entitled to the 20-foot strip? What ethical values are involved? [*Brown v Kelly* (Fla App) 545 So 2d 518]

4. Martin made an oral contract with Cresheim Garage to work as its manager for two years. Cresheim wrote Martin a letter stating that the oral contract had been made and setting forth all its terms. Cresheim later refused to recognize the contract. Martin sued Cresheim for breach of the contract and offered Cresheim's letter in evidence as proof of the contract. Cresheim claimed that the oral contract was not binding because the contract was not in writing and the letter referring to the contract was not a contract but only a letter. Was the contract binding?

5. Lawrence loaned money to Moore, who died without repaying the loan. Lawrence claimed that when he mentioned the matter to Moore's widow, she promised to pay the debt. She did not do so, and Lawrence sued her on her promise. Does she have any defense? [*Moore v Lawrence*, ____ Ark ____, 480 SW2d 941]

6. Jackson signed an agreement to sell 79 acres of land to Devenyns. Jackson owned 80 acres and was apparently intending to keep for himself the acre on which his home was located. The written agreement also stated, "Devenyns shall have the option to buy on property _____," but nothing was stated in the blank space. Devenyns sued to enforce the agreement. Was it binding? [*Re* Jackson's Estate (Wyo) 892 P2d 786]

7. Boeing Airplane Co. contracted with Pittsburgh-Des Moines Steel Co. for the latter to construct a supersonic wind tunnel. R.H. Freitag Mfg. Co. sold materials to York-Gillespie Co., which subcontracted to do part of the work. To persuade Freitag to keep supplying materials on credit, Boeing and the principal contractor both assured Freitag that he would be paid. When Freitag was not paid by the subcontractor, he sued Boeing and the contractor. They defended on the ground that the assurances given Freitag were not written. Decide. What ethical values are involved? [*R.H. Freitag Mfg. Co. v Boeing Airplane Co.* (Wash) 347 P2d 1074]

8. An accounting firm sold out its business to a new firm. The sales contract stated that it was the intention of the parties that the new firm should provide service for clients of the old firm. The new firm agreed to pay the old firm 15 percent of the gross billings for assignments performed by the new firm for a period of 84 months. Later a dispute arose as to whether the 15 percent of gross billings was limited to the billings of those who were originally clients of the old firm or whether it also included billings of new clients of the new firm. In a lawsuit over this point, parol evidence was offered to show what the contract covered. Was this evidence admissible? [*Rullman v LaFrance, Walker, Jackley & Saville*, ____ Neb ____, 292 NW2d 19]

9. With respect to the applicability of the statute of frauds, compare (a) a promise made by an aunt to her niece to pay the niece's bill owed to a department store; (b) a promise made by the aunt to the department store to pay the amount the aunt owes the store for a television set the aunt purchased as a present for her niece; and (c) a promise made by the aunt to the department store that she would pay her niece's bill if the niece did not do so.

10. Louise Pulsifer owned a farm. She desired to sell the farm and ran an ad in the local newspaper. After Russell Gillespie agreed to purchase the farm, Pulsifer wrote him a letter stating that she would not sell it. He sued her to enforce the contract, and she raised the defense of the statute of frauds. The letter signed by her did not contain any of the terms of the sale. Gillespie, however, claimed that the newspaper ad could be combined with her letter to satisfy the statute of frauds. Was he correct? [*Gillespie v Pulsifer* (Mo) 655 SW2d 123]

11. McLarty claimed that he and Wright made an oral contract to start a business under the name of DeKalb Textile Mill, Inc.; to incorporate the business; and to divide the stock equally. The alleged contract was not performed, and McLarty sued Wright for breach of contract. Wright raised the defense of the statute of frauds, asserting that it was not specified that the contract should be performed within one year of making. Was this defense valid? [*McLarty v Wright* (Ala Civ App) 321 So 2d 687]

12. In February or March, Corning Glass Works orally agreed to retain Hanan as management consultant from May 1 of that year to April 30 of the next year for a total fee of $25,000. Was this agreement binding? Is this decision ethical? [*Hanan v Corning Glass Works* 314 NYS2d 804]

13. Levina made a contract with Thompson. She later claimed that she could enforce the terms of an earlier agreement that they had made a week before. Thompson claimed that proof of that agreement was barred by the parol evidence rule. Levina claimed this was not so because (1) she never intended that the written contract should wipe out the earlier oral

agreement, and (2) the written contract did not state it was the entire agreement of the parties and displaced all prior agreements. Were her objections valid?

14. When Holdings and Thriftway borrowed money from the Northland Bank, Filipek and others guaranteed that the loans would be paid back. Touche Ross was appointed to liquidate the assets of the bank. The loans to Holdings and Thriftway were not repaid when due. Touche Ross sued Filipek and the other guarantors on their obligation to repay the loans. They raised the defense that they were not bound by their guarantees because they and the borrower had been induced to enter into the transactions by the bank's fraudulent statements and promises. Touche Ross claimed that the parol evidence rule barred any evidence that the parties had been induced by fraud.

Could the guarantors produce parol evidence to support their claim of fraud? [*Touche Ross Ltd. v Filipek* (Haw App) 778 P2d 721]

15. While Celeste was in New York, the manager of Kendall Corp. of Galveston, Texas, interviewed her for the position of head of the corporate accounting department. The manager told her to send her application to Galveston and that he believed she would be given a five-year contract for the job. Within a few days after the manager left New York, Celeste sold her New York home, quit her New York job, and went to Texas. When she arrived she was told that the vacancy had been filled by someone else. She sued Kendall for breach of contract, and it contended there was no writing to evidence existence of the contract. Celeste raised the counterdefense of promissory estoppel. Decide.

CPA QUESTIONS

1. Which of the following statements is true with regard to the Statute of Frauds?
   a. All contracts involving consideration of more than $500 must be in writing.
   b. The written contract must be signed by all parties.
   c. The Statute of Frauds applies to contracts that can be fully performed within one year from the date they are made.
   d. The contract terms may be stated in more than one document.

   (11/92, Law, #16)

2. With regard to an agreement for the sale of real estate, the Statute of Frauds
   a. Requires that the entire agreement be in a single writing.
   b. Requires that the purchase price be fair and adequate in relation to the value of the real estate.
   c. Does **not** require that the agreement be signed by all parties.
   d. Does **not** apply if the value of the real estate is less than $500.

   (11/87, Law, #3)

3. In negotiations with Andrews for the lease of Kemp's warehouse, Kemp orally agreed to pay one-half of the cost of the utilities. The written lease, later prepared by Kemp's attorney, provided that Andrews pay all of the utilities. Andrews failed to carefully read the lease and signed it. When Kemp demanded that Andrews pay all of the utilities, Andrews refused, claiming that the lease did not accurately reflect the oral agreement. Andrews also learned that Kemp intentionally misrepresented the condition of the structure of the warehouse during the negotiations between the parties. Andrews sued to rescind the lease and intends to introduce evidence of the parties' oral agreement about sharing the utilities and the fraudulent statements made by Kemp. The parol evidence rule will prevent the admission of evidence concerning the

	Oral agreement regarding who pays the utilities	Fraudulent statements by Kemp
a.	Yes	Yes
b.	No	Yes
c.	Yes	No
d.	No	No

Interpretation of Contracts

CHAPTER 17

A. RULES OF CONSTRUCTION AND INTERPRETATION

1. Function of Judge and Jury
2. Intention of the Parties
3. Additional Printed Matter
4. Whole Contract
5. Conditions
6. Contradictory and Ambiguous Terms
7. Implied Terms
8. Conduct and Custom
9. Avoidance of Hardship
10. Joint, Several, and Joint and Several Contracts

B. CONFLICT OF LAWS

11. State Courts
12. Federal Courts

OBJECTIVES

After studying this chapter, you should be able to

1. *Compare the effects of objective and subjective intent of the parties to a contract;*
2. *Distinguish between conditions precedent and conditions subsequent;*
3. *State the rules for interpreting ambiguous terms in a contract;*
4. *State the effect of contradictory terms;*
5. *Define and illustrate implied terms; and*
6. *State what controls the choice of law applicable to an interstate contract.*

When it has been decided that there is a contract between the parties, the next step is to determine what the contract means.

A.   RULES OF CONSTRUCTION AND INTERPRETATION

In interpreting contracts, courts are aided by certain rules.

1.   Function of Judge and Jury

Interpretation is a function of the judge and jury.

When no dispute arises over what a contract stated, the determination of its meaning is a question for the judge. If, however, disagreement arises over what terms were stated or if the terms are ambiguous, there is then a question of fact. Just what the contract provided then needs to be determined and ordinarily such disputes will be determined by the jury.

Once the terms of a contract are determined, the contract must be enforced according to those terms unless there is some factor that makes the contract voidable or void. If valid, the court must enforce the contract according to its terms. It cannot rewrite the contract made by the parties.[1]

2.   Intention of the Parties

The object of interpretation is to determine the intention of the parties.

When persons enter into an agreement, it is to be presumed they intend that their agreement should have some effect. A court will strive to determine the intent of the parties and to give effect to it. A contract is therefore to be enforced according to its terms. A court cannot remake or rewrite the contract of the parties under the pretense of interpreting it.[2] If there is a dispute as to the meaning of a contract, the court examines the contract to determine what the parties intended. It will then give effect to this intent, so long as it is lawful.

No particular form of words is required, and any words manifesting the intent of the parties are sufficient. In the absence of proof that a word has a peculiar meaning or that it was employed by the parties with a particular meaning, a common word is given its ordinary meaning.[3]

A word will not be given its literal meaning when it is clear that the parties did not intend such a meaning. For example, *and* may be substituted for *or, may* for *shall*, and *void* for *voidable*, and vice versa, when it is clear that the parties so intended.

A court must take care to avoid interpreting a contract so narrowly that the intent of the parties is defeated. At the same time, it must avoid an interpretation so loose that it releases a party from an obligation that the contract was intended to impose.[4]

Objective intent controls.

(a) Objective Intent. When it is stated that the law seeks to enforce the intent of the parties, this means the intent that is outwardly manifested. That is, what would a reasonable third person believe the parties intended? It is this **objective intent**

---

[1] *Raines v White* (W Va) 465 SE2d 266 (1995).
[2] *Paddison Builders v Turncliff* (La App) 672 So 2d 1133 (1996).
[3] *Ex parte* Agee (Ala) 669 So 2d 102 (1995).
[4] *Anderson v Horizon Homes, Inc.* (Ind App) 664 NE2d 1281 (1995).

that will be enforced. A party cannot effectively claim that something else was secretly intended. Such secret or **subjective intent** cannot be proven.

The use of the objective intent standard means that an unambiguous contract must be interpreted as written.[5] It cannot be given a different meaning that one party thinks it has.

CASE SUMMARY

Just the Usual Meaning

Facts: Theodore and Barbara Kubala were married and owned a home. They put it up for sale and gave Foxfield Realty the exclusive agency to sell the house under which the realtor was entitled a 6% commission "if any sale or exchange is made by the broker, by the seller or by anyone else." Before the house sold, the couple divorced and as part of the divorce settlement Barbara transferred her interest in the house to Theodore. When Foxfield learned of this settlement, they claimed the 6% commission on the $237,000 list price since the transfer constituted a "sale" of the house.

Decision: Foxfield was only entitled to commissions if there was a sale. In its ordinary usage, a sale is a transfer of title to property by one owner to a buyer for consideration. By this ordinary meaning, the surrender by Barbara of her interest to Theodore was not a sale. Accordingly, Foxfield was not entitled to the commissions that it would have been given had there been a "sale." [*Foxfield Realty, Inc. v Kubala,* _____ Ill App 3d _____, _____ Ill Dec _____, 678 NE2d 1060 (1997)]

Words have ordinary meaning unless there is special reason for assuming otherwise.

(b) Meaning of Words. Ordinary words are to be interpreted according to their ordinary meaning.[6]

When a contract requires the gasoline dealer to pay the supplier for "gallons" supplied, the term *gallons* is unambiguous and does not require that an adjustment of the gallonage be made for the temperature.[7]

If there is a common meaning to a term, that meaning will be followed even though the dictionary may give a different meaning. If technical or trade terms are used in a contract, they are to be interpreted according to the area of technical knowledge or trade from which the terms are taken.

The prior relationships of the parties may give meaning to the words used by the parties.[8]

Writings may be incorporated by reference.

(c) Incorporation by Reference. The contract may not cover all the agreed terms. The missing terms may be found in another document. Frequently, the parties executing the contract will state that it embraces or incorporates the other document. Thus, a contract for storage will simply state that a storage contract is entered into and that the contract applies to the goods that are listed in the schedule that is attached to and made part of the contract. Likewise, a contract for the construction of a building may involve plans and specifications on file in a named city office. The contract will simply state that the building is to be constructed according to those plans and specifications that are "incorporated herein and made part of this contract." When there is such an incorporation by reference, the contract consists of both the original or skeleton document and the detailed statement that is incorporated in it.

---

[5] *Hoggard v City of Carlsbad* (NM App) 909 P2d 726 (1995).
[6] *Thornton v D.F.W. Christian Television, Inc.* (Tex App) 925 SW2d 17 (1995).
[7] *Hopkins v BP Oil, Inc.* (CA11 Ala) 81 F3d 1070 (1996).
[8] See section 6 of this chapter.

ETHICS & THE LAW

John J. Mellencamp, professionally known at various times as John Cougar, John Cougar Mellencamp, or John Mellencamp, is a songwriter, performer, and recording artist who has enjoyed enormous success since the early 1980s.

Through a series of agreements, Mellencamp had assigned the copyrights to his songs to Riva Music. He was not pleased with the arrangement, however, because he felt he had not been paid all the royalties he was entitled to and that Riva had not acted in good faith in promoting his songs.

During a luncheon meeting held in a New York City restaurant in March 1987, Mellencamp's accountant, Sigmund Balaban, Riva owner William Gaff, and Gaff's attorney, Milton Marks, entered into an alleged agreement to sell Mellencamp's copyrights back to him for $3 million.

Gary Baker served as Gaff's attorney for the due diligence process and drafting the oral agreement. Henry Goldstein served as Mellencamp's attorney. Goldstein sent the following letter to Baker on April 1, 1987:

> *I enclose a preliminary Document Request List in connection with our preparation of an agreement pursuant to which, among other things, John Mellencamp will effect the cancellation of his songwriter agreements with Riva Music et al.*
>
> *Please note that the Document Request List is designed for our due diligence investigation and evaluation and, accordingly, is intended to be illustrative rather than exhaustive. It is expected that, during the course of our review of the materials and our preparation of the agreement, we will make requests for additional information.*

On April 27, Baker received a draft agreement from Mr. Goldstein accompanied by a letter that stated the following:

> *I enclose a draft of the proposed agreement between John J. Mellencamp and Riva Music pursuant to which, among other things, John Mellencamp will effect the cancellation of his songwriter agreements with Riva Music et al.*
>
> *Under separate cover, I will shortly be sending you the various Exhibits to the proposed agreement. I would appreciate it if, while you are reviewing the proposed agreement, you prepare the Schedules to the proposed agreement and forward same to me.*
>
> *As soon as you have reviewed the proposed agreement, please call me.*
>
> *Please note that I am simultaneously sending a copy of the proposed agreement to our client for review; therefore, I must reserve the right to make any changes which it may require.*

On April 21, 1987, Balaban sent a letter to Mellencamp that included the following:

> *I have been in frequent communication with Hank Goldstein regarding the proposed contract with Riva Music Ltd. and its associated entities.*
>
> *In that connection Hank forwarded to me a preliminary draft dated April 16, 1987, for my comments. I suggested to Hank that he delete certain words on page 1 of the draft because they do not appear to me to be necessary, and may result in a hostile reaction from Gaff . . . .*
>
> *I have also indicated to Hank that while Gaff and his companies should release you from all obligations under the prior agreements, there does not appear to be any reason for you to release Gaff et al. from anything, except acting as your publisher. This is of course the lawyer's domain.*

Gaff had not signed the agreement. Both Mellencamp and Balaban indicated their intent was to be bound, and Balaban testified as follows at the trial about the luncheon meeting:

At the conclusion of the meeting Milton Marks, William Gaff and I joined hands and Milton Marks solemnly stated the Hebrew words "Mazel Bracha," which literally means "good fortune and good blessing" and which are customarily said in some circles to evidence a firm agreement. I am also aware that in the entertainment business handshake agreements, particularly where there have been extensive negotiations prior to the agreement, are honored and binding.

Would you interpret the letters as indicating there was a binding agreement? Was the conduct at the close of the lunch meeting relevant? Was it ethical for Gaff to withhold his signature from the agreement? Is the fact that the sale fell through after an oral agreement simply just a risk of business?
Mellencamp v Riva Music Ltd. (DC NY) 698 F Supp 1154 (1988)

(d) Expectations Distinguished from Meaning. A contract means what it says. A contracting party must avoid reading into a contract something that it does not say because that is what the party expects, hopes for, or wants. ◆ *For example,* the word *permanent* in a contract provision for permanent employment does not mean that the employment will continue unless the employee is discharged for cause but merely indicates that the employment is not temporary or seasonal.[9] ◆

(e) Economic Realities. In searching for the intent of the parties, a court will view their contract in the context of the economic realities surrounding its execution. Consequently, when uncertainty exists over whether new or used goods are to be sold, or the kind of insurance that is provided, the court may properly consider what is being paid because the payment and performance specified in a contract usually are commensurate.

3. Additional Printed Matter

Frequently a contract is mailed or delivered by one party to the other in an envelope that contains additional printed matter. Similarly, when goods are purchased, the buyer often receives with the goods a manufacturer's manual and various pamphlets. What effect do all these papers have on the contract? The same question arises when a worker gets a new job and the employer hands the new employee a handbook or a set of rules. Is this material accompanying the contract a part of the contract?

(a) Incorporation of Other Statement. The contract itself may furnish the answer. Sometimes the contract will expressly refer to and incorporate into the contract the terms of the other writing or printed statement. For example, the contract may say that the customer will be charged at the rates set forth in the approved tariff schedule, "a copy of which is attached hereto and made part of this contract." ◆ *For example,* Hondras stored furniture with Westgate Warehouse. The receipt given to Hondras stated that the storage contract was subject to the

---

[9] *Friedman v BRW, Inc.* (CA8 Minn) 40 F3d 293 (1994).

terms and conditions that were posted on the bulletin board on the door of the warehouse office. One of these conditions stated that Westgate was not responsible for property left over 30 days. Two months later, Hondras came for his furniture but it could not be found. Westgate denied liability on the basis of the posted limitation, whereas Hondras claimed the limitation had no effect because it was not contained in the storage contract. Hondras is wrong. The incorporation clause in the receipt had the effect of making the limitation clause part of the storage contract.

(b) Exclusion of Other Statement. As the opposite of incorporation, the contract may declare that there is no agreement outside of the contract. This means that either there never was anything else or that any prior agreement was merely a preliminary step that has been canceled out or erased; namely, the contract in its final form is as stated in the writing. For example, the seller of goods may state in the contract that no statements about the goods have been made to the buyer and that the written contract contains all of the terms of the sale.

(c) Reduction of Contract Terms. The effect of accompanying or subsequently delivered printed matter may be to reduce the terms of the written contract; that is, one party may have had a better bargain under the original contract. In this case, the accompanying matter will generally be ignored by a court if it is not shown that the party who would be harmed had agreed that it be part of the contract. This is so because a contract, once made, cannot be changed by unilateral action—that is, by the action of one party or one side of the contract without the agreement of the other.

(d) Employee's Handbook. It is a common practice for large employers to hand a new employee a manual or handbook that sets forth various matters relating to the employment. The question can then arise whether the statements in the handbook are binding terms of the employment contract or whether they are merely statements of the employer's existing policies or practices. If the handbook constitutes part of the contract, it cannot be changed by the action of the employer alone. If the handbook is merely a statement of policies or practices, the terms of the handbook can be changed by the employer at will. Litigation frequently arises when an employee who is fired or denied pension rights claims that this is a violation of the terms of the handbook.

Whether the handbook is part of the employment contract depends on the intent of the parties. If the handbook has been carefully written, it will specify whether it represents terms of the contract or merely policies. The handbook is clearly not part of the employment contract when the employee signed a card so stating and agreeing that the employer could change the handbook at any time.[10]

An employee's handbook may become part of the employment contract when the circumstances surrounding the employee's hiring manifest the intent that the handbook be so regarded. The same conclusion may be reached when a handbook is distributed to existing employees and they continue to work thereafter without any objection.

4. Whole Contract

A contract is to be interpreted as a whole, with effect given to all terms.

The provisions of a contract must be construed as a whole in such a way that every part is given effect. This rule is followed even when the contract is partly written

---

[10] *Hicks v Baylor University Medical Center* (Tex App) 789 SW2d 299 (1990).

and partly oral. Every word of a contract is to be given effect if reasonably possible. The contract is to be construed as a whole, and if the plain language of the contract thus viewed solves the dispute, no further analysis is to made by the court.[11]

CASE SUMMARY

Get the Total Picture

Facts: Avis-Rent-A-Car System gave Southwestern Automotive Leasing Corporation (SALCO) a car and truck rental franchise for three Louisiana cities in 1961. The licensing agreement gave each party the right to terminate with or without cause for a certain period of time and further provided that after "five years from the date Licensee first became an Avis System Licensee ... Licensor may terminate ... only with cause ...." SALCO was not successful, and by common consent its franchise rights were transferred in 1964 to Gulf Shores Leasing Corp. In 1968, Avis notified Gulf that it was terminating without cause the license held by Gulf. Gulf brought suit to prevent termination, claiming that Avis could only terminate for cause because five years had passed from the date of the original franchise agreement.

Decision: Gulf could not add on the term of the prior licensee, and therefore Gulf's license could be terminated without cause. The contract when read as a whole showed that the five-year period was a probationary or trial period and each licensee was required to stand on its own merits and to show five years of satisfactory work. The years of a former licensor could not be counted, particularly when, as in the case of SALCO, the prior years were not satisfactory. [*Gulf Shores Leasing Corp. v Avis Rent-A-Car System, Inc. (CA5 La) 441 F2d 1385 (1971)*]

(a) Divisible Contract. A contract may contain a number of provisions or performances to be rendered. If so, the question arises as to whether the parties intended merely a group of separate contracts (a divisible contract).[12] Possibly they intended a package deal so that complete performance of every provision of the contract was essential.

A significant indication that the parties intended a divisible contract is the fact that the consideration given by one party can be apportioned among the performances to be rendered by the other, or a separate consideration is stated for each performance. ◆ *For example,* an insurer may provide coverage for a house and garage and charge a premium that is the sum of one amount specified for insuring the house and another amount for insuring the garage. In such a case, it will be held that the insurance contract is divisible into two contracts. One contract covers the house, and the other covers the garage. ◆

(b) What Constitutes the Whole Contract. The question may arise whether separate papers or particular parts of a paper constitute part of the contract.

Terms in a printed letterhead or billhead or on the reverse side of a printed contract form are not part of the contract written there unless a reasonable person would regard such terms as part of the contract. An employer's manual that is shown to the job applicant after the signing of an employment contract is not part of that contract. Similarly, provisions in a manufacturer's instruction manual, or in invoices, or on labels that are not seen or called to the attention of a buyer until after a contract of sale has been made are not part of the contract. They do not bind the buyer.

---

[11] *Atlantic Mut. Ins. Co. v Metron Engineering and Construction Co.* (CA7 Ill) 83 F3d 897 (1996).
[12] *Re* Claussen's Estate (Iowa) 482 NW2d 381 (1992).

5. Conditions

When the occurrence or nonoccurrence of an event affects the existence of a contract or the obligation of a party to a contract, the event is called a **condition**.

A contract or duty may be subject to a condition precedent or subsequent.

Courts do not favor conditions because they cause a loss of rights. Therefore, courts will interpret a contract provision as not creating a condition when that interpretation is reasonably possible.

(a) Condition Precedent. An obligation-triggering event may be described as a **condition precedent**. It precedes the existence of the obligation to perform or the existence of any contract. Terms such as *if, provided that, when, after, as soon as, subject to,* and *on condition* that indicate the creation of a condition.[13]

If an obligation to pay money is subject to a condition precedent, no duty to pay exists if the condition is never satisfied. Likewise, when business premises were leased with an option to buy and provided that the owner would not compete with the purchaser, the provision did not protect the lessee until the lessee exercised the option and became the purchaser.

In a fire insurance policy, the insurer has no obligation to make any payment until there is a fire loss. The occurrence of such a loss is thus a condition precedent to the insurer's duty to pay under the policy. Similarly, when an employee is required to give notice to the employer to obtain a particular benefit, giving notice is a condition precedent to the employer's duty to provide the benefit. There must be strict compliance with an express condition precedent.[14]

(b) Condition Subsequent. The parties may specify that the contract shall terminate when a particular event occurs or does not occur. Such a provision is a **condition subsequent**. If government approval is required, the parties may specify that the contract shall not bind them if the government approval cannot be obtained.

A contract for the purchase of land may contain a condition subsequent that cancels the contract if the buyer is not able to obtain a zoning permit to use a building for a particular purpose.

CASE SUMMARY

What Comes After

Facts: Levenson leased a building to Supermarkets. Haynes guaranteed that the rent would be paid by the tenant. The guaranty contract stated that it would be void if any change was made to the terms of the lease. The lease terms were changed by Levenson and Supermarkets.

Decision: The change to the lease released Haynes from the obligation under the guaranty. The making of that change was a condition subsequent that discharged the obligation of Haynes. [*Levenson v Haynes (NM App) 934 P2d 300 (1997)*]

Conditions may be concurrent.

(c) Concurrent Conditions. In most bilateral contracts, the performances by the parties are concurrent conditions. That is, the duty of each party to perform is dependent on the other party's performing. Thus, neither is required to perform until the other performs or tenders performance. Frequently the contract will

---

[13] *Harmon Cable Communications v Scope Cable Television, Inc.* 237 Neb 871, 468 NW2d 350 (1991).
[14] *Oppenheimer & Co., Inc. v Oppenheim, Appel, Dixon & Co.,* ____ NY ____, 660 NE2d 415 (1995).

specify or indicate that one person must perform first. In this case, that performance is a condition precedent and the conditions are not concurrent. ◆ *For example*, in a contract to pay a painter $1,000 for painting a house, the painter must perform the painting work before the owner is required to perform the promise of paying for the work. Performance by the painter is thus a condition precedent to the owner's obligation to pay. ◆

(d) Validity of Condition. A condition must satisfy the same requirements as to validity as any other contract term. If the effect of the condition imposes too great a hardship, a court will refuse to enforce it. ◆ *For example*, a provision expressly stating that a contractor is not required to pay a subcontractor until the contractor receives payment from the owner is void as against public policy. Courts reason that the subcontractor should not bear the risk of default by the owner.[15] ◆

6. Contradictory and Ambiguous Terms

Contradictory terms may show an absence of agreement.

One term in a contract may conflict with another term, or one term may have two different meanings. It is then necessary for the court to determine whether there is a contract and, if so, what the contract really means. When the terms of a contract are contradictory or conflict about a significant matter, this conflict precludes the existence of any contract.

CASE SUMMARY

Collision Course!

Facts: Mohon executed a contract to sell 372.12 acres of land to Moore. One paragraph of the contract stated that the purchase price was $110,000. Another paragraph stated that it was $275 an acre, which would produce a total price of $102,333, which would be $7,667 less than the stated price of $110,000. Which amount was binding?

Decision: Neither amount. There was no contract because the conflict in the terms could not be reconciled. [*Moore v Mohon* (Tex Civ App) 514 SW2d 508 (1974)]

In some instances, conflict between the terms of a contract is eliminated by the introduction of parol evidence or by the application of an appropriate rule of construction.

Conflict of terms may be solved by the nature of writing.

(a) Nature of Writing. When a contract is partly a printed form or partly typewritten and partly handwritten, and the written part conflicts with the printed or typewritten part, the written part prevails. When there is a conflict between a printed part and a typewritten part, the latter prevails. Consequently, when a clause typewritten on a printed form conflicts with what is stated by the print, the conflicting print is ignored and the typewritten clause controls. This rule is based on the belief that the parties had given greater thought to what they typed or wrote for the particular contract as contrasted with printed words already in a form designed to cover many transactions. Thus a typewritten provision to pay 90 cents per unit overrode a preprinted provision setting the price as 45 cents per unit.[16]

---

[15] *West-Fair Electric Contractors v Aetna Casualty & Surety Co.,* ____ NY ____, 661 NE2d 967 (1995).
[16] *Honigsbaum's Inc. v Stuyvesant Plaza, Inc.,* ____ App Div 2d ____, 577 NYS2d 165 (1991).

When there is a conflict between an amount or quantity expressed both in words and figures, as on a check, the amount or quantity expressed in words prevails. Words control because there is less danger that a word will be wrong than a number.

A contract may be ambiguous.

(b) Ambiguity. A contract is **ambiguous** when the intent of the parties is uncertain and the contract is capable of more than one reasonable interpretation. Some courts refuse to look beyond the four corners to the written contract for determining if the contract contains any ambiguity. Other courts reject this "four corners rule" and look at the contract in the light of the situation in which it was made to determine if it is ambiguous.[17]

Disagreement over the legal effect of terms used by the parties does not make the contract ambiguous.[18] This is so because the court, by applying the law to their terms, can reach a conclusion as to the intent manifested by the contract. In contrast, if the intent would still be uncertain even after rules of law were applied, the contract is ambiguous.

CASE SUMMARY

Multiple Meanings Obviously Ambiguous

Facts: Kirk Clemons and his father were living in the house of Kirk's grandfather, Frank Clemons. Kirk was accidentally injured. Frank had insurance with Oregon Mutual Insurance Company. It refused to pay for Kirk's injury because the policy stated to Frank that it did not cover injuries of a person under 21 "in your care." The insurance company claimed that Kirk was in the care of Frank. Frank claimed that he did not have "care" over Kirk because Kirk's father was present.

Decision: The phrase "in your care" was ambiguous because it could be interpreted in two ways. The ordinary purchaser of insurance, however, would interpret "in your care" as meaning the one having responsibility for care. The phrase would therefore be given that meaning. It was accordingly necessary to have a trial to determine from the evidence of the case who had the responsibility of caring for Kirk. [*Oregon Mut. Ins. Co. v Clemons*, 124 Or App 155, 861 P2d 372 (1993)]

Whether a contract is ambiguous cannot always be determined merely by looking at it. In some cases, the written contract will look perfectly clear, and the ambiguity does not become apparent until the contract is applied to the facts or the property concerned.[19]

The fact that a particular situation is not provided for by the contract does not make it ambiguous. ◆ *For example,* a summer camp contract is not ambiguous because it does not contain any provision relating to refunds if cancellation occurs. ◆

The background from which the contract and the dispute arose may help in determining the intention of the parties. Thus, when suit was brought in Minnesota on a Canadian insurance policy, the question arose whether the dollar limit of the policy referred to Canadian or American dollars. The court concluded that Canadian dollars were intended. Both the insurer and the insured were

---

[17] *R.T. Hepworth Co. v Dependable Ins. Co.* (CA7 Ill) 997 F2d 315 (1993).
[18] *Young Dental Manufacturing Co. v Engineered Products, Inc.* (Mo App) 838 SW2d 154 (1992).
[19] *Sparrow v Tayco Construction Co.* (Utah App) 846 P2d 1323 (1993).

Canadian corporations; the original policy, endorsements to the policy, and policy renewals were written in Canada; over the years, premiums had been paid in Canadian dollars; and a prior claim on the policy had been settled by the payment of an amount computed on the basis of Canadian dollars.

An ambiguous contract is interpreted against the drafting party.

(c) Strict Construction against Drafting Party. An ambiguous contract is interpreted strictly against the party who drafted it.[20] Thus, printed forms of insurance policies that are supplied by the insurer are interpreted against the insurer and in favor of the insured when two interpretations are reasonably possible. If the contract is clear and unambiguous, it will be enforced according to its terms even though this benefits the party who drafted the contract.

CASE SUMMARY

When You Prepare the Contract, Watch Out!

Facts: The Dickinson Elks Club conducted an annual Labor Day golf tournament. Charbonneau Buick-Pontiac offered to give a new car as a prize to anyone making a hole in one on hole no. 8. The golf course of the club was only nine holes. To play 18 holes, the players would go around the course twice, although they would play from different tees or locations for the second nine holes. On the second time around, what was originally the 8th hole became the 17th hole. Grove was a contestant in the tournament. On the first day, he scored 3 on the no. 8 hole, but on approaching it for the second time as the 17th hole, he made a hole in one. He claimed the prize car from Charbonneau. The latter claimed that Grove had not won the prize because he did not make the hole in one on the 8th hole.

Decision: Judgment for Grove. The offer made by Charbonneau was ambiguous in that it could refer to the particular cup in the golf course or to the sequence in which the hole in one was made. That is, it could refer either to making the hole in one as the hole on the first time around the course or to making the hole in one in the same cup on the 8th hole or the second time around the course, when it would be the 17th hole. As Charbonneau had specified the terms, this ambiguity would be interpreted against it and in favor of Grove. The prize contract was therefore satisfied by making the hole in one on either the first or second time around the course. Since Grove had done this, he satisfied the terms of the contract and was entitled to the prize. [*Grove v Charbonneau Buick-Pontiac, Inc.* (ND) 240 NW2d 853 (1976)]

---

7. Implied Terms

In some cases, a court will imply a term to cover a situation for which the parties failed to provide or, when needed, to give the contract a construction or meaning that is reasonable.

A term will not be implied in a contract when the court concludes that the silence of the contract on the particular point was intentional.

Reasonable duration of a contract is implied.

(a) Duration of Contract. When a contract is to continue over a period of time but no duration is specified in the contract, courts will imply that the contract is to be performed or will continue for a reasonable time. But either party may terminate the contract by giving notice to the other party. An employment contract that does not specify any duration may be terminated by either party at any time for any reason.[21]

---

[20] *Idaho Migrant Council, Inc. v Warila* (Wyo) 890 P2d 39 (1995).
[21] *Wlasiuk v Whirlpool Corp.*, ____ Wash App ____, 914 P2d 102 (1996).

(b) Details of Performance. Details of performance of a contract not expressly stated in the contract will often be implied by the court. Thus, an obligation to pay a specified sum of money is implied to mean payment in legal tender. In a contract to perform work, there is an implied promise to use such skill as is necessary for the proper performance of the work. In a "cost plus" contract, an undertaking is implied that the costs will be reasonable and proper. When payment is made "as a deposit on account," there is an implied term that if the payment is not used for the purpose stated, the payment will be returned to the person who made the deposit. When a contract does not specify where money is to be paid, it will be implied that the payment is to be made to the creditor at the creditor's office or place of business.

A local custom or trade practice, such as that of allowing 30 days' credit to buyers, may form part of the contract. This occurs when it is clear that the parties intended to be governed by this custom or trade practice, or when a reasonable person would believe that they had so intended.

When a contract does not specify the time for performance, a reasonable time is implied. "Reasonable time for a contract's performance is not measured by hours, days, weeks, months or years, but is to be determined from the surrounding conditions and circumstances which the parties contemplated at the time the contract was executed."[22]

CASE SUMMARY

No Set Performance Time

Facts: William Dolbeer purchased a tract of land from Fred Aldridge. Fred knew that William intended to build a house on the land and in the sales contract specified that "the seller will install water to the property at no cost to purchaser" but did not specify when the water was to be installed. After failing to furnish the water for six years, William sued Fred for breach of contract.

Decision: Judgment for Dolbeer. There was a breach of contract although the contract did not specify when the water was to be installed. Since no date was specified, the seller was required to perform within a reasonable time. The seller's delay clearly ran beyond a reasonable time and therefore was a breach of the contract. *[Aldridge v Dolbeer (Ala) 567 So 2d 1267 (1990)]*

(c) Good Faith. In every contract, there is an implied obligation that neither party shall do anything that will have the effect of destroying or injuring the right of the other party to receive the fruits of the contract. This means that in every contract there exists an implied covenant of good faith and fair dealing. Thus an owner having the right under a contract with a real estate developer to approve or reject the plans submitted by the developer was guilty of a breach of the duty to act in good faith when it was shown that the owner refused to approve the developer's plans, not because the plans were disapproved, but because the owner was trying to get more money from the developer. When the contract expressly gives one party uncontrolled discretion to act, the concept of good faith does not require action in a way that will satisfy the other contracting party.

When the satisfaction of a condition involves action by a party to the contract, the implied duty to act in good faith requires that the party make an honest, good-faith effort to bring about the satisfaction of the condition. For example, when a

---

[22] *Miller v Beales,* ____ Ohio App ____, 608 NE2d 1133 (1992).

contract is made subject to the condition that one of the parties obtain financing, that party must make reasonable, good-faith efforts to obtain financing. The party is not permitted to do nothing and then claim that the contract is not binding because the condition has not been satisfied. Likewise, when a contract requires a party to obtain government approval, the party must use all reasonable means to obtain it.[23] When a contract may reasonably be interpreted in different ways, a court should make the interpretation that is in harmony with good faith and fair dealing. The court should avoid an interpretation that imputes bad faith to a party or produces an inequitable result.

(1) Necessity of a Contract. Ordinarily, no duty of good faith arises unless there is an existing contract.[24] Except in certain insurance cases or when there is a fiduciary relationship between the parties, no duty exists to act in good faith before entering any contract.

(2) Making of a Contract. The duty of good faith and fair dealing does not require a person to enter into any contract. Nor does it impose any duty on a party to extend or renew a contract beyond its stated life.

Thus it does not require a bank to lend money to an applicant. This is true even if the bank had done so in prior years and the applicant expected the bank would continue to make loans.

(3) Enforcement of a Contract. A party does not act in bad faith by enforcing a contract according to its terms. Hence the conduct of a party in demanding payment according to the terms of the contract does not constitute a breach of the covenant of good faith and fair dealing.[25]

The obligation of good faith and fair dealing does not impose any obligation that is not imposed by the contract of the parties. Hence it does not limit the power of an employer under an at-will contract to terminate the contract at any time for any reason.[26]

> Good faith does not require the making of a new contract or the surrender of an existing right.

(4) Modification of a Contract. The obligation to act in good faith does not require a party to agree to a modification of the contract or to surrender any right.[27] When a contract expressly gives a party the right to cancel the contract, the duty to act in good faith does not bar canceling the contract. Similarly, a franchiser having a right to terminate the franchise without cause is not barred from doing so because of the duty of good faith. When a franchisee has been granted a nonexclusive franchise, good faith does not prevent the franchiser from granting another franchise that competes with the original franchise.

(5) Termination of a Contract. When a party to a contract has the power to terminate the contract, the principle of good faith does not bar termination to further a party's economic interest. Thus an employer may reduce the number of employees by discharging those who do not have contracts of employment for fixed periods of time.

---

[23] *Kroboth v Brent,* _____ App Div 2d _____, 625 NYS2d 748 (1995).
[24] *Cimino v Firstier Bank,* _____ Neb _____, 530 NW2d 606 (1995).
[25] *Overseas Private Investment Corp. v Industria de Pesca* (DC Dist Col) 920 F Supp 207 (1996).
[26] *Cook v Zions First National Bank* (Utah App) 919 P2d 56 (1996).
[27] *Metro Communications Co. v Ameritech Mobile Communications, Inc.* (CA6 Mich) 984 F2d 739 (1993).

A party may have a good faith duty to assist another party in obtaining government approval.

(d) Government Approval. In some situations, the ability to perform a contract will depend on obtaining a government permit or approval. When this occurs, the failure to obtain this approval or permit may be made an express condition subsequent. The contract is then discharged by such failure. An implied term generally arises that one party to the contract will cooperate with the other in obtaining any necessary government permit or approval.

(e) Statutory Terms. Statutes commonly require that certain kinds of contracts contain particular clauses. *For example,* automobile insurance contracts are often required by statute to contain clauses relating to no-fault liability and uninsured motorists. When a contract is written that does not contain the required statutory terms, the courts will ordinarily imply the statutory terms and interpret the contract as though it complied with the statute. Similarly, a provision in a contract that would be contrary to a required statutory provision will be ignored.

8. Conduct and Custom

The conduct of the parties and the customs and usages of a particular trade may give meaning to the words of the parties and thus aid in the interpretation of their contract.

The conduct of parties may give definite meaning to a contract.

(a) Conduct of the Parties. The conduct of the parties in carrying out the terms of a contract is the best guide to determining the parties' intent. When performance has been repeatedly tendered and accepted without protest, neither party will be permitted to claim that the contract was too indefinite to be binding. *For example,* a travel agent made a contract with a hotel to arrange for junkets to the hotel. After some 80 junkets had already been arranged and paid for by the hotel at the contract price without any dispute about whether the contract obligation was satisfied, any claim that it was not certain what was intended must be ignored. Moreover, when the conduct of the parties is inconsistent with the original written contract, proof of such conduct may justify concluding that the parties had orally modified the original agreement.

Custom and trade usage may supply missing terms for a contract.

(b) Custom and Usage of Trade. The customs and usages of the trade or commercial activity to which the contract relates may be used to interpret the terms of a contract.[28] *For example,* when a contract for the construction of a house calls for a "turn-key construction," industry usage is admissible to show what this means—a construction in which all the owner needs to do is "turn the key" in the lock to open the building for use and in which all risks are assumed by the contractor.[29]

Special meaning given to words by the customs and usages of the applicable trade may be shown by parol evidence even if the terms of the contract are not ambiguous.[30]

Custom and usage, however, cannot override express provisions of a contract that are inconsistent with custom and usage.

---

[28] *Affiliated FM Ins. Co. v Constitution Reinsurance Corp,* ____ Mass ____, 626 NE2d 878 (1994).
[29] *Blue v R.L. Glossen Contracting, Inc.,* ____ Ga App ____, 327 SE2d 582 (1985).
[30] *Doswell Ltd. v Virginia Electric & Power Co.,* ____ Va ____, 468 SE2d 84 (1996).

Custom as the Background

Facts: Beck & Co., a brewery, gave Gianelli Distributing Company a franchise to distribute Beck's Beer. The franchise agreement specified that it would continue "unless and until terminated at any time by 30 days' written notice by either party to the other." Later, Beck notified Gianelli that the franchise was terminated. Gianelli claimed that the franchise could only be terminated upon proof of reasonable cause for termination. Gianelli offered evidence of trade usage to show that there was a common practice to require cause for termination, and further claimed that such usage should be read into the franchise agreement with Beck.

Decision: The franchise contract was not a complete agreement because it did not state whether termination could be for any cause or only for a good cause. Parol evidence of trade custom was therefore admissible on the ground that the parties naturally intended to do business in the way that was customary and that therefore their actual intent was that termination could only be made for good cause. As a result, a new trial was required in order to determine whether in fact there was a trade usage as claimed. [*Gianelli Distributing Co. v Beck & Co. 172 Cal App 3d 1020, 219 Cal Rptr 203 (1985)*]

9. Avoidance of Hardship

Courts may imply terms to protect the weaker party from hardship.

As a general rule, a party is bound by a contract even though it proves to be a bad bargain. If possible, a court will interpret a contract to avoid hardship, particularly when the hardship will hurt the weaker of the two parties to the contract. Courts will, if possible, interpret a vague contract in a way to avoid any forfeiture. Accordingly, a court will avoid holding that a statement or a promise is a condition precedent, which if unsatisfied would mean that no rights would arise under the contract, or is a condition subsequent, which if satisfied would mean that all rights under the contract would be terminated.

When there is ambiguity about the meaning of a contract, a court will avoid the interpretation that gives one contracting party an unreasonable advantage over the other or that causes a forfeiture of a party's interest. When there is an inequality of bargaining power between the contracting parties, courts will sometimes classify the contract as a contract of adhesion. This means that it was offered on a take-it-or-leave-it basis by the stronger party. The court will then interpret the contract as providing what appeared reasonable from the standpoint of the weaker bargaining party.

In some instances if hardship cannot be avoided in this manner, the court may hold that the contract or a particular provision is not binding because it is unconscionable or contrary to public policy. The extent to which this protection is available is uncertain.

When hardship arises because the contract makes no provision for the situation that has occurred, the court will sometimes imply a term in order to avoid the hardship.

Helping the Small Fry

Facts: Standard Oil Co. made a nonexclusive jobbing or wholesale dealership contract with Perkins, which limited him to selling Standard's products and required Perkins to maintain certain minimum prices. Standard Oil had the right to approve or disapprove Perkins' customers. To be able to perform under his contract, Perkins had to make a substantial monetary investment, and his only income was from the commissions on the sales of Standard's products. Standard Oil

> made some sales directly to Perkins' customers. When Perkins protested, Standard Oil pointed out that the contract did not contain any provision making his rights exclusive. Perkins sued Standard Oil to compel it to stop dealing with his customers.
>
> **Decision:** Judgment for Perkins. In view of the expenditure required of Perkins to operate his business and to perform his part of the contract and because of his dependence on his customers, the interpretation should be made that Standard Oil would not solicit customers of Perkins. This is true even though the contract did not give Perkins an exclusive dealership within the given geographic area. [*Perkins v Standard Oil Co. 235 Or 7, 383 P2d 107 (1963)*]

10. Joint, Several, and Joint and Several Contracts

A modern contract declares joint and several liability.

The obligation of defendants bound by a contract may be **several** (separate), **joint,** or **joint and several.**[31] Defendants are jointly liable when they are indivisibly liable together. When they are liable severally, they are each liable separately, or individually. When they are jointly and severally liable, each is separately liable for the full amount. Printed forms will commonly specify that liability is joint and several. Thus, the modern contract will provide that when a daughter buys a motorcycle and the contract is cosigned by her mother, the liability of each of the two is joint and several. This means that the seller may sue and collect the full amount from either of them or part of the amount from each of them until payment has been made in full.

B.   CONFLICT OF LAWS

Conflict of laws determines which law applies to an interstate transaction.

When a lawsuit is brought on a contract, the court will seek to apply the law under which the contract was made. In other words, a California court in many cases will not apply California law to a foreign (out-of-state) contract. The principle that determines when a court applies the law of its own state—**the law of the forum**—or some foreign law is called **conflict of laws.**

Because there are 50 state court systems and a federal court system, as well as a high degree of interstate activity, conflict of laws questions arise frequently.

11. State Courts

It is important to distinguish between the state in which the parties are **domiciled** or have their permanent home, the state in which the contract is made, and the state in which the contract is to be performed. The law of the state where the contract is made determines whether it is valid in substance and satisfies requirements of form. Matters relating to the performance of the contract, excuse or liability for nonperformance, and the measure of damages for nonperformance are generally governed by the law of the state where the contract is to be performed. Similar considerations apply to the interpretation of international contracts. Thus, a California court will apply Swiss law to a contract made in Switzerland that is to be performed in that country.

When a lawsuit is brought on a contract, the law of the forum determines the procedure and the rules of evidence.

---

[31] *Chun v Chun*, ____ Cal App 3d ____, 235 Cal Rptr 553 (1987).

The place of contracting historically determined which law to apply.

(a) Place of Contracting.

The state in which the contract is made is determined by finding the state in which the last act essential to the formation of the contract was performed. When an acceptance is mailed in one state to an offeror in another state, the state of formation of the contract is the state in which the acceptance is mailed if the acceptance becomes effective at that time.

If acceptance by telephone is otherwise proper, the acceptance takes effect at the place where the acceptance is spoken into the phone. Thus, an employment contract is made in the state in which the job applicant telephones an acceptance. Consequently, the law of that state governs a claim to workers' compensation even though the injuries were sustained in another state.

If an action on a contract made in one state is brought in a court of another state, an initial question is whether that court will lend its aid to the enforcement of a foreign contract. Ordinarily, suit may be brought on a foreign contract. If there is a strong contrary local policy, however, recovery may be denied even though the contract was valid in the state where it was made. But there is also authority that when a contract would be valid by the law of one state but invalid by the law of another, a court will apply the law of the state under which the contract is valid.[32]

The capacity of a natural person to make a contract is governed by the place of contracting. A corporation's capacity to make a contract is determined by the law of the state of incorporation.

The modern view applies the center of gravity to determine which law applies.

(b) Center of Gravity.

It is common for contracts with interstate aspects to specify that they shall be governed by the law of a particular state. In the absence of a law-selecting provision in the contract, there is a growing acceptance of the rule that a contract should be governed by the law of the state that has the most significant contacts with the transaction. This is the state to which the contract may be said to gravitate.

CASE SUMMARY

Common Sense Says, "Forget the Past"

Facts: Lazard Freres & Co. is an investment bank and registered broker. Protective Life Insurance Co. is a large bank debt refinancer. In 1994 Kevin Murphy, a Lazard Freres representative, called Mark Okada, a Protective Life representative, with an offer to purchase new bank debt. The call reached Okada in Florida where he was attending a conference. During their conversation Murphy advised Okada that he had to act quickly on the offer because a report was soon be made public that would make the purchase attractive to other investors. Okada agreed to the purchase. When the report became public, Okada became convinced that Murphy had misrepresented the report's contents. Protective refused to close the deal and Lazard sued Protective for breach of contract. Lazard brought suit in New York and Protective succeeded in removing the case to federal court. Protective sought to have Florida law govern the contract rather than New York's since acceptance of the offer took place in Florida.

Decision: By the traditional rule, the Florida law would apply, but instead New York would apply the modern center of gravity rule and ignore the fact that the contract was made in Florida. The center of gravity of the contract lay in New York, and the law of that state would therefore be applied. [Lazard Freres & Co. v Protective Life Ins. Co. (CA2 NY) 108 F3d 1531 (1997)]

---

[32] *American Home Insurance Co. v Safway Steel Products Co., Inc.* (Tex App) 743 SW2d 693 (1987).

For example, assume the buyer's place of business and the seller's factory are located in state *A*, and the buyer is purchasing to resell to customers in state *A*. Many courts will hold that this is a contract governed by the law of state *A* in all respects. The fact that it is a state *B* contract by virtue of the chance circumstance that the seller's offer was accepted by the buyer in state *B* would not change this result. In determining which state has the most significant contacts, the court is to consider the place of contracting, negotiating, and performing; the location of the subject matter of the contract; and the domicile (residence) and states of incorporation and principal place of business of the parties.

When all states have the same rule of law, it is not important which state's law is followed. If, however, the law of the states involved is not the same, the choice of the state whose law is to govern will determine how the lawsuit will end. With the increasing interstate character of big business, the question of choice of law becomes increasingly important.

12. Federal Courts

A federal court in a diversity action follows the local conflict of laws rule

When the parties to a contract reside in different states and the amount involved is $50,000 or more, an action may be brought in a federal court because of the parties' different citizenship. The federal court must apply the same rules of conflict of laws that would be applied by the courts of the state in which the federal court is sitting. Thus, a federal court in Chicago deciding a case involving parties from different states must apply the same rule of conflict of laws as would be applied by the state courts in Illinois. The state law must be followed by the federal court in such a case, whether or not the federal court agrees with the state law.

SUMMARY

Because a contract is based on the agreement of the parties, courts must determine the intent of the parties manifested in the contract. The intent that is to be enforced is the intent as it reasonably appears to a third person. This objective intent is followed, and the subjective or secret intent is ignored because recognition of secret intention would undermine the stability of contracts and open the door to fraud.

In interpreting a contract, ordinary words are to be given their ordinary meanings. If trade or technical terms have been used, they are interpreted according to their technical meanings. The court must consider the whole contract and not read a particular part out of context. When different writings are executed as part of the same transaction, or one writing refers to or incorporates another, all the writings are to be read together as the contract of the parties. In some cases, the reverse is done, and a contract is held divisible.

When provisions of a contract are contradictory, the court will try to reconcile or eliminate the conflict. If this cannot be done, the conclusion may be that there is no contract because the conflict makes the agreement indefi-

nite as to a material matter. In some cases, conflict is solved by considering the form of conflicting terms. Handwriting prevails over typing and a printed form, and typing prevails over a printed form. Ambiguity will be eliminated in some cases by the admission of parol evidence or by interpreting the provision strictly against the party preparing the contract, particularly when that party has significantly greater bargaining power.

In most cases, the parties are held to their contract exactly as it has been written. In other cases, the courts will imply certain terms to preserve the contract against the objection that essential terms are missing or to prevent hardship. The law will imply that performance is to be made within a reasonable time and that details of performance are reasonable when the contract fails to be specific on these points. Also, the law will imply an obligation to act in good faith.

When a contract has interstate aspects, it is necessary to determine which state's law governs it. The rules that govern that decision are called the law of conflict of laws. The parties may specify the jurisdiction whose law is to govern. If that jurisdiction bears a reasonable relationship to the contract, the choice will be given effect by the court. In the absence of such a provision, some courts will apply the older rule that the law of the state where the contract was made prevails in most matters and the law of the state where performance is to be made prevails in matters relating to performance. The modern, or center-of-gravity, view is to choose the jurisdiction that has the most signif- icant relationship to the parties, the contract, and its performance. When an action is brought in a federal court because it involves citizens of different states (diversity of citizenship), the federal court must apply the conflict of laws principles that would be applied by the courts of the state in which the federal court is sitting.

QUESTIONS AND CASE PROBLEMS

1. What social forces are affected by the rule that a secret intention has no effect?

2. Harrison Builders made a contract to build a house for Kendall on the basis of cost plus 10 percent profit. The cost of the finished house was approximately $100,000. Kendall had expected that it would be $60,000 and claimed that Harrison was careless and extravagant in incurring costs of $100,000. Harrison asserted that since Kendall did not deny that the costs were $100,000, he could not dispute that they were proper. Is Harrison correct?

3. In letters between the two, Rita Borelli contracted to sell "my car" to Viola Smith for $2,000. It was later shown that Borelli owned two cars. Borelli refused to deliver either car to Smith, and Smith sued Borelli for breach of contract. Borelli raised the defense that the contract was too indefinite to be enforced because it could not be determined from the writing which car was the subject matter of the contract. Is the contract too indefinite to be enforced?

4. Quinn of Ohio sues Norman of California in the federal district court for the southern district of New York. Quinn claims that the court should apply the conflict of laws rules of Ohio because he is from Ohio and the plaintiff should have the choice of law. Norman claims that the federal court should apply federal law rather than the law of any particular state. Who is correct?

5. Panasonic Industrial Co. (PIC) made a contract making Manchester Equipment Co., Inc. (MECI), a nonexclusive wholesale distributor of its products. The contract stated that PIC reserves the unrestricted right to solicit and make direct sales of the products to anyone, anywhere. The contract also stated that it contained the entire agreement of the parties and that any prior agreement or statement was superseded by the contract. PIC subsequently began to make direct sales to two of MECI's established customers. MECI claimed that this was a breach of the distribution contract and sued PIC for damages. Decide. What ethical values are involved? [*Manchester Equipment Co. v Panasonic Industrial Co.* ____ App Div 2d ____, 529 NYS2d 532]

6. McGill and his grandson, Malo, made an agreement by which McGill would live with Malo and receive support and maintenance in return for McGill's deeding his house to Malo. After a number of years, McGill left the house because of the threats and physical violence of the grandson. There was no complaint of lack of support and maintenance. Had the grandson broken the contract? [*McGill v Malo* (Conn Super) 184 A2d 517]

7. A contract made for the sale of a farm stated that the buyer's deposit would be returned "if for any reason the farm cannot be sold." The seller later stated that she had changed her mind and would not sell, and she offered to return the deposit. The buyer refused to take the deposit back and brought suit to enforce the contract. The seller contended that the "any reason" provision extended to anything, including the seller's changing her mind. Was the buyer entitled to recover? [*Phillips v Rogers,* ____ W Va ____, 200 SE2d 676]

8. Integrated, Inc., entered into a contract with the state of California to construct a building. It then subcontracted the electrical work to Alec Fergusson Electrical Contractors. The subcontract was a printed form with blanks filled in by typewriting. The printed payment clause required Integrated to pay Fergusson on the 15th day of the month following the submission of invoices by Fergusson. The typewritten part of the contract required Integrated to pay Fergusson "immediately following payment" (by the state) to the general contractor. When was payment required? [*Integrated, Inc. v Alec Fergusson Electrical Contractors,* ____ Cal App 3d ____, 58 Cal Rptr 503]

9. Norwest Bank had been lending money to Tresch to run a dairy farm. The balance due the bank after several years was $147,000. The loan agreement stated that Tresch would not buy any new equipment in excess of $500 without the express consent of the bank. Some time later, Tresch applied to the bank for a loan of $3,100 to purchase some equipment. The bank refused to make the loan because it did not believe the new equipment would correct the condition for which

it would be bought and would not result in significant additional income. Tresch then sued the bank, claiming that its refusal to make the loan was a breach of the implied covenant of good faith and fair dealing. Decide. [*Tresch v Norwest Bank of Lewistown,* ____ Mont ____, 778 P2d 874]

10. Physicians Mutual Insurance Co. issued a policy covering Brown's life. The policy declared that it did not cover any deaths resulting from "mental disorder, alcoholism, or drug addiction." Brown was killed when she fell while intoxicated. The insurance company refused to pay because of the quoted provision. Her executor, Savage, sued the insurance company. Did the insurance company have a defense? [*Physicians Mutual Ins. Co. v Savage* (Ind App) 296 NE2d 165]

11. Tucker was employed by Ashland Oil. Tucker's contract prohibited him from working for a competitor after the termination of his employment. Tucker worked as a district manager of Ashland in Louisiana, Missouri, and Illinois. When his employment ended, he worked for a competitor in Missouri, which would be a breach of the anticompetitive covenant. Tucker claimed, however, that the covenant did not bind him because it was invalid under the law of Louisiana, where the contract of employment had originally been made. Suit was brought in Missouri to enforce the covenant, and under Missouri law the covenant was valid. Which state law should be applied? [*Ashland Oil, Inc. v Tucker* (Mo App) 768 SW2d 595]

12. Carol and John, a married couple, separated and signed an agreement by which John promised to pay Carol $100 a month. A year later they were divorced, and John stopped making payments. Carol sued him for breach of the contract. John offered to testify that it was his intention that the payments would stop when the parties were divorced. Is this testimony admissible? [*Grady v Grady* (NC App) 224 SE2d 282]

13. Suburban Power Piping Corp., under contract to construct a building for LTV Steel Corp., made a subcontract with Power & Pollution Services, Inc., to do some of the work. The subcontract provided that the subcontractor would be paid when the owner (LTV) paid the contractor. LTV went into bankruptcy before making full payment to the contractor, who then refused to pay the subcontractor on the ground that the "pay-when-paid" provision of the subcontract made payment by the owner a condition precedent to the obligation of the contractor to pay the subcontractor. Was the contractor correct? [*Power & Pollution Services, Inc. v Suburban Power Piping Corp.* ____ Ohio App ____, 598 NE2d 69]

14. Beck and Co., a brewery, gave Gianelli Distributing Co. a franchise to distribute Beck's Beer. The franchise agreement specified that it would continue "unless and until terminated at any time by 30 days' written notice by either party to the other." Some time thereafter, Beck notified Gianelli that the franchise was terminated. Gianelli claimed that the franchise could be terminated only upon proof of reasonable cause. He offered evidence of trade usage to show that common practice required cause for termination and further claimed that such usage would be read into the franchise agreement with Beck. Is this evidence admissible?

15. Drews Co. contracted to renovate a building owned by Ledwith. There were many delays in performing the contract, and finally the contractor quit the job. Ledwith sued the contractor for damages for delay and for breach of the contract. The contractor claimed that it was not liable for damages for delay because the contract did not contain any date by which the work was to be completed and did not state that time was of the essence. Did the silence of the contract excuse the delay?

Third Persons and Contracts

CHAPTER 18

OBJECTIVES

After studying this chapter, you should be able to

1. *Distinguish between a third party beneficiary and an incidental beneficiary;*
2. *Define an assignment of contract rights;*
3. *State the limitations on the assignability or a right to performance;*
4. *Describe what constitutes a delegation of duties;*
5. *State the liability of the parties after a proper delegation of duties has been made;*
6. *Describe the status of an assignee with respect to defenses and setoffs available against the assignor;*
7. *State the significance of a notice of assignment; and*
8. *State the liability of an assignor to an assignee.*

In most cases, contracts involve only the parties making the contract. In some cases, third persons may have rights under contracts made by other persons.

A. THIRD PARTY BENEFICIARY CONTRACTS

Generally, only the parties to a contract may sue on it. However, in some cases a third person who is not a party to the contract may sue on the contract.

1. Definition

A third person may sue on a contract when that benefit was intended.

When a contract is intended to benefit a third person, such a person is a **third party beneficiary** and may bring suit on and enforce the contract. In some states, the right of the third party beneficiary to sue on the contract is declared by statute.

Two parties may make a contract by which a promisor promises the other party that the promisor will make a payment of money to a third person. That is, the contracting parties intend to benefit the third person. Because of this intent, if the promisor fails to perform that promise, the third person, who is not the original promisee, may enforce the contract against the promisor.[1] Such an agreement is a **third party beneficiary contract**. A life insurance contract is a third party beneficiary contract because the insurance company promises the insured to make payment to the beneficiary. Such a contract entitles the beneficiary to sue the insurance company upon the insured's death even though the insurance company never made any agreement directly with the beneficiary.

CASE SUMMARY

You Take Care of Them

Facts: Newski purchased Peter Orville's newspaper business for $42,200. Under the terms of the sales contract, Newski agreed to pay the debts Orville owed to other creditors. Newski failed to pay these debts and was sued by Orville and the unpaid creditors. Newski raised the defense that he did not owe any money to Orville's creditors and did not have a contract with them.

Decision: Judgment for Orville and the other creditors. The provision in the sales contract providing for paying creditors made them third party beneficiaries of that contract. As such, they could sue the party to the contract who had promised to pay the debts, even though they had no contract with that person. [*Orville v Newski, Inc.* 155 App Div 2d 799, 547 NYS2d 913 (1989)]

A third person does not have the status of a third pary beneficiary unless it is clear at the time that the contract was formed that the parties intended to impose a direct obligation with respect to the third person.[2]

In determining whether there is an intent to benefit a third party, the surrounding circumstances as well as the contract must be examined. It is immaterial that the third party beneficiary did not have knowledge of the contract at the time that it was made.[3]

---

[1] *Vale Dean Canyon Homeowners Ass'n v Dean,___ Or App ___, 785 P2d 772 (1990).*
[2] *Trient Partners I v Blockbuster Entertainment Corp.* (CA5 Tex) 83 F3d 704 (1996).
[3] *OEC-Diasonics, Inc. v Major* (Ind App) 622 NE2d 1025 (1993).

There is a strong presumption that the parties to a contract intend to benefit only themselves. The fact that they know that performance of the contract will benefit third persons does not overcome this presumption and does not make such third persons third party beneficiaries of the contract.[4]

CASE SUMMARY

The Outsider for Whom Nobody Cared

Facts: The State Highway Department of South Carolina made a contract with Banks Construction to build a portion of an expressway. Banks then subcontracted with Bob Hammond Construction to do part of the work. The Highway Department knew and approved of this subcontract. Later Banks and the Highway Department canceled some of the work that was to be done under the subcontract. Hammond Construction then sued Banks and the Highway Department claiming that the reduction in the contracted for work amounted to a breach of contract. Though not in contractual privity with the Highway Department, Hammond claimed that it had a sufficient relationship with it as a third party beneficiary to the contract to support an action against it.

Decision: The subcontractor was not a third party beneficiary of the contract between the contractor and the Highway Department. That contract showed no intention of benefiting the subcontractor. The fact that the department approved the subcontract did not alter the fact that the original contract was made without any intent to benefit the subcontractor. The subcontractor was therefore merely an incidental beneficiary and had no standing to complain when the parties to the original contract modified the work to be done. [*Bob Hammond Construction Co., Inc. v Banks Construction Co. (SC App) 440 SE2d 890 (1994)*]

A third party beneficiary may be named or described by class.

(a) Description of Third Party Beneficiary. It is not necessary that the third party beneficiary be identified by name. The beneficiary may be identified by class, with the result that any member of that class is a third party beneficiary. For example, a contract between the promoter of an automobile stock car race and the owner of the race track contains a promise to pay specified sums of money to each driver racing a car in certain races. A person driving in one of the designated races is a third party beneficiary and can sue on the contract for the promised compensation.

If the contract does not express an intent to benefit a named person or a described class, a third person cannot be held to be a third party beneficiary of the contract.[5]

(b) Burden of Proof. Parties to a contract are presumed to have contracted to benefit themselves. A stranger to the contract claiming to be a third party beneficiary has the burden of proving that the contracting parties had the intention to benefit the nonparty.

2. Modification or Termination of Third Party Beneficiary Contract

A third party beneficiary's rights may be changed if a contract authorizes this.

Can the parties to the contract modify or terminate it so as to destroy the right of the third party beneficiary? If the contract contains an express provision allowing a change of beneficiaries or cancellation of the contract without the consent of the

---

[4] *Barney v Unity Paving, Inc.* (Ill App) 639 Ne2d 592 (1994).
[5] *Roskowske v Iron Mountain Forge Corp.* (Mo App) 897 SW2d 67 (1995).

third party beneficiary, the parties to the contract may destroy the rights of the third party beneficiary by acting in accordance with such a contract provision.[6]

In addition, the rights of a third party beneficiary are destroyed if the contract is discharged or ended by operation of law, for example, through bankruptcy proceedings.

For example, Roy obtained a life insurance policy from Phoenix Insurance Co. that provided the beneficiary could be changed by the insured. Roy named his son, Harry, as the beneficiary. Later, Roy had a fight with Harry and removed him as beneficiary. Roy could do this because the right to change the beneficiary was expressly reserved by the contract that created the status of the third party beneficiary.

3. Limitations on Third Party Beneficiary

A third party beneficiary is subject to any limitation in a contract.

While the third party beneficiary rule gives the third person the right to enforce the contract, it obviously gives no greater rights than the contract provides. Otherwise stated, the third party beneficiary must take the contract as it is. If there is a time limitation or any other restriction in the contract, the third party beneficiary cannot ignore it but is bound by it. Similarly, a third party beneficiary is required to arbitrate a dispute arising under the contract when the original parties to the contract were bound to arbitrate.

If the contract is not binding for any reason, that defense may be raised against the third party beneficiary suing on the contract.[7]

4. Incidental Beneficiaries

An incidental beneficiary cannot enforce a contract.

Not everyone who benefits from the performance of a contract between other persons is entitled to sue as a third party beneficiary.[8] If the benefit was intended, the third person is a third party beneficiary with the rights described in the preceding sections. If the benefit was not intended, the third person is an incidental beneficiary. The fact that the contracting parties know that the performance of their contract will benefit a third person does not in itself make that person a third party beneficiary.

A direct incidental beneficiary benefits by performance of an original contract.

(a) Direct Incidental Beneficiary. When the performance of the contract will confer a direct, although not intended, benefit on the third person, that person is a **direct incidental beneficiary.** For example, when a private employer makes a contract with the U.S. government to employ and train disadvantaged unemployed persons, such persons are merely incidental beneficiaries. They cannot sue for damages if the contract with the government is broken by the employer. Such persons are direct incidental beneficiaries because the performance of the contract would have directly benefited them.

---

[6] A common form of reservation is the life insurance policy provision by which the insured reserves the right to change the beneficiary. Section 142 of the Restatement (Second) of Contracts provides that the promisor and promisee may modify their contract and affect the right of the third party beneficiary thereby unless the agreement expressly prohibits this or the third party beneficiary has changed position in reliance on the promise or has manifested assent to it.

[7] *XL Disposal Corp. v John Sexton Contractors Co.,* ____ Ill App ____, ____ Ill Dec ____, 659 NE2d 1312 (1995).

[8] *Jahannes v Mitchell* (Ga App) 469 SE2d 255 (1996).

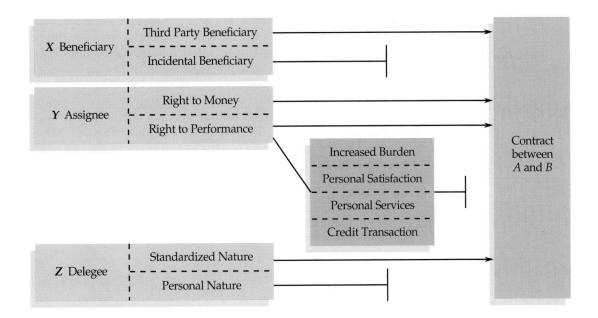

FIGURE 18-1
*Can a Third Person
Sue on a Contract?*

The fact that a contract requires one of the parties to take steps that will protect or benefit a third person does not make such person a third party beneficiary. For example, when a city hired a contractor to do excavation work, the contract specified that the contractor should be careful about underground facilities. Such care benefited the electric power company that had underground facilities. However, that direct benefit did not make the power company a third party beneficiary to the contract. The power company was merely a direct incidental beneficiary.

A contractor who has not been paid by the owner is not the third party beneficiary of the contract between the owner and the institution lending money to the owner for the construction project. Likewise, the patron of a restaurant who is injured in the restaurant cannot sue the restaurant on the theory that the patron is a third party beneficiary of the lease from the building owner to the restaurant.[9]

CASE SUMMARY

Status of Guest as to Management's Contracts

Facts: Admiral Pest Control had a standing contract with Lodging Enterprises to spray its motel every month to exterminate pests. Copeland was a guest in the motel. She was bitten by a spider. She sued Admiral on the ground that she was a third party beneficiary of the extermination contract.

Decision: Judgment against Copeland. There was no intent manifested that guests of the motel were beneficiaries of the extermination contract. That contract was made by the motel to protect itself. The guests were merely incidental beneficiaries of that contract and therefore could not sue for its breach. [*Copeland v Admiral Pest Control Co. (Okla App) 933 P2d 937 (1996)*]

---

[9] *Storts v Hardee's Food Systems, Inc.* (DC Kan) 919 F Supp 1513 (1996).

A contingent incidental beneficiary does not benefit from performance of the contract unless some other action is taken.

(b) Contingent Incidental Beneficiary.

In contrast with the incidental beneficiary who is directly benefited by the performance of the contract, the situation may be such that the third party will benefit only if the obligee of the original contract takes some further action that will benefit the third person. For example, a landlord is not a third party beneficiary of the contract by which a bank agreed to lend money to the tenant even though the tenant intended to use the money to make improvements to the rented premises. In effect, the landlord was an incidental beneficiary once removed. The landlord would benefit only (1) if the bank loaned the money to the tenant and (2) if the tenant used the money to make the improvements. Thus, the bank could perform its duty by making the loan, but if the tenant never used the money to make the improvements, the landlord would never receive any benefit from that loan. The benefit to the landlord was therefore contingent on the tenant's using proceeds of the loan for making improvements.

CASE SUMMARY

Just Too Iffy to Count

Facts: Patrick leased to the State of Michigan a tract of land that the state planned to use for a home for mentally retarded persons. There was local opposition to the construction of the home, and Patrick sold the land to third persons. Frick, and other handicapped persons who had been preliminarily selected to live in the home that would have been built on the land, brought a suit against Patrick and the buyers of the land. Frick and the other plaintiffs claimed that they were third party beneficiaries of the lease between Patrick and the state and that they could sue for the breach of Patrick's lease with the state.

Decision: The plaintiffs were not third party beneficiaries of the lease because the performance of the lease would not benefit them. They would have been benefited only if the state constructed the contemplated home and then if the proper administrative agency finally placed the plaintiffs in the home. They accordingly did not have any standing to sue for breach of the lease contract. [*Frick v Patrick*, 165 Mich App 689, 419 NW2d 55 (1988)]

(c) Ultimate user of product as incidental beneficiary.

A supplier will often sell raw materials or component parts that are used by the buyer in making a product that is sold ultimately to the person making actual use of the product. Such ultimate user is not a third party beneficiary of the contract between the supplying seller and that seller's buyer. If there is a defect in the materials or in the component parts supplied by the seller, the ultimate user cannot sue the supplier for breach of contract. The user's remedy, if any, is to be found in the fields of law governing torts and sales.

CASE SUMMARY

Ultimate User As Incidental Beneficiary

Facts: Caretta Trucking, Inc., made a contract with Colonial Yacht Sales to purchase a yacht. Colonial had the yacht built by Cheoy Lee Shipyards according to the specifications in the contract with Caretta. That contract called for painting the yacht with a specifically numbered paint manufactured by U.S. Paint Corp. The paint supplied by U.S. Paint proved defective, and Caretta was required to repaint the yacht. Caretta sued U.S. Paint for damages on the theory that it was a third party beneficiary of the contract by which U.S. Paint sold the specified paint to Cheoy Lee.

> **Decision:** Judgment against Caretta. It was not a party to the contract. The contract did not manifest any intent to benefit Caretta. The fact that Caretta would ultimately be affected by the paint did not make Caretta a third party beneficiary of the contract. [*Caretta Trucking, Inc. v Cheoy Lee Shipyards, Ltd. (Fla App) 647 So 2d 1028 (1994)*]

Where the product is specifically made for the ultimate user, such user could be a third party beneficiary of the original contract. Where the product is mass produced and mass marketed, the rule of the *Caretta* case would be applied.

(d) Consequence of Incidental Beneficiary Status. An incidental beneficiary cannot sue the parties to the contract that gave rise to the benefit or the possible benefit.

An incidental beneficiary is a stranger to the contract.

The importance of making the distinction between the direct and the contingent incidental beneficiaries lies in the value of the distinction as proof of lack of intent to benefit the third person. For example, when the performance of a contract directly benefits the third person, it is necessary to go further and determine whether the parties to the contract had intended to confer that benefit on the third person. In the case of a contingent incidental beneficiary, it is obvious that the parties to the original contract did not intend to confer a benefit on that person who would benefit only if the obligee in turn would choose to confer a benefit. Consequently, once it is established that the third party is, at best, a contingent incidental beneficiary, the lawsuit is ended, and there is no need to make further inquiry as to the intent of the original parties.

ETHICS & THE LAW

Ruth Bullis, 37, is a waitress at Stanford's Restaurant & Bar in Lake Oswego, Oregon. One evening, Bullis served a lumber broker who ordered a gin and tonic for $3.95. Before leaving, he put the tab for his drink on his American Express card and added a $1,000 tip for Bullis. Bullis verified with him that his intent was to give her the tip. Several other servers verified the tip and the fact that the lumber broker was not tipsy or addled.

After Bullis had spent the $1,000, American Express contacted Stanford's to reclaim the $1,000 because the customer had notified American Express that the tip was a mistake. After you evaluate the legal positions of the four parties (Bullis, Stanford's, American Express, and the lumber broker), consider the ethical issues of giving a tip and then revoking it.

B.   ASSIGNMENTS

The parties to a contract have both rights and duties. Can rights be transferred or sold to another person? Can duties be transferred to another person?

5.   Definitions

An assignment transfers rights.

An **assignment** is a transfer of rights. The party making the assignment is the **assignor**, and the person to whom the assignment is made is the **assignee**. An assignee of a contract may generally sue directly on the contract rather than suing in the name of the assignor.

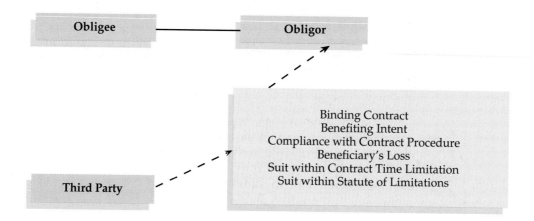

FIGURE 18-2
*What a Third Party
Beneficiary Must Prove*

Assignee's Right to Sue

CASE SUMMARY

Facts: Hendersonville Truck City, Inc., was a licensed and bonded automobile dealer. Western Surety Company was the surety that furnished the bond. NCNB National financed the purchase of new automobiles by different customers of Hendersonville. In making those sales, Hendersonville violated a state statute, and because of this the customers did not obtain clear title and were entitled to sue Western Surety for damages. These customers assigned their rights against Western Surety to NCNB, which then brought suit against Western Surety. Western Surety claimed that NCNB had no standing to sue.

Decision: NCNB had standing to sue because it was the assignee of the claims of the customers. The assignee has all the rights of the assignors and is entitled to bring any lawsuit that could have been brought by the assignors. [*NCNB National Bank v Western Surety Co. 88 NC App 705, 364 SE2d 675 (1988)*]

Contract Distinguished. An assignment is a transfer of ownership of property. It is not a contract and is therefore not required to satisfy the rules of law governing contracts.[10]

Whether or not there is consideration for the assignment does not affect the validity of the assignment. An assignment cannot be challenged by the obligor on the ground that there was no consideration. This is so because an assignment is not a contract. It is a transfer of a property right. An assignment may therefore be made as a gift, although it is usually part of a business transaction.

Every Obligation Not an Assignment

CASE SUMMARY

Facts: Mr. Carol Silverthorne owed Larry Kimes $450,000 for legal representation. Robert Mosley was a lawyer working for Kimes who worked extensively on Silverthorne's case. When Mosley left Kimes' firm, Kimes promised to pay to Mosley 20% of the fees it collected from Silverthorne. Kimes paid Mosley $24,000 of the $90,000 due. Fearing that Kimes would not pay him the remainder due, Mosley contacted Silverthorne and requested that he be paid

---

[10] *Minnesota Mutual Life Ins. Co. v Anderson* (Minn App) 504 NW2d 284 (1993).

directly by him. Silverthorne refused this request and paid his debt to Kimes in full. Kimes shortly thereafter filed for bankruptcy without paying Mosley. Mosley sued Silverthorne for the $66,000 owed him by Kimes on the theory that the amount had been assigned to him.

Decision: Judgment against Mosley. The agreement with Kimes imposed a duty upon Kimes to make payment to Mosley but it did not constitute an assignment of the right against Silverthorne. There was no intent manifested of transferring to Mosley any right held by Kimes against Silverthorne. Accordingly there was no assignment, and Mosley could not sue Silverthorne. [*Silverthorne v Mosley (Tex App) 929 SW2d 680 (1996)*]

6. Form of Assignment

Generally, an assignment may be in any form.

Generally, an assignment may be in any form. Statutes, however, may require that certain kinds of assignments be in writing or be executed in particular form. This requirement is common in statutes limiting the assignment of claims to wages.

Any words, whether written or spoken, that show an intention to transfer or assign will be given the effect of an assignment.[11] It is not necessary to use the word *assign* or *transfer*.

CASE SUMMARY

Anything Goes

Facts: The Heritage-Pulman Bank was entitled to money from certain legal proceedings. The bank's attorney wrote a letter to the attorney for Lorenzetti stating: "Our client, [the bank], has instructed us to allow your client, Carlo Lorenzetti, to collect any payments which may remain due from [plaintiff] in the [judicial proceeding]." Was this letter an assignment?

Decision: Yes. It showed the intent to transfer ownership of an identified right from one person to another. No particular words were required to constitute an assignment. The manifested intent to transfer ownership of the funds was sufficient. [*Department of Transportation v Heritage-Pulman Bank and Trust Co.,* ____ Ill App 3d ____, ____ Ill Dec ____, 627 NE2d 191 (1993)]

Since no particular words are necessary to create an assignment, an authorization to the obligor (the other party to the original contract) to pay a third person is an assignment to such third person. For example, the printed form supplied by the health insurer that reads, "I hereby authorize payment directly to the below named dentist of the group insurance benefits otherwise payable to me," constitutes an assignment to the dentist of such benefits.

7. Assignment of Right to Money

Any right to money may be assigned.

A person entitled to receive money, such as payment for the price of goods or for work done under a contract, may generally assign that right to another person.[12] A claim or cause of action against another person may be assigned. A contractor entitled to receive payment from the owner can assign that right to the bank as security for a loan or can assign it to anyone else. ◆ *For example,* Celeste owed Roscoe Painters $5,000 for painting her house. Roscoe assigned this claim to the

---

11 *Lone Mountain Production Co. v Natural Gas Pipeline Co. of America* (CA10 Utah) 984 F2d 1551 (1992).
12 *Pravin Banker Associates v Banco Popular del Peru* (CA2 NY) 109 F3d 850 (1997).

Main Street Bank. Celeste refused to pay the bank because she had never consented to the assignment. The fact that Celeste had not consented was irrelevant. Roscoe was the owner of the claim and could transfer it.

The owner of a right to money may make a partial assignment. Thus, a tenant who is owed $1,000 may wish to assign $600 of this to pay the rent to the landlord. Such a partial assignment is valid. To protect the person owing the original debt of $1,000 from being sued by two claimants, one for $600 and the other for $400, the law requires that both claimants join in a single suit against the obligor in which the recovery is sought of the original $1,000.

(a) Future Rights. By the modern rule, future and expected rights may be assigned.[13] Thus, the contractor may assign money that is not yet due under the contract because the building has not yet been constructed.

Similarly, an author may assign royalties that are expected to be received from contracts that the author expects to enter into in the future. The fact that there is nothing in existence now does not prohibit the assignment of what is expected to be existing in the future.

(b) Purpose of Assignment. The assignment of the right to money may be a complete transfer of the right that gives the assignee the right to collect and keep the money. In contrast, the assignment may be held for security. In this case, the assignee may hold the money only as security for some specified obligation. Likewise, assignment rights may be limited to collection, in which case the net amount collected is to be paid to the assignor.[14]

Assignment of rights cannot be prohibited by modern law.

(c) Prohibition of Assignment of Rights. A contract may prohibit the assignment of any rights arising under it. Some courts hold that such a prohibition is binding.

This means that an assignment made in violation of the prohibition has no effect. By the modern view, however, a prohibition against assignment has no effect. Thus, an assignment is valid even though prohibited by the contract. By this view, a provision in a construction contract that the contractor may not assign money to become due under the contract without the consent of the other contracting party is not binding. The assignee may recover the amounts due from the obligor. Under the Uniform Commercial Code, the assignment of accounts receivable cannot be prohibited by the parties.[15] A right that is otherwise assignable may be assigned even though the obligor does not consent to the assignment.[16]

8. Assignment of Right to a Performance

The right to performance may be assigned with certain exceptions.

When the contractual right of the obligee is that of receiving a performance by the other party, the obligee may ordinarily assign that right. However, if a transfer of a right to a performance would materially affect or alter a duty or the rights of the obligor, an assignment of the right to the performance is not permitted.[17] When

---

[13] *New Holland, Inc. v Trunk* (Fla App) 579 So 2d 215 (1991).
[14] *DeBenedicts v Hagen*, ____ Wash App ____, 890 P2d 529 (1995).
[15] UCC § 9-318(4), although some cases still follow the contrary pre-Code law. See, for example, *Cordis Corp. v Sonies International, Inc.* (Fla App) 427 So 2d 782 (1983).
[16] *Great Southern National Bank v McCullough Environmental Services, Inc.* (Miss) 595 So 2d 1282 (1992).
[17] *Aslakson v Home Savings Ass'n* (Minn App) 416 NW2d 786 (1987) (increase of credit risk).

an obligee is entitled to assign a right, the assignment may be done by unilateral act. There is no requirement that the obligor consent or agree. Likewise, the act of assigning does not constitute a breach of the contract unless the contract specifically declares so. The assignee of a service contract is subject to any limitations of liability contained in that contract.

The right to performance is not assignable if a burden is increased.

(a) Assignment Increasing Burden of Performance. When the assigning of a right would increase the burden of the obligor in performing, an assignment is ordinarily not permitted. To illustrate, if the assignor has the right to buy a certain quantity of a stated article and to take such property from the seller's warehouse, this right can be assigned. However, if the sales contract stipulated that the seller should deliver to the buyer's premises, and the assignee's premises were a substantial distance from the assignor's place of business, the assignment would not be given effect. In this case, the seller would be required to give a different performance by providing greater transportation if the assignment were permitted. ◆ *For example,* Savannah Roofers had a contract with Dundee Tile Factory for the purchase of roofing tiles. The contract required Dundee to deliver the tile to Savannah's warehouse, which is five miles away. Savannah assigned this contract to Achmed Roofers, located 100 miles away. The assignment is invalid because the delivery of the goods 100 miles away unreasonably increased the burden of the contract on Dundee. ◆

The right to personal performance cannot be assigned if a personal satisfaction is required.

(b) Personal Satisfaction. A similar problem arises when the goods to be furnished must be satisfactory in the personal judgment of the buyer. Because the seller contracted that the performance would stand or fall according to only the buyer's judgment, the buyer may not substitute the personal judgment of an assignee.

The right to personal services cannot be assigned.

(c) Personal Services. An employer cannot assign to another the employer's right to have an employee work.[18] The relationship of employer and employee is so personal that the right cannot be assigned. The performance contracted by the employee was to work for a particular employer at a particular place and at a particular job. To permit an assignee to claim the employee's services would be to change that contract.

The right to credit cannot be assigned.

(d) Credit Transaction. When a transaction is based on extending credit, the person to whom credit is extended cannot assign any rights under the contract to another. For example, when land is sold on credit, the buyer cannot assign the contract unless the seller consents to this. The making of an assignment is prohibited here because the assignee is a different credit risk. Whether the assignee is a better or worse credit risk is not considered.

(e) Personal Nature. A contract cannot be assigned when there is a personal aspect, such as in the case of a golf club membership.[19]

---

[18] *Mail Concepts, Inc. v Foote & Davies, Inc.,* ____ Ga App ____, 409 SE2d 567 (1991).
[19] *In re* Magness (CA6 Ohio) 972 F2d 689 (1992).

9. Rights of Assignee

Unless restricted by the terms of the assignment or applicable law, the assignee acquires all the rights of the assignor.[20]

An assignee holds the rights of the assignor.

An assignee stands exactly in the position of the assignor. The assignee's rights are no greater or less than those of the assignor. If the assigned right to payment is subject to a condition precedent, that same condition exists for the assignee. For example, when a contractor is not entitled to receive the balance of money due under the contract until all bills of suppliers of materials have been paid, the assignee to whom the contractor assigns the balance due under the contract is subject to the same condition.

10. Delegation of Duties

Standardized non-personal performance may be delegated.

A **delegation of duties** is a transfer of duties by a contracting party to another person who is to perform them. Under certain circumstances, a contracting party may obtain someone else to do the work. When the performance is standardized and nonpersonal, so that it is not material who performs, the law will permit the delegation of the performance of the contract. In such cases, however, the contracting party remains liable in the case of default of the person doing the work just as though no delegation had been made.[21] If performance involves a personal element, delegation is barred unless consented to by the person entitled to the performance.

A delegation intention must be found.

(a) Intention to Delegate Duties. An assignment does not in itself delegate the performance of duties to the assignee. In the absence of clear language in the assignment stating that duties are or are not delegated, all circumstances must be examined to determine whether there is a delegation. When the total picture is viewed, it may become clear what was intended. The fact that an assignment is made for security of the assignee is a strong indication that there was no intent to delegate to the assignee the performance of any duty resting on the assignor.[22]

A question of interpretation arises as to whether an assignment of "the contract" is only an assignment of the rights of the assignor or is both an assignment of those rights and a delegation of duties. Whether it does the latter is a question of the intent of the parties.[23] The trend of authority is to regard such a general assignment as both a transfer of rights and a delegation of duties.

CASE SUMMARY

The Package Assignment

Facts: Smith, who owned the Avalon Apartments, a condominium, sold individual apartments under contracts that required each purchaser to pay $15 a month extra for hot and cold water, heat, refrigeration, taxes, and fire insurance. Smith assigned his interest in the apartment house and under the various contracts to Roberts. When Roberts failed to pay the taxes on the building, the purchasers of the individual apartments sued to compel Roberts to do so.

---

[20] *Puget Sound National Bank v Washington Department of Revenue,* ____ Wash ____, 868 P2d 127 (1994).
[21] *Orange Bowl Corp. v Warren* (SC App) 386 SE2d 293 (1989).
[22] *City National Bank of Fort Smith v First National Bank and Trust Co. of Rogers* (Ark App) 732 SW2d 489 (1987).
[23] *Oquirrh Associates v First National Leasing Co.* (Utah App) 888 P2d 659 (1994).

> **Decision:** Judgment against Roberts. In the absence of a contrary indication, it is presumed that an assignment of a contract delegates the performance of the duties as well as transfers the rights. Here there was no indication that a package transfer was not intended, and the assignee was therefore obligated to perform in accordance with the contract terms. [*Radley v Smith and Roberts*, 6 Utah 2d 314, 313 P2d 465 (1957)]

UCC makes assignment of goods contract a delegation.

(b) Delegation of Duties under the UCC. With respect to contracts for the sale of goods, "an assignment of 'the contract' or of 'all my rights under the contract' or an assignment in similar general terms is an assignment of rights and, unless the language or the circumstances (as in an assignment for security) indicate the contrary, it is a delegation of performance of the duties of the assignor, and its acceptance by the assignee constitutes a promise . . . to perform those duties. This promise is enforceable by either the assignor or the other party to the original contract."[24]

11. Continuing Liability of Assignor

An assignor remains liable to an obligor.

The making of an assignment does not relieve the assignor of any obligation of the contract. In the absence of a contrary agreement, an assignor continues to be bound by the obligations of the original contract. Thus, the fact that a buyer assigns the right to goods under a contract does not terminate the buyer's liability to make payment to the seller. Similarly, when an independent contractor is hired to perform a party's obligations under a contract, that party is liable if the independent contractor does not properly perform the contract.

12. Liability of Assignee

Ordinarily, an assignee cannot be sued by another party.

It is necessary to distinguish between the question of whether the obligor can assert a particular defense against the assignee and the question of whether any person can sue the assignee for failing to perform the contract. Ordinarily, the assignee is not subject to suit by virtue of the fact that the assignment has been made.

Consumer protectionism imposes liability on an assignee.

(a) Consumer Protection Liability of Assignee. The assignee of a right to money typically has no relationship to the original debtor except with respect to receiving payments or collecting. Consumer protection laws, however, may subject the assignee to liability for the misconduct of the assignor. When the circumstances are such that the debtor could recover the money paid to the assignor, the debtor may recover that amount from the assignee by virtue of a Federal Trade Commission regulation preserving consumer defenses. Some state statutes go beyond this and declare that the assignee must pay the debtor the same penalties that the seller-assignor would have been required to pay under a consumer protection law.[25]

---

[24] UCC § 2-210(4).
[25] *Home Savings Ass'n v Guerra* (Tex App) 720 SW2d 636 (1986).

Assignment of Right to Money	Assignment of Right to Performance	Delegation of Duties
Prohibition in Government Contracts	Increase of Burden Personal Satisfaction Personal services Credit Transaction	Personal or Nonstandardized Performance

FIGURE 18-3
Limitations on Transfer of Rights and Duties

(b) Assignment "Subject To." The assignee of a right that is "subject to" a claim is not personally bound with respect to the payment of the claim. The "subject to" clause merely means that the other claim comes first and has priority over the rights of the assignee.[26]

An assignee is subject to the defenses and setoffs of an obligor.

(c) Defenses and Setoffs. The assignee's rights are no greater than those of the assignor. If the obligor could successfully defend against a suit brought by the assignor, the obligor will also prevail against the assignee.[27]

CASE SUMMARY

Defenses of Obligor

Facts: Bestways purchased for $50,000 from E.R.S. Technologies (E.R.S.) 10 machines called "Night Clerks" to register guests. Before delivering the machines, E.R.S. made an agreement with Royal Bank to sell the invoices and purchase orders of the Bestways' "Night Clerks" to the Bank in return for ready cash. Royal Bank would then collect the proceeds of the Bestways sale as they came in. Bestways received the machines and then refused to pay for the "Night Clerks" because they were junk. Royal Bank sued. Bestways raised the defense that the products were not merchantable and, thus, it had no obligation to pay either E.R.S. or its assignee, Royal Bank.

Decision: Judgment for Bestways. The bank was merely the assignee of ordinary contract rights. As such, it was subject to any defense of the obligor (Bestways) that the obligor could have raised against the assignor if sued by the assignor. [*Royal Bank Export Finance Co. v Bestways Distributing Co. 299 Cal App 3d 764, 280 Cal Rptr 355 (1991)*]

The fact that the assignee has given value for the assignment does not give the assignee any immunity from defenses that the other party, the obligor, could have asserted against the assignor. The rights acquired by the assignee remain subject to any limitations imposed by the contract.

Modern contract forms commonly provide that the debtor waives or will not assert against an assignee of the contract exemptions and defenses that could have been raised against the assignor. Such waivers are generally valid, although consumer protection statutes often prohibit them. Some statutes take a modified position and permit barring a buyer if, when notified of the assignment, the buyer fails to inform the assignee of the defense against the seller.

---

[26] *Winegor v Froerer Corp.* (Utah) 813 P2d 104 (1991).
[27] *Florida v Family Bank of Hallandale* (Fla App) 667 So 2d 257 (1995).

Assignments of contracts are generally made to raise money. For example, an automobile dealer assigns a customer's credit contract to a finance company and receives cash for it. Sometimes assignments are made when an enterprise closes down and transfers its business to a new owner. The availability of defenses and setoffs is the same for both cases.

13. Notice of Assignment

Assignment is effective without notice.

An assignment, if otherwise valid, takes effect the moment it is made. It is not necessary that the assignee or the assignor give notice to the other party to the contract. As a practical matter, though, the assignee should give prompt notice of the assignment to prevent improper payment of the obligation.[28]

Payment may be made to an assignor until the assignor receives notice of the assignment and direction to pay the assignee.

If the obligor is notified in any manner that there has been an assignment and that any money due must be paid to the assignee, the obligor's obligation can be discharged only by making payment to the assignee. Before the obligor is so notified, any payment made by the obligor to the assignor reduces or cancels the debt even though, as between the assignor and the assignee, it is the assignee who is entitled to the money. The only remedy of the assignee is to sue the assignor to recover the payments that were made by the obligor.

The Uniform Consumer Credit Code (UCCC) restates the protection of the consumer-debtor making payment to the assignor without knowledge of the assignment and imposes a penalty for using a contract term that would destroy this protection of the consumer

CASE SUMMARY

Why Notice of Assignment Is Important

Facts: Jimmie Machado purchased a mobile home from Crestview Mobile Housing. The contract specified that if it was assigned, Machado would pay the balance to the assignee, and that any payments otherwise made shall be at the risk of the Purchaser if not received by the assignee. Crestview assigned the contract to the Commercial Credit Corporation but did not notify Machado. Machado made payments to Crestview. Commercial demanded payment of the full amount and refused to give Machado credit for the payments he had made to Crestview. Machado then brought an action to recover the statutory penalty provided by the UCCC, claiming that the UCCC was violated because it provided that payment made to the assignor without knowledge of an assignment would bind the assignee.

Decision: The provision of the contract was a violation of the UCCC. The clause in the contract with Machado would make him liable for payments made to the assignor although he did not know that there was an assignment if the assignor did not remit those payments to the assignee. Machado was therefore entitled to recover the penalty authorized by the UCCC. [Machado v Crestview Mobile Housing (Tex App) 650 SW2d 494 (1983)]

14. Warranties of Assignor

When the assignment is made for a consideration, the assignor is regarded as impliedly warranting that the right assigned is valid. The assignor also warrants that the assignor is the owner of the claim or right assigned and that the assignor

---

[28] In some cases, an assignee will give notice of the assignment to the obligor in order to obtain priority over other persons who claim the same right or in order to limit the defenses that the obligor may raise against the assignee. UCC § 9-318.

will not interfere with the assignee's enforcement of the obligation. The assignor does not warrant that the other party will pay or perform as required by the contract.

The term *without recourse* or *no recourse* in an assignment means that the assignor does not guarantee that the obligation of the other party will be performed.[29]

SUMMARY

Ordinarily, only the parties to contracts have rights and duties with respect to such contracts. Exceptions are made in the case of third party beneficiary contracts and assignments.

When a contract shows a clear intent to benefit a third person or class of persons, those persons are called third party beneficiaries, and they may sue for breach of the contract. A third party beneficiary is subject to any limitation or restriction found in the contract. A third party beneficiary loses all rights when the original contract is terminated by operation of law or if the contract reserves the right to change beneficiaries and such a change is made.

In contrast, an incidental beneficiary benefits from the performance of a contract, but the conferring of this benefit was not intended by the contracting parties. An incidental beneficiary cannot sue on the contract.

An assignment is a transfer of a right; the assignor transfers a right to the assignee. In the absence of local statute, there are no formal requirements for an assignment. Any words manifesting the intent to transfer are sufficient to constitute an assignment. No consideration is required. Any right to money may be assigned, whether the assignor is entitled to the money at the time of the assignment or will be entitled or expects to be entitled at some time in the future. By the modern view, a contract term prohibiting the assignment of a right to money is invalid and does not prevent the making of an assignment.

A right to a performance may also be assigned except when it would increase the burden of performance, when performance under the contract is to be measured by the personal satisfaction of the obligee, or when the contract involves the performance of personal services or the credit of the person entitled to the performance.

When a valid assignment is made, the assignee has the same rights—and only the same rights—as the assignor. The assignee is also subject to the same defenses and setoffs as the assignor had been.

The performance of duties under a contract may be delegated to another person except when a personal element of skill or judgment of the original contracting party is involved. The intent to delegate duties may be expressly stated. The intent may also be found in an "assignment" of "the contract" unless the circumstances make it clear that only the right to money was intended to be transferred. The fact that there has been a delegation of duties does not release the assignor from responsibility for performance. The assignor is liable for breach of the contract if the assignee does not properly perform the delegated duties. In the absence of an effective delegation or the formation of a third party beneficiary contract, an assignee of rights is not liable to the obligee of the contract for its performance by the assignor.

Notice is not required to effect an assignment. When notice of the assignment is given to the obligor together with a demand that future payments be made to the assignee, the obligor cannot discharge liability by payment to the assignor.

When an assignment is made for a consideration, the assignor makes implied warranties that the right assigned is valid and that the assignor owns that right and will not interfere with its enforcement by the assignee. The assignor does not warrant that the obligor on the assigned right will perform the obligation of the contract.

[29] *Indiana National Bank v Oklahoma* (Okla) 880 P2d 371 (1994).

QUESTIONS AND CASE PROBLEMS

1. What social forces are affected by allowing an obligee to assign the right to obtain payment?

2. Give an example of a third party beneficiary contract.

3. A court order required John Baldassari to make specified payments for the support of his wife and child. His wife needed more money and applied for Pennsylvania welfare payments. In accordance with the law, she assigned to Pennsylvania her right to the support payments from her husband. Pennsylvania then increased her payments. Pennsylvania obtained a court order directing John, in accordance with the terms of the assignment from his wife, to make the support-order payments directly to the Pennsylvania Department of Public Welfare. John refused to pay on the ground that he had not been notified of the assignment or the hearing directing him to make payment to the assignee. Was he correct? [*Pennsylvania v Baldassari*, _____ Pa Super _____, 421 A2d 306]

4. Lee contracts to paint Sally's two-story house for $1,000. Sally realizes that she will not have sufficient money, so she transfers her rights under this agreement to her neighbor Karen, who has a three-story house. Karen notifies Lee that Sally's contract has been assigned to her and demands that Lee paint Karen's house for $1,000. Is Lee required to do so?

5. Assume that Lee agrees to the assignment of the house-painting contract to Karen as stated in question 4. Thereafter, Lee fails to perform the contract to paint Karen's house. Karen sues Sally for damages. Is Sally liable?

6. Jessie borrows $1,000 from Thomas and agrees to repay the money in 30 days. Thomas assigns the right to the $1,000 to Douglas Finance Co. Douglas sues Jessie. Jessie argues that she had agreed to pay the money only to Thomas and that when she and Thomas had entered into the transaction, there was no intention to benefit Douglas Finance Co. Are these objections valid?

7. Washington purchased an automobile from Smithville Motors. The contract called for payment of the purchase price in installments and contained the defense preservation notice required by the Federal Trade Commission regulation. Smithville assigned the contract to Rustic Finance Co. The car was always in need of repairs, and by the time it was half paid for, it would no longer run. Washington canceled the contract. Meanwhile, Smithville had gone out of business. Washington sued Rustic for the amount she had paid Smithville. Rustic refused to pay on the ground that it had not been at fault. Decide.

8. Helen obtained an insurance policy insuring her life and naming her niece Julie as beneficiary. Helen died, and about a year later the policy was found in her house. When Julie claimed the insurance money, the insurer refused to pay on the ground that the policy required that notice of death be given to it promptly following the death. Julie claimed that she was not bound by the time limitation because she had never agreed to it, as she was not a party to the insurance contract. Is Julie entitled to recover?

9. Lone Star Life Insurance Co. agreed to make a long-term loan to Five Forty Three Land, Inc., whenever requested to by that corporation. Five Forty Three wanted this loan to pay off its short-term debts. The loan was never made, as it was never requested by Five Forty Three, who owed the Exchange Bank & Trust Co. on a short-term debt. Exchange Bank then sued Lone Star for breach of its promise on the theory that the Exchange Bank was a third party beneficiary of the contract to make the loan. Was the Exchange Bank correct? [*Exchange Bank & Trust Co. v Lone Star Life Ins. Co.* (Tex App) 546 SW2d]

10. The New Rochelle Humane Society made a contract with the city of New Rochelle to capture and impound all dogs running at large. Spiegler, a minor, was bitten by some dogs while in her schoolyard. She sued the school district of New Rochelle and the Humane Society. With respect to the Humane Society, she claimed that she was a third party beneficiary of the contract that the Humane Society had made with the city. She claimed that she could therefore sue the Humane Society for its failure to capture the dogs that had bitten her. Was she entitled to recover? [*Spiegler v School District of the City of New Rochelle*, 242 NYS2d 430]

11. Zoya operated a store in premises rented from Peerless. The lease required Zoya to maintain liability insurance to protect Zoya and Peerless. Caswell entered the store, fell through a trap door, and was injured. She then sued Zoya and Peerless on the theory that she was a third party beneficiary of the lease requirement to maintain liability insurance. Was she correct? [*Caswell v Zoya International*, _____ Ill App 3d _____, _____ Ill Dec _____, 654 NE2d 552]

12. Henry was owed $10,000 by Jones Corp. In consideration of the many odd jobs performed for him over the years by his nephew, Henry assigned the $10,000 claim to his nephew, Charles. Henry died, and his widow claimed that the assignment was ineffective, so that the claim was part of Henry's estate. She based

her assertion on the ground that the past performance rendered by the nephew was not consideration. Was the assignment effective?

13. Industrial Construction Co. wanted to raise money to construct a canning factory in Wisconsin. Various persons promised to subscribe the needed amount, which they agreed to pay when the construction was completed. The construction company assigned its rights and delegated its duties under the agreement to Johnson, who then built the cannery. Vickers, one of the subscribers, refused to pay the amount that he had subscribed on the ground that the contract could not be assigned. Was he correct?

14. The Ohio Department of Public Welfare made a contract with an accountant to audit the accounts of health care providers who were receiving funds under the Medicaid program. Windsor House, which operated six nursing homes, claimed that it was a third party beneficiary of that contract and could sue for its breach. Was it correct? [*Thornton v Windsor House, Inc.,* ____ Ohio ____, 566 NE2d 1220]

CPA QUESTIONS

1. On August 1, Neptune Fisheries contracted in writing with West Markets to deliver to West 3,000 pounds of lobster at $4.00 a pound. Delivery of the lobsters was due October 1 with payment due November 1. On August 4, Neptune entered into a contract with Deep Sea Lobster Farms which provided as follows: "Neptune Fisheries assigns all the rights under the contract with West Markets dated August 1 to Deep Sea Lobster Farms." The best interpretation of the August 4 contract would be that it was
   a. Only an assignment of rights by Neptune.
   b. Only a delegation of duties by Neptune.
   c. An assignment of rights and a delegation of duties by Neptune.
   d. An unenforceable third-party beneficiary contract.

   (5/90, Law, #22)

2. Graham contracted with the city of Harris to train and employ high school dropouts residing in Harris. Graham breached the contract. Long, a resident of Harris and a high school dropout, sued Graham for damages. Under the circumstances, Long will
   a. Win, because Long is a third-party beneficiary entitled to enforce the contract.
   b. Win, because the intent of the contract was to confer a benefit on all high school dropouts residing in Harris.
   c. Lose, because Long is merely an incidental beneficiary of the contract.
   d. Lose, because Harris did **not** assign its contract rights to Long.

   (5/91, Law, #22)

3. Union Bank lent $200,000 to Wagner. Union required Wagner to obtain a life insurance policy naming Union as beneficiary. While the loan was outstanding, Wagner stopped paying the premiums on the policy. Union paid the premiums, adding the amounts paid to Wagner's loan. Wagner died and the insurance company refused to pay the policy proceeds to Union. Union may
   a. Recover the policy proceeds because it is a creditor beneficiary.
   b. Not recover the policy proceeds because it is a donee beneficiary.
   c. Not recover the policy proceeds because it is **not** in privity of contract with the insurance company.
   d. Not recover the policy proceeds because it is only an incidental beneficiary.

   (5/90, Law, #19)

Discharge of Contracts

CHAPTER 19

A. DISCHARGE BY PERFORMANCE

1. Normal Discharge of Contracts
2. Nature of Performance
3. Time of Performance
4. Adequacy of Performance
5. Guarantee of Performance

B. DISCHARGE BY ACTION OF PARTIES

6. Discharge by Unilateral Action
7. Discharge by Agreement

C. DISCHARGE BY EXTERNAL CAUSES

8. Discharge by Impossibility
9. Economic Disappointment
10. Risk of Economic Instability
11. Temporary Impossibility
12. Discharge by Operation of Law

OBJECTIVES

After studying this chapter, you should be able to

1. *List the ways in which a contract can be discharged;*
2. *Distinguish between the effect of a rejected tender of payment and a rejected tender of performance;*
3. *Define when time is of the essence;*
4. *Compare performance to the satisfaction of the other contracting parties, performance to the satisfaction of a reasonable person, and substantial performance;*
5. *State when a consumer contract may be rescinded by the consumer;*
6. *Compare the discharge of a contract by rescission, cancellation, substitution, and novation;*
7. *State the effect on a contract of the death or disability of one of the contracting parties; and*
8. *Define the concept of economic frustration.*

In the preceding chapters, you studied how a contract is formed, what it means, and who has rights under a contract. In this chapter, attention is turned to how a contract is ended or discharged. In other words, what puts an end to the rights and duties created by the contract?

A. DISCHARGE BY PERFORMANCE

When it is claimed that a contract is discharged by performance, questions arise as to the nature, time, and sufficiency of the performance.

1. Normal Discharge of Contracts

Contracts may be discharged by performance,

A contract is usually discharged by the performance of the terms of the agreement. In most cases, the parties perform their promises, and the contract ceases to exist or is thereby discharged. A contract is also discharged by the expiration of the time period specified in the contract.[1]

FIGURE 19-1
Causes of Contract Discharge

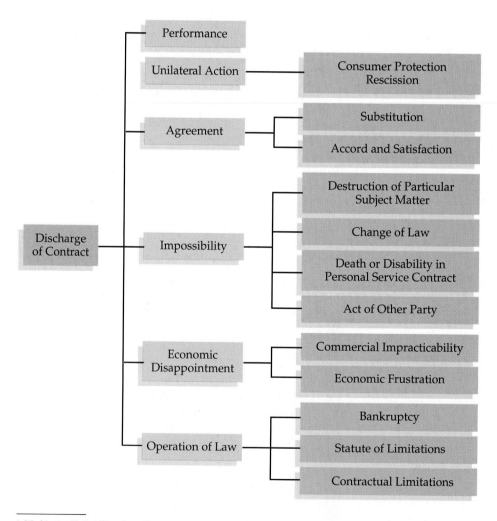

---

[1] *Washington National Ins. Co. v Sherwood Associates* (Utah App) 795 P2d 665 (1990).

2. Nature of Performance

Performance may be the doing of an act or the making of payment.

(a) Tender. An offer to perform is known as a **tender.** If performance of the contract requires the doing of an act, the refusal of a tender will discharge the party offering to perform. If performance requires the payment of a debt, however, a tender that is refused does not discharge the debt. It does stop the running of interest and does prevent the collection of court costs if the party is sued, provided the tender is kept open and the money is produced in court.

A valid **tender of payment** consists of an unconditional offer of the exact amount due on the date when due. A tender of payment is not just an expression of willingness to pay; it must be an actual offer to perform by making payment of the amount owed. The debtor must offer **legal tender** or, in other words, such form of money as the law recognizes as lawful money and declares to be legal tender for the payment of debts. The offer of a check is not a valid tender of payment because a check is not legal tender (even when it is certified). A tender of part of the debt is not a valid tender. In addition to the amount owed, the debtor must tender all accrued interest and any costs to which the creditor is entitled. If the debtor tenders less than the amount due, the creditor may refuse the offer without affecting the right to collect the amount that is due. If the creditor accepts the smaller amount, the question arises as to whether it has been accepted as payment on account or as full payment of the balance that was due.

(b) Payment. When payment is required by the contract, performance consists of the payment of money or, if accepted by the other party, the delivery of property or the rendering of services.

(1) Application of Payments. If a debtor owes more than one debt to the creditor and pays money, a question may arise as to which debt has been paid. If the debtor specifies the debt to which the payment is to be applied and the creditor accepts the money, the creditor is bound to apply the money as specified.[2] Thus, if the debtor specifies that a payment is to be made for a current purchase, the creditor may not apply the payment to an older balance.

(2) Payment by Check. Payment by commercial paper, such as a check, is ordinarily a conditional payment. A check merely suspends the debt until the check is presented for payment. If payment is then made, the debt is discharged; if not paid, the suspension terminates, and suit may be brought on either the debt or the check. Frequently, payment must be made by a specified date. It is generally held that the payment is made on time if it is mailed on or before the final date for payment.

---

2 *Oakes Logging, Inc. v Green Crow, Inc.,* ____ Wash App ____, 832 P2d 894 (1992).

The Mailed Check Payment

Facts: Thomas Cooper was purchasing land from Peter and Ella Birznieks. Cooper was already in possession of the land but was required to pay the amount owed by January 30; otherwise he would have to vacate the property. The attorney handling the transaction for the Birznieks told Cooper that he could mail the payment to him. On January 30th Cooper mailed to the attorney a personal check drawn on an out-of-state bank for the amount due. The check arrived at the Birznieks' attorney's office on February 1. The Birznieks refused to accept the check on the grounds that it was not a timely payment and moved to evict Cooper from the property.

Decision: Because of the general custom to regard a check mailed to a creditor as paying the bill that is owed, payment was made by Cooper on January 30 when he mailed the check. Payment was therefore made within the required time even though received after the expiration of the required time. [*Birznieks v Cooper* 405 Mich 319, 275 NW2d 221 (1979)]

3. Time of Performance

When the date or period of time for performance is specified in the contract, performance should be made on that date or within that time period.

(a) No Time Specified. When the time for performance is not specified in the contract, an obligation to perform within a reasonable time will be implied.[3] The fact that no time is stated neither impairs the contract on the ground that it is indefinite nor allows an endless time in which to perform.

> Performance should be made within the contract time or reasonable time if no time is specified.

(b) When Time Is Essential. If performance of the contract on or within the exact time specified is vital, it is said that "time is of the essence." Time is of the essence when the contract relates to property that is perishable or that is fluctuating rapidly in value.

An express statement in the contract that time is of the essence may not be controlling. When it is obvious that time is not important, such a statement will be ignored by the courts. It is the nature of the subject matter of the contract and the surrounding circumstances rather than the declaration of the parties that control.[4] When time is of the essence, a party who has not made timely performance of the contract cannot obtain its enforcement.[5]

(c) When Time Is Not Essential. Ordinarily, time is not of the essence, and performance within a reasonable time is sufficient. In the case of the sale of property, time will not be regarded as of the essence when there has not been any appreciable change in the market value or condition of the property and when the person who delayed does not appear to have done so for the purpose of speculating on a change in market price.

---

[3] *First National Bank v Clark* (W Va) 447 SE2d 558 (1994).
[4] *O & M Construction, Inc. v Louisiana* (La App) 576 So 2d 1030 (1991).
[5] *Smith v Potter* (Ind App) 652 Ne2d 538 (1995).

CASE SUMMARY

What's Important?

Facts: Lane sold a resort to Crescent Beach Lodge & Resort, Inc. on the installment plan. The contract required Crescent to keep the property insured and specified that the payment of the premiums when due was of the essence. Crescent did not pay the premiums when due, but the insurance company extended credit to Crescent and kept the policies in force. Lane sued Crescent to cancel the installment sale contract on the ground that Crescent had breached the contract by failing to pay the insurance on time and that time was of the essence.

Decision: There was no breach of the contract, because paying the insurance when due was not essential. The essential thing was keeping the insurance protection in force. This had been done because the insurance company had extended credit for the premiums that were due. No policy was canceled because of nonpayment of premiums, nor was any statement made by anyone that there would be a cancellation. Consequently, the late payment of the premiums did not cause Lane any loss, and it therefore was not a breach of the contract. *[Lane v Crescent Beach Lodge & Resort (Iowa) 199 NW2d 78 (1972)]*

(d) Waiver of Essence of Time Limitation. A provision that time is of the essence may be waived. It is waived when the specified time has expired but the party who could complain requests the delaying party to take steps necessary to perform the contract.[6]

4.   Adequacy of Performance

When a party renders exactly the performance called for by the contract, no question arises as to whether the contract has been performed. In other cases, there may not have been a perfect performance, or a question arises as to whether the performance made satisfies the standard set by the contract.

Substantial performance satisfies a contract in some cases.

C P A

(a) Substantial Performance. Perfect performance of a contract is not always required. A party who in good faith has substantially performed the contract may sue to recover the payment specified in the contract. However, because the performance was not perfect, the performing party is subject to a counterclaim for the damages caused the other party. When a building contractor has substantially performed the contract to construct a building, the measure of damages is the cost of repairing or correcting the defects if that can be done at a reasonable cost. If, however, the cost would be unreasonably disproportionate to the importance of the defect, such as when a virtual rebuilding of the finished building would be required to make a minor correction, the measure of damages is the difference between the value of the building as completed and the value that the building would have had if the contract had been performed perfectly.

This rule of substantial performance applies only when departures from the contract or the defects were not made willfully. A contractor who willfully makes a substantial departure from the contract is in default and cannot recover any

---

[6] *Stefanelli v Vitale,* ____ App Div 2d ____, 636 NYS2d 50 (1996).

O
P
A

payment from the other party to the contract. In large construction contracts when the total value of the partial performance is large compared to the damages sustained through incomplete or imperfect performance, the courts tend to ignore whether the breach was intentional or not.

Performance is not substantial when the finished product does not have some use.

(1) What Constitutes Substantial Performance. There is no exact standard or test by which to determine whether a performance is substantial.[7] In connection with a construction contract, "substantial performance" is performance that in spite of deviations or omissions does provide the promisee with the important and essential benefits of the contract. Whether there is such performance is a question of degree to be determined by consideration of all the facts, including the particular type of structure involved, its intended purposes, and the nature and relative expenses of repairs. A performance cannot be regarded as substantial if what has been done is of no use to the defendant. ◆ *For example,* when a contractor failed to follow specifications for the construction of a swimming pool and the result was a pool that was so cracked that it would not hold water, the work of the contractor was not of any use to the other party. Therefore, the contractor could not recover on the ground of substantial performance. The performance of a road contractor was not substantial when the deviations from the contract specifications made the road significantly less durable than it would have been had the specificationsbeen followed.[8] ◆

CASE SUMMARY

When Perfection Not Required

Facts: The Beeson Company made a contract to construct a shopping center for Sartori. Before the work was fully completed, Sartori stopped making the payments to Beeson that were required by the contract. The contract provided for liquidated damages of $1,000 per day if Beeson failed to substantially complete the project within 300 days of the beginning of construction. The contract also provided for a bonus of $1,000 for each day Beeson completed the project ahead of schedule. Beeson then stopped working and sued Sartori for the balance due under the contract, just as though it had been fully performed. Sartori defended on the ground that Beeson had not substantially completed the work. Beeson proved that Sartori had been able to rent most of the stores in the center.

Decision: The fact that the shopping center could be used for its intended purpose, that of renting stores to others, showed that there had been a substantial performance of the contract. The contractor therefore could recover the contract price less any amount required to complete the construction. [*J.M. Beeson Co. v Sartori (Fla App) 553 So 2d 180 (1989)*]

---

(2) Applicability of Substantial Performance Rule. Although most commonly applied in the case of construction contracts, the substantial performance rule is applicable to any contract. ◆ *For example,* it has been held that the publisher of the telephone book Yellow Pages could recover from a customer under this rule, although it had failed to include a discount coupon in the phone book to be used in paying for work done by the customer.[9] ◆

---

[7] *VRT, Inc. v Dutton-Lainson Co.,* ____ Neb ____, 530 NW2d 619 (1995).
[8] *County Asphalt Paving Co. v 1861 Group, Ltd.* (Mo App) 851 SW2d 577 (1993).
[9] *Southwestern Bell Yellow Pages, Inc. v Robbins* (Mo App) 865 SW2d 361 (1993).

(3) Limitations to Substantial Performance Doctrine. The doctrine of substantial performance will not be applied when the contract makes it clear that a literal and exact compliance is required. When a contract requires the payment of a specific sum of money by a certain date, the full amount is not enforceable as substantial performance even though it equals 90 percent of the required amount.[10]

Substantial performance does not apply to a condition precedent.

The doctrine of substantial performance does not apply to a condition precedent. Consequently, a lender, obligated to lend a specified amount for the purchase and renovation of an office building, was excused from making the loan when the duty to lend was subject to a condition precedent that a specific number of office space leases had to be signed but the required number was not obtained. The borrower's claim that the substantial performance rule should be applied to hold that there was a sufficient compliance with the rental condition was rejected.

(b) Fault of Complaining Party. A party cannot complain that a performance was defective when the performance follows the terms of the contract required by the complaining party. Thus, a homeowner who supplied the specifications for poured cement walls cannot hold a contractor liable for damages when the walls that were poured in exact compliance with those specifications proved defective.

A contract may require satisfaction of a promisee or third person.

(c) Satisfaction of Promisee or Third Person. Sometimes an agreement requires that the promisor perform an act to the satisfaction, taste, or judgment of the other party to the contract. The courts are divided over whether the promisor must so perform the contract as to satisfy the promisee or whether it is sufficient that the performance be such as would satisfy a reasonable person under the circumstances. When personal taste is an important element, the courts generally hold that the performance is not sufficient unless the promisee is actually satisfied. However, most courts insist that the dissatisfaction be shown to be in good faith and not merely to avoid paying for the work that has been done.[11] The personal satisfaction of the promisee is generally required under this rule when one promises to make clothes or to paint a portrait to the satisfaction of the other party. There is a similar division of authority when the subject matter involves the fitness or mechanical utility of property. With respect to things mechanical and to routine performances, however, courts are more likely to hold that the promisor has satisfactorily performed if a reasonable person should be satisfied with what was done.

When a building contract requires the contractor to perform the contract to the "satisfaction" of the owner, the owner generally is required to pay if a reasonable person would be satisfied with the work of the contractor.

When performance is to be approved by a third person, the tendency is to apply the reasonable-person test of satisfaction. This is true especially when the third person has wrongfully withheld approval or has become incapacitated. When work is to be done subject to the approval of an architect, engineer, or other expert, the determination of that expert is ordinarily final and binding on the parties in the absence of fraud.

---

[10] *Ujdur v Thompson* (Idaho App) 878 P2d 180 (1994).
[11] *Kohler v Leslie Hindman, Inc.* 80 F3d 1181 (7th Cir 1996).

When You Can't Be Too Choosy

Facts: Repp purchased a used farm combine from McSweeney Tractor Company. The seller stated that the combine would be made field ready and that it would be made to work to the satisfaction of the buyer. On eleven occasions something went wrong with the combine. More often than not it was the harvesting mechanism which broke down, although the drive train sometimes required some sort of repair. Every time a breakdown occurred, it was promptly repaired by the seller at no cost to Repp. However, Repp refused to pay the balance of the purchase price. Empire South purchased the McSweeney Tractor Company and brought suit against Repp for the balance of the purchase price. The trial court determined that a reasonable person would have been satisfied with the combine in view of the no-cost repairing of all defects. Repp claimed that nevertheless he was not satisfied and therefore was not liable.

Decision: Judgment against Repp. Although the combine had been sold on the basis that he would be satisfied, the satisfaction was to be objectively determined. Therefore, his subjective dissatisfaction did not relieve him from liability because the facts were such that a reasonable person would have been satisfied. [*Empire South, Inc. v Repp, 51 Wash App 868, 756 P2d 745 (1988)*]

5. Guarantee of Performance

Performance may be guaranteed by an obligor or a third person.

It is common for an obligor to guarantee the performance. Thus, a builder may guarantee for one year that the work will be satisfactory. The guarantee may be made by a third person. Thus, a surety company may guarantee to the owner that a contractor will perform the contract. In this case, it is clear that the obligation of the surety is in addition to the liability of the contractor and does not take the place of such liability.

B. DISCHARGE BY ACTION OF PARTIES

Contracts may be discharged by the joint action of both contracting parties or, in some cases, by the action of one party alone.

6. Discharge by Unilateral Action

Generally, a contract cannot be discharged by unilateral action.

Ordinarily, a contract cannot be discharged by the action of either party alone. In some cases, the contract will give one or either party the right to cancel the contract by unilateral action, such as by notice to the other party.[12] Insurance policies covering loss commonly provide that the insurer may cancel the policy upon giving a specified number of days' notice.

If the contract does not specify any duration, or it states a duration in such vague terms as "for life," the contract may be terminated by either party at will.

(a) Consumer Protection Rescission. A basic principle of contract law is that a contract between competent persons is a binding obligation. Consumer protection legislation is introducing into the law a contrary concept—that of giving the consumer a chance to think things over and to rescind the contract. Thus, the federal Consumer Credit Protection Act (CCPA) gives the debtor the right to rescind a

---

[12] *Cherokee Communications, Inc. v Skinny's, Inc.* (Tex App) 893 SW2d 313 (1994).

credit transaction within three business days when the transaction would impose a lien on the debtor's home. ◆ *For example,* a homeowner who mortgages the home to obtain a loan may cancel the transaction for any reason by notifying the lender before midnight of the third full business day after the loan is made.[13] ◆

A Federal Trade Commission regulation gives the buyer three business days in which to cancel a home-solicited sale of goods or services costing more than $25.[14]

ETHICS & THE LAW

H&H Concrete, Inc., was awarded the contract for supplying concrete for work at the Consolata Cemetery in the Lake Charles, Louisiana, area. Civicon, Inc., was serving as the subcontractor for all cement work for the general contractor, The Chelsea Group.

Section 8 of the H&H contract provided:

> *The Seller will not, however, be responsible for failure to make delivery when prevented by strikes or other labor troubles, accidents or necessary repairs to machinery, by fire, floods or other adverse weather conditions, by inability to procure transportation, electric power, or operating materials or machinery, by Government regulations, requirements, or orders, by acts of public enemies, mobs or rioters, by acts of God, or by any other causes beyond the Seller's control. The Seller reserves the right to refuse to make deliveries when it believes unsafe or impracticable by reason of any existing or threatened strikes, lockout, picket or other labor dispute.*

H&H delivered concrete to the site according to the terms of the contract until April 1986. In April 1986, H&H was unable to obtain liability insurance for its trucks. H&H officers notified Civicon that it was closing its operations. Civicon sent a letter to H&H with the following language:

> *This correspondence will serve as notice of cancellation of the referenced purchase order. Due to the insurance situation with your company it will be to our best advantage to contract with another supplier for the 3500 PSI concrete needed.*

H&H assumed that the letter was a mutual rescission of its contract with Civicon. Civicon did not pay H&H for its work through April, so H&H brought suit against Civicon seeking payment. Civicon claimed H&H had breached the agreement, that it had hired another concrete supplier resulting in additional cost, and that the quality of the concrete H&H furnished was so poor that much of the work had to be redone. H&H said that paragraph 8 in the contract discharged it from its duty to perform. Do you agree? Did H&H have a legal obligation to lease trucks for delivery? Did H&H have an ethical obligation to do so? Did Civicon mislead H&H with the letter? Do you think H&H was legally and ethically discharged from the contract? *H&H Concrete, Inc. v Civicon, Inc.* (La) 533 So.2d 1294 (1988).

---

[13] If the owner is not informed of this right to cancel, the three-day period does not begin until that information is given. In any case, however, the right to cancel is lost if the owner sells the house or three years elapse after the loan transaction. Consumer Credit Protection Act § 125, 15 USC § 1635 (a), (e), (f).

[14] CFR § 429.1 This displaces state laws making similar provision for rescission, such as UCCC § 2.502.

7. Discharge by Agreement

A contract may be discharged by an agreement contained in an original contract or subsequently made.

A contract may be discharged by the operation of one of its provisions or by a subsequent agreement. Thus, there may be a discharge by (1) the terms of the original contract, such as a provision that the contract should end on a specified date; (2) a mutual cancellation, in which the parties agree to end their contract; (3) a mutual **rescission**, in which the parties agree to annul the contract and return both parties to their original positions before the contract had been made;[15] (4) the substitution of a new contract between the same parties; (5) a novation or substitution of a new contract involving a new party;[16] (6) an accord and satisfaction; (7) a release; or (8) a waiver. To constitute a novation, it must be shown that an obligor to the original contract was released from liability and that the new party to the second contract was accepted in substitution for the original obligor.

CASE SUMMARY

The Escape Hatch and the Contract

Facts: Phoebe Szatmari provided child day care services for Ellen and David Rosenbaum's infant daughter Lorraine. The contract between them provided that Phoebe would care for the child and that either the parents or Phoebe could terminate the arrangement on four weeks' notice. After several years, Phoebe wrote the parents that she gave notice to terminate the arrangement and that she offered them four weeks in which to make other arrangements. The parents replied that they rejected the offer and claimed that Phoebe was breaking the contract.

Decision: The contract between the parties gave both sides the power to terminate at any time upon notice. When this power of termination was exercised by one party, the other party could not reject the termination. The use of the word *offer* by Phoebe was not a correct use of the term because there was no offer in the true sense, in that the parents could not reject or accept as they chose. The parents, having bound themselves by a contract that gave the other party the power to terminate, could only recognize the fact that the contract was terminated and could not insist that the contract was still in force. [*Szatmari v Rosenbaum*, 490 NYS2d 97 (1985)]

Substitution discharges a contract by substituting a new contract between the original parties.

(a) Substitution. The parties may decide that their contract is not the one they want. They may then replace it with another contract. If they do, the original contract is discharged by substitution.[17]

CASE SUMMARY

Do We Have a New Contract?

Facts: Paul Shires made a contract to build a house for Marion Priem. Disputes arose between them as to whether the house had been properly built in a good and workmanlike manner. Shires and Priem executed a contract in which it was agreed that Shires would make repairs to the house's foundation and structure that would correct the defects of which Priem complained. These repairs were not made and Priem then sued Shires for breach of the original construction contract.

---

15 *Agri Careers, Inc. v Jepsen* (Iowa App) 463 NW2d 93 (1990).
16 *Eagle Industries, Inc. v Thompson*, ____ Or ____, 900 P2d 475 (1995). In a few jurisdictions, the term *novation* is used to embrace the substitution of any new contract, whether between the original parties or not.
17 *Shawnee Hospital Authority v Dow Construction, Inc.* (Okla) 812 P2d 1351 (1990).

> **Decision:** Suit could not be brought on the original construction contract. The repair contract clearly showed the intention to replace the original contract with the terms of the new repair contract. The original contract was thus discharged by the making of the subsequent contract, and the only contract on which Priem could sue was the second or repair contract. *[Priem v Shires (Tex App) 697 SW2d 860 (1985)]*

It is not necessary for the parties to state expressly that they are making a substitution. Whenever they make a new contract that is clearly inconsistent with a former contract, the court will conclude that the earlier contract has been superseded by the later. Because the new contract must in itself be a binding agreement, it must be supported by consideration. Any suit brought thereafter must show a breach of the second or subsequent contract.

The fact that a second contract is entered into does not establish that the original contract is canceled. The later contract may merely add to or supplement the original contract, or it may merely modify part of the original contract. For the later contract to displace the first, the later contract must show the intent of the parties to substitute the later contract for the earlier contract. This intent may be shown by an express statement in the later contract that the parties thereby cancel or set aside the earlier contract. Alternatively, the later contract may be so complete and so inconsistent with the earlier writing that the intent is clear that the later writing was a substitute for the earlier one.

The agreement modifying the original contract may be expressed in words or by conduct, but in any event it is essential that an agreement to modify be found.[18] When one party to a contract proposes a modification but the other party ignores the proposal, the contract remains unmodified.[19]

A written contract may be modified by a subsequent oral agreement even though the contract itself prohibits oral modification. However, the modification contract must be evidenced by a writing when the modified contract comes within the statute of frauds.

When a provision may be orally waived, it may be waived by a fax transmission so stating.[20]

(b) Accord and Satisfaction. In lieu of the performance of an obligation specified by a contract, the parties may agree to a different performance. Such an agreement is called an **accord.** When the accord is performed or executed, there is an **accord and satisfaction,** which discharges the original obligation. To constitute an accord and satisfaction, there must be a bona fide dispute, an agreement to settle the dispute, and performance of the agreement.[21] To constitute a bona fide dispute, the parties must assert their respective positions in good faith. If one of the parties to the accord and satisfaction owes a fiduciary duty to the other party, such as an attorney to a client, there must be a full disclosure of all material facts by the party under the fiduciary duty.

The accord that is the basis for the accord and satisfaction must be a binding agreement—that is, a contract. It must therefore meet the basic requirements of a

> An accord and satisfaction discharges a contract when there is an agreement to do so and the terms of the agreement are performed.

---

18 *Medina v Sunstate Realty, Inc.* (MN) 889 P2d 171 (1995)
19 *Solar Motors, Inc. v First National Bank,* ____ Neb ____, 545 NW2d 714 (1996).
20 *Baker v Norman* (App Div) 643 NYS 2d 30 (1996).
21 *S&G, Inc. v Intermountain Power Agency* (Utah) 913 P2d 735 (1996).

simple contract. If it is not a contract (for example, if it is not supported by consideration), there is no binding accord, and the prior contract is not discharged. The making of an accord does not by itself discharge the prior contract. It is not until the terms of the accord are carried out that there is a discharge of the earlier contract.

CASE SUMMARY

It Takes More to Wipe the Slate Clean

Facts: Christopher Bloom received a medical school scholarship created by the U.S. Department of Health and Human Services to increase the number of doctors serving rural areas. In return for this assistance Bloom agreed to practice four years in a region identified as being under-served by medical professionals. After some problems with his post-graduation assignment, Bloom requested a repayment schedule from the agency. Although no terms were offered, Bloom tendered to the agency two checks totalling $15,500 and marked "Final Payment." Neither check was cashed, and the government sued Bloom for $480,000, the value of the assistance provided. Bloom claimed that by tendering the checks to the agency his liability had been discharged by an accord and satisfaction.

Decision: Bloom was wrong. There is no discharge by accord and satisfaction unless the creditor agreed to accept the tendered sum in discharge of a disputed claim and had accepted the sum so tendered. Here there was no agreement to accept or any acceptance by the government of the checks tendered. There was no discharge by accord and satisfaction. *[United States v Bloom (CA7 La) 112 F3d 200 (1997)]*

C.   DISCHARGE BY EXTERNAL CAUSES

Circumstances beyond the control of the contracting parties may discharge the contract.

8.   Discharge by Impossibility

Circumstances beyond control of the parties may discharge a contract by impossibility.

Impossibility of performance refers to external or extrinsic conditions. This is contrasted with the obligor's personal inability to perform.[22] Thus, the fact that a debtor does not have the money to pay and cannot pay a debt does not present a case of impossibility.

CASE SUMMARY

Personal Inability Not an Impossibility

Facts: Frank and Vetra Denis, husband and wife, jointly owned a plot of land in Hawaii. Frank made a contract to sell the land to Cynthia Warner for $455,000. Vetra did not authorize her husband to sell her undivided one-half interest in the property and would not consent to the sale. Warner sued Frank Denis for breach of contract. Frank raised the defense of impossibility since, absent his wife's express authority, he was powerless to contract for the sale of any interest in the property.

---

[22] *Haessly v Safeco Title Ins. Co.* (Idaho) 825 P2d 1119 (1992).

> **Decision:** Without the consent of Vetra, Frank could not convey the title to the buyer. This was not an "impossibility" that discharged Frank from his contract as there was nothing unforeseeable about the necessity of getting the consent of the wife. Frank was therefore liable to Warner for breach of his contract to convey the land to Warner. [*Warner v Dennis (Haw App) 933 P2d 1372 (1997)*]

Riots, shortages of materials, and similar factors, even though external, usually do not excuse the promisor from performing a contract. A seller may have contracted to sell goods to a buyer. The fact that the seller cannot obtain these goods from any supplier does not excuse the seller from liability to the buyer unless the inability to procure the goods was made a condition subsequent to the sales contract. *For example,* if a contractor's contemplated gravel source cannot be used (and it is necessary to transport gravel from a more distant source, making performance more costly) does not discharge the contractor from the obligation to construct a road. If there is nothing in the contract requiring that the gravel be obtained from the unavailable source, no question of impossibility of performance exists. A contract is not discharged merely because performance proves to be more burdensome than was originally contemplated.[23]

The fact that it will prove more costly to perform the contract than originally contemplated or that the obligor has voluntarily gone out of business does not constitute impossibility that excuses performance. No distinction is made in this connection between the acts of nature, people, or governments. For example, the adoption of a new government regulation made performance more costly. The contract was not discharged when the regulation was reasonably foreseeable because it was common in many parts of the country.

The fact that performance is not possible does not discharge the contract when the contract has placed that risk upon the obligor.[24]

CASE SUMMARY

Does the Contract Allocate the Risk?

Facts: The Transatlantic Financing Corp. made a contract with the United States to haul a cargo of wheat from the United States to a safe port in Iran. The normal route lay through the Suez Canal. As the result of the nationalization of the canal by Egypt and a subsequent international crisis that developed, the canal was closed, and it was necessary for Transatlantic to go around Africa to get to the destination. It then sued for additional compensation because of the longer route on the theory that it had been discharged from its obligation to carry to Iran for the amount named in the contract because of what Transatlantic called impossibility.

Decision: Judgment for United States. Although impossibility does not mean literally impossible, it may be apparent from the contract that the risk of performance becoming commercially impracticable was assumed by one of the parties. In that case, such impracticability is necessarily not a defense that the party may raise. Since no route was specified and everyone was aware of the problems of international shipping, the unqualified contract to deliver the cargo at a specified point must be interpreted as indicating that the carrier assumed the risk that the shorter route through the Suez Canal might not be available; the carrier thus assumed the risk of impossibility. [*Transatlantic Financing Corp. v United States (CA Dist Col) 363 F2d 312 (1966)*]

---

[23] *Stasyszyn v Sutton East Associates,* _____ App Div 2d _____, 555 NYS2d 297 (1990).
[24] *Wheelabrator Envirotech Operating Services Inc. v Massachusetts Laborers District Council* (CA1 Mass) 88 F3d 40 (1996).

(a) Destruction of Particular Subject Matter. When parties contract expressly for or with reference to a particular subject matter, the contract is discharged if the subject matter is destroyed through no fault of either party. When a contract calls for the sale of a wheat crop growing on a specific parcel of land, the contract is discharged if that crop is destroyed by blight.

On the other hand, if there is merely a contract to sell a given quantity of a specified grade of wheat, the seller is not discharged when the seller's crop is destroyed by blight. The seller had made an unqualified undertaking to deliver wheat of a specified grade. No restrictions or qualifications were imposed as to the source. If the seller does not deliver the goods called for by the contract, the contract is broken, and the seller is liable for damages.

The parties may by their contract allocate the risk of loss. Thus, a contract for the sale of a building and land may specify that any loss from damage to the building should be borne by the seller.

(b) Change of Law. A contract is discharged when its performance is made illegal by a subsequent change in the law. Thus, a contract to construct a non-fireproof building at a particular place is discharged by the adoption of a zoning law prohibiting such a building within that area. Mere inconvenience or temporary delay caused by the new law, however, does not excuse performance. Similarly, a change of law that merely increases the cost to the promisor is not a "change of law" that discharges the contract. There is authority that the deregulating of an industry is not a change of law that discharges a contract entered into on the assumption of continuing regulation.

CASE SUMMARY

Regulation Change Ignored

Facts: N.C. Coastal Motor Line was authorized by the Interstate Commerce Commission to engage in interstate trucking operations. It made a contract to sell this authority to Everette Truck Line. Payment was to be made in eight annual installments. At the time of making the contract, it was unlawful to engage in interstate trucking without such an authority. Everette made four annual payments. The trucking industry was then deregulated by the government, and the authority of the Interstate Commerce Commission was no longer required to engage in interstate trucking. Everette refused to make any more payments on the ground that what it was paying for was worthless. N.C. Coastal sued Everette.

Decision: Judgment for Coastal. While the authority had no value when the industry was deregulated, that fact did not discharge the contract. There was no implied term that the subject matter of the contract would retain its original economic value. The loss of value therefore did not discharge the contract. [*N.C. Coastal Motor Line, Inc. v Everette Truck Line, Inc.* 77 NC App 149, 334 SE2d 499 (1985)]

(c) Death or Disability. When the contract obligates a party to perform an act that requires personal skill or that contemplates a personal relationship with the obligee or some other person, the death or disability of the obligor, obligee, or other person (as the case may be) discharges the contract.[25] For example, the death of a newspaper cartoonist before the expiration of the contract discharges the contract.

---

[25] *Cazares v Saenz*, 208 Cal App 3d 279, 256 Cal Rptr 209 (1989).

If the act called for by the contract can be performed by others or by the promisor's personal representative, however, the contract is not discharged.

The death of a person to whom personal services are to be rendered also terminates the contract when the death of that person makes impossible the rendering of the services contemplated. Thus, a contract to employ a person as the musical director for a singer terminates when the singer dies.

When the contract calls for the payment of money, the death of either party does not affect the obligation. If the obligor dies, the obligation is a liability of the obligor's estate. If the obligee dies, the right to collect the debt is an asset of the obligee's estate. The parties to a contract may agree, however, that the death of either the obligee or the obligor shall terminate the debt. In any case, the creditor can obtain insurance on the life of the debtor.

(d) Act of Other Party. Every contract contains "an implied covenant of good faith and fair dealing." As a result of this covenant, a promisee is under an obligation to do nothing that would interfere with performance by the promisor. When the promisee prevents performance or otherwise makes performance impossible, the promisor is discharged from the contract. Thus, a subcontractor is discharged from any obligation when unable to do the work because the principal contractor refuses to deliver the material, equipment, or money required by the subcontract. When the default of the other party consists of failing to supply goods or services, the duty may rest on the party claiming a discharge of the contract to show that substitute goods or services could not be obtained elsewhere.

When the conduct of the other contracting party does not make performance impossible but merely causes delay or renders performance more expensive or difficult, the contract is not discharged. The injured party is, however, entitled to damages for the loss incurred.

A promisor is not excused from performing under the contract when it is the act of the promisor that has made performance impossible. Consequently, when a data service contracted with a bank to process the records of its daily operations, the bank was not excused from its obligation under the contract by the fact that it installed its own computers. The bank could not ignore its contract. It could terminate the contract with the data service only by giving the notice required by the contract.

9. Economic Disappointment

A bad bargain does not discharge a contract.

The fact that the contract proves to be a bad bargain does not discharge the contract.[26] Some courts hold that a contract is discharged when, because of a change of circumstances, the performance of the contract has become such an economic disappointment that it would be unjust and oppressive to insist on performance.

(a) Commercial Impracticability. At times, the cost of performance rises suddenly and so greatly that performance of the contract will result in a substantial loss. In this case, some courts hold that the contract is discharged because it is **commercially impracticable** to perform. Although it is possible to perform, it has become such a bad bargain that the courts will not enforce it.

---

[26] *Young v Tate*, 232 Neb 915, 442 NW2d 865 (1989).

When subsequent developments prove to be different than was assumed by the parties, there is a growing trend to find that there is an impossibility that discharges the contract. This doctrine is described as the doctrine of **supervening impracticability**.

After a contract is made, it may happen that a party's performance is made impracticable by the occurrence of an event, the nonoccurrence of which was the basic assumption on which the contract was made. In such a case, the duty to render that performance is discharged unless the language or the circumstances indicate the contrary.[27]

Some courts regard a contract as discharged by economic frustration when value of performance drops greatly.

(b) Economic Frustration. Because of a change of circumstance, the performance of the contract may have no value to the party entitled to receive performance. Some courts sympathize with the disappointed person and hold that the contract is discharged by economic or commercial frustration or frustration of purpose.

Relief for Broken Dreams

Facts: John J. Paonessa Company made a contract with the State of Massachusetts to reconstruct a portion of highway. It then made a contract with Chase Precast Corp. to obtain concrete median barriers for use in the highway. Thereafter, the State Highway Department decided that such barriers would not be used. Paonessa therefore had no reason to go through with the contract to purchase the barriers from Chase because it could not use them and could not get paid for them by the state. Chase sued Paonessa for the profit Chase would have made on the contract for the barriers.

Decision: Judgment for Paonessa. The change to the highway construction plan made by the State Department of Highways made the barriers worthless. There was accordingly a frustration of the purpose for which the contract had been made to purchase the barriers. Therefore, the contract for the median barriers was discharged by such frustration of purpose and did not bind Paonessa. [*Chase Precast Corp. v John J. Paonessa Co., Inc. 409 Mass 371, 566 NE2d 603 (1991)*]

Traditional contract law requires literal impossibility in order to protect the stability of contracts.

(c) The Majority Rule Compared. The majority or traditional common law rule refuses to recognize commercial impracticability or economic frustration. By the common law rule, the losses and disappointments against which commercial impracticability and economic frustration give protection are merely the risks that one takes in entering into a contract. Moreover, the situations could have been guarded against by including an appropriate condition subsequent in the contract. A condition subsequent declares that the contract will be void if a specified event occurs. Or the contract could have provided for a readjustment of compensation if there was a basic change of circumstances. The common law approach also rejects these two new concepts because they weaken the stability of a contract. The net result of these new concepts is that a contract ceases to be binding when there is a significant change in circumstances. That is, when a contract is most needed to give stability, the courts by these new concepts hold that there is no contract.

The common law rule is also opposed to the new concepts because they raise questions of measurement of matters that cannot be measured. How much change is needed in order to make a change "significant"?

---

[27] Restatement (Second) of Contracts, § 261.

In spite of the logical and practical objections to the new doctrines, it is likely that they will be given greater recognition by the courts in the future. The expanded recognition of the doctrine of unconscionability is developing a pattern of the judicial monitoring of contracts to prevent injustice. Further indication of a wider recognition of the concept that "extreme" changes of circumstances can discharge a contract is found in the Uniform Commercial Code. The UCC provides for the discharge of a contract for the sale of goods when a condition that the parties assumed existed, or would continue, ceases to exist.[28]

If a contract clearly places on one of the parties a particular risk, the contract is not discharged when that risk is realized and loss is sustained. Neither the concept of commercial impracticability nor that of economic frustration will be applied to cancel out provisions of a contract that allocate risk.[29]

CASE SUMMARY

Victims of Technology Change

Facts: Twelve railroads coming into Kansas City, Missouri, formed the Kansas City Terminal Railway Company. Each of the railroads owned an equal share of the terminal company. By an agreement with the terminal company made in 1909, the railroads agreed to a plan of contributing to the expenses for maintaining the facilities at the terminal owned by the terminal company. By 1969, competing methods of transportation had caused a serious drop in the mail and passenger service of the railroads. One of the twelve railroads, the Atchison, Topeka and Sante Fe Railway Company, claimed that because of these changed traffic patterns, the agreement had become unreasonable and was not binding.

Decision: The agreement was binding on the railroads as written. There was no ambiguity. The provisions of the clear contract could not be changed by the court merely because transportation conditions proved to be different than had been originally contemplated. [*Kansas City Terminal Railway Co. v Atchison, Topeka and Santa Fe Railway Co.* (Mo App) 512 SW2d 415 (1974)]

(d) Bad Bargain Distinguished. The mere fact that a party to a contract sustained a loss when an expected profit is not realized does not constitute economic frustration. It is immaterial whether the disappointment is caused by the poor way in which the contract was written or by circumstances external to the contract.

◆ *For example,* a contract for the sale of a gasoline station that required the seller to correct contamination caused by gas leakage remained binding although the cleanup cost was much greater than the seller had expected.[30] ◆

10. Risk of Economic Instability

Every long-term commercial transaction is affected by the condition of the national economy. The fact that "times are bad" does not excuse the failure to perform such a contract.

---

[28] UCC § 2-615.
[29] *Alaska v Carpenter* (Alaska) 869 P2d 1181 (1994).
[30] *Bond Drug Co. of Illinois v Amoco Oil Co.,* ____ Ill App 3d ____, ____ Ill Dec ____, 654 NE2d 540 (1995).

Tough Times No Excuse

Facts: Charles Dorr borrowed $271,600 from the Federal Land Bank. He failed to repay the loan. When sued for the money, Dorr raised the defense that he was unable to repay the loan because the U.S. government had adopted a pricing subsidy and trade policy that made it impossible for Dorr to repay the loan.

Decision: Dorr was not excused by the economic conditions. There was nothing in the loan agreement that made repayment conditional upon the state of the economy. When Dorr obtained the loan it was foreseeable that "times" could change, and when they did there was merely the realization of a foreseeable event. That was a risk that Dorr took in obtaining the loan, and he was not excused from performing his part of the contract of repaying the loan. [*Farm Credit Bank v Dorr*, _____ Ill App 3d _____, _____ Ill Dec _____, 620 NE2d 549 (1993)]

11. Temporary Impossibility

Temporary impossibility generally merely delays but does not discharge a contract.

Ordinarily, either a temporary impossibility has no effect on the performance obligation of a party or at most it suspends the duty to perform. If the obligation to perform is suspended, it is revived on the termination of the impossibility. If, however, performance at that later date would impose a substantially greater burden on the obligor, some courts discharge the obligor from the contract.

(a) Weather. Acts of God, such as tornadoes, lightning, and floods, usually do not terminate a contract even though they make performance difficult or impossible. Thus, weather conditions constitute a risk that is assumed by a contracting party in the absence of a contrary agreement. Consequently, extra expense sustained by a contractor because of weather conditions is a risk that the contractor assumes in the absence of an express provision for additional compensation in such a case. ◆ *For example*, Danielo Contractors made a contract to construct a shopping mall for the Rubicon Center, with construction to begin November 1. Because of abnormal cold and blizzard conditions, Danielo was not able to begin work until April 1 and was five months late in completing the construction of the project. Rubicon sued Danielo for breach of contract by failing to perform on schedule. Danielo is liable. As no provision was included in the contract covering delay caused by weather, Danielo bore the risk of the delay and resulting loss. ◆

(b) Weather Clauses. Modern contracts commonly contain a "weather clause." This clause either expressly grants an extension for delays caused by weather conditions or expressly denies the right to any extension of time or additional compensation because of weather difficulties. Some courts hold that abnormal weather conditions excuse what would otherwise be a breach of contract. Thus, nondelivery of equipment has been excused when the early melting of a frozen river made it impossible to deliver.

12. Discharge by Operation of Law

A contract may be discharged by operation of law.

A contract is discharged by operation of law by (1) an alteration or a material change made by a party, (2) the destruction of the written contract with intent to discharge it, (3) bankruptcy, (4) the operation of a statute of limitations, or (5) a contractual limitation.

(a) Bankruptcy. Most insolvent debtors may voluntarily enter into a federal court of bankruptcy or be compelled to do so by creditors. The trustee in bankruptcy then takes possession of the debtor's property and distributes it as far as it will go among the creditors. After this is done, the court grants the debtor a discharge in bankruptcy if it concludes that the debtor has acted honestly and has not attempted to defraud creditors. Even though all creditors have not been paid in full, the discharge in bankruptcy discharges ordinary contract claims against the debtor.

Most debts may be discharged by bankruptcy.

(b) Statutes of Limitations. Statutes of limitations provide that after a certain number of years have passed, a contract claim is barred. The time limitation provided by state statutes of limitations varies widely. The period usually differs with the type of contract—ranging from a relatively short time for open accounts (ordinary customers' charge accounts) and other sales of goods (4 years)[31] through a somewhat longer period for written contracts (usually 5 to 10 years) to a maximum period for judgments of record (usually 10 to 20 years).

Contract claims are discharged by statutes of limitations.

(c) Contractual Limitations. Some contracts, particularly insurance contracts, contain a time limitation within which suit must be brought. This is in effect a private statute of limitations created by the agreement of the parties. A 12-month limitation in an insurance policy for the time for suit is not unconscionable even though a person obtaining the insurance has virtually no chance of successfully negotiating a change of the provision.[32]

Some contracts are discharged if suit is not brought within the contract time.

CASE SUMMARY

No Excuses For Delay

Facts: The State Bank of Viroqua obtained a bankers blanket bond from Capitol Indemnity to protect it from loss by forgery. The bond required that the bank give the insurer notice of any loss at the earliest practicable moment. DeLap borrowed money from the bank by means of paper on which he forged the name of Mellem. This was learned in October 1969. In October 1970, an agent of Capitol was discussing the bond with the bank. The bank then realized for the first time that the bond covered the DeLap forgery loss. Fifteen days later, the bank notified Capitol of that claim. Capitol denied liability because of the delay. The bank sued Capitol.

Decision: The bank was barred, since it had not given notice at the earliest practicable moment after it knew that a loss had been sustained. The failure of the bank to realize sooner that it had a claim under the contract did not excuse it from complying with the contract. *[State Bank of Viroqua v Capitol Indemnity Corp., 61 Wis 2d 699, 214 NW2d 42 (1974)]*

A contract may also require that notice of any claim be given within a specified time. A party who fails to give notice within the time specified by the contract is barred from suing thereon.

A contract provision requiring that suit be brought within one year does not violate public policy although the statute of limitations would allow two years in the absence of such a contract limitation.[33]

---

[31] UCC § 2-725(1).
[32] *Thomas v United Fire and Casualty Co.* (Iowa) 426 NW2d 396 (1988).
[33] *Keiting v Skauge* (Wis App) 543 NW2d 565 (1995).

SUMMARY

Most contracts are discharged by performance. An offer to perform is called a tender of performance. If a tender of performance is wrongfully refused, the duty of the tenderer to perform is terminated. If the performance required was the payment of money, the refusal of a proper tender does not discharge the debt. It does, however, prevent the creditor from recovering interest or costs if suit is thereafter brought against the tenderer to recover the amount owed. When the performance called for by the contract is the payment of money, it must be legal tender that is offered. In actual practice it is common to pay and to accept payment by checks or other commercial paper.

When the debtor owes the creditor on several accounts and makes a payment, the debtor may specify which account is to be credited with the payment. If the debtor fails to specify, the creditor may choose which account to credit.

When a contract does not state when it is to be performed, it must be performed within a reasonable time. If time for performance is stated in the contract, the contract must be performed at the time specified if such time is essential (is of the essence). Performance within a reasonable time is sufficient if the specified time is not essential. Ordinarily, a contract must be performed exactly in the manner specified by the contract. A less-than-perfect performance is allowed if it is a substantial performance and if damages are allowed the other party. The other contracting party or a third person may guarantee a perfect performance. Such a guarantor is then liable if the performance is less than perfect.

A contract cannot be discharged by unilateral action unless authorized by the contract itself or by statute, as in the case of consumer protection rescission.

As a contract arises from an agreement, it may also be terminated by an agreement. This may be a provision in the original contract or a subsequent agreement to rescind the contract. A contract may also be discharged by the substitution of a new contract for the original contract; by a novation, or making a new contract with a new party; by accord and satisfaction; by release; or by waiver.

A contract is discharged when it is impossible to perform. Impossibility may result from the destruction of the subject matter of the contract, the adoption of a new law that prohibits performance, the death or disability of a party whose personal action was required for performance of the contract, or the act of the other party to the contract. Some courts will also hold that a contract is discharged when its performance is commercially impracticable or there is economic frustration. Although increased cost of performance ordinarily has no effect on a contract, if that increase is grossly disproportionate to the original performance cost, some courts will classify the situation as one of commercial impracticability and hold that the contract is discharged. In the case of economic frustration, the contract can be performed, but the performance has ceased to have any significant value to the party who originally contracted to obtain that performance. Temporary impossibility, such as a labor strike or bad weather, has no effect on a contract. It is common, though, to include protective clauses that excuse delay caused by temporary impossibility.

A contract may be discharged by operation of law. This occurs when (1) the liability arising from the contract is discharged by bankruptcy, (2) suit on the contract is barred by the applicable statute of limitations, or (3) a time limitation stated in the contract is exceeded.

QUESTIONS AND CASE PROBLEMS

1. What social forces are affected by the doctrine of economic frustration?
2. McMullen Contractors made a contract with Richardson to build an apartment house for a specific price. A number of serious apartment house fires broke out in the city, and an ordinance was adopted by the city council increasing the fire precautions that had to be taken in the construction of a new building. Compliance with these new requirements would make the construction of the apartment house for Richardson more expensive than McMullen had originally contemplated. Is McMullen discharged from the contract to build the apartment house?
3. Grattan contracted to build a house and garage for Boris for $50,000. The job was completed according to the specifications in all respects except that Grattan forgot to put a tool shed next to the garage, as required by the contract specifications. Boris refused to pay Grattan, and Grattan sued Boris. Boris raised the defense that Grattan was not entitled to any money until the contract was completely performed and that the performance was incomplete because the tool shed had not been constructed. Was Boris correct?
4. American Bank loaned Koplik $50,000 to buy equipment for a restaurant about to be opened by Casual Citchen Corp. The loan was not repaid, and Fast

Foods, Inc., bought out the interest of Casual Citchen. As part of the transaction, Fast Foods agreed to pay the debt owed to American Bank, and the parties agreed to a new schedule of payments to be made by Fast Foods. Fast Foods did not make the payments, and American Bank sued Koplik. He contended that his obligation to repay $50,000 had been discharged by the execution of the agreement providing for the payment of the debt by Fast Foods. Was this defense valid? [*American Bank & Trust Co. v Koplik,* ____ App Div 2d ____, 451 NYS2d 426]

5. Metalcrafters made a contract to design a new earth-moving vehicle for Lamar Highway Construction Co. Metalcrafters was depending on the genius of Samet, the head of its research department, to design a new product. Shortly after the contract was made between Metalcrafters and Lamar, Samet was killed in an auto-mobile accident. Metalcrafters was not able to design the product without Samet. Lamar sued Metalcrafters for damages for breach of the contract. Metalcrafters claimed that the contract was discharged by Samet's death. Is it correct?

6. The Tinchers signed a contract to sell land to Creasy. The contract specified that the sales transaction was to be completed in 90 days. At the end of the 90 days Creasy requested an extension of time. The Tinchers refused to grant an extension and stated that the contract was terminated. Creasy claimed that the 90-day clause was not binding because the contract did not state that time was of the essence. Was the contract terminated? [*Creasy v Tincher* (W Va) 173 SE2d 332]

7. When Jean and Jerry Butner were divorced, their property settlement and divorce decree specified that when their son no longer needed their home, the home would be sold and the proceeds divided equally between Jean and Jerry. Jean died, and Marie Shutt, her mother, was appointed her executrix. Jerry then claimed that the obligation to sell the house had been discharged by the death of Jean. Was he correct? [*Shutt v Butner* (NC App) 303 SE2d 399]

8. Dickson contracted to build a house for Moran. When it was approximately 25 to 40 percent completed, Moran would not let Dickson work any further because he was not following the building plans and specifications, and there were many defects. Moran hired another contractor to correct the defects and fin-ish the building. Dickson sued Moran for breach of contract, claiming that he had substantially per-formed the contract up to the point where he had been discharged. Was Dickson correct? [*Dickson v Moran* (La App) 344 So 2d 102]

9. A lessor leased a trailer park to a tenant. At the time, sewage was disposed of by a septic tank system that was not connected with the public sewage system. The tenant knew this, and the lease declared that the tenant had examined the premises and that the land-lord made no representation or guarantee as to the condition of the premises. Some time thereafter, the septic tank system stopped working properly, and the county health department notified the tenant that he was required to connect the septic tank system with the public sewage system or else the department would close the trailer park. The tenant did not want to pay the additional cost involved in connecting with the public system. The tenant claimed that he was released from the lease and was entitled to a refund of the deposit that he had made. Was he correct? [*Glen R. Sewell Sheet Metal v Loverde,* ____ Cal App 3d ____, 451 P2d 721]

10. Oneal was a teacher employed by the Colton Consolidated School District. Because of a diabetic condition, his eyesight deteriorated so much that he offered to resign if he would be given pay for a speci-fied number of "sick leave" days. The school district refused to do this and discharged Oneal for nonper-formance of his contract. He appealed to remove the discharge from his record. Decide. What ethical values are involved? [*Oneal v Colton Consolidated School District,* ____ Wash App ____, 557 P2d 11]

11. Northwest Construction, Inc., made a contract with the state of Washington for highway construction. Part of the work was turned over under a subcontract to Yakima Asphalt Paving Co. The contract required that any claim be asserted within 180 days. Yakima brought an action for damages after the expiration of 180 days. The defense was that the claim was too late. Yakima replied that the action was brought within the time allowed by the statute of limitations and that the contractual limitation of 180 days was therefore not binding. Was Yakima correct?

12. The Metropolitan Park District of Tacoma gave Griffith a concession to run the district's parks. The agreement gave the right to occupy the parks and use any improvements found therein. The district later wished to set this agreement aside because it was not making sufficient money from the transaction. While it was seeking to set the agreement aside, a boathouse and a gift shop in one of the parks were destroyed by fire. The district then claimed that the concession con-tract with Griffith was discharged by impossibility of performance. Was it correct? [*Metropolitan Park District of Tacoma v Griffith,* ____ Wash ____, 723 P2d 1093]

13. Hutton, as a prospective franchisee, and Mograde, Inc., as a prospective franchisor, entered into a fran-chise agreement. The agreement stated that it would be canceled and the deposit refunded if Hutton could

not obtain satisfactory financing for the balance of the money due the franchisor. A few days later Hutton notified the franchisor that he could not obtain satisfactory financing and was therefore canceling the contract, and he demanded his deposit back. Decide.

14. Ellen borrowed money from Farmers' Bank. As evidence of the loan, she signed a promissory note by which she promised to pay to the bank in installments the amount of the loan together with interest and administrative costs. She was unable to make the payments on the scheduled dates. She and the bank then executed a new agreement that gave her a longer period of time for making the payments. However, after two months she was unable to pay on this new schedule. The bank then brought suit against her under the terms of the original agreement. She raised the defense that the original agreement had been discharged by the execution of the second agreement and could not be sued upon. Decide.

15. Acme Hydraulic Press Co. manufactured large presses and sold them throughout the United States. The agreement of sale contract that Acme would execute with its customers specified that they could make no claim for breach of contract unless notice of the breach had been given within ten days after the delivery of a press in question to the buyer and that no lawsuit could thereafter be brought if notice had not been given. Was this time limitation valid?

CPA QUESTION

1. Parc hired Glaze to remodel and furnish an office suite. Glaze submitted plans that Parc approved. After completing all the necessary construction and painting, Glaze purchased minor accessories that Parc rejected because they did not conform to the plans. Parc refused to allow Glaze to complete the project and refused to pay Glaze any part of the contract price. Glaze sued for the value of the work performed. Which of the following statements is correct?

a. Glaze will lose because Glaze breached the contract by **not** completing performance.
b. Glaze will win because Glaze substantially performed and Parc prevented complete performance.
c. Glaze will lose because Glaze materially breached the contract by buying the accessories.
d. Glaze will win because Parc committed anticipatory breach.

(11/90, Law, #25, 0460)

Breach of Contract and Remedies

CHAPTER 20

A. WHAT CONSTITUTES A BREACH OF CONTRACT

1. Definition of Breach
2. Anticipatory Breach

B. WAIVER OF BREACH

3. Cure of Breach by Waiver
4. Existence and Scope of Waiver
5. Waiver of Breach as Modification of Contract
6. Reservation of Right

C. REMEDIES FOR BREACH OF CONTRACT

7. Remedies upon Anticipatory Repudiation
8. Action for Damages
9. Rescission
10. Action for Specific Performance
11. Action for an Injunction

D. CONTRACT PROVISIONS AFFECTING REMEDIES AND DAMAGES

12. Limitation of Remedies
13. Liquidated Damages
14. Limitation of Liability Clauses
15. Invalid Provision Relating to Remedies or Damages

OBJECTIVES

After studying this chapter, you should be able to

1. *List and define the kinds of damages that may be recovered when a contract is broken;*
2. *Describe the requirement of mitigation of damages;*
3. *State when liquidated damages clauses are valid;*
4. *State when liability-limiting clauses are valid;*
5. *State when a breach of contract is waived; and*
6. *List the steps that may be used to prevent a waiver of breach of contract.*

What can be done when a contract is broken?

A. WHAT CONSTITUTES A BREACH OF CONTRACT

The question of remedies does not become important until it is first determined that the contract has been broken, that is, that there has been a breach.

1. Definition of Breach

A **breach** is the failure to act or perform in the manner called for by the contract. When the contract calls for performance, such as painting an owner's house, the failure to paint or to paint properly is a breach of contract. If the contract calls for a creditor's forbearance, the action of the creditor in bringing a lawsuit is a breach of the contract.

A breach is a failure to perform.

(a) Breach of Contract Distinguished from a Tort or Crime. When the breach of a contract occurs, the only recovery available is damages under contract law. The conduct or failure to act that breaches the contract may, however, also be a crime or a tort. In such a case, the wrongdoer is liable under both contract law and the applicable tort or criminal law. Whether liability exists outside of contract law depends on the facts of the case.

If a person was fraudulently induced to enter into a contract, that person may bring a tort action against the wrongdoer for the fraud. This is a cause of action that is independent of and distinguished from a claim for breach of the contract that occurs when the wrongdoer fails to perform.[1]

2. Anticipatory Breach

When the contract calls for performance, a party may make it clear before the time for performance arrives that the contract will not be performed.

An anticipatory breach is a clear repudiation of a contract before performance time.

(a) Anticipatory Repudiation. When a party expressly declares that performance will not be made when required, this declaration is called an **anticipatory repudiation** of the contract. To constitute such a repudiation, there must be a clear, absolute, unequivocal refusal to perform the contract according to its terms.

A refusal to perform a contract that is made before performance is required, unless the other party to the contract does an act or makes a concession that is not required by the contract, is an anticipatory repudiation of the contract.[2]

CASE SUMMARY

Did the Door Slam Shut?

Facts: Tal Wooten made a contract to buy an office building and land from Harry DeMean for $1,282,000. Payment was to be made at the time of closing. A dispute arose among the parties as to the meaning of a "business day" as used in the contract. This term was important because it was used to determine the actual date of the closing. During a conference to settle

---

[1] *HTP, Ltd. v Linias Aereas Constarricenses* (Fla) 685 So 2d 1238 (1997).
[2] *Chamberlain v Puckett Construction* (Mont) 921 P2d 1237 (1996).

the dispute, both parties agreed orally to the formula of a "business day" meaning "a weekday unless it was a holiday . . . not counting Saturdays or Sundays." Later when this understanding was reduced to writing, Wooten signed the agreement but DeMean refused. On October 16th, the day of closing as computed using the agreed-upon formula, Wooten was prepared to complete the deal. DeMean did not show up. DeMean refused to close claiming that he was released from the contract because Wooten had made an anticipatory repudiation of the contract by requesting a "change" to the contract as to the meaning of a "business day." DeMean shortly thereafter sold the property to someone else for $1,650,000.

Decision: There was no anticipatory repudiation because there was no clear and unequivocal assertion that if the requested changes were not made, the buyer would not go through with the contract. The mere making of requests for changes is not a repudiation. DeMean was therefore not released from his contract. [*Wooten v DeMean (Mo App)* 788 SW2d 522 (1990)]

A party making an anticipatory repudiation may retract or take back the repudiation if the other party has not changed position in reliance on the repudiation. However, if the other party has changed position, the party making the anticipatory repudiation cannot retract it. For example, if a buyer makes another purchase when the seller declares that the seller will not perform the contract, the buyer has acted in reliance on the seller's repudiation. The seller will therefore not be allowed to retract the repudiation.

Anticipatory repudiation may be made by conduct.

(b) Anticipatory Repudiation by Conduct. The anticipatory repudiation may be expressed by conduct that makes it impossible for the repudiating party to perform subsequently. To illustrate, there is a repudiation by conduct if a farmer makes a contract to sell an identified mass of potatoes and then sells and delivers them to another buyer before the date specified for the delivery to the first buyer.

(c) Anticipatory Repudiation and Bad Faith. Some authority exists for the view that when the anticipatory repudiation goes beyond merely refusing to perform and amounts to a bad-faith denial of the existence of a contract and this denial is made without probable cause, the wrongdoer is guilty of the tort of breach of the implied warranty of good faith.[3]

ETHICS & THE LAW

NBC, for the 1994–1995 and 1995–1996 television seasons, had its show *Friends* place consistently among the top ten television programs (as measured by the Nielsen ratings). The show has an ensemble cast of six "Generation X" friends who live in New York City.

In addition to the revenues from advertising on the popular show, NBC had significant profits from brisk sales of *Friends* merchandise including hats, t-shirts, and mugs.

Just prior to the August 12, 1996, start of production for the show for the 1996–1997 season, the six cast members demanded raises from their contract

---

[3] *Stoll v Shuff,* ____ Cal App 3d ____, 27 Cal Rptr 249 (1994). It does not appear likely that this view will be given much recognition, particularly as the Permanent Editorial Board of the Uniform Laws Commissioners for the Uniform Commercial Code has taken the position that no independent cause of action for breach of the implied covenant of good faith can arise in the case of an ordinary contract. Permanent Editorial Board Commentary #10.

salaries of $40,000 per episode to $100,000. The stars of the show also demanded a percentage of profits from the show and any affiliated sales and contracts. The six actors indicated that they would not report for the start of filming if their demands for a raise were not met. None of the six had expired contracts. Their $40,000-per-episode salary was to continue at least through 1997.

NBC had just signed an agreement to sell the *Friends* episodes into syndication beginning in 1998. This syndication deal required NBC to turn over four seasons of episodes, and it was reported NBC received $40 million for the sale of the syndication rights.

When production began for the 1996–1997 season, all the members of the *Friends* cast did report for work. The network issued a statement indicating that no agreement had been reached but negotiations were ongoing.

Was it fair for the stars to threaten to strike unless their demands for higher compensation were met? Suppose that NBC signed new contracts with the six actors, agreeing to all their demands. Would the contracts be enforceable? What defenses could be raised? Do you believe contracts negotiated for the higher salaries with the cast members are supported by consideration? Why or why not?

If the actors had failed to report for filming on August 12, 1996, would their conduct constitute a breach of contract? What damages would NBC experience if the stars failed to report for filming? What damages could NBC recover in the event the actors failed to complete their existing contracts?

When Jay Leno was asked about the tactics of the *Friends* stars, he responded, "You have to get what you can while you can in this business." Is Mr. Leno right? Is such an attitude ethical?

B.   WAIVER OF BREACH

The breach of a contract may have no importance because the other party to the contract waives the breach.

3.   Cure of Breach by Waiver

Breach of contract may be waived.

The fact that one party has broken a contract does not necessarily mean that there will be a lawsuit or a forfeiture of the contract. For practical business reasons, one party may be willing to ignore or waive the breach. When it is established that there has been a waiver of a breach, the party waiving the breach cannot take any action on the theory that the contract was broken. The waiver, in effect, erases the past breach. The contract continues as though the breach had not existed.[4]

A tender of performance will often be defective in some respect. There may be delays, or the product tendered may not be exactly what was ordered. The obligee will frequently accept the performance, although defective, without making any complaint about the defect. Performance may be accepted because the obligee is not really troubled by the defect or because the obligee is in such a position that the defective performance must be accepted as better than none.

The waiver may be express or it may be implied from the continued recognition of the existence of the contract by the aggrieved party. When the conduct of a party shows an intent to give up a right, that right is waived. Once a right is waived, it cannot be revived.

---

[4] *Wheat Belt Public Power District v Batterman*, ____ Neb ____, 452 NW2d 49 (1990).

CASE SUMMARY

Speak Up or Forget About It!

Facts: Digital Resources made a contract for $6,750 to supply Seismic & Digital Concepts with software it needed for oil exploration. Though the contract called for delivery within 45 days of the contract, there was no indication that time was of the essence in the performance of the contract. Digital delivered the software to Seismic a few weeks late whereupon it was discovered that the data provided by Seismic to Digital was erroneous. Seismic asked Digital to rework the program so as to correct the errors. Seismic also asked Digital to modify the program so as to make it run faster even though the program already ran as fast as was called for in the contract. Seismic agreed to pay $800 for the additional work required to speed up the program, and Digital made the agreed-to modifications. Despite the delay, Seismic took the software and used it in its business. Seismic did not make payment as required by the contract. When Digital brought suit against it, Seismic counterclaimed for damages caused by the delay in the delivery of the software.

Decision: Judgment against Seismic. It could not claim damages for delay because it had waived the right to assert the delay by the fact that it took the late delivery and used the software, and even asked the plaintiff to perform additional services. *[Seismic & Digital Concepts Inc. v Digital Resources Corp. (Tex Civ App) 590 SW2d 718 (1979)]*

4. Existence and Scope of Waiver

It is a question of fact whether there has been a waiver.

A waiver is shown by words or conduct.

(a) Existence of Waiver. A party may express or declare that the breach of a contract is waived. A waiver of breach is more often the result of silence or failure to object in timely fashion than the result of an express forgiving of a breach. Thus, a party allowing the other party to continue performance without objecting that the performance is not satisfactory waives the right to raise that objection when sued for payment by the performing party.

A waiver has the scope intended by the parties.

(b) Scope of Waiver. The waiver of a breach of contract extends only to the matter waived. It does not show any intent to ignore other provisions of the contract.

5. Waiver of Breach as Modification of Contract

When the contract calls for a continuing performance, such as making delivery of goods or paying an installment on the first of each month, the acceptance of a late delivery or a late payment may have more significance than merely waiving a claim for damages because of the lateness.

Repeated waivers may show modification of the contract.

(a) Repeated Breaches and Waivers. Repeated breaches and repeated waivers may show that the parties have modified their original contract. For example, the contract calling for performance on the first of the month may have been modified to permit performance in the first week of the month. When there is a modification of the contract, neither party can go back to the original contract without the consent of the other.

A contract may state no modification by waiver.

(b) Antimodification Clause. Modern contracts commonly specify that the terms of a contract shall not be deemed modified by waiver as to any breaches. This means that the original contract remains as agreed to. Either party may therefore return to and insist on compliance with the original contract.

FIGURE 20-1
What Follows the Breach?

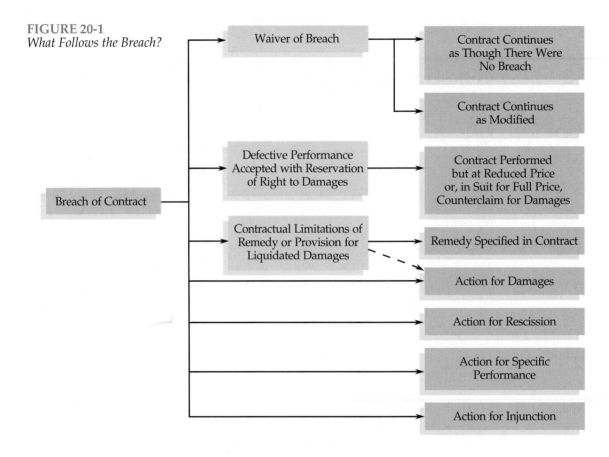

6. Reservation of Right

A reservation of rights bars waiver.

It may be that a party is willing to accept a defective performance but does not wish to surrender any claim for damages for the breach. For example, the buyer of coal may need a shipment of coal so badly as to be forced to accept it although it is defective. At the same time, the buyer does not wish to be required to pay the full purchase price for the defective shipment. The buyer wants to claim a deduction for damages because the shipment was defective. In such a case, the buyer should accept the tendered performance with a **reservation of rights.** In the above illustration, the buyer would state that the defective coal was accepted but that the right to damages for nonconformity to the contract was reserved.[5] Frequently the buyer will express the same thought by stating that the coal is accepted "without prejudice" to a claim for damages for nonconformity, or that the shipment is accepted "under protest." ◆ *For example,* Seaside Hotel ordered Russian caviar from Food Imports, which instead sent Baltic caviar to the hotel. The hotel accepted the caviar on the basis of Food Imports' representation that there was no distinguishable difference between the brand ordered and the brand sent. Seaside Hotel also accepted the caviar because it had to have some brand of caviar. Seaside can protect its rights by making its acceptance of the Baltic brand subject to the reservation of any right to claim damages for breach of contract because of the failure to send the ordered brand. ◆

---

[5] UCC § 1-207.

C.   REMEDIES FOR BREACH OF CONTRACT

When a party has broken a contract, one or more remedies may be available to the injured party. There is also the possibility that arbitration or a streamlined, out-of-court procedure is available for determining the rights of the parties.

7.   Remedies upon Anticipatory Repudiation

On anticipatory repudiation, the other party may wait, sue, or cancel.

When an anticipatory repudiation of a contract occurs, the aggrieved person has several options.[6] He or she may (1) do nothing beyond stating that the performance at the proper time will be required; (2) regard the contract as having been definitively broken and bring a lawsuit against the repudiating party, without waiting to see if there will be a proper performance when the performance date arrives;[7] or (3) regard the repudiation as an offer to cancel the contract. This offer can be accepted or rejected. If accepted, there is a discharge of the original contract by the subsequent cancellation agreement of the parties.

8.   Action for Damages

The object of a suit for damages is to put the plaintiff in the same position as if performance had occurred.

When a breach of contract occurs, the injured party is entitled to bring an action for damages. The amount of damages is the sum of money that will place the injured party in the same position that would have been attained if the contract had been performed.[8]

If the defendant has been negligent in performing the contract, the plaintiff may sue for the damages caused by the negligence. Thus, a person contracting to drill a well for drinking water can be sued for the damage caused by negligently drilling the well so as to cause the water to become contaminated. However, damages representing annoyance ordinarily may not be recovered for breach of contract. Similarly, the mere fact that breaking the contract causes the injured party to be emotionally upset does not ordinarily entitle that person to recover damages for the emotional distress.[9]

(a) Measure of Damages. A plaintiff who has sustained actual loss is entitled to a sum of money that will, so far as possible, compensate for that loss. Such damages are called **compensatory damages,** which compensate the aggrieved party for harm caused by breach of the contract.[10] An injured party who does not sustain an actual loss from the breach of a contract is entitled to a judgment of a small sum, such as $1, known as **nominal damages.** A party seeking to recover damages for breach of contract must produce evidence that affords a basis for determining the monetary value of the damages with reasonable certainty. If the proof is uncertain, conjectural, or speculative, the plaintiff cannot recover compensatory damages.

The fact that damages cannot be established with mathematical certainty is not a bar to their recovery. All that is required is reasonable certainty. The trier of fact is given a large degree of discretion in determining damages.

---

[6] *Jitner v Gersch Development Co.,* ____ Or App ____, 789 P2d 704 (1990).

[7] If the aggrieved party follows alternative (2), the duty to mitigate damages may arise. This duty is described in section 8(a) of this chapter.

[8] *Leingang v City of Mandan Weed Board* (ND) 468 NW2d 397 (1991).

[9] *Hancock v Northcutt* (Alaska) 808 P2d 251 (1991).

[10] *Topco, Inc. v Montana Department of Highways,* ____ Mont ____, 912 P2d 805 (1996).

Punitive damages are
rare for a breach of
contract.

(b) Punitive Damages. Damages in excess of actual loss, imposed for the purpose of punishing or making an example of the defendant, are known as **punitive damages** or **exemplary damages**. In contract actions, punitive damages are not ordinarily awarded, nor are they awarded for mere breach of contract.[11]

In some states, the lawmakers or the courts impose a multiplier limitation of the amount of punitive damages that may be recovered. This is done by imposing a ceiling such that the punitive or exemplary damages cannot be more than three or four times the amount of the compensatory damages awarded the plaintiff.

CASE SUMMARY

When Is It Just a Broken Contract?

Facts: Mr. and Mrs. Floyd made a contract with Video Barn to photograph their daughter's wedding. For no explained reason, Video went to the wrong church and photographed the wrong wedding. The Floyds sued Video for breach of contract and claimed punitive damages because of their mental and emotional distress.

Decision: Punitive damages could not be recovered. The mere fact that there has been an unexplained breach of contract does not entitle the other party to recover punitive damages. It must be shown that the breach was willful, wanton, or malicious, and proof that there was merely negligence is not sufficient. *[Floyd v Video Barn, Inc. (Fla App) 538 So 2d 1322 (1989)]*

Other courts ignore a ratio limitation and require only that the amount of the exemplary damages be reasonable. In determining reasonableness, consideration is given to "(1) the nature of the wrong, (2) the character of the conduct involved, (3) the degree of culpability of the wrongdoer, (4) the situation and sensibilities of the parties concerned, (5) the extent to which such conduct offends a public sense of justice and propriety, and (6) the net worth of the wrongdoer.[12]

In some consumer situations, recovery of punitive damages is allowed to discourage the defendant from breaking the law with other consumers. ◆ *For example*, in cases in which the plaintiff is a consumer and the seller has acted wrongfully and stubbornly, an increasing trend is to award punitive damages to prevent a repetition of such conduct. ◆

The fact that the breaching party made prompt efforts to correct the situation when notified of the breach is strong evidence of the lack of the mental state justifying imposition of punitive damages.

(c) Direct and Consequential Damages. The breach of a contract may cause the other party direct and consequential loss.

Direct loss is necessarily
caused by the breach.
Consequential loss is
caused by the breach
because of the circum-
stances of the case.

(1) Direct and Consequential Loss Distinguished. A **direct loss** is one that necessarily is caused by breach of the contract. A **consequential loss** is one that does not necessarily follow breach of the contract but happens to do so in a particular case because of the injured party's circumstances. For example, if the seller breaks the contract to deliver a truck that operates properly, the buyer sustains the damages of receiving a truck that cannot be used. This is the direct loss. If the

---

[11] *Art's Flower Shop, Inc. v Chesapeake and Potomac Telephone Co.* (W Va) 413 SE2d 670 (1991).
[12] *Formosa Plastics Corporation, USA v Presidio Engineers and Contractors, Inc.* (Tex App) 941 SW2d 138 (1995).

buyer of the truck needed the truck to take a harvest of ripe tomatoes to the cannery, the loss of the crop that could not be transported would be the consequential loss sustained by the farmer-buyer.

(2) Limitation on Consequential Damages. Consequential damages may be recovered if they were within the contemplation of the parties at the time they entered into their contract. This does not mean that the parties must have actually thought of the consequential damages that would follow from a breach of the contract. It is sufficient that a reasonable person in the same position would have foreseen the probability of such damages.

To recover damages for a particular consequential loss, the plaintiff must show that it was within the defendant's contemplation—that is, it was reasonably foreseeable that the kind of loss in question could be sustained by the plaintiff if the contract were broken.

> **CASE SUMMARY**
>
> ## Who Pays the Expenses?
>
> **Facts:** Jerry Birkel was a grain farmer. Hassebrook Farm Service, Inc., made a contract with Jerry to sell to him and install a grain storage and drying bin. Jerry's old dryer was traded in to the seller. The new equipment did not work properly, and Jerry had to pay other persons for drying and storing his grain. Jerry sued Hassebrook for damages and claimed the right to be repaid what he had paid to others for drying and storage.
>
> **Decision:** Jerry was entitled to recover what he had paid others for drying and storage. Since Jerry had traded in his old dryer to the seller, it was obvious to the seller that if the new equipment did not work properly, Jerry would be forced to pay for alternative drying and storage to prevent the total loss of his crops. The cost of such an alternative was therefore within the contemplation of the seller when the contract was made, and so the buyer could recover this cost as an element of damages for the seller's breach of contract. *[Birkel v Hassebrook Farm Service, Inc. 219 Neb 286, 363 NW2d 148 (1985)]*

(d) Mitigation of Damages. The injured party is under the duty to mitigate damages if reasonably possible.[13] In other words, damages must not be permitted to increase if an increase can be prevented by reasonable efforts. This means that the injured party must generally stop any performance under the contract to avoid running up a larger bill. It may require an injured party to buy or rent elsewhere the goods that the wrongdoer was obligated to deliver under the contract. In the case of a breach of an employment contract by the employer, the employee is required to seek other similar employment. The wages earned from other employment must be deducted from the damages claimed. The discharged employee, however, is not required to take employment of an unreasonably inferior nature to the prior work.

(1) Effect of Failure to Mitigate Damages. The effect of the requirement of mitigating damages is to limit recovery by the injured party to the damages that would have been sustained had the injured party mitigated the damages. That is,

---

[13] *West Pinal Family Health Center, Inc. v McBride* (Ariz) 785 P2d 66 (1989).

recovery is limited to the direct loss, and damages for consequential loss are excluded. For example, assume that a commercial hauler makes a contract to buy a truck. Because the seller fails to deliver the truck, the buyer loses a hauling job on which a profit of $500 would have been made. Assume that the hauler could have rented a truck for $150 in time to do the hauling job. The hauler would then be under a duty to rent the truck so that the $500 profit would not be lost. By failing to do this, the hauler permitted the damages to grow from a rental cost of $150 to a loss of profit of $500. When the hauler sues the seller for breach of the sales contract, the rule of mitigation of damages will limit the hauler to recovering only $150, because the additional $350 loss was unnecessarily sustained. If in fact the hauler had rented a truck, the rental of $150 would be recoverable as damages from the seller. Thus, the hauler will receive only $150 in damages whether or not a truck is rented to mitigate the damages.

There is no duty to mitigate damages when this is impossible or unreasonable.

(2) *Excuse for Failure to Mitigate Damages.* If the injured party can reasonably do nothing to reduce damages, there is, by definition, no duty to mitigate damages. ◆ *For example,* a leasing company broke its contract to supply a specified computer and auxiliary equipment by delivering a less desirable computer. Because the specified computer and equipment could not be obtained elsewhere by the customer, the customer was entitled to recover full damages. ◆

A plaintiff is not required to make substantial expenditures in order to mitigate damages.[14]

When the cost of mitigating—for example, by purchasing elsewhere the goods that the seller failed to deliver—is unreasonably great, there is no duty to mitigate damages.

There are conflicting views as to judgments on contracts for payment of foreign money.

(e) Conversion of Foreign Currency. Judgments entered in U.S. state and federal courts must be stated in terms of U.S. currency, that is, American dollars. This raises a problem when an international contract is involved and the plaintiff's damages are measured in terms of a foreign currency. The earlier American rule was to award the plaintiff the number of American dollars that the amount of the foreign currency would buy at the rate of exchange on the day of the defendant's breach. In view of the present fluctuations in world currencies, the modern trend is to award the foreign plaintiff the number of American dollars determined by the rate of exchange on the date of the judgment when the use of that date will produce a more equitable result.

In contrast with the American judgment, the plaintiff may hold a judgment entered in a foreign country that is stated in terms of the currency of that country. A Uniform Foreign Money-Judgments Recognition Act provides for the payment of such judgment in this country in the currency of the foreign country or in American dollars computed at the rate of exchange on the day before the defendant was to make payment.[15]

---

[14] *Tampa Pipeline Transport Co. v Chase Manhattan Service Corp.* (DC Fla) 928 F Supp 1568 (1995).
[15] *Manches & Co. v Gilbey,* 419 Mass 414, 646 NE2d 86 (1995). The uniform act has been adopted in Alaska, California, Colorado, Connecticut, Florida, Georgia, Hawaii, Idaho, Illinois, Iowa, Maryland, Massachusetts, Michigan, Minnesota, Missouri, Montana, New Mexico, New York, North Carolina, Ohio, Oklahoma, Oregon, Pennsylvania, Texas, Virgin Islands, and Washington. It has also been adopted for the District of Columbia.

A contract may be rescinded for material breach.

9.   Rescission

When there has been a material breach of a contract, the aggrieved party may rescind the contract. If the wrongdoing party objects, the aggrieved party may bring an action for rescission.

(a) Right to Rescind. When one party commits a material breach of the contract, the other party may rescind the contract. A breach is material when it is so substantial that it defeats the object of the parties in making the contract.[16]

In some situations, the right to rescind may be governed or controlled by civil service statutes or similar regulations, or by an obligation to submit the matter to arbitration or to a grievance procedure.

The rescinding party may recover the value of the performance.

An injured party who rescinds after having performed or paid money under the contract may recover the reasonable value of the performance rendered or the money paid. This recovery is based not on the contract that has been rescinded but on a quasi contract that the law implies to prevent the defaulter from keeping the benefit received and thus being unjustly enriched. When a contract for the sale of land is rescinded, the buyer is entitled to the return of the purchase price and to compensation for any improvements made to the land. A deduction will be made from such sums for the reasonable rental value of the property during the time that the buyer was in possession.

Rescission is the undoing of the contract. The rescinding party must restore the other party to that party's original position. If the rescinding party's own acts make this impossible, the contract cannot be rescinded. Thus, a buyer who has placed a mortgage on property purchased cannot rescind the sales contract because the property cannot be returned to the seller in its original unmortgaged condition.

Care must be exercised in deciding to rescind a contract. If proper ground for rescission does not exist, the party who rescinds is guilty of repudiating the contract and is liable for damages for its breach.[17] Except in a contract for the sale of goods, rescission and the recovery of money damages are alternative remedies; the two are not concurrently available.[18] *For example*, Carvel Motors, a manufacturer of electric motors for household appliances, purchased a large quantity of switches from Morena Electronics. The switches proved defective, and Carvel returned them to Morena, rescinded the contract, and demanded damages. As the transaction was for the sale of goods, the UCC allows Carvel to rescind the contract concurrently and recover damages for its breach.

(b) Judicial Rescission. If the party breaking the contract does not recognize the right of the aggrieved party to rescind the contract, the aggrieved party may bring an action in which a court will declare that the contract has been rescinded. In that action, the court will also specify what payments or exchanges of property are to be made by the parties in order to return matters to the conditions existing before the contract was made.

---

[16] *Frank Felix Associates v Austin Drugs, Inc.* (CA2 NY) 111 F3d 284 (1997).
[17] *Joshua v McBride* (Ark App) 716 SW2d 215 (1986).
[18] *Newton v Aiken,* ____ Ill App 3d ____, ____ Ill Dec ____, 633 NE2d 213 (1994).

10. Action for Specific Performance

Specific performance
may compel perfor-
mance in limited
cases where money
would not compen-
sate.

C
P
A

Under special circumstances, an injured party may obtain the equitable remedy of specific performance, which compels the other party to carry out the terms of a contract. The plaintiff seeking specific performance must first establish the existence of a binding contract that the defendant has not performed.[19]

CASE SUMMARY

Does the Contract Say Enough?

Facts: June Murray made a contract to sell most of her land to Mark Scheinfeld. The contract called for a transfer of a 33-acre tract less a 25,000 square foot lot on which Murray's home stood. The contract also stated that the actual dimensions of this retained lot would be specified later by Scheinfeld. An "approximation of the Purchaser's designation of lots" was attached to the agreement by Scheinfeld. Before the deal closed Scheinfeld informed Murray that the lot configurations had been redesigned. When Murray saw that the redesigned lot would have her home facing away from the street she decided not to sell her property. Scheinfeld sued for specific performance of the contract.

Decision: Judgment against Scheinfeld. Specific performance will not be granted unless there is a contract that describes the land as definitely as it would be described in a deed. As the retained portion was not described this precisely, specific performance could not be granted. [Scheinfeld v Murray, ____ Ga ____, 481 SE2d 194 (1997)]

C
P
A

Specific performance is ordinarily granted only if the subject matter of the contract is unique, thereby making an award of money damages an inadequate remedy. Money damages may be inadequate because it is not possible to make a reasonable determination of the damages the plaintiff will sustain by the breach of the contract. Money damages may be inadequate because a replacement or substitute performance cannot be obtained in the marketplace. Contracts for the purchase of land will be specifically enforced, as will contracts for the sale of a business and the franchise held by the business.

Specific performance of a contract to sell personal property can generally be obtained only if the article is of unusual age, beauty, unique history, or other distinction. In the case of heirlooms, original paintings, old editions of books, or relics, identical articles could not be obtained in the market. Specific performance is also allowed a buyer in the case of a contract to buy shares of stock essential for control of a close corporation when those shares have no fixed or market value and are not quoted in the commercial reports or sold on a stock exchange. ◆ *For example,* Maurice owned a rare Revolutionary War musket that he agreed to sell to Herb. Maurice then changed his mind because of the uniqueness of the musket. Herb can sue and win, requesting the remedy of specific performance of the contract because of the unique nature of the goods. ◆

Granting specific performance is discretionary with the court and will be refused when it would impose an unreasonable hardship on the defendant. Specific performance will also be refused when the plaintiff has acted inequitably.[20]

---

[19] *Sayer v Bowley,* ____ Neb ____, 503 NW2d 166 (1993).
[20] *Hawthorne's, Inc. v Warrenton Realty, Inc.,* ____ Mass ____, 606 NE2d 908 (1993).

When the damages sustained by the plaintiff can be measured, specific performance will be refused. Consequently, a contract to sell a television station will not be specifically enforced when the buyer had made a contract to resell the station to a third person; the damages caused by the breach of the first contract would be the loss sustained by being unable to make the resale, and such damages would be adequate compensation to the original buyer.[21]

Ordinarily, contracts for the performance of personal services will not be specifically ordered. This is because of the difficulty of supervision by the court and the restriction of the U.S. Constitution's Thirteenth Amendment, prohibiting involuntary servitude except as criminal punishment.

To do complete justice, the court, in awarding specific performance, can also award damages to compensate for the direct and consequential loss caused by the defendant's refusal to perform the contract.

11. Action for an Injunction

There is a limited use of injunction to compel performance.

When a breach of contract consists of doing an act prohibited by the contract, a possible remedy is an injunction against doing the act. For example, when the obligation in an employee's contract is to refrain from competing and the obligation is broken by competing, a court may order or enjoin the employee to stop competing. Similarly, when a singer breaks a contract to record exclusively for a particular company, the singer may be enjoined from recording for any other company. This may have the indirect effect of compelling the singer to record for the plaintiff.

D. CONTRACT PROVISIONS AFFECTING REMEDIES AND DAMAGES

The contract of the parties may contain provisions that affect the remedies available or the recovery of damages.

12. Limitation of Remedies

A contract may limit remedies.

The contract of the parties may limit the remedies of the aggrieved parties. For example, the contract may give one party the right to repair or replace a defective item sold or to refund the contract price. The contract may require both parties to submit any dispute to arbitration or another streamlined out-of-court procedure.

13. Liquidated Damages

The liquidated damages clause specifies the amount recoverable.

The parties may stipulate in their contract that a certain amount should be paid in case of a breach. This amount is known as **liquidated damages** and may be variously measured by the parties. When delay is anticipated, liquidated damages may be a fixed sum, such as $100 for each day of delay. When there is a total default, damages may be a percentage of the contract price or may be the amount of the down payment. ◆ *For example,* the We-Take-Care-of-You store sold household furnishings on credit. The sales contract stated that if the buyer stopped making regular payments, the store could repossess any articles purchased. It also stated

---

21 *Miller v LeSea Broadcasting Inc.* (CA7 Wis) 87 F3d 224 (1996).

that all payments that had been made by the buyer could be retained by the store as liquidated damages. This damages clause constitutes a penalty, not liquidated damages, because the amount paid by the buyer could far exceed the loss sustained by the store. ◆

Proof of actual damages is eliminated by the liquidated damages clause.

(a) Effect. When a liquidated damages clause is held valid, the injured party cannot collect more than the amount specified by the clause. The defaulting party is bound to pay such damages once the fact is established that there has been a default. The injured party is not required to make any proof as to damages sustained, and the defendant is not permitted to show that the damages were not as great as the liquidated sum.

The liquidated damages clause is valid when actual damages are not determinable and the specified amount is not excessive.

(b) Validity. To be valid, a liquidated damages clause must satisfy two requirements: (1) The situation must be one in which it is difficult or impossible to determine the actual damages, and (2) the amount specified must not be excessive when compared with the probable damages that would be sustained.[22] To illustrate, the owner of land made a contract to sell it for $100,000. The buyer made a down payment of $50,000. The contract stated that if the buyer defaulted, the seller could keep the buyer's down payment as liquidated damages. When the buyer subsequently refused to go through with the sale, the seller claimed the right to keep the $50,000. The seller could not do this because the liquidated damages clause was void. Although land does not have any fixed value, it is clear that the seller could not sustain damages of $50,000. That amount was a penalty, the liquidated damages clause was void, and the seller would be required to prove the actual damages that were sustained and return the excess of the down payment to the buyer.

The validity of a liquidated damages clause is determined on the basis of the facts existing when the clause was agreed to. Excessive damages that are subsequently sustained are ignored.[23]

A contract provision that purports to be a liquidated damages clause is not binding when the actual damages can be readily determined—for example, by comparing the contract price and the market price of the subject matter of the contract.

CASE SUMMARY

Can We Freeze the Damages?

Facts: Manny Fakhimi agreed to buy an apartment complex for $697,000 at an auction from David Mason. Fakhimi was obligated to put up 10% of the agreed-to price at the auction as a deposit. The agreement signed by Fakhimi allowed Mason to keep this deposit should Fakhimi fail to come up with the remaining 90% of the auction price as liquidated damages for the default. Shortly after the auction, Fakhimi heard a rumor that the military base located near the apartment complex might be closing. Fakhimi immediately stopped payment on the check and defaulted on the agreement. Mason sued Fakhimi for the liquidated damages specified in the sales contract.

Decision: Yes. Because of the difficulty of forecasting the loss that might be caused by the breach of a real estate purchase contract, it is held that a liquidated damage clause of ten percent of the sale price is valid and is not a penalty. The fact that the damages sustained there-

---

[22] *Southeast Alaska Construction Co. v Alaska* (Alaska) 791 P2d 339 (1990).
[23] *Kendrick v Alexander* (Tenn App) 844 SW2d 187 (1992).

> after were less than ten percent does not convert the ten percent into an unreasonable fore-cast. The ten percent clause remained valid, as it would have remained had the damages on resale been greater than ten percent. [*Mason v Fakhimi*, ____ Neb ____, 865 P2d 333 (1993)]

If the liquidated damages clause calls for the payment of a sum that is clearly unreasonably large and unrelated to the possible actual damages that might be sustained, the clause will be held to be void as a penalty. Thus, a contract term was void as a penalty by providing that a village would be entitled to $100,000 if a cable television franchisee failed to complete installation by a specified date.

In determining the validity of a liquidated damages clause, the court must consider all the surrounding circumstances and the intentions of the parties.[24]

A liquidated damages provision tries to measure the compensation for a breach of the contract. In contrast, a penalty provision punishes the breach. When a liquidated damages clause is held invalid, the effect is merely to erase the clause from the contract. A party injured by breach of the contract may proceed to recover damages for its breach. Instead of recovering the liquidated damages amount, the injured party will recover those damages established by the evidence.

14. Limitation of Liability Clauses

A contract may limit liability.

A contract may contain a provision stating that one of the parties shall not be liable for damages in case of breach. Such a provision is called an **exculpatory clause** or a **limitation-of-liability clause**. *For example*, a construction contract may state that the contractor shall not be liable for damages from delay caused by third persons.[25]

(a) Content and Construction. An exculpatory clause, as in the case of any other contract provision, is to be given the scope intended by the parties. An exculpatory clause must be clear and unambiguous. Moreover, such a clause is strictly construed.[26] *For example*, a limitation of liability for negligence does not bar liability for violation of a consumer protection statute. Likewise, a limitation is not binding when the party breaking the contract showed reckless indifference to the rights of others in so doing or commits fraud during the formulation of the contract.[27]

CASE SUMMARY

Can There Be a Generic Limitation of Liability?

Facts: The Otis Elevator Company was about to install an elevator in a high school building. It made a contract with Don Stodola's Well Drilling Company to drill out sections of the building's foundation and walls so that Otis could install its elevator hardware. The contract stated that Don Stodola assumed no liability for damage to the building. Because of the alleged negligence of Don Stodola, the building cracked where the elevator was installed. When suit was brought against Don Stodola, he raised the defense that the exculpatory clause barred any suit against him. Otis claimed that the clause could not bar liability for negligence because the clause did not expressly refer to negligence.

---

[24] *LeRoy v Sayers*, ____ App Div 2d ____, 635 NYS2d 217 (1995).
[25] *City of Beaumont v Excavators and Constructors, Inc.* (Tex App) 870 SW2d 123 (1993).
[26] *Johnson v Board of County Commissioners*, ____ Kan ____, 913 P2d 119 (1996).
[27] *Lorenzo v Noel*, ____ Mich App ____, 522 NW2d 724 (1994).

Decision: Judgment for Don Stodola. An exculpatory clause is to be given the scope intended by the parties. The subcontractor, Don Stodola, declared in the contract that he assumed no liability for damage to the building. This clearly included liability based on any theory. Therefore, the clause covered and excluded liability based on negligence, even though nothing was expressly said about negligence. [*Otis Elevator Co. v Don Stodola's Well Drilling Co., Inc.* (Minn App) 372 NW2d 77 (1985)]

CASE SUMMARY

Could We Make It Any Clearer?

Facts: Woodside Homes made a contract to build a house for Russ. He and his wife later visited the constriction site, where his wife slipped and fell into a hole in the driveway in front of the house. The fall caused a blood clot to form which caused the wife's death. Russ sued Woodside for damages for his wife's death, claiming that she had been harmed because of Woodside's negligence. There was no evidence of negligence. Woodside raised the defense that the construction contract stated that "the construction site is a dangerous place to visit" and that Woodside would not be liable for any accident, injury, or death resulting from a visit to the job site.

Decision: Judgment for Woodside. The contractor gave adequate warning of the danger and the wife assumed the risk in visiting the site. The exculpation clause therefore shielded the contractor from liability. [*Russ v Woodside Homes, Inc.* (Utah App) 905 P2d 901 (1995)]

The exculpatory clause is valid unless contrary to public policy or avoidable for fraud. The trend is to hold it invalid when there is inequality of bargaining power or an oppressive result.

(b) Validity. When the public interest is not involved, the parties are free to allocate liability for negligence as they choose. If the public interest is involved, it is contrary to public policy to exempt one party from liability for that party's negligence.[28] Exculpatory clauses are generally valid, particularly between experienced business persons. Thus, a telephone company may limit its liability to a nominal amount for the omission of a customer's name and number from the Yellow Pages directory where the limitation is conspicuous, the customer is experienced in business, and the omission was merely the result of simple negligence.[29] Release forms signed by participants in athletic and sporting events declaring that the sponsor, proprietor, or operator of the event shall not be liable for injuries sustained by participants because of its negligence are binding. Such forms are invalid, though, when the harm was caused by "willful or wanton conduct or by gross negligence."[30]

A provision in a stock sales agreement that the officers of the corporation of which the stock was being sold "shall have no liability" was void, as it would allow the officers to escape liability for intentional misconduct.

A growing trend is to hold exculpatory provisions invalid when it is felt that they are oppressive or unconscionable because of the superior bargaining power of the party they protect. This is particularly likely to be the result when the party in question is a public utility. Such an enterprise is under the duty to provide service to the public in a nonnegligent way.

In recent years, the concept has developed that a limitation of liability is invalid when persons in an inferior bargaining position are involved, particularly when

---

[28] *Olsen v Breeze, Inc.,* ____ Cal App 4th, 55 Cal Rptr 2d 818 (1996).
[29] *Pinnacle Computer Services, Inc. v Ameritech Publishing, Inc.* (Ind App) 642 NE2d 1011 (1994).
[30] *New Light Co. v Wells Fargo Alarm Services,* ____ Neb ____, 525 NW2d 25 (1994).

services essential to those persons or to the general public are involved.[31] In any case, a limitation of liability is not binding if obtained by misconduct or deception.

Some courts refuse to recognize provisions releasing a party from liability for negligence when the provisions are so inconspicuous as to raise a question of whether the party knowingly agreed to the release.[32]

15. Invalid Provision Relating to Remedies or Damages

The invalid damages or remedies provision is ignored.

When a contract contains a valid provision governing remedies or damages, the parties are bound by it. That means that they must follow the procedures specified, or the aggrieved person is bound by the provision as to damages. What happens if the provision in question is invalid? The provision is merely ignored. The balance of the contract remains valid. This means that if the limitation of remedies is not valid, an aggrieved person may follow any remedy that would otherwise be available. If a liquidated damages or a limitation-of-damages clause is invalid, the aggrieved person may sue for the damages sustained but must actually prove what those damages were.

SUMMARY

When a party fails to perform a contract or performs improperly, the other contracting party may sue for damages caused by the breach. What may be recovered by the aggrieved person is stated in terms of being direct or consequential damages. Direct damages are those that ordinarily will result from the breach. Consequential damages are those that are in fact caused by the breach but do not ordinarily or necessarily result from every breach of the particular kind of contract. Direct damages may be recovered on proof of causation and amount. Consequential damages can be recovered only if, in addition to proving causation and amount, it is shown that they were reasonably within the contemplation of the contracting parties as a probable result of a breach of the contract. The right to recover consequential damages is lost if the aggrieved party could reasonably have taken steps to avoid such damages. In other words, the aggrieved person has a duty to mitigate or reduce damages by reasonable means.

In any case, the damages recoverable for breach of contract may be limited to a specific amount by a liquidated damages clause. Damages may be canceled out completely by a limitation-of-liability clause.

In a limited number of situations, an aggrieved party may bring an action for specific performance to compel the other contracting party to perform the acts called for by the contract. Specific performance by the seller is always obtainable for the breach of a contract to sell land or real estate on the theory that such property has a unique value. With respect to other contracts, specific per-

formance will not be ordered unless it is shown that there was some unique element present so that the aggrieved person would suffer a damage that could not be compensated for by the payment of money damages.

The aggrieved person also has the option of rescinding the contract if (1) the breach has been made concerning a material term and (2) the aggrieved party returns everything to the way it was before the contract was made. Rescission and recovery of money damages are alternative remedies except when the contract relates to the sale of goods. In the latter case, the aggrieved party may both rescind and obtain money damages.

Although there has been a breach of the contract, the effect of this breach is nullified if the aggrieved person by word or conduct waives the right to object to the breach. Conversely, an aggrieved party may accept a defective performance without thereby waiving a claim for breach if the party makes a reservation of rights. A reservation of rights can be made by stating that the defective performance is accepted "without prejudice," "under protest," or "with reservation of rights."

The continued waiver of a breach of a particular clause may indicate that the parties have modified their contract by abandoning the clause to which the waiver relates. To guard against the unintended modification of a contract by waiver, the contract may contain a clause stating that nothing shall constitute a modification of the contract unless stated in writing.

---

[31] *Bunia v Knight Ridder* (Minn App) 544 NW2d 60 (1996).
[32] *Conradt v Four Star Promotions, Inc.*, ____ Wash App ____, 728 P2d 617 (1986).

QUESTIONS AND CASE PROBLEMS

1. What social forces are affected by the rule governing the mitigation of damages?

2. Anthony makes a contract to sell a rare painting to Laura for $100,000. The written contract specifies that if Anthony should fail to perform the contract, he will pay Laura $5,000 as liquidated damages. Anthony fails to deliver the painting and is sued by Laura for $5,000. Can she recover this amount?

3. Rogers made a contract with Salisbury Brick Corp. that allowed it to remove earth and sand from land he owned. The contract ran for 4 years, with provision to renew it for additional 4-year terms up to a total of 96 years. The contract provided for compensation to Rogers based on the amount of earth and sand removed. By an unintentional mistake, Salisbury underpaid Rogers the amount of $863 for the months of November and December 1986. Salisbury offered this amount to Rogers, but he refused to accept it and claimed that he had been underpaid in other months. Rogers claimed that he was entitled to rescind the contract. Was he correct? [*Rogers v Salisbury Brick Corp.* (SC) 382 SE2d 915]

4. A contractor departed at a number of points from the specifications in a contract to build a house. The cost to put the house in the condition called for by the contract was approximately $1,000. The contractor was sued for $5,000 for breach of contract and emotional disturbance caused by the breach. Decide.

5. Protein Blenders, Inc., made a contract with Gingerich to buy from him the shares of stock of a small corporation. When the buyer refused to take and pay for the stock, Gingerich sued for specific performance of the contract on the ground that the value of the stock was unknown and could not be readily ascertained because it was not sold on the general market. Was he entitled to specific performance? [*Gingerich v Protein Blenders, Inc.* (Iowa) 95 NW2d 522]

6. The buyer of real estate made a down payment. The contract stated that the buyer would be liable for damages in an amount equal to the down payment if the buyer broke the contract. The buyer refused to go through with the contract and demanded his down payment back. The seller refused to return it and claimed that he was entitled to additional damages from the buyer because the damages that he had suffered were greater than the amount of the down payment. Decide. [*Waters v Key Colony East, Inc.* (Fla App) 345 So 2d 367]

7. Kuznicki made a contract for the installation of a fire detection system by Security Safety Corp. for $498. The contract was made one night and canceled at 9:00 the next morning. Security then claimed one-third of the purchase price from Kuznicki by virtue of a provision in the contract that "in the event of cancellation of this agreement . . . the owner agrees to pay 33⅓ percent of the contract price, as liquidated damages." Was Security Safety entitled to recover the amount claimed? [*Security Safety Corp. v Kuznicki,* ____ Mass ____, 213 NE2d 866]

8. Over the telephone, Wagner agreed to sell a farm he owned to Van for $1 million. Wagner later repudiated the agreement, and Van sued him for specific performance of the agreement. Decide.

9. Melodee Lane Lingerie Co. was a tenant in a building that was protected against fire by a sprinkler and alarm system maintained by the American District Telegraph Co. (ADT). Because of the latter's fault, the controls on the system were defective and allowed the discharge of water into the building, which damaged Melodee's property. When Melodee sued ADT, its defense was that its service contract limited its liability to 10 percent of the annual service charge made to the customer. Was this limitation valid? [*Melodee Lane Lingerie Co. v American District Telegraph Co.,* ____ NY ____, 218 NE2d 661]

10. In May, a homeowner made a contract with a roofer to make repairs to her house by July 1. The roofer never came to repair the roof, and heavy rains in the fall damaged the interior of the house. The homeowner sued the roofer for breach of contract and claimed damages for the harm done to the interior of the house. Is the homeowner entitled to recover such damages?

11. Ken Sulejmanagic, aged 19, signed up for a course in scuba diving taught by Madison at the YMCA. Before the instruction began, Ken was required to sign a form releasing Madison and the YMCA from liability for any harm that might occur. At the end of the course, Madison, Ken, and another student went into deep water. After Ken made the final dive required by the course program, Madison left him alone in the water while he took the other student for a dive. When Madison returned, Ken could not be found, and it was later determined that he had drowned. Ken's parents sued Madison and the YMCA for negligence in the performance of the teaching contract. The defendants raised the defense that the release Ken signed shielded them from liability. The plaintiffs claimed that the release was invalid. Who was correct? [*Madison v Superior Court,* ____ Cal App 3d ____, 250 Cal Rptr 299]

12. Wassenaar worked for Panos under a three-year contract stating that if the contract were terminated

wrongfully by Panos before the end of the three years, he would pay as damages the salary for the remaining time that the contract had to run. After three months, Panos terminated the contract, and Wassenaar sued him for pay for the balance of the contract term. Panos claimed that this amount could not be recovered because the contract provision for the payment was a void penalty. Was this provision valid? [*Wassenaar v Panos* (Wis) 331 NW2d 357]

13. Soden, a contractor, made a contract to build a house for Clevert. The sales contract stated that "if either party defaults in the performance of this contract," that party would be liable to the other for attorney fees incurred in suing the defaulter. Soden was 61 days late in completing the contract, and some of the work was defective. In a suit by the buyer against the contractor, the contractor claimed that he was not liable for the buyer's attorney fees because he had made only a defective performance and because "default" in the phrase quoted above meant "non-performance of the contract." Was the contractor liable for the attorney fees? [*Clevert v Soden*, ____ Va ____, 400 SE2d 181]

14. Protection Alarm Co. made a contract to provide burglar alarm security for Fretwell's home. The contract stated that the maximum liability of the alarm company was the actual loss sustained or $50, whichever was the lesser, and that this provision was agreed to "as liquidated damages and not as a penalty." When Fretwell's home was burglarized, he sued for the loss of approximately $91,000, claiming that the alarm company had been negligent. The alarm company asserted that its maximum liability was $50. Fretwell claimed that this was invalid because it bore no relationship to the loss that could have been foreseen when the contract was made or that in fact "had been sustained." Decide.

15. Shepherd-Will made a contract to sell Emma Cousar "5 acres of land adjoining property owned by the purchaser and this being formerly land of Shepherd-Will, Inc., located on north side of Highway 223. This 5 acres to be surveyed at earliest time possible at which time plat will be attached and serve as further description on property." Shepherd-Will owned only one 100-acre tract of land that adjoined Emma's property. This tract had a common boundary with her property of 1,140 feet. Shepherd-Will failed to perform this contract. Emma sued it for specific performance of the contract. Decide. [*Cousar v Shepherd-Will, Inc.* (SC App) 387 SE2d 723]

CPA QUESTIONS

1. Ordinarily, in an action for breach of a construction contract, the statute of limitations time period would be computed from the date the
   a. Contract is negotiated.
   b. Contract is breached.
   c. Contract is begun.
   d. Contract is signed.

   (5/95, Law, #25, 5359)

2. Master Mfg., Inc. contracted with Accur Computer Repair Corp. to maintain Master's computer system. Master's manufacturing process depends on its computer system operating properly at all times. A liquidated damages clause in the contract provided that Accur pay $1,000 to Master for each day that Accur was late responding to a service request. On January 12, Accur was notified that Master's computer system failed. Accur did not respond to Master's service request until January 15. If Master sues Accur under the liquidated damage provision of the contract, Master will
   a. Win, unless the liquidated damage provision is determined to be a penalty.
   b. Win, because under all circumstances liquidated damage provisions are enforceable.
   c. Lose, because Accur's breach was **not** material.
   d. Lose, because liquidated damage provisions violate public policy.

   (5/93, Law, #25)

3. Jones, CPA, entered into a signed contract with Foster Corp. to perform accounting and review services. If Jones repudiates the contract prior to the date performance is due to begin, which of the following is **not** correct?
   a. Foster could successfully maintain an action for breach of contract after the date performance was due to begin.
   b. Foster can obtain a judgment ordering Hones to perform.
   c. Foster could successfully maintain an action for breach of contract prior to the date performance is due to begin.
   d. Foster can obtain a judgment for the monetary damages it incurred as a result of the repudiation.

   (5/89, Law, #35)

Accountant's Liability and Malpractice

CHAPTER 21

After studying this chapter, you should be able to

OBJECTIVES

1. *Define malpractice;*
2. *Distinguish malpractice liability from breach of contract liability;*
3. *State the effect of contributory negligence of a plaintiff suing to impose malpractice liability;*
4. *State the extent to which third persons may enforce the malpractice liability of accountants; and*
5. *State the extent to which statutes have regulated the malpractice liability of accountants.*

When is a professional, such as an accountant, liable for harm caused by improper performance?

A. GENERAL PRINCIPLES

The liability of an accountant for malpractice raises questions of what constitutes malpractice, what remedies are available to enforce liability for malpractice, the effect of the plaintiff's conduct, and the effect of limitations of liability.

1. What Constitutes Malpractice

Malpractice is negligent performance.

When an accountant makes a contract to perform services, there is a duty to exercise the skill and care that are common within the community for persons performing similar services. If the services are not properly rendered in accordance with those standards, there is an improper practicing of the particular profession, or **malpractice,** as it is commonly called.

2. Choice of Remedy

Because performance falls below the proper standard in cases of malpractice, malpractice is classified as negligence and constitutes a tort. In addition, because the services called for by the contract have not been rendered, malpractice is also a breach of contract.

A negligent performer may be sued for breach of contract or for negligence.

(a) Breach of Contract or Tort Action. Because malpractice is both a breach of contract and an independent tort, the client who is harmed has the choice of suing for breach of contract or for the particular tort that is involved. Generally, the client will bring a tort action when justified by the facts because a tort claimant may recover greater damages than a breach of contract plaintiff. Moreover, the tort claimant may have a longer period of time in which to sue. The statute of limitations runs on the tort claim from the date when the harm was discovered. In a contract action, the statute of limitations runs from the date when the contract was broken. This may be very important because in some cases the plaintiff does not realize that any harm has been sustained until a substantially long period of time after a breach of the contract occurred.

A third-person malpractice claim is enforced as a tort.

(b) Action by Third Person. When the malpractice claim is brought by a third person rather than a client of the defendant, the malpractice action will be brought on the tort theory. Suit cannot be brought by the third person on the original contract. The third person is not a party to that contract and ordinarily cannot be classified as a third party beneficiary of that contract.

A nonaccountant may be hired to prepare a report, such as a statement of the condition of a building. If the nonaccountant knows that the owner is selling the building and that the prospective buyers will rely on the report, the buyer may sue the nonaccountant for negligence and recover the losses sustained if the report is false.[1]

---

[1] *Real Estate Support Services, Inc. v Nauman* (Ind App) 644 NE2d 907 (1994).

3.   The Environment of Accountants' Malpractice Liability

During this century, several changes have influenced the law of malpractice liability relating to accountants.

First, an accountant has in many cases moved from being a clerical employee to being an essential participant in planning business strategies. In addition, the accountant in many instances has moved from being an employee of one employer to being an independent contractor performing accounting services for many clients. Also, the accountant is now employed in many cases to produce data on which third persons will rely. For example, an accountant will prepare statements submitted to banks to induce them to lend to the accountant's client. Similarly, such information may be supplied to prospective purchasers of a client corporation's stock.

As these changes took place, it became natural for courts to allow a third person relying on an accountant's work product to sue the accountant when malpractice caused loss to that third person.

At the same time that the changes noted above were taking place in the economy and in the legal status of accountants, changes were taking place in other areas of the law. Manufacturers and remote sellers became liable to ultimate users for damages caused by defective products. Technicians became liable to third persons harmed by the technicians' negligence. Thus, this century brings a rising tide of liability to third persons. This background of liability to third persons in other areas has naturally influenced the law regulating accountants.[2]

4.   Limitation of Liability

Can accountants protect themselves from liability for malpractice claims of clients and third persons? Because the law generally permits any contracting party to limit or disclaim liability for negligence, an accountant may exclude liability for malpractice on a theory of negligence. Influenced by the consumer protection movement and by the law governing product liability, courts will require such disclaimers to be (1) clear and unambiguous and (2) conspicuous. If these requirements are not met, the disclaimers will not be held effective.

(a) Scope of Limitation. Disclaimers are valid when the circumstances are such that it is not reasonable to expect the accountant to stand behind particular data. For example, when a client owns land in a foreign country, it is reasonable for the accountant to accept the valuation placed on the land by someone in that foreign country. If the accountant includes in the financial statement prepared for the client a statement that the valuation of that land was obtained from an identified person in the foreign country and that the accountant assumes no responsibility for the accuracy of that valuation, the accountant is protected from the falsity of that information. Similarly, if the accountant's examination has been restricted, the

---

[2] The interplay between the various areas of malpractice liability and those of accountants is further seen in the fact that the Restatement (Second) of Torts does not contain a separate provision applicable only to accountants but deals with the subject of malpractice liability of accountants to third persons in a general section, 552. Section 552 declares that "one who in the course of his business, profession or employment, or in any other transaction in which he has a pecuniary interest, supplies false information for the guidance of others in their business transactions, is subject to liability for pecuniary loss caused to them by their justifiable reliance on the information, if he fails to exercise reasonable care or competence in obtaining or communicating the information." The section then continues to define what persons can enforce this liability.

accountant is protected from claims of third persons when the accountant makes a certification or statement that certain assets were not examined and that the figures relating to them had not been verified. For example, when the accountant was restricted from examining accounts receivable and the accountant's certificate stated that no opinion was expressed as to accounts receivable, the accountant could not be held liable because the information relating to accounts receivable was not accurate.[3]

> An accountant's disclaimer of liability is valid where it is stated that the accountant lacks actual knowledge.

CASE SUMMARY

Can a Disclaimer Shield the Accountant?

Facts: Etna Leasing Services furnished information about its assets to the accountants Finkle & Ross (F & R). They assembled this information into a report or compilation. In accordance with the regulations of the American Institute of Certified Public Accountants, F & R attached to this compilation a statement that the compilation consisted merely of information provided by management, that nothing was verified or audited by the accountants, and that the accountants did not express any opinion. F & R's statement expressly said that the management had not disclosed much information that was required by generally accepted principles of accounting. On the basis of the compilation, Penvest made a large loan to Etna. Later Penvest went bankrupt and Ris, as the trustee in bankruptcy, attempted to collect the loan. When this failed, he sued F & R, claiming that the compilation was false and misleading and that the accountants were liable for fraud.

Decision: Judgment for F & R. By the covering letter, the accountants made it clear that they were not standing behind the information that had been supplied. They were stating in effect that they were merely relaying the information and that it was up to the person receiving it to determine whether or not it was true. Since there was no intent on the part of the accountants that third persons should rely on the information contained in the compilation, F & R could not be liable for fraud. [*Ris v Finkle*, 148 Misc 2d 773, 561 NYS2d 499 (1989)]

> An accountant is not protected by a false disclaimer.

(b) Limitations on Exculpatory Provisions. A disclaimer based on lack of knowledge does not protect the accountant from liability if the accountant had knowledge or reason to know that the statements made were in fact false. In such a case, a court would hold that the disclaimer was not binding. The theory would be misrepresentation—when the accountant stated that personal knowledge was lacking, the accountant impliedly represented that the accountant did not have any knowledge or reason to know that the statements were not correct.

In some states, a limitation of liability or exculpatory clause will protect the accountant only from a malpractice suit brought by a client, not from a suit brought by a third person. In such cases, courts apply the general rule of contract law that only a party to a contract is bound by an exculpatory or limitation of liability clause.

When the malpractice liability of accountants is based on intentional falsification of data, a limitation of liability will not be binding. This follows from the general rule of law that it is against public policy to permit a limitation of liability to immunize an intentional tort.

---

[3] *Stephans Industries, Inc. v Haskins & Sells* (CA10 Colo) 438 F2d 357 (1971).

5. Contributory Negligence of Plaintiff

When a suit for malpractice is brought against an accountant by a client, the comparative negligence of the client may reduce the liability of the accountant. To do this, it is necessary that the negligence of the client contributed to the accountant's failure or that the client ignored instructions of the accountant.

When suit is brought by a third person for malpractice, the defendant accountant may raise the defense of the plaintiff's contributory negligence. If the plaintiff acted negligently in relying on a financial statement, the plaintiff cannot sue the accountant for negligently preparing the statement. For example, when the statement recites that it is merely a working examination and is not certified by the accountant, the third person is negligent if reliance is placed on the statement. The plaintiff is then barred by such contributory negligence.

In some cases, it may be apparent on the face of the financial statement that the business it represents is in poor financial condition. When a prudent person would see danger in the financial statement, the plaintiff not perceiving such danger cannot sue the accountant on the ground that the statement was negligently prepared.

When the plaintiff is highly sophisticated and a shareholder of the corporate client, and has been warned by its own advisors that the corporate assets have been overvalued, the plaintiff cannot hold the accountant liable for the latter's negligence in overstating the value of the corporate assets. In such case, the plaintiff is not entitled to rely on the audit made by the accountant and is contributorily negligent in so doing. Such negligence bars recovery from the accountant.[4]

Some states ignore the negligence of the client unless it actually contributed to the accountant's negligence or interfered with the accountant's audit. Thus it has been held that the negligence of the client of the accountant in the keeping of its records is not a bar to the accountant's liability to the client for the accountant's failing to discover the true facts unless the negligence of the client contributed to the failure of the accountant to discover and report the truth.[5]

B.   ACCOUNTANTS' MALPRACTICE LIABILITY

Most accountants' malpractice litigation involves the question of whether third persons may sue rather than what standards of conduct accountants should observe.

6. Standards of Conduct for Accountants

Accountants are liable for losses they caused their clients by failing to observe the standards of sound accounting practices. Accountants are also liable if their failure to call attention to a condition causes a client to fail to take preventive steps and to thereby sustain a loss.

"Certified public accountants are liable for damages proximately caused by their negligence just like other skilled professions. . . . Accordingly they owe their clients a duty to exercise the degree of care, skill, and competence that reasonably competent members of their profession would exercise under similar

---

4 *Scottish Heritable Trust v Peat Marwick Main & Co.* (CA5 Tex) 81 F3d 606 (1996).
5 *World Radio Laboratories, Inc. v Coopers & Lybrand*, 4 Neb App 34, 538 NW2d 501 (1995).

circumstances."[6] Basically, the concept is the same as the one applied to doctors and attorneys.

An accountant is liable to the client when the accountant negligently fails to detect or fraudulently conceals signs that an employee of the client is embezzling or the internal audit controls of the client's business are not being observed. An accountant who prepares tax returns and acts as tax manager for the client will be liable when additional taxes or penalties are assessed against the client as a result of negligently given advice. Similarly, a client may recover damages from the accountant when the latter negligently failed to inform the client of the tax consequences of selling of the business.[7]

Comparative Negligence. Can an accountant reduce liability for negligence by proving that the client was also negligent? Some states apply the comparative negligence concept and permit proof of the client's negligence.[8]

7. Liability of Accountant for Client's Liability

In some cases, the accountant's malpractice is followed almost immediately by a loss to the client. In other cases, such as those involving taxes, the misconduct of the accountant causes a tax liability to attach to the client, but there is an interval before the client is required to pay those taxes; that is, there is liability for taxes before there is a loss by payment of taxes. It is uncertain whether the client may sue the accountant as soon as the client becomes subject to the additional taxes or whether the client cannot sue until the additional taxes have been paid.

For example, Joan was a CPA that Smithfield Farms retained to work out a plan to liquidate its business and minimize its liability for federal income taxes. Joan recommended an immediate sale of the business's assets, which imposed a tax liability greater than would other alternative tax minimization plans. The fact that Joan was making an error would have been recognized by competent accountants in the community. Joan is thus liable to Smithfield for the taxes that were paid but that would have been avoided if she had not made the mistake.

8. Nonliability to the Interloper

An interloper cannot sue an accountant for malpractice.

No court imposes liability on the accountant to a total stranger who gets possession of the accountant's work and then sustains a loss because of a false statement in the work. This applies regardless of whether the statement was negligent or intentional. For example, assume that a negligently prepared financial statement of a corporation is thrown in the wastepaper basket and is then retrieved by a security guard. If the guard thinks that the statement is a "hot tip" and invests in the stock of the corporation on the basis of the statement, the guard cannot sue the accountant for negligence in preparing the statement. The courts have struggled to form a rule that will exclude what the court regards as interlopers but permit suits by those the courts regard as proper plaintiffs.

---

[6] *Greenstein, Logan & Co. v Burgess Marketing, Inc.* (Tex App) 744 SW2d 170 (1987).
[7] *Deloitte, Haskins & Sells v Green,* ___ Ga App ___, 403 SE2d 818 (1991).
[8] *American National Bank v Touche Ross & Co.,* ___ Ohio ___, 659 NE2d 1276 (Ohio).

9. Nonliability to Person Affected by the Decision of Accountant's Client

A third person cannot sue an accountant for advice given to a client.

On the basis of information furnished by the accountant to a client, the client may make a decision that affects a third person. For example, a report by an independent auditor may indicate that a fiscal officer of the client has not handled funds properly. The report may indicate that it is economically unsound to enter into a contract with a third person. Assume that the client relies on the accountant's report and fires the employee or refuses to make a contract with the third person. If the report of the accountant was negligently made and the true facts would not have justified the action taken by the client, the question arises as to whether the third person or the discharged employee may sue the negligent accountant. At least one court has held that such a suit may not be brought.[9]

10. Accountants' Negligence Malpractice Liability to Third Persons

In the last century, the negligence of an accountant would impose liability only to the accountant's clients. Today, many states permit third persons to recover damages from the accountant. In some states, a statute specifies when a nonprivity plaintiff may sue an accountant.[10]

Malpractice standards are the same for all kinds of accountants.

(a) Status of Accountant. The accountant sued by a third person for malpractice may be an in-house accountant working full time for a particular employer. The accountant may be an independent contractor who regularly does accounting-related work, such as preparing financial statements and tax returns for different clients, or the accountant may be an independent auditor.

ETHICS & THE LAW

Johns-Manville, Inc., had been a producer of asbestos since the nineteenth century. Since 1936, health issues involving asbestos workers had been developing and included breathing difficulties as well as a cancer linked to asbestos fibers in the lungs. With each passing year, Manville and other producers experienced more litigation and liability.

Prior to 1982, the disclosures in Manville's financial statements had explained the pending and resolved liability suits but concluded that it was impossible, under Financial Accounting Standards Board Directive #5 (FASB-5), to quantify the potential liability: "The company is unable to predict at this time the outcome or liability in these cases." In 1982, Coopers & Lybrand, the auditors for Manville, were given a report from Manville's Litigation Analysis Group that the cost of disposition of all the asbestos suits would be $1.9 billion. Because of this expert opinion, Coopers & Lybrand told Manville that it was now possible to "reasonably estimate" the liability costs and refused to issue a clean audit report unless some form of financial disclosure regarding the asbestos liability was made. It was the opinion of Coopers & Lybrand that, based on its expert analysis, the liability was quantifiable.

Manville fired Coopers & Lybrand and filed appropriate notices with the Securities and Exchange Commission that it was changing audit firms. Manville

[9] *Harper v Inkster Public Schools,* ___ Mich App ___, 404 NW2d 776 (1987).
[10] *Chestnut Corp. v Pestine, Brinati, Gamer, Ltd.,* ___ Ill App ___, 667 NE2d 543 (1996).

then hired Price Waterhouse as its new audit firm. After examining the records and the status of litigation as well as the expert opinions, Price Waterhouse also refused to issue a clean audit statement without the disclosure.

The effect of the refusals of both audit firms to issue clean financial opinions was that Manville declared bankruptcy on August 26, 1982, and was required to sign over $2.5 billion of its assets (mostly stock) and contribute 20 percent of its annual net income to a trust for asbestos workers. The result of the bankruptcy for Manville shareholders was the loss of their investment in the company.

Did the auditors do the right thing? Were their decisions ethical? Didn't their decisions in effect destroy the value of the shareholders' investment? Would you have done the same thing?

What constitutes negligence is the same for all three types of accountants. As a practical matter, a third person would not ordinarily sue the employee-accountant because the claim would probably be much more than the employee could pay. It would be more practical to sue the employer, who would be liable for the negligent performance of the employee.

When the nonprivity plaintiff sues the accountant, it is immaterial that there is no fiduciary relationship between them. The liability of the accountant to the nonprivity plaintiff, when recognized, is based on the reliance of the plaintiff on the work of the accountant.[11]

(b) Conflicting Theories. A number of theories have been developed in this century to determine whether a third person sustaining a loss because of the accountant's negligence can sue the accountant for loss or whether this third person is an interloper who cannot sue. These views may be identified as (1) the privity rule, (2) the contact rule, (3) the known user rule, and (4) the foreseeable user rule. In addition, some courts follow (5) a flexible rule, deciding each case as it arises.

> Conflict exists as to when a third party can sue an accountant.

Each of these views represents an attempt to draw a boundary line between the interloper and the "proper" plaintiff. Each view is supported by honest judges seeking to do justice. They have the same goal and are all guided by ethics, but the resultant rules of law are different.

In some states, statutes have been adopted defining when nonprivity plaintiffs may sue an accountant for negligence.[12]

(1) The Privity Rule. The privity rule excludes a negligence malpractice suit by a third person. This rule holds that only the person in privity with the accountant-that is, the accountant's client-may sue the accountant.[13]

> The privity rule bars a third person from suing for an accountant's malpractice.

When the privity rule is applied, a bank lending money to the accountant's client cannot sue the accountant for malpractice.

---

[11] *Brown v KPMG Peat Marwick* (Tex App) 756 SW2d 742 (1993).

[12] *Deloitte & Touche* (DC Ark) 834 F Supp 1129 (1992). (The court stated "[the statute] moves the State somewhat closer to the Restatement position.")

[13] This rule was originally known as the New York rule, *Ultramares Corp. v Touche,* ___ NY ___, 174 NE 441 (1931). Although it has been replaced in New York by the contact rule, the privity rule is still the law in many jurisdictions.

C· P· A

The contract rule permits a third person to sue an accountant if the third person had contact with the accountant.

(2) The Contact Rule. As a relaxation of the privity requirement, New York now holds that a third person may sue a negligent accountant if there was some contact between the third person and the accountant. *For example*, an accountant may go to a bank to see what information the bank requires for the accountant's client to obtain a loan. In this case, there is a sufficient "link" or "contact" between the bank and the accountant to allow the bank to sue the accountant if it sustains loss because of the accountant's negligence.[14] It appears that the New York contact rule requires that the accountant meet or communicate with the nonprivity plaintiff to establish a relationship equivalent to privity. It also appears that the accountant must know the purpose of the accounting work and foresee the nonprivity plaintiff's reliance on that work.[15]

Thus, there must be enough contact with, or dealings between, the plaintiff and the accountant to give the accountant reason to know that the plaintiff was relying for a particular purpose on the financial statements prepared by the accountant.

The contact rule applies to malpractice defendants generally. It is not limited to suits against accountants.[16]

The known user rule permits a third person to sue an accountant when the accountant knew that the third person would be using a work product.

(3) The Known User Rule. By this rule, the accountant is liable for a third person's negligently caused loss when the accountant knew that the third person would be using the accountant's work product. Thus, a shareholder may bring suit against the accountant negligently preparing and certifying an annual financial report that was prepared for distribution to shareholders.[17]

Under this rule, the fact that the nonprivity plaintiff's reliance on a financial statement was foreseeable does not entitle the plaintiff to sue the accountant for negligent preparation of the statement. It must be shown that the accountant knew the statement would be furnished to that plaintiff. Under the known user rule, the plaintiff's reliance must thus be actually foreseen and not merely reasonably foreseeable.[18]

---

[14] *Credit Alliance Corp. v Arthur Andersen & Co.,* ___ NY ___, 483 NE2d 110 (1985). Some courts are reluctant to turn their backs on the requirement of privity and describe the contact rule not as a different rule but as requiring "a relationship sufficiently intimate to be equated with privity." *Empire of America v Arthur Andersen & Co.,* ___ App Div 2d ___, 514 NYS2d 578 (1987). A further attempt to define the New York rule was made in *William Iselin & Co. v Landau,* ___ NY ___, 522 NE2d 21 (1988) (involving a review report), in which the court declared that it was necessary for a nonprivity plaintiff suing an accountant for negligent misrepresentation to establish "a nexus between them sufficiently approaching privity (Credit Alliance Corp. . . .)." The contact rule has been adopted by a minority of states. *Idaho Bank & Trust Co. v First Bankcorp of Idaho* (Idaho) 772 P2d 720 (1989).

[15] *Security Pacific Business Credit, Inc. v Peat Marwick Main & Co.,* 597 (NY) NE2d 1080 (1992). In *Franko v Mitchell* (Ariz App) 762 P2d 1345 (1988), the court held that when the borrower's attorney met and discussed the proposed loan details with both the lender and the borrower, it could be found that there was an implied contract of employment between the borrower's attorney and the creditor so as to permit the creditor to bring a malpractice action against the attorney. This would have been classified as "equivalent to privity" if the court had followed the New York terminology.

[16] *Ossining Union Free School District v Anderson* (NY) 539 NE2d 91 (1989) ("The long-standing rule is that recovery may be had for pecuniary loss arising from negligent representations where there is actual privity of contract between the parties or a relationship so close as to approach that of privity. Nor does the rule apply only to accountants. We have never drawn that categorical distinction, and see no basis for establishing such an arbitrary limitation now."); *Board of Managers of the Astor Terrace Condominium v Shuman, Lichtenstein, Claman & Efron,* ___ App Div 2d ___, 583 NYS2d 398 (1992).

[17] *Boykin v Arthur Andersen & Co.* (Ala) 639 So 2d 504 (1994).

[18] *Lindner Fund v Abney* (Mo App) 770 SW2d 437 (1989). The rule that the nonprivity plaintiff may recover from the accountant for malpractice negligence only if the accountant's statement was furnished to that plaintiff, or the accountant knew that the client who was given the statement would in turn give the statement to the plaintiff, is often identified as "the Restatement rule." This rule is based on Restatement (Second) Torts (1977) § 522(2). There is, however, some uncertainty as to the exact boundaries of the Restatement rule. See *Selden v Burnett* (Alaska) 754 P2d 256 (1988); *Raritan River Steel Co. v Cherry, Bekaert & Holland* (NC) 367 SE2d 609 (1988).

You Knew Who Would Get Hurt

Facts: Hicks, the president and manager of Intermountain Merchandising, wanted to sell the business to Montana Merchandising, Inc. To provide a basis for the transaction, he retained Bloomgren, an accountant, to make an audit of Intermountain. Bloomgren knew that the audit report was to be used by Montana in making the purchase of the business from Intermountain. Bloomgren's audit report showed the Intermountain business as profitable. Thayer, the president of Montana, relied on this report in agreeing to purchase the business of Intermountain and in agreeing to the terms of the purchase. Some time later, it was discovered that the accountant had made a number of mistakes and that the business that was sold was actually insolvent. Thayer and Montana Merchandising sued Hicks and Bloomgren for damages. Liability of the accountant was claimed on the ground that the accountant had negligently misrepresented the facts. The accountant defended on the basis that Thayer was not in privity of contract with him and therefore could not sue him.

Decision: Lack of privity of contract between the plaintiff and the defendant's accountant is not a bar to suit. While there is a conflict of what will be required in place of privity, there is no reason to deny recovery by a nonprivity plaintiff against a negligent accountant when the accountant made the audit with knowledge that an identified third person would rely on the audit report in connection with a particular transaction. Bloomgren had this knowledge as to Thayer and Montana Merchandising, so the lack of privity of the plaintiff was not a bar to recovering damages for the negligent preparation of the audit report by Bloomgren. [*Thayer v Hicks*, _____ Mont _____, 793 P2d 784 (1990)]

Under the known user rule, it is sufficient if the user is a member of a known class even though the identity of the particular user is not known to the accountant. However, there is authority that when the identity of the intended user is known to the accountant, another person coming within the same class cannot sue the accountant.[19] *For example*, an accountant prepares a financial statement for a client with the knowledge that the client will take it to First National Bank to obtain a loan. First National Bank may sue the accountant for negligent loss even though the bank never had any direct contact or dealings, or was in privity, with the accountant. However, no one other than First National may sue the accountant for negligence. The fact that the plaintiff was a foreseeable user does not give the right to sue in a "known user" state. Accordingly, when the accountant prepared a financial statement for the client and nothing was said about what further use of the statement would be made, creditors of the client could not sue the accountant for negligent preparation of the statement. It was the client who was the known user.

If the court follows the privity rule or the contact rule described in the two preceding sections, the known user cannot sue the accountant for negligent malpractice. Moreover, some courts that follow the known user rule apply it so strictly that a substitute foreseeable user is not allowed to sue. To illustrate, assume that in the example just given the client was refused the loan by First National Bank.

---

[19] *Blue Bell, Inc. v Peat, Marwich, Mitchell & Co.* (Tex App) 715 SW2d 408 (1986) ("If under current business practice and the circumstances of that case, an accountant preparing audited financial statements knows or should know that such statements will be relied upon by a limited class of persons, the accountant may be liable for injuries to members of that class relying on his certification of the audited reports.") Note that to the extent that a court speaks in terms of "should know," there is the inference that the court is embracing "foreseeability" and is thus moving from the known user rule to the foreseeable user rule.

The client might then make an application for a loan to Second National Bank. It has been held that Second National Bank could not sue the accountant because it was not a known user. However, Second National Bank would be allowed to sue under the rules discussed in the section that follows.

(4) The Foreseeable User Rule. The accountant may foresee that a particular class of unknown persons will rely on the accountant's work. For example, when the accountant prepares a financial statement knowing that the client is going to use it to borrow money from some bank or finance company, the accountant foresees a class of lenders. Similarly, the accountant may know that the financial statement will be used to sell the stock of the client corporation. Here again, there is a foreseeable class consisting of unknown persons.

When it is reasonable to foresee there will be persons who will rely on the accountant's statement, the foreseeable user rule imposes liability on the accountant for negligent malpractice. The foreseeable user rule allows these third persons to sue for their loss without regard to the lack of privity of contract between them and the accountants.[20]

CASE SUMMARY

Equal Treatment of All Negligent Defendants

Facts: The auditing firm of Timm, Schmidt & Co. prepared annual financial statements for Clintonville Fire Apparatus, Inc. (CFA). CFA showed these statements to Citizens State Bank and asked for loans. On the basis of the financial statements, Citizens loaned CFA approximately $380,000. Timm later discovered that the financial statements overvalued CFA by more than $400,000. Citizens demanded repayment of the loans. CFA could not pay the balance, and Citizens sued Timm and its malpractice liability insurer. They raised the defense that suit was barred by lack of privity and the fact that no one in the Timm firm knew that CFA intended to use the financial statements to obtain loans from anyone.

Decision: The absence of privity or the lack of knowledge of the intended use did not bar liability of an accountant for negligence to third persons sustaining loss by relying on the statements prepared by the accountant. The liability of an accountant should be determined under accepted principles of negligence law. "The fundamental principle [of that law] is that a tortfeasor is ... liable for all the foreseeable consequences of his act." The client's use of the statements to obtain loans and the harm to the lender were all foreseeable. [*Citizens State Bank v Timm, Schmidt & Co.* 113 Wis 2d 376, 335 NW2d 361 (1983)]

When an accountant made an audit report of a business enterprise and a partnership was formed and invested in the enterprise on the basis of the audit report, the accountant could not be sued for negligence. The accountant had no reason to foresee that the partnership would be formed, that it would invest in the enterprise, or that it would rely on the accountant's report.[21]

---

[20] *Bily v Arthur Young & Co.* 230 Cal App 3d 835, 271 Cal Rptr 470 (1990). This rule is regarded by some courts as representing the majority view. The foreseeable user rule brings the law with respect to accountants into harmony with the tort law relating to other persons and activities.
[21] *ML-Lee Acquisition Fund v Deloitte & Touche* (SC) 463 SE2d 618 (1995).

(5) The Intended User Rule. Fear that the foreseeability rule does not sufficiently restrict the number of potential plaintiffs has led some courts to limit suit to those nonprivity plaintiffs who were not merely foreseeable but also expected or intended to rely on the work of the accountant in a particular transaction or another similar transaction.[22] In this view the accountant must have furnished the information directly to the nonprivity plaintiff or to the client, knowing that the client would transmit the information to the nonprivity plaintiff.

(6) The Flexible Rule. Some courts have rejected the requirement of privity in malpractice suits against accountants but have not adopted any of the rules discussed in the preceding sections. These courts prefer to keep the question open and to decide each case as it arises.

When a malpractice claim relates to advice given to a client, strong arguments can be made for retaining the privity rule. Thus, it has been held that when an accountant orally recommended the client make an investment as a tax shelter, third persons to whom the client repeated the advice could not sue the accountant for malpractice.[23]

(c) Unknown User. When the accountant has no knowledge of, or reason to know of, any third person's making use of the accountant's work, the plaintiff is not able to come within any exception to the requirement of privity. Consequently, a nonprivity plaintiff cannot sue for the accountant's negligence when the accountant had no knowledge of any use that could affect the plaintiff.[24]

11. Accountants' Fraud Malpractice Liability to Third Persons

Society in general condemns fraud more strongly than it does negligence. This is seen in the greater liability of accountants for fraudulent malpractice.

(a) What Constitutes Fraud by Accountants. *Fraud* is defined as a false statement made with knowledge that it was false or with reckless indifference as to whether it was true. This statement was made with the intent that the listener rely on it, and the listener did rely on it and sustained loss. In the field of accounting, the false statement will typically be one of accounting in such a way as to make the client appear to be in a better financial position than is actually the case. For example, the client may own assets that are worthless, but the accountant retains them in the financial statement at cost or some other unreasonable value.

At times, the falsification of the financial statement may be designed to downgrade the financial condition of a corporation. This has been done to induce shareholders to sell their stock to a dominant group of shareholders. The false financial statement purposely undervalued the assets of the corporation to make the shareholders believe their stock had little value and that, therefore, they should sell at the low price offered by the dominant group.

> Fraud of an accountant has the same meaning as in contract law.

---

[22] *Bily v Arthur Young & Co.* 3 Cal 4th 370, 11 Cal Rptr 2d 51, 834 P2d 745 (1992).
[23] *Selden v Burnett* (Alaska) 754 P2d 256 (1988).
[24] *Sudamerican Bank & Trust Co. v Harrison* (Mo App) 851 SW2d 563 (1993).

(b) Fraud Liability of Accountant to Intended Victims. When an accountant commits fraud, it is typically intended to mislead a third person or a class of persons whose identity is known to the accountant. Any such victims, whether an identified person or member of a contemplated class of potential victims, may sue the accountant for loss caused by fraud. The problem of privity (relating to liability for negligence) is ignored when the basis of the malpractice suit is fraud. The social force of preventing fraud overrides concern for creating a hardship on the accountant by allowing third persons to bring suit.

An intended victim may sue an accountant for fraud, regardless of lack of privity.

An accountant might make a false financial statement for a corporate client, with knowledge that it will be used in selling securities of the corporation to third persons. If so, the third persons may sue the accountant for the damages sustained.

For example, an accountant has been held liable for disguising the true character of a hoped-for profit from the sale and resale of real estate. The accountant described it as "deferred income," although there was little reason to believe that the transaction could ever be completed. In this case, the buyer, who was obligated to pay $5 million for the property, had assets of only $100,000. The financial statement would have shown a loss instead of a substantial profit if the true character of the transaction had been disclosed.

For a statutory basis of liability under the Federal Securities Statutes, see Chapter 48.

SUMMARY

When a contract requires a party to perform services, the party must perform with the care exercised by persons performing similar services within the same community. If the party negligently fails to observe those standards, there is both a breach of contract and a tort. This tort of negligent breach of contract constitutes malpractice, and the other party to the contract can sue the wrongdoer either for breach of contract or for the negligence involved.

In the modern view, third persons may also sue the wrongdoer for malpractice. However, when the malpractice suit is brought against an accountant for negligence, courts differ as to when a third person may sue. Some courts refuse to let the third person sue; these courts require privity between the parties. Most courts allow suit by the third person against the wrongdoer but differ over what the plaintiff must show in order to bring such a suit. In New York, the plaintiff must show as a minimum that there was a "contact" with the accountant. In some states, it is sufficient that the third person was a known user of the accountant's information. Other courts go further and allow the third person to sue if it was reasonable to foresee that the third person would make use of the accountant's information. Some courts limit suit to those nonprivity plaintiffs who were intended to rely on the accounting work.

When an accountant is guilty of fraud, the intended victim of the fraud may sue the accountant even though privity of contract is lacking.

To a limited degree, an accountant is protected from malpractice liability by a disclaimer of liability or by the contributory negligence of the plaintiff.

QUESTIONS AND CASE PROBLEMS

1. What social forces are affected by allowing a stranger to a contract to sue for the harm caused by the negligent performance of the contract?

2. The president of Jones Corp. was concerned whether it would be necessary to borrow money to pay taxes. The corporation employed Roanne to prepare a financial statement of the corporation. When the president saw this statement, he decided that money should be borrowed. The lending bank required the corporation to submit a financial statement, and the statement prepared by Roanne was submitted. It contained a number of negligent mistakes that misled the bank into lending the money to Jones. Jones went into bankruptcy shortly after, and the bank recovered only a small percentage of the loan. The bank sued Roanne for the amount it could not collect. Was she liable in a state that followed the known user rule?

3. Thomas & Sons, certified public accountants, prepared a financial statement of Continental Land Development Co. Much of the company's assets consisted of land in foreign countries, some of which had been confiscated by local governments. The financial statement prepared by Thomas said that, based on the best information available, the land described in the statement was owned by Continental and had not been confiscated. The financial statement further recited that Thomas was entirely dependent on foreign sources for the information about the foreign land and had no knowledge of its accuracy. On the strength of this financial statement, Fifth National Bank loaned money to Continental. The recitals as to the land owned by Continental and its value proved false, and the bank could not get back its loan. The bank sued Thomas. Was Thomas liable?

4. The certified public accounting partnership of James, Guinn, and Head prepared a certified audit report of four corporations, known as the Paschal Enterprises, with knowledge that their report would be used to induce Shatterproof Glass Corp. to lend money to those corporations. The report showed the corporations to be solvent when in fact they were insolvent. Shatterproof relied on the audit report, loaned approximately $500,000 to the four corporations, and lost almost all of it because the liabilities of the companies were in excess of their assets. Shatterproof claimed that James and other accountants had been negligent in preparing the report and sued them to recover the loss on the loan. The accountants raised the defense that they had been retained not by the plaintiff but rather by Paschal. Was this defense valid? [*Shatterproof Glass Corp. v James* (Tex App) 466 SW2d 873]

5. Landau made an audit and a financial report of Suits Galore, a clothing manufacturer. The statement prepared by Landau was not certified. It stated that it was a review report only and that no opinion was expressly stated by the accountant. On the basis of this report, William Iselin & Co. extended credit to Suits Galore. Shortly after, Suits Galore went into bankruptcy, and Iselin was not repaid the money it had loaned. Iselin sued Landau on the ground that the financial report had been negligently prepared and that Iselin could sue Landau for the loss sustained. Was it correct? [*William Iselin & Co. v Landau*, ___ App Div 2d ___, 513 NYS2d 3]

6. For almost 13 years, Touche Ross had prepared the annual audit of Buttes Gas and Oil Co. Buttes wanted to obtain a loan from Dimensional Credit Corp. (DCC) and showed DCC its most recent annual audit. DCC made the loan on the basis of what it learned from the audit. The loan was not repaid, and DCC then realized that it had been misled by negligent statements about Buttes' financial condition that appeared in the annual statement prepared by Touche Ross. Suit was brought against Touche Ross for its negligence in preparing this report. Was it liable?

7. Wright, who owned a home, contracted with Orkin Exterminating Co. to exterminate termites in his house. Two years later Wright sold the house to Teunissen, who afterward found that the house was infested with termites. She then found out there had been a termite extermination two years before. She sued Orkin, claiming that the prior inspection had been negligently performed and that Orkin was liable to her for the damage she sustained. Was she correct?

8. Ernst & Whinney made an audit report for W.L. Jackson Mfg. Co. On the basis of this report, Bethlehem Steel sold on credit to Jackson Mfg. The report had been negligently prepared, and Jackson went broke shortly after. Bethlehem Steel did not get paid and then sued Ernst & Whinney for negligent malpractice. It raised the defense that it was not liable because it was not in privity with Bethlehem and did not know the name of Bethlehem in connection with its audit statements. Was this a valid defense? [*Bethlehem Steel Corp. v Ernst & Whinney* (Tenn) 822 SW2d 592]

CPA QUESTIONS

1. In general, the third party (primary) beneficiary rule as applied to a CPA's legal liability in conducting an audit is relevant to which of the following causes of action against a CPA?

	Fraud	Constructive Fraud	Negligence
a.	Yes	Yes	No
b.	Yes	No	No
c.	No	Yes	Yes
d.	No	No	Yes

(11/87, Law, #29)

2. Beckler & Associates, CPAs, audited and gave an unqualified opinion on the financial statements of Queen Co. The financial statements contained misstatements that resulted in a material overstatement of Queen's net worth. Queen provided the audited financial statements to Mac Bank in connection with a loan made by Mac to Queen. Beckler knew that the financial statements would be provided to Mac. Queen defaulted on the loan. Mac sued Beckler to recover for its losses associated with Queen's default. Which of the following must Mac prove in order to recover?

I. Beckler was negligent in conducting the audit.
II. Mac relied on the financial statements.

a. I only.
b. II only.
c. Both I and II.
d. Neither I nor II.

3. In a common law action against an accountant, lack of privity is a viable defense if the plaintiff
a. Is the client's creditor who sues the accountant for negligence.
b. Can prove the presence of gross negligence that amounts to a reckless disregard for the truth.
c. Is the accountant's client.
d. Bases the action upon fraud.

(11/94, Law, #9, 5187)

P A R T 3

Personal Property and Bailments

Personal Property

CHAPTER 22

OBJECTIVES

After studying this chapter, you should be able to

1. *Write a definition of personal property;*
2. *List and explain various types of gifts;*
3. *Identify the public policy reasons behind the law of escheat;*
4. *Identify the four forms of multiple ownership of personal property; and*
5. *Set forth the remedies for violation of property rights.*

What is personal property? Who owns it? How is it acquired?

A.   GENERAL PRINCIPLES

In common usage, the term *property* refers to a piece of land or a thing or an object. As a legal concept, however, property also refers to the rights that an individual may possess in that piece of land or that thing or that object.[1] Property includes the rights of any person to possess, use, enjoy, and dispose of a thing or object of value. A right in a thing is property, without regard to whether this right is absolute or conditional, perfect or imperfect, legal or equitable.

Real property means land and things embedded in the land, such as oil tanks. It also includes things attached to the earth, such as buildings or trees, and rights in any of these things. **Personal property** is property that is movable or intangible, or rights in such things. As described in the next chapter, rights in intellectual property such as writings, computer programs, inventions, and trademarks are valuable business properties that are protected by federal statutes.

1.   Personal Property

Personal property is an expanding concept.

Personal property consists of (1) whole or fractional rights in things that are tangible and movable, such as furniture and books; (2) claims and debts, which are called **choses in action**; and (3) intangible proprietary rights, such as trademarks, copyrights, and patents.

The concept of personal property is expanding. For example, courts now generally include gas and water within the definition of property. Thus, persons who tap water mains and gas pipes to obtain water and gas without paying are guilty of taking property.

2.   Limitations on Ownership

A person who has all possible rights in and over a thing is said to have *absolute ownership* of it. The term *absolute*, however, is somewhat misleading, for one's rights with respect to the use, enjoyment, and disposal of things are subject to certain restrictions. An owner's property is subject to the government's powers to tax, to regulate under the police power, and to take by eminent domain. Property is subject to the creditors of the owner. Above all, the owner may not use property in a way that will unreasonably infringe on the rights of others.

B.   ACQUISITION OF TITLE TO PERSONAL PROPERTY

Title to personal property may be acquired in different ways. For example, property is commonly purchased. The purchase and sale of goods is governed by the law of sales. In this chapter, the following methods of acquiring personal property will be discussed: gift, finding of lost property, transfer by a nonowner, occupation, and escheat.

---

[1] *Presley Memorial Foundation v Crowell* (Tenn App) 733 SW2d 89 (1987).

3. Gifts

Title to personal property may be transferred by the voluntary act of the owner without receiving anything in exchange—that is, by **gift**. The person making the gift, the **donor**, may do so because of things that the recipient of the gift, the **donee**, had done in the past or is expected to do in the future. However, such things are not deemed consideration and thus do not alter the "free" character of the gift. Five types of gifts are discussed below.

(a) Inter Vivos Gifts. The ordinary gift that is made between two living persons is an **inter vivos gift**. For practical purposes, such a gift takes effect when the donor (1) expresses an intent to transfer title and (2) makes delivery, subject to the right of the donee to disclaim the gift within a reasonable time after learning that it has been made.[2] Because there is no consideration for a gift, there is no enforceable contract, and an intended donee cannot sue for breach of contract if the donor fails to complete the gift.

(1) Intent. The intent to make a gift requires an intent to transfer title at that time. In contrast, an intent to confer a benefit at a future date is not a sufficient intent to create any right in the intended donee.

A delivery of property without the intent to make a gift does not transfer title. For example, there is no gift when the owner lends a VCR to another person.

(2) Delivery. Ordinarily, the delivery required to make a gift will be an actual handing over to the donee of the thing that is given.

The delivery of a gift may also be made by a **symbolic or constructive delivery**, such as by the delivery of means of control of property. Such means of control might be keys to a lock or keys to a garden tractor or papers that are essential to or closely associated with the ownership of the property, such as documents of title or a ship's papers. A signed blank check is capable of being delivered and may be a gift after delivery when the donee fills out the check in the amount designated by the donor and cashes the check. However, making out a check to a friend and entering the amount in a checkbook do not create a valid gift when the check is not delivered to the friend before the donor's death.

FIGURE 22-1
Inter Vivos Gift

Law:	Donor	1. Intent and 2. Delivery	Unless the gift is disclaimed, title passes to donee.
Application:	Smith owns the Van Gogh painting *The Irises*.	1. He states, "This is for you, Michael," and 2. Personally presents the painting to his son Michael.	Michael becomes the owner.

---

[2] *Owen v Owen* (SD) 351 NW2d 139 (1984).

CASE SUMMARY

The Check Was Not in the Mail

Facts: Barbara Worrell and Elizabeth Brisendine were longtime friends. The two ladies saw each other at social events and traveled together. During Brisendine's terminal illness, Worrell drove her to and from the hospital and doctors' appointments. On a visit to Brisendine's home during her terminal illness, Brisendine wrote a check for $10,000, made an entry in her checkbook, and attempted to present it to Worrell. Without seeing the actual amount of the check, Worrell refused it, saying she looked out for Brisendine out of friendship and did not desire payment for helping a friend. Brisendine told Worrell that "the check will be in the mail to you." Soon thereafter, Henry Meyer, who took care of Brisendine's finances, discussed the entry for $10,000 to Worrell with Brisendine, who told him she was going to mail the check to Worrell. She died before mailing the check. After her death Meyer told Worrell the amount of the check, and she filed a claim against the estate for $10,000, believing the check was intended as a gift. The personal representative refused the claim.

Decision: Judgment for the personal representative of the estate of Brisendine. In this case there was donative intent to give the gift. However, no evidence was presented to show the check was mailed, or placed in the hands of an agent for delivery. Without evidence of delivery, a gift is not established regardless of the donor's intent. [*Worrell v Lathan (SC App) 478 SE2d 287 (1996)*]

The delivery of a symbol is effective as a gift if the intent to make a gift is established.[3] This is in contrast to merely giving the token's recipient temporary access to the property—for example, until the deliverer comes back from a hospital stay.

(3) Donor's Death. If the donor dies before doing what is needed to make an effective gift, the gift fails.[4] An agent or the executor or administrator of the estate cannot thereafter perform the missing step on behalf of the decedent. ◆ *For example,* Mary Manning, who was in poor health, wanted to give her college-age granddaughter, Phyllis, her valuable 1966 Ford Mustang convertible. She sent her daughter, Nel, to obtain the car's title from a file in the basement but was too tired to sign it upon Nel's return with the title. Mary passed away the next day without signing the document. Nel, the executor under Mary's will, cannot complete the delivery of the gift by signing the title because it is beyond the authority of an executor. Even though donative intent existed, no evidence of transfer of ownership and delivery to Phyllis occurred prior to Mary's death. Therefore, no valid gift was made. ◆

(b) Gifts Causa Mortis. A **gift causa mortis** is made when the donor, contemplating imminent and impending death, delivers personal property to the donee with the intent that the donee shall own it if the donor dies. This is a conditional gift, and the donor is entitled to take the property back if (1) the donor does not die, (2) the donor revokes the gift before dying, or (3) the donee dies before the donor.

---

[3] *Matter of Estate of Monks* (Sur Ct) 655 NY S2d 296 (1997).
[4] *Laverman v Destocki* (Ohio App) 622 NE2d 1122 (1994).

To the surprise of some parents, a completed gift to a minor cannot be revoked.

(c) Gifts and Transfers to Minors. Uniform acts provide for transferring property to a custodian to hold for the benefit of a minor.[5] When property is held by a custodian for the benefit of a minor under one of the uniform acts, the custodian has discretionary power to use the property "for the support, maintenance, education, and benefit" of the minor, but the custodian may not use the custodial property for the custodian's own personal benefit. The gift is final and irrevocable for tax and all other purposes on complying with the procedure of the acts.

CASE SUMMARY

Ignorance Is No Defense

Facts: In 1980, Larry Heath received $10,000 from his father. With interest, these funds grew to $13,381 by 1983, and in March he used this money to establish two custodian bank accounts for his minor children under the Uniform Gifts to Minors Act. Larry was listed as custodian on each account. In August 1984, Larry closed both accounts and returned the proceeds to his mother, since his father was now in Europe. The children's mother, Pamela, brought suit to recover the funds on behalf of the children, contending that the deposits were irrevocable gifts. Larry contended that the money was his father's and was never intended as a gift. Larry testified that he was a mere factory worker and was ignorant of the legal effect of his signing the signature cards for the custodian accounts.

Decision: Judgment for Pamela on behalf of the children. To find that an inter vivos gift has been made, there must be donative intent and delivery. The UGMA expressly deals with "delivery" and provides that this element of a gift is satisfied by documentary compliance with the procedures of the statute. The issue of "donative intent" is not conclusively resolved by making a determination that there was documentary compliance with the statute. However, documentary compliance with the procedures set forth by the UGMA is highly probative on the issue of intent. Larry's testimony that he was ignorant of the legal effect of his signing the signature cards was unworthy of belief and insufficient to rebut the strong documentary showing that he had created irrevocable gifts. [Heath v Heath, 143 Ill App 3d 390, 98 Ill Dec 615, 493 NE2d 97 (1986)]

Under the uniform acts, custodianships terminate and the property is distributed when the minor reaches age 21.

(d) Conditional Gifts. A gift may be made subject to a condition, such as "This car is yours when you graduate" or "This car is yours unless you drop out of school." In the first example, the gift is subject to a condition precedent—graduation. A condition precedent must be satisfied before any gift or transfer takes place. In the second example, the gift is subject to a condition subsequent—dropping out of school. A condition subsequent operates to destroy or divest a title that had already been transferred.

---

5 The Uniform Gifts to Minors Act (UGMA) was originally proposed in 1956. It was reviewed in 1965 and again in 1966. One of these versions is in effect in the following states: Delaware, New York, South Carolina, and Vermont. It has been adopted for the U.S. Virgin Islands.

The Uniform Transfers to Minors Act, which expands the type of property that can be made the subject of a gift, was originally proposed in 1983. It has been adopted, often with minor variations, in the following states: Alabama, Alaska, Arizona, Arkansas, California, Colorado, Connecticut, Florida, Georgia, Hawaii, Idaho, Illinois, Indiana, Iowa, Kansas, Kentucky, Louisiana, Maine, Maryland, Massachusetts, Minnesota, Mississippi, Missouri, Montana, Nebraska, Nevada, New Hampshire, New Jersey, North Carolina, North Dakota, Ohio, Oklahoma, Oregon, Pennsylvania, Rhode Island, South Dakota, Tennessee, Texas, Utah, Virginia, Washington, West Virginia, Wisconsin, and Wyoming. It has also been adopted by the District of Columbia.

Ordinarily, no condition is recognized unless it is expressly stated. However, most courts regard an engagement ring as a conditional gift subject to the condition subsequent of a failure to marry. The inherent symbolism of the gift itself is deemed to foreclose the need to establish an express condition that there be a marriage.

Most jurisdictions require return of engagement rings only if the donor has not unjustifiably broken off the engagement. A few states reject considerations of "fault" in the breaking of an engagement and always require the return of the ring to the donor when an engagement is broken. This view is based on the theory that, in most cases, a change of mind rather than fault occasions the termination of the engagement.[6] Majority rule requires the return of the engagement ring to the donor where the engagement is mutually broken.

CASE SUMMARY

If You Miss the Boat, You Must Return the Ring

Facts: John Vann gave Cindy Vehrs a diamond ring upon their engagement to be married. They mutually agreed to postpone the wedding, which had been set for June 1989. For the next several months, they discussed rescheduling the wedding, but due to Cindy's work-related travel, they were unable to set a new date. In January 1990, John told her at a dinner party that if she was not going to set a new date, she should return the ring. Thereafter, while Cindy never said the engagement was off, she acted "cool" toward him whenever he called her. When John ultimately asked for the ring, she refused, and John sued for the return of the ring in a replevin action.

Decision: Judgment for Vann. In the *Harris v Davis* precedent case, the court relied on a Pennsylvania decision to explain the conditional nature of an engagement ring. That court stated:

> A gift by a man to a woman on condition that she embark on the sea of matrimony with him is no different from a gift based on the condition that the donee sail on any other sea, and if, after receiving the provisional gift, the donee refuses to leave the harbor-if the anchor of contractual performance sticks in the sands of irresolution and procrastination—the gift must be restored to the donor.

So also when the engagement is mutually broken, as in this case, and the condition not fulfilled, the donor of an engagement ring is entitled to the return of the ring. [*Vann v Vehrs*, (Ill App) 633 NE2d 102 (1994)]

(e) Anatomical Gifts. Persons may make gifts of parts of their bodies, as in the case of kidney transplants. Persons may also make postdeath gifts. The Uniform Anatomical Gift Act[7] permits persons 18 years or older to make gifts of their bodies or any parts thereof. The gift takes effect on the death of the donor. The gift may be made to a school, a hospital, an organ bank, or a named patient. Such a gift may also be made, subject to certain restrictions, by the spouse, adult child, parent, adult brother or sister, or guardian of a deceased person. If a hospital misleads family members into consenting to tissue or organ donations that exceed their express wishes, such misconduct is sufficiently outrageous to support a claim for intentional infliction of emotional distress.[8]

---

[6] *McIntire v Raukhorst* (Ohio App) 585 NE2d 456 (1989).
[7] This act has been adopted in every state.
[8] See *Perry v Saint Francis Hospital*, 886 F Supp 1551 (D Kan 1995).

4. Finding of Lost Property

Personal property is lost when the owner does not know where it is located but intends to retain title to or ownership of it. The person finding lost property does not acquire title but only possession. Ordinarily, the finder of lost property is required to surrender the property to the true owner when the latter establishes ownership. Meanwhile, the finder is entitled to retain possession as against everyone else.

Without a contract with the owner or a statute so providing, the finder of lost property usually is not entitled to a reward or to compensation for finding or caring for the property.

(a) Finding in Public Place. If the lost property is found in a public place, such as a hotel, under such circumstances that to a reasonable person it would appear the property had been intentionally placed there by the owner and the owner would be likely to recall where the property had been left and to return for it, the finder is not entitled to possession of the property. The finder must give it to the proprietor or manager of the public place to keep it for the owner. This exception does not apply if it appears that the property was not intentionally placed where it was found. In that case, it is not likely that the owner will recall having left it there.

(b) Statutory Change. In some states, statutes have been adopted permitting the finder to sell the property or keep it if the owner does not appear within a stated period of time. In this case, the finder is required to give notice—for example, by newspaper publication—to attempt to reach the owner.

5. Transfer by Nonowner

Ordinarily, a sale or other transfer by one who does not own the property will pass no title. No title is acquired by theft. The thief acquires possession only; and if the thief makes a sale or gift of the property to another, the latter acquires only possession of the property. The true owner may reclaim the property from the thief or from the thief's transferee.

(a) Automobiles. In some states, the general rule stated above is fortified by statutes that declare that the title to an automobile cannot be transferred, even by the true owner, without a delivery of a properly endorsed title certificate. The states that follow the common law do not make the holding of a title certificate essential to the ownership of an automobile, although as a matter of police regulation, the owner must obtain such a certificate.

(b) Exceptions. As an exception to the rule that a nonowner cannot transfer title, an agent who does not own the property but who is authorized to sell it may transfer the title of the agent's principal.

6. Occupation of Personal Property

In some cases, title to personal property may be acquired by occupation-that is, by taking and retaining possession of the property.

(a) Wild Animals. Wild animals, living in a state of nature, are not owned by any individual. In the absence of restrictions imposed by game laws, the person who acquires dominion or control over a wild animal becomes its owner. What constitutes sufficient dominion or control varies with the nature of the animal and the surrounding circumstances. If the animal is killed, tied, imprisoned, or otherwise prevented from going at its will, the hunter exercises sufficient dominion or control over the animal and becomes its owner. If the wild animal, subsequent to its capture, should escape and return to its natural state, it resumes the status of a wild animal.

As a qualification to the ordinary rule, the following exception developed. If an animal is killed or captured on the land of another while the hunter is on the land without permission of the landowner, the animal, when killed or captured, belongs not to the hunter but to the landowner.

(b) Abandoned Personal Property. Personal property is deemed abandoned when the owner relinquishes possession of it with the intention to disclaim title to it. Yesterday's newspaper that is thrown out in the trash is abandoned personal property. Title to abandoned property may be acquired by the first person who obtains possession and control of it. A person becomes the owner at the moment of taking possession of the abandoned personal property. If, however, the owner of property flees in the face of an approaching peril, property left behind is not abandoned. An abandonment occurs only when the owner voluntarily leaves the property.

CASE SUMMARY

Not an Ordinary Bank

Facts: Charles and Rosa Nelson owned a home in Selma, Iowa, for over a half century. After their deaths, the property was abandoned because of the substantial unpaid real estate taxes. The Selma United Methodist Church purchased the property at a tax sale. When the church razed the dwelling, they found $24,547 in cash and coins that had been buried in the ground in glass jars by Charles many years before. The heirs of the Nelson family claimed the money. The church claimed that since the real estate was abandoned by the estate, the church was now the true owner of the money.

Decision: Judgment for the heirs. Although the real estate was abandoned, the money found by the church had not been abandoned by its owner, Charles Nelson. The fact that it was buried in glass jars indicates that the owner was trying to preserve it. Therefore, the money had not been abandoned and was owned by Nelson's heirs. [Ritz v Selma United Methodist Church (Iowa) 467 NW2d 266 (1991)]

7. Escheat

Who owns unclaimed property? In the case of personal property, the practical answer is that the property will probably "disappear" after a period of time, or, if in the possession of a carrier, hotel, or warehouse, it may be sold for unpaid charges. A growing problem arises with respect to unclaimed corporate dividends, bank deposits, insurance payments, and refunds. Most states have a statute providing for the transfer of such unclaimed property to the state government. This transfer to the government is often called by its feudal name of **escheat**. Funds held by stores for layaway items for customers who fail to complete the layaway purchases are subject to escheat to the state.[9] To provide for unclaimed property, many states have adopted the Uniform Disposition of Unclaimed Property Act (UDUPA).[10]

CASE SUMMARY

The King Is Dead! Who Gets the Unrefunded Ticket Proceeds?

Facts: Elvis Presley contracted with the Mid-South Coliseum Board (City of Memphis) for the rental of the Coliseum and for personnel to sell tickets for concerts on August 27 and 28, 1977. Subsequently, $325,000 worth of tickets were sold. On August 16, 1977, Elvis Presley died. Refunds were given to those who returned their tickets to the coliseum board. Ten years after his death, however, $152,279 worth of ticket proceeds remained unclaimed in the custody of the board. This fund had earned $223,760 in interest. Priscilla Presley and the co-executors of the estate of Elvis Presley brought an action claiming the unrefunded ticket proceeds for the canceled concerts. The state of Tennessee claimed that it was entitled to the proceeds under the Uniform Disposition of Unclaimed Property Act.

Decision: Judgment for the state. Elvis Presley's estate has no legal claim to the ticket proceeds because his death discharged the contract represented by each ticket sold. Ticket holders would have claimed the refunds if it had not been for Presley's legendary status, and they chose to keep the tickets as memorabilia. The drafters of the UDUPA intended that windfalls such as the unrefunded proceeds in this case benefit the public rather than individuals. [*Presley v City of Memphis* (Tenn App) 769 SW2d 221 (1988)]

ETHICS & THE LAW

When you walk into the lobby of a commercial or office building, you will often see painted murals, photography displays, sculptures, or fountains designed with or around works of art. In some cases, the tenant paid an artist to install these designs. In other cases, the building's owner installed the designs during construction or renovation. What happens to the painter's, photographer's, or sculptor's work when the tenant leaves? To whom do those works of art belong? What if they cannot be removed without significant damage to the real estate? Are these works of art real or personal property, and who retains the rights to them?

---

[9] *Rose's Stores Inc. v Boyles* (NC App) 416 SE2d 200 (1992).
[10] The 1954 version of the act has been adopted in Arkansas. A 1966 version of the act has been adopted in Alabama, Georgia, Mississippi, Missouri, Nebraska, and the District of Columbia. A 1985 version of the act has been adopted in Alaska, Arizona, Colorado, Florida, Hawaii, Idaho, Illinois, Kansas, Louisiana, Maine, Michigan, Montana, Nevada, New Hampshire, New Jersey, New Mexico, North Dakota, Oklahoma, Oregon, Rhode Island, South Carolina, Utah, Virginia, Washington, Wisconsin, Wyoming, and the Virgin Islands. A 1995 version of the act is being considered by a number of states.

Congress has been trying to pass legislation to protect the rights of visual artists but has not yet completed the provisions of the latest proposed amendments to the Visual Artists Rights Act (VARA). Artists must still deal with the problems the artistic group JX3 experienced when, while working for the tenant on the redesign of a leased building's lobby, the landlord elected not to renew the tenant's lease. JX3, along with its tools and work materials, was evicted from the premises by the landlord, leaving their completed sculptures behind. The landlord allowed the sculptures to remain in the building. Do they belong to the landlord? Should he be permitted to keep them? Was it honest for the tenant to contract for JX3's services without disclosing that its lease was up for renewal?

C. MULTIPLE OWNERSHIP OF PERSONAL PROPERTY

When all rights in a particular object of property are held by one person, that property is held in **severalty**. However, two or more persons may hold concurrent rights and interests in the same property. In that case, the property is said to be held in **cotenancy**. The various forms of cotenancy include (1) tenancy in common, (2) joint tenancy, (3) tenancy by entirety, and (4) community property.

8. Tenancy in Common

A tenancy in common is a form of ownership by two or more persons. The interest of a tenant in common may be transferred or inherited, in which case the taker becomes a tenant in common with the others. ◆ *For example*, Brandt and Vincent restored an 18-foot 1940 mahogany-hulled Chris Craft runabout and own it as tenants in common. If Brandt sold his interest in the boat to Andrea, then Vincent and Andrea would be co-owners as tenants in common. If Brandt died before Vincent, a one-half interest in the boat would become the property of Brandt's heirs. ◆

9. Joint Tenancy

A joint tenancy is another form of ownership by two or more persons, but a joint tenancy has a right of survivorship.[11] On the death of a joint tenant, the remaining tenants take the share of the deceased tenant. The last surviving joint tenant takes the property as a holder in severalty. ◆ *For example*, in Brandt and Vincent's Chris Craft example, if the boat were owned as joint tenants with a right of survivorship, Vincent would own the boat outright upon Brandt's death, and Brandt's heirs would obtain no interest in it. ◆

A joint tenant's interest may be transferred to a third person, but this destroys the joint tenancy. If the interest of one of two joint tenants is transferred to a third person, the remaining joint tenant becomes a tenant in common with the third person. ◆ *For example*, if Brandt sold his interest to Andrea, Vincent and Andrea would be co-owners as tenants in common. ◆

---

[11] *Estate of Munier v Jacquemin* (Mo App) 899 SW2d 114 (1995).

To create a joint tenancy, statutes in many states require that the instrument contain words of survivorship.

C
P
A

Statutes in many states have modified the common law by adding a formal requirement to the creation of a joint tenancy with survivorship. At common law, such an estate would be created by a transfer of property to "*A* and *B* as joint tenants."[12] Under these statutes, however, it is necessary to add the words "with right of survivorship," or other similar words, if a right of survivorship is desired.

CASE SUMMARY

Honor Thy Mother's Wishes?

Facts: Rachel Auffert purchased a $10,000 certificate of deposit on January 7, 1981, creating a joint tenancy in this bank deposit payable to herself or either of two children, Leo or Mary Ellen, "either or the survivor." When Rachel died, a note dated January 7, 1981, written in Rachel's handwriting and signed by her was found with the certificate of deposit. The note stated:

Leo: If I die this goes to Sr. Mary Ellen,
Wanted another name on it.
s/Rachel Auffert
Jan 7 1981

Mary Ellen cashed the certificate of deposit and retained the proceeds. Leo sued to recover one-half the value of the certificate.

Decision: Judgment for Leo. There was statutory compliance when the certificate of deposit was purchased, and thus a statutory joint tenancy was created. The only means available to Rachel to alter the joint tenants' proportionate interests was to change the names on the account during her lifetime. Because Rachel failed to do so, the law presumes that Leo and Mary Ellen equally owned the certificate of deposit. [*Auffert v Auffert* (Mo App) 829 SW2d 95 (1992)]

C
P
A

If no words of survivorship are used, the transfer of property to two or more persons will be construed as creating a tenancy in common. Under such a statute, a certificate of deposit issued only in the name of "*A* or *B*" does not create a joint tenancy because it does not contain words of survivorship.

10. Tenancy by Entirety

At common law, a **tenancy by entirety** or t**enancy by the entireties** was created when property was transferred to both husband and wife. It differs from joint tenancy in that it exists only when the transfer is to husband and wife. Also, the right of survivorship cannot be extinguished, and one spouse's interest cannot be transferred to a third person. However, in some jurisdictions a spouse's right to share the possession and the profits may be transferred. This form of property holding is popular in common law jurisdictions because creditors of only one of the spouses cannot reach the property while both are living. Only a creditor of both the husband and the wife under the same obligation can obtain execution against the property.

---

12 Some states have modified the common law by creating a condition that whenever two or more persons are listed as owners of a bank account or certificate of deposit, a presumption of joint tenancy with right of survivorship arises unless expressly negated by the signature card or another instrument or by extrinsic proof. Thus when Herbert H. Herring had his bank change the designated owners of a certificate of deposit to read "Herbert H. Herring or [his grandson] Robert J. Herring," and no words indicating survivorship upon the death of either were on the certificate, nevertheless under a 1992 Florida statute creating a presumption of survivorship, which presumption was not rebutted, grandson Robert was declared the owner of the certificate. *In Re* Estate of H.H. Herring (Fla App) 670 So 2d 145 (1996).

◆ *For example,* husband and wife Rui and Carla Canseco, purchased a 1997 Acura Legend for cash. It was titled in the names of "Rui J. *and* Carla T. Canseco." Later that year, State National Bank obtained a money judgment against Rui for $200,000, and the bank claims entitlement to half the value of the Cansecos' car, which it asserts is Rui's share as a joint tenant. A tenancy by entirety was created, and the bank cannot levy against the auto. If, however, the car was titled "Rui *or* Carla T. Canseco," in most states the use of the word "or" would indicate that the vehicle was held in joint tenancy even if the co-owners are husband and wife. As such, Rui's half interest could be reached by the bank. ◆

The tenancy by entirety is, in effect, a substitute for a will because the surviving spouse acquires the complete property interest on the death of the other. There are usually other reasons, however, why each spouse should make a will.

In many states, the granting of an absolute divorce converts a tenancy by the entireties into a tenancy in common.

11. Community Property

In some states, property acquired during the period of marriage is the community property of the husband and wife. Some statutes provide for the right of survivorship; others provide that half of the property of the deceased husband or wife shall go to the heirs of that spouse or permit such half to be disposed of by will. It is commonly provided that property acquired by either spouse during the marriage is prima facie community property, even though title is taken in the spouse's individual name, unless it can be shown that it was obtained with property possessed by the spouse prior to the marriage.

SUMMARY

Personal property consists of whole or fractional ownership rights in things that are tangible and movable as well as rights in things that are intangible.

Personal property may be acquired by purchase. Personal property may also be acquired by gift where the donor has present intent to make a gift and delivers possession to the donee or makes a constructive delivery. Personal property may be acquired by occupation and under some statutes may also be acquired by finding. The state may acquire property by escheat.

All rights in a particular object of property can be held by one individual, in which case it is said to be held in severalty. Ownership rights may be held concurrently by two or more individuals, in which case it is said to be held in cotenancy. The major forms of cotenancy are (1) tenancy in common, (2) joint tenancy, (3) tenancy by entirety, and (4) community property.

QUESTIONS AND CASE PROBLEMS

1. Why shouldn't businesses, banks, and insurance companies be allowed to keep, like other abandoned property, unclaimed funds left in their possession?

2. May a parent reclaim (revoke) a gift of $10,000 to a child made under the Uniform Transfers to Minors Act where the parent's circumstances have changed because of unemployment from corporate downsizing?

3. What social forces give rise to the rule of law requiring that there be an actual or a symbolic delivery in order to make a gift?

4. How does capturing a wild animal on unrestricted land during the hunting season compare with finding lost property?

5. Can a creditor of both the husband and wife under the same obligation obtain an execution against a Winnebago mobile home owned by the husband and wife in tenancy by entirety?

6. Joe obtained a box of antique Lenox china dishes that had been left at the Mashpee town dump. He supplemented the sizable but incomplete set of dishes with

other Lenox pieces found at antique dealers. And at dinner parties he proudly told of the origin of his china. When Marlene discovered that Joe had taken her dishes from the dump, she hired an attorney to obtain their return. What result?

7. Joyce Clifford gave a check for $5,000 to her nephew Carl to help with living expenses for his last year of college. The face of the check stated, "As a loan." Years later, Carl wrote to his aunt asking what he should do about the loan. She responded on her Christmas card simply, "On money—keep it—no return." After Joyce's death, her administrator sued Carl after discovering the "As a loan" canceled check. Decide.

8. Ruth and Stella were sisters. They owned a house as joint tenants with right of survivorship. Ruth sold her half interest to Roy. Thereafter, Stella died, and Roy claimed the entire property by survivorship. Was he entitled to it?

9. Mona found a wallet on the floor of an elevator in the office building where she worked. She posted several notices in the building about her finding the wallet, but no one appeared to claim it. She waited for six months and then spent the money in the wallet in the belief that she owned it. Jason, the person who lost the wallet, subsequently brought suit to recover the money. Mona's defense was that the money was hers because Jason did not claim it within a reasonable time after she posted the notices. Is she correct? (Assume that the common law applies.)

10. In 1971, Harry Gordon turned over $40,000 to his son, Murray Gordon. Murray opened two $20,000 custodial bank accounts under the Uniform Gifts to Minors Act for his minor children, Eden and Alexander. Murray was listed as the custodian of both accounts. On January 9, 1976, both accounts were closed, and a single bank check representing the principal of the accounts was drawn to the order of Harry Gordon. In April 1976, Murray and his wife, Joan, entered into a separation agreement and were later divorced. Thereafter, Joan, on behalf of her children Eden and Alexander, brought suit against Murray to recover the funds withdrawn in January 1976, contending that the deposits in both accounts were irrevocable gifts. Murray contended that the money was his father's and that it was never intended as a gift but was merely a means of avoiding taxes. Decide. [*Gordon v Gordon* (App Div) 419 NYS2d 684]

11. Carol and Robert, both over 21, became engaged. Robert gave Carol an engagement ring. He was killed in an automobile crash before they were married. His estate demanded that Carol return the ring. Was she entitled to keep it? [*Cohen v Bayside Federal Savings and Loan Ass'n* (Sup Ct Trial Term) 309 NYS2d 980]

12. Professor Arland Weiscoff, fearing that he would die as a consequence of a forthcoming lung transplant operation, brought his colleague Professor Joyce Claremont into his office. Pointing to an antique beveled glass bookcase, he said, "If I don't pull through the operation, I want you to have this." A graduate assistant was then instructed to move the bookcase to Claremont's office, and Claremont has come to value this possession since that time. Professor Weiscoff's operation was successful, and he returned to teaching after a sabbatical. Must Professor Claremont legally return the bookcase?

13. New York's banking law provides that a presumption arises that a joint tenancy has been created when a bank account is opened in the names of two persons "payable to either or the survivor." While he was still single, Richard Coddington opened a savings account with his mother, Amelia. The signature card they signed stated that the account was owned by them as joint tenants with the right of survivorship. No statement as to survivorship was made on the passbook. Richard later married Margaret. On Richard's death, Margaret claimed a share of the account on the ground that it was not held in joint tenancy because the passbook did not contain words of survivorship and because the statutory presumption of a joint tenancy was overcome by the fact that Richard had withdrawn substantial sums from the account during his life. Decide. [*Coddington v Coddington* (Sup Ct App Div) 391 NYS2d 760]

14. Kevin stole Juan's Mongoose bicycle and then sold it to Ray for its fair market value. To protect himself, Ray sought and received from Kevin a bill of sale duly notarized by a notary public. Can Juan legally recover the bicycle from Ray?

15. Mark and Estelle, a husband and wife, started a business manufacturing halogen lighting fixtures. Mark took charge of new product development, production, and finance. Estelle handled public relations, marketing, and accounts payable. When the business was incorporated, the couple agreed that Mark would be the sole shareholder. The business prospered, but the marriage broke down, and a divorce is contemplated. Mark believes that in the community property state where he and Estelle live, only their real and personal property, unrelated to the business property, is subject to division in divorce proceedings. Is he correct?

CPA QUESTIONS

1. Sklar, Rich, and Cey own a building as joint tenants with the right of survivorship. Sklar gave Sklar's interest in the building to Marsh by executing and delivering a deed to Marsh. Neither Rich nor Cey consented to this transfer. Rich and Cey subsequently died. After their deaths, Marsh's interest in the building would consist of

    a. A ⅓ interest as a tenant in common.
    b. A ⅓ interest as a joint tenant.
    c. Total ownership due to the deaths of Rich and Cey.
    d. No interest, because Rich and Cey did *not* consent to the transfer.

    (11/92, Law, #52, 3134)

2. Boch and Kent are equal owners of a warehouse. Boch died leaving a will that gave his wife all of his right, title, and interest in his real estate. If Boch and Kent owned the warehouse at all times as joint tenants with the right of survivorship, Boch's interest

    a. Will pass to his wife after the will is probated.
    b. Will *not* be included in his gross estate for federal estate tax purposes.
    c. Could *not* be transferred before Boch's death without Kent's consent.
    d. Passed to Kent upon Boch's death.

    (5/88, Law, #53, 0828)

Bailments

CHAPTER 23

OBJECTIVES

After studying this chapter, you should be able to

1. *Describe how a bailment is created;*
2. *List and distinguish the various classifications of bailments;*
3. *Contrast the renting of space with the creation of a bailment;*
4. *Explain the standard of care a bailee is required to exercise over bailed property;*
5. *State the burden of proof when a bailor sues a bailee for damages to bailed property; and*
6. *Define a bailor's implied warranty concerning goods furnished by the bailor.*

Many instances arise in which the owner of personal property entrusts it to another—a person checks a coat at a restaurant, delivers a watch to a jeweler for repairs, or loans hedge clippers to a neighbor, or a company rents a car to a tourist for a weekend. The delivery of property to another under such circumstances is a bailment.

A. GENERAL PRINCIPLES

A bailment is based on an agreement regarding personal property.

1. Definition

A **bailment** is the relationship that arises when one person delivers possession of personal property to another under an agreement by which the latter is under a duty to return the identical property to the former or to deliver it or dispose of it as agreed. The person who turns over the possession of the property is the **bailor**. The person who accepts possession is the **bailee**.

2. Elements of Bailment

A bailment is created when the following elements are present.

(a) Agreement. The bailment is based on an agreement. This agreement may be express or implied. Generally, it will contain all the elements of a contract. The bailment transaction in fact consists of (1) a contract to bail and (2) the actual bailing of the property. Ordinarily there is no requirement that the contract of bailment be in writing.[1]

The subject of a bailment may be any personal property of which possession may be given. Real property cannot be bailed.

(b) Delivery and Acceptance. The bailment arises when, pursuant to the agreement of the parties, the property is delivered to the bailee and accepted by the bailee as subject to the bailment agreement.[2]

Generally, the act of employees leaving articles in a work area on the employer's premises is not consistent with the delivering of goods to the exclusive possession and control of the employer within the meaning of a bailment. However, when an employee is required to bring his or her own tools to a job site and it is impractical to remove the tools at the end of the workday, such circumstances necessitate "delivery" to the employer for safekeeping, and a bailment is created.

---

[1] Commercial bailments or leases are regulated by the Uniform Commercial Code, Article 2A, in the states listed in the footnote in Appendix 3 of this text.
[2] *Allred v Brown* (Utah App) 893 P2d 1087 (1995).

Q: What Do You Call a 1,000-Pound Toolbox at a Firestone Store?
A: A Bailment

Facts: Service technicians at a Firestone store in Indianapolis were required by their employer to provide their own tools and toolboxes; the toolboxes weighed approximately 1,000 pounds when filled with tools. Employees locked their toolboxes at night and maintained their own keys. Employees, however, did not have access to the premises or their toolboxes after business hours. The store was the scene of several criminal acts; it was then burglarized, and employees' tools and toolboxes were taken. The employees sued Firestone, claiming a bailment existed, that Firestone negligently failed to protect the premises, and that, as a result, the bailed property was stolen. Firestone defended that no bailment existed and it was not negligent.

Decision: Judgment against Firestone. Because it was impractical to remove the tools and toolboxes on a daily basis and employees did not have access to their tools after working hours, it is reasonable to infer that the employees and Firestone understood that Firestone would assume control over the tools after working hours. Thus, there was an agreement, delivery, and acceptance of the bailed property. Under the facts of this case, the bailee, Firestone, did not prove that it was not negligent in protecting the premises and tools. [*Kottlowski v Bridgestone/Firestone* (Ind App) 670 NE2d 78 (1996)]

C P A

Delivery may be **actual**, as when the bailor physically hands a book to the bailee, or it may be **constructive**, as when the bailor points out a package to the bailee, who then takes possession of it. In the absence of a prior agreement to the contrary, a valid delivery and acceptance generally require that the bailee be aware that goods have been placed within the bailee's exclusive possession or control.

◆ *For example,* photography equipment belonging to Bill Bergey, the photographer of Roosevelt University's student newspaper, was stolen from the newspaper's campus office. Bergey believes that the university breached its duty as bailee because records showed that no campus police officer checked the building on the night of the theft. Bergey's case against the university on this bailment theory will fail, however, because the university did not know the equipment was left in the office. Without this knowledge, there was neither a bailment agreement nor acceptance of delivery by the university as a bailee. ◆

Caution: If the bailee does not know that the goods have been delivered to the bailee's exclusive possession and control, there is no "acceptance" and thus no bailment.

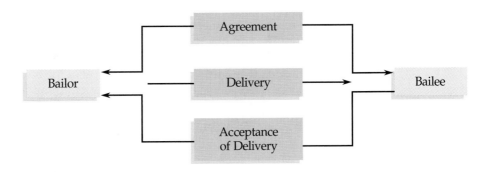

FIGURE 23-1
Bailment of Personal Property

3. Nature of the Parties' Interests

The bailor and bailee have different legal interests in the bailed property.

A bailor need not be the owner of goods to be entitled to the rights of a bailor.

(a) Bailor's Interest. The bailor is usually the owner, but ownership by the bailor is not required. It is sufficient that the bailor have physical possession.[3]

CASE SUMMARY

The Case of the Missing Blue Fox Jacket

Facts: Magee delivered to Walbro a blue fox jacket for summer storage. When it was not returned, she sued Walbro for the fur's replacement cost ($3,400). Magee testified that she bought the jacket from Evans' Furs. Evans' Furs, however, showed no record of having made the sale. Walbro contended that because Magee had not proven that she owned the jacket, Walbro could not be held liable to her.

Decision: Judgment for Magee for the value of the jacket. Ownership on the part of the bailor is not necessary to establish a bailment. Walbro's attack on Magee's assertion of ownership was irrelevant to the bailment transaction. Because Walbro raised no other defense, Magee was entitled to recover. [*Magee v Walbro Inc.*, 171 Ill App 3d 774, 525 NE2d 975 (1988)]

(b) Bailee's Interest. The bailee has only possession of the property. Title to the property does not pass to the bailee, and the bailee cannot sell the property to a third person. If the bailee attempts to sell the property, such sale transfers only possession, and the owner may recover the property from the buyer.

There are some exceptions to the rule that a bailee cannot transfer title. A bailee who is an agent authorized to sell the property may transfer title. As another exception, the bailor may cause third persons to believe that the bailee is the owner of the bailed property. If the bailor does so, the bailor is estopped from denying that the bailee is the owner as against persons who have relied on the bailor's representations. As a further exception, if the bailee is a dealer in goods of the kind entrusted to the bailee by the bailor, a sale by the bailee to a buyer in the ordinary course of business will pass the bailor's title to the buyer.

4. Classification of Bailments

Bailments are classified as ordinary and extraordinary (or special). **Extraordinary bailments** are those in which the law imposes unusual duties and liabilities on the bailee, as in the case of bailments in which a motel or a common carrier is involved. **Ordinary bailments** include all other bailments.

Bailments may or may not provide for compensation to the bailee. On the basis of compensation, bailments may be classified as (1) **contract bailments**, or **bailments for hire**, and (2) **gratuitous bailments**. The fact that no charge is made by the bailor does not necessarily make the transaction a gratuitous bailment. If the bailment is made to further a business interest of the bailor, as when something is loaned free to a customer, the bailment is not gratuitous.

Bailments may also be classified in terms of benefit. A bailment may be for the sole benefit of the bailor. ◆ *For example*, when Fred allows Mary, a college class-

---

[3] *Williams v Boswell* (Minn App) 444 NW2d 887 (1989).

mate from out of state, to store her books and furniture in his basement over the summer, Fred, the bailee, is liable only for gross negligence in storing Mary's belongings. A bailment may be for the sole benefit of the bailee, as when Mary allows Fred to borrow her Les Paul Gibson guitar. Fred, the bailee, is liable even for slight negligence in the case of any damage to the guitar. ◆ Most bailments, however, are mutual benefit bailments. ◆ *For example,* when Harry rents for a fee a trailer from U-Haul, Inc., to transport his son's belongings to college, Harry, the bailee, is responsible for using reasonable care under the circumstances while possessing and using the trailer. U-Haul, the bailor, has a duty to warn Harry of any known defects or defects that could be discovered upon reasonable inspection. ◆

ETHICS & THE LAW

The video rental store has been a rapid-growth industry since 1986. Now dominated by national chains, the industry remains profitable. Typical fees for the rental of late-run movies are $3 per evening; video games can also be rented for fees that range from 99¢ to $2.

There are hidden charges in the video rental arrangement: A penalty of another evening's fee is assessed for the late return of a video, rewind fees range from 50¢ to $2, and fees for damage to the containers can be as high as $20. These fees are simply charged to the customer's credit card, as that card and number must be given to the rental store to rent videos. In some cases, computer errors have caused the assessment of charges on credit cards to the wrong customers. Having those charges removed has proved time-consuming for the wronged customers.

Is a video rental a bailment? Is it a lease arrangement? Does it matter that customers are not always aware of all the potential charges they can incur for renting a video? Should the terms of the arrangement be disclosed? What duties does the customer have with respect to the rented video?

5. Constructive Bailments

In a constructive bailment, all of the elements of a bailment are not present.

When one person comes into possession of personal property of another without the owner's consent, the law treats the possessor as a bailee and calls the relationship a **constructive bailment**. It is thus held that the finder of lost property is a bailee of that property. When a city or state impounds an automobile or water craft, a constructive bailment arises as to such object and its contents. A seller who has not yet delivered the goods to the buyer is treated as bailee of the goods if title has passed to the buyer.

CASE SUMMARY

The Police Are Not Above the Law of Bailments

Facts: The New York State Police seized Terranova's 35-foot pleasure craft as part of a homicide investigation. No incriminating evidence was found by the state in its search. However, when the boat was returned to Terranova four months after the seizure, parts and accessories were missing, destroyed, or damaged, and the engine was inoperable. Terranova sued the state for the damage to his property on the theory that the police had breached the bailee's duty of care for the boat. The defense was raised that the police were not subject to the duties of a bailee because Terranova had not bailed the boat with the police.

> **Decision:** Judgment for Terranova. Although a true bailment did not exist because there was no agreement between Terranova and the state to bail the property, there was a constructive bailment. Therefore, the state was subject to the same duties as a bailee. *[Terranova v State of New York (Ct Cl) 445 NYS2d 965 (1982)]*

C
P
A

6. Renting of Space Distinguished

When a person rents space in a locker or building under an agreement that gives the renter the exclusive right to use that space, the placing of goods by the renter in that space does not create a bailment.[4] In such a case, putting property into the space does not constitute a delivery of goods into the possession of the owner of the space. An example of a nonbailment space rental is the use of a coin-activated package or luggage locker in an airport.

CASE SUMMARY

What Difference Does It Make Whose Lock It Is?

Facts: Sackett entered into an agreement to rent storage space at Public Storage Management (PSM), a self-storage facility. He stored personal belongings valued at $25,000 in the rental unit and secured the unit with his own lock, as required by the rental agreement. When PSM discovered that Sackett's lock had been tampered with, it placed a PSM padlock on the unit, immediately notified Sackett of what had taken place, and advised him to replace the lock with his own. Sackett had a friend verify that nothing was missing from the unit. A new lock purchased by the friend did not fit the unit's hasp, and PSM's lock was placed back on the unit. Five weeks later, when Sackett came to reclaim his belongings, he discovered they were gone. He sued PSM for the value of his belongings, claiming that PSM was a bailee because it took possession of the goods, securing the unit with its lock. PSM responded that it was a mere lessor of space and that no bailment was created.

Decision: Judgment for PSM. PSM only rented space to Sackett and never took possession of Sackett's property. Therefore, no bailment was created. Providing a lock for the unit after it was vandalized was not an assumption of control over bailed items but rather a simple extension of courtesy to a customer who was immediately notified to secure his property with his own lock. *[Sackett v Public Storage Management, 222 Cal App 3d 1080, 272 Cal Rptr 284 (1990)]*

---

7. Bailment of Contents of Container

The question of whether or not the bailment of a container is also a bailment of the contents of the container is determined by the reasonable, objective intentions of the parties.

It is a question of the intention of the parties, as that appears to a reasonable person, whether a bailment of a container also constitutes a bailment of articles contained in it—for example, whether a bailment of a coat is a bailment of articles in the coat. When the contained articles are of a class that is reasonably or normally to be found in the container, they may be regarded as bailed in the absence of an express disclaimer. If the articles are not of such a nature and their presence in the container is unknown to the bailee, there is no bailment of such articles. Consequently, although the circumstances may be such that the parking of a car constitutes a bailment, there is no bailment of valuable drawings and sporting equipment that are on the back seat but not visible from the outside of the car. However, there is ordinarily a bailment of whatever is locked in the trunk.

---

[4] *Magliocco v American Locker Co.* (Cal App) 239 Cal Rptr 497 (1987).

B.   RIGHTS AND DUTIES OF THE PARTIES

A bailment creates certain rights and imposes certain duties on each party. These may be increased or modified by statute, by custom, or by the express agreement of the parties.

8.   Duties of the Bailee

A bailee's lien allows for the retention of the bailed property until the bailor pays the amount due.

The bailee has certain duties concerning performance, care, maintenance, and return of the bailed property. A bailee's lien gives the bailee the right to keep possession of the bailed property until charges are paid. Unauthorized use of the bailed property is forbidden.

(a) Performance. If the bailment is based on a contract, the bailee must perform the bailee's part of the contract and is liable to the bailor for ordinary contract damages arising out of the failure to perform the contract.[5] Thus, if the bailment is for repair, the bailee is under the duty to make the repairs properly. The fact that the bailee used due care in attempting to perform the contract does not excuse the bailee from liability for failing to perform the contract.

(b) Care of Property. The bailee is under a duty to care for the bailed property. If the property is damaged or destroyed, the bailee is liable for the loss (1) if the harm was caused in whole or in part by the bailee's failure to use reasonable care under the circumstances or (2) if the harm was sustained during unauthorized use of the property by the bailee. Otherwise, the bailor bears the loss. Thus, if the bailee was exercising due care and was making an authorized use of the property, the bailor must bear the loss of or damage to the property caused by an act of a third person, whether willful or negligent; by an accident or occurrence for which no one was at fault; or by an act of God. In this connection, the phrase "act of God" means a natural phenomenon that is not reasonably foreseeable, such as a sudden flood or lightning.

(1) Standard of Care. The standard for ordinary bailments is reasonable care under the circumstances—that is, the degree of care that a reasonable person would exercise in the situation to prevent reasonably foreseeable harm. The significant factors in determining what constitutes reasonable care in a bailment are the time and place of making the bailment, the facilities for taking care of the bailed property, the nature of the bailed property, the bailee's knowledge of its nature, and the extent of the bailee's skills and experience in taking care of goods of that kind.

Some courts state the standard of care in terms of the benefit characteristic of the bailment. Thus, when the bailment is for the sole benefit of the bailee, the bailee is held liable for the slightest negligence. When the bailment is for the mutual benefit of the parties, the bailee is held liable for ordinary negligence. In contrast, if the bailment is for the sole benefit of the bailor, the bailee is required only to exercise slight care and will be liable only for gross negligence.

---

[5] *Computer Systems v Western Reserve Life* (Mass App) 475 NE2d 745 (1985).

(2) Contract Modification of Liability. A bailee's liability may be expanded by contract. A provision that the bailee assumes absolute liability for the property is binding.

An ordinary bailee may limit liability, except for willful misconduct, by agreement or contract.[6] If the bailee seeks to limit liability for its own negligence, then the wording of the contract must clearly express this intention so that the other party will know what is being contracted away.[7] In some states, statutes prohibit certain kinds of paid bailees, such as automobile parking garages, from limiting their liability for negligence. And statutes in some states declare that a party cannot bar liability for negligent violations of common law standards of care where a public interest is involved.

CASE SUMMARY

Auto Dealer Named Joe, "We're Not Liable ... It Says So in the Repair Contract."
Customer Named Harry, "I'll See You in Court ... Jack!"

Facts: Gardner took his Porsche automobile to be repaired at Downtown Porsche Audi. Gardner signed a repair order bearing the disclaimer "not responsible for loss (of) cars ... in case of ... theft." While it was parked in the repair garage, the car was stolen because of Downtown's negligence. Gardner sued Downtown for failing to redeliver his car. Downtown defended that the disclaimer absolved it of liability for its negligence.

Decision: Judgment for Gardner. Downtown was negligent in securing the automobile during the bailment. Because it is in the automobile repair business, which is a business of practical necessity to the people of the state and thus involves the public interest, Downtown cannot exempt itself from liability for ordinary negligence. In addition, California Civil Code § 1668 prohibits a party from contracting away liability for its negligence where a public interest is involved. [*Gardner v Downtown Porsche Audi*, 180 Cal App 3d 713, 225 Cal Rptr 757 (1986)]

By definition, a limitation of liability must be a term of the bailment contract before any question arises as to whether it is binding. Thus, a bailor is not bound by a limitation of liability that was not known at the time the bailment was made. *For example,* a limitation contained in a receipt mailed by a bailee after receiving a coat for storage is not effective to alter the terms of the bailment as originally made.

(3) Insurance. In the absence of a statute or contract provision, a bailee is not under any duty to insure for the benefit of the bailor the property entrusted to the bailee.

One of the most common bailments occurs when an automobile is rented. Car rental agencies alter the common law rule that bailees are not responsible for damages unattributable to their fault by setting forth in their standard rental contracts that bailees (lessees) are responsible for any damages however caused. The rental agencies then offer bailees protection against damages, even those caused by the bailees' fault, through the purchase of collision damage waiver (CDW) insurance. In

---

[6] *Eifler v Shurgard Capital Management Corp.* (Wash App) 861 P2d 1071 (1993).
[7] *Hertz v Klein Mfg. Inc.* (Fla App) 636 So 2d 189 (1994).

the fine print of the rental contracts, exclusions commonly exist voiding coverage if, for example, the bailee operates the vehicle while intoxicated. Some courts have refused to enforce these standardized form exclusions because they are unreasonable in that the lessee would not reasonably expect that the coverage would be subject to any exclusion.[8] Other courts have found exclusions related to alcohol use to be invalid as against public policy because the exclusions punish innocent victims of drunk drivers.

CASE SUMMARY

Which Public Policy Argument Prevails?

Facts: Angelique Garrott rented an automobile from Hertz Rent-a-Car in Chicago. In small print on the reverse side of the rental contract, it provided that if the customer permitted the use of the vehicle in a prohibited manner, all liability protection and other insurance coverage would be voided and the customer "may" then be responsible for all losses and damages to the vehicle. One of the prohibited uses was operating the vehicle while under the influence of alcohol. Angelique permitted her husband, Rodney, to operate the vehicle. At 3:00 A.M., while under the influence of alcohol, Rodney was involved in a collision with a taxi, in which the occupants Ferraro and Whitehead were injured. Hertz contended that its obligation to provide liability coverage was voided by the intoxication of the driver under the clear language of the policy. Moreover, it contended that the exclusion served the public policy of preventing driving while intoxicated because lessees will not expose themselves to the risk of loss of coverage by drinking and driving. The Garrotts, Ferraro, and Whitehead contended that the exculpatory clause is contrary to public policy.

Decision: Judgment for Garrott et al. Hertz, a private entity, does not have the ability to separately impose sanctions upon private citizens for driving while intoxicated, in the name of the public policy, when such sanctions work a hardship upon the general public and, at the same time, benefit the rental agency and/or its insurer. That is, members of the general public who were innocent victims of the individuals who drove while intoxicated would not have their losses compensated through the insurance coverage. Also, the rental agency, which was paid by the lessee to provide liability coverage, would be able to avoid large indemnity payments for liability involving the use of the rental vehicle. *[Hertz Corp. v Garrott (Ill App) 606 NE2d 219 (1992)]*

(c) Maintenance of Property. In a bailment for hire, such as when a business rents a truck from a leasing firm for a three-month period, the bailee, in the absence of a contrary contract provision, must bear the expense of maintenance that is ordinary and incidental to the use of the truck. If, however, repairs are required, the bailor is required to make the repairs unless the need for the repairs arose from the fault of the bailee.

(d) Unauthorized Use. The bailee is liable for conversion, just as though the bailee stole the property, if the bailee uses the property without authority or uses it in any manner to which the bailor had not agreed. Ordinarily the bailee will be required to pay compensatory damages, although punitive damages may be imposed when the improper use was deliberate and when the bailee was recklessly indifferent to the effect of the use on the property.

---

[8] *Lauvetz v Alaska Sales and Service Co.* (Alaska) 828 P2d 162 (1991).

(e) Return of Property. The bailee is under a duty to return the identical property that is the subject of the bailment or to deliver it as directed by the bailment agreement. An exception exists for **fungible goods**, which are those goods of a homogeneous nature of which any unit is the equivalent of any other like unit. Examples of fungible goods are grain, potatoes (within the same grade), and petroleum (within the same grade). In the case of fungible goods, if the bailee contracts to return an equal amount of the same kind and quality, the transaction is a bailment. If the bailee has the option of paying an amount of money or returning property other than that which was delivered by the bailor, there is generally no bailment but rather a sale. *For example,* when a farmer delivers wheat to a grain elevator that gives the farmer a receipt that promises to return either a similar amount of wheat or a certain sum of money upon presentment of the receipt, the relationship is generally not a bailment.

(f) Bailee's Lien. By common law or statute, a bailee is given a **lien**, or the right to retain possession of the bailed property, until the bailee has been paid by the bailor for any charges due for storage or repairs.[9] The lien is lost if the property is voluntarily returned to the bailor. If the bailor is guilty of any misconduct in regaining possession of the property, there is no loss of lien, and the bailee may retain possession if possession can be reacquired.

A bailee who is authorized by statute to sell the bailed property to enforce a charge or claim against the bailor must give such notice as is required by the statute. A bailee who sells without giving the required notice is liable for conversion of the property.

In some states, a bailee's lien may be extinguished where the bailee intentionally claims an amount greater than that to which the bailee is entitled. *For example,* an auto stereo seller's lien is extinguished when he knowingly demands in a lien statement an additional charge of $100 per day for storage of the bailor's truck.[10] This charge is clearly excessive and an intentional demand for an amount greater than that due the bailee.

9. Burden of Proof

When the bailor sues the bailee for damages to the bailed property, the bailor has the burden of proving that the bailee was at fault and that such fault was the proximate cause of the loss.[11] A prima facie right of the bailor to recover is established, however, by proof that the property was delivered by the bailor to the bailee and subsequently could not be returned or was returned in a damaged condition. When this is done, the bailee has the burden of proving that the loss or damage was not caused (1) by the bailee's failure to exercise the care required by law or (2) by an unauthorized use of the property.

10. Rights of the Bailor

A commercial bailment is a mutual benefit bailment. Under such a bailment the bailor has the right to compensation, commonly called *rent*, for the bailee's use of

9 *Boyd v Panama City Boatyard Inc.* (Fla App) 522 So 2d 1058 (1988).
10 See *First Bank Southdale v Kinney* (Minn App) 392 NW2d 740 (1986).
11 *Puissegur v Delchamps* (La App) 595 So 2d 691 (1992).

the property. If the bailor is obligated to render a service to the bailee, such as maintenance of the rented property, the bailor's failure to do so will ordinarily bar the bailor from recovering compensation from the bailee. ◆ *For example,* Michael Iemma brought his race-car trailer to Adventure RV Rentals Inc. for repair of a malfunctioning electric step. While in the bailee's possession, the trailer was destroyed by acts of arson committed by Adventure's president, Richard Dorman. Dorman is liable for the full value of Iemma's trailer on the theory of conversion.[12] ◆

(a) Rights against the Bailee. The bailor may sue the bailee for breach of contract if the goods are not redelivered to the bailor or delivered to a third person as specified by the bailment agreement. The bailor may also maintain an action against a bailee for negligence, willful destruction, and unlawful retention or conversion of the goods.

(b) Rights against Third Persons. The bailor may sue third persons who damage or take the bailed property from the bailee's possession even though the bailment is for a fixed period that has not yet expired. In such a case the bailor is said to recover damages for injury to the bailor's **reversionary interest**—that is, the right that the bailor has to regain the property upon the expiration of the period of the bailment.

11. Duties of the Bailor

The bailor has certain duties concerning the bailed property. Sometimes the duty concerning goods furnished by the bailor is described as an implied warranty.

A car rental agency (bailor) may be liable for damages or injury caused by the defective condition of the rented car (the bailed property).

(a) Condition of the Property. In a mutual benefit bailment, such as a bailment for hire, the bailor is under a duty to furnish goods reasonably fit for the purpose contemplated by the parties. If the bailee is injured or the bailee's property is damaged because of the defective condition of the bailed property, the bailor may be held liable. If the bailment is for the sole benefit of the bailee, the bailor is under a duty to inform the bailee of known defects.[13] If the bailee is harmed by a defect that was known by the bailor and not communicated to the bailee, the bailor is liable for damages.[14] If the bailor receives a benefit from the bailment, the bailor must not only inform the bailee of known defects but also make a reasonable investigation to discover defects. The bailor is liable for the harm resulting from the defects that would have been disclosed if the bailor had made such an examination, in addition to the harm stemming from the defects that were known to the bailor. If the defect would not have been revealed by a reasonable examination, the bailor, regardless of the classification of the bailment, is not liable for the harm that results.

In any case, a bailee who is aware of a defective condition of the bailed property but makes use of the property and sustains injury because of its condition is barred from collecting damages from the bailor. This bar may be based on either contributory negligence or assumption of risk.

[12] *Iemma v Adventure RV Rentals Inc.* (Ind App) 632 NE2d 1178 (1994).
[13] *McMaster v Swicker* (Ill App) 551 NE2d 654 (1990).
[14] *Acampora v Acampora* (Sup Ct App Div) 599 NYS2d 615 (1993).

(b) Implied Warranty and Strict Liability. In many cases, the duty of the bailor is described as an implied warranty that the goods will be reasonably fit for their intended use. Apart from an implied warranty, the bailor may make an express warranty as to the condition of the property. The law of strict liability, moreover, provides protection for purchasers of defective products and in many states also applies to the bailment of defective products.

CASE SUMMARY

The Sled That Couldn't

Facts: Richard Gray purchased tickets on an Alpine Slide ride from the owner and operator, Snow King Resort, Inc. The ride involved navigating a wheeled bobsled down a winding, trough-shaped concrete slide. At the top of the slide, Gray was directed by Snow King personnel to select a sled. As he went down the slide, he hit a dip that launched him into the air, causing injury to his back. Gray sued Snow King, alleging that as bailor it is liable for breach of implied warranty and strict product liability. Snow King argued that no bailment was created and that state law does not allow a strict liability theory of recovery from injuries.

Decision: Judgment against Snow King. The transaction in this case constituted a bailment, with Snow King as bailor and Gray as bailee. It was a mutual benefit bailment, with Snow King benefiting from the sale of tickets and Gray presumably receiving the benefit from the amusement of the ride. In this day of expanding leasing and rental enterprises, the mere fact that a person leases rather than purchases does not deny a person injured by a defective product the protection the law affords for defective products, which is strict liability. Snow King, as bailor of the sled, should rightly be held answerable to Gray's accusations that the sled was defective. [Gray v Snow King Resort, Inc., 889 F Supp 1473 (D Wyo 1995)]

---

12. Liability to Third Persons

When injuries resulting from the use of bailed property are sustained by third persons, liability may, under certain circumstances, be imposed on the bailee or the bailor.

A person who rents a car (a bailee) is liable to third persons as though the bailee owned the car.

(a) Liability of Bailee. When the bailee injures a third person with the bailed property—for example, when the bailee runs into a third person while driving a rented automobile—the bailee is liable to the third person to the same extent as though the bailee were the owner of the property. When the bailee repairs bailed property, the bailee is liable to a third person who is injured as a result of the negligent way in which the repairs were made.

(b) Liability of Bailor. The bailor is ordinarily not liable to a third person injured by the bailee while using the bailed property. In states that follow the common law, a person lending an automobile to another is not liable to a third person injured by the bailee when the lender did not know or have reason to know that the bailee was not a fit driver.

The bailor is liable, however, to the injured third person (1) if the bailor has entrusted a dangerous instrumentality to one known to the bailor to be ignorant of its dangerous character; (2) if the bailor has entrusted an instrumentality, such as an automobile, to one known to the bailor to be so incompetent or reckless that injury of third persons is a foreseeable consequence; (3) if the bailor has entrusted property with a defect that causes harm to the third person when the circumstances are such that the bailor would be liable to the bailee if the bailee were injured by the defect; or (4) if the bailee is using the bailed article, such as driving an automobile, as the bailor's employee in the course of employment.

(c) Test Drives. When a prospective purchaser takes an automobile for a test drive unaccompanied by the dealer, the law of bailments applies, and the bailee must exercise due care. In such a case, the customer would not be liable for harm not caused by his or her fault. However, a prospective purchaser (bailee) who promises to return the car in good condition after a test drive is responsible for damage to the car during the test drive.[15] Such a bailee assumes the liability of an insurer for the condition of the car, and it is no defense that the bailee exercised due care. Third persons injured by the negligence of a prospective purchaser during a test drive unaccompanied by the dealer ordinarily have no recourse against the dealer.

The law of bailments applies to test drives unaccompanied by the dealer. Injured parties ordinarily have no recourse against the dealer.

CASE SUMMARY

Not Directing the Operation; Not Liable

Facts: Lougee was considering buying a used Chrysler "Lazer" from Evergreen Chrysler Plymouth. After a brief test drive, Lougee was undecided about buying the car. The salesman suggested that he take it home overnight for an extended test drive. Later that night Lougee asked his best friend, Blackburn, a mechanic, to accompany him on a test drive. During that drive, Lougee struck a power pole, injuring Blackburn. Blackburn sued Lougee and Evergreen for damages. Evergreen denied liability.

Decision: Judgment for Evergreen. No Evergreen representative was present at the time of the accident. Evergreen had wholly surrendered the control of the car to the test driver, Lougee. Because the bailor, Evergreen, was not directing the operation of the car, it was not liable for the bailee's driving. [*Blackburn v Evergreen Chrysler Plymouth*, 53 Wash App 146, 765 P2d 922 (1989)]

(d) Family Purpose Doctrine. Under what is called the **family purpose doctrine**, many courts hold that when the bailor supplies a car for the use of members of his or her family, the bailor is liable for harm caused by a family member who is driving the car negligently. Other jurisdictions reject this doctrine and refuse to impose liability on the bailor of the automobile unless there is an agency relationship between the bailor and the driver.

---

[15] *Universal Ins. Co. v Vallejo* (Mich App) 446 NW2d 510 (1989).

SUMMARY

A bailment is the relationship that exists when tangible personal property is delivered by the bailor into the possession of the bailee under an agreement, express or implied, that the identical property will be returned or delivered in accordance with the agreement. No title is transferred by a bailment. The bailee has the right of possession. When a person comes into the possession of the personal property of another without the owner's consent, the law classifies the relationship as a constructive bailment.

Bailments may be classified in terms of benefit—that is, for the (1) sole benefit of the bailor, (2) sole benefit of the bailee, or (3) benefit of both parties (mutual benefit bailment). Some courts state the standard of care required of a bailee in terms of the class of bailment. Thus, if the bailment is for the sole benefit of the bailor, the bailee is required to exercise only slight care and is liable for gross negligence only. When the bailment is for the sole benefit of the bailee, the bailee is liable for the slightest negligence. When the bailment is for the mutual benefit of the

parties, as in a commercial bailment, the bailee is liable for ordinary negligence. In other states, the courts do not make the above distinctions based on the class of bailment but apply a "reasonable care under the circumstances" standard. An ordinary bailee may limit liability except for willful misconduct or where prohibited by law.

A bailee (1) must perform the bailee's part of the contract; (2) unless otherwise agreed, must bear the repair expenses incidental to the use of property in a bailment for hire situation; and (3) must return the identical property. The bailee has a lien on the bailed property until paid for storage or repair charges.

In a mutual benefit bailment, the bailor is under a duty to furnish goods reasonably fit for the purposes contemplated by the parties. The bailor may be held liable for damages or injury caused by the defective condition of the bailed property. If a bailee injures a third person while driving a rented motor vehicle, the bailee is liable to the third person as though the bailee were the owner of the vehicle.

QUESTIONS AND CASE PROBLEMS

1. What social forces are affected by the recognition of a bailment relationship?

2. Martin Acampora purchased a shotgun at a garage sale in the 1960s and never used the weapon and did not know of any defects in the weapon. His 31-year-old son Marty borrowed the shotgun to go duck hunting. As Marty attempted to engage the safety mechanism, the shotgun fired. The force of the shotgun's firing caused it to fall to the ground and to discharge another shot, which struck Marty in the hand. Classify the bailment in this case. What duty of care was owed by the bailor in this case? Is Martin liable to his son for the injury?

3. What is a bailee's lien?

4. Compare a gift with a bailment.

5. Schroeder parked his car in a parking lot operated by Allright, Inc. The parking stub given him had printed in large, heavy type that the lot closed at 6:00 P.M. Under this information, printed in smaller, lighter type, was a provision limiting the liability of Allright for theft or loss. A large sign at the lot stated that after 6:00 P.M. patrons could obtain their car keys at another location. Schroeder's car was stolen from the lot some time after the 6:00 P.M. closing, and he sued Allright for damages. Allright defended on the basis of the limitation of liability provision contained in the parking stub and the notice given Schroeder that the lot

closed at 6:00 P.M. Decide. [*Allright, Inc. v Schroeder* (Tex Civ App) 551 SW2d 745]

6. Compare a bailment with a constructive bailment.

7. John Hayes and Lynn Magosian, auditors for a public accounting firm, went to lunch at the Bay View Restaurant in San Francisco. John left his raincoat with a coatroom attendant, but Lynn took her new raincoat with her to the dining room, where she hung it on a coat hook near her booth. When leaving the restaurant, Lynn discovered that someone had taken her raincoat. When John sought to claim his raincoat at the coatroom, it could not be found. The attendant advised that it might have been taken while he was on his break. John and Lynn sued the restaurant, claiming that the restaurant was a bailee of the raincoats and had a duty to return them. Are both John and Lynn correct?

8. Before Todd returned to college in late August, he left his Boston Whaler motorboat at Terry's High Tide Marina for land storage during the fall and winter months. On a number of occasions when all of his rental boats were in use, Terry rented the Whaler to customers. Todd discovered this and sued Terry for conversion. Terry stated that he did no harm to anybody in renting the boat. Moreover, he contended that he had the legal status of bailee, that he had proper possession of the boat, and that, accordingly, he could

not have committed conversion. Were Terry's actions ethical? Is Terry liable for conversion?

9. Rhodes parked his car in the self-service park-and-lock lot of Pioneer Parking Lot, Inc. The ticket that he received from the ticket meter stated the following: "NOTICE. THIS CONTRACT LIMITS OUR LIABILITY. READ IT. WE RENT SPACE ONLY. NO BAILMENT IS CREATED." Rhodes parked the car himself and kept the keys. There was no attendant at the lot. The car was stolen from the lot. Rhodes sued the parking lot on the theory that it had breached its duty as a bailee. Was there a bailment? [*Rhodes v Pioneer Parking Lot, Inc.* (Tenn) 501 SW2d 569]

10. Lewis put a paper bag containing $3,000 in cash in a railroad station coin-operated locker. After the period of the coin rental expired, a locker company employee opened the locker, removed the money, and, because of the amount, surrendered it to police authorities as required by local law. When Lewis demanded the return of the money from Aderholdt, the police property clerk, the clerk required Lewis to prove his ownership of the funds because there were circumstances leading to the belief that Lewis had stolen the money. Lewis sued the police property clerk and the locker company. Was the locker company liable for breach of duty as a bailee? [*Lewis v Aderholdt,* 203 A2d 919 (DC)]

11. Newman underwent physical therapy at Physical Therapy Associates of Rome, Inc. (PTAR), in Rome, Georgia, for injuries sustained in an auto accident. At a therapy session on February 6, it was necessary for Newman to take off two necklaces. Newman placed one of the necklaces on a peg on the wall in the therapy room, and the therapist placed the other necklace on the peg. After the session, Newman forgot to retrieve her jewelry from the wall pegs. When she called the next day for the forgotten jewelry, it could not be found. She sued PTAR for the value of the jewelry on a bailment theory. PTAR raised the defense that there was no bailment because Newman retained the right to remove the jewelry from the wall pegs. Decide. [*Newman v Physical Therapy Associates of Rome, Inc.* (Ga App) 375 SE2d 253]

12. Contract Packers rented a truck from Hertz Truck Leasing. The brakes of the truck did not function properly. This resulted in the injuring of Packers' employee Cintrone while he was riding in the truck as it was driven by his helper. Cintrone sued Hertz for breach of the implied warranty that the truck was fit for normal use on public highways. Hertz contended that implied warranties apply only to sales and not to bailments for hire. Decide. [*Cintrone v Hertz Truck Leasing & Rental Service* (NJ) 212 A2d 769]

13. Herbert Pellegrini and Hardie Maloney traveled together to the Georgia Numismatic Association coin show in Atlanta. After the show, Pellegrini suggested that Maloney get their car while Pellegrini checked out of the Waverly Hotel. Maloney agreed to do so, after being assured by Pellegrini that he would watch Maloney's briefcase containing $31,000 in coins. Pellegrini watched as Maloney set the briefcase down beside Pellegrini's three bags. When Maloney returned with the car, Pellegrini was carrying all three pieces of his luggage as he walked up to the vehicle, but he had left Maloney's briefcase in front of the hotel. When they returned for the briefcase, it was gone. Maloney sued Pellegrini, whose defense was that he was not liable for the criminal acts of some unknown person. Decide. [*Simon v Maloney* (La App) 579 So 2d 925]

14. June Southard was employed in the sporting goods department of Kmart. While at work she was struck by a mounted fish that fell from the wall. The fish was owned by taxidermist Marty Hansen and had been delivered to Kmart as a sample of Hansen's work in case customers wanted to contact him directly. Southard sued Hansen for her injuries on the basis that Hansen was vicariously liable for the negligence of his agent, Kmart, in improperly hanging the fish. Hansen contended that his legal relationship with Kmart was that of bailor and bailee, and that as the bailor he was not liable to Southard. Decide. [*Southard v Hansen* (SD) 376 NW2d 56]

15. Charter Apparel, Inc., supplied fabric to Marco Apparel, Inc., in December to manufacture finished articles of clothing at its Walnut Grove, Mississippi, facilities. The fabric arrived just before the Christmas holiday shutdown and was stacked on cutting tables in the old building, which was known to have a roof that leaked. The evidence showed that no precautions were taken to cover the fabric and no guard was posted at the plant during the shutdown. Severe weather and freezing rain occurred during the shutdown, and it was discovered that the rain had leaked through the roof and destroyed over $400,000 of the fabric. Marco denied that it was negligent and argued that it exercised ordinary care. It offered no evidence to rebut Charter's prima facie case or to rebut Charter's evidence of negligence. It asserted, however, that as a bailee it was not an insurer of goods against severe weather conditions. Decide. [*California Union Ins. v City of Walnut Grove,* 857 F Supp 515 (SD Miss)]

CPA QUESTION

1. Which of the following requirements must be met to create a bailment?

   I.   Delivery of personal property to the intended bailee.
   II.   Possession by the intended bailee.
   III. An absolute duty on the intended bailee to return or dispose of the property according to the bailor's directions.

   a.   I and II only.
   b.   I and III only.
   c.   II and III only.
   d.   I, II, and III.

   (5/94, Law, #60, 4815)

Legal Aspects of Warehousing, Transportation, Factoring, and Hotelkeeping

CHAPTER 24

OBJECTIVES

After studying this chapter, you should be able to

1. *Differentiate between negotiable and nonnegotiable warehouse receipts;*
2. *List the three types of carriers of goods;*
3. *State the common carrier's liability for loss or damage to goods;*
4. *Explain the effect of a sale on a consignment; and*
5. *Describe a hotelkeeper's liability for loss of a guest's property.*

All bailments are not created equal. Because of the circumstances under which possession of the bailed property is transferred, the law imposes special duties in some cases on warehousers, common carriers, factors, and hotelkeepers. Documents of title facilitate the transportation, storage, and financing of goods in commerce.

A.   WAREHOUSERS

The storage of goods with a warehouser is a special bailment.

1.   Definitions

A **warehouser** is a person engaged in the business of storing the goods of others for compensation. **Public warehousers** hold themselves out to serve the public generally, without discrimination.

A building is not essential to warehousing. Thus, an enterprise that stores boats outdoors on land is engaged in warehousing, for it is engaged in the business of storing goods for hire.

A warehouser stores the goods of others for compensation and, for the most part, has the rights and duties of the bailee in a mutual benefit bailment.

2.   Rights and Duties of Warehousers

The rights and duties of a warehouser are for the most part the same as those of a bailee under a mutual benefit bailment.[1] A warehouser is not an insurer of goods. A warehouser is liable for loss or damage to goods stored in its warehouse when the warehouser is negligent.

(a) Statutory Regulation. The rights and duties of warehousers are regulated by the UCC, Article 7. In addition, most states have passed warehouse acts defining the rights and duties of warehousers and imposing regulations. Regulations govern charges and liens, bonds for the protection of patrons, maintenance of storage facilities in a suitable and safe condition, inspections, and general methods of transacting business.

(b) Lien of Warehouser. The public warehouser has a lien against the goods for reasonable storage charges.[2] It is a **specific lien** in that it attaches only to the property on which the charges arose and cannot be asserted against any other property of the same owner in the possession of the warehouser. However, the warehouser may make a lien carry over to other goods by noting on the receipt for one lot of goods that a lien is also claimed for charges on the other goods. The warehouser's lien for storage charges may be enforced by sale after due notice has been given to all persons who claim any interest in the stored property.

---

[1] UCC § 7-204.

[2] UCC § 7-209(1). The warehouser's lien provision of the UCC is constitutional as a continuation of the common law lien.

Taking Action Against Action

Facts: Tate hired Action-Mayflower Moving & Storage to ship his belongings. Action prepared a detailed inventory of Tate's belongings, loaded them on its truck, and received the belongings at its warehouse, where they would be stored until Tate asked that they be moved. Months later a dispute arose, and Tate asked Action to release his property to a different mover. Tate had prepaid more than enough to cover all charges to this point. Action refused to release the goods and held them in storage. After allowing storage charges to build up for 15 months, Action sold Tate's property under the warehouser's public sale law.

Decision: Judgment for Tate. At the time Tate demanded the release of his property, he did not owe Action anything for storage. Action therefore had no right to retain possession (a lien) and had no right to sell the property. Action's conduct constituted conversion, for which Action was liable to Tate. [*Tate v Action-Mayflower Moving & Storage Inc.*, 95 NC App 541, 383 SE2d 229 (1989)]

3. Warehouse Receipts

A warehouse receipt is a document issued by a warehouser acknowledging receipt of goods for storage from a depositor. The receipt contains the terms of the contract of storage.

A **warehouse receipt** is a written acknowledgment by a warehouser (bailee) that certain property has been received for storage from a named person called a **depositor** (bailor). The warehouse receipt is a memorandum of the contract between the **issuer**, the warehouser that prepares the receipt, and the depositor. It sets forth the terms of the contract for storage. No particular form is required, but usually the receipt will provide (1) the location of the warehouse where the goods are stored, (2) the date of issuance of the receipt, (3) the number of the receipt, (4) information on the negotiability or nonnegotiability of the receipt, (5) the rate of storage and handling charges, (6) a description of the goods or the packages containing them, and (7) a statement of any liabilities incurred for which the warehouser claims a lien or security interest.[3]

The warehouse receipt is a **document of title**—that is, a document that in the regular course of business or financing is treated as evidencing that a person is entitled to receive, hold, and dispose of the document and the goods it covers.[4] The person holding this receipt or the person specified in the receipt is entitled to the goods represented by the receipt. A warehouse receipt as a document of title can be bought or sold and can be used as security for a loan.

4. Rights of Holders of Warehouse Receipts

The rights of the holders of warehouse receipts differ depending on whether the receipts are nonnegotiable or negotiable.

(a) Nonnegotiable Warehouse Receipts. A warehouse receipt in which it is stated that the goods received will be delivered to a specified person is a **nonnegotiable warehouse receipt**. A transferee of a nonnegotiable receipt acquires only the title and rights that the transferor had actual authority to transfer. Therefore, the transferee's rights may be defeated by a good-faith purchaser of the goods from the transferor of the receipt.

---

[3] UCC § 7-202(2).
[4] UCC § 1-201(15).

(b) Negotiable Warehouse Receipts. A warehouse receipt stating that the goods will be delivered "to the bearer" or "to the order of" any named person is a **negotiable warehouse receipt**.

(1) Negotiation. If the receipt provides for the delivery of the goods "to the bearer," the receipt may be negotiated by transfer of the document. If the receipt provides for delivery of the goods "to the order of" a named individual, the document must be indorsed[5] and delivered by that person in order for the document to be negotiated.

(2) Due Negotiation. If a receipt is duly negotiated, the person to whom it is negotiated may acquire rights superior to those of the transferor. A warehouse receipt is "duly negotiated" when the holder purchases the document in good faith, without notice of any defense to it, for value, in an ordinary transaction in which nothing appears improper or irregular.[6] The holder of a duly negotiated document acquires title to the document and title to the goods.[7] The holder also acquires the direct obligation of the issuer to hold or deliver the goods according to the terms of the warehouse receipt. The rights of a holder of a duly negotiated document cannot be defeated by the surrender of the goods by the warehouser to the depositor.

It is the duty of the warehouser to deliver the goods only to the holder of the negotiable receipt and to cancel this receipt on surrendering the goods.[8]

The rights of a purchaser of a warehouse receipt by due negotiation are not cut off by the fact that (1) an original owner was deprived of the receipt in "bearer" form by misrepresentation, fraud, mistake, loss, theft, or conversion or (2) a bona fide purchaser bought the goods from the warehouser.

A purchaser of a warehouse receipt who takes by due negotiation does not cut off all prior rights. If the person who deposited the goods with the warehouser did not own the goods or did not have power to transfer title to them, the purchaser of the receipt is subject to the title of the true owner. Accordingly, when goods are stolen and delivered to a warehouse and a warehouse receipt is issued for them, the owner of the goods prevails over the due-negotiation purchaser of the warehouse receipt.

Study Figure 24-1, and note all of the features of a negotiable warehouse receipt in the context of the following. *For example,* Latham and Loud (L&L) sporting goods manufacturers' representatives in Cleveland, Ohio, hijacked a truckload of ice skates from Bartlett Shoe and Skate Co. of Bangor, Maine. L&L warehoused the skates at the Northern Transfer Co. warehouse and received a negotiable warehouse receipt. Jack Preston, a large sporting goods retailer who had had previous business dealings with L&L and believed them to be honest individuals, made a bona fide purchase of the receipt. Bartlett, the true owner, discovered that the skates were at Northern's warehouse and informed Northern of the hijacking. Northern delivered the skates to Bartlett; Latham and Loud have fled the country. Preston believes he was entitled to delivery of the skates, as he acquired the

---

[5] The spelling *endorse* is commonly used in business. The spelling *indorse* is used in the UCC.
[6] UCC § 7-501(4).
[7] UCC § 7-502(1).
[8] UCC § 7-403(3).

FIGURE 24-1
Negotiable Warehouse Receipt

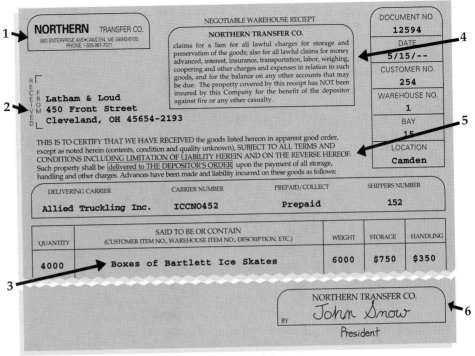

Front of receipt

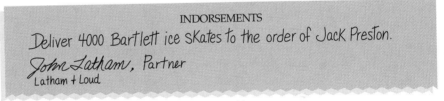

Reverse side

(1) warehouser, (2) depositor, (3) goods, (4) warehouser's lien, (5) negotiable delivery terms, (6) warehouser's authorized agent. A negotiable warehouse receipt contains a promise to deliver to bearer or to depositor's order, unlike a nonnegotiable warehouse receipt, which promises only to deliver to depositor.

negotiable receipt by due negotiation and informed Northern of his status before delivery of the skates to Bartlett. He is contemplating legal action against Northern. Preston, however, is not entitled to the skates. Ordinarily a purchase of a warehouse receipt obtained by due negotiation takes title to the document and title to the goods. However, an exception exists in the case of theft. Thus, because of the theft by L&L, Preston's rights have been cut off by the true owner in this case. When conflicting claims exist, the warehouser can protect itself by instituting proceedings under UCC §7-603 to ascertain the validity of the conflicting claims. ◆

(c) Warranties. The transferor of a negotiable or nonnegotiable warehouse receipt makes certain implied warranties for the protection of the transferee. These warranties are that (1) the receipt is genuine, (2) its transfer is rightful and effective, and (3) the transferor has no knowledge of any facts that impair the validity or worth of the receipt.[9]

5. Field Warehousing

Ordinarily stored goods are placed in a warehouse belonging to the warehouser. In other instances, the owner of goods, such as a manufacturer, keeps the goods in the owner's own storage room or building. The warehouser may then take exclusive control over the room or the area in which the goods are stored and issue a receipt for the goods just as though they were in the warehouse. Such a transaction has the same legal effect with respect to other persons and purchasers of the warehouse receipts as though the property were in fact in the warehouse of the warehouser. This practice is called **field warehousing** because the goods are not taken to the warehouse but remain "in the field."

The purpose of field warehousing is to create warehouse receipts that the owner of the goods may pledge as security for loans. The owner could, of course, have done this by actually placing the goods in a warehouse, but this would have involved the expense of transportation and storage.

6. Limitation of Liability of Warehouser

A warehouser may
limit liability in the
warehouse receipt,
provided

• the customer is
given the right to
store goods without
the limitation for a
higher fee and

• the limitation is
stated as to each
item or each unit of
weight.

A warehouser may limit liability by a provision in the warehouse receipt specifying the maximum amount for which the warehouser can be held liable. This privilege is subject to two qualifications. First, the customer must be given the choice of storing the goods without such limitation if the customer pays a higher storage rate, and, second, the limitation must be stated for each item or for each unit of weight. *For example,* a limitation is proper when it states that the maximum liability for a piano is $3,000 or that the maximum liability per bushel of wheat is a stated amount. Conversely, there cannot be a blanket limitation of liability, such as "maximum liability $100," when the receipt covers more than one item.

General contract law determines whether a limitation clause is a part of the contract between the warehouser and the customer. A limitation in a warehouse receipt is not part of the contract when the receipt is delivered to the customer a substantial period of time after the goods have been left for storage.

B. COMMON CARRIERS

The purpose of a bailment may be transportation. In this case, the bailee may be a common carrier.

7. Definitions

A **carrier** of goods is an individual or organization undertaking the transportation of goods regardless of the method of transportation or the distance covered.

---

[9] UCC § 7-507. These warranties are in addition to any that may arise between the parties by virtue of the fact that the transferor is selling the goods represented by the receipt to the transferee. See chapter 28 covering seller's warranties.

The **consignor** or shipper is the person who delivers goods to the carrier for shipment. The **consignee** is the person to whom the goods are shipped and to whom the carrier should deliver the goods.

A carrier may be classified as a common carrier, a contract carrier, or a private carrier. A **common carrier** holds itself out as willing to furnish transportation for compensation without discrimination to all members of the public who apply, assuming that the goods to be carried are proper and facilities of the carrier are available. A **contract carrier** transports goods under individual contracts, and a **private carrier** is owned and operated by the shipper. For example, a truck fleet owned and operated by an industrial firm is a private carrier. Common carrier law or special bailment law applies to common carriers, ordinary bailment law to contract carriers, and the law of employment to private carriers.

8. Bills of Lading

When the carrier accepts goods for shipment or forwarding, the carrier ordinarily issues to the shipper a **bill of lading** in the case of land or water transportation or an **airbill** for air transportation.[10] This instrument is a document of title and provides rights similar to those provided by a warehouse receipt. A bill of lading is both a receipt for the goods and a memorandum of a contract stating the terms of carriage. Title to the goods may be transferred by a transfer of the bill of lading made with that intention.

Bills of lading for intrastate shipments are governed by the Uniform Commercial Code. For interstate shipments, bills of lading are regulated by the Federal Bills of Lading Act (FBLA).[11]

(a) Contents of Bill of Lading. The form of the bill of lading is regulated in varying degrees by administrative agencies.[12] Negotiable bills of lading must be printed on yellow paper, and nonnegotiable or straight bills of lading must be printed on white paper.[13]

As against the good-faith transferee of the bill of lading, a carrier is bound by the recitals in the bill as to the contents, quantity, or weight of goods.[14] This means that the carrier must produce the goods that are described or pay damages for failing to do so. This rule is not applied if facts appear on the face of the bill that should keep the transferee from relying on the recital.

(b) Negotiation. A bill of lading is a **negotiable bill of lading** when by its terms the goods are to be delivered "to the bearer" or "to the order of" a named person.[15] Any other bill of lading, such as one that consigns the goods to a named person, is a **nonnegotiable** or **straight bill of lading**. Like transferees of warehouse receipts who take by due negotiation, holders of bills of lading who take by due negotiation ordinarily also acquire title to the bills and title to the goods represented by them.

---

[10] *Imitiaz v Emery Airfreight, Inc.* (Tex App) 728 SW2d 897 (1987).
[11] 49 USC §§ 81 et seq.
[12] The UCC contains no provision regulating the form of the bill of lading.
[13] Bill of Lading, 55 ICC 671.
[14] UCC § 7-301(1).
[15] UCC § 7-104(1)(a).

International Intrigue

Facts: Banque de Depots, a Swiss bank, sued Bozel, a Brazilian corporation, for money owed the bank. Banque obtained a writ of attachment from the court against goods being shipped by Bozel from Rio de Janeiro through the Port of New Orleans for transit to purchasers located in three states. Bozel claimed that the writ of attachment must be dissolved because the cargo was shipped under negotiable bearer bills of lading and the bills of lading had been sent to American banks for collection from the purchasers.

Decision: Judgment for Bozel. The writ of attachment must be dissolved. Goods shipped pursuant to a negotiable bill of lading cannot be seized unless the bill of lading is surrendered to the carrier or impounded by a court. On the day of the seizure of the cargo under the writ, the negotiable bills of lading were outstanding. The bills of lading were not in the hands of the carrier, and their negotiation had not been enjoined by the court. The law protects holders of duly negotiated bills of lading from purchasing such bills and then finding out that the goods have been seized by judicial process. The holder of a duly negotiated bill of lading acquires title to the document and title to the goods described therein. [Banque de Depots v Bozel (La App) 569 So 2d 40 (1990)]

Rights of a transferee are defeated by the true owner, however, when a thief delivers the goods to the carrier and then negotiates the bill of lading. The thief had no title to the goods at any time.

(c) Warranties. By transferring for value a bill of lading, whether negotiable or nonnegotiable, the transferor makes certain implied warranties to the transferee. The transferor impliedly warrants that (1) the bill of lading is genuine, (2) its transfer is rightful and is effective to transfer the goods represented by it, and (3) the transferor has no knowledge of facts that would impair the validity or worth of the bill of lading.[16]

9. Rights of Common Carrier

A common carrier of goods has the right to make reasonable and necessary rules for the conduct of its business. It has the right to charge such rates for its services as yield it a fair return on the property devoted to the business of transportation. Under the ICC Termination Act of 1995, rail carriers may set their own rates subject to challenge by shippers on the basis of lack of reasonableness where there is an absence of effective rail competition in the area.[17] The Surface Transportation Board was formed under the 1995 act to decide these and other regulatory questions involving the rail industry. As an incident of the right to charge for its services, a carrier may charge **demurrage**—a charge for the detention of its cars or equipment for an unreasonable length of time by either the consignor or the consignee.

As security for unpaid transportation and service charges, a common carrier has a lien on goods that it transports. The carrier's lien also secures demurrage, the costs of preservation of the goods, and the costs of sale to enforce the lien.[18]

---

[16] UCC § 7-507; FBLA, 49 USC § 114, 116. When the transfer of the bill of lading is part of a transaction by which the transferor sells the goods represented thereby to the transferee, there will also arise the warranties that are found in other sales of goods.

[17] PL 104-88, 109 Stat 804, 49 USC § 10501.

[18] UCC § 7-307(1); FBLA, 49 USC § 105.

10. Duties of Common Carrier

A common carrier is required (1) to receive and carry proper and lawful goods of all persons who offer them for shipment as long as the carrier has space; (2) to furnish facilities that are adequate for the transportation of freight in the usual course of business and to furnish proper storage facilities for goods awaiting shipment or awaiting delivery after shipment; (3) to follow the directions given by the shipper; (4) to load and unload goods delivered to it for shipment (in less-than-carload lots in the case of railroads), but the shipper or consignee may assume this duty by contract or custom; and (5) to deliver the goods in accordance with the shipment contract.

Goods must be delivered at the usual place of delivery at the specified destination. When goods are shipped under a negotiable bill of lading, the carrier must not deliver the goods without obtaining possession of the bill, properly indorsed. When goods are shipped under a straight bill of lading, the carrier may deliver the goods to the consignee or the consignee's agent without receiving the bill of lading unless notified by the shipper to deliver the goods to someone else. If the carrier delivers the goods to the wrong person, the carrier is liable for breach of contract and for the tort of conversion.

CASE SUMMARY

Miami Ice

Facts: Bottoms & Tops International Inc. shipped a package containing jewelry by United Parcel Service (UPS) to its salesman Ed Dwek at the Marco Polo Hotel in Miami Beach, Florida. The package was delivered to the hotel and signed for by the bell captain, who placed it in the package room and alerted Mr. Dwek by illuminating the call light in his room to contact the front desk. The bell captain released the package to an individual bearing a key to Mr. Dwek's room. Mr. Dwek did not receive the package, and Bottoms & Tops sued UPS for failure to deliver the package to the consignee, Mr. Dwek.

Decision: Judgment for UPS. In the circumstances of delivering packages to hotel guests, delivery persons are generally not permitted access to guest rooms. Where the terms of the bill of lading do not mandate delivery only to a named individual, delivery of a package by a common carrier to a bell captain terminates the carrier's duty owed to the shipper. [*Bottoms & Tops International Inc. v UPS (NY City Civ Ct) 610 NYS2d 439 (1994)*]

---

11. Liabilities of Common Carrier

> **CPA**
>
> Common carriers are absolutely liable for any loss or damage to goods unless they can show the loss was caused by an act of God, an act of a public enemy, an act of a public authority, the act of the shipper, or the inherent nature of the goods.

When goods are delivered to a common carrier for immediate shipment and while they are in transit, the carrier is absolutely liable for any loss or damage to the goods unless it can prove that the loss or damage was due solely to one or more of the following excepted causes: (1) an act of God, meaning a natural phenomenon that is not reasonably foreseeable;[19] (2) an act of a public enemy, such as the military forces of an opposing government, as distinguished from ordinary robbers; (3) an act of a public authority, such as a health officer removing goods from the carrier; (4) an act of the shipper, such as fraudulent labeling or defective packing; or (5) the inherent nature of the goods, such as those naturally tending to spoil or deteriorate.

---

[19] *Utilities Pipeline Co. v American Petrofina* (Tex App) 760 SW2d 719 (1988).

(a) Carrier's Liability for Delay. A carrier is liable for losses caused by its failure to deliver goods within a reasonable time. ◆ *For example,* the carrier is liable for losses arising from a fall in price or a deterioration of the goods caused by the carrier's unreasonable delay. ◆ The carrier, however, is not liable for every delay. The risk of ordinary delays incidental to transporting goods is assumed by the shipper.

(b) Limitation of Liability of Carrier. In the absence of a constitutional or statutory prohibition, a common carrier generally has the right to limit its liability by contract.

Common carriers operating interstate may limit their liability for the negligent loss of consigned items to a stated dollar amount, such as $100 per package. Shippers, however, must be allowed the option of selecting a higher value for the shipment, with payment of higher freight charges.

CASE SUMMARY

Did the Shipper Miss the Class on Limitation of Liability by Carriers?

Facts: Richard Trujillo, a jeweler, sent a commercial package valued at $123,490 on American Airlines, Inc., from Los Angeles to Dallas. An American employee prepared a waybill, which limited the carrier's cargo liability to $50 for the package plus the shipping cost, which was $76.50. The package was lost, and Trujillo sued American for breach of contract. American contends that it offered a choice of paying a higher rate for greater protection but that Trujillo left the declared value box on the waybill blank. This was Trujillo's first time using American, and he was confused about their procedures. He denied that he was made aware of the limitation of liability.

Decision: Judgment for American. The carrier properly limited its liability in the waybill, and the shipper, Trujillo, is bound by the terms stated in the waybill even though Trujillo complained he was not aware of the limitation. Trujillo was entitled to only $126.50 for the lost package ($50 plus the amount paid to the air carrier by the shipper). [*Trujillo v American Airlines, Inc.,* 938 F Supp 389 (ND Tex 1995)]

The Carmack Amendment to the Interstate Commerce Act governs the liability of carriers for loss or damage in the interstate shipment of goods.[20] Shippers displeased with liability limitations permitted carriers under the Carmack Amendment may not sue a carrier under any state statute if the statute in any way enlarges the responsibility of a carrier for loss or damage to the goods.[21] The Carmack Amendment provides the exclusive remedy for loss or damage, and its purpose is to provide uniformity in the disposition of claims brought under a bill of lading or waybill.

ETHICS & THE LAW

The life of the long-haul trucker is grueling. Shippers impose deadlines that require round-the-clock time behind the wheel. The U.S. Department of Commerce regulates the maximum number of hours a trucker can log behind the wheel before a break is required. Enforcement of those maximums is difficult because the truckers themselves maintain the logs.

---

[20] 49 USC § 11707.
[21] *Rini v United Van Lines Inc.,* 104 F3d 502 (lst Cir 1997).

The investigation of a 1993 accident involving a semitrailer truck and several autos, in which there were fatalities, revealed that the driver of the truck had driven for 47 hours without sleep. The driver's logs showed that he was in compliance with U.S. mandates for breaks and sleep. A fellow trucker commented, "It's not us. To make a living, you have to meet their deadlines. They screw up and get behind on shipment dates and we're supposed to make up the time."

Who is responsible for violations of the break-and-sleep requirements? Is it just drivers, or do those paying for shipments share some responsibility? Do you think shippers should assume some responsibility for supervision of their drivers? Is it ethical for shippers to ask their drivers to make up the time they themselves lost in fulfilling an order?

(c) Notice of Claim. The bill of lading and applicable government regulations may require that a carrier be given notice of any claim for damages or loss of goods within a specified time, generally within nine months.

(d) COD Shipment. A common carrier transporting goods under a COD (cash on delivery) shipment may not make delivery of the goods without first receiving payment. If it does, it is liable to the shipper for any resulting loss. Thus, if a FedEx or UPS driver were to accept a bad check from a consignee on a COD shipment, the carrier would be liable to the shipper for the amount owed.

(e) Rejected Shipments. When a common carrier tenders delivery of consigned goods to a consignee that refuses to accept the delivery, the carrier is no longer a common carrier but becomes a warehouser. When the carrier-turned-warehouser receives new shipping instructions from the owner, its status again changes to that of a common carrier.

C.   FACTORS

A **factor** is a special type of bailee who sells consigned goods as though the factor were the owner of those goods.

12. Definitions

Entrusting a person with the possession of property for the purpose of sale is commonly called **selling on consignment**.[22] The owner who consigns the goods for sale is the **consignor**. The person or agent to whom they are consigned is the factor or **consignee**; this individual may also be known as a commission merchant. A consignee's compensation is known as a **commission** or **factorage**.

13. Effect of Factor Transaction

A sale by a factor will pass the title of the consignor (owner) to the purchaser.

In a sale on consignment, the property remains the property of the owner or consignor, and the consignee acts as the agent of the owner to pass the owner's title to the buyer. As a factor is by definition authorized by the consignor to sell the

---

[22] *Amoco Oil Co. v DZ Enterprises Inc.*, 607 F Supp 595 (SDNY 1985).

goods entrusted to the factor, such a sale will pass the title of the consignor to the purchaser. Before the factor makes the sale, the goods belong to the consignor, but in some instances creditors of the factor may ignore the consignor and treat the goods as though they belonged to the factor.[23] If the consignor is not the owner, as when a thief delivers stolen goods to the factor, a sale by the factor passes no title and is an unlawful conversion. It is constitutional, however, to provide by statute that the factor who sells in good faith in ignorance of the rights of other persons in the goods is protected from liability.

D. HOTELKEEPERS

A hotelkeeper has a bailee's liability with respect to property specifically entrusted to the hotelkeeper's care. In addition, the hotelkeeper has special duties with respect to a guest's property brought into the hotel. The rules governing the special relationship between a hotelkeeper and a guest arose because of the special needs of travelers.

14. Definitions

The definitions of *hotelkeeper* and *guest* exclude lodging of a more permanent character, such as that provided by boardinghouse keepers to boarders.

(a) Hotelkeeper. A **hotelkeeper** is an operator of a hotel, motel, or tourist home or anyone who is regularly engaged in the business of offering living accommodations to transient persons. In the early law, the hotelkeeper was called an innkeeper or a tavernkeeper.

(b) Guest. A **guest** is a transient. The guest need not be a traveler or come from a distance. A person living within a short distance of a hotel who engages a room at the hotel and remains there overnight is a guest.

In contrast, a person who enters a hotel at the invitation of a guest or attends a dance or a banquet given at the hotel is not a guest. Similarly, the guest of a registered occupant of a motel room who shares the room with the occupant without the knowledge or consent of the management is not a guest of the motel because there is no relationship between that person and the motel.

15. Duration of Guest Relationship

The relationship of guest and hotelkeeper does not begin until a person is received as a guest by the hotelkeeper. The guest-hotelkeeper relationship does not automatically end when the hotel bill is paid.

The relationship terminates when the guest leaves or ceases to be a transient, as when the guest arranges for a more or less permanent residence at the hotel. The transition from the status of guest to the status of boarder or lodger must be clearly indicated. It is not established by the mere fact that one remains at the hotel for a long period, even though it runs into months.

---

[23] UCC § 2-326.

When Does "Guest" Status End?

Facts: Salisbury was a guest at the St. Regis-Sheraton Hotel. He was ready to leave the hotel but wanted to go sightseeing for another day. He checked out of his room and paid the hotel bill. With the consent of the hotel, he left his luggage with the hotel. When he returned, he learned that some of the luggage had been stolen. He claimed that the hotel was liable to him as a guest. The hotel asserted that the guest status had ended and that the hotel was merely a bailee of the luggage.

Decision: The hotel was still a hotel, and Salisbury was still a guest insofar as the luggage was concerned. The holding of luggage temporarily when a guest leaves a hotel is such a normal incident of the hotel-guest relationship that it could not be said that the hotel ceased to have the liability of a hotel with respect to such luggage. Therefore, hotel law applied, and the hotel was not a mere bailee of the luggage. [*Salisbury v St. Regis-Sheraton Hotel Corp., 490 F Supp 449 (SD NY 1980)*]

16. Hotelkeeper's Liability for Guest's Property

At common law, a hotelkeeper was absolutely liable for loss of a guest's property, subject to the same exceptions applicable to common carriers. Most states provide a method of limiting this liability, however.

With respect to property expressly entrusted to the hotelkeeper's care, the hotelkeeper has a bailee's liability. At common law, the hotelkeeper was absolutely liable for damage to, or loss of, a guest's property unless the hotelkeeper could show that the damage or loss was caused solely by an act of God, a public enemy, an act of a public authority, the inherent nature of the property, or the fault of the guest.[24]

In most states, statutes limit or provide a method of limiting the common law liability of a hotelkeeper. The statutes may limit the extent of liability, reduce the liability of a hotelkeeper to that of an ordinary bailee, or permit the hotelkeeper to limit liability by contract or by posting a notice of the limitation. Some statutes relieve the hotelkeeper from liability when the guest has not complied with directions for depositing valuables with the hotelkeeper.[25] When a statute permits a hotel receiving valuables for deposit in its safe deposit box to limit its liability to the amount specified in the agreement signed by the guest, this limitation binds the guest even though the loss was caused by negligence on the part of the hotel.

A hotelkeeper must substantially comply with such a statute in order to obtain its protection.

Bleam Blames Bellmen

Facts: Levi Bleam was in the business of buying and selling baseball cards. He left five large briefcases full of valuable cards, along with several thousand dollars in cash, checks, and credit card receipts, in his room at the Marriott Hotel to go out to dinner after attending a card show at the Nassau County Coliseum in New York. He believed his room was secure against theft. When he returned from dinner, he found that all of his property had been stolen. Marriott, in accordance with the state law that provides a method of limiting the common law liability of a hotelkeeper, posted on the bathroom door and at the hotel registration desk notices requiring guests to store valuables in the hotel's safe. It also notified guests that it provided other safe storage for large items of luggage. The notices informed guests that otherwise the hotelkeeper's

---

24 *Cook v Columbia Sussex Corp.* (Tenn App) 807 SW2d 567 (1991).
25 *Numismatic Enterprise v Hyatt Corp.*, 797 F Supp 687 (D Ind 1992).

liability for the negligent loss of a guest's property was limited to $500. Bleam sued Marriott, contending it was liable for the loss of property due to the gross negligence of Marriott employees in allowing the thief to walk out of the hotel with the five large briefcases. Bleam believed that the notices were not effective to limit liability because he "did not recall" seeing them. Marriott contends that its liability was limited to $500.

Decision: Judgment for Marriott. The hotelkeeper fully complied with the applicable state statute that allowed it to limit its common law liability for the loss of its guests' property when it properly posted the notices in the room and at the registration desk. The hotel presented photographs and testimony showing the placement of the notices. It is of no avail to Bleam that he did not recall seeing them. The hotelkeeper's liability was limited to $500. *[Bleam v Marriott Corp. (App Div) 655 NYS2d 567 (1997)]*

17. Hotelkeeper's Lien

A hotelkeeper has a lien on the luggage of guests until the agreed charges are paid.

The hotelkeeper has a lien on the baggage of guests for the agreed charges or, if no express agreement was made, for the reasonable value of the accommodations furnished. Statutes permit the hotelkeeper to enforce this lien by selling the goods of the guests at a public sale. The lien of the hotelkeeper is terminated by (1) the guest's payment of the hotel charges, (2) any conversion of the guest's goods by the hotelkeeper, or (3) final return of the goods to the guest.

18. Boarders or Lodgers

The hotelkeeper owes only the duty of an ordinary bailee of personal property under a mutual benefit bailment to those persons who are permanent boarders or lodgers rather than transient guests.

A hotelkeeper has no lien on property of boarders or lodgers, as distinguished from guests, in the absence of an express agreement creating such a lien. In a number of states, however, legislation giving a lien to a boardinghouse or a lodging house keeper has been adopted.

SUMMARY

A warehouser stores the goods of others for compensation and has the rights and duties of a bailee in an ordinary mutual benefit bailment. A warehouser issues a warehouse receipt to the depositor of the goods. This receipt is a document of title that ordinarily entitles the person in possession of the receipt to receive the goods. The warehouse receipt can be bought, sold, or used as security to obtain a loan. A nonnegotiable warehouse receipt states that the goods received will be delivered to a specified person. A negotiable warehouse receipt states that the goods will be delivered "to the bearer" or "to the order of" a named person. If a negotiable warehouse receipt is duly negotiated, the transferee may acquire rights superior to those of the transferor. A warehouser may limit its liability for loss or damage to goods due to its own negligence to

an agreed valuation of the property stated in the warehouse receipt provided the depositor is given the right to store the goods without the limitation at a higher storage rate.

A common carrier of goods is in the business of transporting goods received from the general public. It issues to the shipper a bill of lading or an airbill. Both of these are documents of title and provide rights similar to those provided by a warehouse receipt. A common carrier is absolutely liable for any loss or damage to the goods unless the carrier can show that the loss was caused solely by an act of God, an act of a public enemy, an act of a public authority, an act of the shipper, or the inherent nature of the goods. The carrier may limit its liability in the same manner as a warehouser.

A factor is a special type of bailee who has possession of the owner's property for the purpose of sale. The factor, or consignee, receives a commission on the sale.

A hotelkeeper is in the business of providing living accommodations to transient persons called guests.

Subject to exceptions, at common law hotelkeepers were absolutely liable for loss or damage to their guests' property. Most states, however, provide a method of limiting this liability. A hotelkeeper has a lien on the property of the guest for the agreed charges.

QUESTIONS AND CASE PROBLEMS

1. What social forces are involved in the rule of law governing the liability of a common carrier for loss of freight?

2. American Cyanamid shipped 7,000 vials of DPT—a vaccine for immunization of infants and children against diphtheria, pertussis, and tetanus—from its Pearl River, New York, facility to the U.S. Defense Department depot in Mechanicsburg, Pennsylvania, by New Penn Motor Express, a common carrier. Cyanamid's bill of lading included a "release value," which stated the value of the property was declared as not exceeding $1.65 per pound. Cyanamid's shipment weighed 1,260 pounds. The bill of lading accepted by New Penn on picking up the DPT vaccine on February 6 also clearly stated that the shipment contained drugs and clearly warned to "protect from freezing." The bill further recited "rush . . . must be delivered by February 8, 1989." New Penn permitted the vaccine to sit in an unheated uninsulated trailer while it gathered enough other merchandise to justify sending a truck to Mechanicsburg. The DPT vaccine was delivered on February 10 in worthless condition, having been destroyed by the cold. New Penn admitted it owes $2,079 in damages pursuant to the bill of lading ($1.65 x 1,260 lbs.). Cyanamid claimed that the actual loss was much greater, $53,936.75. It stated that because New Penn breached its contract with Cyanamid, it cannot invoke the benefits of that same contract, namely, the release value clause.

   Was it ethical for New Penn to hold the vaccine while waiting for enough merchandise to justify the trip? How would you decide the case? [*American Cyanamid Co. v New Penn Motor Express, Inc.*, 979 F2d 301 (3d Cir)]

3. Compare the liens of carriers, warehousers, and hotels in terms of being specific.

4. Compare the limitations of the liability of a warehouser and of a hotelkeeper.

5. Compare warehouse receipts and bills of lading as to negotiability.

6. Doyle Harms applied to his state's Public Utilities Commission for a Class B permit authorizing performance as a common carrier. Doyle testified that it was not his intention to haul in a different direction than he was already going, stating in part:

   No way, that's not what I'm asking for. I've got enough business of my own, it's just the times when you get done with a sale at the end of the day and you've got a half load and somebody else has a half load, then you'd be able to help each other out. It's kind of the name of the game in my mind.

   He also testified that the application was so he could haul cattle for his own customers. State law defines a common carrier as "a motor carrier which holds itself out to the general public as engaged in the business of transporting persons or property in intrastate commerce which it is accustomed to and is capable of transporting from place to place in this state, for hire." Its property is "devoted to the public service." Should Doyle Harms be issued a common carrier permit? [*In re* Harms (SD) 491 NW2d 760]

7. Welch Brothers Trucking, Inc., a common carrier, made an agreement with B&L Export and Import Co. of San Francisco to transport a shipment of freshly harvested bluefin tuna from Calais, Maine, to the Japan Air Lines freight terminal at New York's Kennedy Airport. The bluefin tuna had been packed in ice and were to be shipped by Japan Air Lines to Tokyo. Fresh bluefin are used in the traditional Japanese raw fish dish sashimi and command very high prices. When transportation charges were not paid by B&L's representative in New York, Welch Brothers refused to release the shipment to Japan Air Lines. B&L's representative in New York explained that he had no check-writing authority but assured Welch that it would be paid and pleaded for the release of the cargo because of its perishable nature. Transportation charges were not paid in the next 12-hour period because the principals of B&L were on a business trip to the Far East and could not be contacted. After waiting the 12-hour period, Welch sent a telegram to B&L's offices in San Francisco, stating the amount due and that it intended to auction the cargo in 24 hours if transportation charges were not paid. Welch also sent telegrams seeking bidders to all fish wholesalers listed in the New York City Yellow Pages. In the telegrams, Welch advised that the cargo would be sold at auction in 24 hours if the charges were not

paid. Welch sold the shipment to the highest bidder at the appointed time for an amount just in excess of the transportation charges plus a demurrage charge for the 36-hour waiting period. When the principals of B&L were later informed of what happened, they sued Welch for the profits they would have earned if the cargo had been shipped and sold in Japan. Decide.

8. Richard Schewe and others placed personal property in a building occupied by Winnebago County Fair Association, Inc. Prior to placing their property in the building, they signed a "Storage Rental Agreement" prepared by the County Fair Association, which stated: "No liability exists for damage or loss to the stored equipment from the perils of fire. . . ." The property was destroyed by fire. Suit was brought against the County Fair Association to recover damages for the losses on the theory of negligence of a warehouser. The County Fair Association claimed that the language in the storage agreement relieved it of all liability. [*Allstate Ins. Co. v Winnebago County Fair Association, Inc.* (Ill App) 475 NE2d 230]

9. Buffett sent a violin to Strotokowsky by International Parcel Service (IPS), a common carrier. Buffett declared the value of the parcel at $500 on the pick-up receipt given him by the IPS driver. The receipt also stated: "Unless a greater value is declared in writing on this receipt, the shipper hereby declares and agrees that the released value of each package covered by this receipt is $100.00, which is a reasonable value under the circumstance surrounding the transportation." When the parcel was not received by Strotokowsky, Buffett sued IPS for the full retail value of the violin— $2,000. IPS's defense was that it was liable for just $100. Decide.

10. Glen Smith contracted with Dave Watson, a common carrier, to transport 720 hives of live bees along with associated equipment from Idabel, Oklahoma, to Mandan, North Dakota. At 9:00 A.M. on May 24, 1984, while en route, Watson's truck skidded off the road and tipped over, severely damaging the cargo. Watson notified Smith what had happened, and Smith immediately set out for the scene of the accident. He arrived at 6:00 P.M. with two bee experts and a Bobcat loader. They were hindered by the turned-over truck on top of the cargo, and they determined that they could not safely salvage the cargo that evening. The next day an insurance adjuster determined that the cargo was a total loss. The adjuster directed a bee expert, Dr. Moffat, to conduct the cleanup; Moffat was allowed to keep the salvageable cargo, valued at $12,326, as compensation. Smith sued Watson for damages. Watson denied liability and further contended that Smith failed to mitigate damages. Decide. [*Smith v Watson* (ND) 406 NW2d 685]

11. A guest in a motel opened the bedroom window at night and went to sleep. During the night, a prowler pried open the screen, entered the room, and stole property of the guest. The guest sued the motel. The motel asserted that it was not responsible for property in the possession of the guest and that the guest had been contributorily negligent in opening the window. Could the guest recover damages? [*Buck v Hankin* (Pa Super) 269 A2d 344]

12. On March 30, Emery Air Freight Corp. picked up a shipment of furs from Hopper Furs, Inc. Hopper's chief of security filled in certain items in the airbill. In the box entitled ZIP Code, he mistakenly placed the figure "61,045," which was the value of the furs. The ZIP Code box is immediately above the Declared Value box. The airbill contained a clause limiting liability to $10 per pound of cargo lost or damaged unless the shipper makes a declaration of value in excess of the amount and pays a higher fee. A higher fee was not charged in this case, and Gerald Doane signed the airbill for the carrier and took possession of the furs. The furs were lost in transit by Emery, and Hopper sued for the value of the furs, $61,045. Emery's offer to pay $2,150, the $10-per-pound rate set forth in the airbill, was rejected. Hopper claimed that the amount of $61,045, which was mistakenly placed in the ZIP Code box, was in fact part of the contract set forth in the airbill and that Emery, on reviewing the contract, must have realized a mistake was made. Decide. [*Hopper Furs, Inc. v Emery Air Freight Corp.*, 749 F2d 1261 (8th Cir)]

13. When de Lema, a Brazilian resident, arrived in New York City, his luggage consisted of three suitcases, an attaché case, and a cylindrical bag. The attaché case and the cylindrical bag contained jewels valued at $300,000. De Lema went from JFK Airport to the Waldorf Astoria Hotel, where he gave the three suitcases to hotel staff in the garage, and then he went to the lobby to register. The assistant manager, Baez, summoned room clerk Tamburino to assist him. De Lema stated, "The room clerk asked me if I had a reservation. I said, 'Yes. The name is José Berga de Lema.' And I said, 'I want a safety deposit box.' He said, 'Please fill out your registration.'" While de Lema was filling out the registration form, paying $300 in cash as an advance, and Tamburino was filling out a receipt for that amount, de Lema had placed the attaché case and the cylindrical bag on the floor. A woman jostled de Lema, apparently creating a diversion, and when he next looked down, he discovered

that the attaché case was gone. De Lema brought suit against the hotel for the value of the jewels stolen in the hotel's lobby. The hotel maintained a safe for valuables and posted notices in the lobby, garage, and rooms as required by the New York law that modifies a hotelkeeper's common law liability. The notices stated in part that the hotel was not liable for the loss of valuables that a guest neglected to deliver to the hotel for safekeeping. The hotel's defense was that de Lema neglected to inform it of the presence of the jewels and to deliver the jewels to the hotel. Is the hotel liable for the value of the stolen jewels? [*De Lema v Waldorf Astoria Hotel, Inc.*, 588 F Supp 19 (SDNY)]

14. Frosty Land Foods shipped a load of beef from its plant in Montgomery, Alabama, to Scott Meat Co. in Los Angeles via Refrigerated Transport Co. (RTC), a common carrier. Early Wednesday morning, December 7, at 12:55 A.M., two of RTC's drivers left the Frosty Land plant with the load of beef. The bill of lading called for delivery at Scott Meat on Friday, December 9, at 6:00 A.M. The RTC drivers arrived in Los Angeles at approximately 3:30 P.M. on Friday, December 9. Scott notified the drivers that it could not process the meat at that time. The drivers checked into a motel for the weekend, and the load was delivered to Scott on Monday, December 12. After inspecting 65 of the 308 carcasses, Scott determined that the meat was in off condition and refused the shipment. On Tuesday, December 13, Frosty Land sold the meat, after extensive trimming, at a loss of $13,529. Frosty Land brought suit against RTC for its loss. Decide. [*Frosty Land Foods v Refrigerated Transport Co.*, 613 F2d 1344 (5th Cir)]

15. Singer Corp. had been storing air conditioners in Stoda warehouses for several years. In May, Singer's transportation manager, Guy Bataglia, went to Stoda's Hoffman Plant warehouse accompanied by Stoda's president, Larry Ellis. While looking over the building, Bataglia noticed the sprinkler system and inquired about it. Ellis, who knew the system had been turned off, said the system was active. Singer stored 133 cartons of air-conditioning units at the Hoffman Plant as of that day. On July 7, a fire broke out in the Hoffman Plant, totally destroying Singer's goods. Singer claimed that it was entitled to recover the value of the destroyed air conditioners from Stoda, as it made out a prima facie case of negligence, which was not rebutted. Stoda claimed that it was not an insurer of the goods. Decide. [*Singer Co. v Stoda* (App Div) 435 NYS2d 508]

CPA QUESTIONS

1. A common carrier bailee generally would avoid liability for loss of goods entrusted to its care if the goods are
   a. Stolen by an unknown person.
   b. Negligently destroyed by an employee.
   c. Destroyed by the derailment of the train carrying them due to railroad employee negligence.
   d. Improperly packed by the party shipping them.
   (11/95, Law, #59, 5928)

2. Under a nonnegotiable bill of lading, a carrier who accepts goods for shipment must deliver the goods to
   a. Any holder of the bill of lading.
   b. Any party subsequently named by the seller.
   c. The seller who was issued the bill of lading.
   d. The consignee of the bill of lading.
   (11/92, Law, #43, 3125)

3. Under the UCC, a warehouse receipt
   a. Is negotiable if, by its terms, the goods are to be delivered to bearer or to the order of a named person.
   b. Will **not** be negotiable if it contains a contractual limitation on the warehouser's liability.
   c. May qualify as both a negotiable warehouse receipt and negotiable commercial paper if the instrument is payable either in cash or by the delivery of goods.
   d. May be issued only by a bonded and licensed warehouser.
   (5/92, Law, #49, 2862)

PART 4

Sales and Leases of Personal Property

Nature and Form of Sales

CHAPTER 25

After studying this chapter, you should be able to

1. *Define a sale of goods and state when UCC Article 2 applies to contracts;*
2. *Distinguish between a sale of goods and other transactions relating to goods;*
3. *Describe how contracts are formed under Article 2 and list the differences between the UCC and common law;*
4. *State when a contract for the sale of goods must be in writing;*
5. *List and explain the exceptions to the requirement that certain contracts be in writing;*
6. *Define and state the purpose of the United Nations Convention on Contracts for the International Sale of Goods; and*
7. *State the distinguishing features of a consumer lease and a finance lease.*

Article 2 is one section of the Uniform Commercial Code that governs contracts for the sale of goods.

The Uniform Commercial Code (UCC) is a set of statutes drafted by experts and business people that has been adopted in some form in nearly all states; governs significant aspects of business transactions, such as contracts for the sale of goods, leases of goods, negotiable instruments for payment, secured transactions for creditors, and transfer of documents of title.

Sales of goods are sales of tangible personal property. Sales of everything from boats to televisions to compact disks are governed by **Article 2** of the Uniform Commercial Code. Article 2 of the UCC is a source of contract law derived from the law merchant, a body of contract law used in common law England to facilitate transactions in goods. Today's UCC Article 2 is the work product of business people, commercial transactions lawyers, and legal experts who have worked together to develop a body of contract law that facilitates the fast pace of business today. Article 2 has been modified and refined to provide a uniform system of laws that continue to facilitate transactions in goods across the country.

In chapters 11 through 20, the common law of contracts was examined. That source of contract law applies to contracts with the subject matter of land or services. However, there is another source of contract law, Article 2 of the Uniform Commercial Code, which applies to contracts for the sale of goods. This chapter and chapters 25 through 29 cover this source of contract law, which businesses rely on each day.

The UCC is applicable to both new and used goods.

A. NATURE AND LEGALITY

The sale of goods is the present transfer of title to tangible personal property for a price.

A **sale of goods** is a present transfer of title to tangible property for a price. This price may be a payment of money, an exchange of other property, or the performance of services.

The parties to a sale are the person who owns the goods and the person to whom the title is transferred. The **transferor** is the seller or vendor, and the **transferee** is the buyer or vendee.

1.   Subject Matter of Sales

Goods are tangible personal property; do not include securities, real estate, or intellectual property.

Goods, the subject matter of a sale under Article 2 of the Uniform Commercial Code, are defined to include tangible personal property.[1] ◆ *For example,* tangible personal property includes everything from a fan to a painting to a yacht. ◆ For purposes of the application of Article 2, goods are not defined to include (1) investment securities, such as stocks and bonds, the sale of which is regulated by Article 8 of the UCC; (2) choses in action, such as insurance policies and promissory notes, because they are assigned or negotiated rather than sold or, because of their personal nature, are not transferable; and (3) real estate, such as houses, factories, farms, and just land itself.

(a) Nature of Goods. Article 2 applies to contracts for the sale of familiar items of personal property, such as automobiles or chairs. But Article 2 also applies to the transfer of commodities, such as oil, gasoline, milk, and grain.

Future goods are goods that are not yet owned by the seller or that are yet to be manufactured by the seller.

(b) Existing and Future Goods. Goods that are already manufactured or crops already grown and owned by the seller at the time of the transaction are called **existing goods**. All other goods are called **future goods**. Future goods include both goods that are physically existing but not owned by the seller and goods that have not yet been produced, as when a buyer contracts to purchase custom-made office furniture.

2.   Sale Distinguished from Other Transactions

There are other types of transactions in goods that are not covered by Article 2 because they are not transfers of title to the goods. If there is a transfer of a lesser interest than title, the transaction is not a sale.

A bailment is a transfer of possession of personal property to another.

(a) Bailment. A **bailment** is not a sale because only possession is transferred to a **bailee**. Title to the property is not transferred. (For more information on bailments, their nature, and the rights of the parties, see chapter 23.) ◆ *For example,* a valet at a hotel parking your car for you is an example of a bailment. ◆ A lease of goods, such as a lease of an automobile, is governed by Article 2A of the UCC. Article 2A is covered later in section D of this chapter.

A gift is a gratuitous transfer of title to property.

(b) Gift. A **gift** is a gratuitous (free) transfer of the title to property. The Article 2 definition of a sale requires that the transfer of title be made for a price. Gifts are not covered under Article 2.

(c) Contract for Services. A contract for services, such as a contract for painting a home, is not a sale of goods and is not covered under Article 2 of the UCC.

---

[1] UCC § 2-105(1)–(2). Goods include minerals, some fixtures (or personal property attached to the land), growing crops, the unborn young of animals, and building materials to be removed by the seller. UCC § 2-105 (1990); *Koch Oil Co. v Wilber* (Tex App) 895 SW2d 854 (1995).

(d) Contract for Goods and Services. If a contract calls for both the rendering of services and the supplying of materials to be used in performing the services, the contract is classified according to its dominant element. ◆ *For example,* a homeowner may purchase a security system. The homeowner is paying for the equipment that is used in the system as well as for the seller's expertise and installation of that system. Is the homeowner's contract governed by Article 2, or is it a contract for services and covered under the common law of contracts? ◆

If the service element is dominant, it is a service contract and is governed by common law rather than Article 2. If the goods make up the dominant element of the contract, then the parties' rights are determined under Article 2. In the home security system contract example, the question requires a comparison of the costs of the system's parts versus the costs of its installation. In some contracts, the equipment costs are minimal, and installation is key for the customer. In more sophisticated security systems, the installation is a small portion of the overall contract price, and the contract is held to be one governed by the UCC.[2]

CASE SUMMARY

The Decaying Relationship between the Dentist and His Patient: When the Dentures Don't Fit, Does the UCC Apply?

Facts: Mrs. Downing was fitted for dentures by a dentist, Dr. Cook. After she received her dentures, Mrs. Downing began experiencing mouth pain she attributed to Dr. Cook's manufacture of dentures that did not fit her properly. Mrs. Downing filed suit against Dr. Cook for breach of warranty under Article 2 of the UCC. Dr. Cook defended on the grounds that his denture work was a service and therefore not covered under Article 2 warranties.

Decision: The court held that Dr. Cook is not a merchant and is not in the business of selling dentures. Rather, Dr. Cook is a professional who renders medical services that are governed by common law contracts provisions as well as the provisions in state law for professional malpractice. Mrs. Downing might have had a suit, but it was one based on negligence and not on the sale of goods because the agreement to produce dentures was a medical service and not a sale of goods. [*Cook v Downing* (Okla App) 891 P2d 611 (1995)]

---

3. Formation of Sales Contracts

(a) Necessary Detail for Formation. Article 2 of the UCC, in order to streamline business transactions, does not have standards as rigid as those the common law has for other contracts. Under the UCC, the formation of a contract can be recognized even though one or more terms are left open so long as the parties clearly intend to contract.[3] The minimum terms required for formation of an agreement under the UCC are the subject matter and quantity (if there is more than one). ◆ *For example,* an agreement that described "the sale of my white Ford Taurus" would be sufficient, but an agreement to purchase "some Ford Tauruses" would require a quantity in order to qualify for formation. ◆ Other provisions under Article 2 can cover any missing terms so long as the parties are clear on their

---

[2] *Central Dist. Alarm, Inc. v Hal-Tuc, Inc.* (Mo App) 886 SW2d 210 (1994).
[3] UCC § 2-204(3); *Synergistic Technologies, Inc. v IDB Mobile Communications, Inc.,* 871 F Supp 24 (DDC 1994). This provision on formation assumes that the agreement the parties do have provides "a reasonably certain basis for giving an appropriate remedy."

intent to contract. Article 2 contains provisions covering price, delivery, time for performance, payment, and other details of performance in the event the parties agree to a sale but have not discussed or reduced to writing their desires in these areas.[4]

(b) The Merchant versus Nonmerchant Parties. Because Article 2 applies to all transactions in goods, it is applicable to sales by both **merchants** and nonmerchants,[5] including consumers. In most instances, the UCC treats all buyers and sellers alike. However, there are some sections in Article 2 that are applicable only to merchants, and, as a result, there are circumstances in which merchants are subject to different standards and rules. Generally, these areas of different treatment constitute the UCC's recognition that merchants are experienced, have special knowledge of the relevant commercial practices, and often need to have greater flexibility and speed in their transactions. The sections under which merchants' rules and rights are different are noted throughout chapters 25 through 28.

(c) Offer. Just as in common law, the **offer** is the first step in formation of a sales contract under Article 2. The common law contract rules on offers are generally applicable in sales contract formation with the exception of the **firm offer**[6] provision, which is a special rule on offers applicable only to merchants: An offer by a merchant cannot be revoked if the offer (1) expresses an intention that it will be kept open, (2) is in a writing, and (3) is signed by the merchant.

The period of irrevocability in a merchant's offer cannot exceed three months. If nothing is said about the duration of the offer, irrevocability continues only for a reasonable time. A firm offer is effective regardless of whether the merchant received any consideration to keep the offer open. *For example*, a rain check given by a store on advertised merchandise is a merchant's firm offer. The rain check guarantees that you will be able to purchase two bottles of Windex at $1.99 each for a period that generally lasts one month.

For nonmerchants and for periods in excess of three months, the parties in a sale of goods contract must have consideration and create an option contract just like those used in common law contracts (see chapters 11 and 12).

(d) Acceptance—Manner. Unlike the common law rules on acceptance, which control with great detail the method of acceptance, the UCC rules on acceptance are much more flexible. Under Article 2, an acceptance of an offer may be in any manner and by any medium that is reasonable under the circumstances.[7] Acceptance can occur through written communication or through performance, as when a seller accepts an offer for prompt shipment of goods by simply shipping the goods.[8] However, if the offer requires a specific manner or medium of acceptance, the offer can be accepted only in that manner.

A merchant is someone who deals in the goods that are the subject matter of the contract or someone who has specialized knowledge in the area of sales related to the contract.

An offer is an initial expression of present intent to contract.

A merchant's firm offer is a written and signed offer by a merchant that states it will be kept open; irrevocable despite no requirement of consideration.

Acceptance is an expression of response and intent to contract from an offeree.

---

[4] For information on terms, see UCC §§ 2-305 (price), 2-307–2-308 (delivery), 2-311 (performance), and 2-310 (payment).
[5] Merchant is defined in UCC § 2-104(1).
[6] UCC § 2-205.
[7] UCC § 2-206(1); *Gulf States Utilities Co. v NEI Peebles Elec. Products, Inc.,* 819 F Supp 538 (MD La 1993).
[8] UCC § 2-206(1)(b).

(e) Acceptance—Timing. The timing rules of the common law for determining when a contract has been formed are used to determine the formation of a contract under Article 2 with one slight modification. The **mailbox rule** for the timing of when an acceptance is effective applies under the UCC so long as the acceptance is communicated by any reasonable method of communication. Under the common law, the same method of communication used by the offeror had to be used by the offeree in order to have the mailbox rule of acceptance be effective upon mailing or dispatch. A UCC offeree can use a reasonable method and still obtain the priority timing, so that his or her acceptance is effective when it is sent.

(f) Acceptance—Language. Under the common law, the mirror image rule applies to acceptances. Acceptances under common law, to be valid, must be absolute, unconditional, and unequivocal; that is, the acceptance under common law must be the mirror image of the offer in order for a contract to be formed. However, the UCC has liberalized this rigid rule and permits formation even in circumstances where the acceptance includes terms that vary from the offer.

(1) Additional Term in Acceptance—Nonmerchants. Under Article 2, unless it is expressly specified that an offer to buy or sell goods must be accepted just as made, the offeree may accept an offer and at the same time propose an additional term. The additional term does not reject the original offer. A contract is formed with the terms of the original offer, and the new term is a counteroffer that does not become binding until accepted by the original offeror. If, however, the offer states that it must be accepted exactly as made, the ordinary contract law rules apply. ◆ *For example,* Joe tells Susan, "I'll sell you my Schwinn bicycle for $150," and Susan responds, "I'll take it. The tire pump is included." Susan has added an additional term in her acceptance. At this point, Joe and Susan have a contract for the sale of the Schwinn bicycle for $150. Whether the tire pump is included is up to Joe; Joe is free to accept Susan's proposal or reject it, but his decision does not control whether he has a contract. There is a contract because Susan has made a definite statement of acceptance. ◆ To avoid being bound by a contract before she is clear on the terms, Susan should make an inquiry before using the language of acceptance, such as "Would you include the tire pump as part of the sale?" Susan's inquiry is not an acceptance and leaves the original offer still outstanding, which she is free to accept or reject.

CASE SUMMARY

If You Use a Credit Card to Buy a Computer— What Are the Contract Terms?

Facts: Rich and Enza Hill ordered a Gateway computer over the telephone using a credit card. The computer arrived with a list of terms in the box along with the notation that these terms apply if the customer keeps the computer longer than 30 days.

The Hills kept the computer longer than 30 days and then began complaining about problems with the computer's performance and component parts. When the problems were not remedied to the Hills' satisfaction, they filed suit against Gateway 2000, Inc., for breach of contract. Gateway asked that the suit be dismissed because one of the terms listed on the paper in the box with the computer requires Gateway customers to submit to arbitration.

The Hills maintain that their phone order was an offer that Gateway accepted by shipping a computer. For the terms in the box to apply to their relationship with Gateway, the phone representative would have had to have read those terms over the telephone and then permitted the Hills to agree to them by going ahead with the order.

Decision: The court held that the shipping of the computer was the offer, with the terms included in the box with the computer. The acceptance occurred when the Hills used the computer for longer than 30 days without objection. There was not an issue of additional terms because the court did not label the placing of the telephone credit card order as the offer, with the shipment as acceptance with additional terms. The shipment was the offer, and the use was the acceptance. That the Hills did not read the terms does not prevent their applicability. [*Hill v Gateway 2000, Inc.,* 105 F3d 1147 (7th Cir, 1997)]

(2) Additional Term in Acceptance—Merchants. Under Article 2, the use of additional terms in acceptances by merchants is treated slightly differently. The different treatment of merchants in acceptances is the result of a commercial practice known as the **battle of the forms**. The battle of the forms results because a buyer sends a seller a purchase order for the purchase of goods. The seller sends back an invoice to the buyer. While the buyer and seller may agree on the front of their documents that the subject matter of their contracts is 500 treadmills, the backs of their forms will have details on the contracts, often called *boiler plate language*, that will never match. Suppose, for example, that the seller's invoice adds a payment term of "10 days same as cash." Is the payment term now a part of the parties' agreement? The parties have a meeting of the minds on the subject matter of the contract but now have a slight difference in performance terms.

> The battle of the forms is merchants' exchanges of invoices and purchase orders with differing boiler plate terms that create issues for formation under Article 2.

Under Article 2, in a transaction between merchants, the additional term or terms sent back in an acceptance become part of the contract if the additional term or terms do not materially alter the offer and the offeror does not object in a timely fashion.[9] *For example,* returning to the Joe and Susan example, suppose that they are both now bicycle merchants negotiating for the sale and purchase of a used bicycle, they would have a contract, and the tire pump would be included as part of the sale. Joe could, however, avoid the problem by adding a limitation to his offer, such as "This offer is limited to these terms." With that limitation, Susan would have a contract, but not for the tire pump. Joe could also object immediately to Susan's proposal for the tire pump and still have a contract without this additional term.

If the proposed additional term in the acceptance is material, a contract is formed, but the material additional term does not become a part of the contract. *For example,* if Susan added to her acceptance, "Repairs free for one year," she has probably added a material term because the bicycle is used and a one-year contract for repairs would probably exceed the contract price in terms of cost. Again, Joe can avoid this problem by limiting his offer so as to strike any additional terms, whether material or immaterial. Figure 25-1 is a graphic picture of the rules on acceptance and contract terms under Article 2 when additional terms are proposed.

---

[9] UCC § 2-207(2).

FIGURE 25-1
*UCC Rules for Additional
Terms in Acceptance*

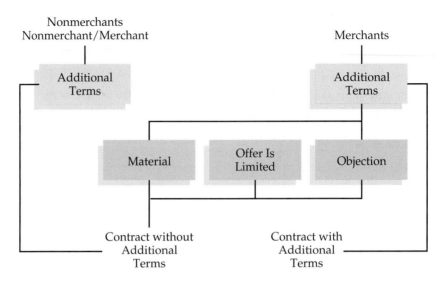

Reprinted with permission from *Business: Its Legal, Ethical and Global Environment* by Marianne M. Jennings.
© South-Western Publishing.

Even without all the UCC provisions on contract terms, an offeror may expressly or by conduct agree to a term added by the offeree to its acceptance of the offer. The offeror may agree orally or in writing to the additional term. There is an acceptance by conduct of the additional term if the performance continues with knowledge that the term has been added by the offeree.

(3) Conflicting Terms in Acceptance. In some situations, the offeree has not added a different term from the original offer but has instead proposed terms that contradict the terms of the offer. For example, a buyer's purchase order may require the seller to offer full warranty protection, while the seller's invoice may include a disclaimer of all warranties. The buyer's purchase order may include a clause that provides payment in 30 days same as cash, while the seller's invoice may include a term that has 10 days same as cash. Once again, it is clear that the parties intended to enter into a contract, and the subject matter is also clear. The task for Article 2 becomes one of establishing the rules that determine the terms of a contract when both sides have used different forms. When a term of an acceptance conflicts with a term of an offer but it is clear that the parties intended to be bound by a contract, the UCC recognizes the formation of a contract. The terms that are conflicting cancel out and are ignored. The contract then consists of the terms of the offer and acceptance that agree, together with any term that the UCC implies in a contract when the parties fail to agree on that particular term, such as the place for delivery. In the above example, where one party's form provided for full warranty protection and the other party's form provided for no warranty protection, the terms cancel each other out, and the parties' contract includes only those warranties provided under Article 2 (see chapter 28 for a discussion of those warranties).

(g) Defenses to Formation. Article 2 incorporates the common law defenses to formation of contracts by reference to the common law defenses in section 1-103 (see chapter 13 for a full discussion of those defenses). For example, a party to a contract who can establish fraud may cancel the contract and recover for losses that result from any damages for goods already delivered or payment already made.

(1) Unconscionability. The UCC includes an additional contract defense for parties to a sale contract called **unconscionability**.[10] This section permits a court to refuse to enforce a sales contract that it finds to be unconscionable, which is generally defined as grossly unfair. A court may also find a clause or portions of a contract to be unconscionable and refuse to enforce those clauses or sections.

◆ *For example,* one contract clause that is currently considered unconscionable is one that a consumer agrees to through a click on a computer program. The clause may require the consumer to submit disputes to arbitration and even dictate where that arbitration will be held. ◆ Because the new computer user may not understand the process of loading programs and working a computer, the acceptance by "click" is an unfair advantage on the part of the computer seller.

> Unconscionability is the quality of unfairness or a lack of bargaining power between the parties to a contract that results in provisions that may be unenforceable.

(2) Illegality. At common law, a contract is void if the subject matter of the contract itself is illegal, such as a contract for hire to murder someone. Under the UCC, a contract for the sale of heroin would be void. Likewide, a contract for the sale of a recalled or banned toy would be void.

(3) The Effect of Illegal Sale. An illegal sale or contract to sell cannot be enforced. As a general rule, courts will not aid either party in recovering money or property transferred under an illegal agreement.

4. Terms in the Formed Contract

As noted earlier, contracts can be formed under Article 2 with terms of performance still missing or open. A contract is formed with just the quantity agreed on, but there are issues that must be resolved if the contract is to be completed. Article 2 has provisions for such missing terms.

(a) Price. If the price for the goods is not expressly fixed by the contract, the price may be an open term, whereby the parties merely indicate how the price should be determined at a later time. In the absence of any reference to price, the price will be a reasonable price at the time of the delivery of the goods, which is generally the market price.

Formulas for determining price are common in sales of goods. The price itself is missing from the contract until the formula is applied at some future time. In recent years, there has been an increase in the use of the **"cost plus" formula** for determining price. Under this formula, the buyer pays the seller a sum equal to the seller's cost of obtaining the goods plus a specified percentage of that cost. The percentage represents the seller's profit.

> A "cost plus" contract is a contract in which the seller is entitled to all costs under the contract plus a percentage of those costs as the profit to be earned.

The UCC allows contracts that expressly provide that one of the parties may determine the price. In such a case, that party must act in good faith.[11]

---

[10] UCC § 2-302.

[11] Good faith requires that the party act honestly and, in the case of a merchant, also requires that the party follow reasonable commercial standards of fair dealing that are recognized in the trade. UCC §§ 1-201(1)(a), 2-103(1)(b); *Uptown Heights Associates Ltd. Partnership v Seafirst Corp.* (Or) 891 P2d 639 (1995).

Output and require-
ments contracts are
agreements in which the
seller agrees to sell all of
its output or the buyer
agrees to purchase all of
its requirements; quan-
tity is left open in the
contract, but it is
enforceable because a
standard of good faith
with respect to the
amount manufactured
or the amount purchased
is assumed.

(b) Output and Requirements Contracts. Somewhat related to the open-term concept concerning price is the concept involved in **output and requirements contracts**[12] that the quantity to be sold or purchased is not a specific quantity. Instead, the contract amount is what the seller produces or the buyer requires. *For example,* a homeowner may contract to purchase propane fuel for her winter heating needs. The propane company agrees to sell her the amount of propane she needs, which will vary from year to year according to the winter weather, her time at home, and other factors. Although the open quantity in contracts such as this introduces an element of uncertainty, such sales contracts are valid, but subject to two limitations: (1) The parties must act in good faith, and (2) the quantity offered or demanded must not be unreasonably disproportionate to prior output or requirements or to a stated estimate. With these restrictions, the homeowner will obtain all the propane she needs for heating but could not use her particularly beneficial price under her open quantity contract to purchase additional propane to sell to others.

(c) Indefinite Duration Term. When the sales contract is a continuing contract, such as one calling for periodic delivery of coal, but no time is set for the life of the contract, the contract runs for a reasonable time. It may be terminated by notice from either party to the other party.

(d) Changes in Terms: Modification of Contract. An agreement to modify a contract for the sale of goods is binding even though the modification is not supported by consideration.[13] The modification is valid so long as the agreement is voluntary. *For example,* suppose that Chester's Drug Store has agreed to purchase 300 bottles of vitamins from Pro-Life, Inc., at a price of $3.71 per bottle. Pro-Life has experienced substantial cost increases from its suppliers and asks Chester to pay $3.74 per bottle. Chester is not required to agree to such a price increase because it has a valid contract for the lower price. But if Chester agrees to the price increase, the agreement for the higher price is valid despite the lack of additional consideration on the part of Pro-Life. Chester may agree to the higher price because Pro-Life's price is still much lower than its competitors and Chester has a longstanding relationship with Pro-Life and values its customer service. However, Pro-Life could not threaten to cut off Chester's supply in order to obtain the price increase because that would be a breach of contract and would also be duress that would invalidate Chester's consent to the higher price (see chapter 13 for a discussion of duress).

Parol evidence is extrinsic
evidence or evidence
beyond the face of the
contract between the
parties.

(e) Contradicting Terms: Parol Evidence Rule. The **parol evidence rule** (see chapter 17 for a complete discussion) applies to the sale of goods, with the slight modification that a writing is not presumed to represent the entire contract of the parties unless the court specifically decides that it does.[14] If the court so decides, parol evidence is not admissible to add to or contradict the terms of the writing. *For example,* suppose that Ralph Rhodes and Tana Preuss negotiate the sale of Ralph's 1965 Mustang to Tana. During their discussions, Ralph agrees to pay for an inspection and for new upholstery for the car. However, Tana and Ralph sign a

---

[12] UCC § 2-306.
[13] UCC § 2-209(1).
[14] UCC § 2-202.

simple sales contract that includes only a description of the Mustang and the price. Tana cannot enforce the two provisions because she failed to have them written into their final agreement. ◆ The parol evidence rule requires the parties to be certain that everything they want is in their agreement before they sign. The courts cannot referee disputes over collateral agreements the parties fail to put in writing.

If the court decides that the writing was not intended to represent the entire contract, the writing may be supplemented by additional extrinsic evidence including the proof of additional terms as long as these terms are not inconsistent with the written terms. Parol evidence may also be admitted to interpret contract terms or show what the parties meant by their words.

(f) Interpreting Contract Terms: Course of Dealing and Usage of Trade. The patterns of doing business the parties develop through their prior contractual transactions, or **course of dealing**, become part of their contract.[15] These patterns may be used to find what was intended by the express provisions in their contract and to supply otherwise missing terms. For example, if the parties had 10 previous agreements and payment was always made on the 30th day following delivery, that conduct could be used to interpret the meaning of a clause "payment due in 30 days" when the start of the 30 days is not specifically agreed to in the contract.

In addition, the customs of the industry, or **usage of trade**, are adopted by courts in their interpretation of contract terms. ◆ *For example,* suppose that a contract provides for the sale of "mohair." There are two types of mohair: adult and kid. Industry custom, because adult mohair is cheaper and easier to find, provides that unless the parties specifically place the term "kid" with the term "mohair" in the contract, the contract is one for the sale of adult mohair. ◆

> Course of dealing is the pattern of performance between two parties to a contract, often used to determine rights under that contract.
>
> Usage of trade is the language and customs of an industry, often used in the interpretation of contracts.

5.   Bulk Transfers

Bulk transfer law, Article 6 of the UCC, was created to deal with situations in which sellers of businesses fail to pay the creditors of the business and instead use the proceeds of the sale for their own use.

In 1989, the National Conference of Commissioners on Uniform State Laws recommended that UCC Article 6 be repealed because it was obsolete and had little value in the modern business world. At the same time, the commissioners adopted a revised version Article 6 (Alternative B) for adoption by those states that desired to retain the concept for bulk sales. The states that have adopted each version are listed in the first footnote in Appendix 3. Rather than relying on the bulk sales law, the trend is for suppliers to use UCC Article 9, Secured Transactions, for protection.

B.   FORM OF SALES CONTRACT

A contract for the sale of goods may be oral or written. However, under the UCC, certain types of contracts must be in writing, or they cannot be enforced in court.

---

[15] UCC § 2-208.

6. Amount

Whenever the sales price of goods is $500 or more, the sales contract must be in writing to be enforceable.[16] The section of the UCC that establishes this requirement is known as the **statute of frauds**. (For more detail on the statute of frauds and its role in common law contracts, see chapter 16.)

7. Nature of the Writing Required

The requirement for a written contract may be satisfied by a complete written contract signed by both parties. However, under Article 2, two merchants can reduce their agreement to writing in much simpler fashion because the detail required under common law is not required in order to satisfy the UCC standards.

(a) Terms. In order to satisfy the UCC statute of frauds, the writing must indicate that there has been a completed transaction covering certain goods. Specifically, the writing must (1) indicate that a sale or contract to sell has been made[17] and (2) state the quantity of goods involved. Any other missing terms may be supplied by reference to Code sections (discussed earlier) or shown by parol evidence.

(b) Signature. The writing must be signed by the person who is being held to the contract or by the authorized agent of that person.[18] The signature must be placed on the paper with the intention of authenticating the writing. The signature may consist of initials or may be a printed, stamped, or typewritten signature placed with the intent to authenticate.

The UCC statute of frauds does provide an important exception to the signature requirement for merchants that enables merchants to expedite their transactions. This exception allows merchants to create a confirmation memorandum of their oral agreement as written evidence of an agreement. A merchant's **confirmation memorandum** is a letter or memo signed by one of the two merchant parties to an oral agreement. This memorandum can be used by either party to enforce the contract. *For example,* suppose that Ralph has orally agreed to purchase 1,000 pounds of T-bone steak from Jane for $2.79 per pound. Jane sends Ralph a signed memo that reads, "This is to confirm our telephone conversation of earlier today. I will sell you 1,000 pounds of T-bone @ $2.79 per pound." The memo can be used by either Ralph or Jane to enforce the contract.

A confirming letter or memo sent by one merchant to another results in a binding and enforceable contract that satisfies the statute of frauds within ten days of its receipt. Such a confirmation binds the nonsigning merchant, just as if he had signed the letter or a contract. A merchant can object when he receives the confirmation memo, but he must do so immediately. This confirmation procedure makes it necessary for merchants to watch their mail and other correspondence and to act within ten days of receiving a mailed confirmation.

(c) Purpose of Execution. A writing can satisfy a statute of frauds even though it was not made for that purpose. Accordingly, when the buyer writes to the seller

[16] UCC § 2-201.
[17] *Nebraska Builders Products Co. v Industrial Erectors, Inc.* (Neb) 478 NW2d 257 (1992).
[18] UCC § 1-201(39).

45 days after delivery and merely criticizes the quality of the goods, the letter satisfies the statute because it indicates that there was a sale of those goods.

(d) Particular Writings. Formal contracts, bills of sale, letters, and telegrams are common forms of writings that satisfy the requirement. Purchase orders, cash register receipts, sales tickets, invoices, and similar papers generally do not satisfy the requirement as to a signature, and sometimes they do not specify any quantity. Two or more writings grouped together may constitute a writing sufficient to satisfy the statute of frauds.[19]

CASE SUMMARY

Is a Crayon-Scrawled Contract Good Enough for the Statute of Frauds?

Facts: Michelle Rosenfeld, an art dealer, alleges she contracted with artist Jean-Michel Basquiat to buy three of his paintings. The works that she claims she contracted to buy were entitled *Separation of the K, Atlas,* and *Untitled Head.* Rosenfeld testified that she went to Basquiat's apartment on October 25, 1982; while she was there, he agreed to sell her three paintings for $4,000 each, and she picked out three. Basquiat asked for a cash deposit of 10 percent; she left his loft and later returned with $1,000 in cash, which she paid him. When she asked for a receipt, he insisted on drawing up a contract and got down on the floor and wrote it out in crayon on a large piece of paper, remarking that some day this contract would be worth money. The handwritten document listed the three paintings, bore Rosenfeld's signature and Basquiat's signature, and stated: "$12,000—$1,000 DEPOSIT—Oct 25 82." Rosenfeld later returned to Basquiat's loft to discuss delivery, but Basquiat convinced her to wait for at least two years so that he could show the paintings at exhibitions. After Basquiat's death, the estate argued that there was no contract because the statute of frauds made the agreement unenforceable. The estate contended that a written contract for the sale of goods must include the date of delivery.

Decision: The crayon-scrawled writing had the specific paintings, the price, the date, and the signature of the seller. Rosenfeld had paid a deposit. The form of the writing is not important so long as all the requirements are present. The crayon document satisfied the statute of frauds. [*Rosenfeld v Basquiat, 78 F3d 184 (2nd Cir 1996)*]

---

8. Effect of Noncompliance

A sales agreement that does not satisfy the statute of frauds cannot be enforced. However, the oral contract itself is not unlawful and may be voluntarily performed by the parties.

9. Exceptions to Requirement of a Writing

The absence of a writing does not always mean that a sales contract is unenforceable. Article 2 provides some exceptions for the enforceability of certain oral contracts.

(a) Specially Manufactured Goods. No writing is required when the goods are specially made for the buyer and are of such an unusual nature that they are not suitable for sale in the ordinary course of the seller's business. ◆ *For example,* a manufacturer who builds a stair lift for a two-story home cannot resell the $4,000

---

[19] *American Dredging Co. v Plaza Petroleum, Inc.,* 799 F Supp 1335 (EDNY 1993).

device to someone else because it is specially built for the stairs in the buyer's home. The manufacturer could enforce the oral contract against the buyer despite the price being in excess of $500.

In order for this nonresellable goods exception to apply, the seller must have made a substantial beginning in manufacturing the goods or, if a distributor is the seller, in procuring them before the buyer indicates he will not honor the oral contract.[20] The stair lift manufacturer must have progressed to a point beyond, for example, simply ordering materials for construction of the lift because those materials could be used for any lift.

(b) Receipt and Acceptance. An oral sales contract may be enforced if it can be shown that the goods were delivered by the seller and were both received and accepted by the buyer even if the amount involved is over $500 and there is no writing. The receipt and acceptance of the goods by the buyer makes the contract enforceable despite the statute of frauds issue. Both receipt and acceptance of the goods by the buyer must be shown. If only part of the goods had been received and accepted, the contract may be enforced only insofar as it relates to those goods received and accepted.[21]   *For example,* suppose that Wayne ordered 500 baseball jackets at a price of $22 each from Pamela. The order was taken over the telephone, and Wayne emphasized urgency. Pamela immediately shipped the 120 jackets she had on hand and assured Wayne the remainder would be finished over the next two weeks. Wayne received the 120 jackets and sold them to a golf tournament sponsor. Wayne refused to pay Pamela because the contract was oral. Wayne must pay for the 120 jackets, but Pamela will not be able to recover for the remaining 380 jackets she went ahead and manufactured.

(c) Payment. An oral contract may be enforced if the buyer has made full payment. In the case of part payment for divisible units of goods, a contract may be enforced only with respect to the goods for which payment has been made and accepted. In the Pamela and Wayne example, if the circumstances were changed so that Pamela agreed to ship only if Wayne sent payment, then Pamela, upon accepting the payment, would be required to perform the contract for the amount of payment received. If part payment is made for indivisible goods, such as an automobile, a part payment avoids the statute of frauds and is sufficient proof to permit enforcement of the entire oral contract.

(d) Admission. An oral contract may be enforced if the party against whom enforcement is sought admits in pleadings, testimony, or otherwise in court that a contract for sale was made. The contract, however, is not enforceable beyond the quantity of goods admitted.[22]

10. Non-Code Requirements

In addition to the UCC requirements for written contracts, other statutes may impose requirements.   *For example,* state consumer protection legislation commonly requires that there be a detailed contract and that a copy of it be given to the consumer.

---

[20] *Adams v Petrade International, Inc.* (Tex App) 754 SW2d 696 (1988).
[21] *Allied Grape Growers v Bronco Wine Co.* (Ct App) 249 Cal Rptr 872 (1988).
[22] *Harvey v McKinney* (Ill App) 581 NE2d 786 (1991).

11. Bill of Sale

A bill of sale is a receipt that reflects a transfer of title to goods.

Regardless of the requirement of the statute of frauds, the parties may wish to execute a writing as evidence or proof of the sale. Through custom, this writing has become known as a **bill of sale**, but it is neither a bill nor a contract. It is merely a receipt or writing signed by the seller reciting the transfer to the buyer of the title to the described property. A bill of sale can be used as proof of an otherwise oral agreement.

C.   UNIFORM LAW FOR INTERNATIONAL SALES

CISG (Contracts for the International Sale of Goods) is a UN set of rules for international sales transactions; varies from both the UCC and the common law.

The United Nations Convention on **Contracts for the International Sale of Goods (CISG)** applies to contracts between parties in the United States and parties in the other nations that have ratified the convention.[23] The provisions of this convention or international agreement have been strongly influenced by Article 2 of the Uniform Commercial Code. The international rules of the convention automatically apply to contracts for the sale of goods if the buyer and seller have places of business in different countries that have ratified the convention. The parties may, however, choose to exclude the convention provisions in their sales contract.

12. Scope of the CISG

The CISG does not govern all contracts between parties in the countries that have ratified it. The CISG does not apply to goods bought for personal, family, or household use. The CISG also does not apply to contracts in which the predominant part of the obligations of the party who furnishes the goods consists of the supply of labor or other services. In addition, the CISG does not apply to the liability of the seller to any person for death or personal injury caused by the goods.

The CISG governs the formation of the contract of sale and the rights and obligations of the seller and the buyer arising from such a contract. The CISG provides a basis for answering questions and settling issues the parties failed to cover in their contract.

13. Irrevocable Offers

An offer under the CISG is irrevocable if it states that it is irrevocable or if the offeree reasonably relies on it as being irrevocable. Such an offer is irrevocable even if there is no writing and no consideration. This provision differs from the common law, which requires consideration for an offer to be irrevocable, and the UCC's merchant's firm offer, which must be in writing to be irrevocable.

14. Statute of Frauds

Under the CISG, a contract for the sale of goods need not be in any particular form and can be proven by any means. The convention, by this provision, has abolished the statute of frauds' requirement of a writing. Countries may, however, retain the UCC requirements of the statute of frauds by requiring certain contracts to be in writing.

---

[23] 52 Fed Reg 6262 (1987). While the list of adopting countries is always increasing, those countries involved in NAFTA, GATT, and the European Union (EU) (see chapter 7) have adopted the CISG.

The former president of Bosnia, Radovan Karadzic, is under indictment for war crimes. Because he is barred by law from holding public office while under indictment, Mr. Karadzic serves as the leader of the Bosnian Serbs in an unofficial fashion. Mr. Karadzic still has the power to negotiate and award contracts for the reconstruction of roads, railroads, and hydroelectric plants in Bosnia. Many U.S. companies have been approached to enter into contracts to furnish goods for the reconstruction effort. Contracts with Mr. Karadzic's regime would provide reconstruction for the country and jobs to help the country's economy.

Most U.S. companies have refused to enter into contracts with Mr. Karadzic. If the goods the companies would sell are legal, why would these companies refuse to enter into a contract with him? Are the political issues and forces in another country a part of contract formation in international business? What ethical issues do you see for companies doing business in countries in which there are controversial issues such as civil war and the conduct of the leaders? Are there sound financial reasons for refusing to enter into contracts in these types of political situations?

D.   LEASES OF GOODS

Article 2A is the portion of the UCC that governs the lease of goods.

Article 2A of the UCC codifies the law of leases for tangible movable goods. Article 2A applies to any transaction, regardless of form, that creates a lease of personal property or fixtures. Many of the provisions of Article 2 were carried over and changed to reflect differences in style, leasing terminology, or leasing practices.[24] As a practical matter, leases will be of durable goods, such as equipment and vehicles of any kind, computers, boats, airplanes, and household goods and appliances. A lease is "a transfer of the right to possession and use of goods for a term in return for consideration."[25]

15. Types of Leases

Article 2A regulates consumer leases, commercial leases, finance leases, nonfinance leases, and subleases. These categories may overlap in some cases, such as when there is a commercial finance lease.

A consumer lease is a lease of goods by a natural person for personal, family, or household use.

(a) Consumer Lease. A **consumer lease** is made by a merchant lessor regularly engaged in the business of leasing or selling the kinds of goods involved. A consumer lease is made to a natural person (not a corporation) who takes possession of the goods primarily for personal, family, or household use. Total rental payments under a consumer lease cannot exceed $25,000.[26]

---

[24] Some states have limited the application of Article 2A to consumer leases. Article 2A has been adopted in Alabama, Alaska, Arizona, Arkansas, California, Colorado, Delaware, District of Columbia, Florida, Georgia, Hawaii, Idaho, Illinois, Indiana, Iowa, Kansas, Kentucky, Maine, Maryland, Massachusetts, Michigan, Minnesota, New Mexico, New York , North Carolina, North Dakota, Ohio, Oklahoma, Oregon, Pennsylvania, Rhode Island, South Carolina, South Dakota, Tennessee, Texas, Utah, Vermont, Virginia, Washington, West Virginia, Wisconsin, and Wyoming.
[25] UCC § 2A-103(1)(j).
[26] UCC § 2A-103(1)(e).

(b) Commercial Lease. When a lease does not satisfy the definition of a consumer lease, it may be called a **nonconsumer** or **commercial lease**. ◆ *For example*, a contractor's one-year rental of a truck to haul building materials is a commercial lease. ◆

A commercial lease is any non-consumer lease.

(c) Finance Lease. A **finance lease** is a three-party transaction involving a lessor, a lessee, and a supplier. Instead of going directly to a supplier for goods, the customer goes to a financier and tells the financier where to obtain the goods and what to obtain. The financier then acquires the goods and either leases or subleases the goods to its customer. The financier/lessor is in effect a paper channel, or conduit, between the supplier and the customer/lessee. The customer/lessee must approve the terms of the transaction between the supplier and the financier/lessor.[27]

A finance lease is a three-party lease agreement in which there is a lessor and a lessee and also a financier, who locates and funds the purchase of the goods to be leased to the lessee.

16. Form of Lease Contract

The lease must be in writing if the total of the payments under the lease will be $1,000 or more. The writing must be signed by the party against whom enforcement is sought. The writing must describe the leased goods, state the term of the lease, and indicate that a lease contract has been made between the parties.[28]

17. Warranties

Under Article 2A, the lessor, except in the case of finance leases, makes all the usual warranties that are made by a seller in a sale of goods. In a finance lease, however, the real parties in interest are the supplier, who supplies the lessor with the goods, and the lessee, who leases the goods. The supplier and the lessee stand in a position similar to that of seller and buyer. The lessee looks to the supplier of the goods for warranties. Any warranties, express or implied, made by the supplier to the lessor are passed on to the lessee, who has a direct cause of action on them against the supplier regardless of the lack of privity.[29] The finance lessor does not make any implied warranty; any warranty liability of a financier/lessor must rest on the lessor's express warranty.

> **CASE SUMMARY**
>
> ## Do I Have Any Rights If My Leased Copier Goes Bad?
>
> **Facts:** Jim Johnson, d/b/a Electric Image, leased a color copier, graphics system, and software from Innovative Office Systems, Inc. After the system and software were delivered to Johnson, he had significant difficulties in getting them to work. The software would not work at all, and Johnson was able to use only the color copier. The programs he needed to run on the machine for his contracts and customers would not work. Johnson had expanded his leased office space to make room for the system, and he had undertaken new contracts assuming the system would work.
>
> Despite repeated repair attempts, the system never did perform as had been demonstrated for Johnson. Johnson filed suit against Innovative for breach of warranty. Innovative claims there is no warranty because there has been no sale of a good.

---

[27] UCC § 2A-103(1)(g).
[28] UCC § 2A-201(b).
[29] UCC § 2A-209.

> **Decision:** All of the warranties applicable to sales of goods under Article 2 are applicable to leases under Article 2A. Johnson collected as damages—for the inability of the color graphics system to perform—all the lease payments made, the costs of his expansion, the additional rent costs for the additional space for the system, the lost profits on the contracts he had that assumed he would have such a system in place, and his attorney fees and costs of litigation plus $20,000 for mental anguish. [*Innovative Office Systems, Inc. v Johnson (Tex App) 906 SW2d 940 (1995)*]

18. Irrevocable Promises: Commercial Finance Leases

A commercial finance lease is a three-party nonconsumer finance lease.

Under ordinary contract law, the obligations of the lessee and lessor are mutually dependent. In contrast, upon a commercial finance lessee's acceptance of the goods, the lessee's promises to the lessor become irrevocable and independent from the obligations of the lessor. This irrevocability and independence require the lessee to perform even if the lessor's performance after the lessee's acceptance is not in accordance with the lease contract. The lessee must make payment to the lessor no matter how badly the leased goods perform. This is known as a **"hell or high water" clause**. It does not apply to consumer leases.[30] In some cases, the lessor assigns the lease contract to a third party, and that third party collects payment from the lessee. Some courts are requiring that the assignee of the lease contract take the lease assignment in good faith and without knowledge of problems with the lease or leased goods.

A hell or high water clause is a clause in a lease agreement that requires the lessee to continue paying under the lease regardless of any problems with the lease .

In a finance lease, the only remedy of the lessee for nonconformity of the goods is to sue the supplier. That is, the lessee can sue the lessor only if it is not a finance lease or if the lessor has made an express warranty or promise.

19. Default

The lease agreement and provisions of Article 2A determine whether the lessor or lessee is in default. If either the lessor or the lessee is in default under the lease contract, the party seeking enforcement may obtain a judgment or otherwise enforce the lease contract by any available judicial or nonjudicial procedure. Neither the lessor nor the lessee is entitled to notice of default or notice of enforcement from the other party. Both the lessor and the lessee have rights and remedies similar to those given to a seller in a sales contract.[31] If the lessee defaults, the lessor is entitled to recover any rent due, future rent, and incidental damages.[32] (See chapter 29 for more information on remedies.)

---

[30] UCC § 2A-407.
[31] UCC §§ 2A-501, 2A-503.
[32] UCC § 2A-529.

SUMMARY

Contracts for services and real estate are governed by the common law. Contracts for the sale of goods are governed by Article 2 of the UCC. Goods are defined as anything movable at the time it is identified as the subject of the transaction. Goods physically existing and owned by the seller at the time of the transaction are existing goods.

A sale of goods is the transfer of title to tangible personal property for a price. A bailment is a transfer of possession and not title and is therefore not a sale. A gift is not a sale because there is no price paid for the gift. A contract for services is an ordinary contract and is not governed by the UCC. If a contract calls for both the rendering of services and the supplying of goods, the contract is classified according to its dominant element.

The common law contract rules for intent to contract apply to formation of contracts under the UCC. However, several formation rules under the UCC differ from common law contract rules. A merchant's firm offer is irrevocable without the payment of consideration. The UCC rules on additional terms in an acceptance permit the formation of a contract despite the changes. These proposals for new terms are not considered counteroffers under the UCC. If the transaction is between nonmerchants, then a contract is formed without the additional terms, which the original offeror is free to accept or reject. If the transaction is between merchants, the additional terms become part of the contract if those terms do not materially alter the offer and no objection is made to them.

The same defenses available to formation under common law are incorporated in Article 2. In addition, the UCC recognizes unconscionability as a defense to formation.

The UCC does not require the parties to agree on every aspect of contract performance in order for the contract to be valid. Provisions in Article 2 will govern the parties' relationship in the event their agreement does not cover all terms. The price term may be expressly fixed by the parties. The parties may make no provision as to price,

or they may indicate how the price should be determined later. In output or requirements contracts, the quantity that is to be sold or purchased is not specified, but such contracts are nevertheless valid. A contract relating to a sale of goods may be modified even though the modification is not supported by consideration. The parol evidence rule applies to a sale of goods in much the same manner as to ordinary contracts that are not for the sale of goods. There is the slight modification in that a writing is not presumed to represent the entire contract of the parties unless the court specifically decides that it does. The UCC permits the introduction of course of dealing and usage of trade as evidence for clarification of contract terms and performance.

The UCC's statute of frauds provides that a sales contract for $500 or more must be evidenced by a writing. The UCC's merchant's confirmation memorandum allows two merchants to be bound to an otherwise oral agreement by a memo or letter signed by only one party that stands without objection for ten days. Several exceptions to the UCC statute of frauds exist: when the goods are specially made or procured for the buyer and are nonresellable in the seller's ordinary market, when the buyer has received and accepted the goods, when the buyer has made either full or partial payment, and when the party against whom enforcement is sought admits in court pleadings or testimony that a contract for sale was made.

Article 2A of the UCC regulates consumer leases, commercial leases, finance leases, nonfinance leases, and subleases of tangible movable goods. A lease subject to Article 2A must be in writing if the lease payments will total $1,000 or more.

Uniform rules for international sales are applicable to contracts for sales between parties in countries that have ratified the CISG. Under the CISG, a contract for the sale of goods need not be in any particular form and can be proven by any means.

QUESTIONS AND CASE PROBLEMS

1. What social forces are affected by the rule that consideration is not required for a modification of a contract for the sale of goods?
2. R-P Packaging manufactured cellophane wrapping material that was used by Kern's Bakery in packaging its product. Kern's decided to change its system

for packaging cookies from a tied bread bag to a tray covered with printed cellophane wrapping. R-P took measurements to determine the appropriate size for the cellophane wrapping and designed the artwork to be printed on the wrapping. After agreeing that the artwork was satisfactory, Kern placed a verbal order for the cellophane at a total cost of $13,000. When the printed wrapping material was received, Kern complained that it was too short for the trays and the artwork was not centered. The material, however, conformed exactly to the order placed by Kern. Kern returned the material to R-P by overnight express. R-P sued Kern. Kern claimed that because there was no written contract, the suit was barred by the statute of frauds. What result? [*Flowers Baking Co. v R-P Packaging, Inc.* (Va) 329 SE2d 462]

3. Smythe wrote to Lasco Dealers, inquiring about the price of a certain freezer. Lasco wrote her a letter signed by its credit manager, stating that Smythe could purchase the freezer in question during the next 30 days for $400. Smythe wrote back the next day ordering a freezer at that price. Smythe's letter was received by Lasco the following day, but Lasco wrote an answering letter, stating that it had changed the price to $450. Smythe claims that Lasco could not change its price. Is she correct?

4. Kucera purchased a refrigerator-freezer from the Elton Appliance Shop for $600. The purchase was made over the phone, after which Elton sent Kucera a letter thanking her for the purchase of the refrigerator-freezer. Before the appliance was delivered to her, Kucera telephoned Elton and canceled the purchase. Elton then sued Kucera for damages, and Kucera raised the defense of the statute of frauds. Elton produced a copy of the letter that it sent to Kucera. Does this letter avoid the defense of the statute of frauds?

5. Meyers was under contract with Henderson to install overhead doors in a factory that Henderson was building. Meyers obtained the disassembled doors from the manufacturer. His contract with Henderson required Meyers to furnish all labor, materials, tools, and equipment to satisfactorily complete the installation of all overhead doors. Henderson felt the doors were not installed properly and paid less than one-half of the contract price after subtracting out his costs for correcting the installation. Because of a business sale and other complications, Meyers did not sue Henderson for the difference in payment until five years later. Henderson raised the defense that because the contract was for the sale of goods, it was barred by the Code's four-year statute of limitations. Meyers claimed that it was a contract for services and that suit could be brought within six years. Decide. [*Meyers v Henderson Construction Co.* (NJ Super) 370 A2d 547]

6. Valley Trout Farms ordered fish food from Rangen. Both parties were merchants. The invoice that was sent with the order stated that a specified charge—a percentage common in the industry—would be added to any unpaid bills. Valley Trout Farms did not pay for the food and did not make any objection to the late charge stated in the invoice. When sued by Rangen, Valley Trout Farms claimed that it had never agreed to the late charge and therefore was not required to pay it. Is Valley Trout Farms correct? [*Rangen, Inc. v Valley Trout Farms, Inc.* (Idaho) 658 P2d 955]

7. Tober Foreign Motors, Inc., sold an airplane to Skinner on installments. Later, it was agreed that the amount of the monthly installments should be reduced by one-half. Thereafter, Tober claimed that the reduction agreement was not binding because it was not supported by consideration. Was this claim correct? [*Skinner v Tober Foreign Motors, Inc.* (Mass) 187 NE2d 669]

8. LTV Aerospace Corp. manufactured all-terrain vehicles for use in Southeast Asia. LTV made an oral contract with Bateman under which Bateman would supply the packing cases needed for the vehicles' overseas shipment. Bateman made substantial beginnings in the production of packing cases following LTV's specifications. LTV thereafter stopped production of its vehicles and refused to take delivery of any cases. When sued by Bateman for breach of contract, LTV argued that the contract could not be enforced because there was no writing that satisfied the statute of frauds. Was this a valid defense? [*LTV Aerospace Corp. v Bateman* (Tex App) 492 SW2d 703]

9. Syrovy and Alpine Resources, Inc., entered into a "Timber Purchase Agreement," whose terms were for two years. Syrovy agreed to sell and Alpine agreed to buy all the timber produced during the two years. The timber to be sold, purchased, and delivered was to be produced by Alpine from timber on Syrovy's land. Alpine continued harvesting for one year and then stopped after making an initial payment. Syrovy sued Alpine. Alpine alleged there was no contract because the writing to satisfy the statute of frauds must contain a quantity term. Decide. [*Syrovy v Alpine Resources, Inc.* (Wash App) 841 P2d 1279]

10. Mary wrote to Ed, "I'll buy your antique table for $325. Ed wrote back, "I'll sell the table for $325, cash or cashier's check." Neither Ed nor Mary are merchants. Is there a contract? If so, what terms would be included?

11. Fastener Corp. sent a letter to Renzo Box Co. that was signed by Ronald Lee, Fastener's sales manager, and read as follows: "We hereby offer you 200 type #14 Fastener bolts at $5 per bolt. This offer will be irrevocable for 10 days." On the fifth day, Fastener informed

Renzo it was revoking the offer, alleging that there was no consideration for the offer. Could Fastener revoke? Explain.

12. Richard, a retailer of video equipment, telephoned Craft Appliances and ordered a $1,000 videotape recorder for his business. Craft accepted Richard's order and sent him a copy of the purchase memorandum that stated the price, quantity, and model ordered and that was stamped "order accepted by Craft." Richard, however, did not sign or return the purchase memorandum and refused to accept delivery of the recorder when Craft delivered it to him three weeks later. Craft sued Richard, who raised the statute of frauds as a defense. Will Richard prevail? Why or why not?

13. REMC furnished electricity to Helvey's home. The voltage furnished was in excess of 135 volts and caused extensive damage to his 110-volt household appliances. Helvey sued REMC for breach of warranty. Helvey argued that providing electrical energy is not a transaction in goods but a furnishing of services, so that he had six years to sue REMC rather than the UCC's four-year statute of limitations, which had expired. Was it a sale of goods or a sale of services? Identify the ethical principles involved in this case. [*Helvey v Wabash County REMC* (Ind App) 278 NE2d 608]

14. Lawrence Fashions, a retail dress merchant, placed a telephone order with Bentley Co. for 240 dresses at a total price of $5,000. The next week, Lawrence Fashions received, inspected, and accepted 120 dresses. Lawrence Fashions refused to accept the balance when tendered and sought to return the other 120 dresses, claiming it was not obligated to keep and pay for them. Decide.

15. Flora Hall went to the Rent-A-Center in Milwaukee and signed an agreement to make monthly payments of $77.96 for nineteen months in exchange for the Rent-A-Center allowing her to have a Rent-A-Center washer and dryer in her home. In addition, the agreement required Hall to pay tax and a liability waiver fee on the washer and dryer. The total amount she would pay under the agreement was $1,643.15. The agreement provided that Hall would return the washer and dryer at the end of the nineteen months, or she could, at that time, pay $161.91 and own the washer and dryer as her own. Is this a sale contract? Is this a consumer lease? At the time Ms. Hall leased her washer and dryer, she could have purchased a set for about $600. What do you think about the cost of her agreement with Rent-A-Center? Is it unconscionable? Refer to chapter 30, and determine whether any other laws apply. Must this contract be in writing? [*Rent-A-Center, Inc. v Hall* (Wis) 510 NW2d 789]

CPA QUESTIONS

1. Webstar Corp. orally agreed to sell Northco, Inc. a computer for $20,000. Northco sent a signed purchase order to Webstar confirming the agreement. Webstar received the purchase order and did not respond. Webstar refused to deliver the computer to Northco, claiming that the purchase order did not satisfy the UCC Statute of Frauds because it was not signed by Webstar. Northco sells computers to the general public and Webstar is a computer wholesaler. Under the UCC Sales Article, Webstar's position is
   a. Incorrect, because it failed to object to Northco's purchase order.
   b. Incorrect, because only the buyer in a sale-of-goods transaction must sign the contract.
   c. Correct, because it was the party against whom enforcement of the contract is being sought.
   d. Correct, because the purchase price of the computer exceeded $500.
   (5/94, Law, #46, 4801)

2. On May 2, Lace Corp., an appliance wholesaler, offered to sell appliances worth $3,000 to Parco, Inc., a household appliances retailer. The offer was signed by Lace's president, and provided that it would not be withdrawn before June 1. It also included the shipping terms: "F.O.B.—Parco's warehouse." On May 29, Parco mailed an acceptance of Lace's offer. Lace received the acceptance June 2. Which of the following is correct if Lace sent Parco a telegram revoking its offer, and Parco received the telegram on May 25?
   a. A contract was formed on May 2.
   b. Lace's revocation effectively terminated its offer on May 25.
   c. Lace's revocation was ineffective because the offer could *not* be revoked before June 1.
   d. No contract was formed because Lace received Parco's acceptance after June 1.
   (5/92, Law, #51, 2864)

3. Bond and Spear orally agreed that Bond would buy a car from Spear for $475. Bond paid Spear a $100 deposit. The next day, Spear received an offer of $575, the car's fair market value. Spear immediately notified Bond that Spear would not sell the car to Bond and returned Bond's $100. If Bond sues Spear and Spear defends on the basis of the Statute of Frauds, Bond will probably

a. Lose, because the agreement was for less than the fair market value of the car.

b. Win, because the agreement was for less than $500.

c. Lose, because the agreement was *not* in writing and signed by Spear.

d. Win, because Bond paid a deposit.

(5/91, Law, #17, 9622)

Passage of Title and Risk of Loss: Rights of Parties

CHAPTER 26

After studying this chapter, you should be able to

1. *State when title and risk of loss pass with respect to goods;*
2. *State who bears the risk of loss when goods are damaged or destroyed;*
3. *Explain why it is important to know when risk of loss and title pass in transactions for the sale of goods;*
4. *Describe the passage of title and risk in special situations, such as a sale or return or a sale on approval; and*
5. *Classify the various circumstances in which title can be passed to a bona fide purchaser.*

In most sales, the buyer receives the proper goods and makes payment, and the transaction is completed. However, problems can arise during performance, and there may be resulting issues of liability. For example, what if the goods are lost in transit? Must the buyer still pay for those lost goods? Can the seller's creditors take goods from the seller's warehouse when they are packed for shipment to buyers? The parties can include provisions in their contract that determine the results, should these types of problems arise. However, if the parties do not cover these types of problems in their contract, then specific rules under UCC Article 2 apply. These rules are covered in this chapter.

A. TYPES OF POTENTIAL PROBLEMS AND TRANSACTIONS

The solution to problems of damage to the contract goods and property rights between the seller and the buyer and their creditors depends on the kind and terms of their transaction. The types of problems that can arise in sales contracts include situations in which a third party makes a claim on the goods and in which the goods themselves have problems that have resulted not through the fault of either the buyer or the seller.

1. Damage to Goods

One potential problem occurs if the goods are damaged or totally destroyed without any fault of either the buyer or the seller. With no goods and a contract performance still required, the parties have questions: Must the seller bear the loss and supply new goods to the buyer? Or is it the buyer's loss, so that the buyer must pay the seller the purchase price even though the goods are damaged or destroyed?[1] The fact that there may be insurance does not avoid this question because the questions of whose insurer is liable and the extent of liability still remain.

2. Creditors' Claims

Another potential problem that can arise that affects the buyer's and seller's rights occurs when creditors of the seller or buyer seize the goods under the belief that their debtor has title. The buyer's creditors may seize them because they believe

---

[1] UCC § 2-509 provides for the allocation of risk of loss in those situations where the goods are destroyed and neither party has breached the contract.

them to be the buyer's. The seller's creditors may step in and take goods because they believe the goods still belong to the seller, and the buyer is left with the dilemma of whether he can get the goods back from the creditors. The question to be resolved is which creditor is correct about who owns the goods. The question of title or ownership is also important in connection with a resale of the goods by the buyer; the parties' liability for, or the computation of, inventory or personal property taxes; and the parties' legal liability under certain registration and criminal law statutes.

3. Insurance

Until the buyer has received the goods and the seller has been paid, both the seller and the buyer have an economic interest in the sales transaction. The question arises as to whether either or both have enough interest to allow them to insure the property involved, that is, whether they have an insurable interest. If both have an insurable interest, the question that remains is, which insurer is responsible for paying for the goods?

B.   DETERMINING RIGHTS: IDENTIFICATION OF GOODS

Identification is the point in a transaction when the buyer acquires an interest in the goods that are the subject matter of the contract.

Until the goods that are the subject matter of a contract are identified, the rights of the buyer with respect to the contract and any damage or creditor claims are minimal. The **identification** of the goods to the contract is a necessary step to provide the buyer with claims for damages and reimbursement. How goods that are the subject matter of a contract are identified varies according to the nature of the contract and the goods themselves.[2]

4. Existing Goods

Existing goods are goods physically in existence at the time of the contract and owned by the seller. When particular goods have been selected by either the buyer or the seller, or both, as being the goods called for by the sales contract, the goods are identified. ◆ *For example*, when you go into a store, point to a particular item, and tell the clerk, "I'll take that one," your sales transaction relates to existing goods that are now identified by you. ◆ This step of identification provides you with certain rights in those goods because of your contract as well as Article 2 protections for buyers when goods are identified.

5. Future Goods

Future goods are goods that are the subject matter of a contract that have not yet been manufactured or that have not yet been acquired by the seller.

Future goods are those not yet owned by the seller or not yet in existence. ◆ *For example*, suppose a wholesaler learns from a woolen mill that certain goods have been manufactured and are available for purchase. Before purchasing any of the woolens from the mill, the wholesaler makes a contract with Burns, a buyer, to sell the to-be-purchased woolens to Burns. These goods are future goods because they are not yet owned by the wholesaler-seller. ◆

---

[2] UCC § 2-501(1)(a).

Likewise, a contract between a seller and a buyer for the seller to manufacture 100 wooden rocking horses is a contract for future goods because the goods are not yet in existence.

Future goods are identified when they are shipped, marked, or otherwise designated for the buyer.[3] The woolens cannot be identified until the wholesaler has purchased them and designated for the buyer whatever portion the buyer has purchased. Similarly, the earliest that the rocking horses can be identified is when they come off the production line and are designated for the buyer. Prior to identification of these goods in which the buyer has only a future interest at the time of the contract, the buyer has few rights with respect to them.[4]

6. Fungible Goods

Fungible goods are goods that, when mixed together, are indistinguishable. *For example,* crops such as corn and oil and dairy products such as milk are fungible goods. A seller who has 10,000 cases of cling peaches has fungible, unidentified goods. Like future goods, these fungible goods are identified when they are shipped, marked, or otherwise designated for the buyer, whichever of these events occurs first. *For example,* if the peach seller sets aside 1,000 cases for Kelcie's Grocery Store, then 1,000 cases of peaches are identified. If the seller had agreed to process 1,000 new cases for Kelcie's with a special Kelcie's label, then the contract would be for future goods that would not be identified until manufactured and set aside for Kelcie's. The seller's act of tagging, marking, labeling, or in some way indicating to those responsible for shipping the goods that certain goods are associated with a particular order means that identification has occurred.

7. Effect of Identification

Once goods that are the subject matter of a contract have been identified, the buyer holds an insurable interest in them. In other words, once the buyer's economic interest and the identity of the goods are clear, the insurance company for the buyer has an obligation to provide coverage for any mishaps that could occur until the contract is performed completely.

Identification is also significant in that the buyer's rights with respect to damage (or risk of loss) and passage of title cannot arise until identification has occurred. Identification is the first step in resolving questions about liability for damaged goods and rights of creditors.

C. DETERMINING RIGHTS: PASSAGE OF TITLE

When title to the goods passes to the buyer (following identification) depends on whether there is a document of title, whether the seller is required to ship the goods, and what the terms of that shipping agreement are. In the absence of an agreement by the parties as to when title will pass, there are several Article 2 rules that govern the timing for passage of title.

---

[3] UCC § 2-501(1)(b).
[4] In re Quality Processing, Inc., 9 F3d 1360 (8th Cir 1993).

8.   Goods Represented by Documents of Title

A document of title is formal paperwork required to transfer title to certain goods such as cars and airplanes.

A bill of lading is a document of title used by carriers to accompany the shipment of goods and ensure proper transfer of goods and title from seller to buyer.

A warehouse receipt is a document of title used to evidence ownership of goods held by a third party.

Instead of calling for the actual delivery of goods, a sales contract may require simply a transfer of the **document of title** for the goods.[5] For example, the goods may be stored in a warehouse, and the seller and the buyer may have no intention of moving the goods. The parties intend that the sale and delivery of the warehouse receipt for the goods are the transfer of title and completion of the sale of the goods. The obligation of the seller under a document transfer transaction is to transfer the proper paperwork, as distinguished from the goods themselves. Goods may be represented by various documents, including a **bill of lading** issued by a carrier and a **warehouse receipt**.

In other situations, a document of title is a necessary part of a sale because the transfer of the particular good is governed by statutes that require documents of title. *For example*, if Gina purchases a car from Phil's Auto Junction, Gina does not have title to the car simply by driving it off the lot with her contract with Phil. She obtains title to the car when all the necessary paperwork for the transfer on state records is complete and Gina receives either a temporary document or an official title for the car.[6]

A document of title can be negotiable or nonnegotiable (for the significance of this distinction, see chapter 24). Merchants dealing in large quantities of goods often prefer to deal only with negotiable documents of title to the goods rather than make a physical delivery of the goods. In fact, the seller may not have the goods but has a third-party warehouse handle storage, shipment, and transfer. In such a transaction, the buyer acquires an insurable interest in the goods at the time and place of contracting, and title passes when the buyer has possession of the negotiable document of title.

9.   Nonshipment Contracts

Unless the parties to the contract agree otherwise, there is no requirement under Article 2 that the seller deliver the contracted-for goods to the buyer. The seller is required only to make the goods available for the buyer. In a situation where the parties do not specifically agree to shipment or delivery of the goods, there is no document of title, and the goods to the contract are identified, then title passes to the buyer at the time the contract is entered into by the buyer and seller.[7]

10. Delivery and Shipment Terms

If delivery is required under the terms of the parties' agreement, the seller is normally required only to make shipment, and the seller's part of the contract is completed by placing the goods in the possession of a carrier for shipment. However, the parties may agree to various shipping provisions that do affect the passage of title under Article 2.[8] Figure 26-1 provides a summary of the shipping terms the parties can use in their sales contracts and the liabilities and responsibilities under each.

---

[5] UCC § 2-401(3).
[6] Other types of transportation, such as a boat, may or may not require a title document to be transferred, and title passes at the time of contracting. *Pierce v First Nat'l Bank* (Tex App) 899 SW2d 365 (1995). But see *Jerry v Second Nat'l Bank* (Mich App) 527 NW2d 788 (1994), where a state *does* require a title.
[7] UCC § 2-401(2).
[8] UCC § 2-401(2).

FIGURE 26-1
Shipping Terms

COD	Cash on delivery (payment term, not shipment term)
CF	Lump sum, price includes cost and freight Risk–buyer upon delivery to carrier Title–buyer upon delivery to carrier Expense–seller includes cost of freight in contract price
CIF	Lump sum, price includes cost, insurance, and freight Risk–buyer upon delivery to carrier Title–buyer upon delivery to carrier Expense–included in contract price (seller buys insurance in buyer's name, and pays freight)
FOB	Free on Board
FAS	Free Along Side (FOB for boats)

FOB (Free on Board) is a shipping term.

FOB place of shipment is a shipping term that requires the seller to deliver the goods to a carrier and make a contract for their shipment; title and risk of loss pass to the buyer upon the seller's delivery of the goods to the carrier.

(a) FOB Place of Shipment. FOB is a shipping term that is an acronym for "Free on Board."[9] If a contract contains a delivery term of "FOB Place of Shipment," then the seller's obligation under the contract is to deliver the goods to a carrier for shipment. ◆ *For example*, if there is a New York buyer and a Los Angeles seller and their contract provides for delivery as "FOB Los Angeles," then the seller's responsibility is to place the goods in the possession of a Los Angeles carrier and enter into a contract to have the goods shipped to New York. ◆

FOB place of destination is a shipping term that requires the seller to ship the goods to the buyer's designated location; title and risk of loss pass to the buyer upon tender of the goods by the carrier to the buyer.

Tender is the time when goods are made available to the buyer for pickup and the buyer has been notified of their availability.

(b) FOB Place of Destination. If a contract contains a delivery term of "FOB Place of Destination," then the seller's responsibility is to get the goods to the buyer. ◆ *For example*, if the contract between the New York buyer and the Los Angeles seller is "FOB New York," then the seller is responsible for getting the goods to New York. ◆ An FOB destination contract holds the seller accountable throughout the journey of the goods across country.

Under an FOB destination contract, the seller's obligation under the contract is not completed until the goods have been delivered to their destination and tendered to the buyer. **Tender** occurs when the goods have arrived and are available for the buyer to pick up and the buyer has been notified of their availability. In the above example, the seller's obligation is complete when the goods are at the rail station in New York and the buyer has been notified that he may come and pick them up at any time during working hours.

---

[9] UCC § 2-319.

(c) FAS. FAS is a shipping term that means "Free Along Side." FAS is the equivalent of FOB for boat transportation.[10] *For example*, a contract between a London buyer and a Norfolk, Virginia, seller that is "FAS Norfolk" requires only that the seller deliver the goods to a ship in Norfolk.

(d) CF and CIF. CF is an acronym for "Cost and Freight," and CIF is an acronym for "Cost, Insurance, and Freight."[11] Under a CF contract the seller will get the goods to a carrier, and the cost of shipping the goods is included in the contract price. Under a CIF contract the seller will get the goods to a carrier and buy an insurance policy in the buyer's name to cover the goods while in transit. The costs of the freight and the insurance policy are included in the contract price.

Often, contracts for the sale of goods provide for **COD**. The acronym stands for "Cash on Delivery." While the term does include the word *delivery*, COD is not a shipping term but rather a payment term that requires the buyer to pay in order to gain physical possession of the goods (see chapter 27 for more details).

11. Shipment Contracts and Passage of Title

The type of shipment contract the parties have agreed to controls when title to the goods has passed and, as a result, the rights of creditors of the buyer and seller in those goods.

(a) Passage of Title in an FOB Place of Shipment Contract. Title to the goods passes from the seller to the buyer in an FOB shipment contract when the seller delivers the goods to the carrier.[12] The title to the goods no longer rests with the Los Angeles seller once the goods are delivered to the carrier if the contract is an "FOB Los Angeles" contract. *For example*, if the Internal Revenue Service received authorization to collect taxes by seizing the seller's property, it could not take those goods once they were delivered to the carrier. Under an FOB shipment contract, the buyer owns the goods once they are in the hands of the carrier.

(b) Passage of Title in an FOB Place of Destination Contract. Title to the goods passes from the seller to the buyer in an FOB destination contract when the goods are tendered to the buyer at the destination. *For example*, when the contract provides for delivery with an "FOB New York" provision, title to the goods passes to the New York buyer when the goods have arrived in New York, they are available for pickup, and the buyer has been notified of their arrival. Thus, the IRS could seize the goods during shipment if the contract is FOB New York because title remains with the seller until actual tender. Figure 26-2 is a summary of the Article 2 rules for passage of title.

CF (Cost and Freight) is a contract term that requires the seller to arrange for delivery to the carrier, with the cost of shipping included in the price of the goods.

CIF (Cost, Insurance, and Freight) is contract term that requires the seller to arrange for delivery to the carrier and to purchase an insurance policy for the buyer, with the cost of all included in the price of the goods.

COD (Cash on Delivery) is a contract term that requires payment in full at or before the time of delivery.

[10] UCC § 2-319.
[11] UCC §§ 2-320, 2-321.
[12] UCC § 2-401(2).

FIGURE 26-2
Passage of Title under Article 2

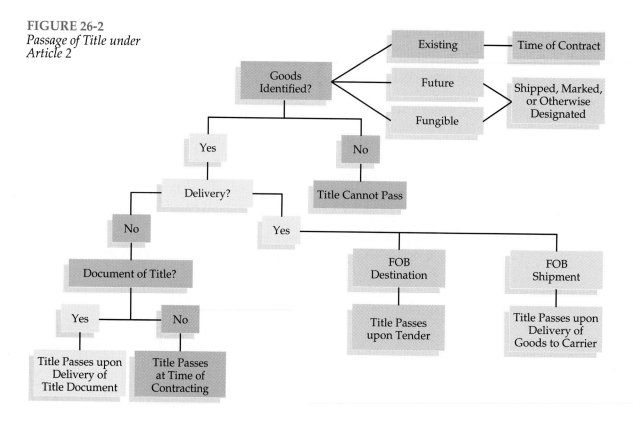

Battle on the High Seas over Computer Contracts and Title

Facts: Future Tech International, Inc., is a buyer and distributor of Samsung monitors and other computer products. In 1993, Future Tech determined that brand loyalty was important to customers, and it sought to market its own brand of computer products. Future Tech, a Florida firm, developed its own brand name of MarkVision and entered into a contract in 1994 with Tael II Media, a Korean firm. The contract provided that Tael II Media would be the sole source and manufacturer for the MarkVision line of computer products.

The course of performance on the contract did not go well. Future Tech alleged that from the time the ink was dry on the contract, Tael II Media had no intention of honoring its commitment to supply computers and computer products to Future Tech. Future Tech alleged that Tael II Media entered into the contract with the purpose of limiting Future Tech's competitive ability because Tael II Media had its own Tech Media brand of computers and computer products.

Future Tech, through threats and demands, was able to have the first line of MarkVision products completed. Tael II Media delivered the computers to a boat but, while in transit, ordered the shipping line to return the computers. The terms of their contract provided for delivery "FOB Pusan Korea." Future Tech filed suit, claiming that Tael II Media could not take the computer products because title had already passed to it.

Decision: The title to the computers passed to Future Tech when they were handed over to the carrier in Pusan because the contract was one with delivery under an FOB place of shipment term. Tael II Media could not take the goods back from the carrier because it no longer held title to them during the course of transit. [*Future Tech International, Inc. v Tael II Media, Ltd., 944 F Supp 1538 (SD Fla 1996)*]

D.   DETERMINING RIGHTS: RISK OF LOSS

Risk of loss in contract
performance is the cost
of damage or injury to
the goods contracted for

Identification determines insurability, and title determines rights of third parties such as creditors. **Risk of loss** determines who must pay under a contract in the event the goods that are the subject of the contract are damaged or destroyed during the course of performance.

12. Nonshipment Contracts

As noted earlier, there is no provision for delivery under Article 2 in the absence of an agreement. Without an agreement on delivery, the place of delivery is the seller's place of business or, in the case of a nonmerchant, the seller's residence. In the absence of a delivery provision in contract, the contract is a nonshipment contract. The rules for passage of risk of loss from the seller to the buyer in a nonshipment contract make a distinction between a merchant seller and a nonmerchant seller. If the seller is a merchant, the risk of loss passes to the buyer upon actual receipt of the goods from the merchant.[13] If the seller is a nonmerchant, the risk of loss passes when the seller makes the goods available to the buyer or upon tender. *For example,* if John buys a refrigerator at Kelvinator Appliances and then leaves it there while he goes to borrow a pickup truck to pick it up and save the $25 delivery fee, the risk of loss has not yet passed to John. He may have had title at the time he entered into the contract for the existing goods, and the goods are identified, but the risk of loss will not pass to John until he has actually received the refrigerator. His receipt will not occur until the refrigerator is placed in the back of his pickup truck. John is fully protected if anything happens to the refrigerator until then.

In the case of a nonmerchant seller, the risk of loss passes to the buyer upon tender. When the goods are available for the buyer to take, the risk of loss passes to the buyer whether the buyer actually does or does not take the goods.[14]

For example, suppose John purchased a refrigerator at a garage sale. John enters into a contract to buy the refrigerator for $200 and then explains to the homeowner/garage sale sponsor that he will go to get a pickup truck to take the refrigerator home. If anything happens to the refrigerator while John is gone, he (or his insurer) must absorb the loss because the risk had already passed to John.

13. Shipment Contracts

If the parties have agreed to delivery or shipment terms as part of their contract, the rules for risk of loss are different.[15]

(a) Contract for Shipment to Buyer. In a contract for "FOB Place of Shipment," the seller performs under the contract by delivering the goods to a carrier for shipment to the buyer. Under such a contract, the risk of loss and the title pass to the buyer when the goods are delivered to the carrier, that is, at the time and place of shipment. After the goods are delivered to the carrier, the seller has no liability for or insurable interest in the goods unless the seller has reserved a security interest

---

[13] UCC § 2-509.
[14] UCC § 2-509.
[15] UCC § 2-509.

in the goods. ◆ *For example,* if the Los Angeles seller has an "FOB Los Angeles" contract, once the goods are in the hands of the carrier, the risk belongs to the buyer or the buyer's insurer. If the goods are hijacked outside of Kansas City, the New York buyer must still pay the Los Angeles seller for the goods according to the contract price and terms. ◆

(b) Contract for Delivery at Destination. When the contract requires the seller to make delivery of the contract goods at a particular destination, the risk of loss does not pass to the buyer until the carrier tenders the goods at the destination. ◆ *For example,* if the contract is "FOB New York" and the goods are hijacked in Kansas City, the seller is required to find substitute goods and perform under the contract because the risk of loss does not pass to the buyer until the goods arrive in New York and are available to the notified buyer.

A provision in the contract directing the seller to "ship to" the buyer does not convert the contract into a destination contract. The general commercial language for delivery to the buyer is "FOB Place of Destination." A "ship to" contract is known as "FOB Place of Shipment."

14. Damage to or Destruction of Goods

In the absence of a contract provision, Article 2 provides for certain rights for the parties in the event of damage to or destruction of goods that are the subject matter in a contract.

(a) Damage to Identified Goods before Risk of Loss Passes.[16] Goods that were identified at the time the contract was made may be damaged or destroyed without the fault of either party before the risk of loss has passed. If so, the contract is avoided if the loss is total. The loss may be partial, or the goods may have so deteriorated that they do not conform to the contract. In this case, the buyer has the option, after inspecting the goods, to either avoid the contract or accept the goods subject to an allowance or a deduction from the contract price. There is no breach by the seller, so the purpose of the law is simply to eliminate the legal remedies, allow the buyer to choose to take the goods, and have the insurers involved cover the losses.[17]

(b) Damage to Identified Goods after Risk of Loss Passes. If partial damage or total destruction occurs after the risk of loss has passed to the buyer, it is the buyer's loss. The buyer may be able to recover the amount of the damages from the carrier, the person in possession of the goods (such as a warehouse), or any third person causing the loss.

(c) Damage to Unidentified Goods. As long as the goods are unidentified, no risk of loss passes to the buyer. If any goods are damaged or destroyed during this period, the loss is the seller's. The buyer is still entitled to receive the goods described by the contract. The seller is therefore liable for breach of contract if the proper goods are not delivered.

---

[16] UCC § 2-613.
[17] *Design Data Corp. v Maryland Casualty Co.* (Neb) 503 NW2d 552 (1993).

The only exceptions to these general rules on damage or destruction arise when the parties have expressly provided in the contract that the destruction of the seller's inventory, crop, or source of supply releases the seller from liability, or when it is clear that the parties contracted for the purchase and sale of part of the seller's supply to the exclusion of any other possible source of such goods. In these cases, destruction of or damage to the seller's supply is a condition subsequent that discharges the contract.

ETHICS & THE LAW

All Merica Export-Import Corporation entered into a contract to purchase several types of knit fabric manufactured by A.M. Knitwear Corporation. All Merica's purchase order included the following language: "Pick up from your plant." The purchase order also had a space for an FOB delivery instruction, but it was left blank. The place on the purchase order labeled "Price" included the following language: "FOB PLANT PER LB. $1.35."

By telephone, All Merica told A.M. that it would send containers to A.M.'s plant and asked A.M. to pack the fabric into the containers. All Merica indicated that it would send an independent carrier to pick up the containers once A.M. notified All Merica that the containers were packed.

When the containers arrived, A.M. packed them with the fabric and notified All Merica. Before the carrier arrived, the containers and the fabric were stolen. A.M.'s factory was located in a high-crime area, and there was no security at the factory at night when the theft occurred. All Merica had never done business with A.M. before and was unaware of the nature of the area where the factory was located. A.M. claimed that the risk of loss had passed to All Merica and it had no responsibility for the stolen goods; A.M. just wanted to get paid. All Merica responded, "If you had just told us about the high crime in the area, we would have had the carrier handle everything. Now we've lost everything. We have no intention of paying you."

Who has the risk of loss in this situation? Do you think sellers should disclose the crime rate in their business areas? Is there any legal obligation to do so? Is there any ethical obligation to do so? Was it unfair for A.M. to pack the goods and leave them without security? Should A.M. have taken precautions because of the boxed fabrics that belonged to someone else? Did they belong to All Merica at that point? Do you think A.M.'s insurance would cover the loss? Will All Merica's insurance cover it? *A.M. Knitwear Corp. v All Merica Export-Import Corp.* (NY) 359 NE2d 342 (1976).

15. Effect of Seller's Breach

When the seller breaches the contract by sending the buyer goods that do not conform to the contract and the buyer rejects the goods, the risk of loss does not pass to the buyer.[18] If there has been a breach, the risk of loss remains with the seller even though the risk, according to the contract terms or the Article 2 rules discussed earlier, would ordinarily have passed to the buyer.

Figure 26-3 provides a summary of all the risk provisions for parties in a sales transaction.

[18] UCC § 2-510.

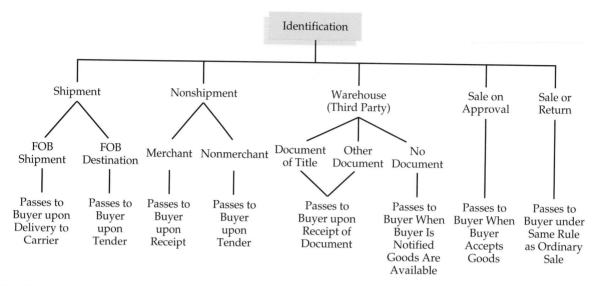

FIGURE 26-3
Risk of Loss

E. DETERMINING RIGHTS: SPECIAL SITUATIONS

16. Returnable Goods Transactions

The parties may agree that the goods to be transferred under the contract can be returned to the seller. This type of arrangement in which goods may be returned will be classified as one of the following: (1) a sale on approval, (2) a sale or return, or (3) a consignment sale. In the first two types of transactions, the buyer is allowed to return the goods as an added inducement to purchase. The consignment sale is used when the seller is actually the owner's agent for the purpose of selling goods.[19]

Classifying the transaction is the first step in determining the rights and risks of the parties as well as who has title.

(a) Sale on Approval. In a **sale on approval**, no sale takes place (meaning there is no transfer of title) until the buyer approves, or accepts, the goods. Title and risk of loss remain with the seller until there is an approval. Because the buyer is not the "owner" of the goods before approval, the buyer's creditors cannot attach or take the goods before the buyer's approval of the goods.

The buyer's approval may be shown by (1) express words, (2) conduct, or (3) the lapse of time. Trying out or testing the goods does not constitute approval or acceptance. Any use that goes beyond trying out or testing, such as repairing the goods or giving them away as a present, is inconsistent with the seller's continued ownership. These types of uses show approval by the buyer. ◆ *For example,* a buyer may order a set of recipe cards through a television ad. The ad allows

---

[19] UCC §§ 2-326, 2-327.

buyers to try the cards for 30 days and then promises, "If you are not completely satisfied, return the cards and we'll refund your money." The offer is one for a sale on approval. If the buyer does not return them or contact the seller within 30 days, the sale is complete.

The contract may give the buyer a fixed number of days for approval. The expiration of that period of time, without any action by the buyer, constitutes an approval. If no time is stated in the contract, the lapse of a reasonable time without action by the buyer constitutes an approval. If the buyer gives the seller notice of disapproval, the lapse of time thereafter has no effect.

If the goods are not approved by the buyer, the seller bears the risk of and expense for their return.

(b) Sale or Return. A **sale or return** is a completed sale with an option for the buyer to return the goods.[20] The buyer sells or transfers back to the seller the title that had already passed to the buyer. The option to return must be exercised within the time specified by the contract or within a reasonable time if none is specified.

> A sale or return is a form of sale in which title and risk of loss do pass to the buyer but which allows the buyer to return the goods to the seller.

In a sale or return transaction, title and risk of loss pass to the buyer as in the case of the ordinary or absolute sale. Until the actual return of the goods is made, title and risk of loss remain with the buyer. The buyer bears the expense for and risk of return of the goods. As long as the goods remain in the buyer's possession, the buyer's creditors may treat the goods as belonging to the buyer.

CASE SUMMARY

Wood, Badgers, and Title Passage

Facts: Badger manufactured wood products. Associated Bank held three of Badger's promissory notes totaling over $3.7 million, which were secured through a security agreement filed with Wisconsin's secretary of state. The security agreement covered a variety of Badger's assets, including all raw materials and work in process.

In September 1993, Badger defaulted on all three notes. Badger surrendered all of its assets to Associated Bank, including three shipments of wood for making cabinets that had been delivered to Badger from Houghton Wood Products in July and August. Associated disposed of the wood and other assets and applied the funds received to cover Badger's indebtedness on the three notes. Houghton sued Badger and Associated Bank to recover the price of the wood because it had been delivered under a sale-on-approval contract. The invoice accompanying the wood stated that acceptance could be accomplished only by payment of the purchase price.

Decision: The court held the arrangement was not a sale on approval. Because the lumber was to be used to manufacture cabinets, there was little opportunity for any return once the wood had been so used. Further, the seller retained a security interest in the wood as a way of preserving its rights, which cuts against the notion that the transaction was one in which the buyer had an out through a return. Because title had already passed to Badger—i.e., it was not a sale on approval—the bank could properly repossess all the assets including the wood. [*Houghton Wood Products v Badger Wood Products* (Wis App) 538 NW2d 621 (1995)]

> A consignment entrusts goods to another for the purposes of sale.

(c) Sale on Consignment. Under a **consignment**, the owner of the goods entrusts them to a dealer for the purpose of selling them. The seller is the **consignor**, and the dealer is the **consignee**. The dealer/consignee is paid a fee for selling the goods on behalf of the seller/consignor. A consignment sale is treated as

---

[20] In re Thomas, 182 BR 347, 26 UCC2d 774 (Bankr SD Fla 1995).

a sale or return under Article 2. For this reason, creditors of the consignee can obtain possession of the goods and have a superior right to them over the consignor. If, however, the consignor complies with the security interest and perfection provisions of Article 9 of the UCC (Secured Transactions—see chapter 35), then there is public notice of the consignment, and the goods will be subject to the claims of the seller's creditors but not those of the consignee.[21]

17. Reservation of a Security Interest

The seller can protect against the danger of a buyer's failure to pay for goods by insisting that the buyer pay cash immediately. Cash payment may not be practical for geographic or business reasons. The seller can allow the buyer to purchase goods on credit but obtain repayment protection by retaining a security interest in the goods. When goods are shipped to the buyer, the creditor can create a temporary security interest so that the buyer must make payment before obtaining the goods from the carrier. Between merchants, this mandatory prepayment can be accomplished through various ways of handling the bill of lading issued by the carrier. In the case of a consumer buyer, it is customary for the seller to make the shipment COD (Cash on Delivery), in which case the buyer must pay for the goods before taking possession of them from the carrier. Under the bill of lading or the COD shipment, the security interest of the seller ends when the goods are delivered to the buyer, who pays prior to being allowed possession. If a seller desires a security interest that will continue as long as the purchase price remains unpaid, a secured transaction under Article 9 of the Uniform Commercial Code could be created. (See chapter 35.)

The fact that a seller has a security interest in the goods, by virtue of a COD provision or any other device, has no effect on the question of whether title or risk of loss has passed to the buyer. Title and risk of loss pass according to the terms of the contract or Article 2 regardless of whether the seller retains a security interest. For example, under a shipment contract of future goods from a distant seller, the risk of loss and the title pass to the buyer on delivery to the carrier. The result is the same even though such shipment is made COD.

18. Sale Authorization and Title

As a general rule, a seller can sell only what the seller owns. If a person in possession of goods is not the owner, as in the case of a finder of stolen property or a thief, a sale by such possessor does not pass title, only possession. It is immaterial that the buyer had purchased from the possessor in good faith and had given value. The attempted sale does not pass any title. Consequently, the buyer of stolen goods must surrender them to the true owner and can be sued by the true owner for damages for conversion of the goods. The fact that the negligence of the owner made the theft possible or contributed to the losing of the goods does not bar the owner from recovering the goods or money damages from the thief, the finder, or the purchaser from either the thief or the finder.

In certain instances, however, because of either the conduct of the owner or the desire of society to protect the good-faith purchaser for value, the law permits

---

[21] *Knight v United States*, 838 F Supp 1243 (MD Tenn 1993).

a greater interest or title than the seller possessed to be transferred to the good-faith purchaser.[22]

(a) Estoppel. If an owner has acted in a way that misleads others, the owner of personal property may be prevented, or estopped, from asserting ownership. The owner would be barred from denying the right of another person to sell the property. *For example*, a minor buys a car and puts it in his father's name so that he can obtain lower insurance rates. If the father then sells the car to a good-faith purchaser, the son would be estopped from claiming ownership.

(b) Powers. In certain circumstances, persons in possession of someone else's property may sell the property. This sale by possessors can occur in the case of pledgees, lienholders, and some finders who, by statute, may have authority to sell the property either to enforce their claim or when the owner cannot be found.

(c) Negotiable Documents of Title. By statute, documents of title, bills of lading, and warehouse receipts are negotiable when executed in proper form. By virtue of such provisions, the holder of a negotiable document of title may transfer to a good-faith purchaser for value such title as was possessed by the person leaving the property with the issuer of the document. In cases of this nature, it is immaterial that the holder had not acquired the document in a lawful manner.

> A voidable title is a title to goods that carries with it the contingency of an underlying problem, or potential problems as when a minor sells goods to another.

(d) Voidable Title. If the buyer has a **voidable title**—for example, when the goods were obtained by fraud—the seller can rescind the sale. However, if the buyer resells the property to a good-faith purchaser before the seller has rescinded the transaction, the subsequent purchaser acquires valid title. It is immaterial whether the buyer with the voidable title had obtained title by fraud as to identity or by larceny by trick, or had paid for the goods with a bad check, or that the transaction was a cash sale and the purchase price had not been paid.

If the transferee from the holder of the voidable title is not a good-faith purchaser, the title remains voidable. The true owner may reclaim the goods.

(e) Sale by Entrustee. If the owner entrusts goods to a merchant who deals in goods of that kind, the latter has the power to transfer the entruster's title to anyone who buys from the entrustee in the ordinary course of business.[23]

It is immaterial why the goods were entrusted to the merchant. *For example*, leaving a watch for repair with a jeweler who sells new and secondhand watches gives the jeweler the power to pass the title of the repair customer's property to a buyer in the ordinary course of business. Goods in inventory thus have a degree of negotiability. The ordinary buyer, whether a consumer or another merchant, buys the goods free of the ownership interest of the person entrusting the goods to the seller. The entrustee is, of course, liable to the owner for damages caused by the entrustee's sale of the goods. The entrustee is also guilty of some form of statutory offense such as larceny or embezzlement if the goods were sold intentionally.

---

[22] UCC § 2-403.
[23] *Thorn v Adams* (Or App) 865 P2d 417 (1993).

In the case of an entrustee who is not a merchant, such as a prospective customer trying out an automobile, there is no transfer of title to the buyer from the entrustee. Similarly, there is no transfer of title when a mere bailee, such as a repairer who is not a seller of goods of that kind, sells the property of a customer.

CASE SUMMARY

The Traveling Ford Pickup Salesman

Facts: In 1989, Michael Heinrich wanted to buy a particular model of a new Ford pickup truck. James Wilson represented himself to Heinrich to be a dealer/broker who was licensed to buy and sell vehicles. Because he did not know that Wilson had lost his Washington vehicle dealer's license a year earlier, Heinrich retained Wilson to make the truck purchase but did not direct Wilson to any particular dealer.

Wilson negotiated with Titus-Will Sales for a pickup truck with the options Heinrich had specified. Wilson had completed hundreds of transactions over the years with Titus-Will, which also was unaware that Wilson had lost his license.

Heinrich made two initial payments to Wilson: an $1,800 down payment and a $3,000 payment when Titus-Will ordered the truck. Wilson gave Heinrich a receipt with his vehicle dealer's license number and then ordered the truck from Titus-Will, using his own check to provide a $7,000 down payment. Wilson told the Titus-Will salesman with whom he placed the order that he was buying the truck for resale.

When the truck arrived, Titus-Will issued a dealer-to-dealer title to it after Heinrich had paid the remaining $15,549.55 due on the sale. However, Wilson's original check for $7,000 failed to clear, and Titus-Will refused to issue the title and took the truck back from Heinrich. Seeking to have his truck returned, Heinrich sued Titus-Will and Wilson.

Decision: Wilson had the power to pass good title to a good-faith purchaser for value. Heinrich purchased the truck and, in this situation of entrustment, did so in good faith. The fact that Wilson paid Titus-Will with a check that was later dishonored by the bank (see chapter 34) does not prevent a good-faith purchaser from taking title. Although Wilson was in a situation of either entrustment or voidable title, he did, under either circumstance, have the authority under Article 2 to pass good title to Heinrich as a good-faith purchaser for value. [*Heinrich v Titus-Will Sales, Inc.* (Wash App) 868 P2d 169 (1994)]

---

19. Self-service Stores

In the case of goods in a self-service store, the reasonable interpretation of the circumstances is that the store, by its act of putting the goods on display on the shelves, makes an offer to sell such goods for cash and confers on a prospective customer a license to carry the goods to the cashier in order to make payment. Most courts hold that there is no transfer of title until the buyer makes payment to the cashier. On this rationale, no warranty liability of the store arises before the buyer pays.

A contrary rule adopts the view that a contract to sell is formed when the customer accepts the seller's offer by taking the item from the shelf.

By another contrary view, a sale actually occurs when the buyer takes the item from the shelf. That is, title passes at that moment to the buyer even though the goods have not yet been paid for. Under this view, if the buyer places the item back on the shelf, this is merely a return by the buyer. By this return, the buyer transfers back to the seller the title that had already passed to the buyer when the item was removed from the shelf.

20. Auction Sales

When goods are sold at an auction in separate lots, each lot is a separate transaction, and title to each passes independently of the other lots. Title to each lot passes when the auctioneer announces by the fall of the hammer or in any other customary manner that the lot in question has been sold to the bidder.

Figure 26-4 provides a summary of the principles covered in this chapter.

FIGURE 26-4
Risk and Property Rights in Sales Contract

Nature of Goods	Terms of Transaction	Transfer of Risk of Loss to Buyer	Transfer of Title to Buyer	Acquisition of Insurable Interest by Buyer
Existing Goods Identified at Time of Contracting	1. Without Document of Title	Buyer's receipt of goods from merchant seller, tender of delivery by nonmerchant seller § 2–509(3)	Time and place of contracting* § 2–401(3)(b)	Time and place of contracting § 2–501(1)(a)
	2. Delivery of Document of Title Only	Buyer's receipt of negotiable document of title § 2–509(2)(a)	Time and place of delivery of documents by seller § 2–401(3)(a)	Time and place of contracting § 2–501(1)(a)
Future Goods	3. Marking for Buyer	No transfer until a later event	No transfer until a later event	At time of marking § 2–501(1)(b)
	4. Contract for Shipment to Buyer	Delivery of goods to carrier § 2–509(1)(a)	Delivery of goods to carrier § 2–401(2)(a)	Delivery to carrier or marking for buyer § 2–501(1)(b)
	5. Contract for Delivery at Destination	Tender of goods at destination § 2–509(1)(b)	Tender of goods at destination § 2–401(2)(b)	Delivery to carrier or marking for buyer § 2–501(1)(b)

*Assumes no document of title

SUMMARY

Problems relating to risk and property rights in sales transactions often involve damage to the goods, the claims of creditors, and insurance. In the absence of an agreement, the solution to these problems depends on the nature of the transaction between the seller and the buyer. Sales transactions may be classified according to the nature of the goods and the terms of the transactions.

Existing goods are physically in existence and owned by the seller. Future goods are not yet owned by the seller or are not yet in existence. The title to existing goods that are identified at the time of the contract passes to the buyer at the time the parties agree to the transaction. Once the goods are identified, both the buyer and the seller have an insurable interest in the goods. If the goods are damaged after the sales agreement has been made, a merchant seller bears the loss occurring until the time the buyer receives the goods. If the seller is not a merchant, the risk of loss passes to the buyer when the goods are tendered or made available to the buyer. In a shipment contract, title and risk of loss pass at the time and place of shipment; in a destination contract, title and risk pass when the goods are made available at the destination. As long as the goods are unidentified, neither title nor risk of loss passes to the buyer.

In cases where the risk of loss would ordinarily pass to the buyer, the risk remains with the seller if the goods do not conform to the contract. Even when the goods do conform to the contract, the buyer and seller could have agreed in their contract that the goods may be returned. The nature of their agreement, such as a sale on approval, sale or return, or consignment sale, determines who has title and who bears the risk of loss.

The reservation of a security interest in goods does not affect the question of whether title or risk of loss has passed to the buyer.

Ordinarily, sellers cannot pass any better title than they possess. In some cases, however, the law permits a greater title to be transferred. These exceptions protect good-faith purchasers.

QUESTIONS AND CASE PROBLEMS

1. What are the costs and implications of the rule that the buyer has an insurable interest when goods that were to be manufactured are finally completed and marked for shipment to the buyer?

2. Stanley borrowed a lawn mower from Rita, his neighbor. He immediately sold it to Jones, who purchased the lawn mower without knowledge that Rita was the true owner. Does Rita have the right to recover the lawn mower from Jones? Explain your answer.

3. Kirk bought a television set from the Janess Television Store. At the time of the sale, Kirk gave Janess a check for the purchase price and obtained a receipt marked "Paid in full." The check was drawn on an account in which the balance was insufficient to cover the amount of the check. Kirk knows of the insufficient funds and the resulting bad check but hopes to leave town with the television set before Janess learns that the check is bad. Is Kirk the owner of the television set?

4. Helen Thomas contracted to purchase a pool heater from Sunkissed Pools. As part of the $4,000 contract, Sunkissed agreed to install the pool heater, which was delivered to Thomas's home and left in the driveway. The heater was too heavy for Thomas to lift, and she was forced to leave it in the driveway because no one from Sunkissed responded to her calls about its installation. Subsequently, the heater disappeared from the driveway. Sunkissed maintained the risk of loss had passed to Thomas. Thomas maintained that the failure to install the heater as promised is a breach of contract. Who should bear the risk for the stolen pool heater? [*In re* Thomas, 182 BR 774 (Bankr SD Fla 1995)]

5. Jamison wants to buy a new truck. Kenton, a dealer, tries to sell him a particular truck. Jamison is not certain that this is the truck he wants. To encourage him to buy, Kenton sells the truck to him on "30-day approval." Jamison owes First National Bank on an overdue debt, and 25 days later the bank has the sheriff seize the truck to sell it to pay off the debt owed by Jamison. Both Kenton and Jamison object that the bank cannot do this. Are they correct?

6. A thief stole a television set and sold it to a good-faith purchaser for value. This person resold the set to another buyer, who also purchased in good faith and for value. The original owner of the set sued the second purchaser for the set. The defendant argued that he had purchased it in good faith from a seller who had sold in good faith. Was this defense valid? [*Johnny*

Dell, Inc. v New York State Police (Misc) 375 NYS2d 545]

7. Using a bad check, *B* purchased a used automobile from a dealer. *B* then took the automobile to an auction at which the automobile was sold to a party who had no knowledge of its history. When *B*'s check was dishonored, the dealer brought suit against the party who purchased the automobile at the auction. Was the dealer entitled to reclaim the automobile? [*Greater Louisville Auto Auction, Inc. v Ogle Buick, Inc.* (Ky) 387 SW2d 17]

8. Coppola, who collected coins, joined a coin club, First Coinvestors, Inc. The club would send coins to its members, who were to pay for them or return them within ten days. What was the nature of the transaction? [*First Coinvestors, Inc. v Coppola* (Misc) 388 NYS2d 833]

9. Sandford signed an agreement to purchase a used calculator from Roberts, a dealer in such equipment. Sandford agreed to pick it up the next day. The Roberts salesperson marked the calculator "Sold," placed Sandford's name on it, and moved it to the storeroom. That night thieves broke into the storeroom and took everything, including the calculator. The burglary was in no way caused by Roberts' negligence. Sandford refuses to pay unless he receives his calculator. Who bears the risk of loss? Why?

10. Does a pawnbroker who purchases property in good faith acquire good title to that property? Can the pawnbroker pass good title? [*Fly v Cannon*, 813 SW2d 458 (Tenn App)]

11. Larsen Jewelers sold a necklace to Conway on a layaway plan. Conway paid a portion of the price and made additional payments from time to time. The necklace was to remain in the possession of Larsen until payment was fully made. The Larsen jewelry store was burglarized, and Conway's necklace and other items were taken. Larsen argued that Conway must bear the risk of loss. Conway sought recovery of the full value of the necklace. Decide. [*Conway v Larsen Jewelers* (Misc) 429 NYS2d 378]

12. Leton Wholesale Co. sold and delivered ten executive desks on consignment to Frelow, the owner and manager of Handy Office Supply Co. Frelow had severe financial problems, and her creditors petitioned the court to allow attachment of her inventory. A marshal seized the entire inventory of Handy Office Supply Co., including the ten executive desks. Explain how Leton Wholesale Co. could have prevented the desks from becoming subject to the claim of Frelow's creditors.

13. Smith operated a marina and sold and repaired boats. Gallagher rented a stall at the marina, where he kept his vessel, the River Queen. Without any authorization, Smith sold the vessel to Courtesy Ford. Gallagher sued Courtesy Ford for the vessel. What was the result? [*Gallagher v Unenrolled Motor Vessel River Queen*, 475 F2d 117 (5th Cir)]

14. Without permission, Grissom entered onto land owned by another and then proceeded to cut and sell the timber from the land. On learning that the timber had been sold, the owner of the land brought an action to recover the timber from the purchaser. The purchaser argued that he was a good-faith purchaser who had paid value and therefore was entitled to keep the timber. Decide. [*Baysprings Forest Products, Inc. v Wade* (Miss) 435 So 2d 690]

15. Brown Sales ordered goods from Everhard Manufacturing Co. The contract contained no agreement about who would bear the risk of loss. There were no shipping terms. The seller placed the goods on board a common carrier with instructions to deliver the goods to Brown. While in transit, the goods were lost. Which party will bear the loss? Explain. [*Everhard Manufacturing Co. v Brown* (Mich App) 232 NW2d 378]

CPA QUESTIONS

1. Bond purchased a painting from Wool, who is not in the business of selling art. Wool tendered delivery of the painting after receiving payment in full from Bond. Bond informed Wool that Bond would be unable to take possession of the painting until later that day. Thieves stole the painting before Bond returned. The risk of loss

   a. Passed to Bond at Wool's tender of delivery.
   b. Passed to Bond at the time the contract was formed and payment was made.
   c. Remained with Wool, because the parties agreed on a later time of delivery.
   d. Remained with Wool, because Bond had **not** yet received the painting.

   (11/93, Law, #55, 4352)

2. Which of the following statements applies to a sale on approval under the UCC Sales Article?
   a. Both the buyer and seller must be merchants.
   b. The buyer must be purchasing the goods for resale.
   c. Risk of loss for the goods passes to the buyer when the goods are accepted after the trial period.
   d. Title to the goods passes to the buyer on delivery of the goods to the buyer.

   (11/93, Law, #49, 4346)

3. If goods have been delivered to a buyer pursuant to a sale or return contract, the
   a. Buyer may use the goods but **not** resell them.
   b. Seller is liable for the expenses incurred by the buyer in returning the goods to the seller.
   c. Title to the goods remains with the seller.
   d. Risk of loss for the goods passed to the buyer.

   (11/88, Law, #46)

Obligations and Performance

CHAPTER 27

OBJECTIVES

After studying this chapter, you should be able to

1. *Define the obligation of good faith as applied to merchants and nonmerchants;*
2. *State what steps can be taken by a party to a sales contract who feels insecure;*
3. *State the obligations of the seller and the buyer in a sales contract; and*
4. *Identify conduct that constitutes an acceptance.*

509

Contracts for the sale of goods impose both obligations and requirements for performance on the parties.

A. GENERAL PRINCIPLES

Good faith means honesty in fact in conduct or in a transaction.

Each party to a sales contract is bound to perform according to the terms of the contract. Each is likewise under a duty to **exercise good faith** in the contract's performance and to do nothing that would impair the other party's expectation that the contract will be performed.

1. Obligation of Good Faith

Every contract or duty within the UCC imposes an obligation of good faith in its performance or enforcement.[1] The UCC defines good faith as "honesty in fact in the conduct or transaction concerned."[2] In the case of a merchant seller or buyer of goods, the UCC carries the concept of good faith further. The UCC imposes the additional requirement that merchants observe "reasonable commercial standards of fair dealing in the trade."[3]

CASE SUMMARY

The Postponed Boeing 777 Jet Engine

Facts: Euralair, a French commercial airline business, entered into a contract with Boeing to purchase two Boeing 777 airplanes, with each plane to be equipped with two jet engines. After a competition among three manufacturers, Euralair selected General Electric (GE) to manufacture the jet engines that would be used in their Boeing planes.

Under the terms of their 1992 agreement, Euralair would purchase the four engines needed for the Boeing planes from GE and in addition order, by April 30, 1995, at least one spare engine. Also, GE financed the jet engine purchase by Euralair. The financing agreement was tied to the engine purchase contract. Under the terms of the financing agreement, Euralair would be declared in default on the financing arrangement if the spare engine order was not received within the time deadline specified by the engine purchase agreement.

Euralair did not place an order for a spare engine by April 30, 1995. In a letter dated August 21, 1995, GE notified Euralair that unless it agreed to a restructuring of the financing arrangement, the entire outstanding principal on the notes for the engine purchase was due and owing. Euralair indicated that its large contract with the French government had been terminated and that it was taking delivery of the Boeing jets later as a result of the decline in business and would not need the spare engine until the planes were delivered. Euralair claimed that GE had breached its obligation of good faith and fair dealing by suddenly declaring the full amount of the loan due. Euralair also claimed that GE's failure to negotiate a restructuring of its debt was a violation of the requirement of good faith.

Decision: There was no breach of good faith. The contract terms and obligations were clear: Either Euralair purchased a spare engine by a given date, or the full amount of the loan was due and owing. Euralair's business setbacks do not mean that GE is required to accept anything less than the rights and protections afforded by the parties' contract. Further, GE had no oblig-

---

[1] UCC § 1-203; *Plaza Terraces, Inc. v QSC Products, Inc.*, 868 F Supp 346 (DDC 1994).
[2] UCC § 1-201(19); *Kotis v Nowlin Jewelry, Inc.* (Tex App) 844 SW2d 920 (1992).
[3] UCC § 2-103(1)(b); *Amoco Oil Co. v Ervin* (Colo) 908 P2d 493 (1995).

> ation to restructure under the terms of the agreement. The loan agreement simply provided for default and acceleration. That the consequences of enforcement of a contract can be harsh does not mean that their enforcement represents a lack of good faith on the part of the enforcer. *[General Electric Co. v Compagnie Euralair, S.A., 945 F Supp 527 (SDNY 1996)]*

2. Time Requirements of Obligations

In a cash sale that does not require the physical moving of the goods, the duties of the seller and buyer are concurrent. Each one has the right to demand that the other perform at the same time. That is, as the seller hands over the goods, the buyer theoretically must hand over the purchase money. If either party refuses to act, the other party has the right to withhold performance. In self-service stores, the performance of the parties is concurrent. The buyer pays as the items are bagged at check-out.

3. Repudiation of the Contract

Repudiation is a party's refusal to perform on a contract when the time for performance arises.

Anticipatory repudiation is a party's refusal to perform on a contract before the time for performance arises.

Demand for adequate assurances is a party's demand for written assurances made based on reasonable grounds for concern about the other party's performance.

Adequate assurances are assurances sufficient to satisfy a reasonable person that performance will occur.

If the seller or the buyer refuses to perform the contract when the time for performance arises, a **repudiation** of the contract results. Often, before the time for performance arrives, one party may inform the other that the contract will never be performed. This repudiation made in advance of the time for performance is called an **anticipatory repudiation**.[4]

4. Adequate Assurance of Performance

A party to a sales contract may become concerned that the other party will not perform the contract.[5] *For example*, if the seller's warehouse is destroyed by fire, the buyer could worry that the seller will not be able to make a delivery scheduled for the following month. Whenever a party to a sales contract has reasonable grounds to be concerned about the future performance of the other party, a written demand may be made for **assurance** that the contract will be performed.[6] *For example*, a seller who is concerned about a buyer's ability to pay for goods could demand an updated credit report, financial statement, or even additional security or payment.

(a) Form of Assurance. The person on whom demand for assurance is made must give "such assurance of due performance as is adequate under the circumstances of the particular case."[7] The exact form of assurance is not specified by the UCC. If the party on whom demand is made has an established reputation, a reaffirmation of the contract obligation and a statement that it will be performed may be sufficient to assure a reasonable person that it will be performed. In contrast, if the party's reputation or economic position at the time is such that mere words and promises would not give any real assurance, it may be necessary to have a third person (or an insurance company) guarantee performance or put up property as security for performance.

---

[4] UCC § 2-610; *Aero Consulting Corp. v Cessna Aircraft Co.*, 867 F Supp 1480 (D Kan 1994).
[5] UCC § 2-609
[6] *S & S, Inc. v Meyer* (Iowa App) 478 NW2d 857 (1991).
[7] UCC § 2-609(4).

(b) Failure to Give Assurance. If adequate assurance is not given within 30 days from the time of demand, the demanding party may treat the contract as repudiated. The demanding party may then sue for damages for breach of contract. In addition, a demanding buyer may make a substitute contract with a third person to obtain goods covered by a broken contract.

CASE SUMMARY

When a Demand for Full Payment Is Unreasonable

Facts: Ward Transformer Co. and Distrigas of Massachusetts Corp. (DOMAC) entered into a contract for the sale of a reconditioned transformer. The date of delivery was left open. DOMAC, the buyer, inquired about the seller's charges for canceling the contract. Ward then sent an invoice to the buyer demanding payment in full within 30 days even though payment was not due under the contract until after delivery. The buyer declined to pay the full purchase price but offered to make a progress payment of 15 percent. Ward demanded 50 percent immediately and the remaining 50 percent within 30 days after delivery. DOMAC refused and canceled the contract.

DOMAC subsequently purchased a transformer from another company for substantially the same price. Ward filed an action for breach of contract, arguing that it had reasonable grounds for insecurity, that its invoice was a demand for adequate assurance, and that the buyer's response was not adequate. DOMAC contended that it never gave Ward reasonable grounds to believe that it would not perform and that even if it did, Ward never made a written demand for adequate assurance in proper form. DOMAC further contended that if demand was in proper form, it called for assurances that were commercially unreasonable.

Decision: Ward's suspension of its performance was commercially unreasonable. Ward demanded payment of the entire purchase price even though the contract terms expressly made payment due 30 days after satisfactory delivery.

DOMAC, in a good-faith effort to avoid a dispute, offered Ward a progress payment of 15 percent of the purchase price even though such a payment was not required under the terms of the contract. Although Ward subsequently reduced its demand to a payment of 50 percent of the purchase price, the fact remains that it was actually entitled to nothing prior to shipment of the transformer. If Ward had truly had reasonable grounds for insecurity, then DOMAC's offer to pay 15 percent of the purchase price was adequate assurance for Ward that DOMAC intended to honor the contract, and it terminated any right Ward may have had under its own theory to suspend performance on its part.

Ward's suspension of its performance pending the payment of 50 percent of the purchase price constituted a violation of the contract of purchase and was commercially unreasonable. [*Ward Transformer Co. v Distrigas of Massachusetts Corp.*, 18 UCC Rep Serv 2d 29 (EDNC 1992)]

B.   DUTIES OF THE PARTIES

The obligations of the parties to a sales contract include (1) the seller's duty to deliver the goods, (2) the buyer's duty to accept the goods, and (3) the buyer's duty to pay for the goods.

5. Seller's Duty to Deliver

The seller has the duty to deliver the goods in accordance with the terms of the contract.

(a) Place, Time, and Manner of Delivery. The terms of the contract determine whether the seller is to send the goods or the buyer is to call for them and whether the goods are to be transported from the seller to the buyer or the transaction is to be completed by the delivery of documents without the movement of the goods. In the absence of a provision in the contract or a contrary course of performance or usage of trade, the place of delivery is the seller's place of business if the seller has one; otherwise, it is the seller's residence. (See chapter 26 for more details on delivery and shipping terms.)[8] However, if the subject matter of the contract consists of identified goods that are known by the parties to be in some other place, that place is the place of delivery. If no time for shipment or delivery is stated, delivery or shipment is required within a reasonable time.

When a method of transportation called for by the contract becomes unavailable or commercially unreasonable, the seller must make delivery by means of a commercially reasonable substitute if available.

(b) Quantity Delivered. The buyer has the right to insist that all the goods be delivered at one time. If the seller delivers a smaller or larger quantity than what is stipulated in the contract, the buyer may refuse to accept the goods.[9]

6. Buyer's Duty upon Receipt of Goods

The buyer must accept goods that conform to the contract, and the refusal to do so is a breach of the contract. However, the buyer has certain rights prior to acceptance.

> Inspection is the buyer's right to review, look at, and test goods prior to acceptance.

(a) Right to Examine Goods—The Buyer's Right of Inspection.[10] To determine whether the goods in fact conform to the contract, the buyer has the right to examine the goods when tendered by the seller. An exception to this rule occurs when goods are sent COD. In a COD shipment, the buyer has no right to examine the goods until payment is made.

The buyer's right of **inspection** includes the right to remove goods from cartons and conduct tests. *For example*, a buyer who is purchasing potatoes for use in making potato chips has the right to peel and test a portion of the potatoes to determine whether they are the appropriate type for "chipping."

> Rejection is the buyer's right to not accept goods that fail to conform in any respect to the terms of the contract.

(b) Right to Refuse or Return the Goods—The Buyer's Right of Rejection.[11] If the goods the seller has tendered do not conform to the contract in any way, the buyer can **reject** the goods. *For example*, the buyer may reject a mobile home when it does not contain an air conditioner with the capacity specified by the contract. The buyer may reject the goods if they are not perfect. The standard for rejection does not require that the defect in the goods or the breach be material. *For example*, a small pressure mark on an ottoman is not material; the ottoman will function just as well. However, the buyer still has the right to reject the ottoman because it has a defect.

The buyer has the right to reject the full shipment, accept the full shipment and seek damages for the goods' diminished value (see chapter 29), or accept any

---

[8] UCC § 2-308.
[9] UCC § 2-307.
[10] UCC § 2-601.
[11] UCC § 2-602.

Commercial unit is the standard of the trade for shipment or packaging of a good.

commercial units and reject the remainder. Commercial units are defined by trade and industry according to the customary size of cartons or containers for the goods shipped. Envelopes come in commercial units of boxes of 500. Computer disks often come in packages of 20 or 50. Rejection by a buyer in these cases would be not of individual envelopes or disks, but of boxes. ◆ *For example,* if Donna purchased a package of 20 disks and 4 of the 20 disks were defective, Donna would return the box of 20 disks for a new box. ◆ Rejection and acceptance in commercial units prevent the problems created when a seller has to open other units and mix and match goods in each.

After rejecting the goods, the buyer may not exercise any right of ownership over the goods. The buyer must hold the goods and await instructions from the seller. If the buyer disposes of the goods before the seller has had a reasonable time in which to give instructions, the buyer is liable for any loss.[12]

The buyer's rejection must be made within a reasonable time after the delivery or tender of the goods. The buyer must notify the seller of the rejection and, in transactions with merchants particularly, provide the seller with the reason for the rejection.[13]

Right to cure is the seller's right to send a new shipment when the buyer rejects the first shipment if there is still time for performance or the buyer agrees to allow it.

(c) Cure of Defective Tender or Delivery. The reason for the notification of rejection to the seller by the buyer is that the UCC gives a right of cure to the seller if the seller tenders or delivers nonconforming goods. The buyer's rejection is not an end to the transaction. The seller is given a second chance, or a **right to cure**, to make a proper tender of conforming goods.[14]

Seasonable means timely.

This right of cure is restricted by whether the seller can make the second tender of the goods within the time remaining for performance under the contract. If the time for making delivery under the contract has not expired, the seller need only give the buyer **seasonable** (timely) notice of the intention to make a proper delivery within the time allowed by the contract. However, if the time for making the delivery has expired, the seller may be given an additional reasonable time in which to make a substitute conforming tender. Additional time is allowed if (1) the seller so notifies the buyer and (2) the seller had acted reasonably in making the original tender, believing that it would be acceptable to the buyer.

CASE SUMMARY

If I Want a Used VCR, I'll Pay Less

Facts: On January 3, 1991, Central District Alarm (CDA) and Hal-Tuc entered into a written sales agreement providing that CDA would sell and install new security equipment described on an equipment list attached to the contract. This list included a Javelin VCR. When the system was installed, CDA installed a used JVC VCR instead of a new Javelin VCR. Hal-Tuc called CDA the day after the installation and complained that the equipment was not the Javelin brand and that the VCR was a used JVC VCR. CDA told Hal-Tuc that the equipment was not used and that a JVC VCR was better than a Javelin. Hal-Tuc telephoned CDA personnel over a two-week period during which they denied that the equipment was used. After two weeks of calls, CDA's installation manager went to the store to see the equipment and admitted that it was used. No

---

[12] UCC § 2-603.
[13] UCC § 2-602(1); *Loden v Drake* (Colo App) 881 P2d 467 (1994).
[14] *Allied Semi-Conductors Int'l v Pulsar Components Int'l, Inc.,* 907 F Supp 618 (EDNY 1995).

one from CDA advised Hal-Tuc in advance that they were installing used equipment temporarily until the right equipment arrived.

CDA offered to replace it with a new Javelin VCR as soon as one arrived, which would take one or two months. Hal-Tuc asked CDA to return its deposit and take the equipment back, but CDA refused. Hal-Tuc put all the equipment in boxes and stored it. CDA filed a petition against Hal-Tuc for damages for breach of contract. Hal-Tuc filed a counterclaim, alleging fraud. CDA asserted it had the right to cure by tendering conforming goods after Hal-Tuc rejected the nonconforming goods.

Decision: CDA did not seasonably notify Hal-Tuc of an intent to cure. CDA did not advise Hal-Tuc in advance that it did not have the new equipment and was installing used equipment. CDA installed the used equipment knowingly and not by mistake. Hal-Tuc notified CDA after it discovered that CDA had installed the wrong equipment. CDA first denied that the equipment it installed was used. Only after inspecting the equipment two weeks later did CDA admit the equipment was used and offer to cure with new equipment. These circumstances support a finding that CDA did not seasonably notify Hal-Tuc of its intention to cure.

Because it did not establish seasonable notification and reasonable grounds, CDA did not have a right to cure. [*Central District Alarm, Inc. v Hal-Tuc, Inc.* (Mo App) 866 SW2d 210 (1994)]

7. Buyer's Duty to Accept Goods

> **Acceptance of goods is the use of the goods or the communication of satisfaction with the goods following the time for inspection and timely rejection.**

Assuming that the buyer has no grounds for rejection of the goods after inspection, the next step in the performance of the contract is the buyer's **acceptance** of the goods.

(a) What Constitutes Acceptance of Goods.[15] Acceptance of goods means that the buyer, pursuant to a contract, has, either expressly or by implication, taken the goods permanently. The buyer's statement of acceptance is an express acceptance. A buyer can accept goods by implication if there is no rejection after a reasonable opportunity to inspect them or after a reasonable time after the buyer has inspected them. Another form of acceptance by implication is conduct by the buyer that is inconsistent with rejection, as when a buyer uses or sells the delivered goods.[16]

A buyer accepts goods by making continued use of them and by not attempting to return them. A buyer, of course, accepts goods by modifying them because such action is inconsistent with a rejection or with the continued ownership of the goods by the seller.

> **Revocation of acceptance is the buyer's right to revoke acceptance of goods when their value is substantially impaired and they were accepted without knowing of a latent defect or with the seller's assurance that the defect would be fixed.**

(b) Revocation of Acceptance. Even after acceptance of the goods, the performance under the contract may not be finished if the buyer exercises the right to revoke acceptance of the goods.[17] The buyer may revoke acceptance of the goods when they do not conform to the contract, the defect is such that it substantially impairs the value of the contract to the buyer, and either the defect is such that the buyer could not discover the problem or the seller has promised to correct a problem the buyer was aware of and pointed out to the seller prior to acceptance.

---

[15] UCC § 2-606.
[16] *Contours, Inc. v Lee* (Haw App) 874 P2d 1100 (1994).
[17] UCC § 2-608.

◆ *For example*, a buyer who purchased an emergency electric power generator found that the generator produced only about 65 percent of the power called for by the contract. This amount of power was insufficient for the operation of the buyer's electrical equipment. The seller's repeated attempts to improve the generator's ouput failed. The buyer, despite having used the generator for three months, could revoke his acceptance of it because its value was substantially impaired and he continued to keep it and use it only because of the seller's assurances that it would be repaired. ◆

Substantial impairment is a higher standard than the one of "fails to conform in any respect" for rejection. Substantial impairment requires proof of more than the mere fact that the goods do not conform to the contract. The buyer is not required to show that the goods are worthless, but the buyer must prove that their use to him is substantially different from what the contract promised.

A revocation of acceptance is not a cancellation of the contract with the seller. After revocation of acceptance, the buyer can choose from the remedies available for breach of contract or demand that the seller deliver conforming goods. (See chapter 29 for more information on remedies for breach.)

(c) Notification of Revocation of Acceptance. To revoke acceptance properly, the buyer must take certain steps. The buyer must give the seller notice of revocation. The revocation of acceptance is effective when the buyer notifies the seller. The buyer need not actually return the goods to make the notification or the revocation effective.

The notice of revocation of acceptance must be given within a reasonable time after the buyer discovers or should have discovered the problems with the goods. The right of revocation is not lost if the buyer gives the seller a longer period of time to correct the defects in the goods. Even the lapse of a year will not cost the buyer the right of revocation of acceptance if the seller has been experimenting during that time trying to correct the problems with the goods.

> Substantial impairment is a material defect in a good.

CASE SUMMARY

Andrew and Rachel—The Two Male Emus Who Were Intended as Breeders

Facts: In 1992, Donna Smith telephoned Clark, the manager of Penbridge Farms in response to an advertisement Clark had placed in the July issue of the Emu Finder about the availability for sale of proven breeder pairs. Clark told Smith he had a breeder pair available for purchase. Clark sold the pair to Smith for $16,500. Some months later, after Smith had had a chance to inspect the pair, she discovered that Clark had sold her two male emus. Smith immediately notified Clark and revoked her acceptance of the animals. Clark said the revocation was too late.

Decision: The gender of an emu is not discernible by mere external observation. The only certain way to tell, apart from internal examination, is to observe them in mating. Smith, upon observing both Rachel and Andrew, her two male breeders, grunting, concluded that she had two male emus and not a male and a female breeder because grunting is a male trait. Rachel may have looked like a female emu and walked like a female emu, but it did not sound like a female emu. When Smith heard the noise, she immediately notified Clark. Her notification was timely, and the problem with the bird was a material and substantial impairment because Smith had paid a high price specifically for breeders, not two male emus for pets. [*Smith v Penbridge Associates, Inc.* (Pa Super) 655 A2d 1015 (1995)]

(d) Buyer's Responsibilities upon Revocation of Acceptance. After a revocation of acceptance, the buyer must hold the goods and await instructions from the seller. If the buyer revokes acceptance after having paid the seller in advance, the buyer may retain possession of the goods as security for the refund of the money that has been paid.

ETHICS & THE LAW

At Saks Fifth Avenue, they call it the "return season." Return season occurs within the week following a major fund-raising formal dance. Women who have purchased formal evening wear return the dresses after the dance. The dresses have been worn, and the tags have been cut, but the women return the dresses with requests for a full refund. Neiman Marcus also experiences the same phenomenon of returns.

Some stores have implemented a policy that formal evening wear may not be returned if the tags are cut from it. Others require a return within a limited period of seven days. Others offer an exchange only after five days.

Are the women covered by a right of rejection under Article 2? What do you think of the conduct of the women? Is it simply revocation of acceptance? Is there good faith on the part of the women?

8. Buyer's Duty to Pay

The buyer must pay the amount stated in the sales contract for accepted goods.

(a) Time of Payment. The sales contract may require payment in advance or may give the buyer credit by postponing the time for payment.[18]

(b) Form of Payment. Unless otherwise agreed, payment by the buyer requires payment in cash.

The seller may accept a check or a promissory note from the buyer. If the check is not paid by the bank, the purchase price remains unpaid. A promissory note payable at a future date gives the buyer credit by postponing the time for payment.

The seller can refuse to accept a check or a promissory note as payment for goods but must give the buyer reasonable time in which to obtain legal tender with which to make payment.

9. When Duties Are Excused

Commercial impracticability is an objective inability to perform under the terms and assumptions of a contract.

Under Article 2, the doctrine of **commercial impracticability** is available as a defense to performance of a contract. The doctrine of commercial impracticability is the modern commercial law version of the common law doctrine of impossibility. If a party to a contract can establish that there has been an occurrence or a contingency not anticipated by the parties and not a basic assumption in their entering into a contract, the party can be excused from performance.

The standard for commercial impracticability is objective, not subjective. *For example,* if a farmer has contracted to sell two tons of peanuts to an airline

---

[18] UCC § 2-310.

and his crop fails, he is not excused on the grounds of commercial impracticability. So long as there are peanuts available for the farmer to buy and then sell to the buyer to satisfy their contract terms, the farmer is not excused. Commercial impracticability refers to those circumstances in which peanuts are not available anywhere because the entire peanut harvest was destroyed rather than just the individual farmer's crop. ◆

CASE SUMMARY

The 1,200 School Buses That Were Never Delivered

Facts: Bobby Murray Chevrolet, Inc., submitted a bid to the Alamance County Board of Education to supply 1,200 school bus chassis to the district. Bobby Murray was awarded the contract and contracted with General Motors (GM) to purchase the chassis for the school board.

In between the time of Bobby Murray's contract with GM and the delivery date, the Environmental Protection Agency (EPA) enacted new emission standards for diesel vehicles, such as school buses. Under the new law, the buses Bobby Murray ordered from GM would be out of compliance, as would the buses Bobby Murray specified in its bid to the school board.

GM asked for several extensions in order to manufacture the buses within the new EPA guidelines. The school board was patient and gave several extensions, but then, due to its needs for buses, purchased them from another supplier after notifying Bobby Murray of its intent to do so. The school board had to pay an additional $150,152.94 for the buses from its alternative source and sued Bobby Murray for that amount. Bobby Murray claimed it was excused from performance on the grounds of commercial impracticability.

Decision: Bobby Murray was not excused on the grounds of commercial impracticability. Ordinarily intervening government regulations do not excuse the parties from performance under a contract. Additionally, in this case, the regulations were pending at the time of the contract bid and should have been considered by a seller in submitting a bid to the school board. The contract did not specify that the buses would be from GM, and hence the ability to acquire the buses elsewhere meant that performance had not become commercially impracticable. Bobby Murray owes the school board the price difference for breach of contract. [*Alamance County Board of Education v Bobby Murray Chevrolet, Inc.* (NC App) 28 UCC Rep Serv 2d 1220 (1996)]

SUMMARY

Every sales contract imposes an obligation of good faith in its performance. Good faith means honesty in fact in the conduct or transaction concerned. For merchants, the UCC imposes the additional requirement of observing "reasonable commercial standards of fair dealing in the trade."

In the case of a cash sale where no transportation of the goods is required, both the buyer and the seller may demand concurrent performance.

A buyer's or a seller's refusal to perform a contract is called a repudiation. A repudiation made in advance of the time for performance is called an anticipatory repudiation and is a breach of the contract. If either party to a contract feels insecure about the performance of the other, that party may demand in writing adequate assurance of performance. If that assurance is not given, the demand-

ing party may treat the contract as repudiated.

The seller has a duty to deliver the goods in accordance with the terms of the contract. This duty does not require physical transportation; it requires that the seller permit the transfer of possession of the goods to the buyer.

With the exception of COD contracts, the buyer has the right to inspect the goods upon tender or delivery. Inspection includes the right to open cartons and conduct tests.

If the inspection by the buyer reveals that the seller has tendered nonconforming goods, the buyer may reject them. Subject to certain limitations, the seller may then offer to replace the goods or cure the problems the buyer has noted.

The buyer has a duty to accept goods that conform to

the contract, and refusal to do so is a breach of contract. The buyer is deemed to have accepted goods either expressly or by implication through conduct inconsistent with rejection or by lapse of time. The buyer must pay for accepted goods in accordance with the terms of the contract. The buyer can reject goods in commercial units, accept the goods and collect damages for their problems, or reject the full contract shipment. The buyer must give notice of rejection to the seller and cannot do anything with the goods that would be inconsistent with the seller's ownership rights. The buyer should await instructions from the seller on what to do with the goods.

Even following acceptance, the buyer may revoke that acceptance if the problems with the goods substantially impair their value and the problems were either not easily discoverable or the buyer kept the goods based on the seller's promises to repair them and make them whole. Upon revocation of acceptance, the buyer should await instructions from the seller on what steps to take.

Performance can be excused on the grounds of commercial impracticability, but the seller must show objective difficulties that create more than cost increases.

QUESTIONS AND CASE PROBLEMS

1. What social forces are involved in the rule of law governing the seller's right to cure?

2. Elkins Appliance Store made a contract to purchase 100 electric toasters from Greystone Electric Co., with delivery to be made on November 1. A week later Greystone informed Elkins that its factory has been severely damaged by fire and that Greystone is not sure whether it will be able to deliver the toasters by November 1 or at any time. Elkins claimed that this statement is an anticipatory repudiation of the contract. Is Elkins correct?

3. Custom Built Homes purchased unassembled prefabricated houses from Page-Hill in Minnesota to be delivered by the seller "FOB building site Kansas." The seller brings the houses to the building site by tractor-trailer, where he unhitches the trailer and unloads the shipment. What rights of inspection and rejection does Custom Built have? Explain some defects that might permit revocation of acceptance. [*Custom Built Homes Co. v Kansas State Commission of Revenue* (Kan) 334 P2d 808]

4. Washington ordered a computer by mail from Grant Co. in Seattle. It was sent to her COD. To be sure that there has been no mistake, Washington has asked to examine the computer before she pays the carrier. Can she do so?

5. Lafer Enterprises sold Christmas decorations to B.P. Development & Management Corp., the owners and operators of the Osceola Square Mall. The package of decorations was delivered to Osceola Square Mall prior to Thanksgiving 1986 for a total cost of $48,775, which B.P. would pay in three installments. Cathy Trivigno, a manager at B.P. who supervised the installation of the decorations, indicated that she and the Osceola Square Mall merchants were not satisfied with the quality of the decorations but that they needed to be in place for the day after Thanksgiving (the start of the holiday shopping season). B.P. complained to Lafer about the quality of the decorations but had the decorations installed. B.P. paid the first installment to Lafer but then stopped payment on the last two checks. B.P. claimed it had rejected the decorations. Lafer claimed breach for nonpayment because B.P. used the decorations. Did B.P. accept the decorations? [*B.P. Dev. & Management Corp. v Lafer Enterprises, Inc.* (Fla App) 538 So 2d 1379]

6. International Minerals and Metals Corp. contracted to sell Weinstein scrap metal that was to be delivered within 30 days. Later the seller informed the buyer that it could not make delivery within that time. The buyer agreed to an extension of time, but no limiting date was set. Within what time must the seller perform? [*International Minerals and Metals Corp. v Weinstein* (NC) 73 SE2d 472]

7. Carlson ordered equipment from Ventresca Foundry in St. Louis, Missouri, to be sent "FOB Chicago, Illinois." The equipment was placed on a motor freight truck under a proper shipment contract. The truck was wrecked before it reached Chicago. Ventresca demands payment of the purchase price from Carlson. Carlson says he has inspected the goods and they are defective. Must he take them?

8. Spaulding & Kimball Co. ordered from Aetna Chemical Co. 75 cartons of window washers. The buyer received them and sold about a third to its customers but later refused to pay for them, claiming that the quality was poor. The seller sued for the price. Decide. [*Aetna Chemical Co. v Spaulding & Kimball Co.* (Vt) 126 A 582]

9. A computer manufacturer promoted the sale of a digital computer as a "revolutionary breakthrough." The manufacturer made a contract to deliver one of these computers to a buyer. The seller failed to deliver the computer and explained that its failure was caused by unanticipated technological difficulties. Was this an excuse for nonperformance by the seller? [*United States v Wegematic Corp.*, 360 F2d 674 (2d Cir)]

10. Economy Farms Corp. sold concrete-forming equip-

ment to Kandy. After using the equipment for over six months, Kandy notified Economy that the equipment was inadequate. Economy Farms alleged that Kandy had accepted the goods. Kandy denied liability. Was there an acceptance? Why? [*Economy Forms Corp. v Kandy, Inc.*, 391 F Supp 944 (ND Ga)]

11. Teeman made a contract to purchase lumber from Oakhill Mill. The contract called for payment to be made on delivery to Teeman. When the truck from the mill arrived to deliver the lumber, Teeman gave the driver a check for the purchase price. The driver refused to take the check or leave the lumber. The driver returned to the mill, and the mill then notified Teeman that the contract was canceled. Was the mill entitled to cancel the contract?

12. Lury has a sales contract with Burns, with whom he has not previously dealt, to make four quarterly deliveries of a product on 30 days' credit. Two months after the first delivery under the contract Burns has not yet paid. Can Lury demand adequate assurance of performance?

13. Matsuda was in the process of furnishing her apartment. She purchased a leather sofa and three leather chairs from Davenport Furniture, Inc., to be delivered in 20 days. She paid part of the purchase price upon executing the order and agreed to pay the balance on delivery. Davenport delivered the sofa and the chairs a week later, but the leather chairs did not match the sofa. Matsuda thereupon rejected the sofa and the chairs. She also demanded the return of her money. What rights, if any, does Davenport have?

14. Harry Ulmas made a contract to buy a new car from Acey Oldsmobile. He was allowed to keep his old car until the new car was delivered. The sales contract gave him a trade-in value of $650 on the old car but specified that the car would be reappraised when it was actually brought to the dealer. When Ulmas brought the trade-in to the dealer, an Acey employee took it for a test drive and said that the car was worth between $300 and $400. Acey offered Ulmas only $50 for his trade-in. Ulmas refused to buy from Acey and purchased from another dealer, who appraised the trade-in at $400. Ulmas sued for breach of contract on the grounds of violation of good faith. Is he right? [*Ulmas v Acey Oldsmobile, Inc.* (NY Civ) 310 NYS 2d 147]

15. Cornelia and Ed Kornfeld contracted to sell a signed Picasso print to David Tunick, Inc. The print, entitled *Le Minotauromachie,* was to be signed "Pablo Picasso." The signature on the print was discovered to be a forgery, and the Kornfelds offered Tunick a substitute Picasso print. Tunick refused the Kornfelds' substituted performance and demanded a return of the contract price. The Kornfelds refused on the grounds that their cure had been refused. Was the substitute print an adequate cure? [*David Tunick, Inc. v Kornfeld*, 838 F Supp 848 (SDNY)]

CPA QUESTIONS

1. Under the sales article of the UCC, which of the following statements is correct?
   a. The obligations of the parties to the contract must be performed in good faith.
   b. Merchants and nonmerchants are treated alike.
   c. The contract must involve the sale of goods for a price of more than $500.
   d. None of the provisions of the UCC may be disclaimed by agreement.

   (11/94, Law, #50, 5227)

2. Rowe Corp. purchased goods from Stair Co. that were shipped COD. Under the sales article of the UCC, which of the following rights does Rowe have?
   a. The right to inspect the goods before paying.
   b. The right to possession of the goods before paying.
   c. The right to reject nonconforming goods.
   d. The right to delay payment for a reasonable period of time.

   (11/94, Law, #56, 5233)

3. Bibbeon Manufacturing shipped 300 designer navy blue blazers to Custom Clothing Emporium. The blazers arrived on Friday, earlier than Custom had anticipated and on an exceptionally busy day for its receiving department. They were perfunctorily examined and sent to a nearby warehouse for storage until needed. On Monday of the following week, upon closer examination, it was discovered that the quality of the blazer linings was inferior to that specified in the sales contract. Which of the following is correct insofar as Custom's rights are concerned?
   a. Custom can reject the blazers upon subsequent discovery of the defects.
   b. Custom must retain the blazers since it accepted them and had an opportunity to inspect them upon delivery.
   c. Custom's only course of action is rescission.
   d. Custom had no rights if the linings were merchantable quality.

Warranties and Other Product Liability Theories

After studying this chapter, you should be able to

1. *List the theories of product liability;*
2. *Say who may sue and who may be sued when a defective product causes harm;*
3. *List and define the implied warranties and distinguish them from express warranties;*
4. *Explain and distinguish between full warranties and limited warranties under federal law;*
5. *State what constitutes a breach of warranty; and*
6. *Describe the extent and manner in which implied warranties may be disclaimed under the UCC and the CISG.*

What happens when goods do not work? Who can sue for injury caused by defective goods? What can you do when the goods are not as promised or pictured?

A. GENERAL PRINCIPLES

When defective goods result in damages or injury to the buyer or other parties, remedies may be found in the common law, the UCC, or newly emerging case law.

1. Theories of Liability

Two centuries ago a buyer was limited to suing a seller for breach of an express guarantee or for negligence or fraud. After the onset of mass production and distribution, however, these remedies had little value. A guarantee was good, but, in the ordinary sales transaction, no one stopped to get a guarantee. One never asked the manager of the supermarket to give a guarantee that the loaf of bread purchased was fit to eat. Further, negligence and fraud have become generally impossible to prove in a mass production world. How can one prove there was a problem in the production process for a can of soup prepared months earlier?

> A warranty is a promise, either express or implied, about the nature, quality, or performance of the goods.

To give buyers protection from economic loss and personal injuries, the concept of warranty liability developed. **Warranties** are either express or implied and can be found in the UCC. Many courts have decided that still broader protection beyond the UCC contract remedies is required and have created the additional concept of strict tort liability for defective goods.

There are five theories in law to protect against economic loss and personal injuries: express warranty, implied warranty, negligence, fraud, and strict tort liability. If the plaintiff is a consumer or an employee, there might also be consumer protection liability or employee protection liability. The plaintiff does not have a choice of all theories in every case; the facts of the case will dictate the choices the plaintiff has available for possible theories of recovery.

2. Nature of Harm

When a product is defective, harm may be caused to (1) a person, (2) property, or (3) economic or commercial interests. ◆ *For example,* the buyer of a truck may be injured when, through a defect, it goes out of control and plunges down the side of a hill. Third persons, such as passengers in the truck, bystanders, or the driver of a car hit by the truck, may also be injured. The defective truck may cause injury to a total stranger who seeks to rescue one of the victims. Property damage occurs when the buyer's truck plunges down the slope of another's land. Another driver's car may be damaged, or a building into which the runaway truck careens may be damaged. Commercial and economic interests of the buyer are affected by the fact that the truck is defective. Even if no physical harm is sustained, the defective truck is not as valuable as it would have been. The buyer who has paid for the truck on the basis of its value as it should have been has sustained an economic loss. If the buyer is required to rent a truck from someone else or loses an opportunity to haul freight for compensation, the fact that the truck was defective also causes economic or commercial loss. ◆

3.   Who May Sue and Be Sued

Until the early part of this century, only the parties to a sales contract could sue each other. A seller could be sued by the buyer, but other persons could not recover from the seller because they were not in privity of contract.

> **Privity is a direct contractual relationship between parties.**

This requirement of privity of contract has now been widely rejected. The law is moving toward the notion that persons harmed because of a defective product may sue anyone who is in any way responsible.

(a) The Plaintiff. According to the modern view, not only the buyer but also customers and employees of the buyer and even third persons or bystanders may recover because of harm caused by a defective product. Most states have abolished the requirement of privity when the plaintiff is a member of the buyer's family or household or is a guest of the buyer and has sustained personal injury because of the product.[1] Some states require privity of contract, particularly when the plaintiff does not sustain personal injury or property damage and seeks to recover only economic loss.

(b) The Defendant. The plaintiff who is injured by a defective product may seek recovery from the seller, a remote seller, the manufacturer of the product, and generally even the manufacturer of the component part of the product that caused the harm.[2] ◆ *For example,* when a person is struck by an automobile because of its defective brakes, the victim may seek recovery from the seller and the manufacturer of the car. The maker of the brake assembly or system that the car manufacturer installed in the car may also be liable. ◆

(c) Direct Sales Contact. In many instances, recovery is allowed by a buyer against a manufacturer because there have been direct dealings between them. These dealings justify the conclusion that the buyer and the manufacturer are in privity, as opposed to those situations in which the buyer was only in privity with the local dealer from whom the product was bought.[3] When the manufacturer enters into direct negotiations with the ultimate buyer with respect to any phase of

---

[1] UCC § 2-318, Alternative A. The Code gives the states the option of adopting the provision summarized in this chapter or of making a wide abolition of the requirement of privity by adopting Alternative B or C of section 2-318. As of January 1, 1997, 30 states had adopted Alternative A, 10 states had adopted Alternative B, and 5 states had adopted Alternative C. The remaining states have adopted various combinations and variations of Alternatives A, B, and C.

[2] *Minnesota Mining & Mfg. Co. v Nishkia, Ltd.* (Tex App) 885 SW2d 603 (1994).

[3] *Bryant v Adams* (NC App) 448 SE2d 832 (1994).

the manufacturing or financing of the transaction, the sale will probably be treated as though it were made directly by the manufacturer to the ultimate purchaser. This is so even though, for the purpose of record keeping, the transaction is treated as a sale by the manufacturer to the dealer and a sale by that dealer to the ultimate purchaser. Likewise, recovery may be allowed when the consumer mails to the manufacturer a warranty registration card that the manufacturer packed with the manufactured article.

CASE SUMMARY

The Case of the Peeling Paint: My Walls Look Like Spaghetti

Facts: The 1143 East Jersey Avenue Associates, Inc., owned a ten-story building. The Associates hired Duall Building Restoration, Inc., to restore the surface of its building. The contract between the Associates and Duall specified that Duall would use Modac, a waterproofing paint, to cover the three brick sides of the building. Modac was a waterproof paint manufactured by Mosey Products.

Shortly after the Modac paint was applied to the three sides of the building, it began to peel disastrously. One of the principals in the Associates described the situation as follows: "The entire building is peeling. It's . . . going wild. I mean . . . the surface is a whole bunch of spaghetti. Maybe noodles, I should say. It's curlicues of surface coming off all over the place." The Associates sued both Duall and Mosey Products. Mosey Products claimed that the Associates were remote purchasers and it was not liable to it due to lack of privity.

Decision: Mosey Products was held to be liable to the Associates. While Mosey did not have privity of contract with the Associates, its relationship was similar to the manufacturer of a car who sells that car to a retailer who then sells it to a consumer. Mosey sold paint that others purchased for their customers. Mosey manufactured a product touted as waterproof. Representatives of Mosey made statements to both Duall and members of the Associates regarding the waterproof quality of the paint, and the contract was negotiated specifically using Mosey's Modac product. [*Duall Bldg. Restoration, Inc. v 1143 East Jersey Avenue Associates, Inc.* (NJ Super) 652 A2d 1225 (1995)]

B.   EXPRESS WARRANTIES

A warranty may be express or implied. Both have the same effect and operate as though the defendant had made an express promise or statement of fact. Both express and implied warranties are governed primarily by the UCC.

4.   Definition of Express Warranty

An express warranty is a statement of fact or promise of performance that is a basis of the bargain.

An **express warranty** is a statement by the defendant relating to the goods; the statement is part of the basis of the bargain.[4] "Basis of the bargain" means that the buyer has purchased the goods on the reasonable assumption that they are as stated by the seller. A statement by the seller regarding the quality, capacity, or other characteristic of the goods is an express warranty. ◆ *For example,* express warranties in sellers' statements are "This cloth is all wool," "This paint is for household woodwork," and "This engine can produce 50 horsepower." ◆

---

[4] UCC § 2-313; *Valleyside Dairy Farms, Inc. v A.O. Smith Corp.,* 944 F Supp 612 (WD Mich 1995).

A representation that an airplane is a 1998 model is an express warranty. A statement that a product was developed for a special purpose is an express warranty that it will achieve that purpose.

5.   Form of Express Warranty

No particular form of words is necessary to constitute an express warranty. A seller need not state that a warranty is being made or that one is intended. It is sufficient that the seller asserts a fact that becomes a basis of the bargain or transaction between the parties.

An express warranty can also be found in conduct. If the buyer asks for a can of outside house paint and the seller hands over a can of paint, the seller's conduct expresses a warranty that the can contains outside house paint.

An express warranty can be written or printed as well as oral. The words on the label of a can and in a newspaper ad for "boned chicken" constitute an express warranty that the can contains chicken that is free of bones.

Descriptions of goods, such as the illustrations in a seller's catalog, are express warranties. The express warranty given is that the goods will conform to the catalog illustrations.

6.   Time of Making Express Warranty

It is immaterial whether the express warranty is made at the time of or after the sale. No separate consideration is required for the warranty when it is part of a sale. If a warranty is made after the sale, no consideration is required because it is regarded as a modification of the sales contract.

7.   Seller's Opinion or Statement of Value

An affirmation merely of the value of goods or a statement purporting to be merely the seller's opinion or commendation of the goods does not create a warranty.[5] A purchaser, as a reasonable person, should not believe such statements implicitly. Therefore, the buyer cannot hold the seller liable for such sales talk, should it prove false.   *For example*, sales talk or puffery by a seller that this cloth is "the best piece of cloth in the market" or that this glassware is "as good as anyone else's" is merely an opinion that the buyer cannot ordinarily treat as a warranty. Statements made by the seller of cosmetics that its products are "the future of beauty" and that they are "just the product for [the plaintiff]" are sales talk arising in the ordinary course of merchandising. They do not constitute warranties.

> **Puffery is sales talk: opinions and hype.**

The UCC does permit an exception to the sales talk liability exemption when the circumstances are such that a reasonable person would rely on such a statement. If the buyer has reason to believe that the seller has expert knowledge of the conditions of the market and the buyer requests the seller's opinion as an expert, the buyer is entitled to accept as a fact the seller's statement as to whether a particular good is the best obtainable. The opinion statement could be reasonably regarded as forming part of the basis of the bargain. A statement by a florist that bulbs are of first-grade quality may be a warranty.

> **Basis of the bargain is an assumption that statements made by the seller to the buyer about the quality, capacity, or characteristics of the goods are true.**

---

5 UCC § 2-313(2); *Jordan v Paccar, Inc.*, 37 F3d 1181 (6th Cir 1994).

The Long-Term Wheelchair That Lasted Only a Few Years

Facts: Paul Parrino purchased a wheelchair manufactured by 21st Century Scientific Inc. from Dave's Professional Wheelchair Service. The sales brochure from 21st Century Scientific stated that the wheelchair would "serve [the buyer] well for many years to come." Parrino had problems with the wheelchair within a few years and filed suit against Dave's and 21st Century for breach of express warranty. Both defended on the grounds that the statement on years of service was puffery and not an express warranty.

Decision: The statement about the wheelchair's service for years to come did not rise to the level of a promise of future performance for purposes of an express warranty. The promise was not specific enough to commit the seller to certain number of years of performance. [Parrino v Sperling (App Div) 648 NYS2d 702 (1996)]

8.   Warranty of Conformity to Description, Sample, or Model

When the contract is based in part on the understanding that the seller will supply goods according to a particular description or that the goods will be the same as the sample or a model, the seller is bound by an express warranty that the goods conform to the description, sample, or model.[6] Ordinarily a sample is a portion of the whole mass that is the subject of the transaction. A model is a replica of the article in question.

9.   Federal Regulation of Express Warranties

A seller who makes a written express warranty for a consumer product costing more than $15 must conform to certain standards imposed by federal statute[7] and by regulations of the Federal Trade Commission (FTC).[8] The seller is not required to make any express warranty. However, if the seller does make an express warranty in a consumer sale, it must be stated in ordinary, understandable language and must be made available for inspection before purchasing so that the consumer may comparison shop.[9]

Full warranty is a Magnuson-Moss Act term that mandates a certain time and scope of coverage in order to label a warranty a full warranty.

(a) Full Warranties. If the seller or the label states that a **full warranty** is made, the seller is obligated to fix or replace a defective product within a reasonable time without cost to the buyer. If the product cannot be fixed or if a reasonable number of repair attempts are unsuccessful, the buyer has the choice of a cash refund or a free replacement. No unreasonable burden may be placed on a buyer seeking to obtain warranty service. ◆ *For example,* a warrantor making a full warranty cannot require that the buyer pay the cost of sending the product to or from a warranty service point. A warrantor making a full warranty cannot require the buyer to return the product to a warranty service point if the product weighs over 35 pounds, to return a part for service unless it can be easily removed, or to fill out and return a warranty registration card shortly after purchase to make the war-

---

[6] *Poly Products Corp. v AT&T Nassau Metals, Inc.,* 839 F Supp 1238 (ED Tex 1993).
[7] The Magnuson-Moss Act, or Federal Consumer Product Warranty Law, can be found at 15 USC §§ 2301 et seq.
[8] 16 CFR §§ 700.1 et seq.
[9] Warranty language applies only in consumer sales, or sales for personal or home use, not in business purchases. *Weaver v Dan Jones Ford, Inc.* (Ala) 679 SO 2d 1105 (1996).

ranty effective. ◆ If the warrantor imposes any of these burdens, the warranty must be called a *limited warranty*. A full warranty runs for its specified life without regard to who owns the product.

(b) Limited Warranties. A **limited warranty** is any warranty that does not provide the complete protection of a full warranty. ◆ *For example,* a warranty is limited if the buyer must pay any cost for repair or replacement of a defective product, if only the first buyer is covered by the warranty, or if the warranty covers only part of the product. ◆ A limited warranty must be conspicuously described as such by the seller.

> A limited warranty is any warranty that does not meet the definitional requirements under the Magnuson-Moss Act for a full warranty.

10. Effect of Breach of Express Warranty

If the express warranty made is revealed to be false, there is a breach of the warranty. The warrantor is then liable just as though the truth of the warranty had been guaranteed. It is no defense that the defendant honestly believed that the warranty was true, had exercised due care in manufacturing or handling the product, or had no reason to believe that the warranty was false.

C.   IMPLIED WARRANTIES

> An implied warranty is a warranty not made by the seller but implied in law unless specifically excluded.

Whenever a sale of goods is made, certain warranties are implied unless they are expressly excluded. Implied warranties differ depending on whether the seller is a merchant or a casual seller.

11. Definition of Implied Warranty

An **implied warranty** is one that was not expressly made by the seller but that is implied by law in certain instances. An implied warranty arises automatically from the fact that a sale has been made regardless of the seller's conduct.

Express warranties arise because they form part of the basis on which the sale has been made. The fact that express warranties are made does not exclude implied warranties. When both express and implied warranties exist, they should be construed as being consistent with each other and cumulative if such construction is reasonable. In case it is unreasonable to construe them as consistent and cumulative, an express warranty prevails over an implied warranty as to the subject matter, except in the case of an implied warranty of fitness for a particular purpose.

12. Implied Warranties of All Sellers

A distinction is made between a merchant seller and a casual seller. There is a greater range of warranties in the case of the merchant seller.

(a) Warranty of Title. Every seller, by the mere act of selling, makes a warranty that the seller's title is good and that the transfer is rightful.[10]

---

[10] UCC § 2-312.

A warranty of title is an implied warranty that title to the goods is good and transfer is proper.

A **warranty of title** may be specifically excluded, or the circumstances may be such as to prevent the warranty from arising. The latter situation is found when the buyer has reason to know that the seller does not claim to hold the title or that the seller is purporting to sell only such right or title as the seller or a third person may have. *For example,* no warranty of title arises when the seller makes the sale in a representative capacity, such as a sheriff, an auctioneer, or an administrator of a decedent's estate. Similarly, no warranty arises when the seller makes the sale as a creditor disposing of a debtor's collateral (security).

A warranty against encumbrances is a warranty that there are no liens or other encumbrances to goods being transferred, with the exception of any noted by the seller.

(b) Warranty against Encumbrances. Every seller, by the mere act of selling, makes a **warranty against encumbrances**, that is, that the goods will be delivered free from any security interest or any other lien or encumbrance of which the buyer at the time of the sales transaction had no knowledge. Thus, there is a breach of warranty if the automobile sold to the buyer is delivered subject to an outstanding encumbrance placed on it by the original owner and unknown to the buyer at the time of the sale.

A warranty of fitness for a particular purpose is a warranty given by a seller with peculiar expertise who advises the buyer on an appropriate purchase based on the buyer's request for advice and on which the buyer relies.

(c) Warranty of Fitness for a Particular Purpose.[11] A buyer may intend to use the goods for a particular or unusual purpose, as contrasted with the ordinary use for which they are customarily sold. If so, the seller states that the goods will be fit for the buyer's purpose—the buyer relies on the seller's skill or judgment to select or furnish suitable goods and the seller, at the time of contracting, knows or has reason to know of both the buyer's particular purpose and the buyer's reliance on the seller's judgment then the seller has created an implied warranty of fitness for a particular purpose.[12] *For example,* when the seller knows that the buyer is purchasing an accounting machine to produce a payroll on time and with reduced work hours, an implied warranty arises that the machine will perform as desired by the buyer.

When the buyer makes the purchase without relying on the seller's skill and judgment, no warranty of fitness for a particular purpose arises.[13]

CASE SUMMARY

North to Alaska and the Problems of Bursting Pipes

Facts: Lewis and Sims, a contracting corporation, was installing a water and sewer system in the town of North Pole, Alaska. The order for the pipe stated the size and quantity and specified that the pipe had to be "coal tar enamel lined." The pipe could not withstand the intense cold, and before the pipelines could be constructed, the enamel lining had pulled away from the pipe. Lewis and Sims then sued the suppliers of the original pipe for damages for breach of warranty of fitness for a particular purpose.

Decision: Judgment for the pipe suppliers. An implied warranty of fitness for a particular purpose arises when (1) the buyer relied on the judgment of the seller and (2) the seller had reason to know the buyer's particular purpose. No warranty of fitness arises, however, when the buyer orders goods according to the buyer's own specifications. Here Lewis and Sims ordered

---

[11] UCC § 2-315.
[12] UCC § 2-315. This warranty applies to every seller, but as a matter of fact, it will ordinarily be a merchant seller who has such skill and judgment that the UCC provision would be applicable.
[13] *Potomac Plaza Terraces, Inc. v QSC Products, Inc.,* 868 F Supp, 346 (DDC 1994).

> a specific size and type of pipe, and any deviation from the coal tar enamel-lined pipe that was manufactured would not have been accepted by Lewis and Sims. The supplier was not asked for its recommendations and did not select the pipe or lining to be used. *[Lewis and Sims, Inc. v Key Industries, Inc. 16 Wash App 619, 557 P2d 1318 (1976)]*

13. Additional Implied Warranties of Merchant Seller

A seller who deals in goods of the kind in question is classified as a merchant by the UCC and is held to a higher degree of responsibility for the product than one who is merely making a casual sale.

(a) Warranty against Infringement. Unless otherwise agreed, every merchant seller warrants that the goods will be delivered free of the rightful claim of any third person by way of patent, copyright, or trademark infringement. *For example,* if a buyer purchases videos from a seller who is later discovered to be a bootlegger of the films on the videos, the buyer has a cause of action against the seller for any damages he experiences for perhaps renting out the bootlegged videos.

(b) Warranty of Merchantability or Fitness for Normal Use. A merchant seller makes an implied warranty of the merchantability of the goods sold.[14] This warranty is in fact a group of promises, the most important of which is that the goods are fit for the ordinary purposes for which they are sold.

14. Implied Warranties in Particular Sales

Particular types of sales may involve special considerations in terms of the seller's liability and the buyer's rights.

(a) Sale on Buyer's Specifications. When the buyer furnishes the seller with exact specifications for the preparation or manufacture of goods, the same warranties arise as in the case of any other sale of such goods by the particular seller. No warranty of fitness for a particular purpose can arise, however. It is clear that the buyer is purchasing on the basis of the buyer's own decision and is not relying on the seller's skill and judgment. Similarly, the manufacturer is not liable for loss caused by a design defect.

(b) Sale of Secondhand or Used Goods. Under the UCC, there is a warranty of merchantability in the sale of both new and used goods unless it is specifically disclaimed. However, with respect to used goods, what is considered "fit for normal use" under the warranty of merchantability will be a lower standard. Some courts still follow their pre-Code law, under which no warranties of fitness arise in the sale of used goods.

A warranty against infringement is a seller's promise that the goods sold do not infringe any copyrights or patents; in other words, the seller is authorized to manufacture the goods either as the owner of the copyright or patent or as someone licensed to sell such goods.

A warranty of merchantability is an implied warranty given by a merchant that promises the goods are fit for ordinary purposes.

C
P
A

---

14 UCC § 2-314. *Ford v Starr Fireworks, Inc.* (Wyo) 874 P2d 230 (1994).

(c) Sale of Food or Drink. The sale of food or drink, whether to be consumed on or off the seller's premises, is a sale. When made by a merchant, a sale of food or drink carries the implied warranty that the food is fit for its ordinary purpose-human consumption.[15] ◆ *For example,* the seller of canned crabmeat has broken this warranty when a can of crabmeat contains a nail. Would it make any difference if the thing that harms the buyer is a crab shell? ◆

Some courts refuse to impose warranty liability if the thing in the food that caused the harm was naturally present, such as crab shell in crabmeat, prune stones in stewed prunes, or bones in canned fish. Other courts reject this foreign substance/natural substance liability test. They hold that there is liability if the seller does not deliver to the buyer goods of the character that the buyer reasonably expected. Under this view, there is a breach of the implied warranty of fitness for normal use if the buyer reasonably expected the food to be free of harm-causing natural things, such as shells and bones that could cause harm.

Foreign substance/natural substance liability tests are tests for determining the liability of a seller of foods for injury caused by the presence of elements in the food sold, such as a bone in chicken, based on the source of the harmful element.

Reasonable expectations liability test is a test for determining the liability of a seller of foods for injury caused by the presence of elements in food sold based on the consumer's expectation.

> **CASE SUMMARY**
>
> ## The Turkey Cube with the Bone
>
> **Facts:** Phillips, a high school senior, was eating in the high school cafeteria. He bit into a cube of turkey that contained a bone that injured him. The turkey was served ladled onto his plate along with mashed potatoes. Phillips's esophagus was injured, and he was hospitalized for four days. He sued the city, as operator of the school, for breach of the implied warranty of merchantability.
>
> **Decision:** The reasonable expectations test has been generally recognized as preferable to the foreign substance/natural substance test. The foreign substance/natural substance test exonerates a seller of food from liability for the lack of fitness of the food for ordinary purposes simply because the injury-causing substance was natural to the food. It fails to focus the seller's attention on the consumer's reasonable beliefs and to recognize that sellers may fairly be held responsible in some instances for natural substances in food that cause injury. The reasonable expectations test is the appropriate one to apply in determining liability for breach of warranty of merchantability under UCC § 2-314(2)(c) by reason of a bone or other substance in food that caused harm to a consumer. Phillips could reasonably expect that the turkey meat was boneless. [*Phillips v West Springfield* (Mass) 540 NE 2d 1331 (1989)]

The following case, a landmark decision, reaches a different result.

> **CASE SUMMARY**
>
> ## Waiter, There's a Bone in My Chowder
>
> **Facts:** Webster ordered a bowl of fish chowder at the Blue Ship Tea Room. She was injured by a fish bone in the chowder, and she sued the tea room for breach of the implied warranty of merchantability. The evidence at trial showed that when chowder is made, the entire unboned fish is cooked.
>
> **Decision:** Because the soup is typically made with whole fish, the presence of fish bones in the soup should be foreseen by a reasonable person. Thus, there was no breach of the warranty of merchantability. [*Webster v Blue Ship Tea Room* 347 Mass 421, 198 NE2d 309 (1964)]

---

[15] *Goldman v Food Lion, Inc.,* 879 F Supp 33 (ED Va 1995).

15. Necessity of Defect

To impose liability for breach of the implied warranty of merchantability, it is ordinarily necessary to show that there was a defect in the product, that this defect made the product not fit for its normal use, and that this caused the plaintiff's harm. A product may be defective because there is (1) a manufacturing defect, (2) a design defect, (3) inadequate instruction on how to use the product, or (4) inadequate warning against dangers involved in using the product.

For example, if the manufacturer's blueprint shows that there should be two bolts at a particular place and the factory puts in only one bolt, there is a manufacturing defect. If the two bolts are put in but the product breaks because four bolts are required to provide sufficient strength, there is no manufacturing defect, but there is a design defect. A product that is properly designed and properly manufactured may be dangerous because the user is not given sufficient instructions on how to use the product. Also, a product is defective if there is a danger that is not obvious and there is no warning at all or a warning that does not describe the full danger.

Many courts are relaxing the requirement of proving the existence of a specific defect. These courts impose liability when the goods are in fact not fit for their normal purpose. These courts allow the buyer to prove that the goods are not fit for their normal purpose with evidence that the goods do not function properly even though the buyer does not establish the specific defect.

In contrast with a breach of the implied warranty of merchantability, it is not necessary under the breach of the implied warranty of fitness for a particular purpose or of an express warranty or a guarantee to show that there was a defect that caused the breach. It is sufficient to show that the goods did not perform to meet the particular purpose or did not conform to the express warranty or to the guarantee. Why they did or did not so conform is immaterial.

16. Warranties in the International Sale of Goods

The warranties of both merchantability and fitness for a particular purpose exist under the Convention on Contracts for the International Sale of Goods (CISG). In most cases, the provisions are identical to those of the UCC. Sellers, however, can expressly disclaim the convention's warranties without mentioning merchantability or making the disclaimer conspicuous.

D.   DISCLAIMER OF WARRANTIES

A disclaimer is a provision that eliminates warranty liability.

The seller and the buyer may ordinarily agree that there will be no warranties. In some states, disclaimers of warranties are prohibited for reasons of public policy or consumer protection.

17. Validity of Disclaimer

Warranties may be disclaimed by agreement of the parties, subject to the limitation that such a provision must not be unconscionable, must be conspicuous, and in certain cases must use certain language.[16]

---

[16] UCC § 2-316.

(a) Conspicuousness. A disclaimer provision is made conspicuous by printing it under a conspicuous heading that indicates there is an exclusion or modification of warranties. A heading cannot be relied on to make such a provision conspicuous when the heading is misleading and wrongfully gives the impression there is a warranty. ◆ *For example,* the heading "Vehicle Warranty" is misleading if the provision that follows contains a limitation of warranties. A disclaimer that is hidden in a mass of printed material handed to the buyer is not conspicuous and is not effective to exclude warranties. Similarly, an inconspicuous disclaimer of warranties under a heading of "Notice to Retail Buyers" has no effect. ◆

When a disclaimer of warranties fails to be effective because it is not conspicuous, the implied warranties that would arise in the absence of any disclaimer are operative.

(b) Unconscionability and Public Policy. An exclusion of warranties made in the manner specified by the UCC is not unconscionable. In some states, warranty disclaimers are invalid because they are contrary to public policy or because they are prohibited by consumer protection laws.

There is authority that when a breach of warranty is the result of negligence of the seller, a disclaimer of warranty liability and a limitation of remedies to refunding the purchase price are not binding. Such limitations are unreasonable, unconscionable, and against public policy.

18. Particular Language for Disclaimers

A statement such as "There are no warranties that extend beyond the description on the face hereof" excludes all implied warranties of fitness. Implied warranties (other than the warranty of title and the warranty against encumbrances) are excluded by the statement "as is" or "with all faults" or by other language that in normal, common speech calls attention to the warranty exclusion and makes it clear there is no implied warranty. For a disclaimer of warranties to be a binding part of an oral sales contract, the disclaimer must be called to the attention of the buyer.

In a sales contract, provisions excluding warranties have that effect only. They do not bar the buyer from recovering damages for fraud, negligence, or strict tort liability.

Figure 28-1 provides a summary of the warranties under Article 2 and the methods for disclaimer.

19. Exclusion of Warranties by Examination of Goods

There is no implied warranty covering defects in goods that an examination should have revealed when the buyer, before making the final contract, has examined the goods or model or sample or has refused to examine them.

The examination of the goods by the buyer does not ordinarily exclude the existence of an express warranty. It may, however, if it can be concluded that the buyer, by the examination, learned of the falsity of the statement claimed to be a warranty. As a result, this statement did not in fact form part of the basis of the bargain.

Name of Warranty	Creation	Restriction	Disclaimer
Express	Affirmation of fact or promise of performance (includes samples, models, descriptions)	Must be part of the basis of the bargain	Cannot make a disclaimer inconsistent with an express warranty
Implied Warranty of Merchantability	Given in every sale of goods by a merchant ("fit for ordinary purposes")	Only given by merchants	(1) Must use "merchantability" or general disclaimer of "as is" or "with all faults" (2) If written, must be conspicuous
Implied Warranty of Fitness for a Particular Purpose	Seller knows of buyer's reliance for a particular use (buyer is ignorant)	Seller must have knowledge Buyer must rely on seller	(1) Must be in writing (2) Must be conspicuous (3) Also disclaimed with "as is" or "with all faults"
Title	Given in every sale	Does not apply in circumstances where apparent warranty is not given	Must say "There is no warranty of title"
Magnuson-Moss (Federal Consumer Product Warranty Law)	Only consumer products of $15 or more	Must label "Full" or "Limited"	

FIGURE 28-1
UCC Warranties

20. Postsale Disclaimer

Frequently, a statement purporting to exclude or modify warranties appears for the first time in a written contract sent to confirm or memorialize an oral contract made earlier. The exclusion or modification may likewise appear in an invoice, a bill, or an instruction manual delivered to the buyer at or after the time the goods are received. Such postsale disclaimers have no effect on warranties that arose at the time of the sale.

An exclusion of warranties in a manufacturer's manual given to the buyer after the sale is not binding on a buyer because it is not a term of the sales contract. If the buyer assents to the postsale disclaimer, however, it is effective as a modification of the sales contract.

ETHICS & THE LAW

The following is language from the inside of a football helmet:

WARNING

Do not strike an opponent with any part of this helmet or face mask. This is a violation of football rules and may cause you to suffer severe brain or neck injury, including paralysis or death.

Severe brain or neck injury may also occur accidentally while playing football.

NO HELMET CAN PREVENT ALL SUCH INJURIES. YOU USE THIS HELMET AT YOUR OWN RISK.

The warning appears in all types of helmets, from those purchased by professional clubs to high school and junior high school team purchases. Is it ethical to sell a product like this that cannot provide the safety players need and may even cause injury? Do you believe that the helmet makers are sued for product liability by injured players regardless of what caused their head, back, or spinal injury? Is it ethical to seek such recovery when the helmet maker is not at fault?

E. OTHER THEORIES OF PRODUCT LIABILITY

In addition to recovery for breach of an express guarantee, an express warranty, or an implied warranty, a plaintiff in a given product liability case may be able to recover for negligence, fraud, or strict tort liability.

21. Negligence

Negligence is a product liability theory that requires proof of a defect, causation, and damages and also proof that the seller knew of the defect.

A person injured because of the defective condition of a product may be entitled to recover from the seller or manufacturer for the damages for negligence. The injured person must be able to show that the defendant was negligent in the preparation or manufacture of the article or failed to provide proper instructions and warnings of dangers. An action for negligence rests on common law tort principles. It does not require privity of contract.

22. Fraud

The UCC expressly preserves the pre-Code law governing fraud. Thus, a person defrauded by a distributor's or manufacturer's false statements about a product will generally be able to recover damages for the harm sustained because of such misrepresentations. False statements are fraudulent if the party who made them did so with knowledge that they were false or with reckless indifference to their truthfulness.

23. Strict Tort Liability

Strict tort liability is a product liability theory incorporated in the Restatement (Third) of Torts that requires proof of a defect but not of prior knowledge of it on the part of the seller or manufacturer.

Independently of the UCC, a manufacturer or distributor of a defective product is liable under strict tort liability to a person who is injured by the product. Strict tort liability exists without regard to whether the person injured is a purchaser, a consumer, or a third person, such as a bystander.[17] It is no defense that privity of contract does not exist between the injured party and the defendant. Likewise, it is no defense that the defect was found in a component part purchased from another manufacturer.[18] *For example*, defective tires sold on a new car were probably purchased from a tire supplier by the auto manufacturer. However, the manufacturer is not excused from liability.

Strict tort liability requires that it first be shown that there was a defect in the product at the time it left the control of the defendant.[19] The defective condition is defined in the same way as under negligence: defective by manufacturing error or oversight, defective by design, or defective by the failure to warn. The defendant is liable if the product is defective and unreasonably dangerous and has caused harm. It is immaterial whether the defendant was negligent or whether the user was guilty of contributory negligence. Knowledge of the defect is not a requirement for liability. Assumption of risk by the injured party, on the other hand, is a defense available to the defendant.[20]

---

[17] The concept of strict tort liability was judicially declared in *Greenman v Yuba Power Products* (Cal) 377 P2d 897 (1963). This concept has been incorporated in the Restatement (Second) of Torts as § 402A.
[18] *Guiffrida v Panasonic Industrial Co., Inc.* (Sup Ct App Div) 607 NYS2d 72 (1994).
[19] *Bittner v American Honda Motor Co., Inc.* (Wis) 533 NW2d 476 (1995).
[20] *Monsanto Co. v Logisticon, Inc.* (Mo App) 736 SW2d 371 (1989).

Liability from Being in Hot Water

Facts: Maria Gonzalez lived in a rental unit with her sons in Queens, New York. The hot water supplied to their apartment was heated by a Morflo water heater, which had a temperature control device on its exterior that was manufactured by Robertshaw and sold to Morflo. Maria Garcia, the owner of the Gonzalezes' apartment, had purchased and installed the water heater. The Morflo heater was located in the basement of the apartment house, which was locked and inaccessible by tenants.

There were extensive warnings on the water heater itself and in the manual given to Garcia at the time of her purchase. The warning on the Robertshaw temperature device read, "CAUTION: Hotter water increases the risk of scald injury." The heater itself contained a picture of hot water coming from a faucet with the word "DANGER" printed above it. Additionally, the water heater had a statement on it:

Water temperature over 120 degrees Fahrenheit can cause severe burns instantly or death from scalds. Children, disabled, and elderly are at highest risk of being scalded. Feel water before bathing or showering. Temperature limiting valves are available, see manual.

In the Morflo manual, the following warning appeared:

DANGER! The thermostat is adjusted to its lowest temperature position when shipped from the factory. Adjusting the thermostat past the 120 degree Fahrenheit bar on the temperature dial will increase the risk of scald injury. The normal position is approximately 120 degrees Fahrenheit.

DANGER: WARNING: Hot water can produce first degree burns in 3 seconds at 140 degrees Fahrenheit (60 degrees Celsius), in 20 seconds at 130 degrees Fahrenheit (54 degrees Celsius), in 8 minutes at 120 degrees Fahrenheit (49 degrees Celsius).

On October 1, 1992, 15-month-old Angel Gonzalez was being bathed by his 15-year-old brother, Daniel. When the telephone rang, Daniel left Angel alone in the bathtub. No one else was at home with the boys, and Daniel left the water running. Angel was scalded by the water that came from the tap.

Angel and his mother brought suit against Morflo and Robertshaw, alleging defects in the design of the water heater and the failure to warn.

Decision: There was no design defect. There was sufficient warning on the product. That the landlord did not extend the warning to the tenants is not the responsibility of the product manufacturer. Hot water is hot—this simple fact does not allow recovery in this case. *[Gonzalez v Morflo Industries, Inc., 931 F Supp 159 (EDNY 1996)]*

24. Cumulative Theories of Liability

The theories of product liability are not mutually exclusive. A given set of facts may give rise to two or more theories of liability.

SUMMARY

There are five theories to protect parties from loss caused by nonconforming goods. They are (1) express warranty, (2) implied warranty, (3) negligence, (4) fraud, and (5) strict tort liability.

Theories of product liability are not mutually exclusive. A given set of facts may give rise to liability under two or more theories.

The requirement of privity of contract (that is, the parties to the sales contract for warranty liability) has been widely rejected. The law is moving toward the conclusion that persons harmed because of an improper product may recover from anyone who is in any way responsible. The requirement of privity has been abolished by most states in cases where the plaintiff is a member of the buyer's family or household or is a guest in the buyer's home and has sustained personal injury because of the product.

Warranties may be express or implied. Both have the same effect and operate as though the defendant had made an express guarantee.

A warranty made after a sale does not require consideration. It is regarded as a modification of the sales contract.

Express warranties are regulated by federal statute and the FTC. These warranties must be labeled as full or limited warranties and must conform to certain standards. A distinction is made between a merchant seller and a casual seller. A merchant seller is responsible for a greater range of warranties.

A seller makes a warranty of good title unless such warranty is excluded. Any description, sample, or model made part of the basis of the bargain creates an express warranty that the goods will conform to the description, sample, or model. Warranties of fitness for a particular purpose and merchantability are implied warranties.

Warranties may be disclaimed by agreement of the parties provided the disclaimer is not unconscionable. A written disclaimer to exclude warranties must be conspicuous. To disclaim the implied warranty of *merchantability*, the term merchantability or appropriate language, such as "as is," must be used. Postsale disclaimers have no effect on warranties that arose at the time of the sale.

The warranties of merchantability and fitness exist under the CISG. However, disclaimers under the CISG need not mention merchantability, nor must the disclaimer be conspicuous.

The strict tort liability plaintiff must show there was a defect in the product at the time it left the control of the defendant. No negligence need be established on the part of the defendant, nor is the plaintiff's contributory negligence a defense. The defendant may show that the injured party assumed the risk.

QUESTIONS AND CASE PROBLEMS

1. Edgmore has a class reunion at his house. There is a substantial amount of food left over. He sells the surplus food to his neighbor Hartranft for a fraction of its price. In eating this food, Hartranft is injured from a piece of glass that was contained in a can of salmon. Hartranft sues Edgmore for the injuries sustained. Is Edgmore liable?

2. Jane Jackson purchased a sealed can of Katydids, chocolate-covered pecan caramel candies manufactured by Nestle. Shortly after, Jackson bit into one of the candies and allegedly broke a tooth on a pecan shell embedded in the candy. She filed a complaint, asserting breach of implied warranty. How would you argue on behalf of the company? How would you argue on behalf of Jackson? In your answer, discuss both the reasonable expectations test and the foreign substance/natural substance test. [*Jackson v Nestle-Beich Inc.* (Ill App) 589 NE2d 547]

3. Webster purchased a used automobile from an automobile dealer, and the contract of sale provided: "This automobile is sold 'AS IS.'" Has the warranty (a) of title or (b) against encumbrances been disclaimed?

4. Steve purchases an electric kitchen range from Shermack Electric Appliance Co. In the instruction manual enclosed in the crate in which the range is delivered to Steve's home is a statement that Shermack makes no warranty, express or implied, with respect to the range. The range works properly for two weeks and then ceases to function. When Steve demands his money back from Shermack, it argues that all warranties, including that of fitness for normal use, were excluded by the statement in the manual. Is Shermack correct?

5. Andy's Sales (owned by Andy Adams) sold a well-built trampoline to Carl and Shirley Wickers. The Wickerses later sold the trampoline to Herbert Bryant. While using the trampoline, Herbert's 14-year-old nephew, Rex, sustained injuries that left him a quadriplegic. Rex's guardian filed suit for breach of express warranty and merchantability. The sales brochure for

the round trampoline described it as "safe" because it had a "uniform bounce" and "natural tendency to work the jumper toward the center." The Wickerses had purchased an oval-shaped trampoline. Discuss Rex's ability to recover. Is privity an issue? [*Bryant v Adams* (NC App) 448 SE2d 832]

6. A buyer purchased a new drive-through car wash machine from a dealer. It washed the cars effectively, but it would knock off external accessories, such as mirrors and radio antennas. When the buyer complained, the seller stated that the contract made no provision for such matters. Was this a valid defense?

7. Avery purchased a refrigerator from a retail store. The written contract stated that the refrigerator was sold "as is" and that the warranty of merchantability and all warranties of fitness were excluded. This was stated in large capital letters printed just above the line on which Avery signed her name. The refrigerator worked properly for a few weeks and then stopped. The store refused to do anything about it because of the exclusion of the warranties made by the contract. Avery claimed that this exclusion was not binding because it was unconscionable. Was Avery correct? [*Avery v Aladdin Products Div., Nat'l Service Industries, Inc.* (Ga App) 196 SE2d 357]

8. A manufacturer advertised its product in national magazines. The advertisement induced a buyer to purchase the product, which did not live up to the statements in the advertisement. The buyer claimed there was a breach of warranty. The manufacturer contended the statements in the advertisement were obviously sales talk and therefore could not constitute a warranty. Was this a valid defense? [*Westrie Battery Co. v Standard Electric Co.,* 482 F2d 1307 (10th Cir)]

9. Clark suffered an injury as a result of a defect in a chain saw he had purchased from Grey Hardware. The saw was manufactured by Lee Tool Corp. Clark commences an action against Lee Tool based on strict tort liability. Lee Tool argues that absent privity, the suit should be dismissed. Is Lee Tool correct? Why?

10. The defendant, Zogarts, manufactured and sold a practice device for beginning golfers. According to the statements on the package, the device was completely safe, and a player could never be struck by the device's golf ball. Hauter was hit by the ball when practicing with the device. He sued Zogarts, which denied liability on the ground that the statements were merely matters of opinion, so liability could not be based on them. Was this a valid defense? [*Hauter v Zogarts* (Cal) 534 P2d 377]

11. A buyer purchased an engine to operate an irrigation pump. The buyer selected the engine from a large number that were standing on the floor of the seller's stockroom. A label on the engine stated that it would produce 100 horsepower. The buyer needed an engine that would generate at least 80 horsepower. In actual use in the buyer's irrigation system, the engine generated only 60 horsepower. The buyer sued the seller for damages. The seller raised the defense that no warranty of fitness for the buyer's particular purpose of operating an irrigation pump had arisen because the seller did not know of the use to which the buyer intended to put the engine. Also, the buyer had not relied on the seller's skill and judgment in selecting the particular engine. Did the seller have any liability based on warranties? [*Potter v Ryndall* (NC) 207 SE2d 762]

12. Some time after Old Fort Trading Post sold an antique pistol to McCoy, the police took the gun from McCoy when they learned it was stolen property. The gun was turned over to its rightful owner. McCoy notified Old Fort and demanded his money back. The refund was denied. What remedy, if any, does McCoy have? Explain. [*Trial v McCoy* (Tex App) 553 SW2d 199]

13. Drehman Paving & Flooring Co. installed a brick floor at Cumberland Farms that its salesman promised would be "just like" another floor Cumberland had installed several years earlier. The bricks in the new floor came loose because Drehman had failed to install expansion joints. Expansion joints were not included in the second floor contract, but were part of the first. Can Cumberland recover? What theory? [*Cumberland Farms, Inc. v Drehman Paving & Flooring Co.,* (Mass App Ct) 520 NE2d 1321]

14. A strict tort liability defendant may raise the defense that there was no negligence involved and that, even if there was negligence, the plaintiff cannot recover because the plaintiff was guilty of contributory negligence. Appraise this statement.

15. Mark went to the Happy Hour Cafe to eat breakfast. While drinking milk, his throat was cut because the milk contained a piece of glass. Mark thereupon brought an action against Happy Hour to recover damages for personal injuries resulting from breach of an implied warranty. Will he be successful?

CPA QUESTIONS

1. Under the UCC Sales Article, the warranty of title may be excluded by
   a. Merchants or non-merchants provided the exclusion is in writing.
   b. Non-merchant sellers only.
   c. The seller's statement that it is selling only such right or title that it has.
   d. Use of an "as is" disclaimer.

   (5/90, Law, #42, 0510)

2. Which of the following factors result(s) in an express warranty with respect to a sale of goods?

   I. The seller's description of the goods as part of the basis of the bargain.
   II. The seller selects goods knowing the buyer's intended use.

   a. I only.
   b. II only.
   c. Both I and II.
   d. Neither I nor II.

   (5/92, Law, #58)

3. Morgan is suing the manufacturer, wholesaler, and retailer for bodily injuries caused by a power saw Morgan purchased. Which of the following statements is correct under the theory of strict liability?
   a. The manufacturer will avoid liability if it can show it followed the custom of the industry.
   b. Morgan may recover even if he **cannot** show any negligence was involved.
   c. Contributory negligence on Morgan's part will always be a bar to recovery.
   d. Privity will be a bar to recovery insofar as the wholesaler is concerned if the wholesaler did **not** have a reasonable opportunity to inspect.

   (5/92, Law, #58)

Remedies for Breach of Sales Contracts

CHAPTER 29

OBJECTIVES

After studying this chapter, you should be able to

1. *List the remedies of the seller when the buyer breaches a sales contract;*
2. *List the remedies of the buyer when the seller breaches a sales contract;*
3. *Determine the validity of clauses limiting damages; and*
4. *Discuss the waiver of and preservation of defenses of a buyer.*

If one of the parties to a sale fails to perform the contract, the nonbreaching party is given remedies under the UCC. In addition, the parties may have included provisions pertaining to remedies in their contract.

A. STATUTE OF LIMITATIONS

Statute of limitations is the the time within which legal action must be commenced in order to preserve the rights and remedies given by law.

Judicial remedies have time limitations. After the expiration of a particular period of time, the party seeking a remedy can no longer resort to the courts. The UCC **statute of limitations** applies to actions brought for remedies on the breach of a sales contract.[1] When a suit is brought on the basis of a tort theory, such as negligence, fraud, or strict tort liability, then other general statutes of limitations apply.

1. Time Limits for Suits under the UCC

Breach is the nonperformance of the obligations under a contract.

An action for breach of a sales contract must be commenced within four years after the cause of action arises. When a cause of action arises depends on the nature of the **breach**. Nonpayment by the buyer is a breach, and the seller's cause of action arises at the time of the buyer's failure to pay.[2] When an express warranty is made as to future performance, the statute of limitations runs not from the time of the tender but from the date when the future performance begins.[3] *For example,* if a generator is guaranteed to be free from defects for five years, the statute of limitations does not begin to run at the time the generator is purchased. The statute of limitations would run from the time the defect arises.

The buyer who sues the seller for damages claimed because of a breach of the sales contract must give the seller notice of the breach within a reasonable time after the buyer discovers or should have discovered it.[4]

2. Time Limits for Other Suits

When the plaintiff sues on a non-Code theory, such as on the basis of strict tort liability, fraud, or negligence, the UCC statute of limitations does not apply. The action is subject to each state's tort statute of limitations. Tort statutes of limitations are found in individual state statutes, and the time limitations vary by state.

---

[1] UCC § 2-725.
[2] *Moncrief v Williston Basin Interstate Pipeline Co.,* 880 F Supp 1495 (D Wyo 1995).
[3] *Grand Island Express v Timpte Indus., Inc.,* 28 F3d 73 (8th Cir. 1994).
[4] UCC § 2-607(3)(a); *United States v Williams,* 827 F Supp 641 (D Or 1993).

B.   REMEDIES OF THE SELLER

When a sales contract is broken by the buyer, the seller has different remedies available that are designed to afford the seller compensation for the losses caused by the buyer's breach.

3.   Seller's Lien

A lien is an interest in property that affords its holder the right to possession and possibly sale of the property to satisfy an obligation.

In the absence of an agreement for the extension of credit to the buyer for the purchase of goods, and until the buyer pays for the goods or performs whatever actions the contract requires, the seller has the right to retain possession of the goods.[5]

4.   Seller's Remedy of Stopping Shipment

When the buyer has breached the contract prior to the time the goods have arrived at their destination, the seller can stop the goods from coming into the possession of the buyer. This remedy is important to sellers because it eliminates the need for sellers to try to recover goods from buyers who have indicated they cannot or will not pay.

A seller has the right to stop shipment of large shipments, such as plane loads, train car loads, and boat loads, if the buyer has not provided assurances as requested or the seller has grounds to believe performance by the buyer will not occur.[6] *For example*, if Lon's Furniture learns that a buyer has just gone out of business, Lon's could contact the shipper of a truck load of patio furniture and ask the shipper to return the furniture to it.

If the buyer is to receive the goods on credit and the seller has learned that the buyer is insolvent, then the seller can stop any size shipment. Also, the right to retrieve the goods in the case of a credit buyer's insolvency continues for ten days after the buyer actually has received the goods. In addition, if the seller has demanded assurances and the buyer has misrepresented his solvency in writing in the three months preceding delivery, the ten-day limitation does not apply and the seller can retrieve the goods without time limitation.[7] *For example*, if Bill's Radiator furnished a financial statement to its paint supplier on August 1, 1998, and that financial statement was materially false, the paint supplier could, upon learning on October 20, 1998, of the false statements in Bill's financial statements reclaim the paint shipped to Bill's on October 6, 1998.

5.   Resale by Seller

Resale is the right of the seller to resell the goods that are the subject matter of a contract that has been breached by a buyer.

When the buyer has breached the contract, the seller may resell any of the goods the seller still holds. After the resale, the seller is not liable to the original buyer on the contract and does not have to surrender any profit obtained on the resale. On the other hand, if the proceeds are less than the contract price, the seller may recover the loss from the original buyer.[8]

---

[5] UCC § 2-703.
[6] UCC § 2-705.
[7] UCC § 2-702.
[8] UCC § 2-706(1),(6); *Eades Commodities v Hoeper* (Mo App) 825 SW2d 34 (1992).

The seller must give reasonable notice to the breaching buyer of the intention to resell the goods. Such notice need not be given if the goods are perishable or could decline rapidly in value. Any method of resale must be conducted by the seller under standards of commercial reasonableness.

CASE SUMMARY

The Tire Inflator Contract That Deflated

Facts: Firwood Manufacturing Company had a contract to sell General Tire 55 model 1225 post-cure inflators (PCIs). PCIs are $30,000 machines used by General Tire in its manufacturing process. The contract was entered into in 1989, and by April 1990, General Tire had purchased 22 PCIs from Firwood. However, General Tire then closed its Barrie, Michigan, plant. Firwood reminded General Tire that it still had the obligation to purchase the 33 remaining PCIs. General Tire communicated to Firwood that it would not be purchasing the remaining PCIs. Firwood then was able, over a period of three years, to sell the remaining PCIs. Some of the PCIs were sold as units, while others were broken down and sold to buyers who needed parts.

Firwood's sales of the remaining 33 units brought in $187,513 less than the General Tire contract provided, and Firwood filed suit to collect the resale price difference plus interest.

Decision: Firwood's resale may have taken three years, and the contract goods may have been sold as parts, but Firwood acted in good faith in trying to mitigate damages because there simply was no market for PCIs at the time of General Tire's breach. Firwood acted in good faith and pursued buyers diligently over that three-year period. While the time period may be less than optimal and the sale of the goods as parts not always desirable, Firwood did the best it could given the market following the breach. Firwood was awarded the contract price difference of $187,513 and $100,476 in interest. [*Firwood Manufacturing Co., Inc. v General Tire, Inc., 96 F3d 163 (6th Cir 1996)*]

---

6. Cancellation by Seller

When the buyer materially breaches the contract, the seller may cancel the contract. Such a cancellation ends the contract and discharges all unperformed obligations on both sides. Following cancellation, the seller has any remedy with respect to the breach by the buyer that is still available.

7. Seller's Action for Damages under the Market Price Formula

When the buyer fails to pay for accepted goods, the seller may resell the goods, as discussed earlier, or bring a contract action to recover damages. One formula for a seller's damages is the difference between the market price at the time and place of the tender of the goods and the contract price.[9] Whether the seller chooses to resell or recover the difference between the contract price and the market price is the seller's decision. The flexibility in the remedies under the UCC is provided because certain goods will have very high market fluctuations. ◆ *For example,* suppose that Sears had agreed to purchase ten refrigerators from Whirlpool at a price of $600 each. Sears notifies Whirlpool that it will not be buying the refrigerators. Whirlpool determines the market price at the time of tender to be $450 per refrigerator. The best Whirlpool can find from an alternate buyer after a search is $400. Whirlpool can select the resale remedy to adequately compensate for the change in the market price between the time of tender and the time damages are sought. ◆

---

[9] UCC § 2-708.

8. Seller's Action for Lost Profits

Lost profits are a damage formula for recovery for sellers in cases where other damage formulas would not provide adequate compensation for the buyer's breach.

If the market price measure of damages does not place the seller in the position in which the seller would have been, had the buyer performed, the seller is permitted to recover lost profits. The recovery of lost profits reimburses the seller for costs incurred in gearing up for contract performance.[10] ◆ *For example*, suppose that a buyer has ordered 200 wooden rocking horses from a seller-manufacturer. Before production on the horses begins, the buyer breaches. The seller has nothing to resell, and the goods have not been identified to even permit a market value assessment. Nonetheless, the seller has geared up for production, counted on the contract, and perhaps bypassed other contracts in order to perform. An appropriate remedy for the seller of the rocking horses would be the profits it would have made had the buyer performed. ◆

9. Other Types of Damages

So far, the discussion of remedies has focused on the damages that result because the seller did not sell the goods. However, there may be additional expenses the seller incurs because of the breach. Some of those expenses can be recovered as damages.

Incidental damages are damages incurred by the nonbreaching party as part of the process of trying to cover or sell; includes storage fees, commissions, and the like.

The seller can also recover, as **incidental damages**, any commercially reasonable charges, expenses, or commissions incurred in recovering damages.[11] ◆ *For example*, the seller may recover expenses for the transportation, care, and storage of the goods after the buyer's breach as well as any costs incurred in the return or resale of the goods. ◆ Such damages are in addition to any others that may be recovered by the seller.

10. Seller's Action for the Purchase Price

If goods are specially manufactured and the buyer refuses to take them, it is possible for the seller to recover as damages the full purchase price and keep the goods.[12] ◆ *For example*, a printing company that has printed catalogs for a retail mail-order merchant will not be able to sell the catalogs to anyone. The remedy for the seller is recovery of the purchase price. ◆

11. Seller's Nonsale Remedies

In addition to the seller's traditional sales remedies, many sellers enter into other transactions that provide protection from buyer breaches. One such protection is afforded when the seller obtains a security interest from the buyer under UCC Article 9. A **secured transaction** is a pledge of property by the buyer-debtor that enables the seller to take possession of the goods if the buyer fails to pay the amount owed. (See chapter 35.)

Figure 29-1 is a summary of the remedies available to the seller under Article 2.

---

[10] UCC § 2-709.
[11] UCC § 2-710.
[12] *Weisz Graphics v Peck Industries, Inc.* (SC App) 403 SE2d 146 (1991).

Remedy	Stop delivery	Resale price	Market price	Action for price	Lost profit
Section Number	2-703	2-706 2-710	2-708 2-710	2-709 2-708	2-708(2)
When Available	Insolvency* Advance breach by buyer	Buyer fails to take goods	Buyer fails to take goods	Specially manufactured goods	Anticipated repudiation Breach
Nature of Remedy	Stop delivery of any size shipment or recover goods if buyer insolvent; Stop delivery of large shipments for other reasons	Contract price — Resale price + Incidental damages —°Expenses saved	Contract price — Market price + Incidental damages —°Expenses saved	Contract price + Incidental damages —°Expenses saved	Profits + Incidental damages — Salvage Value

* Misrepresentation of insolvency (3-mo/10-day rules)

FIGURE 29-1
*Seller's Remedies
Under Article 2*

C. REMEDIES OF THE BUYER

When a sales contract is breached by the seller, the buyer has a number of remedies under Article 2 of the UCC. Additional remedies based on contract or tort theories of liability may also be available.

12. Rejection of Improper Tender

As discussed in chapter 27, if the goods tendered by the seller do not conform to the contract in some way, the buyer may reject the goods. However, the rejection is the beginning of the buyer's remedies. Following rejection, the buyer can proceed to recover under the various formulas provided for buyers under the UCC.

13. Revocation of Acceptance

Also as discussed in chapter 27, the buyer may revoke acceptance of the goods when they do not conform to the contract, the defect substantially impairs the value of the contract to the buyer, and the buyer either could not discover the problem or kept the goods because of a seller's promise of repair. Again, following revocation of acceptance, the buyer has various remedies available under the UCC.

14. Buyer's Action for Damages for Nondelivery— Market Price Recovery

If the seller fails to deliver the goods as required by the contract or repudiates the contract, the buyer is entitled to sue the seller for damages for breach of contract. The buyer is entitled to recover the difference between the market price at the time the buyer learned of the breach and the contract price.[13]

---
[13] UCC § 2-713.

15. Buyer's Action for Damages for Nondelivery— Cover Price Recovery

Cover is the right of the buyer to purchase substitute goods when the seller fails to perform under a contract for the purchase of goods

A buyer may also choose as a remedy for the seller's nondelivery of goods that conform to the contract to purchase substitute goods or **cover** as a remedy.[14] If the buyer acts in good faith, the measure of damages for the seller's nondelivery or repudiation is then the difference between the cost of cover and the contract price. The buyer need only make a reasonable cover purchase as a substitute for the contract goods. The goods purchased need not be identical to the contract goods. *For example,* if the buyer could secure only 350 five-speed blenders when the contract called for three-speed blenders, the buyer's cover would be reasonable despite the additional expense of the five-speed blenders.

16. Other Types of Damages

Consequential damages are damages the buyer experiences as a result of the seller's breach with respect to third parties, as in lost sales or penalties for the buyer's nonperformance on contracts with others.

The buyer is also entitled to collect incidental damages in situations in which he must find substitute goods. Those incidental damages could include additional shipping expenses or perhaps commissions paid in order to find the goods and purchase them. Buyers often also experience **consequential damages.** Consequential damages are those damages the buyer experiences with respect to a third party as a result of the seller's breach.[15] *For example,* a seller's failure to deliver the goods may cause the buyer's production line to come to a halt. The buyer could breach on its sales and delivery contracts with its buyers. In the case of a government contract, the buyer may have to pay a penalty for being late. These types of damages are consequential ones and can be recovered if the seller knew about the consequences or they were foreseeable.

CASE SUMMARY

The Car May Be Stolen, But I Paid for It

Facts: Joseph Perna purchased a 1981 Oldsmobile at a traffic auction conducted by Locascio. The car had been seized pursuant to action taken by the New York City Parking Violation Bureau against Jose Cruz. Perna purchased the car for $1,800 plus tax and towing fees "subject to the terms and conditions of any and all chattel mortgages, rental agreements, liens, conditional bills of sale, and encumbrances that may be on the motor vehicle of the above judgment debtor." The Olds had 58,103 miles on it at the time of Perna's purchase.

On May 7, 1993, Perna sold the car to Elio Marino, a co-worker, for $1,200. The vehicle had about 65,000 miles on it at the time of this sale. During his period of ownership, Marino replaced the radiator ($270), repaired the power steering and valve cover gasket ($117), and replaced a door lock ($97.45). He registered and insured the vehicle.

In February 1994, Marino's son was stopped by the police and arrested for driving a stolen vehicle. His son was kept in jail until his arraignment, and the charges were eventually dropped. The Oldsmobile was never returned to Marino.

Marino filed suit for breach of contract because he had been given a car with a defective title. He asked for damages that included the costs of getting his son out of jail and the theft charges dropped.

---

14 UCC § 2-712; *United States v CBC Enterprises, Inc.*, 820 F Supp 242 (ED Va 1993).
15 UCC § 2-715.

> **Decision:** The damages for breach of warranty (in this case, the breach of the warranty of title) are the difference between the value of the goods as they are and their value had they been as warranted. The value of the car if as warranted is $1,200. While Marino had driven the car for some time, he had added value through the repair work.
>
> Marino could not recover the consequential damages related to the arrest of his son. Neither Perna nor Locascio had any knowledge that there was a problem with the title to the car; and as such, the damages experienced as a result of Marino's son's arrest were not forseeable. [*Marino v Perna (NY Civ) 629 NYS2d 669 (1995)*]

17. Action for Breach of Warranty

A remedy available to a buyer when goods are delivered but fail to conform to warranties is an action for breach of warranty.

(a) Notice of Breach. If the buyer has accepted goods that do not conform to the contract or there has been a breach of any warranties given, the buyer must notify the seller of the breach within a reasonable time after the breach is discovered or should have been discovered.[16]

(b) Measure of Damages. If the buyer has given the necessary notice of breach, the buyer may recover damages measured by the loss resulting in the normal course of events from the breach. If suit is brought for breach of warranty, the measure of damages is the difference between the value of the goods as they were when accepted and the value that they would have had if they had been as warranted.

CASE SUMMARY

The Alpha Chi Omega Battle of the Sweaters

Facts: Emily Lieberman and Amy Altomondo were members of the Alpha Chi Omega sorority at Bowling Green State University. Lieberman and Altomondo negotiated with Johnathan James Furlong for the purchase of custom-designed sweaters for them and their sorority sisters for a total price of $3,612. Lieberman and Altomondo paid Furlong a $2,000 deposit.

Lieberman and Altomondo had a friend pick up the sweaters in Columbus and deliver them to Bowling Green. Upon opening the boxes, they discovered that Furlong had made color and design alterations in the lettering imprinted on the sweaters as part of their custom design. Altomondo, as president of AXO, called Furlong and told him that the sweaters were unacceptable and offered to return them. Furlong refused, stating that any changes were immaterial. Altomondo refused to pay the balance due and demanded the return of the $2,000 deposit. Furlong filed suit for breach of contract.

Decision: Furlong had breached the contract. Upon inspection, the buyers found that the sweaters failed to conform. That Furlong considered the sweaters' changes to be immaterial was not an issue. AXO was entitled to a refund of the $2,000 and could retain the sweaters as security for the return of their deposit. AXO did not have any incidental damages. Furlong had breached an express warranty by not delivering the goods in conformity with AXO's specifications. [*Furlong v Alpha Chi Omega Sorority (Ohio Bowling Green Co Mun Ct) 657 NE2d 866 (1993)*]

---

[16] *Hapag-Lloyd, A.G. v Marine Indemnity Ins. Co. of America* (Fla App) 576 SO 2d 1330 (1991).

(c) Notice of Third-party Action against Buyer. When a buyer elects the remedy of resale and sells the contract goods to a third party, that third party has the right of suit against the buyer for breach of warranty. In such a case, it is the buyer's option whether to give the seller notice of the action and request that the seller defend that action.

18. Cancellation by Buyer

The buyer may cancel or rescind the contract if the seller fails to deliver the goods, if the seller has repudiated the contract, or if the goods have been rightfully rejected or their acceptance revoked.[17] A buyer who cancels the contract is entitled to recover as much of the purchase price as has been paid, including the value of any property given as a trade-in as part of the purchase price. The fact that the buyer cancels the contract does not destroy the buyer's cause of action against the seller for breach of that contract. The buyer may recover from the seller not only any payment made on the purchase price but also damages for the breach of the contract. The damages represent the difference between the contract price and the cost of cover.[18]

The right of the buyer to cancel or rescind the sales contract may be lost by a delay in exercising the right. A buyer who, with full knowledge of the defects in the goods, makes partial payments or performs acts of ownership of the goods inconsistent with an intent to cancel cannot thereafter cancel the contract.

19. Buyer's Resale of Goods

When the buyer has possession of the goods after rightfully rejecting them or after rightfully revoking acceptance, the buyer is treated as is the seller in possession of goods after the default of a buyer. The aggrieved buyer has a security interest in the goods to protect the claim against the seller for breach and may proceed to resell the goods. From the proceeds of the sale, the aggrieved buyer is entitled to deduct any payments made to the seller and any expenses reasonably incurred in the inspection, receipt, transportation, care and custody, and resale of the goods.[19]

20. Action for Conversion or Recovery of Goods

When, as a result of the sales agreement, ownership passes to the buyer and the seller wrongfully refuses or neglects to deliver the goods, the buyer may maintain any action allowed by law for owners of goods wrongfully converted or withheld. The obligation of the seller to deliver proper goods may be enforced by an order for specific performance in certain circumstances, such as when the goods are unique. Distributors have been granted specific performance against suppliers to deliver goods covered by supply contracts.

Specific performance will not be granted, however, merely because the price of the goods purchased from the seller has gone up. In such a case, the buyer can still purchase the goods in the open market. The fact that it will cost more to cover can be compensated for by allowing the buyer to recover that cost increase from the seller.

---

17 UCC § 2-720.
18 UCC § 2-712(1), (2); *Valley Timber Sales, Inc. v Midway Forest Products, Inc.* (Ala App) 563 SO 2d 612 (1990).
19 UCC § 2-715(1); *International Financial Services, Inc. v Franz* (Minn App) 515 NW2d 379 (1994).

21. Nonsale Remedies of the Buyer

In addition to the remedies given the buyer under UCC Article 2, the buyer may have remedies based on contract or tort theories of liability.

The pre-Code law on torts still applies in UCC Article 2 transactions. The seller may therefore be held liable to the buyer for any negligence, fraud, or strict tort liability that occurred in the transaction.

A defrauded buyer may both avoid the contract and recover damages. The buyer also has the choice of retaining the contract and recovering damages for the losses caused by the fraud.

Figure 29-2 provides a summary of the remedies available to buyers under Article 2.

ETHICS & THE LAW

Westinghouse Electric Corporation entered into uranium supply contracts with twenty-two electric utilities during the late 1960s. The contract prices ranged from $7 to $10 per pound. The Arab oil embargo and other changes in energy resources caused the price of uranium to climb to $45–$75 per pound. Supply tightened because of increased demand.

In 1973, Westinghouse wrote to the utilities and explained that it was unable to perform on its uranium sales contracts. The utilities needed uranium. Westinghouse did not have sufficient funds to buy the uranium it had agreed to supply, assuming that it could find a supply. One utility executive commented, after totaling up all twenty-two supply contracts, that Westinghouse could not have supplied the uranium even under the original contract terms. He said, "Westinghouse oversubscribed itself on these contracts. They hoped that not all the utilities would take the full contract amount."

Westinghouse says it is impossible for it to perform. The utilities say they

Remedy	Specific performance (Replevin Identification)	Cover	Market price
Section Number	2-711	2-712 2-715	2-708 2-710
When Available	Rare or unique goods	Seller fails to deliver	Buyer fails to take goods
Nature of Remedy	Buyer gets goods (incidental damages)	Cover price — Contract price + Incidental damages + Consequential damages —Expenses saved	Market price — Contract price + Incidental damages + Consequential damages —Expenses saved

FIGURE 29-2
*Buyer's Remedies
Under Article 2*

are owed damages because they must still find uranium somewhere. What damages would the law allow? What ethical issues do you see in the original contracts? In Westinghouse's refusal to deliver? Should we excuse parties from contracts because it is so expensive for them to perform?

D.   CONTRACT PROVISIONS ON REMEDIES

The parties to a sales contract may modify the remedies provided under Article 2 or limit those remedies.

22. Limitation of Damages

(a) Liquidation of Damages. The parties may specify the exact amount of damages that may be recovered in case of breach. A **liquidated damages** clause in a contract is valid if the amount specified is reasonable in the light of the actual harm that would be caused by the breach, the difficulty of proving the amount of such loss, and the inconvenience and impracticality of suing for damages or enforcing other remedies for breach.

(b) Exclusion of Damages. The sales contract may provide that in case of breach no damages may be recovered or that no consequential damages may be recovered. When goods are sold for consumer use and personal injuries are sustained, such total exclusions are unconscionable and unenforceable. A defendant cannot rely on such a contract limitation unless the defendant is able to prove that the limitation of liability was commercially reasonable and fair rather than oppressive and surprising. If the seller would be liable to the buyer for damages, the seller cannot exclude liability for personal injuries to members of the buyer's family or household or to guests of the buyer.

If neither consumer goods nor personal injuries are involved, the exclusion of damages is binding unless the plaintiff proves that it is unconscionable. When the seller knows that the failure of the product will cause serious economic loss, a limitation of damages to just the purchase price is void as unconscionable.

23. Down Payments and Deposits

A buyer can make a deposit with the seller or an initial or down payment at the time of making the contract. If the contract contains a valid provision for liquidation of damages and the buyer defaults, the seller must return any part of the down payment or deposit in excess of the amount specified by the liquidated damages clause. In the absence of such a liquidated damages clause and in the absence of proof of greater damages, the seller's damages are computed as 20 percent of the purchase price or $500, whichever is smaller. Any part of the down payment that exceeds this amount must be returned to the buyer. ◆ *For example,* if in a contract for sale, where the purchase price is $10,000, the buyer has paid $2,000 and then breaches the contract, the buyer would forfeit $500 of the amount paid and would be entitled to the return of the balance of the payments made under the contract, or $1,500. ◆

C P A

Liquidated damages are damages agreed to in advance by the parties; are valid if reasonable and agreed to in circumstances where damages will be difficult to determine.

24. Limitation of Remedies

The parties may also limit the remedies that are provided by the Code in the case of breach of contract. Thus, a seller may specify that the only remedy of the buyer for breach of warranty will be the repair or replacement of the goods or that the buyer will be limited to returning the goods and obtaining a refund of the purchase price. A limitation of remedies need not be conspicuous.

25. Waiver of Defenses

A buyer can be barred from claiming a breach of the contract by the seller if the sales contract expressly states that the buyer will not assert any defenses against the seller.

26. Preservation of Defenses

Consumer protection law prohibits the waiver of defenses in consumer contracts.

(a) Preservation Notice. Consumer defenses are preserved by a Federal Trade Commission (FTC) regulation. This regulation requires that the papers signed by a consumer contain a provision that expressly states that the consumer reserves any defense arising from the transaction.[20] A defense of the consumer arising from the original transaction may be asserted against any third person who acquires rights by assignment in the contract (see chapter 30).

(b) Prohibition of Waiver. When the FTC preservation notice is included in the paper that is obtained by a third party, a waiver of defenses cannot be made. If the preservation notice is not included, the seller has committed an unfair trade practice. The question then arises as to whether the buyer may assert against an assignee a defense that could have been asserted against the seller. The answer to this question depends on state law. In many states, consumer protection statutes nullify a waiver of defenses by expressly providing that the buyer may assert against the seller's transferee any defense that might have been raised against the seller. Under some statutes, the buyer must give notice of any defense within a specified number of days after being notified of the assignment. Some courts extend consumer protection beyond the scope of the statute by ignoring a time limitation on the notice of defenses and allowing consumers to give late notice of defenses.

E.   REMEDIES IN THE INTERNATIONAL SALE OF GOODS

The United Nations Convention on Contracts for the International Sale of Goods (CISG) provides remedies for breach of a sales contract between parties from nations that have approved the CISG.

---

[20] 16 CFR § 433.1. It is an unfair or deceptive trade practice to take or receive a consumer credit contract that fails to contain such a preservation notice.

27. Remedies of the Seller

Under the CISG, if the buyer fails to perform any obligations under the contract, the seller may require the buyer to pay the price, take delivery, and perform other obligations under the contract. The seller may also declare the contract void if the failure of the buyer to perform obligations under the contract amounts to a fundamental breach of contract.

28. Remedies of the Buyer

Under the CISG, a buyer may reject goods only if the tender is a fundamental breach of the contract. This standard of materiality of rejection is in contrast to the UCC requirement of perfect tender. Under the CISG, a buyer may also reduce the price when nonconforming goods are delivered even though no notice of nonconformity is given. However, the buyer must have a reasonable cause for failure to give notice.

SUMMARY

The law provides a number of remedies for the breach of a sales contract. Remedies based on UCC theories are subject to a four-year statute of limitations. If the remedy sought is based on a non-UCC theory, a tort or contract statute of limitations established by state statute will apply.

Remedies of the seller may include (1) a lien on the goods until the seller is paid, (2) the right to resell the goods, (3) the right to cancel the sales contract, and (4) the right to bring an action for damages or, in some cases, for the purchase price. The seller may also have remedies because of secured transactions.

Remedies of the buyer may include (1) rejection of nonconforming goods; (2) revocation of acceptance; (3) an action for damages for nondelivery of conforming goods; (4) an action for breach of warranty; (5) cancellation of the sales contract; (6) the right to resell the goods; (7) the right to bring an action for conversion, recovery of goods, or specific performance; and (8) the right to sue for damages and cancel if the seller has made a material breach of the contract.

The parties may modify their remedies by a contractual provision for liquidated damages, for limitations on statutory remedies, or for waiver of defenses. When consumers are involved, this freedom of contract is to some extent limited for their protection.

Under the CISG, the seller may require the buyer to pay the price, take delivery, and perform obligations under the contract, or the seller may avoid the contract if there is a fundamental breach.

Under the CISG, a buyer may reject goods only if there is a fundamental breach of contract. The buyer may also reduce the price of nonconforming goods.

QUESTIONS AND CASE PROBLEMS

1. What social forces are involved in the rule of law allowing the buyer to cover upon the seller's breach?
2. Soon after Gast purchased a used auto from a Chevrolet dealer, he experienced a series of mechanical problems with the car. Gast refused to make further payments on the bank note that had financed the purchase. The bank took possession of the automobile and sold it. Gast then brought an action against the dealer, alleging that he had revoked his acceptance. Was Gast correct? Decide. [*Gast v Rodgers-Dingus Chevrolet* (Miss) 585 So 2d 725]
3. Formetal Engineering submitted to Presto a sample and specifications for precut polyurethane pads to be used in making air-conditioning units. The goods were paid for as soon as they were delivered. Formetal subsequently discovered that the pads did not conform to the sample and specifications in that there were incomplete cuts, color variances, and faulty adherence to the pad's paper backing. Presto was then informed of the defects. Formetal notified Presto that the pads would be rejected and returned to Presto, but they were not returned for 125 days. Presto argued that it was denied the right to cure, as the goods were not returned until some 125 days after

defendant promised to do so. Was there a breach of the contract. Did the buyer (Formetal) do anything wrong in seeking its remedies? Explain. [*Presto Mfg. Co. v Formetal Engineering Co.* (Ill App) 360 NE2d 510]

4. Leeper purchased a can of starch from Banks Wonder Market and was injured by it on January 30. On April 4, she notified the manufacturer, Colgate-Palmolive Co. She did not notify Banks until she commenced a lawsuit against him on January 29 of the next year on the ground that there was a defect that breached a warranty of the seller. Banks denied liability. Decide. [*Leeper v Banks* (Ky) 487 So2d 58]

5. Best Card Co. shipped 50 decks of playing cards to the Winner Club in Reno, Nevada. After inspecting the cards, Winner discovered that some of the decks contained five kings instead of four and three aces instead of four. What remedy, if any, does Winner have? Explain.

6. The goods purchased by the buyer were defective. The seller made repeated attempts to correct the defect, but it became apparent that it was impossible to correct the defect. The buyer notified the seller that the buyer was revoking acceptance of the goods. The seller offered to try again to repair the goods. The buyer rejected this offer and repeated that acceptance of the goods was being revoked. The seller claimed that the buyer could not revoke acceptance as long as the seller offered to repair the goods. Was the seller correct? [*Fenton v Contemporary Development Co.* (Wash Ct App) 529 P2d 883]

7. McAuliffe & Burke Co. sold plumbing fixtures to Levine but refused to deliver them unless immediate payment was made in cash. The buyer gave the seller a worthless check that he assured the seller was "as good as gold." On the basis of this statement, the seller surrendered the goods to the buyer. Thereafter, a creditor of Levine's brought an action against him, and the sheriff, Gallagher, seized the delivered goods. The seller, learning that the check was worthless, claimed that it had a lien on the goods and sued Gallagher for their return. Can it recover the goods?

8. Sam wants to buy a car on credit from Henry Motors. He is afraid, however, that Henry will assign his contract to a finance company and that the finance company will be able to collect the balance due on the car even if the car does not run properly. Sam wants to be able to defend himself against the finance company by showing that there are defects in the car. Is this possible?

9. Wolosin purchased a vegetable and dairy refrigerator case from Evans Manufacturing Corp. When Evans sued Wolosin for the purchase price, Wolosin claimed damages for breach of warranty. The sales contract provided that Evans would replace defective parts free of charge for one year; it also stated, "This warranty is in lieu of any and all other warranties stated or inferred, and of all other obligations on the part of the manufacturer, which neither assumes nor authorizes anyone to assume for it any other obligations or liability in connection with the sale of its products." Evans claimed that it was liable only for replacement of parts. Wolosin claimed that the quoted clause was not sufficiently specific to satisfy the limitation of remedies requirement of UCC § 2-719. Decide. [*Evans Mfg. Corp. v Wolosin* (Pa) 47 Luzerne County Leg Reg 238]

10. McInnis purchased a tractor and scraper as new equipment of the current model year from Western Tractor & Equipment Co. The written contract stated that the seller disclaimed all warranties and that no warranties existed except those stated in the contract. Actually, the equipment was not the current model but that of the prior year. The equipment was not new but had been used for 68 hours as a demonstrator model, after which the hour meter had been reset to zero. The buyer sued the seller for damages. The seller's defense was based on the ground that all liability for warranties had been disclaimed. Was this defense valid? [*McInnis v Western Tractor & Equipment Co.* (Wash) 388 P2d 562]

11. Compare or contrast the statute of limitations for a breach of warranty upon tender of goods with the statute of limitations for a breach of express warranty as to future performance.

12. Keenan rejected nonconforming goods delivered to him by Ross. After the rejection, but before Ross had been allowed a reasonable time to give instructions for the disposition of the goods, Keenan arranged a sale of the goods at a substantially reduced price. In the meantime, Ross had sold the goods to another of his customers. What rights, if any, does Ross have against Keenan?

13. Peters, the buyer, received merchandise from Hadley, the seller. Upon looking over the goods, Peters noticed that some of the goods did not conform to the contract. He therefore called Hadley, who stated, "We always take care of our customers." Peters then accepted the goods. Because the nonconformity was not remedied within a reasonable time, Peters informed Hadley that he revoked his acceptance. Hadley refused to take back the goods. Who will prevail?

14. A buyer purchased goods and later telephoned the seller that he revoked his acceptance of the goods. The seller claimed that the revocation of acceptance was

not effective because it was not accompanied by a return or an offer to return the goods. Was the seller correct?

15. Stephan's Machine & Tool, Inc., purchased a boring mill from D&H Machinery Consultants. The mill was a specialized type of equipment and was essential to the operation of Stephan's plant. The purchase price was $96,000, and Stephan's had to borrow this amount from a bank in order to finance the sale. This loan exhausted Stephan's borrowing capacity. The mill was unfit, and D&H agreed to replace it with another one. D&H did not keep its promise, and Stephan's sued it for specific performance of the contract as modified by the replacement agreement. Decide. [*Stephan's Machine & Tool, Inc. v D&H Machinery Consultants, Inc.* (Ohio App) 417 NE2d 579]

CPA QUESTION

1. On April 5, 1987, Anker, Inc., furnished Bold Corp. with Anker's financial statements dated March 31, 1987. The financial statements contained misrepresentations which indicated that Anker was solvent when in fact it was insolvent. Based on Anker's financial statements, Bold agreed to sell Anker 90 computers, "F.O.B.—Bold's loading dock." On April 14, Anker received 60 of the computers. The remaining 30 computers are in the possession of the common carrier and in transit to Anker.

    If on April 28, Bold discovered that Anker was insolvent, then with respect to the computers delivered to Anker on April 14, Bold may

    a. Reclaim the computers upon making a damand.
    b. Reclaim the computers irrespective of the rights of any third party.
    c. Not reclaim the computers since ten days have elapsed from its delivery.
    d. Not reclaim the computers since it is entitled to recover the price of the computers.

2. On Februrary 15, Mazur Corp. contracted to sell 1,000 bushels of wheat to Good Bread, Inc. at $6.00 per bushel with delivery to be made on June 23. On June 1, Good advised Mazur that it would not accept or pay for the wheat. On June 2, Mazur sold the wheat to another customer at the market price of $5.00 per bushel. Mazur had advised Good that it intended to resell the wheat. Which of the following statements is correct?

    a. Mazur can successfully sue Good for the difference between the resale price and the contract price.
    b. Mazur can resell the wheat only after June 23.
    c. Good can retract its anticipatory breach at any time before June 23.
    d. Good can successfully sue Mazur for specific performance.

Consumer Protection

CHAPTER 30

OBJECTIVES

After studying this chapter, you should be able to

1. *State the purpose of truth-in-advertising legislation;*
2. *Explain and apply the more-than-four-installments rule;*
3. *Explain the effect of the federal Warranty Disclosure Act of 1974;*
4. *State the extent to which the holder of a credit card is liable for purchases made by a person finding or stealing the card;*
5. *Explain the Federal Trade Commission regulation for the preservation of consumer defenses;*
6. *Explain what the Fair Credit Reporting Act provides for the protection of consumers' credit standing and reputation; and*
7. *List the remedies available for a breach of a consumer protection law.*

In the last few decades, the consumer protection movement has made a substantial number of changes to traditional law.

A.   GENERAL PRINCIPLES

Consumer protection began with the aim of protecting persons of limited means and limited knowledge.

1. Expansion of Protection

The social forces of protecting the person and guarding against fraud, exploitation, and oppression have expanded the category of protected consumers. Many consumer protection statutes now define *consumer* as any person, partnership, corporation, bank, or government that uses goods or services. The statutes thus go beyond providing protection only for the unsophisticated and uneducated.[1] The word *consumer* has been held to include a collector paying nearly $100,000 for jade art objects, a glass manufacturer purchasing 3 million gallons of diesel oil fuel, and the city of Boston purchasing insurance. In addition, the protected consumer may be a firm of attorneys.[2] In Texas, the protected group of buyers of goods and services includes the state of Texas, its governmental agencies, and businesses with assets under $25 million. In contrast with the foregoing expansive definition of *consumer*, some statutes are worded to apply only to natural persons. Some statutes are interpreted to apply only to consumer transactions and not to commercial transactions.

> Consumer protection is expanding.

When the scope of the consumer protection statute is broadened to condemn unfair trade practices, any business comes within the protection of the statute. It is not required that the complainant be a small, unsophisticated business.[3]

A person violating the provisions of a consumer protection statute is liable even though there was no intention to violate the law. Liability also exists even though the breach was a single occurrence rather than a pattern of repeated conduct.

The mere fact that a seller commits a breach of contract does not violate these statutes when no fraud or similar misconduct is shown.

In order to come within the protection of a consumer protection statute, it is generally held necessary to show that the conduct of the defendant is such as to affect the public generally. A contract dispute that is not likely to affect anyone other than the parties to that contract is thus excluded from the coverage of such statutes.[4]

---

[1] *Boubelik v Liberty State Bank* (Minn App) 527 NW2d 589 (1995).

[2] *Catallo Associates, Inc. v MacDonald & Goren* (Mich App) 465 NW2d 28 (1990). Statutes that broaden the protected group to protect buyers of goods and services are often called deceptive trade practices statutes instead of the earlier consumer protection statutes.

[3] *Damon v Sun Co., Inc.* (CA1 Mass) 87 F3d 1467 (1996).

[4] *Infostar Inc. v Worcester Ins. Co.* (DC NY) 924 F Supp 25 (1996).

CASE SUMMARY

How Bad Must the Seller Be?

Facts: York purchased a truck from Conway Ford. Conway stated that the truck was a "like new" demonstrator. York soon had trouble with the truck. A repairman stated that the truck frame had been bent in a previous accident. York sued Conway under the South Carolina Unfair Trade Practices Act.

Decision: Judgment for York. The Unfair Trade Practices Act does not apply to a mere breach of contract that does not involve the public interest. However, when there is the potential for repetition, there is a danger to the public, and the Act applies. As Conway was in the business of selling trucks, there was the danger to the public that he would repeat the false selling statements. The Act therefore applied. [*York v Conway Ford, Inc.* (SC) 480 SE2d 726 (1997)]

2. Proof of Consumer Status

A consumer claiming that there has been a violation of the consumer protection statute has the burden of proving that the statutory definition of *consumer* has been satisfied. However, the consumer is not required to prove that none of the statutory exceptions or defenses is available to the defendant. *For example,* Patrick purchased an automobile from Ranstead Used Cars. He later brought suit against the dealer for violating the consumer protection statute, which expressly stated that it did not protect persons purchasing for resale. Ranstead claimed that Patrick could not recover because he did not prove that he was not purchasing for resale. The defense is not valid. Ranstead had the burden of proving that Patrick had purchased for resale. Patrick was not required to prove the negative, that is, that he had not purchased for resale.

3. Who Is a Defendant in a Consumer Protection Suit?

The defendant in consumer protection situations is a person or an enterprise that regularly enters into the kind of transaction in which the injured consumer was involved. For example, it is the merchant seller, the finance company, the bank, the leasing company, the home repairer, and any others who enter regularly into a particular kind of transaction.

Under consumer protection statutes, it is immaterial that there is no privity of contract between the consumer and the defendant.[5]

4. Fault of Defendant

Consumer protection laws typically require some fault on the part of the defendant. This ordinarily means that there must be some act or omission that is condemned by general principles of law or by the particular consumer protection statute in question.

For example, Marty Good Cars sold a used car to Xavier. Unknown to Marty, the odometer had been reset so that it showed only a fraction of the total mileage of the car. Xavier claimed that this violated the state consumer protection statute, but he is wrong. Consumer protection statutes generally do not impose

---

[5] *Luker v Arnold* (Tex App) 843 SW2d 108 (1992).

absolute liability. The consumer must show some fault of the defendant. Here nothing showed that Marty knew or could have known of the odometer change or that Marty had been recklessly indifferent whether the odometer showed a true reading. ◆

5. Consumer Fault

Consumer protection law is directed at protecting consumers from the misconduct of others. Disclosure provisions are frequently imposed to give consumers the information they lack and would not have enough experience or bargaining power to demand. In a limited number of situations, consumers are given the power to rescind a transaction if hindsight makes them unhappy with the deal that had been made.

Consumer negligence may bar protection.

Consumer protection, however, does not protect consumers from their own negligence. If a consumer signs a contract without reading or understanding what it means, the consumer is bound. Moreover, when the contract signed by the consumer clearly states one thing, the consumer cannot prove that the other contracting party had made statements contradicting what was stated in the signed contract. Consumers should exercise reasonable care and not blindly trust consumer protection law to rescue them from their own blunders.

CASE SUMMARY

What about the Consumer Who Lies?

Facts: Purtle purchased an automobile on credit from Eldridge Auto Sales. In her application for credit, Purtle made false statements. In making the sale, Eldridge did not make the disclosures that were required by the Truth in Lending Act. Purtle sued Eldridge for the statutory damages authorized by the Act for nondisclosure. Eldridge asserted that Purtle could not recover because of her fraudulent misrepresentations.

Decision: Judgment for Purtle. The fact that Eldridge did not make the required disclosures imposed the statutory liability on it. The statute did not make any exception on the ground of fraudulent misrepresentation by the consumer. Accordingly, Purtle could recover the statutory penalty in spite of her fraudulent misrepresentations. [*Purtle v Eldridge Auto Sales, Inc.* (CA6 Tenn) 91 F3d 797 (1996)]

---

6. Consumer Remedies

The theoretical right of consumers to sue or assert a defense is often of little practical value to them. The amount involved may be small compared with the cost of litigation. Consumer protection legislation provides special remedies.

Some statutes require the complaining consumer to give the defendant written notice of the consumer's complaint. This is required in order to give the defendant the opportunity to examine the case and to work out a solution with the consumer.[6]

Consumers have protection through lawsuits or action of a government agency or official.

(a) Government Agency Action. The Uniform Consumer Credit Code (UCCC) provides for an administrator who will, in a sense, police business practices to ensure conformity with the law.

---

[6] *Fredericks v Rosenblatt,* 40 Mass App 713, 667 NE2d 287 (1996).

(b) Action by Attorney General. A number of states provide that the state attorney general may bring an action on behalf of a particular group of consumers. In these actions, the attorney general sues to obtain cancellation of the consumers' contracts and restitution of whatever they had paid.

Many states permit the attorney general to bring an action to enjoin violation of the consumer protection statute. Consumer protection statutes commonly give the attorney general the authority to seek a voluntary stopping of improper practices before seeking an injunction from a court.

CASE SUMMARY

Who May Sue for What?

Facts: Celebrezze, as attorney general of Ohio, brought an action against Hughes Motors, claiming that Hughes had violated the federal and state consumer protection laws by setting back the odometers of used automobiles. The federal statute authorized the entry of a judgment for $1,500 on proof of such tampering, even though there was no proof that actual harm had been sustained. Hughes defended on the ground that (1) the attorney general could not sue without joining the consumers as co-plaintiffs, and (2) no judgment could be entered in favor of any consumer who did not sustain actual loss because of the tampering.

Decision: Judgment against Hughes on both points. The attorney general was authorized by statute to sue without joining the consumers on whose behalf the suit was brought. The applicable statute allowed a minimum recovery of $1,500 for every violation, even though no specific loss was sustained by a consumer. [*Celebrezze v Hughes,* 18 Ohio 3d 71, 479 NE2d 886 (1985)]

When proof of a consumer law violation is made before an agency or commission, proof of guilt is required only by a preponderance of the evidence. The proceeding is not criminal in nature, requiring proof beyond a reasonable doubt, just because the agency could impose a penalty for a violation.[7]

(c) Action by Consumer. Some consumer protection statutes provide that a consumer who is harmed by a violation of the statutes may sue the enterprise that acted improperly.[8] The consumer may sue to recover a specified penalty or may bring an action on behalf of consumers as a class. Consumer protection statutes are often designed to rely on private litigation as an aid to enforcement of the statutory provisions. The Consumer Product Safety Act of 1972 authorizes "any interested person" to bring a civil action to enforce a consumer product safety rule and certain orders of the Consumer Product Safety Commission. In other cases, however, the individual consumer cannot bring any action, and enforcement of the law is entrusted exclusively to an administrative agency. Likewise, a consumer may have lost the right to a statutory remedy by waiver or delay.[9] However, consumer protection statutes are liberally construed to provide consumers with the maximum protection.[10]

In any case, a consumer who shows only that the defendant had broken a contract is not entitled to recover under a fair business practices or deceptive trade

---

[7] *Minnesota v Alpine Air Products, Inc.* (Minn) 500 NW2d 788 (1993).
[8] *Provident American Ins. Co. v Castaneda* (Tex App) 914 SW2d 273 (1996).
[9] *Frey v Vin Devers, Inc.,* ___ Ohio App 3d ___, 608 NE2d 796 (1992).
[10] *Equity Plus Consumer Finance & Mortgage Co. v Howes* (NM) 861 P2d 214 (1993).

practices act. In addition, the plaintiff must show misconduct of the kind prohibited by the statutes.

(d) Replace or Refund. State statutes may require that the goods be replaced or the purchase price refunded if the defects in the goods are not or cannot be repaired within a reasonable time.[11]

(e) Invalidation of Consumer's Contract. Some statutes declare that when the contract made by a consumer violates the statute, the consumer's contract is void. In such a case, the seller cannot sue the consumer-buyer for any unpaid balance. Likewise, the seller cannot repossess the goods for nonpayment. The consumer keeps the goods without making any further payment.[12]

7. Civil and Criminal Penalties

The seller or lender engaging in improper consumer practices may be subject to civil penalties and criminal punishment. In some instances, the laws in question are the general laws applicable to improper conduct, while in other cases the laws are specifically aimed at particular consumer practices. An example of a violation of a general law is a contractor who falsely stated to a homeowner that certain repairs needed on the roof cost, with labor and materials, $650, when in fact they cost only $200. The contractor was guilty of the crime of obtaining money by false pretenses. As an example of a specific consumer protection statute, the Truth in Lending Act subjects the creditor to a separate claim for damages for each periodic statement that violates the disclosure requirements.[13] Furthermore, consumer protection statutes of the disclosure type generally provide that the creditor cannot enforce the obligation of the debtor if the required information is not set forth in the contract.

Civil and criminal liability may be imposed for improper consumer practices.

Some consumer protection statutes authorize the recovery of compensatory damages to compensate the consumer for the loss. Such statutes do not authorize the recovery of punitive damages.[14]

Although consumer protection statutes are interpreted in favor of the consumer, a consumer cannot claim treble damages authorized by such a statute and at the same time recover punitive damages under the common law, as that would give the consumer duplicating remedies for the same wrong.

B. AREAS OF CONSUMER PROTECTION

The following sections discuss the more important areas of consumer protection.

8. Advertising

Consumers are protected from false advertising.

Statutes commonly prohibit fraudulent advertising. Most advertising regulations are entrusted to an administrative agency, such as the Federal Trade Commission

---

[11] *Buford v General Motors Corp.* (NC App) 435 SE2d 782 (1993). Note that apart from these statutes, the buyer may have protection under a warranty to repair or replace. Likewise, a revocation of acceptance under the Uniform Commercial Code would give the right to a refund of the purchase price.
[12] *Glouster Community Bank v Winchell,* ___ Ohio App 3d ___, 659 NE2d 330 (1995).
[13] 15 USC § 1635 (1976).
[14] *Maberry v Said* (DC Kan) 927 F Supp 1456 (1996).

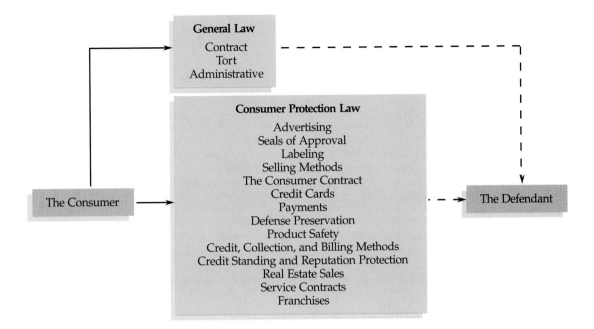

FIGURE 30-1
*The Legal
Environment of
the Consumer*

(FTC). The FTC is authorized to issue orders to stop false or misleading advertising. Statutes prohibiting false advertising are liberally interpreted.

A store is liable for false advertising when it advertises a reduced price sale of a particular item that is out of stock at the time the sale begins. It is no defense that the presale demand was greater than usual.

CASE SUMMARY

Who is the "Public"?

Facts: A Wisconsin statute prohibited sellers from making false and deceptive statements to the public. Automatic Merchandisers advertised its products with truthful statements, but when a salesperson would negotiate with an individual customer, the salesperson would make false statements to that customer. An action was brought by the state of Wisconsin to enjoin the making of the false statements. Automatic defended on the ground that the false statements had not been made to the public but had been made to individual prospective customers.

Decision: Judgment for Wisconsin. The making of the false statements to the individual members of the public who were prospective customers was the making of statements to the public within the scope of the statute. [*Wisconsin v Automatic Merchandisers of America, Inc. 64 Wis 2d 659, 221 NW2d 683 (1974)*]

(a) Deception. Under consumer protection statutes, *deception* rather than *fraud* is the significant element.[15] A breach of these statutes occurs even without proof that the wrongdoer intended to defraud or deceive anyone.

This is a shift in the social point of view. Instead of basing the law in terms of the actor's fault, the law is concerned with the problem of the buyer who is likely

---

15 *Rucker v Huffman* (NC App) 392 SE2d 419 (1990).

to be misled. The good faith of an advertiser or the absence of intent to deceive is immaterial. The purpose of false advertising legislation is to protect the consumer rather than to examine the advertiser's motives.

CASE SUMMARY

Deception Does Not Mean Fraud!

Facts: Miller, the attorney general of Iowa, brought an action to enjoin Hydro Mag from making false claims to advertise its water treatment device. Hydro advertised that the device would produce softer water, sparkling dishes, clean pipes, and better health. There was no scientific evidence to support these statements, but Hydro claimed that no injunction could issue because there was no proof that anyone had relied on its statements or had sustained damage because of them.

Decision: The defense of Hydro was invalid. At common law, reliance and damage were essential elements of fraud liability, but the consumer protection acts do not merely codify or repeat the common law concept of fraud. To make it easier to put a stop to false advertising, such acts provide that false statements may be enjoined merely because they are false. Proof that victims had relied thereon or had sustained harm is not required. [*State ex rel Miller v Hydro Mag (Iowa) 436 NW2d 617 (1989)*]

The FTC requires an advertiser to maintain a file containing the data claimed to support an advertising statement as to safety, performance, efficacy, quality, or comparative price of an advertised product. The FTC can require the advertiser to produce this material. If it is in the interest of the consumer, the FTC can make this information public except to the extent that it contains trade secrets or material that is privileged.

CASE SUMMARY

Appearances Can Be Deceiving

Facts: The Colgate-Palmolive Co. ran a television commercial to show that its shaving cream, Rapid Shave, could soften even the toughness of sandpaper. The commercial showed what was described as the sandpaper test. Actually, what was used was a sheet of Plexiglass on which sand had been sprinkled. The FTC claimed that this was a deceptive practice. The advertiser contended that actual sandpaper would merely look like ordinary colored paper and that Plexiglass had been used to give the viewer an accurate visual representation of the test. Could the FTC prohibit the use of this commercial?

Decision: Yes. The commercial made television viewers believe that they were seeing with their own eyes an actual test, and this would tend to persuade them more than it would if they knew that they were seeing merely an imitation of a test. To that extent, the use of the mockup without disclosing its true character was deceptive. It therefore could be prohibited by the FTC. [*Federal Trade Commission v Colgate-Palmolive Co. 380 US 374 (1965)*]

The FTC may require corrective advertising for false or deceptive statements.

(b) Corrective Advertising. When an enterprise has made false and deceptive statements in advertising, the FTC may require that new advertising be made in which the former statements are contradicted and the truth stated. This corrective advertising required by the FTC is also called retractive advertising.

9. Seals of Approval

Many commodities are sold or advertised with a sticker or tag stating that the article has been approved or is guaranteed by some association or organization. Ordinarily, when a product is sold in this way, it will in fact have been approved by some testing laboratory and will probably have proven adequate to meet ordinary consumer needs. Selling with a seal of approval of a third party makes in effect a guarantee that the product has been approved, and the seller is liable if the product was in fact not approved. In addition, the seller is ordinarily liable for fraud if the statement is not true. ◆ *For example,* the Square Deal Furniture Store sold furniture bearing a tag "Approved by the National Furniture Association." In fact, there was no such association, and the name had been made up by Square Deal, whose deception violated most consumer protection statutes. Square Deal is also liable for common law fraud as well as guilty of the crime of obtaining money by false pretenses. ◆

10. Labeling

Closely related to the regulation of advertising is the regulation of labeling and marking of products. Various federal statutes are designed to give consumers accurate information about a product, while others require warnings about dangers of use or misuse. Consumer protection regulations prohibit labeling or marking products with such terms as *jumbo, giant,* and *full,* which tend to exaggerate and mislead. ◆ *For example,* Eating Well was a health foods store. It sold a number of foods with the label "Fat Free." This label was false, and Eating Well knew that the foods so labeled were ordinary foods not free of fat. Eating Well has violated consumer protection statutes prohibiting false labeling. As for sales made with the false label, it has also committed the tort of fraud and the crime of obtaining money by false pretenses. ◆

The Anticounterfeiting Consumer Protection Act of 1996[16] is designed to protect consumers from counterfeit labels in connection with computer programs and electronic equipment.

11. Selling Methods

Consumer protection statutes prohibit the use of improper and deceptive selling methods.[17] These statutes are liberally construed to protect consumers from improper practices.

(a) Deceptive Practices. Consumer protection statutes and deceptive trade practice acts are violated when the statements or business methods of the defendant are deceptive. It is not necessary to prove that the defendant was guilty of fraud. Hence it is immaterial that the defendant who misrepresented the facts did not intentionally do so. A travel agency commits a deceptive trade practice when it falsely represents that tickets are fully refundable.[18]

---

[16] PL 104-153.

[17] Regarding states adopting the UCCC, see chapter 1, footnote 5. The federal government has expanded the protection of the consumer's food supply by the Nutrition Labeling and Education Act of 1990, Act of November 8, 1990, PL 101-535, 104 Stat 2353, ____ USC § ____; and the Sanitary Food Transportation Act of 1990, Act of November 3, 1990, PL 101-500, 104 Stat 1213, ____ USC § ____. A small number of states have adopted the Uniform Consumer Sales Practices Act, the Uniform Deceptive Trade Practices Act, and the Model Land Sales Practices Act.

[18] *Pellegrini v Landmark Travel Group,* 628 NYS2d 1003 (1995).

(b) Disclosure of Transaction Terms. Federal law requires the disclosure of all interest charges, points or fees for granting loans, and similar charges. These charges must be set forth as an annual percentage rate (APR) so that the consumer can see just how much the transaction costs a year and can compare alternatives.[19] The obligation of disclosure has been further extended by the Fair Credit and Charge Card Disclosure Act of 1988[20] and by the Home Equity Loan Consumer Protection Act of November 23, 1988.[21]

If sellers advertise that they will sell or lease on credit, they cannot state merely the monthly installments that will be due. They must give the consumer additional information: (1) the total cash price; (2) the amount of the down payment required; (3) the number, amounts, and due dates of payments; and (4) the annual percentage rate of the credit charges.[22]

In various ways, consumer protection statutes seek to protect the consumer from surprise or unbargained-for terms and from unwanted contracts. Under consumer protection statutes, it is commonly a deceptive trade practice to fail to disclose to a consumer information that would have prevented the consumer from entering into the transaction if the disclosure had been made. Consumers' savings are protected under the federal Truth in Savings Act.[23]

Federal law requires disclosure when payment is made in more than four installments.

(1) More-Than-Four-Installments Rule. Whenever a consumer sale or contract provides for payment in more than four installments, it is subject to the Truth in Lending Act. This is so even though no service or finance charge is expressly added because of the installment pattern of paying.

When consumer credit is advertised as repayable in more than four installments and no finance charge is expressly imposed, the advertisement must "clearly and conspicuously" state that "the cost of credit is included in the price" quoted for the goods and services.

CASE SUMMARY

No Sneaking around the Rule

Facts: Acting under the Truth in Lending Act, the Federal Reserve Board adopted Regulation Z. Among other things, this regulation declared that whenever a consumer paid the price for goods purchased on credit in more than four installments, the person offering the credit was subject to the Truth in Lending Act. The Family Publications Service sold a magazine to Leila Mourning but failed to disclose the information required by the act, although payment was to be made by her in 30 monthly installments. Family Publications claimed that the four-month rule of Regulation Z was invalid and that the federal Truth in Lending Act could not apply to it because it did not make any extra charge for the making of installment payments.

Decision: The regulation applied to the sale and was valid in so doing. This application of the regulation was necessary to prevent evasion of the statute's disclosure provisions. If it were not applied in this way, a seller could conceal the items of which disclosure was required by increasing the price. The seller could then permit the buyer to pay in installments on a price to which apparently no charges were added. [*Mourning v Family Publications Service, Inc.* 411 US 356 (1973)]

---

[19] Consumer Credit Protection Act (CCPA), 15 USC §§ 1605, 1606, 1636; Regulation Z adopted by the Federal Reserve Board of Governors, § 226.5.
[20] Act of November 3, 1988, PL 100-583, 102 Stat 2960, 15 USC §§ 1601 note, et seq.
[21] Act of November 23, 1988, PL 100-709, 102 Stat 4729, 15 USC §§ 1601 note, et seq.
[22] Regulation Z, § 1210; Consumer Leasing Act of 1976, 15 USC § 1667.
[23] 12 USC §§ 4301-13; Regulation DD, 12 CFR §§ 230.1-.9.

(2) Contract on Two Sides. To be sure that consumers see disclosures required by federal law, special provision is made when the terms of a transaction are printed on both the front and the back of a sheet or contract. In this case, (1) both sides of the sheet must carry the warning "NOTICE: see other side for important information," and (2) the page must be signed at the end of the second side. Conversely, the requirements of federal law are not satisfied if there is no warning of "see other side" and the parties sign the contract only on the face, or the first side, of the paper.

(3) Particular Sales and Leases. The Motor Vehicle Information and Cost Savings Act requires a dealer to disclose to the buyer various elements in the cost of an automobile. The act prohibits selling an automobile without informing the buyer that the odometer has been reset below the true mileage. A buyer who is caused actual loss by odometer fraud may recover from the seller three times the actual loss or $1,500, whichever is greater.[24] The federal statute is breached when the seller knows that the odometer has turned itself at 100,000 miles but the seller states that the mileage is 20,073 miles instead of 120,073. The Consumer Leasing Act of 1976 requires that persons leasing automobiles and other durable goods make a full disclosure to consumers of the details of a transaction.

Although the federal statute imposes liability only when the seller "knowingly" violates the statute, it is not necessary to prove actual knowledge. An experienced auto dealer cannot claim lack of knowledge that the odometer was false when that conclusion was reasonably apparent from the condition of the car.[25]

(c) Home-Solicited Sales. A sale of goods or services for $25 or more made to a buyer at home may be set aside within three business days. This right may be exercised merely because the buyer does not want to go through with the contract. There is no requirement of proving any misconduct of the seller or any defect in the goods or services.[26]

When the buyer has made an oral agreement to purchase and the seller comes to the buyer's home to work out the details, the transaction is not a home-solicited sale and cannot be avoided under the federal regulation.[27]

A sale is not "home solicited" when the seller phoned the consumer at her home for permission to mail her a promotional brochure and she thereafter went to the seller's place of business where the contract was made.[28]

(d) Referral Sales. The technique of giving the buyer a price reduction for customers referred to the seller is theoretically lawful. In effect it is merely paying the buyer a commission for the promotion of other sales. In actual practice, however, the referral sales technique is often accompanied by fraud or exorbitant pricing, so that consumer protection laws variously condemn referral selling. As a result, the referral system of selling has been condemned as unconscionable under the UCC and is expressly prohibited by the UCCC.

24 Act of October 20, 1972, §§ 403, 409, PL 92-513, 86 Stat 947, 15 USC §§ 1901 et seq., as amended; recodified as 49 USC §§ 32701-32711.
25 *Denmon v Nicks Auto Sales* (La App) 537 So 2d 796 (1989).
26 Federal Trade Commission Regulation, 16 CFR § 429.1.
27 *Cooper v Crow* (La App) 574 So 2d 438 (1991).
28 *United Consumers Club v Griffin,* ___ Ohio App 3d ___, 619 NE2d 489 (1993).

(e) Telemarketing Fraud. In recent years, high-pressure selling by telephone has produced a new kind of fraud that is estimated to rob Americans of some $40 billion a year. A regulation of the FTC effective January 1, 1996, is designed to stop such fraud by requiring telemarketers to state truthfully what they are selling and prohibiting access to bank accounts without authorization.[29] Telemarketers are also subject to substantial fines if they continue to call persons who have asked not to be called and are prohibited from calling before 8 A.M. or after 9 P.M. Some states require sellers who solicit orders by telephone to register with a particular government agency.[30]

12. The Consumer Contract

Consumer contracts are affected by consumer protection legislation in several ways.

Consumer protection laws may specify the form of a contract.

(a) Form of Contract. Consumer protection laws commonly regulate the form of the contract, requiring that certain items be specifically listed, that payments under the contract be itemized, and that the allocation to such items as principal, interest, and insurance be indicated. Generally, certain portions of the contract or all of the contract must be printed in type of a certain size, and a copy must be furnished to the buyer. Such statutory requirements are more demanding than the statute of frauds section of the UCC. It is frequently provided that the copy furnished the consumer must be completely filled in. Back-page disclaimers are void if the front page of the contract does not call attention to the presence of such terms.

Consumer protectionism may condemn terms that are too harsh or abusive.

(b) Contract Terms. Consumer protection legislation does not ordinarily affect the right of the parties to make a contract on whatever terms they choose. It is customary, however, to prohibit the use of certain clauses that are believed to bear too harshly on the debtor or that have too great a potential for exploitive abuse by a creditor. For example, the UCCC prohibits provisions permitting a creditor to enter a judgment against a debtor without giving the debtor any chance to make a defense.[31]

The federal Warranty Disclosure Act of 1974 establishes disclosure standards for consumer goods warranties to help consumers understand them.[32]

The parties to a credit transaction may agree that payment should be made in installments but that if there is a default on any installment, the creditor may declare the entire balance due at once. This cancels or destroys the schedule for payments by making the entire balance due immediately. Such acceleration of the debt can cause the debtor great hardship. Because of this, some statutes limit or prohibit the use of acceleration clauses.

A protective ceiling may be placed on the credit of consumers.

(c) Limitation of Credit. Various laws may limit the ability to borrow money or purchase on credit. Some states prohibit **open-end mortgages**, by which the mortgage secures a specified debt and additional loans that may be made later. Consumer protection is also afforded in some states by placing a time limit on smaller loans.

---

[29] CFR § 3100.
[30] *Distributel, Inc. v Alaska* (Alaska) 933 P2d 1137 (1997).
[31] UCCC §§ 2.415, 3.407.
[32] Act of January 4, 1975, PL 93-637, 88 Stat 2183, 15 USC § 2301.

An FTC regulation declares it an unfair trade practice to require a consumer borrowing or buying on credit to give the lender or seller a security interest in all of the consumer's household goods as collateral.[33]

(d) Unconscionability. To some extent, consumer protection has been provided under the UCC by those courts that hold that the "unconscionability" provision protects from "excessive" or "exorbitant" prices when goods are sold on credit.[34]

Some statutes are aimed at preventing price gouging on goods or services for which the demand is abnormally greater than the supply. The New York statute provides: "During any abnormal disruption of the market for consumer goods and services vital and necessary for the health, safety, and welfare of consumers, resulting from stress of weather, convulsion of nature, failure or shortage of electric power or other source of energy . . . no merchant shall sell or offer to sell any such consumer goods or services for an amount which represents an unconscionably excessive price." Consumer goods and services are defined as "those used, bought, or rendered primarily for personal, family, or household purposes." Such a statute protects, for example, purchasers of electric generators for home use during a hurricane-caused blackout.

13. Credit Cards

Regulation of the distribution and use of credit cards protects consumers.

Credit cards permit cardholders to buy on the credit or reputation of card issuers.

(a) Unsolicited Credit Cards. The unsolicited distribution of credit cards to persons who have not applied for them is prohibited.

CASE SUMMARY

The Forged Credit Card Application

Facts: The First National Bank sued Ordoyne on an overdue credit card account. He proved that his wife had obtained the card by forging his name to the application and that he had not approved the issuance or the use of the credit card. He therefore denied liability.

Decision: Judgment for Ordoyne. No liability arises in connection with a credit card unless it is a valid contract between the cardholder and the issuer. Since Ordoyne had not signed or approved the application in any way, he was not bound by any contract and therefore could not be held liable for purchases made using the card. [First National Bank of Commerce v Ordoyne (La App) 528 So 2d 1068 (1988)]

(b) Surcharge Prohibited. Under some statutes, a seller cannot add any charge to the purchase price because the buyer uses a credit card instead of paying with cash or a check.[35]

---

[33] 16 CFR § 444.2(4) (1988).
[34] UCC § 2-302(1).
[35] In contrast, the Truth in Lending Act Amendment of 1976, 15 USC § 1666f, permits a merchant to offer a discount to cash-paying customers but not customers using a credit card.

(c) Unauthorized Use. A cardholder is not liable for more than $50 for the unauthorized use of a credit card. To impose liability up to that amount, the issuer must show that (1) the credit card was an accepted card;[36] (2) the issuer had given the holder adequate notice of possible liability in such case; (3) the issuer had furnished the holder with a self-addressed, prestamped notification form to be mailed by the holder in the event of the loss or theft of the credit card; (4) the issuer had provided a method by which the user of the card could be identified as the person authorized to use it;[37] and (5) unauthorized use of the card had occurred or might occur as a result of loss, theft, or some other event.

The burden of proof is on the card issuer to show that the use of the card was authorized or that the holder is liable for its authorized use.[38]

(d) Unauthorized Purpose Distinguished. There is an unauthorized use of a credit card only when it is used without the permission or approval of the cardholder. In contrast, the holder may authorize another person to use the card but only for a particular purpose, such as to buy a certain item. If the person uses the card for other than the purpose specified by the holder, this is still an authorized use of the card even though it is for an unauthorized purpose.[39] In such a case, the cardholder is liable for all charges made on the card even though they were not intended by the cardholder when the card was loaned. The same rule is applied when an employer has cards issued to employees for making employment-related purchases but an employee uses the card for personal purposes.

(e) Late Payment Fee. The contract between a bank issuing a credit card and a holder may require the holder to pay a late payment fee computed as the rate of interest allowed by the law of the state where the bank is located. The federal Banking Deregulation Act of 1980 cancels out any state consumer protection law that prohibits such a charge.[40]

14. Payments

Consumer legislation may provide that when a consumer makes a payment on an open charge account, the payment must be applied toward payment of the earliest charges. The result is that, should there be a default at a later date, any right of repossession of the creditor is limited to the later, unpaid items. This outlaws a contract provision by which, on the default of the buyer, the seller could repossess all purchases that had been made at any prior time. Such a provision is outlawed by the UCCC and probably would be found unconscionable under the UCC. ◆ *For example*, over the years, Jilda purchased many household articles from the Montparnasse Department Store that were placed on her charge account. Whenever Jilda made a payment on her account, Montparnasse would apply a fraction of it to each item Jilda had purchased so that no item was ever paid for in

---

[36] A credit card is accepted when the cardholder has requested and received or has signed or has used, or authorized another to use, for the purpose of obtaining money, property, labor, or services on credit. CCPA § 103(1).
[37] Regulation Z of the Board of Governors of the Federal Reserve, § 226.13(d), as amended, provides that the identification may be by signature, photograph, or fingerprint on the credit card or by electronic or mechanical confirmation.
[38] *Band v First Bankcard Center* (La App) 644 So 2d 211 (1994).
[39] *American Express Travel Related Services Co. v Web, Inc.* ___ Ga ___, 405 SE2d 652 (1991).
[40] *Stoorman v Greenwood Trust Co.* (Colo) 908 P2d 133 (1995).

full. Montparnasse claimed that it could do this because a creditor can decide how to apply payments when a debtor does not make any specification. Under the ordinary contract law rule, Montparnasse is correct, but consumer protection statutes in many states require the creditor to apply a payment to the oldest debt so that the oldest debts are paid off in full and only the most recent remain unpaid. This means that Montparnasse would have no claim on Jilda's earlier purchases even though Jilda had not paid in full for the more recent ones. ◆

15. Preservation of Consumer Defenses

Consumer protection laws generally prohibit a consumer from waiving or giving up any defense provided by law.

Consumers are protected by preservation of their defenses—as by FTC regulation.

CASE SUMMARY

An Assignee Cannot Duck the Consumer Protection Statute

Facts: Donnelly purchased a television set on credit from D.W.N. Advertising, Inc. He also contracted for service on the set. D.W.N. assigned the sales contract to the Fairfield Credit Corporation, D.W.N. went out of existence, and the service contract was never performed. Fairfield sued Donnelly for the balance due on the purchase price. Donnelly raised the defense that the service contract had never been performed. Fairfield claimed that this defense could not be asserted against it because the sales contract contained a waiver of defenses.

Decision: The assignee (Fairfield) was subject to the defenses that the obligor-consumer could have asserted against the assignor-seller. The waiver of defenses would not be given effect because it was contrary to public policy to permit an assignee to recover from a consumer when the assignor would not be able to do so. Donnelly therefore could assert his defenses against Fairfield Credit Corporation. [*Fairfield Credit Corp. v Donnelly,* 158 Conn 543, 264 A2d 547 (1969)]

In the ordinary contract situation when goods or services purchased or leased by a consumer are not proper or are defective, the consumer is not required to pay the seller or lessor or is only required to pay a reduced amount. With the modern expansion of credit transactions, sellers and lessors have used several techniques for getting paid without regard to whether the consumer had any complaint against them. To prevent this, the FTC has adopted a regulation requiring that, in every sale or lease of goods or services to a consumer, the contract contain a clause giving the consumer the right to assert defenses. These defenses may be asserted not only against the seller or lessor but also against a third person, such as a bank or finance company, to which the seller or lessor transfers the collection rights. The FTC regulation requires the following notice to be included in boldface type at least ten points in size:

> *NOTICE*
> *Any holder of this consumer credit contract is subject to all claims and defenses which the debtor could assert against the seller of goods or services obtained pursuant hereto or with the proceeds hereof. Recovery hereunder by the debtor shall not exceed amounts paid by the debtor hereunder.*

16. Product Safety

Laws protect from dangerous products that may cause injury or create health hazards.

The health and well-being of consumers are protected by a variety of statutes and rules of law, some of which antedate the modern consumer protection era.

Most states have laws governing the manufacture of various products and establishing product safety standards. The federal Consumer Product Safety Act provides for research and the setting of uniform standards for products in order to reduce health hazards. This act also establishes civil and criminal penalties for the distribution of unsafe products, recognizes the right of an aggrieved person to sue for money damages and to obtain an injunction against the distribution of unsafe products, and creates a Consumer Product Safety Commission to administer the act.[41]

A consumer, as well as various nonconsumers, may hold a seller or manufacturer liable for damages when a product causes harm. Liability may be based on guarantees, warranties, negligence, fraud, or strict tort liability.

The federal Anti-Tampering Act makes it a federal crime to tamper with consumer products.[42]

17. Credit, Collection, and Billing Methods

Various provisions have been made to protect consumers from discriminatory and improper credit and collection practices.

Credit discrimination is prohibited.

(a) Credit Discrimination. It is unlawful to discriminate against an applicant for credit on the basis of race, color, religion, national origin, sex, marital status, or age; because all or part of the applicant's income is obtained from a public assistance program; or because the applicant has in good faith exercised any right under the Consumer Credit Protection Act (CCPA). When a credit application is refused, the applicant must be furnished with a written explanation. *For example,* when Eloise applied for a loan from Tradesman Bank, she was told on the phone that the loan would not be made to her unless her husband, Robert, signed as cosigner. The bank violated antidiscrimination law in two respects: (1) The bank was required to give Eloise a written explanation of why it would not make the loan to her, and (2) it is unlawful to refuse to make a loan to a woman merely because she is married and her husband is not a cosigner.

Correction of billing errors is required.

(b) Correction of Errors. When a consumer believes that a billing error has been made by a credit card issuer, the consumer should send the creditor a written statement and explanation of the error. The creditor or card issuer must investigate and make a prompt written reply to the consumer.[43]

Improper collection methods are prohibited, with special regulation of collection agencies.

(c) Improper Collection Methods. Unreasonable methods of debt collection are often expressly prohibited by statute or are held by courts to constitute an unreasonable invasion of privacy.[44] Statutes generally prohibit sending bills in such a form that they give the impression that a lawsuit has been begun against the

---

[41] Act of October 27, 1972, PL 92-573, 86 Stat 1207, 15 USC §§ 2051-2081; as amended by the Consumer Product Safety Improvements Act of 1990, Act of November 16, 1990, PL 101-608, 104 Stat 3110, ____ USC § ____.

[42] Act of October 13, 1983, PL 98-127, 97 Stat 831, 13 USC § 1365.

[43] Fair Credit Billing Act, Act of October 18, 1974, PL 93-495, 15 USC § 1601.

[44] Fair Debt Collection Practices Act, Act of September 20, 1977, PL 95-109, 91 Stat 874, 15 USC §§ 1692 et seq.; Federal Trade Commission Regulation, 16 CFR part 237.

consumer and that the bill is legal process or a warrant issued by the court. The CCPA prohibits the use of extortionate methods of loan collection. A creditor may be prohibited from informing a debtor's employer that the employee owes money.

A creditor is liable for unreasonably attempting to collect a bill that in fact has been paid. This liability can arise under general principles of tort law as distinguished from special consumer protection legislation.

(1) Fault of Agent or Employee. When improper collection methods are used, it is no defense to the creditor that the improper acts were performed by an agent, an employee, or any other person acting on behalf of the creditor.

(2) Fair Debt Collection Practices Act (FDCPA). The FDCPA prohibits improper practices in the collection of debts incurred primarily for personal, family, or household purposes.[45]

(i) Collection Letters. The Act requires that the notice to a debtor state that the debtor has 30 days in which to dispute all or part of the debt.[46]

A debt collector that sends a form letter to debtors that uses the letterhead and the facsimile signature of a lawyer who is not actually representing the collector violates the FDCPA.[47] A letter from a collection agency to a consumer that gives the impression a lawsuit is about to be brought against the consumer when in fact it is not true is a violation of the Fair Debt Collection Practices Act.[48]

A debt collection letter sent to the debtor's place of employment was found to be a violation of the FDCPA when the words "final demand for payment" could be read through the envelope. The fact that it was likely that the debtor would be embarrassed by the delivery of such a letter to the employer's address affected the outcome of the case. In another case, a bank's threat to prosecute depositors if they did not return money that had been paid to them by mistake violated a state debt collection law. No criminal statute prohibited the depositors' conduct.

(ii) What Is Not a Defense. When a collection agency violates the FDCPA, it is liable to the debtor for damages. It is no defense that the debtor owed the money that the agency was seeking to collect. When a creditor uses improper collection methods, it is no defense that the improper acts were performed by an agency, employee, or any other person acting on behalf of the creditor.

(iii) Applicability of Fair Debt Collection Practices Act. The FDCPA applies to lawyers who regularly engage in debt collection whether by means of litigation or not.[49]

CASE SUMMARY

Who is a Debt Collector?

Facts: A consumer made a purchase on a credit card. The card issuer refused to accept the charge and an attorney then sued the consumer for the amount due. In the complaint filed in the lawsuit, the attorney wrongly stated that interest was owed at 18 percent per annum. This was later corrected by an amendment of the complaint to five percent. The case against the consumer was ultimately settled but the consumer then sued the attorney for penalties under the Fair Debt Collection Practices Act claiming that the overstating of the interest due in the

---

45 *Bloom v I.C. System, Inc.* (CA9 Or) 972 F2d 1067 (1992).
46 *Avila v Rubin* (CA7 Ill) 84 F3d 222 (1996).
47 *Taylor v Perrin, Landry, duLauney & Durand* (CA5 La) 103 1232 (1996).
48 *Bentley v Great Lakes Collection Bureau* (CA2 Conn) 6 F3d 60 (1993).
49 *Jenkins v Heintz* (CA7 ___) 25 F3d 536 (1994), aff'd 115 S Ct 1489 (1995).

original complaint was a violation of that Act. The attorney defended on the ground that the Act did not apply.

Decision: Judgment for the attorney. The attorney was not acting as a debt collector but was merely performing normal legal work. The federal statute therefore did not apply to the overstatement of the interest that had been made in the original complaint. *[Green v Hocking (CA6 Mich) 9 F3d 18 (1993)]*

When a collection agency violates the FDCPA, it is liable to the debtor for damages. It is no defense that the debtor in fact owed the money that the agency was seeking to collect.

The FDCPA applies only to those who regularly engage in the business of collecting debts for others—primarily to collection agencies. The act does not apply when a bank attempts to collect debts owed to it by directly contacting the debtors.

(iv) Federal Preemption. In a conflict between collection practices under federal law and a state consumer protection statute, federal law preempts or displaces state law.[50]

(d) Consumer Leases. In some states, the lease of goods to a consumer is treated as a consumer credit sale and is given the same statutory protection as transactions in which the consumer has the option to purchase at the end of the lease or becomes the owner after renting for a specified period of time.[51]

18. Protection of Credit Standing and Reputation

In many instances, one party to a transaction wishes to know certain things about the other party. This situation arises when a person purchases on credit or applies for a loan, a job, or an insurance policy. Between 2,000 and 3,000 private credit bureaus gather such information on borrowers, buyers, and applicants and sell the information to interested persons.

Credit standing and reputation are protected by the FCRA.

The Fair Credit Reporting Act (FCRA)[52] seeks to protect consumers from various abuses that may arise.

CASE SUMMARY

Be Careful with the Credit Standing of Others

Facts: The Credit Bureau of Huntington wrongly reported the entry of a judgment, apparently because an employee with inadequate training had been assigned to the task of entering information. Jones sued Huntington for damages caused him by the erroneous report of the judgment. The jury found in his favor and assessed damages at $4,000. Huntington claimed that this was improper because there was no proof that Jones had suffered that amount of damage because of the wrong information.

Decision: Verdict affirmed. It is not necessary that the exact amount of loss be proven. Moreover, humiliation and mental distress are elements for which a recovery may be obtained. The amount of $4,000 was not an unreasonable amount to compensate for all these elements. *[Jones v Credit Bureau of Huntington, Inc. (W Va App) 399 SE2d 694 (1990)]*

---

[50] *Fischer v Unipac Service Corp.* (Iowa) 519 NW2d 793 (1994).
[51] *Muller v Colortyme, Inc.* (Minn) 518 NW2d 544 (1994); *Rent-A-Center, Inc. v Hall* (Wis App) 510 NW2d 789 (1993), reh'g denied, 515 NW2d 715 (Wis 1994).
[52] Act of October 26, 1970, PL 91-508, 84 Stat 1128, 15 USC §§ 1681 et seq.

The FCRA applies only to **consumer credit**, which is defined as credit for "personal, family, and household" use; it does not apply to business or commercial transactions. The act does not apply to the investigation report made by an insurance company of a policy claim.

(a) Privacy. A report on a person based on personal investigation and interviews is called an **investigative consumer report**. It may not be made without informing the person investigated of the right to discover the results of the investigation. Bureaus are not permitted to disclose information to persons not having a legitimate use for it. It is a federal crime to obtain or to furnish a bureau report for an improper purpose.

On request, a bureau must tell a consumer the names and addresses of persons to whom it has made a credit report during the previous six months. It must also tell, when requested, which employers were given such a report during the previous two years.

A store may not publicly display a list of named customers from whom it will not accept checks; such action is an invasion of the privacy of those persons.

(b) Protection from False Information. Much of the information obtained by credit bureaus is based on statements made by persons, such as neighbors, when interviewed by the bureau's investigator. Sometimes the statements are incorrect. Quite often they are hearsay evidence and would not be admissible in a legal proceeding. Nevertheless, such statements may go on the records of a bureau without further verification and be furnished to a client of the bureau, who will tend to regard them as accurate and true.

A person has a limited right to request that a credit bureau disclose the nature and substance of the information it possesses. The right to know, however, does not extend to medical information. The bureau is not required to identify the persons giving information to its investigators, nor is it required to give the applicant a copy of, or to permit the applicant to see, any file.

When a person claims that the bureau's information is erroneous, the bureau must take steps within a reasonable time to determine the accuracy of the disputed item.

Adverse information obtained by investigation cannot be given to a client after three months unless verified to determine that it is still valid. Most legal proceedings cannot be reported by a bureau after seven years, but a bankruptcy proceeding cannot be reported after ten years.

CASE SUMMARY

No Careless Information Allowed

Facts: The San Antonio Retail Merchants Association (SARMA) was a credit reporting agency. It was asked by one of its members to furnish information on William Douglas Thompson III. It supplied information from a file that contained data on William III and also on William Daniel Thompson, Jr. The agency had incorporated information related to William, Jr. into the file relating to William III, so that all information appeared to relate to William III. This was a negligent mistake because each William had a different social security number, and this should have raised a suspicion that there was a mistake. In addition, SARMA should have used a number of checkpoints to ensure that incoming information would be put into the proper file. William, Jr. had a bad credit standing. Because of its mistake, SARMA gave a bad report on William III, who was denied credit by several enterprises. The federal Fair Credit Reporting Act makes a credit reporting agency liable to any consumer about whom it furnishes a consumer report without following reasonable procedures to assure maximum possible accuracy of information. William III sued SARMA for its negligence in confusing him with William, Jr.

Decision: Judgment for William III. The failure to search for an explanation of the two social security numbers and the failure to establish better filing procedures constituted negligence. This established that the agency had not followed reasonable procedures designed to ensure accuracy of information. Therefore it was liable under the federal statute for the damages sustained by William III. *[Thompson v San Antonio Retail Merchants Ass'n. (CA5 Tex) 682 F2d 509 (1982)]*

Under general principles of agency law, a creditor hiring an individual or an agency to collect a debt is liable to the debtor for damages for unlawful conduct by the collector. It is no defense that the creditor did not intend, or have any knowledge of, this conduct.

19. Protection from Discrimination

Federal law and state laws prohibit improper discrimination against consumers. In addition, a joint policy statement issued by a number of federal agencies and boards prohibits discrimination in consumer lending.[53]

20. Physical Protection of Consumers

Consumers who are natural persons are protected from harm to the same extent as any other natural person. If the consumer is the buyer of goods, the consumer is protected by the various theories of product liability. If the consumer buys or leases an apartment or a building, the consumer will generally be protected by a warranty of habitability and by principles of real property law. A consumer on the premises of a business enterprise will generally have the same protection afforded any other invitee under real property law. However, when using an automated teller machine, a consumer will normally have no protection from physical harm. The provider of the machine is not required to warn consumers of the danger of a criminal attack while using the machine or provide any alarm or security system for protecting users.[54]

For example, High Plains National Bank had automated tellers in many stores throughout the city. Xenia had an account with the bank, and while drawing money from one of the automated tellers one day, she did not notice that a man was watching her. As she left the store, the man assaulted her and stole her money. High Plains is not liable to Xenia for her money lost or for the assault.

21. Expansion of Consumer Protection

Various laws aimed at preventing fraudulent sales of corporate securities, commonly called **blue sky laws**, have been adopted by most states. Other statutes have been adopted to protect purchasers of real estate, buyers of services, and prospective franchisees.

---

[53] Policy statement on discrimination in lending of March 8, 1994, 59 CFR § 18, 266 (1994).
[54] Act of August 1, 1968, as amended, PL 90-448, 82 Stat 590, 15 USC §§ 1701-1720.

Disclosure is required in reals estate development sales.

(a) Real Estate Development Sales. Anyone promoting the sale of a real estate development that is divided into 50 or more parcels of less than five acres each must file with the secretary of Housing and Urban Development (HUD) a **development statement**. This statement must set forth significant details of the development as required by the federal Land Sales Act.[55]

Anyone buying or renting one of the parcels in the subdivision must be given a **property report**, which is a condensed version of the development statement filed with the secretary of HUD. This report must be given to the prospective customer more than 48 hours before the signing of the contract to buy or lease.

If the development statement is not filed with the secretary, the sale or rental of the real estate development may not be promoted through the channels of interstate commerce or by the use of the mail.

If the property report is given to the prospective buyer or tenant less than 48 hours before the signing of a contract to buy or lease, or after it has been signed, the contract may be avoided within 48 hours. If the property report is never received, the contract may be avoided, and there is no statutory limitation on the time in which this may be done.

The federal statute prohibits imposing or receiving unauthorized payments in connection with a real estate settlement.

State statutes frequently require that particular enterprises selling property tell or disclose certain information to prospective buyers.

(b) Service Contracts. The UCCC treats a consumer service contract the same as a consumer sale of goods if (1) payment is made in installments or a credit charge is made and (2) the amount financed does not exceed $25,000. It defines services broadly as embracing work, specified privileges, and insurance provided by a noninsurer. The inclusion of privileges makes the UCCC apply to contracts calling for payment on the installment plan or including a financing charge for transportation, hotel and restaurant accommodations, education, entertainment, recreation, physical culture (such as athletic clubs or bodybuilding schools), hospital accommodations, funerals, and cemetery accommodations.

In some states, it is unlawful for a repair shop to make unauthorized repairs to an automobile and then refuse to return the automobile to the customer until paid for the repairs. In some states, a consumer protection statute imposes multiple damages on a repair shop that delays unreasonably in performing a contract to repair property of the consumer.[56]

Disclosure to a prospective franchisee is required.

(c) Franchises. A franchisee is a consumer entitled to sue the franchisor for violation of a state deceptive practices act. To protect a prospective franchisee from deception, an FTC regulation requires that the franchisor give a prospective franchisee a disclosure statement 10 days before the franchisee signs a contract or pays any money for a franchise. The disclosure statement provides detailed information relating to the franchisor's finances, experience, size of operation, and involvement in litigation. The statement must set forth any restrictions imposed on the franchisee; any costs that must be paid initially or in the future; and the provisions for termination, cancellation, and renewal of the franchise. False statements regarding

[55] *Popp v Cash Station, Inc.,* ___ Ill App 3d ___, ___ Ill Dec ___, 613 NE2d 1150 (1992).
[56] *Crye v Smolak*, 110 Ohio App 3d 504, 674 NE2d 779 (1996).

sales, income, or profits are prohibited. Violators of the regulation are subject to a fine of $10,000.

(d) Automobile Lemon Laws. All of the states have adopted special laws for the protection of consumers buying automobiles that develop numerous defects or defects that cannot be corrected. These statutes protect only persons buying for personal, family, or household use. They generally classify an automobile as a lemon if it cannot be put in proper or warranted condition within a specified period of time or after a specified number of repair attempts. In general, they give the buyer greater protection than is given to other buyers by the Uniform Commercial Code or the other consumer protection statutes. In some states, the seller of a lemon car is required to give the buyer a brand new replacement car. In some states, a government official may also bring an action to collect civil penalties from the seller of a lemon car.

Lemon laws in most states are designed to increase the prelitigation bargaining power of consumers and reduce the greater power of manufacturers to resist complaints or suits by consumers.[57]

For example, Abdul, who owned a paint store, purchased two automobiles from Prime Motors, one for delivering paint to his customers and the second for his wife to use for shopping and taking their children to school. Both cars were defective and in need of constant repair. Abdul claimed that he was entitled to remedies provided by the local automobile lemon law. He is wrong with respect to the store's delivery car, as lemon laws do not cover cars purchased for commercial use, but he is protected by the lemon law for the other car, as it was clearly a family car.

ETHICS & THE LAW The mail-order business is a large part of the retail industry. This segment of retail sales has grown so significantly that state attorneys general have litigated to be able to charge some sales tax within their states despite a mail-order company's out-of-state location and a minimal catalog mailing to in-state residents. With more companies, more catalogs, and more customers, consumer protection issues are increasing.

Currently, the FTC regulates catalog forms and disclosures about merchandise availability and costs. As with the evolving credit laws, however, some areas are not regulated and do present costly problems for consumers. For example, a Talbot's catalog listed the shipment cost for a pair of $12.00 ragg trouser socks as $5.50, or 45.8 percent of the purchase price. If a shopper wanted to send those socks to a daughter at college and thus at a different address than the catalog shopper's, there is an additional $3.00 charge for a "shipped to" address. Then the customer would pay shipping costs of 70.8 percent of the purchase price.

Further, shipping and handling costs are not related to item weights or sizes; they are related to total order amount. And the shipping and handling costs decrease as a percentage of total price the more one buys. The following chart is from a Talbot's catalog:

[57] *Hughes v Chrysler Motors Corp.* (Wis App) 523 NW2d 197 (1994).

Shipping and handling

Total merchandise (exclude tax)	Add	Shipping and Handling %
$20.00 and under	$5.50	27.5%
$20.01 to $30.00	$6.50	22–32.5%
$30.01 to $50.00	$7.50	15–25%
$50.01 to $100.00	$8.50	8.5–17%
$100.01 to $150.00	$9.50	6.3–9.5%
$150.01 to $200.00	$10.50	5.25–7%
$200.01 and over	$11.50	5.7% and less

Please add $3.00 for each additional shipping address.

Some companies, such as L.L. Bean, base their shipping and handling charges on actual weight, and each item in the catalog carries the weight of the item beside the price.

What do you think the basis for catalog shipping and handling charges is? Is it to encourage customers to order more? Do you think companies have determined the most common price ranges for orders and charged the most in those ranges? Do you think this area will be a new focus for consumer protection?

SUMMARY

With the modern era of consumer protection, society has accepted the premise that equality before the law is not appropriate to the marketplace, where modern methods of marketing, packaging, and financing have reduced the ordinary consumer to a subordinate position. To protect the consumer from the hardship, fraud, and oppression that could result from being in such an inferior position, the law has, at many points, limited the freedom of action of the enterprise with which the consumer deals.

Consumer protection laws are directed at false and misleading advertising; misleading or false use of seals of approval and labels; and the methods of selling, requiring the disclosure of terms, permitting consumer cancellation of home-solicited sales, and, in some states, prohibiting referral sales. The consumer is protected in a contract agreement by regulation of its form, prohibition of unconscionable terms, and limitation of the credit that can be extended to a consumer. Credit card protections include prohibition of the unauthorized distribution of credit cards and limited liability of the cardholder for the unauthorized use of a credit card. Included in consumer protection laws are the application of payments; the preservation of consumer defenses as against a transferee of the consumer's contract; product safety; the protection of credit standing and reputation; and (to some extent) real estate development sales, franchises, and service contracts. Lemon laws provide special protection to buyers of automobiles for personal, household, or family use.

When a consumer protection statute is violated, an action may sometimes be brought by the consumer against the wrongdoer. More commonly, an action is brought by an administrative agency or by the state attorney general.

QUESTIONS AND CASE PROBLEMS

1. What is the object of each of the following rules of law? (a) Back-page disclaimers are void if the front page of the contract does not call attention to the presence of such terms. (b) A consumer's waiver of a statute designed for consumer protection is void, but the transaction otherwise binds the consumer.

2. Cora telephoned from her home to Nowlin Music Supply Co. and ordered an electric guitar. The Nowlin employee answering the phone stated that Cora's order was accepted and that the guitar would be sent to her within a few days. That night Cora saw an ad in the newspaper for the same guitar for $100 less than the Nowlin price. She wrote and mailed a letter the next day to Nowlin, stating that she canceled her order. May she do so?

3. Ward purchased an ice-making machine from Kold-Serve Corp. The machine had been sold by Kold-Serve to another buyer but was returned to Kold-Serve. The

president of Kold-Serve sold this machine as a "demonstrator model," but he did not inform Ward of its prior sale and return. Later Ward sued Kold-Serve, claiming that it had "knowingly" committed an unfair trade practice in selling the machine to him. Was Ward correct? [*Kold-Serve Corp. v Ward* (Tex App) 736 SW2d 750]

4. The California consumer protection statute prohibits the use of false or misleading representations in the sale of goods or services. Mayne borrowed money from Bank of America National Trust and Savings Association. He later sued the bank, claiming that it had violated the statute. The bank asserted that Mayne was required to prove that he had been deceived by the information furnished by the bank. Was the bank correct? [*Mayne v Bank of America National Trust and Savings Ass'n*, ___ Cal App 3d ___, 242 Cal Rptr 357]

5. Merit Breakfast Food Co. sold its breakfast cereal in ordinary-sized packages, but the packages were labeled *jumbo size.* Merit was ordered by the FTC to stop using this term. Merit contended that the term *jumbo* was not used with any intent to defraud, so its use was not improper. Was this a valid defense?

6. Thomas was sent a credit card through the mail by a company that had taken his name and address from the telephone book. Because he never requested the card, Thomas left the card lying on his desk. A thief stole the card and used it to purchase merchandise in several stores in Thomas' name. The issuer of the credit card claimed that Thomas was liable for the total amount of the purchases made by the thief. Thomas claimed that he was not liable for any amount. The court decided that Thomas was liable for $50. Who is correct?

7. A federal statute prohibits the interstate shipment of deceptively or fraudulently labeled goods. Acting under the authority of this statute, federal officers seized a shipment of 95 barrels that were labeled *apple cider vinegar.* This vinegar had been made from dried apples that had been soaked in water. The government claimed that the label was false because apple cider vinegar meant to the average person that the vinegar had been made from fresh apples. The shipper claimed that as the barrels in fact contained vinegar that had been made from cider produced from apples, the labels were truthful in calling the contents by the name of apple cider vinegar. Was the shipper correct? [*United States v 95 Barrels of Alleged Apple Cider Vinegar*, 265 US 438]

8. Wilke was contemplating retiring. In response to an advertisement, he purchased from Coinway 30 coin-operated testing machines because Coinway's representative stated that by placing these machines at different public places, Wilke could obtain supplemental income. This statement was made by the representative although he had no experience with the cost of servicing the machines or their income-producing potential. Wilke's operational costs for the machines exceeded the income. Wilke sued Coinway to rescind the contract, alleging that it was fraudulent. Coinway argued that the statements made were merely matters of opinion and did not constitute fraud. Was Wilke entitled to rescission? [*Wilke v Coinway, Inc.* ___ Cal App 3d ___, 64 Cal Rptr 845]

9. Iberlin and others subscribed to the services of TCI Cablevision of Wyoming, which imposed a $2 late charge on any bill not paid when due. Iberlin brought suit against the cable company, claiming that the late charge was for extending credit and thus did not comply with state and federal laws governing credit charges. Was Iberlin correct? [*Iberlin v TCI Cablevision of Wyoming* (Wyo) 855 P2d 716]

10. International Yogurt Co. (IYC) had developed a unique mix for making frozen yogurt and related products. Morris and his wife purchased a franchise from the company but were not told that a franchise was not required to obtain the mix—that the company would sell its yogurt mix to anyone. The Morrises' franchise business was a failure, and they sold it at a loss after three years. They then sued the company for fraud and for violation of the state Franchise Investment Protection Act and the state Consumer Protection Act for failing to inform them that the mix could be obtained without a franchise. IYC claimed that no liability could be imposed for failing to make the disclosure. Was it correct? [*Morris v International Yogurt Co.* ___ Wash ___, 729 P2d 33]

11. A suit was brought against General Foods on the ground that it was violating the state law prohibiting false and deceptive advertising. Its defense was that the plaintiffs had failed to show the public had been deceived by the advertising, that the public in fact had not relied on the advertising, and that there was no proof that anyone had sustained any damage because of the advertising. Were these valid defenses? [*Committee on Children's Television, Inc. v General Foods Corp.* ___ Cal 3d ___, 673 P2d 660]

12. The town of Newport obtained a corporate MasterCard that was given to the town clerk for purchasing fuel for the town hall. The town clerk used the card for personal restaurant, hotel, and gift shop debts. The town refused to pay the card charges on the ground that they were unauthorized. Was the town correct? [*MasterCard v Town of Newport* (Wis App) 396 NW2d 345]

13. How do you explain the rise of consumer protectionism?

14. Stevens purchased a pair of softball shoes manufactured by Hyde Athletic Industries. Because of a defect in the shoes, she fell and broke an ankle. She sued Hyde under the state consumer protection act, which provided that "any person who is injured in . . . business or property . . . could sue for damages sustained." Hyde claimed that the act did not cover personal injuries. Stevens claimed that she was injured in her "property" because of the money that she had to spend for medical treatment and subsequent care. Decide. [*Stevens v Hyde Athletic Industries, Inc.* ___ Wash App ___, 773 P2d 871]

15. How do you justify a large city, a state government, and a millionaire being given the protection of consumer protection statutes?

P A R T 5

Negotiable Instruments

Kinds of Instruments, Parties, and Negotiability

CHAPTER 31

OBJECTIVES

After studying this chapter, you should be able to

1. *Explain the importance and function of negotiable instruments;*
2. *Name the parties to negotiable instruments;*
3. *Describe the concept of negotiability and distinguish it from assignability; and*
4. *List the essential elements of a negotiable instrument.*

A commercial paper is another name given to instruments such as checks and notes used to facilitate payment in transactions.

Over the course of centuries, businesses came to accept certain kinds of paper called **commercial paper** or **negotiable instruments** as substitutes for money or as a means of giving credit. These instruments are now recognized by law and have their own set of rules for their creation and transferring them and for determining the rights of the parties.

A.   TYPES OF NEGOTIABLE INSTRUMENTS AND PARTIES

A negotiable instrument is a written and signed promise or order to pay a specified sum of money at a definite time.

Article 3 of the UCC defines the types of negotiable instruments and the parties for each.

1.   Definition

A negotiable instrument is a written and signed promise or order to pay a specified sum of money.[1] Instruments are negotiable when they contain certain elements required by the UCC. These elements are listed and explained in section 5 of this chapter. However, even those instruments that do not meet the requirements for negotiability are referred to by their UCC name or classification.

2.   Kinds of Instruments

A promissory note is a written promise signed by the maker to pay a sum certain in money.

There are two categories of negotiable instruments: (1) promises to pay, which include promissory notes and certificates of deposit,[2] and (2) drafts, which include checks.

A certificate of deposit (CD) is a "promise to pay" issued by a bank.

(a) Promissory Notes. A **promissory note** is a written promise made and signed by the maker to pay a sum certain in money to the holder of the instrument. (See Figure 31-1.)[3]

A draft is an order by one party to a second party to pay a sum of money.

(b) Certificates of Deposit. A **certificate of deposit (CD)** is a promise to pay issued by a bank.[4] Through a CD, a bank acknowledges the customer's deposit of a specific sum of money and promises to pay the customer that amount plus interest when the certificate is surrendered.

A drawer gives the order to pay a draft.

A drawee is the party on whom the order to pay is drawn.

A payee is the party to whom payment is to be made.

(c) Drafts. A **draft** is an order by one party to a second party to pay a sum of money. (See Figure 31-2.) The party who gives the order is called the **drawer,** and the party on whom the order to pay is drawn is the **drawee.**[5] The party to whom payment is to be made is the **payee.** The drawer may also be named as the payee, as when a seller draws a draft naming a buyer as the drawee. The draft is then used as a means of obtaining payment for goods delivered to that buyer. A drawee is not

---

[1] The law on negotiable instruments has been evolving and changing. The latest version of Article 3 was adopted in 1990. The 1990 version of Article 3 has been adopted in 47 states as of January 1, 1997: Alabama, Alaska, Arizona, Arkansas, California, Colorado, Connecticut, Delaware, the District of Columbia, Florida, Georgia, Hawaii, Idaho, Illinois, Indiana, Iowa, Kansas, Kentucky, Louisiana, Maine, Maryland, Michigan, Minnesota, Mississippi, Missouri, Montana, Nebraska, Nevada, New Hampshire, New Jersey, New Mexico, North Carolina, North Dakota, Ohio, Oklahoma, Oregon, Pennsylvania, Puerto Rico, South Dakota, Tennessee, Texas, Utah, Vermont, Virginia, Washington, West Virginia, Wisconsin, and Wyoming. See UCC § 3-104.

[2] UCC § 3-104(j) (1990).

[3] *Smith v McKeller* (La App) 638 So 2d 1192 (1994).

[4] UCC § 3-104(j).

[5] UCC § 3-103(a)(2)–(3).

FIGURE 31-1
Promissory Note

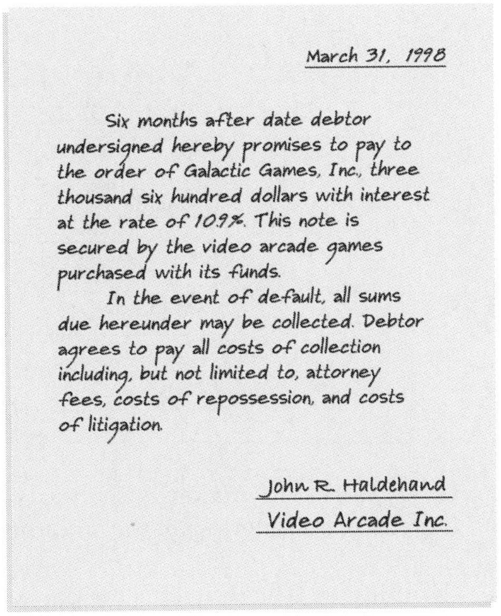

> *March 31, 1998*
>
> Six months after date debtor undersigned hereby promises to pay to the order of Galactic Games, Inc., three thousand six hundred dollars with interest at the rate of 10.9%. This note is secured by the video arcade games purchased with its funds.
>
> In the event of default, all sums due hereunder may be collected. Debtor agrees to pay all costs of collection including, but not limited to, attorney fees, costs of repossession, and costs of litigation.
>
> John R. Haldehand
> Video Arcade Inc.

A check is a draft drawn on a bank or credit union.

A cashier's check is a draft drawn by a bank on itself.

A teller's check is a draft drawn by a bank on another bank in which it has an account.

A traveler's check is payable on demand once it is counter-signed by the original drawer.

A money order is a draft issued by a bank and a nonbank.

bound to pay a draft simply because the drawer has placed his name on it. However, the drawee may agree to pay the draft by accepting it, which then attaches his liability for payment.

(d) Checks. A **check** is a draft drawn on a bank or credit union that is payable on demand. It is an order by a depositor (the drawer) on a bank or credit union (the drawee) to pay a sum of money to the order of another party (the payee).[6]

In addition to the ordinary checks described above, there are also cashier's checks, teller's checks, traveler's checks, and bank money orders. A **cashier's check** is a draft drawn by a bank on itself.[7] A **teller's check** is a draft drawn by a bank on another bank in which it has an account.[8] A **traveler's check** is a check that is payable on demand, provided it is countersigned by the person whose signature was placed on the check at the time those checks were purchased.[9] **Money orders** are issued by both banks and nonbanks. A money order drawn by a bank is also a check.

3.   Parties to Instruments

A note has two original parties—the maker and the payee.[10] A draft or a check has three original parties—the drawer, the drawee, and the payee. The names given to the parties for these instruments are important because their liability on the instrument varies depending on their role. The liability of the various parties to negotiable instruments is covered in chapters 32 and 33.

A party to an instrument may be a natural person or an artificial person, such as a corporation, or an unincorporated enterprise, such as a government agency.

---

[6] UCC § 3-104(f).
[7] UCC § 3-104(g).
[8] UCC § 3-104(h).
[9] UCC § 3-104(i).
[10] UCC § 3-103(a)(5).

FIGURE 31-2
Draft

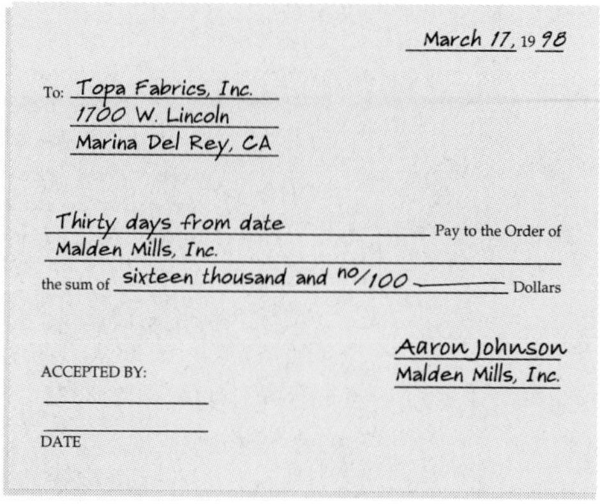
March 17, 19 98

To: Topa Fabrics, Inc.
1700 W. Lincoln
Marina Del Rey, CA

Thirty days from date Pay to the Order of
Malden Mills, Inc.
the sum of sixteen thousand and no/100 Dollars

ACCEPTED BY:

DATE

Aaron Johnson
Malden Mills, Inc.

A maker is obligated under a promissory note or the bank under a certificate of deposit.

CPA

(a) Maker. The **maker** is the party who writes or creates a promissory note, thereby promising to pay the amount specified in the note.

(b) Drawer. The **drawer** is the party who writes or creates a draft or check.

(c) Drawee. The **drawee** is the party to whom the draft is addressed and who is ordered to pay the amount of money specified in the draft. The bank is the drawee on a check, and the credit union is the drawee on a share draft. Again, a drawee on a draft has no responsibility under the draft until it has accepted that instrument.

(d) Payee. The payee is the person named on the face of the instrument to receive payment. ◆ *For example*, on a check with the words "Pay to the order of John Jones" the named person, John Jones, is the payee. ◆

The payee has no rights in the instrument until it has been delivered to the payee by the drawer or the maker. Likewise, the payee is not liable on the instrument in any way until the payee transfers the instrument to someone else.

An acceptor is a drawee who has signified willingness to pay on a draft.

(e) Acceptor. When the drawee of a draft has signified in writing on the draft its willingness to make the specified payment, the drawee has accepted liability and is called the **acceptor.**[11]

An accommodation party is not originally named in an instrument but who assumes some liability thereunder.

(f) Accommodation Party. When a party who is not originally named in an instrument allows his or her name to be added to it for the benefit of another party in order to add strength to the collectability of the instrument, that party becomes an **accommodation party** and assumes the liability such a role imposes.[12]

A guarantor promises to pay an instrument under certain circumstances.

(g) Guarantor. A **guarantor** is a person who promises to pay the instrument under certain circumstances. Ordinarily, a guarantor's promise is made by merely adding "Payment guaranteed" or "Collection guaranteed" to the signature of the guarantor on the paper.

---

11 UCC § 3-103(a)(1).
12 UCC § 3-419.

(1) Nature of Guarantee. The addition of "Payment guaranteed" or similar words to an instrument means that the guarantor will pay when the instrument becomes due. The liability of a **guarantor of payment** is as extensive as that of the original debtor. "**Collection guaranteed**" or similar words mean that the guarantor will not pay the amount due under the instrument until all collection efforts against the original parties to the instrument have been exhausted.

(2) Construction of Guarantee. If the meaning of a guarantee is unclear, it will be construed as a guarantee of payment. *For example,* when an indorser adds a statement that the instrument is guaranteed or adds the word "Guarantor" to the indorsement without specifying whether it is payment or collection that is guaranteed, the indorser is treated as a guarantor of payment.[13]

ETHICS & THE LAW

Fred Dowie was the president and sole stockholder of Fred Dowie Enterprises, Inc., a catering business. Dowie learned that the Pope was coming to visit Des Moines, Iowa, and decided to operate a hot dog concession stand near the site of the Pope's speech. Dowie ordered 325,000 hot dog buns from Colonial Baking Company of Des Moines. Dowie paid for them with a postdated check that had the name "Dowie Enterprises, Inc." imprinted on it. Dowie signed the check "Frederick J. Dowie" in the appropriate place.

The demand for hot dogs during the Pope's visit to Des Moines was not what Dowie had anticipated. As a result, there was nothing left financially to Fred Dowie Enterprises. The check to Colonial did not clear the catering business account. Colonial then presented the check to Dowie for payment. Dowie has told Colonial he is not liable for the amount. Is he correct? What ethical issues do you see in one person running an undercapitalized corporation but enjoying the legal protection afforded this business entity? Apart from his legal obligation, does Dowie have an ethical obligation to pay for the buns? *Colonial Baking Co. of Des Moines v Dowie* (Iowa) 330 NW2d 279 (1983).

B. NEGOTIABILITY

An instrument is a form of contract that, if negotiable, affords certain rights and protections for the parties. **Negotiability** is the characteristic that distinguishes commercial paper and instruments from ordinary contracts.[14] A **nonnegotiable instrument's** terms are enforceable, but it is treated simply as a contract governed by contract law.

4. Definition of Negotiability

If an instrument is negotiable, it is governed by Article 3 of the UCC, and it may be transferred by negotiation. This form of transfer permits the transferee to acquire rights greater than those afforded assignees of contracts under contract law. The quality of negotiability in instruments creates opportunities for transfers

---

13 UCC § 3-205(d) (1990). See Neil B. Cohen, "Suretyship Principles in the New Article 3: Clarification and Substantive Changes," 42 Ala L Rev 595 (1991).
14 UCC § 3-104.

and financings that streamline payments in commerce. Transfers can be made with assurance of payment without the need for investigation of the underlying contract. The process of negotiation is covered in chapter 32. For more information on the rights of assignees of contracts, refer to chapter 18.

5. Requirements of Negotiability

To be negotiable, an instrument must be (1) in writing and (2) signed by the maker or the drawer; it must contain (3) a promise or order (4) of an unconditional character (5) to pay in money (6) a sum certain;[15] it must be (7) payable on demand or at a definite time; and (8) it must be payable to order or bearer. However, a check is negotiable even though not payable to order or bearer, as when a check reads, "Pay to Jane Smith." A bank money order that reads, "Pay to Jones" is negotiable. In contrast, a note that reads, "I promise to pay Jones" is not negotiable.[16]

In addition to these formal requirements for negotiability, the instrument must be delivered or issued by the maker or the drawer to the payee or the payee's agent with the intent that it create a legal obligation.

(a) Writing. A negotiable instrument must be in writing. Writing is defined to include handwriting, typing, printing, and any other method of setting words down in a permanent form. A negotiable instrument may be partly printed and partly typewritten. No particular form is required for an instrument to satisfy the writing requirement although customers of banks may agree to use the banks' forms as part of their contractual agreement with their banks.

(b) Signature. The instrument must be signed by the maker or the drawer. This signature usually appears at the lower right-hand corner of the face of the instrument, but it is immaterial where the signature is placed on the instrument.

The **signature** may consist of the full name or of any symbol placed with the intent to authenticate the instrument. Other means of authentication that are valid as signatures include initials, figures, and marks. A person signing a trade or an assumed name is liable just as if the signer's own name had been used.

> The signature is anything placed on an instrument with the intent to authenticate.

(1) Agent. A signature may be made by the drawer or the maker or by his or her authorized agent. ◆ *For example*, Eileen Smith, the treasurer of Mills Company, could sign a note for her company as an agent. ◆ No particular form of authorization for an agent to execute or sign an instrument is required.

A signing agent should disclose on the instrument (1) the identity of the principal and (2) the fact that the signature was done in a representative capacity.

When this information appears on the face of the instrument, an authorized agent is not liable on it. The representative capacity of an officer of an organization is sufficiently shown by the signature of the officer preceded or followed by the title of the office and the organization's name.[17] ◆ *For example*, a signature of "James Shelton, Treasurer, NorWest Utilities, Inc." on a note sufficiently identifies Shelton's representative capacity. NorWest Utilities, not Shelton, would be liable on the note. ◆

---

[15] *Johnson v Schaub* (Alaska) 867 P2d 812 (1994).
[16] *Amberbox v Societe de Banque Privee* (Tex App) 831 SW2d 793 (1992).
[17] UCC § 3-402.

(2) Absence of Representative Capacity or Identification of Principal. If an instrument fails to show the representative capacity in which the signer acted or fails to identify the represented person, the signing representative is personally liable on the instrument to any person who acquires superior rights, such as the rights of a holder in due course (see chapter 33) who took the instrument without notice that the representative was not intended to be liable on the instrument. Because the instrument is a written agreement, the parol evidence rule applies, and the signer is not permitted to introduce extrinsic evidence that might clarify the representative capacity. The signer, in order to avoid personal liability, must indicate on the face of the instrument his or her role with respect to representation. (For more information about the parol evidence rule, see chapter 16.)

The signing representative is also liable to any other holder or transferee of the instrument unless the representative is able to prove that the original parties to the instrument did not intend the representative to be bound to the instrument. However, an agent is not personally liable on a check that is drawn on the bank account of the principal and signed by him or her even though the agent failed to disclose his or her representative capacity on the check. *For example*, a check that is already imprinted with the employer's name is not the check of the employee, regardless of whether the employee only signs his or her name or also adds a title such as "Payroll Clerk" or "Treasurer" near the signature.

CASE SUMMARY

When Friends Sign Notes, Liability Issues Arise

Facts: George Avery signed a promissory note in the form of a letter addressed to Jim Whitworth as follows:

> This is your note for $45,000 secured individually and by our Company for your security, due February 7, 1984.
>
> Your friend,
>
> /s/ George. S. Avery

The letter was typed on the stationery of Avery's employer, V & L Manufacturing Co., Inc. The name "V & L Manufacturing Co., Inc." was printed at the bottom of the stationery, and the words "George S. Avery, President" were printed at the top. Whitworth brought suit against Avery to recover the amount due on the note. Avery claims he is not liable because he signed the note in a representative capacity.

Decision: The issue is whether the letter from Avery to Whitworth shows on its face that Avery signed for his company in a representative capacity. Even though the stationery on which the note was typed showed that Avery served as president of the corporation, the note itself was signed in an individual and not a representative capacity. It is the form of the signature on the note, and not other printed information appearing on the page, that governs the capacity in which the signer executes the note. The note in this case named the company that Avery represented but did not show that he signed the note in a representative capacity. When an instrument names the person represented (in this case, a corporate entity) but does not show that the representative signed in a representative capacity, the signer is personally obligated. [Avery v Whitworth (Ga) 414 SE2d 725 (1992)]

(c) Promise or Order to Pay. A promissory note must contain a promise to pay money. A mere acknowledgment of a debt, such as a writing stating "I.O.U.," is not a promise. A draft or check must contain an order or command to pay money.

(d) Unconditional Promise or Order. For an instrument to be negotiable, the promise or order to pay must be unconditional.[18] *For example,* when an instrument makes the duty to pay dependent on the completion of the construction of a building, the promise is conditional, and the instrument is nonnegotiable. The instrument is enforceable as a contract, but it is not a negotiable instrument given all the rights and protections afforded under Article 3.

An order for the payment of money out of a particular fund, such as $10 from next week's salary, is conditional. If, however, the instrument is based on the general credit of the drawer and the reference to a particular fund is merely to indicate a source of reimbursement for the drawee, such as "Charge my expense account," the order is considered unconditional. An instrument is not made conditional when payment is to be made only from an identified fund if the issuer is a government, or government unit or agency, or when payment is to be made from the assets of a partnership, unincorporated association, trust, or estate.[19] The standards for negotiability do not require that the issuer of the instrument be personally obligated to pay it.[20]

Money is any medium of exchange adopted or authorized by the United States, a foreign government, or an intergovernmental organization.

(e) Payment in Money. A negotiable instrument must be payable in money. **Money** is defined to include any medium of exchange adopted or authorized by the United States, a foreign government, or an intergovernmental organization. The parties to an instrument are free to decide which currency will be used for payment even though their transaction may occur in a different country.[21] *For example,* two parties in the United States are free to agree that their note will be paid in pesos.

If the order or promise is not for money, the instrument is not negotiable. *For example,* an instrument that requires the holder to take stock or goods in place of money is nonnegotiable. The instrument is enforceable as a contract, but it cannot qualify as a negotiable instrument for purposes of Article 3 rights.

Sum certain is the amount due under an instrument that can be computed from its face with only reference to interest rates.

(f) Sum Certain. This requirement mandates a statement of a **sum certain,** or an exact amount of money, for the instrument. Unless the instrument is definite on its face as to how much is to be paid, there is no way of determining how much the instrument is worth.

Minor variations from the above rule are allowed in certain cases. *For example,* an instrument is not nonnegotiable because its interest rate provisions include changes at maturity or because it provides for certain costs and attorneys' fees to be recovered by the holder in the event of enforcement action or litigation.[22]

In most states, the sum payable under an instrument is certain even though it calls for the payment of a floating or variable interest rate.[23] An instrument is negotiable even though it provides for an interest rate of 1 percent above the prime

---

18 UCC § 3-109(c) (1990).
19 *De Bry v Cascade Enterprises* (Utah) 879 P2d 1353 (1994).
20 UCC § 3-110(c)(1)–(2) (1990); *DH Cattle Holdings Co. v Smith* (App Div) 607 NYS2d 227 (1994).
21 UCC § 3-107.
22 UCC § 3-106.
23 *Means v Clardy* (Mo App) 735 SW2d 6 (1987).

rate of a named bank. It is immaterial that the exact amount of interest that will be paid cannot be determined at the time the paper is issued because the rate may later change. It is also immaterial that the amount due on the instrument cannot be determined without looking at records outside of the face of the instrument.[24]

Can a Credit Application Be a Negotiable Instrument?

Facts: Harold H. Heidingsfelder signed a credit agreement as vice president of J.O.H. Construction Company for a line of credit with Pelican Plumbing Company. The credit agreement contained the following language:

In consideration of an open account privilege, I hereby understand and agree to the above terms. Should it become necessary to place this account for collection I shall personally obligate myself and my corporation, if any, to pay the entire amount due including service charges (as outlined above terms) thirty-three and one third (33 1/3%) attorney's fees, and all costs of collection, including court costs.

Signed [Harold H. Heidingsfelder]

Company J.O.H. Construction Co., Inc.

When J.O.H. Construction failed to make payment, Pelican, claiming it was a holder of a negotiable instrument, sued Harold to hold him personally liable for his failure to indicate a representative capacity on the credit agreement. Harold claims that a credit application is not a negotiable instrument and that he could not be held personally liable.

Decision: The credit application is not a negotiable instrument because it contains no unconditional promise or order to pay a sum certain in money, it is not payable at a definite time or on demand, and it is not payable to order or bearer. The credit application and Pelican's and Harold's rights are not determined under Article 3 of the UCC, but rather are determined by contract law and principles of suretyship. [*Pelican Plumbing Supply, Inc. v J.O.H. Construction Co., Inc.* (La) 653 So 2d 699 (1995)]

(g) Time of Payment. A negotiable instrument must be payable on demand or at a definite time.[25] If an instrument is payable "when convenient," it is nonnegotiable because the day of payment may never arrive. An instrument payable only upon the happening of a particular event that may or may not happen is not negotiable. ◆ *For example,* a provision in a note to pay the sum certain when a person marries is not payable at a definite time because that particular event may never occur. It is immaterial whether the contingency in fact has happened because from an examination of the instrument alone, it still appears to be subject to a condition that might not occur. ◆

A payable on demand instrument is due when presented to the primary party for payment.

(1) Demand. An instrument is payable on **demand** when it expressly states that it is payable "on demand," or at sight, or on presentation.[26] Presentation occurs when a holder demands payment. Commercial paper is deemed to be payable on demand when no time for payment is stated in the instrument.

---

[24] *Goss v Trinity Savings & Loan Ass'n* (Okla) 813 P2d 492 (1991) (holding paper negotiable). But see also *Bankers Trust v 236 Beltway Investment,* 865 F Supp 1186 (ED Va 1994).
[25] UCC § 3-108.
[26] UCC § 3-112.

(2) Definite Time. The time of payment is a **definite time** if an exact time or times are specified or if the paper is payable at a fixed time after sight or acceptance or at a time that is readily ascertainable.

The time of payment is definite even though the instrument provides for prepayment, for acceleration, or for extensions at the option of a party or automatically on the occurrence of a specified contingency. A promissory note is still payable at a definite date when it is payable one year from the date, subject to a six-month automatic extension in case there is a national transportation strike.[27]

(3) Missing Date. Paper that is not dated is deemed dated on the day it is issued to the payee. Any holder may add the correct date to the paper.

(4) Effect of Date on Demand Paper. The date on demand paper controls the time of payment, and the paper is not due before its date. Consequently, a check that is postdated ceases to be demand paper and is not properly payable before the date on the check. A bank making earlier payment does not incur any liability for doing so unless the drawer has given the bank a postdated check notice.

(h) Order or Bearer. An instrument that is not a check must be payable to **order** or **bearer**. This requirement is met by phrases such as "Pay to the order of John Jones," "Pay to John Jones or order," "Pay to bearer," and "Pay to John Jones or bearer." The use of the phrase "to the order of John Jones" or "to John Jones or order" shows that the person executing the instrument had no intention of restricting payment of the instrument to John Jones. These phrases indicate that there is no objection to paying anyone to whom John Jones orders the paper to be paid. Similarly, if the person executing the instrument originally wrote that it will be paid "to bearer" or "to John Jones or bearer," there is no restriction on the payment of the paper to the original payee. However, if the instrument is not a check and it is payable on its face "to John Jones," the instrument is not negotiable.[28] Whether an instrument is bearer or order paper is important because the two instruments are transferred in different ways and because the liability of the transferors can be different.

(1) Order Paper. An instrument is payable to order, or **order paper,** when by its terms it is payable to the order of any person described in it ("Pay to the order of K. Read") or to a person or order ("Pay to K. Read or order").

(2) Bearer Paper. An instrument is payable to bearer, or **bearer paper,** when by its terms it is payable (1) to bearer or the order of bearer; (2) to a specified person or bearer; (3) to "cash," "the order of cash," or any other designation that does not purport to identify a person; or when (4) the last or only indorsement is a blank indorsement (an indorsement that does not name the person to whom the paper is negotiated). An instrument that does not identify any payee is payable to bearer.[29]

Whether an instrument is bearer or order paper is important for determining how the instrument is transferred (see chapter 32), and what the liability of the parties under the instrument is.

[27] *Diamond v T. Rowe Price Associates, Inc.*, 852 F Supp 372 (D Md 1994).
[28] UCC § 3-108.
[29] UCC § 3-104(d).

6. Factors Not Affecting Negotiability

Omitting a date of execution or antedating or postdating an instrument has no effect on negotiability.

Provisions relating to collateral, such as specifying the collateral as security for the debt or a promise to maintain, protect, or give additional collateral, do not affect negotiability. ◆ *For example,* the phrase "This note is secured by a first mortgage" does not affect negotiability. ◆

7. Ambiguous Language

The following rules are applied when ambiguous language exists in words or descriptions:

1. Words control figures where conflict exists.
2. Handwriting supersedes conflicting typewritten and printed terms.
3. Typewritten terms supersede preprinted terms.
4. If there is a failure to provide for the payment of interest or if there is a provision for the payment of interest but no rate is mentioned, the judgment rate at the place of payment applies from the date of the instrument.

8. Statute of Limitations

Statute of limitations is the statutory time limit for bringing an action to enforce one's rights.

The 1990 version of the UCC establishes a three-year statute of limitations for most actions involving negotiable instruments. This limitation also applies to actions for the conversion of such instruments and for breach of warranty. A six-year statute is imposed for suits on certificates of deposit and accepted drafts.

SUMMARY

An instrument or piece of commercial paper is a transferable, written, signed promise or order to pay a specified sum of money. An instrument is negotiable when it contains the terms required by the UCC.

There are two categories of negotiable instruments: (1) promissory notes and (2) drafts. A certificate of deposit is classified as a promissory note. In addition to ordinary checks, there are also cashier's checks and teller's checks. A bank money order is a check even though it bears the words *money order.*

The original parties to a note are the maker and the payee. The original parties to a draft are the drawer, the drawee, and the payee. The term *party* may refer to a natural person or to an artificial person, such as a corporation. It may also mean an unincorporated enterprise, a government, or a bank account.

The requirements of negotiability are that the instrument (1) be in writing, (2) be signed by the maker or the drawer, and (3) contain a promise or order (4) of an unconditional character (5) to pay in money (6) a sum certain (7) on demand or at a definite time (8) to order or bearer. A check may be negotiable without being payable to order or bearer. If an instrument is not negotiable, it is governed by contract law.

The maker of a promissory note and the acceptor of a draft are primarily liable for paying the face value of the instrument. Payment may be demanded from the maker or the acceptor as soon as the paper is due.

QUESTIONS AND CASE PROBLEMS

1. What social forces are affected by the rule of law governing what constitutes a signature on commercial paper?

2. Name the kinds of negotiable instruments.

3. Charter Bank of Gainesville had in its possession a note containing the following provision: "This note with interest is secured by a mortgage on real estate, of even date herewith, made by the maker hereof in favor of said payee. . . . The terms of said mortgage are by this reference made a part hereof." When the bank sued on the note, the defendant contended that the payee was guilty of fraud in obtaining the mortgage. The bank claimed to be a holder in due course. Is the bank precluded from being a holder in due course by the above provision? Why or why not? [*Holly Hill Acres, Ltd. v Charter Bank of Gainesville* (Fla App) 314 So 2d 209]

4. Hampton purchased cloth from Regal Fibres, Inc., on behalf of Twentieth Century Clothing Co., by whom Hampton was employed. Hampton informed Regal that she was acting for Twentieth Century and signed a promissory note for the purchase price of the cloth. The note stated, "I promise to pay," and was signed "Gertrude Hampton." Regal sold the note to Commercial Finance Co., which sued Hampton on the note. Hampton claimed that she was not liable because she had acted as agent for Twentieth Century and had so informed Regal Fibres. Is this a valid defense?

5. The state of Alaska was a tenant in a large office building owned by Univentures, a partnership. The state made a lease payment of $28,143.47 to Univentures with state treasury warrant No. 21045102. Charles LeViege, the managing partner of Univentures, assigned the warrant to Lee Garcia. A dispute then arose among the Univentures partners, and the state was notified that it should no longer pay LeViege the rent. The state placed a stop payment order on the warrant. Garcia claimed that he was a holder of a negotiable instrument and that the state owed him the money. The state claimed that a warrant did not qualify as a negotiable instrument. The warrant is in writing, is signed by the governor of the state, provides a definite sum of $28,143.47, and states that "it will be deemed paid unless redeemed within two years after the date of issue." The warrant states that it is "payable to the order of Univentures." Does the warrant meet the requirements for a negotiable instrument? [*National Bank v Univentures* 1231 (Alaska) 824 P2d 1377]

6. Nation-Wide Check Corp. sold money orders through local agents. A customer would purchase a money order by paying an agent the amount of the desired money order plus a fee. The customer would then sign the money order as the remitter or sender and would fill in the name of the person who was to receive the money following the printed words "Payable to." In a lawsuit between Nation-Wide and Banks, a payee on some of these orders, the question was raised whether these money orders were checks and could be negotiable even though not payable to order or to bearer. Decide. [*Nation-Wide Check Corp. v Banks* (DC) 260 A2d 367]

7. Nelson gave Buchert the following instrument, dated July 6, 1988:

   > One year after date I promise to pay to the order of Dale Buchert one thousand dollars in United States Savings Bonds payable at Last Mortgage Bank. (signed) Ronald K. Nelson

   Does this instrument qualify as a negotiable instrument?

8. Bellino made a promissory note payable in installments that contained the provision that upon default in the payment of any installment, the holder had the option of declaring the entire balance due and payable on demand. The note was negotiated to Cassiani, who sued Bellino for the full debt when there was a default on the installment. Bellino refused to pay, arguing that no notice of acceleration had been given to her prior to suit. Decide. [*Cassiani v Bellino* (Mass) 157 NE2d 409]

9. Money was borrowed from a bank by a corporation whose president negotiated the loan and signed the promissory note. On the first blank signature line of the note, he wrote the name of the corporation. On the second such line, he signed his own name. The note was negotiated by the lending bank to the Federal Reserve Bank. The note was not paid when due, and the Federal Reserve Bank sued the corporation and its president. The president claimed that he was not bound on the note because he did not intend to bind himself and because the money obtained by the loan was used by the corporation. Is the president liable on the note? [*Talley v Blake* (La App) 322 So 2d 877 (non-Code); *Geer v Farquhar* (Or) 528 P2d 1335]

10. Rinehart issues a check that satisfies all the requirements of negotiability. It is payable to the order of cash. Is the instrument payable to order or to bearer?

11. Is the following instrument negotiable?

    > I, Richard Bell, hereby promise to pay to the order of Lorry Motors Ten Thousand Dollars ($10,000) upon the receipt of the final distribution from the estate of my deceased aunt, Rita Dorn. This negotiable instrument is given by me as the down payment on my purchase of a

1986 Buick to be delivered in three weeks.
Richard Bell (signature)

12. Smith has in his possession the following instrument:
September 1, 1986
I, Selma Ray, hereby promise to pay Helen Savit One Thousand Dollars ($1,000) one year after date. This instrument was given for the purchase of Two Hundred (200) shares of Redding Mining Corporation, Interest 6%.
Selma Ray (signature)
What is this instrument? Is this instrument negotiable?

13. Master Homecraft Co. received a promissory note with a stated face value from Sally and Tom Zimmerman. The note was payment for remodeling their home and contained unused blanks for installment payments but contained no maturity date. When Master Homecraft sued the Zimmermans on the note, they argued that they should not be liable on the note because it is impossible to determine from its face the amount due or the date of maturity. Decide. [*Master Homecraft Co. v Zimmerman* (Pa) 22 A2d 440]

14. A check written by Faith Forrest has the following language, "Pay to Super Lock, Inc." Is the check negotiable?

15. A note signed by Barrese and payable to Dreamstreet Holsteins, Inc., provided that "all subsequent payments of principal and interest shall be made as animals are sold from [Barrese's] herd of dairy cattle, but in no event later than December 31, 1990." Is the note negotiable? [*DH Cattle Holdings Co. v Barrese* (App Div) 599 NYS 2d 869]

CPA QUESTIONS

1. A company has in its possession the following instrument:

$500.00   Dayton, Ohio
                                     October 2, 1987

Sixty days after the date I promise to pay to the order of

_____ Cash _____

_____ Five Hundred _____ *Dollars*

at _____ Miami, Florida _____

Value received with interest at the rate of nine percent. This instrument is secured by a conditional sales contract.

No. 11 Due Dec. 1, 1987   Craig Burk
                            Craig Burk

This instrument is
   a. Not negotiable until December 1, 1987.
   b. A negotiable bearer note.
   c. A negotiable time draft.
   d. A nonnegotiable note because it states that it is secured by a conditional sales contract.
                        (11/87, Law, #48, 9911)

2. The instrument below is a

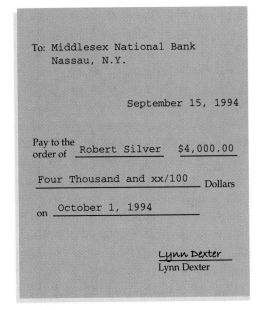

To: Middlesex National Bank
    Nassau, N.Y.

                        September 15, 1994

Pay to the   Robert Silver $4,000.00
order of

Four Thousand and xx/100 _____ Dollars

on   October 1, 1994

                        Lynn Dexter
                        Lynn Dexter

   a. Draft
   b. Postdated check.
   c. Trade acceptance.
   d. Promissory note.
                        (5/95, Law, #42, 5376)

3. Under the commercial paper article of the UCC, for an instrument to be negotiable it must
   a. Be payable to order or to bearer.
   b. Be signed to the payee.
   c. Contain references to all agreements between the parties.
   d. Contain necessary conditions of payment.
                        (5/95, Law, #43, 5377)

Transfer of Negotiable Instruments

CHAPTER 32

OBJECTIVES

After studying this chapter, you should be able to

1. *Distinguish between an assignment and a negotiation;*
2. *Explain the difference between negotiation of order paper and negotiation of bearer paper;*
3. *List the types of indorsements and describe their uses;*
4. *Determine the legal effect of forged and unauthorized indorsements;*
5. *Be familiar with the forged payee impostor exceptions; and*
6. *List the indorser's warranties and describe their significance.*

Much of the commercial importance of negotiable instruments lies in the ease with which they can be transferred. This chapter covers the requirements for and issues in the transfer or negotiation of negotiable instruments.

A. TRANSFER OF NEGOTIABLE INSTRUMENTS

Negotiation is the process whereby a negotiable instrument is transferred so that the transferee becomes a holder.

Negotiable instruments are transferred by a process known as **negotiation**. Negotiation is the transfer of a negotiable instrument so that the transferee becomes a holder.

1. Effect of Transfer

When a contract is assigned, the transferee has the rights of the transferor. The transferee is entitled to enforce the contract but, as assignee, has no greater rights than the assignor.[1] The assignee is in the same position as the original party to the contract and is subject to any defense that could be raised in a suit on an assigned contract.

A holder is a party in possession of an instrument that runs to him: payable to his order, indorsed to him, or bearer paper.

When a negotiable instrument is transferred by negotiation, the transferee becomes the **holder** of the paper. A holder who meets certain additional requirements may also be a **holder in due course**. The status of holder in due course gives immunity from certain defenses that might have been asserted against the transferor (chapter 33 provides a discussion of the rights and role of a holder in due course).

2. Definition of Negotiation

Negotiation is the transfer of a negotiable instrument in such a way that the transferee becomes a holder.[2] A holder is different from a possessor or an assignee of the paper. A holder is a transferee in possession of an instrument that runs to him or her. An instrument runs to a party if it is payable to his or her order, is indorsed to him or her, or is bearer paper.

3. How Negotiation Occurs: The Order or Bearer Character of an Instrument

The order or bearer character of the paper determines how it may be negotiated. The order or bearer character of an instrument is determined according to the words of negotiability used (see chapter 31 for a complete discussion of order and bearer words of negotiation). The character of an instrument is determined as of the time negotiation takes place without regard to the character of the instrument originally or at the time of prior transfers.

---

[1] *Lee v Muller* (Ga App) 407 SE2d 108 (1991).
[2] UCC § 3-201.

B.   HOW NEGOTIATION OCCURS: BEARER INSTRUMENTS

Delivery is the transfer of possession of an instrument; required for negotiation of both bearer and order instruments.

Any bearer instrument is negotiated by a mere transfer of possession. **Bearer paper** is negotiated to a person taking possession of it without regard to whether such possession is lawful. Because **delivery** of a bearer instrument is effective negotiation, it is possible for a thief or an embezzling officer to transfer title to an instrument. Their presence in the chain of transfer does not affect the rights of those who have taken the bearer instrument in good faith.

The types of instruments that qualify as bearer paper include those payable to bearer as well as those payable to the order of "Cash" or payable in blank.

Although a bearer instrument may be negotiated by a mere transfer of possession, the one to whom the instrument is delivered may insist that the bearer indorse the paper. This situation most commonly arises when a check payable to "Cash" is presented to a bank for payment. The reason a transferee of bearer paper would want an indorsement is to obtain the protection of an indorser's warranties from the bearer.

C.   HOW NEGOTIATION OCCURS: ORDER INSTRUMENTS

An indorsement is the signature of the payee on an instrument.

A negotiable instrument that is payable to the order of a specific party is **order paper**, and order paper can be negotiated only through indorsement and transfer of possession of the paper.[3] **Indorsement** and transfer of possession can be made by the person to whom the instrument is then payable or by an authorized agent of that person.[4]

Indorsements vary according to the method of signing and the words used along with the signature. The nature of an indorsement also affects the future of the instrument in terms of its requirements for further negotiation.

4. Blank Indorsement

A blank indorsement is the signature only of the payee used to transfer the instrument.

When the indorser merely signs a negotiable instrument, the indorsement is called a **blank indorsement**. (See Figure 32-1.) A blank indorsement does not indicate the person to whom the instrument is to be paid, that is, the transferee. A blank indorsement turns an order instrument into a bearer instrument. A person who is in possession of an instrument on which the last indorsement is blank is the holder. *For example,* if a check is payable to the order of Jill Barnes and Ms. Barnes indorses the check on the back "Jill Barnes," then the check that was originally an order instrument is now a bearer instrument. The check can now be transferred as bearer paper, which requires only delivery of possession. Once Jill Barnes's signature appears as a blank indorsement on the back, the check becomes transferrable simply by delivery of possession to another party.

---

[3] UCC § 3-201(b) (1990); *J.P. Morgan Del. v Onyx Arabians II*, 825 F Supp 146 (WD Ky 1993).
[4] UCC § 3-204.

FIGURE 32-1
Blank Indorsement

O P A

5. Special Indorsement

A special indorsement is an indorsement that includes a "Pay to" clause, thereby continuing or creating an order instrument.

An indorser is a party who signs an instrument.

An indorsee is a party to whom special indorsement is made.

A **special indorsement** consists of the signature of the **indorser** and words specifying the person to whom the indorser makes the instrument payable, that is, the **indorsee**. (See Figure 32-2.)[5] *For example*, if Jill Barnes wrote on the back of the check payable to her "Pay to Jack Barnes, /s/ Jill Barnes," then the check can be negotiated further only through the signature and possession of Jack Barnes. A special indorsement in this case continues an order instrument as an order instrument. If, after receiving the check, Jack Barnes simply signed it on the back, the check would become bearer paper and could be transferred through possession only.

While words of negotiability are required on the front of negotiable instruments, it is not necessary that indorsements contain the word *order* or *bearer*. Consequently, the paper indorsed as shown in Figure 32-2 continues to be negotiable and may be negotiated further.[6]

An indorsement of "Pay to account [number]" is a special indorsement. In contrast, the inclusion of a notation indicating the debt to be paid is not a special indorsement.

6. Qualified Indorsement

A qualified indorsement is an indorsement in which the indorser limits some liability under the instrument.

A **qualified indorsement** is one that qualifies the effect of a blank or a special indorsement by disclaiming certain liability of the indorser to a maker or a drawee. This disclaimer is given by using the phrase "Without recourse" as part of the indorsement. Any other words that indicate an intent to limit the indorser's

FIGURE 32-2
Special Indorsement

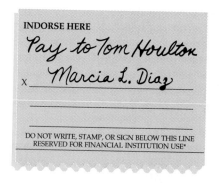

---

[5] UCC § 3-205.

[6] Only a check may use the phrase "Pay to" on its face and remain negotiable. All other instruments require words of negotiability on their faces. Indorsements, however, are sufficient on all instruments with simply "Pay to." UCC § 3-110 (1990).

FIGURE 32-3
Qualified Indorsement

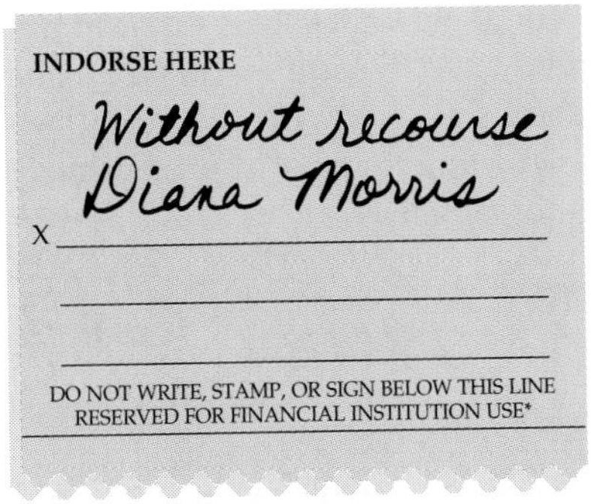

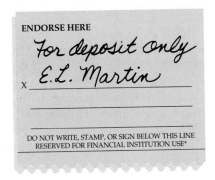

secondary liability in the event the maker or the drawee does not pay on the instrument can also be used.[7] (See Figure 32-3.)

The qualification of an indorsement does not affect the passage of title or the negotiable character of the instrument. It merely disclaims the indorser's secondary liability for payment of the instrument in the event the original parties do not pay as the instrument provides.

This form of indorsement is most commonly used when the qualified indorser is a person who has no personal interest in the transaction. ◆ *For example*, an agent or an attorney who is merely indorsing a check of a third person to a client might make a qualified indorsement because he or she is not actually a party to the transaction. ◆

7. Restrictive Indorsement

A restrictive indorsement is an indorsement such as "For deposit only" that restricts at least the initial use of the instrument.

A **restrictive indorsement** specifies the purpose of the indorsement or the use to be made of the instrument.[8] (See Figure 32-4.) An indorsement is restrictive when it includes words showing that the instrument is to be deposited (such as "For deposit only"), when it is negotiated for collection or to an agent or a trustee, or when the negotiation is conditional.[9]

A restrictive indorsement does not prevent transfer or negotiation of the instrument even when it expressly states that transfer or negotiation is prohibited. The indorsement "For deposit" requires only that the first party who receives the instrument after the restriction is placed on it comply with that restriction. The indorsement "For deposit only" makes an instrument a bearer instrument for any

FIGURE 32-4
Restrictive Indorsement

---

[7] *Florida Coast Bank v Monarch Dodge* (Fla App) 430 So 2d 607 (1983).
[8] UCC § 3-206.
[9] UCC § 3-205 (1990).

bank. If the indorser's account number is added to a "For deposit only" indorsement, then the only party who can take the instrument after this restrictive indorsement is a bank with that account number. A restrictive indorsement reduces the risk of theft or unauthorized transfer by eliminating the bearer quality of a blank indorsement.

CASE SUMMARY

If I Just Write My Account Number on the Back of My Check, Is There a Risk?

Facts: Walcott sent his October paycheck, together with a money order, to Midatlantic Mortgage Co. for his November mortgage installment payment. Walcott alleged that he signed his name to the back of the check and placed his mortgage number and the Midatlantic mailing sticker on the back of the check. He then placed the check and money order in an envelope addressed to Midatlantic Mortgage Co. and dropped the envelope into a U. S. postal box.

Some time later Walcott was notified that he was late with the November payment. Walcott learned that his check had been cashed by Bilko Check Cashing and deposited in Bilko's account with Manufacturers Hanover Trust. The check was finally cleared through Citibank and charged to the account of the original payor, the New York City Transit Authority. Walcott claimed that the check was stolen and Manufacturers Hanover had wrongfully credited it to Bilko's account. Walcott sued Manufacturers and Bilko for the amount of the check. Walcott claimed that his indorsement was either a special or a restrictive indorsement, which should have prevented a thief from cashing the check.

Decision: Uniform Commercial Code § 3-204(1) defines a special indorsement as being one that "specifies the person to whom or to whose order it makes the instrument payable. Any instrument specially indorsed becomes payable to the order of the special indorsee and may be further negotiated only by his indorsement." Examination of the back of the check revealed that Mr. Walcott did not specify any particular indorsee. The numbers written underneath Walcott's signature did not have the effect of restricting his indorsement. An indorsement is restrictive if it includes the words "For collection," "For deposit," or "Pay any bank," or like terms signifying a purpose of deposit or collection. This section of the Uniform Commercial Code is very specific. The series of numbers representing Walcott's mortgage account was insufficient to restrict negotiation of the check. Walcott's indorsement had the effect of converting the check into a bearer instrument, which may be negotiated by delivery alone. The check was properly negotiated by delivery to Bilko and properly cashed. [*Walcott v Manufacturers Hanover Trust (Misc) 507 NYS2d 961 (1986)*]

---

8. Correction of Name by Indorsement

Sometimes the name of the payee or the indorsee of an instrument is spelled improperly. ◆ *For example,* H. A. Price may receive a paycheck that is payable to the order of "H. O. Price." If this error in Price's name was a clerical one and the check is indeed intended for H. A. Price, the employee may ask the employer to write a new check payable to the proper name. ◆ However, under Article 3, a much simpler solution allows the payee or indorsee whose name is misspelled to indorse the wrong name, the correct name, or both. The person giving or paying value or taking it for collection for the instrument may require both forms of the signature.[10]

---

[10] UCC § 3-203.

This correction of name by indorsement may be used only when it was intended that the instrument should be payable to the person making the corrective indorsement. If there were in fact two employees, one named H. A. Price and the other H. O. Price, it would be forgery for one to take the check intended for the other and, by indorsing it, obtain the benefit of the proceeds of the check.

A fictitious, assumed, or trade name is treated the same as a wrong name. The same procedure for correction of a misspelled name with indorsement of both names applies to these forms of payee identifications as well.[11]

9. Bank Indorsement

To simplify the transfer and collection of negotiable instruments from one bank to another, "any agreed method which identifies the transferor bank is sufficient for the item's further transfer to another bank."[12] A bank could simply indorse with its Federal Reserve System number instead of using its name.

Likewise, when a customer has deposited an instrument with a bank but has failed to indorse it, the bank may make an indorsement for the customer unless the instrument expressly requires the payee's personal indorsement. Furthermore, the mere stamping or marking on the item of any notation showing that it was deposited by the customer or credited to the customer's account is effective as an indorsement by the customer.

10. Multiple Payees and Indorsements

Ordinarily, one person is named as the payee in the instrument, but two or more payees may be named. In that case, the instrument may specify that it is payable to any one or more of them or that it is payable to all jointly. *For example,* if the instrument is made payable "to the order of Ferns and Piercy," then Ferns and Piercy are joint payees. The indorsements of both Ferns and Piercy are required to negotiate the instrument.

If the instrument is payable to alternate payees or if it has been negotiated to alternate indorsees, as "Stahl or Glass," or as "Stahl/Glass," it may be indorsed and delivered by either of them.

If it is not clearly stated on the instrument that multiple payees or indorsees are joint, they are considered to be alternative payees. If the instrument is ambiguous, the payees or indorsees are considered payees in the alternative.

> **CASE SUMMARY**
>
> ## Dad Was Helping Me Out by Helping Me Cash My Check—Was It Really My Check?
>
> **Facts:** Jerry O. Peavy, Jr., who did not have a bank account of his own, received a draft from CNL Insurance America in the amount of $5,323.60. The draft was drawn on CNL's account at Bank South, N.A., and was "payable to the order of Jerry Peavy and Trust Company Bank." Jerry O. Peavy, Sr., allowed his son, Jr., to deposit the draft in his account at Bank South, N.A. Bank South accepted the draft and deposited it on December 29, 1992, with only the signature of Jerry Peavy, Jr.

---

[11] UCC § 3-204(d).
[12] UCC § 4-206.

Both Mr. and Mrs. Peavy then wrote checks on the amount of the draft using the full amount to benefit their son. On March 30, 1993, Bank South realized that it had improperly deposited the draft because it was lacking an indorsement from Trust Company Bank and reversed the transaction by debiting Mr. and Mrs. Peavy's account for the full amount of the draft.

A bank officer then called Mr. and Mrs. Peavy, told them what had happened with the draft, and "threatened to send them to jail if they did not immediately deposit the sum of $5,323.60." The Peavys deposited that amount from the sale of some stock they owned and then filed suit against Bank South for its conversion of their son's draft and funds.

Decision: The bank did not convert the draft. The proper indorsement for the draft was lacking because the instrument was order paper with joint payees. The signature of Jerry O. Peavy, Jr., and the indorsement of Trust Company Bank were required before the instrument could be transferred to Bank South. Without the indorsement of Trust Company Bank, Bank South could not be a holder of the instrument, and the Peavys were not entitled to the funds in their account because Bank South had no authority to place the draft funds in that account. [*Peavy v Bank South (Ga App) 474 SE2d 690 (1996)*]

11. Agent or Officer Indorsement

The instrument may be made payable to the order of an officeholder. ◆ *For example*, a check may read "Pay to the order of Receiver of Taxes." Such a check may be received and negotiated by the person who at the time is the receiver of taxes. ◆ This general identification of a payee is a matter of convenience, and the drawer of the check is not required to find out the actual name of the receiver of taxes at that time.

If an instrument is drawn in favor of an officer of a named corporation, the instrument is payable to the corporation, the officer, or any successor to such officer. Any of these parties in possession of the instrument is the holder and may negotiate the instrument.[13]

12. Missing Indorsement

When the parties intend to negotiate an order instrument but for some reason the holder fails to indorse it, there is no negotiation. The transfer without indorsement has only the effect of a contract assignment.[14] If the transferee gave value (see chapter 33 for more information on what constitutes giving value) for the instrument, the transferee has the right to require that the transferor indorse the instrument unqualifiedly and thereby negotiate the instrument.

A forged indorsement is an instrument indorsed by one who is not the payee or the indorsee.

An unauthorized indorsement is an instrument indorsed by an agent for a principal without authorization or authority.

13. Forged and Unauthorized Indorsements

A **forged** or **unauthorized indorsement** is not a valid indorsement.[15] Accordingly, anyone who has possession of a forged instrument is not a holder because the indorsement of the person whose signature was forged was necessary for effective negotiation of the instrument to the possessor.

---

[13] UCC § 3-110(d).
[14] UCC § 3-117 (1990); *Kennerson v FDIC*, 44 F3d19 (1st Cir 1995); *Stickler v Marx* (Va) 436 SE2d 447 (1993).
[15] UCC § 3-403(a) (1990); *Bloom v G.P.F.* (Fla App) 588 So 2d 607 (1991).

If payment of an instrument is made to one claiming under or through a forged indorsement, the payor ordinarily remains liable to the person who is the rightful owner of the paper. Exceptions exist if the rightful owner has been negligent and contributed to the forgery or unauthorized signature problem (see chapter 32 for more information on the rights and liabilities of the parties).

A forged or unauthorized indorsement may be ratified.[16] A ratified signature is effective as though it had been genuine and authorized.

14. Quasi Forgeries: The Impostor Rule

C P A

An impostor rule is an exception to the rules on liability for forgery that covers situations such as the embezzling payroll clerk.

Under the **impostor rule**, there are three exceptions to the rule that a forged indorsement does not serve to validly negotiate an instrument. If one of the three exceptions applies, then even though there may have been a forgery of an indorsement, the instrument is still effectively negotiated.

(a) When Impostor Rule Applicable. The impostor rule applies in cases where an indorser is impersonating a payee and in two cases where the indorser is a dummy payee.[17]

(1) Impersonating Payee. The impersonation of a payee in the impostor rule exception includes impersonation of the agent of the person who is named as payee. ◆ *For example*, if Jones pretends to be the agent of Brown Corp. and thereby obtains a check payable to the order of the corporation, the impostor exception applies. ◆

C P A

(2) Dummy Payee. Another impostor scenario arises when the preparer of the instrument intends that the named payee will never benefit from the instrument. Such a "dummy" payee may be an actual or a fictitious person. This situation arises when the owner of a checking account wishes to conceal the true purpose of taking money from the account at the bank. The account owner makes out a check purportedly in payment of a debt that in fact does not exist.

(3) Dummy Payee Supplied by Employee. The third imposter situation arises when an agent or employee of the maker or the drawer has supplied the name to be used for the payee, intending that payee should not have any interest in the paper. This last situation occurs when an employee fraudulently causes an employer to sign a check made to a customer or another person, whether existing or not. The employee does not intend to send it to that person but rather intends to forge the latter's indorsement, cash the check, and keep the money. This exception to the impostor rule imposes responsibility on employers to have adequate internal controls to prevent employees from taking advantage of an accounting system with loopholes so that others are not required to bear the cost of the employer's lack of appropriate precautions.

---

[16] *White v Moriarty* (Ct App) 19 Cal Rptr 200 (1993).
[17] UCC § 3-404 (1990); *Shearson Lehman Brothers, Inc. v Wasatch Bank,* 788 F Supp 1184 (D Utah 1992).
[18] UCC § 3-404(b) (1990); *Menichini v Grant,* 995 F2d 1224 (3d Cir 1993).

The Bookkeeper Who Found a Loophole: Who Pays for Her Embezzlement?

Facts: C&N and Alabama Siding perform construction work at job sites throughout the southeastern United States. On Wednesday of each week, the foreman at each job site telephoned Bivens and gave her the names of the employees working on the job and the number of hours they had worked. Bivens then conveyed this information to Automatic Data Processing (ADP). Under a contract with C&N and Alabama Siding, ADP prepared payroll checks for the two companies. After preparing the payroll checks based on the information given to it by Bivens, ADP sent the checks to the offices of C&N and Alabama Siding for authorized signatures. Bivens was not an authorized signer. After the checks were signed, Bivens sent the checks to the job site foreman for delivery to the employees.

Bivens soon began conveying false information and hours worked. On the basis of this false information, ADP prepared payroll checks payable to persons who were actually employees but had not worked the hours Bivens had indicated. After obtaining authorized signatures, Bivens intercepted the checks, forged the indorsements of the payees, and either cashed them at Community Bancshares or deposited them into her checking account at Community, often presenting numerous checks at one time. Bivens continued this practice for over a year, forging over 100 indorsements. The vice president of C&N discovered the embezzlement after noticing payroll checks payable to employees who had not recently performed services for the corporations. Bivens later admitted to forging the indorsements. C&N brought suit against the bank for paying on forged indorsements.

Decision: The principle followed is that the loss should fall on the employer as a risk of his business enterprise rather than on the subsequent holder or drawee. The reasons are that the employer is normally in a better position to prevent such forgeries by reasonable care in the selection or supervision of his employees, or if he is not, he is at least in a better position to cover the loss by fidelity insurance, and that the cost of such insurance is properly an expense of his business rather than of the business of the holder or the drawee. [*C&N Contractors, Inc. v Community Bancshares, Inc., 646 So 2d 1357 (Ala. 1994)*]

(b) Effect of Impostor Rule. When the impostor rule is applicable, any person may indorse the name of the payee. This indorsement is treated as a genuine indorsement by the payee and cannot be attacked on the ground that it is a forgery. This recognition of the fictitious payee's signature as valid applies even though the dummy payee of the paper is a fictitious person.[18]

(c) Limitations on Impostor Rule. The impostor rule does not apply when there is a valid check to an actual creditor for a correct amount owed by the drawer and someone later forges the payee's name. The impostor rule does not apply in this situation even if the forger is an employee of the drawer.

Even when the unauthorized indorsement of the payee's name is effective by virtue of the impostor rule, a person forging the payee's name is subject to civil and criminal liability for making such an indorsement.

To claim the protection of the impostor rule, the holder or the taker of the instrument must show that it had been taken (1) in good faith (2) for payment or collection.

(d) Negligence of Drawee Not Required. The impostor rule applies without regard to whether the drawee bank acted with reasonable care.[19]

Russell T. Lund, who suffered from dyslexia, graduated from the University of Minnesota and served as a pilot in the Korean War. He met Wardell M. Montgomery when they were both working on a project for Motorola. Following their work together there, Lund, Montgomery, and four former military pilot friends formed, in 1968, Flight Training Center (FTC), a flight school and aircraft rental business.

Lund had no active role in the management of FTC but did fly its aircraft. Montgomery served as FTC's president but was not active in the company's business affairs. By 1975, all the original owners except Lund and Montgomery had left the business. Montgomery and Lund then hired Janet Karki as a bookkeeper for FTC. Karki told Montgomery and Lund that the company's financial problems stemmed from an unfavorable airplane lease with Rubin. With Montgomery's and Lund's authorization, Karki approached Rubin to renegotiate the lease. Rubin offered instead to work with Karki to make FTC profitable.

Montgomery and Lund, because of their lack of interest in the business end of FTC, handed over the financial reins to Karki and Rubin. Lund, because of his reading difficulties, did not like to review documents. Over the course of the next six years, Karki and Rubin did two public stock offerings in FTC. At the financial closings for the stock offerings, Rubin presented powers of attorney to Chemical Bank and the underwriter. The powers of attorney purported to give him and Karki the authority to indorse the checks for FTC.

At the closing, the first check for $716,946, made payable to Flight Transportation Corporation on the front, was indorsed as follows on the back:

Pay to the order of William Rubin and Russell T. Lund, Jr.
Flight Transportation Corporation
by Janet Karki
*   its secretary*

The second check for $46,056 was indorsed as follows:

Pay to the order of Wardell Montgomery and Janet Karki
Flight Transportation Corporation
by Janet Karki
*   its secretary*

The powers of attorney were forged. Chemical Bank cashed the checks for Karki. Lund and Montgomery became suspicious when their quarterly distributions were low. The stock offering was a fraud, and Rubin and Karki were sentenced to 18 months in prison. Montgomery and Lund said that their signatures were required for the further negotiation of the checks and that Chemical Bank was responsible for their losses. Are they correct? Do you think Montgomery and Lund allowed this scheme to occur because of their failure to supervise Rubin and Karki? Is it unfair to allow them to recover now? *Lund v Chemical Bank*, 797 F Supp 259 (SDNY 1992).

---

[19] *Shearson Lehman Brothers, Inc. v Wasatch Bank*, 788 F Supp 1184 (D Utah 1992).

15. Effect of Incapacity or Misconduct on Negotiation

A negotiation is effective even though (1) it was made by a minor or any other person lacking capacity; (2) it was an act beyond the powers of a corporation; (3) it was obtained by fraud, duress, or a mistake of any kind; or (4) the negotiation was part of an illegal transaction or was made in breach of duty. Under general principles of law apart from the UCC, the transferor in such cases may be able to set aside the negotiation or obtain some other form of legal relief.

However, there are rights of certain parties (holders in due course) that may limit the ability to set aside the negotiation because of incapacity and other contract defenses (see chapter 33).

16. Lost Instruments

The liability on lost instruments depends on who is suing or demanding payment from whom and on whether the instrument was order or bearer paper when it was lost.

(a) Order Instruments. If the lost instrument is order paper, the finder does not become the holder because the instrument has not been indorsed and delivered by the person to whom it was then payable. The former holder who lost it is still the rightful owner of the instrument.

(b) Bearer Instruments. If the lost instrument is in bearer form when it is lost, the finder, as the possessor of a bearer instrument, is the holder and is entitled to enforce payment.

C. NEGOTIATION WARRANTIES

When a negotiable instrument is transferred by negotiation, certain warranties are given by transferors by implication.

17. Warranties of Unqualified Indorser

Transferor warranties are warranties made by those who transfer negotiable instruments, including that the transferor has the right to enforce the instrument, that all signatures are genuine or authorized, that there has been no alteration of the instrument, that there are no defenses or claims to the instrument, and that there are no insolvency proceedings pending against the party responsible for payment.

When the transferor receives consideration for the indorsement and makes an unqualified indorsement, the warranties stated in this section are given by the transferor by implication. No distinction is made between an unqualified blank indorsement and an unqualified special indorsement.

(a) Scope of Warranties. The warranties of the unqualified indorser are as follows:

1. The transferor is entitled to enforce the instrument.
2. All signatures on the instrument are genuine and authorized.
3. The instrument has not been altered.
4. The instrument is not subject to any defense or claim of any party that could be asserted against the transferor.
5. The transferor has no knowledge of any insolvency proceedings against a maker, an acceptor, or the drawer of an unaccepted draft.[20]

---

[20] UCC § 3-416 (1990).

If a forged indorsement has appeared during the transfer of the instrument and there is a refusal to pay because of that problem, the last party who is a holder may turn to his transferor to recover on the basis of these implied warranties. These warranties give those who have transferred and held the instrument recourse against those parties who were involved in the transfer of the instrument although they were not parties to the original instrument. This warranty section of Article 3 of the UCC attaches liability to those who transfer instruments.

(b) What Is Not Warranted. The implied warranties stated here do not guarantee that payment of the paper will be made. Similarly, the holder's indorsement of a check does not give any warranty that the account of the drawer in the drawee bank contains funds sufficient to cover the check.

(c) Beneficiary of Implied Warranties. The implied warranties of the unqualified indorser pass to the transferee and any subsequent transferee. There is no requirement that the subsequent transferee take the instrument in good faith. Likewise, the transferee need not be a holder to enjoy warranty protections.

(d) Disclaimer of Warranties. The unqualified indorser cannot disclaim any warranty when the instrument is a check. Warranties may be disclaimed when the instrument is not a check.

A disclaimer of warranties is ordinarily made by adding "Without warranties" to the indorsement.

(e) Notice of Breach of Warranty. To enforce an implied warranty of an indorser, the party claiming under the warranty must give the indorser notice of the breach. This notice must be given within 30 days after the claimant learns or has reason to know of the breach and the identity of the indorser. If proper notice is not given, the warranty claim is reduced by the amount of the loss that could have been avoided had timely notice been given.

18. Warranties of Other Parties

Warranties are also made by the indorser who indorses "Without recourse" and by one who transfers by delivery only.

(a) Qualified Indorser. The warranty liability of a qualified indorser is the same as that of an unqualified indorser.[21] A qualified indorsement means that the indorser does not assume liability for the payment of the instrument as written. However, a qualified indorsement does not eliminate the implied warranties an indorser makes as a transferor of an instrument.

(b) Transferor by Delivery. When the negotiable instrument is negotiated by delivery without indorsement, the warranty liability of the transferor runs only to the immediate transferee. In all other respects, the warranty liability is the same as in the case of the unqualified indorser. *For example,* Thomas, a minor, gives Craig his note payable to bearer. Craig transfers the note for value and by delivery only to Walsh, who negotiates it to Hall. Payment was refused by Thomas,

---

[21] UCC § 3-416(a).

who chose to disaffirm his contract. Hall cannot hold Craig liable. Craig, having negotiated the instrument by delivery only, is liable on his implied warranties only to his immediate transferee, Walsh. Likewise, because Craig did not indorse the note, he is not secondarily liable for payment of the note. ◆

SUMMARY

Negotiable instruments can be transferred by assignment or negotiation. Typically, negotiable instruments are transferred by negotiation. When a negotiable instrument is assigned, the transferee has the rights of the transferor. The transferee under an assignment is entitled to enforce the instrument as a contract, but the assignee-transferee has no greater rights than the assignor-transferor. The assignee is subject to any defense that could be raised in a suit on an assigned contract. When a negotiable instrument is transferred by negotiation, the transferee becomes the holder of the instrument. If such a holder becomes a holder in due course, the holder will be immune to certain defenses. Negotiation is the transferring of a negotiable instrument in such a way as to make the transferee the holder.

Order instruments are negotiated by an indorsement and delivery by the person to whom it is then payable. Bearer instruments are negotiated by delivery alone. The order or bearer character of an instrument is determined by the face of the instrument, as long as the instrument is not indorsed. If the instrument has been indorsed, the character is determined by the last indorsement.

A number of different kinds of indorsements can be made on negotiable instruments. When an indorser merely signs the instrument, the indorsement is called a blank indorsement. If the last indorsement is a blank indorsement, the instrument is bearer paper, which may be negotiated by change of possession alone. A special indorsement consists of the signature of the indorser and words speci-

fying the person to whom the indorser makes the instrument payable. If the last indorsement is a special indorsement, the instrument is order paper and may be negotiated only by an indorsement and delivery. A qualified indorsement destroys the liability of the indorser to answer for dishonor of the paper by the maker or the drawee. A restrictive indorsement specifies the purpose of the instrument or its use.

A forged or unauthorized indorsement is no indorsement, and the possessor of the instrument cannot be a holder. The impostor rule makes three exceptions to this rule. A negotiation is effective even though (1) it is made by a minor, (2) it is an act beyond the powers of a corporation, (3) it is obtained by fraud, or (4) the negotiation is part of an illegal transaction. However, the transferor may be able to set aside the negotiation under general legal principles apart from the UCC. The negotiation cannot be set aside if the instrument is held by a person paying the instrument in good faith and without knowledge of the facts on which the rescission claim is based.

The warranties of the unqualified indorser who receives consideration are as follows: (1) the transferor is entitled to enforce the instrument; (2) all signatures on the instrument are genuine and authorized; (3) the instrument has not been altered; (4) the instrument is not subject to any defense or claim of any party that could be asserted against the transferor; and (5) the transferor has no knowledge of any insolvency proceedings against a maker, an acceptor, or the drawer of an unaccepted draft.

QUESTIONS AND CASE PROBLEMS

1. What social forces are affected by the law as to qualified indorsements?

2. As soon as Carol Kamiya gets her weekly paycheck, she carefully writes her name on the back so that everyone will know that it is her check. Is Kamiya protected by doing this?

3. Allan pays Bestor $100, which Allan owes Bestor, with a check stating "Pay to the order of Dale Bestor $100." How can Bestor transfer this check to Wickard in such a way as to make Wickard the holder of the check?

4. Higgins owes the Packard Appliance store $100. He

mails a check to Packard. The check is drawn on First National Bank and states "Pay to the order of cash $100." This check is stapled to a letter stating that the $100 is in payment of the debt owed by Higgins. Edwards is employed by Packard in the mailroom. Edwards removes the letter from its envelope, detaches the check, and disappears. No one knows what has become of the check until it is presented at First National Bank by a person identifying himself as Gene Howard. The bank pays this person $100 and debits that amount against the account of Higgins.

Higgins protests that this cannot be done because the check was lost and never belonged to Howard. Is Higgins correct?

5. A thief steals a blank promissory note from Roger, makes it payable to Dodd, and forges Roger's name to it as maker. Dodd gives value for the note and indorses it to Nell, who in turn indorses it to Robert, a holder in due course. Robert attempts to collect against Roger, who proves that his signature was a forgery. Does Robert have any rights against Dodd or Nell? Why?

6. The Gasts owned a building that they contracted to sell to the Hannas. The building was insured against fire with American Casualty Co. Thereafter, when the building was damaged by fire, a settlement was reached with the insurance company through Sidney Rosenbaum, a public fire adjuster. In order to make payment for the loss, the insurance company drew a draft on itself payable to the Hannas, the Gasts, and Sidney Rosenbaum. Apparently the Hannas indorsed the draft, forged the names of the other payees as indorsers, cashed the draft by presenting it to American Casualty Co., and disappeared. Thereafter the Gasts sued American Casualty. Decide. [*Gast v American Casualty Co.* (NJ Super) 240 A2d 682]

7. Snug Harbor Realty Co. had a checking account in First National Bank. When construction work was obtained by Snug Harbor, its superintendent, Magee, would examine the bills submitted for labor and materials. He would instruct the bookkeeper as to what bills were approved, and checks were then prepared by the bookkeeper in accordance with his instructions. After the checks were signed by the proper official of Snug Harbor, they were picked up by Magee for delivery. Instead of delivering certain checks, he forged the signatures of the respective payees as indorsers and cashed the checks. The drawee bank then debited the Snug Harbor account with the amount of the checks. Snug Harbor claimed this was improper and sued the bank for the amount of the checks. The bank claimed it was protected by the impostor rule. Will the bank be successful? Explain. [*Snug Harbor Realty Co. v First National Bank* (NJ Super) 253 A2d 581]

8. Benton, as agent for Savidge, received an insurance settlement check from Metropolitan Life Insurance Co. He indorsed it "For deposit" and deposited it in Bryn Mawr Trust Co. in Savidge's account. What were the nature and effect of this indorsement? [*Savidge v Metropolitan Life Insurance Co.* (Pa) 110 A2d 730]

9. Humphrey drew a check for $100. It was stolen, and the thief forged the payee's indorsement. The check was then negotiated to Miller, who had no knowledge of these facts. Miller indorsed the check to Citizens Bank. Payment of the check was voided on the ground of the forgery. Citizens Bank then sued Miller as indorser. Decide. [*Citizens Bank of Hattiesburg v Miller* (Miss) 11 So 2d 457]

10. When claims filed with an insurance company were approved for payment, they were given to the claims clerk, who would prepare checks to pay those claims and then give the checks to the treasurer to sign. The claims clerk of the insurance company made a number of checks payable to persons who did not have any claims and gave them to the treasurer together with the checks for valid claims, and the treasurer signed all the checks. The claims clerk then removed the false checks, indorsed them with the names of their respective payees, and cashed them at the bank where the insurance company had its account. The bank debited the account of the insurance company with the amount of these checks. The insurance company claimed that the bank could not do this because the indorsements on the checks were forgeries. Is the insurance company correct? [*General Accident Fire & Life Assur. Corp. v Citizens Fidelity Bank & Trust Co.*, 519 SW2d 817 (Ky)]

11. Eutsler forged his brother Richard's indorsement on certified checks and cashed them at First National Bank. When Richard sought to recover the funds from the bank, the bank stated that it would press criminal charges against Eutsler. Richard asked the bank to delay prosecution to give him time to collect directly from his brother. His brother promised to repay him the money but vanished some six months later without having paid any money. Richard sued the bank. What result? [*Eutsler v First National Bank, Pawhuska* (Okla) 639 P2d 1245]

12. Michael Sykes, the president of Sykes Corp., hired Richard Amelung to handle the company's bookkeeping and deal with all its vendors. Amelung entered into an agreement with Eastern Metal Supply to help reduce Sykes' debt to Eastern. Whenever Sykes received a check, Amelung would sign it over to Eastern and allow it to keep 30 percent of the check amount. On 28 checks that totaled $200,000, Amelung indorsed the back as follows: "Sykes & Associates or Sykes Corporation, Richard Amelung." Amelung then turned the checks over to Eastern, and Eastern deposited them into its account at Barnett Bank. Eastern would then write one of its checks to Sykes Corp. for the 70 percent remaining from the checks. When Michael Sykes learned of the arrangement, he demanded the return of the 30 percent from Barnett Bank, claiming that it had paid over an unauthorized signature and that the indorsement was restricted and

had been violated by the deposit into Eastern's account. What type of indorsement did Amelung make? Did he have the authority to do so? Should Sykes be reimbursed by Barnett? [*Sykes Corp. v Eastern Metal Supply Inc.* (Fla App) 659 So 2d 475]

13. J. Minos Simon and Bud Thibodaux were horse breeders who had negotiated a joint venture for breeding and selling horses. Over the course of their relationship, Fasig-Tipton Co. purchased horses from them and issued checks payable to both Simon and Thibodaux. MidSouth Bank cashed the checks for Thibodaux with only his signature as an indorsement. When a dispute arose between Simon and Thibodaux, Simon brought suit against Fasig-Tipton and MidSouth for their participation in allowing Thibodaux to cash checks without Simon's signature. Is MidSouth liable to Simon? What could Fasig-Tipton have done? [*Simon v Fasig-Tipton Co.* (La App) 652 So 2d 1351]

14. Would a bank be liable to a customer who indorsed a check "For deposit only into account #071698570" if that check were deposited into the wrong account? What if the customer's indorsement was "For deposit only"? Would any account qualify? Would any bank qualify? [*Qatar v First American Bank of Virginia*, 885 F Supp 849 (ED Va)]

15. Two employees of the state of New Mexico fraudulently procured and indorsed a warrant (a draft drawn against funds of the state) made out to the Greater Mesilla Valley Sanitation District. There was no such sanitation district. The employees obtained payment from Citizens Bank. Western Casualty, the state's insurer, reimbursed the state for its loss and then brought suit against the bank for negligently paying the warrant. Decide. [*Western Casualty & Surety Co. v Citizens Bank of Las Cruces*, 676 F2d 1344 (10th Cir)]

CPA QUESTIONS

1. Hand executed and delivered to Rex a $1,000 negotiable note payable to Rex or bearer. Rex then negotiated it to Ford and endorsed it on the back by merely signing his name. Which of the following is a correct statement?
   a. Rex's endorsement was a special endorsement.
   b. Rex's endorsement was necessary to Ford's qualification as a holder.
   c. The instrument initially being bearer paper **cannot** be converted to order paper.
   d. The instrument is bearer paper, and Ford can convert it to order paper by writing "pay to the order of Ford" above Rex's signature.

   (11/86, Law, #41, 0556)

2. Jane Lane, a sole proprieter, has in her possession several checks that she received from her customers. Lane is concerned about the safety of the checks since she believes that many of them are bearer paper which may be cashed without endorsement. The checks in Lane's possession will be considered order paper rather than bearer paper if they were made payable (in the drawer's handwriting) to the order of
   a. Cash.
   b. Ted Tint, and endorsed by Ted Tint in blank.
   c. Bearer, and endorsed by Ken Kent making them payable to Jane Lane.
   d. Bearer, and endorsed by Sam Sole in blank.

   (11/85, Law, #37, 0564)

3. West Corp. received a check that was originally made payable to the order of one of its customers, Ted Burns. The following endorsement was written on the back of the check:

   Ted Burns, without recourse, for collection only

   Which of the following describes the endorsement?

	Special	Restrictive
a.	Yes	Yes
b.	No	No
c.	No	Yes
d.	Yes	No

   (11/92, Law, #35, 3117)

Rights of Holders and Defenses

CHAPTER 33

OBJECTIVES

After studying this chapter, you should be able to

1. Distinguish between an ordinary holder and a holder in due course;
2. List the requirements for becoming a holder in due course;
3. Explain the rights of a holder through a holder in due course;
4. List and explain the limited defenses not available against a holder in due course;
5. List and explain the universal defenses available against all holders; and
6. Describe how the rights of a holder in due course have been limited by the Federal Trade Commission.

Chapters 31 and 32 introduced the requirements for negotiable instruments and the methods for transfer of those instruments. However, the requirements of negotiability and transfer are simply preliminary steps for the discovery of the real benefit of using negotiable instruments in commerce, which is to streamline payment in commercial transactions. Article 3 of the UCC allows for that streamlining by providing for special status and rights of certain parties to negotiable instruments. These parties are protected from many of the underlying contract disputes that arise before and after the negotiable instrument is executed and transferred or sold. The extent of the parties' rights and protections is covered in this chapter.

A. PARTIES TO NEGOTIABLE INSTRUMENTS: RIGHTS AND LIABILITIES

The rights and defenses of the parties to negotiable instruments are determined by the types of parties involved.

1. Types of Parties

An assignee is a third party to whom contract benefits are transferred.

The party claiming to have rights in a negotiable instrument can be an **assignee** or a **holder**. A holder may be an **ordinary holder** or a **holder in due course**.

A holder is a party in possession of an instrument that runs to him, i.e., is indorsed to him, is bearer paper, or is payable to him.

2. Ordinary Holders and Assignees

A holder in due course is a holder of an instrument who has taken for value and in good faith and without notice that the instrument is overdue or has been dishonored.

A holder is a party in possession of an instrument that runs to him. An instrument "runs" to a party if it is payable to his order, is bearer paper, or is indorsed to him. Any holder has all the rights given through and under the negotiable instrument. The holder, although only an ordinary holder, is the only party who may demand payment or bring suit for collection on the instrument. A holder is also the only party who can give a discharge or release from liability on the paper or who can cancel the liability of another party to the instrument.

If a holder is forced to bring suit for payment of an instrument, the holder is required only to produce the instrument and show that the signature of the defendant (the maker, drawer, or indorser) is genuine or admitted. If the defendant has no valid defense, the holder is then entitled to a judgment for the full face amount of the instrument. The fact that the holder is merely an ordinary holder has no significance in terms of payment when there are no defenses to the instrument.

The holder can recover from any one or more prior parties liable on the instrument without regard to the order of the signatures on the instrument. A holder could recover from the first indorser on an instrument or the last party to indorse.

The rights of an ordinary holder are no different from the rights of a contract assignee (see chapter 18). The assignee of a negotiable instrument is in the same position and has the same rights as an ordinary holder. It is immaterial whether the person is an assignee by express assignment, by operation of law, or because of the omission of an essential indorsement. ◆ *For example*, if the farmer who signed the note to pay for his tractor has a warranty problem with the tractor, he has a defense to payment on the note. Anyone who is assigned that note as an assignee or holder is also subject to the farmer's defense. ◆

3.   The Holder-in-Due-Course Protections

The law gives certain holders of negotiable instruments preferred status by protecting them from certain defenses when they demand payment under an instrument. This protection makes negotiable instruments more attractive and allows greater ease of transfer. Holders in due course have an immunity not possessed by ordinary holders or assignees. The favored holders are known as holders in due course or holders through holders in due course.

(a) Holder in Due Course. To obtain the preferred status of a holder in due course,[1] a person must first be a holder. However, the preferred status of holder in due course requires these types of holders to meet additional standards. It is easier to understand the requirements for holder-in-due-course status if you substitute modern terminology and think of "due course" as meaning an ordinary transaction. A holder in due course is someone who acquires an instrument as part of an ordinary business transaction.

For purposes of meeting the holder-in-due-course standards for an ordinary business transaction, the holder in due course must have (1) given value; (2) acted in good faith; (3) no notice that the instrument is overdue or dishonored; and (4) no notice of defenses, alteration, forgery, or adverse claims.

(1) Value. Because the law on negotiable instruments is fundamentally a merchant's or businessperson's law, it favors only the holders who have given value for a negotiable instrument. **Value** is similar to consideration (see chapter 14).

For example, a person who receives property under a will does not give value because the property is a gift. An heir who receives her uncle's promissory notes under the provisions in his will is not a holder in due course because the notes are simply a gift and the transfer lacks consideration and value.

A person takes an instrument for value (1) by performing or promising to perform the act for which the instrument was given, such as when a seller delivers the goods for which the buyer's check was sent as payment;[2] (2) by acquiring a security interest in the negotiable instrument—for example, when a note has been pledged as security for another obligation; or (3) by taking the instrument in payment of, or as security for, a prior or current debt, commonly referred to as an **antecedent debt**. When value is given, the courts do not measure or appraise its amount.[3]

A bank does not give value for a deposited check when it credits the depositor's account with the amount of the deposit. The bank gives value to the extent that the depositor is permitted to withdraw funds against that deposit.[4] *For example,* if Janice deposits a $300 check into her account that already has $400 in it, Janice's bank does not give value until Janice has written checks or withdrawn the existing $400. To give value, a bank must allow the customer to draw on the funds deposited.

Value is consideration or antecedent debt or security given in exchange for the transfer of a negotiable instrument.

---

[1] UCC § 3-302.

[2] Because the 1952 version of Article 3 did not recognize a promise of performance as value, many decisions in states not yet under the 1990 version of the Code did not recognize a "promise of performance" as value. *Midfirst Bank v C.W. Haynes & Co.*, 893 F Supp 1304 (DSC 1994).

[3] UCC § 3-303. Although it is an uncommon occurrence, the original payee may also be a holder in due course, provided one of the necessary standards for value is met. *First National Bank v Creston Livestock Auction, Inc.* (Iowa) 447 NW2d 132 (1989).

[4] UCC § 4-211 (1990).

CASE SUMMARY

The Pole Barn Check: I Thought It Had Already Cleared!

Facts: Randy Bocian had a bank account with First of America-Bank (FAB). On October 8, 1990, Bocian received a check for $28,800 from Eric Christenson as payment for constructing a pole barn on Christenson's property. Bocian deposited the check at FAB on October 9, 1990, and was permitted to draw on the funds through October 12, 1990. Bocian wrote checks totaling $12,334.21, which FAB cleared. On October 12, 1990, Christenson stopped payment on the check as the result of a contract dispute over the pole barn. Bocian was then overdrawn in his account once the check was denied clearance by Christenson's bank. FAB brought suit against both Bocian and Christenson to collect its loss. Christenson counterclaimed against Bocian for his contract breach claims on the pole barn construction. FAB maintained that it had given value and was a holder in due course (HDC) and that, as such, it was not required to be subject to the pole barn issues or the stop-payment order.

Decision: The bank is a HDC as a result of the deposit of the check and the subsequent credit applied and advances made. The bank is a HDC because it gave value to the extent that it applied or withdrew credit for it or made advances against the deposited check. The bank took the instrument for "value" because it extended credit, even though provisional, in reliance on the deposited check or allowed its depositor to make withdrawals against the uncollected funds. The bank is not subject to the stop-payment order and can collect the amount due under the check from Christenson. Christenson will be forced to pursue his pole barn claims with Bocian in a separate action, but FAB will be paid under the check. [First of America-Bank Northeast Illinois v Bocian (Ill App Ct) 614 NE2d 890 (1993)]

C
P
A

In a few special cases, a purchaser of a negotiable instrument is not considered a holder in due course even though all the elements for holder-in-due-course status have been satisfied. A holder who acquires a negotiable instrument by legal process or by purchase in an execution, bankruptcy, or creditor's sale or similar proceeding cannot be a holder in due course. A holder who acquires a negotiable instrument as part of a bulk transaction not in the ordinary course of the transferor's business or as the successor in interest to an estate or other organization is also not a holder in due course. [5]

Good faith is the absence of knowledge of any defects or problems.

(2) Good Faith. The element of **good faith** requires that the taker of the negotiable instrument have acted honestly in acquiring the instrument. In addition, the taker must have observed reasonable standards of fair dealing.[6]

Bad faith can sometimes be established when a holder gives only a small value. The transferee need not give value equal to the face of the negotiable instrument; however, a gross disparity between the value given and the value of the instrument may be evidence of bad faith. Bad faith is established by proof that the transferee had knowledge of facts that made it improper to acquire the instrument under the circumstances.

The fact that a transferee acted carelessly does not establish bad faith.[7] If the transferee takes the instrument in good faith, it is immaterial whether the transferor acted in good faith.

---

[5] UCC § 3-302(c) (1990).
[6] UCC § 3-103(a)(4) (1990).
[7] *Carnegie Bank v Shallegl* (NJ Super) 606 A2d 389 (1992).

(3) *Ignorance of the Instrument's Being Overdue or Dishonored.* An instrument can be negotiated even though (1) it has been dishonored, whether by nonacceptance or nonpayment; (2) it is overdue, whether because of lapse of time or the acceleration of the due date;[8] or (3) it is demand paper that has been outstanding more than a reasonable time.[9] Ownership of the instrument may still be transferred. Nevertheless, the fact that the instrument is circulating at a late date or after it has been dishonored is a suspicious circumstance that should alert the person acquiring the instrument that there may be some adverse claim or defense. A person who acquires title to the instrument under such circumstances cannot be a holder in due course. ◆ *For example,* buying a discounted note after its due date is notice that something may be wrong with the instrument. ◆ Such a person is a holder with rights afforded any other contract holder, but the rights and protections afforded a holder in due course are not available to him.

(4) *Ignorance of Defenses and Adverse Claims.* Prior parties on an instrument may have defenses that they could raise if sued by a person who has had the instrument transferred to them. ◆ *For example,* the drawer of a check, if sued by the payee, might have the defense that the merchandise delivered by the payee was defective. ◆ In addition, third persons, whether prior parties or not, may be able to assert that the instrument belongs to them and not to the possessor. A person who acquires an instrument with notice or knowledge that any person might have a defense or that there is any adverse claim of ownership of the instrument cannot be a holder in due course. The holder of an instrument cannot be a holder in due course when the holder acquired the instrument with knowledge that there had been a failure of consideration with respect to the contract for which the instrument had been given. In general, transferees who are aware of facts that would make a reasonable person ask questions are deemed to know what they would have learned if they had asked questions.[10]

The fact that there are documents of record filed in a public office does not give notice of any defense or claim that would bar a taker from being a holder in due course. Knowledge that a party to the instrument has been discharged from the obligation bars suit against that party, but it does not bar the taker from being a holder in due course.[11]

Knowledge acquired by the taker after acquiring the instrument does not prevent the taker from being a holder in due course. Consequently, the fact that the taker, after acquiring the instrument, learns of a defense does not operate retroactively to destroy the taker's character as a holder in due course.

CASE SUMMARY

Can A "Checks Cashed Here" Store Ever Be a Holder in Due Course?

Facts: Cronin, an employee of Epicycle, cashed his final paycheck at Money Mart Check Cashing Center. Epicycle had issued a stop-payment order on the check. Money Mart deposited the check through normal banking channels. The check was returned to Money Mart marked "Payment Stopped." Money Mart brought an action against Epicycle, claiming that, as a holder in due course, it was entitled to recover against Epicycle. Epicycle argued that

---

[8] *St. Bernard Savings & Loan Ass'n v Cella,* 826 F Supp 985 (ED La 1993).
[9] UCC § 3-304.
[10] *Joint Venture Asset Acquisition v Zellner,* 808 F Supp 289 (SDNY 1992).
[11] UCC § 3-302(b) (1990). An exception exists if the discharge occurred in insolvency proceedings.

Money Mart could not be a holder in due course because it failed to verify the check as good prior to cashing it.

Decision: A determination of whether a holder has "reason to know" is based on "all the facts and circumstances known to him." A person "knows" of a fact when he has "actual knowledge" of it. The question therefore is whether Money Mart had actual knowledge of facts giving it reason to know that a defense existed. There is nothing to distinguish the facts of this case from any other of the thousands of checks that Money Mart and others cash each year: A man came to Money Mart to cash his paycheck; Money Mart is in the business of cashing paychecks; the face of the check disclosed nothing to raise even a suspicion that there was something wrong with it.

There is nothing in using a check-cashing service instead of a bank that would lead to a rule imposing different standards on the two kinds of institutions. Money Mart is a holder in due course and, as such, is not subject to the defenses Epicycle may have against Cronin. *[Money Mart Check Cashing Center Inc. v Epicycle Corp. (Colo) 667 P2d 1372 (1983)]*

A holder through a holder in due course is a holder who may not meet the requirements for becoming a holder in due course but who acquired the instrument from a holder in due course and thereby attains the rights thereto.

(b) Holder through a Holder in Due Course. Those persons who become holders of the instrument after a holder in due course has held it are given the same protection as the holder in due course, provided they are not parties to fraud or illegality that affects the instrument. This status of **holder through a holder in due course** is given even if the transferee from a holder in due course does not satisfy one or more of the elements required for holder-in-due-course status. This status is given under Article 3's "shelter rule," and it allows a person who is not a holder in due course to hide under the "umbrella" with a holder in due course and be sheltered from claims and defenses as if actually being a holder in due course. *For example,* a person who acquires an instrument from an estate does not give value and is missing one of the requirements for being a holder in due course. However, if the estate was a holder in due course, then that status does transfer to the heir. Further, suppose that Avery is a holder in due course of a $5,000 promissory note due May 31, 1998. Avery gives the note to his nephew Aaron for Aaron's birthday on June 1, 1998. Aaron did not give value because the note was a gift, and he has taken the note as a holder after it has already become due. Nonetheless, because Avery was a holder in due course, Aaron assumes that status under Article 3's shelter provision.

B. DEFENSES TO PAYMENT OF A NEGOTIABLE INSTRUMENT

One of the key reasons for attaining holder-in-due-course status is to be able to obtain payment free of any underlying problems between the original parties to the instrument. A holder in due course does take an instrument free from certain types of defenses to payment. Whether a defense may be raised against a holder in due course claiming under a negotiable instrument depends on the nature of the defense. While holders take subject to all forms of defenses, holders in due course often enjoy freedom from their assertion.

4. Classification of Defenses

Limited defenses are defenses such as those common to formation of contracts that cannot be used as defenses to payment of a holder in due course.

Universal defenses are defenses such as insolvency that are good against all parties including a holder in due course.

The importance of being a holder in due course or a holder through a holder in due course is that such holders are not subject to certain defenses called **limited defenses**. Another class of defenses, **universal defenses**, may be asserted against any party, whether an assignee, an ordinary holder, a holder in due course, or a holder through a holder in due course.[12]

5. Defenses against Assignee or Ordinary Holder

An assignee suing on a negotiable instrument is subject to every defense raised by the party from whom payment is sought. Similarly, a holder who is neither a holder in due course nor a holder through a holder in due course is subject to every payment defense just as though the instrument were not negotiable. Thus, an ordinary holder suing on the promissory note of a buyer is subject to the buyer's defense of breach of warranty.[13]

ETHICS & THE LAW

Barrett Bank loaned Just Clothes Corporation a total of $150,000, which consisted of a $100,000 promissory note and a $50,000 line of credit.

First American Bank & Trust (FABT) contacted Jason and Geri Zahn, the owners of Just Clothes Corporation, and asked them to consider transferring these loans to FABT. FABT would then loan the Zahns and their company $150,000. On October 29, 1985, FABT sent the Zahns a letter describing the terms of their new $150,000 loan. The first $100,000 of the loan was to be applied as a capital loan to repay Barrett Bank, and the remaining $50,000 would be used as a revolving line of credit. The $50,000 would be deposited into the Just Clothes account and would be secured by a CD and life insurance policy owned by the Zahns.

The Zahns explained to FABT officials that they needed the line of credit funded because they had a December buying trip scheduled. The Zahns signed all the FABT loan papers on November 26, 1985. However, unbeknownst to the Zahns, the line of credit was not funded until January 8, 1986.

Meanwhile, the Zahns had enjoyed a successful buying trip and had made purchases from several wholesale merchants. The Zahns paid for their purchases with checks from the Just Clothes FABT account. All of the checks were dishonored by FABT. Twelve checks in total were not paid. In less than a year, because they did not have timely merchandise, the Zahns and Just Clothes were in Chapter 7 bankruptcy.

The Zahns feel they were treated unfairly. Do you agree? Did FABT act ethically in these circumstances? What legal arguments could you make to help the Zahns? Why was it important for FABT to have the Zahns' loan at their bank at the end of the calendar year? Did FABT not care once the loan was in its portfolio? *In re* Geri Zahn, Inc. (Fla) 16 UCC Rep Serv 2d 731 (1991).

---

[12] Under the pre-Code law and under the 1952 Code, the universal defense was called a *real defense*, and the limited defense was call a *personal defense*. The terms have now been abandoned, but some licensing and CPA examinations may continue to use these pre-Code terms.

[13] *Pascal v Tardera* (App Div) 507 NYS2d 225 (1986).

6. Limited Defenses Not Available against a Holder in Due Course

O·P·A

Neither a holder in due course nor one having the rights of such a holder is subject to any of the following defenses.

(a) Ordinary Contract Defenses. In general terms, the defenses that could be raised in a breach of contract claim cannot be raised against a holder in due course. The defenses of lack, failure, or illegality of consideration with respect to the instrument's underlying transaction cannot be asserted against the holder in due course. Misrepresentation about the goods underlying the contract is also not a defense. ◆ *For example,* a businessperson cannot refuse to pay a holder in due course on the note on his copy machine just because his copy machine does not have the speed he was promised. ◆

O·P·A

(b) Incapacity of Defendant. Ordinarily, the incapacity of the defendant, other than that of minority, may not be raised against a holder in due course. Such incapacity is a defense, however, if by general principles of law that incapacity makes the instrument a nullity. ◆ *For example,* a promissory note made by an insane person for whom a court has appointed a guardian is void. In the case of a lawsuit on the note by a holder in due course, the incapacity of the maker would be a defense. ◆

Fraud in the inducement is fraud in the obtaining of a promise to an instrument, not fraud as to the nature of the instrument itself.

O·P·A

(c) Fraud in the Inducement. If a person is persuaded or induced to execute the instrument because of fraudulent statements, such **fraud in the inducement** cannot be raised against a party with holder-in-due-course status. ◆ *For example,* suppose Mills is persuaded to purchase an automobile because of Pagan's statements concerning its condition. Mills gives Pagan a note, which is negotiated until it reaches Han, who is a holder in due course. Mills meanwhile learns that the car is not as represented and that Pagan's statements were fraudulent. When Han demands payment of the note, Mills cannot refuse to pay on the ground of Pagan's fraud. Mills must pay the note because Han, as a holder in due course, does not take the note subject to any fraud or misrepresentation in the underlying transaction. Mills is left with the remedy of recovering from Pagan for misrepresentation or fraud. ◆

(d) Miscellaneous Defenses.[14] The limited defenses listed in the preceding three subsections are those most commonly raised against demands or suits by holders in due course for payment. The following limited defenses may also be asserted: (1) prior payment or cancellation of the instrument, (2) nondelivery, (3) conditional or special purpose delivery, (4) breach of warranty, (5) duress consisting of threats, (6) unauthorized completion, and (7) theft of a bearer instrument.

---

[14] UCC § 3-305.

CASE SUMMARY

Can I Trust My Banker To Fill In the Blanks?

Facts: William Martin was a business customer of Pisgah Saving Bank from 1975 until he quit farming in March 1984. He would sign blank notes when he purchased cattle and rely on the banker to fill in the correct amount later when the bank learned the purchase price. In 1988, the bank became insolvent. In April 1989, the FDIC sold some of the bank's assets, including two promissory notes signed by Martin to the plaintiff. The notes show the signature of William L. Martin as maker. The amount of the two notes was close to $100,000. The notes were dated after 1984, and both contained erasures and suspicious-looking type. The FDIC sued Martin on the notes. Martin claimed he had not authorized the notes' completions. The FDIC responded that it was a holder in due course and was not subject to the defense of unauthorized completion.

Decision: Even though the notes were filled in inappropriately by the Pisgah Bank, a holder in due course may enforce instruments as completed. The FDIC, as a holder in due course, is entitled to collect the amount due under the notes from Martin. A holder in due course is not subject to the defense of unauthorized completion. [*National Loan Investors, L.P. v Martin (Iowa App)* 488 NW2d 163 (1992)]

7. Universal Defenses Available against All Holders

Certain defenses are regarded as so basic that the social interest in preserving them outweighs the social interest of giving negotiable instruments the freely transferable qualities of money. Accordingly, such defenses are given universal effect and may be raised against all holders, whether ordinary holders, holders in due course, or holders through a holder in due course. These defenses are called universal defenses.

(a) Fraud as to the Nature or Essential Terms of the Instrument. The fact that a person signs an instrument because the person is fraudulently deceived as to its nature or essential terms is a defense available against all holders.[15]

When one person induces another to sign a note by falsely representing that, for example, it is a contract for repairs or that it is a character reference, the note is invalid, and the defense of the misrepresentation of the character of the instrument can be used against a holder in due course. This defense, however, cannot be raised when the defending party was negligent in examining and questioning the true nature and terms of the instrument.

(b) Forgery or Lack of Authority. The defense that a signature was forged or signed without authority can be raised by a drawer or maker against any holder unless the drawer or maker whose name was signed has ratified it or is estopped by conduct or negligence from denying it.[16] The fact that the negligence of the drawer helped the wrongdoer does not prevent the drawee from raising the defense of forgery.

---

[15] UCC § 3-305(a)(1)(iii)(1990).
[16] *Bank of Hoven v Rausch* (SD) 382 NW2d 39 (1986).

(c) Duress Depriving Control. A party may execute or indorse a negotiable instrument in response to a force of such a nature that, under general principles of law, there is duress that makes the transaction void rather than merely voidable. Duress of this type and level may be raised as a defense against any holder.

(d) Incapacity. The fact that the defendant is a minor, who under general principles of contract law may avoid the obligation, is a matter that may be raised against any kind of holder. Other kinds of incapacity may be raised as a defense if the effect of the incapacity is to make the instrument void.[17]

(e) Illegality. If the law declares that an instrument is void when executed in connection with certain conduct, such as gambling or usury, that defense may be raised against any holder.

An alteration is a material change in the terms of an instrument by a party to it.

(f) Alteration. An **alteration** is an unauthorized change or completion of a negotiable instrument designed to modify the obligation of a party to the instrument.[18]
◆ For example, changing the amount of an instrument from $150.00 to $450.00 is an alteration. ◆

(1) Person Making Alteration. By definition an alteration is a change made by a party to the instrument. A change of the instrument made by a nonparty has no effect. Recovery on the instrument is still possible under the terms of the instrument as though the change had not been made, provided it can be proven how the instrument existed in its original form.

(2) Effect of Alteration. If the alteration to the instrument was made fraudulently, the person whose obligation is affected by it is discharged from liability on the instrument. The instrument, however, can be enforced according to its original terms or its terms as completed. This right of enforcement is given to those taking the instrument for value, in good faith, and without notice of the change or improper completion, to payor banks, and to drawees.[19] While a holder in due course would come within the protected class on alteration, such status is not required for this recovery provision in the event of alteration. ◆ For example, Ryan signed a negotiable demand note for $100 made payable to Long. A subsequent holder changed the amount from $100 to $700. A later holder in due course presented the note to Ryan for payment. Ryan would still be liable for the original amount, $100. ◆

8. Avoidance of Holder-in-Due-Course Protection

In certain situations, the taker of a negotiable instrument is denied the status of a holder in due course or is denied the protection of a holder in due course.

(a) Participating Transferee. The seller of goods on credit frequently assigns the sales contract and buyer's promissory note to the manufacturer who made the goods, to a finance company, or to a bank. In such a case, the assignee of the seller

---

[17] UCC § 3-305(a)(1)(ii) (1990).
[18] UCC § 3-407(a) (1990).
[19] UCC § 3-407(b), (c) (1990).

will be a holder in due course of the buyer's note if the paper is properly negotiated and the transferee satisfies all the elements of being a holder in due course. The transferee, however, may take such an active part in the sale to the seller's customer or may be so related to the seller that it is possible to conclude that the transferee was in fact a party to the original transaction. When this conclusion is reached, the transferee is held to have had notice or knowledge of any defense of the buyer against the seller. This close-connection doctrine prevents a transferee with intimate knowledge of the transferor's business practices from becoming a holder in due course under a guise of good faith and lack of knowledge.[20]

CASE SUMMARY

The Holder In Due Course with the Same Name as My Seller: Is This Good Faith?

Facts: Warmus purchased an airplane from Cessna Aircraft and executed an installment sales contract and promissory note. The note was then transferred to Cessna Finance Corp. After allegedly encountering mechanical difficulties with the plane, Warmus ceased payments on the note. Cessna Finance, claiming holder-in-due-course status, sued Warmus. Warmus claimed that the sole consideration for the execution of the installment contract failed. He also claimed that Cessna Finance was so closely connected with the sales transaction that it could not be a holder in due course.

Decision: The court held that there were significant issues of material fact surrounding the close connection between Cessna Aircraft and Cessna Finance and that a trial was required to determine the validity of Mr. Warmus's claim that Cessna Finance was not a holder in due course and thus subject to his contract defenses about the plane's performance. Cessna Finance's name was preprinted on the Cessna Aircraft forms. Cessna Finance did its own credit check before Cessna Aircraft had even agreed to extend credit to Warmus. Cessna Aircraft and Cessna Finance had common boards of directors and officers. There was at least some indication of close connections and a possible loss of the holder-in-due-course status of Cessna Finance. [*Cessna Finance Corp. v Warmus*, 407 NW 2d 66 (Mich Ct App 1987)]

The Federal Trade Commission Rule is the 1976 FTC rule that eliminates the protection of holder-in-due-course status in consumer credit contracts.

(b) The Federal Trade Commission Rule. In 1976, the Federal Trade Commission (FTC) adopted a rule that limits the rights of a holder in due course in a consumer credit transaction. The rule protects consumers who purchase goods or services for personal, family, or household use.[21] When the buyer is sued by a transferee of the note the buyer gave the seller, the buyer may raise any defense that could have been raised against the seller if the consumer's contract contains the notice required by the FTC regulation. The FTC regulation requires that the following notice be included in boldface type at least ten points in size:

> *Notice*
> *Any holder of this consumer credit contract is subject to all claims and defenses which the debtor could assert against the seller of goods or services obtained with the proceeds hereof. Recovery hereunder by the debtor shall not exceed amounts paid by the debtor hereunder.*

---

[20] *Midfirst Bank v C.W. Haynes & Co.*, 893 F Supp 1304 (DSC 1994).

[21] The regulation does not cover purchases of real estate, securities, or consumer goods or services for which the purchase price is more than $25,000. *Roosevelt Federal Savings & Loan Ass'n v Crider* (Mo App) 722 SW2d 325 (1986).

FIGURE 33-1
The Defenses to Payment under Negotiable Instruments

When a notice preserving consumer defenses is stated in a negotiable instrument, no subsequent person can be a holder in due course of the instrument.[22] A summary of the universal and limited defenses is presented in Figure 33-1.

UNIVERSAL (Available against Assignees, Holders, and Holders in Due Course)	LIMITED (Available against Assignees and Holders but Not against Holders in Due Course)	MIXED (Circumstances Vary the Availability)
Fraud as to the Nature of the Instrument	Fraud in the Inducement	Duress
Forgery	Misrepresentation	Incapacity
Unauthorized Signature	Lack of Consideration	
Incapacity (Declaration)	Breach of Warranty	
Illegality	Cancellation	
Alteration	Failure of Delivery	
Consumer Credit Contracts with FTC Notice	Unauthorized Completion	
	All Ordinary Contract Defenses	

SUMMARY

A holder of a negotiable instrument can be either an ordinary holder or a holder in due course. The ordinary holder has the same rights that an assignee would have. Holders in due course and holders through a holder in due course are protected from certain defenses. To be a holder in due course, a person must first be a holder; that is, the person must have acquired the instrument by a proper negotiation. The holder must then also take for value, in good faith, without notice that the paper is overdue or dishonored, and without notice of defenses and adverse claims. Those persons who become holders of the instrument after a holder in due course are given the same protection as the holder in due course through the shelter provision, provided they are not parties to any fraud or illegality affecting the instrument.

The importance of being a holder in due course or a holder through a holder in due course is that those holders are not subject to certain defenses when they demand payment or bring suit on the instrument. These defenses are limited defenses and include ordinary contract defenses, incapacity unless it makes the instrument void, fraud in the inducement, prior payment or cancellation, nondelivery of an instrument, conditional delivery, duress consisting of threats, unauthorized completion, and theft of a bearer instrument. Universal defenses may be asserted against any plaintiff whether that party is an assignee, an ordinary holder, a holder in due course, or a holder through a holder in due course. Universal defenses include fraud as to the nature or essential terms of the paper, forgery or lack of authority, duress depriving

---

22 UCC § 3-106(d) (1990). This goes beyond the scope of the FTC regulation. The latter merely preserves the defenses of the consumer but does not bar holder-in-due-course protection for other parties, such as an accommodation party to a consumer's note.

control, infancy, illegality that makes the instrument void, and alteration. Alteration is only a partial defense; the favored holder may enforce the instrument according to its original terms.

The Federal Trade Commission rule on consumer credit contracts limits the immunity of a holder in due course from defenses of consumer buyers against their sellers. Immunity is limited in consumer credit transactions if the notice specified by the FTC regulation is included in the sales contract. When a notice preserving consumer defenses is stated in a negotiable instrument, no subsequent person can be a holder in due course.

QUESTIONS AND CASE PROBLEMS

1. What social forces are affected by the holder-in-due-course rule?

2. Holton, who owes Zeigler $100, draws a check on her bank payable to the order of Zeigler for $100 and delivers the check to Zeigler. Holton argues that Zeigler did not give anything in return for the check and therefore has not given value. Is this argument correct?

3. Halleck executed a promissory note payable to the order of Leopold. Halleck did not pay the note when due, and Leopold brought suit on the note, producing it in court. Halleck admitted that he had signed the note but claimed the plaintiff was required to prove that the note had been issued for consideration and that the plaintiff was in fact the holder. Decide. [*Leopold v Halleck* (Ill App) 436 NE2d 29]

4. Johnson issued an order promissory note to James but did not fill in James' name. Henry knew this but still took the note from James for value after James inserted his name and indorsed the note. Johnson did not pay on the due date, alleging lack of consideration, which was a fact. Henry brings suit. Will he recover? Why?

5. Statham drew a check. The payee indorsed it to Kemp Motor Sales. Statham then stopped payment on the check on the ground that there was a failure of consideration for the check. Kemp sued Statham on the check. When Statham raised the defense of failure of consideration, Kemp replied that he was a holder in due course. Statham claimed that Kemp could not recover because Stratham learned of his defense before Kemp deposited the check in its bank account. Decide. [*Kemp Motor Sales v Statham* (Ga App) 171 SE2d 389]

6. Compare the rights of (a) an assignee, (b) a holder, (c) a holder in due course, and (d) a holder through a holder in due course when the original party to the instrument is 17 years old.

7. Jones, wishing to retire from a business enterprise that he had been conducting for a number of years, sold all of the assets of the business to Jackson Corp. Included in the assets were a number of promissory notes payable to the order of Jones that he had taken from his customers. Upon the maturity of one of the notes, the maker refused to pay because there was a failure of consideration. Jackson Corp. sued the maker of the note. Who should succeed? Explain.

8. Elliot, an officer of Impact Marketing, drew six post-dated checks on Impact's account. The checks were payable to Bell for legal services to be subsequently performed for Impact. Financial Associates purchased them from Bell and collected on four of the checks. Payment was stopped on the last two when Bell's services were terminated. Financial argued that it was a holder in due course and had the right to collect on the checks. Impact claimed that because the checks were postdated and issued for an executory promise, Financial could not be a holder in due course. Who was correct? Why? [*Financial Associates v Impact Marketing* (Misc) 394 NYS2d 814]

9. *D* drew a check to the order of *P*. It was later claimed that *P* was not a holder in due course because the check was postdated and because *P* knew that *D* was having financial difficulties and that the particular checking account on which this check was drawn had been frequently overdrawn. Do these circumstances prevent *P* from being a holder in due course? [*Citizens Bank, Booneville v National Bank of Commerce*, 334 F2d 257 (10th Cir); *Franklin National Bank v Sidney Gotowner* (NY Sup) 4 UCC Rep Serv 953]

10. At the time that *H* acquired a check by indorsement, he knew of all the circumstances surrounding the original issue of the check. If *H* had known the legal significance of those circumstances, he would have realized that the drawer of the check had a valid defense. Because *H* did not know the law, he did not realize that the drawer had a defense. He took the check in good faith, believing that everything was proper. In a subsequent lawsuit on the check, the question arose whether *H* was a holder in due course. The defendant claimed that *H* was not because *H* knew of the defense based on the surrounding circumstances and *H*'s ignorance of the law did not excuse him from the consequence of that knowledge

because ignorance of the law is no excuse. Was *H* a holder in due course? [*Hartford Life Ins. Co. v Title Guarantee Co.*, 520 F2d 1170 (DC Cir)]

11. A bank customer purchased a bank money order and paid for it with a forged check. The money order was negotiable and was acquired by *N*, who was a holder in due course. When *N* sued the bank on the money order, the bank raised the defense that its customer had paid with a bad check. Could this defense be raised against *N*? [*Bank of Niles v American State Bank* (Ill App) 303 NE2d 186]

12. Clary received a check whose amount was incomplete from Sanders. The check was given as advance payment on the purchase of 100 LT speakers. The amount was left blank because Clary had the right to substitute other LT speakers if they became available and the substitution would change the price. It was agreed that in no event would the purchase price exceed $5,000. Desperate for cash, Clary wrongfully substituted much more expensive LT speakers, thereby increasing the price to $5,700. Clary then negotiated the check to Lawrence, one of his suppliers. Clary filled in the $5,700 in Lawrence's presence, showing him the shipping order and the invoice applicable to the sale to Sanders. Lawrence accepted the check in payment of $5,000 worth of overdue debts and $700 in cash. Can Lawrence recover the full amount? Why or why not?

13. France fraudulently obtained a negotiable promissory note from Frey by misrepresentation of a material fact. France subsequently negotiated the note to Smith, a holder in due course. David, a business associate of France, was aware of the fraud perpetrated by France and purchased the note for value from Smith. Upon presentment, Frey defaulted on the note. What are David's rights? Why?

14. Shade asked Dow to give him a check for $100 in return for Shade's delivery the next day of a television set. Dow gave the check, but Shade never delivered the television set. Does Dow have a defense if sued on the instrument (a) by Shade; (b) by Shade's brother, to whom Shade gave the unindorsed check as a gift; and (c) by a grocer to whom Shade's brother gave the instrument for value in the ordinary course of business the next day (the grocer took the check without knowledge of the defense and while acting in good faith)? Explain your answers.

15. Dorsey was negligent in not determining that the paper he was signing was actually a promissory note. The note was negotiated by proper indorsement and delivery to New Jersey Mortgage & Investment Co., a holder in due course. Dorsey refused to pay, alleging fraud in the nature of essential terms. Decide. [*New Jersey Mortgage & Investment Co. v Dorsey* (NJ) 165 A2d 297]

CPA QUESTIONS

1. Under the Commercial Paper Article of the UCC, which of the following requirements must be met for a person to be a holder in due course of a promissory note?
   a. The note must be payable to bearer.
   b. The note must be negotiable.
   c. All prior holders must have been holders in due course.
   d. The holder must be the payee of the note.

   (5/95, Law, #46, 5380)

2. A maker of a note will have a real defense against a holder in due course as a result of any of the following conditions **except**
   a. Discharge in bankruptcy.
   b. Forgery.
   c. Fraud in the execution.
   d. Lack of consideration.

   (11/92, Law, #40, 3122)

3. Under the commercial paper article of the UCC, in a nonconsumer transaction, which of the following are real defenses available against a hold in due course?

	Material alteration	Discharge in bankruptcy	Breach of contract
a.	No	Yes	Yes
b.	Yes	Yes	No
c.	No	No	Yes
d.	Yes	No	No

   (5/95, Law, #49, 5383)

Checks and Funds Transfers

CHAPTER 34

627

OBJECTIVES

After studying this chapter, you should be able to

1. *Discuss the significance of certification;*
2. *List and explain the duties of the drawee bank;*
3. *Set forth the methods for, and legal effect of, stopping payment;*
4. *State when a check must be presented for payment in order to charge secondary parties;*
5. *Describe the liability of a bank for improper payment and collection;*
6. *Discuss the legal effect of forgeries and material alterations;*
7. *Specify the time limitations for reporting forgeries and alterations; and*
8. *Describe the electronic transfer of funds and laws governing it.*

The three previous chapters have focused on the characteristics, parties, and transfer of all negotiable instruments. This chapter covers checks as negotiable instruments and the issues related to their transfer and payment because of the involvement of banks and special rules applicable to banks as drawees. New technology has also enhanced the ability of banks and consumers to make rapid commercial transactions through the use of electronic funds transfers. Special rules and rights have been developed to govern these forms of payment that serve to facilitate everything from a consumer withdrawing money from an automated teller machine to a buyer wiring money to a seller whose business is located continents away.

A. CHECKS

A check is a draft payable on demand that is drawn on a bank.

As discussed in chapter 31, a **check** is a draft payable on demand that is drawn on a bank. However, checks, because of the involvement of banks as drawees and in their payment, have some characteristics that make them different from drafts and require additional provisions in law.[1] Figure 34-1 summarizes the differences between checks and drafts.

---

[1] Checks are governed by both Article 3 of the UCC relating to negotiable instruments and Article 4 governing bank deposits and collections. The 1990 version of Article 4 is covered in this chapter. The following states have adopted the 1990 version of Article 4: Alabama, Arizona, Arkansas, California, Colorado, Connecticut, Delaware, District of Columbia, Florida, Hawaii, Idaho, Illinois, Indiana, Iowa, Kansas, Louisiana, Maine, Michigan, Minnesota, Mississippi, Missouri, Montana, Nebraska, Nevada, New Hampshire, New Jersey, New Mexico, North Carolina, North Dakota, Ohio, Oregon, Pennsylvania, South Dakota, Tennessee, Texas, Utah, Vermont, Virginia, Washington, West Virginia, and Wyoming.

Check	Draft
1. Drawee is always a bank	1. Drawee is not necessarily a bank
2. Check is drawn on assumption money is in bank to cover check	2. No assumption drawee has any of drawer's money to pay instrument
3. Check is payable on demand	3. Draft may be payable on demand or at future date

FIGURE 34-1
Differences between a Check and a Draft

1. Nature of a Check

(a) Sufficient Funds on Deposit. As a practical matter, a check is drawn on the assumption that the bank has on deposit in the drawer's account an amount sufficient to pay the check. In the case of other drafts, there is no assumption that the drawee has any of the drawer's money with which to pay the instrument.

If a draft is dishonored, the drawer is civilly liable. If a check is drawn with intent to defraud the person to whom it is delivered, the drawer is also subject to criminal prosecution in most states. The laws under which such drawers are prosecuted are known as bad check laws. Most states provide that if the check is not made good within a stated period, such as ten days, there is a presumption that the drawer originally issued the check with the intent to defraud.

(b) Demand Paper. A draft may be payable either on demand or at a future date. A check is a form of demand draft. The standard form of check does not specify when it is payable, and it is therefore automatically payable on demand.

One exception arises when a check is **postdated**—that is, when the check shows a date later than the actual date of execution. Postdating a check means that the check is not payable until the date arrives, and it changes the check from a **demand draft** to a **time draft**.[2]

(c) Form of the Check. A check can be in any form of writing.[3] However, a bank customer may agree, as part of the contract with her bank, to use certain forms for check-writing.

(d) Delivery Not Assignment. The delivery of a check is not an assignment of the money on deposit, so it does not automatically transfer the rights of the depositor against the bank to the holder of the check. A check written by a drawer on his drawee bank does not result in a duty on the part of the drawee bank to the holder to pay the holder the amount of the check.[4] An ordinary check drawn on a customer's account is direction from a customer to the bank for payment, but it does not impose absolute primary liability on the bank at the time the check is written.

> Postdated means an instrument has a later date than its date of execution.
>
> A demand draft is a draft that is payable upon presentment.
>
> A time draft is a draft that is payable not on demand but at a given date in the future.
>
> Trade acceptance is another name for a time draft.

---

[2] *In re* Channel Home Centers, Inc., 989 F2d 682 (3d Cir 1993).
[3] Although not required for negotiation or presentment, a printed bank check is preferable because it generally carries magnetic ink figures that facilitate sorting and posting.
[4] *Roy Supply, Inc. v Wells Fargo Bank* (Ct App) 46 Cal Rptr 2d 309 (1995).

There are some types of checks for which banks assume more responsibility than for the ordinary customer's check. ◆ *For example,* a bank "money order" payable to John Jones is a check and has the bank as both the drawer and the drawee.[5] A cashier's check is a check or draft drawn by a bank again on itself. If a cashier's check is drawn on another bank in which the drawer bank has an account, it is a teller's check. ◆ Although the drawer and drawee may be the same on a money order or a cashier's check, the instrument does not lose its three-party character or its status as a check.

2. Certified Checks

The drawee bank may certify or accept a check drawn on it. The certification must be written on the check and signed by an authorized representative of the bank. When a bank certifies a check, the bank will set aside in a special account maintained by the bank as much of the drawer's account as is needed to pay the certified check. The certification is a promise by the bank that when the check is presented for payment, the bank will make payment according to the terms of the check. Payment is made regardless of the status of the drawer's account at that time.

A holder or drawer may request that a check be certified by a bank. When certification is at the request of the holder, all prior indorsers and the drawer are released from liability. When certification is at the request of the drawer, the indorsers and drawer, as secondary parties, are not released. Unless otherwise agreed, the delivery of a certified check, a cashier's check, or a teller's check discharges the debt for which the check is given, up to the amount of that check.

3. Presentment for Obtaining Payment on a Check

There are required steps a holder of a check must take in order to obtain payment. As discussed in chapter 32, there are primary and secondary parties for every negotiable instrument. In order to attach that liability and obtain payment, the holder is required to take certain steps within certain amounts of time. The holder must first seek payment from the drawee through **presentment**. No secondary party, including drawers and indorsers, is liable on a check until presentment has been made.

(a) Presentment Requirements. Presentment occurs when the holder of a check exhibits it to the drawee bank and demands payment.[6] The party to whom presentment is made can require that the presenter exhibit identification. The holder is required to present the check during normal business hours; banks can treat the presentment as having occurred the following day when presentment is made after 2 P.M. If a check is presented to the drawee bank for payment and paid, the drawer has no liability because payment has been made.

A certified check is a check for which a bank withdraws the funds from the drawer's account and deposits them in a special account until payment is demanded.

Presentment is the formal request for payment on an instrument.

---

[5] UCC § 3-104 (f) (1990).

[6] In addition to the UCC restrictions on times for presentment, banks must comply with federally imposed time constraints. Under the Expedited Funds Availability Act, PL 100-86, 101 Stat 650, 15 USC §§ 401 et seq., banks are required to lift provisional credits on customer accounts within certain time limits. Holds on customer accounts for clearance or audits are also limited in time.

(b) Time for Presentment of a Check for Payment.[7] Under the UCC, presentment must be made within a reasonable time after the drawers and indorsers have signed the check. What constitutes a reasonable time is determined by the nature of the instrument, by commercial usage, and by the facts of the particular case.

Failure to make timely presentment discharges all prior indorsers of the instrument. It also discharges the drawer to the extent that the drawer has lost, through the bank's failure, money that was on deposit at the bank to make the payment due under the check.[8]

The UCC establishes two presumptions as to what is a reasonable time for presentment of checks. If the check is not certified and is both drawn and payable within the United States, it is presumed that 30 days after the date of the check or the date of its issuance, whichever is later, is the reasonable period in which to make presentment for payment in order to attach secondary liability to the drawer. With respect to attachment of the liability of an indorser, seven days after indorsement is presumed to be a reasonable time.

If a check is dated with the date of issue, it may be presented immediately for payment. If it is postdated, it may ordinarily not be presented until that date arrives. If the holder delays in making presentment, the delay discharges the drawer if the bank itself fails during such delay.[9]

A check is overdue the day after the demand for payment has been made or 90 days after the date of the check if no demand has been made, whichever date is the earlier. If the holder of the check does not present it for payment or collection within 30 days after an indorsement was made, the indorser is discharged from liability to the extent that the drawer has lost, through the bank's failure, money that was on deposit at the bank to meet the payment under the check.

4. Dishonor of a Check

Dishonor is the refusal by the primary party liable on an instrument to pay it.

If the bank refuses to make payment, the drawer is then subject to the same secondary liability as the drawer of an ordinary draft.[10] To be able to attach that secondary liability, the holder of the instrument must notify the drawer of the dishonor by the drawee. The notice of dishonor may be oral, written, or electronic.

Notice of dishonor is a requirement of notification when a party does not pay on an instrument

(a) Time for Notice of Dishonor. Banks in the chain of collection for a check must give notice of dishonor by midnight of the next banking day. Others, including the payee or holder of the check, must give notice of dishonor within 30 days after they learn that the instrument has been dishonored. If proper notice of dishonor is not given to the drawer of the check, the drawer will be discharged from liability to the same extent as the drawer of an ordinary draft.[11]

---

7 UCC § 3-501.
8 UCC § 3-605.
9 UCC § 4-208(c).
10 UCC § 3-414.
11 UCC § 4-213. Under Federal Reserve regulations, notice of dishonor may be given by telephone. *Security Bank and Trust Co. v Federal Nat'l Bank,* 554 P2d 119 (Okla Ct App 1976). But see *General Motors Acceptance Corp. v Bank of Richmondville,* 611 NYS2d 338 (App Div 1994).

An overdraft is a negative balance in a drawer's account created when a bank honors a check that is more than the amount of funds on deposit.

(b) Overdraft. If the bank pays the check but the funds in the account are not sufficient to cover the amount, the excess of the payment over the amount on deposit is an **overdraft**. This overdraft is treated as a loan from the bank to the customer, and the customer must repay that amount to the bank.

If the bank account from which the check is drawn is one held by two or more persons, the joint account holder who does not sign the check that creates an overdraft is not liable for the amount of the overdraft if he or she received no benefit from the proceeds of that check.[12] Additional issues on overdrafts and dishonor of checks are covered in section 5.

5. The Customer-Bank Relationship

The relationship between banks and customers is governed by Articles 3 and 4 of the UCC as well as by several federal statutes. These laws impose duties and liabilities on both banks and customers.

(a) Privacy. The bank owes its customer the duty of maintaining the privacy of the information that the bank acquires in connection with its relationship with the customer. Law enforcement officers and administrative agencies cannot require the disclosure of information relating to a customer's account without first obtaining the customer's consent or a search warrant or without following the statutory procedures designed to protect customers from unreasonable invasions of privacy.[13]

(b) Payment. A bank is under a general contractual duty to its customers to pay on demand all checks to the extent of the funds in a depositor's account.

A stale check is a check whose date is longer than six months ago.

(1) Stale Checks. A bank acting in good faith may pay a check presented more than six months after its date (commonly known as a **stale check**), but unless the check is certified, the bank is not required to do so.[14] The fact that a bank may refuse to pay a check that is more than six months old does not mean that it must pay a check that is less than six months old or that it is not required to exercise reasonable care in making payment of any check.

(2) Payment after Depositor's Death. Subject to certain exceptions, the authority of a bank to act on a customer's check terminates with the death of the customer. An exception to this general rule is that for the first ten days after a customer's death, the bank may continue to pay or certify checks of the customer even though it knows of the customer's death unless ordered to stop such payments or certifications by a person claiming an interest in the account.[15] If the bank does not know of the death of the customer, its power to pay and certify the customer's checks drawn on it continues for ten days after the bank actually receives notification of the death.

---

[12] UCC § 4-214 and UCC § 4-401(b).
[13] Right to Financial Privacy Act of 1978, PL 95-630, 92 Stat 3697, 12 USC §§ 3401 et seq.
[14] UCC § 3-304; § 4-404.
[15] UCC § 4-405 (1990); *Hieber v Uptown Nat'l Bank of Chicago* (Ill App) 557 NE2d 408 (1990).

6. Stopping Payment of a Check

A stop payment order is an order by a drawer to his bank to not make payment on a check.

A drawer may stop payment of a check by appropriately notifying the drawee bank of his or her desire.[16] This procedure is useful when a check is lost or mislaid. A duplicate check can be written, and, to make sure that the payee does not receive payment twice or that an improper person does not receive payment on the first check, payment on the first check can be stopped. Likewise, if payment is made by check and then the payee defaults on the contract so that the drawer would have a claim for breach of contract, payment on the check can be stopped provided the check has not been paid. (See chapter 33 and the rights of holders in due course.)

There are some forms of checks for which stop payments orders are invalid even when properly executed. Neither the drawer nor a bank customer can stop payment of a certified check. A bank customer cannot stop payment of a cashier's check.

(a) Form of Stop Payment Order. The **stop payment order** may be either oral or written. If oral, however, the order is binding on the bank for only 14 calendar days unless confirmed in writing within that time. A written stop payment order or confirmation is effective for six months. A stop payment order can be renewed for an additional six months if the customer provides the bank with a written extension.

(b) Liability to Holder for Stopping Payment. The act of stopping payment may in some cases make the drawer liable to the holder of the check. If the drawer has no proper ground for stopping payment, the drawer is liable to the holder of the check. In any case, the drawer is liable for stopping payment with respect to any holder in due course or any other party having the rights of a holder in due course unless payment was stopped for a reason that may be asserted as a defense against a holder in due course (see chapter 33). The fact that payment of a check has been stopped does not affect its negotiable character.[17]

7. Wrongful Dishonor of a Check

Wrongful dishonor is an error by a bank in refusing to pay a check

A check is **wrongfully dishonored** by the drawee bank if the bank refuses to pay the amount of the check although (1) it is properly payable and (2) the account on which it is drawn is sufficient to pay the item.

Dishonor for lack of funds is also wrongful if the customer has an agreement with the bank that it will pay overdraft items.

(a) Bank's Liability to Drawer of Check. The contract between the customer (drawer) and the bank (drawee) obligates the drawee bank to pay in accordance with the orders of its customer as long as there is sufficient money on deposit to make such payment. If the bank improperly refuses to make payment, it is liable to the drawer for damages sustained by the drawer as a consequence of such dishonor.

---

16 UCC § 4-403.
17 *Perini Corp. v First Nat'l Bank*, 553 F2d 398 (5th Cir 1977).

(b) Bank's Liability to Holder. If a check has not been certified, the holder has no claim against the bank for the dishonor of the check regardless of the fact that the bank acted in breach of its contract with its customer. The bank that certifies a check is liable to the holder when it dishonors the check. The certification imposes primary liability on the bank and requires it to pay the face amount of the check.

(c) Holder's Notice of Dishonor of Check. When a check is dishonored by nonpayment, the holder must follow the procedure for notice to the secondary parties discussed earlier. Notice of dishonor need not be given to the drawer who has stopped payment on a check. Notice is also excused under any circumstances that would excuse notice. ◆ *For example,* no notice need be given a drawer or an indorser who knows that there are insufficient funds on deposit to cover the check. Such party has no reason to expect that the check will be paid by the bank. ◆

8. Agency Status of Collecting Bank

When a customer deposits negotiable instruments in a bank, the bank is regarded as being merely an agent even though the customer may be given the right to make immediate withdrawals against the deposited item.

Because of the bank's agency status, the customer remains the owner of the item and is subject to the risks of ownership involved in its collection.

When a bank cashes a check deposited by its customer or cashes a check drawn by its customer based on an amount from a deposited check, it is a holder of the check deposited by its customer. The bank may still sue to collect from the parties on the check even though the bank is an agent for collection and has the right to charge back the amount of the deposited check if it cannot be collected.

9. A Bank's Duty of Care

A bank is required to exercise ordinary care in the handling of items. The liability of a bank is determined by the law of the state where the bank, branch, or separate office involved is located.

(a) Modification of Bank Duties. The parties in the bank collection process may modify their rights and duties by agreement. However, a bank cannot disclaim liability for lack of good faith or failure to exercise ordinary care, nor can it limit the measure of damages for such lack of care.

When a bank handles checks by automated processes, the standard of ordinary care does not require the bank to make a physical examination of each item unless the bank's own procedures require such examination or general banking usage regards the absence of physical examination of the items as a lack of ordinary care.

An encoding warranty is a warranty made by any party who encodes electronic information on an instrument; a warranty of accuracy.

(b) Encoding Warranty and Electronic Presentment. In addition to transfer and presentment warranties, an **encoding warranty** is also given by those who transfer instruments. Under this warranty, anyone placing information on an item or transmitting the information electronically warrants that the information is correct. When there is an agreement for electronic presentment, the presenter warrants that the transfer is made in accordance with the terms of the agreement for such transmissions.[18]

---

[18] UCC § 4-207–4-209 (1990).

B. LIABILITY OF A BANK

Banks can make mistakes in the payment and collection of items presented to them by their customers. ◆ *For example*, a check may slip through and be cashed over a customer's properly executed stop payment order. The bank would be liable for this improper payment and may also be liable for improperly collecting, paying, or refusing to pay a check. ◆

10. Premature Payment of a Postdated Check

A check may be postdated, but the bank is not liable for making payments on the check before the date stated unless the drawer had given the bank prior notice. This notice must inform the bank that postdated checks would thereafter be presented and that the bank should not make payment on them until the stated date.[19]

11. Payment over a Stop Payment Order

A bank must be given a reasonable time to put a stop payment order into effect. However, if the bank makes payment of a check after it has been properly notified to stop payment, it is liable to the drawer (customer) for the loss the drawer sustains in the absence of a valid limitation of the bank's liability.[20] The burden of establishing losses that result from the bank's failure to stop payment rests with the customer.

CASE SUMMARY

Jail Time for a Stop Payment?

Facts: On August 24, 1989, Karrer and her son opened a joint checking account with Georgia State Bank. The signature card agreement contained a provision that the customer, Karrer, should report any account problems to the bank within 60 days of her statement or lose her rights to assert this problem against the bank. On August 15, 1990, Karrer tendered a check signed by her in the amount of $1,510 to Casey Construction. At the time the check was tendered, Karrer knew there were insufficient funds in her account to cover the check. Casey, who had an account at the same bank, deposited the check to its account along with another check and received $965 in cash. On Saturday, August 18, 1990, Karrer went to the main office of the bank and for the first time notified it that she wanted to stop payment on the check because of Casey's defective work. Her account did not have sufficient funds to honor the check, so the bank assured her that it would do everything to stop payment. The stop payment order was not implemented before the check was returned to Casey for insufficient funds. Karrer was notified on August 24 by Casey's attorney by registered mail that the check was dishonored and that if she failed to pay the full amount of the check, both civil and criminal actions would be filed against her. The letter was returned "Unclaimed." The letter was sent to the same address that Karrer and her son used when they opened the account. Karrer was arrested on October 9 for issuance of a bad check. She never tried to make good the check prior to her arrest or communicate to the bank any problems she had with the requested stop payment order or the return of the check for insufficient funds until June 4, 1991, almost eight months after her arrest. Even on closing her account in February 1991, she said nothing to the bank about its handling of the check or the stop payment order. In August 1991, Karrer filed suit against the bank, alleging that its return of the check for insufficient funds was wrongful, unlawful, and improper.

---

[19] Note that a "postdated check" is not a check but a draft. UCC §§ 4-401–4-402 (1990).
[20] UCC § 4-403(c) (1990).

> She also alleged a breach of the agreement between herself and the bank and demanded damages for her arrest, imprisonment, and indictment on charges of issuing a bad check.
>
> **Decision:** The bank acted in good faith in attempting to notify Karrer that the check had been dishonored. The check had already been sent through by the time Karrer issued her stop payment order. While the notice that the check had been dishonored did not reach Karrer in actuality, the bank sent it to the only address it had for her. Karrer raised no issues despite other contact with the bank. The bank is not liable for the resulting damages Karrer experienced when the stop payment order was not honored because the bank had acted with commercial reasonableness and expediency. [*Karrer v Georgia State Bank of Rome* (Ga App) 452 SE2d 120 (1994)]

12. Payment on a Forged Signature of Drawer

A forgery of the signature of the drawer occurs when the name of the drawer has been signed by another person without authority to do so with the intent to defraud by making it appear that the check was signed by the drawer. The bank is liable to the drawer if it pays a check on which the drawer's signature has been forged, as a forgery ordinarily has no effect as a signature. The risk of loss caused by the forged signature of the drawer is thus placed on the bank without regard to whether the bank could have detected the forgery.[21] The reasoning behind the bank's liability for a forged drawer's signature is that the bank is presumed to know its own customer's signature even if it does not regularly review the checks for authenticity of the signature.

The bank's customer whose signature was forged may be barred from holding the bank liable if the customer's negligence substantially contributed to the making of the forgery. This preclusion rule prevents or precludes the customer from making a forgery claim against the bank. However, to enjoy the protection of the preclusion rule, the bank, if negligent in its failure to detect the forgery or alteration, must have cashed the check in good faith or have taken it for value or collection.[22]

Article 4 of the UCC extends forgery protections and rights to alterations and unauthorized signings (those made with no fraudulent intent). When an officer with authority limited to signing $5,000 checks signs a check for $7,500, the signature is unauthorized. If the principal for the drawer account is an organization and has a requirement that two or more designated persons sign negotiable instruments on its behalf, signatures by fewer than the specified number are also classified as unauthorized signatures.

13. Payment on a Forged or Missing Indorsement

A drawee bank that honors a customer's check bearing a forged indorsement must recredit the customer's account upon the drawer's discovery of the forgery and notification to the bank. A drawee bank is liable for the loss when it pays a check that lacks an essential indorsement.[23] In such a case, the instrument is not properly payable. Without proper indorsements for an order instrument and special

---

[21] *Sun Bank v Merrill Lynch, Pierce, Fenner & Smith, Inc.* (Fla App) 637 So 2d 279 (1994).
[22] UCC § 4-406(e) (1990).
[23] *First Guaranty Bank v Northwest Georgia Bank* (Ga App) 417 SE2d 348 (1992).

indorsements, the person presenting the check for payment is not the holder of the instrument and is not entitled to demand or receive payment.

When a customer deposits a check but does not indorse it, the customer's bank may make an indorsement on behalf of the depositor unless the check expressly requires the customer's indorsement. A bank cannot add the missing indorsement of a person who is not its customer when an item payable is deposited in a customer's bank account.[24]

14. Alteration of a Check

If the face of a check has been altered so that the amount to be paid has been increased, the bank is liable to the drawer for the amount of the increase when it makes payment of the greater amount.

The drawer may be barred from claiming that there was an alteration if there was negligence in writing the check or reporting its alteration. A drawer is barred from claiming alteration if the check was written negligently, the negligence substantially contributed to the making of the material alteration, and the bank honored the check in good faith and observed reasonable commercial standards in doing so. ◆ *For example,* the drawer is barred from claiming alteration when the check was written with blank spaces that readily permitted a change of "four" to "four hundred" and the drawee bank paid out the latter sum because the alteration was not obvious. A careful drawer will write figures and words close together and run a line through or cross out any blank spaces. ◆

15. Unauthorized Collection of a Check

Although a bank acts as agent for its customer in obtaining payment of a check deposited with it by its customer, the bank may be liable to a third person when its customer's action toward that third person is unauthorized or unlawful. If a customer has no authority to deposit the check, some banks, in obtaining payment from the drawee of the check and later depositing the proceeds of the check in the account of its customer, may be liable for conversion of the check to the person lawfully entitled to the check and its proceeds.

A collecting bank, or a bank simply collecting an item for a customer, is protected from liability when it follows the instructions of its customer. It is not required to inquire or verify that the customer had the authority to give such instructions. In contrast, instructions do not protect a payor bank. It has an absolute duty to make proper payment. If it does not, it is liable unless it is protected by estoppel or by the preclusion rule. The person giving wrongful instructions is liable for the loss caused by those instructions.

16. Time Limitations

The liability of the bank to its depositor is subject to certain time limitations.

(a) Forgery and Alteration Reporting Time. A customer must examine with reasonable care and promptness a bank statement and relevant checks that are paid

---

[24] *Krump Construction Co. v First Nat'l Bank,* 655 P2d 524 (Nev 1982).

in good faith and sent to the customer by the bank and must try to discover any unauthorized signature or alteration on the checks. The customer must notify the bank promptly after discovering either a forgery or an alteration. If the bank exercises ordinary care in paying a forged or an altered check and suffers a loss because the customer fails to discover and notify the bank of the forgery or alteration, the customer cannot assert the unauthorized signature or alteration against the bank.[25]

Further, there are some cases of forgery that are the result of the customer's lack of care, as when an employee is given too much authority and internal controls are lacking, with the result that the employee is able to forge checks on a regular basis not easily detected by the bank. Referred to as the fictitious payee exception, this issue was covered in chapter 32.

Customers are precluded from asserting unauthorized signature or alterations if they do not report such within one year from the time the bank statement is received.[26] A forged indorsement must be reported within three years.

(b) Unauthorized Signature or Alteration by Same Wrongdoer. If there is a series of improperly paid items and the same wrongdoer is involved, the customer is protected only as to those items that were paid by the bank before it received notification from the customer and during that reasonable amount of time that the customer has to examine items or statements and to notify the bank. The time limit on the customer's duty to examine the bank statement and report forgeries is 30 days. If the customer failed to exercise reasonable promptness and failed to notify the bank, but the customer can show that the bank failed to exercise ordinary care in paying the item, the loss will be allocated between the customer and the bank.[27]

(c) Statute of Limitations. An action to enforce a liability imposed by Article 4 must be commenced within three years after the cause of action accrued.

C. CONSUMER FUNDS TRANSFERS

Electronic funds transfer (EFT) is a method for payment that involves teller machines, point-of-sale transactions, and automatic deposits and withdrawals.

Consumers have begun to use electronic methods of payment at an increasing rate. From the swipe of the card at the grocery store check-out to the retrieval of funds from the local automated teller machine, **electronic funds transfers** are a way of life for many consumers. A federal statute protects consumers making electronic funds transfers.

17. Electronic Fund Transfers Act

Electronic Funds Transfer Act (EFTA) is a federal law governing consumers' rights and liabilities for electronic funds transactions.

Congress passed the **Electronic Fund Transfers Act (EFTA)** to protect consumers making electronic transfers of funds.[28]

The term *electronic funds transfer (EFT)* means any transfer of funds (other than a transaction originated by check, draft, or similar paper instrument) that is initiated through an electronic terminal, telephone, computer, or magnetic tape that

---

[25] *Vending Chattanooga v American Nat'l Bank and Trust* (Tenn) 730 SW2d 624 (1987).
[26] UCC § 4-406.
[27] UCC § 4-406 (1990).
[28] Act of November 10, 1978, PL 95-630, 92 Stat 3728, 15 USC §§ 1693 et seq.

authorizes a financial institution to debit or credit an account. The service available from an automated teller machine is a common form of EFT.

18. Kinds of Electronic Funds Transfer Systems

There are currently four common kinds of EFT systems in use. In some of these systems, the consumer has a card to access the machine. The consumer usually has a private code that prevents others who wrongfully obtain the card from using it.

(a) Automated Teller Machine. The automated teller machine (ATM) performs many of the tasks once performed exclusively by bank employees. Once a user activates an ATM, he or she can deposit and withdraw funds from his or her account, transfer funds between accounts, make payments on loan accounts, and obtain cash advances from bank credit cards.[29]

An ATM (automated teller machine) is a machine that facilitates electronic banking transactions.

(b) Pay-by-Phone System. This system facilitates paying telephone and utility bills without writing checks. The consumer calls the bank and directs the transfer of funds to a designated third party.

(c) Direct Deposit and Withdrawal. Employees may authorize their employers to deposit wages directly to their accounts. A consumer who has just purchased an automobile on credit may elect to have monthly payments withdrawn from a bank account to be paid directly to the seller.

A point-of-sale transaction is an electronic means of payment whereby funds are withdrawn by a merchant at the point of the sale for the buyer's benefit from the buyer's account.

(d) Point-of-sale Terminal. The **point-of-sale terminal** allows a business with such a terminal to transfer funds from a consumer's account to the store's account. The consumer must be furnished in advance with the terms and conditions of all EFT services and must be given periodic statements covering account activity. Any automatic EFT from an individual's account must be authorized in writing in advance.

Financial institutions are liable to consumers for all damages proximately caused by the failure to make an EFT in accordance with the terms and conditions of an account. Exceptions exist if the consumer's account has insufficient funds, the funds are subject to legal process, the transfer would exceed an established credit limit, or insufficient cash is available in an ATM.

19. Consumer Liability

A consumer who notifies the issuer of an EFT card within two days after learning of a loss or theft of the card can be held to a maximum liability of $50 for unauthorized use of the card. Failure to notify within this time will increase the consumer's liability for losses to a maximum of $500.

The consumer has a responsibility to examine periodic statements provided by the financial institution. If it is established that a loss would not have occurred but for the failure of the consumer to report within 60 days of the transmittal of the statement any unauthorized transfer, then the loss is borne by the consumer.

---

[29] *Curde v Tri-City Bank & Trust Co.* (Tenn App) 826 SW2d 911 (1992).

CASE SUMMARY

I Missed That $20 ATM Withdrawal!

Facts: The Krusers, who had a checking account with the Bank of America, received a Versatel plastic card that enabled them to obtain cash from an automatic teller machine. They believed that Mr. Kruser's card had been destroyed, but it actually had been lost. The account statement for December showed that an unauthorized $20 withdrawal had been made with Mr. Kruser's card. However, the Krusers did not notice this until August or September of the following year. The bank statements for July and August showed 47 unauthorized withdrawals totaling over $9,000. The Krusers promptly notified the bank and demanded that their account be recredited with the amount of the withdrawals.

Decision: The court held that the failure of the Krusers to notify the bank of the $20 withdrawal was the cause of the future losses. Notification of that $20 withdrawal could have prevented the withdrawals that occurred during July and August. The bank is entitled to judgment under the law and need not credit the Krusers' account. [*Kruser v Bank of America (Ct App) 281 Cal Rptr 463 (1991)*]

ETHICS & THE LAW

Electronic funds transfer technology has made life very convenient. You can withdraw cash from teller machines at the bank, the university, the airport, or the mall. You can use your debit card to pay for your groceries just by swiping your card through a machine at the check-out counter. The ease of credit card use finds us using the cards for even our fast food purchases.

However, these electronic devices keep perfect records. Every cash withdrawal amount and location is recorded. Every grocery purchase can be traced. Your location can be determined by the last business where you used your credit card. The electronic age brings convenience, but it also brings a certain amount of privacy loss. With the information gained about you through the use of electronic funds transfers, a firm could put together a profile that estimates your income, outlines your budget and expenditures, specifies your shopping preferences, and provides an itemized list of grocery store purchases.

This extensive information is invaluable for effective marketing. Knowing when, where, and how much households and individual consumers spend can help target customers. Metromail is a consumer information firm that sells lists of customers to businesses. Those lists are customized ones developed from Metromail's consumer data base (which it says covers 90 percent of all U.S. households) following criteria the buyer establishes. For example, a *Los Angeles Times* reporter requested a mailing list for children. Metromail sold the reporter a list with 5,000 names. The reporter used the name of Richard Allen Davis, the convicted murderer of 12-year-old Polly Klaas. Should there be restrictions on the use of EFT information? Do you think its use should be regulated? What policies would you implement to prevent misuse of information about customers?

D. FUNDS TRANSFERS

The funds transfers made by businesses are governed by the UCC and Federal Reserve regulations.

20. What Law Governs

In states that have adopted Article 4A of the Uniform Commercial Code, funds transfers are governed by that article.[30] In addition, whenever a Federal Reserve bank is involved, the provisions of Article 4A apply by virtue of Federal Reserve regulations.

21. Characteristics of Funds Transfers

The transfers regulated by Article 4A are characteristically made between highly sophisticated parties dealing with large sums of money. Speed of transfer is often an essential ingredient. An individual transfer may involve many millions of dollars, and the national total of such transfers on a business day can amount to trillions of dollars.

22. Pattern of Funds Transfers

In the simplest form of funds transfer, both the debtor and the creditor have a separate account in the same bank.[31] In this situation, the debtor can instruct the bank to pay the creditor a specified sum of money by subtracting that amount from the debtor's account and adding it to the creditor's account. As a practical matter, the debtor will merely instruct the bank to make the transfer, and the bank, upon making the transfer, will debit the debtor's account.

A more complex situation is involved if each party has an account in a different bank. In that case, the funds transfer could involve only these two banks and no clearinghouse. The buyer could instruct the buyer's bank to direct the seller's bank to make payment to the seller. Here there would be direct communication between the two banks. In a more complex situation, the buyer's bank may relay the payment order to another bank, called an *intermediary bank,* and that bank, in turn, would transmit it to the seller's bank.

Further complexity is found when there are two or more intermediary banks or when a clearinghouse is involved.

23. Scope of UCC Article 4A

Article 4A applies to all funds transfers except as expressly excluded by its own terms, by federal preemption, or by agreement of the parties or clearinghouse rules.

---

[30] The following states have adopted the 1990 version of Article 4A: Alabama, Arizona, Arkansas, California, Colorado, Connecticut, Delaware, District of Columbia, Florida, Georgia, Hawaii, Idaho, Illinois, Indiana, Iowa, Kansas, Kentucky, Louisiana, Maine, Maryland, Massachusetts, Michigan, Minnesota, Mississippi, Missouri, Montana, Nebraska, Nevada, New Hampshire, New Jersey, New Mexico, New York, North Carolina, North Dakota, Ohio, Oklahoma, Oregon, Pennsylvania, Rhode Island, South Dakota, Tennessee, Texas, Utah, Vermont, Virginia, Washington, West Virginia, Wisconsin, and Wyoming.

[31] The text refers to debtor and creditor in the interest of simplicity and because that situation is the most common in the business world. However, a gift may be made by a funds transfer. Likewise, a person having separate accounts in two different banks may transfer funds from one bank to another.

Some funds transfers are excluded from Article 4A because of their nature or because of the parties involved.

(a) EFTA and Consumer Transactions. Article 4A does not apply to consumer transaction payments to which the EFTA applies. If any part of the funds transfer is subject to the EFTA, the entire transfer is expressly excluded from the scope of UCC Article 4A.[32]

A credit transfer (in commercial EFTs) is the buyer's request of payment to a beneficiary's bank.

A debit transfer (in commercial EFTs) is the beneficiary's request of payment.

(b) Debit Transfers. When the person making payment, such as the buyer, requests that payment be made to the beneficiary's bank, the transaction is called a **credit transfer**. If the beneficiary entitled to money goes to the bank according to a prior agreement and requests payment, the transaction is called a **debit transfer**. The latter kind of transfer is not regulated by Article 4A. Article 4A applies only to transfers begun by the person authorizing payment to another.

(c) Nonbank Transfers. In order for Article 4A to apply to a money transfer, it is necessary that, once the transfer is begun, all communication be between banks. Thus, sending money by Western Union does not come under 4A because there is no bank-to-bank communication. Payment by check is also not covered because the drawer of the check sends the check directly to the payee. There is no involvement of banks until the payee deposits the check or presents it for payment. Likewise excluded under Article 4A is payment by credit card even when the transaction does not come within the scope of the EFTA.

24. Definitions

Article 4A employs terms that are peculiar to Article 4A or are used in a particular context.

(a) Funds Transfer. A funds transfer is more accurately described as a communication of instructions or requests to pay a specific sum of money to, or to the credit of, a specified account or person. There is no actual physical transfer or passing of money.

An originator (in commercial EFTs) is the party who originates the funds transfer.

A beneficiary (in commercial EFTs) is the party to whom the transfer of funds is made.

(b) Originator. The person starting the funds transfer is called the **originator** of the funds transfer.[33]

(c) Beneficiary. The **beneficiary** is the ultimate recipient of the benefit of the funds transfer. Whether it is the beneficiary personally, an account owned by the beneficiary, or a third person to whom the beneficiary owes money is determined by the payment order.

(d) Beneficiary's Bank. The beneficiary's bank is the final bank in the chain of transfer that carries out the transfer by making payment or application as directed by the payment order.

---

[32] UCC § 4A-108 (1990). This exclusion applies when any part is subject to Regulation E adopted under the authority of that statute.
[33] UCC § 4A-201 (1990).

(e) Payment Order. The **payment order** is the direction given by the originator to the originator's bank or by any bank to a subsequent bank to make the specified funds transfer. Although called a payment order, it is in fact a request. No bank is required or obligated to accept a payment order unless it is so bound by a contract or clearinghouse rule that operates independently of Article 4A.

(f) Acceptance of Payment Order. When a receiving bank other than the beneficiary's bank receives a payment order, it accepts or executes that order by issuing a payment order to the next bank in the transfer chain. When the beneficiary's bank agrees to, or actually makes, the application of funds as directed by the payment order, the order has been accepted by that bank.

25. Form of Payment Order

There are no specific legal requirements for the form of the payment order. There is no requirement that funds transfer orders or documents be in writing. As a practical matter, it is probable there will be a written contract between an originator and the originator's bank. There may be agreements between parties and banks as well as clearinghouse and funds transfer system rules that do mandate a writing.

26. Manner of Transmitting Payment Order

Article 4A makes no provisions for the manner of transmitting a payment order. As a practical matter, most funds transfers under Article 4A are controlled by computers, and payment orders will be electronically transmitted. Article 4A, however, applies to any funds transfer payment order even if made orally, such as by telephone, or in writing.

   The agreement of the parties or the clearinghouse and funds transfer system rules may impose some restrictions on the methods for communicating orders.

27. Security Procedure

Because there is no writing and no face-to-face contact in the typical funds transfer, Article 4A contemplates that the banks in the transfer chain will agree on a commercially reasonable security procedure. Reasonable commercial practice would require that a bank receiving a payment order be able to verify that a payment order was authorized by the purported sender and that it is free from error.[34]

   A bank that receives a payment order that passes the security procedure may act on the basis of the order. It is immaterial that the order was not authorized or was fraudulent.

28. Regulation by Agreement and Funds Transfer System Rule

Article 4A, with minor limitations, permits the parties to make agreements that modify or change the provisions of Article 4A that would otherwise govern. Likewise, the rules of a clearinghouse or a funds transfer system through which the banks operate may change the provisions of the Code.

---

[34] Id § 4A-201. But see *Credit Lyonnais-New York v Washington Strategic Consulting Group*, 886 F Supp 92 (D DC 1995).

(a) Choice of Law. When the parties enter into an agreement for a funds transfer, they may designate the law that is to apply in interpreting the agreement. The parties are given a free hand to select a jurisdiction. Contrary to the rule applicable in other Code transactions, there is no requirement that the jurisdiction selected bear any relationship to the transaction.

(b) Clearinghouse Rules. The banks involved in a particular funds transfer may be members of the same clearinghouse. In such a case, they will be bound by the lawful rules and regulations of the house. The rights of the parties involved in a funds transfer may be determined by the rules of FedWire, a clearinghouse system operated by the Federal Reserve system, or by CHIPS, which is a similar system operated by the New York clearinghouse.

29. Acceptance of Payment Order

A bank receiving a payment order accepts the order when it complies with the order's terms. What acceptance means depends on whether the receiving bank is an intermediary bank or the beneficiary's bank.

An intermediary bank is a bank in between the originator and the beneficiary bank in the transfer of funds.

(a) Intermediary Bank. An **intermediary bank** accepts a payment order when it carries out or executes the order by transmitting a similar payment order to the next bank in the transfer chain. Unlike a check sent through bank collection channels, the original payment order is not transferred, but a new payment order by the intermediary bank is dispatched.

(b) Beneficiary's Bank. The beneficiary's bank accepts a payment order when it notifies the beneficiary that it holds the amount of the payment order at the disposal of the beneficiary. The payment order may require the beneficiary's bank to credit the amount to an account or to a named person. The person so named may be the beneficiary, as when a buyer uses a funds transfer to pay the purchase price to the seller. A beneficiary can also be a designated third person. *For example*, a buyer could direct the crediting of the bank account of a manufacturer in order to discharge or reduce the debt of the seller to the manufacturer. The transfer to the manufacturer would reduce or discharge the debt of the buyer to the seller by the amount transferred.

When the beneficiary's bank complies with the payment order, it accepts the order. When the bank does so, it takes the place of the originator as the debtor owing the beneficiary. In such a case, the originator no longer owes the beneficiary, and the debt to the beneficiary is discharged or reduced by the amount of the payment order.[35]

30. Reimbursement of the Bank

After the beneficiary's bank accepts the payment order, it, and every bank ahead of it in the funds transfer chain, is entitled to reimbursement of the amount paid to or for the beneficiary. This reimbursement is due from the preceding bank. By going back along the funds transfer chain, the originator's bank, and ultimately the originator, makes payment of this reimbursement amount.

---

[35] UCC § 4A-406.

31. Refund on Noncompletion of Transfer

If the funds transfer is not completed for any reason, the sender or originator is entitled to a refund of any payment that has been made in advance to the originator's bank. The sender or originator is not required to reimburse any bank for payment made by it.

32. Error in Funds Transfer

There may be an error in a payment order. The effect of an error depends on its nature.

(a) Kind of Error. The error in a payment order may consist of a wrong identification or a wrong amount.

(1) Wrong Beneficiary or Account Number. The payment order received by the beneficiary's bank may contain an error in the designation of the beneficiary or in the account number. This error may result in payment being made to or for the wrong person or account.

(2) Excessive Amount. The payment order may call for the payment of an amount that is greater than it should be. For example, the order may wrongly add an additional zero to the specified amount.

(3) Duplicating Amount. The payment order may be issued after a similar payment order has already been transferred, so that the second order duplicates the first. This duplication would result in doubling the proper amount paid by the beneficiary's bank.

(4) Underpayment. The payment order may call for the payment of a smaller sum than was ordered. For example, the order may drop off one of the zeros from the amount ordered by the originator.

(b) Effect of Error. When the error is one of the first three classes noted above, the bank committing the error will bear the loss because it will not be reimbursed for any amount that it caused to be wrongfully paid. In contrast, when the error is merely underpayment, the bank making the mistake can cure the fault by making a supplementary order for the amount of the underpayment. If verification by the agreed-upon security procedure would disclose an error in the payment order, a bank is liable for any loss caused by the error if it failed to verify the payment order by such a procedure. In contrast, if the security procedure was followed but did not reveal any error, there is no liability for accepting the payment order.

When an error of any kind is made, the possibility also exists that there may be liability under a collateral agreement of the parties, a clearinghouse or funds transfer system rule, or general principles of contract law. However, the right of the originator to complain that there is an error may be lost in certain cases by failure to notify the involved bank that the mistake had been made.

33. Liability for Loss

Unless otherwise regulated by agreement or clearinghouse rule, very slight liability is imposed on a bank in the funds transfer chain that follows the agreed-upon security procedure.

(a) Unauthorized Order. If a bank executes or accepts an unauthorized payment order, it is liable to any prior party in the transfer chain for the loss caused. However, as a practical matter, such loss will rarely be imposed because the transfer is typically made under an agreement establishing a security procedure. If a bank acts on the basis of an unauthorized order that nevertheless is verified by the security procedure, the bank is not liable for the loss that is caused.

The customer, however, can avoid this effect of verification by a security procedure by proving that the security procedure was not commercially reasonable or that the payment order was initiated by a total stranger. The latter requires the customer to show that the initiator was not an employee or agent of the customer's having access to confidential security information or a person who obtained that information from a source controlled by the customer. However, it is immaterial whether the customer was at fault.

(b) Failure to Act. A bank that fails to carry out a payment order is usually liable at the most for interest loss and expenses. There is no liability for the loss sustained by the originator or for consequential damages suffered because payment was not made to satisfy the originator's obligation to the beneficiary. A person seeking to exercise an option by forwarding money to the optionor cannot recover for the loss of the option when the failure of a bank to act results in the optionor's not receiving the money in time.

SUMMARY

A check is a particular kind of draft; it is drawn on a bank and payable on demand. A delivery of a check is not an assignment of money on deposit with the bank on which it is drawn. A check does not automatically transfer the rights of the depositor against the bank to the holder of the check, and there is no duty on the part of the drawee bank to the holder to pay the holder the amount of the check.

A check may be an ordinary check, a cashier's check, or a teller's check. The name on the paper is not controlling. Unless otherwise agreed, the delivery of a certified check, a cashier's check, or a teller's check discharges the debt for which it is given, up to the amount of the check.

Certification of a check by the bank is the acceptance of the check—the bank becomes the primary party. Certification may be at the request of the drawee or the holder. Certification by the holder releases all prior indorsers and the drawer from liability.

Notice of nonpayment of a check must be given to the drawer of a check. If no notice is given, the drawer is discharged from liability to the same extent as the drawer of an ordinary draft.

A depositor may stop payment on a check. However, the depositor is liable to a holder in due course unless such stop payment was for a reason that may be raised against a holder in due course. The stop payment order may be oral (binding for 14 calendar days) or written (effective for six months).

Liability of a secondary party cannot be enforced unless that party was given proper notice of the dishonor.

The depository bank is the agent of the depositor for the purpose of collecting a deposited item. The bank may become liable when it pays a check contrary to a stop payment order or when there has been a forgery or an alteration. The bank is not liable, however, if the drawer's negligence has substantially contributed to the forgery. A bank that pays on a forged instrument must recredit the drawer's account. A depositor is subject to certain time limitations in order to enforce liability of the bank.

A customer and a bank may agree that the bank should retain canceled checks and simply provide the customer with a list of paid items. The customer must examine canceled checks or paid items to see if any were improperly paid.

An electronic funds transfer is a transfer of funds (other than a transaction originated by check, draft, or other commercial paper) that is initiated through an electronic terminal, telephone, computer, or magnetic tape so as to authorize a financial institution to debit or credit an account. The Electronic Fund Transfers Act requires that a financial institution furnish consumers with specific information containing all the terms and conditions of all EFT services. Under certain conditions, the financial institution will bear the loss for unauthorized transfers. Under other circumstances, the loss will be borne by the consumer.

Funds transfers regulated by UCC Article 4A are those made between highly sophisticated parties who deal with large sums of money. If any part of the funds transfer is subject to the EFTA, such as consumer transactions, the entire transfer is expressly excluded from the scope of Article 4A. A funds transfer is simply a request or an instruction to pay a specific sum of money to, or to the credit of, a specified person. The person who originates the funds transfer is called the funds transfer originator. The beneficiary is the ultimate recipient of the funds transfer.

QUESTIONS AND CASE PROBLEMS

1. What social forces are involved in the common statutory provision that it will be presumed a check was issued with intent to defraud if the drawer does not pay the amount of the check within ten days after its dishonor?

2. Helen was a very forgetful person, so she had placed her bank code (PIN number) on the back of her debit card. A thief stole Helen's card and was able to take $100 from an automatic teller machine the day of the theft. That same day Helen realized that the card was gone and phoned her bank. The following morning the thief withdrew another $100. For how much, if anything, is Helen responsible? Why?

3. Shirley drew a check on her account in First Central Bank. She later telephoned the bank to stop payment on the check, and the bank agreed to do so. Sixteen days later the check was presented to the bank for payment and was paid by the bank. Shirley sued the bank for violating the stop payment order. The bank claimed it was not liable. Is Shirley entitled to recover?

4. Arthur Odgers died, and his widow, Elizabeth Odgers (Elizabeth Salsman by remarriage), retained Breslow as the attorney for her husband's estate. She received a check payable to her drawn on First National City Bank. Breslow told her to deposit it in her husband's estate. She signed an indorsement "Pay to the order of Estate of Arthur J. Odgers." Breslow deposited this check in his trustee account in National Community Bank, which collected the amount of the check from the drawee, First City National Bank. Thereafter, Elizabeth, as administratrix of the estate of Arthur J. Odgers, sued National Community Bank for collecting this check and crediting Breslow's trustee account with the proceeds. Was National Community Bank liable? Explain. [*Salsman v National Community Bank* (NJ Super) 246 A2d 162]

5. Shipper was ill for 14 months. His wife did not take care of his affairs carefully, nor did she examine his bank statements as they arrived each month. One of Shipper's acquaintances had forged his name to a check in favor of himself for $10,000. The drawee bank paid the check and charged Shipper's account. Shipper did not notify the bank for 13 months after he received the statement and the forged check. Can he compel the bank to reverse the charge? Why?

6. Gloria maintains a checking account at First Bank. On the third day of January the bank sent Gloria a statement of her account for December accompanied by the checks that the bank had paid. One of the checks had her forged signature, which Gloria discovered on the 25th of the month, when she prepared a bank reconciliation. Upon discovering this, Gloria immediately notified the bank. On January 21, the bank had paid another check forged by the same party who had forged the December item. Who must bear the loss on the forged January check?

7. Dean bought a car from Cannon. As payment, Dean gave him a check drawn on South Dorchester Bank of Eastern Shore Trust Co. Cannon cashed the check at

the Cambridge Bank of Eastern Shore Trust Co. The drawee bank refused payment when the check was presented on the ground that Dean had stopped payment because of certain misrepresentations made by Cannon. Will Eastern Shore Trust Co. succeed in an action against Dean for payment? [*Dean v Eastern Shore Trust Co.* (Md) 150 A 797]

8. A depositor drew a check and delivered it to the payee. Fourteen months later the check was presented to the drawee bank for payment. The bank had no knowledge that anything was wrong and paid the check. The depositor then sued the person receiving the money and the bank. The depositor claimed that the bank could not pay a stale check without asking the depositor whether payment should be made. Was the depositor correct? [*Advanced Alloys, Inc. v Sergeant Steel Corp.* (Queens Co. Civ Ct) 340 NYS2d 266]

9. Siniscalchi drew a check on his account in Valley Bank of New York. About a week later the holder cashed the check at the bank on a Saturday morning. The following Monday morning Siniscalchi gave the bank a stop payment order on the check. The Saturday morning transaction had not yet been recorded, and neither the bank nor Siniscalchi knew that the check had been cashed. When that fact was learned, the bank debited Siniscalchi's account for the amount of the check. He claimed that the bank was liable because the stop payment order had been violated. Was the bank liable? [*Siniscalchi v Valley Bank of New York* (Nassau Co. Dist Ct) 359 NYS2d 173]

10. Bogash drew a check on National Safety Bank and Trust Co., payable to the order of Fiss Corp. At the request of Fiss Corp., the bank certified the check. The bank later refused to make payment on the check because of a dispute between Bogash and the corpo-

ration over the amount due the corporation. The corporation sued the bank on the check. Decide. [*Fiss Corp. v National Safety Bank and Trust Co.* (City Ct) 77 NYS2d 293]

11. Compare the differences between certification of a check by a bank at the request of the depositor and certification at the request of a holder.

12. Norris, who was ill in the hospital, was visited by his sister during his last days. Norris was very fond of his sister and wrote a check to her that she deposited in her bank account. Before the check cleared, Norris died. Can the sister collect on the check even though the bank knew of the depositor's death? Explain. [*In re Estate of Norris* (Colo) 532 P2d 981]

13. After Tusso sent a check for $1,000 drawn on Security National Bank payable to Adamson Construction Co., he realized that he had already paid Adamson. At 9 A.M. the next morning he notified the bank to stop payment. Later that morning the check was brought to the bank, and at 10:40 A.M. the bank certified the check and charged it to Tusso's account. Tusso sued the bank to recover the amount of the first check charged. The bank claimed that he was required to prove that the bank was negligent. Decide. [*Tusso v Security National Bank* (Suffolk Co. Dist Ct) 349 NYS2d 914]

14. Hixson paid Galyen Petroleum Co. money he owed with three checks. The bank refused to cash the three checks because of insufficient funds in the Hixson account to pay all three. Galyen sued the bank. What was the result? Why? [*Galyen Petroleum Co. v Hixson* (Neb) 331 NW2d 1]

15. What is the maximum liability of a consumer who fails to notify the issuer of an EFT card after learning of the loss or theft of the card?

1. A check has the following endorsements on the back:

    > *Paul Frank*
    > without recourse
    >
    > *George Hopkins*
    > payment guaranteed
    >
    > *Ann Quarry*
    > collection guaranteed
    >
    > *Rachell Ott*

    Which of the following conditions occurring subsequent to the endorsements would discharge all of the endorsers?
    a. Lack of notice of dishonor.
    b. Late presentment.
    c. Insolvency of the maker.
    d. Certification of the check.
    (11/92, Law, #41, 3123)

2. Blare bought a house and provided the required funds in the form of a certified check from a bank. Which of the following statements correctly describes the legal liability of Blare and the bank?
    a. The bank has accepted; therefore, Blare is without liability.
    b. The bank has **not** accepted; therefore, Blare has primary liability.
    c. The bank has accepted, but Blare has secondary liability.
    d. The bank has **not** accepted, but Blare has secondary liability.
    (11/89, Law, #43, 0541)

3. In general, which of the following statements is correct concerning the priority among checks drawn on a particular account and presented to the drawee bank on a particular day?
    a. The checks may be charged to the account in any order convenient to the bank.
    b. The checks may be charged to the account in any order provided **no** charge creates an overdraft.
    c. The checks must be charged to the account in the order in which the checks were dated.
    d. The checks must be charged to the account in the order of lowest amount to highest amount to minimize the number of dishonored checks.
    (11/88, Law, #39, 9911)

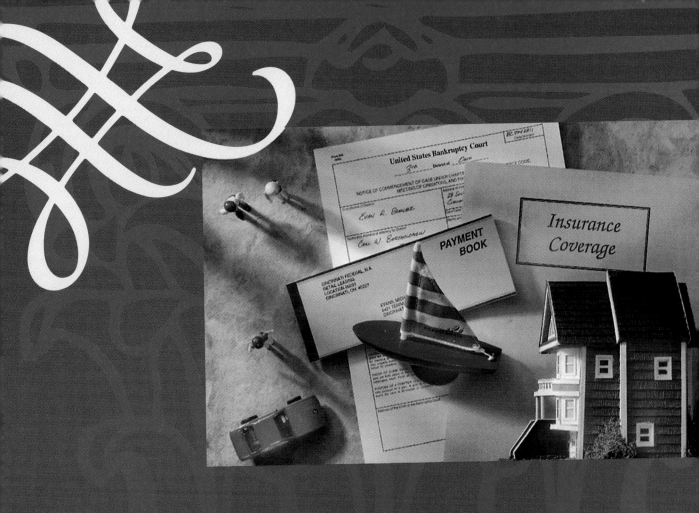

PART 6

Debtor-Creditor Relations and Risk Management

Secured Transactions in Personal Property

After studying this chapter, you should be able to

1. *Describe a secured transaction in personal property;*
2. *Explain the requirements for creating a valid security interest;*
3. *List the four major types of collateral;*
4. *Define perfection and explain its significance in secured transactions;*
5. *Discuss the priorities of parties with conflicting interests in collateral when default occurs; and*
6. *State the rights of the parties upon the debtor's default.*

Money is loaned, and sales are made on credit. Lenders and sellers hope that the borrowers and buyers can repay the money or pay for their purchases. To provide creditors with additional assurance that money will be repaid, legal rights in property can be assigned to creditors so that in the event the person obligated to pay does not pay, the creditor can turn to the property as a means of satisfying the obligation.

A. CREATION OF SECURED TRANSACTIONS

A secured transaction is one means by which personal property is used to provide a back-up plan or security for the creditor in the event the borrower does not pay. Secured transactions are governed by Article 9 of the Uniform Commercial Code.[1]

1. Definitions

A **secured interest is a property right given to a creditor that allows the creditor to take possession of the property in the event the debtor does not pay.**

Collateral is property subject to a security interest.

A secured party is the creditor or lender (person who is owed the money) in a secured transaction.

A debtor is a borrower or buyer who purchases on credit.

A **secured transaction** in personal property is created by giving the creditor a security interest in that property.

A **security interest** is a property right that enables the creditor to take possession of the property if the debtor does not pay the amount owed. ◆ **For example,** if you borrow money from a bank to buy a car, the bank will take a security interest in the car. If you do not repay the loan, the bank can take possession of the car and resell it to recover the money the bank has loaned you. If you purchase a side-by-side refrigerator from Kelvin's Appliances on credit, Kelvin's will take a security interest in the refrigerator. If you do not repay Kelvin's, Kelvin's can take possession of the refrigerator and sell it to cover the amount you still owe. ◆

The property that is subject to the security interest is called **collateral**. In the preceding examples, the car was the collateral for the loan, and the refrigerator was Kelvin's collateral.

(a) Parties. The person owed the money, whether as a seller or a lender, is called the **creditor** or **secured party**. The buyer on credit or the borrower is called the **debtor**.

---

[1] All 50 states, including Louisiana, have some version of Article 9 as law.

(b) Nature of Creditor's Interest. The creditor does not own the collateral, but the security interest is a property right. That property right can ripen into possession and the right to transfer title as the section in this chapter on default discusses. However, the creditor also has certain present property interests and rights even prior to default. For example, having a security interest gives the creditor standing to sue a third person who damages, destroys, or improperly repossesses the collateral.

If the creditor has possession of the collateral, the UCC imposes a duty of care on the creditor. The UCC provides that reasonable care must be exercised in preserving the property. The creditor is liable for damage that results from failing to do so.

(c) Nature of Debtor's Interest. A debtor who is a borrower will ordinarily own the collateral.[2] As such, the debtor has all the rights of any property owner to recover damages for the loss or improper seizure of, or damage to, the collateral.

2. Creation of a Security Interest

A security interest is created, or **attaches**, when the following three conditions are satisfied: there is a security agreement, value has been given, and the debtor has rights in the collateral. These three conditions can occur in any order. A security interest will attach when the last of these conditions has been met.[3] When the security interest attaches, it is then enforceable against the debtor and the collateral.

(a) Agreement. There must be an agreement between the creditor and the debtor that the creditor will have a security interest. The **security agreement** is the agreement of the creditor and the debtor that the creditor will have a security interest. The agreement must identify the parties, contain a reasonable description of the collateral, indicate the parties' intent that the creditor have a security interest in it, and describe the debt or the performance that is secured thereby.

If the creditor has possession of the collateral, the security agreement may be oral regardless of the amount involved.[4] ◆ *For example,* if you pledge your stereo system to a friend as security for the loan and the friend will keep it at his home until you have repaid him, your friend has possession of the collateral, and your oral security agreement is valid and enforceable by your friend. ◆ If the creditor does not have possession of the collateral, as in the case of credit sales and most secured loans, the security agreement must be written and signed by the debtor.

In addition to being signed by the debtor, the agreement must contain a description of the collateral pledged to the creditor.[5]

(b) Value. The creditor gives **value** either by lending money to the debtor or by delivering goods on credit. The value may be part of a contemporaneous exchange or given previously as a loan. ◆ *For example,* a debtor who already owes a

---

Attachment is the creation of a valid security interest.

Security agreement is a contract between a debtor and a creditor giving the creditor an interest in the collateral.

Value is a loan of money or goods delivered; a requirement for a valid security interest although it need not be contemporaneous with the pledge of collateral.

---

2 *Gibson County Farm Bureau Co-op. Ass'n v Greer* (Ind App) 643 NE2d 313 (1994); *Belke v M & I First Nat'l Bank* (Wis App) 525 NW2d 737 (1994).

3 UCC § 9-203; *Alpine Paper Co. v Lontz* (Mo App) 856 SW2d 940 (1993).

4 UCC § 9-207; *Myers v Fifth Third Bank* (Ohio App) 624 NE2d 748 (1993). If there is no written security agreement, the security interest itself is destroyed when the collateral is surrendered.

5 UCC §§ 9-201, 9-110.

creditor $5,000 could later pledge a water scooter as collateral for that loan and give the debtor a security interest in the scooter. ◆ In fact creditors who become nervous about repayment often request collateral later during the course of performance of a previously unsecured loan.

(c) Rights in the Collateral. The debtor must have rights in the collateral for a security interest to attach. These rights could include everything from title to the right to possession.[6]

CASE SUMMARY

The Creditor, the Seller, the Landlord, and the Citrus-Sorter

Facts: Charles Lakin, who did business as Sun Country Citrus, owned a citrus-packing plant in Yuma, Arizona. In 1985, the packing plant was leased to Sunco Partners. Under the terms of the lease, Sunco had the right to replace existing packing, sizing, and grading equipment with "state-of-the-art" equipment.

In 1986, PKD, Inc., purchased Sunco. Sunco signed a bill of sale for all of its "personal property, including but not limited to, packing equipment, boilers, compressors, and packinghouse-related supplies." The bill of sale was secured by an Article 9 security interest executed by PKD as the debtor and Lakin/Sunco as the creditors.

In February 1987, PKD changed its name to Amcico and negotiated for the purchase and lease of citrus-sorting equipment from Pennwalt Corporation, now Elf Atochem. The documents for the transaction specifically provided that title to the equipment would remain with Elf Atochem until all payments were made under the terms of the sale and lease agreement.

In December 1987, Amcico defaulted on its payments to Lakin and Sunco. Lakin and Sunco took possession of all of the equipment in the Yuma plant. Elf Atochem objected, claiming its title to the citrus-sorting equipment. Lakin and Sunco produced the security agreement giving them such equipment as collateral. Elf Atochem claimed that because it retained title in the citrus-sorting equipment, there was no interest in it on the part of Amcico and the security interest of Sunco and Lakin never attached.

Decision: Elf Atochem was correct. Attachment of the security interest was a problem in that the equipment was not in existence at the time of the sale and lease to Amcico. Further, the future acquisition could not be included when Elf Atochem never surrendered its rights in the citrus-sorter, thereby preventing Amcico from acquiring an interest. [*Elf Atochem North America, Inc. v Celco, Inc.* (Ariz App) 927 P2d 355 (1996)]

---

3. Purchase Money Security Interest

Purchase money security interest (PMSI) is the interest of a seller who sells on credit or a lender who lends money for the purchase of the goods.

When a seller sells on credit and is given a security interest in the goods, that interest is called a **purchase money security interest (PMSI)**. If the buyer borrows money from a third person so that the purchase can be made for cash, a security interest given the lender in the goods is also called a purchase money security interest.[7] There are certain special priority rights given in some circumstances to creditors who hold a purchase money security interest.

---

[6] UCC § 9-112.
[7] UCC § 9-107; *In re* Freeman, 956 F2d 252 (11th Cir 1992).

4.   The Nature and Classification of Collateral

The nature of the collateral in a credit transaction as well as its classification under Article 9 affects the procedural obligations and rights of creditors. The basic types of collateral are consumer goods, equipment, inventory, general intangibles, farm products, and fixtures.[8] Other issues with respect to these general categories of collateral arise, such as whether the security interest covers the collateral when its changes form, as when the inventory is sold in exchange for a promissory note.

(a) Consumer Goods. Collateral is classified as **consumer goods** if it is used or bought primarily for personal, family, or household use. It is the use of the good and not its properties that controls its classification. ◆ *For example,* a computer purchased by an architect for her office is not a consumer good. That same computer purchased by the same architect for use by her children at their home is a consumer good. A refrigerator purchased for the kitchen near an office conference center is not a consumer good. A refrigerator purchased for a home is a consumer good. ◆ It is the use that controls the label for the collateral.

Consumer goods are goods purchased for home or personal use.

(b) Equipment. Collateral is **equipment** if it is used or bought primarily for use in a business—for example, a fax machine used in a business office.

Equipment is collateral used in the operation of a business.

(c) Inventory. Collateral is **inventory** if it is held primarily for sale or lease to others or if it consists of raw materials, work in process, or materials consumed in a business. ◆ *For example,* inventory includes a clothing retailer's dresses and suits or crates of vegetables in a grocery store. Keyboards and processing units used by a computer manufacturer in assembling its final product would also be inventory. ◆

Inventory is collateral used for sale or lease to others.

(d) General Intangibles. **General intangibles** include forms of intellectual property as well as accounts receivable, notes, and negotiable instruments. Property rights evidenced by documents would fall into the general intangibles category.

(e) Farm Products. **Farm products** that can be used as collateral include crops, livestock, or supplies used or produced in farming operations.

Farm products are goods such as crops, livestock, and the byproducts from such.

(f) Fixtures. **Fixtures** are a form of collateral that consists of goods that were once personal property but that now are attached to real property (see chapter 50 for more details on fixtures).

Fixtures are personal property attached or affixed in a permanent fashion to real property.

(g) Attachment in Future Transactions. When the security interest is intended to cover future loans or advances, the interest already existing expands to cover any future advance when received by the debtor. If the security agreement so provides, the security interest attaches to **after-acquired goods**.[9] This attachment occurs as soon as the debtor acquires rights in those goods. ◆ *For example,* a security interest can cover the current inventory of the debtor and any future replenishments if a clause in the security agreement adds "after-acquired

After-acquired goods are goods acquired after a security interest has attached.

C · P · A

---

8 UCC §§ 9-106, 9-109; *Octagon Gas Systems, Inc. v Rimmer,* 995 F2d 948 (10th Cir 1993), *cert den* 114 S Ct 554 (1994).
9 UCC § 9-108.

Floating lien is a security interest with an after-acquired property clause.

property" to the description of the inventory. ◆ Referred to in lay terms as a **floating lien**, the creditor's interest attaches to the inventory regardless of its form or time of arrival in terms of the attached security interest.

An after-acquired property clause in a security agreement cannot cover all consumer goods that the debtor may ever acquire. It can only cover goods acquired by the debtor within ten days after the creditor gave value to the debtor.

Proceeds are the value received for the sale of the collateral, such as cash, checks, or notes.

(h) Proceeds. The debtor may receive payments for selling or leasing the collateral to a third person. If the collateral has been insured and is damaged or destroyed, the debtor will receive money from the insurance company. All of these payments are called **proceeds** of the collateral and are automatically subject to the creditor's security interest unless the contrary was stated in the security agreement. The proceeds may be in any form, such as cash, checks, or other property.

B. PERFECTION OF SECURED TRANSACTIONS

Perfected security interest is a secured interest that gives public notice of the creditor's rights through possession, filing, or statutory protection.

Attachment of the security interest makes it enforceable against the debtor. Attachment allows the secured party to resort to the collateral to enforce the debt upon default. The creditor holding a security interest in collateral may face competing claims of other creditors of the debtor or persons to whom the debtor has sold the collateral. However, a creditor who obtains a **perfected security interest** enjoys priority over unperfected interests and may in some cases enjoy priority over other perfected interests. A security interest is valid against the debtor even though it is not perfected. However, perfection provides creditors with rights superior to unperfected interests. Attachment provides creditors with rights; perfection provides them with priority.

The nature of the goods or the transaction determines what must be done to obtain perfection.

5. Perfection by Creditor's Possession

If the collateral is in the possession of the creditor, the security interest in the possessed goods is perfected.[10] It remains perfected until that possession is surrendered. ◆ *For example,* when a creditor has taken a security interest in 50 gold coins and has those gold coins in his vault, his possession of the coins is perfection. ◆

Field warehousing is an arrangement whereby the seller's agent has possession of the collateral at the buyer's place of business, or "in the field."

A more complex example of possession as a means of perfection is found in the commercial tool of **field warehousing**. In this arrangement, a creditor actually has an agent on site at a buyer's place of business, and the creditor's agent controls the buyer's access to, use of, and transfer of the collateral. ◆ *For example,* an aircraft manufacturer may have an agent on site at a aircraft dealership. That agent decides when the planes can be released to buyers and who will receive the buyer's payment or note. ◆

---

[10] UCC § 9-305; *Royal Bank of Pennsylvania v Selig* (Pa Super) 644 A2d 516 (1994).

6. Perfection for Consumer Goods

A purchase money security interest in consumer goods is perfected from the moment it attaches.[11] Known as **automatic perfection**, no other action is required for perfection as against other creditors. Because there are so many consumer purchases on credit, the UCC simplifies perfection so that merchant seller-creditors are not overly burdened with paperwork. However, as discussed in the section on priorities, the automatic perfection of a PMSI in consumer goods does have some limitations. It may be destroyed by the debtor-consumer's resale of the goods to a consumer who does not know of the security interest.

7. Perfection for Motor Vehicles

In most states, a non-Code statute provides that a security interest in a noninventory motor vehicle must be noted on the vehicle title registration. When so noted, the interest is perfected. In states that do not have a separate motor vehicle perfection system, there must be a filing of a financing statement, as described in the next section.

8. Perfection by Filing a Financing Statement

The **financing statement** is a brief statement that gives sufficient information to alert third persons that a particular creditor may have a security interest in the collateral described. (See Figure 35-1.)

The financing statement must be signed by the debtor. It must give an address of the secured party from which information concerning the security interest may be obtained. The financing statement must give a mailing address of the debtor, and it must contain a statement indicating the kind, or describing the items, of collateral.[12]

The financing statement need not include the terms of the agreement between the parties. However, a security agreement can be filed as a financing statement if it contains all of the above-required information.

Because the financing statement is intended as notice to third parties, it must be filed in a public place. The location for filing a financing statement is either central or local.[13] A typical central filing location in many states is the office of the secretary of state. A typical local filing location is the recorder or other office that handles land and property tax records. Whether a filing is required to be central or local depends upon the nature of the collateral. ◆ *For example*, financing statements for consumer goods and fixtures are generally filed locally. Financing statements for inventory, equipment and general intangibles are usually filed centrally. ◆

---

[11] UCC § 9-302; *Thompson v Danner* (ND) 507 NW2d 550 (1993).
[12] UCC § 9-402; *Farmers & Merchants State Bank v Teveldal* (SD) 524 NW2d 874 (1994).
[13] UCC § 9-401; *Mastro v Witt*, 39 F3d 238 (9th Cir 1994).

FIGURE 35-1
*Financing
Statement*

Uniform Commercial Code – FINANCING STATEMENT

This FINANCING STATEMENT is presented to a Filing Officer for filing pursuant to the Uniform Commercial Code	No. of Additional Sheets Presented:	3. ☐ The Debtor is a transmitting utility.
1. Debtor(s) (Last Name First) and Address(es):	2. Secured Party(ies) Name(s) and Address(es):	4. For Filing Officer: Date, Time, No. Filing Office:

5. This Financing Statement covers the following types (or items) of property:

6. Assignee(s) of Secured Party and Address(es):

☐ Products of the Collateral are also covered.

7. ☐ The described crops are growing or to be grown on:*
☐ The described goods are or are to be affixed to:*
☐ The lumber to be cut or minerals or the like (including oil and gas) is on:*
*(Describe Real Estate Below)

8. Describe Real Estate Here: ☐ This statement is to be indexed in the Real Estate Records: 9. Name of a Record Owner

No. & Street	Town or City	County	Section	Block	Lot

10. This statement is filed without the debtor's signature to perfect a security interest in collateral (check appropriate box)
☐ under a security agreement signed by debtor authorizing secured party to file this statement, or
☐ which is proceeds of the original collateral described above in which a security interest was perfected, or
☐ acquired after a change of name, identity or corporate structure of the debtor, or ☐ as to which the filing has lapsed, or already subject to a security interest in another jurisdiction:
☐ when the collateral was brought into the state, or ☐ when the debtor's location was changed to this state.

By _____   By _____
Signature(s) of Debtor(s)   Signature(s) of Secured Party(ies)

ETHICS & THE LAW

Beach 40 Limited Partnership is a real estate partnership that owns and develops real property and is now in bankruptcy. One of its assets is a parking garage in which spaces are "licensed" in three different ways. Some are licensed in bulk; that is, a group ranging from 10 to 120 spaces is leased to a corporation or other entity. Other spaces are licensed individually on a month-to-month basis, generally to commuters who need a regular place to park. A final group of spaces is licensed daily, as the garage is open to the public, who can park for a fee on the basis of the time vehicles are parked in the garage.

One of Beach 40's creditors has an Article 9 security interest in all "licenses and resulting fees" owned by Beach 40 and is entitled to priority on the funds collected from the parking garage because it has a perfected security interest in those licenses and fees. Beach 40's other creditors maintain that the fees paid by those using the parking garage are "rent" and that, as such, they are real property interests in which the other creditors have priority as real property creditors. Without the parking garage licenses and resulting fees, the creditors have no asset as security. Beach 40 refers to the interest as licenses in its contracts with the companies and individuals who have long-term parking arrangements.

Do you think the parking garage fees are rent or licenses? What do you think the parties intended? Is it fair to deny the license fees to the creditors when there is no other pledged security interest?

(a) Errors in Financing Statement. Errors in the financing statement have no effect unless they are seriously misleading. If they are seriously misleading, the filing has no effect and does not perfect the security interest.

(b) Defective Filing. When the filing of the financing statement is defective either because the statement is so erroneous or incomplete that it is seriously misleading or the filing is made in a wrong county or office, the filing fails to perfect the security interest. The idea of perfection by filing is to give public notice of a creditor's interest. To the extent that the notice cannot be located or does not give sufficient information, the creditor then cannot rely on it in order to obtain the superior position of perfection. When there is a question about where a financing statement should be filed, the creditor should file in both central and local locations to avoid a possible loss of perfected status.[14]

CASE SUMMARY

The Magical Carpet Sign: Its Perfection Disappeared

Facts: In 1983, Carpet Contracts owned a commercial lot and building, which it operated as a retail carpet outlet. In April of that year, Carpet Contracts entered into a credit sales agreement with Young Electric Sign Corporation (Yesco) for the purchase of a large electronic sign for the store. The total cost of the sign was $113,000, with a down payment of $25,000 and 60 monthly payments of $2,100 each.

In August 1985, Carpet Contracts agreed to sell the property to Interstate. As part of the sale, Carpet Contracts gave Interstate an itemized list showing that $64,522 of the proceeds from the sale would be used to pay for the "Electronic Sign." The property was transferred to Interstate, and the Carpet Contracts store continued to operate there, but now it paid rent to Interstate. In June 1986, Carpet Contracts asked Yesco to renegotiate the terms of the sign contract. Yesco reduced Carpet Contracts' monthly payments and filed a financing statement on the sign at the Utah Division of Corporations and Commercial Code.

In December 1986, Interstate agreed to sell the property and the sign to the Webbs. The Webbs conducted a title search on the property, which revealed no interest with respect to the electronic sign. Interstate conveyed the property to the Webbs. Carpet Contracts continued its operation but was struggling financially and had not made its payments to Yesco for some time. By 1989, Yesco declared the sign contract in default and contacted the Webbs, demanding the balance due of $26,100. The Webbs then filed suit, claiming Yesco had no priority as a creditor because its financing statement was not filed in the real property records where the Webbs had done their title search before purchasing the land.

Decision: The court held that the sign was not equipment but a fixture. As a fixture, the proper place for the filing of a security interest in it was the recorder's office, where land records are located. The central filing at the Division of Corporations and Commercial Code was not sufficient public notice to give Yesco a perfected interest. The Webbs purchased the property in good faith without notice of any interest of Yesco. Yesco has no priority due to its failure to file in the proper location. [Webb v Interstate Land Corp. (Utah) 920 P2d 1187 (1996)]

9. Other Means of Perfection

Temporary perfection is the state of perfection given for a limited period of time to creditors.

Under Article 9, there are other forms of perfection. Some creditors are given **temporary perfection** for the collateral.[15] For example, a creditor is generally given four months to refile its financing statement in a state to which a debtor has

---

[14] UCC § 9-403.
[15] UCC § 9-304.

relocated. During that four-month period, the interest of the creditor is temporarily perfected in the new state despite no filing of a financing statement in that state's public records. Most creditors' agreements provide that the failure of the debtor to notify the creditor of a move constitutes a default under the credit agreement. Creditors need to know of the move so that they can refile in the debtor's new state.

10. Loss of Perfection

The perfection of the security interest can lost if the creditor does not comply with the Article 9 requirements for continuing perfection.

(a) Possession of Collateral. When perfection was obtained because the creditor took possession of the collateral, that perfection is lost if the creditor voluntarily surrenders the collateral to the debtor without any restrictions.

(b) Consumer Goods. The perfection obtained by the automatic status of a PMSI is lost in some cases by removal of the goods to another state. The security interest may also be destroyed by resale of the goods to a consumer. To protect against these types of losses of protection, the creditor would need to file a financing statement. In the case of a PMSI, the perfection is good against other creditors but is not superior when it comes to buyers of the goods.

(c) Lapse of Time. The perfection obtained by filing a financing statement lasts five years. The perfection may be continued for successive five-year periods by filing a continuation statement within six months before the end of each five-year period.[16]

(d) Removal from State. In most cases, the perfection of a security interest lapses when the collateral is taken by the debtor to another state unless, as noted earlier, the creditor makes a filing in that second state within the four-month period of temporary perfection.

(e) Motor Vehicles. If the security interest is governed by a non-Code statute creating perfection by title certificate notation, the interest, if so noted, remains perfected without regard to lapse of time or removal to another state. The perfection is lost only if a state issues a new title without the security interest rotation.

C. RIGHTS OF PARTIES BEFORE DEFAULT

The rights of parties to a secured transaction are different in the time preceding the debtor's default from those in the time following the default.

11. Status of Creditor before Default

The status of a creditor who loaned money to the debtor is determined by ordinary principles of contract law. A creditor who is a seller of goods has the rights granted

---

[16] UCC § 9-403.

by Article 2, Sales, of the Uniform Commercial Code. If the creditor is the lessor of goods, that status is determined by Article 2A, Leases, of the Uniform Commercial Code.

12. Status of Debtor before Default

The status of the debtor before default depends on whether there is a loan, a sale, or a lease.

The status of a debtor who borrowed money from the creditor is determined by ordinary principles of contract law. If the debtor is a buyer or lessee of goods, the debtor's status is determined by Article 9, Secured Transactions, and by either Article 2 or 2A of the Uniform Commercial Code.

13. Statement of Account

To keep the record straight, the debtor may send the creditor a written statement of the amount the debtor thinks is due and an itemization of the collateral together with the request that the creditor approve the statement as submitted or correct and return the statement. Within two weeks after receiving the debtor's statement, the creditor must send the debtor a written approval or correction. If the secured creditor has assigned the secured claim, the creditor's reply must state the name and address of the assignee.

14. Termination Statement

Termination statement is a creditor's statement that the debt has been satisfied and that the collateral is now owned free and clear by the debtor.

A debtor who has paid his or her debt in full may make a written demand on the secured creditor, or the latter's assignee if the security interest has been assigned, to send the debtor a **termination statement**.[17] A termination statement states that a security interest is no longer claimed under the specified financing statement. The debtor may present this statement to the filing officer, who marks the record terminated and returns to the secured party the various papers that had been filed. The termination statement clears the debtor's record so subsequent buyers or lenders will not be subject to the now-satisfied security interest.

D.   PRIORITIES

Two or more parties may have conflicting interests in the same collateral. However, the seller must file a financing statement to protect its security interest in the event of sale of the collateral to a buyer or repledge of the same collateral to a different creditor. In this section, the rights of creditors and buyers with respect to each other and to collateral that carries a secured interest or perfected secured interest are discussed.

---

[17] UCC § 9-404; *In re* Kitchin Equipment Co. of Virginia, 960 F2d 1242 (4th Cir 1992).

15. Unsecured Party vs. Unsecured Party

When creditors are unsecured, they have equal priority. In the event of insolvency or bankruptcy of the debtor, all the unsecured creditors stand at the end of the line in terms of repayment of their debts. In the event the assets of the debtor are insufficient to satisfy all unsecured debtors, the unsecured debtors simply receive a **pro rata** share of their debts.

Pro rata means a proportionate share.

16. Secured Party vs. Unsecured Party

A secured creditor has a right superior to that of an unsecured creditor because the secured creditor can take back the collateral from the debtor's assets, while an unsecured creditor simply waits for the leftovers once all secured creditors have taken back their collateral. If the collateral is insufficient to satisfy the secured creditor's debt, the secured debtor can still stand in line with the unsecured creditors and collect an additional amount or pro rata share. *For example,* suppose that Linens Galore has a security interest in Linens R Us's inventory. Linens Galore has the right to repossess the inventory and sell it to satisfy the debt Linens R Us owes. Suppose that Linens R Us owes Linens Galore $22,000, and the sale of the inventory brings $15,000. Linens Galore still has a claim as an unsecured creditor for the remaining $7,000 due.

17. Secured Party vs. Secured Party

If two creditors have a secured interest in the same collateral, their priority is determined according to a **first-in-time provision**; that is, the creditor whose interest attached first has priority in the collateral.[18] The secured party whose interest was last to attach must then proceed against the debtor as an unsecured creditor because the collateral was given to the creditor whose interest attached first. *For example,* if Bob pledged his antique sign collection to Bill on October 30, 1998, with a signed security agreement in exchange for a $5,000 loan and then pledged the same collection to Jane on November 1, 1998, with a signed security agreement, Bill has priority because his security agreement attached first.

18. Perfected Secured Party vs. Secured Party

The perfected secured creditor will take priority over the unperfected secured creditor and will be entitled to take the collateral. The unperfected secured party is then left to seek remedies as an unsecured creditor because the collateral has been given to the perfected creditor. *For example,* with respect to Bob's sign collection, if Jane filed a financing statement on November 2, 1998, then she would have priority over Bill because her perfected interest is superior to Bill's unperfected interest even though Bill's interest attached before Jane's.

The perfected secured party's interest as against other types of creditors, such as lienors, mortgagees, and judgment creditors, is also determined on a **first-to-perfect basis**. If the secured party perfects before a judgment lien or mortgage is recorded, the perfected secured creditor has priority.

---

[18] UCC § 9-312; *Melcher v Bank of Madison, Neb* (Neb App) 529 NW2d 814 (1995).

19. Perfected Secured Party vs. Perfected Secured Party

The general rule for priority among two perfected secured creditors in the same collateral is also a first-in-time rule: The creditor who perfected first is given priority. *For example,* again with respect to Bob's sign collection, if Bill filed a financing statement on November 3, 1998, Jane would still have priority because she perfected her interest first. If, however, Bill filed a financing statement on October 31, 1998, then he would have priority over Jane. There are, however, three exceptions to this rule of first-in-time, first-in-right for perfected secured creditors.

(a) The Purchase Money Security Interest in Inventory. If the collateral is inventory, the purchase-money secured creditor must do two things to prevail even over prior perfected secured creditors. The creditor must perfect before the debtor receives possession of the goods that will be inventory, and the creditor must also give written notice to any other secured party who has previously filed a financing statement with respect to that inventory. The other secured parties must receive this notice before the debtor receives possession of the goods covered by the purchase money security interest. Compliance with these notice requirements gives the last creditor to extend credit for inventory priority, which is a rule of law based on the notion that a debtor must be able to replenish its inventory is order to stay in business and keep creditors paid in a timely fashion. With this priority for subsequently perfected creditors, the opportunity to replenish is open for debtors. *For example,* suppose that First Bank has financed the inventory for Roberta's Exotic Pets, taken a security interest in the inventory, and filed a financing statement covering Roberta's inventory. Two months later Animal Producers sells reptiles on credit to Roberta, taking a security interest in Roberta's inventory. In order to take priority over First Bank, Animal Producers would have to file the financing statement on the inventory before Roberta has the reptiles and notify First Bank at the same time. The commercial rationale for this priority exception is to permit businesses to replenish their inventories by giving new suppliers a higher priority.

(b) Purchase Money Security Interest—Noninventory Collateral. If the collateral is noninventory collateral, such as equipment, the purchase-money secured creditor will prevail over all others as to the same collateral if a financing statement is filed within ten days after the giving of possession to the debtor. *For example,* First Bank loans money to debtor Kwik Copy and properly files a financing statement covering all of Kwik Copy's present and after-acquired copying equipment. Second Bank then loans money to Kwik Copy to enable Kwik Copy to purchase a new copier. Second Bank's interest in the copier will be superior to First Bank's interest if Second Bank perfects its interest by filing either before the debtor receives the copier or within ten days thereafter.

(c) Status of Repair or Storage Lien. What happens when the debtor does not pay for the repair or storage of the collateral? In most states, a person repairing or storing goods has a lien or right to keep possession of the goods until paid for such services. The repairer or storer also has the right to sell the goods to obtain payment if the customer fails to pay and if proper notice is given.[19]

---

19 UCC § 9-310; *ITT Commercial Finance Corp. v Kallmeyer & Sons Truck Tire Service, Inc.* 593 NYS2d 951 (S Ct/Trial/Special Term/Suffolk Co. 1993).

Article 9 makes a lien for repairs or storage superior to the perfected security interest in the collateral. The only exception to this rule makes the perfected security interest superior if the lien was created by statute rather than by common law and that statute expressly states that the lien is subordinate to a perfected security interest in the collateral.

Figure 35-2 provides a summary of the priorities of various parties with respect to secured and unsecured creditor interests.

20. Secured Party vs. Buyer of Collateral from Debtor

The debtor may sell the collateral to a third person. How does this sale affect the secured creditor?

(a) Sales in the Ordinary Course of Business. A buyer who buys goods from the debtor in the ordinary course of business is not subject to any creditor's security interest regardless of whether the interest was perfected or unperfected and regardless of whether the buyer had actual knowledge of the security interest.

FIGURE 35-2
Priority of Secured Interest Under Article 9

PRIORITY OF SECURED INTEREST UNDER ARTICLE 9	
CONFLICT	**PRIORITY**
Secured Party vs. Secured Party	First to attach
Unsecured Party vs. Secured Party	Secured party
Perfected Secured Party vs. Secured Party	Perfected secured party
Perfected Secured Party vs. Perfected Secured Party	Party who is first to perfect
Perfected Secured Party vs. Lienor	Party who filed (financing statement or lien) first [9-307(2)]
Exceptions	
PMSI in Fixtures vs. Perfected Secured Party	PMSI creditor if perfected before annexation or within ten days after annexation (PMSI will have priority even over prior perfected secured party) (9-313, 9-314)
PMSI in Equipment vs. Perfected Security Party	PMSI is perfected within ten days after delivery [9-301(2), 9-312(4)]
PMSI in Inventory vs. Perfected Security Party	PMSI is perfected before delivery and if perfected secured party given notice before delivery[9-312(3)]
PMSI in Consumer Goods vs. Buyer	Buyer unless perfection is by filing before purchase [9-302(1)(d)]
Perfected Security Party vs. Buyer	Buyer in ordinary course wins even with knowledge [9-306(1)(d)]

The reason for this protection of buyers in the ordinary course of business is that subjecting buyers to a creditor's reclaim of goods would cause great delay and hesitation in commercial and consumer sales transactions.

(b) Sales Not in the Ordinary Course of Business: The Unperfected Security Interest. A sale not in the ordinary course of business is one in which the seller is not usually a seller of such merchandise. *For example*, if a buyer purchases a computer desk from an office supply store, the sale is in the ordinary course of business. If that same buyer purchases that same computer desk from a law firm that is going out of business, that buyer is not purchasing in the ordinary course of business. If a buyer is purchasing the collateral and the purchase is not in the ordinary course of business but the security interest is unperfected, such a security interest has no effect against a buyer who gives value and buys in good faith, i.e., not knowing of the security interest. A buyer who does not satisfy these conditions is subject to the security interest.

(c) Sales Not in the Ordinary Course of Business: The Perfected Security Interest. If the security interest was perfected, the buyer of the collateral is ordinarily subject to the security interest unless the creditor had consented to the sale.

(d) Sales Not in the Ordinary Course of Business: The Consumer-Debtor's Resale of Consumer Goods. When the collateral constitutes consumer goods in the hands of the debtor, a resale of the goods to another consumer destroys the automatically perfected PMSI of the consumer-debtor's creditor. Assuming the buyer from the consumer-debtor has no knowledge of a security interest, he or she will take the collateral free and clear from the creditor's security interest even though there was perfection by that creditor. Thus, the perfection without filing option afforded consumer PMSI creditors has a flaw in its coverage when it comes to a consumer-debtor selling his refrigerator to a neighbor. Without a filed financing statement, the neighbor-buyer takes free and clear of the creditor's security interest in the refrigerator. However, consumer creditors can avoid the loss of this perfected interest by going ahead and additionally perfecting by filing. With filing, consumer PMSI creditors will enjoy continuation of their interests even when the neighbor has paid the consumer-debtor for the refrigerator.

Figure 35-3 offers a summary of the rights of buyers of collateral with respect to the creditors who hold security interests in that collateral.

F.   RIGHTS OF PARTIES AFTER DEFAULT

Repossession is the creditor's taking of the collateral for the debtor's default.

When a debtor defaults on an obligation in a secured transaction, the secured creditor has the option of suing the debtor to enforce the debt or of proceeding against the collateral.

FIGURE 35-3
*Priorities in Transfer
of Collateral by Sale*

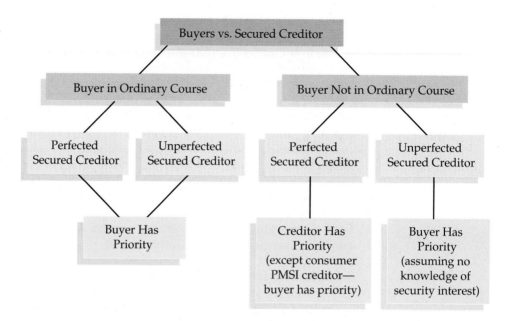

21. Creditor's Possession and Disposition of Collateral

Self-help is the creditor's right of repossession of the collateral without judicial proceedings.

Breach of the peace is a violation of the law in the repossession of the collateral.

Upon the debtor's default, the secured party is entitled to take the collateral from the debtor.[20] **Self-help** repossession is allowed if this can be done without causing a breach of the peace. If a **breach of the peace** might occur, the seller must use court action to obtain the collateral.

The secured creditor may sell, lease, or otherwise dispose of the collateral to pay the defaulted debt. The sale may be private or public, at any time and place, and on any terms provided that the sale is done in a manner that is commercially reasonable. The creditor's sale eliminates all the debtor's interest in the collateral.

CASE SUMMARY

I Was in My Driveway in My Underwear Protesting, and They Still Took My Car

Facts: Koontz entered into an agreement with Chrysler to purchase a 1988 Sundance in exchange for 60 monthly payments of $185.92. When Koontz defaulted on the contract in early 1991, Chrysler notified him that it would repossess the vehicle if he did not make up the missed payments. Koontz notified Chrysler that he would make every effort to catch up on the payments, that he did not want the vehicle to be repossessed, and that Chrysler was not to enter his private property to repossess the car. Chrysler repossessed the car, however, according to the self-help repossession statute of the UCC.

When Koontz heard the repossession in progress, he rushed outside in his underwear and hollered, "Don't take it," to the repossessor. The repossessor did not respond and proceeded to take the vehicle. Chrysler sold the car and filed a complaint against Koontz, seeking a deficiency judgment for the balance due on the loan. Koontz alleged that the repossession was a breach of the peace.

---

20 UCC § 9-503.

> **Decision:** The circumstances of the repossession did not amount to a breach of the peace. To find otherwise would be to invite the ridiculous situation whereby a debtor could avoid a deficiency judgment by merely stepping out of his house and yelling once at a nonresponsive repossessor. Such a narrow definition of the conduct necessary to breach the peace would render the self-help repossession remedies of Article 9 useless. Chrysler's entering upon the private real property of Koontz and taking possession of the secured collateral, without more, did not constitute a breach of the peace. So long as the entry was limited to repossession and so long as no gates, barricades, doors, enclosures, buildings, or chains were breached or cut, no breach of the peace occurred. [*Chrysler Credit Corp. v Koontz (Ill App) 661 NE2d 1171 (1996)*]

22. Creditor's Retention of Collateral

Retention is the creditor's right to keep the collateral, as opposed to selling it.

Instead of selling the collateral, the creditor may wish to keep it and cancel the debt owed.[21]

(a) Notice of Intention. To retain the collateral in satisfaction of the debt, the creditor must send the debtor written notice of this intent.

(b) Compulsory Disposition of Collateral. In two situations, the creditor must dispose of the collateral. A creditor must sell the collateral if the debtor makes a written objection to retention within 21 days after the retention notice was sent.

The creditor must also dispose of the collateral if it consists of consumer goods and the debtor has paid 60 percent or more of the cash price or of the loan secured by the security interest. The sale must be held within 90 days of the repossession. However, the debtor, after default, may sign a writing surrendering the right to require the resale.

A creditor who fails to dispose of the collateral when required to do so is liable to the debtor for conversion of the collateral or for the penalty imposed by the Code for violation of Article 9.[22]

23. Debtor's Right of Redemption

Right of redemption is the debtor's right to pay all amounts due under a contract and reclaim the repossessed property.

The debtor may redeem the collateral at any time prior to the time the secured party has disposed of the collateral or entered into a binding contract for resale. To redeem, the debtor must tender the entire obligation that is owed plus any legal costs and expenses incurred by the secured party.[23]

24. Disposition of Collateral

Upon the debtor's default, the creditor may sell the collateral at a public or private sale or may lease it to a third party. The creditor must give any required notice and act in a commercially reasonable manner. The UCC does not specify the form of notice, and any form of notice that is reasonable is sufficient. A letter to the debtor can satisfy this requirement.

---

[21] UCC § 9-505.
[22] UCC § 9-507.
[23] UCC § 9-506.

25. Postdisposition Accounting

When the creditor disposes of the collateral, the proceeds are applied in the following order. Proceeds are first used to pay the expenses of disposing of the collateral. Next, proceeds are applied to the debt owed the secured creditor making the disposition. Remaining proceeds are applied to any debts owed other creditors holding security interests in the same collateral that are subordinate to the interest of the disposing creditor.

(a) Distribution of Surplus.
If there is any money remaining, the surplus is paid to the debtor.

(b) Liability for Deficit.
If the proceeds of the disposition are not sufficient to pay the costs and the debt of the disposing creditor, the debtor is liable for the deficiency. However, the disposition of the collateral must have been conducted in the manner required by the Code. This means that proper notice was given, if required, and that the disposition was made in a commercially reasonable manner.

SUMMARY

A security interest is an interest in personal property or fixtures that secures payment or performance of an obligation. The property that is subject to the interest is called the collateral, and the party holding the interest is called the secured party. Attachment is the creation of a security interest. To secure protection against third parties' claims to the collateral, the secured party must perfect the security interest. Tangible collateral is divided into classes: consumer goods, equipment, inventory, general intangibles, farm products, and fixtures. These classifications are based on the debtor's intended use, not on the physical characteristics of the goods.

Perfection of a security interest is not required for its validity, but it does provide the creditor with certain superior rights and priorities over other types of creditors and creditors with an interest in the same collateral. Perfection can be obtained through possession; filing; automatically, as in the case of a PMSI in consumer goods; or temporarily, when statutory protections are provided for creditors for limited periods of time.

Priority among creditors is determined according to their status. Unperfected, unsecured creditors simply wait to see if there will be sufficient assets remaining after priority creditors are be paid. Secured creditors have the right to take the collateral on a priority basis. As between secured creditors, the first creditor's interest to attach takes priority in the event the creditors hold security interests in the same collateral. A perfected secured creditor takes priority over an unperfected secured creditor.

Perfected secured creditors with interests in the same collateral take priority generally on a first-to-perfect basis. Exceptions include PMSI inventory creditors who file a financing statement before delivery and notify all existing creditors, and equipment creditors who perfect within ten days of attachment of their interests.

A buyer in the ordinary course of business always takes priority even over perfected secured creditors who have knowledge of the creditor's interest. A buyer not in the ordinary course of business will lose out to a perfected secured creditor but will extinguish the rights of a secured creditor unless the buyer had knowledge of the security interest. A buyer from a consumer-debtor takes free and clear of the debtor's creditor's perfected security interest unless the creditor has filed a financing statement and perfected beyond just the automatic PMSI consumer goods perfection.

Upon default, a secured party may repossess the collateral from the buyer if this can be done without a breach of the peace. If a breach of the peace might occur, the secured party must use court action to regain the collateral. If the buyer has paid 60 percent or more of the cash price of the consumer goods, the seller must resell them within 90 days after repossession unless the buyer, after default, has waived this right in writing. Notice to the debtor of the sale of the collateral is usually required. A debtor may redeem the collateral prior to the time the secured party disposes of it or contracts to resell it.

QUESTIONS AND CASE PROBLEMS

1. What social forces are affected by the destruction of a security interest in consumer goods when a consumer-debtor resells the goods to another consumer who does not know of the security interest?

2. Name the ways a creditor can perfect a security interest.

3. Wayne Smith purchased a computer from Lee Sounds, Inc., for personal use. Smith signed an installment purchase note and a security agreement. Under the terms of the note, Smith was to pay $100 down and $50 a month for 20 months. The security agreement included a description of the computer; however, Lee did not file a financing statement. Did Lee fulfill the requirements necessary for the attachment and perfection of its security interest in the computer? Why?

4. When Johnson Hardware Shop borrowed $20,000 from First Bank, it used its inventory as collateral for the loan. First Bank perfected its security interest by filing a financing statement. The inventory was subsequently damaged by fire, and Flanders Insurance Co. paid Johnson Hardware $5,000 for the loss, but First Bank claimed the proceeds of the insurance. Is First Bank correct? Why?

5. Gold and Finance Co. entered into a security agreement whereby Gold borrowed $20,000 from Finance. The financing statement contained a description of the collateral by item, the name of Finance Co., and Gold's signature and address. Does the financing statement comply with the formal requisites of a financing statement. Why?

6. Compare and contrast attachment of a security interest with perfection of a security interest.

7. Rawlings purchased a typewriter from Kroll Typewriter Co. for $600. At the time of the purchase, he made an initial payment of $75 and agreed to pay the balance in monthly installments. A security agreement was prepared that complied with the UCC, but no financing statement was ever filed for the transaction. Rawlings, at a time when he still owed a balance on the typewriter and without the consent of Kroll, sold the typewriter to a neighbor. The neighbor, who had no knowledge of the security interest, used the typewriter in her home. Can Kroll repossess the typewriter from the neighbor?

8. Kim purchased on credit a $1,000 freezer from Silas Household Appliance Store. After she had paid approximately $700, Kim missed the next monthly installment payment. Silas repossessed the freezer and billed Kim for the balance of the purchase price of $300. Kim claimed that the freezer, now in the possession of Silas, was worth much more than the balance due and requested that Silas sell the freezer in order to wipe out the balance of the debt and to leave something for her. Silas claimed that as Kim had broken her contract to pay the purchase price, she had no right to say what should be done with the freezer. Was Silas correct? Explain.

9. Benson purchased a new Ford Thunderbird automobile. She traded in her old car and used the Magnavox Employees Credit Union to finance the balance. The credit union took a security interest in the Ford. Subsequently the Ford was involved in a number of accidents and was taken to a dealer for repairs. Benson was unable to pay for the work done. The dealer claimed a lien on the car for services and materials furnished. The Magnavox Employees Credit Union claimed priority. Which claim has priority? [*Magnavox Employees Credit Union v Benson* (Ind App) 331 NE2d 46]

10. Lockovich borrowed money from a bank to purchase a motorboat. The bank took a security interest in the boat but never filed a financing statement. A subsequent default on the loan occurred, and the debtor was declared bankrupt. The bank claimed priority in the boat, alleging that no financing statement had to be filed. Do you agree? Why? [*In re* Lockovich, 124 BR 660 (Bankr WD Pa)]

11. Hull-Dobbs sold an automobile to Mallicoat and then assigned the sales contract to Volunteer Finance & Loan Corp. Later Volunteer repossessed the automobile and sold it. When Volunteer sued Mallicoat for the deficiency between the contract price and the proceeds on resale, Mallicoat argued that he had not been properly notified of the resale. The loan manager of the finance company testified that Mallicoat had been sent a registered letter stating that the car would be sold. He did not state, however, whether the letter merely declared in general terms that the car would be sold or specified a date for its resale. He admitted that the letter never was delivered to Mallicoat and was returned to the finance company "unclaimed." The loan manager also testified that the sale was advertised by posters, but, on cross-examination, he admitted that he was not able to state when or where

it was advertised. It was shown that Volunteer knew where Mallicoat and his father lived and where Mallicoat was employed. Mallicoat claimed that he had not been properly notified. Volunteer asserted that sufficient notice had been given. Was the notice of the resale sufficient? [*Mallicoat v Volunteer Finance & Loan Corp.* (Tenn App) 415 SW2d 347]

12. *A* borrowed money from *B*. He orally agreed that *B* had a security interest in certain equipment that was standing in *A*'s yard. Nothing was in writing, and no filing of any kind was made. Nine days later *B* took possession of the equipment. What kind of interest did *B* have in the equipment after taking possession of it? [*Transport Equipment Co. v Guaranty State Bank*, 518 F2d 373 (10th Cir)]

13. Cook sold Martin a new tractor truck for approximately $13,000 with a down payment of approximately $3,000 and the balance to be paid in 30 monthly installments. The sales agreement provided that "on default in any payment, Cook could take immediate possession of the property . . . without notice or demand. For this purpose vendor may enter upon any premises on which the property may be." Martin failed to pay the installments when due, and Cook notified him that the truck would be repossessed. Martin left the tractor truck attached to a loaded trailer and locked on the premises of a company in Memphis. Martin intended to drive to the West Coast with the trailer. When Cook located the tractor truck, no one was around. To disconnect the trailer from the truck (as Cook had no right to the trailer), Cook removed the wire screen over a ventila-

tor hole by unscrewing it from the outside with his penknife. He next reached through the ventilator hole with a stick and unlocked the door of the tractor truck. He then disconnected the trailer and had the truck towed away. Martin sued Cook for unlawfully repossessing the truck by committing a breach of the peace. Decide. [*Martin v Cook* (Miss) 114 So 2d 669]

14. Muska borrowed money from the Bank of California and secured the loan by giving the bank a security interest in equipment and machinery at his place of business. To perfect the interest, the bank filed a financing statement that contained all the information required by the Code except for the residence address of the debtor. Muska later filed for bankruptcy. The trustee in bankruptcy claimed that the security interest of the bank was not perfected because the omission of the residence address from the financing statement made it defective. Decide. [*Lines v Bank of California*, 467 F2d 1274 (9th Cir)]

15. Kimbrell's Furniture Co. sold a new television set and tape player to Charlie O'Neil and his wife. Each purchase was on credit, and, in each instance, a security agreement was executed. Later on the same day of purchase O'Neil carried the items to Bonded Loan, a pawnbroker, and pledged the television and tape deck as security for a loan. Bonded Loan held possession of the television set and tape player as security for its loan and contended that its lien had priority over the unrecorded security interest of Kimbrell. Decide. [*Kimbrell's Furniture Co. v Sig Friedman, d/b/a Bonded Loan* (SC) 198 SE2d 803]

CPA QUESTIONS

1. On March 1, Green went to Easy Car Sales to buy a car. Green spoke to a salesperson and agreed to buy a car that Easy had in its showroom. On March 5, Green made a $500 down payment and signed a security agreement to secure the payment of the balance of the purchase price. On March 10, Green picked up the car. On March 15, Easy filed the security agreement. On what date did Easy's security interest attach?

    a. March 1.
    b. March 5.
    c. March 10.
    d. March 15.

    (5/93, Law, #46)

2. Carr Corp. sells VCRs and video tapes to the public. Carr sold and delivered a VCR to Sutter on credit. Sutter executed and delivered to Carr a promissory note for the purchase price and a security agreement covering the VCR. Sutter purchased the VCR for personal use. Carr did not file a financing statement. Is Carr's security interest perfected?

    a. No, because the VCR was a consumer good.
    b. No, because Carr failed to file a financing statement.
    c. Yes, because Carr retained ownership of the VCR.
    d. Yes, because it was perfected at the time of attachment.

    (5/91, Law, #58)

3. On July 8, Ace, a refrigerator wholesaler, purchased 50 refrigerators. This comprised Ace's entire inventory and was financed under an agreement with Rome Bank that gave Rome a security interest in all refrigerators on Ace's premises, all future-acquired refrigerators, and the proceeds of sales. On July 12, Rome filed a financing statement that adequately identified the collateral. On August 15, Ace sold one refrigerator to Cray for personal use and four refrigerators to Zone Co. for its business. Which of the following statements is correct?

    a. The refrigerators sold to Zone will be subject to Rome's security interest.
    b. The refrigerator sold to Zone will **not** be subject to Rome's security interest.
    c. The security interest does **not** include the proceeds from the sale of the refrigerators to Zone.
    d. The security interest may **not** cover after-acquired property even if the parties agree.

    (11/92, Law, #49)

Other Security Devices

OBJECTIVES

After studying this chapter, you should be able to

1. *Distinguish a contract of suretyship from a contract of guarantee;*
2. *Define the parties to a contract of suretyship and a contract of guarantee;*
3. *List and explain the rights of sureties to protect themselves from loss;*
4. *Explain the defenses available to sureties; and*
5. *Explain the nature of a letter of credit and the liabilities of the various parties to a letter of credit.*

In chapter 35, the additional security of a pledge of collateral and Article 9 of the UCC were highlighted as a means of ensuring payment for creditors. There are, however, other forms of security devices creditors can use that can be coupled with collateral as security or simply used by themselves.

A.   SURETYSHIP AND GUARANTEE

A debtor can make a separate contract with a third party under which that third party agrees to pay the debtor's creditor if the debtor does not pay or defaults in the performance of an obligation. This relationship, in which a third party agrees to be responsible for the debt or undertaking of the debtor, is used most commonly to ensure that a debt will be paid or that a contractor will perform the work called for by a contract. ◆ *For example,* a third-party arrangement occurs when a corporate officer agrees to be personally liable if his corporation does not pay a note by which the corporation borrowed money. ◆ Contractors are generally required to obtain a surety bond, in which a third party agrees to pay damages or complete performance of the construction project in the event the contractor fails to perform in a timely manner or according to the contract terms.

1.   Definitions

One kind of agreement to answer for the debt or default of another is called a **suretyship**. The **obligor** is called a **surety**. The other kind of agreement is called a **guarantee**, and the obligor is called a **guarantor**. In both cases, the person who owes the money or is under the original obligation to pay or perform is called the **principal**, **principal debtor**, or **debtor**.[1] The person to whom the debt or obligation is owed is the **obligee** or **creditor**.

Suretyship and guarantee undertakings have the common feature of a promise to answer for the debt or default of another. The terms are often used interchangeably. However, there is one distinction that qualifies certain forms of guarantee. A surety is liable from the moment the principal is in default. The creditor or obligee can demand performance or payment from the surety without first proceeding against the principal debtor. A **guarantee of collection** is one in which the creditor generally cannot proceed directly against the guarantor and must first attempt to collect from the principal debtor. An exception is an **absolute guarantee**, which creates the same obligation as a suretyship. A **guarantee of payment** creates an absolute guarantee and requires the guarantor to pay upon default by the principal debtor.

2.   Indemnity Contract Distinguished

Both suretyship and guarantee differ from an **indemnity contract**. An indemnity contract is an undertaking by one person, for a consideration, to pay another

---

1 Unless otherwise stated, *surety* as used in the text includes guarantor as well as surety, and *guarantee* is limited to a conditional guarantee. The word *principal* is also used in law to identify the person who employs an agent. The term *principal* in suretyship should be distinguished from the term *principal* as used in a principal/agent relationship. In suretyship, the term *principal* refers to the debtor.

A suretyship is a three-party relationship in which a surety agrees to stand liable to a creditor for the debt of the principal debtor in the event of default.

Obligor is the debtor in a surety or guarantee relationship.

Surety is the third party who has agreed to stand liable for another's debt.

Guarantee is a three-party relationship in which a guarantor agrees to stand liable to a creditor for the debt of the principal debtor in the event of default.

Guarantor is the third party who has agreed to stand liable for another's debt.

Principal debtor is the original borrower or debtor.

Obligee is the creditor in a guarantee or surety relationship.

Guarantor of collection is a guarantee form that allows collection of the principal debt from the guarantor only after the creditor has pursued all avenues of collection.

Absolute guarantee is a guarantee form that allows collection of the principal debt from the guarantor upon the debtor's default.

Indemnity contract is a three-party relationship (e.g., fire insurance) in which one party agrees to pay losses incurred upon the occurrence of certain events.

person a sum of money in the event that the other person sustains a specified loss. ◆ *For example*, a fire insurance policy is an indemnity contract. The insurance you obtain when you use a rental car is also an example of an indemnity contract. ◆

3. Creation of the Relation

Suretyship, guarantee, and indemnity relationships are based on contract. The principles relating to capacity, formation, validity, and interpretation of contracts are applicable. Generally, the ordinary rules of offer and acceptance apply. Notice of acceptance must usually be given by the obligee to the guarantor.

In most states, the statute of frauds requires that contracts of suretyship and guarantee be in writing to be enforceable. No writing is required when the promise is made primarily for the promisor's benefit.

When the contract of suretyship or guarantee is made at the same time as the original transaction, the consideration for the original promise that is covered by the guarantee is also consideration for the promise of the guarantor. When the suretyship or guarantee contract is entered into subsequent to and separate from the original transaction, there must be new consideration for the promise of the guarantor.

CASE SUMMARY

The Sole Proprietors of Blind Ambition

Facts: On August 1, 1987, Dori Leeds signed a "guarantee of credit" with Sun Control Systems, which guaranteed "the prompt payment, when due, of every claim of [Sun Control Systems] against [Dori Leeds dba 'Blind Ambitions']." At the time she signed the guarantee of credit, Blind Ambitions was in the business of installing window treatments and installed only Faber brand blinds, which were purchased from Sun Control Systems.

In 1991, Sun Control Systems sold and assigned all of its assets to Faber. Shortly thereafter Dori assigned her interest in Blind Ambitions to David and Judith Leeds, who continued to do business as Blind Ambitions. In 1994 and 1995, Blind Ambitions made credit purchases from Faber and did not pay under the terms of those contracts. Faber brought suit against Dori Leeds as the guarantor of credit for Blind Ambitions. Dori refused to pay on the grounds that she was acting as a personal guarantor for her business and not for Blind Ambitions.

Decision: The plain language in the guarantee of credit was one intended to cover Dori Leeds while she owned and operated Blind Ambitions. The language did not cover the business itself and thereby carry Dori's liability as a guarantor to any subsequent owners or operators. She was in essence only a personal guarantor for her sole proprietorship and not a guarantor for a separate entity. *[Faber Industries, Ltd. v Dori Leeds Witek (NC App) 483 SE2d 443 (1997)]*

---

4. Rights of Sureties

Sureties have a number of rights to protect them from loss, to obtain their discharge because of the conduct of others that would be harmful to them, or to recover money that they were required to pay because of the debtor's breach.

(a) Exoneration. If the position of the surety becomes endangered, such as when the debtor is about to leave the state, the surety may call on the creditor to take action against the debtor. If at that time the creditor could proceed against the

Exoneration is the right of a surety to be discharged in the event the creditor fails to take action against the debtor upon the creditor's notification of risk, such as the debtor leaving the jurisdiction.

Subrogation is the right a of surety to step into the creditor's shoes and collect the debt or take the collateral pledges once the surety pays the obligation for the principal debtor.

Indemnity is the right of a surety to be repaid by the principal debtor if the surety pays the creditor upon the debtor's default.

Contribution is the right of a surety in a situation in which more than one surety guaranteed the same debt to be paid to have each surety pay a pro rata share of the obligation.

Co-sureties are sureties for the same debtor and obligation.

debtor and fails to do so, the surety is released or **exonerated** from liability to the extent that the surety has been harmed by such failure.

(b) Subrogation. When a surety pays a claim that it is obligated to pay, it automatically acquires the claim and the rights of the creditor. This is known as **subrogation**. That is, once the creditor is paid in full, the surety stands in the same position as the creditor and may sue the debtor or enforce any security that was available to the creditor in order to recover the amount it has paid. The effect is the same as if the creditor, on being paid, made an express assignment of all rights to the surety.

(c) Indemnity. A surety that has made payment of a claim for which it was liable as surety is entitled to **indemnity** from the principal debtor; that is, it is entitled to demand from the principal reimbursement of the amount that it has paid.

(d) Contribution. If there are two or more sureties, each is liable to the creditor or claimant for the full amount of the debt until the claim or debt has been paid in full. Between themselves, however, each is liable only for a proportionate share of the debt. Accordingly, if a surety has paid more than its share of the debt, it is entitled to demand **contribution** from its **co-sureties**. In the absence of a contrary agreement, co-sureties must share the debt repayment on a prorata basis. *For example,* Aaron and Bobette are sureties of $40,000 and $60,000, respectively, for Christi's $60,000 loan. If Christi defaults, Aaron owes $24,000 and Bobette owes $36,000.

5. Defenses of Sureties

The surety's defenses include those that may be raised by a party to any contract and also special defenses that are peculiar to the suretyship relation.

(a) Ordinary Contract Defenses. Because the relationship of suretyship is based on a contract, the surety may raise any defense that a party to an ordinary contract may raise. For example, a surety may raise the defense of lack of capacity of parties, absence of consideration, fraud, or mistake.

Fraud and concealment are common defenses. Fraud on the part of the principal that is unknown to the creditor and in which the creditor has not taken part does not ordinarily release the surety.

Because the risk of the principal debtor's default is thrown on the surety, it is unfair for a creditor to conceal from the surety facts that are material to the surety's risk. Under common law, the creditor was not required to volunteer information to the surety and was not required to disclose that the principal was insolvent. There is a growing modern view that the creditor should be required to inform the surety of matters material to the risk when the creditor has reason to believe that the surety does not possess such information.

(b) Suretyship Defenses. Perhaps the most important thing for a surety to understand is the type of defense that does not result in a discharge of his or her obligation in the suretyship. The insolvency or bankruptcy of the principal debtor does not discharge the surety. The financial risk of the principal debtor is why a surety was obtained from the outset. The lack of enforcement of the debt by the

C·P·A

creditor is not a defense to the surety's obligation or a discharge. The creditor's failure to give the surety notice of default is not a defense. The creditor's right, absent a specific guarantee of collection, is simply to turn to the surety for payment.

In some cases, the creditor may have also taken a pledge of collateral for the debt in addition to the commitment of a surety. It is the creditor's choice as to whether to proceed against the collateral or the surety. If, however, the creditor proceeds first against the surety, the surety then has the right of exoneration and can step into the shoes of the creditor and repossess that collateral.

Changes in the terms of the loan agreement do not serve to discharge a compensated surety. A surety who is acting gratuitously would, however, be discharged in the event of such changes. Changes in the loan terms that would discharge a gratuitous surety's obligation include extension of the loan terms and acceptance of late payments.

A surety is discharged when the principal debtor performs his or her obligations under the original debt contract. If a creditor refuses to accept payment from a debtor, a surety is discharged.

A surety is also discharged, to the extent of the value of the collateral, if a creditor releases back to the debtor any collateral in his possession. ◆ *For example,* suppose that Bank One has in its possession $10,000 in gold coins as collateral for a loan to Janice in the amount of $25,000. Albert has agreed to serve as a surety for the loan to Janice in the amount of $25,000. If a Bank One manager returns the $10,000 in coins to Janice, then Albert is discharged on his suretyship obligation to the extent of that $10,000. Following the release of the collateral, the most that Albert could be held liable for in the event of Janice's default is $15,000. ◆

A surety is also discharged from his or her obligation if the creditor substitutes a different debtor. A surety and a guarantor make a promise that is personal to a specific debtor and do not agree to assume the risk of an assignment or a delegation of that responsibility to another debtor.

A surety also enjoys the discharge rights afforded all parties to contracts, such as the statute of limitations. If the creditor does not enforce the suretyship agreement within the time limits provided for such contract enforcement in the surety's jurisdiction, the obligation is forever discharged.

Figures 36-1 and 36-2 provide summaries of the defenses and release issues surrounding suretyship and guarantee relationships.

FIGURE 36-1
No Release of Surety

1. Fraud by Debtor
2. Misrepresentation by Debtor
3. Changes in Loan Terms (e.g., extension of payment, compensated surety)
4. Release of Principal Debtor
5. Bankruptcy of Principal Debtor
6. Insolvency of Principal Debtor
7. Death of Principal Debtor
8. Incapacity of Principal Debtor
9. Lack of Enforcement by Creditor
10. Creditor's Failure to Give Notice of Default
11. Failure of Creditor to Resort to Collateral

FIGURE 36-2
Release of Surety

1. Proper Performance by Debtor
2. Release, Surrender, or Destruction of Collateral (to extent of value of collateral)
3. Substitution of Debtor
4. Fraud/Misrepresentation by Creditor
5. Refusal by Creditor to Accept Payment from Debtor
6. Change in Loan Terms (uncompensated surety only)
7. Statute of Frauds
8. Statute of Limitations

CASE SUMMARY

My Boats and My Liability

Facts: Continental Airlines (plaintiff) is an airline operating in the United States and around the world. In 1989, Continental established an Air Travel Plan Account that permitted Regency Cruises to purchase air travel and other related services from Continental and charge those services to the Air Travel Plan Account. Regency Cruises is an owner and operator of a fleet of pleasure ships and a wholly owned subsidiary of Regency Holdings, Inc., which is incorporated in the Cayman Islands. Antonio Lelakis is the chairman of the board of Regency Holdings.

To establish the account, Regency signed a contract with Continental providing that Regency would be billed on a monthly basis and would be required to make payments on the account. From July 1994 through October 1994, Regency fell behind on its payments to Continental. Officials of Continental and Regency Holdings signed an addendum to the travel account agreement in which Regency Holdings agreed to be jointly and severally liable for any existing and future Regency Cruises debt on the account. Regency Holdings also executed a promissory note payable to Continental in the amount of $10,476,992.23, to be paid by June 30, 1995. Mr. Lelakis signed an individual guarantee to Continental for the $10,476,992.23 note.

During 1995, Continental renegotiated the payment schedule for the note with Regency Holdings. However, by March 2, 1995, Regency Holdings had made only two payments on the note, and Continental declared Regency Holdings in default, accelerated the amount due, and demanded full payment of the note. Both Regency Holdings and Regency Cruises filed for Chapter 11 bankruptcy in November 1995. Continental demanded payment of the note from Mr. Lelakis as a surety. Mr. Lelakis refused on the grounds of misrepresentation, duress, and changes in the surety's obligations under the original agreement. Mr. Lelakis alleged that his spoken and written English skills are limited and, as a result, he did not understand all that transpired at the October 5, 1994, meeting at which the guarantee was negotiated. He further contended that Continental represented that the guarantee was only an "assurance" that Regency Cruises would meet its obligations under the Air Travel Plan Account and that he was asked to sign as chairman of Regency Holdings, not as a personal guarantor who would pay if Regency Cruises did not. Under Greek law, such an assurance exposes the signer to liability only after corporate assets are exhausted.

Decision: Mr. Lelakis remains liable as a surety for the obligation. While he may not have the best English skills in the world, he did allow meetings to be conducted in English and had advisors with him who did speak English. Mr. Lelakis understood the nature of the agreements he signed. If he wanted liability only following exhaustion of his company's assets, he should have negotiated a contract for a guarantee of collection. *[Continental Airlines, Inc. v Lelakis, 943 F Supp 300 (SDNY 1996)]*

Very often the creditors of a business can exercise a great deal of authority over the operation of the business when it has missed a payment on its debt or has experienced some business or market setbacks. Without owning any stock in a corporation, creditors will, in over 50 percent of all cases in which they express concern about repayment, succeed in having both boards and officers replaced in part or in toto.

For example, Worlds of Wonder, Inc., a creative and innovative toy manufacturer that was responsible for the first talking toy, Teddy Ruxpin, was required by demands from its secured and unsecured creditors to obtain the resignation of its founder and CEO, Donald Kingsborough. Kingsborough was paid $212,500 upon his departure for "emotional distress."

Studies show that creditors also have input on the following corporate actions:

Type of decision	Percentage of creditors with vote
Declaration of dividends	48%
Increased security	73%
Restructuring of debt	55%
Cap on borrowing	50%
Cap on capital expenses	25%
Restrictions on investment	23%

Is it fair to have creditors control corporate governance? Will they always make the choices that are best for the shareholders? Is it unconscionable to have these control covenants in loan agreements? Why do creditors need them in their loan agreements?

B.   LETTERS OF CREDIT

Letter of credit is a three-party arrangement in which the beneficiary is paid according to the terms of a document drawn on a third party, as when a bank issues a letter of credit for a buyer in order to allow the seller to ship the goods or turn them over to the buyer.

Issuer is the party on whom the letter of credit is drawn.

Standby letter of credit is a letter of credit for a contractor, for example, ensuring that the contractor will perform by completing the project as contracted for.

A **letter of credit** is a three-party arrangement with a payor, a beneficiary, and a party on whom the letter of credit is drawn, or **issuer**. A letter of credit is an agreement that the issuer of the letter will pay drafts drawn by the beneficiary of the letter. Letters of credit are a form of advance arrangement for financing. Sellers of goods, for example, know in advance how much money may be obtained from the issuer of the letter. It may also be used by a creditor as a security device because the creditor knows that the drafts that the creditor draws will be accepted or paid by the issuer of the letter.

The use of letters of credit arose in international trade. While international trade continues to be the primary area of use, there is a growing use of letters in domestic sales and in transactions in which the letter of credit takes the place of a surety bond. Thus, a letter of credit has been used to ensure that a borrower would repay a loan, that a tenant would pay the rent due under a lease, and that a contractor would properly perform a construction contract. This kind of letter of credit is known as a **standby letter**.

There are few formal requirements for creating a letter of credit. Although banks often use a standardized form for convenience, they may draw up individualized letters of credit for particular situations. (See Figure 36-3.)

FIGURE 36-3
Letter of Credit

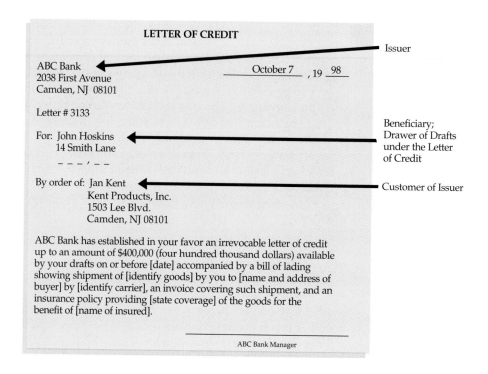

LETTER OF CREDIT

Issuer

ABC Bank
2038 First Avenue
Camden, NJ 08101

October 7 , 19 98

Letter # 3133

For: John Hoskins
      14 Smith Lane

Beneficiary;
Drawer of Drafts
under the Letter
of Credit

By order of: Jan Kent
             Kent Products, Inc.
             1503 Lee Blvd.
             Camden, NJ 08101

Customer of Issuer

ABC Bank has established in your favor an irrevocable letter of credit up to an amount of $400,000 (four hundred thousand dollars) available by your drafts on or before [date] accompanied by a bill of lading showing shipment of [identify goods] by you to [name and address of buyer] by [identify carrier], an invoice covering such shipment, and an insurance policy providing [state coverage] of the goods for the benefit of [name of insured].

ABC Bank Manager

6. Definition

A letter of credit is an engagement by its issuer that it will pay or accept drafts when the conditions specified in the letter are satisfied. The issuer is usually a bank.

Three contracts are involved in letter-of-credit transactions: (1) the contract between the issuer and the customer of the issuer; (2) the letter of credit itself; and (3) the underlying agreement, often a contract of sale, between the beneficiary and the customer of the issuer of the letter of credit. (See Figure 36-4.) The letter of credit is completely independent from the other two contracts. Consideration is not required to establish or modify a letter of credit.

The issuer of the letter of credit is in effect the obligor on a third-party-beneficiary contract made for the benefit of the beneficiary of the letter. The key to the commercial success of letters of credit is their independence. ◆ *For example,* a bank obligated to issue payment under a letter of credit "when the goods are

FIGURE 36-4
Three Contracts Involved in Letter-of-credit Transactions

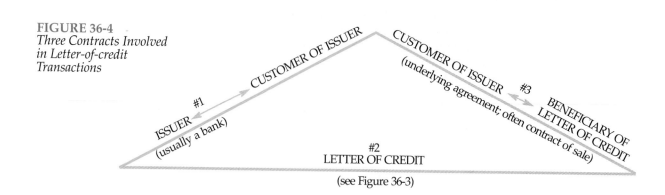

CUSTOMER OF ISSUER

CUSTOMER OF ISSUER
(underlying agreement; often contract of sale)

#1

#3

ISSUER
(usually a bank)

BENEFICIARY OF
LETTER OF CREDIT

#2
LETTER OF CREDIT

(see Figure 36-3)

delivered" must honor that obligation even if the buyer has complaints about the goods. ◆ It is the terms of the letter of credit that control the payment and not the relationship, contract, or problems of the beneficiary or issuer of the letter of credit.

CASE SUMMARY

The Great Trucking Fraud and the Letter of Credit

Facts: First Interstate Bank issued a letter of credit in favor of Comdata Network, Inc. Comdata is engaged in money transfer services. It provides money to truckers on the road by way of cash advances through form checks written by truckers. When Comdata enters into a business relationship with a trucking company, it requires a letter of credit. This requirement is to secure advances made on behalf of the trucking company. One of the trucking companies defrauded the bank that issued the letter of credit. Comdata demanded that the bank make payment to it under the letter of credit for cash advances that the trucking company had not repaid. The bank, alleging fraud by the trucking company, refused. Comdata filed suit.

Decision: A letter of credit "constitutes an enforceable obligation" in the nature of a contract by the issuer "in favor of the beneficiary." The duty created in the letter of credit is wholly independent of the underlying contract between the issuer's customer and the beneficiary. Thus, the bank was obligated to pay Comdata. [*Comdata Network, Inc. v First Interstate Bank of Fort Dodge (Iowa App) 497 NW 2d 807 (1993)*]

The key to the commercial vitality and function of a letter of credit is that the issuing bank's promise is independent of the underlying contracts, and the bank should not resort to them in interpreting a letter of credit. The respective parties are protected by careful description of the documents that will trigger payment.

Misconduct is not relevant to the above dispute, which is between Comdata and the bank. The claim of a beneficiary of a letter of credit is not subject to defenses normally applicable to third-party contracts.

7. Parties

> Advising bank is the bank that advises the seller that the letter of credit is available.

> Correspondent bank will honor the letter of credit from the domestic bank of the buyer.

The parties to a letter of credit are (1) the issuer; (2) the customer who makes the arrangements with the issuer; and (3) the beneficiary, who will be the drawer of the drafts that will be drawn under the letter of credit. There may also be (4) an **advising bank**[2] if the local issuer of the letter of credit requests its **correspondent bank**, where the beneficiary is located, to notify or advise the beneficiary that the letter has been issued. ◆ *For example,* an American merchant may want to buy goods from a Spanish merchant. There may have been prior courses of dealing between the parties, so that the seller is willing to take the buyer's commercial paper as payment or to take trade acceptances drawn on the buyer. If the foreign seller is not willing to do this, the American buyer, as customer, may go to a bank, the issuer, and obtain a letter of credit naming the Spanish seller as beneficiary. The American bank's correspondent or advising bank in Spain will notify the Spanish seller that this has been done. The Spanish seller will then draw drafts on the American buyer. Under the letter of credit, the issuer is required to accept or pay these drafts. ◆

---

2 *See* UCC § 5-107; *Artoc Bank & Trust v Sun Marine Terminals* (Tex App) 760 SW2d 311 (1988).

8. Duration

A letter of credit continues for any length of time it specifies. Generally, a maximum money amount is stated in the letter, so that the letter is exhausted or used up when drafts aggregating that maximum have been accepted or paid by the issuer. A letter of credit may be used in installments as the beneficiary chooses. A letter of credit cannot be revoked or modified by the issuer or the customer without the consent of the beneficiary unless that right is expressly reserved in the letter.

9. Form

Documentary draft is a letter of credit that requires the delivery of certain documents to the issuer before the letter of credit will be paid.

A letter of credit must be in writing and signed by the issuer. If the credit is issued by a bank and requires a documentary draft or a documentary demand for payment,[3] or if the credit is issued by a nonbank and requires that the draft or demand for payment be accompanied by a document of title, the instrument is presumed to be a letter of credit (rather than a contract of guarantee). Otherwise, the instrument must conspicuously state that it is a letter of credit.[4]

10. Duty of Issuer

The issuer is obligated to honor drafts drawn under the letter of credit if the conditions specified in the letter have been satisfied. The issuer takes the risk that the papers submitted are the ones required by the letter. If they are not, the issuer cannot obtain reimbursement for payment made in reliance on such documents. The issuer has no duty to verify that the papers are properly supported by facts or that the underlying transaction has been performed. It is thus immaterial that the goods sold by the seller in fact do not conform to the contract as long as the seller tenders the documents specified by the letter of credit. If the issuer dishonors a draft without justification, it is liable to its customer for breach of contract.[5]

11. Reimbursement of Issuer

When the issuer of a letter of credit makes proper payment of drafts drawn under the letter of credit, it may obtain reimbursement from its customer for such payment. No reimbursement can be obtained if the payment was not proper. This will be the case if the payment is made after the letter has expired or if the payment is in an amount greater than that authorized by the letter. Reimbursement cannot be obtained if the payment is made without the proper presentation of required documents or if the payment is made in violation of a court injunction against payment.

---

3 A *documentary draft* or a *documentary demand for payment* is one for which honor is conditioned on the presentation of one or more documents. A document could be a document of title, security, invoice, certificate, notice of default, or other similar paper. UCC § 5-103(1)(b).

4 *Hendry Const. Co. v Bank of Hattiesburg* (Miss) 562 So 2d 100 (1990).

5 Ibid.

SUMMARY

Suretyship and guarantee undertakings have the common feature of a promise to answer for the debt or default of another. The terms are used interchangeably, but a guarantor of collection is ordinarily only secondarily liable, which means that the guarantor does not pay until the creditor has exhausted all avenues of recovery. If the guarantor has made an absolute guarantee, then its status is the same as that of a surety, which means that both are liable for the debt in the event the debtor defaults regardless of what avenues of collection, if any, the creditor has pursued. The surety and guarantee relationships are based on contract. Sureties have a number of rights to protect them. They are exoneration, subrogation, indemnity, and contribution. In addition to those rights, sureties also have certain defenses. They include ordinary contract defenses as well as some defenses peculiar to the suretyship relationship, such as release of collateral, change in loan terms, substitution of debtor, and fraud by the creditor.

A letter of credit is an agreement that the issuer of the letter will pay drafts drawn on the issuer by the beneficiary of the letter. The issuer of the letter of credit is usually a bank. There are three contracts involved in letter-of-credit transactions: (1) the contract between the issuer and the customer of the issuer, (2) the letter of credit itself, and (3) the underlying agreement between the beneficiary and the customer of the issuer of the letter of credit. The parties to a letter of credit are the issuer, the customer who makes the arrangement with the issuer, and the beneficiary, who will be the drawer of the drafts to be drawn under the letter of credit. The letter of credit continues for any time it specifies. The letter of credit must be in writing and signed by the issuer. Consideration is not required to establish or modify a letter of credit. If the conditions in the letter of credit have been complied with, the issuer is obligated to honor drafts drawn under the letter of credit.

QUESTIONS AND CASE PROBLEMS

1. What social forces are affected by the use of a letter of credit?

2. Kiernan Construction Co. makes a contract with Jackson to build a house for her. Century Surety Co. executes a bond to protect Jackson from loss if Kiernan should fail to construct the house or pay labor and materials bills. Kiernan fails to build the house, and Jackson sues Century Surety, which claims that Jackson must first sue Kiernan. Is it correct?

3. Identify the parties to a letter of credit.

4. Fern Schimke's husband, Norbert, was obligated on two promissory notes in favor of Union National Bank. Some time prior to his death, Union National Bank prepared a guarantee contract that was given to Norbert to be signed by his wife. She signed the guarantee at the request of her husband without any discussion with him about the provisions of the document she was signing. Upon Norbert's death, the bank brought suit against Fern on the basis of the guarantee. Fern argued that because there was no consideration for the guarantee, she could not be liable. Decide. [*Union National Bank v Fern Schimke* (ND) 210 NW2d 176]

5. In May 1989, Alma Equities Corp., owned by its sole shareholder and president, Lewis Futterman, purchased a hotel and restaurant in Vail, Colorado, from Alien, Inc., for $3,900,000. Alma paid $600,000 in cash to Alien, and Alien provided a purchase money loan to Alma for the remaining amount of the sale price, with the loan secured by a deed of trust on the hotel and restaurant. The hotel and restaurant did not do well, and Futterman negotiated a friendly foreclosure on the property in 1991 whereby Alma would continue to operate the hotel and restaurant on a lease basis, with Futterman providing a personal guarantee for the lease. Alma failed to make the lease payments for the months of November and December 1991 and, following an unlawful detainer action filed by Alien for possession of the hotel and restaurant, was forced into bankruptcy. Alien turned to Futterman for satisfaction on the lease payments. Futterman said he should not have been forced to pay because Alien's unlawful detainer forced Alma into bankruptcy. Was Futterman correct? Did he have a defense? [*Alien, Inc. v Futterman* (Colo) 924 P2d 1063]

6. Eberstadt owed Terence $500 and gave his note for that amount to Terence. At the same time, an agreement signed by Reid and given to Terence was as follows: "I agree to be surety for the payment of Eberstadt's note for $500." On maturity of the note, Eberstadt paid $200 on account and gave a new note for $300 due in three months. Reid was not informed of this transaction. The new note was not paid at maturity. Terence sued Reid. Does Reid have any defense?

7. Gilbert signed a guarantee for the benefit of his son with Cobb Exchange Bank. The guarantee included all extensions and renewals of the son's obligation. Subsequently, a renewal of the note added an additional $600 to the original obligation. On the son's default, Cobb Bank brought suit on the guarantee. Who should win? Why? [*Gilbert v Cobb Exchange Bank* (Ga App) 231 SE2d 508]

8. Keller made a contract to purchase goods from Conti Co. To assure Conti that it would be paid, Keller obtained a letter of credit from Enterprise Bank. The letter was irrevocable and provided that Enterprise would honor drafts for the purchase price of goods shipped to Keller on presentment to the bank of the drafts, the bill of lading showing shipment to Keller, and the invoice showing the nature and price of the goods shipped. Because of financial difficulties, Keller did not want to receive the goods under the contract and made an agreement with Enterprise that no drafts would be honored pursuant to the letter of credit. Conti shipped goods to Keller under the contract and presented drafts, the proper bills of lading, and invoices to Enterprise. Enterprise refused to honor the drafts, and Conti sued Enterprise, which claimed that it was not liable because the letter of credit that had obligated it to accept the drafts had been terminated by the agreement of its customer. Was this a valid defense?

9. The Kitsap County Credit Bureau held against Alderman a claim whose payment had been guaranteed by Richards. When Richards was sued on his guarantee, he proved that the claim against Alderman had been settled by compromise upon Alderman's paying $100 to the creditor. What was the result? [*Kitsap County Credit Bureau v Richards* (Wash) 325 P2d 292]

10. Hugill agreed to deliver shingles to W.I. Carpenter Lumber Co. and furnished a surety bond to secure the faithful performance of the contract on his part. After a breach of the contract by Hugill, the lumber company brought an action to recover its loss from the surety, Fidelity & Deposit Co. of Maryland. The surety denied liability on the grounds that there was concealment of (a) the price to be paid for the shingles and (b) the fact that a material advance had been made to the contractor equal to the amount of the profit that he would make by performing the contract. Decide. [*W.I. Carpenter Lumber Co. v Hugill* (Wash) 270 P 94]

11. Donaldson sold plumbing supplies. The St. Paul–Mercury Indemnity Co., as surety for him, executed and delivered a bond to the state of California for the payment of all sales taxes. Donaldson failed to pay, and the surety paid the taxes that he owed and then sued him for the taxes. What was the result? [*St. Paul–Mercury Indemnity Co. v Donaldson* (SC) 83 SE2d 159]

12. Paul owed Charles a $1,000 debt due September 1. On August 15, George, for consideration, orally promised Charles to pay the debt if Paul did not. On September 1, Paul did not pay, so Charles demanded $1,000 from George. Is George liable? Why?

13. First National Bank hired Longdon as a secretary and obtained a surety bond from Belton covering the bank against losses up to $100,000 resulting from Longdon's improper conduct in the performance of his duties. Both Longdon and the bank signed the application for the bond. After one year of service, Longdon was promoted to teller, and the original bond remained in effect. Shortly after Longdon's promotion, examination showed that after his promotion Longdon had taken advantage of his new position and stolen $50,000. He was arrested and charged with embezzlement. Longdon had only $5,000 in assets at the time of his arrest. (a) If the bank demands a payment of $50,000 from Belton, what defense, if any, might Belton raise to deny any obligation to the bank? (b) If Belton fully reimburses the bank for its loss, under what theory or theories, if any, may Belton attempt to recover from Longdon?

14. Jack Smith was required by his bank to obtain two sureties for his line of credit of $100,000. Ellen Weiss has agreed to act as a surety for $50,000, and Allen Fox has agreed to act as a surety for $75,000. Smith has used the full $100,000 in the line of credit and is now in bankruptcy. What is the maximum liability of Weiss and Fox if the bank chooses to collect from them for Smith's default? How should the $100,000 be allocated between Weiss and Fox?

15. Partridge lends $1,000 to Fazio, who agrees to repay the amount in three months. A month after the loan is made, Partridge requests security. Shank, without asking for or receiving payment, gives Partridge a written promise to answer in the event of default by Fazio. Fazio defaults. Partridge sues Fazio and obtains judgment; execution is issued and returned unsatisfied. Partridge then sues Shank, who claims there is no consideration for her promise. Is this defense valid? Explain.

CPA QUESTIONS

1. Marbury Surety, Inc., agreed to act as a guarantor of collection of Madison's trade accounts for one year beginning on April 30, 1980, and was compensated for same. Madison's trade debtors are in default in payment of $3,853 as of May 1, 1981. As a result
   a. Marbury is liable to Madison without any action on Madison's part to collect the amounts due.
   b. Madison can enforce the guarantee even if it is **not** in writing because Marbury is a del credere agent.
   c. The relationship between the parties must be filed in the appropriate county office because it is a continuing security transaction.
   d. Marbury is liable for those debts for which a judgment is obtained and returned unsatisfied.
   (11/81, Law, #27)

2. Queen paid Pax and Co. to become the surety on a loan that Queen obtained from Squire. The loan is due, and Pax wishes to compel Queen to pay Squire. Pax has not made any payments to Squire in its capacity as Queen's surety. Pax will be most successful if it exercises its right to
   a. Reimbursement (Indemnification).
   b. Contribution.
   c. Exoneration.
   d. Subrogation.
   (11/86, Law, #28)

3. Which of the following defenses by a surety will be effective to avoid liability?
   a. Lack of consideration to support the surety undertaking.
   b. Insolvency in the bankruptcy sense of the debtor.
   c. Incompetency of the debtor to make the contract in question.
   d. Fraudulent statements by the principal debtor that induced the surety to assume the obligation and that were unknown to the creditor.
   (5/82, Law, #23)

Bankruptcy

CHAPTER 37

After studying this chapter, you should be able to

1. *List the requirements for the commencement of a voluntary bankruptcy case and an involuntary bankruptcy case;*
2. *Describe the rights of a trustee in bankruptcy;*
3. *Explain the procedure for the administration of a debtor's estate;*
4. *List a debtor's duties and exemptions;*
5. *Explain the significance of a discharge in bankruptcy; and*
6. *Explain when a business reorganization and an extended-time payment plan might be used.*

What can a person or business do when overwhelmed by debts? Bankruptcy proceedings can provide temporary and sometimes permanent relief from those debts.

A. BANKRUPTCY LAW

Bankruptcy is a statutory proceeding for relief from debts when a debtor is unable to pay those debts as they become due.

Bankruptcy is a statutory proceeding with detailed procedures and requirements.

1. The Federal Law

Bankruptcy law is based on the Bankruptcy Reform Act of 1994[1] and on the Bankruptcy Rules adopted by the U.S. Supreme Court. Jurisdiction over bankruptcy proceedings is vested in the federal district courts. The district courts have the authority to transfer such matters to courts of special jurisdiction called **bankruptcy courts**.

2. Kinds of Bankruptcy Proceedings

Liquidation is a form of bankruptcy in which all assets are liquidated for distribution to creditors.

Chapter 7 is the liquidation form of bankruptcy under federal law.

Reorganization is a form of bankruptcy in which debt payments and debts are restructured to allow repayment according to agreements and schedules.

Chapter 11 is the reorganization form of bankruptcy under federal law.

Three kinds of bankruptcy proceedings are available to individuals and businesses.

(a) Liquidation or Chapter 7 Bankruptcy. A **Chapter 7 bankruptcy** is one in which all of the debtor's assets (with some exemptions) will be **liquidated** in order to pay debts. Those debts that remain unpaid or are paid only partially are discharged, with some exceptions. The debtor who declares Chapter 7 bankruptcy begins again with a nearly clean slate.

Chapter 7 bankruptcy is available to individuals, partnerships, and corporations. However, farmers, insurance companies, savings and loans, municipalities, small business investment companies, and railroads are not entitled to declare Chapter 7 bankruptcy because they are specifically governed by other statutes or specialized sections of the Bankruptcy Code.[2]

(b) Reorganization or Chapter 11 Bankruptcy. **Chapter 11 bankruptcy** is a means for a debtor to reorganize and continue a business with protection from

---

[1] PL 104-18, 11 USC §§ 301 et seq., as amended (1994).

[2] For example, the Small Business Investment Act governs the insolvency of small business investment companies, 11 USC § 109(b). Municipalities' bankruptcies are governed by Chapter 9 of the bankruptcy code, and farmers' bankruptcies are covered under Chapter 12.

overwhelming debts and without the requirement of liquidation. Anyone who qualifies for Chapter 7 liquidation bankruptcy qualifies for a Chapter 11 bankruptcy. The same exemptions also apply, with the exception of railroads that may declare Chapter 11 bankruptcy. Stockbrokers, however, are not eligible for Chapter 11 bankruptcy.

Chapter 13 is the consumer debt readjustment plan bankruptcy proceeding.

Payment plans/consumer debt adjustment plans are part of Chapter 13 bankruptcy and are similar to a Chapter 11 reorganization.

(c) Chapter 13 Bankruptcy or Payment Plans or Consumer Debt Adjustment Plans. Chapter 13 of the federal Bankruptcy Code provides consumers with an individual form of reorganization. Chapter 13 works with consumer debtors to develop a plan for repayment of debt. To be eligible for Chapter 13 bankruptcy, the individual must owe unsecured debts of $269,250, owe secured debts of less than $807,750, and have regular income.[3]

B. HOW BANKRUPTCY IS DECLARED

There are different ways in which bankruptcy can be declared. The exact requirements and process for declaration are also spelled out in detail in the federal Bankruptcy Code.

3. Declaration of Voluntary Bankruptcy

Voluntary bankruptcy is a proceeding in which the debtor files the petition for relief.

A **voluntary bankruptcy** is begun when the debtor files a petition with the bankruptcy court. A joint petition may be filed by a husband and wife. When a voluntary case is begun, the debtor must file a schedule of current income and current expenditures unless the court excuses this filing.

The voluntary petition simply requires the debtor to swear that he, she, or it has debts. When a voluntary petition is filed, the debtor automatically obtains an order of relief, which happens without a hearing or court decree.[4]

ETHICS & THE LAW

TLC was an Atlanta rhythm, blues, and hip-hop band that performed at clubs in 1991. The three-woman group signed a recording contract with LaFace Records. The group's first album that LaFace produced, *Oooooooohhh on the TLC Tip,* in 1992 sold almost three million albums. The group's second album, *Crazysexycool,* also produced by LaFace, sold 5 million albums through June 1996. The two albums together had 6 top-of-the-chart singles.

LaFace had the right to renew TLC's contract in 1996 following renegotiation of the contract terms. Royalty rates in the industry for unknown groups, as TLC was in 1991, are generally 7 percent of the revenues for the first 500,000 albums and 8 percent for sales on platinum albums (albums that sell over one million copies). The royalty rate increases to 9.5 percent for all sales on an eighth album.

Established artists in the industry who renegotiate often have royalty rates of 13 percent, and artists with two platinum albums can command an even higher royalty.

The three women in TLC—Tionne Watkins (T-Boz), Lisa Lopes (Left-Eye), and Romanda Thomas (Chili)—declared bankruptcy in July 1995. All three

---

3 The amounts of $250,000 and $750,000 originally in the Bankruptcy Reform Act increase each year to allow for inflation.
4 PL 104-18, 11 USC § 301.

listed debts that exceeded their assets, which included sums owed to creditors for their cars and to Zale's and The Limited for credit purchases. Lopes is being sued by Lloyd's of London, which claims Lopes owes it $1.3 million it paid on a policy held by her boyfriend on his home. Lopes has pleaded guilty to one count of arson in the destruction of the home but denies that she intended to destroy the house.

Lopes has asked that the Lloyd's claim be discharged in her bankruptcy. All three members of TLC have asked that their contract with LaFace be discharged in bankruptcy because being bound to their old contract could impede their fresh financial starts.

Do the three women meet the standards for declaring bankruptcy? Evaluate whether Lopes' Lloyd's claim should be discharged. Determine whether the record contract should be discharged.

During 1996, the members of three music groups declared bankruptcy just before their contracts were due for renegotiation. One record company executive has noted that record company owners are frightened by the trend: "You invest all the money and time in making them stars. Then they leave for the bigger companies and a higher take on sales. It has all of us scared."

Is declaring bankruptcy by the members of these musical groups legal? Is it ethical? Are the musicians using bankruptcy as a way to avoid contract obligations? Are the musicians using bankruptcy as a way to maximize their income?

Pop singer Billy Joel also had a record contract with a small company during the initial stages of his career. When the company refused, during renegotiations, to increase his royalty rate, Joel did not produce another album during the period of the contract renewal option. Instead, he used a clause in the contract that limited him to night club and piano bar appearances in the event another album was not produced. For three years, Joel played small clubs and restaurants and did not produce an album. At the end of that period when his contract had expired, he negotiated a contract with Columbia. His first album with Columbia was *Piano Man*, a multiplatinum album. Did Joel take an ethical route? Is his solution more ethical than bankruptcy?

4. Declaration of Involuntary Bankruptcy

(a) Eligibility. An **involuntary bankruptcy** is begun when creditors file a petition with the bankruptcy court. An involuntary case may be commenced against any individual, partnership, or corporation, except those excluded from filing voluntary petitions. Nonprofit corporations are also exempt from involuntary proceedings.[5]

> **Involuntary bankruptcy is a proceeding in which a creditor or creditors file the petition for relief.**

(b) Number and Claims of Petitioning Creditors. If there are 12 or more creditors, at least 3 whose unsecured claims total $10,775 or more must sign the involuntary petition. If there are fewer than 12 creditors, excluding employees or insiders (that is, the debtor's relatives, partners, directors, and controlling persons), any creditor whose unsecured claim is at least $10,775 may sign the petition.

If the creditor holds security for the claim, only the amount of the claim in excess of the value of the security is counted. The holder of a claim that is the subject of a bona fide dispute may not be counted as a petitioning creditor.[6]

---

[5] 11 USC § 303(a).
[6] 11 USC § 303(b)(1).

◆ *For example*, David, a CPA, is an unsecured creditor of Arco Co. for $11,000. Arco has a total of 10 creditors, all of whom are unsecured. Arco has not paid any of the creditors for three months. The debtor had fewer than 12 creditors. Anyone may file the petition if the unsecured portion of the amount due that creditor is at least $10,775.[7] Because David is owed $11,000 in unsecured debts, he may file the petition. ◆

(c) Grounds for Relief for Involuntary Case. The mere filing of an involuntary case petition does not constitute an order for relief. The debtor may contest the bankruptcy petition. If the debtor does not contest the petition, the court will enter an order of relief if at least one of the following grounds exists: (1) The debtor is generally not paying debts as they become due, or (2) within 120 days before the filing of the petition, a custodian has been appointed for the debtor's property.

5. Automatic Stay

Just the filing of either a voluntary or an involuntary petition operates as an **automatic stay**. An automatic stay prevents creditors from taking action, such as filing suits or foreclosure actions, against the debtor.[8] The stay freezes all creditors in their filing date positions so that no one creditor gains an advantage over other creditors. This automatic stay ends when the bankruptcy case is closed or dismissed or when the debtor is granted a discharge. An automatic stay means that all activity by creditors with respect to collection must stop. All litigation with the debtor is halted, and any judgments in place cannot be executed.

> Automatic stay is a court order that halts all collections and court actions against the debtor once the bankruptcy petition is filed

---

CASE SUMMARY

Who Has the Mercedes and Why?

Facts: Charles Carte obtained a judgment against Sultan Shabazz in the amount of $40,442.78. Mr. Carte's lawyers levied the judgment against two Mercedes vehicles owned by Shabazz. Jennings Enterprises, Inc. (JEI), a towing and storage yard, took possession of the two cars, a grey Mercedes and a red 1987 Mercedes, in March 1992.

J. Nevin Smith, counsel for Mr. Carte, called Robbie Jennings the day after JEI took possession of the cars and told him that he should use caution because they were responsible for the cars until the sheriff's sale could be held and that Mr. Shabazz might try to take the cars.

Mr. Smith was informed shortly after JEI took the cars that Mr. Shabazz had declared bankruptcy. Upon entry of the stay of relief, Mr. Smith postponed the sheriff's sale of the Mercedes indefinitely but did not contract JEI.

In December 1992, when JEI had heard nothing further from Mr. Smith, Robbie Jennings sold the 1987 red Mercedes to Elizabeth Ramey for the amount of JEI's lien on the car for storage fees. Elizabeth Ramey, the next day, sold the car back to Robbie Jennings.

In April 1994, Mr. Smith asked for the return of the red car, and Robbie Jennings refused, noting that the car had been sold. Mr. Carte filed suit against JEI to obtain the value of the red car. Robbie Jennings says his lien took priority and he was free to sell the car to satisfy the lien.

Decision: The sale of the red Mercedes for JEI's lien on it for storage fees violated the bankruptcy stay of relief. JEI could not countermand the declaration of bankruptcy by conducting a sale to satisfy its lien. All efforts of all creditors must stop when a debtor declares bankruptcy. Mr. Carte is entitled to receive the fair market value of the car from JEI, which the court determined to be $20,000. [*Jennings Enterprises, Inc. v Carte (Ga App) 481 SE2d 541 (1997)*]

---

7 The amount of $10,000 originally in the Bankruptcy Reform Act increases each year to allow for inflation.
8 11 USC § 362.

6. If the Creditors Are Wrong: Rights of Debtor in an Involuntary Bankruptcy Case

If an involuntary petition is dismissed other than by consent of all petitioning creditors and the debtor, the court may award costs, reasonable attorney fees, or damages to the debtor. The damages are those that were caused by taking possession of the debtor's property. The debtor may also recover damages against any creditor who filed the petition in bad faith.[9]

Figure 37-1 provides a summary of the requirements for declaration of bankruptcy and the standards for relief.

C. ADMINISTRATION OF THE BANKRUPTCY ESTATE

The administration of the bankruptcy estate varies according to the type of bankruptcy declared. This section of the chapter focuses on the process for liquidation or Chapter 7 bankruptcy. Figure 37-2 provides a flowchart view of the Chapter 7 liquidation process.

7. The Order of Relief

Order of relief is a court finding that creditors have met the standards for bankruptcy petition filing in an involuntary bankruptcy.

The **order of relief** is granted by the bankruptcy court and is the procedural step required for the case to proceed in bankruptcy court. An order of relief is entered automatically in a voluntary case and in an involuntary case when those filing the petition have established that the debtor is unable to pay his, her, or its debts as they become due.

FIGURE 37-1
Declaration of Bankruptcy

	Chapter 7	Chapter 11	Chapter 13
Trustee	Yes	No	Yes
Eligible persons: **Individuals** **Partnerships** **Corporations**	Yes Yes Yes	Yes Yes Yes	Yes No No
Voluntary	Yes	Yes	Yes
Involuntary	Yes, except Farmers and Nonprofits	Yes, except Farmers and Nonprofits	No
Exemptions	Railroads, insurance companies, S & Ls, small businesses (under SBA), municipalities*, farmers*	Same as Chapter 7 except that railroads are eligible for Chapter 11 and stock-brokers are ineligible for Chapter 11	Only individuals
Requirements ± **Voluntary**	Debts	Debts	Income <$269,250 unsecured <$807,750 secured*
Requirements ± **Involuntary**	<12 = 1/$10,775 ≥12 = 3/$10,775	<12 = 1/$10,775 ≥12 = 3/$10,775	N/A

*Special sections (chapter 9 – municipalities; Chapter 12 – farmers)

---

[9] *Arizona Public Service v Apache County* (Ariz App) 847 P2d 1339 (1993).

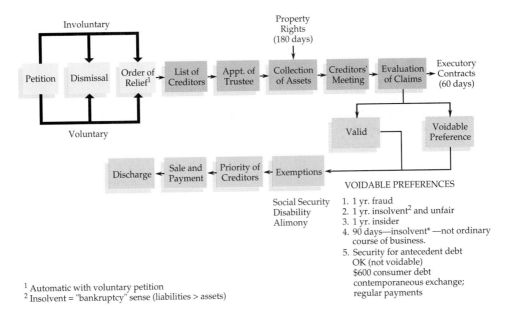

¹ Automatic with voluntary petition
² Insolvent = "bankruptcy" sense (liabilities > assets)

FIGURE 37-2
Anatomy of
Bankruptcy Case

8. List of Creditors

It is the debtor's responsibility to furnish the bankruptcy court with a list of creditors. While imposing the responsibility for disclosing debts on the debtor may not seem to be effective, the debtor has an incentive for full disclosure. Those debts not disclosed by the debtor will not be discharged in bankruptcy.

9. Trustee in Bankruptcy

The trustee in bankruptcy is elected by the creditors. An interim trustee will be appointed by the court or by the U.S. trustee if a trustee is not elected by the creditors.

   The trustee is the successor to the property rights of the debtor. By operation of law, the trustee automatically becomes the owner of all the property of the debtor in excess of the property to which the debtor is entitled under exemption laws. Everyone is charged with notice that the trustee is the owner of rights formerly owned by the debtor.

10. The Bankrupt's Estate

All of the debtor's property, with certain exceptions discussed below, is included in the bankrupt's estate. Property inherited by the debtor within six months after the filing of the petition also passes to the trustee.

   In many cases where a debtor knows that insolvency is a problem and bankruptcy is imminent, the debtor attempts to hang onto property or reputation by making transfers to friends, relatives, and creditors. However, trustees have the authority to set aside or avoid (1) transfers by the debtor that a creditor holding a valid claim under state law could have avoided at the commencement of the bankruptcy case; (2) **preferences**, that is, transfers of property by the debtor to a creditor, the effect of which is to enable the creditor to obtain payment of a greater percentage of the creditor's claim than the creditor would have received if the

Voidable preference is a payment within a certain time frame prior to bankruptcy that can be set aside by the trustee if it can be shown to place a creditor above the position it should have.

debtor's assets had been liquidated in bankruptcy; and (3) statutory liens that became effective against the debtor at the commencement of the bankruptcy.

11. Voidable Transfers

A debtor may not transfer property to prevent creditors from satisfying their legal claims. The trustee may avoid any such transfer made or obligation incurred by the debtor within one year of bankruptcy when the debtor's actual intent was to hinder, delay, or defraud creditors by doing so.

The trustee may also avoid certain transfers of property made by a debtor merely because their effect is to make the debtor insolvent or to reduce the debtor's assets to an unreasonably low amount.[10]

(a) The Insolvent Debtor. A debtor is insolvent for purposes of determining voidable transfers when the total fair value of all the debtor's assets does not exceed the debts owed by the debtor. This test for insolvency under voidable transfers is commonly called the **balance sheet test**, because it is merely a comparison of assets to liabilities without considering whether the debtor will be able to meet future obligations as they become due.

Balance sheet test is a solvency test that shows that assets are greater than liabilities.

(b) Preferential Transfers. A transfer of property by the debtor to a creditor may be set aside as **preferential** and the property recovered by the debtor's trustee in bankruptcy if (1) the transfer was made to pay a debt incurred at some earlier time, (2) the transfer was made when the debtor was insolvent and within 90 days before the filing of the bankruptcy petition, and (3) by the transfer the creditor received more than the creditor would have received in a liquidation of the debtor's estate. A debtor is presumed to be insolvent on and during the 90 days immediately preceding the date of the filing of the bankruptcy petition.[11]

Preferential transfers are certain transfers of money or security interests in the time frame just prior to bankruptcy that can be set aside if voidable.

Transfers made to insiders within the 12 months prior to the filing of the petition may be set aside.[12] *For example*, if a building contractor transferred title to one of his model homes to the company accountant just six months before declaring bankruptcy, the transfer would be a preferential one that would be set aside. However, a transfer by an insider to a noninsider is not subject to recovery by the trustee. The sale of that same model home to a good-faith buyer just three days before bankruptcy would be valid.

Certain transfers by a debtor may not be attacked by the trustee as preferences. A transaction for a present consideration, such as a cash sale, is not subject to attack.[13] A payment by a debtor in the ordinary course of business, such as the payment of a utility bill, is not subject to attack. A payment by an individual debtor whose debts are primarily consumer debts is not subject to attack if the aggregate value of the transfer is less than $600. Child support and alimony payments are not subject to the preferential provisions.

---

[10] 11 USC § 548.
[11] 11 USC § 547(f).
[12] 11 USC § 547(b)(4)(B).
[13] In re Tolona Pizza Product Corp., 3 F3d 1029 (7th Cir 1993).

The Debtor Who Paid, Bounced, and Then Declared

Facts: Hall-Mark regularly supplied electronic parts to Peter Lee. On September 11, 1992, Lee gave Hall-Mark a $100,000 check for parts it had received. Hall-Mark continued to ship parts to Lee. On September 23, 1992, Lee's check was dishonored by the bank. On September 25, 1992, Lee delivered to Hall-Mark a cashier's check for $100,000. Hall-Mark shipped nothing more to Lee after receipt of the cashier's check.

On December 24, 1992, Lee filed a voluntary petition for bankruptcy. The trustee filed a complaint to have the $100,000 payment to Hall-Mark set aside as a voidable preference. Hall-Mark said it was entitled to the payment because it gave value to Lee. The trustee said that the payment was not actually made until the cashier's check was delivered on September 25, 1992, and that Hall-Mark gave no further value to Lee after that check was paid.

Decision: The court held that a transfer by an ordinary check takes place not on the day the check is delivered but on the day it is honored by the bank. The personal check, delivered more than 90 days prior to the filing for bankruptcy, was never honored. The cashier's check was the transfer, and for Hall-Mark to be entitled to keep it, it had to give new value *after* it received the cashier's check, and it did not because no new shipments were made. The transfer of $100,000 to Hall-Mark was set aside as a voidable preference. *[In re Lee, 108 F3d 239 (9th Cir 1997)]*

12. Proof of Claim

Bankruptcy law regulates the manner in which creditors present their claims, and the assets of the debtor are distributed in payment of these claims.

After the debtor has filed a list of creditors, the court will then send a notice of the bankruptcy proceedings to listed creditors. The creditors who wish to participate in the distribution of the proceeds of the liquidation of the debtor's estate must file a proof of claim. A **claim** is a right to payment, whether liquidated (certain and not disputed), unliquidated, contingent, unmatured, disputed, legal, or equitable. A **proof of claim** is a written statement, signed by the creditor or an authorized representative, setting forth any claim made against the debtor and the basis for it. It must ordinarily be filed within 90 days after the first meeting of creditors.[14] A creditor must file within that time even though the trustee in bankruptcy in fact knows of the existence of the creditor's claim.

> Proof of claim is a creditor's paperwork filed in bankruptcy to show the amount of the debt owed

13. Priority of Claims

Creditors who hold security for payment, such as a lien or a mortgage on the debtor's property, are not affected by the debtor's bankruptcy. Secured creditors may enforce their security to obtain payment of their claims. ◆ *For example,* suppose that First Bank holds a mortgage on a company's office building. The mortgage amount is $750,000. The building is sold for $700,000. First Bank is entitled to the $700,000 from the sale. ◆ Unsecured creditors with unsecured debts that have priority and their order of priority following the secured creditors' rights in their collateral are covered in the following sections.[15] Once the bottom of the priority list is reached, any remaining unsecured creditors share on a pro rata basis

---

14 Bankruptcy Code 11 USC § 302(c).
15 11 USC § 507(1)-(6).

any remaining assets of the debtor. Any balance remaining after all creditors have been paid is paid to the debtor. The following is a list of the priorities for unsecured creditors following the satisfaction of any secured creditors from the debtors' pledged property.

1. Costs and expenses of administration of the bankruptcy case, including fees to trustees, attorneys, and accountants, and the reasonable expenses of creditors in recovering property transferred or concealed by the debtor
2. Claims arising in the ordinary course of a debtor's business or financial affairs after the commencement of the case and before the appointment of a trustee
3. Claims for wages, salaries, or commissions, including vacation, severance, or sick leave pay earned within 90 days before the filing of the petition or the date of cessation of the debtor's business, whichever occurred first, limited, however, to $4,300 for each person.
4. Claims arising for contributions to employee benefit plans, based on services rendered within 180 days before the filing of the petition or when the debtor ceased doing business, whichever occurred first; maximum amount is $4,300
5. Farm producers and fisherman against debtors who operate grain storage facilities or fish produce storage or processing facilities, up to $4,300 per claim
6. Claims by consumer creditors, not to exceed $1,950 for each claimant, arising for the purchase of consumer goods or services when such property or services were not delivered or provided
7. Allowed claims for debts to a spouse, former spouse, or child of the debtors and for alimony to, maintenance for, or support of such spouse or child
8. Certain taxes and penalties due government units, such as income and property taxes
9. All other unsecured creditors
10. Remainder (if any) to debtor

Each claim must be paid in full before any lower claim is paid anything. If a class of claims cannot be paid in full, the claims in that case are paid on a pro rata basis.
For example, suppose that following the payment of all secured creditors, there is $10,000 left to be distributed. The accountants who performed work on the bankruptcy are owed $15,000, and the lawyers who worked on it are owed $10,000. Because there is not enough to pay two parties in the same priority ranking, the $10,000 is split proportionately. The accountants will receive 15/25 or 3/5 of the $10,000 or $6,000, and the lawyers will receive 10/25 or 2/5 of the $10,000 or $4,000.

D. DEBTOR'S DUTIES AND EXEMPTIONS

Bankruptcy law imposes certain duties on the debtor and provides for specific exemptions of some of the debtor's estate from the claims of creditors.

14. Debtor's Duties

A debtor must file with the court a list of creditors, a schedule of assets and liabilities, and a statement of the debtor's financial affairs. The debtor must also appear for examination under oath at the first meeting of creditors.

15. Debtor's Exemptions

Exemptions are debtor's assets that are given protection from the bankruptcy trustee by state or federal law.

A debtor is permitted to claim certain property of the estate in the trustee's possession and keep it free from claims of creditors. The debtor may choose either the **exemptions** permitted by the law of the debtor's state of domicile or those permitted by the Bankruptcy Code.[16] The principal exemptions provided by the Bankruptcy Code are the debtor's interest in real or personal property used as a residence to the extent of $16,150; the debtor's interest in a motor vehicle to the extent of $2,575; household furnishings of the debtor or the debtor's dependents, not to exceed $425 per item or $8,675 in aggregate value; payments under a life insurance contract; alimony and child support payments; and awards from personal injury causes of action.[17]

16. Debtor's Protection against Discrimination

Federal, state, or local law may not discriminate against anyone on the basis of a discharge in bankruptcy. For example, a state could not refuse to issue a new license to an individual if the license fees on a previous one had been discharged as a debt in the individual's declaration of bankruptcy.

E.   DISCHARGE IN BANKRUPTCY

Discharge is court-ordered relief from debts, which is permanent.

The main objectives of a bankruptcy proceeding are the collection and distribution of the debtor's assets and the **discharge** of the debtor from obligations. The decree terminating the bankruptcy proceeding is generally a discharge that releases the debtor from most debts.

17. Denial of Discharge

The court will refuse to grant a discharge if the debtor has (1) within one year of the filing of the petition fraudulently transferred or concealed property with intent to hinder, delay, or defraud creditors; (2) failed to keep proper financial records; (3) made a false oath or account; (4) failed to explain satisfactorily any loss of assets; (5) refused to obey any lawful order of the court or refused to testify after having been granted immunity; (6) obtained a discharge within the last six years; or (7) filed a written waiver of discharge that is approved by the court.[18]

A discharge releases the debtor from the unpaid balance of most debts. However, a discharge does not release a person from all debts. A tax, customs duty, or tax penalty is not discharged by bankruptcy. Likewise, a release is not given for student loans unless the loan first became due more than seven years before bankruptcy or unless excepting the loan from discharge would impose undue hardship on the debtor.

In addition, the following debts are not discharged by bankruptcy: (1) loans obtained by use of a false financial statement made with intent to deceive and on

---

[16] The law of the state of the debtor's domicile may prohibit making such an election and limit the debtor to the exemptions allowed by state law.

[17] 11 USC § 522(d) (including automatic adjustments effective 4/1/98). Again, the exemption amounts increase each year.

[18] 11 USC § 523.

which the creditor reasonably relied; (2) debts not scheduled or listed with the court in time for allowance; (3) debts arising from fraud while acting in a fiduciary capacity or by reason of embezzlement or larceny; (4) alimony and child support; (5) a judgment for willful and malicious injury to property (*For example,* the finding of malice in *Goldman v O.J. Simpson* precludes the discharge by bankruptcy of Simpson's $8.5 million damage award to the Goldmans and Browns); (6) judgments against the debtor for liability for driving while intoxicated; (7) a consumer debt to a single creditor totaling more than $1,075 for luxury goods or services and cash advances exceeding $1,075 based on consumer open-end credit, such as a credit card (both must be incurred within 60 days of the order of relief); and (8) loans used to pay taxes (including credit cards). See Figure 37-3.

CASE SUMMARY

Riches, Bankruptcy, and the Eye of the Needle

Facts: Robert Z. Gergely, an obstetrician, performed an amniocentesis on Jordan Lee-Benner's mother during her pregnancy with him. As a result of difficulties with the amniocentesis, Lee-Benner was blinded in one eye.

After his birth, Lee-Benner, through his guardian, brought suit against Gergely. Lee-Benner claimed that Gergely had misrepresented the need for amniocentesis and that he had performed the procedure negligently. The court awarded a judgment in the amount of $780,282 to Lee-Benner but did not specify on which legal theory the judgment was rendered.

Three years later, but before Lee-Benner was paid the judgment, Gergely filed a Chapter 7 bankruptcy petition. Lee-Benner moved to have the amount due him, now nearly $1 million with interest, declared a nondischargeable debt. Lee-Benner asserted three theories for nondischarge of the debt: (1) There was a false representation, (2) Gergely had committed fraud as a fiduciary, and (3) Gergely had inflicted willful and malicious injury. The bankruptcy court dismissed Lee-Benner's claim, and he appealed.

Decision: The debt owed by Dr. Gergely falls within the fraud exception for discharge because Gergely intentionally misrepresented the need for amniocentesis to Lee-Benner's mother. *[Lee-Benner v Gergely, 110 F3d 1448 (9th Cir 1997)]*

FIGURE 37-3
Nondischargeable Debts in Bankruptcy

1. Taxes within Three Years of Filing Bankruptcy Petition
2. Liability for Obtaining Money or Property by False Pretenses
3. Willful and Malicious Injuries
4. Debts Incurred by Driving DWI
5. Alimony, Maintenance, or Child Support
6. Unscheduled Debts (unless actual notice)
7. Debts Resulting from Fraud as a Fiduciary (embezzlement)
8. Government Fines or Penalties Imposed within Three Years Prior
9. Educational Loans Due within Seven Prior Years (unless hardship)
10. Prior Bankruptcy Debts in Which Debtor Waived Discharge
11. Presumption on Luxury Goods: $1,075 Goods; $1,075 Cash
12. Reaffirmation Agreements
    - Writing
    - Filed with Court
    - Not Rescinded prior to Discharge

F.   REORGANIZATION PLANS UNDER CHAPTER 11

In addition to liquidation under Chapter 7, the Bankruptcy Code permits debtors to restructure the organization and finances of their businesses so that they may continue to operate. In these rehabilitation plans, the debtor keeps all the assets (exempt and nonexempt), continues to operate the business, and makes a settlement that is acceptable to the majority of the creditors. This settlement is binding on the minority creditors.

Individuals, partnerships, and corporations in business may all be reorganized under the Bankruptcy Code. The first step is to file a plan for the reorganization of the debtor. This plan may be filed by the debtor or by any party in interest or by a committee of creditors.

18. Contents of the Plan

The plan divides ownership interests and debts into those that will be affected by the adoption of the plan and those that will not. It then specifies what will be done to those interests and claims that are affected. *For example*, where mortgage payments are too high for the income of a corporation, a possible plan would be to reduce the mortgage payments and give the mortgage holder preferred stock to compensate for the loss sustained.

All persons within a particular class must be treated the same way. For example, the holders of first mortgage bonds must all be treated similarly.

A plan can also provide for the assumption, rejection, or assignment of executory contracts. Thus, the trustee or debtor can, under certain circumstances, suspend performance of a contract not yet fully performed. *For example*, collective bargaining agreements may be rejected with the approval of the bankruptcy court.[19]

19. Confirmation of the Plan

After the plan is prepared, it must be approved or confirmed by the court. A plan will be confirmed if it has been submitted in good faith and if its provisions are reasonable.[20] After the plan is confirmed, the owners and creditors of the enterprise have only the rights that are specified in the plan. They cannot go back to their original contract positions.

G.   PAYMENT PLANS UNDER CHAPTER 13

The Bankruptcy Code also provides for the adoption of extended-time payment plans for individual debtors who have regular income. These debtors must owe unsecured debts of less than $269,250 and secured debts of less than $807,750.

An individual debtor who has a regular income may submit a plan for the installment payment of outstanding debts. If approved by the court, the debtor may then pay the debts in the installments specified by the plan even if the creditors had not originally agreed to such installment payments.

---

[19] 11 USC § 1113.
[20] 11 USC § 1129.

20. Contents of the Plan

The individual debtor plan is in effect a budget of the debtor's future income with respect to outstanding debts. The plan must provide for the eventual payment in full of all claims entitled to priority under the Bankruptcy Code. All creditors holding the same kind or class of claim must be treated the same way.

21. Confirmation of the Plan

The plan has no effect until it is approved or confirmed by the court. A plan will be confirmed if it was submitted in good faith and is in the best interests of the creditors.[21] When the plan is confirmed, debts are payable in the manner specified in the plan.

22. Discharge of the Debtor

After all the payments called for by the plan have been made, the debtor is given a discharge. The discharge releases the debtor from liability for all debts except those that would not be discharged by an ordinary bankruptcy discharge.[22] If the debtor does not perform under the plan, the creditors can move to transfer the debtor's case to a Chapter 7 proceeding.

WHAT'S BEHIND THE LAW?

Bankruptcy: Rising Debt, Luxury Goods, and Increasing Numbers of Personal Bankruptcies

In 1980, there were 287,570 personal bankruptcies filed in the United States. In 1996, the number of personal bankruptcies topped one million for the first time in history. In 1997, the number of personal bankruptcies continued above the one million mark at 1,178,555. That number translates to a bankruptcy for 1 of every 100 households in the United States. The rate of bankruptcy filing in the United States for 1997 was eight times higher than the bankruptcy rate during the Great Depression.

The number one reason for bankruptcy declaration in 1997 was not loss of job or health problems or divorce. Nearly 30 percent of all bankruptcy filings were attributed by the petitioner to simply being "overextended." The average credit card debt is now $7,000 per family. Over 70 percent of those filing for personal bankruptcy chose Chapter 7, or full bankruptcy, as opposed to Chapter 13 for a consumer debt adjustment plan.

Most consumer debt is owed by those who earn between $50,000 and $100,000 a year. As one lender remarked, "These are people who could afford to save and buy later." Many members of Congress and federal bankruptcy judges feel that current laws are too permissive and make the declaration of bankruptcy very easy and very tempting. Other lawmakers note that forgiveness of debt is an important part of the willingness of entrepreneurs to take risks and invest in a business. Judging the reasons for debt was never part of the federal Bankruptcy Code. Changing the laws and requiring different standards could hamper investment. Yet the average loss of $11,000 in debt write-off per bankruptcy costs each family in the United States $100 in higher prices as creditors try to cover the losses of bankruptcy.

For more information on bankruptcy courts, the Bankruptcy Code, and policy issues, visit the Emory University bankruptcy law site at http://www.law.emory.edu/FOCAL/bank.html

---

[21] 11 USC § 1325.
[22] 11 USC § 1328.

SUMMARY

Jurisdiction over bankruptcy cases is in U.S. district courts, which may refer all cases and related proceedings to adjunct bankruptcy courts.

Three bankruptcy proceedings are available: liquidation, reorganization, and extended-time payment.

A liquidation proceeding under Chapter 7 may be either voluntary or involuntary. A voluntary case is commenced by the debtor's filing a petition with the bankruptcy court. An involuntary case is commenced by the creditors' filing a petition with the bankruptcy court. If there are 12 or more creditors, at least 3 whose unsecured claims total $10,775 or more must sign the involuntary petition. If there are fewer than 12 creditors, any creditor whose unsecured claim is at least $10,775 may sign the petition. If the debtor contests the bankruptcy petition, it must be shown that the debtor is not paying debts as they become due or that within 120 days before the date of the filing of the petition a custodian had been appointed for the debtor's property.

An automatic stay prevents creditors from taking legal action against the debtor after a bankruptcy petition is filed. The trustee in bankruptcy is elected by the creditors and is the successor to, and acquires the rights of, the debtor. In certain cases, the trustee can avoid transfers of property to prevent creditors from satisfying their claims. Preferential transfers may be set aside. A transfer for a present consideration, such as a cash sale, is not a preference.

Bankruptcy law regulates the way creditors present their claims and the assets of the debtor are to be distributed in payment of the claims.

Secured claims are not affected by the bankruptcy of the debtor. Unsecured claims are paid in the following order of priority: (1) administrative expenses; (2) claims arising in the ordinary course of the debtor's business; (3) wage claims, limited to $4,300 for each claimant and to wages earned within 90 days before the filing of the petition; (4) claims for contributions to employee benefit plans; (5) claims by consumer creditors; (6) certain taxes; and (7) general creditors. Certain property of the debtor is exempt from the claims of creditors.

The decree terminating bankruptcy proceedings is generally a discharge that releases the debtor from most debts. Certain debts, such as income taxes, student loans, loans obtained by use of a false financial statement, alimony, and debts not duly scheduled, are not discharged.

Individuals, partnerships, and corporations in business may be reorganized so that the business may continue to operate. A plan for reorganization must be approved by the court.

Individual debtors with a regular income may adopt extended-time payment plans for the payment of debts. A plan for extended-time payment must also be confirmed by the court.

Federal, state, or local law may not discriminate against anyone on the basis of a discharge in bankruptcy.

QUESTIONS AND CASE PROBLEMS

1. What social forces are affected by permitting a debtor to avoid paying debts by going into bankruptcy?

2. What are the requirements for filing an involuntary petition by creditors?

3. Barron sold goods on credit to Charles by relying on a false financial statement issued by Charles. Charles later filed for voluntary bankruptcy, still owing a debt to Barron. Barron claimed that Charles was not entitled to a discharge from this particular debt because of the fraud. Was Barron correct?

4. Carl owes the following unsecured creditors: Richard, $2,000; Val, $6,000; Yates, $11,000; and Vail, $2,500. Carl has not paid any creditor since January 31, 1998. On July 31, 1998, Richard, Val, and Vail involuntarily petitioned Carl into bankruptcy. Carl opposed the petition. Will the petition be upheld? Why?

5. Anita, who knows Jean is insolvent, sells Jean her car for $500 and receives cash in payment. Some time later an involuntary bankruptcy case is commenced against Jean by her creditors. The trustee in bankruptcy attempts to recover the $500 on the ground that it was a preferential transfer. Will the trustee be successful?

6. Okamoto owed money to Hornblower and Weeks-Hemphill, Noyes. Hornblower filed an involuntary bankruptcy petition against Okamoto, who moved to dismiss the petition on the ground that he had more than 12 creditors and the petition could not be filed by only 1. Hornblower replied that the claims of the other creditors were too small to count and therefore the petition could be filed by 1 creditor. Decide. [*In re Okamoto*, 491 F2d 496 (9th Cir)]

7. Which of the following, if any, will survive Rogers' discharge in bankruptcy? (a) Wages amounting to $400 owed to three employees and earned within 60 days of the bankruptcy, (b) a judgment against Rogers

for injuries received because of Rogers' negligent operation of an automobile, (c) a judgment against Rogers by Landers for breach of contract, (d) Rogers' obligation for alimony and child support.

8. Kentile sold goods over an extended period of time to Winham. The credit relationship began without Winham's being required to furnish any financial statement. After some time payments were not made regularly, and Kentile requested a financial statement. Winham submitted a statement for the year that had just ended. After that, Kentile requested a second statement. The second statement was false. Kentile objected to Winham's discharge in bankruptcy because of the false financial statement. Should the discharge be granted? Why or why not?

9. Essex is in serious financial difficulty and is unable to meet current unsecured obligations of $40,000 to some 20 creditors, who are demanding immediate payment. Essex owes Stevens $5,000, and Stevens has decided to file an involuntary petition against Essex. Can Stevens file the petition?

10. Sonia, a retailer, has the following assets: a factory worth $1 million; accounts receivable amounting to $750,000, which fall due in four to six months; and $20,000 cash in the bank. Sonia's sole liability is a $200,000 note falling due today, which Sonia is unable to pay. Can Sonia be forced into involuntary bankruptcy under the Bankruptcy Code?

11. Samson Industries, Inc., ceased doing business and is in bankruptcy proceedings. Among the claimants are five employees seeking unpaid wages. Three of the employees are owed $3,500 each, and two are owed $1,500 each. These amounts became due within 90 days preceding the filing of the petition. Where, in the priority of claims, will the employees' wage claims fall?

12. Vega Baja Lumber Yard owed money to First City National Bank. The bank sued the lumber yard and attached some of its property. Bankruptcy proceed-

ings were then begun, and the lumber yard was adjudicated a bankrupt. The bank filed a claim in bankruptcy, but the referee rejected the bank's claim because it had been filed more than 90 days after the debtor had been adjudicated a bankrupt. The bank claimed that the 90-day limitation did not bar it because the trustee knew of the claim. What result? Why? [*In re Vega Baja Lumber Yard, Inc.,* 285 F Supp 143 (DCPR)]

13. Carol Cott, doing business as Carol Cott Fashions, is worried about an involuntary bankruptcy proceeding being filed by her creditors. Her net worth, using a balance sheet approach, is $8,000 ($108,000 in assets minus $100,000 in liabilities). However, her cash flow is negative, and she has been hardpressed to meet current obligations as they mature. She is in fact some $12,500 in arrears in payments to her creditors on bills submitted during the past two months. Will the fact that Cott is solvent in the balance sheet sense result in the court's dismissing the creditors' petition if Cott objects to the petition? Explain.

14. The Guaranteed Student Loan Program provides funds for students attending college. Some time after a student borrowed money under the program to attend school, she filed a petition in bankruptcy and listed the student loans on her list of obligations. Is she entitled to a discharge from the loan? Under what conditions, if any, can such an obligation be discharged? Explain. [*Massachusetts Higher Education Assistance Corporation v Taylor* (Mass) 459 NE2d 807]

15. On July, 1 Roger Walsh, a sole proprietor operating a grocery, was involuntarily petitioned into bankruptcy by his creditors. At that time, and for at least 90 days prior to that time, Walsh was unable to pay current obligations. On June 16, Walsh paid the May electric bill that was incurred in his business. The trustee in bankruptcy claims that this payment was a voidable preference. Is the trustee correct? Explain.

1. Which of the following statements is correct concern-

CPA QUESTIONS

1. Which of the following statements is correct concerning the voluntary filing of a petition of bankruptcy?
   a. If the debtor has 12 or more creditors, the unsecured claims must total at least $10,775.
   b. The debtor must be solvent.
   c. If the debtor has less than 12 creditors, the unsecured claims must total at least $10,775 .
   d. The petition may be filed jointly by spouses. (AICPA adapted)

2. On February 28, 1996, Master, Inc. had total assets with a fair market value of $1,200,000 and total liabilities of $990,000. On January 15, 1996, Master made a monthly installment note payment to Acme Distributors Corp., a creditor holding a properly perfected security interest in equipment having a fair market value greater than the balance due on the note. On March 15, 1996, Master voluntarily filed a petition in bankruptcy under the liquidation provisions of Chapter 7 of the Federal Bankruptcy Code. One year later, the equipment was sold for less than the balance due on the note to Acme.

   If a creditor challenged Master's right to file, the petition would be dismissed
   a. If Master had less than 12 creditors at the time of filing.
   b. Unless Master can show that a reorganization under Chapter 11 of the Federal Bankruptcy Code would have been unsuccessful.
   c. Unless Master can show that it is unable to pay its debts in the ordinary course of business or as they come due.
   d. If Master is an insurance company.

3. A voluntary petition filed under the liquidation provisions of Chapter 7 of the Federal Bankruptcy Code
   a. Is **not** available to a corporation unless it has previously filed a petition under the reorganization provisions of Chapter 11 of the Federal Bankruptcy Code.
   b. Automatically stays collection actions against the debtor **except** by secured creditors collateral only.
   c. Will be dismissed unless the debtor has 12 or more unsecured creditors whose claims total at least $10,000.
   d. Does **not** require the debtor to show that the debtor's liabilities exceed the fair market value of assets.

4. Which of the following conditions, if any, must a debtor meet to file a voluntary bankruptcy petition under Chapter 7 of the Federal Bankruptcy Code?

	Insolvency	Three or more creditors
a.	Yes	Yes
b.	Yes	No
c.	No	Yes
d.	No	No

Items 5a and 5b are based on the following:

Knox operates an electronics store as a sole proprietor. On April 5, 1997, Knox was involuntarily petitioned into bankruptcy under the liquidation provisions of the Bankruptcy Code. On April 20, a trustee in bankruptcy was appointed and an order for relief was entered.

Knox's non-exempt property has been converted to cash, which is available to satisfy the following claims and expenses as may be appropriate:

Claims and Expenses

Claim by Dart Corp (one of Knox's suppliers) for computers ordered on April 6, 1997 and delivered on credit or Knox on April 10, 1997.	$20,000
Fee earned by the bankruptcy trustee.	$15,000
Claim by Boyd for a deposit given to Knox on April 1, 1997, for a computer Boyd purchased for personal use but that had not yet been received by Boyd.	$1,500
Claim by Noll Co. for the delivery of stereos to Knox on credit. The stereos were delivered on March 4, 1997, and a financing statement was properly filed on March 5, 1997. These stereos were sold by the trustee with Noll's consent for $7,500, their fair market value.	$5,000
Fees earned by the attorneys for the bankruptcy estate.	$10,000
Claims by unsecured general creditors.	$1,000

The cash available for distribution includes the proceeds from the sale of the stereos.

5a. What amount will be distributed to the trustee as a fee if the cash available for distribution is $15,000?
    a. $6,000
    b. $9,000
    c. $10,000
    d. $15,000

5b. What amount will be distributed to Dart if the cash available for distribution is $41,000?
    a. $10,100
    b. $11,000
    c. $16,000
    d. $20,000

6. On May 1, 1997, 2 months after becoming insolvent, Quick Corp., an appliance wholesaler, filed a voluntary petition for bankruptcy under the provisions of Chapter 7 of the Federal Bankruptcy Code. On October 15, 1996, Quick's board of directors had authorized and paid Erly $50,000 to replay Erly's April 1, 1996, loan to the corporation. Erly is a sibling of Quick's president. On March 15, 1996, Quick paid Kray $100,000 for inventory delivered that day.

    Which of the following is **not** relevant in determining whether the repayment of Erly's loan is a voidable preferential transfer?
    a.   Erly is an insider.
    b.   Quick's payment to Erly was made on account of an antecedent debt.
    c.   Quick's solvency when the loan was made by Erly.
    d.   Quick's payment to Erly was made within on eyear of the filing of the bankruptcy petition.

Insurance

CHAPTER 38

OBJECTIVES

After studying this chapter, you should be able to

1. *Define insurable interest;*
2. *Compare contracts of insurance with ordinary contracts;*
3. *Explain the purpose of business liability insurance, marine insurance, fire and homeowners insurance, automobile insurance, and life insurance; and*
4. *Explain the effect of an incontestability clause.*

By means of insurance, protection from loss and liability may be obtained.

A. THE INSURANCE CONTRACT

Insurance is a contract by which one party for a stipulated consideration promises to pay another party a sum of money on the destruction of, loss of, or injury to something in which the other party has an interest or to indemnify that party for any loss or liability to which that party is subjected.

1. The Parties

The promisor in an insurance contract is called the **insurer** or **underwriter**. The person to whom the promise is made is the **insured**, the assured, or the policyholder. The promise of the insurer is generally set forth in a written contract called a **policy**.

Insurance contracts are ordinarily made through an agent or broker. The **insurance agent** is an agent of the insurance company, generally working exclusively for one company. For the most part, the ordinary rules of agency law govern the dealings between this agent and the applicant for insurance.[1]

An **insurance broker** is generally an independent contractor who is not employed by any one insurance company. When a broker obtains a policy for a customer, the broker is the agent of the customer for the purpose of that transaction. Under some statutes, the broker is made an agent of the insurer with respect to transmitting the applicant's payments to the insurer.

2. Insurable Interest

An insurable interest in property exists when damage to it will cause a direct monetary loss to the insurance purchaser at the time of the loss.

C·P·A

A person obtaining insurance must have an insurable interest in the subject matter insured. If not, the insurance contract cannot be enforced.

(a) Insurable Interest in Property. A person has an insurable interest in property whenever the destruction of the property will cause a direct pecuniary loss to that person.

It is immaterial whether the insured is the owner of the legal or equitable title, a lien holder, or merely a person in possession of the property.[2] ◆ *For example,* Vin Harrington, a builder, maintained fire insurance on a building he was remodeling under a contract with its owner, Chestnut Hill Properties. The building was destroyed by fire before renovations were completed. Harrington had an insurable interest in the property to the extent of the amount owed him under the renovation contract. ◆

C·P·A

To collect on property insurance, the insured must have an insurable interest at the time the loss occurs.

---

[1] *Tidelands Life Insurance Co. v France* (Tex App) 711 So 2d 728 (1986).
[2] *Hunter v State Farm Fire & Casualty Co.* (Ala) 543 So 2d 679 (1989).

She Lost Interest When He Got the House

Facts: While Dorothy and James Morgan were still married, Dorothy purchased insurance on their home from American Security Insurance Co. The policy was issued on November 3, 1981, listing the "insured" as Dorothy L. Morgan. Shortly thereafter the Morgans entered into a separation agreement under which Dorothy deeded her interest in the house to James. The Morgans were divorced on August 26, 1982. On November 28, 1982, the house was destroyed by fire. American Security refused to pay on the policy, claiming that Dorothy had no insurable interest in the property at the time of the loss. The Morgans sued the insurer, contending that they were entitled to payment under the policy issued to Dorothy.

Decision: Judgment for American Security. In the case of property insurance, the insurable interest must exist at the time of the loss. If the insured parts with all interest in the property prior to the loss, that individual is not covered. Dorothy had conveyed her interest in the property prior to the loss. She did not have an insurable interest at the time of the loss and therefore could not recover on the policy. James Morgan was not insured under the policy. [*Morgan v American Security Insurance Co. (Fla App) 522 So 2d 454 (1988)*]

(b) Insurable Interest in Life. A person who obtains life insurance can name anyone as beneficiary regardless of whether that beneficiary has an insurable interest in the life of the insured. A beneficiary who obtains a policy, however, must have an insurable interest in the life of the insured. Such an interest exists if the beneficiary can reasonably expect to receive pecuniary gain from the continued life of the other person and, conversely, would suffer financial loss from the latter's death. Thus, a creditor has an insurable interest in the life of the debtor because he or she may not be paid the amount owed upon the death of the debtor.

A partner or partnership has an insurable interest in the life of each of the partners because the death of any one of them will dissolve the firm and cause some degree of loss to the partnership. A business enterprise has an insurable interest in the life of an executive or a key employee because that person's death would inflict a financial loss on the business to the extent that a replacement might not be readily available or could not be found.

> A beneficiary who obtains a policy on another's life must have an insurable interest in the insured when the policy is purchased.

In the case of life insurance, the insurable interest must exist at the time the policy is obtained. It is immaterial that the interest no longer exists when the loss is actually sustained. Thus, the fact that a husband (insured) and wife (beneficiary) are divorced after the life insurance policy was procured does not affect the validity of the policy. Also, the fact that a partnership is terminated after a life insurance policy is obtained by one partner on another does not invalidate the policy.

Proceeds to the Surviving Partner or the Deceased Partner's Wife?

Facts: Jewell Norred's husband James Norred was the business partner of Clyde Graves for ten years. On May 7, 1979, Graves and Norred took out life insurance policies, with Graves being the beneficiary of Norred's policy and Norred being the beneficiary of Graves's policy. Premiums were paid out of partnership funds. On February 28, 1983, Graves and Norred divided the partnership assets, but they did not perform the customary steps of dissolving and winding up the partnership. Graves became the sole owner of the business and continued to pay the premiums on both insurance policies until James Norred died on December 5, 1983. Jewell Norred

> sued Graves, seeking the proceeds of the insurance policy for herself, alleging that Graves had no insurable interest in the life of James Norred at the time of his death. From a judgment on behalf of the estate, Graves appealed.
>
> Decision: Judgment for Graves. A partner or partnership has an insurable interest in the life of one of the partners. This interest continues even if the partnership is discontinued prior to the death of one of the partners. Thus, Graves was entitled to the proceeds of the policy. [*Graves v Norred* (Ala) 510 So 2d 816 (1987)]

3. The Contract

An insurance policy is a contract, and general contract law applies.

The formation of a contract of insurance is governed by the general principles applicable to contracts. By statute, it is now commonly provided that an insurance policy must be written. To avoid deception, many statutes also specify the content of certain policies, in whole or in part. Some statutes specify the size and style of type to be used in printing the policies. Provisions in a policy that conflict with statutory requirements are generally void. Frequently, a question arises as to whether advertising material, estimates, and statistical projections constitute a part of the contract.

(a) The Application as Part of the Contract. The application for insurance is generally attached to the policy when issued and is made part of the contract of insurance by express stipulation of the policy.

The insured is bound by all statements in the attached application if the policy and the attached application are retained without objection to such statement.[3]

Common standards of interpretation are that
- terms in conflict with a statute are void,
- terms required by statute are implied in the policy, and
- exceptions and restrictions must be expressly stated.

(b) Statutory Provisions as Part of the Contract. When a statute requires that insurance contracts contain certain provisions or cover certain specified losses, a contract of insurance that does not comply with the statute will be interpreted as though it contained all the provisions required by the statute. When a statute requires that all terms of the insurance contract be included in the written contract, the insurer cannot claim that a provision not stated in the written contract was binding on the insured.

CASE SUMMARY

What Happens When an Exception Clearly Stated in the Master Policy is not Contained in the Certificate of Insurance?

Facts: In 1975, Edwin Domke submitted an application for mortgage disability insurance, under an employer group insurance plan, to cover his house. On his application, he set forth his medical history and indicated that he had a hearing impairment. Domke was issued a four-page certificate of insurance, but he was not given a copy of the group master policy, which excluded from coverage "preexisting conditions." A state law required that each certificate of insurance set forth "any exceptions, limitations and restrictions." In 1977, Domke resigned his employment because of his hearing problem and applied for benefits under the mortgage disability policy. The insurance company denied benefits because the master policy excluded coverage for preexisting conditions and his hearing impairment was a preexisting condition.

---

[3] *Old Line Life Ins. Co. v Superior Court*, Ct of App, 1st Dist, 281 Cal Rptr 15 (1991).

> **Decision:** Judgment for Domke. The certificate of insurance issued to Domke by the insurance company constituted the insurance contract. The exclusion of "preexisting conditions" from coverage is clearly an exception that must be set forth in the certificate to be binding on the insured. *[Domke v F & M Savings Bank & N.C. Life Insurance Company (Minn App) 363 NW2d 898 (1985)]*

4. Antilapse and Cancellation Statutes and Provisions

If the premiums are not paid on time, the policy under ordinary contract law would lapse because of nonpayment. However, with life insurance policies, by either policy provision or statute, the insured is allowed a grace period of 30 or 31 days in which to make payment of the premium due. When there is a default in the payment of a premium by the insured, the insurer may be required by statute to (1) issue a paid-up policy in a smaller amount, (2) provide extended insurance for a period of time, or (3) pay the cash surrender value of the policy.

The contract of insurance may expressly declare that it may or may not be canceled by the insurer's unilateral act. By statute or policy provision, the insurer is commonly required to give a specific number of days' written notice of cancellation.[4]

5. Modification of Contract

If a policy term and an endorsement conflict, the endorsement controls.

As is the case with most contracts, a contract of insurance can be modified if both insurer and insured agree to the change. The insurer cannot modify the contract without the consent of the insured when the right to do so is not reserved in the insurance contract.

To make changes or corrections to the policy, it is not necessary to issue a new policy. An endorsement on the policy or the execution of a separate rider is effective for the purpose of changing the policy. When a provision of an endorsement conflicts with a provision of the policy, the endorsement controls because it is the later document.

6. Interpretation of Contract

A contract of insurance is interpreted by the same rules that govern the interpretation of ordinary contracts. Words are to be given their ordinary meaning and interpreted in light of the nature of the coverage intended. Thus, an employee who has been killed is not regarded as disabled within the meaning of a group policy covering employees.

The courts are increasingly recognizing the fact that most persons obtaining insurance are not specially trained. Therefore, the contract of insurance is to be read as it would be understood by the average person or by the average person in business rather than by one with technical knowledge of the law or of insurance.[5]

If there is an ambiguity in the policy, the provision is interpreted against the insurer.

---

[4] *Transamerican Ins. Co. v Tab Transportation*, Sup Ct 48 Cal Rptr 2d 159 (1995).
[5] *Bering Strait School District v RLT Insurance Co.* (Alaska) 872 P2d 1292 (1994).

Why Insurers Must Say What They Mean!

Facts: R.F. Baurer purchased a White Freightliner tractor and agreed that his son-in-law, Britton, could use it in the trucking business. In return, Britton agreed to haul Baurer's hay and cattle, thus saving Baurer approximately $30,000 per year. Baurer insured the vehicle with Mountain West Farm Bureau Insurance Co. The policy contained an exclusionary clause that provided: "We don't insure your [truck] while it is rented or leased to others. ... This does not apply to the use of your [truck] on a share expense basis." When the vehicle was destroyed, Mountain West refused to pay on the policy. Mountain West contended that the arrangement between Baurer and Britton was a lease of the vehicle, which was excluded under the policy. Baurer sued, contending that it was a "share expense basis" allowed under the policy.

Decision: Judgment for Baurer. The tractor was covered by the policy. The relationship between the parties could be construed as being either a renting out of the truck or a cooperative use of the truck on a share expense basis. Ambiguous language in an insurance policy is construed in a way that is most favorable to the insured. This rule of interpretation particularly applies to exclusionary clauses. Such a construction of the language in this case would result in the conclusion that the tractor was destroyed while used on a share expense basis. The loss was therefore covered by the policy. [*Baurer v Mountain West Farm Bureau Ins.* 215 Mont 196, 695 P2d 1307 (1985)]

ETHICS & THE LAW

On April 19, 1995, the federal building in downtown Oklahoma City was nearly leveled by a bomb detonated in a truck parked on the street at the front of the building. The bombing was similar to the 1993 explosion at the World Trade Center in New York City in that businesses in and around the explosion were forced to close and relocate.

Many of these businesses also discovered that their insurance policies might not cover either their physical property damage or their indirect losses. Some businesses discovered that their policies were not business interruption policies that provided payments for lost profits during the time that it took to relocate and initiate business activity. Most discovered that there was confusion about what their policies really covered. The questions that arose were these: Who pays for the office clean up in those businesses where things were messy but did not require reconstruction? Who pays for the overtime of employees needed to restart a business? Who pays for the security guards needed to prevent looting? Who pays for the rent at a temporary location? Who pays for third-party suits against the business when its damage has caused damage to surrounding property?

One insurance executive commented, "These two tragedies showed us that no one had really thought through the kinds of losses and coverage a business really needs."

Should insurers cover all the losses for the businesses harmed by these terrorist types of attacks? Do businesses rely on the advice of insurers? What about an insurer's excluding coverage altogether for these types of events? Is that fair? Is it the insurer's fault that businesses do not check the scope of their coverage? Would it be best to just have the community absorb the losses, or is it best to have individuals and individual businesses cover the losses?

7. Burden of Proof

When an insurance claim is disputed by the insurer, the person bringing suit has the burden of proving that there was a loss, that it occurred while the policy was in force, and that the loss was of a kind that was within the coverage or scope of the policy.

A policy will contain exceptions to the coverage. This means that the policy is not applicable when an exception applies to the situation.[6] Exceptions to coverage are generally strictly interpreted against the insurer. The insurer has the burden of proving that the facts were such that there was no coverage because an exception applied. Although an exception is literally applicable, it will be ignored by some courts and coverage sustained if there is no cause-and-effect relationship between the loss and the conduct that was the violation of the exception.

8. Insurer Bad Faith

An insurer's negligent or bad-faith refusal to defend an insured or settle within policy limits may render it liable for
- a statutory penalty in some states,
- damages, and
- any excess judgment, in some states.

As is required in the case of all contracts, an insurer must act in good faith in processing and paying claims under its policy. In some states, laws have been enacted making an insurer liable for a statutory penalty and attorney fees in case of a bad-faith failure or delay in paying a valid claim within a specified period of time. A bad-faith refusal is generally considered to be any frivolous or unfounded refusal to comply with the demand of a policyholder to pay according to the policy.[7]

When it is a liability insurer's duty to defend the insured and the insurer wrongfully refuses to do so, the insurer is guilty of breach of contract and is liable for all consequential damages resulting from the breach. In some jurisdictions, an insured can recover for an excess judgment rendered against the insured when it is proven that the insurer was guilty of negligence or bad faith in failing to defend the action or settle the matter within policy limits.

If there is a reasonable basis for the insurer's belief that a claim is not covered by its policy, its refusal to pay the claim does not subject it to liability for a breach of good faith or for a statutory penalty.[8] This is so even though the court holds that the insurer is liable for the claim.

For example, the following illustrates an insurer's bad-faith failure to pay a claim, as opposed to an insurer's reasonable basis for failure to pay. Carmela Garza's home and possessions were destroyed in a fire set by an arsonist on August 19, 1990. Carmela's husband, Raul, who was no longer living at the home, had a criminal record. An investigator for the insurer stated that while he had no specific information to implicate the Garzas in the arson, Carmela may have wanted the proceeds to finance relocation to another city. By October of 1990, however, Aetna's investigators ruled out the possibility that Garza had the motive or the opportunity to set the fire. The insurer thus no longer had a reasonable basis to refuse to pay the claim after this date. Yet it took over a year and a half and court intervention for Aetna to allow Carmela to see a copy of her policy, which had been destroyed in the fire. Two years after the fire, Aetna paid only $28,624.55 for structural damage to the fire-gutted home, which was insured for $111,000. The court held that Aetna's actions constituted a bad-faith failure to pay by the insurer.[9]

---

6 *Fireman's Fund Ins. v Fireboard Corp.,* Ct of App, 1st Dist, 227 Cal Rptr 203 (1986).
7 *Ingals v Paul Revere Life Ins. Group* (ND) 561 NW2d 273 (1997).
8 *Shipes v Hanover Ins. Co.,* 884 F2d 1357 (11th Cir 1989).
9 See *Aetna Casualty & Surety Co. v Garza* (Tex App) 906 SW2d 543 (1995).

9. Time Limitations on Insured

The insured must comply with a number of time limitations in making a claim. For example, the insured must promptly notify the insurer of any claim that may arise, submit a proof-of-loss statement within the time set forth in the policy, and bring any court action based on the policy within a specified time period.

10. Subrogation of Insurer

In some instances, the insured has a claim against a third person for the harm covered by the insurance policy. ◆ *For example,* A sells an automobile insurance policy to B, which provides collision coverage. C "rear ends" B's car at a traffic rotary in the city. A pays B the full amount of the property damage repair costs. A is then subrogated to B's claim against C, the person who caused the harm. See Figure 38-1. When the insurer is subrogated to the insured's claim, the insurer may enforce that claim against the third person.[10] ◆

FIGURE 38-1
Subrogation

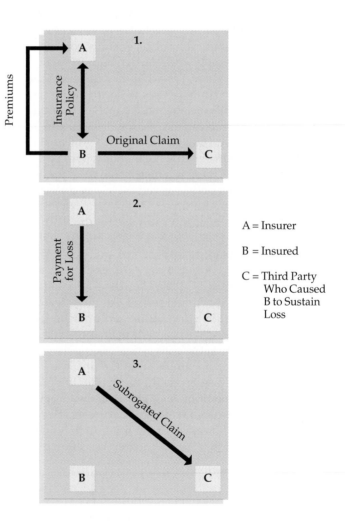

A = Insurer

B = Insured

C = Third Party
Who Caused
B to Sustain
Loss

---

[10] *Julson v Federated Mutual Ins. Co.* (SD) 562 NW2d 117 (1997).

B.   KINDS OF INSURANCE

Businesses today have specialized risk managers who identify the risks to which individual businesses are exposed, measure those risks, and purchase insurance to cover those risks (or decide to self-insure in whole or in part).

Insurance policies can be grouped into certain categories. Five major categories of insurance are considered below: (1) business liability insurance, (2) marine and inland marine insurance, (3) fire and homeowners insurance, (4) automobile insurance, and (5) life insurance.

11. Business Liability Insurance

Businesses may purchase "Comprehensive[11] General Liability" (CGL) policies. This insurance is a broad, "all-risk" form of insurance providing coverage for all sums that the insured may become legally obligated to pay as damages because of "bodily injury" or "property damage" caused by an "occurrence." The insurer is obligated to defend the insured business and pay damages under CGL policies for product liability cases, actions for wrongful termination of employees, sexual harassment cases, damages caused by the business advertising, and trademark infringement suits.[12] The insurer may also be obligated to pay for damages in the form of cleanup costs imposed for contamination of land, water, and air under environmental statutes.[13]

CASE SUMMARY

EPA's PRP Suits the Court Just Fine

Facts: Anderson Development Co. (ADC) manufactures and sells specialty organic materials in Adrian, Michigan. It built a lagoon to handle the occasional accidental discharge of Curene 442 process water, believing it to be insoluble in water. Curene 442, which it manufactured between 1970 and 1979, was a known animal carcinogen, and it turned out to be soluble. The lagoon's discharge piping was connected to the sewer system and the Curene 442 found its way to the city's sewage treatment plant. In 1985, the Environmental Protection Agency (EPA) sent ADC a formal notification that it was considered a "potentially responsible party" (PRP) for the release of hazardous substances into the soil and ground water. This notice was called a PRP letter. ADC notified Travelers Indemnity Co., its insurer, of the letter, and Travelers contended that it was not prepared to defend or cover ADC in the matter. ADC did a study that revealed contamination on its property. The EPA and ADC entered a consent decree wherein ADC agreed to the cleanup activities required by the EPA, spending over $6 million on the cleanup. ADC brought an action against its insurer, seeking coverage under its general liability insurance policies for the cost of its defense and the cost of the cleanup. Travelers alleged that it was not liable under the policies.

Decision: Judgment for insured. The state's highest court has held that a PRP letter issued by the EPA is the functional equivalent of a "suit" brought in a court of law because the EPA's

---

11 Insurers today have in many cases substituted the term "Commercial" for "Comprehensive" on many new policies, believing that the courts were interpreting Comprehensive General Liability policies to cover almost any liability associated with a business.

12 *Lebase Fashion Imports of USA v ITT Hartford Insurance Group* (Cal App) 54 Cal Rptr 2d 36 (1996).

13 *Chemical Leaman Tank Lines Inc. v Aetna Casualty Co.*, 788 F Supp 846 (DNJ 1992); *United States v Pepper's Steel Inc.*, 823 F Supp 1574 (SD Fla 1993). But see *Northville Industries v National Union Fire Ins. Co.* (Sup Ct App Div) 636 NYS2d 359 (1995); *Aydin Corp. v First State Insurance Co.* (Cal App) 62 Cal Rptr 2d 825 (1997).

> extensive authority to determine and apportion liability allows it to essentially usurp the traditional role of a court. Thus, Travelers had an obligation to defend the insured under the contractual terms used in the policy, "defend any suit." Travelers is also liable for "damages" as that term is used in the insurance contract because state court decisions hold that EPA-mandated cleanup costs constitute damages. [*Anderson Development Co. v Travelers Indemnity Co.*, 49 F3d 1128 (6th Cir 1995).

Businesses may purchase policies providing liability insurance for their directors and officers. Manufacturers and sellers may purchase product liability insurance. Professional persons, such as accountants, physicians, lawyers, architects, and engineers, may obtain liability insurance protection against malpractice suits.

12. Marine Insurance

Ocean marine insurance covers transportation of goods at sea. Inland marine insurance covers the domestic transportation of goods other than at sea.

Marine insurance policies cover perils relating to the transportation of goods. **Ocean marine** insurance policies cover the transportation of goods in vessels in international and coastal trade. **Inland marine** insurance principally covers domestic shipments of goods over land and inland waterways.

(a) Ocean Marine. Ocean marine insurance is a form of insurance that covers ships and their cargoes against "perils of the sea." Four classes of ocean marine insurance are generally available: (1) hull, (2) cargo, (3) liability, and (4) freight. **Hull insurance** covers physical damage to the vessel. **Cargo insurance** protects the cargo owner against financial loss if the goods being shipped are lost or damaged at sea.

<table>
<tr><td>CASE SUMMARY</td><td>

This Coverage Is Worth a Hill of Beans

Facts: Commodities Reserve Co. (CRC) contracted to sell 1,008 tons of beans and 50 tons of seed to purchasers in Venezuela. CRC purchased the beans and seeds in Turkey and chartered space on the ship MV West Lion. The cargo was insured under an ocean marine policy issued by St. Paul Fire & Marine Insurance Co. The Sue & Labor Clause in CRC's ocean marine policy with St. Paul provided: "In case of any loss or misfortune, it shall be lawful and necessary to and for the Assured . . . to sue, labor and travel for, in and about the defense, safeguard and recovery of the said goods and merchandise . . . to the charges whereof, the [insurer] will contribute according to the rate and quantity of the sum hereby insured." While the ship was sailing through Greek waters, Greek authorities seized the vessel for carrying munitions. CRC had to go to the expense of obtaining an order from a court in Crete to release the cargo. When St. Paul refused to pay the costs of the Cretan litigation to release the cargo, CRC brought suit against St. Paul.

Decision: Judgment for CRC. The Sue and Labor Clause required CRC to sue for "recovery of the said goods and merchandise." The clause also requires the insurer to reimburse the insured for those expenses. [*Commodities Reserve Co. v St. Paul Fire & Marine Ins. Co.*, 879 F2d 640 (9th Cir 1990)]

</td></tr>
</table>

Cargo insurance does not cover risks prior to the loading of the insured cargo on board the vessel.[14] An additional warehouse coverage endorsement is needed to insure merchandise held in a warehouse prior to import or export voyages.

---

[14] *S.P. Duggal Corp. v Aetna Casualty Co.*, Sup Ct App Div 580 NYS2d 767 (1992).

Liability insurance covers the shipowner's liability if the ship causes damage to another ship or its cargo. **Freight insurance** insures that the shipowner will receive payment for the transportation charges.

(b) Inland Marine. Inland marine insurance evolved from marine insurance. It protects goods in transit over land, by air, or on rivers, lakes, and coastal waters. Inland marine insurance can be used to insure property held by a bailee. Moreover, it is common for institutions financing automobile dealers' new car inventories to purchase inland marine insurance policies to insure against damage to the automobiles while in inventory.[15]

13. Fire and Homeowners Insurance

A **fire insurance policy** is a contract to indemnify the insured for property destruction or damage caused by fire. In almost every state, the New York standard fire insurance form is the standard policy. A **homeowners insurance** policy is a combination of the standard fire insurance policy and comprehensive personal liability insurance. It thus provides fire, theft, and certain liability protection in a single insurance contract.

(a) Fire Insurance. In order for fire loss to be covered by fire insurance, there must be an actual, hostile fire that is the immediate cause of the loss. A hostile fire is one that becomes uncontrollable, burns with excessive heat, or escapes from the place where it is intended to be. To illustrate, when soot is ignited and causes a fire in the chimney, the fire is hostile. On the other hand, if a loss is caused by the smoke or heat of a fire that has not broken out of its ordinary container or become uncontrollable, the loss results from a friendly fire. Damage from a friendly fire is not covered by the policy.

By policy endorsement, the coverage may be extended to include loss by a friendly fire.

CASE SUMMARY

Excuse Me? The Fire Wasn't Hostile?

Facts: Youse owned a ring that was insured with the Employers Fire Insurance Co. against loss, including "all direct loss or damage by fire." The ring was accidentally thrown by Youse into a trash burner and was damaged when the trash was burned. He sued the insurer.

Decision: Judgment for insurer. A fire policy only covers loss caused by a hostile fire. The fire was not hostile, because it burned in the area in which it was intended to burn. [*Youse v Employers Fire Insurance Co.* 172 Kan 111, 238 P2d 472 (1951)]

An insurer's obligations may be reduced by a co-insurance clause in a fire policy.

(1) Co-insurance. The insurer is liable for the actual amount of the loss sustained up to the maximum amount stated in the policy. An exception exists when the policy contains a co-insurance clause. A **co-insurance clause** requires the insured to maintain insurance on the covered property up to a certain amount or a certain percentage of the value (generally 80 percent). Under such a provision, if the policyholder insures the property for less than the required amount, the insurer

---

[15] *Boyd Motors Inc. v Employers Ins. of Wausau*, 880 F2d 270 (10th Cir 1989).

is liable only for the proportionate share of the amount of insurance required to be carried. Suppose the owner of a building with a value of $200,000, for example, insures it against loss to the extent of $120,000. The policy contains a co-insurance clause requiring that insurance of 80 percent of the value of the property be carried (in this case, $160,000). Assume that an $80,000 loss is then sustained. The insured would receive not $80,000 from the insurer but only three-fourths of that amount, which is $60,000, because the amount of the insurance carried ($120,000) is only three-fourths of the amount required ($160,000).

In some states, use of a co-insurance clause is prohibited.

(2) Assignment. Fire insurance is a personal contract, and in the absence of statute or contractual authorization, it cannot be assigned without the consent of the insurer.

(3) Occupancy. Provisions in a policy of fire insurance relating to the use and occupancy of the property are generally strictly construed because they relate to the hazards involved.

(b) Homeowners Insurance. In addition to providing protection against losses resulting from fire, the homeowners policy provides liability coverage for accidents or injuries that occur on the premises of the insured. Moreover, the liability provisions provide coverage for unintentional injuries to others away from home for which the insured or any member of the resident family is held responsible, such as injuries caused others by golfing, hunting, or fishing accidents.[16] Generally, motor vehicles, including mopeds and recreational vehicles, are excluded from such personal liability coverage.

A homeowners policy also provides protection from losses caused by theft. In addition, it provides protection for all permanent residents of the household, including all family members living with the insured. Thus, a child of the insured who lives at home is protected under the homeowner's policy for the value of personal property lost when the home is destroyed by fire.[17]

14. Automobile Insurance

Associations of insurers, such as the National Bureau of Casualty Underwriters and the National Automobile Underwriters Association, have proposed standard forms of automobile insurance policies. These forms have been approved by the association members in virtually all states. The form used today by most insurers is the Personal Auto Policy (PAP).

(a) Perils Covered. Part A of the policy provides liability coverage that protects the insured driver or owner from the claims of others for bodily injuries or damage to their property. Part B of the policy provides coverage for medical expenses sustained by a covered person or persons in an accident. Part C of the PAP provides coverage for damages the insured is entitled to recover from an **uninsured motorist**. Part D provides coverage for loss or damage to the covered automobile. Coverage under Part D includes collision coverage and coverage of "other than collision" losses, such as fire and theft.

---

16 *American Concept Ins. Co. v Lloyds of London* (SD) 467 NW2d 480 (1991).
17 *Gulf Ins. Co. v Mathis* (GA App) 358 SE2d 307 (1987).

(b) Covered Persons. Covered persons include the named insured or any family member (a person related by blood, marriage, or adoption or a ward or foster child who is a resident of the household). If an individual is driving with the permission of the insured, that individual is also covered.

(c) Use and Operation. The coverage of the PAP policy is limited to claims arising from the "use and operation" of an automobile. The term *use and operation* does not require that the automobile be in motion. Thus, the term embraces loading and unloading as well as actual travel.[18]

CASE SUMMARY

Is Carrying a Transmission Down a Driveway "Loading or Unloading" a Truck? A Liberal Interpretation.

Facts: Gerhard Schillers was assisting his friend J.L. Loethen in removing a transmission from the bed of the Loethens' truck on the Loethens' property. While Schillers was carrying the transmission down a driveway, he fell and was seriously injured. J.L. was insured under his parents' automobile insurance policy with Shelter Mutual Insurance Co., which insured for liability, including "the loading and unloading" of the vehicle.

Decision: Schillers's injuries were incidental to and a consequence of the unloading of the Loethens' pickup truck. The injuries would not have occurred if the men had not been unloading the truck. The unloading activity continued until the removed property was put in the place to which it was to be taken. Therefore, Schillers's injury was covered by the motor vehicle liability policy issued by Shelter Mutual. [*American Family Mutual Insurance Co. v Shelter Mutual Insurance Co.* (Mo App) 747 SW2d 174 (1988)]

(d) Notice and Cooperation. The insured is under a duty to give notice of claims, to inform, and to cooperate with the insurer. Notice and cooperation are conditions precedent to the liability of the insurer.

(e) No-Fault Insurance. Traditional tort law (negligence law) placed the economic losses resulting from an automobile accident on the one at fault. The purpose of automobile liability insurance is to relieve the wrongdoer from the consequences of a negligent act by paying defense costs and the damages assessed. Under no-fault laws, injured persons are barred from suing the party at fault for ordinary claims. When the insured is injured while using the insured automobile, the insurer will make a payment without regard to whose fault caused the harm. However, if the automobile collision results in a permanent serious disablement or disfigurement, or death, or if the medical bills and lost wages of the plaintiff exceed a specified amount, suit may be brought against the party who was at fault.

There are three major types of life insurance:
• term,
• whole life, and
• endowment.

15. Life Insurance

There are three basic types of life insurance: term insurance, whole life insurance, and endowment insurance.

---

[18] *State Farm Ins. v Whitehead* (Mo App) 711 SW2d 198 (1986).

Term insurance is written for a specified number of years and terminates at the end of that period. If the insured dies within the time period covered by the policy, the face amount is paid to the beneficiary. If the insured is still alive at the end of the time period, the contract expires, and the insurer has no further obligation. Term policies have little or no cash surrender value.

Whole life insurance (or ordinary life insurance) provides lifetime insurance protection. It also has an investment element.

Part of every premium covers the cost of insurance, and the remainder of the premium builds up a **cash surrender value** of the policy.

An **endowment insurance** policy is one that pays the face amount of the policy if the insured dies within the policy period. If the insured lives to the end of the policy period, the face amount is paid to the insured at the end of the period.

Many life insurance companies pay double the amount of the policy, called **double indemnity**, if death is caused by an accident and death occurs within 90 days after the accident. A comparatively small additional premium is charged for this special protection.

In consideration of an additional premium, many life insurance companies also provide insurance against total permanent disability of the insured. **Disability** is usually defined in a life insurance policy as any "incapacity resulting from bodily injury or disease to engage in any occupation for remuneration or profit."

(a) Exclusions. Life insurance policies frequently provide that death is not within the protection of the policy and that a double indemnity provision is not applicable when death is caused by (1) suicide,[19] (2) narcotics, (3) the intentional act of another, (4) execution for a crime, (5) war activities, or (6) operation of aircraft.

(b) The Beneficiary. The recipient of life insurance policy proceeds that are payable upon the death of the insured is called the **beneficiary**. The beneficiary may be a third person or the estate of the insured, and there may be more than one beneficiary.

The beneficiary named in a policy may be barred from claiming the proceeds of the policy. It is generally provided by statute or stated by court decision that a beneficiary who has feloniously killed the insured is not entitled to receive the proceeds of the policy.

The customary policy provides that the insured reserves the right to change the beneficiary without the latter's consent. When the policy contains such a provision, the beneficiary cannot object to a change that destroys all of that beneficiary's rights under the policy and that names another person as beneficiary.

An insurance policy will ordinarily state that to change the beneficiary, the insurer must be so instructed in writing by the insured and the policy must then be endorsed by the company with the change of the beneficiary. These provisions are construed liberally. If the insured has notified the insurer but dies before the endorsement of the change by the company, the change of beneficiary is effective.[20] However, if the insured has not taken any steps to comply with the policy requirements, a change of beneficiary is not effective even though a change was intended.

---

[19] *Mirza v Maccabees Life and Annuity Co.* (Mich App) 466 NW2d 340 (1991).
[20] *Zeigler v Cardona*, 830 F Supp 1395 (MD Ala 1993).

Under an incontestability clause, an insurer cannot refuse to pay a claim after a contestability period regardless of fraud or misrepresentation by the insured when the policy was purchased.

(c) Incontestability Clause. Statutes commonly require the inclusion of an **incontestability clause** in life insurance policies. Ordinarily this clause states that after the lapse of two years the policy cannot be contested by the insurance company. The insurer is free to contest the validity of the policy at any time during the contestability period. Once the period has expired, the insurer must pay the stipulated sum upon the death of the insured and cannot claim that in obtaining the policy, the insured had been guilty of misrepresentation, fraud, or any other conduct that would entitle it to avoid the contract of insurance.[21]

CASE SUMMARY

The Substitute with Different Attributes—No Contest

Facts: Jose Morales applied for a life insurance policy from Amex in January 1991. Although he was HIV positive, he lied on the application form and denied having the AIDS virus. As part of the application process, Amex required him to have a medical examination. In March 1991, a paramedic working for Amex met a man claiming to be Morales and took blood and urine samples. On his application, Morales listed his height as 5'6" and weight as 142 pounds. The examiner stated that the man he examined was 5'10" tall and weighed 172 pounds. The man produced no identification and appeared to be older than the stated age. His blood sample was HIV negative. Amex issued Morales a policy in May 1991, and all premiums were paid. Just over two years later on June 11, 1993, Morales died of AIDS-related causes on. Thereafter Amex investigated and found gross differences between the signature of the person examined and tested and that of the person who applied for and signed the insurance policy. It is conceded that Morales substituted another person to take the medical examination so that Morales would be issued a life insurance policy. The beneficiary sued, and Amex raised the "imposter" defense.

Decision: The insurer was liable. Incontestability clauses are strictly construed. The named insured, Morales, himself applied for the policy and did everything except take the medical examination. The policy insured him, not someone else. The fraud, although abhorrent and clearly justifying rescission of the policy during the two-year contestability period, is not quantitatively different from other types of fraud that courts have held may not be used to contest coverage once the contestability period has expired, if the premiums have been paid. Thus, Amex, which did nothing to protect its interests but collect premiums, may not now challenge coverage on an imposter defense. [*Amex Life Assurance Co. v Superior Court (Sup Ct) 60 Cal Rptr 2d 898 (1997)*]

SUMMARY

Insurance is a contract, called a policy. Under an insurance policy, provision is made by the insurer, in consideration of premium payments, to pay the insured or beneficiary a sum of money if the insured sustains a specified loss or is subjected to a specified liability. These contracts are made through an insurance agent, who is an agent for the insurance company, or through an insurance broker. An insurance broker is the agent of the insured when obtaining a policy for the latter.

The person purchasing an insurance contract must have an insurable interest in the insured life or property. An insurable interest in property exists when the damage or destruction of the property will cause a direct monetary loss to the insured. In the case of property insurance, the insured must have an insurable interest at the time of loss. An insurable interest in the life of the insured exists if the purchaser would suffer a financial loss from the insured's death. This interest must exist as of the time the policy is obtained.

Ocean marine policies insure ships and their cargoes against the perils of the sea. Inland marine policies insure goods being transported by land, by air, or on inland and coastal waterways.

In order for a fire loss to be covered by fire insurance, there must be an actual, hostile fire that is the immediate cause of the loss. The insurer is liable for the actual

---

[21] *Rapak v Companion Life Ins. Co.* (SC) 424 SE2d 486 (1992).

amount of the loss sustained up to the maximum amount stated in the policy. An exception exists when the policy contains a co-insurance clause requiring the insured to maintain insurance up to a certain percentage of the value of the property. To the extent this is not done, the insured is deemed a co-insurer with the insurer, and the insurer is liable for only its proportional share of the amount of insurance required to be carried. A homeowners insurance policy provides fire, theft, and liability protection in a single contract.

Automobile insurance may provide protection for collision damage to the insured's property and injury to persons. It may also cover liability to third persons for injury and property damage, and loss by fire or theft.

A life insurance policy requires the insurer to pay a stated sum of money to a named beneficiary upon the death of the insured. It may be a term insurance policy, a whole life policy, or an endowment policy. State law commonly requires the inclusion of an incontestability clause, whereby, at the conclusion of the contestability period, the insurer cannot contest the validity of the policy.

QUESTIONS AND CASE PROBLEMS

1. What social forces are affected by requiring an insurable interest?

2. Compare (a) a contract of insurance and (b) an ordinary contract.

3. What time limits may bar an insured from recovering on an insurance policy?

4. On April 6, 1988, Luis Serrano purchased for $75,000 a 26' 8"-long Carrera speed boat named *Hot Shot*. First Federal Savings Bank provided $65,000 financing for this purchase. Serrano obtained a marine yacht policy for hull insurance on the boat for $75,000 from El Fenix, with First Federal being named as payee under the policy. On May 2, 1988, Serrano sold the boat to Reinaldo Polito, and Serrano furnished First Federal with documents evidencing the sale. Polito assumed the obligation to pay off the balance due First Federal. On October 6, 1989, Serrano again applied to El Fenix for a new yacht policy, covering the period from October 6, 1989, through October 6, 1990, and the coverage extended to peril of confiscation by a governmental agency. Serrano did not have ownership or possession of the boat on October 6, 1989. First Federal, the named payee, had not perfected or recorded a mortgage on *Hot Shot* until July 5, 1990. On November 13, 1989, in the waters off Cooper Island in the British Virgin Islands (BVI), *Hot Shot* was found abandoned after a chase by governmental officials. A large shipment of cocaine was recovered, although no one was arrested. When Serrano and First Federal were informed that *Hot Shot* was subject to mandatory forfeiture under BVI law, they both filed claims under the October 6, 1989, insurance policy. What defenses would you raise on behalf of the insurer in this case? Decide. [*El Fenix v Serrano Gutierrez*, 786 F Supp 1065 (DPR)]

5. From the United Insurance Co., Rebecca Foster obtained a policy insuring the life of Lucille McClurkin and naming herself as beneficiary. McClurkin did not live with Foster, and Foster did not inform McClurkin of the existence of the policy. Foster paid the premiums on the policy and, upon the death of McClurkin, sued the United Insurance Co. for the amount of the insurance. At the trial, Foster testified vaguely that her father had told her that McClurkin was her second cousin on his side of the family. Was Foster entitled to recover on the policy? [*Foster v United Ins. Co.* 250 SC 423, 158 SE2d 201]

6. Dr. George Allard and his brother-in-law, Tom Rowland, did not get along after family land that was once used solely by Rowland was partitioned among family members after the death of Rowland's father. Rowland had a reputation in the community as a bully and a violent person. On December 17, Allard was moving cattle down a dirt road by "trolling" (leading the cattle with a bucket of feed, causing them to follow him). When he saw a forestry truck coming along the road, he led the cattle off the road onto Rowland's land to prevent frightening the cattle. When Rowland saw Allard, Rowland ran toward him screaming at him for being on his land. Allard, a small older man, retreated to his truck and obtained a 12-gauge shotgun. He pointed the gun toward the ground about an inch in front of Rowland's left foot and fired it. He stated that he fired the shot in this fashion to bring Rowland to his senses and that Rowland stepped forward into the line of fire. Allard claimed that if Rowland had not stepped forward, he would not have been hit and injured. Allard was insured by Farm Bureau homeowners and general liability policies, which did not cover liability resulting

from intentional acts by the insured. Applying the policy exclusion to the facts of this case, was Farm Bureau obligated to pay the $100,000 judgment against Allard? [*Southern Farm Bureau Casualty Co. v Allard* (Miss) 611 So 2d 966]

7. Assistant manager trainee R.G. Smith suspected Bowen of shoplifting at Broad & Marshall Department Store. After getting permission from the store manager to follow her, he observed Bowen driving out of the store's parking lot. Smith followed her in his car and forced her into a ditch, where her car overturned and was destroyed. Bowen received the fair market value for her car from her insurance company, General National Mutual (GNM), and executed a subrogation agreement in connection with this payment. GNM brings suit against Smith and the store to obtain reimbursement for the amount paid by it for the damage to the car. They argue that GNM is not the proper party plaintiff. Decide.

8. Linda Filasky held policies issued by Preferred Risk Mutual Insurance Co. Following an injury in an automobile accident and storm damage to the roof of her home, Filasky sustained loss of income, theft of property, and water damage to her home. These three kinds of loss were covered by the policies with Preferred, but the insurer delayed unreasonably in processing her claims and raised numerous groundless objections to them. Finally the insurer paid the claims in full. Filasky then sued the insurer for the emotional distress caused by the bad-faith delay and obstructive tactics of the insurer. The insurer defended that it had paid the claims in full and that nothing was owed Filasky. Decide. [*Filasky v Preferred Risk Mut. Ins. Co.* (Ariz) 734 P2d 76]

9. Collins obtained from South Carolina Insurance Co. a liability policy covering a Piper Colt airplane he owned. The policy provided that it did not cover loss sustained while the plane was being piloted by a person who did not have a valid pilot's certificate and a valid medical examination certificate. Collins held a valid pilot's certificate, but his medical examination certificate had expired three months before. Collins was piloting the plane when it crashed, and he was killed. The insurer denied liability because Collins did not have a valid medical certificate. It was stipulated by both parties that the crash was in no way caused by the absence of the medical certificate. Decide. [*South Carolina Ins. Co. v Collins* (SC) 237 SE2d 358]

10. Marshall Produce Co. had insured its milk- and egg-processing plant against fire. When smoke from a fire near its plant permeated the environment and was absorbed into the company's egg powder products, cans of powder delivered to the U.S. government were rejected as contaminated. Marshall Produce sued the insurance company for a total loss, but the insurer contended there had been no fire involving the insured property and no total loss. Decide. [*Marshall Produce Co. v St. Paul Fire & Marine Ins. Co.* (Minn) 98 NW2d 280]

11. Amador Pena, who had three insurance policies on his life, wrote a will in which he specified that the proceeds from the insurance policies should go to his children instead of to Leticia Pena Salinas and other beneficiaries named in the policies. He died the day after writing the will. The insurance companies paid the proceeds of the policies to the named beneficiaries. The executor of Pena's estate sued Salinas and the other beneficiaries for the insurance money. Decide. [*Pena v Salinas* (Tex App) 536 SW2d 671]

12. Spector owned a small automobile repair garage in rural Kansas that was valued at $40,000. He purchased fire insurance coverage against loss to the extent of $24,000. The policy contained an 80 percent co-insurance clause. A fire destroyed a portion of his parts room, causing a loss of $16,000. Spector believes he is entitled to be fully compensated for this loss, as it is less than the $24,000 of fire protection that he purchased and paid for. Is Spector correct?

13. Carman Tool & Abrasives, Inc., purchased two milling machines, FOB Taiwan, from the Dah Lih Machinery Co. Carman obtained ocean marine cargo insurance on the machines from St. Paul Fire and Marine Insurance Co. and authorized Dah Lih to arrange for the shipment of the two machines to Los Angeles, using the services of Evergreen Lines. Dah Lih booked the machinery for shipment on board Evergreen's container ship, the *M/V Ever Giant*; arranged for the delivery of the cargo to the ship; provided all the shipping information for the bill of lading; and was the party to whom the bill was issued. Dah Lih then delivered the bill of lading to its bank, which, in turn, negotiated it to Carman's bank to authorize payment to Dah Lih. After the cargo was removed from the vessel in Los Angeles but before it was delivered to Carman, the milling machines were damaged to the extent of $115,000. Is the insurer liable to Carman? Can the insurer recover from Evergreen? [*Carman Tool & Abrasives, Inc. v Evergreen Lines*, 871 F2d 897 (9th Cir)]

14. Vallot was driving his farm tractor on the highway. It was struck from the rear by a truck, overturned, exploded, and burned. Vallot was killed, and a death

claim was made against All American Insurance Co. The death of Vallot was covered by the company's policy if Vallot had died from "being struck or run over by" the truck. The insurance company claimed that the policy was not applicable because Vallot had not been struck; the farm tractor had been struck, and Vallot's death occurred when the overturned tractor exploded and burned. The insurance company also claimed that it was necessary that the insured be both struck and run over by another vehicle. Decide. [*Vallot v All American Ins. Co.* (La App) 302 So 2d 625]

15. When Jorge de Guerrero applied for a $200,000 life insurance policy with John Hancock Mutual Life Insurance Co., he stated on the insurance application that he had not seen a physician within the past five years. In fact he had had several consultations with his physician, who three weeks prior to the application had diagnosed him as overweight and suffering from goiter. His response to the question on drug and alcohol use was that he was not an alcoholic or user of drugs. In fact he had been an active alcoholic since age 16 and was a marijuana user. De Guerrero died within the two-year contestability period included in the policy, and John Hancock refused to pay. The beneficiary contended that all premiums were fully paid on the policy and that any misstatements in the application were unintentional. John Hancock contended that if the deceased had given the facts, the policy would not have been issued. Decide. [*de Guerrero v John Hancock Mutual Life Ins. Co.* (Fla App) 522 So 2d 1032]

CPA QUESTIONS

1. Beal occupies an office building as a tenant under a 25-year lease. Beal also has a mortgagee's (lender's) interest in an office building owned by Hill Corp. In which capacity does Beal have an insurable interest?

	Tenant	Mortgagee
a.	Yes	Yes
b.	Yes	No
c.	No	Yes
d.	No	No

(5/88, Law, #60, 9911)

2. With respect to property insurance, the insurable interest requirement
   a. Need only be satisfied at the time the policy is issued.
   b. Must be satisfied both at the time the policy is issued and at the time of the loss.
   c. Will be satisfied only if the insured owns the property in fee simple absolute.
   d. Will be satisfied by an insured who possesses a leasehold interest in the property.

(11/87, Law, #59, 9911)

3. Lawfo Corp. maintains a $200,000 standard fire insurance policy on one of its warehouses. The policy includes an 80% coinsurance clause. At the time the warehouse was originally insured, its value was $250,000. The warehouse now has a value of $300,000. If the warehouse sustains $30,000 of fire damage, Lawfo's insurance recovery will be a maximum of
   a. $20,000.
   b. $24,000.
   c. $25,000.
   d. $30,000.

(5/90, Law, #59, 9911)

P A R T 7

Agency and Employment

Agency

CHAPTER 39

After studying this chapter, you should be able to

1. *Differentiate between an agent and an independent contractor;*
2. *Explain and illustrate who may be a principal and who may be an agent;*
3. *State the three classifications of agents;*
4. *Differentiate between express authority, incidental authority, customary authority, and apparent authority;*
5. *Explain the effect of the proper exercise of authority by an agent;*
6. *Describe the duty of a third person to determine the extent of an agent's authority;*
7. *List the four ways an agency relationship may be created;*
8. *List six ways an agency may be terminated by an act of one or both of the parties to the agency agreement; and*
9. *List five ways an agency may be terminated by operation of law.*

One of the most common business relationships is that of agency.

By virtue of the agency device, one person can make contracts at numerous places with many different parties at the same time.

A.   NATURE OF THE AGENCY RELATIONSHIP

Agency is ordinarily based on the consent of the parties and for that reason is called a *consensual relationship*. However, the law sometimes imposes an agency relationship. If consideration is present, the agency relationship is contractual.

1. Definitions and Distinctions

An agency is based on an express or implied agreement whereby the agent is authorized to negotiate and make contracts by and for a principal with a third party.

Agency is a relationship based on an express or implied agreement by which one person, the **agent**, is authorized to act under the control of and for another, the **principal**, in negotiating and making contracts with third persons.[1] The acts of the agent obligate the principal to third persons and give the principal rights against third persons.

The term *agency* is frequently used with other meanings. It is sometimes used to denote the fact that one has the right to sell certain products, such as when a dealer is said to possess an automobile agency. In other instances, the term is used to mean an exclusive right to sell certain articles within a given territory. In these cases, however, the dealer is not an agent in the sense of representing the manufacturer.[2] Courts are sometimes called on to determine if an agency relationship existed although the term *agent* had not been used.

It is important to be able to distinguish agencies from other relationships because there are certain rights and duties in agencies that are not present in other relationships.

(a) Employees and Independent Contractors. Control and authority are characteristics that distinguish ordinary employees and independent contractors from agents.

---

[1] Restatement (Second) of Agency § 1; *Union Miniere, S.A. v Parday Corp.* (Ind App) 521 NE2d 700 (1988).
[2] *Professional Lens Plan, Inc. v Polaris Leasing Corp.* (Kan) 710 P2d 1297 (1985).

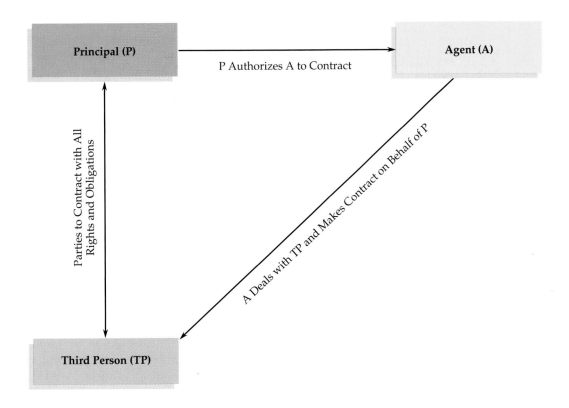

FIGURE 39-1
Agency Relationship

(1) Employees. An agent is distinguished from an ordinary employee, who is not hired to represent the employer in making contracts with third persons. It is possible, however, for the same person to be both an agent and an employee. For example, the driver of a milk delivery truck is an agent in making contracts between the milk company and its customers but is an employee with respect to the work of delivering milk.

(2) Independent Contractors. An independent contractor is bound by a contract to produce a certain result—for example, to build a house. The actual performance of the work is controlled by the contractor, not the owner. An agent or employee differs from an independent contractor in that the principal or employer has the right to control the agent or employee, but not the contractor, in the performance of the work. ◆ *For example,* Ned and Tracy Seizer contract with Fox Building Co. to build a new home on Hilton Head Island, South Carolina, according to referenced plans and specifications. Individuals hired by Fox to work on the home are subject to the authority and control of Fox, the independent contractor, not the Seizers. However, Ned and Tracy could decide to build the home themselves, hiring two individuals from nearby Beaufort, Ted Chase and Marty Bromley, to do the work the Seizers will direct each day. Because Ted and Marty would be employees of the Seizers, the Seizers would be held responsible for any wrongs committed by these employees within the scope of their employment. But, as a general rule, on the other hand, the Seizers are not responsible for the torts of Fox, the independent contractor, and the contractor's employees. ◆

A "right to control" test determines whether an individual is an agent, an employee, or an independent contractor.

Why Some Businesses Use Independent Agents Rather Than Employees!

Facts: Patricia Yelverton died from injuries sustained when an automobile owned and driven by Joseph Lamm crossed the center line of a roadway and struck the automobile driven by Yelverton. Yelverton's executor brought suit against Lamm and Lamm's alleged employer, Premier Industrial Products Inc. The relationship between Lamm and Premier was governed by a written contract entitled "Independent Agent Agreement," wherein Lamm, as "Independent Agent," was given the right to sell Premier's products in a designated territory. The agreement provided that all orders were subject to acceptance by Premier and were not binding on Premier until so accepted. Lamm was paid by commission only. He was allowed to work on a self-determined schedule, retain assistants at his own expense, and sell the products of other companies not in competition with Premier. The executor claimed Lamm was an agent or employee of Premier. Premier stated Lamm was an independent contractor.

Decision: Judgment for Premier. Lamm had no authority to make contracts for Premier but simply took orders. Therefore, he was not an agent. Lamm was not an employee of Premier. Premier had no right to control the way he performed his work and did not in fact do so. Lamm was an independent contractor. [*Yelverton v Lamm*, 94 NC App 536, 380 SE2d 621 (1989)]

A person who appears to be an independent contractor may in fact be so controlled by the other party that the contractor is regarded as an agent of, or employee of, the controlling person.[3] The separate identity of an independent contractor may be concealed so that the public believes that it is dealing with the principal. When this situation occurs, the principal is liable as though the contractor were an agent or employee.

2. Who May Be a Principal

Any person who is competent to act may act through an agent. The appointment of an agent by a person lacking capacity is generally void or voidable to the same extent that a contract made by such a person would be. Thus, a minor acting through an agent will effect a contract that will be voidable to the same extent as though made by the minor.

3. Who May Be an Agent

Since a contract made by an agent is, in law, the contract of the principal, it is immaterial whether the agent has legal capacity to make a contract. Therefore, it is permissible to employ as agents persons who are minors and others who are under a natural or legal disability.

Ordinarily, an agent is one person acting for another, but an agent may be a partnership or a corporation.

4. Classification of Agents

Agents may be classified as
• general agents,
• special agents, or
• universal agents.

A **special agent** is authorized by the principal to handle a definite business transaction or to do a specific act. One who is authorized by another to purchase a particular house is a special agent.

---

[3] *Dague v Fort Wayne Newspapers, Inc.* (Ind App) 641 NE2d 1138 (1995).

A **general agent** is authorized by the principal to transact all affairs in connection with a particular kind of business or trade or to transact all business at a certain place. To illustrate, a person who is appointed as manager by the owner of a store is a general agent.

A **universal agent** is authorized by the principal to do all acts that can be delegated lawfully to a representative. This form of agency arises when a person absent because of being in the military service gives another person a blanket power of attorney to do anything that must be done during such absence.

5. Agency Coupled with an Interest

An agent has an **interest in the authority** when consideration has been given or paid for the right to exercise the authority. To illustrate, when a lender, in return for making a loan of money, is given, as security, authority to collect rents due the borrower and to apply those rents to the payment of the debt, the lender becomes the borrower's agent with an interest in the authority given to collect the rents.

An agent has an **interest in the subject matter** when, for a consideration, the agent is given an interest in the property with which the agent is dealing. Hence, when the agent is authorized to sell property of the principal and is given a lien on such property as security for a debt owed to the agent by the principal, the agent has an interest in the subject matter.

B.   CREATING THE AGENCY

An agency may arise by appointment, conduct, ratification, or operation of law.

6. Authorization by Appointment

The usual method of creating an agency is by express authorization; that is, a person is appointed to act for or on behalf of another.

In most instances, the authorization of the agent may be oral. However, some appointments must be made in a particular way. A majority of the states, by statute, require the appointment of an agent to be in writing when the agency is created to acquire or dispose of any interest in land. A written authorization of agency is called a **power of attorney**. An agent acting under a power of attorney is referred to as an **attorney in fact**.[4]

> The usual method of creating an agency is by express authorization, either orally or in writing, with a written authorization being called a power of attorney.

CASE SUMMARY

Who Gets to Call the Homeplace Home?

Facts: George W. Pittman, Jr., was concerned about what would happen to his North Carolina property, called the Homeplace, when he died. He wanted to be assured that it would not be taken from his wife, and he wanted to be sure that neither his own daughter nor his wife's daughter by a previous marriage could take the property upon his death. He explained these concerns to his attorney, who then prepared a power of attorney giving his wife authority to act for Mr. Pittman, including the power to transfer real property "including the power to transfer real estate known as the Homeplace that I inherited from my mother." Shortly after Mr. Pittman

---

[4] *Lamb v Scott* (Ala) 643 So 2d 972 (1994).

signed the power of attorney, the attorney drafted a deed to the property conveying the property from Mr. Pittman to his two sisters. Mr. Pittman signed the deed in the presence of the attorney and a notary public. The sisters did not pay Mr. Pittman any consideration for the property. Mr. Pittman died without a will, and his daughter, Diane Whitford, brought suit, challenging the validity of the conveyance of the real estate to Mr. Pittman's sisters without consideration, contending that an attorney in fact lacks authority to make a gift of real estate (transfer property without consideration). Mrs. Pittman died during the litigation, and thus, Mr. Pittman's daughter and Mrs. Pittman's daughter would inherit the Homeplace under the State Intestate Succession Act.

Decision: Judgment against Diane Whitford. An attorney in fact, acting pursuant to a broad general power of attorney, lacks authority to make a gift of the principal's real estate unless that power is expressly conferred. However, the power of attorney executed by Mr. Pittman provided that Mrs. Pittman had the power to "transfer" the Homeplace. The word transfer is ordinarily used to represent a conveyance of property by sale or gift, and she thus was expressly granted the power to make the gift. [*Whitford v Goshill (NC) 480 SE 2d 690 (1997)*]

Ordinarily no agency arises from the fact that two people are married to each other or that they are co-owners of property. Consequently, when a check is made payable to the order of husband and wife, it is necessary for each to endorse the check. The fact that both names are on the check does not create an agency by which the husband can endorse the wife's name and deposit the money into the husband's own bank account.

7. Authorization by Conduct

Apparent authority arises when a principal creates the appearance of authority in the "agent" by words or conduct and the third person reasonably believes the "agent" has authority, even though the "agent" has no actual authority.

Conduct consistent with the existence of an agency relationship may be sufficient to show authorization. The principal may have such dealing with third persons as to cause them to believe that the "agent" has authority. Thus, if the owner of a store places another person in charge, third persons may assume that the person in charge is the agent for the owner in that respect. The "agent" then appears to be authorized and is said to have **apparent authority**, and the principal is stopped from contradicting the appearance that has been created.[5]

The term *apparent authority* is used when there is only the appearance of authority, but no actual authority, and that appearance of authority was created by the principal.[6] The test for the existence of apparent authority is an objective test determined by the principal's outward manifestations through words or conduct that lead a third person reasonably to believe that the "agent" has authority. A principal's express restriction on authority not made known to a third person is no defense.

Apparent authority extends to all acts that a person of ordinary prudence, familiar with business usages and the particular business, would be justified in believing that the agent has authority to perform. It is essential to the concept of apparent authority that the third person reasonably believe that the agent has authority. The mere placing of property in the possession of another does not give that person either actual or apparent authority to sell the property.

---

[5] *Intersparex Leddin KG v Al-Haddad* (Tenn App) 852 SW2d 245 (1992).
[6] *Raclaw v Fay, Conmy and Co., Ltd.* (Ill App) 668 NE2d 114 (1996).

A principal may ratify
an unauthorized
action by an agent.

C
P
A

8. Agency by Ratification

An agent may attempt, on behalf of the principal, to do an act that was not authorized, or a person who is not the agent of another may attempt to act as such an agent. Generally, in such cases the principal for whom the agent claimed to act has the choice of ignoring the transaction or of ratifying it. Ordinarily any unauthorized act may be ratified.

(a) Intention to Ratify. Initially ratification is a question of intention. Just as in the case of authorization, when there is a question of whether the principal authorized the agent, so there is a question of whether the principal intended to approve or ratify the action of the unauthorized agent.

The intention to ratify may be expressed in words, or it may be found in conduct indicating an intention to ratify.[7]

CASE SUMMARY

Why Friends Should Not Let Friends Use Their Names and Credit Histories

Facts: Daniels and Julian were employed by the Marriott Hotel in New Orleans and were close personal friends. One day after work Daniels and Julian went to Werlein's music store to open a credit account. Julian, with Daniels's authorization and in her presence, applied for credit using Daniels's name and credit history. Later Julian went to Werlein's without Daniels and charged the purchase of a television set to Daniels's account, executing a retail installment contract by signing Daniels's name. Daniels saw the new television in Julian's home and was informed that it was charged to the Werlein's account. Daniels told Julian to continue making payments. When Werlein's credit manager first contacted Daniels and informed her that her account was delinquent, she claimed that a money order for the television was in the mail. On the second call, she asked for a "payment balance." Some four months after the purchase, she informed Werlein's that she had not authorized the purchase of the television, nor had she ratified the purchase. Werlein's sued Daniels for the unpaid balance.

Decision: Judgment for Werlein's. While Daniels did not authorize the purchase of the television set, the evidence shows that she ratified the unauthorized signing of her name to the contract for the purchase of the television set by Julian. Instead of taking immediate action to repudiate what had been done in her name, Daniels simply told Julian to continue making payments. And when contacted by Werlein's credit manager, she replied that a money order was in the mail. Daniels's conduct manifested a clear intent to ratify, and she is bound by the unauthorized signature. [*Philip Werlein, Ltd. v Daniels* (La App) 538 So 2d 722 (1989)]

If the conditions for ratification are satisfied, a principal ratifies an agent's act when, with knowledge of the act, the principal accepts or retains the benefit of the act.[8] A principal also ratifies an act when the principal brings an action to enforce legal rights based on the agent's act, defends an action by asserting the existence of a right based on the unauthorized transaction, or fails to repudiate the agent's act within a reasonable time. The receipt, acceptance, and deposit of a check by the principal with knowledge that it arises from an unauthorized transaction is a common illustration of ratification of the unauthorized transaction by conduct.

---

7 *Richardson Greenshield Securities Inc. v Lau*, 819 F Supp 1246 (SDNY 1993).
8 *MSP Industries Inc. v Diversified Mortgage Services Inc.* (Colo App) 777 P2d 237 (1989).

(b) Conditions for Ratification. In addition to the intent to ratify, expressed in some instances with a certain formality, the following conditions must be satisfied for the intention to take effect as a ratification:

1. The agent must have purported to act on behalf of or as agent for the identified principal.
2. The principal must have been capable of authorizing the act both at the time of the act and at the time it was ratified.
3. The principal must ratify the act before the third person withdraws.
4. The act to be ratified must generally be legal.
5. The principal must have full knowledge of all material facts. If the agent conceals a material fact, the ratification of the principal that is made in ignorance of such fact is not binding. Of course, there can be no ratification when the principal does not know of the making of the contract by the alleged agent. Consequently, when the owner's agent and a contractor make unauthorized major changes to an installation contract without knowledge of the owner, the fact that the owner had no knowledge of the matter bars any claim of ratification of the agent's act.

It is not always necessary, however, to show that the principal had actual knowledge. Knowledge will be imputed if a principal knows of other facts that would lead a prudent person to make inquiries or if that knowledge can be inferred from the knowledge of other facts or from a course of business. ◆ *For example*, Stacey, without authorization but knowing William needed money, contracted to sell one of William's paintings to Courtney for $298. Stacey told William about the contract that evening; William said nothing and helped her wrap the painting in protective plastic for delivery. A favorable newspaper article about William's art appeared the following morning and drastically increased the value of all of his paintings. William cannot recover the painting from Courtney on the theory that he never authorized the sale because he ratified the unauthorized contract made by Stacey by his conduct in helping her wrap the painting with full knowledge of the terms of the sale. The effect is a legally binding contract between William and Courtney. ◆

Knowledge is likewise not an essential factor when the principal does not care to know the details and is willing to ratify the contract regardless of this lack of knowledge.

(c) Form of Ratification. An agreement that is binding although oral may be ratified orally or by conduct. If a contract cannot be enforced unless evidenced by a writing, it is generally held that a ratification of the contract must be in writing.

(d) Effect of Ratification. When an unauthorized act is ratified, the effect is the same as though the act had been originally authorized. Ordinarily this means that the principal and the third party are bound by the contract made by the agent.[9] When the principal ratifies the act of the unauthorized person, such ratification releases that person from the liability that would otherwise be imposed for having acted without authority.

---

[9] *Bill McCurley Chevrolet v Rutz* (Wash App) 808 P2d 1167 (1991).

9. Proving the Agency Relationship

The burden of proving the existence of an agency relationship rests on the person who seeks to benefit by such proof. The third person who desires to bind the principal because of the act of an alleged agent has the burden of proving that the latter person was in fact the authorized agent of the principal and possessed the authority to do the act in question.[10] For example, when a buyer asserts that there has been a breach of an express warranty made by the seller's agent, the buyer must establish that there was actual or apparent authority to make the warranty. In the absence of sufficient proof, the jury must find that there was no authority.

What duties do the principal and agent owe each other?

C.   AGENT'S AUTHORITY

When there is an agent, it is necessary to determine the scope of the agent's authority.

10. Scope of Agent's Authority

The scope of an agent's authority may be determined from the express words of the principal to the agent, or it may be implied from the principal's words or conduct or from the customs of the trade or business.

(a) Express Authority. If the principal tells the agent to perform a certain act, the agent has **express authority** to do so. Express authority can be given orally or in writing.

(b) Incidental Authority. An agent has implied incidental authority to perform any act reasonably necessary to execute the express authority given to the agent. *For example,* if the principal authorizes the agent to purchase goods without furnishing funds to the agent to pay for them, the agent has the implied incidental authority to purchase the goods on credit.[11]

(c) Customary Authority. An agent has implied customary authority to do any act that, according to the custom of the community, usually accompanies the transaction for which the agent is authorized to act. An agent who has express authority to receive payments from third persons, for example, has the implied authority to issue receipts.

(d) Apparent Authority. A person has apparent authority as an agent when the principal's words or conduct leads a third person to reasonably believe that the person has that authority and the third person relies on that appearance.[12]
Apparent authority is not available where the third person has notice of the limitations on the agent's powers.

---

[10] *Fleck v Jaques Seed Co.* (ND) 445 NW2d 649 (1989).
[11] *Badger v Paulson Investment Co.* (Or) 803 P2d 1178 (1991).
[12] *Draemal v Rufenacht, Dromagen & Hertz, Inc.* (Neb) 392 NW2d 759 (1986).

CASE SUMMARY

The Super Mario Brothers Were Hot. The Streetmans Were Not.

Facts: Michael Streetman and his wife, Laura, were in the video rental business. They decided to expand their business by opening a Nintendo distributorship because Nintendo was flourishing at that time. Needing more money than their original bank could authorize due to lending limits based on the Streetmans' collateral, they approached Mr. Watts of Benchmark Bank and sought assurance that all their overdraft checks would be honored by the bank. The Streetmans claim that Watts agreed to honor all of their overdrafts, in addition to providing a loan authorized by the bank at the lending limits. Over the next several months, the Streetmans wrote some 500 overdraft checks, and their checking account was overdrawn $204,863.10. After some eight months of doing business with the Streetmans, the bank stopped honoring overdraft checks. As a result of a lack of cash, the Streetmans were unable to purchase Nintendo cartridges as soon as they became available, and they lost their Nintendo distributorship. The bank sued them for $440,770.47, the amount due on the Streetmans' promissory notes, and the Streetmans counterclaimed for the bank's failure to honor its agent's promise to pay all overdrafts. From a judgment for the Streetmans, the bank appealed.

Decision: Judgment for the bank. In order for the bank to be liable for a promise by Watts "to pay all overdrafts," there must be evidence that Watts had authority to make such an agreement—either actual authority or apparent authority. Watts testified that he did not have authority, and there was no evidence that he had such actual authority. The theory of apparent authority is not available to third persons who know of limitations on the agent's powers. The Streetmans knew from their dealings with their prior bank that banks have lending limits. Consequently, they knew that Watts' authority to bind the bank was limited and that he could not pay "all overdrafts" drawn on their account without any limitations. [*Streetman v Benchmark Bank* (Tex App) 890 SW2d 212 (1995)]

11. Effect of Proper Exercise of Authority

Where an agent properly exercises authority to make a contract, the agent is not a party to that contract and is not liable on it.

When an agent with authority properly makes a contract with a third person that purports to bind the principal, there is by definition a binding contract between the principal and the third person. The agent is not a party to this contract. Consequently, when the owner of goods is the principal, the owner's agent is not liable for breach of warranty with respect to the goods "sold" by the agent. The owner-principal, not the agent, was the "seller" in the sales transaction.

12. Duty to Ascertain Extent of Agent's Authority

C.P.A.

A third person who deals with a person claiming to be an agent cannot rely on the statements made by the agent concerning the extent of authority.[13] If the agent is not authorized to perform the act or is not even the agent of the principal, the transaction between the alleged agent and the third person will have no legal effect between the principal and the third person.

Remember: An attorney lacks authority to settle a case without a client's consent.

Third persons who deal with an agent whose authority is limited to a special purpose are bound at their peril to find out the extent of the agent's authority. An attorney is such an agent. Unless the client holds the attorney out as having greater authority than usual, the attorney has no authority to settle a claim without approval from the client.

---

[13] *Bells Banking Co. v Jackson Centre Inc.* (Tenn App) 938 SW2d 421 (1996).

Nevertheless, Auvil Is Not a Nice Person

Facts: Auvil gave his attorney Melvin Synder III authority to negotiate a settlement of a lawsuit with his former employer, Grafton Homes Inc. After the attorneys for both sides agreed to the terms of a settlement, Synder met with Auvil and his wife and recommended that they accept the settlement. He testified that "Mr. Auvil said go ahead and do that." The attorneys then drafted the settlement papers. Synder testified that when Auvil received the settlement papers, he requested some additional terms. Several days later Auvil refused to go forward. Auvil testified that he had never authorized Synder to settle the case and that although he requested some modifications to the settlement papers, this was done to "tog and tease" in order to find time to hire another attorney. The district court enforced the settlement agreement, ruling that Auvil had "clothed" Synder with apparent authority to settle and that Auvil was bound by the settlement with Grafton Homes Inc. even though Auvil denies he gave Synder actual authority. Auvil appealed.

Decision: The district court's order enforcing the settlement was vacated. Those who deal with an agent whose authority is limited to special purposes, such as an attorney, are bound at their peril to find out the extent of the agent's authority. Auvil manifested to Grafton Homes Inc. that Synder had authority to conduct settlement *negotiations* on behalf of Auvil. And while Auvil directed Synder to inquire about additional terms after receiving settlement papers, Auvil never manifested to Grafton Homes Inc. or its attorneys that Synder was authorized to consummate a settlement or that Auvil was relinquishing his right to approve a settlement. Indeed Grafton Homes Inc. forwarded settlement papers for "Auvil's approval." [*Auvil v Grafton Homes Inc.*, 92 F3d 226 (4th Cir 1996)]

(a) Agent's Acts Adverse to Principal. The third person who deals with an agent is required to take notice of any acts that are clearly adverse to the interest of the principal. Thus, if the agent is obviously making use of funds of the principal for the agent's personal benefit, persons dealing with the agent should recognize that the agent may be acting without authority and that they are dealing with the agent at their peril.

> A third person cannot claim that apparent authority existed when the person observes the agent acting against the principal's interests.

The only certain way that third persons can protect themselves is to inquire of the principal whether the agent is in fact the agent of the principal and has the necessary authority. If the principal states that the agent has the authority, the principal cannot later deny this authorization unless the subject matter is such that an authorization must be in writing to be binding.

13. Limitations on Agent's Authority

> A third person's rights are not affected by secret limitations on an agent's authority.

A person who has knowledge of a limitation on the agent's authority cannot ignore that limitation. When the third person knows that the authority of the agent depends on whether financing has been obtained, the principal is not bound by the act of the agent if the financing in fact was not obtained. If the authority of the agent is based on a writing and the third person knows that there is such a writing, the third person is charged with knowledge of limitations contained in it.

(a) Obvious Limitations. In some situations, it will be obvious to third persons that they are dealing with an agent whose authority is limited. When third persons know that they are dealing with an officer of a private corporation or a representative of a government agency, they should recognize that such a person will ordinarily have limited authority. Third persons should recognize that a contract made with such an officer or representative may not be binding unless ratified by the principal.

(b) Secret Limitations. If the principal has clothed an agent with authority to perform certain acts but the principal gives secret instructions that limit the agent's authority, the third person is allowed to take the authority of the agent at its face value. The third person is not bound by the secret limitations of which the third person has no knowledge.

ETHICS & THE LAW

The Seattle rock group Pearl Jam has earned three platinum albums. In 1994, Pearl Jam refused to allow its concert tickets to be sold through Ticketmaster, which is a national company that controls two-thirds of the U.S. concert market through both its ticket sales and its exclusive contracting arrangements with concert facilities.

According to the members of Pearl Jam, Ticketmaster charges a service fee of 12 percent on its tickets, with the fee going up to 55 percent for such choice events as a Pearl Jam concert. When members of Pearl Jam testified before Congress about their boycott and the prices, they noted that their fans could not afford to pay $50 per ticket for their concerts.

Promoters for Pearl Jam are permitted to schedule concerts for the group only if the venues for those concerts do not have exclusive ticket arrangements with Ticketmaster. This restriction means that Pearl Jam plays parks and other open-air facilities.

What type of restriction is placed on the Pearl Jam promoters? Are these promoters agents of Pearl Jam? What would happen if one of the promoters set up a concert in a facility handled exclusively by Ticketmaster? Would Pearl Jam be obligated to play the concert? What legal and ethical issues do you see in Ticketmaster's control of two-thirds of the concert arenas?

D. DUTIES AND LIABILITIES OF PRINCIPAL AND AGENT

The creation of the principal-agent relationship gives rise to duties and liabilities.

14. Duties and Liabilities of Agent during Agency

While the agency relationship exists, the agent owes certain duties to the principal.

An agent owes the following duties to the principal:
* loyalty,
* obedience and performance,
* reasonable care,
* accounting, and
* information.

(a) Loyalty. An agent must be loyal or faithful to the principal. The agent must not obtain any secret benefit from the agency. If the principal is seeking to buy or rent property, the agent cannot secretly obtain the property and then sell or lease it to the principal at a profit.

An agent who owns property cannot sell it to the principal without disclosing that ownership to the principal. If disclosure is not made, the principal may avoid the contract even if the agent's conduct did not cause the principal any financial loss. Alternatively, the principal can approve the transaction and sue the agent for any secret profit obtained by the agent.

A contract is voidable by the principal if the agent who was employed to sell the property purchases the property, either directly or indirectly, without full disclosure to the principal.

An agent cannot act as agent for both parties to a transaction unless both know of the dual capacity and agree to it. If the agent does act in this capacity without the consent of both parties, any principal who did not know of the agent's double status can avoid the transaction.

An agent must not accept secret gifts or commissions from third persons in connection with the agency. If the agent does so, the principal may sue the agent for those gifts or commissions. Such practices are condemned because the judgment of the agent may be influenced by the receipt of gifts or commissions.

It is a violation of an agent's duty of loyalty to make and retain secret profits.

CASE SUMMARY

Would an Agent Fail to Inform His Principal of a Better Deal Just to Avoid Sharing His Commission?

Facts: Joan Kulwin owned Allen Industries, Inc., which owned a commercial building in Evanston, Illinois. She granted the Sheldon Co. the exclusive right to sell the building and agreed to pay a commission to Sheldon on the sale. This commission was to be divided in half between Sheldon and a cooperating broker if a cooperating broker secured the purchaser. On August 21, 1985, Sheldon Co. presented Kulwin a written offer in final contract form from J.W. Collier. Kulwin rejected this offer of $335,000 and made a counteroffer of $350,000, which Collier accepted. Kulwin had not been informed by Sheldon Co. that Sheldon knew the TLC Company was going to make a bid for the property that was much better for Kulwin than her counteroffer. When Kulwin later learned that she could have made a better deal if Sheldon had told her about TLC, she sued Sheldon for breach of an agent's duty of disclosure. Kulwin asserted that Sheldon Co. failed to inform her of all facts material to the sale to avoid sharing the commission with the cooperating broker who showed TLC the property.

Decision: Judgment for Kulwin. On the day Kulwin received Collier's offer from her agent, Sheldon Co., the agent knew that TLC was preparing a cash offer. Because these facts might have influenced the principal in accepting or rejecting Collier's offer, they were material facts that the agent had a duty to disclose to Kulwin. [*Allen Industries v Sheldon Co.*, 153 Ill App 3d 120, 106 Ill Dec 313, 505 NE2d 1104 (1987)]

An agent is, of course, prohibited from aiding the competitors of a principal or disclosing to them information relating to the business of the principal. It is also a breach of duty for the agent to knowingly deceive a principal.[14]

(b) Obedience and Performance. An agent is under a duty to obey all lawful instructions.[15] The agent is required to perform the services specified for the period and in the way specified. An agent who does not is liable to the principal for any harm caused. For example, if an agent is instructed to take cash payments only but accepts a check in payment, the agent is liable for the loss caused the principal if a check is dishonored by nonpayment. Similarly, when an insurance broker undertakes to obtain an insurance policy for a principal to provide a specified

---

15 *Koontz v Rosener* (Colo App) 787 P2d 192 (1990).
16 *Stanford v Neiderer* (Ga App) 341 SE2d 892 (1986).

coverage but fails to obtain a policy with the proper coverage, the broker, as agent of the principal, is liable to the principal for any loss caused.

(c) Reasonable Care. It is the duty of an agent to act with the care that a reasonable person would exercise under the circumstances. In addition, if the agent possesses a special skill, as in the case of a broker or an attorney, the agent must exercise that skill.

(d) Accounting. An agent must account to the principal for all property or money belonging to the principal that comes into the agent's possession. The agent must, within a reasonable time, give notice of collections made and render an accurate account of all receipts and expenditures. The agency agreement may state at what intervals or on what dates such accountings are to be made. An agent must keep the principal's property and money separate and distinct from that of the agent.

(e) Information. It is the duty of an agent to keep the principal informed of all facts relating to the agency that are relevant to protecting the principal's interests.[16]

CASE SUMMARY

This "Option" Quarterback Is Out of Bounds!

Facts: Real estate broker Donald Alley, Sr., had a listing contract that gave him the exclusive right to sell Wayman Ellison's farm for at least $200,000. Ellison was told that a buyer was found. The buyer, Cora Myers, who had been paid $585,000 for a small farm because the land was needed for a commercial development, agreed to pay $380,000 for the large Ellison farm. The closing of the transaction was orchestrated in such a way by Alley that the buyer believed the purchase price of $380,000 was being paid to Ellison. Ellison signed a warranty deed conveying his farm to Myers, and he received $200,000. Alley received $180,000 for an assignment of his "option" at the closing, unbeknownst to either Ellison or Myers. When Ellison later learned of these details, he sued Alley for the $180,000. Alley defended that Ellison received the full price he sought, $200,000. He contended that he was entitled to the "option" money as well as the commission on the sale.

Decision: Judgment for Ellison. An agent's fiduciary obligation is not satisfied by obtaining a minimum price. The agent's obligation is to obtain the best possible price for the principal. Alley breached his fiduciary duty to Ellison by obtaining the secret profit of $180,000, which must be returned to the principal. Since Alley acted beyond the bounds of ethical conduct in this case, he is not entitled to a reasonable commission on the sale, for such would be an undeserved reward for avarice. [*Ellison v Alley* (Tenn) 841 SW2d 605 (1992)]

---

15. Duties and Liabilities of Agent after Termination of Agency

When the agency relationship ends, the duties of the agent continue only to the extent necessary to perform prior obligations. For example, the agent must return to the former principal any property that had been entrusted to the agent for the purpose of the agency. With the exception of such "winding-up" duties, the agency relationship is terminated, and the former agent can deal with the principal as freely as with a stranger.[17]

---

[16] Restatement (Second) of Agency § 381; *Cole v Jennings* (Colo App) 847 P2d 200 (1991).
[17] *Corron & Black of Illinois, Inc. v Magner* (Ill App) 494 NE2d 785 (1986).

16. Enforcement of Liability of Agent

When the agent's breach of duty causes harm to the principal, the amount of the loss may be deducted from any compensation due the agent or recovered in an ordinary lawsuit. When the agent handles money for the principal, the contract of employment may provide that the amount of any shortages in the agent's account may be deducted from the compensation to which the agent would otherwise be entitled.

If the agent has made a secret profit, the principal may recover that profit from the agent. In addition, the agent may forfeit the right to all compensation without regard to whether the principal benefited from some of the actions of the agent and without regard to whether the principal had actually been harmed.

E.   TERMINATION OF AGENCY

An agency may be terminated by the act of one or both of the parties to the agency agreement or by operation of law. When the authority of an agent is terminated, the agent loses all right to act for the principal.

17. Termination by Act of Parties

The duration of the agency relationship is commonly stated in the contract creating the relationship. In most cases, either party has the power to terminate the agency relationship at any time. However, the terminating party may be liable for damages to the other if the termination is in violation of the agency contract.

When a principal terminates an agent's authority, it is not effective until the notice is received by the agent. Since a known agent will have the appearance of still being an agent, notice must be given to third persons of the termination, and the agent may have the power to bind the principal and third persons until this notice is given.

18. Termination by Operation of Law

Termination by operation of law results upon
- **death, insanity, or bankruptcy;**
- **impossibility;**
- **war.**

The agency relationship is a personal one, and anything that renders one of the parties incapable of performing will result in the termination of the relationship by operation of law. The death of either the principal or the agent ordinarily terminates the authority of an agent automatically even if the death is unknown to the other.[18]

An agency is also terminated by operation of law on the (1) insanity of the principal or agent; (2) bankruptcy of the principal or agent; (3) impossibility of performance, such as the destruction of the subject matter; or (4) when the country of the principal is at war with that of the agent.

---

[18] *New York Life Ins. Co. v Estate of Haelen* (Sup Ct AD) 521 NYS2d 970 (1987).

Missing Out by Minutes

Facts: William Moore, a fire chief for the city of San Francisco, suffered severe head injuries in a fall while fighting a fire. Moore sued the building owner, Lera, for negligence. The attorneys for the parties held a conference and reached a settlement at 5:15 P.M. Unknown to them, Moore had died at 4:50 P.M. on that day. Was the settlement agreement binding?

Decision: No. The death of either the principal or the agent terminates the agency. Thus, the death of a client terminates the authority of his agent to act on his behalf. Because Moore died at 4:50 P.M., Moore's attorney no longer had authority to act on his behalf, and the settlement was not enforceable. [Moore v Lera Development Inc. (Cal App) 274 Cal Rptr 658 (1990)]

19. Disability of the Principal under the UDPAA

The Uniform Durable Power of Attorney Act (UDPAA) permits the creation of an agency by specifying that "this power of attorney shall not be affected by subsequent disability or incapacity of the principal." Alternatively, the UDPAA permits the agency to come into existence upon the disability or incapacity of the principal. For this to be effective, the principal must designate the attorney in fact in writing. The writing must contain words showing the intent of the principal that the authority conferred shall continue notwithstanding the disability or incapacity of the principal. The UDPAA, which has been adopted by most states,[19] changes the common law and the general rule that insanity of the principal terminates the agent's authority to act for the principal. Society today recognizes that it may be in the best interest of a principal and good for the business environment for a principal to designate another as an attorney in fact to act for the principal when the principal becomes incapacitated.[20]

Durable powers of attorney grant only those powers that are specified in the instrument. A durable power of attorney may be terminated by revocation by a competent principal and by the death of the principal.

The Flanders Fleece Flinn

Facts: Tillie Flinn executed a durable power of attorney designating her nephew James C. Flanders and/or Martha E. Flanders, his wife, as her attorney in fact. Seven months later Martha Flanders went to the Capitol Federal Savings and Loan Association office. She had the durable power of attorney instrument, five certificates of deposit, and a hand-printed letter identifying Martha as an attorney in fact and stating that Tillie wished to cash her five CDs that Martha had with her. At approximately 10:31 A.M., five checks were given to Martha in the aggregate amount of $135,791.34, representing the funds in the five CDs less penalties for early withdrawal. Some of the checks were drawn to the order of Martha individually and some to the order of James and Martha, as individuals. Tillie was found dead of heart disease later that day. The time of her death stated on her death certificate was 11:30 A.M. The Flanderses spent the

---

[19] The Uniform Durable Power of Attorney Act has been adopted in some fashion in all states except Georgia, Louisiana, and Illinois.

[20] The Uniform Probate Code and the Uniform Durable Power of Attorney Act provide for the coexistence of durable powers and guardians or conservators. These acts allow the attorney in fact to continue to manage the principal's financial affairs, while the court-appointed fiduciary would take the place of the principal in overseeing the actions of the attorney in fact. See Rice v Flood (Ky) 768 SW2d 57 (1989).

money on themselves. Bank IV, as administrator of Tillie's estate, sued Capitol Federal to recover the amount of the funds paid to the Flanderses. It contended that Capitol Federal breached its duty to investigate before issuing the checks. Capitol Federal contended it did all that it had a duty to do.

Decision: Judgment for Capitol Federal. Capitol Federal was presented with a power of attorney that it is agreed was signed by Tillie, its depositor. Martha Flanders was properly identified as being the Martha Flanders designated as attorney in fact. The request to cash the CDs and the issuance of the checks in the individual name(s) of the attorney(s) in fact were within the scope of the power of attorney. Absent an act or acts amounting to participation in the wrongdoing, Capitol Federal's issuance of the checks in the names of the attorneys in fact imposed no liability on Capitol Federal. Were Tillie incompetent at the time of the request to transfer funds, such would not defeat the exercise of the durable power of attorney, for its very purpose is to allow the orderly transaction of a person's business during contemplated disability or incompetence. [*Bank IV, Olathe v Capitol Federal Savings and Loan Ass'n* (Kan) 828 P2d 355 (1992)]

20. Termination of Agency Coupled with an Interest

An agency coupled with an interest is an exception to the general rule as to the termination of an agency. Such an agency cannot be revoked by the principal before the expiration of the interest. It is not terminated by the death or insanity of either the principal or the agent.

21. Protection of Agent from Termination of Authority

The modern world of business has developed several methods of protecting an agent from the termination of authority for any reason.[21]

These methods include use of an exclusive agency contract, a secured transaction, an escrow deposit, a standby letter of agreement, or a guarantee agreement.

22. Effect of Termination of Authority

Caution: An agent may have apparent authority to bind a principal after termination. That is why notice must be given to third parties who have dealt with the agent.

If the agency is revoked by the principal, the authority to act for the principal is not terminated until the agent receives notice of revocation. As between the principal and the agent, the *right* of the agent to bind the principal to third persons generally ends immediately upon the termination of the agent's authority. This termination is effective without the giving of notice to third persons.

When the agency is terminated by the act of the principal, notice must be given to third persons. If this notice is not given, the agent may have the *power* to make contracts that will bind the principal and third persons. This rule is predicated on the theory that a known agent will have the appearance of still being the agent unless notice to the contrary is given to third persons. ◆ *For example,* Seltzer owns property in Boca Raton that he uses for the month of February and leases the remainder of the year. O'Neil has been Seltzer's rental agent for the past seven years, renting to individuals like Ed Tucker under a power of attorney that gives

---

[21] These methods generally replace the concept of an agency coupled with an interest because of the greater protection given to the agent. Typically the rights of the agent under these modern devices cannot be defeated by the principal, by operation of law, or by claims of other creditors.

him authority to lease the property for set seasonal and off-season rates. O'Neil's right to bind Seltzer on a rental agreement ended when Seltzer faxed O'Neil a revocation of the power of attorney on March 1. A rental contract with Ed Tucker signed by O'Neil on behalf of Seltzer on March 2 will bind Seltzer, however, because O'Neil still appeared to be Seltzer's agent and Tucker had no notice to the contrary. ◆

When the law requires the giving of notice in order to end the power of the agent to bind the principal, individual notice must be given or mailed to all persons who had prior dealings with the agent. In addition, notice to the general public can be given by publishing in a newspaper of general circulation in the affected geographic area a statement that the agency has been terminated.

If a notice is actually received, the power of the agent is terminated without regard to whether the method of giving notice was proper. Conversely, if proper notice is given, it is immaterial that it does not actually come to the attention of the party notified. Thus, a member of the general public cannot claim that the principal is bound on the ground that the third person did not see the newspaper notice stating that the agent's authority had been terminated.

SUMMARY

An agency relationship is created by an express or implied agreement whereby one person, the agent, is authorized to make contracts with third persons on behalf of and subject to the control of another person, the principal. An agent differs from an independent contractor in that the principal, who controls the acts of an agent, does not have control over the details of performance of work by the independent contractor. Likewise, an independent contractor does not have authority to act on behalf of the other contracting party.

A special agent is authorized by the principal to handle a specific business transaction. A general agent is authorized by the principal to transact all business affairs of the principal at a certain place. A universal agent is authorized to perform all acts that can be lawfully delegated to a representative.

The usual method of creating an agency is by express authorization. However, an agency relationship may be found to exist when the principal causes or permits a third person to reasonably believe that an agency relationship exists. In such a case, the "agent" appears to be authorized and is said to have apparent authority.

An unauthorized transaction by an agent for a principal may be ratified by the principal.

An agent acting with authority has the power to bind the principal. The scope of an agent's authority may be determined from the express words of the principal to the agent; this is called express authority. An agent has incidental authority to perform any act reasonably necessary to execute the authority given the agent. An agent's authority may be implied so as to enable the agent to perform any act in accordance with the general customs or usages in a business or an industry. This authority is often referred to as customary authority.

The effect of a proper exercise of authority by an agent is to bind the principal and third person to a contract. The agent, not being a party to the contract, is not liable in any respect under the contract. A third person dealing with a person claiming to be an agent has a duty to ascertain the extent of the agent's authority and a duty to take notice of any acts that are clearly adverse to the principal's interests. The third person cannot claim that apparent authority existed when that person has notice that the agent's conduct is adverse to the interests of the principal. A third person who has knowledge of limitations on an agent's authority is bound by those limitations. A third person is not bound by secret limitations.

While the agency relationship exists, the agent owes the principal the duties of (1) being loyal, (2) obeying all lawful instructions, (3) exercising reasonable care, (4) accounting for all property or money belonging to the principal, and (5) informing the principal of all facts relating to the agency that are relevant to the principal's interests. An agency relationship can be terminated by act of either the principal or the agent. However, the terminating party may be liable for damages to the other if the termination is in violation of the agency contract.

Since a known agent will have the appearance of still being an agent, notice must be given to third persons of the termination, and the agent may have the power to bind the principal and third persons until this notice is given.

An agency is terminated by operation of law upon (1) the death of the principal or agent; (2) insanity of the principal or agent; (3) bankruptcy of the principal or agent; (4) impossibility of performance, caused, for example, by the destruction of the subject matter; or (5) war.

In states that have adopted the Uniform Durable Power of Attorney Act (UDPAA), an agency may be created that is not affected by subsequent disability or incapacity of the principal. In UDPAA states, the agency may also come into existence upon the "disability or incapacity of the principal." The designation of an attorney in fact under the UDPAA must be in writing.

QUESTIONS AND CASE PROBLEMS

1. What social forces are affected by allowing an agent to make a contract that will bind the agent's principal and a third person?

2. How does an agent differ from an independent contractor?

3. Compare authorization of an agent by (a) appointment and (b) ratification.

4. Ernest A. Kotsch executed a durable power of attorney when he was 85 years old, giving his son Ernie the power to manage and sell his real estate and personal property "and to do all acts necessary for maintaining and caring for [the father] during his lifetime." Thereafter Mr. Kotsch began "keeping company" with a widow, Margaret Gradl. Ernie believed that the widow was attempting to alienate his father from him, and he observed that she was exerting a great deal of influence over his father. Acting under the durable power of attorney and without informing his father, Ernie created the "Kotsch Family Irrevocable Trust," to which he transferred $700,000, the bulk of his father's liquid assets, with the father as grantor and initial beneficiary and Ernie's three children as additional beneficiaries. Ernie named himself trustee. His father sued to avoid the trust. Ernie defended his action on the ground that he had authority to create the trust under the durable power of attorney. Decide. [*Kotsch v Kotsch* (Fla App) 608 So 2d 879]

5. Ken Jones, the number-one-ranked prizefighter in his weight class, signed a two-year contract with Howard Stayword. The contract obligated Stayword to represent and promote Jones in all business and professional matters, including the arrangement of fights. For these services, Jones was to pay Stayword 10 percent of gross earnings. After a year, when Stayword proved unsuccessful in arranging a title match with the champion, Jones fired Stayword. During the following year, Jones earned $4 million. Stayword sued Jones for $400,000. Jones defended himself on the basis that a principal has the absolute power at any time to terminate an agency relationship by discharging the agent, so he was not liable to Stayword. Was Jones correct?

6. Paul Strich did business as an optician in Duluth, Minnesota. Paul used only the products of the Plymouth Optical Co., a national manufacturer of optical products and supplies with numerous retail outlets and some franchise arrangements in areas other than Duluth. To increase business, Paul renovated his office and changed the sign on it to read "Plymouth Optical Co." Paul did business this way for more than three years—advertised under that name, paid bills with checks bearing the name of Plymouth Optical Co., and listed himself in the telephone and city directories by that name. Plymouth immediately became aware of what Paul was doing. However, because Paul used only Plymouth products and Plymouth did not have a franchise in Duluth, it saw no advantage at that time in prohibiting Paul from using the name and losing him as a customer. Paul contracted with the *Duluth Tribune* for advertising, making the contract in the name of Plymouth Optical Co. When the advertising bill was not paid, the *Duluth Tribune* sued Plymouth Optical Co. for payment. Plymouth's defense was that it had never authorized Paul to do business under the name, nor had it authorized him to make a contract with the newspaper. Decide.

7. Beck, president of Anita Beck Cards & Such, Inc., and Hutton, a national sales director for Mary Kay Cosmetics, agreed that Beck would manufacture calendars and stationery to be sold at Mary Kay conventions. To finance the project, Hutton gave $20,000 to Beck. Beck and Hutton prepared and signed a document to reflect the quantity and prices of goods shipped from Beck to the Dallas convention for sale under Hutton's supervision. The document stated, "Commission is 15% on all but calendars." The unsold goods were shipped back to Beck's business at Beck's expense. The undertaking proved to be a substantial failure. Hutton sued Beck for the return of the $20,000, claiming that she was Beck's agent and that the money had been a loan. Beck claimed that the money was the down payment on the actual purchase of the goods by Hutton. Decide. [*Hutton v Anita Beck Cards and Such, Inc.* (Minn App) 366 NW2d 358]

8. Gilbert Church owned Church Farms, Inc., in Manteno, Illinois. Church advertised its well-bred stallion Imperial Guard for breeding rights at $50,000, directing all inquiries to "Herb Bagley, Manager." Herb Bagley lived at Church Farms and was the only person available to visitors. Vern Lundberg answered the ad and, after discussions in which Bagley stated that Imperial Guard would remain in Illinois for at least a two-year period, Lundberg and Bagley executed a two-year breeding rights contract. The contract was signed by Lundberg and by Bagley as "Church Farms, Inc., H. Bagley, Mgr." When Gil Church moved Imperial Guard to Oklahoma prior to the second year of the contract, Lundberg brought suit for breach of contract. Church testified that Bagley had no authority to sign contracts for Church Farms. Decide. [*Lundberg v Church Farms, Inc.* (Ill) 502 NE2d 806]

9. Mrs. Bird, although a woman of means, was living in deplorable conditions. Neighbors got in contact with her cousin, Logan Ledbetter, who, in turn, had Mrs. Bird examined by Dr. Phillips, a psychiatrist. Dr. Phillips determined that Mrs. Bird was suffering from "an organic brain syndrome, chronic," that "her mental function was very impaired," and that, in his opinion, Mrs. Bird was "mentally incompetent at the time of the examination." Ledbetter planned to deal with the situation by selling off a number of valuable real estate holdings owned by Mrs. Bird and using the proceeds to pay for proper care for Mrs. Bird. Soon thereafter Mrs. Bird executed a power of attorney designating Logan Ledbetter as her attorney in fact, and Ledbetter entered into a contract to sell a large parcel of her land to Andleman Associates. Mrs. Bird's niece, Barbara, who disliked Ledbetter, filed a petition to have Mrs. Bird declared incompetent and herself named guardian of her estate. The court appointed Barbara as guardian, and she refused to allow the sale of the land to Andleman. In the lawsuit that resulted, Ledbetter and Andleman contended that Ledbetter acted in good faith and had a properly executed power of attorney and that therefore his signing the sales contract with Andleman was binding on Mrs. Bird (the principal). Atkins (the real estate agent who produced the ready, willing, and able buyer) sought his 10 percent commission under the listing agreement signed by Ledbetter as agent for Mrs. Bird. Barbara contended that the power of attorney was void and that Ledbetter owed the real estate commission because he breached his implied warranty that he had a principal with capacity. Decide.

10. Jane Byrne, while a candidate for reelection as mayor of the city of Chicago, told Stanley Gapshis, president of Progress Printing Corp., "You will have my campaign. . . . Mr. Griffin will get in touch with you." Shortly thereafter Griffin called Gapshis and said, "You have the Byrne campaign" and "you will get your copy from [Mary] Pitz." One week later Gapshis went to Pitz's office at her request. There Pitz told him she would be "handling all the artwork and copy for the campaign." Shortly after completion of each printing job, Progress prepared an invoice, which described the items printed and the quantity; these invoices were sent to Griffin on Pitz's instructions. Griffin testified that he never reviewed these invoices. According to Gapshis, the candidate called him in November 1983, nine months after her unsuccessful reelection bid, to say that she was sending a check for $10,000 and would have more later. When the full printing bill was not paid, Progress sued the candidate for $91,000. Byrne argued that she could not be held personally liable for the campaign committee's debts because she was not a party to the transactions. Progress responded that she had ratified the actions of her agents Griffin and Pitz. Decide. [*Progress Printing v Jane Byrne Political Committee* (Ill App) 601 NE2d 1055]

11. Lew owns a store on Canal Street in New Orleans. He paid a person named Mike and other individuals commissions for customers brought into the store. Lew testified that he had known Mike for less than a week. Boulos and Durso, partners in a wholesale jewelry business, were visiting New Orleans on a business trip when Mike brought them into the store to buy a stereo. While Durso finalized the stereo transaction with the store's manager, Boulos and Mike negotiated to buy 2 cameras, 3 videos, and 20 gold Dupont lighters. Unknown to the store's manager, Mike was given $8,250 in cash and was to deliver the merchandise later that evening to the Marriott Hotel, where Boulos and Durso were staying. Mike gave a receipt for the cash, but it showed no sales tax or indication that the goods were to be delivered. Boulos testified that he believed Mike was the store owner. Mike never delivered the merchandise and disappeared. Boulos and Durso contended that Lew is liable for the acts of his agent, Mike. Lew denied that Mike was his agent, and the testimony showed that Mike had no actual authority to make a sale, to use a cash register, or even to go behind a sales counter. What ethical principle applies to the conduct of Boulos and Durso? Decide. [*Boulos v Morrison* (La) 503 So 2d 1]

12. Martha Christiansen owns women's apparel stores bearing her name in New Seabury, Massachusetts; Lake Placid, New York; Palm Beach, Florida; and Palm Springs, California. At a meeting with her four

store managers, she discussed styles she thought appropriate for the forthcoming season, advised them as always to use their best judgment in the goods they purchased for each of their respective stores, and cautioned "but no blue jeans." Later Jane Farley, the manager of the Lake Placid store, purchased a line of high-quality blue denim outfits (designer jeans with jacket and vest options) from Women's Wear, Inc., for the summer season. The outfits did not sell. Martha refused to pay for them, contending that she told all of her managers "no blue jeans" and that if it came to a lawsuit, she would fly in three managers to testify that Jane Farley had absolutely no authority to purchase denim outfits and was, in fact, expressly forbidden to do so. Women's Wear sued Martha, and the three managers testified for her. Is the fact that Martha had explicitly forbidden Farley to purchase the outfits in question sufficient to protect her from liability for the purchases made by Farley?

13. Fred Schilling, the president and administrator of Florence General Hospital, made a contract, dated August 16, 1989, on behalf of the hospital with CMK Associates to transfer the capacity to utilize 25 beds from the hospital to the Faith Nursing Home. Schilling, on behalf of the hospital, had previously made a contract with CMK Associates on May 4, 1987. Schilling had been specifically authorized by the hospital board to make the 1987 contract. The hospital refused to honor the 1989 contract because the board had not authorized it. CMK contended that Schilling had apparent authority to bind the hospital because he was president and administrator of the hospital and he had been the person who negotiated and signed a contract with CMK in 1987. Thus, according to CMK, the hospital had held out Schilling as having apparent authority to make the contract. The hospital disagreed. Decide. [*Pee Dee Nursing Home v Florence General Hospital* (SC Ct App) 419 SE2d 843]

14. Barbara Fox was the agent of Burt Hollander, a well-known athlete. She discovered that Tom Lanceford owned a '57 Chevrolet convertible, which had been stored in a garage for the past 15 years. After demonstrating to Lanceford that she was the authorized agent of Hollander, she made a contract with Lanceford on behalf of Hollander to purchase the Chevrolet. Lanceford later discovered that the car was much more valuable than he originally believed, and he refused to deliver the car to Fox. Fox sued Lanceford for breach of contract. Can she recover?

15. Francis Gagnon, an elderly gentleman, signed a power of attorney authorizing his daughter Joan "to sell any of my real estate and to execute any document needed to carry out the sale . . . and to add property to a trust of which I am grantor or beneficiary." This power was given in case Gagnon was not available to take care of matters personally because he was traveling. When Joan learned that Gagnon intended to sell his Shelburne property to Cosby for $750,000, she created an irrevocable trust naming Gagnon as beneficiary and herself as trustee. Acting then on the basis of the authority set forth in the power of attorney, she conveyed the Shelburne property to herself as trustee of the irrevocable trust, thus blocking the sale to Cosby. When Gagnon learned of this, he demanded that Joan return the Shelburne property to him, but she refused, saying she had acted within the authority set forth in the power of attorney. Did Joan violate any duty owed to Gagnon? Must she reconvey the property to Gagnon? [*Gagnon v Coombs* (Mass App) 654 NE2d 54]

CPA QUESTIONS

1. Generally, an agency relationship is terminated by operation of law in all of the following situations except the
   a. Principal's death.
   b. Principal's incapacity.
   c. Agent's renunciation of the agency.
   d. Agent's failure to acquire a necessary business license.

   (5/90, Law, #1, 0650)

2. Able, on behalf of Pix Corp., entered into a contract with Sky Corp., by which Sky agreed to sell computer equipment to Pix. Able disclosed to Sky that she was acting on behalf of Pix. However, Able had exceeded her actual authority by entering into the contract with Sky. If Pix wishes to ratify the contract with Sky, which of the following statements is correct?

   a. Pix must notify Sky that Pix intends to ratify the contract.
   b. Able must have acted reasonably and in Pix's best interest.
   c. Able must be a general agent of Pix.
   d. Pix must have knowledge of all material facts relating to the contract at the time it is ratified.

   (5/88, Law, #5, 9911)

3. Which of the following actions requires an agent for a corporation to have a written agency agreement?
   a. Purchasing office supplies for the principal's business.
   b. Purchasing an interest in undeveloped land for the principal.
   c. Hiring an independent general contractor to renovate the principal's office building.
   d. Retaining an attorney to collect a business debt owed the principal.

   (11/94, Law, #16, 5193)

4. Simmons, an agent for Jensen, has the express authority to sell Jensen's goods. Simmons also has the express authority to grant discounts of up to 5% of list price. Simmons sold Hemple a 10% discount. Hemple had not previously dealt with either Simmons or Jensen. Which of the following courses of action may Jensen properly take?
   a. Seek to void the sale to Hemple.
   b. Seek recovery of $50 from Hemple only.
   c. Seek recovery of $50 from Simmons only.
   d. Seek recovery of $50 from either Hemple or Simmons.

   (5/89, Law, #13)

5. Ogden Corp. hired Thorp as a sales representative for nine months at a salary of $3,000 per month plus 4% of sales. Which of the following statements is correct?
   a. Thorp is obligated to act solely in Ogden's interest in matters concerning Ogden's business.
   b. The agreement between Ogden and Thorp formed an agency coupled with an interest.
   c. Ogden does not have the power to dismiss Thorp during the nine-month period without cause.
   d. The agreement between Ogden and Thorp is not enforceable unless it is in writing and signed by Thorp.

   (5/91, Law, #9)

6. Frost's accountant and business manager has the authority to
   a. Mortgage Frost's business property.
   b. Obtain bank loans for Frost.
   c. Insure Frost's property against fire loss.
   d. Sell Frost's business.

   (5/91, Law, #3)

Third Persons in Agency

CHAPTER 40

OBJECTIVES

After studying this chapter, you should be able to

1. *Describe how to execute a contract as an agent on behalf of a principal;*
2. *Identify when an agent is liable to a third person on a contract;*
3. *State the effect of a payment made by a third person to an authorized agent;*
4. *Explain and illustrate the doctrine of respondeat superior;*
5. *Contrast the liability of an owner for a tort committed by an independent contractor with the liability of an employer for a tort committed by an employee; and*
6. *Distinguish between the authority of a soliciting agent and that of a contracting agent.*

The rights and liabilities of the principal, the agent, and the third person with whom the agent deals are generally determined by contract law. In some cases, tort or criminal law may be applicable.

A. LIABILITY OF AGENT TO THIRD PERSON

The liability of the agent to the third person depends on the existence of authority and the manner of executing the contract.

1. Action of Authorized Agent of Disclosed Principal

An agent of a disclosed principal is not liable on a contract made for a principal if the agent was authorized to make the contract or, if unauthorized, the contract was ratified by the principal.

If an agent makes a contract with a third person on behalf of a disclosed principal and has proper authority to do so, and if the contract is executed properly, the agent has no personal liability on the contract. Whether the principal performs the contract or not, the agent cannot be held liable by the third party.

In speaking of an agent's action as authorized or unauthorized, it must be remembered that *authorized* includes action that, though originally unauthorized, was subsequently ratified by the principal. Once there is an effective ratification, the original action of the agent is no longer treated as unauthorized.

2. Unauthorized Action

An agent is personally liable to a third person for unauthorized actions.

If a person makes a contract as agent for another but lacks authority to do so, the contract does not bind the principal. When a person purports to act as agent for a principal, an implied warranty arises that that person has authority to do so.[1] If the agent lacks authority, there is a breach of this warranty.

If the agent's act causes loss to the third person, that third person may generally hold the agent liable for the loss.

CASE SUMMARY

The Company President Was Personally Liable When the Charcoal Plant Deal Did Not Ignite

Facts: Craig Industries Inc. was in the business of manufacturing charcoal. Craig, the corporation's president, contracted in the name of the corporation to sell the company's plants to Husky Industries. Craig did not have authority from the board of directors to make the contract, and later the board of directors voted not to accept the contract. Husky Industries sued Craig on the theory that he, as agent for the corporation, exceeded his authority and should be held personally liable for damages.

Decision: Judgment for Husky Industries. An agent who purports to contract in the name of a principal without or in excess of authority to do so is personally liable to the other contracting party for the agent's breach of implied warranty of authority. This liability is implied unless the agent manifests that no warranty of authority is made or the other contracting party knows the agent is not authorized. There was no discussion by the contracting parties concerning a limitation of Craig's warranty of authority to contract for the corporation, and Husky Industries was not aware that Craig was not authorized to make the contract. [*Husky Industries v Craig (Mo App) 618 SW2d 458 (1981)*]

---

[1] *Walz v Todd & Honeywell Inc.*, 599 App Div NYS2d 638 (1993).

It is no defense for the agent in such a case that the agent acted in good faith or misunderstood the scope of authority. The purported agent is not liable for conduct in excess of authority when the third person knows that the agent is acting beyond the authority given by the principal.

An agent with a written authorization may avoid liability on the implied warranty of authority by showing the written authorization to the third person and permitting the third person to determine the scope of the agent's authority.

3.   Disclosure of Principal

There are three degrees to which the existence and identity of the principal may be disclosed or not disclosed. An agent's liability as a party to a contract with a third person is affected by the degree of disclosure.

(a) Disclosed Principal. When the agent makes known the identity of the principal and the fact that the agent is acting on behalf of that principal, the principal is called a **disclosed principal**. The third person dealing with an agent of a disclosed principal ordinarily intends to make a contract with the principal, not with the agent. Consequently the agent is not a party to and is not bound by the contract that is made.[2]

> An agent is liable on contracts made for partially disclosed and undisclosed principals.

(b) Partially Disclosed Principal. When the agent makes known the existence of a principal but not the principal's identity, the principal is a **partially disclosed principal**. Because the third party does not know the identity of the principal, the third person is making the contract with the agent, and the agent is therefore a party to the contract.

(c) Undisclosed Principal. When the third person is not told or does not know that the agent is acting as an agent for anyone else, the unknown principal is called an **undisclosed principal**.[3] In this case, the third person is making the contract with the agent, and the agent is a party to that contract.

CASE SUMMARY

You've Got to Tell Them You're Contracting on Behalf of the Corporation, Silly

Facts: Richard Pawlus was an owner of Dutch City Wood Products, Inc., which did business as "Dutch City Marketing." Pawlus purchased merchandise from Rothschild Sunsystems Inc. from April 24 to June 24, using the designation "Richard Pawlus Dutch City Marketing" on orders and correspondence. In October, Rothschild was notified that Pawlus was acting on behalf of the corporation when the merchandise was purchased. Rothschild sued Pawlus for payment for the merchandise. Pawlus contended that he was an agent of the corporation and was thus not personally liable.

Decision: Judgment for Rothschild. The contracts were made between April and June. Pawlus did not inform Rothschild until October that he was an agent acting on behalf of Dutch City Wood Products, Inc. Because Pawlus did not make known that he was acting as an agent for the corporation at the time the contracts were made, he is liable on the contracts. [*Rothschild Sunsystems Inc. v Pawlus, (App Div) 514 NYS2d 572 (1987)*]

---

2 *New York Times v Glynn-Palmer Inc.* (NY City Civ Ct) 525 NYS2d 565 (1988).
3 *Southwest Slopes, Inc. v Lum* (Haw App) 918 P2d 1157 (1996).

During the 1970s, large tracts of land in south Tempe, Arizona, were owned by dairy farmers. The land was used by the farmers for grazing. Economic growth in this suburb of Phoenix was limited because of the state's inability at that time to attract large businesses to the area for relocation or location of new facilities.

In 1973, three farmers who owned adjoining parcels of land in the south Tempe area were approached by a local real estate agent with an offer for the purchase of their property. The amount of the offer was approximately 10 percent above the property's appraised value. The three farmers discussed the offer and concluded that, with their need to retire, it was best to accept the offer and sell the land. All three signed contracts for the sale of their lands.

After the contracts were entered into, but before the transactions had closed, the three farmers learned that the land was being purchased by a real estate development firm from southern California. The development firm had planned and would be proposing to the Tempe City Council a residential community called the Lakes. The Lakes would consist of upper-end homes in a community laced with parks, lakes, and ponds, with each house in the developed area backing up to its own dock and water recreation. The development firm had begun the project because it had learned of the plans of American Express, Rubbermaid, and Dial to locate major facilities in the Phoenix area.

The three farmers objected to the sale of their land when they learned of the identity of the buyer. "If we had known who was coming in here and why, we never would have sold for such a low price." The farmers wish to know if their contracts are binding. Is it ethical to use the strategy of an undisclosed principal? What is the role of an agent in a situation in which the third party is making a decision not as beneficial to him or her as it could or should be? Can the agent say anything?

4. Assumption of Liability

Agents may intentionally make themselves liable on contracts with third persons.[4] This situation frequently occurs when the agent is a well-established local brokerage house or other agency and when the principal is located out of town and is not known locally.

Pay the Air Tiger

Facts: For five years, Air Tiger Express Inc., a freight shipper, transported goods from overseas to New York for Farrell Forwarding Corporation's clients. Air Tiger billed Farrell, a customs agent, for these services. Farrell then billed its clients for both Air Tiger's and its services and remitted payment to Air Tiger based on a pricing agreement it had negotiated with Air Tiger. When Air Tiger was not paid for certain services in the amount of $82,732, it sued Farrell for payment. Farrell defended that it acted as agent for its consignees, who were disclosed principals, and being an agent, it was not liable for the debts of the principals.

Decision: Judgment for Air Tiger. It was Farrell's intent to substitute itself for the personal liability of its principals, the consignees. The course of dealings between Air Tiger and Farrell, including the method of billing and payment and the pricing agreement, makes it clear that Farrell intentionally made itself liable to Air Tiger for the service to the principals. [*Air Tiger Express Inc. v Farrell Forwarding Corp. (App Div) 611 NYS2d 242 (1994)*]

---

[4] *Fairchild Publications v Rosston* (NY Country Sup) 584 NYS2d 389 (1992).

In some situations, the agent will make a contract that will be personally binding. If the principal is not disclosed, the agent is necessarily the other contracting party and is bound by the contract. Even when the principal is disclosed, the agent may be personally bound if it was the intention of the parties that the agent assume a personal obligation even though this was done to further the business of the principal. To illustrate, if an attorney hires an expert witness to testify on behalf of a client, the attorney is an agent acting on behalf of a disclosed principal and is not personally liable for an expert witness fee.

However, where an expert witness asks the attorney about payment and the attorney states, "Don't worry, I will take care of it," the attorney (agent) has assumed a personal obligation and is liable for the fee.[5]

5. Execution of Contract

A simple contract that would appear to be the contract of the agent can be shown by other evidence, if believed, to have been intended as a contract between the principal and the third party.

CASE SUMMARY

If You Sign As an Agent, *You* Don't Have to Pay

Facts: Beverly Baumann accompanied her mother to Memorial Hospital, where her mother was placed in intensive care for heart problems. A nurse asked Baumann to sign various documents, including one that authorized the hospital to release medical information and to receive the mother's insurance benefits directly. This form stated, "I understand I am financially responsible to the hospital for charges not covered by this authorization." Baumann's mother died during the course of her hospitalization. The hospital later sued Baumann to recover $19,013.42 in unpaid hospital charges based on the form she signed, which the hospital called a "guarantee of payment." Baumann contended that she signed the document as an agent for her mother and was thus not personally liable.

Decision: Judgment for Baumann. She acted as an agent for a disclosed principal, her mother. Unless the contract clearly states otherwise, an agent has no personal liability on a contract executed for a disclosed principal. [*Memorial Hospital v Baumann*, 474 NYS2d 636 (1984)]

To avoid problems, an agent should sign contracts writing the principal's name and *by* or *per* the agent's name.

To avoid any question of interpretation, an agent should execute an instrument by signing the principal's name and either *by* or *per* and the agent's name. For example, if Jane R. Craig is an agent for B.G. Gray, Craig should execute instruments by signing either "B.G. Gray, by Jane R. Craig" or "B.G. Gray, per Jane R. Craig." Such a signing is in law a signing by Gray, and the agent is therefore not a party to the contract. The signing of the principal's name by an authorized agent without indicating the agent's name or identity is likewise in law the signature of the principal.

If the instrument is ambiguous as to whether the agent has signed in a representative or an individual capacity, parol evidence is admissible as between the original parties to the transaction for establishing the character in which the agent was acting. If the body of the contract states an obligation that clearly refers only to the principal, then the agent is not bound by the contract even though it is signed in the agent's individual name without indicating any agency.

---

5 *Boros v Carter* (Fla App) 537 So 2d 1134 (1989).

6. Torts and Crimes

Agents are liable for harm caused third persons by the agents' fraudulent, intentional, or negligent acts.[6] The fact that persons were acting as agents at the time or that they acted in good faith under the directions of a principal does not relieve them of liability if their conduct would impose liability on them when acting for themselves.

Employees Are Not Personally Liable for Roadway Accidents While at Work, Are They?

Facts: Ralls was an employee of the Arkansas State Highway Department. While repairing a state highway, he negligently backed a state truck onto the highway, causing a collision with Mittlesteadt's car. Mittlesteadt sued Ralls, who raised the defense that, because he was acting on behalf of the state, he was not liable for his negligence.

Decision: The fact that an employee or agent is acting on behalf of someone else does not excuse or exonerate the agent or employee from liability for torts committed by the agent or employee. Ralls was therefore liable for his negligence even though it occurred within the scope of his employment by the state. [*Ralls v Mittlesteadt*, 268 Ark 471, 596 SW2d 349 (1980)]

If an agent commits a crime, such as stealing from a third person or shooting the third person, the agent is liable for the crime without regard to the fact of acting as an agent. The agent is liable without regard to whether the agent acted in self-interest or sought to advance the interest of the principal.

C.   LIABILITY OF PRINCIPAL TO THIRD PERSON

The principal is liable to the third person for the properly authorized and executed contracts of the agent and, in certain circumstances, for the agent's unauthorized contracts.

7. Agent's Contracts

The liability of a principal to a third person on a contract made by an agent depends on the extent of disclosure of the principal and the form of the contract that is executed.

(a) Simple Contract with Principal Disclosed. When a disclosed principal with contractual capacity authorizes or ratifies an agent's transaction with a third person, and when the agent properly executes a contract with the third person, a binding contract exists between the principal and the third person. The principal and the third person may each sue the other in the event of a breach of the contract.

---

[6] *Mannish v Lacayo* (Fla App) 496 So 2d 242 (1986).

The agent is not a party to the contract, is not liable for its performance, and cannot sue for its breach.[7]

The liability of a disclosed principal to a third person is not discharged by the fact that the principal gives the agent money with which to pay the third person. Consequently the liability of a buyer for the purchase price of goods is not terminated by the fact that the buyer gave the buyer's agent the purchase price to remit to the seller.

(b) Simple Contract with Principal Partially Disclosed. A partially disclosed principal is liable for a simple contract made by an authorized agent. The third person may recover from either the agent or the principal.

(c) Simple Contract with Principal Undisclosed. An undisclosed principal is liable for a simple contract made by an authorized agent. Although the third person initially contracted with the agent alone, the third person upon learning of the existence of the undisclosed principal may sue that principal. In some states, the third person must elect whether to hold the agent or the previously undisclosed principal liable for the debt. Under this "election of remedies rule," if the third person elects to hold the principal liable and the principal turns out to be insolvent, the third person may not collect from the agent.[8] The trend in the law is to reject this rule. The modern rule allows judgments to be entered simultaneously against the agent and the undisclosed principal. It allows a third person to collect from the agent, the principal, or both until the judgment is fully satisfied (joint and several liability).[9]

(d) Commercial Paper with Principal Undisclosed. An undisclosed principal whose name or description does not appear on commercial paper is not liable as a party on that paper.[10] Thus, an undisclosed principal is not liable on commercial paper executed by an agent in the agent's own name.

8. Payment to Agent

Payment to an agent with actual or apparent authority to receive such is deemed payment to the principal even though it is not remitted to the principal.

When the third person makes payment to an authorized agent, the payment is deemed made to the principal. Even if the agent never remits or delivers the payment to the principal, the principal must give the third person full credit for the payment so long as the third person made the payment in good faith and had no reason to know that the agent would be guilty of misconduct.[11]

---

[7] *Levy v Gold & Co. Inc.* (App Div) 529 NYS2d 133 (1988).

[8] *Orruck v Crouse Realtors Inc.* (Mo App) 823 SW2d 40 (1991).

[9] *Crown Controls Inc. v Smiley* (Wash) 756 P2d 717 (1988).

[10] UCC §§ 3-401, 3-403 of the 1952 version and UCC §§ 3-401, 3-402 of the 1990 version. The 1990 version changes prior law covering when an agent or employee authorized to sign checks signs with only the agent's or employee's name. In such a case, if the check shows on its face that it is drawn on the account of the employer or principal, the employee or agent is not liable for the payment of the check. § 3-402(c) (1990).

[11] This general rule of law is restated in some states by Section 2 of the Uniform Fiduciaries Act, which is expressly extended by Section 1 of the act to agents, partners, and corporate officers. Similar statutory provisions are found in a number of other states.

But We Already Paid!

Facts: E.I. duPont de Nemours & Co. licensed Enjay Chemical Company (now Exxon) and Johnson & Johnson to use certain chemical processes, in return for which royalty payments by check were to be made to duPont. By agreement between the companies, the royalty payments to be made to duPont were to be made by check sent to a specified duPont employee, C.H.D., in its Control Division. These checks were sent during the next nine years. C.H.D. altered some of them so that he was named thereon as the payee. He then cashed them and used the money for his own purposes. Liberty Mutual Insurance Company, which insured the fidelity of duPont's employees, and duPont sued Enjay and Johnson & Johnson on the basis that they still owed the amounts embezzled by C.H.D.

Decision: Judgment for Enjay and Johnson & Johnson. Payment to an authorized agent has the legal effect of payment to the principal regardless of whether the agent remits the payment to the principal or embezzles it. C.H.D. was the agent authorized to receive the royalty checks. Therefore, the defendants had effectively paid the royalties when they sent C.H.D. the checks. His misconduct did not revive the debts that were paid by sending him the checks. *[Liberty Mutual Insurance Co. v Enjay Chemical Co. (Del Super) 316 A2d 219 (1974)]*

Because apparent authority has the same legal effect as actual authority, a payment made to a person with apparent authority to receive the payment is deemed a payment to the apparent principal.

When payment is made by a debtor to a person who is not the actual or apparent agent of the creditor, such a payment does not discharge the debt unless that person in fact pays the money over to the creditor.

9. Agent's Statements

A principal is bound by a statement made by an agent while transacting business within the scope of authority.[12] This means that the principal cannot later contradict the statement of the agent and show that it is not true. Statements or declarations of an agent, in order to bind the principal, must be made at the time of performing the act to which they relate or shortly thereafter.

10. Agent's Knowledge

The principal is bound by knowledge or notice of any fact that is acquired by an agent while acting within the scope of actual or apparent authority.

When a commercial paper is endorsed to the principal and the agent acting for the principal has knowledge of a matter that would be a defense to the paper, such knowledge of the agent is imputed to the principal and bars the principal from being a holder in due course. When a fact is known to the agent of the seller, the sale is deemed made by the seller with knowledge of that fact. When an employee knows that there has been water pollution contrary to law, such knowledge is imputed to the corporate employer even if no officer or director in fact had any knowledge of it.

The rule that the agent's knowledge is imputed to the principal is extended in some cases to knowledge gained prior to the creation of the agency relationship.

---

[12] *Potomac Leasing Co. v Bulger* (Ala) 531 So 2d 307 (1988).

The notice and knowledge in any case must be based on reliable information. Thus, when the agent hears only rumors, the principal is not charged with notice.

(a) Exceptions. If the subject matter is outside the scope of the agent's authority, the agent is under no duty to inform the principal of the knowledge, and the principal is not bound by it. The principal is not charged with knowledge of an agent (1) when the agent is under a duty to another person to conceal such knowledge, (2) when the agent is acting adversely to the principal's interest, or (3) when the third party acts in collusion with the agent for the purpose of cheating the principal. In such cases, it is not likely that the agent would communicate knowledge to the principal. The principal is therefore not bound by the knowledge of the agent.

(b) Communication to Principal. As a consequence of regarding the principal as possessing the knowledge of the agent, when the law requires that a third person communicate with the principal, that duty may be satisfied by communicating with the agent. Thus, an offeree effectively communicates the acceptance of an offer to the offeror when the offeree makes such communication to the offeror's agent. An offeror effectively communicates the revocation of an offer to the offeree by communicating the revocation to the offeree's agent.

C.   LIABILITY OF PRINCIPAL FOR TORTS AND CRIMES OF AGENT

Under certain circumstances, the principal may be liable for the torts or crimes of the agent or the employee.

11. Vicarious Liability for Torts and Crimes

Assume that an agent or an employee causes harm to a third person. Is the principal or the employer liable for this conduct? If the conduct constitutes a crime, can the principal or the employer be criminally prosecuted? The answer is that in many instances the principal or the employer is liable civilly and may also be prosecuted criminally. That is, the principal or the employer is liable although personally free from fault and not guilty of any wrong. This concept of imposing liability for the fault of another is known as **vicarious liability**.

The situation arises both when an employer has an employee and when a principal has an agent who commits the wrong. The rules of law governing the vicarious liability of the principal and the employer are the same. In the interest of simplicity, this section will be stated in terms of employees acting in the course of employment. Remember that these rules are equally applicable to agents acting within the scope of their authority. As a practical matter, some situations will arise only with agents. *For example,* the vicarious liability of a seller for the misrepresentations made by a salesperson will arise only when the seller appointed an agent to sell. In contrast, both the employee hired to drive a truck and the agent being sent to visit a customer could negligently run over a third person. In many situations, a person employed by another is both an employee and an agent, and the tort is committed within the phase of "employee work."

The rule of law imposing vicarious liability on an innocent employer for the wrong of an employee is also known as the doctrine of *respondeat superior*. In modern times, this doctrine can be justified on the grounds that the business should pay

The legal doctrine of *respondeat superior* holds an employer or principal vicariously liable for torts committed by an employee or an agent acting within the scope of employment or authority.

for the harm caused in the doing of the business, that the employer will be more careful in the selection of employees if made responsible for their actions, and that the employer may obtain liability insurance to protect against claims of third persons.

(a) Nature of Act. The wrongful act committed by the employee may be a negligent act, an intentional act, a fraudulent act, or a violation of a government regulation. It may give rise only to civil liability of the employer, or it may also subject the employer to prosecution for crime.

(1) Negligent Act. Historically the act for which liability would be imposed under the doctrine of *respondeat superior* was a negligent act committed within the scope of employment.

(2) Intentional Act. Under the common law, a master was not liable for an intentional tort committed by a servant. The modern law holds that an employer is liable for an intentional tort committed by an employee for the purpose of furthering the employer's business. Thus, an employer is not liable for an intentional unprovoked assault committed by an employee on a third person or customer of the employer because of a personal grudge or for no reason. However, the employer will be held liable under the modern view when the employee's assault was committed in the belief that the employee was advancing the employer's interest.[13] ◆ *For example,* an employee may be hired to retake property, as in the case of an employee of a finance company hired to repossess automobiles on which installment payments have not been made. In such a case, the employer is generally liable for any unlawful force used by the employee in retaking the property or in committing an assault on a debtor. ◆

(3) Fraud. Modern decisions hold the employer liable for fraudulent acts or misrepresentations. The rule is commonly applied to a principal-agent relationship. To illustrate, when an agent makes fraudulent statements in selling stock, the principal is liable for the buyer's loss. In states that follow the common law rule of no liability for intentional torts, the principal is not liable for the agent's fraud when the principal did not authorize or know of the fraud of the agent.

(4) Government Regulation. The employer may be liable because of the employee's violation of a government regulation. These regulations are most common in the areas of business and of protection of the environment. In such cases, the employer may be held liable for a penalty imposed by the government. In some cases, the breach of the regulation will impose liability on the employer in favor of a third person who is injured as a consequence of the violation.

(b) Course of Employment. The mere fact that a tort or crime is committed by an employee does not necessarily impose vicarious liability on the employer. It must also be shown that the individual was acting within the scope of authority if an agent or in the course of employment if an employee. If an employee was not acting within the scope of employment, there is no vicarious liability.[14]

---

[13] Restatement (Second) of Agency § 231; *Carrero v New York City Housing Authority,* 668 F Supp 196 (SDNY 1987).
[14] *DDZ v Molerway Freight Lines, Inc.* (Utah App) 880 P2d 1 (1994).

He Was Back to Nettie's Business When He Hit the Studebaker

Facts: Judith Studebaker was injured when a van owned and driven by James Ferry collided with her vehicle. On the morning of the incident, Ferry made his usual runs for the florist for whom he delivered flowers, Nettie's Flower Garden Inc. Studebaker brought an action against Nettie's on a *respondeat superior* theory on the belief that Ferry was Nettie's employee at the time of the accident. Nettie's defended that Ferry was an independent contractor, not an employee. From a judgment in favor of Studebaker for $125,000, Nettie's appealed.

Decision: Judgment against Nettie's. Applying a "right to control" test, it is clear that Nettie's controlled or had the right to control Ferry at the time of the collision. Nettie's set standards for Ferry's dress and conduct, determined his territory, and set standards for his van. While Ferry made a slight detour prior to the accident to conduct personal business at a pawn shop, this did not relieve the employer from liability because he was clearly back to Nettie's business at the time of the accident. [*Studebaker v Nettie's Flower Garden Inc. (Mo App) 842 SW2d 227 (1992)*]

(c) Employee of the United States. The Federal Tort Claims Act (FTCA) declares that the United States shall be liable vicariously whenever a federal employee driving a motor vehicle in the course of employment causes harm under such circumstances that a private employer would be liable. Contrary to the general rule, the statute exempts the employee driver from liability.[15]

12. Negligent Hiring and Retention of Employees

In addition to a complaint against the employer based on the doctrine of *respondeat superior*, a lawsuit may often raise a second theory, that of negligent hiring or retention of an employee.[16] Unlike the *respondeat superior* theory, by which the employer may be vicariously liable for the tort of an employee, the negligent hiring theory is based on the negligence of the employer in the hiring process. Under the *respondeat superior* rule, the employer is liable only for those torts committed within the scope of employment or in the furtherance of the employer's interests. The negligent hiring theory has been used to impose liability in cases where an employee commits an intentional tort, almost invariably outside the scope of employment against a customer or the general public, and the employer knew or should have known that the employee was incompetent, violent, dangerous, or criminal.[17]

(a) Need for Due Care in Hiring. An employer may be liable on a theory of negligent hiring when it is shown that the employer knew, or in the exercise of ordinary care should have known, that the job applicant would create an undue risk of harm to others in carrying out job responsibilities. Moreover, it must also be shown that the employer could have reasonably foreseen injury to the third party. Thus, an employer who knows of an employee's preemployment drinking problems and violent behavior may be liable to customers assaulted by that employee.

---

[15] Claims of negligent hiring are not permissible under the FTCA. See *Tonelli v United States,* 60 F3d 492 (8th Cir 1995).
[16] *Medina v Graham's Cowboys Inc.* (NM App) 827 P2d 859 (1992).
[17] *Rockwell v Sun Harbor Budget Suites* (Nev) 925 P2d 1175 (1996).

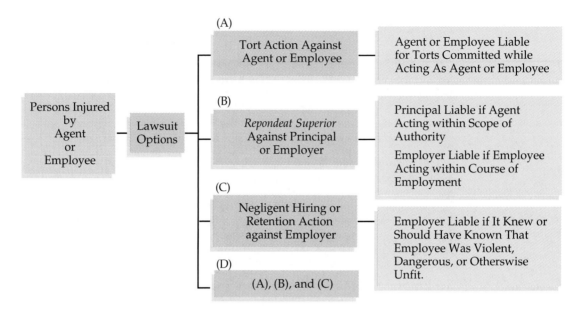

FIGURE 40-1
*Liability for Torts of
Agent or Employee*

Employers might protect themselves from liability in a negligent hiring case by having each prospective employee fill out an employment application form and then checking into the applicant's work experience, background, character, and qualifications. This would be evidence of due care in hiring. Generally, the scope of preemployment investigation should correlate to the degree of opportunity the prospective employee would have to do harm to third persons. A minimum investigation consisting of the filling out of an application form and a personal interview would be satisfactory for the hiring of an outside maintenance person, but a full background inquiry would be necessary for the hiring of a security guard. However, such inquiry does not bar *respondeat superior* liability.

(b) Employees with Criminal Records. The hiring of an individual with a criminal record does not by itself establish the tort of negligent hiring.[18] An employer who knows that an applicant has a criminal record has a duty to investigate to determine if the nature of the conviction in relationship to the job to be performed creates an unacceptable risk to third persons.

(c) Negligent Retention. Courts assign liability under negligent retention on a basis similar to that of negligent hiring. That is, the employer knew, or should have known, that the employee would create an undue risk of harm to others in carrying out job responsibilities.

CASE SUMMARY

1) Alcohol, 2) Battery, and 3) Negligent Retention: Three Strikes and You're Out!

Facts: Mark Livigni was manager of the National Super Markets, Inc., store in Cahokia, Illinois. After drinking alcoholic beverages one evening, he stopped by the store to check the premises when he observed a ten-year-old boy's unacceptable behavior outside the store. Livigni chased the boy to a car, where he pulled another child, a four-year-old named Farris Bryant, from the car

---

[18] *Connes v Molalla Transportation Systems* (Colo) 831 P2d 1316 (1992).

and threw him through the air. A multicount lawsuit was brought against National and Livigni. The evidence revealed that some eight years before the incident with Farris Bryant, Livigni had thrown an empty milk crate at a subordinate employee, striking him on the arm and necessitating medical treatment, and that some two years before the incident, he threw his 13-year-old son onto a bed while disciplining him, causing the boy to sustain a broken collarbone. Livigni was promoted to store manager subsequent to the milk crate incident, and he pled guilty to aggravated battery to his child and was sentenced to two years' probation. A verdict was rendered against National for $20,000 under a *respondeat superior* theory for the battery of Farris Bryant. A verdict was also rendered against National for $15,000 for negligent retention of Livigni and for $115,000 in punitive damages for willful and wanton retention. National appealed the trial court's denial of its motions for directed verdicts on these counts.

Decision: Judgment for Bryant. Employers that wrongfully hire or retain unfit employees expose the public to the acts of these employees, and it is not unreasonable to hold the employer accountable when the employee causes injury to another. The principle is not *respondeat superior;* rather, it is premised on the wrongful conduct of the employer itself. Additionally the employer in this case is responsible under *respondeat superior* because Livigni was prompted to act, in part, to protect store property. A dissenting opinion stated that the wrong message is sent to employers on the negligent retention issue and will cause them to terminate any employee who has ever had an altercation on or off company premises, which is contrary to the state's public policy of rehabilitating criminal offenders. *[Bryant v Livigni, (Ill App)619 NE 2d 550 (1993)]*

A hospital is liable for negligent retention when it continues the staff privileges of a physician that it knew or should have known had sexually assaulted a female patient in the past.[19]

13. Agent's Crimes

A principal is liable for the crimes of an agent committed at the principal's direction. When not authorized, however, the principal is ordinarily not liable for an agent's crime merely because it was committed while the agent was otherwise acting within the scope of the latter's authority or employment. As an exception to the rule of nonliability just stated, courts now hold an employer criminally liable when the employee has in the course of employment violated environmental protection laws, liquor sales laws, pure food laws, or laws regulating prices or prohibiting false weights. ◆ *For example*, an employer may be held criminally responsible for an employee's sale of liquor to a minor in violation of the liquor law even though the sale was not known to the employer and violated instructions given to the employee. ◆

14. Owner's Liability for Acts of an Independent Contractor

Ordinarily an owner is not liable for the torts caused by an independent contractor or that contractor's employees.

If work is done by an independent contractor rather than by an employee, the owner is not liable for harm caused by the contractor to third persons or their property. Likewise, the owner is not bound by the contracts made by the independent contractor. The owner is ordinarily not liable for harm caused to third persons by the negligence of the employees of the independent contractor.[20]

---

[19] *Capithorne v Framingham Union Hospital* (Mass) 520 NE2d 139 (1988).
[20] *King v Lens Creek Ltd. Partnership* (W Va) 483 SE2d 265 (1996).

Hauling Hobbs' Heifers

Facts: Joan Kime was seriously injured when her vehicle was struck from the rear by a tractor–livestock trailer unit driven by Edward Yelli as her vehicle was preparing to turn left into a farm driveway. Yelli was hauling a load of cattle belonging to Hobbs, a large-scale farmer, rancher, and cattle feeder. Hobbs owned eight livestock trailers but did not own any tractor units, utilizing a number of truckers on an as-needed basis. Yelli owned his own grain trailer, and prior to the job at issue, he had been hauling corn for another rancher. Between October 1 and October 22, when the accident occurred, he made four trips for Hobbs. Kime sued both Yelli and Hobbs, contending that Yelli was an employee of Hobbs rather than an independent contractor. Kime also contended that Hobbs may not escape liability for Yelli's negligence, even if Yelli was an independent contractor, under the "inherently dangerous work" doctrine. Hobbs contended that he was not liable for the harm caused by the independent contractor, Yelli.

Decision: Judgement for Hobbs. Hobbs did not retain control over Yelli's activities as a trucker; he did not control the route taken or who would drive the tractor, either Yelli or someone hired by Yelli. Yelli was engaged in a distinct occupation or business as a trucker, owned his own tractor and a trailer, and provided all of the instrumentalities of the work, including maintenance and insurance on the tractor, and he decided what jobs to take. As a matter of law, he was an independent contractor. The transportation of cattle in a tractor–livestock trailer unit is not an inherently dangerous activity such as to impose a nondelegable duty on Hobbs, the employer of the independent contractor, Yelli. [*Kime v Hobbs (Neb) 562 NW2d 705 (1997)*]

(a) Exceptions to Owner's Immunity. There is a trend toward imposing liability on the owner when work undertaken by an independent contractor is inherently dangerous.[21] That is, the law is taking the position that if the owner wishes to engage in a particular activity, the owner must be responsible for the harm it causes. The owner cannot be insulated from such liability by the device of hiring an independent contractor to do the work.

Regardless of the nature of the activity, the owner may be liable for the torts and contracts of the independent contractor when the owner controls the conduct of the independent contractor.[22] ◆ *For example,* when a franchisor exercises a high degree of control over a franchisee, the relationship will be recognized as an agency relationship, and the franchisor is bound by the action of the franchisee. ◆

In certain circumstances, such as providing security for a business, collecting bills, and repossessing collateral, there is an increased risk that torts may be committed by the individuals performing such duties. The trend of the law is to refuse to allow the use of an independent contractor for such work to insulate the employer.

When the immunity based on use of an independent contractor would make it possible for the enterprise engaging the contractor to avoid liability under copyright laws or to defraud others, the immunity will be ignored.

(b) Undisclosed Independent Contractor. In some situations, the owner appears to be doing the act in question because the existence of the independent contractor is not disclosed or apparent. This situation occurs most commonly when a franchisee does business under the name of the franchisor; when a concession-

---

[21] *Hinger v Parker & Parsley Petroleum Co.* (NM App) 902 P2d 1033 (1995).
[22] *Parish v Omaha Public Power District* (Neb) 496 NW2d 902 (1993).

aire, such as a restaurant in a hotel, appears to be the hotel restaurant, although in fact it is operated by an independent concessionaire; or when the buyer of a business continues to run the business in the name of the seller. In such cases of an undisclosed independent contractor, it is generally held that the apparent owner (that is, the franchisor, the grantor of the concession, or the seller) is liable for the torts and contracts of the undisclosed independent contractor.

15. Enforcement of Claim by Third Person

A lawsuit may be brought by a third person against the agent or the principal if each is liable. In most states and in the federal courts, the plaintiff may sue either or both in one action when both are liable. If both are sued, the plaintiff may obtain a judgment against both, although the plaintiff is allowed to collect the full amount of the judgment only once.

E.   TRANSACTIONS WITH SALES PERSONNEL

Many transactions with sales personnel do not result in a contract with the third person with whom the salesperson deals.

16. Soliciting and Contracting Agents

A salesperson is ordinarily an agent whose authority is limited to soliciting orders, and no contract is made until accepted by the principal.

The giving of an order to a salesperson often does not give rise to a contract. Ordinarily a salesperson is a **soliciting agent**, whose authority is limited to soliciting offers from third persons and transmitting them to the principal for acceptance or rejection. Such an agent does not have authority to make a contract that will bind the principal to the third person. The employer of the salesperson is not bound by a contract until the employer accepts the order. And the third person (customer) may withdraw the offer at any time prior to acceptance.

In contrast, if the person with whom the buyer deals is a **contracting agent** with authority to make contracts, there is by definition a binding contract between the principal and the customer from the moment that the agent agrees with the customer. In other words, the contract arises when the agent accepts the customer's order.

SUMMARY

An agent of a disclosed principal who makes a contract with a third person within the scope of authority has no personal liability on the contract. It is the principal and the third person who may each sue the other in the event of a breach. A person purporting to act as an agent for a principal warrants by implication that there is an existing principal with legal capacity and that the principal has authorized the agent to act. The person acting as an agent is liable for any loss caused the third person for breach of these warranties. An agent of a partially disclosed or an undisclosed principal is a party to the contract with the

third person. The agent may enforce the contract against the third person and is liable for its breach. To avoid problems of interpretation, an agent should execute a contract "Principal, by Agent." Agents are liable for harm caused third persons by their fraudulent, malicious, or negligent acts.

An undisclosed or a partially disclosed principal is liable to a third person on a simple contract made by an authorized agent. When a third person makes payment to an authorized agent, it is deemed paid to the principal.

A principal or an employer is vicariously liable under

the doctrine of *respondeat superior* for the torts of an agent or an employee committed within the scope of authority or the course of employment. The principal or the employer may also be liable for some crimes committed in the course of employment. An owner is not liable for torts caused by an independent contractor to third persons or their property unless the work given to the independent contractor is inherently hazardous.

A salesperson is ordinarily an agent whose authority is limited to soliciting offers (orders) from third persons and transmitting them to the principal. The principal is not bound until he or she accepts the order. The customer may withdraw an offer at any time prior to acceptance.

QUESTIONS AND CASE PROBLEMS

1. What social forces are affected by the rule that an agent receiving an overpayment is not liable for that amount when the payment was received in ignorance of the mistake and was remitted to the principal?

2. Myles Murphy was appointed by Cy Sinden, a famous developer, to purchase land for a shopping center near the intersection of I-95 and Route 1. Mary Mason, the property owner, contracted with Murphy for the sale of the property. Because of an economic downturn, Sinden was unable to provide the planned behind-the-scenes financing for the venture, and the contract was not performed. Mason's real estate experts determined that she lost $2 million because of the breach of contract. Mason also discovered that Sinden was "behind the deal." If Mason elects to sue Sinden, who turns out to be unable to pay the judgment because of the collapse of his business "empire," can she later bring suit against Murphy?

3. Compare a third-party beneficiary contract with a contract made by an agent on behalf of an undisclosed principal.

4. What is the justification for the doctrine of *respondeat superior*?

5. Compare the liability of an agent's undisclosed principal to a third person on (a) a promissory note and (b) an oral contract.

6. Mills Electric Co. signed a contract with S&S Horticulture Architects, a two-person landscaping partnership operated by Sullivan and Smyth, to maintain the grounds and flowers at the Mills Electric Co. plant in Jacksonville, Florida. Mills checked references of S&S and found the company to be highly reputable. The contract set forth that S&S would select the flowers for each season and would determine when to maintain the lawns so long as the lawns were properly maintained. The contract called for payments to be made to S&S on the first workday of each month, and the contract stipulated that "nothing herein shall make S&S an agent of the company." The contract also required that S&S personnel wear uniforms identifying them as employees of S&S. S&S had other accounts, but the large Mills Electric plant took up most of its time. While working on a terraced area near the visitors' entrance to the plant, Sullivan lost control of his large commercial mower, and the mower struck Gillespie, a plant visitor, causing her serious injury. A witness heard Sullivan apologizing to Gillespie and saying that "running that mower on the terrace is a two-person job." Gillespie brought suit against Mills Electric Co., contending Mills should be held vicariously liable. Decide.

7. A.D. McLeod contacted Thompson's agent and agreed that certain property would be leased for a period of two years at a rental of $700 per month for the first year and $800 per month for the second year. The first month's rent was paid with McLeod's personal check. McLeod and his associates manufactured mattresses on the premises under the trademark Sleep, and the business was incorporated as Sleep System Inc. After some six months of operation during which the rent was paid by the corporation, McLeod informed Thompson that he had been "kicked out" of the company. When the subsequent rent was not paid, Thompson sued McLeod for the back rent. McLeod alleged that Thompson knew or should have known that McLeod was acting as an agent of Sleep System Inc. and that after he was "kicked out" of the company, it should have been very clear that he would no longer be responsible for rent. Thompson responded that if McLeod were an agent, he had an obligation to disclose that he was acting in a representative capacity when the lease was made, not six months later. Decide. [*McLeod v Thompson* (Ala Civ App) 615 So 2d 90]

8. On July 11, 1984, José Padilla was working as a vacation-relief route salesperson for Frito-Lay. He testified that he made a route stop at Sal's Beverage Shop, where he was told by Mrs. Ramos that she was dissatisfied with Frito-Lay service and no longer wanted its products in the store. He asked if there was any-

thing he could do to change her mind. She said no and told him to pick up his merchandise. He took one company-owned merchandise rack to his van and was about to pick up another rack when Mr. Ramos said that the rack had been given to him by the regular route salesperson. Padilla said the route salesperson had no authority to give away Frito-Lay racks. A confrontation occurred over the rack, and Padilla pushed Mr. Ramos against the cash register, injuring Ramos's back. Frito-Lay has a company policy, clearly communicated to all employees, that prohibits them from getting involved in any type of physical confrontation with a customer. Frito-Lay contended that Padilla was not acting within the course and scope of his employment when the pushing incident took place and that the company was therefore not liable to Ramos. Ramos contended that Frito-Lay was responsible for the acts of its employee Padilla. [*Frito-Lay Inc. v Ramos* (Tex App) 770 SW2d 887]

9. Jason Lasseigne, a Little League baseball player, was seriously injured at a practice session when he was struck on the head by a poorly thrown baseball from a team member, Todd Landry. The league was organized by American Legion Post 38. Claude Cassel and Billy Johnson were the volunteer coaches of the practice session. The Lasseignes brought suit on behalf of Jason against Post 38, claiming that the coaching was negligent and that Post 38 was vicariously liable for the harm caused by such negligence. Post 38 contended that it had no right to control the work of the volunteer coaches or the manner in which practices were conducted and as a result should not be held vicariously liable for the actions of the coaches. Decide. [*Lasseigne v American Legion Post* 38, (La App) 543 So 2d 1111]

10. Moritz, a guest at the Pines Hotel, was sitting in the lobby when Brown, a hotel employee, dropped a heavy vacuum cleaner on her knee. When she complained, he insulted her and hit her with his fist, knocking her unconscious. She sued the hotel for damages. Was the hotel liable? [*Moritz v Pines Hotel, Inc.* (App Div) 383 NYS2d 704]

11. Steve Diezel, an employee of Island City Flying Service in Key West, Florida, stole a General Electric Credit Corp. (GECC) aircraft and crashed the plane while attempting to take off. GECC brought suit against Island City on the theory that it had negligently hired Diezel as an employee and was therefore legally responsible for Diezel's act of theft. Diezel had a military prison record as a result of a drug offense and had been fired by Island City twice previously but was immediately reinstated each time. Island City claimed that the evidence was insufficient to establish that it had been negligent in employing Diezel. Decide. [*Island City Flying Service v General Electric* (Fla) 585 So 2d 274]

12. The Bay State Harness Horse Racing and Breeding Association conducted horse races at a track where music for patrons was supplied by an independent contractor hired by the association. Some of the music played was subject to a copyright held by Famous Music Corp. The playing of that music was a violation of the copyright unless royalties were paid to Famous Music. No royalties were paid, and Famous Music sued the association, which raised the defense that the violation had been committed by an independent contractor specifically instructed not to play Famous Music's copyrighted material. Decide. [*Famous Music Corp. v Bay State Harness Horse Racing and Breeding Association, Inc.*, 554 F2d 1213 (1st Cir)]

13. Steven Trujillo, told by the assistant door manager of Cowboys Bar "to show up to work tonight in case we need you as a doorman," came to the bar that evening wearing a jacket with the bar logo on it. Trujillo "attacked" Rocky Medina in the parking lot of the bar, causing him serious injury. Prior to working for Cowboys, Trujillo was involved in several fights at that bar and in its parking lot and Cowboys knew of these matters. Medina sued Cowboys on two theories of liability: (1) *respondeat superior* and (2) negligent hiring of Trujillo. Cowboys' defense was that *respondeat superior* theory should be dismissed because the assault was clearly not within the course of Trujillo's employment. Concerning the negligent hiring theory, Cowboys asserted that Trujillo was not on duty that night as a doorman. Decide. [*Medina v Graham's Cowboys Inc.* (NM App) 827 P2d 859]

14. Neal Rubin, while driving his car in Chicago, inadvertently blocked the path of a Yellow Cab Co. taxi driven by Robert Ball, causing the taxi to swerve and hit Rubin's car. Angered by Rubin's driving, Ball got out of his cab and hit Rubin on the head and shoulders with a metal pipe. Rubin sued Yellow Cab Co. for the damages caused by this beating, contending that the employer was vicariously liable for the beating under the doctrine of *respondeat superior* because the beating occurred in furtherance of the employer's business, which was to obtain fares without delay. The company argued that Ball's beating of Rubin was not an act undertaken to further the employer's business. Is the employer liable under respondeat superior? [*Rubin v Yellow Cab Co.* (Ill App) 507 NE2d 114]

15. Brazilian & Colombian Co. (B&C), a food broker, ordered 40 barrels of olives from Mawer-Gulden-

Annis, Inc. (MGA). MGA's shipping clerk was later told to make out the bill of lading to B&C's customer Pantry Queen; the olives were shipped directly to Pantry Queen. Eight days after delivery the president of B&C wrote MGA to give it the name of its principal, Pantry Queen, and advised MGA to bill the principal directly. Pantry Queen was unable to pay for the olives, and MGA sued B&C for payment. B&C contended that it was well known to MGA that B&C was a food broker (agent) and the olives were shipped directly to the principal by MGA. It stated that as an agent it was not a party to the contract and was thus not liable. Decide. [*Mawer-Gulden-Annis, Inc. v Brazilian & Colombian Coffee Co.* (Ill App) 199 NE2d 222]

CPA QUESTIONS

1. Frey entered into a contract with Cara Corp. to purchase televisions on behalf of Lux, Inc. Lux authorized Frey to enter into the contract in Frey's name without disclosing that Frey was acting on behalf of Lux. If Cara repudiates the contract, which of the following statements concerning liability on the contract is **not** correct?
   a. Frey may not hold Cara liable and obtain money damages.
   b. Frey may hold Cara liable and obtain specific performance.
   c. Lux may hold Cara liable upon disclosing the agency relationship with Frey.
   d. Cara will be free from liability to Lux if Frey fraudulently stated that he was acting on his own behalf.

   (11/87, Law, #24, 0662)

2. A principal will **not** be liable to a third party for a tort committed by an agent
   a. Unless the principal instructed the agent to commit the tort.
   b. Unless the tort was committed within the scope of the agency relationship.
   c. If the agency agreement limits the principal's liability for the agent's tort.
   d. If the tort is also regarded as a criminal act.

   (11/89, Law, #2, 0655)

3. Cox engaged Datz as her agent. It was mutually agreed that Datz would **not** disclose that he was acting as Cox's agent. Instead, he was to deal with prospective customers as if he were a principal acting on his own behalf. This he did and made several contracts for Cox. Assuming Cox, Datz, or the customer seeks to avoid liability on one of the contracts involved, which of the following statements is correct?
   a. Cox must ratify the Datz contracts in order to be held liable.
   b. Datz has **no** liability once he discloses that Cox was the real principal.
   c. The third party can avoid liability because he believed he was dealing with Datz as a principal.
   d. The third party may choose to hold either Datz or Cox liable.

   (5/86, Law, #60)

Regulation of Employment

OBJECTIVES

After studying this chapter, you should be able to

1. *Explain the contractual nature of the employment relationship;*
2. *Identify the five employer unfair labor practices;*
3. *Identify the nine union unfair labor practices;*
4. *State the four ways in which ERISA provides protection for the pension interests of employees;*
5. *Set forth the eligibility requirements for unemployment compensation;*
6. *Explain how the Occupational Safety and Health Act is designed to reach the goal of ensuring safe and healthful working conditions; and*
7. *List the three types of benefits provided by workers' compensation statutes.*

Employment law involves the law of contracts and the law established by lawmakers, courts, and administrative agencies.

A. THE EMPLOYMENT RELATIONSHIP

The relationship of an employer and an employee exists when, pursuant to an express or implied agreement of the parties, one person, the employee, undertakes to perform services or to do work under the direction and control of another, the employer, for compensation. In older cases, this relationship was called the master-servant relationship.

1. Characteristics of Relationship

An employee is hired to work under the control of the employer. An employee differs from an agent, who is to negotiate or make contracts with third persons on behalf of and under the control of a principal. However, a person may be both an employee and an agent for the other party. An employee also differs from an independent contractor, who is to perform a contract independent of, or free from, control by the other party.[1]

---

[1] *Ost v West Suburban Travelers Limousine, Inc.*, 88 F3d 435 (7th Cir 1996).

2. Creation of Employment Relationship

The relationship of employer and employee can be created only with the consent of both parties. Generally, the agreement of the parties is a contract. It is therefore subject to all of the principles applicable to contracts. The contract will ordinarily be express, but it may be implied, such as when the employer accepts the rendering of services that a reasonable person would recognize as being rendered with the expectation of receiving compensation.

(a) Individual Employment Contracts. As in contracts generally, both parties must assent to the terms of an employment contract. Subject to statutory restrictions, the parties are free to make a contract on any terms they wish.

(b) Collective Bargaining Contracts. Collective bargaining contracts govern the rights and obligations of employers and employees in many private and public areas of employment. Under collective bargaining, representatives of the employees bargain with a single employer or a group of employers for an agreement on wages, hours, and working conditions. The agreement worked out by the representatives of the employees, usually union officials, is generally subject to a ratification vote by the employees. Terms usually found in collective bargaining contracts are (1) identification of the work belonging exclusively to designated classes of employees; (2) wage and benefits clauses; (3) promotion and layoff clauses, which are generally tied in part to seniority; (4) a management's rights clause; and (5) a grievance procedure. A grievance procedure provides a means by which persons claiming that the contract was violated or that they were disciplined or discharged without just cause may have their cases decided by impartial labor arbitrators.

3. Duration and Termination of Employment Contract

In many instances, the employment contract does not state any time or duration. In such a case, it may be terminated at any time by either party. In contrast, the employment contract may expressly state that it shall last for a specified period of time; an example would be an individual's contract to work as general manager for five years. In some instances, a definite duration may be implied by the circumstances.

(a) Employment-at-Will Doctrine and Developing Exceptions. Ordinarily a contract of employment may be terminated in the same manner as any other contract. If it is to run for a definite period of time, the employer cannot terminate the contract at an earlier date without justification. If the employment contract does not have a definite duration, it is terminable at will. Under the **employment-at-will doctrine**, the employer has historically been allowed to terminate the employment contract at any time for any reason or for no reason.[2] Recent court decisions—and in some instances, statutes—have changed the rule in some states by limiting the power of the employer to discharge the employee. Some courts have carved out exceptions to the employment-at-will doctrine when the discharge violated an established public policy.

---

[2] *Brown v Hammond*, 810 F Supp 644 (ED Pa 1993).

CASE SUMMARY

"Restructuring" Your Accountant Out of Her Job Because She Won't Bend the Rules

Facts: Diana Mariani is a licensed certified public accountant. She was hired by Rocky Mountain Hospital and Medical Sources, doing business as Blue Cross and Blue Shield of Colorado (BCBS), as an at-will manager of accounting. Mariani complained to her supervisor about irregular practices in connection with a proposed merger between BCBS and other health care providers, and her supervisor ordered her to turn her work papers over to someone else. Soon thereafter she was told of her termination due to "a restructuring within the finance department." Mariani sued BCBS for wrongful discharge in violation of public policy, contending she was fired because she refused to go along with the employer's questionable accounting practices, which would result in her violating the state board of accountancy Rules of Professional Conduct. These rules mandate accuracy in financial reporting in order to establish public confidence in financial reporting. BCBS defended that the sources of public policy must be limited to constitutional or statutory provisions.

Decision: Judgment for Mariani. A professional person forced to choose between violating his or her ethical obligations and being terminated is placed in an intolerable position. Professional ethical codes may be a source of public policy for purposes of a claim of wrongful discharge in violation of public policy. Mariani presented evidence to satisfy a prima facie case, and the matter should be resolved by a jury. [*Rocky Mountain Hospital and Medical Sources v Mariani* (Colo) 916 P2d 519 (1996)]

Public policy exceptions are often made to the employment-at-will doctrine when an employee is discharged in retaliation for insisting that the employer comply with the state's food and drug act[3] or for filing a workers' compensation claim.[4] In some states, so-called whistleblower laws have been enacted to protect employees who disclose employer practices that endanger public health or safety.

The obligation to act in good faith and deal fairly has been held by some courts to bar an employer from terminating an at-will contract when done to benefit the employer financially at the expense of the employee. Thus, an employer may not discharge an at-will employee to avoid paying commissions or pension benefits to the employee.[5]

The right to fire an employee may be limited if contrary to
• public policy
• good faith and fair dealing
• written policies of the employer
• federal laws

The contract of employment may be construed to bar a discharge of the employee except for cause. If so construed, good cause would then be required for the discharge of an at-will employee. Written personnel policies used as guidelines for supervisors have also been interpreted as being part of the employment contract. These policies have thus been held to restrict the employer's right to discharge at-will employees without proof of good or just cause. Moreover, employee handbooks that provide for "proper notice and investigation" before termination may bar employers from terminating employees without providing such notice and an investigation.[6]

---

[3] *Sheets v Teddy's Frosted Foods* (Conn) 427 A2d 385 (1980); *Lynch v Blanke Baer Inc.* (Mo App) 901 SW2d 147 (1985).
[4] *Brigham v Dillon Companies, Inc.* (Kan) 935 P2d 1054 (1997).
[5] *Metcalf v Intermountain Gas Co.* (Idaho) 778 P2d 744 (1989).
[6] *Duldalao v St. Mary Nazareth Hospital Center* (Ill) 505 NE2d 314 (1987). But see *Varrallo v Hammond Inc.*, 94 P3d 842 (3d Cir 1996).

Call 1-800-Collect—Hurley Must Pay the Charges

Facts: Mary O'Brien was a nonmanagement, nonunion employee of New England Telephone and Telegraph Co. (NET). Her employment relationship was covered by NET's company-wide personnel manual, which applied to employees in her classification. The manual granted each employee the right to expect that she or he would be treated fairly and that, except for gross violation of rules, shortcomings would not be grounds for immediate discharge but would be handled in a "progressive" manner. The manual provided a grievance procedure, which allowed an employee to file a complaint about unfair treatment. After 16 years in other departments where she had an unblemished record, O'Brien went to work in the marketing department, headed by Edwin Hurley. After a year Hurley asked her to transfer, and she refused. She filed a grievance under the personnel manual, which upheld O'Brien's right to refuse a transfer. Thereafter Hurley became very hostile to her. He swore and yelled at her over small things in front of other people in the office on a regular basis, calling her the "Nitwit in the Northend," "The Blessed Mother," and "Looney Tunes." A witness heard him call O'Brien a "whore" and described the outburst as a temper tantrum making O'Brien cry. Hurley gave O'Brien's work to other employees and refused to let her do work she was trained to do. After some six years in the department Hurley gave some of O'Brien's secretarial work to a female salesperson. O'Brien believed that Hurley was spending time with the salesperson, and she confirmed her suspicions by making "hang up" telephone calls to Hurley's office and his home and to the salesperson's office and once to her home. She was afraid that the salesperson was taking over her job. The phone calls were traced to O'Brien, and she was fired. O'Brien did not file a grievance over her termination but sued NET for wrongful termination; she also sued Hurley for interference with her contractual relations with her employer. NET defended that O'Brien was an employee at will and therefore could be discharged without cause. Hurley defended that he did not intentionally interfere with O'Brien's employment.

Decision: The idea that an employer may ignore promises made in a personnel manual is in increasing disfavor in this country. NET's personnel manual granted O'Brien rights beyond those of an at-will employee, and they can be enforced. However, because she did not pursue her rights through the grievance procedure required by the manual, she lost these rights. Hurley's conduct toward O'Brien was motivated by actual malice and not related to NET's legitimate corporate interests. The jury was warranted in finding that Hurley's treatment of O'Brien caused her to commit the misconduct that led to her discharge. Judgment against Hurley for interference with O'Brien's employment relationship. [*O'Brien v New England Telephone and Telegraph Co.* (Mass) 664 NE2d 843 (1996)]

Other courts still follow the common law at-will rule because they believe that a court should not rewrite the contract of the parties to provide employee protection that was never intended. Some courts favor the view limiting the employer from making an at-will discharge but will not adopt such a rule by decision because it is felt that such a significant change should be made (if at all) by the legislature.[7]

If an employment contract provides that an employee can be fired only for "good cause" or "just cause," an at-will discharge will not be allowed.

(b) Justifiable Discharge. An employer may be justified in discharging an employee because of the employee's (1) nonperformance of duties, (2) misrepresentation or fraud in obtaining the employment, (3) disobedience of proper

---

[7] *D'Avino v Trachtenburg* (App Div) 539 NYS2d 755 (1989); *Fiammetta v St. Francis Hospital* (App Div) 562 NYS2d 777 (1990).

directions, (4) disloyalty, (5) theft or other dishonesty, (6) possession or use of drugs or intoxicants, (7) misconduct, or (8) incompetence.

Employers generally have the right to lay off employees because of economic conditions, including a lack of work. Such actions are sometimes referred to as reductions in force (RIFs).

Employers, however, must be very careful not to make layoffs based on age, for that is a violation of the Age Discrimination in Employment Act.

In some states, a "service letter" statute requires an employer on request to furnish to a discharged employee a letter stating the reason for the discharge.

4. Duties of the Employee

The duties of an employee are determined primarily by the contract of employment with the employer. The law also implies certain obligations.

(a) Services. Employees are under the duty to perform such services as may be required by the contract of employment.

(b) Trade Secrets. An employee may be given confidential trade secrets by the employer but must not disclose this knowledge to others. An agreement by the employee to refrain from disclosing trade secrets is binding. Even in the absence of such an agreement, an employee is prohibited from disclosing the trade secrets of the employer. If the employee violates this obligation, the employer may enjoin the use of the information by the employee and by any person to whom it has been disclosed by the employee.

Former employees who are competing with their former employer may be enjoined from using information about suppliers and customers that they obtained while employees when this information is of vital importance to the employer's business. Injunctive relief is denied, however, if the information is not important or not secret.

(c) Inventions. Employment contracts commonly provide that an employer will own any invention or discovery made by an employee, whether during work hours, after work hours, or for a period of one or two years after leaving the employment. In the absence of an express or implied agreement to the contrary, the inventions of an employee usually belong to the employee. This is true even though the employee used the time and property of the employer in the discovery. In this case, however, the employer has what is known as a shop right to use the invention without cost in its operations.

5. Rights of the Employee

The rights of an employee are determined by the contract of employment and by the law as declared by courts, lawmakers, and administrative agencies.

Employees who successfully sue for unpaid wages are entitled to attorney fees and may be awarded statutory penalties for negligent or bad-faith failure to pay the wages.

(a) Compensation. The rights of an employee with respect to compensation are governed in general by the same principles that apply to the compensation of an agent. In the absence of an agreement to the contrary, when an employee is discharged, whether for cause or not, the employer must pay wages to the expiration of the last pay period.[8] State statutes commonly authorize employees to sue employers for wages improperly withheld and to recover penalties and attorney fees. In addition to hourly wages, payments due for vacations and certain bonuses are considered "wages" under state statutes.[9]

CASE SUMMARY

A "Whopper" in Penalty Wages

Facts: Diane Garrison started her employment with Burger King on October 6, 1978. She resigned from this employment as of July 30, 1987. When her final paycheck did not contain payment for her accumulated vacation benefits, she made a formal demand for this pay and thereafter initiated a lawsuit. Burger King defended that Garrison had not worked the necessary "service year" qualifying time.

Decision: Judgment for Garrison. Burger King failed to give employees notice of its alleged "service year" policy. Penalty wages are properly assessed when an employer arbitrarily refuses to pay wages. Burger King's conduct constituted an impermissible forfeiture of earned wages. Garrison is entitled to her vacation wages, plus penalty wages equal to 90 days' wages and attorney fees. Penalty wages punish the employer for not paying full wages and make it worthwhile for a worker to pursue her just compensation. *[Garrison v Burger King Corp. (La App) 537 So 2d 834 (1989)]*

(b) Federal Wage and Hour Law. Workers at enterprises engaged in interstate commerce are covered by the Fair Labor Standards Act (FLSA),[10] popularly known as the Wage and Hour Act. These workers cannot be paid less than a specified minimum wage.

CASE SUMMARY

What is a "Willful" Violation?

Facts: An action against an employer for violating the Fair Labor Standards Act must be brought within two years unless the violation was willful, in which case it may be brought within three years. McLaughlin, the secretary of labor, brought suit against the Richland Shoe Company for failing to pay the minimum wage. Richland claimed that the suit was barred because more than two years had elapsed. McLaughlin claimed that the violation was willful, in which case the action was properly brought because three years had not expired. The parties disagreed as to what proof was required to establish that the violation was "willful."

Decision: To be "willful" within the statute, the violation must be intentional or made with reckless indifference as to whether the statute has been satisfied. Because the case had not been tried on the basis of this standard, the case was remanded to the lower court to determine the matter in the light of the new definition of willful. *[McLaughlin v Richland Shoe Co., 486 US 128 (1988)]*

The FLSA has been amended to cover domestic service workers, including housekeepers, cooks, and full-time baby sitters. Executive, administrative, and professional employees and outside salespersons are exempt from both the minimum wage and overtime provisions of the law.

---

8 *Lorentz v Coblentz* (La App) 600 So 2d 1376 (1992).
9 *Knutson v Snyder Industries, Inc.* (Neb) 436 NW2d 496 (1989).
10 PL 75-718, 52 Stat 1060, 29 USC §§ 201 et seq.

(1) Subminimum Wage Provisions. The FLSA allows for the employment of full-time students at institutions of higher education at wage rates below the statutory minimum. Also, individuals whose productive capacity is impaired by age, physical or mental deficiency, or injury may be employed at less than the minimum wage to prevent the curtailment of work opportunities for these individuals. In these cases, however, a special certificate is needed by the employer from the Department of Labor's Wage and Hour Division, which has offices throughout the United States.

(2) Wage Issues. Deductions made from wages as a result of cash or merchandise shortages and deductions for tools of the trade are not legal if they reduce wages below the minimum wage. An employer's requiring employees to provide uniforms or tools of their own is a violation of the law to the extent that the expenses for these items reduce wages below the minimum wage.

(3) Overtime Pay. Overtime must be paid at a rate of one and a half times the employee's regular rate of pay for each hour worked in excess of 40 hours in a work week.

(4) Child Labor Provisions. The FLSA child labor provisions are designed to protect educational opportunities for minors and prohibit their employment in occupations detrimental to their health and well-being. The FLSA restricts hours of work for minors under 16 and lists hazardous occupations too dangerous for minors to perform.

ETHICS & THE LAW

Sports Illustrated cover model Kathy Ireland has a line of swimsuits and active wear at Kmart. Actress Connie Selleca has a line of clothing at Montgomery Ward. Actress Jaclyn Smith has had her clothing line at Kmart since 1985. Weight-loss guru Richard Simmons has his own line of clothing. Chicago Bulls' superstar Michael Jordan has his own signature pair of basketball shoes as well as athletic clothing with Nike. Talk-show host Kathie Lee Gifford has her line of clothing through Wal-Mart.

This combination of stars with clothing serves both the star and the sponsors well. The stars' endorsements and appearances in ads attract attention to products in an increasingly crowded market.

In June 1996, labor activists revealed to the press that Ms. Gifford's clothing was manufactured in Honduran sweatshops, where the pay was 31 cents per hour and children were employed extensively. Within weeks of the Gifford disclosures, activists revealed that Nike used factories in Indonesia that paid wages of $2.23 per day. Such low labor costs allowed Nike to produce its Pegasus running shoe for $18.75; it sells for $75.

The final revelation in the stream of attacks by labor activists was that Ms. Gifford's clothing was also manufactured in sweatshops in the United States, where workers are paid on a per item basis. Six dollars is generally the payment for completing a suit. Suits bearing the Ann Taylor and J.C. Penney labels were sewn by Nancy Penaloza for $6 each, selling at retail for $120. Actress Cheryl Tiegs, with a clothing line at Sears, said, "To please consumers, you have to keep lowering prices-lower and lower and lower."

Michael Jordan, when confronted with the news that some workers in the plants used by Nike were 11 years old and made 14¢ per hour, said, "I don't know the complete situation . . . . Hopefully, Nike will do the right thing."

What is the "right thing"? Should Nike not use the factories? Aren't companies just minimizing costs for shareholders? None of the companies has violated any labor laws with these sweatshops. Is it ethical to use them? Would inspections of their contractors help?

Some companies, such as Wal-Mart, Nordstrom, and Levi Strauss, have now signed labor codes of ethics that prohibit the use of child labor anywhere in the world. Should companies sign such a code? What do they accomplish by doing so?

B.   LABOR RELATIONS LAWS

Even if employers are not presently unionized, they are subject to certain obligations under federal labor relations law. It is important to both unionized and nonunionized employers to know their rights and obligations under the National Labor Relations Act (NLRA).[11] Employee rights and obligations are also set forth in this act. The Labor-Management Reporting and Disclosure Act regulates internal union affairs.[12]

6.   The National Labor Relations Act

The National Labor Relations Act, passed in 1935, was based on the federal government's power to regulate interstate commerce granted in Article 1, Section 8, of the Constitution. Congress, in enacting this law, explained that its purpose was to remove obstructions to commerce caused by employers who denied their employees the right to join unions and refused to accept collective bargaining.[13] Congress stated that these obstructions resulted in depression of wages, poor working conditions, and diminution of purchasing power.

Section 7 of the amended NLRA is the heart of the act, stating in part that "[e]mployees shall have the right to self organization . . . to bargain collectively through representatives of their own choosing and to engage in other concerted activities for the purpose of collective bargaining or other mutual aid or protection . . . and shall have the right to refrain from such activities . . . ."

Section 8 of the NLRA contains employer and union unfair labor practices, set forth in Figure 41-1, and authorizes the National Labor Relations Board to conduct proceedings to stop such practices.

The act applies to private-sector employers with gross incomes of $500,000 or more. The Railway Labor Act applies to employees of railroad and air carriers.

7.   National Labor Relations Board

Administration of the NLRA is entrusted to the five-member National Labor Relations Board (NLRB or Board) and the general counsel of the Board. The

---

11   29 USC §§ 141-169. Note that in the *Lechmere* and *Transportation Management* cases presented in this section, the employers were not unionized.
12   29 USC §§ 401-531.
13   NLRA § 1, 29 USC § 141.

Unfair Labor Practices Charges Against Employers	Section of the NLRA*
1. Restrain or coerce employees in the exercise of their rights under Section 7; threat of reprisals or promise of benefits	8(a)(1); 8(c)
2. Dominate or interfere with the formation or administration of a labor organization or contribute financial or other support to it.	8(a)(2) 8(a)(2)
3. Discriminate in regard to hire or tenure of employment or any term or condition of employment in order to encourage or discourage membership in any labor organization.	8(a)(3)
4. Discharge or otherwise discriminate against employees because they have given testimony under the Act.	8(a)(4)
5. Refuse to bargain collectively with representatives of its employees.	8(a)(5)

Unfair Labor Practices Charges Against Unions	Section of the NLRA
1. Restrain or coerce employees in the exercise of their rights under Section 7.	8(b)(1)(A)
2. Restrain or coerce an employer in the selection of its representatives.	8(b)(1)(B)
3. Cause or attempt to cause an employer to discriminate against an employee.	8(b)(2)
4. Refuse to bargain collectively with the employer.	8(b)(3)
5. Require employees to pay excessive fees for membership.	8(b)(5)
6. Engage in "featherbed practices" of seeking pay for services not performed.	8(b)(6)
7. Use secondary boycotts (banned, except for publicity proviso).	8(b)(4)
8. Allow recognitional and organizational picketing by an uncertified union.	8(b)(7)
9. Enter into "hot cargo" agreements, except for construction and garment industries	8(e)

* 29 U.S.C. § 151.

FIGURE 41-1
Employer and Union Unfair Labor Practices Charges

general counsel is responsible for investigating and prosecuting all unfair labor practice cases. The five-member Board's major function is to decide unfair labor practice cases brought before it by the general counsel.

The Board is also responsible for conducting representation and decertification elections. This responsibility is delegated to the regional directors of the 32 regional offices located throughout the United States, who (1) determine the appropriateness of each proposed bargaining unit for the purpose of collective bargaining, (2) investigate petitions for the certification or decertification of unions, and (3) conduct elections to determine the choice of the majority of those employees voting in the election. Should a majority of the employees voting select a union, the NLRB will certify that union as the exclusive representative of all employees within the unit for the purpose of bargaining with the employer to obtain a contract with respect to wages, hours, and other conditions of employment.

8. Election Conduct

The Board has promulgated preelection rules restricting electioneering activities so that the election will express the true desire of employees. The NLRA prohibits employer interference or coercion during the preelection period. The act also prohibits during this period employer statements that contain threats of reprisal or promises of benefits.

   The Board prohibits all electioneering activities at polling places and has formulated a "24-hour rule," which prohibits both unions and employers from making speeches to captive audiences within 24 hours of an election. The rationale is to preserve free elections and prevent any party from obtaining undue advantage.

9. Union Activity on Private Property

While section 7 of the NLRA gives employees the statutory right to self-organization, employers have the undisputed right to make rules to maintain discipline in their establishments. Generally speaking, employers may prohibit union solicitation by employees during work periods. During nonworking time, employers may prohibit activity and communications only for legitimate efficiency and safety reasons and only if the prohibitions are not manifestly intended to impede employees' exercise of their rights under the law. Nonunion employers, moreover, may not refuse to interview or retain union members because of their union membership. And even if a union pays an individual working for a nonunion employer to help organize the company, that individual is still protected under the NLRA.[14]

   An employer may validly post its property against all nonemployee solicitations, including distribution of union literature, if reasonable efforts by the union through other available channels of communication would enable it to reach the employees with its message.

CASE SUMMARY

The Supreme Court Is Always Right

Facts: Lechmere, Inc., owned and operated a retail store located in a shopping plaza in Newington, a suburb of Hartford, Connecticut. Lechmere was also part owner of the plaza's parking lot, which was separated from a public highway by a 46-foot-wide grassy strip. Almost all of the strip was public property. In a campaign to organize Lechmere employees, nonemployee union organizers from Local 919 of the United Food and Commercial Workers placed handbills on the windshields of cars parked in the employees' part of the parking lot. After Lechmere denied the organizers access to the lot, they picketed from the grassy strip. In addition, they were able to contact directly some 20 percent of the employees. The union filed an unfair labor practice charge with the Board, alleging that Lechmere had violated the NLRA by barring the organizers from its property. An administrative law judge ruled in the union's favor. The Board affirmed, and the court of appeals enforced the Board's order. The matter was heard by the Supreme Court.

---

14 *NLRB v Town & Country Electric Inc.*, 116 S Ct 450 (1995).

> **Decision**: Judgment for Lechmere. A two-stage test is used in evaluating the accommodation between the employees' right to learn of the advantages of unionization from outside union organizers and an employer's property rights. Stage 1 considers whether the outsiders have reasonable access to employees off the employer's property. Stage 2 applies if the access is infeasible. In such a case the employer's property rights must yield to the extent needed to communicate information on organizational rights. The Court majority determined that the outsiders had reasonable access from the grassy strip. The dissent believed that holding up signs from the grassy strip was not sufficient to learn of advantages of unionization. [*Lechmere, Inc. v NLRB,* 502 US 527 (1992)]

10. Firing Employees for Union Activity

Although employers and supervisors often feel betrayed by individual employees who take leadership roles in forming organizations, the NLRA prohibits discrimination against such employees because of their union activity.

The NLRB has found evidence of discrimination against active union supporters where the employer

1.   discharges on the strength of past misdeeds that were condoned,
2.   neglects to give customary warnings prior to discharge,
3.   discharges for a rule generally unenforced,
4.   applies disproportionately severe punishment to union supporters, or
5.   effects layoffs in violation of seniority status with disproportionate impact on union supporters.

The NLRA preserves the right of the employer to maintain control over the workforce in the interest of discipline, efficiency, and pleasant and safe customer relations. Employees, on the other hand, have the right to be free from coercive discrimination resulting from union activity.

At times these two rights may collide. For example, an employee may be discharged for apparently two reasons: (1) violation of a valid company rule and (2) union activity. The former is given by the employer as the reason for termination; the latter remains unstated on the employer's part, causing the filing of a section 8(a)(3) unfair labor practice charge against the employer. These are known as *dual motive cases*. The general counsel must present on behalf of the dismissed employee a prima facie case that such protected conduct as union activity was a motivating factor in the dismissal. After this showing, the burden shifts to the employer, who must prove that the employee would have been dismissed for legitimate business reasons even absent the protected conduct.

CASE SUMMARY

The Sam Santillo Story

Facts: Prior to his discharge, Sam Santillo was a bus driver for Transportation Management Corp. On March 19, Santillo talked to officials of the Teamster's Union about organizing the drivers who worked with him. Over the next four days Santillo discussed with his fellow drivers the possibility of joining the Teamsters and distributed authorization cards. On the night of March 23, George Patterson, who supervised Santillo and the other drivers, told one of the drivers that he had heard of Santillo's activities. Patterson referred to Santillo as two-faced and promised to get even with him. Later that evening Patterson talked to Ed West, who was also a bus driver. Patterson asked, "What's with Sam and the Union?" Patterson said that he took Santillo's actions personally, recounted several favors he had done for Santillo, and added that he would remember Santillo's activities when Santillo again asked for a favor. On Monday, March 26, Santillo was discharged. Patterson told Santillo that he was being fired for leaving his keys in the bus and taking unauthorized breaks. Santillo filed charges with the Board, and the general counsel issued a complaint, contending that Santillo was discharged because of his union activities in distributing authorization cards to fellow employees. The evidence revealed that the practice of leaving keys in buses was commonplace among company employees and the company tolerated the practice of taking coffee breaks. The company had never taken disciplinary action against an employee for the behavior in question.

Decision: Judgment for Santillo and the NLRB. The general counsel established a prima facie case by showing that Santillo was involved in union-organizing activities just prior to his discharge. The employer did not meet its burden of proving that Santillo was fired for a legitimate business reason. The infractions involved were commonplace, and no discipline had ever been issued to any employee previously. The reasons given by the company were pretextual. Santillo would not have been fired had the employer not considered his effort to establish a union. [*NLRB v Transportation Management Corp.,* 462 US 393 (1983)]

11. Duty of Employer to Bargain Collectively

Once a union wins a representative election, the Board certifies the union as the exclusive bargaining representative of the employees. The employer then has the obligation under the NLRA to bargain with the union in good faith over wages, hours, and working conditions. These matters are *mandatory subjects of bargaining* and include seniority provisions, promotions, layoff and recall provisions, no-strike no-lockout clauses, and grievance procedures. Employers also have an obligation to bargain about the "effects" of the shutdown of a part of a business[15] and may have an obligation to bargain over the decision to relocate bargaining unit work to other plants.[16]

Permissive subjects of bargaining are those over which an employer's refusal to bargain is not a section 8(a)(5) unfair labor practice. Examples are the required use of union labels, internal union affairs, union recognition clauses, and benefits for already retired workers.

12. Right to Work

The NLRA allows states to enact *right to work laws*. These laws restrict unions and employers from negotiating clauses in their collective bargaining agreements that make union membership compulsory.[17]

Advocates of such laws contend that compulsory union membership is contrary to the First Amendment right of freedom of association. Unions have attacked these laws as unfair because unions must represent all employees, and in right to work states where a majority of employees vote for union representation, nonunion employees receive all the benefits of collective bargaining contracts without paying union dues.

---

15 *First National Maintenance v NLRB,* 452 US 666 (1981).
16 *Dubuque Packing Co. and UFCWIU, Local 150A,* 303 NLRB 66 (1991).
17 Right to work statutes declare unlawful any agreement that denies persons the right to work because of nonmembership in a union or the failure to pay dues to a union as a condition of employment. These laws have been adopted in Alabama, Arizona, Arkansas, Florida, Georgia, Idaho, Iowa, Kansas, Louisiana, Mississippi, Nebraska, Nevada, North Carolina, North Dakota, South Carolina, South Dakota, Tennessee, Texas, Utah, Virginia, and Wyoming.

13. Strike and Picketing Activities

If the parties reach an impasse in the negotiation process for a collective bargaining agreement, a union may call a strike and undertake picketing activity to enforce its bargaining demands. Strikers in such a situation are called **economic strikers**. Although the strike activity is legal, the employers may respond by hiring temporary or permanent replacement workers.

(a) Rights of Strikers. Economic strikers who unconditionally apply for reinstatement at a time when their positions are filled by permanent replacements are not entitled to return to work at the end of the economic strike. They are, however, entitled to full reinstatement when positions become available.

CASE SUMMARY

Avoiding the Sack—The Pilots Returned Before Their Positions Were Filled

Facts: Striking pilots of Eastern Airlines made an unconditional offer to return to work on November 22, 1989. As of that date some 227 new-hire replacement pilots were in training and had not obtained certificates from the Federal Aviation Administration permitting them to fly revenue flights. The striking pilots contended that the trainees were not permanent replacement pilots on the date they offered to go back to work because the trainees could not lawfully fly revenue flights. Eastern contended that the new-hire pilots were permanent employees and as such should not be displaced.

Decision: The pilots' positions were not filled by permanent replacements at the time the striking pilots unconditionally applied to return to work. The new-hire replacement pilots were not qualified to fill the positions at that time. Giving preference to trainees over returning strikers would discourage employees from exercising their right to strike. [*Eastern Airlines Inc. v Airline Pilots Association International*, 970 F2d 722 (11th Cir 1990)]

Strikers responsible for misconduct while out on strike may be refused reemployment by the employer.

When employees strike to protest an unfair labor practice of an employer, such as the firing of an employee for union organizing activity, these unfair labor practice strikers have a right to return to their jobs immediately at the end of the strike. This right exists even if the employer has hired permanent replacements.

(b) Picketing. Placing persons outside a business at the site of a labor dispute so that they may, by signs or banners, inform the public of the existence of a labor dispute is called **primary picketing**. Such picketing is legal. Should the picketing employees mass together in great numbers in front of the gates of the employer's facility to effectively shut down the entrances, such coercion is called **mass picketing** and is illegal. **Secondary picketing** is picketing an employer with whom a union has no dispute to persuade the employer to stop doing business with a party to the dispute. Secondary picketing is generally illegal under the NLRA. An exception exists for certain product picketing at supermarkets or other multiproduct retail stores provided it is limited to asking customers not to purchase the struck product at the neutral employer's store.[18]

14. Regulation of Internal Union Affairs

To ensure the honest and democratic administration of unions, Congress passed the Labor-Management Reporting and Disclosure Act (LMRDA).[19] Title IV of the LMRDA establishes democratic standards for all elections for union offices, including

1. secret ballots in local union elections,
2. opportunity for members to nominate candidates,
3. advance notice of elections,
4. observers at polling and at ballot-counting stations for all candidates,
5. publication of results and preservation of records for one year,
6. prohibition of any income from dues or assessments to support candidates for union office, and
7. advance opportunity for each candidate to inspect the membership name and address lists.

C. PENSION PLANS AND FEDERAL REGULATION

The Employees Retirement Income Security Act (ERISA)[20] was adopted in 1974 to protect employee pensions.

15. ERISA

The act sets forth fiduciary standards and requirements for vesting, funding, and termination insurance.

(a) Fiduciary Standards and Reporting. Persons administering a pension fund must handle it so as to protect the interest of employees.[21]

CASE SUMMARY

Placing a Conglomerate's Money-Losing Eggs in One Financially Rickety Basket

Facts: Charles Howe and others worked for Massey-Ferguson, Inc., a wholly owned subsidiary of Varity Corporation. These employees were beneficiaries of Massey-Ferguson's self-funded employee welfare benefit plan, an ERISA-protected plan that Massey-Ferguson itself administered. In the mid-1980s Varity became concerned that some of Massey-Ferguson's money-losing divisions were losing too much money, and it developed a business plan to deal with the problem that amounted to placing many of Varity's money-losing eggs in one financially rickety basket. It called for a transfer of Massey-Ferguson's money-losing divisions, along

---

18 *NLRB v Fruit and Vegetable Packers, Local 760* (Tree Fruits Inc.), 377 US 58 (1964); but see *NLRB v Retail Clerks, Local 1001* (Safeco Title Ins. Co.), 477 US 607 (1980).
19 29 USC §§ 401–531.
20 PL 93-406, 88 Stat 829, 29 USC §§ 1001–1381.
21 *John Hancock Mutual Life Ins. Co. v Harris Trust*, 510 US 86 (1993).

with other debts, to a newly created, separately incorporated subsidiary called Massey Combines. The plan foresaw the possibility that Massey Combines would fail. But it viewed such a failure, from Varity's business perspective, as closer to a victory than to a defeat because failure would eliminate several poorly performing divisions and eradicate various debts that Varity would transfer to Massey Combines. Among the obligations that Varity hoped the reorganization would eliminate were those arising from the benefits plan's promises to pay medical and other nonpension benefits to employees of Massey-Ferguson's money-losing divisions. To persuade the employees of the failing divisions to accept the change of employer and benefits, Varity called them together at a special meeting and talked to them about its likely financial viability and the security of their employee benefits. The thrust of Varity's remarks was that the employees' benefits would remain secure if they voluntarily transferred to Massey Combines. As Varity knew, however, the reality was very different. The evidence showed that Massey Combines was insolvent from the day of its creation and that it hid its $46 million negative net worth by overvaluing its assets and underestimating its liabilities. After Massey Combines went into receivership, the employees lost their benefits, and Howe and others sued for reinstatement of the old plan. Varity defended that individuals did not have a right to bring an ERISA lawsuit for individual relief. It also contended that when its managers talked to employees at the special meeting, they did so in their capacity as employer and not as plan administrators.

Decision: Judgment for Howe and the other employees restoring plan benefits. When an employer runs a benefits plan and its managers or agents, regardless of their job titles, talk about those benefits to employees, painting a false picture of security to induce them to transfer to the new company by saying "your benefits are secure," they are fiduciaries, and their breach of fiduciary duties in making false and misleading statements is binding on the employer. ERISA § 502(a)(3) authorizes lawsuits for individual equitable relief for breach of fiduciary duties. [*Varity Corp. v Howe*, 116 S Ct 1065 (1996)]

The fact that an employer contributed all or part of the money to the pension fund does not entitle the employer to use the fund as though it were still owned by the employer. Persons administering pension plans must make detailed reports to the secretary of labor.

(b) Vesting. Vesting is the right of an employee to pension benefits paid into a pension plan in the employee's name by the employer. Prior to ERISA, many pension plans did not vest accrued benefits until an employee had 20 to 25 years of service. Thus, an employee who was forced to terminate service after 18 years would not receive any pension rights or benefits at all. Under ERISA, employees' rights must be fully vested within five or seven years in accordance with the two vesting options available under the law.

In the past, it was common for pension plans to contain break-in-service clauses, whereby employees who left their employment for a period longer than one year for any reason other than an on-the-job injury lost pension eligibility rights. Under the Retirement Equity Act of 1984,[22] an individual can leave the workforce for up to five consecutive years and still retain eligibility for pension benefits.

(c) Funding. ERISA requires that employers make contributions to their pension funds on a basis that is actuarially determined so that the pension fund will be large enough to make the payments that will be required of it.

---

[22] PL 98-397, 29 USC § 1001.

The Pension Benefit Guaranty Corporation ensures that employees will receive their pension benefits.

(d) Termination Insurance. ERISA established an insurance plan to protect employees when an employer goes out of business. To provide this protection, the statute created a Pension Benefit Guaranty Corporation (PBGC). In effect, this corporation guarantees that employees will receive benefits in much the same way as the Federal Deposit Insurance Corporation protects bank depositors. The PBGC is financed by small payments made by employers for every employee covered by a pension plan.

(e) Enforcement. ERISA authorizes the secretary of labor and employees to bring court actions to compel the observance of statutory requirements.

D. UNEMPLOYMENT BENEFITS, FAMILY LEAVES, AND SOCIAL SECURITY

Generally, when employees are without work through no fault of their own, they are eligible for unemployment compensation benefits. Twelve-week maternity, paternity, or adoption leaves and family and medical leaves are available for qualifying employees. Social Security provides certain benefits, including retirement and disability benefits.

16. Unemployment Compensation

Unemployment compensation today is provided primarily through a federal-state system under the unemployment insurance provisions of the Social Security Act of 1935.[23] All of the states have laws that provide similar benefits, and the state agencies are loosely coordinated under the federal act. Agricultural employees, domestic employees, and state and local government employees are not covered by this federal-state system. Federal programs of unemployment compensation exist for federal civilian workers and former military service personnel. A separate federal unemployment program applies to railroad workers.

Unemployment benefits may be denied if the employee
• quits without cause
• is fired for misconduct
• refuses to take a new job with comparable pay.

(a) Eligibility. In most states, an unemployed person must be available for placement in a similar job and willing to take such employment at a comparable rate of pay. Full-time students generally have difficulty proving that they are available for work while they are still going to school.

CASE SUMMARY

Priority of Necessity: Work Comes Before School

Facts: Robert Evjen was full-time employee for Boise Cascade. At the same time, he was a full-time student at Chemata Community College. He was laid off as part of a general economy move by the employer. He applied for unemployment compensation. His claim was opposed on the ground that he was not available for work because he was going to school. The referee found that Robert never missed work in order to go to classes, that he could not afford to go to school without working, and that, in case of any conflict between work and school, work came first.

Decision: Judgment for Robert. To obtain unemployment benefits, an unemployed individual must prove, among other things, that he or she is "available for work" and is unable to obtain suit-

---

[23] 42 USC §§ 301-1397e.

> able work. A student's unavailability for work during school hours is contrary to the concept of "available for work," which requires availability for all shifts of suitable work. However, Robert's uncontroverted testimony that his education was secondary to his employment was sufficient to overcome either an inference or a presumption of nonavailability. He was available for work and therefore entitled to unemployment compensation. *[Evjen v Employment Agency, 22 Or App 372, 539 P2d 662 (1975)]*

If an employee quits a job without cause or is fired for misconduct, the employee is ordinarily disqualified from receiving unemployment compensation benefits.

For example, stealing property from an employer constitutes misconduct for which benefits will be denied. Moreover, an employee's refusal to complete the aftercare portion of an alcohol treatment program has been found to be misconduct connected with work, disqualifying the employee from benefits.

(b) Funding. Employers are taxed for unemployment benefits based on each employer's "experience rating" account. Thus, employers with a stable workforce with no layoffs, who therefore do not draw on the state unemployment insurance fund, pay lower tax rates. Employers whose experience ratings are higher pay higher rates. Motivated by the desire to avoid higher unemployment taxes, employers commonly challenge the state's payment of unemployment benefits to individuals whom they believe are not properly entitled to benefits.

17. Family and Medical Leaves of Absence

The Family and Medical Leave Act of 1993[24] (FMLA) entitles an eligible employee, whether male or female, to a total of 12 workweeks of unpaid leave during any 12-month period (1) because of the birth or adoption of the employee's son or daughter; (2) to care for the employee's spouse, son, daughter, or parent with a serious health condition; or (3) because of a serious health condition that makes the employee unable to perform the functions of his or her position. In the case of an employee's serious health condition or that of a covered family member, an employer may require the employee to use any accrued paid vacation, personal, medical, or sick leave toward any part of the 12-week leave provided by the act. When an employee requests leave because of the birth or adoption of a child, the employer may require the employee to use all available paid personal, vacation, and medical leave, but not sick leave, toward any FMLA leave.

To be eligible for FMLA leave, an employee must have been employed by a covered employer for at least 12 months and worked at least 1,250 hours during the 12-month period preceding the leave. Upon return from FMLA leave, the employee is entitled to be restored to the same or an equivalent position with equivalent pay and benefits.

18. Social Security

Employees and employers are required to pay Social Security taxes, which provide employees with four types of insurance protection-retirement benefits, disability

---

[24] 29 USC §§ 2601-2654.

benefits, life insurance benefits, and health insurance (Medicare). The federal Social Security Act established a federal program of aid for the aged, the blind, and the disabled. This is called the Supplemental Security Income (SSI) program. Payments are administered directly by the Social Security Administration, which became an independent government agency in 1995.

E.   EMPLOYEES' HEALTH AND SAFETY

The Occupational Safety and Health Act of 1970 (OSHA) was passed to assure every worker, so far as possible, safe and healthful working conditions and to preserve the country's human resources.[25] OSHA provides for (1) the establishment of safety and health standards and (2) effective enforcement of these standards and the other employer duties required by OSHA.

19. Standards

The secretary of labor has broad authority under OSHA to promulgate occupational safety and health standards.[26] Except in emergency situations, public hearings and publication in the *Federal Register* are required before the secretary can issue a new standard. Any person adversely affected may then challenge the validity of the standard in a U.S. court of appeals. The secretary's standards will be upheld if they are reasonable and supported by substantial evidence. The secretary must demonstrate a need for a new standard by showing that it is reasonably necessary to protect employees against a "significant risk" of material health impairment. The cost of compliance with new standards may run into billions of dollars. The secretary is not required to do a cost-benefit analysis for a new standard but must show that the standard is economically feasible.

20. Employer Duties

Employers have a "general duty" to furnish to each employee a place of employment that is free from hazards that are likely to cause death or serious physical injuries.

Employer record keeping required by OSHA has been a valuable aid in identifying areas of risk.

Employers are required by OSHA to maintain records of occupational illness and injuries if they result in death, loss of consciousness, or one or more lost workdays or if they require medical treatment other than first aid. Such records have proven to be a valuable aid in recognizing areas of risk. They have been especially helpful in identifying the presence of occupational illnesses.

21. Enforcement

The Occupational Safety and Health Administration (also identified as OSHA) is the agency within the Department of Labor that administers the act. OSHA has authority to conduct inspections and to seek enforcement action where there has been noncompliance. Worksite inspections are conducted when employer records indicate incidents involving fatalities or serious injuries. These inspections may also

25 29 USC §§ 651 et seq.
26 *Martin v OSHRC*, 499 US 144 (1991).

result from employee complaints. The act protects employees making complaints from employer retaliation. Employers have the right to require that an OSHA inspector secure a warrant before inspecting the employer's plant.

If OSHA issues a citation for a violation of workplace health or safety standards, the employer may challenge the citation before the Occupational Safety and Health Review Commission. Judicial review of a commission ruling is obtained before a U.S. court of appeals.

The Occupational Safety and Health Act provides that no employer shall discharge or in any manner discriminate against employees because they filed a complaint with OSHA, testified in any OSHA proceeding, or exercised any right afforded by the act.[27] A regulation issued by the secretary of labor under the act provides that if employees with no reasonable alternative refuse in good faith to expose themselves to a dangerous condition, they will be protected against subsequent discrimination. The secretary of labor may obtain injunctive and other appropriate relief in a U.S. district court against an employer who discriminates against employees for testifying or exercising any right under the act.

CASE SUMMARY

To Work or Not to Work? Empowering Employees to Refuse to Expose Themselves to Dangerous Duties

Facts: Virgil Deemer and Thomas Cornwell, employees at a Whirlpool Corporation plant, refused to comply with a supervisor's order that they perform maintenance work on certain mesh screens located some 20 feet above the plant floor. Twelve days before this incident, a fellow employee had fallen to his death from the screens. After their refusal to work on the screens, the men were ordered to stop work and leave the plant. They were not paid for the remaining six hours of their shift, and written reprimands for insubordination were placed in their employment files. The secretary of labor filed suit against Whirlpool, contending that Whirlpool's actions against Deemer and Cornwell constituted "discrimination" under the secretary's regulation and section 11(C)(1) of the act. Whirlpool contended that the regulation encouraged workers to engage in "self-help" and unlawfully permitted a "strike with pay."

Decision: Judgment against Whirlpool. The Occupational Safety and Health Act's "general duty" clause requires an employer to furnish a workplace free from hazards that are likely to cause death or serious injury to employees. OSHA inspectors cannot be present around the clock in every workplace to enforce this clause. Thus, each worker has the power to make a good-faith decision that there is danger. In the unusual circumstances Deemer and Cornwell faced, when in good faith and without reasonable alternatives they refused to expose themselves to the dangerous work on the mesh screens, the secretary's regulation protects them against subsequent discrimination by the employer for the refusal. The secretary's regulation is consistent with the act's "general duty" clause, and the employer violated this regulation when it placed reprimands in the personnel files of Deemer and Cornwell. [*Whirlpool v Marshall,* 445 US 1 (1980)]

---

22. State "Right-to-Know" Legislation

Laws that guarantee individual workers the "right to know" if there are hazardous substances in their workplaces have been enacted by many states in recent years. These laws commonly require an employer to make known to an employee's physician the chemical composition of certain workplace substances in connec-

---

[27] *Reich v Cambridgeport Air Systems,* 26 F3d 1187 (1st Cir 1994).

tion with the employee's diagnosis and treatment by the physician. Further, local fire and public health officials, as well as local neighborhood residents, are given the right to know if local employers are working with hazardous substances that could pose health or safety problems.

F.   COMPENSATION FOR EMPLOYEES' INJURIES

For most kinds of employment, workers' compensation statutes govern compensation for injuries. These statutes provide that an injured employee is entitled to compensation for accidents occurring in the course of employment from a risk involved in that employment.

23. Common Law Status of Employer

In some employment situations, common law principles apply. Workers' compensation statutes commonly do not apply to employers with fewer than a prescribed minimum number of employees or to agricultural, domestic, or casual employment. When an exempted area of employment is involved, it is necessary to consider the duties and defenses of employers apart from workers' compensation statutes.

(a) Duties. The employer is under the common law duty to furnish an employee with a reasonably safe place in which to work, reasonably safe tools and appliances, and a sufficient number of competent fellow employees for the work involved. The employer is also under the common law duty to warn the employee of any unusual dangers particular to the employer's business.

(b) Defenses. At common law, the employer is not liable to an injured employee if the employee is harmed by the act of a fellow employee. Similarly, an employer is not liable at common law to an employee harmed by an ordinary hazard of the work because the employee assumed such risks. If the employee is guilty of contributory negligence, regardless of the employer's negligence, the employer is not liable at common law to an injured employee.

24. Statutory Changes

The rising incidence of industrial accidents resulting from the increasing use of more powerful machinery and the growth of the industrial labor population led to a demand for statutory modification of common law rules relating to the liability of employers for industrial accidents.

(a) Modification of Employer's Common Law Defenses. One kind of change by statute was to modify the defenses that an employer could assert when sued by an employee for damages. For example, under the Federal Employer's Liability Act (FELA), which covers railroad workers, the injured employee must still bring an action in court and prove the negligence of the employer or other employees. However, the burden of proving the case is made lighter by limitations on employers' defenses. Under FELA, contributory negligence is a defense only in mitigation of damages; assumption of the risk is not a defense.[28]

---

[28] 45 USC §§ 1 et seq.

(b) Workers' Compensation. A more sweeping development was made by the adoption of workers' compensation statutes in every state. In addition, civil employees of the U.S. government are covered by the Federal Employees' Compensation Act. When an employee is covered by a workers' compensation statute and the injury is job connected, the employee's remedy is limited to that provided in the workers' compensation statute.

Workers' compensation proceedings are brought before a special administrative agency or workers' compensation board. In contrast, a common law action for damages or an action for damages under an employer's liability statute is brought in a court of law.

CASE SUMMARY

Locked In

Facts: Bryant is the administrator of the estate of the deceased and the guardian of the deceased's minor child. Bryant sued Wal-Mart for damages following the death of the deceased based on the theory of false imprisonment. While working on the night restocking crew, the deceased suffered a stroke. Medical personnel arrived six minutes later but could not enter the store because management had locked all doors of the store for security reasons and no manager was present to open a door. By the time the medical crew entered the store to assist her, they were unable to revive her, and she died 15 hours later. Bryant contended that the false imprisonment occurred between the time the deceased became ill and the time the medical team was unable to enter the store. Wal-Mart contended that Bryant's exclusive remedy is the Workers' Compensation Act.

Decision: Judgment for Wal-Mart. It is well settled that a claim under the Workers' Compensation Act is the sole and exclusive remedy for injury or occupational disease incurred in the course of employment. In exchange for the right to recover scheduled compensation without proof of negligence on the part of the employer, employees forgo other rights and remedies they once had. Injuries to an employee's peace, happiness, and feelings are not compensable under the act. [*Bryant v Wal-Mart Stores, Inc. (Ga App) 417 SE2d 688 (1992)*]

Without proof of employer fault, workers' compensation pays injured employees
• medical benefits
• a percentage of lost wages
• limited death benefits

For injuries arising within the course of the employee's work from a risk involved in that work, workers' compensation statutes usually provide (1) immediate medical benefits; (2) prompt periodic wage replacement, often computed as a percentage of weekly wages (ranging from 50 to 80 percent of the injured employee's wage) for a specified number of weeks; and (3) a death benefit of a limited amount. In such cases, compensation is paid without regard to whether the employer or the employee was negligent. However, no compensation is generally allowed for a willful, self-inflicted injury or one sustained while intoxicated.

There has been a gradual widening of the workers' compensation statutes, so compensation today is generally recoverable for both accident-inflicted injuries and occupational diseases. In some states, compensation for occupational diseases is limited to those named in the statute. These diseases may include silicosis, lead poisoning, or injury to health from radioactivity. In other states, any disease arising from an occupation is compensable.

G.   EMPLOYEE PRIVACY

Employers may want to monitor employee telephone conversations in the ordinary course of their business to evaluate employee performance and customer service; to document business transactions between employees and customers; or to meet special security, efficiency, or other needs. Employers may likewise want to monitor E-mail for what they perceive to be sound business reasons. Or employers may seek to test employees for drug use or search employee lockers for illicit drugs. Litigation may result because employees may believe that such activities violate their right to privacy.

25. Source of Privacy Rights

The Bill of Rights contained in the U.S. Constitution, including the Fourth Amendment, which protects against unreasonable search and seizure, provides a philosophical and legal basis for individual privacy rights for federal employees. The Fourteenth Amendment applies this privacy protection to actions taken by state and local governments that affect their employees. The privacy rights of individuals working in the private sector are not directly controlled by the Bill of Rights, however, because challenged employer actions are not government actions. Limited employee privacy rights in the private sector are provided by statute, case law, and collective bargaining agreements.

26. Monitoring Employee Telephone Conversations

The Federal Wiretapping Act[29] makes it unlawful to intercept oral and electronic communications and provides for both criminal liability and civil damages against the violator. There are two major exceptions, however. The first allows an employer to monitor a firm's telephones in the "ordinary course of business" through the use of extension telephones; a second exception applies when there is prior employee consent to the interception. If employer monitoring results in the interception of a business call, it is within the ordinary-course-of-business exception. Personal calls can be monitored, however, only to the extent necessary to determine that the call is personal, and the employer must then cease listening. ◆ *For example*, Newell Spears taped all phone conversations at his store in trying to find out if an employee was connected to a store theft. He listened to virtually all 22 hours of intercepted and recorded telephone conversations between his employee Sibbie Deal and her boyfriend Calvin Lucas without regard to the conversations' relation to Spears's business interest. While Spears might well have legitimately monitored Deal's call to the extent necessary to determine that the calls were personal and made or received in violation of store policy, the scope of the interception in this case was well beyond the boundaries of the ordinary-course-of-business exception and in violation of the act.[30] ◆

Employer monitoring of employee phone calls can be accomplished without fear of violating the act if consent is established. Consent may be established by prior written notice to employees of the employer's monitoring policy. It is prudent, as well, for the employer to give customers notice of the policy through a recorded message as part of the employer's phone-answering system.

---

[29] Title III of the Omnibus Crime Control and Safe Streets Act of 1968, 18 USC §§ 2510–2520.
[30] *Deal v Spears*, 580 F2d 1153 (8th Cir 1992).

27. E-mail Monitoring

Electronic mail (E-mail) is a primary means of communication in many of today's businesses, serving for some employers as an alternative to faxes, telephones, or the U.S. Postal Service. Employers may want to monitor employees' E-mail messages to evaluate the efficiency and effectiveness of their employees or for corporate security purposes, including the protection of trade secrets and other intangible property interests. When employees are disciplined or terminated for alleged wrongful activities discovered as a result of E-mail searches, however, the issue of privacy may be raised.

The Electronic Communications Privacy Act of 1986 (ECPA)[31] amended the federal wiretap statute and was intended in part to apply to E-mail. However, ordinary-course-of-business and consent exceptions apply to E-mail, and it would appear that employers have broad latitude to monitor employee E-mail use.

For example, Alana Shoars, an E-mail administrator for Epson America Inc., was fired after complaining about her supervisor's reading of employee E-mail messages. Her state court invasion of privacy case was unsuccessful.[32] Very few cases involving E-mail issues have been adjudicated so far under the ECPA.

An employer can place itself within the consent exception of the act by issuing a policy statement to all employees that informs them of the monitoring program and its purposes and justification.

28. Property Searches

In the case of a public-sector employee whose office, desk, or file cabinets are searched, the Supreme Court has determined that the balance of interests should favor the public employer because its interests in supervision, control, and the efficient operation of the workplace outweigh an employee's privacy interest.[33]

In the private sector, employers may create a reasonable expectation of privacy by providing an employee with a locker and allowing the employee to provide his or her own lock. A search of that locker could be an invasion of privacy.[34] If, however, the employer provides a locker and lock but retains a master key and this is known to employees, then the lockers may be subject to legitimate reasonable searches by the employer. Ultimately, if a private-sector employer notifies all employees of its policy on lockers, desks, and office searches and the employer complies with its own policy, employees will have no actionable invasion of privacy case.

29. Drug and Alcohol Testing

Drug and alcohol testing is an additional source of privacy concerns for employees. Public-sector employees may see drug and alcohol testing as potentially infringing on their Fourth and Fifth Amendment rights, although they may be subject to this testing on the basis of reasonable suspicion. In ordinary circumstances, however, random drug testing is not permissible in the public sector except for mass transit workers and some safety-sensitive positions. The Federal Omnibus Transportation

---

[31] 18 USC §§ 2510–2520.
[32] See *Shoars v Epson America, Inc.,* 1994 Cal LEXIS 3670 (June 29, 1994).
[33] *O'Conner v Ortega,* 480 US 709 (1987).
[34] *Kmart Corp. v Trotti* (Tex App) 677 SW2d 632 (1984).

Employee Testing Act,[35] which covers certain classes of employees working in the airline, railroad, and trucking industries, makes covered employees subject to random drug and alcohol testing. Random drug and alcohol testing of employees working in safety-sensitive positions in the private sector also is permissible, as is the testing of private-sector employees on the basis of reasonable suspicion.

H.   EMPLOYER-RELATED IMMIGRATION LAWS

The Immigration and Naturalization Act (INA), the Immigration Reform and Control Act of 1986 (IRCA), and the Immigration Act of 1990[36] are the principal employer-related immigration laws.

30. Employer Liability

The IRCA was designed to stop illegal immigration through the elimination of job opportunities by means of employer sanctions.

The IRCA sets forth criminal and civil penalties against employers who knowingly hire aliens who have illegally entered the United States. The IRCA was designed to stop illegal immigration through the elimination of job opportunities for these aliens.

31. Employer Verification

Upon hiring a new employee, an employer must verify that the employee is legally entitled to work in the United States. Both the employer and the employee must fill out portions of Form I-9. Verification documents include a U.S. passport, a certificate of U.S. citizenship, or an Alien Registration Card ("green card"). In lieu of these documents, a state driver's license and a Social Security card are sufficient to prove eligibility to work. The 1990 act prohibits employers from demanding other documentation. Thus, if a prospective employee with a "foreign accent" offers a driver's license and Social Security card and the employer seeks a certificate of U.S. citizenship or a green card, the employer has committed an unfair immigration practice. The employer will be ordered to hire the individual and provide back pay.

WHAT'S BEHIND THE LAW?

Worker's Compensation for Stress Illnesses

Since 1983, the number of worker's compensation claims for anxiety and other mental disorders has increased fivefold. Workers file claims not for actual physical injuries but for breathing, hearing, or sleeping problems. The claims are based on "cumulative traumas" in the workplace, such as deadline pressures, earnings goals, or understaffing due to downsizing. The claims are difficult to challenge in court because the employees offer their statements plus those of their physicians or chiropractors to substantiate their poor mental states.

Very often employers' insurance companies do not investigate these types of stress-related claims because the cost of an investigation exceeds the cost of simply paying the claim. However, an employer's workers' compensation insurance rates are determined by the number of claims per year. When the number of claims jumps, the insurer increases the employer's premium. If claims triple, then the employer's next year's premium will triple as well.

---

[35] PL 102-143, 105 Stat 952, 49 USC § 1301 nt.
[36] PL 101-649, 8 USC § 1101.

Kerry Mortensen, the chief financial officer for Big Yank, a jeans manufacturer for the Gap and Levi Strauss, noted that increases in stress-related claims caused the closure of one of his company's plants: "People don't realize that the abuse of workers' comp is causing the loss of our own jobs." However, trial lawyer Lloyd B. Rowe supports fully an employee's right to workers' compensation for stress-related illnesses: "There are many people who are not totally dysfunctional, but they are the working hurt."

In Michigan, over 50 percent of workers' compensation claims are for stress-related injuries. Both New Jersey and Louisiana note large increases in stress-related claims by workers at plants where an announcement of closure has been made. "They're too hard to dispute," an insurer explained. For statistics on business and the labor force visit the Business, Economics and Finance site at http://www.law.emory.edu/FOCAL/bus.html

SUMMARY

The relationship of employer and employee is created by the agreement of the parties and is subject to the principles applicable to contracts. If the employment contract sets forth a specific duration, the employer cannot terminate the contract at an earlier date unless just cause exists. If no definite time period is set forth, the individual is an at-will employee. Under the employment-at-will doctrine, an employer can terminate the contract of an at-will employee at any time for any reason or for no reason. Courts in many jurisdictions, however, have carved out exceptions to this doctrine when the discharge violates public policy or is contrary to good faith and fair dealing in the employment relationship. The Fair Labor Standards Act regulates minimum wages, overtime hours, and child labor.

Under the National Labor Relations Act, employees have the right to form a union to obtain a collective bargaining contract or to refrain from organizational activities. The National Labor Relations Board conducts elections to determine whether employees in an appropriate bargaining unit desire to be represented by a union. The NLRA prohibits employers' and unions' unfair labor practices and authorizes the NLRB to conduct proceedings to stop such practices. Economic strikes have limited reinstatement rights. Federal law sets forth democratic standards for the election of union offices.

The Employees Retirement Income Security Act (ERISA) protects employees' pensions by requiring (1) high standards of those administering the funds, (2) reasonable vesting of benefits, (3) adequate funding, and (4) an insurance program to guarantee payments of earned benefits.

Unemployment compensation benefits are paid to persons for a limited period of time if they are out of work through no fault of their own. Persons receiving unemployment compensation must be available for placement in a job similar in duties and comparable in rate of pay to the job they lost. Twelve-week maternity, paternity, and adoption leaves are available under the Family and Medical Leave Act. Employers and employees pay Social Security taxes to provide retirement benefits, disability benefits, life insurance benefits, and Medicare.

The Occupational Safety and Health Act provides for (1) the establishment of safety and health standards and (2) the effective enforcement of these standards. Many states have enacted "right-to-know" laws, which require employers to inform their employees of any hazardous substances present in the workplace.

Workers' compensation laws provide for the prompt payment of compensation and medical benefits to persons injured in the course of employment without regard to fault. An injured employee's remedy is generally limited to the remedy provided by the workers' compensation statute. Most states also provide compensation to workers for occupational diseases.

The Bill of Rights is the source of public sector employees' privacy rights. Private sector employees may obtain limited privacy rights from statutes, case law, and collective bargaining agreements. Employers may monitor employee telephone calls, although once it is determined that the call is personal, the employer must stop listening or be in violation of the federal wiretap statute. The ordinary-course-of-business and consent exceptions to the Electronic Communications Privacy Act of 1986 (ECPA) give private employers a great deal of latitude to monitor employee E-mail. Notification to employees of employers' policies on searching lockers, desks, and offices reduces employees' expectations of privacy, and a search conducted in conformity with a known policy is generally not an invasion of privacy. Drug and alcohol testing is generally permissible if it is based on reasonable suspicion; random drug and alcohol testing may also be permissible in safety-sensitive positions.

Immigration laws prohibit the employment of aliens who have illegally entered the United States.

QUESTIONS AND CASE PROBLEMS

1. What social forces are affected by the shop right rule applicable to employee inventions?

2. Michael Smyth was an operations manager at the Pillsbury Co., and his employment status was that of an employee at will. Smyth received certain E-mail messages at home, and he replied to his supervisor by E-mail. His messages contained some provocative language including the phrase "kill the backstabbing bastards" and a reference to an upcoming company party as the "Jim Jones Koolaid affair." Later Smyth was given two weeks' notice of his termination, and he was told that his E-mail remarks were inappropriate and unprofessional. Smyth believes that he is the victim of invasion of privacy because the E-mail messages caused his termination, and the company had promised that E-mail communications would not be intercepted and used as a basis for discipline or discharge. The company denies that it intercepted the E-mail messages and points out that Smyth himself sent the unprofessional comments to his supervisor. Is Smyth entitled to reinstatement and back pay because of the invasion of privacy? [*Smyth v Pillsbury Co.*, 914 F Supp 97 (ED PA)]

3. What remedies does an employee who has been wrongfully discharged have against an employer?

4. Michael Hauck claimed that he was discharged by his employer, Sabine Pilot Service, Inc., because he refused its direction to perform the illegal act of pumping the bilges of the employer's vessel into the waterways. Hauck was an employee at will, and Sabine contends that it therefore had the right to discharge him without having to show cause. Hauck brought a wrongful discharge action against Sabine. Decide. [*Sabine Pilot Service, Inc. v Hauck* (Tex) 687 SW2d 733]

5. Jeanne Eenkhoorn worked as a supervisor at a business office for the New York Telephone Co. While at work, she invented a process for terminating the telephone services of delinquent subscribers. The telephone company used the process but refused to compensate her for it, claiming a shop right. Eenkhoorn then sued for damages on a quasi-contract theory. Decide. [*Eenkhoorn v New York Telephone Co.* (Sup) 568 NYS2d 677]

6. One Monday a labor organization affiliated with the International Ladies Garment Workers Union began an organizational drive among the employees of Whittal & Son, Inc. On the following Monday six of the employees who were participating in the union drive were discharged. Immediately after the firings the head of the company gave a speech to the remaining workers in which he made a variety of antiunion statements and threats. The union filed a complaint with the NLRB, alleging that the six employees were fired because they were engaging in organizational activity and were thus discharged in violation of the NLRA. The employer defended its position, arguing that it had a business to run and that it was barely able to survive in the global economy against cheap labor from third world countries. It asserted that the last thing it needed was "union baloney." Was the NLRA violated?

7. David Stark submitted an application to the maintenance department of Wyman-Gordon Co. Stark was a journeyman millwright with nine years' experience at a neighboring company at the time of his application to Wyman-Gordon. Stark was vice president of the local industrial workers union. In his preliminary interview with the company, Ms. Peevler asked if Stark was involved in union activity, and Stark detailed his involvement to her. She informed Stark that Wyman-Gordon was a nonunion shop and asked how he felt about this. Peevler's notes from the interview characterize Stark's response to this question as "seems to lean toward third-party intervention." Company officials testified that Stark's qualifications were "exactly what we were looking for," but he was not hired. Stark claimed that he was discriminated against. Wyman-Gordon denied that any discrimination had occurred. Is a job applicant (as opposed to an employee) entitled to protection from antiunion discrimination? On the facts of this case, has any discrimination taken place? [(*Wyman-Gordon Co. v NLRB*, 108 LRRM 2085 (1st Cir.)]

8. Juan Ortiz was regularly employed by Donegan Productions Co. as an actor on an afternoon television series. A dispute arose as to how much Donegan owed Juan. Donegan claimed that the dispute must be resolved solely on the basis of the written individual employment contract that Juan and Donegan had signed. Donegan claimed that past practice, usages of the profession, and an existing collective bargaining contract with the American Federation of Television and Radio Artists were not relevant. Was Donegan correct?

9. Jane Richards was employed as the sole crane operator of Gale Corp. and also held the part-time union position of shop steward for the plant. On May 15 Richards complained to OSHA concerning what she contended were seven existing violations of the Occupational Safety and Health Act that were brought to her attention by members of the bargaining unit.

On May 21 she stated to the company's general manager at a negotiating session: "If we don't have a new contract by the time the present one expires on June 15, we will strike." On May 22 an OSHA inspector arrived at the plant, and Richards told her supervisor, "I blew the whistle." On May 23 the company rented and later purchased two large electric forklifts that were used to do the work previously performed by the crane, and the crane operator's job was abolished. Under the existing collective bargaining contract, the company had the right to lay off for lack of work. The contract also provided for arbitration, and it prohibited discipline or discharge without "just cause." On May 23 Richards was notified that she was being laid off "for lack of work" within her classification of crane operator. She was also advised that the company was not planning on using the crane in the future and that, if she were smart, she would get another job. Richards claimed that her layoff was in violation of the National Labor Relations Act, the Occupational Safety and Health Act, and the collective bargaining agreement. Was she correct?

10. Samuel Sullivan, president of the Truck Drivers and Helpers International Union, also holds the position of president of the union's pension fund. The fund consists of both employer and employee contributions, which are forwarded quarterly to the fund's offices in New York City. Sullivan ordered Mark Gilbert, the treasurer of the fund, not to give out any information to anyone at any time concerning the fund because it was union money and because the union was entitled to take care of its own internal affairs. Was Sullivan correct?

11. In May the nurses union at Waterbury Hospital went on strike, and the hospital was shut down. In mid-June the hospital began hiring replacements and gradually opened many units. In order to induce nurses to take employment during the strike, the hospital guaranteed replacement nurses their choice of positions and shifts. If a preferred position was in a unit that was not open at that time, the hospital guaranteed that the individual would be placed in that position at the end of the strike. The strike ended in October, and as the striking workers returned to work, the hospital began opening units that had been closed during the strike. It staffed many of these positions with replacement nurses. The nurses who had the positions prior to the strike and were waiting to return to work believed that they should have been called to fill these positions rather than the junior replacements who had held other positions during the strike. Decide. [*Waterbury Hospital v NLRB*, 950 F2d 849 (2d Cir)]

12. Buffo was employed by the Baltimore & Ohio Railroad. Along with a number of other workers, he was removing old brakes from railroad cars and replacing them with new brakes. In the course of the work, rivet heads and scrap from the brakes accumulated on the tracks under the cars. This debris was removed only occasionally when the workers had time. Buffo, while holding an air hammer in both arms, was crawling under a car when his foot slipped on scrap on the ground, causing him to strike and injure his knee. He sued the railroad for damages under the Federal Employers Liability Act. Decide. [*Buffo v Baltimore & Ohio Railroad Co.* (Pa) 72 A2d 593]

13. Mark Phipps was employed as a cashier at a Clark gas station. A customer drove into the station and asked him to pump leaded gasoline into her 1976 Chevrolet, an automobile equipped to receive only unleaded gasoline. The station manager told Phipps to comply with the request, but he refused, believing that his dispensing leaded gasoline into the gas tank was a violation of law. Phipps stated that he was willing to pump unleaded gas into the tank, but the manager immediately fired him. Phipps sued Clark for wrongful termination. Clark contended that it was free to terminate Phipps, an employee at will, for any reason or no reason. Decide. [*Phipps v Clark Oil & Refining Corp.* (Min App) 396 NW2d 588]

14. Reno, Nevada, police officers John Bohach and Jon Catalano communicated with each other on the Alphapage computer system, typing messages on a keyboard and sending them to each other by use of a "send" key. The computer dials a commercial paging company, which receives the message by modem, and the message is then sent to the person paged by radio broadcast. When the system was installed, the police chief warned that every Alphapage message was logged on the network, and he barred messages that were critical of department policy or discriminatory. The two police officers sought to block a department investigation into their messages and prevent disclosure of the messages' content. They claimed that the messages should be treated the same as telephone calls under federal wiretap law. The department contended that the system was essentially a form of E-mail, whose messages are by definition stored in a computer, and the storage was itself not part of the communication. Was the federal wiretap law violated? [*Bohach v City of Reno* (DC Nev) No. 96-403-ECR].

15. Michael Kittell was employed at Vermont Weatherboard Inc. While operating a saw at the plant, Kittell was seriously injured when a splinter flew into his eye and penetrated his head. Kittell sued Vermont Weatherboard, seeking damages on a common law

theory. His complaint alleged that he suffered severe injuries solely because of the employer's wanton and willful acts and omissions. The complaint stated that he was an inexperienced worker, put to work without instructions or warning on a saw from which the employer had stripped away all safety devices. Vermont Weatherboard made a motion to dismiss the complaint on the ground that the Workers' Compensation Act provided the exclusive remedy for his injury. Decide. [*Kittell v Vermont Weatherboard, Inc.* (Vt) 417 A2d 926]

Equal Employment Opportunity Law

CHAPTER 42

OBJECTIVES

After studying this chapter, you should be able to

1. *Explain and illustrate the difference between disparate treatment employment discrimination and disparate impact employment discrimination;*
2. *Recognize and remedy sexual harassment problems in the workplace;*
3. *Evaluate the legality of voluntary affirmative action programs by applying five court-approved principles;*
4. *State the consequences of discriminating against employees and job applicants because of their age; and*
5. *State and illustrate an employer's legal obligation to make reasonable accommodations for individuals with disabilities.*

United States laws reflect our society's concern that all Americans, including minorities, women, and persons with disabilities, have equal employment opportunities and that the workplace is free from discrimination and harassment. Title VII of the Civil Rights Act of 1964, as amended in 1972, 1978, and 1991, is the principal law regulating equal employment opportunities in the United States. Other federal laws require equal pay for men and women doing substantially the same work and forbid discrimination because of age or disability.

A. TITLE VII OF THE CIVIL RIGHTS ACT OF 1964, AS AMENDED

Title VII of the Civil Rights Act of 1964[1] seeks to eliminate employer and union practices that discriminate against employees and job applicants on the basis of race, color, religion, sex, or national origin. The law applies to the hiring process and to discipline, discharge, promotion, and benefits.

1. Theories of Discrimination

The Supreme Court has created, and the Civil Rights Act of 1991 has codified, two principal legal theories under which a plaintiff may prove a case of unlawful employment discrimination: disparate treatment and disparate impact (see Figure 42-1).

Disparate treatment is intentional discrimination.

A *disparate treatment* claim exists where an employer treats some individuals less favorably than others because of their race, color, religion, sex, or national origin. Proof of the employer's discriminatory motive is essential in a disparate treatment case.[2]

Disparate impact exists when an employer's facially neutral employment practices, such as hiring or promotion examinations, though neutrally applied and making no adverse reference to race, color, religion, sex, or national origin, have a significantly adverse or disparate impact on a protected group. In addition, the employment practice in question is not shown by the employer to be job related and consistent with business necessity. Under the disparate impact theory, it is not a defense for an employer to demonstrate that the employer did not intend to discriminate.

For example, if plant manager Jones is heard telling the personnel director that the vacant welder's position should be filled by a male because "this is man's work," a qualified female applicant turned down for the job would prevail in a *disparate treatment* theory case against the employer because she was not hired because of her gender. Necessary evidence of the employer's discriminatory motive would be satisfied by testimony about the manager's "this is man's work" statement.

If a Generic Airlines policy required new pilots to have a minimum height of 5 feet 7 inches, and no adverse reference to gender was stated in this employment policy, nevertheless the 5 feet 7 inch minimum height policy has an adverse or

---

[1] 42 USC §§ 2000(e) et seq.
[2] *Woodson v Scott Paper Co.,* 109 F3d 913 (3d Cir 1997).

disparate impact on women since far fewer women than men reach this height. Such an employment policy would be set aside on a *disparate impact* theory, and a minimum height for the position would be established by the court based on evidence of job relatedness and business necessity. A 5 feet 5 inch height requirement was set by one court for the pilots.

FIGURE 42-1
Unlawful Discrimination under Title VII of the Civil Rights Act of 1964 as Amended by the Civil Rights Act of 1991

Discriminatory Treatment in Employment Decisions on the Basis of Race Color Religion Sex National Origin	
Disparate Treatment Theory	**Disparate Impact Theory**
Nonneutral practice or Nonneutral application	Facially neutral practice and Neutral application
Requires proof of discriminatory intent	Does not require proof of discriminatory intent Requires proof of adverse effect on protected group and Employer is unable to show that the challenged practice is job related for the position in question and is consistent with business necessity
Either party has a right to require a jury trial when seeking compensatory or punitive damages	No right to a jury trial
Remedy: Reinstatement, hiring, or promotion Back pay less interim earnings Retroactive seniority Attorneys and expert witness fees **plus** Compensatory* and punitive damages. Damages capped for cases of sex and religious discrimination depending on size of employer:	**Remedy:** Reinstatement, hiring, or promotion Back pay less interim earnings Retroactive seniority Attorneys and expert witness fees

Number of employees	Damages cap
100 or fewer	$ 50,000
101 to 200	100,000
201 to 500	200,000
Over 500	300,000

No cap on damages for race cases.

* Compensatory damages include future pecuniary losses and nonpecuniary losses such as emotional pain and suffering.

Number 1 on the Charts! The Case That Created the Disparate Impact Theory

Facts: Griggs and other black employees of the Duke Power Company's Dan River Station challenged Duke Power's requirement of a high school diploma and the passing of standardized general intelligence tests in order to transfer to more desirable "inside" jobs. The district court and court of appeals found no violation of Title VII because the employer did not adopt the diploma and test requirements with the purpose of intentionally discriminating against black employees. The Supreme Court granted certiorari.

Decision: Judgment for Griggs. The absence of any intent on the part of the employer to discriminate was not a defense. Title VII prohibits not only overt discrimination but also practices that are fair in form but discriminatory in operation. If any employment practice, such as a diploma or testing requirement, that operates to exclude minorities at a substantially higher rate than white applicants cannot be shown to be "job related" and consistent with "business necessity," the practice is prohibited. [*Griggs v Duke Power Co., 401 US 424 (1971)*]

2. The Equal Employment Opportunity Commission

The Equal Employment Opportunity Commission (EEOC) is a five-member commission appointed by the president to establish equal employment opportunity policy under the laws it administers. The EEOC supervises the conciliation and enforcement efforts of the agency.

The EEOC administers Title VII of the Civil Rights Act, the Equal Pay Act (EPA), the Age Discrimination in Employment Act (ADEA), section 501 of the Rehabilitation Act (which prohibits federal-sector discrimination against persons with disabilities), and Title I (the employment provisions) of the Americans with Disabilities Act (ADA).

(a) Procedure. Where there is a state or local EEO agency with the power to act on claims of discriminatory practices, the charging party must file a complaint with that agency. The charging party must wait 60 days or until the termination of the state proceedings, whichever occurs first, before filing a charge with the EEOC. If no state or local agency exists, a charge may be filed directly with the EEOC so long as the charge is filed within 180 days of the occurrence of the discriminatory act. The commission conducts an investigation to determine whether reasonable cause exists to believe that the charge is true. If such cause is found to exist, the EEOC attempts to remedy the unlawful practice through conciliation. If the EEOC does not resolve the matter to the satisfaction of the parties, it may decide to litigate the case where unusual circumstances exist, including a "pattern or practice of discrimination." In most instances, however, the EEOC will issue the charging party a *right-to-sue* letter. Thereafter the individual claiming a violation of EEO law has 90 days to file a lawsuit in a federal district court.[3]

An individual must file a lawsuit within 90 days after issuance of a right to sue letter by the EEOC.

(b) Damages. Damages available to victims of discrimination under Title VII are set forth in Figure 42-1.

---

[3] When an individual misses the filing deadline of Title VII, the individual may be able to bring a race discrimination case under the two-year time limit allowed under section 1981 of the Civil Rights Act of 1866, codified at 42 USC § 1981, and sometimes called a section 1981 lawsuit.

B. PROTECTED CLASSES AND EXCEPTIONS

To successfully pursue a Title VII lawsuit, an individual must belong to a protected class and meet the appropriate burden of proof. Exceptions exist for certain employment practices.

3. Race and Color

The legislative history of Title VII of the Civil Rights Act demonstrates that a primary purpose of the act is to provide fair employment opportunities for black Americans. The protections of the act are applied to blacks based on race or color.

CASE SUMMARY

The Money-Back Guarantee

Facts: David Gwin, an African-American, sold cars as Chesrown Chevrolet, Inc. Gwin and two other salesmen from Chesrown took the opportunity to attend an eight-hour seminar by a motivational speaker, and Chesrown agreed to pay for half of the seminar fee of $150. The speaker assured them that if they were not satisfied with the seminar they would receive a full refund on the spot. The three salesmen attended the seminar on their own time, and at a break they told the speaker they wanted their money back. The speaker gave them the runaround but eventually promised to send them refund checks. The next morning at the regular sales staff meeting, the manager, who had just found out about the demand for refunds, stormed into the room shouting expletives and fired Gwin in front of his peers. The two other salesmen were permitted to apologize and keep their jobs. The evidence revealed that the manager had on occasion used racial slurs on the car lot. Gwin sued Chesrown asserting a racially discriminatory firing in violation of Title VII of the Civil Rights Act. Chesrown asserted that Gwin had been drinking and was belligerent in his confrontation with the motivational speaker, and it also contended that Gwin was fired for poor sales performance. At the trial Gwin demonstrated that his sales record was average to above average, and this reason was not a supportable ground for dismissal. He asserted the other reason offered by Chesrown was a pretext.

Decision: Judgment for Gwin. While the manager's termination of Gwin may have been motivated in part by Gwin's actions at the seminar, the jury believed the termination was motivated by race in violation of Title VII and section 1981. Gwin was therefore entitled to compensatory and punitive damages and to attorney fees. [*Gwin v Chesrown Chevrolet, Inc. (Colo App) 931 P2d 466 (1996)*]

The word *race* as used in the act applies to all members of the four major racial groupings: white, black, native American, and Asian-Pacific. Native Americans can file charges and receive the protection of the act on the basis of national origin, race, or, in some instances, color. Individuals of Asian-Pacific origin may file discrimination charges based on race, color, or, in some instances, national origin. Whites are also protected against discrimination because of race and color. ◆ *For example*, two white professors at a predominately black university were successful in discrimination suits against the university when it was held that the university had discriminated against them on the basis of race and color in tenure decisions.[4] ◆

---

[4] *Turgeon v Howard University*, 571 F Supp 679 (DDC 1983).

4. Religion

Title VII requires employers to accommodate their employees' or prospective employees' religious practices. Most cases involving allegations of religious discrimination revolve around the determination of whether an employer has made reasonable efforts to accommodate religious beliefs.

CASE SUMMARY

The Book of Isaiah

Facts: Isaiah Brown, who identifies himself as a born-again Christian, was director of the information services department for Polk County, Iowa, supervising some 50 employees. Brown directed his secretary to type his Bible study notes for him, and several employees said prayers in Brown's office before work and in addressing one meeting of employees Brown affirmed his Christianity and referred to Bible passages related to slothfulness and "work ethics." Subsequently Brown was reprimanded and told to cease religious activities on county time. Brown was also told to remove from his office all items with religious connotations, including a Bible in his desk. Several months later Brown was reprimanded for lack of judgment relating to financial constraints on the county budget, and asked to resign. When he refused to resign, he was fired. Brown claimed discrimination based on religion; the county claimed he was fired for his poor work performance.

Decision: Judgment for Brown. An employer must accommodate an employee's religious activities on the job to the extent the activities do not create undue hardship to the public employer by disrupting the work environment and forcing the employer to sustain real nonhypothetical costs. It was not a violation of Title VII for the employer to prohibit the typing of Bible study notes on paid county work time, or to refuse to open the building before the start of a work day for nonwork purpose such as a prayer meeting. However, allowing a county supervisory employee to conduct an occasional spontaneous prayer, and making references to his Christian belief did not impose undue hardship on the employer. Since the county did not demonstrate that it would have fired Brown anyway, absent his religious activities, the county was liable for firing Brown under Title VII. [*Brown v Polk County, Iowa, 61 F3d 650 (8th Cir 1995 en banc 6-5 decision)*]

> *Reasonable accommodation for an employee's religious belief requires an employer to seek a volunteer to allow the employee time off for religious observances, but it does not require the employer to expend more than a de minimis cost.*

If an employee's religious beliefs prohibit working on Saturday, an employer's obligation under Title VII is to try to find a volunteer to cover for the employee on Saturdays. The employer would not have an obligation to violate a seniority provision of a collective bargaining agreement or call in a substitute worker if such accommodation would require more than a *de minimis* or very small cost.

Title VII permits religious societies to grant hiring preferences in favor of members of their religion. It also provides an exemption for educational institutions to hire employees of a particular religion if the institution is owned, controlled, or managed by a particular religious society. The exemption is a broad one and is not restricted to the religious activities of the institution.

5. Sex

Employers who discriminate against female or male employees because of their sex are held to be in violation of Title VII. The EEOC and the courts have determined that the word sex as used in Title VII means a person's gender and not the person's sexual orientation. State and local legislation, however, may provide specific protection against discrimination based on sexual orientation.

(a) Height, Weight, and Physical Ability Requirements. Under the *Griggs v Duke Power* precedent, an employer must be able to show that criteria used to make an employment decision that has a disparate impact on women, such as minimum height and weight requirements, are in fact job related. All candidates for a position requiring physical strength must be given an opportunity to demonstrate their capability to perform the work. Women cannot be precluded from consideration just because they have not traditionally performed such work.

Under the PDA, women unable to work as a result of pregnancy-related medical conditions or childbirth may not be given lesser disability insurance coverage or sick leave than is provided the employer's other workers.

(b) Pregnancy-Related Benefits. Title VII was amended by the Pregnancy Discrimination Act (PDA) in 1978. The amendment prevents employers from treating pregnancy, childbirth, and related medical conditions in a manner different from the manner in which other medical conditions are treated. Thus, women unable to work as a result of pregnancy, childbirth, or related medical conditions must be provided with the same benefits as all other workers. These include temporary and long-term disability insurance, sick leave, and other forms of employee benefit programs. An employer who does not provide disability benefits or paid sick leave to other employees is not required to provide them for pregnant workers.

6. Sexual Harassment

Quid pro quo sexual harassment involves supervisors seeking sexual favors from their subordinates in return for such job benefits as continued employment, promotions, raises, or favorable performance evaluations.[5] In cases of supervisors' actions affecting job benefits, Title VII's prohibition against sex discrimination has been violated. The employer is then liable to the employee for the loss of benefits plus punitive damages because of a supervisor's misconduct.

There are two kinds of sexual harassment, (1) "quid pro quo" where a supervisor seeks sexual favors in exchange for job benefits, and (2) "hostile work environment" harassment where "unwelcome" sexual conduct poisons the work environment.

A second form of sexual harassment is *hostile working environment* harassment. With this type of harassment, an employee's economic benefits have not been affected by a supervisor's conduct, but the supervisor's sexually harassing conduct has nevertheless caused anxiety and "poisoned" the work environment. Such conduct may include unwelcome sexual flirtation, propositions, or other abuses of a sexual nature, including the use of degrading words or the display of sexually explicit or suggestive pictures. An injunction against such conduct can be obtained and attorney fees awarded. Moreover, if such conduct drives the employee to quit, the employer may be responsible for all economic losses caused the employee plus punitive damages.

---

5 According to EEOC Guidelines § 1604.11(f), unwelcome sexual advances, requests for sexual favors, and other verbal or physical conduct of a sexual nature constitute sexual harassment when (1) submission to such conduct is made either explicitly or implicitly a term or condition of an individual's employment, [and] (2) submission to or rejection of such conduct has the purpose or effect of unreasonably interfering with an individual's work performance or creating an intimidating, hostile, or offensive working environment.

You'll Know It When You See It! A Hostile Work Environment Is Determined by Looking at All the Circumstances

Facts: Teresa Harris sued her former employer, Forklift Systems Inc., under Title VII of the Civil Rights Act of 1964, claiming that the company's president, Charles Hardy, created "an abusive work environment" with a constant stream of sexually offensive jokes and remarks. When Hardy's conduct continued after Harris complained to him, she quit her job. A federal district court denied Harris's case because she had not shown severe psychological injury, and the Sixth Circuit affirmed. The U.S. Supreme Court granted certiorari.

Decision: Judgment in favor of Harris. The district court erred in relying on whether the conduct seriously affected Harris's psychological well-being. Title VII comes into play before the harassing conduct leads to a nervous breakdown. Rather, whether a work environment is "hostile" or "abusive" can be determined only by looking at all the circumstances included in the particular case. These may include the frequency of the discriminatory conduct; its severity; whether it is physically threatening or humiliating, or a mere offensive utterance; and whether it unreasonably interferes with an employee's work performance. [*Harris v Forklift Systems Inc.,* 510 US 17 (1993)]

In determining whether the conduct complained of was so pervasive as to alter the conditions of employment and create an abusive working environment, one federal circuit has applied a "reasonable woman" standard in determining that the complainant was the victim of sexual harassment.[6] Subsequently the EEOC's 1994 guidelines adopted a "reasonable person in the same or similar circumstances as the victim" test.[7]

An employer is liable for the sexual harassment caused its employees by co-workers or its customers only when it fails to take remedial action after being informed of the misconduct. Employers may avoid liability for "hostile environment" sexual harassment by affirmatively raising the subject with all of the employees, expressing strong disapproval of such conduct, advising employees how to inform the employer of instances of sexual harassment, and taking disciplinary action against wrongdoers. (See Figure 42-2.)

7. National Origin

Title VII protects members of all nationalities from discrimination. The judicial principles that have emerged from cases involving race, color, and gender employment discrimination are generally applicable to cases involving allegations of national origin discrimination. Thus, physical standards, such as minimum height requirements, that tend to exclude persons of a particular national origin because of the physical stature of the group have been found unlawful when these standards cannot be justified by business necessity.

Adverse employment action based on an individual's lack of English language skills violates Title VII when the language requirement bears no demonstrable relationship to the successful performance of the job to which it is applied.

---

[6] *Ellison v Brady,* 924 F2d 872 (9th Cir 1991).
[7] EEOC Notice 915.002 (Mar. 8, 1994).

FIGURE 42-2
Employer Procedure

A. Develop and implement an equal employment policy that specifically prohibits sexual harassment and imposes discipline up to and including discharge. Set forth specific examples of conduct that will not be tolerated such as

- unwelcome sexual advances, whether they involve physical touching or not;

- sexual epithets and jokes; written or oral references to sexual conduct; gossip regarding one's sex life; comments on an individual's body; comments about an individual's sexual activity, deficiencies, or prowess;

- the displaying of sexually suggestive objects, pictures, and cartoons;

- unwelcome leering, whistling, brushing against the body, sexual gestures, and suggestive or insulting comments;

- inquiries into one's sexual experiences; and

- discussion of one's sexual activities.

B. Establish ongoing educational programs, including role playing and films to demonstrate unacceptable behavior.

C. Designate a responsible senior official to whom complaints of sexual harassment can be made. Avoid any procedure that requires an employee to first complain to the employee's supervisor, because that individual may be the offending person. Make certain complainants will know that there will be no retaliation for filing a complaint.

D. Investigate all complaints promptly and thoroughly.

E. Keep the complaint and investigations as confidential as possible and limit all information to only those who need to know.

F. If a complaint has merit, impose appropriate and consistent discipline.

CASE SUMMARY

A Close Call

Facts: Manuel Fragante applied for a clerk's job with the City and County of Honolulu. Although he placed high enough on a civil service eligibility list to be chosen for the position, he was not selected because of a perceived deficiency in oral communication skills caused by his "heavy Filipino accent." Fragante brought suit, alleging that the defendants discriminated against him on the basis of his national origin in violation of Title VII of the Civil Rights Act.

Decision: Judgment for the City and County of Honolulu. Accents and national origin are inextricably intertwined in many cases. Courts take a careful look at nonselection decisions based on foreign accents because an employer may unlawfully discriminate against someone based on national origin by falsely stating that it was the individual's inability to measure up to the communication skills demanded of the job. Because the record showed that the ability to speak clearly was one of the most important skills required for the clerk's position and because the judge confirmed that Fragante was difficult to understand, the court dismissed his complaint. *[Fragante v City and County of Honolulu 888 F2d 591 (9th Cir 1989)]*

8.   Title VII Exceptions

Section 703 of Title VII defines which employment activities are unlawful. This same section, however, also exempts several key practices from the scope of Title VII enforcement. The most important are the bona fide occupational qualification exception, the testing and educational requirement exception, and the seniority system exception.

A "BFOQ" is a narrowly applied employer defense.

(a) Bona Fide Occupational Qualification Exception. It is not an unlawful employment practice for an employer to hire employees on the basis of religion, sex, or national origin in those certain instances where religion, sex, or national origin is a bona fide occupational qualification (BFOQ) reasonably necessary to the normal operation of a particular enterprise. ◆ *For example*, a valid BFOQ is a men's clothing store's policy of hiring only males to do measurements for suit alterations. An airline's policy of hiring only female flight attendants is not a valid BFOQ because such a policy is not reasonably necessary to safely operate an airline. ◆ Note that there is no BFOQ for race or color.

CASE SUMMARY

It's A Woman's Choice

Facts: Johnson Controls, Inc. (JCI), manufactures batteries. A primary ingredient in the battery-manufacturing process is lead. Occupational exposure to lead entails health risks, including the risk of harm to any fetus carried by a female employee. After eight of its employees became pregnant while maintaining blood lead levels exceeding levels set by the Centers for Disease Control as dangerous for a worker planning to have a family, respondent JCI announced a policy barring all women, except those whose infertility was medically documented, from jobs involving lead exposure exceeding the OSHA standard. The United Auto Workers (UAW) brought a class action in the district court, claiming that the policy constituted sex discrimination violative of Title VII of the Civil Rights Act of 1964, as amended. The court granted summary judgment for JCI based on its BFOQ defense, and the court of appeals affirmed. The Supreme Court granted certiorari.

Decision: Judgment for the UAW. JCI's fetal protection policy discriminated against women because the policy applied only to women and did not deal with the harmful effect of lead exposure on the male reproductive system. JCI's concerns about the welfare of the next generation do not suffice to establish a BFOQ of female sterility. Title VII, as amended, mandates that decisions about the welfare of future children be left to the parents who conceive, bear, support, and raise them rather than to the employers who hire those parents or to the courts. Moreover, an employer's tort liability for potential fetal injuries does not require a different result. If, under general tort principles, Title VII bans sex-specific fetal-protection policies, the employer fully informs the woman of the risk, and the employer has not acted negligently, the basis for holding an employer liable seems remote at best. *[UAW v Johnson Controls, 499 US 187 (1991)]*

(b) Testing and Educational Requirements. Section 703(h) of the act authorizes the use of "any professionally developed ability test [that is not] designed, intended, or used to discriminate." Employment testing and educational requirements must be "job related"; that is, the employers must prove that the tests and educational requirements bear a relationship to job performance.

Tests validated by one court may be subsequently accepted by other courts if the jobs are essentially the same.

Courts will accept prior court-approved validation studies developed for a different employer in a different state or region so long as it is demonstrated that the job for which the test was initially validated is essentially the same job function for which the test is currently being used. ◆ *For example*, a firefighters' test that had been validated in a study in California will be accepted as valid when later used in Virginia. ◆ Such application is called *validity generalization*.

The Civil Rights Act of 1991 makes it an unlawful employment practice for an employer to adjust scores or use different cutoff scores or otherwise alter the results of employment tests in order to favor any race, color, religion, sex, or national origin. This provision addresses the so-called race-norming issue, whereby the results of hiring and promotion tests are adjusted to assure that a minimum number of minorities are included in application pools.

(c) Seniority System. Section 703(h) provides that differences in employment terms based on a bona fide seniority system are sanctioned so long as the differences do not stem from an intention to discriminate. The term *seniority system* is generally understood to mean a set of rules that ensures that workers with longer years of continuous service for an employer will have a priority claim to a job over others with fewer years of service. Because such rules provide workers with considerable job security, organized labor has continually and successfully fought to secure seniority provisions in collective bargaining agreements.

ETHICS & THE LAW

T.J. Rodgers is the founder and CEO of Cypress Semiconductors. In early 1996, Mr. Rodgers received a form letter from Sister Doris Gromley, the director of corporate social responsibility for the Sisters of St. Francis of Philadelphia, stating that her order would use its shareholder votes against the Cypress board (including Mr. Rodgers) to attempt to remove them because of a lack of women and minorities on the Cypress board. Mr. Rodgers responded with a detailed letter to Sister Gromley." Part of the letter appears below:

> *Thank you for your letter criticizing the lack of racial and gender diversity of Cypress's Board of Directors. I received the same letter from you last year. I will reiterate the management arguments opposing your position. Then I will provide the philosophical basis behind our rejection of the operating principles espoused in your letter, which we believe to be not only unsound, but even immoral . . .*
>
> *The semiconductor business is a tough one with significant competition from the Japanese, Taiwanese, and Koreans. There have been more corporate casualties than survivors. For that reason, our Board of Directors is not a ceremonial watchdog, but a critical management function. The essential criteria for Cypress board membership are as follows:*
> —*Experience as a CEO of an important technology company*
> —*Direct expertise in the semiconductor business based on education and management experience*
> —*Direct experience in the management of a company that buys from the semiconductor industry*
>
> *A search based on these criteria usually yields a male who is 50-plus years old, has a Master's degree in engineering science, and has moved up the managerial ladder to the top spot in one or more corporations. Unfortunately, there are currently few minorities and almost no women who chose to be engineering graduate students 30 years ago (This picture will be dramatically different in 10 years, due to the greater diversification of graduate students in the 80s.). Bluntly stated, a "woman's view" on how to run our semiconductor company does not help us, unless that woman has an advanced technical degree and experience as a CEO. I do realize there are other industries in which the last statement does not hold true. We would quickly embrace the opportunity to include any woman or minority person who could help us as a director, because we pursue talent and we don't care in what package that talent comes.*
>
> *I believe that placing arbitrary racial or gender quotas on corporate boards is fundamentally wrong.*

Do you agree with Mr. Rodgers or Sister Doris Gromley? Do you agree that Cypress should have women and minorities on its board? Has Mr. Rodgers violated any laws with his posture? Is the board an appropriate place for affirmative action programs?

9. Affirmative Action and Reverse Discrimination

Employers have an interest in *affirmative action* because it is fundamentally fair to have a diverse and representative workforce. Employers, under affirmative action plans (AAPs), may undertake special recruiting and other efforts to hire and train minorities and women and help them advance within the company. The plan may also provide job preferences for minorities and women. Such aspects of affirmative action plans have resulted in numerous lawsuits contending that Title VII, the Fifth and Fourteenth Amendments, or collective bargaining contracts have been violated.[8]

(a) Permissible AAPs. A permissible AAP should conform to the following criteria:

1. The affirmative action must be in connection with a "plan."
2. There must be a showing that affirmative action is justified as a remedial measure.
3. The plan must be voluntary.
4. The plan must not unnecessarily trammel the interests of whites.
5. The plan must be temporary.[9]

(b) Reverse Discrimination. When an employer's AAP is not shown to be justified or "unnecessarily trammels" the interests of nonminority employees, it is often called *reverse discrimination*. For example, a city's decision to rescore police promotional tests to achieve specific racial and gender percentages unnecessarily trammeled the interests of nonminority police officers.[10]

Debra Williams and Sharon Taxman were hired on the same day as teachers for the Township of Piscataway, New Jersey. The public employer had no past history of unlawful racial bias. Faced with having to lay off one of the two teacher, the employer decided under its AAP to retain black school teacher Debra Williams. Sharon Taxman challenged the decision as reverse discrimination. The U.S. Court of Appeals for the Third Circuit decided in favor of Taxman, determining in part that the AAP violated Title VII because it was adopted for the purpose of promoting racial diversity rather than to remedy discrimination or the effects of past discrimination. The Supreme Court of the United States agreed to hear the case.[11] However, the case was withdrawn from the Court after a $433,500 out of court settlement was reached with Taxman, with a coalition of national civil rights organizations agreeing to pay $308,500 of the settlement. The coalition was fearful that the Supreme Court would overturn its AAP precedents.[12]

---

[8] In *Adarand Constructors, Inc. v Pena,* 115 S Ct 2097 (1995), the U.S. Supreme Court held that a subcontractor had standing to receive relief where a federal program provided financial incentives to prime contractors to hire "disadvantaged" subcontractors and race-based presumptions were used to identify such individuals. The program was found to violate the equal protection component of the Fifth Amendment's Due Process Clause. After this decision, the EEOC issued a statement on affirmative action, stating in part: "Affirmative action is lawful only when it is designed to respond to a demonstrated and serious imbalance in the workforce, is flexible, time-limited, applies only to qualified workers, and respects the rights of non-minorities and men." (Daily Lab Rep (BNA) No. 147, at S-47 (August 1, 1995).)

[9] *Steelworkers v Weber,* 443 US 193 (1979); *Johnson v Santa Clara County Transportation Agency,* 480 US 616 (1987).

[10] *San Francisco Police Officers Ass'n v San Francisco,* 812 F2d 1125 (9th Cir 1987).

[11] *Taxman v Board of Education of Piscataway,* 91 F3d 1547 (3d Cir 1996), cert. granted 117 S Ct 2506 (1997).

[12] Daily Labor Report (BNA) No. 226, AA-1 (Nov. 24, 1997).

(c) Executive Order. Presidential Executive Order 11246 regulates contractors and subcontractors doing business with the federal government. This order forbids discrimination against minorities and women and in certain situations requires affirmative action to be taken to offer better employment opportunities to minorities and women. The secretary of labor has established the Office of Federal Contract Compliance Programs (OFCCP) to administer the order.

C.   OTHER EQUAL EMPLOYMENT OPPORTUNITY (EEO) LAWS

Major federal laws require equal pay for men and women doing equal work and forbid discrimination against older people and those with disabilities.

10. Equal Pay

The Equal Pay Act requires equal pay for woman doing substantially equal work as men.

The Equal Pay Act prohibits employers from paying employees of one gender a lower wage rate than the rate paid employees of the other gender for equal work or substantially equal work in the same establishment, for jobs that require substantially equal skill, effort, and responsibility and that are performed under similar working conditions.[13] The Equal Pay Act does not prohibit all variations in wage rates paid men and women but only those variations based solely on gender. The act sets forth four exceptions. Variances in wages are allowed where there is (1) a seniority system, (2) a merit system, (3) a system that measures earnings by quantity or quality of production, or (4) a differential based on any factor other than gender.

11. Age Discrimination

The Age Discrimination in Employment Act (ADEA) forbids discrimination by employers, unions, and employment agencies against persons over 40 years of age.[14] Section 4(a) of the ADEA sets forth the employment practices that are unlawful under the act, including the failure to hire because of age and the discharge of employees because of age. Section 7(b) of the ADEA allows for the doubling of damages in cases of willful violations of the act. Consequently, an employer who willfully violates the ADEA is liable not only for back wages and benefits but also for an additional amount as liquidated damages.

CASE SUMMARY

Miffed at Being RIF-ed

Facts: Calvin Rhodes began his employment with Dresser Industries in 1955 as an oil industry salesman. In the throes of a severe economic downturn, Rhodes took a job selling oil field equipment at another Dresser company that became Guiberson Oil Tools. After seven months he was discharged and told that the reason was a reduction in force (RIF) but that he would be eligible for rehiring. At that time he was 56 years old. Within two months Guiberson hired a 42-year-old salesperson to do the same job. Rhodes sued Guiberson for violating the ADEA.

---

13   29 USC § 206(d)(1).
14   29 USC § 623.

> At the trial Lee Snyder, the supervisor who terminated Rhodes, testified in part that Jack Givens, Snyder's boss who instructed Snyder to fire Rhodes, once said that he could hire two young salesmen for what some of the older salesmen were costing.
>
> **Decision**: Judgment for Rhodes. The official reason given Rhodes, that he was being terminated under a RIF, was false. Every other reason given by the employer was countered with evidence that Rhodes was an excellent salesman. Based on all of the evidence, including the statement about hiring two young salesmen for what some of the older salesmen were costing, a reasonable jury could find that Guiberson Oil discriminated against Rhodes on the basis of age. [Rhodes v Guiberson Oil Tools, Inc., 75 F3d 989 (5th Cir 1996)]

The ADEA protects persons over 40 from failure to hire or discharge because of their age.

The Older Workers Benefit Protection Act (OWBPA) of 1990[15] amends the ADEA by prohibiting age discrimination in employee benefits and establishing minimum standards for determining the validity of waivers of age claims. The OWBPA amends the ADEA by adopting an "equal benefit or equal cost" standard, providing that older workers must be given benefits at least equal to those provided for younger workers unless the employer can prove that the cost of providing an equal benefit would be more for an older worker than for a younger one.

Employers commonly require that employees electing to take early retirement packages waive all claims against their employers, including their rights or claims under the ADEA. The OWBPA requires that employees be given a specific period of time to evaluate a proposed package.

Enforcement of the ADEA is the responsibility of the EEOC. Procedures and time limitations for filing and processing ADEA charges are the same as those under Title VII.

12. Discrimination against Persons with Disabilities

The right of persons with disabilities to enjoy equal employment opportunities was established on the federal level with the enactment of the Rehabilitation Act of 1973.[16] Although designed not specifically as an employment discrimination measure but rather as a comprehensive plan to meet many of the needs of persons with disabilities, the act contains three sections that provide guarantees against discrimination in employment. Section 501 is applicable to the federal government itself, section 503 applies to federal contractors, and section 504 applies to the recipients of federal funds.

The ADA prohibits discrimination against disabled workers who, with or without reasonable accommodations, are qualified to perform the essential functions of the job.

The Americans with Disabilities Act[17] extends protection beyond the federal level. It prohibits all private employers with 15 or more employees from discriminating against individuals with disabilities who, with or without reasonable accommodations, are qualified to perform the essential functions of the job. Enforcement of the ADA is the responsibility of the EEOC.

An employer may make preemployment inquiries into the ability of a job applicant to perform job-related functions. Under new "user friendly" EEOC Guidelines on Preemployment Inquiries under the ADA, an employer may ask applicants whether they will need reasonable accommodations for the hiring process. If the answer is yes, the employer may ask for reasonable documentation

---

15 29 USC § 623. This law reverses the Supreme Court's 1989 ruling in *Public Employees Retirement System of Ohio v Betts,* 492 US 158 (1989), which had the effect of exempting employee benefit programs from the ADEA.

16 29 USC §§ 701–794.

17 42 USC §§ 12101–12117.

of the disability.[18] In general, the employer may not ask questions about whether an applicant will need reasonable accommodations to do the job.

(a) Reasonable Accommodations under the ADA. Section 101(9) of the ADA defines an employer's obligation to make "reasonable accommodations" for individuals with disabilities to include (1) making existing facilities accessible to and usable by individuals with disabilities and (2) restructuring jobs, providing modified work schedules, and acquiring or modifying equipment or devices. An employer is not obligated under the ADA to make accommodations that would be an "undue hardship" on the employer.

For example, before passage of the ADA, a supermarket meatcutter unable to carry meat from a refrigerator to a processing area might have been refused clearance to return to work after a back injury until he was able to perform all job functions. Today under the ADA, it would be the employer's obligation to provide that worker with a disability with a cart to assist him perform the job even if the cart cost $500. However, if the meatcutter was employed by a small business with limited financial resources, an "accommodation" costing $500 might be an undue hardship that the employer could lawfully refuse to make.

(b) Contagious Diseases. A person with a contagious disease may be protected under the Rehabilitation Act and the Americans with Disabilities Act. The courts determine if the employee can work on the basis of individualized medical judgments. Considerations include (1) how the disease is transmitted, (2) the duration of the risk, (3) the severity of the risk, (4) the probability that the disease will be transmitted, and (5) whether the individual is otherwise qualified.

Persons with AIDS are within the protection of both the Rehabilitation Act and the Americans with Disabilities Act. Such persons must be treated like anyone else with a disability.[19]

(c) Exclusions from Coverage of the ADA. The act excludes from its coverage employees or applicants who are "currently engaging in the illegal use of drugs." The exclusion does not include an individual who has been successfully rehabilitated from such use or is participating in or has completed supervised drug rehabilitation and is no longer engaging in the illegal use of drugs.

Title V of the act states that behaviors such as transvestitism, transsexualism, pedophilia, exhibitionism, compulsive gambling, kleptomania, pyromania, and psychoactive substance use disorders resulting from current illegal use of drugs are not in and of themselves considered disabilities.

D.   EXTRATERRITORIAL EMPLOYMENT

The Civil Rights Act of 1991 amended both Title VII and the ADA to protect U.S. citizens employed in foreign countries by American-owned or -controlled companies against discrimination based on race, color, religion, national origin, sex, or disability.[20] The 1991 act contains an exemption if compliance with Title VII or the ADA would cause a company to violate the law of the foreign country in which it is located.

---

[18] EEOC Guidelines on Preemployment Inquiries under the ADA (October 10, 1995).
[19] *Chalk v U.S. District Court*, 840 F2d 701 (9th Cir 1988).
[20] Section 109 of the Civil Rights Act of 1991, PL 102-166, 105 Stat 1071.

WHAT'S BEHIND THE LAW?

BFOQs: Inside Hollywood

Hunter Tylo was hired by Spelling Entertainment Group to play a character who would "strut in a bikini to steal actress Heather Locklear's husband on the show," *Melrose Place*. Ms. Tylo never began work on the contract because she was fired after she disclosed to the show's executives that she was pregnant.

Mr. Spelling, owner of the Spelling Entertainment Group, explained that Ms. Tylo was fired because he did not think it was fair to have scripts rewritten around a character and an actress who had not yet appeared on the show. Mr. Spelling noted that he had worked with Ms. Locklear during her pregnancy, using various camera angles to avoid revealing Ms. Locklear's pregnancy.

In a letter to Mr. Spelling, actress Gabrielle Carteris, who plays a character on Mr. Spelling's other show, *Beverly Hills 90210*, expressed support for Mr. Spelling, "I just had to let you know how sorry I am with regards to the trial. It was particularly upsetting, when for me you were so very supportive of my getting pregnant."

Mr. Spelling also said that following Ms. Tylo's termination, he offered her a contract for the following season that would have paid more than her fee of $13,500 per episode on the terminated contract and that would have run for more episodes. Ms. Tylo refused the offer and filed suit.

Is there a distinction between Ms. Tylo's circumstances and Ms. Locklear's? Is not being pregnant a BFOQ for playing a "vixen" on a television series? Did Mr. Spelling give sufficient justification for Ms. Tylo's termination?

For information on women's rights, visit Women and the Law at
http://www.law.emory.edu/FOCAL/women.html.

SUMMARY

Title VII of the Civil Rights Act of 1964, as amended, forbids discrimination on the basis of race, color, religion, sex, or national origin. The EEOC administers the act. Intentional discrimination is unlawful where there is disparate treatment of individuals because of their race, color, religion, gender, or national origin. Also, employment practices that make no reference to race, color, religion, sex, or national origin, but that nevertheless have an adverse or disparate impact on the protected group, are unlawful. In disparate impact cases, the fact that an employer did not intend to discriminate is no defense. The employer must show that there is a job-related business necessity for the disparate impact practice in question. Employers have several defenses they may raise in a Title VII case to explain differences in employment conditions. They are (1) bona fide occupational qualifications reasonably necessary to the normal operation of the business, (2) job-related professionally developed ability tests, and (3) bona fide seniority systems. If a state EEO agency or

the EEOC is not able to resolve the case, the EEOC issues a right-to-sue letter that enables the person claiming a Title VII violation to sue in a federal district court. An affirmative action plan is legal under Title VII provided there is a voluntary "plan" justified as a remedial measure and provided it does not unnecessarily trammel the interests of whites.

Under the Equal Pay Act (EPA), employers must not pay employees of one gender a lower wage rate than the rate paid to employees of the other gender for substantially equal work. Workers over 40 years old are protected from discrimination by the Age Discrimination in Employment Act (ADEA). Employment discrimination against persons with disabilities is prohibited by the Americans with Disabilities Act (ADA). Under the ADA, employers must make reasonable accommodations without undue hardship on them to enable individuals with disabilities to work.

QUESTIONS AND CASE PROBLEMS

1. What social forces gave rise to laws requiring equal employment opportunity for all individuals entitled to work in the United States?

2. List the major federal statutes dealing with the regulation of equal rights in employment.

3. State the general purpose of Title VII of the Civil Rights Act of 1964.

4. Continental Photo, Inc., is a portrait photography company. Alex Riley, a black man, applied for a position as a photographer with Continental. Riley submitted an application and was interviewed. In response to a question on a written application, Riley indicated that he had been convicted for forgery (a felony) six years before the interview, had received a suspended sentence, and was placed on five-year probation. He also stated that he would discuss the matter with his interviewer if necessary. The subject of the forgery conviction was subsequently not mentioned by Continental's personnel director in his interview with Riley. Riley's application for employment was eventually rejected. Riley inquired about the reason for his rejection. The personnel director, Geuther, explained to him that the prior felony conviction on his application was a reason for his rejection. Riley contended that the refusal to hire him because of his conviction record was actually discrimination against him because of his race in violation of Title VII. Riley felt that his successful completion of a five-year probation without incident and his steady work over the years qualified him for the job. Continental maintained that because its photographers handle approximately $10,000 in cash per year, its policy of not hiring applicants whose honesty was questionable was justified. Continental's policy excluded all applicants with felony convictions. Decide. Would the result have been different if Riley had been a convicted murderer? [*Continental Photo, Inc.,* 26 Fair Empl Prac Cas (BNA) 1799 (EEOC)]

5. What are the guidelines to be used in determining whether an affirmative action plan is permissible under Title VII?

6. Mohen is a member of the Sikh religion. The practice of Sikhism forbids cutting or shaving facial hair and also requires wearing a turban that covers the head. In accordance with the dictates of his religion, Mohen wore a long beard. He applied for a position as breakfast cook at the Island Manor Restaurant. He was told that the restaurant's policy was to forbid cooks to wear facial hair for sanitary and good grooming reasons and that he would have to shave his beard or be denied a position. Mohen contended that the restaurant had an obligation to make a reasonable accommodation to his religious beliefs and let him keep his beard. Is he correct?

7. Sylvia Hayes worked as a staff technician in the radiology department of Shelby Memorial Hospital. On October 1 Hayes was told by her physician that she was pregnant. When Hayes informed the doctor of her occupation as an X-ray technician, the doctor advised Hayes that she could continue working until the end of April so long as she followed standard safety precautions. On October 8 Hayes told Gail Nell, the director of radiology at Shelby, that she had discovered she was two months' pregnant. On October 14 Hayes was discharged by the hospital. The hospital's reason for terminating Hayes was its concern for the safety of her fetus given the X-ray exposure that occurs during employment as an X-ray technician. Hayes brought an action under Title VII, claiming that her discharge was unlawfully based on her condition of pregnancy. She cited scientific evidence and the practice of other hospitals where pregnant women were allowed to remain in their jobs as X-ray technicians. The hospital claimed that Hayes's discharge was based on business necessity. Moreover, the hospital claimed that the potential for future liability existed if an employee's fetus was damaged by radiation encountered at the workplace. Decide. [*Hayes v Shelby Memorial Hospital,* 546 F Supp 259 (ND Ala)]

8. Overton suffered from depression and was made sleepy at work by medication taken for this condition. Also, because of his medical condition, Overton needed a work area away from public access and substantial supervision to complete his tasks. His employer terminated him because of his routinely sleeping on the job, his inability to maintain contact with the public, and his need for supervision. Overton argued that he is a person with a disability under the ADA and the Rehabilitation Act, fully qualified to perform the essential functions of the job, and that the employer had an obligation to make reasonable accommodations, such as allowing some catnaps as needed and providing some extra supervision. Decide. [*Overton v Reilly,* 977 F2d 1190 (7th Cir)]

9. A teenage female high school student named Salazar was employed part-time at Church's Fried Chicken Restaurant. Salazar was hired and supervised by Simon Garza, the assistant manager of the restaurant. Garza had complete supervisory powers when the restaurant's manager, Garza's roommate, was absent. Salazar claimed that while she worked at the restaurant, Garza would refer to her and all other females by

a Spanish term that she found objectionable. According to Salazar, Garza once made an offensive comment about her body and repeatedly asked her about her personal life. On another occasion, Garza allegedly physically removed eye shadow from Salazar's face because he claimed it was unattractive. Salazar also claimed that one night she was restrained in a back room of the restaurant while Garza and another employee fondled her. Later that night, when Salazar told a customer what had happened, she was fired. Salazar brought suit under Title VII against Garza and Church's Fried Chicken, Inc., alleging sexual harassment. Church's, the corporate defendant, maintained that it should not be held liable under Title VII for Garza's harassment. Church's based its argument on the existence of a published fair treatment policy. Decide. [*Salazar v Church's Fried Chicken, Inc.*, 44 Fair Empl Prac Cas (BNA) 472 (SD Tex)]

10. John Chadbourne was hired by Raytheon on February 4, 1980. His job performance reviews were uniformly high. In December 1983, Chadbourne was hospitalized and diagnosed with AIDS. In January 1984, his physician informed Raytheon that Chadbourne was able to return to work. On January 20, 1984, Chadbourne took a return-to-work physical examination required by Raytheon. The company's doctor wrote the County Communicable Disease Control Director, Dr. Juels, seeking a determination of the appropriateness of Chadbourne's returning to work. Dr. Juels informed the company that "contact of employees to an AIDS patient appears to pose no risk from all evidence accumulated to date." Dr. Juels also visited the plant and advised the company doctor that there was no medical risk to other employees at the plant if Chadbourne returned to work. Raytheon refused to reinstate Chadbourne to his position until July 19, 1984. Its basis for denying reinstatement was that co-workers might be at risk of contracting AIDS. Was Raytheon entitled to bar Chadbourne from work during the six-month period of January through July? [*Raytheon v Fair Employment and Housing Commission* (Ct App) 261 Cal Rptr 197]

11. Connie Cunico, a white woman, was employed by the Pueblo, Colorado, School District as a social worker. She and other social workers were laid off in seniority order because of the district's poor financial situation. However, the school board thereafter decided to retain Wayne Hunter, a black social worker with less seniority than Cunico, because he was the only black on the administrative staff. No racial imbalance existed in the relevant workforce, with black persons constituting 2 percent. Cunico, who was rehired over two years later, claimed that she was the victim of reverse discrimination. She stated that she lost $110,361 in back wages plus $76,000 in attorney fees and costs. The school district replied that it was correct in protecting with special consideration the only black administrator in the district under the general principles it set forth in its AAP. Did the employer show that its affirmative action in retaining Hunter was justified as a remedial measure? Decide. [*Cunico v Pueblo School District No. 6*, 917 F2d 431 (10th Cir)]

12. Della Janich was employed as a matron at the Yellowstone County Jail in Montana. The duties of the position of matron resemble those of a parallel male position of jailer. Both employees have the responsibility for booking prisoners, showering and dressing them, and placing them in the appropriate section of the jail depending on the sex of the offender. Because 95 percent of the prisoners at the jail were men and 5 percent were women, the matron was assigned more bookkeeping duties than the jailer. At all times during Della's employment at the jail, her male counterparts received $125 more per month as jailers. Della brought an action under the Equal Pay Act, alleging discrimination against her in her wages because of her sex. The county sheriff denied the charge. Decide. [*Janich v Sheriff*, 29 Fair Empl Prac Cas (BNA) 1195 (D Mont)]

13. Following a decline in cigarette sales, L & M, Inc., hired J. Gfeller as vice president of sales and charged him to turn around the sales decline. After receiving an analysis of the ages of sales personnel and first-line management, Gfeller and his assistant, T. McMorrow, instituted an intensive program of personnel changes that led to the termination of many older managers and sales representatives. If a top manager sought to justify keeping an older manager, he was informed that he was "not getting the message." Gfeller and McMorrow emphasized that they wanted young and aggressive people and that the older people were not able to conform or adapt to new procedures. R.E. Moran, who had been rated a first-rate division manager, was terminated and replaced by a 27-year-old employee. Gfeller and McMorrow made statements about employees with many years' experience: "It was not twenty years' experience, but rather one year's experience twenty times." The EEOC brought suit on behalf of the terminated managers and sales representatives. The company vigorously denied any discriminatory attitude in regard to age. Decide. [*EEOC v Liggett and Meyers, Inc.*, 29 FEP 1611 (EDNC)]

14. Mazir Coleman had driven a school bus for the Casey County, Kentucky, Board of Education for four years. After that time, Coleman's left leg had to be amputated. Coleman was fitted with an artificial leg and

underwent extensive rehabilitation to relearn driving skills. When his driving skills had been sufficiently relearned over the course of four years, Coleman applied to the county board of education for a job as a school bus driver. The board refused to accept Coleman's application, saying that it had no alternative but to deny Coleman a bus-driving job because of a Kentucky administrative regulation. That regulation stated in part: "No person shall drive a school bus who does not possess both of these natural bodily parts: feet, legs, hands, arms, eyes, and ears. The driver shall have normal use of the above named body parts." Coleman brought an action under the Rehabilitation Act, claiming discrimination based on his physical handicap. The county board of education denied this charge, claiming that the reason they rejected Coleman was because of the requirement of the state regulation. Could Coleman have maintained an action for employment discrimination in light of the state regulation on natural body parts? Decide. [*Coleman v Casey County Board of Education,* 510 F Supp 301 (ND Ky)]

15. Marcia Saxton worked for Jerry Richardson, a supervisor at AT&T's International Division. Richardson made advances to Saxton on two occasions over a three-week period. Each time Saxton told him she did not appreciate his advances. No further advances were made, but thereafter Saxton felt that Richardson treated her condescendingly and stopped speaking to her on a social basis at work. Four months later Saxton filed a formal internal complaint, asserting sexual harassment, and went on "paid leave." AT&T found inconclusive evidence of sexual harassment but determined that the two employees should be separated. Saxton declined a transfer to another department, so AT&T transferred Richardson instead. Saxton still refused to return to work. Thereafter AT&T terminated Saxton for refusal to return to work. Saxton contended she was a victim of hostile working environment sexual harassment. AT&T argued that while the supervisor's conduct was inappropriate and unprofessional, it fell short of the type of action necessary for sexual harassment under federal law (the Harris case). Decide. [*Saxton v AT&T Co.,* 10 F3d 526 (7th Cir)]

P A R T 8

Business Organizations

Forms of Business Organizations

OBJECTIVES

After studying this chapter, you should be able to

1. *List the advantages and disadvantages of the three principal forms of business;*
2. *Determine if a business arrangement is a franchise;*
3. *State the reasons for FTC disclosure requirements;*
4. *Distinguish a joint venture from a partnership; and*
5. *Compare an unincorporated association with a cooperative.*

What form of legal organization should you have for your business? The answer will be found in your needs for money, personnel, control, tax and estate planning, and protection from liability.

A.   PRINCIPAL FORMS OF BUSINESS ORGANIZATIONS

The law of business organizations may be better understood if the advantages and disadvantages of proprietorships, partnerships, and corporations are first considered.

1.   Individual Proprietorships

The sole proprietor controls add decisions and is entitled to all profits. However, the proprietor has unlimited liability, and the business terminates upon the owner's death.

A **sole** or **individual proprietorship** is a form of business ownership in which one individual owns the business. The owner may be the sole worker of the business or may employ as many others as needed to run the concern. Individual proprietorships are commonly used in retail stores, service businesses, and agriculture.

(a) Advantages. The proprietor or owner is not required to expend resources on organizational fees. The proprietor, as the sole owner, controls all of the decisions and receives all of the profits. The business's net earnings are not subject to corporate income taxes but are taxed only as personal income.

(b) Disadvantages. The proprietor is subject to unlimited personal liability for the debts of the business and cannot limit this risk. The investment capital in the business is limited by the resources of the sole proprietor. Because all contracts of the business are made by the owner or in the owner's name by agents of the owner, the authority to make contracts terminates upon the death of the owner, and the business is subject to disintegration.

2.   Partnerships, LLPs, and LLCs

The partnership form allows individuals to pool resources. Yet there is unlimited liability, and the business is of uncertain duration.

A **partnership** involves the pooling of capital resources and the business or professional talents of two or more individuals whose goal is making a profit. Law firms, medical associations, and architectural and engineering firms may operate under the partnership form. Today, however, these firms may convert to the newly created form of business organization called a *limited liability partnership* (LLP). A wide range of small manufacturing, retail, and service businesses operate as partnerships. These businesses may operate under the new form of organization called a *limited liability company* (LLC), which allows for tax treatment as a partnership with limited liability for the owners.

(a) Advantages. The partnership form of business organization allows individuals to pool resources and then initiate and conduct their business without the requirement of a formal organizational structure.

(b) Disadvantages. Major disadvantages of a partnership are the unlimited personal liability of each partner and the uncertain duration of the business because the partnership is dissolved by the death of one partner. Unlimited personal liability is remedied by the LLC form of business organization. Professional partnerships that convert to an LLP shield innocent partners from personal liability beyond their investment in the firm.

3. Corporations

Business corporations exist to make a profit and are created by government grant. State statutes regulating the creation of corporations require a corporate structure consisting of shareholders, directors, and officers. The shareholders, as the owners of the business, elect a board of directors, which is responsible for the management of the business. The directors employ officers, who serve as the agents of the business and run day-to-day operations. Corporations range in size from incorporated one-owner enterprises to large multinational concerns.

> A key advantage of the corporate form is that shareholders have limited liability.

(a) Advantages. The major advantage to the shareholder, or investor, is that the shareholder's risk of loss from the business is limited to the amount of capital he or she invested in the business or paid for shares. This factor, coupled with the free transferability of corporate shares, makes the corporate form of business organization attractive to investors.

By purchasing shares, a large number of investors may contribute the capital assets needed to finance large business enterprises. As the capital needs of a business expand, the corporate form becomes more attractive.

A corporation is a separate legal entity capable of owning property, contracting, suing, and being sued in its own name. It has perpetual life. In other words, a corporation is not affected by the death of any of its shareholders or the transfer of their shares. In contrast to the case of a partnership or proprietorship, the death of an owner has no legal effect on the corporate entity.

> Corporations incur organizational expenses, exposure to double taxation, and reporting requirements.

(b) Disadvantages. A corporation is required to pay corporate income taxes. Shareholders, when they receive a distribution of profits for the corporation, are required to pay personal income taxes on the amount received. This is a form of double taxation, which may be significant if the corporation is owned by a small group.

Incorporation involves the expenditure of funds for organizational expenses. Documents necessary for the formation of a corporation, which are required by state law, must be prepared, and certain filing fees must be paid. State corporation laws may also require filing an annual report and other reports.

B.   SPECIALIZED FORMS OF ORGANIZATIONS

4. Joint Ventures

A **joint venture**, or joint adventure, is a relationship in which two or more persons combine their labor or property for a single business undertaking and share profits and losses equally, or as otherwise agreed.[1] When several contractors pool all their assets to construct one tunnel, the relationship is a joint venture.

---

[1] See *Latiolais v BFI of Louisiana, Inc.* (La App) 567 So 2d 1159 (1990).

CASE SUMMARY

Joint Venture

Facts: Three corporations and two individuals pooled their equipment, services, and assets for the performance of a contract to construct a tunnel. When Wheatley brought suit against them, he claimed that they were a joint venture.

Decision: The corporations and individuals had formed a joint venture because they had pooled everything and had limited their associating to the performance of the one tunnel construction contract. *[Wheatley v Halvorson, 213 Or 228, 323 P2d 49 (1958)]*

ETHICS & THE LAW

Guess? brand jeans began a longstanding fashion phenomenon in 1981. Georges Marciano, the CEO of a new company, Guess?, owned by him and his brothers sold 2 dozen pairs of supertight, superfaded jeans to Bloomingdale's. The 24 pairs of jeans sold within just hours, and Bloomingdale's wanted more. The small company did not have the financing or factories to keep up with the demand and sold stock through an initial public offering in order to raise funds for expansion.

The Nakash brothers, the Israeli owners of Jordache Jeans, purchased a 51% interest in Guess? through that offering. The Marciano brothers combined their hot new product with the funds the Nakash brothers had accumulated from their now fading Jordache label jeans. The Nakash brothers bought their shares for $5 million, but by 1985 the shares were worth $100 million.

The Marciano brothers wished to regain control of the company. Signing over that control was necessary for growth, but they looked at the Nakash interest as a "temporary joint venture." The Nakash brothers were not interested in selling their shares back to the Marciano brothers. The Marciano brothers then began a series of attempts over the next five years to drive out the Nakash brothers. A judge found that the Marciano brothers hid earnings from the Nakashes by requiring all contractors to overbill the corporation $1 per garment. The extra $1 was funneled to other companies the Marcianos owned. There were two trials over trademark infringement, accusations about labor disputes, and even misconduct by a former IRS agent that was eventually investigated by Congress. The Nakash brothers settled out of court on the pending cases and sold their shares to the Marcianos. Following the settlement of the cases and the reacquisition of control of the company, the Marciano brothers and Guess? have experienced setbacks. The market has new competition from CK Jeans and Tommy Hilfiger. The Guess? percentage of the market share has declined dramatically. By 1996, one fashion industry analyst said, "They're fading."

Did the Marcianos use the Nakash capital that they needed and then try to eliminate their obligations to them? Would you want to negotiate a joint venture with the Marciano brothers? Why or why not? Should the Marciano brothers have focused more on their business and less on their partners? Would you invest on a joint venture? Why or why not?

A joint venture is similar in many respects to a partnership. It differs primarily in that the joint venture typically involves the pursuit of a single enterprise or transaction, although its accomplishment may require several years. A partnership is generally a continuing business or activity but may be expressly created for a single transaction. Because the distinction is so insubstantial, most courts hold that joint ventures are subject to the same principles of law as partnerships.[2] Thus, the duties owed by the joint venturers to each other are the same as those that partners owe to each other.

A joint venture is similar to a general partnership, although the joint venture is formed to accomplish a single enterprise.

It is essential that the venturers have a common purpose and that each has an equal right to control the operations or activities of the undertaking.[3] The actual control of the operations may be entrusted to one of the joint venturers. Thus, the fact that one joint venturer is placed in control of the farming and livestock operations of an undertaking, for example, and appears to be the owner of the land does not destroy the joint venture relationship.

(a) Duration of Joint Venture. A joint venture continues for the time specified in the agreement of the parties. In the absence of a fixed-duration provision, a joint venture is ordinarily terminable at the will of any participant. When the joint venture clearly relates to a particular transaction, such as the construction of a specified bridge, the joint venture ordinarily lasts until the particular transaction or project is completed or becomes impossible to complete.

(b) Liability to Third Persons. The conclusion that persons are joint venturers is important when a suit is brought by or against a third person for personal injuries or property damage. If there is a joint venture, the fault or negligence of one venturer will be imputed to the other venturers.[4]

5. Unincorporated Associations

An **unincorporated association** is a combination of two or more persons for the furtherance of a common purpose.[5] No particular form of organization is required. Any conduct or agreement indicating an attempt to associate or work together for a common purpose is sufficient.

The authority of an unincorporated association over its members is governed by ordinary contract law. An association cannot expel a member for a ground that is not expressly authorized by the contract between the association and the member.

An unincorporated association does not have legal existence apart from the members who make up the organization.

Except when otherwise provided by statute, an unincorporated association does not have any legal existence apart from its members. Thus, an unincorporated association cannot sue or be sued in its own name.

Generally, the members of an unincorporated association are not liable for the debts or liabilities of the association by the mere fact that they are members. It must usually be shown that they authorized or ratified the act in question. If either authorization or ratification by a particular member can be shown, that member has unlimited liability for the act.

---

[2] *Pardco v Spinks* (Tex App) 836 SW2d 649 (1992).
[3] *Dunbar v RKG Engineering, Inc.* (Tex App) 746 SW2d 314 (1988).
[4] *Kim v Chamberlain* (Ala App) 504 So 2d 1213 (1987).
[5] The National Conference of Commissioners on Uniform State Law has adopted a Uniform Unincorporated Nonprofit Association Act. In addition, community associations are being widely formed, primarily for the purpose of community planning and environmental protection.

Batters with Two Strikes Should Never Trust the Umpire, and Their Parents Should Have Little Faith That the Association Will Pay the Bills

Facts: Golden Spike Little League was an unincorporated association of persons who joined together to promote a little league baseball team in Ogden, Utah. They sent one of their members to arrange for credit at Smith & Edwards, a local sporting goods store. After getting credit, various members went to the store and picked up and signed for different items of baseball equipment and uniforms, at a total cost of $3,900. When Mr. Smith, the owner, requested payment, the members arranged a fundraising activity that produced only $149. Smith sued the Golden Spike Little League as an entity and the members who had picked up and signed for the equipment individually. The individual defendants denied that they had any personal liability, contending that only the Golden Spike Little League could be held responsible.

Decision: Judgment for Smith against the individual members. The association could not be held liable because it did not have any legal existence. The persons who purchased the goods from the seller were personally liable as buyers even though they had purported to act on behalf of the unincorporated association. [Smith & Edwards v Golden Spike Little League (Utah) 577 P2d 132 (1978)]

6. Cooperatives

A **cooperative** consists of a group of two or more independent persons or enterprises that cooperate for a common objective or function. Thus, farmers may pool their farm products and sell them. Consumers may likewise pool their orders and purchase goods in bulk.

(a) Incorporated Cooperatives. Statutes commonly provide for the special incorporation of cooperative enterprises. Such statutes often provide that any excess of payments over the cost of operation shall be refunded to each participant member in direct proportion to the volume of business that the member has done with the cooperative. This contrasts with the payment of a dividend by an ordinary business corporation, in which the payment of dividends is proportional to the number of shares held by the shareholder and is unrelated to the extent of the shareholder's business activities with the enterprise.

A farmers' cooperative is exempt from the Sherman Antitrust Act as long as it does not conspire with outsiders to fix prices.

(b) Antitrust Law Exemption. The agreement by the members of sellers' cooperatives that all products shall be sold at a common price is an agreement to fix prices. Therefore, the sellers' cooperative is basically an agreement in restraint of trade and a violation of antitrust laws. The Capper-Volstead Act of 1922 expressly exempts normal selling activities of farmers' and dairy farmers' cooperatives from the operation of the federal Sherman Antitrust Act so long as the cooperatives do not conspire with outsiders to fix prices.

C. THE FRANCHISE BUSINESS FORMAT

Franchising in individual situations is a method of doing business, not a form of business organization. A franchisor or franchisee could be a sole proprietor, a partnership, a limited liability company, or a corporation. It is a "business format," as opposed to a business organization. Franchising relies on contract law to set forth the rights and obligations of the parties. However, the Federal Trade Commission Act and certain state laws require disclosure. And federal and/or state laws regulating securities, intellectual property, antitrust violations, sales, agency, and tort law apply to franchises.

Section 5 of the Federal Trade Commission Act prohibits deceptive, manipulative, or unfair business practices[6], and state deceptive trade practices acts similarly prohibit such practice.

CASE SUMMARY

Not Going to Have to Pay a Lot for This Muffler Shop?

Facts: Kelly Broussard and other franchisees brought a class action lawsuit against their franchisor, Meineke Discount Muffler Shops Inc. for violation of North Carolina's Deceptive Trade Practices Act (DTPA). Under terms of their Franchise and Trademarks Agreements (FTAs) Meineke was obligated to purchase and place advertising for its franchisees in exchange for their franchise fees. Franchisees testified that Meineke told them that the fund created under the FTA was exclusively for the benefit of its franchisees and it took no revenue from it. The franchisees presented evidence that the franchisor used the advertising fund for improper purposes such as settling a lawsuit, paying other business expenses, and advertising to attract franchisees as opposed to advertising to generate business for existing franchisees and that Meineke had negotiated volume discounts for advertising and kept the discounts for itself. Meineke raised procedural defenses and denied it had done anything improper.

Decision: Judgment for the franchisees who had not signed releases. Meineke breached its fiduciary duty to its franchisees and violated the state DTPA by using the advertising account to settle a lawsuit, by securing large volume discounts for advertising and keeping the discounts, and by spending the franchisees' advertising funds to attract new franchisees rather than to advertise to generate business. Treble charges were allowed the franchisees under the DTPA. [*Broussard v Meineke Discount Muffler Shops, Inc.*, 958 F Supp 1087 (WDNC 1997)]

---

7. Definition and Types of Franchises

The Federal Trade Commission (FTC) has defined a franchise as "an arrangement in which the owner of a trademark, trade name, or copyright licenses others, under specified conditions or limitations, to use the trademark, trade name, or copyright in purveying goods or services." The **franchisor** is the party granting the franchise, and the **franchisee** is the person to whom the franchise is granted. There are three principal types of franchises. The first is a *manufacturing* or *processing franchise*, in which the franchisor grants the franchisee authority to manufacture and sell products under the trademark(s) of the franchisor. The franchisor may supply an essential ingredient in a processing franchise, such as the syrup for an independent regional Coca-Cola bottling company. The second type of franchise is a *service franchise*, whereby the franchisee renders a service to customers under the terms of a franchise agreement. The drain-cleaning service provided by Roto-Rooter is an example of a service franchise. The third type is a *distribution franchise*, in which the franchisor's products are sold to a franchisee, who then resells to customers in a geographical area. Mobil Oil Co.'s products are often sold to retail customers through independent distribution franchises.

---

[6] 15 USC § 45.

A common issue in litigation under state laws protecting franchisees is whether or not the business arrangement of the parties is a franchise, or a businessperson is a franchisee, under the applicable state law.

CASE SUMMARY

A Rabbit's Foot Case

Facts: In order to establish that a business is a "franchisee" qualifying for protection under the Illinois Franchise Disclosure Act, the business must demonstrate that it paid a franchise fee either directly or indirectly to the "franchisor" to enter the business. To-Am Equipment Co. Inc. believed it had paid an implied fee in excess of $500 to enter the forklift business as a dealer for Mitsubishi-Caterpillar Forklift of America (MCFA) by paying $1,658 for service manuals, which MCFA had commanded it to possess. MCFA denied that it had charged To-Am a franchise fee and asserted that it is not obligated to To-Am under the state Franchise Disclosure Act.

Decision: Judgment for To-Am. A required purchase at a price exceeding the item's value is an indirect franchise fee. A franchisor of rabbits' feet would be indifferent between receiving a franchise "fee" of $1,000 and a price of $1 for a rabbit's foot, which was the franchisor's cost, or a "price" of $1,001 for a rabbit's foot it cost $1 for the franchisor to supply. The evidence supported the jury's finding that To-Am paid a fee in excess of $500 for the right to enter the business and is therefore protected under the Franchise Disclosure Act. *[To-Am Equipment Co. v Mitsubishi-Caterpillar Forklift of America, 953 F Supp 987 (ND Ill 1997)]*

---

8. The Franchise Agreement

> A franchise is a business relationship between independent contractors governed by a franchise contract.

The relationship between the franchisor and the franchisee is ordinarily an arm's-length relationship between two independent contractors. Their respective rights are determined by the contract existing between them, called the **franchise agreement**. The agreement sets forth the rights of the franchisee to use the trademarks, trade name, trade dress, and trade secrets of the franchisor. ◆ *For example*, Burger King Corp. licenses franchisees to use the trademarks Burger King, Whopper, Croissanwich, and Whopper Jr.[7] ◆ The franchise agreement commonly requires the franchisor to provide training for the franchisees' employees, including processing or repair training. Thus, a new Chili's Bar and Grill franchise can expect to have its employees taught how to prepare and serve the food on its menu. And in a distribution franchise, an Acura dealer can expect the franchisor to train its mechanics to repair the automobiles it sells. The franchise agreement also deals with terms for payment of various fees by the franchisee and sets forth compliance requirements for quality control set by the franchisor.

The duration of a franchise is a critical element of the franchise agreement. The franchise may last for as long as the parties agree. The laws in some states may require advance written notice of cancellation.[8] Franchise contracts generally specify the causes for which the franchisor may terminate the franchise, such as the franchisee's death, bankruptcy, failure to make payments, or failure to meet sales quotas. Implied obligations of good faith and fair dealing apply to these contracts.[9]

---

[7] *Burger King Corp. v Agad,* 1996 Bus. Franchise Guide (CCH) ¶ 1082 (D Fla 1996).
[8] See, for example, Mo Rev Stat § 407.405; *Ridings v Thoele* (Mo) 739 SW2d 547 (1987).
[9] *Dunkin Donuts of America v Minerva, Inc.,* 956 F2d 1566 (11th Cir 1992).

If You're Not Making Monthly Payments, Then You Must Stop Making Big Macs

Facts: McDonald's Corporation entered into a contract with Robert A. Makin, Inc., to lease and operate a McDonald's restaurant in Clarence, New York. The franchise agreement required Makin to make monthly payments of license and lease fees to McDonald's, and the agreement provided for the termination of the franchise if Makin should fail to make all payments under the agreement. Makin failed to make monthly payments from October 1985 through February 10, 1986. McDonald's gave notice that it had terminated the lease and the franchise. Makin refused to stop operations and to surrender the premises. McDonald's brought suit for the amount due for the period and sought a court order granting it the right to enter and take possession of the restaurant.

Decision: Judgment for McDonald's. Makin's failure to pay the monthly franchise fees was a breach of contract. When Makin refused to pay the amounts owed, McDonald's had a contractual right to terminate the lease and the franchise agreement. McDonald's had the immediate right to enter and take possession of the restaurant. [*McDonald's Corp. v Makin, Inc.,* 653 F Supp 401 (WNDY 1986)]

Franchise agreements frequently contain an arbitration provision under which a neutral party is to make a final and binding determination whether there has been a breach of the contract sufficient to justify cancellation of the franchise. The arbitration provision may provide that the franchisor can appoint a trustee to run the business of the franchisee while arbitration proceedings are pending.

9. Special Protections under Federal Laws

Holders of automobile dealership franchises are protected from bad-faith termination of their dealerships by the federal Automobile Dealers' Franchise Act.[10] When an automobile manufacturer makes arbitrary and unreasonable demands and then terminates a dealer's franchise for failure to comply with the demands, the manufacturer is liable for the damages caused. However, a manufacturer is justified in terminating an automobile dealership when the dealership fails to maintain the required sales quota after the manufacturer has given the dealer repeated warnings, when the quota is reasonable, and when the quota has been reduced to reflect local economic conditions.

The Petroleum Marketing Practices Act (PMPA) gives gas station franchisees the opportunity to continue in business by purchasing the entire premises used in selling motor fuel when the franchisor decides to sell the property and not renew a lease.[11]

10. Disclosure

The FTC has adopted a franchise disclosure rule that requires franchisors to give prospective franchisees a full disclosure statement ten days before a franchisee signs a contract or pays any money for a franchise. Fourteen states also have

---

[10] 15 USC § 1222. A number of states have similar statutes.
[11] *Baker v Amoco Oil Co.,* 956 F2d 639 (7th Cir 1992).

protective regulations requiring disclosure in the sale of franchises. Effective on and after December 21, 1995, all 14 states and the FTC accepted the 1993 revised version of the Uniform Franchise Offering Circular as full compliance with state and FTC disclosure rules.

The disclosure statement must include (1) the business experience of the franchisor and its brokers, (2) any current and past litigation against the franchisor, (3) any previous bankruptcy, (4) the material terms of the franchise agreement, (5) initial and recurring payments, (6) restrictions on territories, (7) grounds for termination of the franchise, and (8) actual, average, or projected sales, profits, or earnings.

Under the FTC disclosure rule, a franchisor must pay a civil penalty of as much as $10,000 for each violation when it is shown that a sale of a franchise subject to the FTC rule was made, the franchisor knew or should have known of the disclosure rule, and no disclosure statement was given to the buyer. Also, the franchisor may be required to make the buyer whole for any losses suffered.

CASE SUMMARY

Why a Franchise Disclosure Rule is Necessary

Facts: Wolf, King, and others sold business "opportunities" in vending machines by taking out ads in newspapers throughout the country. When investors responded, telemarketers called "fronters" would tell the investors of false earnings estimates, and those who could afford $16,000 to $25,000 for vending machines were turned over to "closers" who promised exclusive, very desirable territories to the investors. References were provided who were "shills" who did not own vending machines but were paid to tell "stories" that were monitored by Wolf, King, and other supervisors. None of the investors received the franchise disclosure documents required by the FTC or a copy of an earnings claim document. King induced one investor to mortgage her house so that she could pay $70,000 for a sham business opportunity. In three years Wolf, King, and others took in some $31.3 million from the sale of business opportunities. The FTC alleged that the defendants violated the FTC franchise disclosure rule.

Decision: Judgment for the FTC. The FTC's franchise disclosure rule requires a franchisor to provide prospective franchisees with a complete and accurate disclosure document containing information about the history, terms, and conditions of the franchise. The rule also requires that the franchisor have a reasonable basis for all representations concerning earnings or profits. The defendants violated the rule. A receiver was appointed to collect all of the defendants' assets up to the sum of $31,362,576, and to formulate a plan for redress to investors. [*FTC v Wolf*, 1996 (USDC Fla) Bus. Franchise Guide (CCH) ¶ 27,655]

---

11. Vicarious Liability Claims against Franchisors

Ordinarily a franchisor is not liable for the contracts or torts of a franchisee.

In theory, a franchisor is not liable to a third person dealing with or affected by the franchise holder. This freedom from liability is one of the main reasons franchisors use franchises. If the negligence of the franchisee causes harm to a third person, the franchisor is not liable because the franchisee is an independent contractor.[12] However, franchisors continue to be subject to lawsuits based on the wrongful conduct of their franchisees under the theory of either authority or apparent authority.

---

[12] *Cislaw v 7-Eleven, Inc.* (Cal App) 6 Cal Rptr 2d 386 (1992); *Ciup v Chevron USA Inc.* (NM) 928 P2d 263 (1886).

Special Damages

Facts: For a five-year period Laurie Henry worked for James Doull, the owner of four Taco Bell franchises. During that time she had an affair with Doull. He was the father of her two illegitimate children. Enraged over a domestic matter Doull physically assaulted her and then fired her and ordered her off the premises. Later, on Doull's recommendation, she was hired by a "company store" in an adjoining state. Henry brought suit against Doull, his corporate entity Taco Tia, Inc., and the Taco Bell Corporation (TBC). She did not characterize her suit as one for sexual harassment. Rather, she contended that TBC was responsible for Doull's actions because he was TBC's agent. She sought damages for the loss of romantic and material satisfactions a person might expect from a traditional courtship and wedding. TBC denied that Doull was an employee or agent of TBC. The evidence showed that Henry knew that Doull's stores were not owned by TBC and that his stores differed from TBC "company" stores.

Decision: Judgment for Taco Bell Corporation. Laurie Henry's employer was the franchise owner, James Doull, not the franchisor, Taco Bell Corporation. She had actual knowledge that Doull was a franchisee and not an agent of TBC. No basis exists to believe that Doull was an apparent agent of TBC. [*Henry v Taco Tia, Inc. (La App) 606 So2d 1376 (1992)*]

In order to maintain uniform systems for processing or distributing goods or rendering services, franchisors often place very significant controls on their franchisees' businesses. These controls are set forth in franchise agreements and operating manuals. In a lawsuit brought against a franchisor for the wrongful conduct of its franchisee, the franchise agreement and operations manuals may be used as evidence of the franchisor's right to control the franchisee and the existence of an agency relationship rather than an independent contractor relationship.[13]

To avoid negating its franchisees' independent contractor status and being liable for the wrongful conduct of a franchisee, the franchisor should make certain that the franchise agreement minimizes the number and kind of provisions that authorize the franchisor to control the "means" of operating the business. *For example,* the franchisor should not exercise control over employment-related matters.[14]

Franchisors may also insulate themselves from liability by requiring individual franchisees to take steps to publicly maintain their own individual business identities. *For example,* a gas station may post a sign stating that it is "dealer owned and operated," or a real estate franchise may list on its business sign the franchise name and the name of the local owner, such as Century 21, L & K Realty Co. All invoices, purchase orders, paychecks, and notices to employees should contain notice of the independent ownership and operation of the business. Finally,

---

[13] *J.M. v Shell Oil Co.* (Mo App) 1996 Bus. Franchise Guide (CCH) ¶ 10,817.
[14] Consider the degree of control exercised by McDonald's Corp. over its franchises. Only designated food and beverages may be served, and franchisees are required to use prescribed buildings and equipment. The franchisor dictates the level of quality, service, and cleanliness. All franchisees' employees must wear the uniforms designated by the franchisor with McDonald's logos. McDonald's dictates management, advertising, and personnel policies and requires that managers be trained at its "Hamburger University." The Illinois Court of Appeals has held that the question of whether the franchisee was an apparent agent of McDonald's was an issue of material fact that should go to a jury in a lawsuit involving a slip and fall by a customer on ice in a franchised restaurant's bathroom. The court stated that the employees responsible for maintaining the bathroom wore "McDonald's uniforms" and were required to follow McDonald's standards of "quality, service, and cleanliness." *O'Banner v McDonald's Corp.* (Ill App) 653 NE2d 1267 (1995). On further appeal to the Supreme Court of Illinois, the court of appeals was reversed because in order to recover on an apparent agency theory the customer had to show that he actually relied on the apparent agency in going to the restaurant where he was injured. The customer failed to do so, thus losing the right to hold McDonald's Corp. liable for his injuries. *O'Banner v McDonald's Corp.* (Ill) 670 NE2d 632 (1996).

franchisors should require their franchisees to maintain appropriate comprehensive general liability insurance, workers' compensation insurance, and other appropriate insurance.

SUMMARY

The three principal forms of business organizations are sole proprietorships, partnerships, and corporations. A sole proprietorship is a form of business organization in which one person owns the business, controls all decisions, receives all profits, and has unlimited liability for all obligations and liabilities. A partnership involves the pooling of capital resources and talents of two or more persons whose goal is making a profit; the partners are subject to unlimited personal liability. However, newly created forms of business organizations-the limited liability company and the limited liability partnership-allow for tax treatment as a partnership with certain limited liability for the owners. A business corporation exists to make a profit. It is created by government grant, and its shareholders elect a board of directors, who are responsible for managing the business. A shareholder's liability is limited to the capital the shareholder invested in the business or paid for shares. Corporate existence continues without regard to the death of shareholders or the transfer of stock by them.

The selection of the form of organization is determined by the nature of the business, tax considerations, the financial risk involved, the importance of limited liability, and the extent of management control desired.

A joint venture exists when two or more persons combine their labor or property for a single business undertaking and share profits and losses as agreed. An unincorporated association is a combination of two or more persons for the pursuit of a common prupose.

A cooperative consists of two or more persons or enterprises, such as farmers, who cooperate to achieve a common objective, such as the distribution of farm products.

By a franchise, the owner of a trademark, trade name, or copyright licenses others to use the mark or copyright in selling goods or services. To protect against fraud, the FTC requires that franchisors provide prospective franchisees with a disclosure statement ten days prior to any transaction. The Automobile Dealers' Franchise Act and the Petroleum Marketing Practices Act are federal laws that provide covered franchisees with protection from bad-faith terminations. State laws also protect franchisees in a wide range of businesses. A franchisor is not liable to third persons dealing with its franchisees. Liability of the franchisor may, however, be imposed on the ground of the apparent authority of the franchisee or the latter's control by the franchisor. Liability of the franchisor may also arise in cases of product liability.

QUESTIONS AND CASE PROBLEMS

1. What social forces are affected by the federal Automobile Dealers' Franchise Act?
2. When is a franchisor held liable to a third person dealing with or affected by the franchisee?
3. Jerome, Sheila, Gary, and Ella agreed to purchase a tract of land and make it available for use as a free playground for neighborhood children. They called the enterprise Meadowbrook Playground. One of the playground swings was improperly hung by Jerome and Gary, and a child was injured. Suit was brought against Meadowbrook Playground. Can damages be recovered?
4. Morris Friedman was president of Tiny Doubles International, Inc. He sold business opportunities for Tiny Doubles Studios, which made small photographic statues of people for customers. Friedman was the primary negotiator with prospective buyers

of these studio business opportunities. He advised buyers up front that the opportunities were not franchises, and, accordingly, he did not provide all of the information set forth in the disclosure rule on franchising, although he did provide full answers to all questions asked. Many businesses closed, however, because of lack of success. The FTC claims Friedman violated its disclosure rule. Friedman disagrees. Decide. [*FTC v Tiny Doubles International, Inc.*, 1996 Bus. Franchise Guide (CCH) ¶ 10,831]
5. Katherine Apostoleres owned the rights to Dunkin Donuts franchises in Brandon and Temple Terrace, Florida. In early 1982 the franchisor offered all its franchisees the right to renew their existing franchise agreements if they agreed to abide by advertising decisions favored by two-thirds of the local franchise owners in a given television market. Apostoleres

refused the offer because she did not want to be bound by the two-thirds clause. Soon thereafter Dunkin Donuts audited her two stores, and, using a "yield and usage" analysis, it concluded that gross sales were being underreported. Based on these audits and a subsequent audit, Dunkin Donuts gave notice of immediate termination of Apostoleres's franchises, contending that the franchise agreement had been violated. Apostoleres stated that an implied obligation of good faith exists by operation of law in every contract, and she asserted that the 1982 audits were in retaliation for her refusal to accept the renewal agreement. The yield and usage test used in the audit was not specified in the franchise agreement as a measure to be used to enforce the franchisor's rights, and certain accounting experts testified as to the unreliability of this test. Was Dunkin Donuts liable for breach of its implied obligation of good faith in this case? [*Dunkin Donuts of America v Minerva, Inc.*, 956 F2d 1566 (11th Cir)]

6. If a group of farmers agrees among themselves to pool their products and set a common price for the sale of these products, would this be price fixing in violation of federal antitrust laws?

7. Compare and contrast a franchise and a contract.

8. The Armory Committee was composed of officers from various National Guard units. They organized a New Year's Eve dance at a charge of $2 per person to defray costs. Perry, along with others, was a member of the Armory Committee. Libby was a paying guest at the dance who was injured by slipping on frozen ruts in the immediate approaches to the steps leading to the armory building, where the dance was held. He sued Perry, Turner, and the other committee members. The evidence showed that every member of the committee had taken some part in planning or running the dance with the exception of Turner. Was the Armory Committee an unincorporated association or a joint venture? Decide. [*Libby v Perry* (Me) 311 A2d 527]

9. The Kawasaki Shop of Aurora, Illinois (dealer), advised Kawasaki Motors Corp. (manufacturer) that it intended to move its Kawasaki franchise from New York Street to Hill Avenue, which was in the same market area. The Hill Avenue location was also the site of a Honda franchise. The manufacturer's sales manager advised the dealer that he did not want the dealer to move in with Honda at the Hill Avenue site. In February 1982, the dealer moved to the Hill Avenue location. Effective May 1, 1982, the manufacturer terminated the dealer's franchise. The dealer brought suit against the manufacturer under the state's Motor Vehicle Franchise Act, which made it unlawful to terminate franchises for site control (requiring that the

dealer's site be used exclusively as a Kawasaki dealership). The manufacturer argued that it had a right to have its products sold by a dealer who was not affiliated with a competitor. Decide. [*Kawasaki Shop v Kawasaki Motors Corp.* (Ill App) 544 NE2d 457]

10. Goodward, a newly hired newspaper reporter for the Cape Cod News, learned that the local cranberry growers had made an agreement under which they pooled their cranberry crops each year and sold them at what they determined to be a fair price. Goodward believes that such an agreement is in restraint of trade and a violation of the antitrust laws. Is he correct?

11. Food Caterers, Inc., of East Hartford, Connecticut, obtained a franchise from Chicken Delight, Inc., to use that name at its store. Food Caterers agreed to the product standards and controls specified by the franchisor. The franchise contract required the franchisee to maintain a free delivery service to deliver hot, freshly prepared food to customers. The franchisee used a delivery truck that bore no sign or name. Its employee Carfiro was driving the truck in making a food delivery when he negligently struck and killed McLaughlin. The victim's estate sued Chicken Delight on the theory that Carfiro was its agent because he was doing work that Chicken Delight required and that benefited Chicken Delight. Was Carfiro the agent of Chicken Delight? [*McLaughlin's Estate v Chicken Delight, Inc.* (Conn) 321 A2d 456]

12. Groseth had the International Harvester (IH) truck franchise in Yankton, South Dakota. The franchise agreement Groseth signed required dealers to "cooperate with the Company by placing orders for goods in accordance with advance ordering programs announced by the Company." IH wanted to terminate Groseth's franchise because Groseth refused to comply with IH's requirement that a computerized "dealer communication network" (DCN) be set up. Under the DCN, each dealer was required to obtain a computer terminal, display screen, and software. The DCN was initially used for ordering parts and allowed IH to reduce the number of employees needed for manual processing of "parts" orders. Groseth refused to set up the DCN because of the expense. Moreover, he contended that the task of ordering parts was easily accomplished by telephone or written orders. Did IH have good cause to terminate Groseth's franchise? [*Groseth International Harvester, Inc. v International Harvester* (SD) 442 NW2d 229]

13. Brenner was in the scrap iron business. Almost daily Plitt lent Brenner money with which to purchase scrap iron. The agreement of the parties was that when the scrap was sold, Plitt would be repaid and would

receive an additional sum as compensation for making the loans. The loans were to be repaid in any case without regard to whether Brenner made a profit. A dispute arose over the nature of the relationship between the two men. Plitt claimed that it was a joint venture. Decide. [*Brenner v Plitt* (Md) 34 A2d 853]

14. Donald Salisbury, William Roberts, and others purchased property from Laurel Chapman, a partner of Chapman Realty, a franchisee of Realty World, Inc. The purchasers made payments directly to Laurel Chapman at the Realty World office, and Chapman was to make payments on the property's mortgage. However, Chapman did not make the payments and absconded with the funds. Salisbury and Roberts sued the franchisor, Realty World, claiming that Realty World was liable for the wrongful acts of the apparent agent, Chapman. Realty World and Chapman Realty were parties to a franchise agreement stating that the parties were franchisor and franchisee. The agreement contained a clause that required Chapman to prominently display a certificate in the office setting forth her status as an independent franchisee. Chapman displayed such a sign, but the plaintiffs did not recall seeing it. Chapman Realty hires, supervises, and sets the compensation for all of its employees. The plaintiffs pointed out that Chapman Realty used the service mark Realty World on its signs, both outside and inside its offices. They pointed out that a Realty World manual sets forth the general standards by which franchisees must run their businesses and that this represents clear control over the franchise. They contended that, all things considered, Realty World held out Chapman Realty as having authority to bind Realty World. Realty World disagreed, stating that both were independent businesses. Decide. [*Salisbury v Chapman and Realty World, Inc.* (Ill App) 65 NE2d 127]

15. H.C. Blackwell Co. held a franchise from Kenworth Truck Co. to sell its trucks. After 12 years, the franchise was nearing expiration. Kenworth notified Blackwell that the franchise would not be renewed unless Blackwell sold more trucks and improved its building and bookkeeping systems within the next 90 days. Blackwell spent $90,000 attempting to meet the demands of Kenworth but could not do so because a year was required to make the specified changes. Kenworth refused to renew the franchise. Blackwell sued Kenworth for damages under the federal Automobile Dealers' Franchise Act. Blackwell claimed that Kenworth had refused to renew in bad faith. Decide. [*Blackwell v Kenworth Truck Co.*, 620 F2d 104 (5th Cir)]

CPA QUESTION

1. A joint venture is a(an)
   a. Association limited to no more than two persons in business for profit.
   b. Enterprise of numerous co-owners in a nonprofit undertaking.
   c. Corporate enterprise for a single undertaking of limited duration.
   d. Association of persons engaged as co-owners in a single undertaking for profit.

   (11/89, Law, #4)

Creation and Termination of Partnerships

CHAPTER 44

OBJECTIVES

After studying this chapter, you should be able to

1. *Describe the characteristics of a partnership;*
2. *Distinguish between general and special partnerships and trading and nontrading partnerships;*
3. *List the seven rules that aid in determining whether the parties have created a partnership;*
4. *Explain the effect of a dissolution of a partnership;*
5. *Describe how a partnership may be dissolved by the acts of the partners, by operation of law, and by order of a court; and*
6. *Describe the extent of a partner's authority during the winding up of a partnership's business.*

What can you do if a sole proprietorship does not meet your business needs? You might form a partnership.

A. NATURE AND CREATION

Partnerships are created by agreement. A codification of general partnership law is found in the Uniform Partnership Act (UPA), which has been revised (Revised Uniform Partnership Act or RUPA). Together the UPA and the RUPA are in effect in 49 states.[1] Limited partnerships (LPs) and limited liability partnerships (LLPs) differ significantly from general partnerships and are discussed in the next chapter. The 1994 version of the Revised Uniform Partnership Act is being phased in in twelve states.[2] Like the UPA, most of the provisions of the RUPA apply only when the partners do not have partnership agreement language that deals with the matter at issue. Certain features of the RUPA that differ from those of the UPA are identified in the text.

1. Definition

A **partnership** (also called a *general partnership*) is a relationship created by the voluntary "association of two or more persons to carry on as co-owners a business for profit."[3] The persons so associated are called **partners** or **general partners**. A partner is the agent of the partnership and of each partner with respect to partnership matters. A partner is not an employee of the partnership even when doing work that would ordinarily be done by an employee.

> **CASE SUMMARY**
>
> ## A Partner Is Not an Employee
>
> **Facts:** Ford and Mitcham were partners engaged in construction. Ford was killed at work. His widow made a claim for workers' compensation against the partnership. Mitcham opposed the claim on the ground that Ford was a partner and not an employee.
>
> **Decision:** Workers' compensation denied. While a working partner does work, a partner is not an employee. The essential element of an employment relationship is the right of the employer to control the employee. Although a partner is required to act in a proper manner, a partner is not subject to the control of the partnership in the same sense as an employee and therefore is not an "employee" of the partnership for the purpose of workers' compensation. [*Ford v Mitcham (Ala Civ App) 298 So 2d 34 (1974)*]

2. Characteristics of a Partnership

A partnership has distinguishing characteristics:

1. A partnership is a voluntary, consensual relationship.

2. A partnership involves partners' contributions of capital, services, or a combination of these.

Partners are the co-owners of a business and are agents of the partnership and each other. Note the agency principles that are interwoven into the partnership law chapters.

---

[1] The UPA or the RUPA is in effect in all states except Louisiana.

[2] The RUPA or versions of it have been adopted by Alabama, Arizona, California, Connecticut, Florida, Montana, New Mexico, North Dakota, Texas, Virginia, West Virginia, and Wyoming. The RUPA was approved in 1992 and amended in 1993 and 1994. It provides for a transition period after passage, during which only newly created partnerships come under the new law, with all partnerships in the state eventually being governed by the RUPA (see RUPA § 1206(a)).

[3] UPA § 6(1).

3. The partners are associated as co-owners to transact the business of the firm for profit.

If profit is not the object, the group will commonly be an unincorporated association.

The UPA does not make the partnership a separate entity, and therefore suit cannot be brought by the firm in its name in the absence of a special statute or procedural rule so providing. However, in RUPA states partnerships are recognized as "entities."

3. Rights of Partners

The rights of partners are determined by the partnership agreement. If written, this agreement is interpreted by the same rules that govern the interpretation of any other written document. Any matter not covered by the partnership agreement may be covered by a provision of the applicable UPA.

CASE SUMMARY

No Discounts for Partners

Facts: Marshall and Olsen were partners. The partnership agreement provided that upon the death of a partner, the survivor could purchase the interest of the deceased partner. Olsen died, and Seattle-First National Bank was appointed the executor for Olsen's estate. A dispute arose as to how the interest of Olsen was to be valued. Marshall claimed that certain discounts should be allowed to reduce the purchase price.

Decision: The agreement of the partners did not provide for any discount in computing the valuation. No such discount was authorized by the UPA. Therefore, the survivor was not entitled to any discount. [*Seattle-First National Bank v Marshall, 31 Wash App 339, 641 P2d 1194 (1982)*]

ETHICS & THE LAW

Gin Miller, a nationally known fitness instructor, tore a knee ligament in 1986. During her recovery, a physical therapist suggested that she step up and down on a wooden step to strengthen her knee. Miller discovered that there was an aerobic component to this physical therapy, and she began using the wooden step-up in teaching her aerobic classes. Using music and choreographed routines, Miller began an aerobic trend with what she called the "Bench Blast."

Richard Boggs, the owner of seven Atlanta health clubs, noticed the "Bench Blast" and formed a partnership with several Atlanta businessmen to market The Step, a plastic platform that was marketed to health clubs. The Step was available in three versions, ranging in price from $59 to $199, and included a video tape.

Reebok noticed The Step and formed a joint venture with Boggs to market the product nationally. The Step carried Reebok's name and was included in Reebok's national marketing plan. Sales of The Step went from $7.8 million annually to $40 million annually within two years.

As his health club sales dropped off, Boggs wanted to sell directly to the in-home market, but Reebok wanted that market for itself. Boggs began marketing The Step through television infomercials, but his product did not have the Reebok name and thus was offered at a lower price than the Reebok in-home model.

Was it proper for Boggs to sell The Step in the home market without Reebok? Was it proper for Reebok to sell to the in-home market without Boggs? Both sides argued that they did not contemplate the in-home market when they formed their partnership. How would you respond to that point? What about Boggs's initial partnership without Miller? Did he steal her idea?

4. Purposes of a Partnership

A partnership may be formed for any lawful purpose but cannot be formed to commit immoral or illegal acts or acts that are contrary to public policy.

CASE SUMMARY

Morelli Was No Doctor and Thus No Partner

Facts: Ehsan, a physician, and Morelli, a nonphysician, were general partners running a family care clinic. Morelli acted as director of operations. In a subsequent dispute between the partners, Ehsan claimed that the partnership agreement was illegal and void because Morelli's activities constituted the unlawful practice of medicine.

Decision: Judgment for Ehsan. Under state law, no unlicensed person may engage, through a licensed partner or licensed employees, in the practice of the learned professions that affect the public health and welfare, including law, medicine, dentistry, and optometry. The court would not enforce the illegal partnership agreement. [*Morelli v Ehsan*, 110 Wash 2d 555, 756 P2d 129 (1988)]

---

5. Firm Name

In the absence of a statutory requirement, a partnership need not have a firm name, although it is customary to have one. The partners may, as a general rule, adopt any firm name they desire, including a fictitious name. There are, however, certain limitations on the adoption of a firm name:

1. The name cannot be the same as, or deceptively similar to, the name of another enterprise for the purpose of attracting its patrons.
2. Some states prohibit the use of the words *and Company* unless they indicate an additional partner.
3. Most states provide for the registration of a fictitious partnership name. For example, Ken and Steve Swain transact business under a partnership name: The Berkshire Dairy Farm. Because such a name does not reveal the names of the partners, a certificate stating the names and addresses of the partners can be filed at the public office designated by state law, usually a city or town clerk's office.

6. Classification of Partners

Partners are classified according to their activity.

1. **General partners** are those who publicly and actively engage in the transaction of firm business.
2. **Nominal partners** hold themselves out as partners or permit others to hold them out as such, but they are not in fact partners.
3. **Silent partners** are those who, although they may be known to the public as partners, take no active part in the business.
4. **Secret partners** are those who take an active part in the management of the firm but who are not known to the public as partners.
5. **Dormant partners** are ones who take no active part in transacting the business and who remain unknown to the public.

7. Who May Be Partners

Any competent person may be a partner.

In the absence of statutory provisions to the contrary, persons who are competent to contract may form a partnership. A minor may be a partner but may avoid the contract of partnership and withdraw.

In general, the capacity of a mentally incompetent person to be a partner is similar to that of a minor except that an adjudication of incompetence makes subsequent agreements void rather than merely voidable. At common law, a corporation could not be a partner. However, statutes for certificates of incorporation now typically permit corporations to become partners.

8. Creation of a Partnership

In determining if a partnership has been created, the law looks to the substance of the relationship, rather than the name used.

If the parties agree that the legal relationship between them shall be such that they in fact operate a business for profit as co-owners, a partnership is created even though the parties may not have labeled their new relationship a partnership.[4] The law is concerned with the substance of what is done, rather than the name.[5] Conversely, a partnership does not arise if the parties do not agree to the elements of a partnership even though they call it a partnership.

9. Partnership Agreement

Because of the complexity of the problems involved, partnership agreements are typically written. However, there is no requirement that they be in writing unless compliance with a statute of frauds is required. ◆ *For example*, the world's highest-paid performers in the early 1990s, the New Kids on the Block, who grossed $74.1 million in one year, were a group started by promoter Maurice Starr. He obtained $60,000 from James Martorano, who was connected with organized crime, and $50,000 from businessman Jeffrey Furst to finance the initial recording and promotion of the group. Martorano and Furst testified that ultimately all three agreed with a handshake that 50 percent of the profits from the group would be shared between Martorano as a silent partner and Furst, who would also provide limousine service and security. They testified that Starr would keep half of the

---

[4] *Halbersbery v Berry* (SC App) 394 SE2d 7 (1990).
[5] *Weinig v Weinig* (Ind App) 674 NE2d 991 (1996).

profits. Starr denied that a partnership existed because he believed that such an alleged business arrangement would have had to be reduced to writing with great detail. However, based on the evidence, which included damaging testimony that Starr tried to buy some witnesses' silence, a jury decided that a binding oral partnership agreement existed.[6]

To reduce or avoid disputes and litigation, partnership agreements should be in writing.

The formal document that is prepared to evidence the contract of the parties is termed a **partnership agreement**, **articles of partnership**, or **articles of copartnership**. The partnership agreement will govern the partnership during its existence and may also contain provisions relating to dissolution.

10. Determining the Existence of a Partnership

A partnership is shown to exist when it is established that the parties have agreed to the formation of a business organization that has the characteristics of a part-

PARTNERSHIP AGREEMENT

This is a partnership agreement executed at Cincinnati, Ohio, this 9th day of September, 1998 by and among Louis K. Hall, Sharon B. Young, and C. Lynn Mueller, individuals residing in Cincinnati, Ohio, hereinafter sometimes referred to individually as "Partner" and collectively as "Partners."

RECITALS

The Partners to this agreement desire to acquire a certain parcel of real estate and to develop such real estate for lease or sale, all for investment purposes. This agreement is being executed to delineate the basis of their relationship.

PROVISIONS

1. Name; and Principal Offices. The name of the partnership shall be: Hall, Young and Mueller, Associates. Its principal place of business shall be at: 201 River Road, Cincinnati, Ohio 45238.

2. Purpose. The purpose of the partnership shall be to purchase and own for investment purposes, a certain parcel of real estate located at 602 Sixth Street, Cincinnati, Ohio, and to engage in any other type of investment activities that the partnership may from time to time hereinafter unanimously agree upon.

3. Capital Contributions. The capital of the partnership shall be the aggregate amount of cash and property contributed by the Partners. A capital account shall be maintained for each Partner.

A. Capital Contributions. Any additional capital which may be required by the partnership shall be contributed to the partnership by the Partners in the same ratio as that Partner's original contribution to capital as to the total of all original capital contributions to the partnership unless otherwise agreed by the Partners.

FIGURE 44-1
Partnership Agreement

---

[6] *The Boston Globe*, November 13, 1995, at 13.

The following factors are considered in determining whether or not the parties intended to form a partnership:
- control,
- the sharing of profits and losses, and
- the sharing of profits.

nership. The burden of proving the existence of a partnership is on the person who claims that one exists.[7]

When the nature of the relationship is not clear, the following rules aid in determining whether the parties have created a partnership.

(a) Control. The presence or absence of control of a business enterprise is significant in determining whether there is a partnership and whether a particular person is a partner.

CASE SUMMARY

The Oral Sawmill Partnership Agreement Muddied with the Passage of Time

Facts: Thomas Smith and Jackie Lea were partners in the logging business. In January 1981, they joined Gordon Redd and went into business running a sawmill, calling the business Industrial Hardwood Products (IHP). Smith and Lea used their logging equipment at the mill site. Smith hauled 400 loads of gravel, worth some $26,000, from his father's land for the mill yard in the process of getting the mill operational. Smith and Lea received $300 a week compensation for their work, which was reported on federal W-2 forms. They worked up to 65 hours per week and were not paid overtime. All three discussed business decisions. Smith and Lea had check-writing authority and the authority to hire and fire employees. Lea left the business in 1983 and was paid $20,000. The testimony indicated that the three individuals agreed in January 1981 that as soon as the bank was paid off and Redd was paid his investment, Lea and Smith would be given an interest in the mill. No written agreement existed. Redd invested $410,452 in the business and withdrew $500,475 from the business. As of December 31, 1986, IHP had sufficient retained earnings to retire the bank debt. In April 1987, Smith petitioned the Chancery Court for the dissolution of the "partnership" and an accounting. Redd denied that any partnership agreement was formed and asserted that Smith was an employee because he was paid wages. He offered to pay Smith $50,000 for the gravel and use of equipment.

Decision: Judgment for Smith. The fact that Smith received wages does not per se defeat the existence of a partnership and the position that Smith was a partner. Smith worked long hours, sometimes 25 overtime hours in a week without pay, to establish the business and to pay off debts. Other facts, such as the control exercised by Smith, the admission of Redd that an ownership interest was intended, the contribution of $26,000 worth of gravel to the firm, and the prior payment of $20,000 to buy out Lea's interest, indicated that Smith was a partner. [*Smith v Redd* (Miss) 593 So 2d 989 (1991)]

(b) Sharing Profits and Losses. The fact that the parties share profits and losses is strong evidence of a partnership.

(c) Sharing Profits. An agreement that does not provide for sharing losses but does provide for sharing profits is evidence that the parties are partners. If the partners share profits, it is assumed that they will also share losses. Sharing profits is prima facie evidence of a partnership. However, a partnership is not to be inferred when profits are received in payment (1) of a debt, (2) of wages, (3) of an annuity to a deceased partner's surviving spouse or representative, (4) of interest, or (5) for

---

[7] *MacArthur v Stein* (Mont) 934 P2d 214 (1997).

the goodwill of the business.[8] The fact that one doctor receives one-half of the net income does not establish that doctor as a partner of another doctor when the former was guaranteed a minimum annual amount. Also, federal income tax and Social Security contributions were deducted from the payments to the doctor, thus indicating that the relationship was employer and employee. If there is no evidence of the reason for receiving the profits, a partnership of the parties involved exists.

(d) Gross Returns. The sharing of gross returns is itself very slight, if any, evidence of partnership. ◆ *For example*, in a case in which one party owned a show that was exhibited on land owned by another under an agreement to divide the gross proceeds, no partnership was proven. There was no co-ownership or community of interest in the business. ◆ Similarly, it was not established that there was a partnership when it was shown that a farmer rented an airplane to a pilot to do aerial chemical spraying under an agreement by which the pilot would pay the farmer, as compensation for the use of the plane, a share of the fees that the pilot received.

(e) Co-Ownership. Neither the co-ownership of property nor the sharing of profits or rents from property that two or more persons own creates a partnership. Thus, the fact that a person acquires a 49 percent interest in a trailer park does not establish that such person is a partner. This in itself does not establish that the co-owners are together conducting the trailer park business for profit. Conversely, the mere fact that there is a sharing of the income from property by joint owners does not establish that they are partners.

(f) Contribution of Property. The fact that all persons have not contributed capital to an enterprise does not establish that the enterprise is not a partnership. A partnership may be formed even though some of its members furnish only skill or labor.

CASE SUMMARY

Can You Fire Your Partner?

Facts: Upon graduating from Vanderbilt University with a degree in economics, James Pettes began working for Video Magic, a video rental business. In 1987, Dr. Gordon Yukon, a pediatrician, wanted to invest in a two-store video business called Rent-a-Flick, with one store located on Quince Road and the other in Germantown. Pettes testified that Dr. Yukon paid $42,000 for the business. Pettes testified that they agreed that they would be partners, with Pettes managing the two stores and earning the same amount he earned at Video Magic. Pettes testified that he worked 70 to 80 hours a week and his capital contribution was "sweat equity." He also testified that many times Yukon told him and others that Pettes and Yukon were partners. Pettes testified that in the middle of 1992, the parties agreed to divide the business so that the Germantown store would go to Dr. Yukon and the Quince Road store would go to Pettes. In December 1992, Pettes made a written demand for an accounting. On January 5, 1993, Yukon "fired" Pettes. Sutherland, an employee, testified that she questioned Dr. Yukon about this action because Pettes was a partner, and Yukon's reply was not a denial of the partnership but rather a claim that in the absence of written proof Pettes could not prove such an arrangement. Pettes sued for breach of an oral partnership agreement and an accounting.

---

[8] UPA § 7(4).

> **Decision:** Judgment for Pettes. From the totality of the proof in this case, the parties intended a partnership and co-ownership to the extent that a dissolution agreement would result in Yukon acquiring the Germantown store and Pettes acquiring the Quince Road store. The implied partnership and agreed dissolution thereof are binding on the parties, and Pettes is entitled to the value of the Quince Road store as of January 3, 1993. [*Pettes v Yukon (Tenn App) 912 SW2d 709 (1995)*]

(g) Fixed Payment. When a person who performs continuing services for another receives a fixed payment that is not dependent on the existence of profit and not affected by losses, that person is not a partner.

11. Partners as to Third Persons

In some instances, persons who are in fact not partners may be held liable to third persons as though they were partners. This liability arises when they conduct themselves in such a manner that others are reasonably led to believe that they are partners and to act in reliance on that belief to their injury.[9] A person who is held liable as a partner under such circumstances is termed a *nominal partner*, a *partner by estoppel*, or an *ostensible partner*.

Partnership liability may arise by estoppel when a person who in fact is not a partner is described as a partner in a document filed with the government provided the person so described has in some way participated in the filing of the document and the person claiming the benefit of the estoppel had knowledge of that document and relied on the statement. *For example*, suppose that the partnership of Holt and Schwark, in registering its fictitious name, specifies Holt, Schwark, and Collins as partners and that the registration certificate is signed by all of them. If a creditor who sees this registration statement extends credit to the firm in reliance in part on the fact that Collins is a partner, Collins is estopped from denying that she is a partner. She has a partner's liability, along with the other partners insofar as that creditor is concerned.

Under the RUPA, an apparent partnership or partnership by estoppel is called a "purported" partnership, and a third person who relies on the partnership's representations that the purported partner had authority to bind the partnership can hold it liable as if the purported partner was an actual partner with authority.[10] Under the RUPA, a partnership can limit potential liability with a publicly recorded statement of partnership authority or limitation on partner authority.[11]

12. Partnership Property

In general, partnership property consists of all the property contributed by the partners or acquired for the firm or with its funds.

There is usually no limitation on the kind and amount of property that a partnership may acquire. The firm may own real as well as personal property unless it is prohibited from doing so by statute or by the partnership agreement.

---

[9] UPA § 16(1).
[10] RUPA § 308.
[11] RUPA § 303.

C P A

The parties may agree that real estate owned by one of the partners should become partnership property. When this intent exists, the particular property constitutes partnership property even if it is still in the name of the original owner.

CASE SUMMARY

Who Owns the Dagmar Bar?

Facts: Two brothers, Eugene and Marlowe Mehl, formed a partnership to operate the family farm. One year Eugene Mehl withdrew $7,200 from the partnership account and bought the Dagmar Bar. The warranty deed and the liquor license to the bar were obtained in the names of Eugene Mehl and his wife, Bonnie. In a subsequent lawsuit, Marlowe claimed that the bar was a partnership asset.

Decision: Judgment for Marlowe. The bar had been purchased with partnership funds and therefore belonged to the partnership. There was no agreement of the partnership that Eugene and his wife could acquire title. [Mehl v Mehl (Mont) 786 P2d 1173 (1990)]

Article 2 of the RUPA recognizes that partnerships are "entities" that can acquire and own property in the partnership's name.

C P A

13. Tenancy in Partnership

Partners hold title to firm property by **tenancy in partnership**.[12]
The characteristics of such a tenancy are as follows:

A creditor of a partner cannot proceed against any specific item of partnership property but must obtain a charging order to receive a partner's share of the partnership's profits.

1. Each partner has an equal right to use firm property for partnership purposes in the absence of a contrary agreement.
2. A partner possesses no divisible interest in any specific item of partnership property that can be voluntarily sold, assigned, or mortgaged by a partner.
3. A creditor of a partner cannot proceed against any specific items of partnership property. The creditor can proceed only against the partner's interest in the partnership. This is done by applying to a court for a **charging order**. By this procedure, the share of any profits that would be paid to the debtor-partner is paid to a receiver on behalf of the creditor, or the court may direct the sale of the interest of the debtor-partner in the partnership.
4. Upon the death of a partner, the partnership property vests in the surviving partners for partnership purposes and is not subject to the rights of the surviving spouse of the deceased partner.

14. Assignment of a Partner's Interest

Although a partner cannot transfer specific items of partnership property in the absence of authority to so act on behalf of the partnership, a partner's interest in the partnership may be voluntarily assigned by the partner.[13] The assignee does not become a partner without the consent of the other partners. Without this consent, the assignee is entitled to receive only the assignor's share of the profits during the continuance of the partnership and the assignor's interest upon the dissolution of the firm. The assignee has no right to participate in the management of the partnership or to inspect the books of the partnership.

---

[12] UPA § 25(1); *Krause v Vollmar*, 83 Ohio App 3d 378, 614 NE2d 1136 (1992).
[13] *Farmers State Bank v Mikesell*, 51 Ohio App 3d 69, 554 NE2d 900 (1988).

B.   DISSOLUTION AND TERMINATION

The end of a partnership's existence is marked by dissolution and termination.

15. Effect of Dissolution

Dissolution ends the right of the partnership to exist as a going concern, but it does not end the existence of the partnership.[14] Dissolution is followed by a winding-up period, at the conclusion of which the partnership's legal existence terminates.

Dissolution reduces the authority of the partners. From the moment of dissolution, the partners lose authority to act for the firm, "except so far as may be necessary to wind up partnership affairs or to complete transactions begun but not then finished."[15] The vested rights of the partners are not extinguished by dissolving the firm, and the existing liabilities remain. Thus, when the partnership is dissolved by the death of a partner, the estate of the deceased partner is liable to the same extent as the deceased partner.

16. Dissolution by Act of the Parties

A partnership may be dissolved by action of the parties. However, certain acts of the parties do not cause a dissolution.

A partnership is dissolved by act of the parties by
- agreement,
- expulsion, or
- withdrawal.

(a) Agreement. A partnership may be dissolved in accordance with the terms of the original agreement of the parties. This may be by the expiration of the period for which the relationship was to continue or by the performance of the object for which the partnership was organized.[16] The relationship may also be dissolved by subsequent agreement. The partners may agree to dissolve the firm before the lapse of the time specified in the articles of partnership or before the attainment of the object for which the firm was created.

(b) Expulsion. A partnership is dissolved by the expulsion of any partner from the business, whether or not authorized by the partnership agreement.[17]

(c) Alienation of Interest. Neither a voluntary sale of a partner's interest nor an involuntary sale for the benefit of creditors works a dissolution of the partnership.

(d) Withdrawal. A partner has the power to withdraw from the partnership at any time. However, if the withdrawal violates the partnership agreement, the withdrawing partner becomes liable to the co-partners for damages for breach of contract.[18] When the relationship is for no definite purpose or time, a partner may withdraw without liability at any time. Restrictive provisions on later employment are commonly found in professional and marketing partnership agreements.

---

[14] *Sheppard v Griffin* (Tenn App) 776 SW2d 119 (1989).
[15] UPA § 33.
[16] UPA § 31(1)(a).
[17] *Susman v Cypress Venture*, 187 Ill App 3d 312, 134 Ill Dec 901, 543 NE2d 184 (1989).
[18] *Tabco Exploration Inc. v Tadlock Pipe Co.* (La App) 617 So 2d 606 (1993).

17. Dissolution by Operation of Law

A partnership is dissolved by operation of law in the following instances.

(a) Death. A partnership is dissolved immediately upon the death of any partner. Thus, when the executor of a deceased partner carries on the business with the remaining partner, there is legally a new firm.

(b) Bankruptcy. Bankruptcy of the firm or of one of the partners causes the dissolution of the firm; insolvency alone does not.

(c) Illegality. A partnership is dissolved by an event which makes it unlawful for the business of the partnership to be carried on or for the members to carry it on in partnership. To illustrate, when it is made unlawful by statute for judges to engage in the practice of law, a law firm is dissolved when one of its members becomes a judge.

18. Dissolution by Decree of Court

A court may decree the dissolution of a partnership for proper cause. A court will not order the dissolution for trifling causes or temporary grievances that do not involve a permanent harm or injury to the partnership.

The filing of a complaint seeking a judicial dissolution does not in itself cause a dissolution of the partnership; it is the decree of the court that has that effect.

A partner may obtain a decree of dissolution for any of the following reasons.

(a) Insanity. A partner has been judicially declared insane or of unsound mind.

(b) Incapacity. One of the partners has become incapable of performing the terms of the partnership agreement.

(c) Misconduct. One of the partners has been guilty of conduct that substantially prejudices the continuance of the business. The habitual drunkenness of a partner is a sufficient cause for judicial dissolution.

(d) Impracticability. One of the partners persistently or willfully acts in such a way that it is not reasonably practicable to carry on the partnership business. Dissolution will be granted when dissensions are so serious and persistent that continuance is impracticable or when all confidence and cooperation between the partners have been destroyed.

(e) Lack of Success. The partnership cannot continue in business except at a loss.

(f) Equitable Circumstances. A decree of dissolution will be granted under any other circumstances that equitably call for a dissolution. Such a situation exists when one partner had been induced by fraud to enter into the partnership.

19. Application under the RUPA

Under the RUPA and it "entity" concept, a partner can leave the firm and not disrupt the partnership's legal existence. The RUPA uses the term *disassociation* for the departure of a partner[19] and reserves the term *dissolution* for those instances when a partner's departure results in the winding up and termination of the business.[20] A partner has an absolute power to disassociate at will, just like a partner has the power to withdraw under the UPA, even if it is wrongful.[21] And if wrongful, the partner is liable for damages for breach of contract.

20. Notice of Dissolution

Under some circumstances, one partner may continue to possess the power to make a contract that binds the partnership even though the partnership has been dissolved.

(a) Notice to Partners. When the firm is dissolved by the act of a partner, notice must be given to the other partners unless that partner's act clearly shows an intent to withdraw from or to dissolve the firm. If the withdrawing partner acts without notice to the other partners, that partner is bound by contracts created for the firm.

Where the dissolution is caused by the act, death, or bankruptcy of a partner, each partner is liable to the co-partners for a share of any liability created by any other partner acting for the partnership without knowledge or notice of the act, death, or bankruptcy of the partner who caused the dissolution.

(b) Notice to Third Persons. When dissolution is caused by the act of a partner or of the partners, notice must be given to third parties. A notice should expressly state that the partnership has been dissolved. Circumstances from which a termination may be inferred are generally not sufficient notice.

Thus, the fact that the partnership checks added the abbreviation *Inc.* after the partnership name was not sufficient notice that the partnership did not exist and that the business had been incorporated.

Actual notice of dissolution must be given to persons who have dealt with the firm.

CASE SUMMARY

Notice Necessary!

Facts: Paul Babich ran a business under the name of House of Paul. The business became a partnership among Babich, Dyson, and Schnepp but continued under the same name. The partners arranged for the printing of advertising material with Philipp Lithographing Co., making contracts on three separate occasions for such printing. During the course of these dealings, the House of Paul became a corporation. When the printing bills were not paid in full, Philipp sued the partners as individuals. They claimed they were not liable because the corporation had made the contracts.

---

19 RUPA § 601 cmt 1.
20 RUPA § 801.
21 RUPA §§ 601(1), 602(a).

> **Decision:** Whether or not the House of Paul was a corporation with respect to a particular contract was not important because no notice had been given of its change from a partnership to a corporation. Having originally done business with the defendant as a partnership, Philipp could hold the individual persons liable as partners until notice to the contrary was given to the plaintiff. [*Philipp Lithographing Co. v Babich, 27 Wis 2d 645, 135 NW2d 343 (1965)*]

For persons who have had no dealings with the firm, a publication of the fact of dissolution is sufficient. Such notice may be by newspaper publication, by the posting of a placard in a public place, or by any similar method. Failure to give proper notice continues the power of each partner to bind the others with respect to third persons on contracts within the scope of the business.

When dissolution has been caused by operation of law, notice to third persons is not required. As between the partners, however, the UPA requires knowledge or notice of dissolution by death and bankruptcy.

21. Winding Up Partnership Affairs

In the absence of an express agreement permitting the surviving partners to continue the business, they must wind up the business and account for the share of any partner who has withdrawn, been expelled, or died. If the remaining partners continue the business and use the partner's distributive share, that partner is entitled to that share, together with interest or the profit earned on it.

Partners have no authority after dissolution to create new obligations. They have authority only to do acts necessary to wind up the business.

The Walnut Kernel Case

Facts: The Stoddard family-father, mother, and son-formed a partnership that published a newspaper, the *Walnut Kernel*. The parents died, and the son kept running the paper. King performed accounting services for the paper. When he was not paid, he sued the son and the executors of the estates of the deceased partners, the parents, claiming that his bill was a partnership liability for which each was liable. The executors defended on the ground that the son as surviving partner did not have authority to employ an accountant but was only authorized to wind up the partnership business. To this defense, it was answered that the newspaper was continued in order to preserve its asset value as a going concern so that it could be sold and that the running of the paper was therefore part of the winding-up process.

Decision: The accountant was not entitled to recover the value of his services because the son had no authority to continue the publishing of the newspaper indefinitely. The operation of the paper by the son was not a winding up of the estate but was merely a continuing of the business as usual. [*King v Stoddard, 28 Cal App 3d 708, 104 Cal Rptr 903 (1972)*]

When dissolution is obtained by court decree, the court may appoint a receiver to conduct the winding up of the partnership business. This may be done in the usual manner, or the receiver may sell the business as a going concern to those partners who wish to continue its operation.

With a few exceptions, all partners have the right to participate in the winding up of the business.[22]

When the firm is dissolved by the death of one partner, the partnership property vests in the surviving partners for the purpose of administration. They must collect and preserve the assets, pay the debts, and make an accounting to the representative of the deceased partner's estate. A partner cannot purchase any of the partnership property without the consent of the other partners.

22. Distribution of Assets

Partnership assets are distributed as follows:
- **Debts are paid to creditors,**
- **Partners are paid for loans,**
- **Capital is returned to partners, and**
- **Remaining assets are divided equally as profits.**

Creditors of the firm have first claim on the assets of the partnership.[23] Difficulty arises when there is a contest between the creditors of the firm and the creditors of the individual partners. The general rule is that firm creditors have first claim on assets of the firm. The individual creditors share in the remaining assets, if any.

After the firm's liabilities to nonpartners have been paid, the assets of the partnership are distributed as follows: (1) Each partner is entitled to a refund of advances made to or for the firm; (2) contributions to the capital of the firm are then returned; and (3) the remaining assets, if any, are divided equally as profits among the partners unless there is some other agreement. A partner who contributes only services to the partnership is not considered to have made a capital contribution, absent an agreement to the contrary.

CASE SUMMARY

Are Time and Labor Capital Contributions? Fred Ott Says They Ought to Be

Facts: Fred Ott and Charles Corley were partners doing business as "Lakewood Associates, a general partnership." Corley provided the capital to purchase the land to be sold by the partnership, called Lakewood Estates. Corley brought suit for the dissolution of the partnership, and Ott contended that his contributions of time and labor in improving Lakewood Estates should be credited to him as capital contributions in the distribution of assets.

Decision: Judgment for Corley. There was no evidence of any agreement between the partners that Ott's services should be credited as capital contributions. Therefore, the value of the services could not be credited as capital contributions in the distribution of assets. [*Corley v Ott* (SC) 485 SE2d 97 (1997)]

If the partnership has sustained a loss, the partners bear it equally in the absence of a contrary agreement. Distribution of partnership assets must be made on the basis of actual value when it is clear that the book values are merely nominal or arbitrary amounts.

A provision in a partnership agreement that upon the death of a partner the interest of the partner shall pass to that partner's surviving spouse is valid. Such a provision takes effect as against the contention that it is not valid because it does not satisfy the requirements applicable to wills.

---

[22] UPA § 37.
[23] *Holmes v Holmes*, 119 Or App 36, 849 P2d 1140 (1993).

23. Continuation of Partnership Business

As a practical matter, the business of the partnership is commonly continued after dissolution and winding up. In all cases, however, there is a technical dissolution, winding up, and termination of the life of the original partnership.

If the business continues, either with the surviving partners or with them and additional partners, it is a new partnership. Again, as a practical matter, the liquidation of the old partnership may in effect be merely a matter of bookkeeping entries, with all partners contributing again or relending to the new business any payment to which they would be entitled from the liquidation of the original partnership.

SUMMARY

A partnership is a relationship created by the voluntary association of two or more persons to carry on as co-owners a business for profit.

A partnership agreement governs the partnership during its existence and may also contain provisions relating to dissolution. The partnership agreement will generally be in writing, and this may be required by the statute of frauds. The existence of a partnership may be found from the existence of shared control in the running of the business and the fact that the parties share profits and losses. The sharing of gross returns, as opposed to profits, is very slight evidence of a partnership.

Partners hold title to firm property by tenancy in partnership. A creditor of a partner cannot proceed against any specific item of partnership property but must obtain a charging order to seize the debtor-partner's share of the profits. An assignee of a partner's interest does not become a partner without the consent of the other partners and is entitled only to a share of the profits and the assignor's interest upon dissolution.

Dissolution ends the right of the partnership to exist as a going concern. Dissolution is followed by a winding-up period and the distribution of assets. A partnership may be dissolved by the parties themselves in accordance with the terms of the partnership agreement, by the expulsion of a partner, by the withdrawal of a partner, or by the bankruptcy of the firm or one of the partners. A court may order dissolution of a partnership upon the petition of a partner because of the insanity, incapacity, or major misconduct of a partner. Dissolution may be decreed because of lack of success, impracticability, or other circumstances that equitably call for dissolution. Notice of dissolution, except dissolution by operation of law, must be given. Actual notice must be given to those who have dealt with the firm as a partnership.

All partners generally have a right to participate in the winding up of the business. After the firm's liabilities to nonpartners have been paid, the assets are distributed among the partners as follows: (1) refund of advances, (2) return of contributions to capital, and (3) division of remaining assets in accordance with the partnership agreement or, if no agreement is stated, division of net assets equally among the partners.

QUESTIONS AND CASE PROBLEMS

1. What social forces are affected by the rule that distribution of partnership assets must be made on the basis of actual value when it is clear that the book values are merely nominal or arbitrary amounts?
2. What is the effect of dissolution on a partnership?
3. In proving that Powell and Castillo are partners, compare the effect of proof that they (a) share gross returns, (b) are co-owners of property used in or by the business, or (c) share profits of the business.
4. Ray, Linda, and Nancy form a partnership. Ray and Linda contribute property and cash. Nancy contributes only services. Linda dies and the partnership is liquidated. After all debts are paid, the surplus is not sufficient to pay back Linda's estate and Ray for the property and cash originally contributed by Linda and Ray. Nancy claims that the balance should be divided equally among Ray, Linda's estate, and Nancy. Is she correct?
5. Compare the requirement of notice to third persons when (a) an agency is terminated and (b) a partnership is dissolved.
6. Baxter, Bigelow, Owens, and Dailey were partners in a

New York City advertising agency. Owens, who was in poor health and wanted to retire, advised the partners that she had assigned her full and complete interest in the partnership to her son, Bartholomew, a highly qualified person with ten years of experience in the advertising business. Baxter, Bigelow, and Dailey refused to allow Bartholomew to attend management meetings and refused his request to inspect the books. Bartholomew pointed out that his mother had invested as much in the firm as any other partner. He believed, as assignee of his mother's full and complete partnership interest, that he is entitled to (a) inspect the books as he sees fit and (b) participate fully in the management of the firm. Is Bartholomew correct?

7. Amy Gargulo and Paula Frisken operated as a partnership Kiddies Korner, an infants' and children's clothing store. They operated the business very successfully for three years, with both Paula and Amy doing the buying and Paula keeping the books and paying the bills. Amy and Paula decided to expand the business when an adjoining store became vacant. At the same time, they incorporated the business. Children's Apparel, Inc., was a major supplier to the business before the expansion. After the expansion, business did not increase as anticipated, and when a nationally known manufacturer of children's apparel opened a factory outlet nearby, the business could no longer pay its bills. Children's Apparel, which had supplied most of the store's stock after expansion, sued Amy and Paula as partners for bills due for expansion stock. Children's Apparel did not know that Amy and Paula had incorporated. Amy and Paula contended that the business was incorporated and that they therefore were not liable for business debts occurring after incorporation. Are Amy and Paula correct?

8. Calvin Johnson and Rudi Basecke did business as the Stockton Cheese Co., a partnership, which owned a building and equipment. The partners agreed to dissolve the partnership but never got around to completing the winding-up process. Calvin continued to use the building and to pay insurance on it but removed Rudi's name as an insured on the policy. When the building was later destroyed by fire, Calvin claimed the proceeds of the fire insurance policy, as he and his wife were the named insureds on the policy and they had paid the premiums. Rudi claimed that although the partnership was dissolved before the fire, the winding up of the partnership was not completed at the time of the fire. He therefore claimed that he was entitled to half of the net proceeds of the pol-

icy. Decide. [*State Casualty v Johnson* (Mo App) 766 SW2d 113]

9. Samuel Shaw purchased a ticket through Delta Airlines to fly a "Delta Connection" flight on SkyWest Airlines to Elko, Nevada. He was seriously injured when the SkyWest plane crashed near Elko. SkyWest's relationship with Delta is a contractual business referral arrangement, whereby Delta benefits through its charges for issuing tickets to connecting passengers to and from smaller communities, and SkyWest benefits from revenue generated by passengers sent to it by Delta. Both firms make a profit from this arrangement. SkyWest and Delta are often mentioned together by Delta in national print advertisements. Shaw believes that regardless of how the airlines characterize themselves, these airlines are in fact partners because they share profits from their combined efforts. Delta contended that it had no control over SkyWest's airplane operations and that sharing profits as compensation for services does not create a partnership. Decide. [*Shaw v Delta Airlines, Inc.*, 798 F Supp 1453 (D Nev)]

10. Larson entered into a Special Manager Incentive Agreement (SMIA) with Tandy Corp. He agreed to manage a Radio Shack store for compensation equal to one-half of the adjusted gross profit of the store as computed by a specific formula and to provide the company with a $20,000 "security deposit" on equipment used to set up the store. The agreement was for a period of two years, automatically renewable annually until either party gave notice of termination 30 days prior to the end of a fiscal year. After some eight and one-half years of operating under renewed agreements, Tandy gave Larson notice of his termination. Larson sued Tandy, claiming that the SMIA was a partnership agreement because there were shared risks, expenses, profits, and losses. He sought an accounting for his reasonable share in the value of the store. Tandy argued that under the SMIA Larson was an employee-manager, not a partner, and that the ultimate decision making on all matters was Tandy's. Decide. [*Larson v Tandy Corp.* (Ga App) 371 SE2d 663]

11. In 1974, Weeks joined an accounting firm as a partner. In 1980, a new partner was admitted, and a new partnership agreement was executed by all the partners. In early 1983, two partners retired, and the partners agreed to admit two other persons as partners, but no new partnership agreement was executed. Later, on July 31, 1984, Weeks gave notice of his election to dissolve the partnership. The remaining partners denied Weeks access to the firm's records, and Weeks sued for confirmation of the dissolution and for an accounting. The partners counterclaimed for enforcement of the

1980 partnership agreement, which would preclude a dissolution. The partners also claimed that Weeks violated a noncompetition clause in the 1980 agreement. Decide whether the 1980 partnership agreement should be controlling. [*Weeks v McMillan* (SC App) 353 SE2d 289]

12. Bowen, who owned and operated the Havana Club in a rented building, owned all the physical assets of the business. He made an agreement with Cutler, the bartender, that she would operate the club, purchase supplies, pay bills, keep the books, and hire and fire employees. Cutler and Bowen were each to receive $100 a week and divide the net profits. A partnership form of income tax return was filed for the business. At a later date when the Redevelopment Agency took the building in which the Havana Club was operated, the club went out of business because it could not find a new location. The Redevelopment Agency paid the club $10,000 damages for disruption of business. Cutler sued Bowen for one-half of the sum paid by the Redevelopment Agency on the theory that they had been a partnership. Bowen claimed that he was the sole owner of the business because he was the owner of the physical assets. Decide. [*Cutler v Bowen* (Utah) 543 P2d 1349]

13. Chaiken and two others ran a barber shop. The Delaware Employment Security Commission claimed that the other two persons were employees of Chaiken and that Chaiken had failed to pay the unemployment compensation tax assessed against employers. His defense was on the ground that he had not "employed" the other two and that all three were partners. The evidence showed that Chaiken owned the barber shop; he continued to do business under the same trade name as he had before he was joined by the two additional barbers; and he had a separate contract with each of the two, which specified the days for work and the days off. It was also shown that Chaiken had registered the partnership name and the names of the three partners and that federal tax returns used for partnerships had been filed. Decide. [*Chaiken v Employment Security Commission* (Del Super Ct) 274 A2d 707]

14. Gus Jebeles and his brother-in-law Gus Costellos

entered into an oral partnership agreement on September 2, 1977, to conduct a business under the name of Dino's Hot Dogs at a location on the Montgomery highway. Jebeles, who had expertise in this kind of business, arranged for the lease and furnished the logo used by the partnership. From the beginning, Costellos devoted himself to the business full time, and Jebeles devoted relatively little time to the business. Marital difficulties developed between Jebeles and his wife, who was Costellos's sister. Divorce proceedings began in January 1979. At that time, Costellos ceased to pay any money to Jebeles and changed the locks on the doors of the premises. Jebeles filed suit, seeking a dissolution of the partnership and an accounting of all profits. As judge, you believe that it would be ill advised to dissolve the partnership and lose the valuable lease to the business premises and the future profits of the business. Instead, you are considering ordering that the partnership continue with Costellos as the sole active partner and Jebeles as a silent partner. You plan on ordering an accounting. Would your decision be upheld on appeal? [*Jebeles v Costellos* (Ala) 391 So 2d 1024]

15. Friedman, the "O" Street Carpet Shop, Inc., and Langness formed a partnership known as NFL Associates. "O" Street Carpet's net contribution to capital was $5,004; Langness contributed $14,000 in cash; and Friedman contributed his legal services, on which no value was placed by the articles of partnership. The articles stated that Friedman was entitled to 10 percent of the profits and that Langness was to receive payments of $116.66 per month. The partnership's accountant treated the payments to Langness as a return of her capital. Years later the partnership sold the rental property owned by the partnership, and the partnership was wound up. Friedman claimed that he was entitled to 10 percent of the partnership capital upon dissolution. Langness claimed that Friedman was not entitled to a capital distribution and that the monthly payments to her should not have been treated as a return of capital. Decide. [*Langness v "O" Street Carpet, Inc.* (Neb) 353 NW2d 709]

CPA QUESTIONS

1. A partnership agreement must be in writing if
   a. Any partner contributes more than $500 in capital.
   b. The partners reside in different states.
   c. The partnership intends to own real estate.
   d. The partnership's purpose **cannot** be completed within one year of formation.

   (5/92, Law, #10)

2. Which of the following is **not** necessary to create an express partnership?
   a. Execution of a written partnership agreement.
   b. Agreement to share ownership of the partnership.
   c. Intention to conduct a business for profit.
   d. Intention to create a relationship recognized as a partnership.

   (11/90, Law, #11)

3. Cobb, Inc., a partner in TLC Partnership, assigns its partnership interest to Bean, who is not made a partner. After the assignment, Bean asserts the rights to

   I. Participate in the management of TLC
   II. Cobb's share of TLC's partnership profits.

   Bean is correct as to which of these rights?
   a. I only.
   b. II only.
   c. I and II.
   d. Neither I **nor** II.

   (5/93, Law, #15)

Partnerships, Limited Partnerships, and Limited Liability Companies

CHAPTER 45

After studying this chapter, you should be able to

1. *Distinguish between express authority and customary authority of a partner to act for the partnership;*
2. *Identify the situations that indicate the existence of limitations on a partner's authority;*
3. *Name six transactions that a partner cannot undertake unless expressly authorized to do so;*
4. *List the duties of partners to one another;*
5. *State the rights of partners as owners of the business;*
6. *Explain the nature and extent of a partner's liability for the debts of the firm;*
7. *Recognize what actions of a limited partner will cause the loss of protection from limited liability; and*
8. *Explain the advantages of a limited liability company.*

What is the authority of a partner? What are the duties of partners?

A. AUTHORITY OF PARTNERS

The scope of a partner's authority is determined by the partnership agreement and by the nature of the partnership.

1. Authority of Majority of Partners

The decisions of the majority prevail in ordinary partnership matters not in contravention of the partnership agreement.

When there are more than two partners in a firm, the decision of the majority prevails in matters involving how the ordinary functions of the business will be conducted. To illustrate, a majority of the partners of a firm decide to increase the firm's advertising. They subsequently enter into a contract for that purpose. The transaction is valid and binds the firm and all of the partners.

Majority action is not binding if it contravenes the partnership agreement. For such matters, unanimous action is required.[1] Thus, the majority of the members cannot change the nature of the business against the protests of the minority.

When there are an even number of partners, an even division on a matter that requires majority approval is always a possibility. In such a case, the partnership is deadlocked. When the partners are evenly divided on any question, one partner has no authority to act.

CASE SUMMARY

Strictly Business, or Trashing Your Partner?

Facts: Summers and Dooley formed a partnership to collect trash. Summers became unable to work, and he hired a third man to do his work and paid him out of his personal funds. Summers suggested to Dooley that the third man be paid from the partnership funds, but Dooley refused to do so. Finally Summers sued Dooley for reimbursement for the money he had spent to pay the third man.

Decision: Judgment for Dooley. Summers had no authority to employ the third man at the expense of the firm. Because the partners were evenly divided on the question of such employment, Summers had no authority to act. *[Summers v Dooley, 94 Idaho 87, 481 P2d 318 (1971)]*

---

[1] Uniform Partnership Act (UPA) § 18(h).

If the division is over a basic issue and the partners persist in the deadlock so that it is impossible to continue the business, any one of the partners may petition the court to order the dissolution of the firm.

2.   Express Authority of Individual Partners

An individual partner may have express authority to perform certain acts either because the partnership agreement provides for this or because a sufficient number of partners have agreed to it.

Remember that a partner's authority to act for the firm is similar to that of an agent to act for a principal.

A partner's authority to act for the firm is similar to that of an agent to act for a principal. Thus, in addition to express authority, a partner has the authority to do those acts that are customary for a member of a partnership conducting the particular business of that partnership.[2] As in the case of an agent, the acts of a partner in excess of authority do not ordinarily bind the partnership.

3.   Customary Authority of Individual Partners

A partner, by virtue of being a co-manager of the business, customarily has certain powers necessary and proper for carrying out that business. The scope of such powers varies with the nature of the partnership and also with the business customs and usages of the area in which the partnership operates.

A partner may make any contract necessary to transact the firm's business.

CASE SUMMARY

"Jerry Should Have Run It by Me," Silvio Seethed

Facts: Silvio Giannetti and his daughter and son-in-law, Anne Marie and Jerry Pruzinsky, are partners in a general partnership known as Giannetti Investment Company (GIC) which owns and operates Brougham Manor Apartments. Jerry entered into an access agreement with Omnicom, a provider of cable television services, giving Omnicom the right to enter Brougham Manor for purposes of installing, maintaining, and promoting cable service. Some time later, when Silvio learned of the contract he denied Omnicom access to the property, and Omnicom was unable to repair a signal leakage problem and was forced to discontinue cable service. Omnicom sued GIC for breach of contract. GIC contended that Jerry did not sign the agreement in the partnership name, and thereby failed to bind GIC.

Decision: Judgment for Omnicom. A contract executed in the name of a partner is binding on the partnership. The contract was executed by Jerry in the usual course of GIC's business, for it is a typical activity for an apartment complex to contract for cable television. [*Omnicom v Giannetti Investment Co.* 561 NW2d 138 (Mich App 1997)]

Some common customary powers of individual partners are the powers to
- *make ordinary contracts to buy and sell goods and hire employees,*
- *borrow money for partnership purposes,*
- *handle insurance matters and claims, and*
- *make admissions and receive notice.*

A partner can sell the firm's goods in the regular course of business, make purchases within the scope of the business, and borrow money for firm purposes. When borrowing money, a partner may execute commercial paper in the firm's name or give security such as a mortgage.[3] A partner may purchase insurance, hire employees, and adjust claims for or against the firm. Notice given to a partner is effective notice to the partnership.[4]

---

2 *Ball v Carlson* (Colo App) 641 P2d 303 (1981).
3 *U.S. Leather v H&W Partnership*, 60 F3d 222 (5th Cir 1995).
4 *Cham, Hill Inc. v Block & Veatch* (Wis App) 557 NW2d 829 (1996).

4. Limitations on Authority

The partners may agree to limit the powers of each partner. When a partner, contrary to such an agreement, executes a contract on behalf of the firm with a third person, the firm is bound if the third person was unaware of the limitation. In this case, the partner violating the agreement is liable to the other partners for any loss caused by the breach of the limitation. If the third person knew of the limitation, the firm would not be bound.[5]

CASE SUMMARY

Bound by Your Partner

Facts: David Cassilly and Joseph Mason were partners in the real estate development business, doing business as Glen Park Properties. Schnucks Markets brought an action against the partners for breach of contract. Schnucks testified that Cassilly and Schnucks agreed that Glen Park and the market would split the cost of extending a sewer line to the market and that Glen Park did not pay its share of $25,263.36. Glen Park asserted that it was not liable on the ground that Cassilly had no authority to contract for Glen Park.

Decision: Judgment for Schnucks Markets. Cassilly, as a partner in Glen Park Properties, was an agent of the partnership for the purposes of its business. A partner's negotiating and reaching an agreement about the installation of a sewer was within the ordinary course of real estate development partnership business. Glen Park was thus liable for half of the cost of extending the sewer line to the market. [*Schnucks Markets, Inc. v Cassilly (Mo App) 724 SW2d 664 (1987)*]

A third person must not assume that a partner has all the authority that the partner purports to have. If there is anything that would put a reasonable person on notice that the partner's powers are limited, the third person is bound by that limitation.

The third person must be on the alert for the following situations because they warn that the partner with whom the third person deals has either restricted authority or no authority at all.

FIGURE 45-1
*Limitations on
Authority of Individual
Partner to Bind
Partnership*

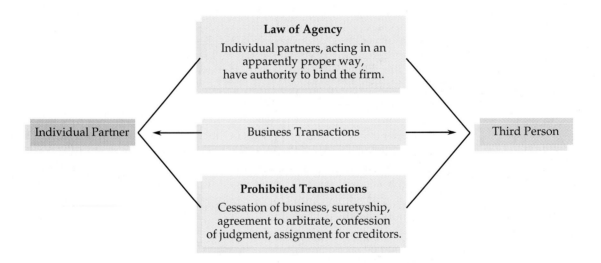

---

5 UPA § 9(4); *First National Bank & Trust Co. v Scherr* (ND) 467 NW2d 427 (1991).

5. Prohibited Transactions

Prohibited transactions
include
• cessation of business,
• suretyship,
• arbitration and confession
  of judgment,
• assignment for creditors,
  and
• discharge of personal
  obligations with firm
  assets.

There are certain transactions into which a partner cannot enter on behalf of the partnership unless the partner is expressly authorized to do so. A third person entering into such a transaction does so at the risk that the partner has not been authorized.

The following are prohibited transactions.

(a) Cessation of Business. A partner cannot bind the firm by a contract that would make it impossible for the firm to conduct its usual business.[6]

CASE SUMMARY

Family Feud

Facts: The Patel family, consisting of parents and a son, was a partnership that owned and operated a motel. The parents made a contract to sell the motel, but thereafter the son refused to sell. He claimed that the contract of sale was not binding.

Decision: Judgment for the son. The motel was not an asset held by the partnership for sale. It was an asset that was essential for the running of the partnership/business. Accordingly, neither one partner nor a majority had implied authority to sell the motel. To the contrary, the unanimous consent of all the partners was required for the sale of the motel because such a sale would make it impossible to continue the partnership business. [Patel v Patel, 212 Cal App 3d 6, 260 Cal Rptr 255 (1989)]

(b) Suretyship. A partner has no implied authority to bind the firm by contracts of surety, guarantee, or indemnity for purposes other than firm business.[7]

(c) Arbitration. A partner cannot submit controversies of the firm to arbitration "unless authorized by the other partners or unless they have abandoned the business."[8]

(d) Confession of Judgment. All partners should have an opportunity to defend in court. Because of this, a partner cannot confess judgment against the firm on one of its obligations. Exceptions exist when the other partners consent or when they have abandoned the business.

(e) Assignment for Creditors. A partner cannot make a general assignment of firm property for the benefit of creditors unless authorized by the other partners or unless they have abandoned the business.

(f) Personal Obligations. A partner cannot discharge personal obligations or claims of the firm by interchanging them in any way.

---

[6] *Wales v Roll* (Wyo) 769 P2d 899 (1989).
[7] *First Interstate Bank of Oregon v Bergendahl* (Or App) 723 P2d 1005 (1986).
[8] UPA § 9(3)(e).

B. DUTIES, RIGHTS, REMEDIES, AND LIABILITIES OF PARTNERS

The rights and duties of partners are based on their dual capacity of agent and co-owner.

6. Duties of Partners

In many respects, the duties of a partner are the same as those of an agent.

Each partner has the
following duties:
• loyalty and good faith
• obedience
• reasonable care
• information
• accounting

(a) Loyalty and Good Faith. Each partner must act in good faith toward the partnership. One partner must not take any advantage over the other(s) by the slightest misrepresentation or concealment. Each partner owes a duty of loyalty to the firm. This duty requires a partner's devotion to the firm's business and bars the making of any secret profit at the expense of the firm.

CASE SUMMARY

Honesty Is the Best Policy—Even for Managing Partner of Hotels

Facts: Rogers and Leatherman were managing partners of the Howard Johnson's Riverfront Enterprises partnership, which operated a hotel in Charleston, South Carolina. Houck and Lawson were nonmanaging partners. Rogers and Leatherman instructed the hotel's manager, Alan Harrison, to collect all miscellaneous cash revenues and split the money three ways. This "cash fund" included commissions from telephone calls, VCR rentals, arcade machines, and soda and snack machines. An accountant estimated that over a fifteen-month period some $39,278 was split between the three individuals. In September of 1989 the hotel sustained severe damage from Hurricane Hugo. Over $46,000 of partnership funds were spent in cash disbursements over the next few months. Few receipts and no records were kept. According to the managing partners, an engineer was paid up to $22,000 in cash to inspect the building for structural damage. However, no one remembered his last name, no records were kept, and no reports were ever made by the engineer. Lawson and Houck brought an accounting action against the managing partners for the cash disbursements wrongfully appropriated by them. Rogers and Leatherman defended that the cash fund was to pay their expenses in managing the hotel. Moreover, they claim they had the right to make cash disbursements after the hurricane because of the emergency.

Decision: Judgment for the nonmanaging partners. Rogers and Leatherman breached their fiduciary duty to their other partners by their appropriation of cash from the firm. The "cash fund" was not tied to any specific expenses, and the $39,278 must be restored to the firm. It is one of the ordinary duties of partners to keep true and correct books showing the firm's accounts. And where there are managing partners, this duty is on them. There was not a proper accounting of $32,000 of the $46,000 disbursed after the hurricane. Rogers and Leatherman also must return this amount to the partnership. [Lawson v Rogers (SC) 435 SE3d 853 (1993)]

Moreover, the duty of loyalty bars the use of the firm's property for personal benefit or the exploitation of a business opportunity of the partnership for personal gain.[9] ◆ *For example,* when one partner renewed a lease of the building occupied by the firm but the lease was renewed in the name of that partner alone, that partner was compelled to hold the lease for the firm. The failure to renew the lease in the name of the firm was a breach of the duties of good faith and loyalty owed to the firm. ◆

---

[9] *Lutz v Schmillen* (Wyo) 899 P2d 861 (1995).

A partner cannot promote a competing business. If the partner does so, he or she is liable for damages sustained by the partnership.

Each partner also owes a fiduciary duty of good faith to all other partners. This duty extends to any transaction connected with the formation, conduct, or liquidation of the partnership.

The obligation of a partner to refrain from competing with the partnership continues after the termination of the partnership if the partnership agreement contains a valid anticompetitive covenant. If there is no such restriction or if the restriction agreed on is held invalid, a partner is free to compete with the remaining partners even though they continue the partnership business.

(b) Obedience. Each partner is obligated to perform all duties and to obey all restrictions imposed by the partnership agreement or by the vote of the required number of partners.[10] Consequently each partner must observe any limitation imposed by a majority of the partners with respect to the ordinary details of the partnership business. ◆ *For example*, if a majority of the partners operating a retail store decide that no sales shall be made on credit, a partner who is placed in charge of the store must obey this limitation. If a third person does not know of the limitation, the managing partner has the power to make a binding sale on credit to that person. If the third person does not pay the bill and the firm suffers a loss as a result, the partner who violated the no-credit limitation is liable to the firm for the loss caused by such disobedience. ◆

(c) Reasonable Care. A partner must use reasonable care in transacting the business of the firm and is liable for any loss resulting from a failure to do so. A partner is not liable, however, for honest mistakes or errors of judgment.

(d) Information. A partner has the duty to inform the partnership of matters relating to the partnership. A partner must "render on demand true and full information of all things affecting the partnership to any partner or the legal representative of any deceased partner or partner under legal disability."[11]

The obligation to inform embraces matters relating to the purchase by one partner of the interest of another and to matters relating to the liquidation of the partnership.

(e) Accounting. A partner transacting any business for the firm must make and keep, or turn over to the proper person, correct records. If the partners have delegated to one of the partners the task of keeping the books and accounts for all the business of the firm, that partner must keep proper records. If the records are disputed, the record keeper has the burden of proving their accuracy.[12] If it is not shown that the records are correct, the record keeper is held liable.

When an action is brought to compel a partner to account, the court may require the making of an audit by a disinterested third person.

When a partnership is organized for an illegal purpose or for conducting a lawful business in an unlawful manner, a wrongdoing partner cannot obtain an accounting by the partnership. For example, when the members of an engineering

---

[10] *Cobin v Rice,* 823 F Supp 1419 (D Ind 1993).
[11] UPA § 20.
[12] *Laurence v Floshner Medical Partnership,* 206 Ill App 3d 777, 151 Ill Dec 875, 565 NE2d 146 (1990).

partnership did not have the license required for engineering work, one of the partners, an unlicensed engineer, could not require the other partners to account.

7. Rights of Partners as Owners

Each partner, in the absence of a contrary agreement, has the following rights. These rights stem from the fact that the partner is a co-owner of the partnership business.

(a) Management. Each partner has a right to take an equal part in transacting the business of the firm. It is immaterial that one partner contributed more than another or that one contributed only services.

Incidental to the right to manage the partnership, each partner has the right to possession of the partnership property for the purposes of the partnership.

(b) Inspection of Books. All partners are equally entitled to inspect the books of the firm. "The partnership books shall be kept, subject to any agreement between the partners, at the principal place of business of the partnership, and every partner shall at all times have access to and may inspect and copy any of them."[13]

(c) Share of Profits. Each partner is entitled to a share of the profits. The partners may provide, if they so wish, that profits shall be shared in unequal proportions. In the absence of such a provision in the partnership agreement, each partner is entitled to an equal share of the profits without regard to the amount of capital contributed or services performed for the partnership.

The right to profits is personal property regardless of the nature of the partnership assets. Upon the death of a partner, the right to a share of the profits and an accounting passes to the deceased partner's executor or administrator.

(d) Compensation. In the absence of a contrary agreement, a partner is not entitled to compensation for services performed for the partnership. There is no right to compensation even if the services are unusual or more extensive than the services rendered by other partners. Consequently, when one partner becomes seriously ill and the other partners transact all of the firm's business, they are not entitled to compensation for those services. The sickness of a partner is considered a risk assumed in the relationship. No agreement can be inferred that the active partners are to be compensated even though the services rendered by them are such that they would ordinarily be rendered in the expectation of receiving compensation. As an exception, "a surviving partner is entitled to reasonable compensation for services performed in winding up the partnership affairs."[14]

Contrary to the above, the partners may agree that one of the partners will devote full time as manager of the business and receive for such services a salary in addition to the managing partner's share of the profits.

(e) Repayment of Loans. A partner is entitled to the return of any money advanced to or for the firm. Such amounts must be separate and distinct from original or additional contributions to the capital of the firm.

---

[13] UPA § 19. See *Smith v Brown & Jones* (Sup Ct) 633 NYS2d 436 (1995).
[14] UPA § 18(f).

C
P
A

(f) Payment of Interest. In the absence of an agreement to the contrary, contributions to capital do not draw interest. The theory is that the profits constitute sufficient compensation. Advances by a partner in the form of loans are treated as if they were made by a stranger and bear interest from the date the advance is made.

(g) Contribution and Indemnity. A partner who pays more than a proportionate share of the debts of the firm has a right to contribution from the other partners. Under this principle, if an employee of a partnership negligently injures a third person while acting within the scope of employment and if the injured party collects damages from one partner, the latter may enforce contribution from the other partners in order to divide the loss proportionately among them.

The partnership must indemnify every partner for payments made and personal liabilities reasonably incurred in the ordinary and proper conduct of its business or for the preservation of its business or property. A partner has no right, however, to indemnity or reimbursement if the partner has (1) acted in bad faith, (2) negligently caused the necessity for payment, or (3) previously agreed to bear the expense alone.[15]

(h) Distribution of Capital. After the payment of all creditors and the repayment of loans made to the firm by partners, every partner is entitled to receive a share of the firm property upon dissolution. Unless otherwise stated in the partnership agreement, all partners are entitled to the return of their capital contributions.

After such distribution is made, each partner is the sole owner of the fractional part distributed to that partner rather than a co-owner of all the property, as during the existence of the partnership.

8. Liability of Partners and Partnership

The liability of a partnership and of the partners for the acts of individual partners and of employees is governed by the same principles that apply to the liability of an employer or a principal for the acts of an employee or agent.

(a) Nature and Extent of Partner's Liability. Partners are jointly liable on all firm contracts. They are jointly and severally liable for all torts committed by an employee or one of the partners in the scope of the partnership business. When partners are liable for the wrongful injury caused a third person, the latter may sue all or any of the members of the firm.

> *Each member of the firm has individual and unlimited liability for the debts of the partnership.*

CASE SUMMARY

"But the Jury Found Me Not Guilty of Malpractice," Dr. Antenucci Complained

Facts: Daniel Zuckerman, a minor, and Elaine, his mother, brought a medical malpractice action against Dr. Joseph Antenucci and Dr. Jose Pena. Although the summons did not state that the two defendants were partners, the undisputed evidence at the trial established that this was their relationship and that the alleged acts of malpractice were done in the course of partnership

---

[15] *Gramacy Equities Corp. v DuMont*, 72 NY2d 560, 531 NE2d 629 (1988).

business. The jury returned a verdict finding that Pena was guilty of malpractice but that Antenucci was not guilty of malpractice. The amount of the verdict was $4 million. Antenucci contended that he should not be held liable on a partnership theory for the act of his partner when the plaintiffs had not named the partnership entity on the summons and when the summons did not designate him as a partner.

Decision: Judgment against Antenucci. When Antenucci was served with a summons that named him as a defendant, jurisdiction was acquired over him. This gave the court the right to decide his personal liability and any liability that he might have for the action of a partner. Antenucci, as a partner, was jointly and severally liable for the malpractice of the other partner. The court could enforce that liability by entering judgment against Antenucci. [*Zuckerman v Antenucci, 124 Misc 2d 971, 478 NYS2d 578 (1984)*]

Partners who have satisfied a claim against the partnership have the right to contribution from the other partners, whereby the liability is apportioned among all the partners.[16] Unlike the UPA, partners under the Revised Uniform Partnership Act (RUPA) are jointly and severally liable for both tort and contract obligations of the firm.[17] However, the RUPA alters the traditional applications of "joint and several" liability by requiring that the creditors and tort victims satisfy their claims against the partnership before pursuing the personal assets of a partner.

(b) Liability for Breach of Duty. When a partner violates a duty owed to the partnership, the partner's liability is determined by the general principles of contract, tort, or agency law that may be applicable to such conduct. When one partner breaches a duty owed to another partner, the injured partner may recover damages.

(c) Liability of New Partners. A person admitted as a partner into an existing partnership has limited liability for all the obligations of the partnership arising before such admission. This is a limited liability in that the preadmission claim may be satisfied only out of partnership property and does not extend to the individual property of the newly admitted partner.[18] The incoming partner does not become personally liable for preadmission claims unless the incoming partner expressly promises to pay such claims.

(d) Effect of Dissolution on Partner's Liability. A partner remains liable after dissolution of the partnership unless expressly released by the creditors or unless all claims against the partnership have been satisfied. The dissolution of the partnership does not of itself discharge the existing liability of any partner. The individual property of a deceased partner is liable for the obligations of the partnership that were incurred while the deceased partner was alive. However, the individual creditors of the deceased partner have priority over the partnership creditors with respect to such property.[19]

---

[16] *U.S. Trust Co. v Bamco18* (App Div NY) 585 NYS2d 186 (1992).
[17] RUPA § 307(d).
[18] UPA § 17; see also UPA § 41(1), (7).
[19] UPA § 36.

9. Enforcement and Satisfaction of Creditor's Claims

The firm may have been sued in the name of all the individual partners doing business as the partnership, as in the case of "Plaintiff v *A, B, C,* doing business as the Ajax Warehouse." The partners named are bound by the judgment against the firm if they have been properly served in the suit.

If a debt is contractual in origin, common law requires that the partnership's assets be resorted to and exhausted before partnership creditors can reach a partner's individual assets.[20]

Personal creditors of a partner must first pursue the assets of that partner for satisfaction of their claims. After a partner's personal assets are exhausted, the creditor may enforce the unpaid portion of a judgment by obtaining a **charging order** against the partner's interest in the partnership.[21] Under such an order, a court requires that the partner's share of the profits be paid to the creditor until the debt is discharged.

C. LIMITED PARTNERSHIPS

A limited partnership is a special kind of partnership.

10. Formation of Limited Partnerships

A limited partnership can
be created only by com-
plying with the applicable
state law, either the
ULPA or the RULPA.

A limited partnership can be created only by complying with the appropriate local statute. Vermont follows the Uniform Limited Partnership Act (ULPA).[22] Most other states have adopted a version of the Revised Uniform Limited Partnership Act (RULPA) or the RULPA as amended in 1985.

General partners have
unlimited personal liability for partnership obligations. Limited partners'
liability is "limited" to
their contributions.

(a) Members of a Limited Partnership. In a limited partnership, certain members contribute capital but have limited liability for firm debts. The most these members can lose is their investment. These members are known as **limited partners**. The partners who manage the business and are personally liable for the firm debts are **general partners**.[23] A limited partnership can be formed by "one or more general partners and one or more limited partners."[24]

(b) Certificate of Limited Partnership. Unlike a general partnership, a limited partnership can be created only by executing a certificate of limited partnership. Under the ULPA, the certificate must set forth the name and business address of each partner, specifying which partners are general partners and which are limited partners. The essential details of the partnership and the relative rights of the partners must also be specified. The certificate, when executed, must be recorded locally in the office of the official in charge of public records. Ordinarily this will be the office of the county clerk or recorder of deeds of the county in which the principal place of business of the partnership is located.

---

[20] *McCune & McCune v Mountain Bell Tel. Co.* (Utah) 758 P2d 914 (1988); *Midwood Development Corp. v K 12th Associates,* 146 App Div 2d 754, 537 NYS2d 237 (1989).
[21] *Nigri v Lotz* (Ga App) 453 SE2d 780 (1995).
[22] Only Louisiana has not enacted either the ULPA or the RULPA.
[23] *Brooke v Mt. Hood Meadows Ltd.* (Or App) 725 P2d 925 (1986).
[24] ULPA § 1; RULPA § 101(7).

Under the 1985 amendments to the RULPA, the certificate need only include (1) the limited partnership's name, (2) the address of the partnership's registered office and the name and business address of its agent for service of process, (3) the name and business address of each general partner, (4) the partnership's mailing address, and (5) the latest date on which the limited partnership is to dissolve. The names of the limited partners (the investors) are not required. This allows for the preservation of the confidentiality of the investors' names from competitors. Moreover, new investors may be admitted as limited partners without the significant administrative burden involved in amending the certificate, as is required under the ULPA. The RULPA provides for the filing of the certificate with the office of the secretary of state, as opposed to the local filing required under the ULPA.

When there is no filing of the limited partnership certificate, all participants have the status and liability of general partners in a general partnership. However, technical defects in the certificate do not prevent formation of a limited partnership if there has been substantial, good-faith compliance with the filing requirements.[25]

11. Characteristics of Limited Partnerships

A limited partnership has the following characteristics.

(a) Capital Contributions. Under the ULPA, a limited partner contributes cash or property but not services. Under the RULPA, however, a limited partner may contribute services.

(b) Firm Name. With certain exceptions, a limited partner's name cannot appear in the firm name. If the name of a limited partner is used in the firm name so as to give the impression that the limited partner is an active partner, the limited partner loses the protection of limited liability and becomes liable without limit as a general partner. Under the RULPA, the words *limited partnership* must appear without abbreviation in the firm name.

(c) Management and Control of the Firm. The general partners manage the business and are personally liable for firm debts. Limited partners (the investors) have the right to a share of the profits and a return of capital upon dissolution and have limited liability. The limitation of liability is lost, however, if they participate in the control of the business.

CASE SUMMARY

The Problem of Limited Partners in Control

Facts: Gilroy, Sims & Associates, Ltd., was a limited partnership engaged in real estate development whose original general partners were Richard Gilroy and William Sims. Thomas Green and John Murphy, Jr., were listed as limited partners along with certain other individuals on the certificate of limited partnership. Green and Murphy took an active role in the day-to-day operations of the real estate developed by the limited partnership. Financing was obtained to construct the venture's building in St. Louis in 1968, and a mortgage was payable to American National Insurance Co. over 27 years. In 1976 the partnership executed a Restated Agreement, and Green and Murphy became general partners of Gilroy, Sims, agreeing to "unlimited liability for the debts of the partnership." In the fall of 1990, the partnership stopped making mortgage

---

[25] ULPA § 2(2); RULPA § 201(b); *Fabry Partnership v Christensan* (Nev) 794 P2d 719 (1990).

payments. After foreclosure by American National, a deficiency of $1,437,840 was outstanding. Green and Murphy believed that as limited partners when the debt was incurred in 1968, they were absolved from any personal liability beyond the assets of the firm. American National disagreed.

Decision: Judgment for American National Insurance Co. Green and Murphy expressly adopted the partnership obligation in the Restated Agreement executed in 1976. Moreover, although Green's and Murphy's limited partner status would ordinarily limit their personal liability to creditors to the amount of their investment, their active roles in taking part in the control of the business subjected them to potential general partner liability. [*American National Ins. Co. v Gilroy Associates, Ltd., 847 F Supp 971 (ED Mo 1995)*]

The RULPA lists a number of "safe harbor" activities in which limited partners may engage without losing their protection from liability. These activities include

1. being a contractor for or an agent or employee of the limited partnership or of a general partner,
2. consulting with and advising a general partner regarding the partnership business,
3. acting as a surety for the limited partnership, and
4. voting on partnership matters, such as dissolving and winding up the limited partnership or removing a general partner.

(d) Right to Sue. A limited partner may bring a derivative action on behalf of the limited partnership to enforce a claim that the limited partnership possesses against others but that the partnership refuses to enforce. This derivative suit is filed in the name of the limited partner, and the partnership is named as a defendant, with the limited partnership deriving the benefits of the action. Also, limited partners may sue the general partners to protect the limited partners' interests.

CASE SUMMARY

Why Limited Partnerships Have Fallen into Disfavor

Facts: Dolan formed a limited partnership in which Labovitz and others invested as limited partners. The limited partnership agreement gave Dolan "sole discretion" as to whether there were profits and whether they should be distributed. In two successive years, the partnership had large gross earnings ($34 million in one year and $18 million the next). Dolan refused to make any cash distributions. The limited partners had heavy personal income tax obligations as a result of the high earnings and had to pay their taxes from their own or borrowed resources. Dolan then offered to buy out their interests at two-thirds of book value. The limited partners brought suit, claiming Dolan breached his fiduciary duty to them by coercing them to sell their interests to him by unreasonably refusing to distribute cash.

Decision: Dolan was required to show that he had acted in good faith rather than to further his own personal interests at the expense of the limited partners. The fact that he was given "sole discretion" did not mean that he could do whatever he wanted to do. This discretion was subject to an implied duty to act in good faith for the protection and benefit of all participants in the limited partnership. The court said the general partner's discretion "was encumbered by a supreme fiduciary duty of fairness, honesty, good faith, and loyalty to his limited partners." The case was therefore remanded to the lower court to determine if Dolan had breached his duty to the limited partners. [*Labovitz v Dolan, 189 Ill App 3d 403, 136 Ill Dec 708, 545 NE2d 304 (1989)*]

(e) Dissolution. The dissolution and winding up of limited partnerships is governed by the same principles applicable to general partnerships.

D. LIMITED LIABILITY COMPANIES

Limited liability company (LLC) acts were rapidly adopted by state legislatures throughout the country following a favorable tax ruling on this form of organization by the Internal Revenue Service.[26] This corporate-sounding entity is considered in this chapter because it is a form of limited partnership.

12. Characteristics of LLCs

The IRS has determined that an LLC may qualify for partnership federal tax treatment. Unlike a corporation, an LLC pays no federal taxes on its income as an entity. Instead, the income (or losses, deductions, and credits) flows through to the LLC's owners (called members) based on their proportionate interest in the company. The members report the income on their personal tax returns. The LLC combines this tax advantage with the limited liability feature of the corporate form of business organization. The owners and managers are not personally liable for the debts and obligations of the entity.[27]

(a) Formation. An LLC is formed by filing articles of organization with the secretary of state in a manner similar to the filing of articles of incorporation by a corporation. The articles must contain the name, purpose, duration, registered agent, and principal office of the LLC. An LLC must use the words "limited liability company" or "LLC" in the company's name. The LLC is a legal entity with authority to conduct business in its own name.

(b) Capital Contributions. An ownership interest in an LLC may be issued for cash, property, or services. The owners of the entity are known as members.

(c) Management. Management of an LLC is vested in its members. An *operating agreement*, equivalent to the bylaws of a corporation or a partnership agreement, sets forth the specific management authority of members and managers.

The operating agreement need not be in writing. All amendments must be unanimous unless otherwise agreed to by the members. Oral amendments may modify written terms unless otherwise set forth in the operating agreement. To promote certainty in management, it is recommended that the operating agreement be in writing and that it be changed only by written amendments adopted by a specified percentage or number of members.

The management structure created in the operating agreement may provide for the company to be member-managed. However, members commonly delegate authority to run the entity to managers who may or may not be required to be members of the LLC. A member is not entitled to compensation for services

---

[26] IRS Rev Rul 88-76. LLCs have been adopted by every state and the District of Columbia. A Uniform Limited Liability Company Act was approved by the National Conference of Commissioners on Uniform State Law in August 1994.

[27] Some LLC statutes provide that courts may disregard the LLC entirely and hold the owners personally liable beyond their investments to the same extent as is done in corporate law when exceptional circumstances warrant.

performed by an LLC unless it is stipulated in the operating agreement. (Members receive profits and losses according to the terms of the operating agreement.)

In a member-managed company, each member has equal rights in management, with decisions made by a majority vote of the members. In a manager-managed company, nonmanager members have no rights in management, except for extraordinary matters, such as amending the operating agreement or consenting to merge with another entity.

Managers have the same fiduciary duties to the entity as corporate officers have to a corporation.

FIGURE 45-2
Comaprison of General Partnership, Limited Partnership, Limited Liability Company, and Limited Liabiity Partnership

	General Partnership	Limited Partnership	Limited Liability Company (LLC)	Limited Liability Partnership (LLP)
Creation	No formality required.	Filing a certificate of limited partnership with appropriate state office.	Filing articles of organization with secretary of state.	Registration of LLP filed with state government.
Liability	Unlimited liability of each partner for firm debts.	General partners: unlimited liability for firm debts. Limited partners: no liability beyond loss of investment.	All members are liable for LLC debts to the extent of their capital contributions and equity in firm. No personal liability beyond such.	No liability for partners beyond their contributions and equity in firm, except unlimited personal liability for their own wrongful acts and those of persons whom they supervise.
Management	All partners according to their partnership agreement or the UPA or RUPA.	General partners according to their partnership agreement or the UPA or RUPA. Limited partners excluded.	By members of firm, who may delegate authority to managers.	All partners according to partnership agreement or the UPA.
Dissolution	As set forth in the partnership agreement or the UPA or RUPA.	As set forth in the partnership agreement or the ULPA or RULPA.	As set forth in LLC statute or articles of organization.	As set forth in partnership agreement or the UPA or RUPA.

(d) Distributions. Profits and losses are shared according to the terms of the operating agreement.

Liquidating distributions must first be applied to return all contributions not previously returned, and the remainder is distributed per capita to members unless members alter these rules in the operating agreement.

Any distribution made when the company is insolvent is unlawful. Each member or manager who votes for the making of an unlawful distribution is in violation of his or her fiduciary duty to the firm and is personally liable for the amount of distribution improperly paid. However, they may compel contribution from all other responsible members and managers.

(e) Assignment. An interest in an LLC is personal property and is generally assignable. However, LLC members cannot transfer the right to participate in management without the consent of the other members of the LLC.

(f) Dissolution. Statutes creating LLCs commonly limit the existence of the entity to no more than 30 years. And most statutes provide that an LLC will dissolve by the consent of the members or upon the death, retirement, resignation, expulsion, or bankruptcy of a member. Statutes also provide, however, that the business of the LLC may be continued with the consent of all of the remaining members.

Upon the winding up of an LLC, the assets are distributed according to the operating agreement. Should the agreement fail to provide for this event, then the assets will be distributed according to the state's LLC statute.

(g) Tax Classification. The IRS applied a four-factor corporate characteristics test in determining whether an LLC would be taxed as a partnership or a corporation, allowing no more than two characteristics to exist in order to qualify for taxation as a partnership. The factors were continuity of life, centralized management, limited liability, and free transferability of interest. Effective January 1, 1997, the four-factor test became obsolete upon the implementation by the IRS of its so-called check-the-box entity classification election procedure available to unincorporated associations that are not publicly traded.[28] Now, if an LLC wants to be classified as a partnership, all it needs to do is make that election by checking the box on the appropriate IRS form.

13. LLCs and Other Entities

LLCs are distinguishable from Subchapter S corporations and limited partnerships.

(a) LLC Distinguished from a Subchapter S corporation. Under a Subchapter S corporation (so named from Subchapter S of the Internal Revenue Code), shareholders of a close corporation may be treated as partners for tax purposes and retain the benefit of limited liability under the corporate form. An S corporation is limited to 75 shareholders who must be U.S. citizens or resident aliens. While partnerships and corporations may generally not be shareholders, employee stock ownership plans (ESOPs) and nonprofit entities may be. In contrast, an LLC has no limit on the number of owners, and there is no restriction on the types of entities or persons that may own an LLC. Thus, partnerships, corporations,

---

[28] Treas Reg 301.7701 et seq.

and foreign investors may be owners of an LLC. Because substantial taxes on appreciated assets are payable upon the liquidation of an S corporation, it is generally not feasible to convert an existing S corporation to an LLC.

(b) LLC Distinguished from a Limited Partnership. Limited partners in a limited partnership have the advantage of limited liability. However, every limited partnership must have a general partner who manages the business, and this partner is subject to unlimited liability. This structural feature is a major disadvantage of the limited partnership form that does not exist in a limited liability company (LLC). Also, limited partners may lose their limited liability if they participate in the control of the business. Under an LLC, the members may actively participate in the control of the business and still receive limited liability protection.

(c) Usage. It is expected that the LLC will in many instances replace general and limited partnerships as well as close corporations and S corporations. The LLC will not replace the publicly traded corporation, however, because publicly traded partnerships must be classified as corporations for tax purposes.[29]

E.   LIMITED LIABILITY PARTNERSHIPS

As part of the limited liability trend established by the swift enactment of LLC laws throughout the country, most states have recently enacted limited liability partnership (LLP) acts. Like LLCs, they provide businesses and those offering professional services the benefit of single taxation as a partnership as well as limited liability.[30]

14. Extent of Limited Liability

In a general partnership, partners are jointly liable for partnership debts and jointly and severally liable for partnership torts. LLP statutes were initially drafted to shield innocent partners from vicarious negligence or malpractice liability of their partners. Some states now provide "full shields" for innocent partners that eliminate the vicarious personal liability of these partners for the obligations of the partnership and free them from any obligation to contribute personal assets beyond their investments in the partnership. In every state, however, LLP partners remain fully liable for their own negligence and continue to have unlimited liability for the wrongful acts of those whom they directly supervise and control.

Professional LLPs continue to be subject to professional regulations, and the appropriate regulating boards set the amount and type of malpractice insurance firms must carry to operate as an LLP.

◆ *For example,* to illustrate the effects of a change from a general partnership to an LLP, surgeons Jones, Smith, and Gray are partners. Jones inadvertently removed Miller's healthy kidney rather than his diseased kidney, and a jury

---

29 See IRS Notice 88-75, 1988, 1988-2 CB 386. The traditional corporation retains many advantages, such as the low corporate income tax on corporate profits, which allows for the accumulation of capital for expansion or the distribution of all corporate earnings as compensation, as well as providing fringe benefits for employee-owners with pretax dollars (IRC §§ 79, 119, 162).

30 The 1994 Revised Uniform Partnership Act (RUPA) was amended in 1996 to include two new articles: Article 10 dealing with limited liability partnerships and Article 11 dealing with foreign limited liability partnerships. Articles 1 through 11 constitute the Uniform Limited Liability Partnership Act.

returned a verdict of $2 million. Smith and Gray, although innocent partners, are jointly and severally liable along with Jones under general partnership law, and their personal assets can be reached to pay the judgment if necessary. Under an LLP, only partnership assets and the personal assets of Jones are available to pay the judgment. Smith's and Gray's personal assets cannot be reached. ◆

15. Registration and Usage

LLP statutes are designed to permit the conversion of existing general partnerships into limited liability partnerships. The statutes require registration with the secretary of state, and the name of the partnership must contain the term "limited liability partnership" or "LLP."

Traditional partnership agreements, like those used by many accounting and law firms and other professional partnerships, can be converted into limited liability partnership agreements without major redrafting or renegotiating of the underlying agreements. It is thus expected that many of these professional firms will organize under this new form of partnership.

ETHICS & THE LAW

When the Office of the Special Counsel concluded its work in both civil and criminal litigation against officers, directors, and consultants involved with failed savings and loans in the late 1980s, it released a report on its work. On the civil side, the Office of the Special Counsel had obtained settlements from defendants in civil suits of $2.9 billion in restitution. Accounting firms, along with lawyers and consultants, comprised 71 percent of the defendants.

Because most accounting firms were organized as partnerships, the result was that many partners were required to dig into their personal assets to meet the restitution requirements imposed by the federal government. Since the creation of LLPs, all of the largest accounting firms in the United States have restructured, with most choosing the LLP for conducting business. All forms of restructuring will ensure limited personal liability for their principals.

Was the restructuring undertaken to avoid liability? Does limited liability insulate those who make decisions from liability for those decisions? Financiers attempt to determine what stake the officers in a corporation have in the corporation. Stock ownership and exposure to losses through the value of those shares are seen as a positive influence. Do liability limitations reduce the stake a principal has? Is it good to have decision makers separated from the costs of those decisions?

SUMMARY

When there are more than two partners in a firm, the decisions of the majority prevail on ordinary matters relating to the firm's business unless the decisions are contrary to the partnership agreement. A partner's authority to act for the firm is similar to that of an agent to act for a principal. A partner may have express authority to act as set forth in the partnership agreement or as agreed to by a suffi-

cient number of partners. A partner has the customary or implied power to make contracts to transact the firm's business, to sell the firm's goods in the regular course of business, to make purchases within the scope of the business, and to borrow money for firm purposes. Further, a partner may purchase insurance, hire employees, and adjust claims for and against the firm. A partner may not bind the firm by a contract that makes it impossible for the firm to conduct its business. In the absence of express authority from the firm, an individual partner cannot enter into a suretyship contract or an agreement to submit a partnership dispute to arbitration. Nor can a partner confess judgment against the firm, make an assignment of the firm's assets for the benefit of its creditors, or discharge personal obligations of the partner by paying them with obligations of the firm.

A partner's duties are the same as those of an agent. These duties include loyalty and good faith, obedience, reasonable care, the provision of full information on all matters affecting the firm, and the keeping of proper and correct records. If there is no contrary agreement, each partner has the right to take an equal part in the management of the business, to inspect the books, to share in the profits, and, after payment of all of the firm's debts and the return of capital, to share in the firm's property or surplus upon dissolution.

Partners have unlimited personal liability for partnership liabilities. Partners are jointly liable on all firm contracts. They are jointly and severally liable for all torts committed by one of the partners or by a firm employee within the scope of the partnership's business. A partner remains liable after dissolution unless expressly released by creditors. An incoming partner is not liable for the existing debts of the partnership unless the new partner expressly assumes those debts.

A limited partnership consists of one or more limited partners, who contribute cash, property, or services without liability for losses beyond their investment, and one or more general partners, who manage the business and have unlimited personal liability. A certificate must be properly executed and filed when a limited partnership is formed.

A limited liability company is a hybrid form of business organization that combines the tax advantages of a partnership with the limited liability feature of the corporation.

A limited liability partnership is a new form of business organization that allows existing partnerships to convert to this new form without major renegotiation of the underlying partnership agreement. Innocent partners in a limited liability partnership are not personally liable for the torts of other partners beyond their investment in the firm.

QUESTIONS AND CASE PROBLEMS

1. What social forces are affected by the rule giving the majority of partners authority to bind the firm in routine business matters?

2. Compare the right of a partner to engage in a business that competes with the firm (a) while still a partner and (b) after leaving the partnership.

3. Ross, Marcos, and Albert are partners. Ross and Marcos each contributed $60,000 to the partnership; Albert contributed $30,000. At the end of the fiscal year, distributable profits total $150,000. Ross claims $60,000 as his share of the profits. Is he entitled to this sum?

4. What is the effect of dissolution on a partner's liability?

5. Leland McElmurry was one of three partners of MHS Enterprises, a Michigan partnership. Commonwealth Capital Investment Corp. sued the partnership and obtained a judgment of $1,137,285 against it, but the partnership could not pay the judgment. Commonwealth then sued McElmurry for the entire debt on the theory that, as a partner of MHS, he was liable for its debts. What, if any, is McElmurry's liability? [*Commonwealth Capital Investment Corp. v McElmurry* (Mich App) 302 NW2d 222]

6. A judgment creditor is owed $100,000 by a partnership, but no partnership assets exist to satisfy this obligation. Of the partnership's two partners, Partner *A* has $100,000 in personal assets, and Partner *B* has no personal assets. How would the $100,000 obligation be apportioned between the partners under "joint liability" and under "joint and several" liability?

7. Brothers Charles and Sonny Monin formed a partnership in 1967 for hauling milk for Dairymen Incorporated (DI), an organization of milk producers. The brothers had a falling out in 1984, and Sonny notified Charles that he was dissolving the partnership in July 1984. The partnership's contract with DI expired on October 16, 1984. On September 24, 1984, the brothers executed an agreement to conclude their business arrangement, whereby they would hold a private auction between themselves for all the assets of the partnership, including equipment and milk routes. The agreement contained a covenant not to compete. Charles was the successful bidder at $86,000. The value of the milk-hauling equipment was $22,000 and the milk routes $64,000. Sonny notified DI that he wanted to apply for the right to haul milk after the expiration of the partnership's contract. Charles was the only other applicant for milk routes. Sonny was selected over Charles for the new DI contract. Charles sued Sonny for breach of his fiduciary duty because Sonny failed to withdraw his application with DI for

the milk routes after agreeing to allow Charles to buy his interest in those milk routes. Sonny contended that the partnership had no interest in the milk routes after the contract expired on October 16, 1984, and that he was therefore free to pursue the contract. Decide. [*Monin v Monin* (Ky App) 785 SW2d 499]

8. Compare the effect of a secret limitation on the authority of (a) an agent and (b) a partner.

9. George and James McCune did business as McCune & McCune, a general law partnership. Mountain Bell provided telephone service to McCune & McCune through November 1983, when the partnership dissolved and its telephone service was discontinued. Mountain Bell transferred the unpaid balance of the partnership's account to the individual business account of George McCune. George brought suit against Mountain Bell to enjoin it from suspending his service when this transferred bill was not paid. He contended that partnership law requires that partnership assets be marshaled and exhausted before a partnership creditor can reach a partner's individual assets. Mountain Bell contended that it had the right to cross-bill customers' accounts for unpaid bills, and if the bill remained unpaid, it had a right to suspend service on the account to which the debt had been transferred. Decide. [*McCune & McCune v Mountain Bell Tel. Co.* (Utah) 758 P2d 914]

10. Mason and Phyllis Ledbetter operated a business in Northbrook, Illinois, as a partnership called Ledbetters' Nurseries that specialized in the sale of garden lilies. The grounds of the nurseries were planted with numerous species of garden lilies, and hundreds of people toured the Ledbetters' gardens every day. After a tour, Sheila Clark offered to buy the facilities at a "top-notch price." Mason felt he could not refuse the high offer, and he signed a contract to sell all the facilities, including all flowers and the business name. When Phyllis refused to go along with the contract, Clark sued the Ledbetters' Nurseries partnership, seeking to obtain specific performance of the sales contract. Decide.

11. Holmes and Clay are partners in a medical partnership. Each had invested $25,000 in the practice; the total market value of all firm assets was $50,000. Marsh, a former patient of Holmes, sued Holmes and Clay for malpractice involved in surgery performed by Holmes. Marsh's suit was successful, and a judgment was entered for $150,000 against the two partners. Holmes had suffered a prior financial setback, and he did not have funds or property other than partnership assets to pay the judgment. Arrangements were made by Holmes and Clay to pay $50,000 using the firm assets. Marsh now seeks to collect $100,000 from Clay. Clay objects that it is absurd to seek payment from her out of her own personal assets when she was not at fault. Is Clay liable to Marsh for the unpaid balance of the judgment?

12. Hacienda Farms, Ltd., was organized as a limited partnership with Ricardo de Escamilla as the general partner and James L. Russell and H.W. Andrews as limited partners. The partnership raised vegetables and truck crops that were marketed principally through a produce concern controlled by Andrews. All three individuals decided which crops were to be planted. The general partner had no power to withdraw money from the partnership's two bank accounts without the signature of one of the limited partners. After operating for some seven and one-half months under these procedures, the limited partners demanded that the general partner resign as farm manager, which he did. Six weeks later the partnership went into bankruptcy. Laurance Holzman, as trustee in bankruptcy, brought an action against Russell and Andrews, claiming that they had become liable to the creditors of the partnership as general partners because they had taken part in the control of the partnership business. How would you decide the case under the ULPA? Would the outcome be different under the RULPA? [*Holzman v de Escamilla* (Cal App) 195 P2d 833]

13. St. John Transportation Co., a corporation, made a contract with the partnership of Bilyeu and Herstel, contractors, by which the latter was to construct a ferryboat. Herstel, a member of the firm of contractors, executed a contract in the firm name with Benbow for certain materials and labor in connection with the construction of the ferryboat. In an action brought by Benbow to enforce a lien against the ferryboat, the James Johns, it was contended that all members of the firm were bound by the contract made by Herstel. Do you agree? [*Benbow v The Ferryboat James Johns* (Or) 108 P 634]

14. Jerome Micco was a major shareholder and corporate officer of Micco and Co., Inc., which was a limited partner in Harbor Creek Ltd., a limited partnership formed to build a condominium complex. Hommel, an electrical contractor, was the successful bidder on certain electrical work for the project. For several months, Hommel worked under the direction of the construction supervisor and was paid by the limited partnership for his work. Because of financial difficulties, the supervisor was released. Thereafter, Jerome Micco played a major role in the building of the project, directing what work was to be performed. Hommel submitted payment invoices directly to Micco. When Hommel was not paid, he sued Micco,

contending that Micco was a limited partner who ran the operation personally and was personally responsible for the debt. Micco argued that he was an employee or agent of a corporation (Micco and Co., Inc.) and thus could not be held liable for the debt. The evidence reveals that Micco had no occasion to tell Hommel that he was acting as a corporate officer. Is it ethical for a corporate officer and shareholder to seek to avoid individual liability in this case? How would you decide the case? [*Hommel v Micco* (Ohio App) 602 NE2d 1259]

15. Zemelman and others did business as a partnership under the name of Art Seating Co. which obtained a fire insurance policy from Boston Insurance Co. There was a fire loss, and a claim was filed under the policy. The claim was prepared by one of the partners, Irving Zemelman. The insurance company asserted that false statements were made by Zemelman and that the insurer was therefore not liable on the policy. The policy contained an express provision stating that it was void if a false claim was made. The partnership replied that it was not bound by any fraudulent statement of Zemelman because the making of fraudulent statements was not within the scope of his authority. Is the partnership correct? [*Zemelman v Boston Ins. Co.* (Ct App) 84 Cal Rptr 206]

CPA QUESTIONS

1. Acorn and Bean were general partners in a farm machinery business. Acorn contracted, on behalf of the partnership, to purchase ten tractors from Cobb Corp. Unknown to Cobb, Acorn was not authorized by the partnership to make such contracts. Bean refused to allow the partnership to accept delivery of the tractors, and Cobb sought to enforce the contract. Cobb will

   a. Lose, because Acorn's action was beyond the scope of Acorn's implied authority.
   b. Prevail, because Acorn had implied authority to bind the partnership.
   c. Prevail, because Acorn had apparent authority to bind the partnership.
   d. Lose, because Acorn's express authority was restricted, in writing, by the partnership agreement.

   (11/90, Law, #13)

2. Upon dissolution of a general partnership, distributions will be made on account of

   I. Partners' capital accounts,
   II. Amounts owed partners with respect to profits, and
   III. Amounts owed partners for loans to the partnership in the following order:
   a. III, I, II.
   b. I, II, III.
   c. II, III, I.
   d. III, II, I.

   (11/91, Law, #17)

3. Which of the following statements is correct with respect to a limited partnership?

   a. A limited partner may **not** be an unsecured creditor of the limited partnership.
   b. A general partner may **not** also be a limited partner at the same time.
   c. A general partner may be a secured creditor of the limited partnership.
   d. A limited partnership can be formed with limited liability for all partners.

   (5/92, Law, #11)

Introduction to Corporation Law

CHAPTER 46

A. NATURE AND CLASSES

1. The Corporation as a Person
2. Classifications of Corporations
3. Corporations and Governments
4. Ignoring the Corporate Entity

B. CREATION AND TERMINATION OF THE CORPORATION

5. Promoters
6. Incorporation
7. Application for Incorporation
8. The Certificate of Incorporation
9. Proper and Defective Incorporation
10. Insolvency, Bankruptcy, and Reorganization
11. Forfeiture of Charter
12. Judicial Dissolution

C. CORPORATE POWERS

13. Particular Powers
14. *Ultra Vires* Acts

D. CONSOLIDATIONS, MERGERS, AND CONGLOMERATES

15. Definitions
16. Legality
17. Liability of Successor Corporations

OBJECTIVES

After studying this chapter, you should be able to

1. *Classify corporations according to their nature, state of incorporation, and functions performed;*
2. *State why/when the corporate entity will be ignored;*
3. *List the steps to be taken in forming a corporation;*
4. *Compare corporations de jure, de facto, and by estoppel;*
5. *List and describe the ways in which corporate existence may be terminated; and*
6. *Compare consolidations, mergers, and conglomerates.*

The corporation is one of the most important forms of business organization.

A. NATURE AND CLASSES

A corporation is an artificial person that is created by government action.

1. The Corporation as a Person

A **corporation** is an artificial person created by government action and granted certain powers. It exists in the eyes of the law as a person, separate and distinct from the persons who own the corporation.

CASE SUMMARY

You See, a Corporation Has a Separate Legal Existence from Those Who Own It

Facts: On September 1, 1987, Kettlewell, Inc., was granted an operating license by the Department of Natural Resources (DNR) to run the Fort Gratiot Sanitary Landfill in Port Huron. In July 1988, Bill Kettlewell, the sole stockholder of this company, sold all of his stock to Stanwix Corporation. The DNR notified the new owners of Kettlewell, Inc., that the sale of stock required the corporation to obtain a new operating license. Kettlewell, Inc., contended that it was properly licensed to run the landfill and that the sale of the stock affected neither its legal existence nor the rights it held.

Decision: Judgment for Kettlewell, Inc. Kettlewell, Inc., at all times retained its distinct legal existence apart from its prior or current shareholders. Therefore, it continued to be a duly licensed disposal operator irrespective of the sale of stock. *[Kettlewell, Inc. v St. Clair County, 187 Mich App 633, 468 NW2d 326 (1991)]*

A corporation is a separate legal entity.
• It can own property.
• Its debts are not the debts of the officers or shareholders.

The concept that the corporation is a distinct legal person means that property of the corporation is owned not by the persons who own shares in the corporation but by the corporation. Debts of the corporation are debts of this artificial person, not of the persons running the corporation or owning shares of stock in it.[1] The corporation can sue and be sued in its own name, but shareholders cannot be sued or be held liable for corporate actions or obligations.

A corporation is formed by obtaining approval of a **certificate of incorporation, articles of incorporation,** or a **charter** from the state or national government.[2]

2. Classifications of Corporations

Corporations may be classified in terms of their relationship to the public, the source of their authority, and the nature of their activities.

---

[1] *American Truck Lines, Inc. v Albino* (Ga App) 424 SE2d 367 (1992).
[2] *Charter, certificate of incorporation,* and *articles of incorporation* are all terms used to refer to the documents that serve as evidence of a government's grant of corporate existence and powers. Most state incorporation statutes now provide for a certificate of incorporation issued by the secretary of state, but a Revised Model Business Corporation Act (RMBCA) has done away with the certificate of incorporation. Under the RMBCA, corporate existence begins when articles of incorporation are filed with the secretary of state. An endorsed copy of the articles together with a fee, receipt, or acknowledgment replaces the certificate of incorporation. See RMBCA §§ 1.25 and 2.03 and footnote 6 in this chapter.

(a) Public, Private, and Quasi-Public Corporations. A public corporation is one established for governmental purposes and for the administration of public affairs. A city is a public or municipal corporation acting under authority granted to it by the state.

A **private corporation** is one organized for charitable and benevolent purposes or for purposes of finance, industry, and commerce. Private corporations are often called "public" in business circles when their stock is sold to the public.

A **quasi–public corporation,** sometimes known as a public service corporation or a public utility, is a private corporation furnishing services on which the public is particularly dependent. An example of a quasi-public corporation is a gas and electric company.

(b) Public Authorities. The public increasingly demands that government perform services. Some of these are performed directly by government. Others are performed by separate corporations or **authorities** that are created by government.

For example, a city parking facility may be organized as a separate municipal parking authority, or a public housing project may be operated as an independent housing authority.

(c) Domestic and Foreign Corporations. A corporation is called a **domestic corporation** with respect to the state under whose law it has been incorporated. Any other corporation going into that state is called a **foreign corporation.** Thus, a corporation holding a Texas charter is a domestic corporation in Texas but a foreign corporation in all other states.

(d) Special Service Corporations. Corporations formed for transportation, banking, insurance, and savings and loan operations and similar specialized functions are subject to separate codes or statutes with regard to their organization. In addition, federal and state laws and administrative agencies regulate in detail the way these businesses are conducted.

(e) Close Corporations. A corporation whose shares are held by a single shareholder or a small group of shareholders is known as a **close corporation.** Its shares are not traded publicly. Many such corporations are small firms that in the past would have operated as proprietorships or partnerships but are incorporated to obtain either the advantage of limited liability or a tax benefit, or both.

In many states, statutes have liberalized the corporation law as it applies to close corporations. For example, some statutes permit incorporation by a smaller number of persons, allow a one-person board of directors, and eliminate the requirement of formal meetings.[3]

(f) Subchapter S Corporations. Subchapter S is a subdivision of the Internal Revenue Code. If corporate shareholders meet the requirements of this subdivision, they may elect Subchapter S status, which allows the shareholders to be treated as partners for tax purposes and retain the benefit of limited liability under the corporate form. A Subchapter S corporation is limited to 75 shareholders.

The most common forms of corporations are private business corporations and close corporations.

---

[3] This distinction between large and small corporations is part of the same current of legal development that in the Uniform Commercial Code has given rise to the distinction between the merchant seller or buyer, on the one hand, and the casual seller or buyer on the other.

Under the Small Business Job Protection Act of 1996, employee stock ownership plans (ESOPs) and tax-exempt entities may be shareholders, subject to certain special taxation rules.[4] Other reforms in this act make it easier for small businesses to comply with S corporation rules.

(g) Professional Corporations. A corporation may be organized for the purpose of conducting a profession.

(h) Nonprofit Corporations. A **nonprofit corporation** (or an eleemosynary corporation) is one that is organized for charitable or benevolent purposes. Nonprofit corporations include hospitals, nursing homes, and universities.[5] Special procedures for incorporation are prescribed, and provision is made for a detailed examination of and hearing regarding the purpose, function, and methods of raising money for the enterprise.

3. Corporations and Governments

Problems arise about the power of governments to create and regulate corporations.

(a) Power to Create. Because by definition a corporation is created by government, the right to be a corporation must be obtained from the proper governmental agency. The federal government may create corporations whenever appropriate to carry out the powers granted to it.

Generally, a state by virtue of its police power may create any kind of corporation for any purpose. Most states have a **general corporation code,** which lists certain requirements, and anyone who satisfies the requirements and files the necessary papers with the government may automatically become a corporation. In 1950, the American Bar Association (ABA) published a Model Business Corporation Act (MBCA) to assist legislative bodies in the modernization of state corporation laws. An updated version was published in 1969. Statutory language similar to that contained in the 1969 version of the MBCA has been adopted in whole or in part by 35 states. The 1984 revision of the model act (RMBCA) represents the first complete revision in more than 30 years.[6] Jurisdictions following the model act have made numerous modifications to reflect their differing views about balancing the interests of public corporations, shareholders, and management. Caution must therefore be exercised in making generalizations about model act jurisdictions. There is no *uniform* corporation act.

---

[4] PL 104-188 (August 20, 1996).

[5] The Committee on Corporate Laws of the American Bar Association has prepared a Model Nonprofit Corporation Act. The Nonprofit Corporation Act has formed the basis for nonprofit corporation statutes in Alabama, Iowa, Nebraska, North Carolina, North Dakota, Ohio, Oregon, Texas, Virginia, Washington, Wisconsin, and the District of Columbia. A revised Model Nonprofit Corporation Act was approved in 1986.

[6] The Revised Model Business Corporation Act (1984) was approved by the Committee on Corporate Laws of the Section of Corporation, Banking and Business Law of the American Bar Association. The committee approved revisions to Sections 6.40 and 8.33 on March 27, 1987, and to Section 7.08 on June 16, 1996; changes to Subchapters B and D of Chapter 1 of the model act, which will accommodate the use of electronic means for transmitting and filing required corporate documents with the secretary of state, are pending. Excerpts of the 1984 act, as revised, are found in Appendix 6 to this book. Model act citations are to the 1984 Revised Model Business Corporation Act (RMBCA) unless designated otherwise.

(b) Power to Regulate. Subject to constitutional limitations, corporations may be regulated by statutes.

(1) Protection of the Corporation as a Person.

The Constitution of the United States prohibits the national government and state governments from depriving any person of life, liberty, or property without due process of law. Many state constitutions contain a similar limitation on their respective state governments. A corporation is regarded as a "person" within the meaning of such provisions.

The federal Constitution prohibits a state from denying to any person within its jurisdiction the equal protection of the laws. No such express limitation is placed on the federal government, although the Due Process Clause binding the federal government is liberally interpreted so that it prohibits substantial inequality of treatment.

(2) Protection of the Corporation as a Citizen.

For certain purposes, such as determining the right to bring a lawsuit in a federal court, a corporation is a citizen of any state in which it has been incorporated and of the state where it has its principal place of business.

4.   Ignoring the Corporate Entity

Ordinarily a corporation will be regarded and treated as a separate legal person, and the law will not look behind a corporation to see who owns or controls it.

The fact that two corporations have identical shareholders does not justify a court's regarding the two corporations as one. Similarly, the fact that there is a close working relationship between two corporations does not in itself constitute any basis for ignoring their separate corporate entities when they in fact are separately run enterprises.

Shareholders are not personally liable for corporate obligations except when extreme circumstances warrant a court to pierce the corporate veil.

(a) "Piercing the Corporate Veil." A court may disregard the corporate entity, or figuratively "pierce the corporate veil," when exceptional circumstances warrant. The decision whether to disregard the corporate entity is made on a case-by-case basis, weighing all factors before the court. Factors that may lead to piercing the corporate veil and imposing liability on its owners (the shareholders) are (1) the failure to maintain adequate corporate records and the commingling of corporate and other funds, (2) grossly inadequate capitalization,[7] (3) the diversion by shareholders of corporate funds or assets, (4) the formation of the corporation to evade an existing obligation, (5) the formation of the corporation to perpetrate a fraud or conceal illegality, and (6) a determination that injustice and inequitable consequences would result if the corporate entity were recognized.[8]

---

[7] An example of grossly inadequate capitalization is found in *Klokke Corp. v Classic Exposition Inc.*, 912 P2d 929 (Or App 1996), in which Classic's two shareholders invested $1,000 of capital to start a business and immediately took out a $200,000 loan. The business remained undercapitalized until part of it was sold. However, the two shareholders effectively withdrew all of the proceeds of the sale in October 1991, and the business was again without sufficient capital, leaving it unable to meet its financial obligations. The court held that the shareholders were personally liable up to the amount withdrawn in October 1991 after the partial sale of the business.

[8] *Barton v Moore* (Minn) 558 NW2d 746 (1997).

The Case of the Rough Roofer

Facts: Russell Nugent was involved in the roofing business in Kansas City, incorporating his business as Russell Nugent Roofing, Inc. In 1985, the name was changed to On Top Roofing, Incorporated. On August 27, 1987, On Top, Inc., ceased to exist, and RNR, Inc., was incorporated. RNR, Inc., went out of business in 1988, and RLN Construction, Inc., was incorporated. In 1989, the business was organized as Russell Nugent, Inc. Nugent and his wife were the sole shareholders, officers, and directors of each corporation. When one roofing company was incorporated, the prior roofing company ceased doing business. All of the companies were located at the same business address and used the same telephone number. Nugent paid himself and his wife over $100,000 in salaries in 1986. In 1986, the corporation paid $99,290 in rent for property that was owned by the Nugents. Nugent testified that he changed to a new corporation every time he needed to get a "fresh start." The evidence showed that he used the "On Top Roofing" logo on his trucks and Yellow Pages advertisements throughout the period of the successive corporations. Suppliers who were not paid for materials in 1986 and 1987 by the insolvent corporations sought to pierce the corporate veils and hold Nugent personally liable. Nugent defended that as a shareholder he had no personal liability.

Decision: Judgment for the suppliers. Nugent was operating an intricate corporate shell game in which he would cease doing business as one corporate entity when he was unable to pay creditors. It would be unfair and unjust to allow him to hide behind the corporate shield and avoid his legal obligations to the suppliers. The corporate veil should be pierced to prevent injustice to the suppliers. Accordingly, Nugent was liable for the debts owed by the various corporations. [*K.C. Roofing Center v On Top Roofing, Inc.* (Mo App) 807 SW2d 545 (1991)]

(b) Wrongful Use by Controlling Persons. Some courts express their reasons for disregarding the corporate entity by stating that the corporation is the "alter ego" of the wrongdoer. A corporation is a separate and distinct person from the person or persons who own the corporation. However, where a corporation is so dominated and controlled by a shareholder(s), officer(s), or director(s) that the separate personalities of the individual and the corporation no longer exist and there is a wrongful use of that control, the courts will disregard the corporate entity so as not to sanction a fraud or injustice. Thus, where a controlling shareholder failed to observe corporate formalities and maintain corporate records, and personally received monetary benefits from the corporation at a time when the corporation was defaulting on its debt to a creditor, the controlling shareholder was held personally liable on this debt.[9]

Justice Prevails

Facts: Adjimi negotiated and executed a lease of premises in the name of Crayons, Inc. This corporation had no assets, income, bank accounts, or elected officers or directors and was utilized by Adjimi solely for the purpose of obtaining a lease for his business in the corporate form. The landlord, Fern, Inc., sought to pierce the veil of the corporate tenant so as to impose personal liability on Adjimi for $38,488 in unpaid rent obligations. Adjimi defended that the rent due was a corporate, not a personal, obligation.

[9] *Ferguson v Strader* (Ohio App) 641 NE2d 728 (1994).

> **Decision:** Judgment for Fern, Inc. Adjimi exercised complete dominion and control over the corporate entity, Crayons, Inc. It was a mere alter ego of Adjimi, having no assets or income or any business other than entering the lease in question. Adjimi used his control to obtain the corporate lease, and it would be an injustice to Fern, Inc., to allow Adjimi to avoid payment of the rental obligations. [*Fern, Inc. v Adjimi (App Div) 602 NYS2d 615 (1993)*]

Limited liability is important to our economy by encouraging investors to make investments in high-risk ventures. It should be disregarded only in exceptional circumstances. When fraud or deceit is absent, other circumstances for piercing the corporate veil must be so strong as to clearly indicate that the corporation is the alter ego of the controlling person.[10]

(c) Obtaining Advantages of Corporate Existence. Courts will not go behind the corporate identity merely because the corporation has been formed to obtain tax savings or to obtain limited liability for its shareholders. Similarly, the corporate entity will not be ignored merely because the corporation does not have sufficient assets to pay the claims against it.

One-person, family, and other closely held corporations are permissible and entitled to all of the advantages of corporate existence. The fact that the principal shareholder runs or oversees the day-to-day operations does not justify ignoring the corporate entity.

B.   CREATION AND TERMINATION OF THE CORPORATION

All states have general laws governing the creation of corporations.

5.   Promoters

A corporation is not liable on a contract made by its promoter unless it takes some affirmative action to adopt it.

Corporations come into existence as the result of the activities of one or more persons known as promoters. The **promoter** brings together persons interested in the enterprise, aids in obtaining subscriptions to stock, and sets in motion the machinery that leads to the formation of the corporation itself.

A corporation is not liable on a contract made by its promoter for its benefit unless the corporation takes some affirmative action to adopt such a contract. This action may be express words of adoption, or it may be acceptance of the contract's benefits. A corporation may also become bound by such contracts through assignment or novation.

The promoter is personally liable for all contracts made on behalf of the corporation before its existence unless the promoter is exempted by the terms of the agreement or by the circumstances surrounding it.

[10] *Lopez v TDI Services Inc.* (La App) 631 So 2d 670 (1994).

The Promoter is Personally Liable

Facts: Clinton Investors Co., as landlord, entered into a three-year lease with the Clifton Park Learning Center as tenant. The lease was executed by Bernie Watkins, who represented himself to be the treasurer of the Learning Center. On May 31, 1984, the day before the lease term began, Watkins signed a rider to the lease. He again signed as treasurer of the tenant but identified the tenant as "the Clifton Park Learning Center, Inc." Watkins had not consulted an attorney regarding the formation of the corporation. He mistook the reservation of the business name with the secretary of state for the filing of a certificate of incorporation. On February 11, 1985, a certificate of incorporation was filed. By March 1986, the Learning Center had become delinquent in rental payments and other fees in the amount of $18,103. Clinton sued Watkins and the Learning Center for the amounts due. Watkins claimed that only the corporation was liable.

Decision: Judgment against Watkins. Because no corporation existed when Watkins signed the lease with Clinton, his legal status was that of a promoter. The subsequent formation of a corporation and adoption of the lease did not relieve Watkins from liability on the lease. Rather, it gave rise to corporate liability in addition to his individual liability as a promoter. [Clinton Investors Co. v Watkins, 146 App Div 2d 861, 536 NYS2d 270 (1989)]

A promoter is liable for all torts committed in connection with the promoter's activities. The corporation is not ordinarily liable for the torts of the promoter, but it may become liable by its conduct after incorporation. If a promoter induces the making of a contract by fraud, the corporation is liable for the fraud if it assumes or ratifies the contract with knowledge or notice of such fraud.

A promoter stands in a fiduciary relation to the corporation and to stock subscribers and cannot make secret profits at their expense. Accordingly, if a promoter makes a secret profit on a sale of land to the corporation, the promoter must surrender the profit to the corporation.

The corporation is not liable in most states for the expenses and services of the promoter unless it subsequently promises to pay for them or the corporation's charter or a statute imposes such liability on it.

6.   Incorporation

One or more natural persons or corporations may act as **incorporators** of a corporation by signing and filing appropriate forms with a designated government official.[11] These papers are filed in duplicate, and a filing fee must be paid. The designated official (usually the secretary of state), after being satisfied that the forms conform to statutory requirements, stamps "Filed" and the date on each copy. The official then retains one copy and returns the other copy, along with a filing fee receipt, to the corporation.[12]

Statutes may require incorporators to give some form of public notice, such as by advertising in a newspaper, of their intention to form a corporation, stating its name, address, and general purpose.

---

[11] RMBCA § 2.01.
[12] RMBCA § 1.25.

7. Application for Incorporation

In most states, the process of forming a corporation is begun by filing an application for a certificate of incorporation. This application will contain or be accompanied by articles of incorporation. The instrument is filed with the secretary of state and sets forth certain information about the new corporation. The articles of incorporation must contain (1) the name of the corporation, (2) the number of shares of stock the corporation is authorized to issue, (3) the street address of the corporation's initial registered office and the name of its initial registered agent, and (4) the name and address of each incorporator.[13] The articles of incorporation may also state the purpose or purposes for which the corporation is organized. If there is no "purpose clause," the corporation will automatically have the purpose of engaging in any lawful business.[14] Also, if no reference is made to the duration of the corporation in the articles of incorporation, it will automatically have perpetual duration.[15]

8. The Certificate of Incorporation

Most state incorporation statutes now provide for a certificate of incorporation to be issued by the secretary of state after articles of incorporation that conform to state requirements have been filed. The Revised Model Business Corporation Act (RMBCA) has eliminated the certificate of incorporation in an effort to reduce the volume of paperwork handled by the secretary of state.

Under the RMBCA, corporate existence begins when the articles are filed with the secretary of state.[16] In some states, corporate existence begins when the proper government official issues a certificate of incorporation. In other states, it does not begin until an organizational meeting is held by the new corporation.

9. Proper and Defective Incorporation

If the procedure for incorporation has been followed, the corporation has a legal right to exist. It is then called a **corporation de jure,** meaning that it is a corporation by virtue of law.

Assume that there is some defect in the corporation that is formed. If the defect is not a material one, the law will usually overlook the defect and hold that the corporation is a corporation de jure.

The RMBCA abolishes objections to irregularities and defects in incorporating. It provides that the "secretary of state's filing of the articles of incorporation is conclusive proof that the incorporators satisfied all conditions precedent to incorporation. . . ."[17] Many state statutes follow this pattern. Such an approach is based on the practical consideration that when countless persons are purchasing shares of stock and entering into business transactions with thousands of corporations, it becomes an absurdity to expect that anyone is going to make the detailed search that would be required to determine whether a given corporation is a corporation de jure.[18]

---

13 RMBCA § 2.02.
14 RMBCA § 3.01.
15 RMBCA § 3.02.
16 RMBCA § 2.03(a).
17 RMBCA § 2.03(b).
18 This trend and the reasons for it may be compared to those involved in the concept of the negotiability of commercial paper. Note the similar protection from defenses given to the person purchasing shares of stock for value and without notice. UCC § 8-202.

(a) De Facto Corporation.
The defect in the incorporation may be so substantial that it cannot be ignored and the corporation will not be accepted as a corporation de jure. Yet compliance may be sufficient for recognizing there is a corporation. When this occurs, the association is called a **de facto corporation.**

Although conflict exists among authorities, the traditional elements of a de facto corporation are that (1) a valid law exists under which the corporation could have been properly incorporated, (2) an attempt to organize the corporation has been made in good faith, (3) a genuine attempt to organize in compliance with statutory requirements has been made, and (4) corporate powers have been used.

(b) Corporation by Estoppel.
The defect in incorporation may be so great that by law the association cannot be accepted as a de facto corporation. In such a case then, there is no corporation. If the individuals involved proceed to run the business in spite of such irregularity, they may be held personally liable as partners for the business's debts.[19] This rule is sometimes not applied when a third person has dealt with the business as though it were a corporation.[20] In such instances, the third person is estopped from denying that the "corporation" had legal existence. In effect, there is **corporation by estoppel** with respect to that person.

Several jurisdictions that follow the 1969 MBCA have expressly retained the doctrine of corporation by estoppel and de facto corporations.[21] Numerous courts interpreting the language of the 1969 MBCA, however, have held that the doctrines of de facto corporation and corporation by estoppel no longer exist.

CASE SUMMARY

No Estoppel Here

Facts: Wayne and Diane Morse built a car wash in 1984 and operated it for approximately 11 months. Thereafter they entered into a contract with Douglas Durbano and Kevin Garn, both licensed attorneys acting as officers of American Vending Services, Inc. (AVSI), to purchase the car wash for $65,000—$20,000 down and the remainder to be paid off monthly. Durbano and Garn claimed that they represented to the Morses that the corporate entity would purchase and operate the car wash. At the time the parties executed the contract on July 10, 1985, Durbano had not filed articles of incorporation for AVSI, although he had received permission from the Utah Division of Corporations to use the name American Vending Services, Inc. Durbano claimed a delay in filing the articles occurred because of a name conflict. The articles of incorporation for AVSI were finally executed on August 1, 1985, and subsequently filed on August 19, 1985. Durbano's explanation for not filing them before the parties executed the contract on July 10, 1985, was that he was "moving offices and was too busy and distracted to file the articles." AVSI operated the car wash for three years but never made any monthly payments to the Morses because of financial difficulties. The Morses sued AVSI as well as Durbano and Garn because the corporation did not legally exist when the parties executed the contract. The trial court dismissed the Morses' claims against Durbano and Garn, finding that Durbano's efforts to file articles of incorporation "constitute[d] a bona fide attempt to organize the corporation." A judgment was issued against AVSI for $76,832, but AVSI had no assets or income to satisfy the judgment. The court's decision was appealed by both parties.

---

[19] In a minority of states, a court will not hold individuals liable as partners but will hold liable the person who committed the act on behalf of the business on the theory that that person was an agent who acted without authority and is therefore liable for breach of the implied warranties of the existence of a principal possessing capacity and of proper authorization.

[20] *Am South Bank v Holland* (Ala Civ App) 669 So 2d 151 (1994).

[21] See Ga Bus Corp Code § 22-5103; Minn Bus Corp Act § 301:08. See also *H. Rich Corp. v Feinberg* (Fla App) 518 So 2d 377 (1987).

Decision: Judgment for the Morses. Section 146 of the MBCA imposes joint and several liability on Durbano and Garn for all of the debts and liabilities that arose as a result of their actions before the corporation legally existed. The corporation did not exist when Durbano and Garn executed the contract to purchase the Morses' car wash of July 10. Their argument that the Morses dealt with a corporation, AVSI, and did not intend to bind them personally, and are therefore estopped to deny AVSI's corporate existence is rejected, as the doctrine of corporation by estoppel does not exist in the state. Durbano and Garn are liable for the judgment amount of $76, 832. *[American Vending Services, Inc. v Morse (Utah) 881 P2d 967 (1994)]*

With respect to preincorporation debts, the 1984 act imposes liability only on persons who act as, or on behalf of, a corporation while knowing that no corporation exists.[22]

10. Insolvency, Bankruptcy, and Reorganization

When a corporation has financial troubles so serious that it is insolvent, the best thing may be to go through bankruptcy or reorganization proceedings. The law with respect to bankruptcy and reorganizations is discussed in chapter 37.

11. Forfeiture of Charter

Remember that owners and officers of a dissolved corporation are no longer shielded from personal liability even though they continue to use the corporate name when making contracts.

In states that have adopted the RMBCA, the secretary of state may commence proceedings to administratively dissolve a corporation if (1) the corporation does not pay franchise taxes within 60 days after they are due, (2) the corporation does not file its annual report within 60 days after it is due, or (3) the corporation is without a registered agent or registered office for 60 days or more.[23] In other states, judicial proceedings may be brought to forfeit a corporate charter when the corporation repeatedly acts beyond the powers granted it or engages in illegal activity. After a corporate charter has been forfeited, the owners and officers of the dissolved corporation are not shielded from personal liability by using the corporate name when making contracts.   *For example*, Todd Crosland was president, director, and principal shareholder of Crosland Industries. Even though Crosland's corporate status was suspended and subsequently discontinued, Todd authorized a guarantee on a note in the name of the corporation. A default occurred and Crosland failed to honor its guarantee. Todd was personally liable on the guarantee.[24]

12. Judicial Dissolution

Judicial dissolution of a corporation may be decreed when its management is deadlocked and the deadlock cannot be broken by the shareholders. In some states, a "custodian" may be appointed for a corporation when the shareholders are unable to break a deadlock in the board of directors and irreparable harm is threatened to or sustained by the corporation because of the deadlock.

---

[22] RMBCA § 2.04.
[23] RMBCA § 14.20.
[24] *Murphy v Crosland* (Utah) 915 P2d 491 (1996).

Corporate Gridlock

Facts: Graham and Black were each 50 percent shareholders of a building supply business. When Graham filed a petition to dissolve the corporation under RMBCA § 14.30, the court appointed a custodian with full powers to run the corporation's day-to-day operations. Subsequently the court concluded that Black and Graham functioned as directors, they were deadlocked within the meaning of RMBCA § 14.30(2)(l), and adequate grounds existed to dissolve the corporation because of the lack of cooperation between Black and Graham and its probable irreparable harm to the business. The court entered an order directing that within one week of receiving an expected appraisal, each would submit a sealed bid in writing for the other's stock. The custodian was to accept the high bid, and the purchaser was to immediately tender the purchase price. In the event neither stockholder made a bona fide offer, the custodian would be redesignated the receiver and proceed to dissolve the corporation (RMBCA § 14.32(c)–(e)). The sale was unsuccessful, and by subsequent order, the court converted the custodianship into a receivership, directing that the receiver wind up and liquidate the business affairs of the corporation. Black did not believe that the successful business should be liquidated, and he appealed.

Decision: Judgment against Black. A deadlock existed between Black and Graham as sole and equal shareholders, who were wholly unable to agree on the management of the business. Neither had the authority to prevail in his view, and irreparable injury was threatened with the sale being unsuccessful. Dissolution was thus warranted. [Black v Graham (Ga) 464 SE2d 814 (1996)]

C.   CORPORATE POWERS

All corporations do not have the same powers. Those that operate banks, insurance companies, and railroads, for example, generally have special powers and are subject to special restrictions.

Except for limitations in the federal Constitution or the state's own constitution, a state legislature may give corporations any lawful powers. The RMBCA contains a general provision on corporate powers granting a corporation "the same powers as an individual to do all things necessary or convenient to carry out its business and affairs."[25]

13. Particular Powers

Modern corporation codes give corporations a wide range of powers.

(a) Perpetual Life. One of the distinctive features of a corporation is its perpetual or continuous life—the power to continue as an entity forever or for a stated period of time regardless of changes in stock ownership or the death of any shareholders.

(b) Corporate Name. A corporation must have a name to identify it. As a general rule, it may select any name for this purpose. Most states require that the corporate name contain some word indicating the corporate character[26] and that the name

---

[25] RMBCA § 3.02. State statutes generally contain similar broad catchall grants of powers.
[26] RMBCA § 4.01(a) declares that the corporate name must contain the word *corporation, company, incorporated,* or *limited* or an abbreviation of one of these words.

not be the same as or deceptively similar to the name of any other corporation. Some statutes prohibit the use of a name that is likely to mislead the public.

(c) Corporate Seal. A corporation may have a distinctive seal. However, a corporation need not use a seal in the transaction of business unless this is required by statute or a natural person in transacting that business would be required to use a seal.

(d) Bylaws. Bylaws are the rules and regulations enacted by a corporation to govern the affairs of the corporation and its shareholders, directors, and officers.

Bylaws are adopted by shareholders, although in some states they may be adopted by the directors of the corporation. Approval by the state or an amendment of the corporate charter is not required to make the bylaws effective.

The bylaws are subordinate to the general law of the state, the statute under which the corporation is formed, and the charter of the corporation.[27] Bylaws that conflict with such superior authority or that are in themselves unreasonable are invalid. Bylaws that are valid are binding on all shareholders regardless of whether they know of the existence of those bylaws or were among the majority that consented to their adoption. Bylaws are not binding on third persons, however, unless they have notice or knowledge of them.

(e) Stock. A corporation may issue certificates representing corporate stock. Under the RMBCA, authorized, but unissued, shares may be issued at the price set by the board of directors. Under UCC Article 8 (1978 and 1994 versions), securities may be "uncertificated," or not represented by an instrument.

(f) Making Contracts. Corporation codes give corporations the power to make contracts.

(g) Borrowing Money. Corporations have the implied power to borrow money in carrying out their authorized business purposes.

(h) Executing Negotiable Instruments. Corporations have the power to issue or indorse negotiable instruments and to accept drafts.

(i) Issuing Bonds. A corporation may exercise its power to borrow money by issuing bonds.

(j) Transferring Property. The corporate property may be leased, assigned for the benefit of creditors, or sold. In many states, however, a solvent corporation may not transfer all of its property without the consent of all or a substantial majority of its shareholders.

A corporation, having power to incur debts, may mortgage or pledge its property as security for those debts. This rule does not apply to public service companies, such as street transit systems and gas and electric companies.

(k) Acquiring Property. A corporation has the power to acquire and hold such property as is reasonably necessary for carrying out its express powers.

---

[27] *Roach v Bynum* (Ala) 403 So 2d 187 (1981).

Yes, Corporations Can Acquire Property

Facts: The state of Oklahoma sued the International Paper Company for the statutory penalty for unlawfully owning rural land. This was in violation of the state constitutional provision that no corporation should own rural land "except such as shall be necessary and proper for carrying on the business for which it was chartered." The paper company claimed that it was reforesting the rural land it owned. It was shown that the reforested area would not develop a timber crop for 40 to 70 years.

Decision: Judgment for International Paper Company. The concept of "necessary and proper" does not mean absolutely necessary, and it is satisfied if the conduct in question is proper, useful, and conducive to the accomplishment of the corporation's objectives. The acquisition of the rural land that the paper company was reforesting was a reasonable step to ensure a continuous supply of wood pulp necessary for making paper. In view of the scarcity of wood and the time required to grow a timber crop, the acquisition of the timberland by the corporation was reasonable and so was not prohibited by the Oklahoma Constitution. *[Oklahoma v International Paper Co. (Okla) 342 P2d 565 (1959)]*

(l) Buying Back Stock. Generally, a corporation may purchase its own stock if it is solvent at the time and the purchase does not impair capital. Stock that is reacquired by the corporation that issued it is commonly called **treasury stock.**

Although treasury stock retains the character of outstanding stock, it has an inactive status while it is held by the corporation.[28] Thus, the treasury shares cannot be voted, nor can dividends be declared on them.

(m) Doing Business in Another State. A corporation has the power to engage in business in other states. However, this does not exempt the corporation from satisfying valid restrictions imposed by the foreign state in which it seeks to do business.

(n) Participating in an Enterprise. Corporations may generally participate in an enterprise to the same extent as individuals. Not only may they enter into joint ventures, but also the modern statutory trend is to permit a corporation to be a member of a partnership, and a corporation may be a limited partner. The RMBCA authorizes a corporation "to be a promoter, partner, member, associate, or manager of any partnership, joint venture, trust, or other entity."[29]

(o) Paying Employee Benefits. The RMBCA empowers a corporation "to pay pensions and establish pension plans, pension trusts, profit-sharing plans, share bonus plans, share option plans, and benefit or incentive plans for any or all of its current or former directors, officers, employees, and agents."[30]

(p) Charitable Contributions. The RMBCA authorizes a corporation, without any limitation, "to make donations for the public welfare or for charitable, scientific, or educational purposes."[31] In some states, a limitation is imposed on the amount that can be donated for charitable purposes.

---

[28] When a corporation reacquires its own shares, it has the choice of retiring them and thus restoring them to the status of authorized, but unissued, shares or of treating them as still issued and available for transfer. It is the latter that are described as treasury shares.
[29] RMBCA § 3.02(9).
[30] RMBCA § 3.02(12).
[31] RMBCA § 3.02(13).

14. *Ultra Vires* Acts

When a corporation acts in excess of or beyond the scope of its powers, the corporation's act is described as *ultra vires*. Such an action is improper in the same way that it is improper for an agent to act beyond the scope of the authority given by the principal. It is also improper with respect to shareholders and creditors of the corporation because corporate funds have been diverted to unauthorized uses.

> Modern business corporations have such broad powers that it is most unusual for a corporation to act beyond its powers or *ultra vires*.

The modern corporation statute will state that every corporation formed under it will have certain powers unless the articles of incorporation expressly exclude some of the listed powers, and then the statute will list every possible power that is needed to run a business. In some states, the legislature makes a blanket grant of all the power that a natural person running the business would possess.[32] The net result is that the modern corporation possesses such a broad scope of powers that it is difficult to find an action that is *ultra vires*. If a mining corporation should begin to manufacture television sets, that might be an *ultra vires* transaction, but such an extreme departure rarely happens.

Because nonprofit corporations have a more restricted range of powers than business corporations, actions not authorized by the charters of nonprofit corporations are more likely to be found *ultra vires*.[33]

D.   CONSOLIDATIONS, MERGERS, AND CONGLOMERATES

Two or more corporations may be combined to form a new structure or enterprise.

15. Definitions

Enterprises may be combined by a consolidation or merger of corporations or by the formation of a conglomerate.

(a) Consolidation. In a **consolidation** of two or more corporations, their separate existences cease, and a new corporation with the property and assets of the old corporations comes into being.

FIGURE 46-1
Consolidation

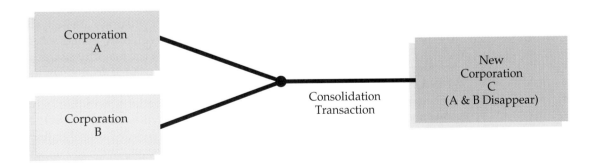

---

32 Note the broad powers granted under RMBCA § 3.02; see also Cal Corp Code §§ 202(b), 207, 208 for an all-purpose clause granting all of the powers of a natural person in carrying out business activities.
33 *Lovering v Seabrook Island Property Owners Association*, 289 SC App 77, 344 SE2d 862 (1986). But see *St. Louis v Institute of Med. Ed. & Res.* (Mo App) 786 SW2d 885 (1990).

When a consolidation occurs, the new corporation ordinarily succeeds to the rights, powers, and immunities of its component parts. However, limitations may be imposed by constitution, statute, or certificate of incorporation.

(b) Merger. When two corporations merge, one absorbs the other. One corporation retains its original charter and identity and continues to exist; the other disappears, and its corporate existence terminates.

(1) Objection of Shareholder. A stockholder who objects to a proposed consolidation or merger or who fails to convert existing shares into stock of the new or continuing corporation may apply to a court to appraise the value of the stock he or she holds. Should either party act arbitrarily, vexatiously, or not in good faith in the appraisal process, the courts have the right to assess court costs and attorney fees.[34] The new or continuing corporation is then required to pay the value of the stock to the stockholder, and the stockholder is required to transfer the stock to the new or continuing corporation.

CASE SUMMARY

"Fair Value," Not Book Value

Facts: In order to avoid being taken over by another bank, Security Bank initiated a reverse stock split, which had the planned effect of squeezing out minority shareholders. The bank paid Ziegeldorf and Allen, two shareholders who dissented from the reverse stock split, the book value of their shares. State law required that dissenters be paid "not less than the fair value of their shares," and they sued Security. Security contested that the book value was fair value because there was no market value for shares of a closely held bank stock.

Decision: Judgment for Ziegeldorf and Allen. The court properly determined the value of the dissenting shareholders' shares by giving weight to the adjusted earnings values and net present values of future income computed by three experts. This resulted in an increase of $764.40 per share over the book value paid by the bank. Because the bank decided to offer book value without consideration of any other factor that might reflect the true value of the bank, the bank was required to pay the dissenting shareholders' attorney fees and expert witness fees. [*Security Bank v Ziegeldorf* (Iowa) 554 NW2d 884 (1996)]

(2) Origin of Plan. In some cases, the plan to merge or consolidate will originate within the corporations involved. In other cases, it will originate with an outside investor. In that situation, the transaction is frequently called a *two-step* merger. First, an outside investor purchases control of the majority shares of the target corporation. Then this newly acquired control is used to arrange for the target and a second corporation controlled by the outside investor to merge.

Statutes commonly regulate mergers and consolidations by requiring disclosure of the details a stated number of days before any action can be taken. The purpose of these statutes is not to prohibit or restrain mergers and consolidations but only to make certain that all stockholders are fully informed about the nature and effect of the proposed action.

---

[34] RMBCA § 3.31; see *Santa's Workshop v A.B. Hirschfeld Press Inc.* (Colo App) 851 P2d 264 (1993).

(c) Conglomerate. Conglomerate describes the relationship of a parent corporation to subsidiary corporations engaged in diversified fields of activity unrelated to the field of activity of the parent corporation. For example, a wire manufacturing corporation that owns all the stock of a newspaper corporation and of a drug manufacturing corporation would be described as a conglomerate. In contrast, if the wire manufacturing company owned a mill that produced the metal used in making the wire and a mine that produced the ore that was used by the mill, the relationship would probably be described as an *integrated industry* rather than as a conglomerate. This term is merely a matter of usage rather than of legal definition. Likewise, when the parent company is not engaged in production or the rendering of services, it is customary to call it a *holding company.*

Without regard to whether the enterprise is a holding company or whether the group of corporations constitutes a conglomerate or an integrated industry, each part is a distinct corporation to which ordinary corporation law applies. In some instances, additional principles apply because of the nature of the relationships existing among the several corporations involved.

16. Legality

Consolidations, mergers, and asset acquisitions between enterprises are prohibited by federal antitrust legislation when the effect is to lessen competition in interstate commerce. A business corporation may not merge with a charitable corporation because this combination would divert the assets of the respective corporations to purposes not intended by their shareholders.

ETHICS & THE LAW

Celestial Seasonings Tea Company was founded in the late 1960s by Mo Siegel. Mr. Siegel gathered herbs from around Aspen and put together a line of herbal teas that were sold only in health food stores initially. The teas grew in popularity, and by 1982, Celestial enjoyed a dominant position in the international market. Celestial was known for its free-wheeling approach in managing employees, and Mr. Siegel was famous for developing new ideas and products while lunching with employees, who were given free hot lunches as part of their jobs.

In 1984, Kraft Foods approached Mr. Siegel about purchasing the privately held Celestial for $40 million. Mr. Siegel accepted the offer and retired as president of Celestial. The new Kraft management team ended the Rocky Mountain casual approach to corporate management and terminated birthday bonuses, required drug testing of all employees, and assigned parking spaces. Barney Feinblum, Siegel's vice president of finance and president of Celestial under Kraft, was unhappy with the changes Kraft implemented and the "big-time corporate structure" Kraft demanded. The disagreements in philosophies resulted in new products that flopped and problems with sales and marketing of the original herbal teas.

Feinblum made an offer to Kraft to buy back Celestial. Kraft refused, and Thomas J. Lipton made an offer to purchase the company. A competitor stopped the combination of the Lipton tea giant with the giant of herbal teas. Feinblum made another offer to Kraft, and Kraft accepted Feinblum's $60 million offer. Siegel returned as president, and the company was forced to "go public" with two stock offerings in 1993 and 1994 totaling $38 million in order to pay back the debt to Kraft. Today, Celestial holds about 54 percent of the herbal tea market but has had trouble breaking into the bottled iced tea market, the industry's growth area.

Trace the history of Celestial's ownership. Explain the takeovers and relationships among Kraft, Lipton, and Celestial. What are the ethical issues in taking over a company like Celestial? What are the management problems in taking over a company like Celestial?

17. Liability of Successor Corporations

When corporations are combined in any way, the question arises of who is liable for the debts and obligations of the predecessor corporations.

(a) Mergers and Consolidations. Generally, the enterprise engaging in or continuing the business after a merger or consolidation succeeds to all of the rights and property of the predecessor, or disappearing, corporation. The enterprise continuing the business is also subject to all of the debts and liabilities of the predecessor corporation.[35] Thus, a successor corporation is liable for the contracts of a predecessor corporation. When the successor corporation is sued on such an inherited liability, it cannot raise the defense that the plaintiff did not have a contract with it.

Because asset sales do not obligate the purchaser to pay the debts of the predecessor businesss, some firms try to cast a transaction as an asset sale while actually structuring a merger. The courts may be expected to look through the form and see the substance of the transaction.

(b) Asset Sales. In contrast with a merger or consolidation, a corporation may merely purchase the assets of another business. In that case, the purchaser does not become liable for the obligations of the predecessor business.

Corporations may seek to avoid liability for the obligations of a predecessor corporation by attempting to disguise a consolidation or merger as being merely a sale of assets. Courts will not recognize such a sham and will impose a successor's liability on the successor corporation.

FIGURE 46-2
Merger

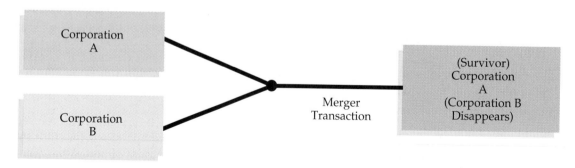

---

[35] *Eagle Pacific Insurance Co. v Christensen Motor Yacht Co. Inc.* (Wash App) 934 P2d 715 (1997).

CASE SUMMARY

Corporate Shell Games Not Allowed

Facts: Since 1976, McGhan/Cal. Inc., a manufacturer of prostheses used in breast augmentation surgery, and later McGhan/Del., received numerous complaints about their implants. They also received inquiries from the Food and Drug Administration. In April 1977, Mary Marks had surgery; two McGhan implants were used. Because of defects in the McGhan implants, Marks underwent three additional operations, eventually having the McGhan products replaced with implants manufactured by another company. In June 1977, McGhan/Cal. was acquired by a Delaware subsidiary of 3M, called McGhan/Del. Inc. McGhan/Del. removed the implants from the market in April 1979. On January 1, 1981, 3M's wholly owned subsidiary McGhan/Del. Inc. was reorganized as a division of 3M and dissolved. In January 1982, following her fourth surgery, Marks brought a product liability suit against 3M. 3M contended that it was not liable for the actions of the predecessor corporation.

Decision: The transaction between the 3M subsidiary McGhan/Del. Inc. and McGhan/Cal. Inc. amounted to a de facto merger of the seller and the purchaser. McGhan/Cal. changed its name, distributed 3M stock to its shareholders, and dissolved, and all key employees signed employment contracts to work for the purchaser. No cash was paid for the business. The transaction was not an assets sale. The second reorganization amounted to a continuation of the de facto merger. Public policy requires that 3M, having accepted the benefits of a going concern, should also assume the costs that all other going concerns must bear. It should not be allowed to avoid liability to an injured person by merely shuffling paper and manipulating corporate entities. [*Marks v Minnesota Mining and Manufacturing Co.*, 187 Cal App 3d 1429, 232 Cal Rptr 594 (1986)]

SUMMARY

A corporation is an artificial person created by government action. It exists as a separate and distinct entity possessing certain powers. In most states, the corporation comes into existence when the secretary of state issues a certificate of incorporation. The most common forms of corporations are private business corporations whose stock is sold to the public (publicly held) and close corporations, which are business firms whose shares are not traded publicly. Corporations may be formed for purposes other than conducting a business. For example, there are nonprofit corporations, municipal corporations, and public authorities for governmental purposes.

Ordinarily each corporation will be treated as a separate person, and the law will not look beyond the corporate identity merely because the corporation had been formed to obtain tax savings or limited liability. The fact that two corporations have the same shareholders does not justify disregarding the separate corporate entities. However, when a corporation is formed to perpetrate a fraud, a court will ignore the corporate form, or "pierce the corporate veil." The corporate form will also be ignored to prevent injustice or because of the functional reality that the two corporations in question are one.

A promoter is a person who brings together the persons interested in the enterprise and sets in motion all that must be done to form a corporation. A corporation is not liable on contracts made by its promoter for the corporation unless it adopts the contracts. The promoter is personally liable for contracts made for the corporation before its existence. A promoter stands in a fiduciary relation to the corporation and stockholders.

The procedures for incorporation are set forth in the statutes of each state. In most states, the corporation comes into existence upon issuance of the certificate of incorporation. When all requirements have been satisfied, the corporation is a corporation de jure. When there has not been full compliance with all requirements for incorporation, a de facto corporation may be found to exist. Or when sufficient compliance for a de facto corporation does not exist, in some jurisdictions a third person may be estopped from denying the legal existence of the "corporation" with which it did business (corporation by estoppel).

A corporation has the power to continue as an entity forever or for a stated period of time regardless of changes in the ownership of the stock or the death of a shareholder.

It may make contracts, issue stocks and bonds, borrow money, execute commercial paper, transfer and acquire property, acquire its own stock if it is solvent and the purchase does not impair capital, and make charitable contributions. Subject to limitations, a corporation has the power to do business in other states. A corporation also may participate in a business enterprise to the same extent as an individual. That is, it may be a partner in a partnership, or it may enter a joint venture or other enterprise. Special service corporations, such as banks, insurance companies, and railroads, are subject to separate statutes with regard to their organization and powers.

An *ultra vires* act occurs when a corporation acts beyond the scope of the powers given it. Because states now grant broad powers to corporations, it is unlikely that a modern corporation would act beyond the scope of its powers.

Two or more corporations may be combined to form a new enterprise. This combination may be a consolidation, with a new corporation coming into existence, or a merger, in which one corporation absorbs the other.

QUESTIONS AND CASE PROBLEMS

1. What social forces are affected by the recognition of a corporation as a distinct legal entity?
2. Edwin Edwards and Karen Davis owned EEE, Inc., which owned three convenience stores, all of which sold gasoline. Reid Ellis delivered to the three convenience stores $26,675.02 worth of gasoline for which he was not paid. Ellis proved that Edwards and Davis owned the business, ran it, and in fact personally ordered the gasoline. He claimed that they were personally liable for the debt owed him by EEE, Inc. Decide. [*Ellis v Edwards*, 180 Ga App 301, 348 SE2d 764]
3. What are common grounds for forfeiture of a corporate charter?
4. Compare and contrast consolidations, mergers, and conglomerates.
5. On January 27, 1982, Joe Walker purchased a wheelloader machine from the Thompson & Green Machinery Co. (T&G). Walker signed a promissory note for $37,886.30 on behalf of "Music City Sawmill, Inc. by Joe Walker, President." When Sawmill was unable to make payments on the loader, the machine was returned to T&G. T&G brought suit against Sawmill and subsequently discovered that Sawmill had not been incorporated on January 27, 1982, when the machine was purchased, but had been incorporated the next day. T&G then sued Walker individually. The lawsuit was Walker's first notice that Sawmill was not incorporated on the date of the sale. Walker's defense was that T&G dealt with Sawmill as a corporation and did not intend to bind him personally on the note, and therefore was estopped to deny Sawmill's corporate existence. Decide based on the 1969 MBCA. What would be the result if the RMBCA applied? [*Thompson & Green Machinery Co. v Music City Lumber Co.* (Tenn App) 683 SW2d 340]
6. North Pole Inc. approved a plan to merge with its subsidiary, Santa's Workshop Inc. The merger plan provided that certain of Workshop's shareholders would receive $3.50 per share. The highest independent appraisal of the stock was $4.04 per share. Hirschfeld Inc., a shareholder, claimed the fair value was $16.80 per share. Workshop offered to make its corporate books and records available to Hirschfeld in order to assess the validity of the $16.80 demand. This offer was declined. Hirschfeld did not attempt to base the $16.80 demand on any recognizable method of stock valuation. Hirschfeld contended it had a right to get the asking price. Refer to RMBCA §§ 13.02, 13.28, and 13.31. Could Hirschfeld have blocked the merger until Workshop paid the $16.80? Decide. [*Santa's Workshop v Hirschfeld Inc.* (Colo App) 851 P2d 264]
7. Norman was organizing a new corporation: the Collins Home Construction Co. Fairchild knew the corporation was not yet formed but made a contract by which he agreed to sell certain goods to Collins. The corporation was later organized and ratified the contract that Norman had made with Fairchild. Fairchild, however, did not perform the contract and was sued by Collins. Fairchild raised the defense that he had never made any contract with Collins and that a corporation that did not exist could not have made a contract. Were these defenses valid?
8. In 1977, Morris Gray leased waterfront property on the Ross Barnett Reservoir to a restaurant, Edgewater Landing Inc., for a 10-year term. After a year and a half, Edgewater's original shareholder, Billy Stegall, sold all of his shares in the corporation to Tom Bradley. As of 1986, Tom Bradley and Bradley's bookkeeper, Sandra Martin, owned all the shares in the restaurant. Sandra's husband, Randy, acted as its manager. Gray visited the property in September 1986 and found many problems with the condition of the property. He claimed that the lease required the tenant to make necessary repairs. Gray sued Edgewater Landing Inc. and Tom Bradley and Sandra Martin

individually for breach of the lease. Bradley and Martin replied that they were not liable for the debt of the corporation. Decide. [*Gray v Edgewater Landing Inc.* (Miss) 541 So 2d 1044]

9. Emmick was a director and shareholder of Colonial Manors, Inc. (CM). He organized another corporation named Oahe Enterprises, Inc. To obtain shares of the Oahe stock, Emmick transferred CM shares arbitrarily valued by him at $19 per share to Oahe. The CM shares had a book value of $.47 per share, but Emmick believed that the stock would increase to a value of $19. The directors of Oahe approved Emmick's payment with the valuation of $19 per share. Golden sued Emmick on the ground that he had fraudulently deceived Oahe Corp. about the value of the CM shares and thus had made a secret profit when he received the Oahe shares that had a much greater value than the CM shares he gave in exchange. Emmick contended that his firm opinion was that the future potential value of CM shares would surely reach $19 per share. Decide. [*Golden v Oahe Enterprises, Inc.* (SD) 295 NW2d 160]

10. Branmar Theatre Co., a family corporation, leased a theater from Branmar, Inc. The lease prohibited it from assigning the lease. The holders of the stock of Branmar Theatre Co. sold their stock to the Schwartzes. The lessor, Branmar, Inc., claimed that this sale of stock was a prohibited assignment and threatened to cancel the lease. Branmar Theatre Co. subsequently brought an action for a declaratory judgment to enjoin the cancellation of the lease. Should the court have enjoined the cancellation of the lease? [*Branmar Theatre Co. v Branmar, Inc.* (Del Ch) 264 A2d 526]

11. In May 1985, Ed Klein was the sole shareholder, director, and chief executive officer of The Gun Exchange, Inc., a retail firearms dealership. The inventory of The Gun Exchange had been pledged as security for a $622,500 debt owed to InterFirst Bank. It also owed $231,484.60 to Sporting Goods, Inc.; this debt was unsecured. On May 20, 1985, InterFirst Bank notified Klein of its intention to foreclose on the inventory and sell it at public auction. InterFirst Bank further advised Klein that, pursuant to his personal guarantee, he would be responsible for any deficiency following the sale. Klein immediately incorporated The Gun Store Inc. for the purpose of purchasing the assets of The Gun Exchange at the foreclosure sale. Before the foreclosure sale, Klein obtained a $650,000 line of credit from CharterBank on behalf of The Gun Store. At the sale, Klein purchased the assets of The Gun Exchange for $650,000 even though the highest prior bid was $175,000. (Had the $175,000 bid been accepted, Klein would have been personally liable for the deficiency to InterFirst Bank.) After the foreclosure sale, no funds existed to pay the unsecured creditors of The Gun Exchange. Following the sale, The Gun Store began operating as a retail firearms dealer with the inventory purchased from the foreclosure sale. It operated in the same location and with the same personnel as The Gun Exchange. Sporting Goods, Inc., sued Klein individually for the $231,484.60. Klein contended that the corporate form under which he did business insulated him as a shareholder from liability for corporate obligations. Decide. Is it ethical to seek limited liability under the corporate form, as was done by Klein in this case? [*Klein v Sporting Goods, Inc.* (Tex Civ App) 772 SW2d 173]

12. The Seabrook Island Property Owners Association, Inc., is a nonprofit corporation organized under state law to maintain streets and open spaces owned by property owners of Seabrook Island. Seabrook Island Co. is the developer of Seabrook Island and has majority control of the board of directors of the association. The association's bylaws empower the board of directors to levy an annual maintenance charge. Neither the association's charter nor its bylaws authorize the board to assess any other charges. When the board levied, in addition to the annual maintenance charge, an emergency budget assessment on all members to rebuild certain bridges and to revitalize the beach, the Loverings and other property owners challenged in court the association's power to impose the assessment. Decide. [*Lovering v Seabrook Island Property Owners Ass'n*, 289 SC App 77, 344 SE2d 862]

13. Adams and two other persons were promoters for a new corporation, Aldrehn Theaters Co. The promoters retained Kridelbaugh to perform legal services in connection with the incorporation of the new business and promised to pay him $1,500. Aldrehn was incorporated through Kridelbaugh's services, and the promoters became its only directors. Kridelbaugh attended a meeting of the board of directors at which he was told that he should obtain a permit for the corporation to sell stock because the directors wished to pay him for his previous services. The promoters failed to pay Kridelbaugh, and he sued the corporation. Was the corporation liable? [*Kridelbaugh v Aldrehn Theaters Co.*, 195 Iowa 147, 191 NW 803]

14. On August 19, 1980, Joan Ioviero injured her hand when she slipped and fell while leaving the dining room at the Hotel Excelsior in Venice, Italy. This hotel was owned by an Italian corporation, Cigahotels, S.p.A. (The designation *S.p.A.* stands for *Societa per Azionean,* the Italian term for corporation.) In 1973, a firm called Ciga Hotels, Inc., was incorporated in New York. Its certificate of incorporation was amended in

1979, changing the name of the firm to Landia International Services, Inc. This New York corporation was employed by the Italian corporation Cigahotels, S.p.A., to provide sales and promotional services in the United States and Canada. Ioviero sought to hold the New York corporation liable for her hand injury at the Venice hotel. She pointed to the similarity of the first corporate name used by the New York firm to the name Cigahotels, S.p.A., and the fact that the New York firm represented the interests of the Italian firm in the United States as clear evidence that the two firms were the same single legal entity. She asked that the court disregard the separate corporate entities. The New York corporation moved that the case be dismissed because it was duly incorporated in New York and did not own the Excelsior Hotel in which Ioviero was injured. Decide. [*Ioviero v CigaHotel, Inc. aka Landia I.S. Inc.,* 101 App Div 2d 852, 475 NYS2d 880]

15. William Sullivan was ousted from the presidency of the New England Patriots Football Club, Inc. Later the borrowed $5,348,000 to buy 100 percent control of the voting shares of the corporation. A condition of the loan was that he reorganize the Patriots so that the income from the corporation could be devoted to repayment of the personal loan and the team's assets could be used as collateral. Sullivan therefore arranged for a cash freeze-out merger of the holders of the 120,000 shares of nonvoting stock. David Coggins, who owned 10 shares of nonvoting stock and took special pride in the fact that he was an owner of the team, refused the $15-a-share buyout and challenged the merger in court. He contended that the merger was not for a legitimate corporate purpose but rather to enable Sullivan to satisfy his personal loan. Sullivan contended that legitimate business purposes were given in the merger proxy statement, such as the National Football League's policy of discouraging public ownership of teams. Coggins responded that before the merger Sullivan had 100 percent control of the voting stock and thus control of the franchise, and that no legal basis existed to eliminate public ownership. Decide. [*Coggins v New England Patriots Football Club,* 397 Mass 525, 492 NE2d 1112]

CPA QUESTIONS

1. Which of the following statements is correct concerning the similarities between a limited partnership and a corporation?
   a. Each is created under a statute and must file a copy of its certificate with the proper state authorities.
   b. All corporate stockholders and all partners in a limited partnership have limited liability.
   c. Both are recognized for federal income tax purposes as taxable entitites.
   d. Both are allowed statutorily to have perpetual existence.

   (11/92, Law, #1)

2. Rice is a promoter of a corporation to be known as Dex Corp. On January 1, 1985, Rice signed a nine-month contract with Roe, a CPA, which provided that Roe would perform certain accounting services for Dex. Rice did not disclose to Roe that Dex had not been formed. Prior to the incorporation of Dex on February 1, 1985, Roe rendered accounting services pursuant to the contract. After rendering accounting services for an additional period of six months pursuant to the contract, Roe was discharged without cause by the board of directors of Dex. In the absence of any agreements to the contrary, who will be liable to Roe for breach of contract?
   a. Both Rice and Dex.
   b. Rice only.
   c. Dex only.
   d. Neither Rice nor Dex.

   (11/85, Law, #5)

3. In general, which of the following must be contained in articles of incorporation?
   a. The names of the states in which the corporation will be doing business.
   b. The name of the state in which the corporation will maintain its principal place of business.
   c. The names of the initial officers and their terms of office.
   d. The classes of stock authorized for issuance.

   (5/87, Law, #3)

Corporate Stocks and Bonds

CHAPTER 47

After studying this chapter, you should be able to

1. *Distinguish between subscriptions for stock and transfers of stock;*
2. *Describe the mechanics of transferring stock;*
3. *Describe the rights of shareholders;*
4. *State the exceptions to the limited liability of shareholders; and*
5. *Distinguish between stocks and bonds.*

The two most common instruments used to provide funds for a corporation are stocks and bonds.

A. CORPORATE STOCK

Ownership of a corporation is represented by stock.

1. Nature of Stock

Membership in a corporation is based on ownership of one or more shares of stock of the corporation. Each share represents a fractional interest in the total property of the corporation. The shareholder does not own or have an interest in any specific property of the corporation; the corporation is the owner of all of its property. The terms share, stock, and share of stock mean the same thing.

(a) Capital and Capital Stock. Capital refers to the net assets of the corporation. Shares that have been issued to holders are said to be **outstanding**. **Capital stock** refers to the value received by the corporation for its outstanding stock.

(b) Valuation of Stock. Corporate stock may have a specified par value. This means that the person subscribing to the stock and acquiring it from the corporation must pay that amount. When stock is issued by the corporation for a price greater than the **par value**, some statutes provide that only the par value amount is to be treated as stated capital, the excess being allocated to surplus.

Shares may be issued with no par value. In that case, no amount is stated in the certificate, and the amount that the subscriber pays the corporation is determined by the board of directors. The Revised Model Business Corporation Act (RMBCA) eliminates the concept of par value, so stock issued by corporations in states following the RMBCA is always no par.

The value found by dividing the value of the corporate assets by the number of shares outstanding is the **book value** of the shares. The **market value** of a share of stock is the price at which that stock can be voluntarily bought or sold in the open market.

2. Certificates of Stock and Uncertificated Shares

Ownership of a corporation is evidenced by shares of stock issued by the corporation.

A corporation ordinarily issues a **certificate of stock** or **share certificate** as evidence of the shareholder's ownership of stock. The issuance of such certificates is not essential either to the existence of a corporation or to the ownership of its stock.

In states that have adopted the 1978 and 1994 amendments to Article 8 of the UCC, uncertificated shares may be issued. Uncertificated shares are not represented by instruments. Their ownership and transfer are registered on the books maintained by, or on behalf of, the issuer corporation.[1]

3.   Kinds of Stock

The stock of a corporation may be divided into two or more classes.

Kinds of stock include
• common stock and
• preferred stock—
   cumulative and
   noncumulative.

C
P
A

(a) Classification by Preferences. Common stock is ordinary stock that has no preferences. Each share usually entitles the holder to have one vote, to receive a share of the profits in the form of dividends when declared, and to participate in the distribution of capital upon dissolution of the corporation. **Preferred stock** has a priority over common stock. The priority may be with respect to either dividends or the distribution of capital upon dissolution of the corporation, or both. Preferred stock is ordinarily nonvoting.

(1) Cumulative Preferred Stock. The right to receive dividends is dependent on the declaration of dividends by the board of directors for a particular period of time. If there is no fund from which the dividends may be declared or if the directors do not declare them from an available fund, the shareholder has no right to dividends. The fact that a shareholder has not received dividends for the current year does not in itself give the right to accumulate or carry over into the next year a claim for those dividends. However, in the absence of a statement that the right to dividends is noncumulative, courts frequently hold that preferred stock has the right to accumulate dividends for each year in which there was a surplus available for dividend payment but dividends were not declared.

(2) Participating Preferred Stock. Sometimes the preferred stock is given the right of participation. If it is, then after the common shares receive dividends or a capital distribution equal to that first received by the preferred stock, both kinds participate or share equally in the balance.

(b) Duration of Shares. Ordinarily shares continue to exist for the life of the corporation. However, any kind of share, whether common or preferred, may be made terminable at an earlier date. **Convertible shares** entitle the shareholder to exchange owned shares for a different kind of share or for bonds of the corporation.

(c) Fractional Shares. A corporation may issue fractional shares or scrip or certificates representing fractional shares. These can be sold or combined for the acquisition of whole shares.

---

[1] UCC § 8-102(1)(b). The 1978 and 1994 amendments to Article 8 of the UCC have been adopted in all of the states except Alabama.

B. ACQUISITION OF SHARES

Shares may be acquired from the corporation or from an existing shareholder.

4. Nature of Acquisition

Shares of stock may be acquired (1) from the corporation by subscription, either before or after the corporation is organized, or (2) by transfer of existing shares from a shareholder or from the corporation. The transfer may be voluntary, as by a sale, gift, or bequest by will; or involuntary, as by an execution sale to pay the judgment of a creditor. The transfer may also take place by operation of law—as when the stock of a shareholder passes to the shareholder's trustee in bankruptcy.

5. Statute of Frauds

Under the 1978 version of Article 8, a contract for the sale of corporate shares must be evidenced by a writing, or it cannot be enforced.[2] The writing must show that there has been a contract for the sale of a stated quantity of described securities at a defined or stated price. The writing must be signed in the manner required by the statute of frauds for the sale of goods.

The 1994 version of Article 8 renders the statute of frauds inapplicable to contracts for the sale or purchase of securities.[3] The commentary notes explain that the 1978 statute's potential for filtering out fraudulent claims is outweighed by the obstacles the statute presents to the development of modern commercial practices in the securities business.

No writing is required for a contract by which a broker agrees with a customer to buy or sell securities for the customer. That is an agency agreement and not a sale made between the customer and the broker.

6. Subscription

> A stock subscription is a contract to buy a designated number and kind of shares when they are issued.

A **stock subscription** is a contract or an agreement to buy a specific number and kind of shares when they are issued by the corporation. As in the case of any other contract, the agreement to subscribe to shares of a corporation may be avoided for fraud.

(a) Subscription before Incorporation. In many states, a preincorporation subscription of shares is an offer to the corporation. According to this view, it is necessary for the corporation to accept the subscription offer either expressly or by conduct. A few states hold that subscriptions automatically become binding contracts when the organization of the corporation has been completed. In some states, the preincorporation subscription is irrevocable for a stated period. The RMBCA provides that "a subscription for shares entered into before incorporation is irrevocable for six months unless the subscription agreement provides a longer or shorter period or all the subscribers agree to revocation."[4]

---

[2] UCC § 8-319(a); *Goldfinger v Brown* (App Div) 564 NYS2d 461 (1991).
[3] UCC § 8-113 (1994).
[4] RMBCA § 6.20(a).

(b) Subscription after Incorporation. Subscriptions may be made after incorporation. In that event, the transaction is like any other contract with the corporation. The offer of the subscription may come from the subscriber or from the corporation. In either case, there must be an acceptance. Upon acceptance, the subscriber immediately becomes a shareholder with all the rights, privileges, and liabilities of a shareholder even though he or she has not paid any of the purchase price. Moreover, the subscriber is a shareholder even though no share certificate has been issued. In contrast with a contract for immediate subscription to shares, the contract may be one for the future issue of shares. In that case, the contracting party has only a contract and is not a shareholder as of the formation of the contract.

7. Transfer of Shares

In the absence of a valid restriction, a shareholder may transfer shares to anyone.

(a) Restrictions on Transfer. Restrictions on the transfer of stock are valid if they are not unreasonable. It is lawful to require that the corporation or other stockholders be given the first right to purchase stock before a shareholder may sell stock to an outsider.[5]

CASE SUMMARY

Restrictions on Transfer of Stock Are Legal, Morris

Facts: In 1974 Billy Fought, Brady Morris, Clayton Strong, and John Peyton organized Vicksburg Mold and Die, Inc., for the purpose of designing and manufacturing plastic and metal products. Each individual was issued 25 shares of stock. The shareholders entered into a stock redemption agreement requiring a stockholder wishing to sell his stock to offer proportionate shares to each stockholder. Morris was elected president and Fought vice president, and all four individuals worked at the plant. Strong retired in 1979 and sold his shares in accordance with the stock redemption plan. In 1983, Peyton decided to sell his shares and agreed to sell them all to Morris, thus giving Morris control of the corporation. Fought sued Morris for breach of his fiduciary duty to Fought and for the value of Fought's pro rata share of Peyton's stock.

Decision: Judgment for Fought. Section 2 of the stock redemption agreement was designed to maintain a balance of power in the four-person close corporation. Before stock could be sold to others, it had to be offered to each shareholder on a pro rata basis. Each individual had an opportunity to maintain the initial balance of power. By purchasing all of Peyton's stock, Morris bought control of the corporation. In doing so, he violated the stock redemption agreement and thus breached his fiduciary duty as a director, officer, and shareholder. *[Fought v Morris (Miss) 543 So 2d 167 (1989)]*

A provision giving a corporation the right to purchase a shareholder's shares upon the death of the shareholder is valid.

A restriction on the right of a certificate's purchaser to transfer his or her stock is not valid unless the restriction is conspicuously noted on the certificate or the transferee had actual knowledge of the restriction. A restriction on the transfer of stock is strictly interpreted.

---

[5] *Hardy v South Bend Sash & Door Co.* (Ind App) 603 NE2d 895 (1992).

Where no restrictions exist, the issuer has a duty to register the transfer. To illustrate, Richard Jones purchased 1,000 certificated shares of International Generic Corp. (IGC) from Madison Tucker on March 30, 1997, at fair market value. Tucker properly indorsed the certificates to Jones on that date, and her signatures were duly notarized. On September 15, 1997, Jones presented the securities to IGC to register the transfer of shares and also to collect dividends for the second quarter (April 1 through June 30) and the third quarter (July 1 through September 30). IGC refused to register the shares in Jones's name, believing him to be a person of questionable integrity that it did not want as an "owner" of IGC. Under either the 1978 or 1994 version of Article 8 of the UCC, it was improper for IGC to fail to register the stock that had been transferred to a bona fide purchaser, Jones.[6] No restrictions existed on the certificate, and IGC had a duty to register the transfer and was liable for its failure to do so. Jones was entitled to the dividends from the date of presentation of the stock for transfer. Prior to that date, the issuer, IGC, was entitled to treat the registered owner, Madison Tucker, as exclusively entitled to exercise the rights of ownership, including the right to dividends.[7] Thus, IGC was not liable to Jones for the second-quarter dividends. However, dividends declared after the date of presentment, which included the third-quarter dividend declared in October 1997 with a record date in October, must be paid to Jones by IGC.

(b) Interest Transferred. The transfer of shares may be absolute; that is, it may divest all ownership and make the transferee the full owner. The transfer may be of only a partial interest in the stock, or the transfer may be for security, such as when stock is pledged to secure the repayment of a loan.

8. Mechanics of Transfer

When stock is represented by a certificate, the ownership of shares is transferred by the delivery of the certificate of stock, indorsed by its owner in blank or to a specified person. Ownership may also be transferred by the delivery of the certificate accompanied by a separate assignment or power of attorney executed by the owner.[8]

A delivery from the owner of the shares directly to the transferee is not required. It can be made to an intermediary.[9] When there is no delivery of the share certificate to anyone, however, there is no transfer of ownership of the shares.

A physical transfer of the certificate without a necessary indorsement is effective as between the parties. Thus, a gift of shares is binding even though no indorsement has been made. An indorsement is required to make the transferee a bona fide purchaser.

9. Effect of Transfer

The transfer of existing shares of stock may raise questions as between the parties to the transfer and between them and the corporation.

---

[6] UCC § 8-401 (1978); UCC § 8-401 (1994).

[7] UCC § 8-207(1) (1978); UCC § 8-207 (a) (1994).

[8] UCC § 8-309. The second alternative of a delivery of an unindorsed certificate is designed to keep the certificate clean—for example, when the transfer is for a temporary or special purpose, as in the case of a pledge of the certificate as security for a loan.

[9] *Broadcourt Capital Corp. v Summa Medical Corp.*, 972 F2d 1183 (10th Cir 1992).

(a) Validity of Transfer. Because a transfer of shares is a transfer of ownership, the transfer must satisfy the requirements governing any other transfer of property or agreement to transfer property. As between the parties, a transfer may be set aside for any ground that would warrant similar relief under property law. If the transfer has been obtained by duress, the transferor may obtain a rescission of the transfer.

(b) Negotiability. Under common law, the transferee of shares of stock had no greater right than the transferor because the certificate and the shares represented by the certificate were nonnegotiable. By statute, the common law rule has been changed by imparting negotiability to certificated stock. Just as various defenses cannot be asserted against the holder in due course of a commercial paper, statutory law provides that similar defenses cannot be raised against the person acquiring the certificate in good faith and for value. As against such a person, the defense cannot be raised that the transferor did not own the shares or did not have authority to deliver the certificate or that the transfer was made in violation of a restriction on transfer not known to the person and not noted conspicuously on the certificate.

Statements sent by the issuer identifying the ownership of uncertificated securities are neither certificated securities nor negotiable instruments. Although certificated securities have the quality of negotiability, they are not commercial paper within Article 3 of the UCC.

(c) Secured Transaction. Corporate stock is frequently delivered to a creditor as security for a debt owed by the shareholder. Thus, a debtor borrowing money from a bank may deliver shares of stock to the bank as collateral security for the repayment of the loan. A broker's customer purchasing stock on margin may leave the stock in the possession of the broker as security for the payment of any balance due. The delivery of the security to the creditor is a pledge. This gives rise to a perfected security interest without any filing by the creditor. In itself, the pledge does not make the pledgee of the corporate stock the owner of the stock.

(d) Effect of Transfer on Corporation. The corporation is entitled to treat as the owner of shares the person whose name is on the corporation's books as the owner. Therefore, until there is a transfer on its books, the corporation may still treat a transferor of shares as the owner. The corporation may properly refuse to recognize a transferee when the corporation is given notice or has knowledge that the transfer is void or in breach of trust. In such a case, the corporation properly refuses to register a transfer until the rights of the parties have been determined. The corporation may also refuse to register the transfer of shares when the outstanding certificate is not surrendered to it or there is a lack of satisfactory proof that the certificate has been lost, destroyed, or stolen.

CASE SUMMARY

UCC Rules!

Facts: Equivest Associates, a partnership, owned 10,000 shares of Altec International Inc. Equivest pledged these shares to secure loans by Lloyds Bank. Sometime after pledging the stock, Equivest transferred beneficial ownership of 350 shares of Altec stock to Thorn Hoffman and 350 shares to John Erikson. Thereafter, in 1988, Altec elected to be treated as a Subchapter S corporation, which necessitated that shareholders return their old stock certificates and be issued new certificates. Neither Erikson nor Hoffman had certificates to return because their stock had been pledged by Equivest to Lloyds Bank. Altec had knowledge that Erikson and Hoffman were the beneficial owners of 700 shares of Altec stock. However, Altec distributed cash dividends to Equivest, the registered owner of the 10,000 shares during the period from 1988 until March 14, 1990, when Equivest defaulted on its loan to Lloyds Bank and Lloyds sold all of the pledged stock, including Hoffman's and Erikson's 700 shares, at public auction. Hoffman and Erikson contend that Altec should have made all cash distributions to them as shareholders and not Equivest. Altec contends it complied with the UCC by making distributions to the owner of record.

Decision: Judgment for Altec. UCC § 8-207(1) permitted Altec to treat Equivest as the owner of the 700 shares because it was the registered owner according to Altec's corporate books and Hoffman and Erikson had not made the due presentment to Altec for registration of the transfer of the 700 shares. *[Hoffman v Altec International Inc. (Wis App) 546 NW2d 162 (1996)]*

10. Lost, Destroyed, and Stolen Share Certificates

The owner of a lost, destroyed, or stolen share certificate is entitled to a replacement if the owner files a sufficient indemnity bond and requests the new certificate within a reasonable time before the issuer has notice that the original certificate has been acquired by a bona fide purchaser. If, after the new security is issued, a bona fide purchaser appears with the original certificate, the corporation must register a transfer of the security to that person and accept that person as the owner of the shares.

C.   RIGHTS OF SHAREHOLDERS

The rights of shareholders stem from their status as owners.

11. Ownership Rights

Shareholder control over the corporation is indirect. Periodically (ordinarily once a year) the shareholders elect directors and by this means control the corporation. At other times, however, the shareholders have no right or power to control corporate activity so long as it is conducted within lawful channels.

(a) Certificates of Stock. A shareholder has the right to have a properly executed certificate as evidence of ownership of shares. An exception is made when the corporation is authorized to issue uncertificated securities.

(b) Transfer of Shares. Unless limited by a valid restriction, a shareholder has the right to transfer his or her shares. The shareholder may sell the shares at any price or transfer them as a gift. The fact that the seller sells at a price higher than the market price is not unlawful even if the seller is a director or an officer.

It's the Real Thing, Controlling Shares in Coke-Anderson, and You Have to Pay a Premium

Facts: Paul Warlick, Jr., was the president and chief executive officer and a stockholder of Coca-Cola Bottling Co. of Anderson, S.C. (Coke-Anderson). He controlled a majority of the shares of stock of the company. Warlick agreed to sell this controlling interest in Coke-Anderson to Coke-Asheville for a price greater than the market value of such shares. Wayne Shoaf, a minority shareholder, brought suit against Warlick, contending that Warlick had violated his fiduciary duty to the corporation by receiving an unlawful premium for the sale of the majority interest in Coke-Anderson.

Decision: Judgment for Warlick. Paying or receiving a premium for the controlling shares of stock in a corporation is not unlawful. A majority shareholder who is also a director and an officer is generally under no duty to minority shareholders to refrain from receiving a premium on the sale of the controlling stock. *[Shoaf v Warlick (SC App) 380 SE2d 865 (1989)]*

Owners of common stock control the corporation indirectly through the election of the directors.

12. Right to Vote

The right to vote means the right to vote at shareholders' meetings for the election of directors and on other special matters that shareholders must vote on. For example, a proposal to change the capital structure of the corporation or a proposal to sell all or substantially all the assets of the corporation must be approved by the shareholders.

(a) Who May Vote. Ordinarily only **shareholders of record**—those common shareholders in whose name the stock appears on the books of the corporation—are entitled to vote. The board of directors may fix a date for closing the corporate books for this purpose.

(b) Number of Votes. Unless there is a provision to the contrary, for each share owned each shareholder is entitled to one vote on each matter to be voted. This procedure is called **straight voting**, and it is the normal method for shareholder voting on corporate matters. However, in the case of voting to elect directors only, cumulative voting is mandatory in nearly half of the states. This requirement is imposed by either state constitution or state statute. Cumulative voting is permitted by law in other states when provided for in the articles of incorporation or bylaws.

Cumulative voting is a form of voting that is designed to give proportional representation on the board of directors to minority shareholders. Under a cumulative voting plan, each shareholder has as many votes as the number of shares owned multiplied by the number of directors to be elected. A shareholder may cast all of these votes for one candidate or may divide the votes between two or more candidates. This system enables minority shareholders to cast all of their votes for a candidate who will represent their interests on the board of directors.

Under straight voting, minority shareholders would always be outvoted. For example, assume that minority shareholder Susan Jones owned 400 shares of stock and majority shareholder C.J. Katz controlled the remaining 600 shares. Also assume that five directors are to be elected to the board. If straight voting were used for the election of directors, C.J., with 600 shares, would always outvote Susan's 400 shares. However, under cumulative voting, Susan would be allowed 2,000 votes (400 shares times five directors), and C.J. would be allowed 3,000 votes

(600 shares times five directors). The five candidates with the highest number of votes will be elected. If Susan casts 1,000 votes for each of two directors and C.J. casts 1,000 votes for each of three directors, Susan, who owns 40 percent of the stock, is able to elect two-fifths of the board to represent her interests.

(c) Voting by Proxy. A shareholder has the right to authorize another to vote the shares owned by the shareholder. This procedure is known as **voting by proxy**. In the absence of restrictions to the contrary, any person, even someone who is not a shareholder, may act as a proxy. The authorization from the shareholder may be made by any writing.[10] The authorization is also commonly called a *proxy*.

(d) Voting Agreements and Trusts. Shareholders, as a general rule, are allowed to enter into an agreement by which they concentrate their voting strength for the purpose of electing directors or voting on any other matter.

A **voting trust** is created when by agreement a group of shareholders, or all of the shareholders, transfers their shares in trust to one or more persons as trustees. The trustees are authorized to vote the stock during the life of the trust agreement.[11] In general, such agreements are upheld if their object is lawful. In some jurisdictions, such trusts cannot run beyond a stated number of years. There are some signs of a relaxation as to time. Several states have abandoned all time limitations, several have extended the time limitation, and many provide for an extension or renewal of the agreement.

13. Preemptive Offer of Shares

If the capital stock of a corporation is increased, shareholders ordinarily have the preemptive right to subscribe to the same percentage of the new shares that their old shares represented of the former total of capital stock. This right is given to enable shareholders to maintain their relative interests in the corporation.

The existence of a preemptive right may make it impossible to conclude a transaction in which the corporation is to transfer a block of stock as consideration. Moreover, practical difficulties arise as to how stock should be allocated among shareholders of different classes.

The RMBCA provides that shareholders do not have preemptive rights unless the articles of incorporation provide for them.

14. Inspection of Books

Shareholders have the right to inspect the books of their corporation if done in good faith for a proper purpose.

A shareholder has the right to inspect the books of the shareholder's corporation. In some states, there are no limitations on this right. In most states, the inspection must be made in good faith, for proper motives, and at a reasonable time and place.[12] In many states, a shareholder must own a certain percentage of the outstanding stock of a corporation (commonly 5 percent) or must own at least one share of stock for a minimum amount of time (commonly six months) in order to have the right to inspect the books.

The purpose of inspection must be reasonably related to the shareholder's interest as a shareholder. A shareholder is entitled to inspect the records to deter-

---

[10] RMBCA § 7.07.
[11] *Bettner Trust v Bettner* (Ind App) 495 NE2d 194 (1986).
[12] RMBCA § 16.02(c); *State v Davis* (Mo App) 932 SW2d 885 (1996).

mine the financial condition of the corporation, the quality of its management, and any matters relating to rights or interests in the corporate business, such as the value of stock.

A shareholder is entitled to inspect the books to obtain information needed for a lawsuit against the corporation or its directors or officers, to organize the other shareholders into an "opposition" party to remove the board of directors at the next election, or to buy the shares of other shareholders.

Inspection has frequently been refused when it was sought merely from idle curiosity or for "speculative purposes." Inspection has sometimes been denied on the ground that it was sought merely to obtain a mailing list of persons who would be solicited to buy products of another enterprise. Inspection has also been refused when the object of the shareholder was to advance political or social beliefs without regard to the welfare of the corporation. Cases that deny the right of inspection do so when it would be harmful to the corporation[13] or is sought only for the purpose of annoying, harassing, or causing vexation or of aiding competitors of the corporation.

(a) Form of Books. There are generally no requirements regarding the form of corporate books and records. The RMBCA recognizes that corporate books and records may be stored in modern data storage systems. "A corporation shall maintain its records in written form or in any other form capable of conversion into written form within a reasonable time."[14]

(b) Financial Statements. The RMBCA requires a corporation to furnish annual financial statements. These statements include a balance sheet as of the end of the fiscal year, an income statement for that year, and a statement of changes in shareholders' equity for that year.[15] A number of state statutes contain similar provisions and also set forth a statutory penalty for any officer responsible for providing the financial statements who fails to perform such duties after written request.

CASE SUMMARY

No Excuses

Facts: Joseph Cousins was a shareholder of Mark VI Pipeline Co. Inc. He brought an action against Lyman Brownfield, the president and sole director. On September 18, 1985, Cousins made a written request to Brownfield for the financial statements of the company. Cousins made subsequent written requests for this information. The financial statements were not furnished to him until February 22, 1990. Cousins brought suit, contending that Brownfield should be assessed a statutory penalty for failure to provide the financial statements. Brownfield defended that no financial statements existed; all that existed were unaudited statements.

Decision: Judgment for Cousins in the amount of $2,000. Brownfield, an officer responsible for providing the financial statements under state law, was not excused from this performance because the financial statements were unaudited. State law did not require that the statements be audited or be prepared based on generally accepted accounting principles. Brownfield could have simply stated that the statements were unaudited. *[Cousins v Brownfield, 83 Ohio App 3d 782, 615 NE2d 1064 (1992)]*

---

13 *Retail Property Investors Inc. v Skeens* (Va) 471 SE2d 181 (1996).
14 RMBCA § 16.01(d).
15 RMBCA § 16.20.

15. Dividends

A shareholder has the right to receive a proportion of dividends as they are declared, subject to the relative rights of other shareholders to preferences, accumulation of dividends, and participation. There is no absolute right that dividends be declared, but dividends, when declared, must be paid in the manner indicated.

(a) Funds Available for Declaration of Dividends. Statutes commonly provide that no dividends may be declared unless there is an "earned surplus" for their payment. Earned surplus, also known as "retained earnings," consists of the accumulated profits earned by the corporation since its formation less prior dividend distributions. Dividend payments are prohibited if the corporation is insolvent or would be rendered insolvent by the payment of the dividend.

As an exception to these rules, a wasting assets corporation may pay dividends out of current net profits without regard to the preservation of the corporate assets. **Wasting assets corporations** are those designed to exhaust or use up the assets of the corporation (for example, by extracting oil, coal, iron, and other ores), as compared with manufacturing plants, where the object is to preserve the plant as well as to continue to manufacture. A wasting assets corporation may also be formed for the purpose of buying and liquidating a stock of merchandise from a company that has received a discharge in bankruptcy court.

In some states, statutes provide that dividends may be declared from earned surplus or from current net profits, without regard to the existence of a deficit from former years.

(b) Discretion of Directors. Assuming that a fund is available for the declaration of dividends, it is then a matter primarily within the discretion of the board of directors whether a dividend shall be declared. The fact that there is an earned surplus that could be used for dividends does not mean that they must be declared. This rule is not affected by the nature of the shares. Thus, the fact that the shareholders hold cumulative preferred shares does not give them any right to demand a declaration of dividends or to interfere with an honest exercise of discretion by the directors.

Maintaining an adequate cash and working capital position is an important practical consideration in determining whether to declare a cash dividend. In general, a court will refuse to substitute its judgment for the judgment of the directors of the corporation and will interfere with their decision on dividend declaration only when it is shown that their conduct is harmful to the welfare of the corporation or its shareholders.[16]

(c) Form of Dividends. Customarily a dividend is paid in money. However, it may be paid in property, such as a product manufactured by the corporation; in shares of other corporations held by the corporation; or in shares of the corporation itself.

(d) Effect of Transfer of Shares. When a corporation declares a cash or property dividend, the usual practice is for the board of directors to declare a dividend as of a certain date—the *declaration date*—payable to shareholders of record on a

---

[16] *Gabelli & Co. v Liggett Group, Inc.* (Del Super) 479 A2d 276 (1984).

stated future date—the *record date*—with a payment date following the record date, usually by some 30 days. The person who is the owner of the shares on the record date is entitled to the dividend even if the shares are transferred prior to the payment date.

If the dividend consists of shares in the corporation declaring the dividend, ownership of the dividend is determined by the date of distribution. Whoever is the owner of the shares when the stock dividend is distributed is entitled to the stock dividend. The reason for this variation from the cash dividend rule is that the declaration of a stock dividend has the effect of diluting the existing corporate assets among a larger number of shares. The value of the holding represented by each share is diminished as a result. Unless the person who owns the stock on the distribution date receives a proportionate share of the stock dividend, the net effect will be to lessen that person's holding.

16. Capital Distribution

Upon dissolution of the corporation, shareholders are entitled to receive any balance of the corporate assets that remains after the payment of all creditors. Certain classes of stock may have a preference or priority in this distribution.

17. Shareholders' Actions

Shareholders may bring a derivative action on behalf of the corporation for damages to it if the corporation refuses to do so.

When the corporation has the right to sue its directors, officers, or third persons for damages caused by them to the corporation or for breach of contract, one or more shareholders may bring such action if the corporation refuses to do so. This is a **derivative** (secondary) **action** in that the shareholder enforces only the cause of action of the corporation and any money recovery is paid into the corporate treasury.[17]

In a derivative action, when a corporation has failed to enforce a right, a shareholder bringing such a suit must show that a demand was made on the directors to enforce the right in question. The shareholder must show that the directors refused to enforce the right[18] or that it would obviously have been useless to demand that they enforce the right. And the shareholder must show that he or she fairly and adequately represents the interests of other "similarly situated" shareholders.

CASE SUMMARY

No Way around the Rules on Shareholder Actions

Facts: Six members of the Weston family, who owned 6.8 percent of the stock of Weston Paper and Manufacturing Co., brought suit against three corporate directors and CFIS, a firm hired by the company to make the annual evaluation of the company's stock for allocating stock options to their employees. The Westons stated that their claims against the defendants were personal claims, alleging that they were injured by CFIS and the three directors who kept the price of the stock low to obtain more shares of stock through the stock option plan. From an adverse ruling on their right to maintain a direct action against the directors, the Westons appealed.

---

[17] *Brown v Tenny* (Ill App) 532 NE2d 230 (1988).
[18] *Marx v Akers*, 88 NY2d 189, 666 NE2d 1034 (1996).

> **Decision:** Judgment for the corporation. If any injuries occurred, they occurred to all the shareholders alike. And such is precisely the situation in which a derivative action is required. However, the Westons meet none of the criteria for bringing a derivative action: (1) They made no effort to have the directors take the action they demanded, (2) they did not explain why they failed to make this effort, and (3) they did not show that they "fairly and adequately" represented the interests of the shareholders "similarly situated." *[Weston v Weston Paper and Manufacturing Co., 74 Ohio St 377 (1996)]*

C P A

Shareholders may also intervene or join in an action brought against the corporation when the corporation refuses to defend the action against it or is not doing so in good faith. Otherwise, the shareholders may take no part in an action by or against the corporation.

Lawsuits may be brought by minority shareholders against majority shareholders who are oppressive toward minority shareholders. Oppressive conduct may include payment of grossly excessive salaries and fringe benefits to the majority stockholders who are also officers of the corporation. Shareholders may bring a derivative action to obtain a dissolution of the corporation by judicial decree.[19]

ETHICS & THE LAW

Derivatives are contracts between two parties that have their value tied to some underlying transaction or measure. That underlying measure could be one to supply electricity at a specified and locked-in price, or the underlying measure could be bond rates or interest rates. Parties enter into derivative investments to protect their market positions. If someone, believing that interest rates are going to rise, has a variable rate loan, he or she buys a derivative interest in a fixed interest rate to be covered when rates rise. If interest rates fall, this person has not hedged his or her position very well and will absorb the cost of the fixed rate loan, as opposed to the cost of his or her variable loan, which would now be less. Derivatives are sophisticated financial instruments that permit parties to gamble on underlying transactions and trends.

Derivatives are interests that trade like stocks and bonds. However, as you can see from the example above, the financial exposure if an investor is wrong can be quite high. If an investor borrows money to invest in derivatives, the exposure if the investor is wrong on his or her hedging can be devastating. England's Barings Bank and Orange County, California, filed bankruptcy during the 1990s after facing heavy losses from leveraged derivative investments. Procter & Gamble and Gibson Greetings, a greeting card company, lost $157 million and $20 million, respectively, on their derivative portfolios during this period.

When Procter & Gamble and Gibson Greetings made their derivative investments, there were no requirements for disclosure of these risky instruments to shareholders. Information about derivatives did not have to be disclosed in financial reports, prospectuses, or proxy materials. Was it fair to allow this type of investment without letting shareholders know the risk? Should the derivative investments have been disclosed?

---

[19] *Lasday v Weiner* (Ill App) 652 NE2d 1198 (1996).

D.   LIABILITY OF SHAREHOLDERS

A shareholder is ordinarily protected from the liabilities of the corporation. Some exceptions are made by statute.

18. Limited Liability

The liability of a shareholder is generally limited. This means that the shareholder is not personally liable for the debts and liabilities of the corporation. The capital contributed by shareholders may be exhausted by the claims of creditors, but there is no personal liability for any unpaid balance.

19. Exceptions to Limited Liability

Shareholders ordinarily do not have personal liability for corporate debts except for
• certain wage claims,
• unpaid subscriptions, and
• unauthorized dividends.

Liability may be imposed on a shareholder as though there were no corporation when the court ignores the corporate entity either because of the particular circumstances of the case or because the corporation is so defectively organized that it is deemed not to exist.

(a) Wage Claims. Statutes sometimes provide that the shareholders shall have unlimited liability for the wage claims of corporate employees. This exception has been abandoned in some states in recent years or has been confined to corporate officers who are active in corporate decision making.[20]

(b) Unpaid Subscriptions. Most states prohibit the issuance of par value shares for less than par or except for "money, labor done, or property actually received." Whenever shares issued by a corporation are not fully paid for, the original subscriber receiving the shares, or any transferee who does not give value or who knows that the shares were not fully paid for, is liable for the unpaid balance if the corporation is insolvent and the money is required to pay its creditors.[21]

CASE SUMMARY

You've Got to Pay for Your Stock, Silly

Facts: On July 19, 1984, Keith and Joan Bryan incorporated Bryan's Inc. The corporation was authorized to issue 100 shares of stock with a par value of $1,000 per share. The corporation issued 50 shares to Keith and 50 shares to Joan, although it did not receive any payment in labor, services, money, or property for the stock. On August 30, 1984, Bryan's Inc. bought Hanewald's dry goods store, giving him a promissory note for part of the purchase price. The business was not successful, and after four months, Keith and Joan Bryan decided to close the store. They disbursed all the corporation's funds in payment of all bills except for the debt owed Hanewald. There were no corporate funds available to pay this debt. Hanewald sued the Bryans individually for the amount owed. The Bryans contended that they were not personally liable for the corporation's debts.

Decision: Judgment for Hanewald. Organizing a corporation to avoid personal liability is legitimate and a primary advantage to doing business in the corporate form. But proper capitalization is the principal prerequisite for this limited liability. Keith and Joan Bryan's failure to

---

[20] *Cusimano v Metro Auto Inc.* (Colo App) 860 P2d 532 (1993).
[21] *Frasier v Trans-western Land Corp.* (Neb) 316 NW2d 612 (1982). But see *Brunfield v Horn* (Ala) 547 So 2d 415 (1989).

pay for their stock makes them liable to Hanewald, the corporate creditor, to the extent that the stock was not paid for. Because the debt to Hanewald, $36,000, was less than the par value of their stock, $100,000, the Bryans are personally liable for the entire corporate debt owed to Hanewald. [Hanewald v Bryan's Inc. (ND) 429 NW2d 414 (1988)]

If the corporation has issued the shares as fully paid for, has given them as a bonus, or has agreed to release the subscriber for the unpaid balance, the corporation cannot recover that balance. The fact that the corporation is thus barred does not prevent creditors of the corporation from bringing an action to compel payment of the balance. The same rules are applied when stock is issued as fully paid for in return for property or services that were overvalued, so that the stock is not actually paid for in full. A conflict of authority exists, however, as to whether the shareholder is liable from the mere fact that the property or service given for the shares was in fact overvalued by the directors or whether it must also be shown that the directors had acted in bad faith in making the erroneous valuation. The trend of modern statutes is, in the absence of proof of fraud, to prohibit disputing the valuation placed by the corporation on services or property.

(c) Unauthorized Dividends. If dividends are improperly paid out of capital, shareholders are generally liable to creditors to the extent of such depletion of capital. In some states, the liability of a shareholder depends on whether the corporation was insolvent at the time and whether debts were existing at the time.

20. The Professional Corporation

The extent to which incorporation limits the liability of shareholders of a professional corporation depends on the interpretation of the statute under which the corporation was formed.

(a) Act of Shareholder in Creating Liability. The statutes that authorize the formation of professional corporations usually require that share ownership be limited to duly licensed professionals. If a shareholder in a professional corporation, such as a corporation of physicians, negligently drives the professional corporation's automobile in going to attend a patient or is personally obligated on a contract made for the corporation or is guilty of malpractice, the physician-shareholder is liable without limit for the liability that has been created. This is the same rule of law that applies in the case of the ordinary business corporation.

Professional corporation statutes generally repeat the rule governing malpractice liability by stating that the liability of a shareholder for malpractice is not affected by the fact of incorporation.

(b) Malpractice Liability of an Associate. The liability of a shareholder in a professional corporation for the malpractice of an associate varies from state to state depending on the language of the professional corporation statute in effect and on the court decisions under the statute.[22]

---

[22] ABA Model Professional Corporation Act Amendments (1984) § 34 offers three alternative positions regarding the liability of shareholders: (1) limited liability, as in a business corporation; (2) vicarious personal liability, as in a partnership; and (3) personal liability limited in amount and conditioned on financial responsibility in the form of insurance or a surety bond.

If the statute provides for limited liability, as in a business corporation, then where doctors *A, B,* and *C* are a professional corporation, *A* and *B* will not be liable for the malpractice of *C* beyond the extent of corporate assets. If the statute provides for vicarious personal liability, as in a partnership, and doctors *A, B,* and *C* are a professional corporation, each will have unlimited liability for any malpractice liability incurred by the other. Often the statutory reference to malpractice liability is not very clear, and the courts are called on to resolve the question of the liability of a professional-shareholder for the malpractice of an associate.

E.   BONDS

Bonds are instruments issued by a corporation to persons lending money to it.

21. Characteristics of Bonds

A **bond** is an instrument promising to repay a loan of money to a corporation. Typically the loan is for a relatively long period of time, generally five years or longer. A bond obligates the corporation to pay the bondholder the amount of the loan, called the **principal**, at a stated time, called the **maturity date**, and to pay a fixed amount of **interest** at regular intervals, commonly every six months. The relationship between the bondholder and the issuing corporation is that of creditor and debtor. And unlike dividends, which are discretionary, bond interest must be paid. A bond may be secured by a mortgage or lien on corporate property. A **debenture** is an unsecured bond of the corporation with no specific corporate assets pledged as security for payment.

Bonds are negotiable securities.[23] Bonds held by owners whose names and addresses are registered on the books of the corporation are called **registered bonds**.

22. Terms and Control

While bond-holders have no voting rights to elect directors to watch out for their interests, the indenture trustee represents their interest to make sure the terms of the issue are met.

The contractual terms of a particular bond issue are set forth in an agreement called a **bond indenture** or **deed**. An **indenture trustee**, usually a commercial banking institution, represents the interests of the bondholders in making sure that the terms and covenants of the bond issue are met by the corporation.[24] For example, the terms of the bond indenture may require a **sinking fund**, by which the borrowing corporation is required to set aside a fixed amount of money each year toward the ultimate payment of the bonds. The indenture trustee makes certain that such terms are complied with in accordance with its responsibilities set forth in the bond indenture.

Bondholders do not vote for directors or have the right to vote on matters on which shareholders vote. However, where the debt is risky, it is highly likely that significant restraints on the corporation's freedom of action will be imposed by the terms of the indenture.

---

[23] UCC § 8-105.
[24] *Lorenc v CSX Corp.,* CCH Sec L Rep 95298 (WD Pa 1990).

SUMMARY

The ownership of a corporation is evidenced by a holder's shares of stock that have been issued by the corporation. Common stock is ordinary stock that has no preferences but entitles the holder to (1) participate in the control of the corporation by exercising one vote per share of record, (2) share in the profits in the form of dividends, and (3) participate, upon dissolution, in the distribution of net assets after the satisfaction of all creditors (including bondholders). Other classes of stock exist, such as preferred stock, which has priority over common stock with regard to distribution of dividends and/or assets upon liquidation. Shares may be acquired by subscription of an original issue or by transfer of existing shares.

Shareholders control the corporation, but this control is indirect. Through their voting rights, they elect directors, and, by this means, they can control the corporation.

Preemptive rights, if they exist, allow shareholders to maintain their voting percentages when the corporation issues additional shares of stock. Shareholders have the right to inspect the books of the corporation unless it would be harmful to the corporation. Shareholders also have the right to receive dividends when declared at the discretion of the directors. Shareholders may bring a derivative action on behalf of the corporation for damages to the corporation. Shareholders are ordinarily protected from liability for the acts of the corporation.

Bonds are debt securities, and a bondholder is a creditor rather than an owner of the corporation. Bondholders' interests are represented by an indenture trustee, who is responsible for ensuring that the corporation complies with the terms of the bond indenture.

QUESTIONS AND CASE PROBLEMS

1. What social forces are affected by the rule requiring that a transfer restriction be known to the transferee or conspicuously noted on the share certificate?

2. What is the distinction between capital and capital stock?

3. Barbara, Joel, and Edna each own less than 5 percent of the stock of Enrico Storm Door Corp. Individually their holdings are too small to be significant in any shareholder's election. Barbara suggests that they and other small shareholders combine their votes by transferring their shares to trustees who will vote the aggregate of their shares as a block. Joel agrees with the idea but says he is afraid this is an illegal conspiracy. Is he correct?

4. Compare the effect of an oral contract (a) by Stone to sell 100 shares of Liberty Corp. stock to Coffey and (b) by stockbroker Mendez to sell Stone's stock in Liberty Corp. when the market price reaches $10 a share.

5. The stock of West End Development Co. was subject to a transfer restriction. This restriction required that any shareholder selling shares first offer every other shareholder the right to purchase a proportion of the shares being sold. The proportions were to be the same as the percentages of the outstanding shares that the other shareholders already owned. This restriction was stated in the articles of incorporation but was not stated on the stock certificate of the corporation. The Taylors owned stock in the company and sold their stock to Vroom, an officer of the corporation, without first offering any stock to the other shareholders, as required by the restriction. The other shareholders brought an action against Vroom to recover from him the percentages of the shares they would have been entitled to if the Taylors had followed the transfer restriction. Decide. [*Irwin v West End Development Co.*, 481 F2d 34 (10th Cir)]

6. Siebrecht organized a corporation called Siebrecht Realty Co. and then transferred his building to the corporation in exchange for its stock. The corporation rented different parts of the building to different tenants. Elenkrieg, an employee of one of the tenants, fell and was injured because of the defective condition of a stairway. She sued Siebrecht individually on the ground that the corporation had been formed by him for the purpose of securing limited liability. Decide. [*Elenkrieg v Siebrecht* (NY) 144 NE 519]

7. William Carter, a former officer and employee of Wilson Construction Co., Inc., owned 317 shares of stock in Wilson. Carter left Wilson to become part owner and employee of C&L Contracting Co., which was a direct competitor of Wilson. Carter requested access to Wilson's corporate books to determine the value of his shares. Wilson refused, not wanting to divulge its business practices to a direct competitor. Decide. [*Carter v Wilson Construction Co., Inc.* (NC App) 348 SE2d 830]

8. Ken and Charlotte Maschmeier were the majority shareholders of Southside Press; each owned 1,300 shares. Marty and Larry Maschmeier, who each owned 1,200 shares of the corporation, had a falling out with Ken and Charlotte and were terminated as employees of the business in the summer of 1985. Ken and Charlotte started a new corporation, which employed most of the employees of the old corporation and which took most of its former customers. Gross receipts of Southside Press went from $613,258 in 1985 to $18,172 in 1987. The $18,172 figure was from the lease of equipment. Ken and Charlotte continued to draw from Southside annual salaries of $20,000, which were in excess of the gross receipts of the business. Marty and Larry brought suit against Ken and Charlotte, alleging "oppressive" conduct. Ken and Charlotte stated that they paid Marty and Larry excellent salaries when they were employed by the corporation. Ken and Charlotte contended they had a right to start a new corporation as they saw fit. Decide. [*Maschmeier v Southside Press, Inc.* (Iowa App) 435 NW2d 377]

9. Harper owned corporate stock, and telling O'Brien that he was going to give the stock to O'Brien, he handed the stock certificate to O'Brien. O'Brien requested Harper to indorse the certificate. Harper refused. Who was the owner of the stock? [*Smith v Augustine*, 82 Misc 2d 326, 368 NYS2d 675]

10. Shares of stock represent debts owed by the corporation to its shareholders. Is this statement correct?

11. Ibanez owned shares of stock in Farmers Underwriters. He left the stock certificate lying on top of his desk in his office. Many persons continually passed through the office, and one day Ibanez realized that someone had taken the certificate from the top of his desk. Ibanez applied to Farmers Underwriters for a duplicate stock certificate. The corporation refused to issue a duplicate on the ground that it was Ibanez's own fault that the original certificate had been stolen. Ibanez claimed that he was entitled to a new certificate even though he had been at fault. Was he correct? [*Ibanez v Farmers Underwriters Ass'n* (Cal) 534 P2d 1336]

12. On March 3, 1995, pursuant to a public offering, First All State Trucking Corp. (FAST) issued securities to investors in denominations of $1,000. The interest rate was 11 percent per year payable semiannually, and the maturity date was March 3, 2005. The rights and obligations of the issuer, FAST, and the holders of the securities were set forth in an indenture agreement. Because the securities were not secured by a mortgage or lien on corporate property, Alec believes they are shares of preferred stock. Is Alec correct? Fully explain the type of security involved, and discuss the extent of the holders' voting rights.

13. Linhart owned shares of stock in First National Bank. She borrowed money from the bank and pledged the stock as security. She later decided to transfer 70 head of cattle and the shares of stock to her son, but she could not deliver the share certificate to him because it was held by the bank. She therefore executed a bill of sale reciting the transfer of the cattle and the stock to the son. She gave him the bill of sale, and he had the bill recorded. After her death, the son brought an action to determine the ownership of the stock. Was the son the owner of the shares?

14. Birt was a hospital patient. The doctor who treated him was a shareholder of a professional corporation organized under the Indiana Medical Professional Corporation Act. Birt claimed that the doctor who treated him was guilty of malpractice, and he sued the doctor. He also sued the professional corporation and all of its officers, directors, and shareholders. These other defendants asserted that they were not liable because the corporate entity shielded them. The plaintiff claimed that the corporation was not a shield because in fact all the persons were rendering medical services and should therefore be held liable as in a partnership. The statute did not expressly regulate the matter of limited liability beyond declaring that it did not change the law between a person supplying medical services and the patient. Decide. [*Birt v St. Mary Mercy Hospital*, 175 Ind App 32, 370 NE2d 379]

15. Ronald Naquin, an employee of Air Engineered Systems & Services, Inc., owned one-third of its outstanding shares. After six years he was fired, and an offer was made to buy out his interest in Air Engineered at a price that Naquin thought inadequate. He then formed a competing business and made a written request to examine the corporate records of Air Engineered. This request was denied. Naquin filed suit to require Air Engineered to allow him to examine the books. Air Engineered raised the defense that he was a competitor seeking to gain unfair competitive advantage. Decide. [*Naquin v Air Engineered Systems & Services, Inc.* (La App) 463 So 2d 992]

CPA QUESTIONS

1. A stockholder's right to inspect books and records of a corporation will be properly denied if the stockholder
   a. Wants to use corporate stockholder records for a personal business.
   b. Employs an agent to inspect the books and records.
   c. Intends to commence a stockholder's derivative suit.
   d. Is investigating management misconduct.

   (11/92, Law, #2, 3084)

2. The limited liability of a stockholder in a closely held corporation may be challenged successfully if the stockholder
   a. Undercapitalized the corporation when it was formed.
   b. Formed the corporation solely to have limited personal liability.
   c. Sold property to the corporation.
   d. Was a corporate officer, director, or employee.

   (5/91, Law, #6, 0697)

3. Price owns 2,000 shares of Universal Corp.'s $10 cumulative preferred stock. During its first year of operations, cash dividends of $5 per share were declared on the preferred stock but were never paid. In the second year, dividends on the preferred stock were neither declared nor paid. If Universal is dissolved, which of the following statements is correct?
   a. Universal will be liable to Price as an unsecured creditor for $10,000.
   b. Universal will be liable to Price as a secured creditor for $20,000.
   c. Price will have priority over the claims of Universal's bond owners.
   d. Price will have priority over the claims of Universal's unsecured judgment creditors.

   (5/92, Law, #19, 9653)

Securities Regulation

OBJECTIVES

After studying this chapter, you should be able to

1. *Determine whether state or federal securities laws apply to a transaction;*
2. *Define a security;*
3. *Compare and distinguish between the Securities Act of 1933 and the Securities Exchange Act of 1934;*
4. *Discuss the factors that subject an individual to liability for insider trading;*
5. *List the reasons for the regulation of cash tender offers; and*
6. *Identify the sections of the federal securities laws under which accountants may be subject to liability.*

Is there anything that protects you when you buy corporate securities?

A.   STATE REGULATION

To protect the public from the sale of fraudulent securities, many states have adopted statutes regulating the intrastate sale of securities.

1.   State Blue Sky Laws

State laws regulating securities are called **blue sky laws**. The term *blue sky* is derived from the purpose of such laws, which is to prevent the sale of speculative schemes that have no more value than the blue sky. The state statutes vary in detail. They commonly contain (1) an antifraud provision prohibiting fraudulent practices and imposing criminal penalties for violations; (2) broker-dealer licensing provisions regulating the persons engaged in the securities business; and (3) provisions for the registration of securities, including disclosure requirements, with a designated government official.

A Uniform Securities Act, covering the foregoing three categories of regulations, exists to provide guidance to states in updating their securities laws. This act contains alternative regulations that can be adopted by states with different regulatory philosophies.

> Blue sky laws are state laws that regulate the intrastate sale of securities.

2.   National Securities Markets Improvement Act

Congress reallocated responsibility between state and federal security regulators in the National Securities Markets Improvement Act of 1996 (NSMIA),[1] recognizing that the dual system of state and federal regulation of securities resulted in duplicative regulation and expenses. Title I of the act exempts from state review and registration securities offered by mutual funds and stocks listed on the New York Stock Exchange, the American Stock Exchange, the NASDAQ National Market System, and other stock exchanges identified by the SEC. The act preserves the states' authority to investigate and bring enforcement actions for fraud or deceit or for unlawful conduct by a broker or dealer in connection with securities transactions.[2] Also the states may continue to collect filing fees for securities in effect as of October 25, 1996. The act also eliminates duplicative registration requirements for investment advisors by dividing regulatory authority between the SEC, which exclusively regulates investment advisors with assets under management of $25 million or more, and the states, which have the responsibility to regulate all investment advisors managing lesser sums of money.[3]

B.   FEDERAL REGULATION

The stock market crash of 1929 and the Great Depression that followed led to the enactment of federal legislation to regulate the securities industry.

---

[1] PL 104-290, 110 Stat 3416, 15 USC § 78a nt.
[2] The 1996 act amends section 18(c) of the 1933 Securities Act to accomplish this result.
[3] NSMIA § 303(a), which adds a new section 203A to the Investment Advisors Act of 1940.

3. Federal Laws Regulating the Securities Industry

Six federal securities regulation laws were passed between 1933 and 1940. The two principal laws that provide the basic framework for the federal regulation of the sale of securities in interstate commerce are the Securities Act of 1933 and the Securities Exchange Act of 1934.

The 1933 act deals with the original distribution of securities by the issuing corporations. The 1934 act is concerned with the secondary distribution of securities in the national securities markets and in the over-the-counter markets. That is, the 1933 act regulates the issuance of securities by a corporation to the first owner. The 1934 act regulates the sale of securities from one owner to another. Four other federal laws deal with specific aspects of the securities industry.[4] These aspects include holding companies in utility businesses, trustees for debt securities, mutual funds, and investment advisors.

The Securities Enforcement Remedies and Penny Stock Reform Act of 1990[5] (Remedies Act) expands the enforcement remedies of the Securities and Exchange Commission (SEC) to reduce fraudulent financial reporting and financial fraud. Under the Remedies Act, the SEC may start administrative proceedings against any person or entity, whether regulated by the SEC or not, and may issue a temporary cease-and-desist order prior to notice and a hearing. The SEC may also order an accounting and disgorgement of ill-gotten gains.

The Remedies Act also authorizes courts to bar individuals who have engaged in fraudulent activities from serving as officers and directors of public corporations.

The Securities Acts Amendments of 1990[6] authorize sanctions against SEC-regulated persons for violation of foreign laws. The amendments facilitate the ability of the SEC and foreign regulators to exchange information and cooperate in international securities law enforcement.

The Market Reform Act of 1990[7] was enacted to provide the SEC with powers to deal with market volatility. Under the law, the SEC has the power to suspend all trading when markets are excessively volatile. Also, the SEC may require "large traders" to identify themselves and provide information concerning their trading.

The Private Securities Litigation Reform Act of 1995[8] (the Litigation Reform Act) was passed to alleviate abuses in private securities litigation. It is expected that the act will reduce the number of lawsuits brought against issuers of securities and accounting firms, who have complained about the explosion of litigation against them. This law applies only to private securities litigation, and the SEC's enforcement activities are not affected by the act.

The NSMIA, previously referred to in regard to the allocation of responsibility for securities regulation between the states and the federal government, also

---

4 The Public Utility Holding Company Act of 1935 (15 USC §§ 79-792-6) provides comprehensive regulation of holding companies and their subsidiaries in interstate gas and electric utilities businesses. The Trust Indenture Act of 1939 (15 USC §§ 77aaa to 77bbb) was enacted to protect the interests of the holders of bonds and other debt securities offered to the public in interstate commerce by requiring the appointment of independent institutional trustees. The Investment Company Act of 1940 (15 USC §§ 80a-1 to 80a-52) provides for the registration and comprehensive regulation of mutual funds and all other investment companies. The Investment Advisors Act of 1940 (15 USC §§ 80b-1 to 80b-21) requires registration with the Securities and Exchange Commission of all persons engaged in the business of providing investment advice in interstate commerce. In 1970 the Securities Investors Protection Act was enacted to protect investors from the business failures of brokers and dealers.
5 PL 101-429, 104 Stat 931, 15 USC § 77g.
6 PL 101-550, 104 Stat 2713, 15 USC § 78a.
7 PL 101-432, 104 Stat 963, 15 USC § 78a.
8 PL 104-67, 109 Stat 737, 15 USC § 78a nt.

provides for national standards allowing brokers and dealers to improve their ability to borrow funds to finance market-making and underwriting activities.[9] This act also provides new national standards regulating margin restriction.

C
P
A

The term *security* is sufficiently broad to encompass virtually any instrument that might be sold as an investment.

4. Definition of Security

In order for the securities acts to apply, the transaction must involve a "security" within the meaning of the acts.[10] Congress adopted a definition of *security* sufficiently broad to encompass virtually any instrument that might be sold as an investment.

The definition of *security* includes not only investment instruments such as stocks and bonds but also "investment contracts." The definition of an *investment contract* developed by the Supreme Court is sufficiently broad to allow the securities acts to apply to a wide range of investment transactions or schemes, including the sale of bottled whiskey, cattle breeding programs, and of limited partnerships for oil and gas exploration. Under the Supreme Court's definition, an investment contract exists if the following elements are present: (1) an investment of money, (2) a common enterprise, and (3) an expectation of future profits from the efforts of others. ◆ *For example,* the sale of citrus groves to investors, coupled with the execution of service contracts to plant, harvest, and sell the fruit and the distribution of the profits of the venture to the investors, is an investment contract. ◆

CASE SUMMARY

Sour Notes or Protected Securities?

Facts: To raise money to support its general business operations, the Farmer's Cooperative of Arkansas and Oklahoma (Co-Op) sold uncollateralized and uninsured promissory notes, payable on demand by the holder. Offered to both Co-Op members and nonmembers and marketed as an "Investment Program," the notes paid a variable interest rate higher than those paid by local financial institutions. The Co-Op filed for bankruptcy. Bob Reves and the other holders of the notes filed suit in the U.S. district court against the Co-Op's auditor, claiming the Securities Exchange Act of 1934 had been violated. The defense was made that the notes were not "securities."

Decision: Judgment for the noteholders. A "note" is presumed to be a "security" unless that presumption is rebutted through analysis of the following four factors: (1) motivation to enter the transaction, (2) plan of distribution, (3) reasonable expectations of the investing public, and (4) existence of another regulatory scheme that would render application of the securities laws unnecessary. Applying the four factors to this case, the notes are clearly "securities." The motivation for the seller was to raise capital, and the motivation for the buyers was to earn a profit in the form of interest. The notes were sold to the general public. The investing public reasonably believed the notes were investments, and the seller called it an "Investment Program." If the securities laws did not apply, the notes would escape federal regulation. *[Reves v Ernst & Young, 494 US 56 (1990)]*

---

[9] NSMIA § 104, PL 104-290, 110 Stat 3416, 15 USC § 776.
[10] The Supreme Court has consistently held that the definition of a security set forth in section 3(a)(10) of the 1934 act is identical to the definition set forth in section 2(1) of the 1933 act. The definition of security under these acts is not to be confused with the narrower definition in Article 8 of the Uniform Commercial Code.

5. Securities Act of 1933

The 1933 act deals with the original issue of securities. It prohibits the offer or sale of securities to the public in interstate commerce before a registration statement is filed with the SEC. A **registration statement** is a document disclosing specific financial information regarding the security, the issuer, and the underwriter. The seller must also provide a prospectus to each potential purchaser of the securities. The **prospectus** sets forth the key information contained in the registration statement. The object is to provide the interested investor with detailed information about the security and the enterprise. The SEC does not approve or disapprove the securities as being good or bad investments but only reviews the form and content of the registration statement and the prospectus to ensure full disclosure. The requirements of advance disclosure to the public through the filing of the registration statement with the SEC and the sending of a prospectus to each potential purchaser are commonly referred to as the **registration requirements** of the 1933 act.

(a) Applicability. The 1933 act applies to (1) stocks, (2) corporate bonds, and (3) any conceivable kind of corporate interest or instrument that has the characteristics of an investment security, including convertible securities and variable annuities. The act applies to all such instruments that have investment characteristics.

(b) The Registration Process. Section 5 of the 1933 act provides for the division of the registration process into three time periods: (1) the prefiling period; (2) the waiting period, from the date of filing with the SEC to the date the registration statement becomes effective (a minimum of 20 days but commonly extended for additional 20-day periods after each amendment by the issuer in compliance with SEC requirements for additional information); and (3) the posteffective period. The time divisions allow the public an opportunity to study the information disclosed in the registration process before a sale can be made. Permissible, required, and prohibited activities during these time periods are set forth in Figure 48-1.

(c) Regulation A Offerings. Regulation A provides a simplified registration process for small issues of securities by small businesses. Although technically exempt from the 1933 act registration requirements, a Regulation A offering involves a "mini-registration" with the SEC. Under the SEC's Small Business Initiative, which became effective in August of 1992, the SEC expanded Regulation A to facilitate the offerings of securities from the previous $1.5 million in a 12-month period to $5 million in a 12-month period. Under the new procedures, disclosure requirements are simplified by the use of the small corporate offerings registration (SCOR) form, with its question-and-answer "fill-in-the-blank" format. Also, the financial statements required in a Regulation A offering are less extensive than those required for a registered public offering.

Issuers may broadly solicit indications of interest from prospective investors before filing an *offering statement* with the SEC. This allows the issuer to "test the waters" and explore investor interest before incurring the expenses associated with a Regulation A offering. Solicitation of interest documents must be factual and comply with the antifraud provisions of the securities acts. No sales may be made until the SEC qualifies the offering statement and the seller delivers the final-offering circular, including the offering price, to the investor.

FIGURE 48-1
Registration Periods

	Prohibited or Required Activities	Permitted Activities
Prefiling Period	Issuer must not sell or offer for sale a security before registration statement is filed.	Issuer may plan with underwriters the distribution of the security.
Waiting Period	No final sale of a security permitted during this period.	Preliminary prospectus* containing information from the registration statement being reviewed by the SEC may be distributed to investors, who may make offers. Advertisements may be placed in financial publications, identifying particulars of the security, from whom a prospectus can be obtained, and by whom orders will be executed.**
Posteffective Period	Must provide a copy of final prospectus with every written offer, confirmation of sale, or delivery of security. Must update prospectus whenever important new developments occur or after nine months.	Sales of the security may be completed.

* The preliminary prospectus is commonly called the "red herring" prospectus because of the red ink caption required by the SEC, informing the public that a registration statement has been filed but is not yet effective, and that no final sale can be made until after the effective date.

** These advertisements are sometimes called "tombstone ads" because they are commonly framed by a black ink border.

(d) Registration Exemptions. Certain private and limited offerings of securities are exempt from the registration requirements of the act. Under SEC Regulation D, offerings of any amount made solely to accredited investors, such as banks, insurance companies, investment companies, or directors and executive officers of the issuing corporation, are exempt from the registration requirements of the act. These accredited investors generally have access to the kinds of information disclosed in a registration statement and prospectus.

Offerings of securities restricted to residents of the state in which the issuing corporation is organized and doing business are exempt from federal regulation. This intrastate offering exemption is applied very narrowly by the SEC and the courts, and such offerings are subject to state laws.

(1) Rule 505 Exemption. SEC Rule 505 of Regulation D exempts from registration offerings of less than $5 million to fewer than 35 nonaccredited purchasers (not offerees) over a 12-month period. No limit exists on the number of accredited investors who may participate. No general solicitation or general advertising is permitted under Rule 505. If any prospective investors are nonaccredited, the issuer must furnish all investors with specific information on the issuer, its business, and the securities offered for sale.

(2) Rule 506 Exemption. SEC Rule 506, the so-called private placement exemption, has no limitation on the amount that may be raised by the offering. As in Rule 505, specific information must be provided to all buyers if any buyers are nonaccredited investors and the number of nonaccredited investors is limited to fewer than 35. Further, the rule requires that the issuer reasonably believe that each nonaccredited investor has enough experience in investments to be capable of evaluating the merits and risks of the investment.

(3) Restrictions. Securities acquired under Rules 505 and 506 exemptions from registration are considered **restricted securities**. Their resale may require registration. Rules requiring registration of these Regulation D securities prior to resale ensure that investors purchase these securities as an investment rather than for public distribution. When there is no attempt to make public distributions, investors ordinarily fit within one of several exemptions to registration upon resale.

(4) Rule 504 Exemption. Under SEC Rule 504 of Regulation D, as amended in 1992, an issuer may offer and sell securities up to $1 million within a 12-month period without registration and without the restrictions contained in Rules 505 and 506.[11] No limitations exist concerning the number of investors being solicited or the method of soliciting investors. Also no restrictions exist on the resale of the securities. The Rule 504 exemption is commonly used by small business issuers in raising seed money to start or expand a business.

Rule 504 differs from a Regulation A offering in that no registration whatsoever is required when the Rule 504 exemption is used, while a "mini registration" with the SEC is required under a Regulation A offering. The SEC's antifraud provisions apply to both.

(e) Liability. Issuers, sellers, and "aiders and abettors" may be subject to civil and criminal liability under the 1933 act.

(1) Issuer's Civil Liability for False or Misleading Statements. The Securities Act of 1933 imposes civil liability under section 11 for making materially false or misleading statements in a registration statement and for omitting any required material fact. An issuing company has virtually no defense if there has been a false statement and a loss.

(2) Civil Liability of Sellers of Securities. Section 12 of the 1933 act applies to those who "offer or sell" securities and employ any device or scheme to defraud or obtain money by means of untrue statements of material facts. This section makes such persons or firms liable to purchasers for damages sustained. Where there are untrue statements of material facts, purchasers may recover under section 12(2) unless they have actual knowledge of the untruth or omission.[12]

---

[11] 17 CFR §§ 230.504 et seq.

[12] As codified, section 12(2) provides: "Any person who . . . (2) offers or sells a security . . . by means of a prospectus or oral communication, which includes an untrue statement of a material fact or omits to state a material fact necessary in order to make the statements, in the light of circumstances under which they were made, not misleading (the purchaser not knowing of such untruth or omission), and who shall not sustain the burden of proof that he did not know, and in the exercise of reasonable care could not have known, of such untruth or omissions, shall be liable to the person purchasing such security from him, who may sue either at law or in equity in any court of competent jurisdiction, to recover the consideration paid for such security with interest thereon, less the amount of any income received thereon, upon the tender of such security, or for damages if he no longer owns the security." 15 USC § 77l(2).

C
P
A

The application of section 12(2) of the 1933 act is limited to initial public offerings (IPOs) of securities and does not apply to privately negotiated transactions subsequent to an IPO.[13]

(3) Criminal Liability. Section 24 of the 1933 act imposes criminal penalties on anyone who willfully makes untrue statements of material facts or omits required material facts from a registration statement. Section 17 of the act makes it unlawful for any person to employ any device, scheme, or artifice to defraud in the offer or sale of securities.

6. Securities Exchange Act of 1934

The 1934 act deals with the secondary distribution of securities. It was designed to prevent fraudulent and manipulative practices on the security exchanges and in over-the-counter markets. The act requires the disclosure of information to buyers and sellers of the securities. Furthermore, the act controls credit in these markets.

C
P
A

(a) Registration Requirements. Exchanges, brokers, and dealers who deal in securities traded in interstate commerce or on any national security exchange must register with the SEC unless exempted by it.

Companies whose securities are listed on a national securities exchange and unlisted companies with assets in excess of $3 million and 500 or more shareholders are subject to the reporting requirements of the act.[14]

Form 10-K is the principal annual report form used by commercial and industrial companies required to file under the 1934 act. The reports require nonfinancial information about the registrant's activities during the year, such as the nature of the firm's business, the property or businesses it owns, and a statement concerning legal proceedings by or against the company. The report requires the submission of financial statements, with management's analysis of the financial condition of the company, and a report and analysis of the performance of corporate shares. It requires a listing of all directors and executive officers and disclosure of executive compensation information.

Registrants who are required to file 10-K reports must also file quarterly reports, called 10-Q reports. The 10-Q reports are principally concerned with financial information relevant to the quarterly period.

The SEC requires that annual shareholder reports be submitted to shareholders in any proxy solicitation on behalf of management. These reports contain essentially the same information provided in the 10-K.

The 1934 act was designed to prevent fraud or manipulative practices on the exchanges. SEC Rule 10b-5 is the principal antifraud rule relating to the secondary distribution of securities.

(b) Antifraud Provision. Section 10(b) of the 1934 act makes it unlawful for any person to use any manipulative or deceptive device in contravention of SEC rules.[15] Under the authority of section 10(b) of the 1934 act, the SEC has promulgated Rule 10b-5. This rule is the principal antifraud rule relating to the secondary distribution of securities. The rule states:

> *It shall be unlawful for any person, directly or indirectly, by use of any means or instrumentality of interstate commerce, or of the mails or of any facility of any national securities exchange,*

---

[13] *Gustafson v Alloyd Co.,* 115 S Ct 1061 (1995).
[14] SEC Release No. 34-18647 (April 15, 1982).
[15] 15 USC § 78j(b).

(a) To employ any device, scheme, or artifice to defraud,

(b) To make any untrue statement of a material fact or to omit to state a material fact necessary in order to make the statements made, in the light of the circumstances under which they were made, not misleading, or

(c) To engage in any act, practice, or course of business that operates or would operate as a fraud or deceit upon any person, in connection with the purchase or sale of any security.[16]

(1) Private Actions. Rule 10b-5 applies to all securities, whether registered or not, as long as use is made of the mail, interstate commerce, or a national stock exchange. Under this rule, a civil action for damages may be brought by any private investor who purchased or sold a security and was injured because of false, misleading, or undisclosed information.

(2) Liability for "Material Misstatements or Omissions of Fact." Rule 10b-5 prohibits the making of any untrue statement of a "material" fact or the omission of a material fact necessary to render statements made not misleading. In every Rule 10b-5 case, the plaintiff must show "reliance" on the misrepresentation and resulting injury.

In a merger context, "materiality" depends on the probability that the transaction will be consummated and on the significance to the issuer of the securities. That is, "materiality" depends on the facts and must be determined on a case-by-case basis. ◆ *For example*, assume that corporation *A* was involved in merger discussions with corporation *B*. During this time, corporation *A* made public statements denying that any merger negotiations were taking place or that it knew of any corporate developments that would account for heavy trading activity in its stock. Corporation *A* may be held liable for damages to its shareholders who sold their stock after the public denial of merger activity and before a later merger announcement. ◆

CASE SUMMARY

Why Silence Is Golden

Facts: In December 1978, Combustion Engineering, Inc., and Basic Inc. agreed to merge. During the preceding two years, representatives of the two companies had meetings regarding the possibility of a merger. During this time, Basic made three public statements denying that any merger negotiations were taking place or that it knew of any corporate developments that would account for the heavy trading activity in its stock. Certain former shareholders who sold this stock between Basic's first public denial of merger activity and the public announcement of the merger brought a section 10(b) and Rule 10b-5 action against Basic and some of its directors. The former shareholders contended that Basic had made material misrepresentation in its public statements denying merger activity. Basic raised the defense that the alleged misrepresentations were not material and that there was no showing of reliance by the shareholders on Basic's statements.

Decision: The standard for materiality applicable to preliminary merger discussions is to be decided on a case-by-case basis depending on the probability that the transaction will be consummated and on its significance to the issuer. There is a presumption of reliance by the shareholders on the misstatements of the corporations. This presumption is supported by the policy

---

[16] 17 CFR § 240.10b-5.

> of the 1934 act, which is to foster reliance on market integrity. However, the presumption may be rebutted by showing that the market price was not affected by the misrepresentation. The case is remanded for further proceedings consistent with this opinion. *[Basic Inc. v Levinson, 405 US 224 (1988)]*

(3) SEC Actions. Overturning 30 years of court precedent, the Supreme Court has ruled that private investors may not bring action under section 10(b) of the 1934 securities act against aiders or abettors, such as accountants, lawyers, and investment bankers, who provide assistance to the primary violator.[17] However, the SEC itself has authority to bring civil and criminal enforcement actions against aiders and abettors who *knowingly* provide substantial assistance to the primary violator.[18]

(c) Litigation Reform Act of 1995. The Private Securities Litigation Reform Act of 1995 (the Litigation Reform Act) was passed because of (1) congressional concern over an excess of frivolous private securities lawsuits, (2) the financial burdens placed on accountants and other professional advisors by such litigation, and (3) concern that the investors in a class-action lawsuit have their interests fairly represented. Important features of the act are as follows.

(1) Safe Harbor Rules. Issuers of securities frequently believed that lawsuits against them under Rule 10b-5 occurred simply because the corporation made a projection that failed to materialize. The Litigation Reform Act provides shelter for issuers from private liability for forward-looking statements that were not known to be false when made and were accompanied by "meaningful" cautionary statements informing investors of contingencies that could cause actual results to differ from projected results. ◆ *For example,* in a January 1998 prospectus for its initial public offering of shares, Apex Oil Discovery Co. (AODC) estimated a sizable volume of oil production based on the studies of two geologists and a test well. A cautionary statement advised that the projections were only estimates based on the opinion of two experts and a test well and that actual production could vary significantly. Lutz, who bought 10,000 shares in May 1998 at $20 per share, could not successfully bring a Rule 10b-5 securities fraud action against AODC when later in the year AODC's forward-looking statement turned out to be erroneous and the price of the stock fell to $6 per share on October 16, 1998. The safe harbor provisions of the Litigation Reform Act will shelter the AODC in any such litigation. ◆

(2) Litigation Reform. The Litigation Reform Act provides for proportionate liability, as opposed to joint and several liability, for defendants who are found not to have knowingly committed a violation of the security laws. Also, securities fraud is eliminated as a predicate for private RICO actions absent a prior criminal conviction. Under the act, frivolous private securities lawsuits require payment of the defendant's reasonable attorney fees.

---

[17] *Central Bank of Denver v First Interstate Bank of Denver,* 511 US 164 (1994). See, however, *McGann v Ernst & Young,* 95 F3d 821 (9th Cir 1996), where the Ninth Circuit Court of Appeals held that an accounting firm could be subject to "primary liability" under section 10(b) for preparing a fraudulent audit report that it knew its client would include in a Form 10-K annual report.

[18] Civil actions may be brought by the SEC under section 20(f) of the 1934 act. Criminal prosecution may be pursued under 18 USC section 2 (1994).

C
·
P
·
A

(3) *Class-action Reforms.* Reforms were necessary to protect against "lawyer-driven lawsuits" in which a class-action counsel would direct a "professional" plaintiff to buy a security so as to have standing to bring a class-action lawsuit. Thereafter, the class-action counsel would race to the courthouse to file before any other plaintiff and thus be able to claim enhanced standing to represent the class. The Litigation Reform Act provides that the status of lead plaintiff is offered to the person with the largest financial interest in the case, who then selects the lead counsel.

(4) *Auditor Disclosure.* The Litigation Reform Act amends the 1934 act by requiring auditors who discover illegal acts to notify management and the board of directors and, in some cases, to notify the SEC if the issuer does not.[19] Auditors are relieved from liability for any such disclosure to the SEC.

7.   Trading on Insider Information

Section 10(b) and Rule 10b-5 form a basis for imposing sanctions for trading on **insider information**. The Insider Trading Sanctions Act of 1984,[20] which amended the 1934 act, gave the SEC authority to bring an action against an individual purchasing or selling a security while in possession of material inside information. The court may impose a civil penalty of up to three times the profit gained or loss avoided as a result of the unlawful sale. Persons who "aid or abet" in the violation may also be held liable under the act.

Under the 1988 Insider Trading Act, "controlling persons," including employers whose lax supervision may allow employees to commit insider trading violations, are subject to civil penalties.[21] The SEC must prove "knowing" or "reckless" behavior by the controlling person. The 1988 law establishes bounty programs that allow the SEC to reward informants giving information on insider trading activity. The reward is up to 10 percent of any penalty imposed.

(a) Trading by Insiders and Tippees. An **insider** may be a director or corporate employee. A **temporary insider** is someone retained by the corporation for professional services, such as an attorney, accountant, or investment banker. Insiders or temporary insiders are liable for inside trading when they fail to disclose material nonpublic information before trading on it and thus make a secret profit. A **tippee** is an individual who receives information from an insider or a temporary insider. A tippee is subject to the insider's fiduciary duty to shareholders when the insider has breached the fiduciary duty to shareholders by improperly disclosing the information to the tippee and when the tippee knows or should know there has been a breach.[22] Such a breach occurs when an insider benefits personally from his or her disclosure. Where the insider does not breach a fiduciary duty, a tippee does not violate the securities laws.

---

19 PL 104-671, 109 Stat 763, 15 USC 78j-l nt.
20 PL 98-376, 98 Stat 1264, 15 USC 78a.
21 PL 100-704, 102 Stat 4677, 15 USC § 78 u A (b)(2).
22 *United States v Chestman*, 974 F2d 564 (2d Cir 1991).

No Secrets from Secrist!

Facts: On March 6, Dirks, an investment analyst, received information from Secrist, a former officer of Equity Funding of America, alleging that the assets of Equity Funding were vastly overstated as the result of fraudulent corporate practices. On investigation by Dirks, certain corporation employees corroborated the charges of fraud. Neither Dirks nor his firm owned or traded any Equity Funding stock, but throughout his investigation, he openly discussed the information he had obtained with a number of clients and investors. The information from Dirks induced them to sell Equity Funding stock in excess of $16 million. On March 27, the New York Stock Exchange halted trading of Equity Funding stock, and a subsequent investigation revealed the vast fraud that had taken place. The SEC, investigating Dirks's role in the exposure of the fraud, claimed that Dirks had aided and abetted violations of the Securities Act of 1933, the Securities Exchange Act of 1934, and SEC Rule 10b-5 by repeating the allegations of fraud to members of the investment community who later sold their Equity Funding stock.

Decision: Judgment for Dirks. Secrist, the insider, did not violate any fiduciary duty to shareholders when he disclosed information about the fraudulent practices to the tippee, Dirks. Secrist received no monetary or personal benefit for the information but was motivated by the desire to expose the fraud. Because the insider did not breach his fiduciary duty when he gave nonpublic information to Dirks, Dirks breached no duty when he passed the information on to investors. [*Dirks v SEC, 463 US 646 (1983)*]

(b) Misappropriators. Individuals who misappropriate or steal valuable nonpublic information in breach of a fiduciary duty to their employer and trade in securities on that information are guilty of insider trading as "misappropriators."[23]

For example, an employee working for a financial printing firm was found guilty of insider trading under section 10(b) and Rule 10b-5.[24] While proofreading a financial document being prepared for a client firm, he figured out the identity of tender offer targets. Soon after that, he traded on this valuable nonpublic information to his advantage.

It is no defense to a section 10(b) and Rule 10b-5 criminal charge of participating in a "scheme to defraud" that the victim of the fraud (an employer) had no economic interest in the securities traded. The convictions of a stockbroker and a columnist for the *Wall Street Journal* were upheld under section 10(b) of the 1934 act. The columnist violated his fiduciary duty to his employer by revealing prepublication information about his column to the stockbroker. The stockbroker then used the information to trade in the securities identified in the column.[25]

Where an individual misappropriates confidential information for security trading purposes in breach of a fiduciary duty owed to the source of the information rather than to the shareholders who sold securities to the individual, that individual may be convicted of security fraud in violation of section 10(b) and Rule 10b-5.

---

[23] *United States v Willis,* 737 F Supp 269 (SDNY 1990).
[24] *SEC v Materia,* 745 F2d 197 (2d Cir 1984).
[25] *Carpenter v United States,* 484 US 19 (1987).

CASE SUMMARY

The Case of the Dastardly Misappropriator

Facts: James O'Hagan was a partner in the law firm of Dorsey & Whitney in Minneapolis, Minnesota. In July 1988, Grand Metropolitan PLC, a company based in London, England, retained Dorsey & Whitney as local counsel to represent Grand Met regarding a potential tender offer for the common stock of the Pillsbury Company, headquartered in Minneapolis. O'Hagan did no work on the Grand Met representation. Dorsey & Whitney withdrew from representing Grand Met on September 9, 1988. Less than a month later, on October 4, 1988, Grand Met publicly announced its tender offer for Pillsbury stock. Previously, on August 18, 1988, while Dorsey & Whitney was still representing Grand Met, O'Hagan began purchasing call options for Pillsbury stock. Each option gave him the right to purchase 100 shares of Pillsbury stock by a specified date in September 1988. Later in August and September O'Hagan purchased additional Pillsbury call options. By the end of September he owned 2,500 unexpired Pillsbury options, apparently more than any other individual investor. O'Hagan also purchased, in September 1988, some 5,000 shares of Pillsbury common stock, at a price just under $39 per share. When Grand Met announced its tender offer in October, the price of Pillsbury stock rose to nearly $60 per share. O'Hagan then sold his Pillsbury call options and common stock, making a profit of more than $4.3 million. O'Hagan was charged and convicted of securities fraud in violation of section 10(b) and Rule 10b-5. On appeal he claimed that he was not a "misappropriator," for he had no fiduciary duty to the Pillsbury shareholders from whom he purchased calls and stock; in fact, he had not even worked on the transaction at the law firm.

Decision: Judgment against O'Hagan. "Misappropriation" requires that there be "deceptive" conduct "in connection with" a securities transaction. A fiduciary who pretends loyalty to the principal while secretly converting the principal's information for personal gain dupes or defrauds the principal. O'Hagan's failure to disclose his personal trading to his law firm and its client, Grand Met, was a breach of his fiduciary duty and was "deceptive" conduct "in connection with" a securities transaction. The misappropriation theory is designed to protect the integrity of the securities market against "outsiders" like O'Hagan, who have access to confidential information that will affect a company's stock price when revealed but have no fiduciary or other duty to the company's shareholders. [*United States v O'Hagan*, 117 SCt 2199 (1997)]

Investor victims of insider trading may recover damages against the insiders through a civil action based on Rule 10b-5.

(c) Remedy for Investors. Investors who lack the inside information possessed by the insider and sell their stock during the relevant time period may recover damages from any insider who had made use of undisclosed information. Recovery is by a civil action based on Rule 10b-5.

8.   Disclosure of Ownership and Short-swing Profit

Corporate directors and officers owning equity securities in their corporation and any shareholder owning more than 10 percent of any class of the corporation's equity securities must file with the SEC a disclosure statement regarding such ownership. This is required under section 16(a) of the 1934 act.

Section 16 of the 1934 act is designed to prevent insiders from participating in short-term trading of their corporation's stocks.

Section 16 is designed to prevent the unfair use of information available to these corporate insiders. This section prevents insiders from participating in short-term trading in their corporation's securities.

If such a person sells at a profit any of these securities less than six months after their purchase, the profit is called a **short-swing profit**. Under section 16(b), the corporation may sue a director, officer, or major stockholder for a short-swing profit. The corporation may recover that profit even without a fraudulent intent in acquiring and selling the securities.[26]

---

[26] *Synalloy Corp. v Gray*, 816 F Supp 963 (D Del 1993).

9. Tender Offers

A corporation or group of investors may seek to acquire control of another corporation by making a general offer to all shareholders of the target corporation to purchase their shares for cash at a specified price. This is called a **cash tender offer**. The offer to purchase is usually contingent on the tender of a fixed number of shares sufficient to ensure takeover. The bid price is ordinarily higher than the prevailing market price. Should more shares be tendered than the offeror is willing to purchase, the tender offeror must purchase shares from each shareholder on a pro rata basis.

The Williams Act, which amended the 1934 act, is the principal law regulating cash tender offers.

The Williams Act, which amended the 1934 act,[27] was passed to ensure that public shareholders who are confronted with a cash tender offer will not be required to act without adequate information. Under section 14(d) of the Williams Act, a person making a tender offer must file appropriate SEC forms. These forms provide information about the background and identity of the person filing, the source of funds used to make purchases of stock, the amount of stock beneficially owned, the purpose of the purchases, any plan the purchaser proposes to follow if it gains control over the target corporation, and any contracts or understandings that it has with other persons concerning the target corporation.[28]

Section 14(e) of the Williams Act is the antifraud section. It prohibits fraudulent, deceptive, or manipulative practices. SEC Rule 14e-1 requires any tender offer to remain open for a minimum of 20 business days from the date it is first published or given to security holders. Federal and state legislation, as well as administrative regulation, is aimed at requiring disclosure of information and allowance of a reasonable length of time for consideration of the facts. These requirements are designed to make agreement to takeovers the result of voluntary action based on full knowledge of material facts.

As far as the courts are concerned, takeovers must be regarded with a neutral eye. If there is misrepresentation or other misconduct, the law will interfere. Otherwise, freedom of contract requires that courts not interfere with the judgment of the contracting parties.

10. Regulation of Accountants by the SEC

Accountants have an important role in financial reporting and have exposure to liability under numerous provisions of the 1933 act and under section 10(b) of the 1934 act.

Accountants play a vital role in financial reporting under the federal securities laws administered by the SEC. Sections 1, 12, 17, and 24 of the 1933 act and section 10(b) of the 1934 act are the sections under which accountants may be subject to liability.

The SEC responds to newly developing regulatory needs through its rule-making procedures, as is demonstrated in its disclosure rule on derivatives, which follows. It also regulates professionals who practice before the SEC.

---

[27] PL 90-439, 82 Stat 454, 15 USC §§ 78m(d), (e).

[28] Section 14(d) requires a filing by any person making a tender offer that, if successful, would result in the acquisition of 5 percent of any class of an equity security required to be registered under the 1934 act. Section 13(d) of the act requires disclosure to the issuer, the SEC, and the appropriate stock exchange when a person acquires 5 percent of a class of equity security through stock purchases on exchanges or through private purchases. The person may have acquired the stock for investment purposes and not for control but must still file disclosure forms under section 13(d). See *SEC v Bilzerian*, 814 F Supp 116 (DDC 1993). Section 14(d) applies only to shares to be acquired by tender offer.

(a) SEC Derivative Disclosure Requirement. A derivative investment is one that derives its earnings and value from a contractual agreement that is based on underlying market-risk-sensitive assets, such as commodities, currencies, stocks, bonds, or mutual funds. Because they are contracts based on future commodity prices, conversion rates of currencies, interest rates, or market prices, they may result in big gains or catastrophic losses. Due to losses suffered by numerous publicly traded companies in the mid-1990s as a result of their derivative investments, the SEC has adopted new disclosure requirements on derivatives to be contained in company financial reports. The rule requires accountants to include quantitative and qualitative market risk information, and it requires a description of the accounting policies used to account for derivatives.[29]

(b) Regulation and Discipline. An accountant who prepares any statement, opinion, or other legal paper filed with the SEC with the preparer's consent is deemed to be practicing before the SEC.[30] Because it relies so heavily on accountants, the SEC has promulgated Rule 2(e), which regulates and provides the basis for discipline of accountants, attorneys, and consultants who practice before the SEC. Under Rule 2(e), the SEC may suspend or disbar from practice before it those who are unqualified or unethical or who have violated federal securities laws or SEC rules.[31]

C.   INDUSTRY SELF-REGULATION

To protect the public from unprofessional or negligent conduct of securities salespersons, the securities industry itself has provided means to resolve controversies relating to the sale of securities.

11. Arbitration of Securities Disputes

Member firms of the National Association of Securities Dealers (NASD), a self-regulatory organization, have adopted a code of arbitration that allows customers of NASD members to submit disputes to arbitration. The arbitration rights are contractual and are set forth in writing upon opening an account with a dealer.

Securities firms with seats on the New York Stock Exchange have a similar arbitration code. Parties who have agreed to arbitrate their securities disputes can be compelled to arbitrate rather than sue in courts.[32] Courts are very reluctant to vacate an arbitration award.

---

[29] SEC Release No. 33-7386 (February 1997).
[30] 17 CFR § 201.2e.
[31] Rule 2(e) provides: "Suspension and disbarment. (1) The Commission may deny, temporarily or permanently, the privilege of appearing or practicing before it in any way to any person who is found by the Commission after notice of an opportunity for hearing in the matter (i) not to possess the requisite qualifications to represent others, or (ii) to be lacking in character or integrity or to have engaged in unethical or improper professional conduct, or (iii) to have willfully violated, or willfully aided and abetted, the violation of any provision of the federal securities laws (15 USC § 77a to 80B-20), or the rules and regulations thereunder." 17 CFR § 201.2(e).
[32] *99 Commercial Street, Inc. v Goldberg,* 811 F Supp 900 (SDNY 1992).

CASE SUMMARY

The Sting of Justice—Punitive Damages

Facts: In 1985 petitioners Antonio Mastrobuono, then an assistant professor of medieval literature, and his wife, Diane Mastrobuono, an artist, opened a securities trading account with respondent Shearson Lehman Hutton, Inc. (SLH), by executing Shearson's standard client's agreement form. Respondent Nick DiMinico, a vice president of SLH, managed the Mastrobuonos' account until they closed it. The Mastrobuonos sued SLH for the fraudulent conduct of DiMinico, and the matter was referred to arbitration under NASD rules. A panel of three arbitrators convened hearings in Chicago, Illinois, where the Mastrobuonos lived, and the panel awarded them $115,274 for commissions and $44,053 for margin interest "as satisfaction for their claims." The panel also awarded them $400,000 as punitive damages. SLH refused to pay the punitive damages and was able to get this portion of the award vacated in a federal court action that was affirmed on appeal to the U.S. Court of Appeals for the Seventh Circuit. Under the terms of the customer agreement, the agreement was to be "governed by the laws of the State of New York," and disputes between the broker-dealer and the customer were to be "settled by arbitration" conducted under NASD rules. New York decisional law follows the "*Garrity* rule," which prohibits arbitrators from awarding punitive damages even in cases where courts may award such damages. By contrast, NASD arbitration rules anticipate that arbitrators will award a broad range of relief, including punitive damages. The Supreme Court decided to hear the case because of differing views held by the courts of appeals.

Decision: Judgment for Mastrobuono. NASD's Code of Arbitration Procedure indicated that arbitrators may award "damages and other relief," and a manual provided to NASD arbitrators recognizes that "arbitrators may consider punitive damages as a remedy." The arbitration award should have been fully enforced, including the award for punitive damages. [*Mastrobuono v Shearson Lehman Hutton* 115 SCt 1212 (1995)]

ETHICS & THE LAW

Dan Dorfman is a former *Wall Street Journal* reporter and respected commentator on the financial markets. He is a commentator for CNBC and has written commentaries for *USA Today* and *Money*.

During late 1995 and early 1996, financial press reports revealed that Douglas A. Kass and Dorfman were good friends; Kass is the chief of research and institutional trading at J.W. Charles Securities of Boca Raton, Florida. Dorfman has been a speaker at J.W. Charles's top-producer weekends. He was not paid a fee, but his hotel room and travel expenses for himself and his girlfriend were paid by J.W. Charles. Dorfman recommended several of J.W. Charles's securities in 1994, securities that performed poorly.

CNBC investigated the relationship of the friends and concluded that Dorfman had done nothing wrong, and they supported him and the integrity of his reporting.

Assume that Dorfman has done nothing illegal. Do you see any ethical breaches in his conduct? Did Dorfman create suspicions even if they were unjustified?

Approximately 300 companies are sued by their shareholders each year following drops in their share prices. The suits are based on shareholders' allegations that the drops in share prices were caused by the failure of management in these companies to make adequate disclosures about events and issues affecting the company and its earnings. Because of the expense incurred by companies and their auditors in defending such suits, Congress passed the Private Securities Litigation Reform Act. The act controls who files securities suits, how much can be recovered in such suits, and who holds the burden of proof.

One portion of the Litigation Reform Act places a limit on the number of securities lawsuits any one individual can file within a three-year period. The act has been criticized for the limitations it places on shareholders; however, in hearings on the act, witnesses testified that in some lawsuits, the plaintiffs named in the suit were unaware that the lawsuit had been filed. In some situations, the plaintiffs had purchased stock for the purpose of bringing litigation.

The Litigation Reform Act, passed by a congressional override of a presidential veto, is one of the first federal laws to limit litigation by controlling both the plaintiffs who can file and the amount of recovery.

For more information on investors and disputes visit SEC Law at http://www.seclaw.com

SUMMARY

State blue sky laws, which apply only to intrastate transactions, protect the public from the sale of fraudulent securities. The term security is defined sufficiently broadly to encompass not only stocks and bonds but also any conceivable kind of corporate interest that has investment characteristics. There are two principal laws providing the basic framework for federal regulation of the sale of securities in interstate commerce. The Securities Act of 1933 deals with the issue or original distribution of securities by issuing corporations. The Securities Exchange Act of 1934 regulates the secondary distribution or sale of securities on exchanges. These acts are administered by the Securities and Exchange Commission. Except for certain private and limited offerings, the 1933 act requires that a registration statement be filed with the SEC and that a prospectus be provided to each potential purchaser. Criminal and civil penalties exist for fraudulent statements made in this process. The 1934 act provides reporting requirements for companies whose securities are listed on a national exchange and unlisted companies that have assets in excess of $3 million and 500 or more shareholders. Rule 10b-5 is the principal antifraud rule under the 1934 act. Trading on "inside information" is unlawful and may subject those involved to a civil penalty of three times the profit made on the improperly disclosed information. Cash tender offers are regulated by the SEC under authority of the Williams Act. The securities industry provides arbitration procedures to resolve disputes between customers and firms.

QUESTIONS AND CASE PROBLEMS

1. What social forces are affected by the rule of law that prohibits corporate insiders from making a short-term sale of their company's stock?

2. What is the major distinction between the Securities Act of 1933 and the Securities Exchange Act of 1934?

3. On what rationale does the SEC allow for the private placement of securities with accredited investors without any limitation on the amount that may be raised?

4. Minnesota Prostate Research Labs Inc. (MPRL) made an inital public offering of its shares in August 1993. It stated in its prospectus that research on laboratory animals indicated that the lab may have discovered a cure for prostate cancer in humans. MPRL pointed out as well that results in animal testing did not necessarily mean that the same positive result would occur in humans. MPRL shares initially traded at $10 per share in 1994 and rose to $18 in August 1996, when the MPRL prostate cancer drug was finally approved for sale to the public. Tuttle reviewed the initial prospectus and analysts' reports on the drug and purchased 10,000 shares at $18 per share on August 18, 1996. In September of 1997 an independent study of the four leading prostate medicines indicated that MPRL's

product was as effective as sugar pills in curing prostate cancer and other prostate symptoms. The price of MPRL shares plummeted to $6 per share. Tuttle is contemplating a Rule 10b-5 securities fraud class-action lawsuit against MPRL. Advise him of his chances of success in this lawsuit and any expenses that he would be exposed to other than the cost of his attorney.

5. The following transactions in Heritage Cosmetics Co., Inc., stock took place: On January 21, Jones, the corporation's vice president of marketing, purchased 1,000 shares of stock at $25 per share. On January 24, Sylvan, a local banker and director of Heritage, purchased 500 shares of stock at $26 per share. On January 30, McCarthy, a secretary at Heritage, purchased 300 shares of stock at $26½. On February 12, Winfried, a rich investor from New England, purchased 25,000 shares at an average price of $26 per share. At that time, Heritage had a total of 200,000 shares of stock outstanding. On June 14, Winfried sold his entire holding in Heritage at an average price of $35 per share. In a local newspaper interview, Winfried was quoted regarding his reasons for selling the stock: "I have not had the pleasure of meeting any person from Heritage, but I have the highest regard for the Heritage Company. . . . I sold my stock simply because the market has gone too high and in my view is due for a correction." After independently reading Winfried's prediction on the stock market, Jones, Sylvan, and McCarthy sold their shares on June 15 for $33 per share. On June 20, Heritage Co. demanded that Jones, Sylvan, McCarthy, and Winfried pay the corporation the profits made on the sale of the stock. Was the corporation correct in making such a demand on each of these people?

6. The Canadian Express Club solicited buyers to purchase shares in a group comprised of shareholders whose money is pooled to purchase lottery tickets in Canada. Total winnings from tickets are split among shareholders, with Canadian Express administering the purchasing, record keeping, and disbursements. The state securities commission claimed that Canadian Express was selling securities on the theory that the lottery ticket purchase agreement was an investment contract. Canadian Express contended that playing the lottery was not an investment of money. Decide. [*Ontario, Inc. v Mays* (Kan App) 780 P2d 1126]

7. Mary Dale worked in the law office of Emory Stone, an attorney practicing securities law. While proofreading Mary's keying of a document relating to the merger of two computer software companies, Emory joked to her, "If I weren't so ethical, I could make a few bucks on this info. Nomac Software stock prices are going to take off when this news hits 'The Street.'" That evening Mary told her friend Rick Needleworth, a stockbroker, what her boss had said. Needleworth bought 500 shares of Nomac Software stock the next day and sold it three days later when the news of the merger was made public. He made a profit of $3,500. Did Dale, Stone, or Needleworth violate any securities law(s) or ethical principles with respect to the profit made by Needleworth?

8. International Advertising Inc. (IA) would like to raise $10 million in new capital to open new offices in eastern Europe. It believes it could raise the capital by selling shares of stock to its directors and executive officers as well as to its bank and a large insurance company whose home office is located near IA's headquarters. Opposition to the financing plan exists because of the trouble, time, and cost involved with registering with the SEC. Advise IA how best to proceed with the registration of the new issue of stock.

9. Dubois sold Hocking a condominium that included an option to participate in a rental pool arrangement. Hocking elected to participate in the arrangement. Under it, the rental pool's agent rented condominiums, pooled the income, and, after deducting a management fee, distributed the income to the owners on a pro rata basis. Hocking brought a Rule 10b-5 fraud action against Dubois. Dubois contended that the sale of the condominium was not a security under the securities acts, so Hocking could not bring a securities suit against her. Was Dubois correct? [*Hocking v Dubois*, 839 F2d 290 (9th Cir)]

10. William Rubin, president of Tri-State Mining Co., sought a loan from Bankers Trust Co. To secure the loan, he pledged worthless stock in six companies and represented that the stock was worth $1.7 million. He also arranged for fictitious quotations to appear in an investment reporting service used by the bank to value the pledged securities. The bank loaned Rubin $475,000 and took the securities as pledged collateral. In a criminal action against Rubin under section 17(a) of the 1933 act, Rubin's defense was that the pledging of securities did not constitute an offer or sale of securities under the act. Was Rubin correct? [*Rubin v United States*, 449 US 424]

11. J.C. Cowdin, a director of Curtis-Wright Co., phoned Robert Gintel, a partner of Cady, Roberts & Co., a stock brokerage house, and advised him that Curtis-Wright's quarterly dividend had been cut. Gintel immediately entered orders selling Curtis-Wright shares for his customers' accounts. The stock was selling at over $40 a share when the orders were executed but fell to $30 soon after the dividend cut was

announced to the public. The SEC contended that the firm, Cady, Roberts & Co., and Gintel violated section 10(b) of the 1934 act, Rule 10b-5, and section 17(a) of the 1933 act. Gintel and Cady, Roberts & Co. disagreed. Decide. *In re* Cady, Roberts & Co., 40 SEC 907]

12. The Baileys bought shares in a real estate limited partnership from Blarney Castle, Ltd., in reliance on false representations by Joan Casey that "Blarney Castle is qualified by the IRS as an IRS-approved tax shelter" and that "Blarney Castle will return your investment plus a profit in a reasonable period of time . . . it is a secure investment, a sure thing." The offering memorandum Casey provided to the Baileys stated that Blarney Castle limited partnership interests were a risky investment, the IRS had not approved and would probably challenge some of the deductions, and buyers should not rely on oral descriptions of this security. The Baileys did not read this document before investing. The limited partnership went into bankruptcy, and the Baileys sued Casey for making material misrepresentations in violation of section 12(2) of the 1933 act. Casey argued that her statements were innocuous "puffery" or mere statements of opinion and were not actionable. Casey asserted that the Baileys are bound by the offering memorandum, which fully informed the Baileys of all relevant facts. Decide.

13. Douglas Hansen, Leo Borrell, and Bobby Lawrence were three psychiatrists who recognized the need for an inpatient treatment facility for adolescents and children in their community. They became limited partners in the building of a for-profit psychiatric facility. Each had a 6.25 percent interest in the partnership. Healthcare International Inc., the general partner with a 75 percent interest, had expertise in hospital construction, management, and operation. Hansen, Borrell, and Lawrence asserted that the managerial control of the partnership was undertaken and operated by the general partner to the exclusion of the limited partners. The doctors claimed that their interest was a security—"an investment contract"—so as to give them status to file a securities suit against the general partner under the 1934 act. The general partner disagreed. Decide. [*L & B Hospital Ventures Inc. v Healthcare International Inc.*, 894 F2d 150 (5th Cir)]

14. Texas International Speedway, Inc. (TIS), filed a registration statement and prospectus with the Securities and Exchange Commission offering a total of $4,398,900 in securities to the public. The proceeds of the sale were to be used to finance the construction of an automobile speedway. The entire issue was sold on the offering date. TIS did not meet with success, and the corporation filed a petition for bankruptcy. Huddleston and Bradley instituted a class action in U.S. district court on behalf of themselves and other purchasers of TIS securities. Their complaint alleged violations of section 10(b) of the 1934 act. The plaintiffs sued most of the participants in the offering, including the accounting firm of Herman & MacLean. Herman & MacLean had issued an opinion concerning certain financial statements and a pro forma balance sheet that were contained in the registration statement and prospectus. The plaintiffs claimed that the defendants had engaged in a fraudulent scheme to misrepresent or conceal material facts regarding the financial condition of TIS, including the costs incurred in building the speedway. Herman & MacLean contended that the case should be dismissed because section 11 of the 1933 act provides an express remedy for a misrepresentation in a registration statement, so an action under section 10(b) of the 1934 act is precluded. Decide. [*Herman & MacLean v Huddleston*, 459 US 375]

15. Melvin J. Ford, president of International Loan Network, Inc. (ILN), promoted ILN's financial enrichment programs to ILN members and prospective members with evangelical fervor at revival-style "President's Night" gatherings. His basic philosophy was this:

> *The movement of money creates wealth. What we believe is that if you organize people and get money moving, it can actually create wealth.*

One ILN program was the Maximum Consideration Program, which, somewhat like a chain letter, provided $5,000 awards to members who sold $3,000 worth of new memberships called PRAs and made a deposit on the purchases of nonresidential real estate. According to Ford, an individual purchasing $16,000 worth of PRAs could receive an award of up to $80,000 because "all of a sudden the velocity of money increases to such a point, the ability to create wealth expands to such a degree, that we could come back and give somebody an award for up to $80,000." The SEC contended that ILN was selling unregistered investment contracts in violation of the 1933 act. ILN disagreed, contending that the program never guaranteed a return and was thus not an investment contract. Decide. Could ILN have provided full disclosure to investors concerning the program in a prospectus if required by the 1933 act? [*SEC v ILN, Inc.*, 968 F2d 1304 (DC Cir)]

1. Which of the following is **least** likely to be considered a security under the Securities Act of 1933?
   a. Stock options.
   b. Warrants.
   c. General partnership interests.
   d. Limited partnership interests.

   (5/93, Law, #30)

2. When a common stock offering requires registration under the Securities Act of 1933,
   a. The registration statement is automatically effective when filed with the SEC.
   b. The issuer would act unlawfully if it were to sell the common stock without providing the investor with a prospectus.
   c. The SEC will determine the investment value of the common stock before approving the offering.
   d. The issuer may make sales 10 days after filing the registration statement.

   (11/91, Law, #36)

3. Hamilton Corp. is making a $4,500,000 securities offering under Rule 505 of Regulation D of the Securities Act of 1933. Under this regulation, Hamilton is
   a. Required to provide full financial information to accredited investors only.
   b. Allowed to make the offering through a general solicitation.
   c. Limited to selling to **no** more than 35 nonaccredited investors.
   d. Allowed to sell to an unlimited number of investors both accredited and nonaccredited.

   (11/90, Law, #44)

Management of Corporations

CHAPTER 49

OBJECTIVES

After studying this chapter, you should be able to

1. *State the requirements with respect to meetings of shareholders and directors;*
2. *Define and illustrate the liability of corporate officers and directors to the corporation;*
3. *Define and illustrate the liability of corporate officers and directors to third persons;*
4. *State the criminal liability of officers and directors of a corporation; and*
5. *State when an officer, director, or employee of a corporation may obtain indemnification from the corporation.*

937

A corporation is managed, directly or indirectly, by its shareholders, board of directors, and officers.

A.   SHAREHOLDERS

As owners, the shareholders have the right to control the corporation.

1.   Extent of Management Control by Shareholders

As a practical matter, control of the shareholders is generally limited to voting at shareholders' meetings to elect directors. In this sense, shareholders indirectly determine the management policies of the business. At shareholders' meetings, they may also vote to amend bylaws, approve shareholder resolutions, or vote on so-called extraordinary corporate matters. Extraordinary matters include the sale of corporate assets outside the regular course of the corporation's business or the merger or dissolution of the corporation.

2.   Meetings of Shareholders

To have legal effect, action by the shareholders must ordinarily be taken at a regular or special meeting.

> Shareholder action is effective only if taken at a properly called regular or special meeting, with a quorum of shareholders present and a majority of those present voting in the affirmative.

(a) Regular Meetings. The time and place of regular or stated meetings are usually prescribed by the articles of incorporation or the bylaws. Notice to shareholders of such meetings is ordinarily not required, but it is usually given as a matter of good business practice. Some statutes require that notice be given of all meetings.

(b) Special Meetings. Generally, notice must be given specifying the subject matter of special meetings. Unless otherwise prescribed, special meetings are called by the directors. It is sometimes provided that a special meeting may be called by a certain percentage of shareholders.[1] Notice of the day, hour, and place of a special meeting must be given to all shareholders. The notice must include a statement of the nature of the business to be transacted, and no other business may be transacted at this meeting.

(c) Quorum. A valid meeting requires the presence of a quorum of the voting shareholders. A **quorum** is the minimum number of persons (shareholders or persons authorized to vote a stated proportion of the voting stock) required to transact business. If a quorum is present, a majority of those present may act on any matter unless there is an express requirement of a greater affirmative vote.

When a meeting opens with a quorum, the quorum is generally not broken if shareholders leave the meeting and those remaining are not sufficient to constitute a quorum.

---

[1] NY Bus Corp Law § 603.

3. Action without Meeting

A number of statutes provide for corporate action by shareholders without holding a meeting. The Revised Model Business Corporation Act (RMBCA) provides that "action required or permitted by this Act to be taken at a shareholders' meeting may be taken without a meeting if the action is taken by all shareholders entitled to vote on the action."[2] The action must be evidenced by a written consent describing the action taken, signed by all the shareholders entitled to vote on the action, and delivered to the corporation for inclusion in the minutes.

B.   DIRECTORS

The management of a corporation is usually under the control of a board of directors elected by the shareholders. Most states now permit the number of directors to be fixed by the bylaws. Many specify that the board of directors shall consist of not less than three directors; a few authorize one or more.[3] Professional corporation legislation often authorizes or is interpreted as authorizing a one- or two-person board of directors.

4. Qualifications

Eligibility for membership on a board of directors is determined by statute, articles of incorporation, or bylaws. In the absence of a contrary provision, any person (including a nonresident, a minor, or a person who is not a shareholder) is eligible for membership. Bylaws may require that a director own stock in the corporation, although this requirement is not ordinarily imposed.

5. Powers of Directors

The board of directors has authority to manage the corporation. Courts will not interfere with the board's discretion in the absence of (1) illegal conduct or (2) fraud harming the rights of creditors, shareholders, or the corporation.

The board of directors may enter into any contract or transaction necessary to carry out the business for which the corporation was formed. The board may appoint officers and other agents to act for the company, or it may appoint several of its own members as an executive committee to act for the board between board meetings.

Broad delegation of authority may, however, run the risk of being treated as an unlawful abdication of the board's management power.

> **CASE SUMMARY**
>
> ## The Case of Medoff, the Marathon Man
>
> **Facts:** The Boston Athletic Association (BAA) is a nonprofit corporation created to sponsor the annual Boston Marathon. In 1981, the BAA authorized William Cloney, president of the BAA, to negotiate contracts for it. Cloney executed a contract with attorney Marshall Medoff, giving Medoff exclusive power to promote the marathon. The BAA transferred to Medoff all rights to use the marathon name and logos. The contract's financial terms were extremely favorable to

---

[2] RMBCA § 7.04(a).
[3] Del Code § 141(b). *See also* RMBCA § 8.03.

Medoff, who could renew the contract from year to year. When the BAA's board members learned of the contract, they declared that it was beyond the authorization vested in Cloney. The board brought an action to have the contract set aside. Medoff contended that Cloney had authority to make the contract and that therefore the contract bound the corporation.

Decision: Judgment for the BAA. It is the obligation of the board to direct the corporation. Consistent with this obligation, a board may delegate general managerial functions to corporate officers. But certain powers cannot be delegated. The contract made with Medoff surrendered virtually complete control of the marathon to Medoff. The board in this case improperly delegated to Cloney the authority to make such a contract, which prevented accomplishment of the BAA's corporate purpose, that of sponsoring the marathon. Authority to make such a contract was beyond the power of the board to delegate. *[Boston Athletic Association v International Marathon, Inc., 392 Mass 356, 467 NE2d 58 (1984)]*

6. Conflict of Interest

C-P-A

The conflict of interest of a director does not impair the transaction if there is disclosure and the transaction is fair and reasonable.

A director is disqualified from taking part in corporate action involving a matter in which the director has an undisclosed conflicting interest. Because it cannot be known how the other directors would have acted if they had known of the conflict of interest, the corporation generally may avoid any transaction because of a director's secret disqualification.

A number of states provide by statute that a director's conflict of interest does not impair the transaction or contract entered into or authorized by the board of directors if the disqualified director disclosed the interest and if the contract or transaction is fair and reasonable with respect to the corporation. Thus, a director may lend money to a corporation if the board of directors is informed of the transaction and the terms approximate the market rate for businesses with similar credit ratings.

FIGURE 49-1
Powers of Directors

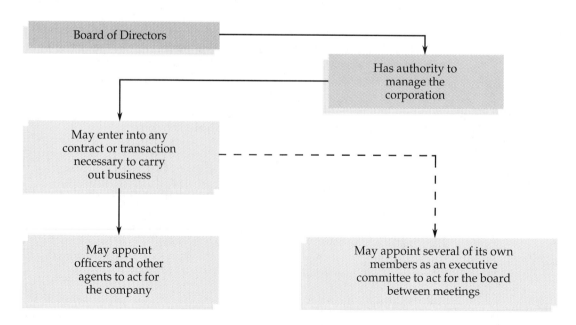

7. Meetings of Directors

Action by directors is ordinarily taken at a meeting of the board of directors. Bylaws sometimes require the meeting to be held at a particular place. Most states expressly provide that the directors may meet either in or out of the state of incorporation. Directors who participate without objection in a meeting irregularly held at a place or time other than as specified in the bylaws cannot object later. Generally, a director is not allowed to vote by proxy.

Most states permit action to be taken by the board of directors without the holding of an actual meeting. It is required when such action is taken that it be set forth in writing and signed by all the directors.

8. Liability of Directors

In dealing with the corporation, the directors act in a fiduciary capacity. It is to their care that the stockholders have entrusted the control of the corporate property and the management of the business.

(a) The Business Judgment Rule. Courts recognize that the decisions of corporate directors often involve weighing and balancing legal, ethical, commercial, promotional, public relations, and other factors. Accordingly, courts will not sit in judgment on the wisdom of decisions made by directors. If the directors have acted in good faith on the basis of adequate information, courts will not enjoin the course of action taken by the directors.[4] Moreover, even though such action causes loss to the corporation, the directors will not be held personally liable for it. This principle is called the **business judgment rule**.

> Under the business judgment rule, directors are not personally liable for erroneous decisions if such decisions were made
> • on an informed basis,
> • in good faith, and
> • in the honest belief that the action was in the best interest of the corporation.

(1) The Traditional Rule. Courts apply the business judgment rule as a presumption that in making a business decision the directors acted (1) on an informed basis, (2) in good faith, and (3) in the honest belief that the action taken was in the best interest of the corporation. The party challenging the directors' actions has the burden of proving they did not act on an informed basis or in good faith or in the best interest of the corporation.[5]

(2) Application in Corporate Control Transactions. When a corporation receives a takeover bid, the target board of directors may tend to take actions that are in their own interest and not in the interest of the shareholders. Courts have recognized the potential for director self-interest in this situation.

CASE SUMMARY

Directors—Independent Evaluators, Not Pawns

Facts: Jerome Van Gorkom was chairman and chief executive officer of Trans Union Inc. On September 13, Van Gorkom arranged a meeting with Jay Pritzker, a well-known takeover specialist and a social acquaintance, to determine his interest in acquiring Trans Union. On Thursday, September 18, Pritzker made an offer of $55 per share (a price suggested by Van Gorkom). Pritzker wanted a decision to be made by the board no later than Sunday, September 21. On Friday, Van Gorkom called a special meeting of the board of directors for noon the following

---

4 *Lewis v Playboy Enterprises, Inc.* (Ill App) 664 NE2d 133 (1996).
5 *Gaillard Katz v Chevron Corp.* (Ct App) 27 Cal Rptr 2d 681 (1994).

day; no agenda was announced. At the directors' meeting, Van Gorkom made a 20-minute oral analysis of the merger transaction. He showed that the company was having difficulty generating sufficient income to offset its increasingly large investment tax credits. Van Gorkom discussed his meeting with Pritzker and the reasons for the meeting. Copies of the proposed merger agreement were delivered too late to be studied before or during the meeting. No consultants or investment advisors were called on to support the merger price of $55 per share. The merger was approved at the end of the two-hour meeting. Certain shareholders brought a class action suit against the directors, contending that the board's decision was not the product of informed business judgment. The directors responded that their good-faith decision was shielded by the business judgment rule.

Decision: Judgment for the shareholders. Directors cannot claim the protection of the business judgment rule if they have been grossly negligent in exercising their judgment. The directors approved the merger based on a 20-minute oral analysis by the president, Van Gorkom, at a hastily called board meeting with no prior notice of its purpose. No investment consultants or other experts were employed to assess the intrinsic value of the company, nor were the merger documents containing the terms of the merger available for study by the directors. Deciding to sell the company without any information and deliberation was gross negligence. The directors therefore could not claim the protection of the business judgment rule when they voted to "sell" the company for $55 per share. The directors are personally liable for damages. [Smith v Van Gorkom (Del) 488 A2d 858 (1985)]

(3) Protection of Directors. In the wake of court decisions holding directors personally liable for damages for gross negligence and in the wake of the resulting general reluctance of individuals to serve as directors, states have passed statutes to protect directors. The aim of the various state laws is essentially the same: to reduce the risk of personal liability for directors who act in good faith when their decisions are challenged. The laws permit a corporation, by a stockholder-approved amendment to its charter or certificate of incorporation, to protect its directors from monetary liability for duty-of-care violations (gross negligence) provided they have not acted in bad faith, breached their duty of loyalty, or gained an improper personal benefit.[6] The laws provide for indemnification and advancement of expenses.

For example, to avoid supervision by the Office of Thrift Supervision (OTS), the directors of Oak Tree Savings Bank, a subsidiary of Landmark Land Co., Inc., which had loaned subsidiary land development companies $986 million, placed the bank in bankruptcy. Because of this, director Bernard Ille resigned. In civil proceedings brought against all of the bank directors, Ille successfully defended himself against the OTS charges. He thus would be entitled to mandatory indemnification from the bank. In addition, employees Trapani and Braun, who were subpoenaed and deposed under adversarial circumstances but were not charged, were deemed to have succeeded on the merits in their defense and were entitled to mandatory indemnification for legal expenses under state law. The other directors and employees charged were found not to have acted in good faith and were not entitled to indemnification.[7]

---

[6] See Del Code § 102(b)(7) (1987); NY Bus Corp Law §§ 721–723 (1987); Ohio Gen Corp Law § 1701.59 (1986); Ind Bus Corp Law, ch 35, § 1(e) (1986); Mo Gen Bus Corp Law 351.355 §§ 2, 7.
[7] *In re* Landmark Land Co. of California, 76 F3d 553 (4th Cir 1996).

(b) Action against Director. Actions against directors should be brought by the corporation. If the corporation fails to act, as is the case when the directors alleged to be liable control the corporation, shareholders may bring the action in a representative capacity for the corporation.

(c) Removal of Director. Ordinarily, directors are removed by vote of the shareholders. In some states, the board of directors may remove a director and elect a successor on the ground that the removed director (1) did not accept office; (2) failed to satisfy the qualifications for office; (3) was continually absent from the state without a leave of absence granted by the board, generally for a period of six months or more; (4) was discharged in bankruptcy; (5) was convicted of a felony; (6) was unable to perform the duties of director because of any illness or disability, generally for a period of six months or more; or (7) has been judicially declared of unsound mind.[8]

The RMBCA provides for removal of directors "with or without cause" by a majority vote of the shareholders unless the articles of incorporation provide that directors may be removed only for cause.[9] Directors may always be voted out of office at a regular meeting of shareholders held for the election of directors.

C.   OFFICERS, AGENTS, AND EMPLOYEES

Corporations generally have a president, at least one vice president, a secretary, a treasurer, and frequently a chief executive officer (CEO). The duties of these officers are generally set forth in the corporation's bylaws. The duty of the secretary to keep minutes of the proceedings of shareholders and directors is commonly included. Corporation codes generally expressly permit the same person to be both secretary and treasurer. In larger corporations, there is often a recording secretary and a corresponding secretary.

Sometimes the officers are elected by the shareholders, but usually they are appointed by the board of directors. The RMBCA follows the general pattern of providing for the appointment of officers by the board of directors.[10] Ordinarily, no particular formality is required to make such appointments. Unless prohibited, a director may hold an executive office.

Officers ordinarily hire the employees and agents of the corporation.

9. Powers of Officers

The officers of a corporation are its agents. Consequently, their powers are controlled by the laws of agency.[11] As in the case of any other agency, a third person has the burden of proving that a particular officer had the authority he or she purported to have.

The fact that the officer or employee acting on behalf of the corporation is a major shareholder does not give either any greater agency powers. Moreover, the person dealing with the officer or employee is charged with knowledge of any limitation on authority contained in the recorded corporate charter or articles of incorporation.

---

[8] See California Corp Code § 807, recognizing grounds (1), (2), (5), and (7).
[9] RMBCA § 8.08(a).
[10] RMBCA § 8.40(a).
[11] *IFC Credit Corp. v Nuova Pasta Co.*, 815 F Supp 268 (ND Ill 1993).

When the nature of the transaction is unusual, that unusual nature should alert a third person to the necessity of specific authorization from the corporation.

A president does not have authority to do anything that requires action by the board of directors, such as all unusual transactions.

(a) President. It is sometimes held that, in the absence of some limitation on authority, the president of a corporation has by virtue of that office the authority to act as agent on behalf of the corporation within the scope of the business in which the corporation is empowered to engage. It has also been held, however, that the president has such broad powers only when the president is the general manager of the corporation. In instances in which a corporation has a president and chief executive officer, the CEO has authority to exercise personal judgment and discretion in the administrative and executive functions of the corporation as endowed by its bylaws and the resolutions of the board of directors. Where a corporation has both a CEO and a president, the CEO is ordinarily the officer entrusted with the broader decisional powers, whereas the president is the executing officer. The president does not have authority by virtue of that office to make a contract that, because of its unusual character, would require action by the board of directors or shareholders.

CASE SUMMARY

Authority and How It Is Used Tells the Story of Most Organizations: Jones Rode Roughshod over Muleshoe Water

Facts: Springer Jones, the president of Muleshoe Water Co. Inc., settled litigation with the Wheatland Irrigation District by selling it Muleshoe's land situated under a reservoir operated by Wheatland. A May 30, 1983 resolution adopted by Muleshoe's board of directors authorized Jones to "initiate such legal action, on behalf of the Company, as he in his sole and absolute discretion deemed necessary, against Wheatland Irrigation District. . . ." Pat Bowen and other minority shareholders brought a derivative action against Jones. Bowen contended that Jones had no authority to settle the case and that by state law the sale of land could not be made without a two-thirds majority vote of the shareholders because the land was substantially all of the assets of the corporation. Jones contended that the May 30 resolution gave him authority to make the sale. He also contended that as president he had authority to make the sale.

Decision: Judgment against Jones. The May 30 resolution authorized President Jones to commence such legal action as he deemed necessary. The resolution did not grant Jones authority to settle the legal action for any amount and in any manner he chose. Jones also lacked authority as president to settle the lawsuit by selling the land to Wheatland. *[Squaw Mountain Cattle Co. and Jones v Bowen (Wyo) 804 P2d 1292 (1991)]*

The president cannot make a contract to fix long-term or unusual contracts of employment, release a claim of the corporation, promise that the corporation will later repurchase shares issued to a subscriber, or mortgage a corporate property.[12]

It is ordinarily held that the president of a business corporation is not authorized to execute commercial paper in the name of the corporation. However, the president may do so when authorized by the board of directors to borrow money for the corporation.

---

[12] *Schmidt v Farm Credit Services,* 977 F2d 511 (10th Cir 1992).

(b) Other Officers and Employees. The authority of corporate employees and other officers, such as the secretary or treasurer, is generally limited to the duties of their offices. However, the authority may be extended by the conduct of the corporation in accordance with the general principles governing apparent authority based on the conduct of the principal. An unauthorized act may, of course, be ratified. The authority of the general manager of the corporation is determined by principles of ordinary agency law.

10. Liability Relating to Fiduciary Duties

The relationship of officers to the corporation, like that of directors, is a fiduciary one. Because corporate officers devote all or most of their time to a corporation's business and receive a salary as officers, their fiduciary duties are more extensive than those of directors, who do not work for the corporation on a daily basis and also receive little or no salary.[13] Officers, because of their access to corporate information developed in the pursuit of their daily duties on behalf of the corporation, have an obligation to inform the directors of material information relating to the business. Officers have an obligation to not make any secret financial gain at the expense of the corporation. Because of their level of knowledge of the business, officer-directors have a high fiduciary duty to the corporation.

> An officer may not divert a corporate business opportunity away from the corporation. If this occurs, the corporation may recover lost profits from the officer.

(a) Corporate Opportunities. If an officer diverts a corporate opportunity, the corporation may recover from the officer the profits of which the corporation has been deprived.

CASE SUMMARY

Ruling Wisely and Decently?

Facts: Demoulas Super Markets Inc. (DSM) was owned by brothers George and Telemachus Demoulas, each owning an equal number of shares of stock. From 1964 through May 1971, the company grew from 5 stores to a chain of 14 supermarkets, including 2 stores in New Hampshire. George died suddenly on June 27, 1971, and, at his death, Telemachus assumed control of DSM under the terms of a voting trust. In 1990, George's son Arthur, age 22 and a shareholder of DSM, brought a shareholder derivative action on behalf of DSM, contending that since George's death Telemachus had diverted business opportunities away from DSM into other businesses that were solely owned by Telemachus's branch of the family. The evidence showed that in the 1970s two new corporations were formed and operated supermarkets in New Hampshire; DSM supplied the financing and management, but ownership was held in Telemachus's sister's and daughter's names. By 1986, these stores grew into a single supermarket chain operating under the Market Basket name and entirely owned by members of Telemachus's branch of the family. The trial court judge determined that Telemachus diverted these corporate opportunities from DSM, and the court ordered the transfer back to DSM of the assets and liabilities of the new corporations. In her decision, the judge cited lines from *Ulysses*, by Alfred, Lord Tennyson, in which Ulysses speaks lovingly of his son, Telemachus, expressing the belief that he would rule wisely and decently after his death. Telemachus denied that any acts were improper or gave rise to liability and charged that the judge was not impartial, as evidenced by her quotation from Tennyson's poem.

Decision: Judgment against Telemachus. Judicial bias was not present, and the literary reference was simply the judge's stylistic way of stating the theme of her decision against Telemachus,

---

13 Fletcher Cyc. Corp. § 991 (perm ed 1986). See also *Geller v Allied-Lyons PLC* (Mass App) 674 NE2d 1334 (1997).

based on the facts she had found. Telemachus had a fiduciary duty to DSM. A fiduciary violates his duty of loyalty by advancing the pecuniary interests of a child or a sibling in a manner that would constitute a breach if he had acted for himself. The record is clear that the New Hampshire companies were set up under Telemachus's direction and were independent in name only, with DSM managing and financing them. The return to DSM of the assets and liabilities of the diverted business was the proper remedy. [*Demoulas v Demoulas Super Markets Inc. (Mass) 677 NE2d 159 (1997)*]

An opportunity that would be advantageous to the corporation must first be offered to the corporation before an officer or a director, who owes a fiduciary duty to the corporation, can take advantage of the opportunity. Full disclosure is required. Only if the opportunity is rejected by a majority of disinterested directors may the officer then take advantage of the opportunity. *For example,* when two officers, unknown to the board of directors, purchased in their own names a building that their corporation was negotiating to purchase, they were held liable for usurping this corporate opportunity.[14]

Officers may avail themselves of all opportunities lying outside the field of their duties as officers when business opportunities come to them in an individual capacity.[15]

(b) Secret Profits. Officers are liable to the corporation for secret profits made in connection with, or at the expense of, the business of the corporation.

CASE SUMMARY

Secret Profits—Serious Sanctions

Facts: Richard Grassgreen was executive vice president and then president and chief operating officer of Kinder-Care Inc., the largest proprietary provider of child care in the country. The company was restructured in 1989 and changed its name to the Enstar Group Inc. Between 1985 and 1990, while Grassgreen served as the corporation's investment manager, he invested millions of dollars of company money in junk bond deals with Michael Milken, and he secretly retained some $355,000 in commitment fees. When the corporation discovered this, Grassgreen repaid the corporation. It sued him to recover any compensation paid him over the five-year period during which the secret payments were made, and it sought punitive damages. Grassgreen defended that his conduct caused little, if any, damage to the corporation because the corporation did not lose any money on any of the investments for which he received personal fees.

Decision: Judgment against Grassgreen. The corporation did lose the commitment fees over the five-year period before it was discovered, and only after he was caught did Grassgreen return the fees to the corporation. Clearly the fact that Grassgreen elected to secretly divert the fees to himself was a violation of his fiduciary duty of loyalty to the corporation to act solely for the benefit of the corporation. Under basic agency law, an officer found to have violated the duty of loyalty may be required to forfeit all compensation during the period in question, including salary and bonuses. In this case, because the violations were so flagrant, the court ordered that Grassgreen forfeit all compensation paid him by the corporation during the period, some $5,197,663.30. [*Enstar Group Inc. v Grassgreen, 812 F Supp 1562 (MD Ala 1993)*]

---

[14] *Case v Murdock* (SD) 488 NW2d 885 (1992).
[15] *Hill v Southeastern Floor Covering Co.* (Miss) 596 So 2d 874 (1992).

11. Agents and Employees

The authority, rights, and liabilities of an agent or employee of a corporation are governed by the same rules as those applicable when the principal or employer is a natural person. The authority of corporate employees is also governed by general agency principles.

The fact that a person is acting on behalf of a corporation does not serve as a shield from the liability that would be imposed for acts done on behalf of a natural person.[16]

ETHICS & THE LAW

For the past five years, one of the concerns shareholders and others have raised about corporate officers is their level of compensation. The following figures are some examples of CEO compensation for 1997:

Company	CEO	
Travelers Group	Sanford Weill	$230,725,000
Coca-Cola Co.	Roberto Goizueta	111,832,000
Healthsouth	Richard Scrushy	106,790,000
Occidental Petroleum	Ray Irani	101,505,000
Nabors Industries	Eugene Isenberg	84,547,000
Cadence Design Systems	Joseph Costello	66,842,000
Intel	Andrew Grove	52,214,000

Other CEOs have taken compensation packages that emphasize stock. Lee Iacocca, for example, agreed to take $1 in salary and the right to stock options when he assumed the CEO position at Chrysler.

On gross sales of $2 billion, is $5 million for a CEO's salary out of line? Is it troublesome to shareholders and perhaps employees that downsizing and cost-cutting occur but CEO salaries remain at the same levels or higher? If the board members approve the salaries, aren't they accountable to the shareholders?

D. LIABILITY

Limited liability is a major reason for incorporating. But management is not free from all civil and criminal liability simply because the corporate form is used.

12. Liability of Management to Third Persons

Officers and managers of a corporation are not liable for the economic consequences of their advice for third persons as long as they acted in good faith to advance the interests of the corporation, even if they cause the corporation to refuse to deal with or break its contract with these third persons.

Ordinarily, the management of a corporation (its directors, officers, and executive employees) is not liable to third persons for the effect of their management or advice. The liability of a director or an officer for misconduct may usually be

---

[16] *Smith v NiteLife, Inc.* (Ky) 777 SW2d 912 (1989).

enforced only by the corporation or by shareholders bringing a derivative action on behalf of the corporation. Ordinarily, directors or officers are not liable to a third person for loss caused by the negligent performance of their duties as directors or officers even if, because of such negligence, the corporation is in turn liable to the third person to whom the corporation owed the duty to use care or was under a contract obligation to render a particular service.

However, in those rare cases when a director or an officer has in some way participated in or directed the tortious act, personal liability will attach.

CASE SUMMARY

The Bungled Beach Bungee

Facts: Zack Steinke was killed at an attraction called Beach Bungee near Myrtle Beach, South Carolina, when the ride operator became distracted and failed to stop the cage carrying Zack and an employee when it reached the top. This caused the single cable to snap and resulted in the cage falling 160 feet to the ground. Charles Vereen and Billy Player were corporate shareholders of the attraction along with the operator, Harold Morris. Rather than wait to have a qualified engineer set up the operation, all three hired a shrimp boat mechanic to do the job so they would not lose out on the busy summer season. They relied on a single cable structure and winch that carried a warning that it was not to be used to lift persons. Also they did not have the device inspected as required by state law. Vereen and Player maintain that they were not involved in the accident and are protected from personal liability by the fact that their company was incorporated. From a judgment for Steinke's estate for $12,000,000, Vereen and Player appealed.

Decision: Judgment against Vereen and Player. The finding of personal liability for a corporate officer or director is an unusual and extraordinary event. However, in this case, the three shareholders personally directed the use of a lift system they knew to be dangerous, chose to have the device installed on the cheap by an unqualified shrimp boat mechanic, and did not have the operation inspected by the state. The jury's finding of individual liability against Vereen and Player was fully justified. [Steinke v Beach Bungee Inc., 105 F3d 192 (4th Cir 1997)]

---

13. Criminal Liability

Officers and directors, as well as the corporation itself, may be criminally accountable for business regulatory offenses.

(a) Active Participation. Officers and directors, as in the case of agents, are personally responsible for any crimes committed by them even when they act on behalf of the corporation.[17] At the local level, they may be criminally responsible for violation of ordinances relating to sanitation, safety, and hours of closing.

> Officers and directors are individually criminally liable for their crimes, even if they were acting for the corporation.

At the state level, they may be criminally liable for conducting a business without obtaining necessary licenses or after the corporate certificate of incorporation has been forfeited.

At the federal level, officers and directors may be criminally liable for tax and securities laws violations as well as egregious environmental protection law and worker safety law violations. International transactions may lead to potential

---

[17] *Joy Management Co. v City of Detroit* (Mich App) 455 NW2d 55 (1990).

criminal exposure. Under the Foreign Corrupt Practices Act, it is a crime to make payments or gifts to a foreign officer to obtain business for an American firm. Not only is the American corporation subject to a fine but also the officers and individuals involved are subject to fine and imprisonment.

(b) Liability of Controlling Persons. Officers and directors may be criminally liable under a number of federal and state statutes for failure to prevent the commission of a crime if they are found to be the "responsible corporate officer." These statutes include the Food, Drug and Cosmetic Act; the Federal Hazardous Substances Act; the Occupational Safety and Health Act; the Federal Water Pollution Act; and, at the state level, the California Corporate Criminal Liability Act. *For example,* the president of a national food retail corporation was found to be a controlling person under the "responsible corporate officer" doctrine and was held criminally liable for a violation of the Food, Drug and Cosmetic Act (FDCA) because of his failure to implement measures to prevent rodent contamination at a warehouse, as required by the FDCA.[18] The California Corporate Criminal Liability Act requires managers in control of corporate operations who have knowledge of "serious concealed dangers" to employees or customers to notify the appropriate regulatory authority or be subject to criminal liability.[19]

(c) Liability of the Corporation Itself. A corporation itself may be convicted of a criminal offense if the offense was committed by its agent acting within the scope of the agent's authority.[20] Thus, an incorporated nursing home may be found guilty of criminal recklessness for the neglect of a patient.

Moreover, a corporation itself may be convicted of a crime involving specific intent, such as theft by swindle or forgery, when (1) the agent was acting at least in part in furtherance of the corporation's business interests and (2) corporate management authorized, tolerated, or ratified the criminal activity.

(d) Punishment of Corporations. With the enactment of the Organizational Federal Sentencing Guidelines in 1991, organizations, including corporations, trusts, pension funds, unions, and nonprofit organizations, are subject to greatly increased fines for criminal convictions. However, corporations and other covered organizations that implement an effective compliance program designed to prevent and detect corporate crimes and voluntarily disclose such crimes to the government will be subject to much lower fines under the guidelines.[21] Figure 49-2 provides an outline of a compliance program.

14. Indemnification of Officers, Directors, Employees, and Agents

While performing what they believe to be their duty, officers, directors, employees, and agents of corporations may commit acts for which they are later sued or criminally prosecuted. The RMBCA broadly authorizes the corporation to indemnify these persons if they acted in good faith and in a manner reasonably believed to be in, or not opposed to, the interests of the corporation and had no reason to

---

[18] *United States v Peck,* 421 US 658 (1975).
[19] Cal Penal Code § 387 (West 1993).
[20] *People v Film Recovery Systems, Inc.* (Ill App) 550 NE2d 1090 (1990).
[21] U.S. Sentencing Commission Guidelines Manual §§ 8C2.5(f), 8C2.6 (1991).

FIGURE 49-2
Program for Crime Prevention and Detection

A. Develop and implement a crime prevention and detection program that must be followed by all employees and agents to reduce the prospect of criminal conduct.

B. Establish ongoing educational programs to communicate the requirements and standards of the program.

C. Designate a responsible senior official to be in charge of the program. Encourage employees to report criminal activities without fear of retribution.

D. Implement an auditing program to detect criminal conduct by employees or agents.

E. Should criminal conduct be detected, adjust standards to prevent a recurrence of the conduct.

believe that their conduct was unlawful.[22] In some states, statutory provision is made requiring the corporation to indemnify directors and officers for reasonable expenses incurred by them in defending unwarranted suits brought against them by shareholders.

15. Liability for Corporate Debts

In general, neither officers nor directors are individually liable for the debts of the corporation.

Because the corporation is a separate legal person, debts that it owes are ordinarily the obligations of the corporation only. Consequently, neither directors nor officers are individually liable for corporate debts, even though it may have been their acts that gave rise to the debts.

In some states, liability for corporate debts is imposed on the corporation's officers and directors when the corporation improperly engages in business.

16. Protection of Shareholders

Shareholders may obtain protection from misconduct by management and by the majority of the shareholders. Shareholders may protect themselves by voting at the next annual election for new directors and also for new officers if the latter are elected. Shareholders may take remedial action at a special meeting called for that purpose. Objecting shareholders may bring a legal action when the management misconduct complained of constitutes a legal wrong.[23]

17. Civil Liability of the Corporation

The rules of agency law determine the extent to which the corporation is liable to third persons for breached contracts made or torts committed by employees, officers, directors, or agents.

A corporation is liable to third persons for the acts of its officers, employees, and agents to the same extent that a natural person is liable for the acts of agents and employees. This means that the ordinary rules of agency law determine the extent to which the corporation is liable to a third person for a contract made or a tort committed by management personnel, employees, and agents.

---

[22] Subchapter 8E, added in 1980 and revised in 1994.
[23] *Christner v Anderson, Nietzke & Co.* (Mich) 444 NW2d 779 (1989).

WHAT'S BEHIND THE LAW?

Institutional Investors, Their Demands, Their Power

In 1993, Medical Care America's acquisition of another company caused its stock price to drop from $60 to $22 a share. Executives of Medical Care America (MCA) then received a merger offer but refused to meet and discuss the proposal. After seven shareholders who owned 40 percent of MCA's outstanding stock demanded the offer be considered, this and many other offers were then evaluated, and MCA merged in what some have called a "premature" sale of the company.

The State of Wisconsin Investment Board, a large institutional investor handling the state's retirement and pension funds, was able to halt Kmart's plan to issue "alphabet stock," or shares, tied to Kmart's specialty divisions.

In most states, any shareholder with a 10 percent or greater share of ownership in a company may call a special shareholder meeting. The management of companies will often hold one-on-one meetings with shareholders who own 5 percent or more of a company's stock.

Studies show that institutional investors have the resources, time, and skills necessary to monitor company performance. Their information about the companies in which they own stock is generally more current and in-depth than the public information available to other shareholders. The larger investors provide other investors with the valuable service of monitoring share and company performance. However, these large investors are also able to organize themselves quickly and efficiently and place sufficient pressure on company management to take action that may help them but could also harm the company or other shareholders over the long term.

The law balances the interests of large and small investors by requiring disclosure of ownership, filing of proxy solicitation materials, and notice of acquisition of more shares. This balance allows other investors a full view of the actions of large investors.

For more information on investor and shareholder rights and issues, visit the securities law Web site at http://www.seclaw.com

SUMMARY

Ordinarily, stockholder action is taken at a regular or special meeting of the stockholders. The presence of a quorum of the voting shareholders is required.

Management of a corporation is under the control of a board of directors elected by the shareholders. Courts will not interfere with the board's judgment in the absence of unusual conduct such as fraud. A director is disqualified from taking part in corporate action when the director has a conflict of interest. Action by directors is usually taken at a properly called meeting of the board. Directors act in a fiduciary capacity in dealing with the corporation. Directors who act in good faith and have exercised reasonable care are not liable for losses resulting from their management decisions. Ordinarily, directors are removed by shareholders.

Officers of a corporation, including a CEO, president,

vice president, secretary, and treasurer, are usually selected and removed by the board of directors. Officers are agents of the corporation, and their powers are governed by the law of agency. Their relations with the corporation are fiduciary in nature, and they are liable for any secret profits and for diverting corporate opportunities to their own advantage.

Directors and officers, as in the case of agents generally, are personally responsible for any torts or crimes they commit even if they act on behalf of the corporation. The corporation itself may be prosecuted for crimes and is subject to fines if convicted. The ordinary rules of agency law determine the extent to which a corporation is liable for a contract made or tort committed by a director, officer, corporate agent, or employee.

1. What social forces are affected by the rule that a person dealing with a corporate officer is charged with knowledge of any limitation on the officer's authority contained in the recorded corporate charter?

2. What constitutes a quorum at a meeting of shareholders?

3. The majority shareholder and president of Dunaway Drug Stores, Inc., William B. Dunaway, was structuring and executing the sale of virtually all the corporation's assets to Eckerd Drug Co. While doing this, he negotiated a side noncompete agreement, with Eckerd giving him $300,000 plus a company car in exchange for a covenant not to compete for three years. He simultaneously amended two corporate leases with Eckerd, thereby decreasing the value of the corporation's leasehold estates. The asset sale was approved by the board of directors. Minority shareholders brought a derivative action against William Dunaway, claiming breach of his fiduciary duty in negotiating the undisclosed noncompete agreement, which did not require him to perform any service for buyer Eckerd Drug. Did William Dunaway make sufficient disclosure about all of the negotiations of the asset sale to Eckerd Drug? Did William Dunaway violate any fiduciary duty to the corporation? Decide. [*Dunaway v Parker* (Ga App) 453 SE2d 43]

4. Larry Phillips was hired for a two-year period as executive secretary of the Montana Education Association (MEA). Six months later he was fired. He then sued MEA for breach of contract and sued the directors and some of the other employees of MEA on the theory that they had caused MEA to break the contract with him and were therefore guilty of the tort of maliciously interfering with his contract with MEA. The evidence showed that the individual defendants, without malice, had induced the corporation to break the contract with Phillips but that this had been done to further the welfare of the corporation. Was MEA liable for breach of contract? Were the individual defendants shielded from personal liability? [*Phillips v Montana Education Association* (Mont) 610 P2d 154]

5. Christy Pontiac, a corporation, was indicted for theft by swindle and forgery involving a GM cash rebate program. Hesli, a middle-management employee of Christy Pontiac, had forged the cash rebate applications for two cars so that the rebate money was paid to Christy Pontiac instead of to its customers. When confronted by a customer who should have received a rebate, the president of the dealership attempted to negotiate a settlement. The president did not contact GM headquarters until after an investigation was begun by the state attorney general. Christy Pontiac argued that it could not be held responsible for a crime involving specific intent because only natural persons, as opposed to corporations, can form such intent. Decide. [*State v Christy Pontiac-GMC, Inc.* (Minn) 354 NW2d 17]

6. Directors must always own stock of the corporation to ensure they will be attentive to their duties. Appraise this statement.

7. Discuss the power of a corporation president to employ a sales manager and to agree that the manager should be paid a stated amount per year plus a percentage of any increase in the dollar volume of sales that might take place.

8. Thywissen owned 60 percent of Flexbin Corp., and Cron owned 40 percent. When they formed the corporation, Thywissen obtained a right of first refusal on a note, which was taken in his own name. He saw this right as a means of protecting Flexbin Corp. and increasing the value of Flexbin's corporate stock. As a result of poor business, Flexbin Corp. was liquidated. The "right of first refusal" was worth $92,000. Cron expected to receive 40 percent of the proceeds. Thywissen claimed that because the right of first refusal was in his own name, it was a personal right, not a corporate asset. He claimed that he had no legal obligation to Cron, only a "moral obligation" to him. He offered him $7,200. Cron brought suit against Thywissen, claiming that Thywissen had breached his fiduciary duty to him by taking this corporate asset for himself. Decide.

9. Danny Hill, the general manager of Southeastern Floor Covering Co., Inc. (SE), had full authority to run the business. His responsibilities included preparing and submitting bid proposals to general contractors for floor coverings and ceilings on construction projects. Hill prepared and submitted a bid for a job for Chata Construction Co. for asbestos encapsulation, ceramic tile, ceilings, carpets, and vinyl tile flooring. However, because SE was not licensed by the EPA, the asbestos work was withdrawn. In the past, SE had used Larry Barnes's company, which was EPA licensed, to do asbestos work under a subcontract agreement. Hill did not pursue a subcontract with Barnes for the Chata job. Rather, Hill and Barnes worked up a bid together and submitted it to Chata for the asbestos work. The bid was accepted, and Hill made $90,000 from the Chata job. Two years later SE found out about Hill's role in the asbestos work done for Chata, and the corporation sued him for the lost profits. Hill argued that SE was not licensed by the

EPA to do asbestos work and thus could not claim a lost corporate opportunity where it was not qualified to do the work. Decide. Are any ethical principles applicable to this case? [*Hill v Southeastern Floor Covering Co.* (Miss) 596 So 2d 874]

10. A director of a corporation cannot lend money to the corporation because that would create the danger of a conflict of interest between the director's status as a director and as a creditor. Appraise this statement.

11. Hamway and other minority shareholders brought an action against majority shareholders of Libbie Rehabilitation Center, Inc., including Frank Giannotti, CEO-director; Alex Grossman, president-director; Henry Miller, vice president-director; Ernest Dervishian, secretary and corporate attorney; and Lewis Cowardin, treasurer-director. The minority shareholders contended that the corporation paid excessive salaries to these director-officers and was wasting corporate assets. Prior to coming to Libbie, Giannotti had been a carpet and tile retailer, Grossman a pharmacist, Miller a real estate developer, Dervishian a lawyer, and Cowardin a jeweler. The evidence showed that the extent of their work for the corporation was very limited. For example, Cowardin, Libbie's finance officer, who was paid $78,121 in 1985, demonstrated no knowledge of the Medicare and Medicaid programs, the principal source of Libbie's income. Although he claimed to have spent 20 to 25 hours a week on corporate duties, he reported on the tax return for his jewelry business that he spent 75 percent of his working time in that business in 1984. One expert witness of the plaintiff's testified that the five men were performing the management functions of one individual. The director-officers contended that the business was making a profit and that all salaries were approved by a board of directors that had extensive business experience. Were the directors within their rights to elect themselves officers and set pay for themselves as they saw fit? Did they violate any legal or ethical duty to their shareholders?

12. Anthony Yee was the president of Waipahu Auto Exchange, a corporation. As part of his corporate duties, he arranged financing for the company. Federal Services Finance Corp. drew 12 checks payable to the order of Waipahu Auto Exchange. These were then indorsed by its president, "Waipahu Auto Exchange, Limited, by Anthony Yee, President," and were cashed at two different banks. Bishop National Bank of Hawaii, on which the checks were drawn, charged its depositor, Federal Services, with the amount of the checks. Federal Services then sued Bishop National Bank to restore to its account the amount of the 12 checks on the ground that Bishop National Bank had improperly made payment on the checks because Anthony Yee had no authority to cash them. Did Yee have authority to indorse and cash the checks? [*Federal Services Finance Corp. v Bishop National Bank of Hawaii*, 190 F2d 442 (9th Cir)]

13. Klinicki and Lundgren incorporated Berlinair, Inc., a closely held Oregon corporation. Lundgren was president and responsible for developing business. Klinicki served as vice president and director responsible for operations and maintenance. Klinicki owned one-third of the stock, and Lundgren controlled the rest. They both met with BFR, a consortium of Berlin travel agents, about contracting to operate some charter flights. After the initial meeting, all contracts with BFR were made by Lundgren, who learned that there was a good chance that the BFR contract would be available. He incorporated Air Berlin Charter Company (ABC) and was its sole owner. He presented BFR with a contract proposal, and it awarded the contract to ABC. Although Lundgren was using Berlinair's working time and facilities, he managed to keep the negotiations a secret from Klinicki. When Klinicki discovered Lundgren's actions, he sued him for usurping a corporate opportunity for Berlinair. Lundgren contended that it was not a usurpation of corporate opportunity because Berlinair did not have the financial ability to undertake the contract with BFR. Decide. Are any ethical principles applicable to this case? Consider the applicability of Chief Justice Cardozo's statement in *Meinhard v Salmon*, 249 NY 458, 164 NE 545 (1928), concerning the level of conduct for fiduciaries: "A trustee is held to something stricter than the morals of the marketplace. Not honesty alone, but the punctillo of an honor the most sensitive, is then the standard of behavior. . . . " [*Klinicki v Lundgren* (Or) 695 P2d 906]

14. Rudolph Redmont, the president of Abbott Thinlite Corp., left Abbott to run Circle Corp. in competition with his former employer. It was claimed that he diverted contracts from his former employer to his new one, having gained the advantage of specific information about the deals in progress while employed by Abbott. Abbott sued Redmont and Circle Corp. to recover lost profits. Redmont contended that all of the contracts in question were made after he left Abbott, at which time his fiduciary duty to Abbott had ceased. Decide. [*Abbott Thinlite Corp. v Redmont*, 475 F2d 85 (2d Cir)]

15. William Gurtler was president and a board member of Unichem Corp., which produced and sold chemical laundry products. While president of Unichem, he encouraged his plant manager to leave to join a rival business, which Gurtler was going to join in the near

future. Moreover, Gurtler sold Unichem products to his son, G. B. Gurtler, in January 1982 at a figure substantially below their normal price and on credit even though G. B. had no credit history. Gurtler made the sales with full knowledge that G. B. was going to start a rival business. Also at that time, Gurtler was aware that his wife was soliciting Unichem employees to join the new Gurtler Chemical Co., and he helped her design Gurtler's label so that it would look like Unichem's. On February 9, 1982, Gurtler guaranteed a $100,000 loan for Gurtler Chemical Co. with funds to be disbursed after he left Unichem, which occurred on March 12, 1982. On March 15, 1982, he became president of Gurtler Chemical Co. Unichem sued Gurtler for breach of fiduciary duty and for the loss of profits that resulted. Gurtler contended that his sales to G. B. guaranteed needed revenue to Unichem and constituted a sound business decision that should be applauded and that was protected under the business judgment rule. Decide. Are any ethical principles applicable to this case? [*Unichem Corp. v Gurtler* (Ill App) 498 NE2d 724]

CPA QUESTIONS

1. Davis, a director of Active Corp., is entitled to
   a. Serve on the board of a competing business.
   b. Take sole advantage of a business opportunity that would benefit Active.
   c. Rely on information provided by a corporate officer.
   d. Unilaterally grant a corporate loan to one of Active's shareholders.

   (5/91, Law, #5)

2. Absent a specific provision in its articles of incorporation, a corporation's board of directors has the power to do all of the following, **except**
   a. Repeal the bylaws.
   b. Declare dividends.
   c. Fix compensation of directors.
   d. Amend the articles of incorporation.

   (5/90, Law, #7)

3. Which of the following statements is correct regarding fiduciary duty?
   a. A director's fiduciary duty to the corporation may be discharged by merely disclosing his self-interest.
   b. A director owes a fiduciary duty to the shareholders but **not** to the corporation.
   c. A promoter of a corporation to be formed owes no fiduciary duty to anyone, unless the contract engaging the promoter so provides.
   d. A majority shareholder as such may owe a fiduciary duty to fellow shareholders.

   (5/85, Law, #12)

P A R T 9

Real Property and Estates

Real Property

CHAPTER 50

G.   MORTGAGES

25. Characteristics of a Mortgage
26. Property Subject to Mortgage
27. Form of Mortgage
28. Creative Forms of Financing
29. Recording or Filing of Mortgage
30. Responsibilities of the Parties
31. Transfer of Interest
32. Rights of Mortgagee after Default
33. Rights of Mortgagor after Default

OBJECTIVES

After studying this chapter, you should be able to

1. *List the kinds of real property;*
2. *Distinguish among liens, licenses, and easements;*
3. *List and illustrate the forms of co-ownership of real property;*
4. *Define a deed and describe its operation;*
5. *Describe and illustrate the warranties of the grantor and the grantee of real estate; and*
6. *Describe the characteristics and effect of a mortgage.*

The law of real property is technical and to a large extent uses a vocabulary drawn from the days of feudalism. Much of the earlier law of real property is no longer of practical importance in the modern business world. This chapter focuses on a modified and simplified presentation of the law of real property.

A.   NATURE OF REAL PROPERTY

Real property is land and what is above it, below it, and on it.

Real property has special characteristics of permanence and uniqueness. These characteristics have strongly influenced the rules that society has developed to resolve disputes concerning real property.

1.   Land

Land means more than the surface of the earth. It comprises the soil and all things of a permanent nature affixed to the ground, such as herbs, grass, or trees and other growing, natural products. The term also includes the waters on the ground and things that are embedded beneath the surface.

Technically land extends downward to the earth's center and upward indefinitely. The general view is that the owner of the land owns the space above that land subject to the right of flying aircraft that do not interfere with the use of the land and are not dangerous to persons or property lawfully on the land.

Easement is the right of use of another's land; it can be a means of ingress and egress.

2.   Easements

An **easement** is the right to use another's property, such as the right to cross another's land. Rights in another person's land also include profits. The easement belongs to the land that is benefitted. The benefitted land is called the **dominant tenement**, and the land that is subject to the easement is called the **servient tenement**.[1]

(a) Creation of Easement. Because an easement is an interest in land, an oral promise to create an easement is not binding because of the statute of frauds. An easement created by agreement is transferred by deed. However, an easement may also be created by implication. An **easement by implication** arises when one conveys part of the land that has been used as a dominant estate in relation to the part retained. *For example*, if water pipes or drain pipes run from the part of the land conveyed through the part retained, there is an implied right to continue using the pipes. In order for an easement to be implied, the use, as in this case with the pipes, must be apparent, continuous, and reasonably necessary.

An easement may also be created by implication when the easement is necessary to the use of the land conveyed. This situation occurs when one subdivides land and sells a portion to which no entry can be made except over the land retained or over the land of a stranger. The grantee's right to use the land retained by the grantor for the purpose of going to and from the land conveyed is known as a **way of necessity**.

An easement may be created by **estoppel**, such as when the grantor conveys a plot of land bounded by what the deed describes as a street. In such a case, if the grantor owns the adjoining land, the public cannot be denied the right to use the area for access to the street.

An easement may be created by **prescription**. Under prescription, a person acquires an easement by adverse use, or use contrary to the landowner's use, for a statutory period. No easement is acquired by prescription if the use of the land is with the permission of the owner. The adverse use by which an easement is acquired is similar to the adverse possession by which title is acquired, discussed later in this chapter.

(b) Termination of Easement. Once an easement has been granted, it cannot be destroyed by the act of the grantor. A "revocation" attempted without the easement owner's consent has no effect.

An easement may be lost by nonuse when surrounding circumstances show an intent to abandon the easement.[2] *For example*, when a surface transit system had an easement to maintain trolley tracks, it could be found that there was an abandonment of the easement when the tracks were removed and when all surface transportation was discontinued. Likewise, when the owner of the easement planted a flower bed on the land across the end of the path of the easement, the intent to abandon the easement was evident.

3. Profits

Profits are rights to take part of the soil or produce of the land belonging to another. *For example*, profits include the right to remove coal from the land of another and the right to use the water from another's land.

Dominant tenement is the tract of land that enjoys the benefit of an easement.

Servient tenement is the tract of land subject to an easement.

Easement by implication is an easement not specifically created by deed that arises from the circumstances of the parties and the land location and access.

Easement by estoppel is an easement that arises when there is no land interest but there is reliance on access prior to the transfer of land without the necessary easement for access.

Easement by prescription is an easement acquired through use of the easement for the statutory period of time required for adverse possession.

Profit is the right to remove something from another's land, such as the right to remove timber.

---

1 *Tipperman v Tsiatos* (Or App) 915 P2d 446 (1996).
2 *Louis W. Espstein Family Partnership v Kmart Corp.*, 13 F3d 762 (3d Cir 1993).

4. Licenses

A **license** is a personal, revocable privilege to perform an act or series of acts on the land of another. Unlike an easement, a license is not an interest in land. ◆ *For example*, the person allowed to come into the house to use the telephone has a license. The advertising company that has permission to paint a sign on the side of a building also has a license. ◆

A license may be terminated at the will of the licensor. It continues only as long as the licensor is the owner of the land.

5. Liens

Real property may be subject to **liens** that arise by the voluntary act of the owner of the land. For example, the lien of a mortgage is created when the owner borrows money and uses the land as security for repayment of the debt.

Liens may also arise involuntarily, as in the case of **tax liens**, **judgment liens**, and **mechanics' liens**. In the case of taxes and judgments, the liens provide a means for enforcing the obligations of the owner of the land to pay the taxes or the judgment. Mechanics' liens give persons furnishing labor and materials in the improvement of real estate the right to proceed against the real estate for the collection of the amounts due them.

6. Fixtures

Under the laws relating to fixtures, personal property becomes real property.

(a) Definition. A **fixture** is personal property that is attached to the earth or placed in a building in such a way or under such circumstances that it is considered part of the real property.

A person may buy a refrigerator, an air conditioner, a furnace, or some other item that is used in a building and then have the item installed. The question of whether such an item is a fixture, and therefore part of a building, can arise in a variety of situations: (1) The real estate tax assessor assesses the building and adds in the value of the item on the theory that it is part of the building. (2) The buyer of the item owns and then sells the building, and the new owner of the building claims that the item stays with the building. (3) The buyer places a mortgage on the building, and the mortgagee claims that the item is bound by the mortgage. (4) The buyer is a tenant in the building in which the item is installed, and the landlord claims that the item must stay in the building when the tenant leaves. (5) The buyer does not pay in full for the item, and the seller of the item has a security interest that the seller asserts against the buyer of the item or against the landlord of the building in which the buyer installs the item. The seller of the item may also be asserting a claim against the mortgagee of the building or against the buyer of the building. The determination of the rights of these parties depends on the common law of fixtures, as occasionally modified by statute.

Carolee and Harold Brown purchased a 4,200-square-foot home from Hal and Jeanette Lindstrom. The Lindstrom house had been built eight years ago, and the Browns purchased it for $380,000. Between the time when the purchase contract was signed and the closing of the sale, the Browns had the house appraised. The appraised value of the home was $393,000.

The Browns conducted several walk-through inspections of the Lindstrom home before the closing occurred. The Lindstroms still resided in the house until the date of closing, and all of the Browns' walk-throughs took place with the Lindstroms' furniture, paintings, and other belongings in the house.

After closing, the Browns went to their newly purchased home and discovered that in each place on the carpet where the Lindstroms' furniture had rested, the carpet was a different color. The wall-to-wall carpet was a chocolate brown color, and the spots, formed in the shape of whatever item had been resting there, were a butterscotch color. Even the places where the four legs of the dining room table had rested had spots on the carpet that were the size and shape of the table legs.

The Browns were dismayed and disappointed about the carpet problem. Friends and family who visited immediately raised questions about the curiously spotted carpet. No carpet cleaner was able to remove the spots. The Browns requested compensation for the carpet damage in the amount of $10,000, the cost of replacing the carpet.

The Lindstroms responded, "Look, you got the house at $13,000 below appraisal, so you've been compensated."

Are the Lindstroms correct? Is there any remedy for the Browns? Despite the legal issues, do the Lindstroms have any ethical obligations with respect to the carpeting flaws?

(b) Tests of a Fixture. In the absence of an agreement between the parties, the courts apply three tests to determine whether personal property has become a fixture.

(1) Annexation. Generally, personal property becomes a fixture if it is so attached to the realty that it cannot be removed without materially damaging the real property or destroying the personal property itself. If the property is so affixed as to lose its specific identity, such as bricks in a wall, it becomes part of the realty. When railroad tracks are so placed as to be immovable, they are fixtures.

(2) Adaptation. Personal property especially adapted or suited to the use made of the building may constitute a fixture.

(3) Intent. The true test is the intention of the person affixing the property.[3] Intent is considered as of the time the property was affixed. In the absence of direct proof of such intent, it is necessary to resort to the nature of the property, the method of its attachment, and all the surrounding circumstances to determine the intent.

---

[3] *Hubbard v Hardeman County Bank* (Tenn) 868 SW2d 656 (1993).

The fact that machinery installed in a plant would be very difficult and expensive to move or is so delicate that the moving would cause damage and unbalancing is significant in reaching the conclusion that the owner of the plant had installed the equipment as a permanent addition and thus had the intent to make the equipment fixtures. ◆ *For example*, when the floors in a large apartment house are of concrete covered with a thin sheet of plywood to which wall-to-wall carpeting is stapled, the carpeting constitutes a fixture that cannot be removed from the building. Removal would probably destroy the carpeting because it was cut to size. In addition, the carpeting is necessary to make the building livable as an apartment. ◆

(c) Movable Machinery and Equipment. Machinery and equipment that are movable are ordinarily held not to be fixtures even though, in order to move them, it is necessary to unbolt them from the floor or to disconnect electrical wires or water pipes. ◆ *For example*, it is ordinarily held that refrigerators, freezers, and gas and electric ranges are not fixtures. They do not lose their character as personal property when they are readily removable after disconnecting pipes or unplugging wires. A portable window air conditioner that rests on a rack that is affixed to the window sill by screws and is connected directly to the building only by an electric cord plug is not a fixture. ◆

The mere fact that an item may be unplugged, however, does not establish that it is not a fixture. ◆ *For example*, a computer and its related hardware constitute fixtures when there is such a mass of wires and cables under the floor that the installation gives the impression of permanence. ◆

(d) Trade Fixtures. Equipment that a tenant attaches to a rented building and uses in a trade or business is ordinarily removable by the tenant when the tenant permanently leaves the premises. Such equipment is commonly called a **trade fixture**.[4]

B. NATURE AND FORM OF REAL PROPERTY OWNERSHIP

Fee simple estate is the highest level of land ownership—full interest of unlimited duration.

Life estate is a land interest held only for the life of the grantee.

Freehold is a land interest that is uncertain or unlimited in duration.

A person's interest in real property may be defined in terms of the period of time for which the person will remain the owner, as (1) a **fee simple estate** or (2) a **life estate**. These estates are termed **freehold estates**, which are interests of uncertain duration. At the time of creation of a freehold estate, a termination date is not known. When a person owns property for a specified period of time, this interest is not regarded as a freehold estate; it is a **leasehold estate**, subject to special rules of law.

7. Fee Simple Estate

An estate in fee, a fee simple, or a fee simple absolute lasts forever. The owner of such a land interest held in fee simple has the absolute and entire interest in the land. The important characteristics of this estate are these: (1) It is alienable, or transferable, during life; (2) it is alienable by will; (3) it passes to heirs of the owner if it is not specifically devised (transferred by will); (4) it is subject to rights of the owner's surviving spouse; and (5) it can be attached or used to satisfy debts of the owner before or after death.

---

[4] *Bence v Sanato* (Wis App) 538 NW2d 614 (1995).

Fee simple defeasible is a fee simple interest that can be lost if restrictions on its use are violated.

There are other forms of the fee simple estate generally used for control of land use. **Fee simple defeasibles** are interests that give the grantee all the rights of a fee simple holder provided that the grantee complies with certain restrictions. *For example*, the grant "To Ralph Watkins so long as he uses the property for school purposes" is an example of a fee simple defeasible. Watkins will have all the rights of a fee simple holder provided he uses the property for school purposes. If Watkins ever stops using the property for school purposes, the property reverts back to the grantor.

8. Life Estate

A life estate (or life tenancy), as its name indicates, lasts only during the life of a person (ordinarily its owner). Upon the death of the person by whose life the estate was measured, the owner of the life estate has no interest remaining to pass to heirs or by will. *For example*, a grant of a life estate would be "To my husband, Nathan Jones, for life, and then to my children." Jones would hold title to the property only for the time he is alive. When Jones dies, he cannot give the property away by will. If Jones conveys the property while he is alive, the grantee for the property holds title to the land only until Jones's death.

9. Future Interests

Future interest is a land interest that will vest at some time in the future.

Remainder is the land interest that follows a life estate.

In several of the examples given to illustrate fee simple and life estates, there has been an interest created in more than one person. *For example*, in the life estate example above, the children of the grantor are given an interest in the land at the same time as Jones. However, the interests of the children will not take effect until Jones dies. The children have a **future interest** in the land. Their interest is referred to as a **remainder** interest because they have the remaining interest in the land once the life estate ends.

In the Watkins fee simple defeasible example, the grantor has a future interest if Watkins violates the restriction. The grantor's interest is called a **possibility of reverter**. It is a future interest because it cannot exist unless and until Watkins violates the use restriction placed on his present interest.

C. LIABILITY TO THIRD PERSONS FOR CONDITION OF REAL PROPERTY

Trespasser is one on the property of another without authorization.

Licensee is a holder of a license for access or use of another's real property; can be revoked at any time.

Invitee is a person expressly permitted to enter property of another, e.g., a customer in a retail establishment.

A person entering the land of another may be injured by the condition of the land. Who is liable for such harm?

10. Status-of-Plaintiff Common Law Rule

Under the common law, liability to a person entering onto land was controlled by the status of the injured person—that is, whether the person injured was a . **trespasser**, a **licensee**, or an **invitee**. A different duty was owed by the owner (or occupier, as when a tenant is leasing property) of land to persons in each of these three categories.

(a) Trespassers. For a trespasser, the landowner ordinarily owes only the duty of refraining from causing intentional harm once the presence of the trespasser is known. The landowner is not under any duty to warn of dangers or to make the premises safe to protect the trespasser from harm. The most significant exception to this rule arises in the case of small children. Even when children are trespassers, they are generally afforded greater protection through the **attractive nuisance doctrine**. *For example,* the owner of a tract of land was held liable for the death of a seven-year-old child who drowned in a creek on that land. Snow had covered the ice on the creek, and children running across the land did not know of the creek's location or the danger of the ice. The landowner had a duty to fence the creek, put up warnings, or control the children's access.[5]

Attractive nuisance doctrine is the rule of law that holds landowners liable for injuries to children on their properties even though the children were trespassers and even though the dangers would be obvious to adults.

(b) Licensees. Licensees are on the premises with the permission of the landowner, who owes the duty of warning of nonobvious dangers that are known to the owner. A host must warn a guest of such dangers. *For example,* when a sliding glass door is "invisible" if the patio lights are on and the house lights are off, the owner must warn guests of the presence of the glass. The owner is liable if he has not warned guests of the danger and a guest is injured in shattering the glass. However, the owner owes no duty to the licensee to take any steps to learn of the presence of dangers that are unknown to him or her.

(c) Invitees. Invitees are persons who enter another's land by invitation. The entry is connected with the owner's business or with an activity the occupier conducts on the land. Business customers, for example, are invitees.

Owners have a duty to take reasonable steps to discover any danger and a duty to warn the invitee or to correct the danger. *For example,* a store must make a reasonable inspection of the premises to determine that there is nothing on the floor that would be dangerous, such as a slippery substance that might cause a patron to fall. The store must correct the condition, appropriately rope off the danger area, or give suitable warning. If the owner of the premises fails to conform to the degree of care described and if harm results to an invitee on the premises, the owner is liable for such harm.

In most states, the courts have expanded the concept of invitees beyond the category of those persons whose presence will economically benefit the occupier. Invitees now usually include members of the public who are invited when it is apparent that such persons cannot be reasonably expected to make an inspection of the premises before using them and that they would not be making repairs to correct any dangerous condition. Some courts have also made inroads into the prior law by treating a recurring licensee, such as a letter carrier, as an invitee.

11. Status of Plaintiff—Modern Changes

A number of courts have begun ignoring the common law distinctions among trespassers, licensees, and invitees. These courts hold the owner liable according to ordinary negligence standards. That is, when the owner as a reasonable person should foresee from the circumstances that harm would be caused to a third person, the owner has the duty to take reasonable steps to prevent such harm. This duty exists regardless of whether the potential victim would be traditionally classified as a trespasser, a licensee, or an invitee.

Some courts have taken an intermediate position. They have merely abolished the distinction between licensees and invitees, so that the owner owes the same

---

5 *Pasierb v Hanover Park Park District* (Ill App) 431 NE2d 1218 (1981).

duty of care to all lawful visitors. Whether one is a licensee or an invitee is merely a circumstance to be considered by the jury in applying the ordinary rule of negligence.

12. Recreational Use Statutes

Recreational use statute is a statute that grants immunity to landowners who permit the use of their land by others for recreational purposes without the requirement of the payment of a fee.

Most states have enacted a statute commonly referred to as a **recreational use statute**. Such statutes provide that landowners who allow use of their property for recreational purposes and without charge owe no duty to keep the property safe for entry or use. In addition, no duty is imposed on the landowner to give any warning of a dangerous condition or structure on the property.[6]

D. CO-OWNERSHIP OF REAL PROPERTY

Real property may be owned by one or several persons, and the method of co-ownership determines the extent of the owners' rights.

13. Multiple Ownership

Several persons may have concurrent interests (or interests that exist at the same time) in the same real property. The forms of multiple ownership for real property are the same as those for personal property. Real property can be held by tenants in common, by joint tenants with right of survivorship, by tenants by the entirety, or under community property rights. When co-owners sell property, they hold the proceeds of sale by the same kind of tenancy as that in which they held the original property.

14. Condominiums

Condominium is a form of land ownership in which individuals own a unit within a building.

A **condominium** is a combination of co-ownership and individual ownership. *For example,* persons owning an office building or an apartment house by condominium are co-owners of the land and of the halls, lobby, elevators, stairways, exits, surrounding land, incinerator, laundry rooms, and other areas used in common. Each apartment or office in the building, however, is individually owned and is transferred in the same way as other forms of real property.

(a) Control and Expense. In some states, owners of the various units in the condominium have equal voice in its management and share an equal part of its expenses. In others, control and liability for expenses are shared by a unit owner in the same ratio that the value of the unit bears to the value of the entire condominium project. In all states, unit owners have equal rights to use the common areas. An owners' association is created by the condominium owners to operate the common areas of the condominium property and resolve any disputes among owners.

The owner of each condominium unit makes the repairs required by the owner's deed or contract of ownership. The owner is prohibited from making any major change that would impair or damage the safety or value of an adjoining unit.

---

6 *Monteville v Terrebonne Parish Con. Gov.* (La) 567 So 2d 1097 (1990).

(b) Collection of Expenses from Unit Owner. When a unit owner fails to pay the owner's share of taxes, operating expenses, and repairs, the owners' association generally has the right to a lien against that owner's unit for the amount due.

(c) Tort Liability. Most condominium projects fail to make provision for the liability of unit owners for a tort occurring in the common areas. A few states expressly provide that when a third person is injured in a common area, a suit may be brought only against the condominium association. Any judgment recovered is a charge against the association to be paid off as a common expense. When the condominium association is incorporated, the same result should be obtained by applying ordinary principles of corporation law. Under principles of corporation law, liability for torts occurring on the premises of the corporation would not be the liability of individual shareholders.

> Cooperatives are a form of land ownership in which cooperative owners hold their interest by holding title to shares of stock in the corporation that owns their building.

(d) Cooperatives Distinguished. Ownership in a condominium is to be distinguished from ownership in a **cooperative**. An apartment cooperative is typically a corporation that owns an apartment complex. The persons who live in that complex are also owners of stock of the corporation. The "ownership" interests of the apartment occupants are as stockholders of the corporation.

E.   TRANSFER OF REAL PROPERTY BY DEED

> Deed is an instrument used to convey title to land.

Although many of the technical limitations of the feudal system and earlier common law on transfer of land have disappeared, much of the law relating to the modern deed originated in those days.

> Grantor is the party granting or transferring land to another.

15. Definitions

> Grantee is the party to whom land is granted or transferred.

A **deed** is an instrument or writing by which an owner or **grantor** transfers or conveys an interest in land to a new owner. The new owner is called a **grantee** or **transferee**.

In contrast to the situation with a contract, no consideration is required to make a deed effective. Although consideration is not required to make a deed valid or to transfer title by deed, the absence of consideration may show that the transfer is made by the owner in order to defraud creditors. The creditors may then be able to set aside the fraudulent transfer.

> Quitclaim deed is a deed that conveys title, if any, held by the grantor but that makes no warranties as to the quality of the title.

Real property may be either sold or given as a gift. A deed, however, is necessary to transfer title to land, even if it is a gift.

16. Classification of Deeds

> Warranty deed is a deed that provides the grantee with the highest level of warranty protection: that title is good, that the transfer is proper, and that there are no liens or encumbrances other than those noted.

Deeds may be classified according to the interest conveyed as **quitclaim deeds** or **warranty deeds**. A quitclaim deed merely transfers whatever interest, if any, the grantor may have in the property without specifying that interest in any way. A warranty deed transfers a specified interest and warrants or guarantees that such interest is transferred. Figure 50-1 is a sample warranty deed.

THIS DEED, made the twentieth day of November, nineteen hundred and . . . between James K. Damron, residing at 132 Spring Street in the Borough of Manhattan, City and State of New York, party of the first part, and Terrence S. Bloemker, residing at 14 Steinway Street in the Borough of Queens, City and State of New York, party of the second part,

WITNESSETH, that the party of the first part, in consideration of the sum of one dollar ($1), lawful money of the United States, and other good and valuable consideration paid by the party of the second part, does hereby grant and release unto the party of the second part, his heirs and assigns forever,

ALL that certain lot, piece, and parcel of land situated in the Borough of Manhattan, City and County of New York, and State of New York, and bounded and described as follows:

Beginning at a point on the northerly side of Spring Street, distant two hundred (200) feet westerly from the corner formed by the intersection of the northerly side of Spring Street with the westerly side of 6th Avenue, running thence northerly parallel with 6th Avenue one hundred (100) feet, thence westerly and parallel with said Spring Street one hundred (100) feet; thence southerly, again parallel with said 6th Avenue one hundred (100) feet to the northerly side of Spring Street, and thence easterly along the said northerly side of Spring Street one hundred (100) feet to the point or place of beginning.

Together with the appurtenances and all the estate and rights of the party of the first part in and to said premises.

TO HAVE AND TO HOLD the premises herein granted unto the party of the second part, his heirs and assigns forever.

AND the party of the first part covenants as follows:

First. That the party of the first part is seised of the said premises in fee simple, and has good right to convey the same;

Second. That the party of the second part shall quietly enjoy the said premises;

Third. That the said premises are free from encumbrances except as expressly stated;

Fourth. That the party of the first part will execute or procure any further necessary assurance of the title to said premises;

IN WITNESS WHEREOF, the party of the first part has hereunto set his hand and seal the day and year first above written.

JAMES K. DAMRON (L.S.)

In presence of:

DIANA L. REILMAN

State of New York } s.s.:
County of New York }

On the twentieth day of November in the year nineteen hundred and . . . , before me personally came James K. Damron, to me known and known to me to be the individual described in, and who executed, the foregoing instrument, and he acknowledged that he executed the same.

DIANA L. REILMAN
Notary Public, New York County

[NOTE: ACKNOWLEDGMENT BEFORE A NOTARY PUBLIC IS NOT ESSENTIAL TO THE EFFECTIVENESS OF A DEED, BUT IT IS TYPICALLY REQUIRED TO QUALIFY THE DEED FOR RECORDING.]

FIGURE 50-1
Form of Warranty Deed

17. Execution of Deeds

Ordinarily a deed must be signed, by signature or mark, by the grantor. In order to have the deed recorded, statutes generally require that two or more witnesses sign the deed and that the grantor then acknowledge the deed before a notary public or other officer. In the interest of legibility, the signatures of the parties are followed by their printed or typewritten names. The deed remains binding between the grantor and the grantee even if it has not been acknowledged or recorded.

A deed must be executed and delivered by a person having capacity. It may be set aside by the grantor on the ground of the fraud of the grantee provided that innocent third persons have not acquired rights in the land.

18. Delivery and Acceptance of Deeds

A deed has no effect, and title does not pass, until the deed has been delivered. Delivery is a matter of intent as shown by words and conduct; no particular form of ceremony is required. The essential intent in delivering a deed is not merely that the grantor intends to hand over physical control and possession of the paper on which the deed is written but also that the grantor intends thereby to transfer the ownership of the property described in the deed. That is, the grantor must deliver the deed with the intent that it should take effect as a deed and convey an interest in the property.

A deed is ordinarily made effective by handing it to the grantee with the intention that the grantee should then be the owner of the property described in the deed. A delivery may also be made by placing the deed, addressed to the grantee, in the mail or by giving it to a third person with directions to hand it to the grantee.

An effective delivery of a deed may be made symbolically, or constructively, such as by delivering to the grantee the key to a locked box and informing the grantee that the deed to the property is in the box. ◆ *For example*, the delivery of a safety deposit box key has been held to constitute delivery of a deed that was in the box. ◆

When a deed is delivered to a third person for the purpose of delivery to the grantee upon the happening of some event or contingency, the transaction is called a **delivery in escrow**. No title passes until the fulfillment of the condition or the happening of the event or contingency.

CASE SUMMARY

The Intervening Death and the Daughter's Deed

Facts: John Smith executed a quitclaim deed in favor of his daughter, Connie Sargent. He instructed his attorney, Freedman, not to record the deed, saying he would be back in touch regarding recording. Freedman testified that he would not record the deed without further instructions from Smith. Before his death, Smith asked his nephew Gerald Buscemi to have Freedman record the deed. However, Buscemi did not contact Freedman before Smith's death. Freedman's office mailed the unrecorded deed to Sargent, who recorded it. Later the personal representative of Smith's estate executed a quitclaim deed to the same property to himself, individually, and recorded it. The trial court ruled that the Smith deed to Sargent failed for lack of delivery. Both deeds were declared void, and the court left title to be determined in pending probate proceedings. Sargent appealed the decision finding both deeds void and alleged that she was the rightful owner of the property.

Decision: Delivery of a deed is essential to its effectiveness. Without delivery, nothing passes to the grantee. A deed is essentially worthless as an instrument of title without delivery, even if delivery may have been intended but failed due to an accident.

A grantor's recording of a deed, in the absence of fraud on the grantor, is generally presumed equivalent to delivery. But in this case, Smith did not record the deed, or cause it to be recorded, during his life. What Smith intended to do cannot be inferred on the basis of what Sargent did after Smith's death. Delivery is not effective when made to a third person pending further instructions from the grantor. In such circumstances, obviously the deed remains subject to the grantor's control, and the grantor can revoke or annul it at will.

> There may be constructive delivery of a deed. However, Smith's continuing retention of control supports the conclusion that Smith did not intend a delivery pending a subsequent decision, if any, to relinquish control. The delivery would have been effective by having it recorded, but without the recording the grantor's intention to transfer was not fulfilled. *[Sargent v Baxter (Fla App) 673 So 2d 979 (1996)]*

Generally, there must be an acceptance by the grantee. In all cases, an acceptance is presumed. However, the grantee may disclaim the transfer if the grantee acts within a reasonable time after learning that the transfer has been made.

19. Recording of Deeds

The owner of land may record the deed in the office of a public official, sometimes called a **recorder** or **commissioner of deeds**. The recording is not required to make the deed effective to pass title, but it is done so that the public will know that the grantee is the present owner and thereby prevent the former owner from making any future transfer or transaction relating to the property. The recording statutes provide that a person purchasing land from the last holder of record will take title free of any unrecorded claim to the land of which the purchaser does not have notice or knowledge.

The fact that a deed is recorded charges everyone with knowledge of its existence even if they in fact do not know of it because they have neglected to examine the record. The recording of a deed, however, is only such notice if the deed was properly executed. Likewise, the grantee of land cannot claim any protection by virtue of the recording of a deed when (1) a claim is made by one whose title is superior to that of the owner of record, (2) the grantee had notice or knowledge of the adverse claim when title was acquired, (3) a person acting under a hostile claim was then in possession of the land, (4) the grantee received the land as a gift, or (5) the transfer to the grantee was fraudulent.

20. Additional Protection of Buyers

Abstract of title is a summary of the history of title to a tract of land.

Apart from the protection given to buyers and third persons by the recorded title to property, a buyer may generally also be protected by procuring title insurance or an **abstract of title**. An abstract of title is a summarized report of the title to the property as shown by the records, together with a report of all judgments, mortgages, and similar recorded claims against the property.

21. Grantor's Warranties

The warranties of the grantor relate to the title transferred by the grantor and to the fitness of the property for use.

(a) Warranties of Title. In the common law deed, the grantor may expressly warrant or make certain covenants as to the title conveyed. The statutes authorizing a short form of deed provide that, unless otherwise stated in the deed, the grantor is presumed to have made certain warranties of title.

The more important of the covenants or warranties of title that the grantor may make are (1) covenant of seisin, or guarantee that the grantor owns the estate conveyed; (2) covenant of right to convey, or guarantee that the grantor, if not the owner, as in the case of an agent, has the right or authority to make the conveyance; (3) covenant against encumbrances, or guarantee that the land is not subject to any right or interest of a third person, such as a lien or an easement; (4) covenant of quiet enjoyment, or guarantee by the grantor that the grantee's possession of the land will not be disturbed either by the grantor, in the case of a limited covenant, or by the grantor or any person claiming title under the grantor, in the case of a general covenant; and (5) covenant of further assurances, or guarantee that the grantor will execute any additional documents that may be required to perfect the title of the grantee.

(b) Fitness for Use. Courts in most states hold that when a builder or real estate developer sells a new house to a home buyer, an implied warranty that the house and foundation are fit for occupancy or use arises. This warranty arises regardless of whether the house was purchased before, during, or after completion of construction.[7] This warranty will not be implied against the first buyer when the house is resold. However, there is authority that the second buyer may sue the original contractor for breach of the implied warranty even though there is no privity of contract.[8]

22. Grantee's Covenants

Covenants running with the land are restrictions on land use that all grantees take subject to when title to the land is passed.

In a deed, the grantee may agree to do or to refrain from doing certain acts. Such an agreement becomes a binding contract between the grantor and the grantee. The grantor may sue the grantee for its breach.

The right to enforce the covenant also **runs with the land** owned by the grantor to whom the promise was made. ◆ *For example,* a promise not to use a tract of land for a parking lot between two adjoining landowners would pass to any buyers who subsequently acquire these tracts. ◆ For more information on covenants, see chapter 51 Environmental Law and Land Use Controls.

F.   OTHER METHODS OF TRANSFERRING REAL PROPERTY

Title to real property can also be acquired by eminent domain and by adverse possession.

23. Eminent Domain

Eminent domain is the taking of private property by the government with a proper purpose and for just compensation.

Under **eminent domain**, property is taken from its private owner for a public purpose. The title is then taken by a government or public authority. Two important questions arise: whether there is a taking of property and whether the property is taken for a public use. With respect to whether a taking has occurred, it is not necessary that the owner be physically deprived of the property. It is sufficient that the normal use of the property has been impaired or lost. As to the second, it is not necessary that the public at large actually use the property. It is sufficient that it is appropriated for public benefit. ◆ *For example,* property can be taken to build a freeway, but it could also be taken for preservation of a historic site. ◆

---

[7] *Richards v Powercraft Homes, Inc.* (Ariz) 678 P2d 427 (1984).
[8] Many states have passed statutes that govern the extent of the implied warranty of habitability. Although the statutes vary, the types of defects covered include defects in construction, design, and appearance.

I Can Sell That Used Car, But Not on My Own Property

Facts: Restigouche, Inc., operated an automobile sales lot on its property located along the main street in Jupiter, Florida. Following a land use study, the town of Jupiter adopted a comprehensive zoning plan. Under the terms of the plan, auto sales were prohibited along the main street, including the Restigouche property and those surrounding it. Restigouche applied for a zoning exception, but it was denied. Restigouche then filed suit, claiming Jupiter was taking property without compensation because Restigouche could no longer continue to operate its business.

Decision: Jupiter's zoning plan does prohibit auto sales along its main street, but in the area where the Restigouche property was located, the plan also permitted 27 other commercial uses. The zoning plan may have outlawed the sale of autos, but it did not render the property useless. The town's goal was one of establishing an aesthetically pleasing corridor along its main street and creating a traditional, identifiable downtown area. Maintenance of community aesthetics is a legitimate government purpose. The town of Jupiter wanted to encourage retail uses that would attract nearby residents and promote pedestrian traffic. The purchase of an automobile is not an everyday need, and the typically large auto lot would break up the pedestrian flow between retailers. Car dealerships with their bright lights, red flags, and flashy signage disrupt the residential character of the traditional downtown street. Jupiter had a legitimate purpose, and the land could be put to alternative and valuable uses that did not result in a taking without compensation. [*Restigouche, Inc. v Town of Jupiter*, 59 F3d 1208 (11th Cir 1995)]

24. Adverse Possession

Title to land may be acquired by possessing it adversely for a statutorily prescribed period of time. A possessor who complies with the physical and time requirements gains title by adverse possession. If such possession is maintained, the possessor automatically becomes the owner of the property, even though the possessor admittedly had no lawful claim to the land.

To acquire title in this manner, possession must be (1) actual, (2) visible and notorious, (3) exclusive, (4) hostile, and (5) continuous for a required period of time.[9]

Commonly the period of time is 21 years, but state statutes may provide 10 to 20 years. Occupation of land in the mistaken belief that one is the owner is a "hostile" possession.

The Warring Tobiases and Johnsons: Adverse Possession through Mistake and Oversight

Facts: Steven and Constance Tobias and Harry and Jolene Johnson, Jr., dispute the compensation the U.S. government has offered to pay to each of them for its taking of property known as McAfee's Knob in northern Roanoke County, Virginia. The Tobiases and their ancestors owned part of the land, with their tract adjoining the land owned by the Johnsons and their ancestors. The government had split payment for the land according to the land records, which showed the Tobiases as having superior paper title to a segment of land at the point where the two tracts met (referred to as the interlock). However, the Johnsons had been using the land and claimed title through adverse possession. The jury found the Tobiases had title and that the Johnsons did not meet the requirements for title by adverse possession. The Johnsons filed a motion for judgment notwithstanding the verdict.

---

[9] *Garringer v Wingard* (Ala) 585 So 2d 898 (1991).

Decision: The facts in this case present a situation where Tobias, who has superior paper title to the interlock, had only constructive possession of the property, while Johnson, who has actual possession of the property, had inferior paper title. The issue to be resolved, then, is whether Johnson's actual possession was of sufficient quality and duration to oust Tobias's constructive possession, thereby allowing Johnson to gain title to the property by adverse possession.

Very little dispute exists between the parties that Johnson's possession was hostile, under color of title, and exclusive. Tobias's challenge to Johnson's claim of adverse possession focuses on the remaining three elements of adverse possession: actual, visible and notorious, and continuous possession.

The evidence clearly indicates that Johnson actually occupied the house on the interlock. The undisputed evidence is that after Johnson, Sr., acquired his tract of land in 1945, the Johnson family made extensive use of the house on the interlock on a regular basis until the mid-to-late 1950s. Johnson's occupancy of the house served to constitute his actual possession of the entire tract commencing in 1945.

There is no question that the interlock was rugged, uncultivated, and by-and-large unimproved land. The question becomes therefore whether the interlock remained completely in a state of nature or whether the changes wrought were sufficient to take it out of that classification.

Johnson put this land to the use for which it was most readily adaptable, i.e., outdoor recreational purposes. This being the case, one would not expect to see the boundary fenced, cultivated, or cleared. Short of fencing the property, it is doubtful that Johnson could reasonably have done more to indicate his claim of ownership. *[United States v 369.31 Acres of Land in Roanoke County, VA, 696 F Supp 185 (WD Va 1988)*

G.   MORTGAGES

> Mortgage is a pledge of property as security for an underlying debt.
>
> Mortgagor is the owner who pledges property as security for a debt.
>
> Mortgagee is the lender who holds the mortgage as security for repayment of a debt.

An agreement that creates an interest in real property as security for an obligation, an interest that is to cease upon the performance of the obligation, is a **mortgage**. The property owner, whose interest in the property is given as security, is the **mortgagor**. The person who receives the security is the **mortgagee**.

25. Characteristics of a Mortgage

There are three characteristics of a mortgage: (1) the termination of the mortgagee's interest upon the performance of the obligation secured by the mortgage, (2) the right of the mortgagee to enforce the mortgage by foreclosure upon the mortgagor's failure to perform, and (3) the mortgagor's right to redeem or regain the property.

26. Property Subject to Mortgage

In general, any form of property that may be sold or conveyed may be mortgaged. It is immaterial whether the right is a present right or a future interest, or merely a right in the land of another. It is not necessary that the mortgagor have complete or absolute ownership in the property. Mortgagors may mortgage any type of land interest they own.

27. Form of Mortgage

Because a mortgage of real property transfers an interest in the property, it must be in writing by virtue of the statute of frauds.

As a general rule, no particular form of language is required if the language used expresses the intent of the parties to create a mortgage. Many state statutes provide a standardized form of mortgage that may be used.

28. Creative Forms of Financing

Adjustable rate mortgage (ARM) is a mortgage with variable financing charges over the life of the loan.

Reverse mortgage is a mortgage in which the owners get their equity out of their home over a period of time and then return the house to the lender upon their deaths.

In many situations in which a buyer seeks to purchase property, the conventional methods for obtaining a mortgage are not available because of affordability or qualifications required for a loan. Many creative forms of financing have been developed to help buyers purchase property. For example, residential land buyers often use an **adjustable rate mortgage (ARM)**, in which the lower interest rates applied at the beginning of the mortgage increase gradually with market interest rates. Other buyers may have the seller finance their purchase through the use of a land or an installment contract. Some new forms of financing, such as the **reverse mortgage**, permit those who have paid off their mortgages on their property to get the value out of their property by having a mortgage company take a mortgage out on the property and pay them money over time. Many senior citizens are able to obtain the additional monthly income they may need by this form of financing, which permits them to draw on their equity in their land.

29. Recording or Filing of Mortgage

An unrecorded mortgage is valid and binding between the parties to it. The heirs or donees of a mortgagor cannot defend against the mortgage on the ground that it has not been recorded. Recording statutes in most states, however, provide that purchasers or creditors who give value and act in good faith in ignorance of an unrecorded mortgage may enforce their respective rights against the property without regard to the existence of the unrecorded mortgage. Accordingly, the purchaser of the land in good faith for value from the mortgagor holds the land free of the unrecorded mortgage. The mortgagee's only remedy is against the mortgagor on the debt due the mortgagee. The mortgagee can proceed against the transferee only if the mortgagee can prove that the transferee of the land did not purchase it in good faith, for value, and without knowledge of the unrecorded mortgage.

30. Responsibilities of the Parties

The mortgagor and mortgagee have the following duties and liabilities when a mortgage is placed on real property.

(a) Repairs and Improvements. In the absence of an agreement to the contrary, a mortgagor is under no duty to make improvements or to restore or repair parts of the premises that are destroyed or damaged through no fault of the mortgagor.

A mortgagee, when in possession, must make reasonable and necessary repairs in order to preserve the property. The mortgagee is entitled to reimbursement for such repairs. Ordinarily, however, the mortgagee may not charge to the mortgagor expenditures for valuable or enduring improvements.

(b) Taxes, Assessments, and Insurance. The duty to pay taxes and assessments rests with the mortgagor. In the absence of an agreement, neither party is under a duty to insure the mortgaged property. Both parties, however, may insure their respective interests. It is common practice for the mortgagor to obtain a single policy of insurance on the property payable to the mortgagee and the mortgagor generally according to the standard mortgagee clause that pays the outstanding loan balance first.

(c) Impairment of Security. The mortgagor is liable to the mortgagee for any damage to the property caused by the mortgagor that impairs the security of the mortgage by materially reducing the value of the property. Both the mortgagor and the mortgagee have a right of action against a third person who wrongfully injures the property.

31. Transfer of Interest

Questions arise as to transfers by the mortgagor and the mortgagee of their respective interests and of the liability of a transferee of the mortgagor.

(a) Transfer by Mortgagor. The mortgagor may ordinarily transfer the property without the consent of the mortgagee. Such a transfer passes only the interest of the mortgagor and does not divest or impair a properly recorded mortgage.

The transfer of the property by the mortgagor does not affect the liability of the mortgagor to the mortgagee. Unless the latter has agreed to substitute the mortgagor's grantee for the mortgagor, the latter remains liable for the mortgage debt as though no transfer had been made.[10]

(b) Liability of the Parties in a Transfer by a Mortgagor. There are two ways to transfer mortgaged property, and each way has differing results in terms of personal liability for the transferee. In an assumption of a mortgage, the transferee agrees to assume liability. In an **assumption**, the mortgagor remains liable, the transferee is liable, and the property is subject to foreclosure by the mortgagee in the event the payments are not made. *For example,* if Bob sold his house with a $175,000 mortgage for $200,000 to Jane, Jane could pay Bob $25,000 cash and then agree to assume Bob's mortgage. Jane may get the benefit of a lower interest rate by assuming Bob's mortgage. Both Bob and Jane are personally liable, and the mortgagee may foreclose on the property if the payments are not made.

The second method of transfer is called a **"subject to" transfer**. In this type of a transfer, the property is subject to foreclosure, but the transferee does not agree to assume the mortgage personally. The mortgagor remains liable in this type of a transfer, too.

(c) Transfer by Mortgagee. In most states, a mortgage may be transferred or assigned by the mortgagee.

---

[10] *In re* Argianis, 156 BR 683 (MD Fla 1993).

32. Rights of Mortgagee after Default

Foreclosure is the right of a mortgagee to sell property to satisfy an unpaid debt.

Upon the mortgagor's default, the mortgagee in some states is entitled to obtain possession of the property and collect the rents or to have a receiver appointed for that purpose. In all states, the mortgagee may enforce the mortgage by **foreclosure**, a judicial procedure resulting in sale of the mortgaged property.

Generally, it is provided that upon any default under the terms of the mortgage agreement, the mortgagee has the right to accelerate the debt or declare that the entire mortgage debt is due. The mortgagee generally has this right even though the default related only to paying an installment or to doing some act, such as maintaining insurance on the property or producing receipts for taxes.

A sale resulting from the foreclosure of the mortgage destroys the mortgage, and the property passes free of the mortgage to the buyer at the sale. However, the extinction of the mortgage by foreclosure does not destroy the debt that was secured by the mortgage. The mortgagor remains liable for any unpaid balance or deficiency. By statute, the mortgagor is generally given credit for the fair value of the property if it was purchased by the mortgagee.

33. Rights of Mortgagor after Default

After default, the mortgagor may seek to stop or stay foreclosure or to redeem the mortgaged land.

Right of redemption is the debtor's right to redeem property after the foreclosure sale but before the deed is conveyed (generally six months).

(a) Stay of Foreclosure. In certain cases authorized by statute, a stay (or delay) of foreclosure may be obtained by the mortgagor to prevent undue hardship.

(b) Redemption. The right of **redemption** is the right of the mortgagor to free the property of the mortgage lien after default. By statute in many states, the right may be exercised during a certain time following foreclosure and sale of the mortgaged land.

SUMMARY

Real property includes land, buildings and fixtures, and rights in the land of another.

The interest held by a person in real property may be defined in terms of the period of time for which the person will remain the owner. The interest may be a fee simple estate, which lasts forever, or a life estate, which lasts for the life of a person. These estates are known as freehold estates. If the ownership interest exists for a specified number of days, months, or years, the interest is a lease-hold estate.

Personal property may be attached to or associated with real property in such a way that it becomes real property. In such a case, it is called a fixture. To determine whether property has in fact become a fixture, the courts look to the method of attachment, to how the property is adapted to the realty, and to the intent of the person originally owning the personal property.

Under common law, the liability of an occupier of land for injury to third persons on the premises is depen-dent on the status of the third persons as trespassers, licensees, or invitees. Many jurisdictions, however, are ignoring these common law distinctions in favor of an ordinary negligence standard or are giving licensees the same protection as invitees. Recreational use statutes limit or eliminate a landowner's liability for personal injuries to a person using the owner's land for recreational purposes.

Real property may be the subject of multiple owner-ship. The forms of multiple ownership are the same as those for personal property. In addition, there are special forms of co-ownership for real property, such as condo-miniums and cooperatives.

A deed is an instrument by which a grantor transfers an interest in land to a grantee. A deed can be a quitclaim deed or a warranty deed. To be effective, a deed must be signed or sealed by the grantor and delivered to the grantee. Recording the deed is not required to make the deed effective to pass title, but recording provides notice to the public that the grantee is the present owner. The warranties of the grantor relate to the title transferred by the grantor and to the fitness of the property for use. In the absence of any express warranty in the deed, no warranty of fitness arises under the common law in the sale or the conveyance of real estate. Most states today hold that when a builder or real estate developer sells a new home to a buyer, an implied warranty of habitability arises. Title to real estate may also be acquired by eminent domain and adverse possession.

An agreement that creates an interest in real property as security for an obligation and that ends upon the performance of the obligation is a mortgage. A mortgage must be in writing under the statute of frauds. If the mortgage is unrecorded, it is valid between the parties. The mortgage should be recorded to put good-faith purchasers on notice of the mortgage. A purchaser of the mortgaged property does not become liable for the mortgage debt unless the purchaser assumes the mortgage. The mortgagor still remains liable unless the mortgagee agrees to a substitution of parties. If the mortgagor defaults, the mortgagee may enforce the mortgage by foreclosure. Such foreclosure may be delayed because of undue hardship.

QUESTIONS AND CASE PROBLEMS

1. What legal issues arise when aircraft are permitted to fly over land at a height that interferes with the use of the land? What real property rights would help the landowner disturbed by the flight?

2. Bunn and his wife claimed that they had an easement to enter and use the swimming pool on neighboring land. A contract between the former owners of the Bunns' property and the adjacent apartment complex contained a provision that the use of the apartment complex's swimming pool would be available to the purchaser and his family. No reference to the pool was made in the contract between the former owners and the Bunns, nor was there any reference to it in the deed conveying the property to the Bunns. Decide. [*Bunn v Offutt*, 216 Va 681, 222 SE2d 522]

3. Richard sold land to Smith by a warranty deed, but Smith did not record the deed. Sometime thereafter, Richard sold the same land to Wayne by a warranty deed. Wayne, a good-faith purchaser for value who had no knowledge of the prior unrecorded deed, recorded his deed. Who owns the land, Smith or Wayne? Why?

4. Kenneth Corson, 10, lived with his mother, Lynda Lontz, in an apartment building owned by Bruno and Carolyn Kosinski. While playing with other children who lived in the same building, Corson was drawn to a stairwell that provided access to the building's laundry room and roof. Corson and the other children climbed to the roof and discovered an area where they could jump from the roof of their building to that of the building next door. The children engaged in roof hopping for several days. On the last day, Corson misjudged his jump and fell the three stories to the ground below. Corson and his mother filed suit against the Kosinskis to collect damages for Corson's injuries. What theory might be used to hold the Kosinskis liable? [*Corson by Lontz v Kosinski*, 801 F Supp 75 (ND Ill 1992)]

5. Compare the status of a condominium owner and a cooperative owner.

6. What is the duty of a landowner with respect to trespassers? Licensees? Invitees? Why are land users distinguished?

7. Bradham and other members and trustees of the Mount Olivet Church brought an action to cancel a mortgage on the church property. The mortgage had been executed previously by Davis and other former trustees of the church and given to Robinson as mortgagee. The court found that the church was not indebted to the mortgagee for any amount. Should the mortgage be canceled? [*Bradham v Robinson*, 236 NC 589, 73 SE2d 555]

8. Miller executed a deed to real estate, naming Zieg as grantee. He placed the deed in an envelope on which was written "To be filed at my death" and put the envelope and deed in a safe deposit box in the National Bank that had been rented in the names of Miller and Zieg. After Miller's death, Zieg removed the deed from the safe deposit box. Moseley, as executor under Miller's will, brought an action against Zieg to declare the deed void. Decide. [*Moseley v Zieg*, 180 Neb 810, 146 NW2d 72]

9. Henry Lile owned a house. When the land on which it was situated was condemned for a highway, he moved the house to the land of his daughter, Sarah Crick. In the course of construction work, blasting damaged the house. Sarah Crick sued the contractors, Terry & Wright, who claimed that Lile should be joined in the action as a plaintiff and that Sarah could not sue by herself because it was Lile's house. Were the defendants correct? [*Terry & Wright v Crick* (Ky) 418 SW2d 217]

10. Bradt believed his backyard ran all the way to a fence. Actually, a strip on Bradt's side of the fence belonged to his neighbor Giovannone, but Bradt never intended to take land away from anyone. Bradt later brought an

action against Giovannone to determine who owned the strip on Bradt's side of the fence. Who is the owner? Why? [*Bradt v Giovannone*, 35 App Div 2d 322, 315 NYS2d 961]

11. Larry Wiersema was building a house for himself in the country. He made a contract with Workman Plumbing, Heating & Cooling, Inc., to do most of the plumbing and heating work, which included the installation of a septic tank. Workman performed the contract correctly. However, because of the peculiar kind of clay surrounding the house, the drainage from the septic tank system was very poor, and the basement of Larry's house was frequently flooded. He sued Workman for breach of the implied warranty of habitability. Was Workman liable? [*Wiersema v Workman Plumbing, Heating & Cooling, Inc.*, 87 Ill App 3d 535, 42 Ill Dec 664, 409 NE2d 159]

12. Davis Store Fixtures sold certain equipment on credit to Head, who installed it in a building that was later owned by the Cadillac Club. When payment was not made, Davis sought to repossess the equipment. If the equipment constituted fixtures, this could not be done. The equipment consisted of a bar for serving drinks, a bench, and a drain board. The first two were attached to the floor or wall with screws, and the drain board was connected to water and drainage pipes. Did the equipment constitute fixtures?

13. Smikahl sold Hansen a tract of land on which were two houses and four trailer lots equipped with concrete patios and necessary connections for utility lines. The tract Hansen purchased was completely surrounded by the land owned by Smikahl and third persons. To get onto the highway, it was necessary to cross the Smikahl tract. Several years after the sale, Smikahl put a barbed wire fence around his land. Hansen sued to prevent obstruction to travel between his land and the highway over the Smikahl land. Smikahl's defense was that no such right of travel had been given to Hansen. Was he correct? [*Hansen v Smikahl*, 173 Neb 309, 113 NW2d 210]

14. Martin Manufacturing decided to raise additional long-term capital by mortgaging an industrial park it owned. First National Loan Co. agreed to lend Martin $1 million and to take a note and first mortgage on the land and building. The mortgage was duly recorded. Martin sold the property to Marshall, who took the property and assumed the mortgage debt. Does Marshall have any personal liability on the mortgage debt? Is Martin still liable on the mortgage debt? Explain.

15. In 1980, Ortleb, Inc., a Delaware corporation, purchased certain land in Montana from the Alberts but neglected to record the deed. In 1988, the Alberts sold the same property to Bently, a resident of Montana, who purchased in good faith and recorded his deed. Ortleb sued Bently to determine who owned the land. Decide and explain.

CPA QUESTIONS

1. Which of the following statements is correct with respect to a real estate mortgage?
   a. It must be signed only by the mortgagor (borrower).
   b. It must be recorded in order to be effective between the mortgagor and the mortgagee.
   c. It does **not** have to be recorded to be effective against third parties without notice if it is a purchase money mortgage.
   d. It is effective even if **not** delivered to the mortgagee.
   (11/86, Law, #53)

2. To be enforceable against the mortgagor, a mortgage must meet all the following requirements **except**
   a. Be delivered to the mortgagee.
   b. Be in writing and signed by the mortgagor.
   c. Be recorded by the mortgagee.
   d. Include a description of the debt and land involved.
   (11/90, Law, #55)

3. Ritz owned a building in which there was a duly recorded first mortgage held by Lyn and a recorded second mortgage held by Jay. Ritz sold the building to Nunn. Nunn assumed the Jay mortgage and had no actual knowledge of the Lyn mortgage. Nunn defaulted on the payments to Jay. If both Lyn and Jay foreclosed, and the proceeds of the sale were insufficient to pay both Lyn and Jay,
   a. Jay would be paid after Lyn was fully paid.
   b. Jay and Lyn would be paid proportionately.
   c. Nunn would be personally liable to Lyn but **not** to Jay.
   d. Nunn would be personally liable to Lyn and Jay.
   (11/90, Law, #58)

Environmental Law and Land Use Controls

CHAPTER 51

OBJECTIVES

After studying this chapter, you should be able to

1. *List and describe the federal statutes that regulate various aspects of the environment;*
2. *Explain how environmental laws are enforced;*
3. *Describe the criminal penalties for violation of environmental laws;*
4. *Define nuisance and list the remedies available;*
5. *Distinguish between restrictive covenants and zoning; and*
6. *Explain the role and application of zoning laws.*

Businesses and regulators alike now recognize that resources should be conserved and the environment protected from pollution.

A. STATUTORY ENVIRONMENTAL LAW

As America changed from a rural, agricultural society to an urban, industrial one, new laws were needed to prevent the pollution of the environment.

1. Air Pollution Regulation

The first legislation that dealt with air pollution, passed in 1955, was the Air Pollution Control Act, which was simply a statutory recognition of a concern about air quality. Even the first statute regulating air pollution, the **Clean Air Act**, passed in 1963, produced no response from the states, which were charged with the responsibility of developing pollution standards and enforcement mechanisms. It was not until the 1970 amendments to the Clean Air Act that the federal law on air pollution got some teeth, for it was in those amendments that Congress established the federal agency that was to be responsible for enforcement of the law, the **Environmental Protection Agency** (EPA). The EPA was authorized to establish national air quality standards and see that the states developed plans for the implementation of those standards. Under the 1970 Clean Air Act,[1] as well as the 1977 and 1990 amendments to it, states must measure their air content of sulfur dioxide, carbon monoxide, and hydrocarbons and then take appropriate steps to bring their air quality within the federal limits established for each of these. States that do not meet federal standards are called **nonattainment areas**, or dirty areas, and their plans for implementation are strictly reviewed by the EPA, which can halt federal highway funding in the event the implementation plan is not followed. Those states that do meet the federal standards must still have a plan to remain at that level.

For nonattainment areas the EPA developed an **emissions offset policy**, which controls whether new factories can be built. For a new plant to obtain a permit to begin operations in a nonattainment area, the business proposing the new plant must be able to show (1) that the plant will have the greatest possible emissions controls, which means better than existing emissions standards; (2) that the business has all of its other plants and operations in compliance with federal emissions standards; and (3) that the new plant's emissions will be offset by reductions in emissions in other facilities in the area. This last requirement is often referred to as the **bubble concept**, which requires an examination of all emissions from all sources in an area. Before any new operations with emissions can be permitted, the business seeking approval must be able to show that overall emissions in the area will not increase.

The 1990 amendments to the Clean Air Act increased the role of the bubble concept with the ability of businesses to transfer their emissions permits. Those businesses that can reduce their emissions below their allowable amounts or that can eliminate their emissions are free to transfer their permit rights to emit to someone else who can then use them without affecting total emissions in the bubble

The Clean Air Act is a federal law that establishes standards for air pollution levels and prevents further deterioration of air quality.

The Environmental Protection Agency (EPA) is the federal agency responsible for the administration and enforcement of federal environmental standards.

Nonattainment areas (under the Clean Air Act) or so-called dirty areas, are those that do not meet federal standards for maximum levels of sulfur dioxide, carbon monoxide, and hydrocarbons.

The bubble concept is a method used to allow new plant operations; any new plant can be operated only if emissions capacity is obtained through a reduction in the operation of other plants in the area.

---

[1] 42 USC §§ 1857 et seq.

area. There is a market exchange for emissions permits because the EPA will not, under the 1990 act, be issuing any additional permits beyond the rights to emission that already exist. Today, approximately 10 percent of all the emissions permit rights are owned by environmental groups.

2. Water Pollution Regulation

The first meaningful regulation in water pollution began at about the same time as effective air pollution regulation. The first legislation with enforcement power was passed in 1972 as the Federal Water Pollution Control Act and then amended and renamed in 1977 as the **Clean Water Act**.[2] Under the Clean Water Act, the EPA has developed **effluent guidelines**, which are ranges for discharges organized according to industrial groups and for specific plants in each of these groups. The guidelines establish the maximum amounts that can be discharged, and those maximums are coupled with a permit system that requires each plant to obtain a permit from the EPA before discharging anything into any type of pool, pond, river, lake, stream, or ocean. ◆ *For example*, a plant that releases hot water from a steam generator must still have a permit just to release hot water into the stream near the plant. ◆ The EPA also has standards for the treatment of water that is used in a plant for whatever processes are employed in that plant before that water can be discharged. The treatment and permit regulations apply to all plants. ◆ *For example*, a plant must still have a permit to discharge water even though that water is cleaner as it is discharged from the plant than it was when it was brought in to be used in production or manufacturing. ◆

3. Solid Waste Disposal Regulation

The disposal of solid waste (garbage) has also been regulated since the 1960s, but the initial legislation simply provided money for research by state and local governments on how to dispose of solid waste.[3] In 1970, the **Resource Recovery Act** provided federal money for cities and states with recycling programs.

After several major open-dumping problems that produced community-wide illnesses, including that in the Love Canal area near Buffalo, New York, Congress passed the **Toxic Substances Control Act (TOSCA)**, which controls the manufacture, use, and disposal of toxic substances, with the EPA developing a list of toxic substances. Along with TOSCA, Congress passed the **Resource Conservation and Recovery Act (RCRA)**, which regulates the disposal of potentially harmful substances through a permit system and also uses federal grants to encourage the restoration of damaged resources.[4] ◆ *For example*, many strip mine locations were restored following the passage of RCRA. ◆

In 1980, Congress passed the **Comprehensive Environmental Response, Compensation, and Liability Act (CERCLA)**,[5] which authorizes the president to issue funds for the cleanup of areas that were once disposal sites for hazardous

The Clean Water Act is federal legislation that regulates water pollution through a control system of permits for discharge of materials and liquids into water.

Effluent guidelines are EPA standards for maximum ranges of discharge into water.

The Resource Recovery Act (early solid waste disposal legislation at the federal level) provided money for states and local governments with recycling programs.

The Toxic Substances Control Act (TOSCA) was the first federal law to control the manufacture, use, and disposal of toxic substances.

The Resource Conservation and Recovery Act (RCRA) is a federal law that regulates the disposal of potentially harmful substances and encourages resource conservation and recovery.

The Comprehensive Environmental Response, Compensation, and Liability Act (CERCLA) is a federal law that authorizes the president to issue funds for the cleanup of areas that were once disposal sites for hazardous wastes.

---

2 33 USC §§ 1251 et seq. The pollution of navigable waters had been regulated by the Rivers and Harbors Act of 1899, which required a permit for discharging into navigable rivers, streams, and lakes, but which was limited in its effect because only the permit was required—there were no limits on the amount or type of discharge into the waters. The act remains in effect today, although other, more recent federal laws are utilized for preventing unauthorized discharges.
3 See the Solid Waste Disposal Act, 42 USC §§ 3251 et seq., and the Resource Recovery and Policy Act of 1970, 42 USC §§ 3251 et seq.
4 42 USC §§ 6901 et seq.
5 42 USC §§ 9601 et seq.

wastes. The act set up a trust fund that is used for cleanups and is reimbursed for those costs by the company responsible for the hazardous wastes on the site. The funds in the trust are available for government use, but are not subject to attachment by private citizens who seek to get an area cleaned up by removing the hazardous waste. Under the CERCLA, the EPA has the authority to designate **Superfund sites**, or parcels of land that are deemed to have or potentially have hazardous wastes that require cleanup.

> A Superfund site is an area designated by the EPA for cleanup of hazardous waste.

The **Superfund Amendment and Reauthorization Act**, passed in 1986, authorizes the EPA to bring suit for the purpose of collecting the costs of cleanup from those who are responsible for the hazardous wastes on the site. The act and its judicial interpretations provide a very broad definition of who is responsible under CERCLA for the costs of cleanup. There are four classes of parties who can be held liable under CERCLA. "Owners and operators" of contaminated property are liable under the statute. Owners include present owners as well as past owners, whether or not they are responsible for the hazardous wastes being dumped on the property. Operators include those who are leasing the property, again whether or not they are responsible for the hazardous waste being dumped. ◆ *For example,* many gas stations have been designated as Superfund sites because the underground tanks have leaks, resulting in gas seeping into the soil. One who owns such a station presently as well as past owners is responsible under CERCLA—even one who has converted the gas station into some other use is responsible. ◆

> The Superfund Amendment and Reauthorization Act is a federal law that authorizes the EPA to collect cleanup costs from those responsible for the ownership, leasing, dumping, or security of hazardous waste sites.

Other responsible parties under CERCLA include anyone who transported hazardous waste to a site and anyone who hired another or arranged to transport hazardous waste to the site. Even lenders who take back property that is designated as a Superfund site can have liability for its cleanup in certain circumstances.[6] CERCLA is an all-encompassing strict liability statute (see chapter 9 for more details on strict liability) that is designed to force the cleanup of hazardous waste from all types of property by holding private landowners responsible.

Dumping Batteries versus Selling Batteries for Dumping Makes a Big Liability Difference

Facts: General Automotive operates Grand Auto Parts Stores, which receive used automotive batteries from customers as trade-ins. General's policy in disposing of these batteries had been to drive a screwdriver through each spent battery and then sell them to a battery-cracking plant operated by Morris P. Kirk & Sons, Inc., which extracted and smelted the lead.

After the lead was extracted from the batteries, Kirk washed and crushed the battery casings, loaded them into a dump truck, and then dumped them. Tons of pieces of crushed batteries were dumped onto Catellus Development Corporation's property. Under CERCLA Catellus sought to recover from General the costs of cleaning up the hazardous battery parts from its property. General maintained that it is not liable because it sold the batteries to Kirk and Kirk did the dumping.

Decision: Catellus could seek to recover the costs from General as a private party. However, General was not an owner or operator and did not arrange for the disposal of the batteries. General simply sold the batteries to Kirk, and Kirk was responsible for their disposal and could be held liable under CERCLA. [*Catellus Development Corp. v United States*, 34 F3d 748 (9th Cir 1994)]

---

[6] *United States v Fleet Factors Corp.,* 901 F2d 1550 (11th Cir 1990).

4. Environmental Quality Regulation

The National Environmental Policy Act (NEPA) is a federal law that mandates study of a federal project's impact on the environment before it can be undertaken by any federal agency.

An environmental impact statement (EIS) is a formal report prepared by a federal agency under NEPA to document findings on the impact of a proposed federal project on the environment.

The federal statutes on air, water, and solid waste pollution are directed at private parties in their use of land. However, the federal government also regulates itself in terms of its operations and impact on the environment. The **National Environmental Policy Act (NEPA)** requires federal agencies to take into account the impact on the environment of their proposed projects.[7] An agency must prepare a report, called an **environmental impact statement (EIS)**, that documents the impact of the proposed federal project on the environment and covers consideration of practical and feasible alternatives with a lesser impact.[8] ◆ *For example*, the federal government has been required to file an EIS for the Alaska oil pipeline, the extermination of wild horses, the construction of a post office, the implementation of a change in national park airport procedures that would permit jets to land, and highway construction. ◆

CASE SUMMARY

Not So Fast! Don't Forget the EIS!

Facts: Henry Street Partners wished to build a high-rise luxury condominium building on a vacant lot in the Chinatown section of New York City. The appropriate city and federal agencies issued a permit allowing the construction of the building. The issuance of the permit was then attacked by a lawsuit brought by the Chinese Staff and Workers Association and others. They protested on the ground that the proposed building would have a harmful effect on the Chinatown section by driving out poorer residents and businesses and that this had not been considered in an environmental impact statement.

Decision: The agency had acted improperly in issuing the building permit without the filing of a proper EIS considering the effect of the project on the character of the neighborhood and the displacement of residents and businesses. The action of issuing the permit without the proper EIS was invalid. [*Chinese Staff and Workers Ass'n v New York*, 68 NY2d 359, 509 NYS2d 499, 502 NE2d 176 (1986)]

---

5. Other Environmental Regulations

The Noise Control Act is a federal law that controls noise emissions from low-flying aircraft.

The Endangered Species Act is a federal law that identifies and protects species that are endangered from development or other acts that threaten their existence.

In addition to the major categories of environmental laws just covered, there are several other important statutes that regulate specific areas of the environment. The **Noise Control Act** sets standards for noise from low-flying aircraft for the protection of landowners who are in flight paths.[9] The **Endangered Species Act** gives the secretary of the interior the responsibility of identifying and protecting endangered terrestrial species and the secretary of commerce the responsibility of identifying and protecting endangered marine species.[10] These cabinet-level federal officers have the authority to curtail any development, noise, or other act that threatens those species on their endangered lists.

---

[7] 42 USC §§ 4321 et seq.
[8] An EIS "functions as an environmental 'alarm bell' whose purpose it is to alert the public and its responsible officials to environmental changes before they have reached ecological points of no return . . . and to demonstrate to an apprehensive citizenry that the agency has in fact analyzed and considered ecological implications of its action." *Silveira v Las Gallina Valley Sanitary District*, 63 Cal Rptr 244 (1997).
[9] 42 USC § 4901.
[10] 16 USC §§ 1530 et seq.

CASE SUMMARY

Home, Sweet Home for the Spotted Owl and Red Woodpecker

Facts: Two federal agencies halted logging in the Pacific Northwest because of its impact on the habitats of the northern spotted owl and the red cockaded woodpecker, both endangered species. Sweet Home Chapter, a group of landowners, logging companies, and the families of loggers, brought suit challenging the authority of federal agencies to halt logging in the Northwest. The secretary of the interior and the Fish and Wildlife Service both had these two birds on their endangered species lists and maintained that the destruction of the trees through logging was a destruction of the habitats of these birds.

Decision: The two federal agencies had clear authority under the Endangered Species Act to halt the logging activities. The extent of federal authority under the act will be determined on a case-by-case basis. [*Babbitt v Sweet Home Chapter of Communities for a Great Oregon*, 115 S Ct 2407 (1995).]

Note: Congress intervened and reinstated logging in the Pacific Northwest by suspending the application of environmental laws there. The Endangered Species Act enjoys continual congressional attention and review.

ETHICS & THE LAW

In September 1996, President Bill Clinton, by executive order, declared 9,000 square miles of land in southern Utah a national monument. Using the 1906 Antiquities Act, President Clinton was able to designate the area as a preserve. The area now cannot be used for logging or mining or for the extraction of other natural resources.

Andalax Resources, Inc., a Dutch coal company, owns the mining lease rights to the Kaiparowits plateau located in the area. Referred to by the settlers in the area as the "badlands," the plateau has remained undeveloped because of its rocky surface and lack of water. However, the coal resources beneath the surface are extensive. The declaration of the area as a national monument does not terminate the Andalax leases, but it does mean the company cannot obtain the permits it will need from the federal government for access to the surface in order to build the roads needed to get the mined coal out of the area. An EPA official stated, "The lease clearly conveys the right to explore for and develop and mine the coal. It doesn't say they necessarily have the right to get coal off the lease."

Environmental groups praised the action as necessary to preserve the natural beauty in certain areas. The logging and mining industries and their employees noted that this act destroys their livelihood. Community leaders in southern Utah expressed concern about the impact of the ban on the economies of the towns and the state.

Who has a stake in the Utah badlands? Who is affected by the declaration of a large area as a national monument? Should such declarations be permitted, or do they destroy economic bases? Is this decision based in environmental law? Is this declaration a possibility for other areas?

WHAT'S BEHIND THE LAW?

Jobs v Spotted Owl: Economics and Environmentalism

In 1789, Jeremy Bentham wrote in favor of animal rights and asked the following question, which has become the value-based inquiry of today's animal rights activists: "The question is not can they *reason*? Nor, can they *talk*? But, can they *suffer*?"

As Congress and various courts have struggled with inherent conflicts between the need for development and economic growth and the presence of animals and endangered species in those areas to be developed, various positions have been advanced. The House of Representatives issued a report along with its passage of the Endangered Species Act indicating the importance of balance and compromise.

> Some . . . groups [formed to advocate stronger protection measures] have been criticized as unrealistic; as failing to recognize that the principal significance of these animals lies in their usefulness to men, and by inference, that *any* use by man is therefore justifiable. The attitude, it seems to the committee, is not more realistic than that of those on the other end of the spectrum—that animals must be left alone altogether. Both fail to recognize that man's thumb is already on the balance of Nature, and that solicitous and decent treatment for the animals may well also be in the long-term interest of man.
>
> H.R. No. 92-707, 92d Cong. 2d Session 2 (1972)

The balance between the lumber-based economies and the wood-dwelling spotted owl is a delicate one. It is a balance involving economics, law, and the environment.

For more on the Endangered Species Act and environmental groups, visit Emory University's environmental law Web site at http://www.law.emory.edu/FOCAL/env.html See also Environmental Law around the World at http://www.igc.org/igc/econet/index.html

---

The **Safe Drinking Water Act** is a federal law that establishes national standards for contaminants in drinking water.

The **Oil Pollution Act** is a federal law that assigns cleanup liability for oil spills in U.S. waters.

The **Safe Drinking Water Act** requires the EPA to establish national standards for contaminants in drinking water. The **Oil Pollution Act** is a federal law that came about following the oil spill from the *Exxon Valdez* off the coast of Alaska, which resulted in damage to the waters, fish, and birds in that area. Under this law companies are financially responsible for the cleanup of their spills that occur in U.S. waters. There are also substantial penalties provided under the act for the failure to take action to clean up the spill, and those penalties can be as high as $25,000 per day or $3,000 per barrel if the spill is the result of negligence or willful misconduct.[11]

6. State Environmental Regulation

All states have some form of environmental regulation, and their environmental agencies work closely with the EPA on enforcement and standards. All states have some form of hazardous waste controls that define hazardous waste differently and carry a range of penalties for violations. ◆ *For example*, Oregon imposes a fine of $3,500 per animal killed as a result of hazardous waste dumping. ◆ Other states mandate disclosure of the history of property use before that property can be sold, transferred, or mortgaged.

---

[11] 33 USC §§ 2701 et seq. The act also establishes a cleanup fund for those spills in which the party to blame is unknown or is financially unable to pay the cost of cleanup. All boats must be double-hulled under the act as well.

B. ENFORCEMENT OF ENVIRONMENTAL LAWS

Federal environmental laws can be enforced through criminal sanctions, penalties, injunctions, and suits by private citizens. In addition to the federal enforcement rights, certain common law remedies exist for the protection of property rights, such as the remedies for nuisance.

7. Parties Responsible for Enforcement

The EPA is the primary federal agency responsible for the enforcement of federal environmental laws, including those on air and water pollution, solid waste disposal, toxic substance control, and noise pollution. The EPA establishes the emissions standards through regulation and then enforces those with a system of permits and sanctions for violations. The EPA works closely with the state environmental agencies in enforcement.

The **Council on Environmental Quality (CEQ)** was established in 1966 as a part of the executive branch to establish national policy on environmental quality and then make recommendations for legislation for the implementation of that policy.

Other federal agencies with responsibility for enforcement of federal environmental laws include the Department of Commerce, the Department of the Interior, the U.S. Forest Service, the Bureau of Land Management, and the Federal Power Commission.

Private citizens also have the right to enforce federal environmental laws through private litigation. ◆ *For example*, a private citizen can bring a suit to halt the construction of a dam by the federal government if the agency responsible failed to conduct an environmental impact study or if the EIS is inadequate. ◆

The Council on Environmental Quality (CEQ) is a federal agency that is part of the executive branch and that establishes national policies on environmental quality and then recommends legislation to implement those policies.

8. Criminal Penalties

Most of the federal environmental laws carry criminal penalties for violations. Figure 51-1 provides a summary of those penalties. Both companies and their employees are subject to these penalties.

FIGURE 51-1
*Penalties for
Violations of Federal
Environmental Laws*

ACT	PENALTIES	PRIVATE SUIT
Clean Air Act	$25,000 per day, up to 1 year imprisonment, or both; $5,000 field citations, $10,000 rewards	Citizen suits authorized, EPA suits for injunctive relief
Clean Water Act	$25,000 per day, up to 1 year imprisonment, or both;	Citizen suits authorized, EPA suits for injunctive relief
Resource Conservation and Recovery Act	$25,000 per day, up to 1 year imprisonment, or both;	No private suits, Hazardous Substance/Response Trust Fund for cleanup, EPA suits for injunctive relief and reimbursement of trust funds
Oil Pollution Act	$25,000 per day, or $1,000 per barrel ($3,000 per barrel if willful or negligent), $250,000 and/or 5 years for failure to report	Private actions in negligence

CASE SUMMARY

Can a Foreman Violate Federal Environmental Laws?

Facts: Johnson and Towers repairs and overhauls large motor vehicles. In its operations, Johnson uses degreasers and other industrial chemicals that contain methylene chloride and trichloroethylene, which are classified as "hazardous wastes" under federal law and as pollutants under the Clean Water Act.

The waste chemicals from Johnson and Towers' cleaning operations were drained into a holding tank and, when the tank was full, pumped into a trench. The trench flowed from the property where Johnson and Towers' plant was located into Parker's Creek, a tributary of the Delaware River.

Johnson and Towers did not have a discharge permit. The EPA charged Johnson and Towers; Jack Hopkins, its foreman; and Peter Angel, its service manager, with violations of the Clean Water Act. Johnson and Towers entered a guilty plea and paid a fine. Hopkins and Angel said they were not responsible because they were just employees and did not know the federal law on discharges into water.

Decision: Both Hopkins and Angel were criminally liable for the plant's discharges. Ignorance of the law is no excuse, and the two knew that the discharges were being made from the plant into the creek. Criminal penalties exist in federal environmental law to stop violations in the interest of public health and welfare. Individuals with responsible positions in companies can be held personally and criminally liable for violations of federal law. [*United States v Johnson & Towers, 741 F2d 662 (3d Cir 1984)*]

9. Civil Remedies

Although criminal remedies are costly to businesses, the EPA also has the authority to have the polluting activity halted through the use of injunctions. The EPA simply brings suit against a business and shows that it is engaged in unauthorized dumping, the release of emissions in excess of a permit, or discharge without a permit. A court can then order the business to halt the activity that is resulting in the violation. In some cases the effect of the injunction is to shut down the business. The business will then be required to negotiate with the EPA to meet certain standards before the EPA will agree to have the injunction lifted.

Private citizens can also sue for injunctions against companies that are in violation of federal law or not in compliance with statutory procedures. ◆ *For example,* private citizens have filed suit against developers to stop construction when there is an issue of possible violation of the Endangered Species Act. ◆

10. Private Remedies: Nuisance

A nuisance is conduct that unreasonably interferes with the enjoyment or use of land.

Conduct that unreasonably interferes with the enjoyment or use of land is a **nuisance**.[12] A nuisance may be smoke from a chemical plant that damages the paint on neighboring houses. It may be noise, dirt, or vibration from passing heavy trucks. Some conduct is clearly so great an interference that it is easy to conclude it constitutes a nuisance but not every interference is a nuisance. Furthermore, it is frequently difficult to determine whether the interference is sufficiently great to be condemned as unreasonable. The fact that the activity or business of the defendant is lawful and is conducted in a lawful manner does not establish that it is not a nuisance. It is the effect on others that determines whether there is a nuisance.

---

[12] *Ardis Mobile Home Park v Tennessee* (Tenn App) 910 SW2d 863 (1995).

A landfill may be a nuisance even though operated by a city in a nonnegligent manner and in accordance with the state's solid waste disposal statutes.[13]

The courts attempt to balance the social utility of the protection of a plaintiff

---

CASE SUMMARY

Too Close Equals a Nuisance

Facts: United Seeds constructed a grain bin on its land so close to the boundary line that the building constituted a nuisance with respect to the building of Omega Chemical Company on the neighboring land. When sued by Omega to end the nuisance, United raised the defense that it had exercised due care in the construction of the grain bin.

Decision: The exercise of due care was not a defense to a claim of nuisance. Once it was established that the grain bin was an unreasonable interference with the use of Omega's land, it was immaterial whether United had acted carefully in creating that interference. [*Omega Chemical Co. v United Seeds, Inc.*, 252 Neb 137, 560 NW2d 820 (1997)]

---

with the social utility of the activity of the defendant. The mere fact that there is harm does not establish that the defendant's conduct is a nuisance. When community welfare outweighs the harm to land and owners, the activity is not deemed a nuisance.[14] The court may believe that the conduct is socially desirable and therefore should be allowed to continue at the expense of the affected landowner. For example, it has been held that smoke, fumes, and noise from public utilities and power plants were not nuisances, although they did create harm. The interests of the community in the activity of the public utilities outweighed the interests of those affected. Similarly, the proper use of land does not constitute a nuisance to a neighbor even though the neighbor does not like the use. In any case, to constitute a nuisance, there must be a harm that goes beyond mere inconvenience or annoyance with the activity. When trees and underbrush on a landowner's property served as a screen to hide the neighbor's backyard from public view, the neighbor had no legal ground for objecting to the landowner's removing the trees and underbrush even though the neighbor lost the privacy they had given.

CASE SUMMARY

A Right Thing in the Wrong Place Can Be Wrong

Facts: O'Cain owned a home in a rural community. To spite him, his neighbor began raising hogs on a strip of land in front of the O'Cain residence. The odor and flies that this caused made it impossible for the O'Cains to enjoy their property, they were ashamed to bring anyone to the house, and it was practically impossible to sell the property. O'Cain sued to stop the hog raising. The defense was raised that hog raising was lawful and the community was rural.

Decision: The facts that hog raising was lawful and that the community was rural did not give the defendant the right to so use his property as to interfere unreasonably with the plaintiff's house or his property. While the mere fact that a neighbor complains is not proof that there is a nuisance, the circumstances here lead to the conclusion that reasonable persons would regard the interference caused by the hog raising as a nuisance. The court issued an injunction. [*O'Cain v O'Cain* (SC) 473 SE2d 460 (1996)]

---

13 *Williams v Great Falls* (Mont) 732 P2d 1315 (1987).
14 *Kopecky v National Farms, Inc.*, 244 Neb 846 510 NW2d 41 (1994).

The fact that neighbors do not approve of the aesthetics of a building or fence does not make that structure a nuisance.[15]

If conduct is held to constitute a nuisance, the persons affected may be awarded money damages for the loss of the use of the land caused by the conduct and may obtain an injunction or court order to stop the offending conduct. If the nuisance is permanent, the measure of damages is the reduction in the fair market value of the affected property. If the nuisance can be stopped, the measure of damages is the reduction in rental value of the property during the time that the nuisance was allowed to continue.[16]

(a) Private and Public Nuisances. When a nuisance affects only one or a few persons, it is called a **private nuisance**. When it affects the community or public at large, it is called a **public nuisance**. At this point, the law of nuisance is very close to environmental protection, although there is a difference between the two. Environmental protection law is more concerned with harm to the environment and less concerned with the social utility of the defendant's conduct than is the law of nuisance.

Planting trees or erecting a fence, although otherwise lawful, constitutes a public nuisance when it creates a traffic hazard by obscuring an intersection. However, a landowner does not create a public nuisance by allowing trees to grow tall even though the height of the trees required the neighboring county airport to alter its approach patterns, which, in turn, triggered the Federal Aviation Administration to order the airport to shorten the usable portion of its runways.[17]

The existence of a statutory environmental protection procedure may bar or supersede the prior common law of nuisance.

(b) Criminal Nuisance. Distinct from the nuisance that is harmful to other persons or to the enjoyment of the use of their land is the nuisance classified as such because it is a place where criminal acts repeatedly occur. By virtue of either common law principles or express provisions of statute, places conducting illegal gambling or the illegal sale of liquor or narcotics are declared to be nuisances.

The reason for this classification is one of practical expediency. Not only can individuals involved in crime be prosecuted, but also the place may be shut down in the same way that any nuisance may be stopped or closed by the police.

(c) Permanent and Continuing Nuisances. If the interference is caused by a construction or a method of operation that can be remedied at a reasonable expense, it is classified as a **temporary nuisance**. If it cannot be so remedied, it is a permanent nuisance.[18] A **permanent nuisance** consists of a single act that has caused permanent harm. A **continuing nuisance** is a series of related acts or a continuation of an activity, such as the emission of smoke from a factory. ◆ *For example,* the Devon Gun and Skeet Club owned a tract of land on which it maintained rifle and skeet ranges. Bullets from the rifles and shot from the skeet guns would repeatedly go beyond the boundaries of the Devon land and onto land owned by Sergio. Sergio sought an injunction to prevent bullets from straying onto

A private nuisance is a nuisance that affects only one or a few persons.

A public nuisance is a nuisance that affects the community at large.

---

15 *Indiana State Board of Registration v Norde* (Ind App) 600 NE2d 124 (1992).
16 *City of Warner Robins v Holt,* 220 Ga App 794, 470 SE2d 238 (1996).
17 *County of Westchester v Town of Greenwich, Connecticut,* 76 F3d 42 (2d Cir 1996).
18 *Huffman v United States,* 82 F3d 703 (6th Cir 1996).

his land. A court will hold that the action of the Devon Club constitutes a continuing nuisance because it unreasonably interferes with the use and enjoyment of the neighboring land. It is probable that a court would not enjoin all shooting on the Devon land but would require that the direction of shooting be changed or that a barricade be erected on the boundary line of Sergio's property so that bullets would not cross the boundary line. ◆

(d) Nuisances Per Se and Nuisances in Fact. Nuisances may also be classified as nuisances per se and nuisances in fact. A **nuisance per se** is an act, occupation, or structure that is a nuisance at all times and under any circumstances. In contrast, a **nuisance in fact** is situational. Whether there is a nuisance in fact depends on the surrounding circumstances viewed objectively; that is, whether there is a nuisance is determined by the effect on a normal person of ordinary sensitivity.[19] Noise is not a nuisance per se, but it may be of such a character or so excessive as to become one even though it arises from a lawful activity or business.[20]

The fact that neighbors are afraid of fire or explosions does not make an activity a nuisance per se. Such fears do not condemn a gasoline filling station with ground fuel storage tanks as a nuisance per se.[21]

(e) Remedy for Nuisance. A criminal nuisance may be terminated by abatement or closure by police authority. A civil nuisance may be stopped by an injunction, and the injured person may sue for money damages for the harm caused.

When an injunction is issued, the court must exercise great care to fully enjoin the nuisance, while avoiding going too far by enjoining conduct that is otherwise lawful.[22]

(f) The Technological Environment of the Law of Nuisance. As technology changes, new ways of manufacturing, new methods of transportation, and new ways of living develop. As the environment changes, corresponding changes are reflected in the law.

CASE SUMMARY

Solar Energy Heats Up Nuisance Litigation

Facts: Prah brought an action to prevent the construction of his neighbor's house. Prah had constructed a house heated by solar energy. Maretti later purchased the adjoining lot and proposed to build a house. Prah requested that Maretti change his building plans so that Maretti's house would be moved a few feet farther away from the boundary line. In this location, it would not interfere with the path of the sunlight to Prah's house. If Maretti built his house as originally planned, it would seriously interfere with the solar energy system of Prah's house. Maretti raised the defense that he could not be prevented from building as he desired because his building conformed to the restrictions in his deed and to the local zoning and building laws. Prah claimed that locating Maretti's house so as to interfere with the solar energy system of Prah's house was a

---

19 *Statler v Catalano*, 167 Ill App 3d 397, 118 Ill Dec 283, 521 NE2d 565 (1988).
20 *Racine v Glendale Shooting Club, Inc.* (Mo App) 755 SW2d 369 (1988).
21 *Milligan v General Oil Co., Inc.*, 293 Ark 401, 738 SW2d 404 (1987).
22 *Fowler v First Federal Savings & Loan Ass'n of Defuniak Springs* (Fla App) 643 So 2d 30 (1994).

nuisance, even though the construction of Maretti's house was by itself lawful. There was no evidence that the change in the building location desired by the plaintiff would have any effect on the defendant or the use of the defendant's house.

Decision: Maretti could be prevented from locating his house where he originally desired because at that location it would constitute a private nuisance. A use of one's land so as to interfere with the lawful use of another's land constitutes a private nuisance. The fact that the defendant's proposed building was itself otherwise lawful, being in conformity with restrictions in the deed and with building and zoning laws, did not give the defendant the right to interfere unnecessarily with the solar energy system of the plaintiff. *[Prah v Maretti, 108 Wis 2d 223, 321 NW2d 182 (1982)]*

(g) The Computer as a Nuisance. Because any electrical current sets up a magnetic field, computers and wire transmissions to and from computers set up magnetic fields that might affect electrical equipment in buildings on neighboring land. The stronger the current, the greater the magnetic field. Also, if there is a loose or broken circuit that sparks, the interference with neighbors is increased. If that interference rises to an unreasonable level, it may be stopped as a nuisance and damages recovered for the harm caused.

◆ *For example,* the Meridian Data Processing Center was an independent contractor that did all the data processing for a large number of banks and stockbrokers within the state. Because of the large number of computers and direct wire lines to its customers, the center's operation set up a substantial magnetic field that interfered with some of the electronic display equipment in several neighboring stores. The stores sued the data processing center to obtain an injunction against it for maintaining a nuisance. Unless the stores can show there was some negligence in the maintenance of the center's equipment that produced unnecessary sparking or a similar cause of electrical disturbance, they cannot establish a nuisance. Because of the social utility of the center's business, a court would be very unwilling to condemn its activity as a nuisance. If the stores could suggest a reasonable method of shielding the equipment, it is possible that the court would order the center to take such protective measures. ◆

11. Private Remedies: Due Diligence

Due diligence is the process of checking the environmental history and nature of land prior to purchase.

Another method by which problems with land are remedied is through sales transactions in which the buyer demands that a situation or problem on the land be fixed before the buyer will sign a contract for purchase. **Due diligence** is the name given to the process by which the buyer conducts a thorough investigation of the property and its current and former uses to determine whether there are any problems with respect to environmental law or nuisance. Due diligence is conducted through a search of public records, an inspection of the land, and often, when problems appear in these first two steps, some soil testing.

This advance determination of problems is a civil means for land cleanup because sellers will be unable to transfer their properties until they meet the buyers' standards, determined by a close examination of the property for violations.

C.   LAND USE CONTROLS

Apart from environmental laws, there are other restrictions, both private and public, that place controls and limits on how land can be used.

12. Restrictive Covenants in Private Contracts

A restrictive covenant is a private restriction on land use that appears in deeds and transfers from owner to owner.

In the case of private planning, a real estate developer will take an undeveloped tract or area of land, map out on paper an ideal community, and then construct the buildings shown on the plan. These buildings are then sold to private purchasers. The buyers' deeds will contain **restrictive covenants** that obligate the buyers to observe certain limitations in the use of their property, the nature of buildings that will be maintained or constructed on the land, and so on. If a restrictive covenant is valid, it binds any prospective buyer of the land if he or she had actual notice or knowledge of the restriction from the previous owner or the restriction was recorded with the deed.[23] Consequently the owner of any one of the tracts may sue another owner for violating the covenant even though there is no contract between the property owners. If a restrictive covenant violates a statute, rule of law, or public policy, it is not valid and will not be enforced.

A restrictive covenant is to be construed by the same rules of construction that are applied in interpreting contracts. A restrictive covenant will be given its ordinary meaning. A restrictive covenant will be given effect according to its terms but will not be extended beyond them.

CASE SUMMARY

Could the Satellite Dish Stay?

Facts: Payak purchased a home in the Woodstream development. His property was subject to the restriction that "no pole ... for use in connection with television, shall be erected ... on any lot ... without the consent of the developer." Without obtaining such consent, Payak erected a pole-mounted satellite dish on his house. The developer sued to compel him to remove the satellite dish.

Decision: Payak had to remove the pole from the satellite dish, as the erection of a pole was clearly prohibited by the restrictive covenant. However, he could mount the dish in any other way. There was nothing in the restrictive covenant that prohibited the erection of a satellite dish, and the prohibition of a pole would not be extended beyond its terms. [*Woodstream Development Co. v Payak*, 93 Ohio App 3d 25, 637 NE2d 391 (1994)]

As in the case of an ordinary contract, the fundamental objective in construing restrictive covenants is to determine the intention of the parties. This requires consideration not only of the words of the covenant but also of the surrounding circumstances and the objectives which the covenant was designed to accomplish.[24]

---

[23] *McIntyre v Baker* (Ind App) 660 NE2d 348 (1996).
[24] *Jubb v Letterle* (WV App) 446 SE2d 182 (1994).

What's a Dwelling?

Facts: Carpenter purchased a lot in a subdivision. The lots were subject to a restrictive covenant that no one-story "dwelling" could be constructed on a lot unless it covered 1150 square feet. Davis and other neighboring lot owners sued to enjoin Carpenter from building a smaller house. He claimed that he met the size requirement for a "dwelling" when a carport and a storage room were included.

Decision: A "dwelling" is a structure in which people live. They could not live in a carport or in a storage room. Therefore, those two areas could not be included in determining the size of Carpenter's proposed dwelling. Accordingly, he was enjoined from building the undersized dwelling. [*Carpenter v Davis* (Ala) 688 So 2d 256 (1997)]

A restrictive covenant must be clearly stated in order to be effective. If there is any uncertainty, the covenant will be construed strictly in favor of the free use of the land. When there is no uncertainty and no reason to depart from the meaning of the words of the covenant, a court will enforce those words.

The social forces favoring freedom of action and the free use of property cause courts to interpret restrictive covenants narrowly so as to permit the greatest possible use of the land. However, courts often disagree as to what is permitted by a restrictive covenant. Thus, there is a conflict of authority as to whether the use of a home for the day care of children violates a restrictive covenant prohibiting any but a residential use.[25]

A restrictive covenant that violates any statute or administrative regulation is void. Thus, a restrictive covenant that discriminates against persons with disabilities is void because it violates the Fair Housing Act.[26]

A restrictive covenant may also be ignored when it has not been observed. Thus, a requirement that no house could be built without first obtaining the approval of the architectural control committee will be ignored when it is shown that such a committee had never had any meetings and that houses had been built on other lots of the subdivision without any committee approval.[27]

13. Public Zoning

Zoning is public restrictions on land use generally imposed through ordinances.

By **zoning**, a governmental unit such as a city adopts an ordinance imposing restrictions on the use of the land. The object of zoning is to ensure an orderly physical development of the regulated area. In effect, zoning is the same as restrictive covenants; the difference is in the source of authority. In most cases, zoning is based on an ordinance of a local political subdivision, such as a municipality or a county. Restrictive covenants, on the other hand, are created by agreement of the parties.

The zoning power permits any regulation that is conducive to advancing public health, welfare, and safety. The object of a particular zoning regulation may be to prevent high-density population.

---

[25] *Stewart v Jackson* (Ind App) 635 NE2d 186 (1994).
[26] *Hill v Community of Damien of Molokai* (NM) 911 P2d 861 (1996).
[27] *Stuart v Chawney* (Mich App) 560 NW2d 336 (1997).

Be Careful How You Draw Those Lines

Facts: The zoning ordinance for the city of Cleburne, Texas, prohibited homes for the mentally retarded unless a special use permit was obtained from the city to run such a home. The Cleburne Living Center applied for such a special use permit. The permit was denied. The center then claimed that the requirement of a special use permit was unconstitutional.

Decision: The special use requirement was unconstitutional because it denied those who were mentally retarded the equal protection of the law that is guaranteed by the Constitution. There was no evidence a number of mentally retarded persons living in one home would in any way harm or threaten the legitimate interests of the city. Therefore, there was no reason for requiring a special use permit. The requirement could not be justified on the ground that it was necessary in order to protect the city or the public. The zoning ordinance made the distinction between those who are mentally retarded and those who are not. But because there was no sound reason for such a classification, the classification was invalid as an unconstitutional denial of equal protection. [*City of Cleburne v Cleburne Living Center, 473 US 432 (1985)*]

Some zoning ordinances may be conservation inspired. Thus, an ordinance may prohibit or regulate the extraction of natural resources from any land within the zoned area.

The fact that a house is designed for the landowner by an internationally known architect does not give the landowner the right to build the house when it violates the local zoning ordinance on a number of points.[28]

The fact that a zoning restriction limits the owner in the use of a property does not amount to a "taking" of property for which compensation must be made.[29]

A zoning ordinance may make it impossible for landowners to make any economically feasible use of their land. As long as that restriction advances the health, safety, or welfare of the community, it is valid. If it does not advance the community interest, the zoning restriction is unconstitutional.[30]

Nonconforming use is a preexisting use that does not comply with zoning laws but that is grandfathered in and permitted to remain.

(a) Nonconforming Use. When the use of land is in conflict with a zoning ordinance at the time the ordinance goes into effect, such use is described as a **nonconforming use**. For example, when a zoning ordinance that requires a setback of 25 feet from the boundary line is adopted, an existing building that has a 10-foot setback is a nonconforming use.

A nonconforming use has a constitutionally protected right to continue, but if the nonconforming use is discontinued, it cannot be resumed.[31] The right to a nonconforming use may thus be lost by abandonment. If a garage is a nonconforming use and its owner stops using it as a garage and uses it for storing goods, a return to the use of the property as a garage will be barred by abandonment.

At times a real estate development or building construction is only partly completed when a zoning ordinance that would prohibit such development or building is adopted. In order to avoid hardship for the persons involved, it is customary to exempt such partly finished projects from the zoning ordinance just as though they were existing nonconforming uses.[32]

---

[28] *Burroughs v Town of Paradise Valley* (Ariz) 724 P2d 1239 (1986).
[29] *Longview of St. Joseph, Inc. v City of St. Joseph* (Mo App) 918 SW2d 364 (1996).
[30] *W.O. Brisben Co. v City of Montgomery* (Ohio App) 837 NE2d 347 (1994).
[31] *Hansen Brothers Enterprises* (Cal) 907 P2d 1325 (1996).
[32] See, for example, *Cuseo v Horry County Planning Commission* (SC App) 445 SE2d 644 (1994).

A variance is an exception to zoning granted by the governing body charged with enforcing zoning ordinances.

(b) Variance. The administrative agency charged with the enforcement of a zoning ordinance may grant a **variance**. This permits the owner of the land to use it in a specified manner that is inconsistent with the zoning ordinance.

The agency will ordinarily be reluctant to permit a variance when neighboring property owners object because, to the extent that variation is permitted, the basic plan of the zoning ordinance is defeated. Likewise, the allowance of an individual variation, or **spot zoning**, may result in such inequality as to be condemned by the courts.[33] In addition, there is a consideration of practical expediency. If variances are readily granted, every property owner will request a variance and thus flood the agency with these requests.

When the desired use of land is in harmony with the general nature of surrounding areas, it is probable that a zoning variance will be granted. A zoning variance will not be granted on the ground of hardship, however, when the landowner created the hardship by purchasing land that was subject to a zoning ordinance.

CASE SUMMARY

Zoning and Lot Size

Facts: The local zoning ordinance required that every lot have a minimum number of feet of street frontage. The owner of a lot that satisfied this requirement desired to divide his lot because the two smaller lots would have a greater total value than the value of the one undivided lot. However, the subdivided lots would not have the required street frontage. The owner of the lot applied for a zoning variance to allow smaller street frontage.

Decision: Variance refused. The fact that two smaller lots would have greater value than the one larger lot was not sufficient justification for departing from the zoning standard. *[Paniccia v Volker, 133 App Div 2d 404, 519 NYS2d 398 (1987)]*

SUMMARY

There are public and private regulations of land use. The public regulations consist of environmental laws and zoning. Environmental laws exist at both the state and the federal levels. At the federal level, there are regulations that govern air pollution through limits on emissions and permits for discharges; water pollution with permit requirements, discharge prohibitions, and treatment standards; solid waste disposal with limitations on dumping and liability for cleanup when hazardous materials are found on property; and environmental quality through the use of advance studies on projects and their impact on the environment. Other federal regulations on the environment protect endangered species, set standards for drinking water, and impose liability for oil spills as well as safety standards for oil tankers.

Environmental laws are primarily enforced at the federal level by the Environmental Protection Agency (EPA), but other federal agencies as well as state agencies work together to enforce the environmental laws, using criminal and civil penalties and injunctions to halt pollution. Private citizens also have the right to bring suit under federal statutes to enforce the requirements imposed.

A nuisance is a public or private interference with the use and enjoyment of land, and individuals can bring suit to halt nuisances. Courts perform a balancing test in deciding how to handle concerns about nuisances. That balance is one between the use and enjoyment of land and the economic interests of all of the parties involved.

Restrictive covenants in deeds are valid land use restrictions that pass from owner to owner and are enforceable so long as they do not violate any constitutional rights. Zoning is a public means of regulating land use. Zoning laws are part of an overall plan for development adopted by a governmental entity. Some landowners can obtain variances from zoning laws, and some preexisting uses are permitted to continue with the protection of a nonconforming use.

---

[33] *Gullickson v Stark County Board* (ND) 474 NW2d 890 (1991).

QUESTIONS AND CASE PROBLEMS

1. The Arizona Mines Supply Co. was prosecuted for violating the county air pollution regulations. It raised the defense that it did not intentionally violate the law and offered evidence that it had installed special equipment to meet the standards imposed by the law. The prosecution objected to the admission of this evidence on the ground that the absence of any intent to violate the law was not a defense and that, accordingly, evidence of an attempt to comply with the law was irrelevant. Is this correct? [*Arizona v Arizona Mines Supply Co.*, 107 Ariz 199, 484 P2d 619]

2. Federal Oil Co. was loading a tanker with fuel oil when the loading hose snapped for some unknown reason and about 1,000 gallons of oil poured into the ocean. Federal Oil was prosecuted for water pollution. It raised the defense that it had exercised due care, was not at fault in any way, and had not intended to pollute the water. Was it guilty?

3. Philip Carey Company owned a tract of land in Plymouth Township, Pennsylvania, on which it deposited a large pile of manufacturing waste containing asbestos. Carey sold the land to Celotex, and Celotex sold the land to Smith Land & Improvement Corporation. The EPA notified Smith that unless it took steps to eliminate the asbestos hazard, the EPA would do the work and pursue reimbursement. Smith cleaned up the land to the EPA's satisfaction at a cost of $218,945.44. Smith asked Celotex and Carey for reimbursement. Which firms have liability for the cleanup costs? [*Smith Land & Improvement Corp. v Celotex*, 851 F2d 86 (3d Cir)]

4. The McConnells bought a home in Sherwood Estates. The land was subject to a restrictive covenant that "no building, fence, or other structure" could be built on the land without the approval of the developer of the property. The McConnells built a dog pen in their yard that consisted of a cement base with fencing surrounding the base. They claimed that approval was not required on the theory that the restrictive covenant did not apply because it showed an intent to restrict only major construction, not minor additions to the landscape. A lawsuit was brought to compel the McConnells to remove the dog pen because prior approval had not been obtained. Decide. [*Sherwood Estates Homes Ass'n, Inc. v McConnell* (Mo App) 714 SW2d 848]

5. Mark divides a large tract of land into small lots and then sells the lots. In the deed to each buyer is a provision stating that the buyer will not build a house closer than six feet to any boundary line of the lot.

Madeline buys one of these lots and begins to build two feet from the boundary line. Her neighbor Jason protests that Madeline cannot do this because of the six-foot restriction in her deed. Madeline replies that this restriction was made with Mark and has no effect between Jason and Madeline. Is Madeline correct?

6. A zoning ordinance of the city of Dallas, Texas, prohibited the use of property in a residential district for gasoline filling stations. Lombardo brought an action against the city to test the validity of the ordinance. He contended that the ordinance violated the rights of the owners of property in such districts. Do you agree with this contention? [*Lombardo v City of Dallas* (Tex) 73 SW2d 475]

7. Taback began building a vacation home on a parcel of wooded land. It was to be a three-story house, 31 feet high. This violated the local zoning ordinance that limited residential homes to two and one-half stories, not exceeding 35 feet. When Taback learned of this violation, he applied for a zoning variance. Because of the delay of the zoning board and because winter was approaching, Taback finished the construction of the building as a three-story house. At a later hearing before the zoning board, he showed that it would be necessary for him to rebuild the third floor in order to convert the house into a two-and-one-half-story house. The zoning board recognized that Taback's violation could not be seen from neighboring properties. Was Taback entitled to a zoning variance? [*Taback v Town of Woodstock Zoning Board of Appeals*, 134 App Div 2d 733, 521 NYS2d 838]

8. Bermuda Run Country Club, Inc., developed a tract of land, formed a country club, and sold some of the lots to individual buyers. Following various sales and litigation, an agreement was executed giving the board of governors power to veto club members' assessments. The agreement declared that this was a restrictive covenant that would run with the land and bind subsequent owners. The corporation that later purchased the country club claimed it did not have that effect. Was the provision in question a restrictive covenant that ran with the land? [*Bermuda Run Country Club, Inc. v Atwell* (NC App) 465 SE2d 9]

9. The Stallcups lived in a rural section of the state. In front of their house ran a relatively unused, unimproved public county road. Wales Trucking Co. transported concrete pipe from the plant where it was made to a lake where the pipe was used to construct a water line to bring water to a nearby city. In the course of four months, Wales made 825 trips over the

road, carrying from 58,000 to 72,000 pounds of pipe per trip and making the same number of empty return trips. Because Wales's heavy use of the road cut up the dirt and made it like ashes, the Stallcups sued Wales for damages caused by the deposit of dust on their house and for the physical annoyance and discomfort caused by the dust. Wales defended its position on the ground that it had not been negligent and that its use of the road was not unlawful. Decide. [*Wales Trucking Co. v Stallcup* (Tex Civ App) 465 SE2d 44]

10. Some sections of the city of Manitou Springs have hills of varying degrees of slope. To protect against water drainage and erosion, the city adopted a hillside zoning ordinance that required homes on hillsides to be surrounded by more open land than in the balance of the city. Sellon owned land on a hillside and claimed that the hillside ordinance was unconstitutional because it did not treat all homeowners equally. Was the ordinance valid? [*Sellon v City of Manitou Springs* (Colo) 745 P2d 229]

11. Patrick Bossenberry owned a house in a planned community area. Each lot in the area was limited by a restrictive covenant to use for a single-family dwelling. The covenant defined family so as to require blood or marital relationship between most of the occupants. Bossenberry rented his building to Kay-Jan, Inc., which wanted to use the building as a care home for not more than six adult mentally retarded persons. The neighbors sought to enjoin this use as a breach of the covenant. A number of Michigan statutes had been adopted that advanced the public policy of providing care for mentally retarded persons. Could the neighbors prevent the use of the property as a care home for mentally retarded adults? [*Craig v Bossenberry,* 134 Mich App 543, 351 NW2d 596]

12. Kenneth and Mary Norpel purchased a house, and Kenneth attached a 35-foot flagpole to it. He did not obtain the permission of the architectural committee of the Stone Hill Community Association. This consent was required by a restrictive covenant to which the Norpel house was subject. The association objected to the flagpole, and Norpel then flew the American flag from the pole. The association brought an action to compel the removal of the pole. Norpel claimed that as a combat veteran of World War II he had a constitutionally protected right to fly the American flag. Can he be compelled to remove the flagpole?

13. Drabik owned a tract of land. He used the eastern fifth of the land as an automobile junkyard. At just about that time, the county adopted a zoning ordinance that zoned for agricultural use the part of the county in which Drabik's land was located. Drabik expanded his junkyard business so that in a few years it covered almost the entire tract of his land. The county then brought an action to compel him to confine his junkyard business to its former area. He claimed that he could make a nonconforming use of his land. Was he correct?

CPA QUESTIONS

1. Which of the following remedies is available against a real property owner to enforce the provisions of federal acts regulating air and water pollution?

	Citizen suits against the Environmental Protection Agency to enforce compliance with the laws	State suits against violators	Citizen suits against violators
a.	Yes	Yes	Yes
b.	Yes	Yes	No
c.	No	Yes	Yes
d.	Yes	No	Yes

(5/94, Law, #59, 4814)

2. Under the Comprehensive Environmental Response, Compensation, and Liability Act (CERCLA), commonly known as Superfund, which of the following parties would be liable to the Environmental Protection Agency (EPA) for the expense of cleaning up a hazardous waste disposal site?

I. The current owner or operator of the site
II. The person who transported the wastes to the site
III. The person who owned or operated the site at the time of the disposal

a. I and II
b. I and III
c. II and III
d. I, II, and III

(5/95, Law, #56, 5390)

Leases

CHAPTER 52

OBJECTIVES

After studying this chapter, you should be able to

1. *Define a lease and list its essential elements;*
2. *List the ways in which a lease may be terminated;*
3. *List and explain the rights and duties of the parties to a lease;*
4. *Describe the remedies of a landlord for breach by the tenant;*
5. *Describe a landlord's liability for a tenant's and a third person's injuries sustained on the premises; and*
6. *Define and distinguish between a sublease and an assignment of a lease.*

If you cannot buy a house or piece of business property, leasing such a property from someone who does own it may be the answer.

A.   CREATION AND TERMINATION

Leases are governed by the common law of property as modified by judicial decisions and statutes.[1]

1.   Definition and Nature

A **lease** is the relationship in which one person is in lawful possession of real property owned by another. In common speech, the term *lease* also refers to the agreement that creates that relationship.

The person who owns the real property and permits the occupation of the premises is known as the **lessor**, or **landlord**. The **lessee**, or **tenant**, is the one who occupies the property. A lease establishes the relationship of landlord and tenant.

Basically a lease parallels bailments in personal property, in which there is an agreement to make the bailment and a subsequent transfer of possession to carry out that agreement. In the case of a lease, there is the lease contract and the interest thereafter acquired by the tenant when possession is delivered under the lease contract. Common law looked at the transfer of possession and regarded the lease as merely the creation of an interest in land. Modern law looks at the contract and regards the lease to be the same as renting an automobile. With this new approach, typical contract law concepts of unconscionability, mitigation of damages, and warranties are brought into the law on leases of real property.

> A lease is the lawful possession of the property of another and the document representing this relationship.
>
> A lessor is the owner of the property who transfers possession.
>
> A landlord is the lessor.
>
> A lessee is the party in possession of the property of another pursuant to a lease.
>
> A tenant is the lessee.

2.   Creation of the Lease Relationship

The relationship of landlord and tenant is created by an express or implied contract. An oral lease is valid at common law, but statutes in most states require written leases for certain tenancies. Many states provide that a lease for a term exceeding three years must be in writing. Statutes in other states require written leases when the term exceeds one year.

(a) Antidiscrimination. Statutes in many states prohibit an owner who rents property for profit from discriminating against prospective tenants on the basis of race, color, religion, or national origin. Enforcement of such statutes is generally entrusted to an administrative agency.

(b) Covenants and Conditions. Some obligations of the parties in the lease are described as **covenants**. Thus, a promise by the tenant to make repairs is called a covenant to repair. Sometimes it is provided that the lease shall be forfeited or terminated upon a breach of a promise. That provision is then called a **condition** rather than a covenant.

---

[1] A uniform act, the Uniform Residential Landlord and Tenant Act (URLTA), has been adopted in Alaska, Arizona, Florida, Hawaii, Iowa, Kansas, Kentucky, Montana, Nebraska, New Mexico, Oregon, Rhode Island, South Carolina, Tennessee, and Virginia.

(c) Other Agreements. The lease may be the only agreement between the parties. However, some parties to a lease also enter into a separate guarantee or a letter of credit to protect the landlord from breach by the tenant. The tenant, in addition to being a lessee, may hold a franchise from the lessor.

(d) Unconscionability. At common law, the parties to a lease had relatively uncontrolled freedom to include such terms as they chose. Some states require that leases conform to the concept of unconscionability and follow the pattern of UCC Section 2-302.[2] *For example,* a provision in a residential lease stating that curtailment of services by the landlord will not constitute an eviction and that such interruption of service will not entitle the tenant to any compensation is unconscionable. Such a clause does not bar the tenant from recovering for breach of the implied warranty of habitability because of the interruptions. Similarly, a provision in a lease declaring that the landlord is not responsible for interruptions in various services provided to tenants will not protect the landlord from liability under the doctrine of unconscionability when the air-conditioning system is out of operation for six weeks in midsummer.

3.   Classification of Tenancies

Tenancies are classified by duration as tenancies for years, from year to year, at will, and by sufferance.

(a) Tenancy for Years. A **tenancy for years** is one under which the tenant has a leasehold estate of definite duration. The expression "for years" is used to describe such a tenancy even if the duration of the tenancy is for only six months or as long as ten years.

> A tenancy for years is a lease for a fixed period of time.

(b) Periodic Tenancy. A **periodic tenancy** is one under which a tenant, holding an estate in land for an indefinite duration, pays an annual, monthly, or weekly rent. This tenancy does not terminate at the end of a year, month, or week except upon proper notice.

> A periodic tenancy is a lease that runs from period to period, as in a month-to-month tenancy.

In almost all states, a periodic tenancy is implied if the tenant, with the consent of the landlord, stays in possession of property after a tenancy for years. Consent may be shown by an express statement or by conduct, such as continuing to accept rent.[3] The lease frequently states that the tenant's holding over gives rise to a tenancy from year to year unless written notice to the contrary is given.

(c) Tenancy at Will. When a lease is to run for an indefinite period, which may be terminated at any time by the landlord or the tenant, a **tenancy at will** exists. A person who enters into possession of land for an indefinite period with the owner's permission, but without any agreement as to rent, is a tenant at will. Statutes in some states and decisions in others require advance notice of termination of this kind of tenancy.

> A tenancy at will is a lease that can be terminated at any time by either party.

(d) Tenancy at Sufferance. When a tenant remains in possession after the termination of the lease without permission of the landlord, the landlord may treat

---

[2] *Flam v Herrman,* 90 Misc 2d 434, 395 NYS2d 136 (1977); URLTA § 1.303.
[3] *Roosen v Schaffer,* 127 Ariz App 346, 621 P2d 33 (1980).

A tenancy at sufferance is a lease arrangement in which tenant occupies the property at the discretion of the landlord. A valid lease no longer exists.

the tenant as either a trespasser or a tenant. Until the landlord elects to do one or the other, a **tenancy at sufferance** exists. ◆ *For example*, if John's one-year lease expired on January 31, 1998, and John remained in the apartment for a week, he is a tenant at sufferance during that week. If John's landlord accepts a rental payment at the end of the first week, John is a periodic or month-to-month tenant. John was a tenant for years, a tenant at sufferance, and then a periodic tenant. ◆

4. Termination of Lease

A lease is generally not terminated by the death, insanity, or bankruptcy of either party except in the case of a tenancy at will. Leases may be terminated in the following ways.

(a) Termination by Notice. A lease may give the landlord the power to terminate it by giving notice to the tenant. In states that follow the common law on termination by notice, it is immaterial why the landlord terminates. A provision giving the landlord the right to terminate the lease by notice if specified conditions exist is strictly construed against the landlord.

(b) Expiration of Term in a Tenancy for Years. When a tenancy for years exists, the relation of landlord and tenant ceases upon the expiration of the term. There is no requirement that one party give the other any notice of termination. Express notice to end the term may be required of either or both parties by provisions of the lease except when a statute prohibits the landlord from imposing such a requirement.

(c) Notice in a Periodic Tenancy. In the absence of an agreement of the parties, notice for termination of a periodic tenancy is now usually governed by statute. It is common practice for the parties to require 30 or 60 days' notice to end a tenancy from year to year. As to tenancies for periods of less than a year, statutory provisions commonly require notice of only one week.

(d) Forfeiture. The landlord may terminate the lease because of the tenant's misconduct or breach of a condition if a term of the lease or a statute so provides. In the absence of such a provision, the landlord may claim damages only for the breach. Terminating the relationship by forfeiture is not favored by the courts.

(e) Destruction of Property. If a lot and a building on it are leased, either an express provision in the lease or a statute generally releases the tenant from liability to pay rent if the building is destroyed. Alternatively, the amount of rent may be reduced in proportion to the loss sustained. Such statutes do not impose on the landlord any duty to repair or restore the property to its former condition.

When the lease covers rooms or an apartment in a building, a destruction of the leased premises terminates the lease.

(f) Fraud. Because a lease is based on a contract, a lease may be avoided when the circumstances are such that a contract could be avoided for fraud. (See chapter 13.)

(g) Transfer of the Tenant. Residential leases may contain a provision for termination upon the tenant's being transferred by an employer to another city or upon the tenant's being called into military service. Such provisions are strictly construed against the tenant. Therefore, when entering a lease, the tenant should exercise care to see that the provision is sufficiently broad to cover personal situations that may arise.

5.   Notice of Termination

When notice of termination is required, no particular words are necessary to constitute a sufficient notice provided the words used clearly indicate the intention of the party. The notice, whether given by the landlord or the tenant, must be definite. Statutes sometimes require that the notice be in writing. In the absence of such a provision, however, oral notice is generally sufficient.

6.   Renewal of Lease

When a lease terminates for any reason, the landlord and the tenant ordinarily enter into a new agreement if they wish to extend or renew the lease. The power to renew the lease may be stated in the original lease by declaring that the lease runs indefinitely, as from year to year, subject to being terminated by either party's giving written notice of a specified number of days or months before the termination date. Renewal provisions are strictly construed against the tenant.

The lease may require the tenant to give written notice of intention to renew the lease. In such a case, there is no renewal if the tenant does not give the required notice but merely remains on the premises after the expiration of the original term.[4]

B.   RIGHTS AND DUTIES OF PARTIES

The rights and duties of the landlord and tenant are based on principles of real estate law and contract law. With the rising tide of consumer protectionism, there is an increasing tendency to treat the relationship as merely a contract and to govern the rights and duties of the parties by general principles of contract law.

7.   Possession

Possession involves both the right to acquire possession at the beginning of the lease and the right to retain possession until the lease is ended.

(a) Tenant's Right to Acquire Possession. By making a lease, the lessor covenants by implication to give possession of the premises to the tenant at the agreed time. If the landlord rents a building that is being constructed, there is an implied covenant that it will be ready for occupancy at the commencement of the term of the lease.

(b) Tenant's Right to Retain Possession. After the lease begins and the tenant takes possession, that possession and control of the premises are the exclusive right of the tenant during the term of the lease. This right exists so long as the lease

---

[4] *Ahmed v Scott*, 65 Ohio App 2d 271, 418 NE2d 406 (1979).

continues or until a default under the lease. Under the exclusive right of possession, a tenant could refuse to allow the lessor to show the property to prospective tenants, so most leases expressly give this right to the landlord.

If the landlord interferes with this possession by evicting the tenant, the landlord has breached the lease agreement, and legal remedies are available to the tenant. An eviction occurs when the tenant is deprived of the possession, use, and enjoyment of the premises by the interference of the lessor or the lessor's agent. If the landlord wrongfully deprives the tenant of the use of one room when the tenant is entitled to use an entire apartment or building, there is a partial eviction.

(c) Covenant of Quiet Enjoyment. Most written leases today contain an express promise by the landlord to respect the possession of the tenant. This promise is called a **covenant of quiet enjoyment**. Such a provision protects the tenant from interference with possession by the landlord or the landlord's agent, but it does not impose liability on the landlord for the unlawful acts of third persons.[5]

> Constructive eviction is a landlord's forced ouster of the tenant because of uninhabitable property conditions.

(d) Constructive Eviction. A **constructive eviction** occurs when some act or omission of the landlord substantially deprives the tenant of the use and enjoyment of the premises.

To establish a constructive eviction, the tenant must show that the landlord intended to deprive the tenant of the use and enjoyment of the premises. This intent may, however, be inferred from conduct. There is no constructive eviction unless the tenant leaves the premises. If the tenant continues to occupy the premises for more than a reasonable time after the acts claimed to constitute a constructive eviction, the tenant waives or loses the right to object to the landlord's conduct. The tenant cannot thereafter abandon the premises and claim to have been evicted.[6] ◆ *For example*, a condition of constructive eviction would be sewage backing up through the bathtub. ◆

CASE SUMMARY

Jewelry and Stereos May Not Mix If the Walls Vibrate

Facts: Paolucci opened a jewelry store in 1978 in an Illinois mall owned and operated by JMB Properties. Barretts Audio and Video Store moved in next door in November 1984. Barretts and Paolucci shared a common wall. In December 1985, Paolucci began complaining to the landlord, Carlyle, about the high level of noise emanating from Barretts. When Barretts' employees conducted demonstrations of their stereo equipment, the walls of the jewelry store literally shook, causing pictures on the walls to rattle. The vibrations caused merchandise in display cases to move or topple over so that the display cases had to be reset almost daily. The stereo store refused to lower the volume, even after many requests. One employee had to resort to wearing ear plugs. Barretts insulated the wall at the landlord's direction, but the problem was not alleviated. Paolucci failed to pay rent for July 1990 and vacated the premises in August 1990, some two years prior to the end of the lease he had renewed in 1986. The landlord filed an action against Paolucci, seeking recovery of past due rent and penalties for violating the lease. Paolucci filed a counterclaim, alleging he had been constructively evicted as a result of the failure of the landlord to control the noise generated by Barretts. Barretts had moved out in February 1990.

---

[5] *Rittenbert v Donohoe Construction Co.* (DC) 426 A2d 338 (1981).

[6] Some states prohibit a landlord of residential property from willfully turning off the utilities of a tenant for the purpose of evicting the tenant. *Kinney v Viccari*, 23 Cal 3d 348, 165 Cal Rptr 787, 612 P2d 877 (1980) (imposing civil penalty of $100 a day for every day utilities are shut off). Such conduct is also a violation of URLTA §§ 2.104 and 4.105.

Decision: The tenant must abandon the premises within a reasonable time after the untenantable condition occurred in order to claim constructive eviction. If the tenant fails to vacate within a reasonable time, the tenant is considered to have waived the landlord's breach of covenant. The reasonableness of a delay is generally a question of fact. The untenantable condition in this case first arose in December of 1985. Paolucci remained on the leasehold premises until August of 1990, nearly five years after the condition arose and six months after Barretts moved out of the mall. Paolucci said that he remained on the premises for six months after Barretts left because his new store was still under construction. One factor to be considered in determining the reasonableness of the delay is the time required to find a new location. Paolucci has no explanation for why he tolerated the alleged untenantable condition for more than four years. There is no constructive eviction when the tenant is able to remain in the premises. [JMB Properties v Paolucci (Ill App) 604 NE2d 967 (1992)

8. Use of Premises

The lease generally specifies the uses authorized for the tenant. In addition, the lease may provide the landlord with authorization to adopt regulations covering the use of the premises. These regulations are binding on the tenant as long as they are reasonable, lawful, and not in conflict with the terms of the lease. In the absence of express or implied restrictions, a tenant is entitled to use the premises for any lawful purpose for which they are adapted or for which they are ordinarily employed or in a manner contemplated by the parties in executing the lease. A provision specifying the use to be made of the property is strictly construed against the tenant.

(a) Change of Use. The modern lease will, in substance, make a change of use a condition subsequent. That is, if the tenant uses the property for any purpose other than the one specified, the landlord has the option of declaring the lease terminated.

(b) Continued Use of Property. The modern lease will ordinarily require the tenant to give the landlord notice of nonuse or vacancy of the premises. This is because of the increased danger of damage to the premises by vandalism or fire when a building is vacant. Also, there is commonly a provision in the landlord's fire insurance policy making it void if a vacancy continues for a specified time.

(c) Rules. The modern lease generally contains a blanket agreement by the tenant to abide by the provisions of rules and regulations adopted by the landlord. These rules are generally binding on the tenant whether they exist at the time the lease was made or are adopted afterward.

(d) Prohibition of Pets. A lease restriction prohibiting pet ownership is valid.

9. Rent

The tenant is under a duty to pay rent as compensation to the landlord. The amount of rent agreed to by the parties may be subject to government regulation, as when a city or county has enacted rent control laws.

(a) Time of Payment. The time of payment of rent is ordinarily fixed by the lease. When the lease does not specify, rent generally is not due until the end of the term. However, statutes or custom may require rent to be paid monthly or may require a substantial deposit before the lease begins.

Assignment is the transfer of the rights under a lease.

Sublease is the transfer of a portion of the time left under a lease.

(b) Assignment. If the lease is assigned (the tenant's entire interest is transferred to a third person), the assignee is liable to the landlord for the rent. However, the assignment does not in itself discharge the tenant from the duty to pay the rent.

If the assignee of the lease does not make the lease payments, the landlord may bring an action for the rent against either the original tenant or the assignee, or both, but is entitled to payment of only what is due under the lease, not a double amount as collected from each party. A **sublessee** (a person to whom part of a tenant's interest is transferred) ordinarily is not liable to the original lessor for rent unless that liability has been expressly assumed or is imposed by statute.

An escalation clause is a provision in the lease that permits rent increases.

(c) Rent Escalation. When property is rented for a long term, it is common to include some provision for the automatic increase of the rent at periodic intervals. Such a provision is often tied to increases in the cost of living or in the landlord's operating costs, and is called an **escalation clause**.

10. Repairs and Condition of Premises

In the absence of an agreement to the contrary, the tenant has no duty to make repairs. When the landlord makes repairs, reasonable care must be exercised to make them in a proper manner. The tenant is liable for any damage to the premises caused by his or her willful or negligent acts.

(a) Inspection of Premises. Under the URLTA, the landlord has the right to enter the leased premises for emergency purposes or with notice to the tenant for repairs, evaluations, and estimates.

(b) Housing Laws. Various laws protect tenants, such as by requiring landlords to observe specified safety, health, and fire prevention standards. Some statutes require a landlord who leases a building for dwelling purposes to keep it in a condition fit for habitation. Leases commonly require the tenant to obey local ordinances and laws relating to the care and use of the premises.

Warranty of habitability is an implied warranty that the leased property is fit for dwelling by tenants.

(c) Warranty of Habitability. At common law, a landlord was not bound by any obligation that the premises be fit for use unless the lease contained an express warranty to that effect. Most jurisdictions now reject this view and have created a **warranty of habitability** to protect tenants. The warranty of habitability requires, in most states, that the premises have running water, have heat in winter, and are free from structural defects and infestation. If the landlord breaches a warranty of habitability, the tenant is entitled to damages. These damages may be set off against the rent that is due, or if no rent is due, the tenant may bring an independent lawsuit to recover damages from the landlord.[7]

---

[7] *Lawrence v Triangle Capital Corp.*, 90 Ohio App 105, 628 NE2d 74 (1993).

Moe's Pizza has leased commercial space for the operation of a pizzeria on Watts Street in New York City from Manhattan Mansions. After moving into the premises and beginning business operations, Moe finds that water from the bathtub located in the residential apartment above his facility leaks down through the floor and emerges just above the grill in the pizzeria. Water drips down onto the grill and, on some days, onto the customer counter. When the customers see the water dripping from the ceiling, they often leave. Several times Moe has had to close the restaurant in order to clean up the water.

Moe complains to Manhattan Mansions, but he is told that commercial leases do not provide any warranties for property conditions. Moe withholds his rent of $3,418.76 for the month of February, and Manhattan brings suit for nonpayment of rent and eviction.

Is there no remedy for Moe's problems with the condition of his leased property? Was it ethical for Manhattan to lease the property without disclosure of the leak problem? Was it ethical for Moe to withhold his rent? What would you have done if you were leasing the premises? *Manhattan Mansions v Moe's Pizza* (Civ. Ct. NY, NY County) 561 NYS2d 331 (1990).

(d) Abatement and Escrow Payment of Rent. To protect tenants from unsound living conditions, statutes sometimes provide that a tenant is not required to pay rent as long as the premises are not fit to live in. As a compromise, some statutes require the tenant to continue to pay the rent but require that it be paid into an escrow or agency account. The money in the escrow account is paid to the landlord only upon proof that the necessary repairs have been made to the premises.

11. Improvements

In the absence of a special agreement, neither the tenant nor the landlord is under a duty to make improvements, as contrasted with repairs. Either party may, as a term of the original lease, agree or covenant to make improvements, in which case a failure to perform will result in liability in an action for damages for breach of contract brought by the other party. In the absence of an agreement to the contrary, improvements become part of the realty and belong to the landlord.

12. Taxes and Assessments

In the absence of an agreement to the contrary, the landlord, not the tenant, is usually under a duty to pay taxes or assessments. The lease may provide for an increase in rent if taxes on the rented property are increased.[8]

If taxes or assessments are increased because of improvements made by the tenant, the landlord is liable for such increases if the improvements remain with the property. If the improvements can be removed by the tenant, the amount of the increase must be paid by the tenant.

13. Tenant's Deposit

A landlord may require a tenant to make a deposit to protect the landlord from any default on the part of the tenant. In some states, protection is given the tenant who

[8] *Brazelton v Jackson Drug Co., Inc.* (Wyo) 796 P2d 808 (1990).

is required to make a payment to the landlord as a deposit to ensure compliance with the lease. Some states require the landlord to hold payment as a trust fund and inform the tenant of the bank in which the money is deposited. The landlord becomes subject to a penalty if the money is used before the tenant has breached the lease. Other states limit the amount the landlord may require the tenant to deposit for the lease.

14. Protection from Retaliation

The modern trend is to protect tenants from retaliation by the landlord for the tenants' exercise of their lawful rights or reporting the landlord for violations of housing and sanitation codes. The retaliation by the lessor may take the form of refusing to renew a lease or evicting the tenant.

15. Remedies of Landlord

If a tenant fails to pay rent, the landlord may bring an ordinary lawsuit to collect the amount due and in some states may seize and hold the property of the tenant.

(a) Landlord's Lien. In the absence of an agreement or a statute, the landlord does not have a lien on the personal property or crops of the tenant for money due for rent. The parties may create by express or implied contract a lien in favor of the landlord for rent and also for advances, taxes, or damages for failure to make repairs.

In the absence of a statutory provision, the lien of the landlord is superior to the claims of all other persons except prior lienors and good-faith purchasers.

(b) Suit for Rent. Whether or not the landlord has a lien for unpaid rent, the landlord may sue the tenant on the latter's obligation to pay rent as specified in the lease. In some jurisdictions, the landlord is permitted to bring a combined action to recover the possession of the land and the overdue rent at the same time.

(c) Recovery of Possession. A lease commonly provides that upon the breach of any of its provisions by the tenant, such as the failure to pay rent, the lease terminates or the landlord may exercise the option to declare the lease terminated. When the lease is terminated for any reason, the landlord then has the right to evict the tenant and retake possession of the property.

Modern cases hold that a landlord cannot lock out a tenant for overdue rent. The landlord must employ legal process to regain possession even if the lease expressly gives the landlord the right to self-help.

The landlord may resort to legal process to evict the tenant in order to enforce the right to possession of the premises. Statutes in many states provide a summary remedy to recover possession that is much more efficient than the slow common law remedies. Often referred to as a **forcible entry and detainer**, this action restores the property to the landlord's possession unless the tenant complies with payment requirements.

Forcible entry and detainer is an action by the landlord to have the tenant removed for nonpayment of rent.

(d) Landlord's Duty to Mitigate Damages. If the tenant leaves the premises before the expiration of the lease, is the landlord under any duty to rent the premises again in order to reduce the rent or damages for which the departing tenant will be liable? By common law and majority rule, a tenant owns an estate in land, and if the tenant abandons it, there is no duty on the landlord to find a new tenant for the premises. A growing minority view, on the other hand, places greater emphasis on the contractual aspects of a lease. Under this new view, when the tenant abandons the property and thereby defaults or breaks the contract, the landlord is under the duty to seek to mitigate the damages caused by the tenant's breach and must make a reasonable effort to rent the abandoned property.

C.   LIABILITY FOR INJURY ON PREMISES

When the tenant, a member of the tenant's family, or a third person is injured because of the condition of the premises, the question arises as to who is liable for the damages sustained by the injured person.

16. Landlord's Liability to Tenant

In the absence of a covenant to keep the premises in repair, the landlord is ordinarily not liable for the tenant's personal injuries caused by the defective condition of the premises that, by the lease, are placed under the control of the tenant. Likewise, the landlord is not liable for the harm caused by an obvious condition that was known to the tenant at the time the lease was made.[9] A landlord is not liable when a tenant falls from an apartment balcony because the balcony is an obvious danger to the tenant.

(a) Crimes of Third Persons. Ordinarily the landlord is not liable to the tenant for crimes committed on the premises by third persons, such as when a third person enters the premises and commits larceny or murder. The landlord is not required to establish a security system to protect the tenant from crimes of third persons.

In contrast, when the criminal acts of third persons are reasonably foreseeable, the landlord may be held liable for the harm caused a tenant. *For example,* when a tenant has repeatedly reported that the deadbolt on the apartment door is broken, the landlord is liable for the tenant's loss when a thief enters through the door because such criminal conduct was foreseeable. Likewise, when the landlord of a large apartment complex does not take reasonable steps to prevent repeated criminal acts, the landlord is liable to the tenant for the harm caused by the foreseeable criminal act of a third person.

CASE SUMMARY

Death at an Office Complex: Who Is Liable?

Facts: Alexis Gale was shot and killed while working in the rented business offices of her employer, Mon Ami International. Gale's husband sued the property owners and managers of the office complex where Mon Ami's rented offices were located, claiming the lessor breached a duty to provide adequate security at the complex. The lease provided that the lessor would provide security services in the common areas of the complex and that the lessee was given exclusive control of the portion of the premises rented as office space. Gale was shot and killed by

---

[9] *English v Kienke* (Utah) 848 P2d 153 (1993).

a co-worker, not in a common area over which the lessor had control, but in the Mon Ami office space over which the lessee had exclusive control and in which the lessor had no duty to provide security.

Gale's husband also alleged that the lessor knew an attack was about to take place because of some strange happenings that took place earlier that day. That morning, a maintenance worker noticed a man opening the back door of the Mon Ami office from the inside. This man appeared to be acting strangely: He took a handkerchief out of his suit pocket and picked up a briefcase sitting outside the door. He was wearing what the worker described as a costume-type wig on his head but looked vaguely familiar. Later that day Gale's body was discovered. The maintenance worker reported what he had seen to the lessor and to the police. It was eventually determined that this was the co-worker who had shot Gale, and it was also determined that the lessor knew of numerous arguments between Gale and the co-worker. Gale's spouse alleged that the lessor had a duty to prevent the shooting.

Decision: A landlord's duty to keep safe portions of the leased premises designated as common areas, in which the landlord has reserved a qualified right of possession, does not extend to the leased areas of the premises over which the tenant has exclusive possession and control. Even retention of the right to enter the leased premises in emergencies and during business hours for landlord-related purposes does not evidence such dominion and control of the premises as to warrant holding the landlord liable. The landlord here had no duty to provide security in the office space where the shooting occurred, which was in the exclusive possession and control of the tenant, Mon Ami.

The observations of the landlord's maintenance worker created no duty on the part of the lessor to foresee or prevent the attack on Gale. The activity witnessed by the maintenance worker was insufficient to have caused any reasonable person to foresee what happened to Gale. The maintenance worker was obviously not trained as or expected to perform the duties of a security guard. Because the lessor could not have reasonably foreseen the attack, there is no basis for claiming it should have done anything to try to prevent it. [*Gale v North Meadow Associates (Ga App) 466 SE 2d 648 (1995)*]

(b) Limitation of Liability. A provision in a lease excusing or exonerating the landlord from liability is generally valid regardless of the cause of the tenant's loss. A number of courts, however, have restricted the landlord's power to limit liability in the case of residential, as distinguished from commercial, leasing. A provision in a residential lease that the landlord shall not be liable for damage caused by water, snow, or ice is void. A modern trend holds that clauses limiting liability of the landlord are void with respect to harm caused by the negligence of the landlord when the tenant is a residential tenant generally or is in a government low-cost housing project.

Third persons on the premises, even with the consent of the tenant, are generally not bound by a clause exonerating the landlord. Such third persons may therefore sue the landlord when they sustain injuries. Members of the tenant's family, employees, and guests are not bound to such a liability limitation when they do not sign the lease. However, there is authority to the contrary.

(c) Indemnification of Landlord. The modern lease commonly contains a provision declaring that the tenant will indemnify the landlord for any liability of the landlord to a third person that arises from the tenant's use of the rented premises.

17. Landlord's Liability to Third Persons

A landlord is ordinarily not liable to third persons injured because of the condition of any part of the rented premises that is in the possession of a tenant by virtue of a lease.

If the landlord retains control over a portion of the premises, such as hallways or stairways, however, a landlord's liability exists for injuries to third persons caused by failure to exercise proper care in connection with that part of the premises. The modern trend of cases imposes liability on the landlord when a third person is harmed by a condition that the landlord was obligated, under a contract with the tenant, to correct or when the landlord was obligated, under a contract with the tenant, to keep the premises in repair.

18. Tenant's Liability to Third Persons

A tenant in possession has control of the property and is liable when his or her failure to use due care under the circumstances causes harm to (1) licensees, such as a person allowed to use a telephone, and (2) invitees, such as customers entering a store. For both classes, the liability is the same as that of an owner in possession of property. It is likewise immaterial whether the property is used for residential or business purposes.

The liability of the tenant to third persons is not affected by the fact that the landlord may have contracted in the lease to make repairs that, if made, would have avoided the injury. The tenant can be protected, however, in the same manner that the landlord can by procuring liability insurance for indemnity against loss from claims of third persons.

CASE SUMMARY

Where There's Smoke, There's Fire and Maybe Liability

Facts: Johnny C. Carpenter and Harvey E. Hill died of asphyxiation when a fire broke out in their Hattiesburg, Mississippi, apartment on the morning of February 20, 1983. There were no smoke detectors in the apartment at the time of the fire, as required under Hattiesburg City Ordinance 2021. The administrators of the estates of Carpenter and Hill filed suit against London, Stetelman, and Kirkwood, the owners and managers of the apartment complex.

Decision: Because there was a statutory requirement for the presence of smoke detectors and the landlord failed to have them installed, there was negligence *per se*. The landlord, in its failure to comply with the law, was a cause of the deaths. The landlord is liable in negligence to the estates of the two men. [*Hill v London, Stetelman, and Kirkwood, Inc.*, 906 F2d 204 (5th Cir 1990)]

D.   TRANSFER OF RIGHTS

Both the landlord and the tenant have property and contract rights with respect to the lease. Can they be transferred or assigned?

19. Transfer of Landlord's Reversionary Interest

The reversionary interest of the landlord may be transferred voluntarily by the landlord or involuntarily by a judicial or an execution sale. The tenant then becomes the tenant of the new owner of the reversionary interest, and the new owner is bound by the terms of the lease.

20. Tenant's Assignment of Lease and Sublease

An assignment of a lease is a transfer by the tenant of the tenant's entire interest in the premises to a third person. A tenancy for years may be assigned by the tenant unless the latter is restricted from doing so by the terms of the lease or by a statute. A sublease is a transfer to a third person, the sublessee, of less than the tenant's entire interest, or full lease term.

(a) Limitations on Rights. The lease may contain provisions denying the right to assign or sublet or provisions imposing specified restrictions on the privilege of assigning or subletting. Such restrictions enable the landlord to obtain protection from new tenants who would damage the property or be financially irresponsible.

Restrictions in the lease are construed liberally in favor of the tenant. No violation of a provision prohibiting assignment or subleasing occurs when the tenant merely permits someone else to use the premises.

(b) Effect of Assignment or Sublease. An assignee or a sublessee has no greater rights than the original lessee.[10] An assignee becomes bound by the obligations of the lease by the act of taking possession of the premises. In contrast, a sublessee is not obligated to the lessor in the absence of an express contract imposing such liability.

Neither the act of subletting nor the landlord's agreement to it releases the original tenant from liability under the terms of the original lease. When a lease is assigned, the original tenant remains liable for the rent that becomes due thereafter.

It is customary and desirable for the tenant to require the sublessee to covenant or promise to perform all obligations under the original lease and to indemnify the tenant for any loss caused by the default of the sublessee. An express covenant or promise by the sublessee is necessary to impose such liability. The fact that the sublease is made "subject to" the terms of the original lease merely recognizes the superiority of the original lease but does not impose any duty on the sublessee to perform the tenant's obligation under the original lease. If the sublessee promises to assume the obligations of the original lease, the landlord, as a third-party beneficiary, may sue the sublessee for breach of the provisions of the original lease.

SUMMARY

The agreement between a lessor and a lessee by which the latter holds possession of real property owned by the former is a lease. Statutes in many states prohibit discrimination by an owner who rents property. Statutes in some states require that the lease not be unconscionable. Tenancies are classified according to duration as tenancies for years, from year to year, at will, and at sufferance. A lease is generally not terminated by the death, insanity, or bankruptcy of either party except for a tenancy at will.

Leases are usually terminated by the expiration of the specified term, notice, surrender, forfeiture, or destruction of the property or because of fraud. A tenant has the right to acquire possession at the beginning of the lease and has the right to retain possession until the lease is ended. Evictions may be either actual or constructive. The tenant is under a duty to pay rent as compensation to the landlord.

An assignment of a lease by the tenant is a transfer of

---

[10] *Gulden v Newberry Wrecker Service, Inc.*, 154 Ga App 130, 267 SE2d 763 (1980).

the tenant's entire interest in the property to a third person; a sublease is a transfer of less than an entire interest—in either space or time. A lease may prohibit both an assignment and a sublease. If the lease is assigned, the assignee is liable to the landlord for the rent. Such an assignment, however, does not discharge the tenant from the duty to pay rent. In a sublease, the sublessee is not liable to the original lessor for rent unless that liability has been assumed or is imposed by statute.

The tenant need not make repairs to the premises, absent an agreement to the contrary. A warranty of habitability was not implied at common law, but most states now reject this view and imply in residential leases a warranty that the premises are fit for habitation.

A landlord is usually liable to the tenant only for injuries caused by latent defects or by defects that are not apparent but of which the landlord had knowledge. Some states apply a strict tort liability, holding the landlord liable to a tenant or a child or guest of the tenant when there is a defect that makes the premises dangerously defective even if the landlord does not have any knowledge of the defect. The landlord is not liable to the tenant for crimes of third persons unless they are reasonably foreseeable.

QUESTIONS AND CASE PROBLEMS

1. What social forces are affected by the rule governing the duty of a landlord to relet premises wrongfully abandoned by a tenant?

2. King leased a single dwelling to Moorehead. King brought an action against Moorehead to recover the premises because of nonpayment of rent and to collect the unpaid rent. Moorehead raised the defense that the house was not habitable and that it violated the housing code. The defense was established at the trial. What result? Explain. [*King v Moorehead* (Mo App) 495 SW2d 65]

3. Rod had a five-year lease in a building owned by Darwood and had agreed to pay $800 a month rent. After two years, Rod assigned his rights under the lease to Kelly. Kelly moved in and paid the rent for a year and then moved out without Darwood's knowledge or consent, owing two months' rent. Darwood demanded that Rod pay him the past due rent. Must Rod do so? Why or why not?

4. Williams, who had leased a building from Jones for ten years, subleased the building to various tenants with Jones's consent. Many of the tenants failed to pay rent as it became due, and Jones brought an action against the sublessees to collect the rent. Will Jones recover? Why or why not?

5. Compare (a) an actual eviction of the tenant, (b) a constructive eviction of the tenant, and (c) a breach of the warranty of habitability.

6. Clay, who owned a tract of land, permitted Hartney to live in a cabin on the land. Nothing was said about the length of time that it could be used by Hartney or about Hartney's paying anything for the use of the cabin. When Hartney died, Clay closed up the cabin the next day and put Hartney's possessions outside the door. Paddock was appointed the executor of Hartney's will and claimed the right to use the cabin. Was he entitled to do so?

7. Phillips Petroleum, Inc., leased a service station to Prather. McWilliam, a customer at the station, was injured when a rusted window fell from the wall. She sued Phillips Petroleum. There was no evidence to show that Phillips knew of the rusted condition of the window. Was Phillips liable? [*McWilliam v Phillips Petroleum, Inc.*, 269 Or 526, 525 P2d 1011]

8. Morgan, who rented an apartment in the Melrose Apartments, wanted Melrose to hire additional security guards to protect the lessees from possible crimes. Was Melrose required to do so when crimes by third persons were not reasonably foreseeable?

9. Old Dover Tavern, Inc., rented a building from Amershadian to conduct a "business under the style and trade name of 'Old Dover Tavern, Inc.' engaging in the serving and selling [of] cigars, tobacco and all kinds of drinks and beverages of any name, nature and description." Thereafter the tenant claimed that it was entitled to sell cold foods, such as sandwiches, on the theory that such sale was "incidental to the sale of beverages" and brought suit to establish that it was so entitled. Was it? [*Old Dover Tavern, Inc. v Amershadian*, 2 Mass App 882, 318 NE2d 191]

10. Cantanese leased a building for operation of his drug store from Saputa. He moved his drug store from Saputa's building to another location but continued to pay rent to Saputa. Saputa, fearing that he was losing his tenant, entered the premises without Cantanese's permission and made extensive alterations to the premises to suit two physicians who had agreed to rent the premises from Saputa. Cantanese informed Saputa that he regarded the making of the unauthorized repairs as ground for canceling the lease. Saputa then claimed that Cantanese was liable for the difference between the rent that Cantanese had agreed to pay and the rent that the doctors would pay for the remainder of the term of the Cantanese lease. Was

Cantanese liable for such rent? [*Saputa v Cantanese* (La App) 182 So 2d 826]

11. Sargent rented a second-floor apartment in a building owned by Ross. Anna, the four-year-old daughter of Sargent, fell from an outdoor stairway and was killed. Suit was brought against Ross for her death. Ross contended that she did not have control over the stairway and therefore was not liable for its condition. Was this defense valid? [*Sargent v Ross,* 113 NH 388, 308 A2d 528]

12. Charles leased a house from Donald for four years. The rent agreed upon was $850 per month. After two years, Charles assigned his rights under the lease to Smith, who moved in and paid rent regularly for a year. Owing rent, Smith moved out sometime later without Donald's knowledge or consent. Donald demanded that Charles pay the rent. Is Charles liable?

13. Green rented an apartment from Stockton Realty. The three-story building had a washroom and clothesline on the roof for use by the tenants. The clothesline ran very near the skylight, and there was no guard rail between the clothesline and the skylight. Mrs. Green's friend, who was 14 years old, was helping Mrs. Green remove clothes from the line when she tripped on an object and fell against the skylight. The glass was too weak to support her weight, and she fell to the floor below, sustaining serious injuries. Is the landlord responsible for damages for the injury sustained?

Decide. [*Reiman v Moore,* 42 Cal 2d 130, 180 P2d 452]

14. Suzanne Andres was injured when she fell from the balcony of her second-floor apartment in the Roswell-Windsor Village Apartments. Andres was leaning against the railing on the balcony when it gave out, and she and the railing fell to the ground. Andres filed suit against Roswell-Windsor for its failure to maintain the railing. Roswell-Windsor maintains that the railing was not in a common area and was in Andres's exclusive possession and that she was responsible for its maintenance or at least letting the manager know the railing needed repairs. Should Andres recover from the landlord for her injuries? [*Andres v Roswell-Windsor Village Apartments,* 777 F2d 671 (11th Cir)]

15. Williams rented an apartment in the Parker House. He was an elderly man who was sensitive to heat. His apartment was fully air-conditioned, which enabled him to stand the otherwise unbearable heat of the summer. The landlord was dissatisfied with the current rent and, although the lease had a year to run, insisted that Williams agree to an increase. Williams refused. The landlord attempted to force Williams to pay the increase by turning off the electricity and thereby stopping the apartment's air conditioners. He also sent up heat on the hot days. After one week of such treatment, Williams, claiming that he had been evicted, moved out. Has there been an eviction? Explain.

CPA QUESTIONS

1. Which of the following provisions must be included to have an enforceable written residential lease?

	A description of the leased premises	A due date for the payment of rent
a.	Yes	Yes
b.	Yes	No
c.	No	Yes
d.	No	No

(11/95, Law, #53, 5922)

2. Bronson is a residential tenant with a 10-year written lease. In the absence of specific provisions in the lease to the contrary, which of the following statements is correct?
   a. The premises may **not** be sublet for less than the full remaining term.
   b. Bronson may **not** assign the lease.
   c. The landlord's death will automatically terminate the lease.
   d. Bronson's purchase of the property will terminate the lease.

(11/90, #52, 0813)

Decedent's Estates and Trusts

CHAPTER 53

OBJECTIVES

After studying this chapter, you should be able to

1. *Define testamentary capacity and testamentary intent;*
2. *Distinguish among signing, attesting, and publishing a will;*
3. *Explain how a will may be modified or revoked;*
4. *Describe briefly the probate and contest of a will;*
5. *Describe the ordinary pattern of distribution by intestacy; and*
6. *Explain the nature of a trust.*

The Uniform Probate Code (UPC) is a uniform statute on wills and the administration of estates drafted by the ABA and ALI and adopted in about one-third of the states.

A will is a document that provides for the distribution of one's property upon death.

A decedent is the person whose estate is being administered.

What happens to your property after you die?

Public policy dictates that your debts be settled, that property owned at the time of your death be applied to the payment of estate administration expenses and your debts, and that any remainder be distributed among those entitled to receive it.

The law of decedents' estates is governed by state statutes and court decisions. The general principles and the procedures that will be discussed in this chapter may be considered typical, but state variations exist. A step toward national uniformity has been taken by the American Bar Association and the National Conference of Commissioners on Uniform State Law by approving a **Uniform Probate Code** (UPC) and submitting it to the states for adoption.[1]

A. WILLS

Testate is a death with a will.

Intestate is a death without a will.

If a **decedent** made a valid **will**, described as having died **testate**, the will determines which persons are entitled to receive the estate property following payment of obligations. If the decedent did not make a valid will, the distribution is determined by laws for **intestate** distribution.

1. Definitions

Testator/testatrix is a person (male/female) who died with a valid will.

A beneficiary is a named person who will receive a property from a decedent.

A legacy is a gift of personal property by will.

A bequest is a gift of personal property by will.

A legatee is a beneficiary of personal property.

A devise is a gift of real property by will.

A devisee is a beneficiary of real property.

Testate distribution describes the distribution that is made when the decedent leaves a valid will. A will is ordinarily a writing that provides for a distribution of property upon death but that confers no rights prior to that time. A man who makes a will is called a **testator**; a woman, a **testatrix**.

The person to whom property is left by a will is a **beneficiary**. A gift of personal property by will is a **legacy** or bequest, in which case the beneficiary may also be called a **legatee**. A gift of real property by will is a **devise**, and the beneficiary may be called a **devisee**.

2. Parties to Will

Each state has variations on the qualifications of persons who wish to make a will. The following requirements are typical.

---

[1] The Uniform Probate Code has been adopted in Alaska, Arizona, Colorado, Florida, Hawaii, Idaho, Maine, Michigan, Minnesota, Montana, Nebraska, New Mexico, North Dakota, South Carolina, South Dakota, and Utah. Twenty other states have adopted portions of the UPC: Arkansas, California, Georgia, Illinois, Indiana, Kansas, Kentucky, Maryland, Missouri, New Jersey, Ohio, Oklahoma, Oregon, Pennsylvania, Texas, Virginia, Washington, West Virginia, Wisconsin, and Wyoming.

Testamentary capacity is the requisite mental capacity for a valid will.

(a) Testator. Generally, the right to make a will is limited to persons 18 or older. The testator must have testamentary capacity.[2] To have **testamentary capacity**, a person must have sufficient mental capacity to understand that the writing that is being executed is a will—that is, that it disposes of the person's property after death. The testator must also have a reasonable appreciation of the identity of relatives and friends and of the nature and extent of the property that may exist at death.

The excessive and continued use of alcohol, producing mental deterioration, may be sufficient to justify the conclusion that the decedent lacked testamentary capacity.

CASE SUMMARY

Rose's Will, Roger's Good Fortune, and Donald's Objections

Facts: Rose Lakatosh was a woman in her seventies in March 1988 when she hired Roger Jacobs to do odd jobs for her around her home in Northampton, Pennsylvania. Rose, who had no contact with her family except for an occasional visit from her sister, Margaret, became very dependent on Jacobs for her physical care, and he began to assist her with her financial affairs. In late 1988, at Jacobs's suggestion, Rose executed a power of attorney making Roger her attorney-in-fact. At the same time she executed the power of attorney, Rose executed a will leaving all of her property, with the exception of $10,000 to her church, to Roger.

Rose was, at the time of Jacobs's involvement with her, also the defendant in a slander lawsuit brought against her by her nephew. Three days after Rose had executed her will leaving her property to Jacobs, her attorney in the slander lawsuit petitioned the court to have her evaluated for competency. Her lawyer said she could not provide information for discovery in the case, did not remember things, and could not seem to grasp how much property she owned.

While the lawsuit progressed and the competency issue remained unresolved by the court, Rose died with the will leaving her property to Jacobs still valid. Rose's relative, Donald Spry, challenged the will on the grounds of mental incapacity and undue influence by Jacobs.

Decision: Although testamentary capacity is to be determined by the condition of the testator at the very time he executes a will, evidence of incapacity for a reasonable time before and after the making of a will is admissible as an indication of lack of capacity on the day the will is executed.

Although Roger testified that Rose was in good physical and mental health on the day the will was executed and that he had no difficulty communicating with her, he also testified that, around the time of the will's execution, Rose had trouble remembering things and had no understanding of her estate or assets. Significantly, it was Roger himself who suggested that Rose execute a power of attorney so that someone could help her if it was necessary.

Although the mental evaluation requested by Attorney Jacobs was never actually conducted, his concern three days after the will's execution that Rose lacked the mental capacity to meaningfully participate in the lawsuit is evidence of her weakened intellect three days before.

Rose made several comments on an audio tape made by Jacobs on the day the will was executed that indicate that she had a weakened intellect and that she was somewhat out of touch with reality. Specifically Rose referred to Roger as "an angel of mercy" who "saved her life" because, before she met him, she had been "so low in hell." Rose also repeatedly claimed that her nephew, Dean Berg, threatened to rob and kill her and that he was persecuting and torturing her.

---

[2] *In the Matter of the Estate of Herbert* (Haw) 935 P2d 130 (1997).

> Rose was living in filth with her bills not having been paid, and after a house fire, it was discovered that her house was in shambles, with trash throughout and dead cats found in her freezer and bathtub.
>
> Rose clearly suffered from a weakened intellect at the time her will was executed. *[Estate of Lakotosh (Pa Super) 656 A2d 1378 (1995)]*

(b) Beneficiary. Generally, no restrictions apply to the capacity of the beneficiary. However, when part of a decedent's estate passes to a minor, it is ordinarily necessary to appoint a guardian to administer that interest for the minor. If a will directs that any share payable to a minor be held by a particular person as trustee for the minor, the minor's interest will be so held, and a guardian is not required. Statutes often provide that if the estate or interest of the minor is not large, it may be paid directly to the minor or to the parent or person by whom the minor is maintained.

3. Testamentary Intent

Testamentary intent is the proper state of mind for making a valid will.

There cannot be a will unless the testator manifests an intention to make a provision that will be effective only upon death. This is called **testamentary intent**.[3] Ordinarily this is an intention that certain persons become the owners of certain property upon the death of the testator. However, a writing also manifests a testamentary intent when the testator only designates an executor and does not make any disposition of property.

4. Form

Because the privilege of disposing of property by will is purely statutory, the will must be executed in the manner required by state statutes. Unless statutory requirements are met, the will is invalid, and the testator is considered to have died intestate. In such a case, the decedent's property will be distributed according to the laws of intestacy of the particular state.

(a) Writing. Ordinarily a will must be in writing. Some state statutes, however, permit oral wills in limited circumstances, and the use of videotaped wills is gaining some legal ground.

(b) Signature. A written will must be signed by the testator. In case of physical incapacity, the testator may be assisted in signing the will. Witnesses to the will can then verify that simple marks were indeed made by the testator while experiencing a physically debilitating condition.

Generally, a will must be signed at the bottom or end. The purpose of this requirement is to prevent unscrupulous persons from taking a will that has been validly signed and writing or typing additional provisions in the space below the signature.

---

[3] *Burns v Adamson* (Ark) 854 SW2d 723 (1993).

Attestation is the witnesses' signatures on a will.

(c) Attestation. Attestation is the act of witnessing the execution of a will. Generally, it includes signing the will as a witness after a clause that recites that the witness has observed either the execution of the will or the testator's acknowledgment of the writing as the testator's will. This clause is commonly called an *attestation clause*. Statutes often require that attestation be made by the witnesses in the presence of the testator and in the presence of each other. Most states and the UPC require two witnesses; a few states require three.

Self-proved wills are wills with notarized witnesses' signatures that do not require the testimony of witnesses to prove the validity of the signatures.

Self-proved wills are wills that eliminate some formalities of proof by being executed in the way set forth by statute. Self-proved wills are recognized in those states following the Uniform Probate Code. A will may be simultaneously executed, attested, and made self-proved by acknowledgment by the testator and by affidavits of the witnesses. The acknowledgment and affidavits must each be made before an officer authorized to administer oaths under the laws of the state in which execution occurs. They must be evidenced by the officer's certificate under official seal.

The self-proving provisions attached to the will are not a part of the will. The only purpose served by self-proving provisions is to admit a will to probate without requiring the testimony of the witnesses to the will. It was not the purpose of legislatures, upon enacting the statute permitting self-proving wills, to amend or repeal the requirement that the will itself meet the requirements of the law. The execution of a valid will is a condition precedent to use of the self-proving provisions.

In some jurisdictions, a witness cannot be a beneficiary under the will. Use of a beneficiary as a witness will not affect the will, but the witness's share is limited to whatever would have been received if there had been no will. Under the UPC, a will or any provision therein is not invalid because the will is signed by an interested person.

(d) Date. There is generally no requirement that a testator must date a will, but it is advisable to do so. When there are several wills, the most recent prevails with respect to conflicting provisions.

5.   Modification of Will

Codicil is an addition to a will.

A will may be modified by executing a **codicil**. A codicil is a separate writing that amends a will. The will, except as changed by the codicil, remains the same. The result is as though the testator rewrote the will, substituting the provisions of the codicil for those provisions of the will that are inconsistent with the codicil. A codicil must be executed with all the formality of a will and is treated in all other respects the same as a will.

Interlineation is the testator's act of revoking a portion of a will by drawing lines through certain portions.

A will cannot be modified merely by crossing out a clause and writing in what the testator wishes. Such an **interlineation** is not operative unless it is executed with the same formality required of a will or, in some states, unless the will is republished in its interlineated form.

6.   Revocation of Will

Revocation is the testator's act of taking back his or her will and its provision.

At any time during the testator's life, the testator may **revoke** the will made or make changes in its terms. It may be revoked by act of the testator or by operation of law. A testator must have the same degree of mental capacity to revoke a will as is required to make a will.

1020 Part 9   Real Property and Estates

(a) Revocation by Act of Testator. A will or a codicil is revoked when the testator destroys, burns, or tears it or crosses out the provisions of the will or codicil with the intention to revoke them. The revocation may be in whole or in part.

Tearing Up the Wrong Thing: The Case of the Revoked Copy

Facts: In 1984, Alexander Tolin executed a will under which the residue of his estate was to be devised to his friend Adair Creaig. The will was prepared by Steven Fine, Tolin's attorney, and executed in Fine's office. The original will was retained by Fine, and a blue-backed photocopy was given to Tolin. In 1989, Tolin executed a codicil to the will that changed the residuary beneficiary from Creaig to Broward Art Guild, Inc. The codicil was also prepared by Fine, who retained the original and gave Tolin a blue-backed photocopy of the original executed codicil. Tolin died in 1990. Six months before his death, he told his neighbor Ed Weinstein, who was a retired attorney, that he made a mistake and wished to revoke the codicil and reinstate Creaig as the residuary beneficiary. Weinstein told Tolin he could do this by tearing up the original codicil. Tolin handed Weinstein a blue-backed document that Tolin said was the original codicil. Tolin then tore up and destroyed the document with the intent and for the purpose of revocation. Sometime after Tolin's death, Weinstein spoke with Fine and found out for the first time that the original will and codicil had been held by Fine. The document that Tolin tore up was an exact photocopy of the will. Tolin's personal representative petitioned the court to have the will and codicil admitted to probate. Creaig filed a petition to determine if there had been a revocation of the codicil.

Decision: It is clear that the testator did not effectively revoke the codicil. The parties' stipulation shows that the testator destroyed a document which "was an exact copy of the fully executed original codicil and was in all respects identical to the original except for the original signatures." Because the testator destroyed a copy of the codicil rather than the original codicil, his attempted revocation was ineffective. [In re Estate of Tolin (Fla App) 622 So 2d 988 (1993)]

(b) Revocation by Operation of Law. In certain instances, statutes provide that a change of circumstances has the effect of a revocation. ◆ *For example*, when a person marries after executing a will, the will is revoked or is presumed revoked unless it was made in contemplation of marriage or unless it provided for the future spouse. ◆ In some states, the revocation is not total but is effective only to the extent of allowing the spouse to take such share of the estate as that to which the spouse would have been entitled had there been no will.

The birth or adoption of a child after the execution of a will commonly works a revocation or partial revocation of the will as to that child. In the case of a partial revocation, the child is entitled to receive the same share as if the testator had died intestate.

The divorce of the testator does not in itself work a revocation. However, the majority of courts hold that if a property settlement is carried out on the basis of the divorce, a prior will of the testator is revoked, at least to the extent of the legacy given to the divorced spouse.

7. Election to Take against the Will

To protect the husband or wife of a testator, the surviving spouse may generally ignore the provisions of a will and elect to take against the will. In such a case, the surviving spouse receives the share of the estate he or she would have received had the testator died without leaving a will or receives a fractional share specified by statute.

The right to take against the will is generally barred by certain kinds of misconduct by the surviving spouse. If a spouse is guilty of desertion or nonsupport that would have justified the decedent's obtaining a divorce, the surviving spouse usually cannot elect to take against the will.

8. Disinheritance

Disinheritance is the distribution of property by will in a manner that contradicts the statutory intestate distribution, as when one leaves nothing to his children.

With some exceptions,[4] any person may be **disinherited** or excluded from sharing in the estate of a decedent. A person who would inherit if there were no will is excluded from receiving any part of a decedent's estate if the decedent has left a will giving everything to other persons.

9. Special Kinds of Wills

In certain situations, special kinds of wills are used.

A holographic will is a will entirely in the handwriting of the testator.

(a) Holographic Wills. A holographic will is an unwitnessed will that is written by the testator entirely by hand. In some states, no distinction is made between holographic and other wills. In other states, the general body of the law of wills applies, but certain variations are established. It may be required that a holographic will be dated.

Under the UPC, a holographic will is valid, whether witnessed or not, if the signatures and the material provisions are in the handwriting of the testator.

A living will is a document that establishes the terms and conditions for life support and treatment in the event of critical illness or accident.

(b) Living Wills. Living wills are documents by which individuals may indicate that, if they become unable to express their wishes and they are in an irreversible, incurable condition, they do not want life-sustaining medical treatments. (See Figure 53-1.) Living wills are legal in most states. Such personal wishes are entitled to constitutional protection as long as they are expressed clearly.

B. ADMINISTRATION OF DECEDENTS' ESTATES

A decedent's estate consists of the assets the decedent owned at death, and it must be determined who is entitled to receive that property. If the decedent owed debts, those debts must be paid first. After that, any balance is to be distributed according to the terms of the will or by the intestate law if the decedent did not leave a valid will.

---

[4] One exception, for example, is that for a surviving spouse. A surviving spouse has marital property rights and cannot be disinherited completely.

FIGURE 53-1
Living Will

Living Will

INSTRUCTIONS:

This is an important legal document. It sets forth your directions regarding medical treatment. You have the right to refuse treatment you do not want. You may make changes in any of these directions, or add to them, to conform them to your personal wishes.

I, _John Jones_ , being of sound mind, make this statement as a directive to be followed if I become permanently unable to participate in decisions regarding my medical care. These instructions reflect my firm and settled commitment to decline medical treatment under the circumstances indicated below:

I direct my attending physician to withhold or withdraw treatment that serves only to prolong the process of my dying, if I should be in an incurable or irreversible mental or physical condition with no reasonable expectation of recovery.

These instructions apply if I am a) in a terminal condition; b) permanently unconscious; or c) if I am conscious but have irreversible brain damage and will never regain the ability to make decisions and express my wishes.

I direct that treatment be limited to measures to keep me comfortable and to relieve pain, including any pain that might occur by withholding or withdrawing treatment.

While I understand that I am not legally required to be specific about future treatments, if I am in the condition(s) described above I feel especially strongly about the following forms of treatment:

I do not want cardiac resuscitation.
I do not want mechanical respiration.
I do not want tube feeding.
I do not want antibiotics.
I do want maximum pain relief.
Other directions (insert personal instructions): _NONE_

These directions express my legal right to refuse treatment, under the law of [name of state]. I intend my instructions to be carried out, unless I have rescinded them in a new writing or by clearly indicating that I have changed my mind.

Sign and date here in the presence of two adult witnesses, who should also sign.

Keep the signed original with your personal papers at home. Give copies of the signed original to your doctor, family, lawyer and others who might be involved in your care.

Signed: _John Jones_
Witness: _Earl Hummel_
Address: _7852 Bailey Avenue_
Buffalo, New York
Witness: _Ramona Valey_
Address: _8921 Clinton Street_
Buffalo, New York

Executor/executrix is the party (male/female) responsible for overseeing the administration of an estate of a testate decedent.

Administrator/administratrix is the party (male/female) responsible for overseeing the administration of an estate of an intestate decedent.

Personal representative is, under the UPC, the party responsible for administering the estate of a decedent, whether testate or intestate.

Probate is the the admission of a will for review and distribution; the processing of the claims of the decedent.

10. Definitions

The decedent has the privilege of naming in the will the person who will administer the estate. A man named in a will to administer the estate of the decedent is an **executor**; a woman, an **executrix**. If the decedent failed to name an executor or executrix or did not leave a will, the law permits another person, usually a close relative, to obtain the appointment of someone to wind up the estate. This person is an **administrator** or **administratrix**. Administrators and executors are referred to generally under the UPC as **personal representatives** of the decedents, because they represent the decedents or stand in their place

11. Probate of Will

Probate is the act by which the proper court or official accepts a will and declares that the instrument satisfies the statutory requirements as the will of the testator. Until a will is probated, it has no legal effect.

When witnesses have signed a will, generally they must appear and state that they saw the testator sign the will (unless the will is self-proving). If those witnesses cannot be found, have died, or are outside the jurisdiction, the will may be probated nevertheless. When no witnesses are required, it is customary to require two or more persons to identify the signature of the testator at the time of probate.

After the probate witnesses have made their statements under oath, the official or court will ordinarily admit the will to probate in the absence of any particular circumstances indicating that the writing should not be probated. A certificate or decree that officially declares that the will is the will of the testator and has been admitted to probate is then issued.

Any qualified person wishing to object to the probate of the will on the ground that it is not a proper will may appear before the official or court prior to the entry of the decree of probate. A person may petition after probate to have the probate of the will set aside.

12. Will Contest

A will contest is litigation over the validity of a decedent's will.

The probate of a will may be refused or set aside on the ground that the will is not the free expression of the intention of the testator. It may be attacked on the ground of (1) a lack of mental capacity to execute a will; (2) undue influence, duress, fraud, or mistake existing at the time of the execution of the will that induced or led to its execution; or (3) forgery. With the exception of mental capacity, these terms mean the same as they do in contract law.

If any one of these elements is found to exist, the probate of the will is refused or set aside. The decedent's estate is then distributed as if there had been no will unless an earlier will can be probated.

CASE SUMMARY

Aunt Naomi Got Everything Dad Owned

Facts: Marilyn Milhoan, the daughter of the decedent, Robert Milhoan, appealed the decision that her father's will was valid. Naomi Evelyn Koenig, Robert Milhoan's sister, was the executrix under the will. Because Robert had developed various health problems, his daughter and her boyfriend had moved into his house to help care for him. Disagreements developed between Koenig and Marilyn. Robert signed a will devising his house to his daughter and bequeathing the residue to Koenig. He prepared a new will leaving all of his property to Koenig. Robert's treating physician testified that although the decedent was receiving medication and was depressed, his mental status was normal, and he had no extraordinary memory problems. Marilyn Milhoan argued that because of undue influence both wills should be set aside in favor of an earlier will bequeathing everything to her.

Decision: Ms. Koenig presented testimony from three witnesses who were present at the execution of Mr. Milhoan's October 5, 1988, will. Both attesting witnesses said that although Mr. Milhoan was obviously physically ill, he was mentally competent to understand the nature and extent of his will. One witness said that although Mr. Milhoan was in pain, he answered questions about who was to inherit his property. Another said that after he read various sections of the will, he looked Mr. Milhoan in the eye, and it was clear to him that Mr. Milhoan understood that under the will his sister, and not his daughter, would inherit all his property.

It is not necessary that a testator possess high quality or strength of mind in order to make a valid will, nor that he then have as strong mind as he formerly had. The mind may be debilitated, the memory enfeebled, the understanding weak; the character may be peculiar and eccentric; and he may even want capacity to transact many of the business affairs of life. Still it is sufficient if he understands the nature of the business in which he is engaged and, when making a will, has a recollection of the property he means to dispose of, the object or objects of his bounty, and how he wishes to dispose of his property.

> Although Ms. Milhoan argues that her father's inability to read the will and to affix his normal signature to the will shows a lack of mental competency, the testimony shows that these circumstances were caused by Mr. Milhoan's physical illness and not a lack of mental capacity or a lack of understanding of the effect of his will. [*Milhoan v Koenig (W Va) 469 SE2d 99 (1996)*]

ETHICS & THE LAW

Josephine Kapp was the aunt of William Kapp and the great-aunt of Keith Kapp, William's son. William lived approximately one and one-half miles from Josephine, and he farmed a 71-acre tract of land owned by Josephine. William advised Josephine on matters such as whether to take a penalty on a certificate of deposit in order to reinvest it at a higher rate and whether to take advantage of stock options.

Josephine spoke with a lawyer in July 1980 and inquired about how to make a will. Based on the lawyer's advice, Josephine drew up her own holographic will on August 13, 1980, in which she stated, "William H. Kapp and Michael Keith Kapp to buy the land (the 71-acre tract) at a reasonable price and to pay it to my estate."

William took Josephine to her lawyer's office four times between September 1980 and January 1981. Sometimes William was present for part of these discussions, and at other times he left. Josephine's will was executed on January 21, 1981. The will directed that William and Keith were to be able to purchase the 71-acre tract of land even if they were acting as the executors of her estate. She also executed an option that permitted William to purchase the tract at $500 per acre or for $35,705 during her lifetime and for six months after her death.

Josephine died on March 11, 1986. William exercised his option within six months after her death and then sold the property in 1988 for $1,423,000. Josephine's remaining heirs challenged the will on the grounds of undue influence and the purchase of the property by William as executor as a breach of his fiduciary duty.

Do you think the court should allow William to keep the property? Would you allow him to keep the property? What things would the heirs point to in order to raise issues of impropriety? Could William and Josephine have done anything differently to prevent the challenge by the heirs? *Kapp v Kapp (NC) 442 SE2d 499 (1994).*

13. When Administration Is Not Necessary

No administration is required when the decedent did not own any property at the time of death. In some states, special statutes provide for a simplified administration when the decedent leaves only a small estate. Likewise, when all the property owned by the decedent was jointly owned with another person who acquired the decedent's interest by right of survivorship, no administration is required.

14. Appointment of Personal Representative

Both executors and administrators must be appointed to act as such by a court or an officer designated by law. The appointment is made by granting to the personal representative **letters testamentary**, in the case of an executor, or **letters of administration**, in the case of an administrator.

15. Proof of Claims against the Estate

Letters testamentary/ letters of administration— authority given by a court to the party responsible for the administration of the decedent's estate.

Statutes vary widely with respect to the presentation of claims against a decedent's estate. In very general terms, statutes provide for some form of public notice of the grant of letters testamentary or letters of administration, as by advertisement. Creditors are then required to give notice of their claims within a period specified by either statute or a court order (for example, within six months). In most states, failure to present a claim within the specified time bars the claim.

16. Construction of a Will

The will of a decedent is to be interpreted according to the ordinary or plain meaning evidenced by its words. The court will strive to give effect to every provision of the will in order to avoid concluding that any part of the decedent's estate was not disposed of by the will.[5]

17. Testate Distribution of an Estate

If the decedent died leaving a valid will, the last phase of the administration of the estate by the decedent's personal representative is the distribution of property remaining after the payment of all debts and taxes in accordance with the provisions of the will.

The testator will ordinarily bequeath to named persons certain sums of money called **general legacies** because no particular money is specified. The testator may bequeath identified property called **specific legacies** or **specific devises**. ◆ *For example*, a testator may give "$1,000 to A; $1,000 to B; my automobile to C." The first two bequests are general; the third is specific. ◆ After such bequests, the testator may make a bequest of everything remaining, called a **residuary bequest** such as "the balance of my estate to D."

A residuary is that part of the decedent's estate not specifically devised or bequeathed.

Abatement is the process of distribution of an estate when the assets are insufficient.

(a) Abatement of Legacies. Assume in the preceding example that after all debts are paid, only $1,500 and the automobile remain. What disposition is to be made? Legacies abate or bear loss in the following order: (1) residuary, (2) general, (3) specific. The law also holds that legacies of the same class abate proportionately. ◆ *For example*, in the hypothetical case, C, the specific legatee, would receive the automobile; A and B, the general legatees, would each receive $750; and D, the residuary legatee, would receive nothing. ◆

Ademption is the cancellation of a gift when the property is no longer part of the decedent's estate.

(b) Ademption of Property. When specifically bequeathed property is sold or given away by the testator prior to death, the bequest is considered adeemed, or canceled. The specific legatee in this instance is not entitled to receive any property or money. **Ademption** has the same consequence as though the testator had formally canceled the bequest. ◆ *For example*, if Aunt Claire left her 1995 Honda Accord to her niece, Helen, but Aunt Claire sold the Honda Accord in 1997 and died in 1998, Helen receives nothing from Aunt Claire's estate because the bequest of the Honda is adeemed or canceled. ◆

---

5 *In the Matter of the Estate of Lubins* (NY Sur) 656 NYS2d 851 (1997).

Antilapse statute is a
statute that prevents the
lapse of a gift in the event
the beneficiary dies
before the decedent.

(c) Antilapse Statutes. If the beneficiary named in the testator's will died before the testator and the testator did not make any alternate provision applicable in such a case, the gift ordinarily does not lapse. **Antilapse statutes** commonly provide that the gift to the deceased beneficiary shall not lapse but that the children or heirs of that beneficiary may take the legacy in the place of the deceased beneficiary. An antilapse statute does not apply if the testator specified a disposition that should be made of the gift if the original legatee had died.

18. Intestate Distribution of an Estate

Intestate succession is a
statutory formula for
distribution of the prop-
erty of an intestate decedent or the property not
covered by a testate
decedent's will.

If the decedent does not effectively dispose of all property by will or does not have a will, the decedent's property is distributed to certain relatives. Because such persons acquire or succeed to the rights of the decedent and because the circumstances under which they do so is the absence of an effective will, it is said that they acquire title by **intestate succession**.

The right of intestate succession or inheritance is not a basic right of the citizen or an inalienable right. It exists only because the state legislature so provides. It is within the power of the state legislature to modify or destroy the right to inherit property.

Although wide variations exist among statutory provisions of the states, there is a common pattern of intestate distribution.

(a) Spouses. The surviving spouse of the decedent, whether husband or wife, shares in the estate. Generally, the amount received is a fraction that varies with the number of children. If no children survive, the spouse is generally entitled to take the entire estate. Otherwise, the surviving spouse ordinarily receives a one-half or one-third share of the estate.

Lineal descendants are
blood descendants of a
decedent.

(b) Lineals. Lineals or **lineal descendants** are blood descendants of the decedent. Lineal descendants include children and grandchildren. That portion of the estate that is not distributed to the surviving spouse is generally distributed to lineals.

(c) Parents. If the estate has not been fully distributed by this time, the remainder is commonly distributed to the decedent's parents.

(d) Collateral Heirs. These are persons who are not descendants of the decedent but are related through a common ancestor. Generally, brothers and sisters and their descendants share any part of the estate that has not already been distributed. Statutes vary as to how far distribution will be made to the descendants of brothers and sisters. Under some statutes, a degree of relationship is specified, such as first cousins, and no person more remotely related to the decedent is permitted to share in the estate.

Escheat is the process
of the property of the
decedent passing to the
state government when
there are no relatives to
inherit it.

If the entire estate is not distributed within the permitted degree of relationship, the property that has not been distributed is given to the state government. This right of the state to take the property is the right of **escheat**. Under some statutes, the right of escheat arises only when there is no relative of the decedent, however remotely related.

(e) Distribution per Capita and per Stirpes. The fact that different generations of distributees may be entitled to receive the estate creates a problem of determining the proportions in which distribution is to be made. (See Figure 53-2.) When all the distributees stand in the same degree of relationship to the decedent, distribution is made **per capita**, each receiving the same share. ◆ *For example*, if the decedent is survived by three children—A, B, and C—each of them is entitled to receive one-third of the estate. ◆

Per capita is a method of distributing estate assets on an equal-per-person basis.

Per stirpes (stirpital) is a method of distributing estate assets on a relationship-to-the-decedent basis.

If the distributees stand in different degrees of relationship, distribution is made in as many equal parts as there are family lines, or **stirpes**, represented in the nearest generation. Parents take to the exclusion of their children or subsequent descendants, and when members of the nearest generation have died, their descendants take by way of representation. This is called **distribution per stirpes** or **stirpital distribution**. ◆ *For example*, Thomas dies leaving two living children, A and B, and one child, C, who predeceased him but left two children (Thomas's grandchildren, D and E). A and B would each take one-third of Thomas's estate, and D and E would, under a per stirpes distribution, split a one-third interest, each receiving one-sixth of the estate. ◆

(f) Murder of Decedent. Statutes generally provide that a person who murders the decedent cannot inherit from the victim by intestacy. In the absence of such a statute, courts are divided over whether the heir may inherit.

(g) Death of Distributee after Decedent. The persons entitled to distribution of a decedent's estate are determined as of the date of death. If a distributee dies after that, the rights of the distributee are not lost but pass from the original decedent's estate to the deceased distributee's estate.

FIGURE 53-2
Distribution Per Capita and Per Sirpes

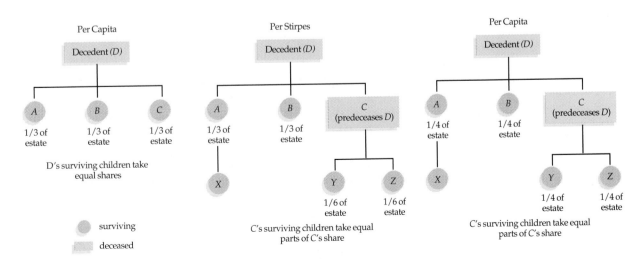

(h) Simultaneous Death. The Uniform Simultaneous Death Act[6] provides that when survivorship cannot be established, the property of each person shall be disposed of as if he or she had survived the other.

E.   TRUSTS

> Trust is a legal device by which title to property, real or personal, is held for the benefit of another.

A **trust** is a legal device by which property, real or personal, is held by one person for the benefit of another. Legal problems in the area of trusts invariably require a determination of the nature of the relationship created by the trust and the rights and obligations of the parties with respect to that relationship.

19. Definitions

> Settlor is the owner of property who transfers it to a trust.
>
> Trustee is the holder of legal title of trust property and the manager of it.
>
> Beneficiary is the party for whom a trust is created.
>
> Trust corpus is the property that is placed in trust and is the body of the trust.
>
> Trust res is the trust corpus.
>
> Principal is the property held in trust.
>
> Income is the earnings from the trust principal.
>
> Living (inter vivos) trust is a trust created while the settlor is alive.
>
> Testamentary trust is a trust created by the settlor's will.

The property owner who creates the trust is the **settlor.** (The word *settlor* is taken from the old legal language of "settling the property in trust.") The settlor is sometimes called the **donor** or **trustor.** The person to whom the property is transferred in trust is the **trustee.** The person for whose benefit the trustee holds the property is the **beneficiary** (or **cestui que trust**).

Property held in trust is sometimes called the **trust corpus, trust fund, trust estate,** or **trust res.** A distinction is made between the **principal,** or the property in trust, and the **income** that is earned by the principal and distributed by the trustee.

Although an express trust is ordinarily created by a transfer of property, the settlor may retain the property as trustee for the beneficiary. The fact that there is a duty to make a payment does not create a trust.

If the trust is created to take effect within the lifetime of the settlor, it is a **living trust** or an **inter vivos trust.** If the trust is provided for in the settlor's will and is to become effective only when the will takes effect after death, the trust is called a **testamentary trust.**

20. Creation of Trusts

The requirements to create a trust are not uniform, but there are certain typical requirements.

(a) Legality. A trust may generally be created for any lawful purpose, but a trust is invalid when it is for an unlawful purpose or is in fraud of creditors.

(b) Capacity of Beneficiary. The capacity of the beneficiary of the trust to hold property or to contract is immaterial. Many trusts are created because the beneficiary lacks legal or actual capacity to manage the property. The trustee, as the holder of legal title, must have capacity.

(c) Formality. In creating a trust, it is common practice to execute a writing, called a **trust agreement** or **deed of trust.** No particular form of language is necessary to create a trust so long as the property, the trust purpose, and the beneficiaries are

---

6 The 1940 version of this act has been adopted in all states except Louisiana and Ohio, The newest version of the act (1993) has been adopted in Arizona, Colorado, Hawaii, Kansas, Montana, New Mexico, North Dakota, South Dakota, and Virginia.

designated. If an inter vivos trust relates to an interest in land, the statute of frauds requires that the trust be evidenced by a writing setting forth the details of the trust. A writing signed by the trustee and referring to a deed from the trustor can satisfy this requirement. When the trust depends on a transfer of title to land, there must be a valid transfer of the title to the trustee.

A trust in personal property may be declared orally without any writing. If a trust is created by the will of the settlor, there must be a writing that meets the requirements of a will. The same is true when the trust is not intended to come into existence until the death of the settlor.

In the absence of a specific requirement of the statute of frauds as to land or of the statutes setting forth the formal requirements for wills, any conduct or writing that shows an intent to create a trust will be given effect.

(d) Intention. An intention to impose a duty on the trustee with respect to specific property must be expressed. It is not necessary, however, that the word trust or *trustee* be used. The settlor will ordinarily name a trustee, but failure to do so is not fatal to the trust because a trustee will be appointed by the court.

(e) Active Duty. A trust does not exist unless an active duty is placed on the trustee to manage the property in some manner or to exercise discretion or judgment. A bare direction to hold the property in trust without any direction for its use or distribution is not sufficient for an active duty. When a decedent transfers $5,000 to a trustee to be held in trust for *A*, no trust is created. In such a case, the intended beneficiary is entitled to receive the property outright as though the decedent had not attempted to create a trust.

(f) Identity of Beneficiary. Every trust must have a beneficiary. In a private trust, the beneficiaries must be identified by name, description, or designation of the class to which the beneficiaries belong. In a charitable trust, it is sufficient that the beneficiaries be members of the public at large or a general class of the public.

(g) Acceptance of Trust. Because the performance of a trust imposes duties on the trustee, a trustee may renounce or reject the trust. Acceptance will be presumed in the absence of a disclaimer. A renunciation does not affect the validity of the trust because a court will appoint a substitute trustee if the settlor does not do so.

21. Nature of Beneficiary's Interest

Legal title is the title held by the trustee in a trust situation.

Equitable title is the title held by the beneficiaries of a trust.

Spendthrift trust is a trust protected from attachment by the beneficiary's creditors.

The effect of a transfer in trust is to divide the property so that the **legal title** is given to the trustee and the **equitable title**, or beneficial interest, is given to the beneficiary. The beneficiary may ordinarily transfer or assign such interest in the trust. The beneficiary's creditors may reach that interest in satisfaction of their claims. An exception arises when the settlor has restricted the trust in such a way that the beneficiary cannot assign, and creditors cannot reach, the interest. This type of trust is called a **spendthrift trust**.

22. Powers of Trustee

A trustee can exercise only those powers that are given by law or the trust instrument or those that the court will construe as being given by implication. Modern trusts commonly give the trustee discretion to make decisions on matters that could not be foreseen by the settlor. ◆ *For example,* the trustee may be authorized to expend principal as well as income when, in the trustee's opinion, it is necessary for the education or medical care of a beneficiary. ◆ The trustee must exercise discretion in a reasonable manner.

23. Duties of Trustee

The duty of a trustee is to administer the trust. The trustee who accepts the appointment must take all the necessary steps to carry out the trust in a proper manner.

(a) Performance. A trustee is under a duty to carry out the trust according to its terms and is personally liable for any loss sustained from an unjustified failure to perform such duties. A trustee cannot delegate the performance of personal duties.

(b) Due Care. The trustee is under a duty to use reasonable skill, prudence, and diligence in the performance of trust duties. More simply stated, the trustee must use the care that would be exercised by a reasonable person under the circumstances.

(c) Loyalty. A trustee is not permitted to profit personally from the position of trustee other than to receive the compensation allowed by contract or law.

(d) Possession and Preservation of Trust Property. The trustee is under a duty to take possession of trust property and to preserve it from loss or damage. If the property includes accounts receivable or outstanding debts, the trustee is under the duty to collect them.

(e) Defense of Trust. The trustee must defend the trust when its validity is disputed in court.

(f) Production of Income. By either express or implied direction, the trustee is required to invest the money or property in enterprises or transactions that will yield an income to the estate.

In the absence of specific investment instructions, a trustee is charged with investing the trust property under the standards of a reasonable and prudent investor.

(g) Accounting and Information. A trustee must keep accurate records so that it can be determined whether the trust has been properly administered. Upon request by a beneficiary, the trustee must furnish information with respect to the trust. Periodically, or at certain times, as determined by the law in each state, a trustee must file an account in court. At such time, the court examines the stewardship of the trust.

C
P
A

In some trusts, the trustee must balance the interests of the life beneficiary (the party entitled to the income from the trust while he or she is alive) with those of the eventual recipients of the trust res. ◆ *For example,* a testator might put this provision in her will: "To my husband in trust for his life, and upon his death in fee simple to my children." How does the trustee account for rental income? What if the rental properties need repairs? Do the repairs come from the income, or are they taken from principal? There are clear rules for the allocation of income and principal and the expenses of operation of the trust and the trust properties. ◆ These rules are summarized in Figure 53-3.

24. Remedies for Breach of Trust

A breach of trust may occur in a variety of ways, which, in turn, affects the remedies available. These remedies include

1. a money judgment against the trustee for the loss caused by him or her,
2. an injunction or order to compel the trustee to do or refrain from doing an act,
3. criminal prosecution of the trustee for misconduct,
4. the tracing and recovery of trust property that has been converted by the trustee unless the property had been acquired by a bona fide purchaser who gave value and purchased without notice of the breach of trust,
5. a judgment against the surety on the trustee's bond for the loss caused the trust by the trustee's default,
6. removal of the trustee for misconduct, and
7. a suit against third persons who participated in a breach of trust.

Principal	**Payable From Principal**
Original Trust Property	Loans (Principal)
Proceeds and Gains from Sale	Litigation Expenses
Insurance Payments	Permanent Improvements
New Property Purchased with Principal	Costs of Purchase
Stock Dividends	
Stock Splits	

Income	**Payable From Income**
Rent	Loans (Interest)
Interest	Taxes
Cash Dividends	Insurance Premiums
Royalties	Repairs

FIGURE 53-3
Trust Principal/Income Allocation

Could I Just See the Trust Agreement?

Facts: Joseph McKinley Bryan was an elderly, wealthy, and eccentric man. Prior to his death, he had made provisions for a testamentary trust for his grandchildren and great-grandchildren. Under the terms of the trust, each grandchild who survived him was to receive $500,000, and each great-grandchild who survived him was to receive $100,000.

By the time of Bryan's death on April 26, 1995, there had been at least five versions of the trust's provisions. His will was originally dated June 29, 1990, but the trust agreement was originally made in 1985, with two changes in 1988, one in 1990, and another in 1992. In May 1995, the grandchildren of Bryan were notified by letter from NationsBank Corporation, the trustee, that they would be receiving only $100,000. Because the grandchildren had understood that they were to receive $500,000, they asked to see the trust agreements. The trustee refused, contending that there was no duty to share the agreement with the trust beneficiaries.

Decision: While the court could find no specific statutory authority or case precedent on the issue, it ruled that the beneficiaries of the trust, the grandchildren, did have a right to see the trust agreements. They would need access to such agreements in order to determine whether the trustee was carrying out its fiduciary duties and responsibilities under that agreement. In the absence of a provision in a trust agreement that prohibits access by beneficiaries, they have a right to see the trust documents themselves. *[Taylor v Nationsbank Corp. (NC App) 481 SE2d 358 (1997)]*

25. Termination of Trust

A trust may be terminated (1) in accordance with its terms, (2) because of the impossibility of attaining the object of the trust; (3) via revocation by the settlor when allowed by the terms of the trust, (4) by merger of all interests in the same person (as when there is only one trustee and one beneficiary and they are the same person), or (5) upon the request of all the beneficiaries when there is no express purpose that requires continuation of the trust.

SUMMARY

A will is a writing that provides for a disposition of property to take effect upon death. A man who makes a will is called a testator; a woman, a testatrix. The person to whom property is left by will is a beneficiary. A legacy is a gift of personal property by will; a gift of real property by will is a devise.

A testator must have testamentary capacity to make a will and must manifest some intention that the will is to be effective only upon death. The will must be signed by the testator and be witnessed.

A will may be modified by a codicil or revoked either by the act of the testator or by operation of law.

Probate is the process by which a proper court official accepts a will. Probate may be refused or set aside on grounds that the will is not the free expression of the testator.

A holographic will is an unwitnessed will written entirely in the handwriting of the testator. A self-proved will may be admitted to probate without the testimony of subscribing witnesses. A living will allows a person to make wishes known regarding life-sustaining medical treatment.

If there is a valid will, the last phase of administration of the estate is the distribution of property after the payment of all debts and taxes. General legacies are bequests of money, whereas specific legacies or specific devises are gifts of identified personal or real property. Legacies abate in the following order: residuary, general, and specific. If a beneficiary named in the will has died before the testator and no alternate provision has been made for such beneficiary, antilapse statutes provide that the gift will not lapse. In that event, the children or heirs of the beneficiary may take the legacy in the place of the deceased beneficiary.

If the decedent does not dispose of all property by will or does not have a will, the property will be distributed according to state intestacy statutes. A surviving spouse may generally elect to take the statutory allocation instead of that provided in the will.

The estate of the testator will be administered by the person appointed in the will (the executor) or, if there is no will, by a person appointed by the court (an administrator). Creditors who have claims against the estate are required to give notice of their claims to the personal representative; otherwise, the claims will be barred.

A trust is a legal device by which property is held by one person for the benefit of another. The settlor creates the trust, and the person for whose benefit the trustee holds the property is the beneficiary. Property held in trust is called the trust corpus, trust fund, trust estate, or trust res.

A trust is usually created by a writing called a trust agreement or deed of trust. No particular form or language is required. A trust is not created unless an active duty is placed on the trustee to manage the property in some manner. A trustee's acceptance of duties is presumed.

Legal title to trust property is given to the trustee, but equitable title is held by the beneficiary. A beneficiary may transfer an interest in the trust except in the case of a spendthrift trust.

The trustee can exercise only those powers that are given by law or the trust instrument. The trustee must administer the trust and carry out the trust in a proper manner. A trustee may be sued for breach of the terms of the trust agreement. A trust comes to an end when its terms so provide or when it becomes impossible to attain the object of the trust.

QUESTIONS AND CASE PROBLEMS

1. What social forces are affected by allowing a person to give property after death by means of leaving a will?

2. Jean repeatedly told her best friend, Diane, and their neighbors that Jean would leave her house to Diane when she died. Jean died without having written any will. Diane claimed the house, and the neighbors testified in court that Jean had repeatedly declared that she would leave the house to Diane. Is Diane entitled to the house?

3. Iona wrote her will. The following year she wrote another will that expressly revoked the earlier will. Later, while cleaning house, she came across the second will. She mistakenly thought that it was the first will and tore it up because the first will had been revoked. Iona died shortly thereafter. The beneficiaries named in the second will claimed that the second will should be probated. The beneficiaries named in the first will claimed that the second will had been revoked when it was torn up. Had the second will been revoked?

4. Logsdon, who had three children, disliked one of them without any reason. In his will, he left only a small amount to the child he disliked and gave the bulk of his estate to the remaining two. Upon his death, the disliked child claimed that the will was void and had been obtained by undue influence. Do you agree? [*Logsdon v Logsdon*, 412 Ill 19, 104 NE2d 622]

5. Field executed a will. Upon her death, the will was found in her safe deposit box, but the part of the will containing the fifth bequest was torn from the will. This torn fragment was also found in the box. There was no evidence that anyone other than Field had ever opened the box. A proceeding was brought to determine whether the will was entitled to be probated. Decide. [*Flora v Hughes*, 312 Ky 478, 228 SW2d 27]

6. Miller wrote a will 11 pages long and enclosed it in an envelope, which she sealed. She then wrote on the envelope "My last will & testament" and signed her name below this statement. This was the only place where she signed her name on any of the papers. Was this signature sufficient to allow this writing to be admitted to probate as her will? [*Miller's Executor v Shannon* (Ky) 299 SW2d 103]

7. Probate of Lingenfelter's will was opposed. It was shown that the testatrix was sick, highly nervous, and extremely jealous and that she committed suicide a week after executing the will. In support of the will, it was shown that she understood the will when she discussed it with an attorney, that her husband was seriously ill when she wrote the will, that he died the following day, and that she grieved his death. A proceeding was brought to determine whether the will was entitled to probate. Decide. [*Lingenfelter's Estate*, 38 Cal 2d 571, 241 P2d 990]

8. Copenhaver wrote a will in ink, which was found with her other papers in her bedroom at her death. Pencil lines had been drawn through every provision of the will and the signature. There was no evidence as to the circumstances under which this had been done. Was the will revoked? Why? [*Franklin v Maclean*, 192 Va 684, 66 SE2d 504]

9. Dolores states in her will, "I leave $10,000 to the First National Bank in trust for my niece, Clara." After the death of Dolores, the will is probated. Is the trust for Clara valid?

10. Jeanette Wall worked for D. J. Sharron for many years.

Sharron executed a will leaving his entire estate to Jeanette. He reexecuted the same will sometime thereafter with the same provisions. Sharron's children contested the will, offering evidence that Sharron was a very sick man, physically as well as mentally, and that Wall was active in Sharron's business as well as his personal life. They offered no evidence that Wall had any involvement in the procurement of the original or the reexecuted will. Who is entitled to the estate? Why? [*Wall v Hodges* (Ala App) 465 So 2d 359]

11. Smith died without leaving a will. He was survived by his widow, two children, and a brother. How will the estate be distributed in most states?

12. Rachael conveyed certain land to Roland in trust for her daughter, Mary. Roland refused to accept the trust. What effect does this refusal have on the rights of her daughter, Mary?

13. By her will, Hendricks provided: "I give, devise, and bequeath [the balance of my estate] to the City of Brookfield, Missouri, for the sole purpose of building and equipping and maintaining a city hospital." The city claimed that this was an absolute gift to the city, subject to a condition as to its use. Do you agree? [*Ramsey v City of Brookfield,* 361 Mo 857, 237 SW2d 143]

14. The Pioneer Trust and Savings Bank was trustee of certain land for the benefit of Harmon. Under the terms of the trust, Harmon could require the trustee to sell the land as he directed. Schneider wrote Pioneer Trust, offering to buy the land. Harmon made a written notation on the letter that he accepted the offer and sent it back to Schneider. Schneider withdrew his offer and claimed that there was no contract. Harmon claimed that Schneider was bound by a contract. Decide. [*Schneider v Pioneer Trust and Savings Bank,* 26 Ill App 2d 463, 168 NE2d 808]

15. Craig delivers bonds in the amount of $100,000 to White in trust to hold and pay over the income in quarterly payments to Craig's niece, Helen, during her minority. Who is the settlor or creator of the trust? Who is the trustee? Who is the beneficiary?

CPA QUESTIONS

1. A decedent's will provided that the estate was to be divided among the decedent's issue, per capita and not per stirpes. If there are two surviving children and three grandchildren who are children of a predeceased child at the time the will is probated, how will the estate be divided?
   a. ½ to each surviving child
   b. ⅓ to each surviving child and ⅑ to each grandchild
   c. ¼ to each surviving shild and ⅛ to each grandchild
   d. ⅕ to each curviving child and grandchild
   (11/92, Law, #9, 3091)

2. To properly create an inter vivos trust funded with cash, the grantor must
   a. Execute a written trust instrument.
   b. Transfer the cash to the trustee.
   c. Provide for payment of fees to the trustee.
   d. Designate an alternate trust beneficiary.
   (5/91, Law, #8, 0856)

3. If not expressly granted, which of the following implied powers would a trustee have?
   I.   Power to sell trust property
   II. Power to borrow from the trust
   III. Power to pay trust expenses

   a. I and II
   b. I and III
   c. II and III
   d. I, II, and III
   (11/92, Law, #7, 3089)

Qualitex Co. v Jacobsen Products Co., Inc.

115 S Ct 1300 (1995)

Since the 1950s, Qualitex Company colored the dry cleaning press pads it manufactures with a special shade of green-gold. In 1991, it registered its green-gold color on press pads as a trademark. Qualitex sued a competitor, Jacobson Products Co., for trademark infringement when Jacobson began to manufacture and sell press pads with a similar green-gold color. Qualitex won the lawsuit in the U.S. District Court, but the Ninth Circuit set the judgment aside because in its view the Lanham Act does not permit a manufacturer to register "color alone" as a trademark. The Federal Circuit had allowed Owens-Corning Fiberglass Corp. to register the color pink as a trademark for its insulation product. Because Ninth Circuit and Federal Circuit courts of appeals differed as to whether or not the law recognizes the use of color alone as a trademark, the U.S. Supreme Court granted certiorari.

BREYER, J. . . .

I. The Lanham Act gives a seller or producer the exclusive right to "register" a trademark, 15 U.S.C. § 1052 (1988 ed. and Supp. V), and to prevent his or her competitors from using that trademark, § 1114(1). Both the language of the Act and the basic underlying principles of trademark law would seem to include color within the universe of things that can qualify as a trademark. The language of the Lanham Act describes that universe in the broadest of terms. It says that trademarks "includ[e] any word, name, symbol, or device, or any combination thereof." § 1127. Since human beings might use as a "symbol" or "device" almost anything at all that is capable of carrying meaning, this language, read literally, is not restrictive. The courts and the Patent and Trademark Office have authorized for use as a mark a particular shape (of a Coca-Cola bottle), a particular sound (of NBC's three chimes), and even a particular scent (of plumeria blossoms on sewing thread). . . .

We cannot find in the basic objectives of trademark law any obvious theoretical objection to the use of color alone as a trademark, where that color has attained "secondary meaning" and therefore identifies and distinguishes a particular brand (and thus indicates its "source"). In principle, trademark law, by preventing others from copying a source-identifying mark, "reduce[s] the customer's costs of shopping and making purchasing decisions," 1 J McCarthy, McCarthy on Trademarks and Unfair Competition § 2.01[2], p. 2–3 (3d ed. 1994) (hereinafter McCarthy), for it quickly and easily assures a potential customer that *this* item—the item with this mark—is made by the same producer as other similarly marked items that he or she liked (or disliked) in the past. At the same time, the law helps assure a producer that it (and not an imitating competitor) will reap the financial, reputation-related rewards associated with a desirable product. The law thereby "encourage[s] the production of quality products," *ibid*, and simultaneously discourages those who hope to sell inferior products by capitalizing on

a consumer's inability quickly to evaluate the quality of an item offered for sale. . . .

. . . [We cannot] find a principled objection to the use of color as a mark in the important "functionality" doctrine of trademark law. The functionality doctrine prevents trademark law, which seeks to promote competition by protecting a firm's reputation, from instead inhibiting legitimate competition by allowing a producer to control a useful product feature. It is the province of patent law, not trademark law, to encourage invention by granting inventors a monopoly over new product designs or functions for a limited time, 35 U.S.C §§ 154, 173, after which competitors are free to use the innovation. If a product's functional features could be used as trademarks, however, a monopoly over such features could be obtained without regard to whether they qualify as patents and could be extended forever (because trademarks may be renewed in perpetuity). . . .

See, *e.g., Kellogg Co.,* 305 U.S., at 119–120, (trademark law cannot be used to extend monopoly over "pillow" shape of shredded wheat biscuit after the patent for that shape had expired). This Court consequently has explained that, "[i]n general terms, a product feature is functional," and cannot serve as a trademark, "if it is essential to the use or purpose of the article or if it affects the cost or quality of the article," that is, if exclusive use of the feature would put competitors at a significant non-reputation-related disadvantage. *Inwood Laboratories, Inc.* 456 U.S., at 850, n. 10, 102 S.Ct., at 2186, n. 10. Although sometimes color plays an important role (unrelated to source identification) in making a product more desirable, sometimes it does not. And, this latter fact—the fact that sometimes color is not essential to a product's use or purpose and does not affect cost or quality—indicates that the doctrine of "functionality" does not create an absolute bar to the use of color alone as a mark. See *Owens-Corning,* 774 F.2d, at 1123 (pink color of insulation in wall "performs no nontrademark function").

It would seem . . . that color alone, at least sometimes,

can meet the basic legal requirements for use as a trademark. It can act as a symbol that distinguishes a firm's goods and identifies their source, without serving any other significant function. See U.S. Department of Commerce, Patent and Trademark Office, Trademark Manual of Examining Procedure § 1202.04(e), p. 1202–13 (2d ed. May, 1993) (hereinafter PTO Manual) (approving trademark registration of color alone where it "has become distinctive of the applicant goods in commerce," provided that "there is [no] competitive need for colors to remain available in the industry" and the color is not "functional"); see also 1 McCarthy §§ 3.01[1], 7.26 ("requirements for qualification of a word or symbol as a trademark" are that it be (1) a "symbol," (2) "use(d) . . . as a mark," (3) "to identify and distinguish the seller's goods from goods made or sold by others," but that it not be "functional"). Indeed, the District Court, in this case, entered findings, (accepted by the Ninth Circuit) that show Qualitex's green-gold press pad color has met these requirements. The green-gold color acts as a symbol. Having developed secondary meaning (for customers identified the green-gold color as Qualitex's), it identifies the press pads' source. And, the green-gold color serves no other function. (Although it is important to use some color on press pads to avoid noticeable stains, the court found "no competitive need in the press pad industry for the green-gold color, since other colors are equally usable." Accordingly, unless there is some special reason that convincingly militates against the use of color alone as a trademark, trademark law would protect Qualitex's use of the green-gold color on its press pads.

II. Respondent Jacobson Products says that there are . . . special reasons why the law should forbid the use of color alone as a trademark. We shall explain, in turn, why we, ultimately, find them unpersuasive. . . .

We . . . Courts traditionally decide quite difficult questions about whether two words or phrases or symbols are sufficiently similar, in context, to confuse buyers. . . . Legal standards exist to guide courts in making comparisons. See, *e.g.*, 2 McCarthy § 15.08; ("[S]trong" marks, with greater secondary meaning, receive broader protection than "weak" marks). . . .

Second, Jacobson argues, as have others, that colors are in limited supply. See, *e.g.*, *NutraSweet Co.*, 917 F.2d, at 1028; *Campbell Soup Co. v. Armour & Co.*, 175 F.2d 795, 798 (CA3 1949). Jacobson claims that, if one of many competitors can appropriate a particular color for use as a trademark, and each competitor then tries to do the same, the supply of colors will soon be depleted. Put in its strongest form, this argument would concede that "[h]undreds of color pigments are manufactured and thousands of colors can be obtained by mixing." L. Cheskin, Colors: What

They Can Do For You 47 (1947). But, it would add that, in the context of a particular product, only some colors are usable. By the time one discards colors that, say, for reasons of customer appeal, are not usable, and adds the shades that competitors cannot use lest they risk infringing a similar, registered shade, then one is left with only a handful of possible colors. And, under these circumstances, to permit one, or a few, producers to use colors as trademarks will "deplete" the supply of usable colors to the point where a competitor's inability to find a suitable color will put that competitor at a significant disadvantage.

This argument is unpersuasive, however, largely because it relies on an occasional problem to justify a blanket prohibition. When a color serves as a mark, normally alternative colors will likely be available for similar use by others. See, *e.g.*, *Owens-Corning*, 774 F.2d, at 1121 (pink insulation). Moreover, if that is not so—if a "color depletion" or "color scarcity" problem does arise—the trademark doctrine or "functionality" normally would seem available to prevent the anticompetitive consequences that Jacobson's argument posits, thereby minimizing that argument's practical force.

The functionality doctrine, as we have said, forbids the use of a product's feature as a trademark where doing so will put a competitor at a significant disadvantage because the feature is "essential to the use or purpose of the article" or "affects [its] cost or quality." Inwood Laboratories, Inc., 456 U.S., at 850, n. 10, 102 S.Ct., at 2186, n. 10. The functionality doctrine thus protects competitors against a disadvantage (unrelated to recognition or reputation) that trademark protection might otherwise impose, namely their inability reasonably to replicate important non-reputation-related product features. . . . And, the federal courts have demonstrated that they can apply this doctrine in a careful and reasoned manner, with sensitivity. . . . Although we need not comment on the merits of specific cases, we note that lower courts have permitted competitors to copy the green color of farm machinery (because customers wanted their farm equipment to match) and have barred the use of black as a trademark on outboard boat motors (because black has the special functional attributes of decreasing the apparent size of the motor and ensuring compatibility with many different boat colors). See *Brunswick Corp. v British Seagull Ltd.*, 36 F.3d 1527, 1532 (CA Fed.1994).

Jacobson points to many older cases—including Supreme Court cases—in support of its position. . . .

These Supreme Court cases, however, interpreted trademark law as it existed *before* 1946, when Congress enacted the Lanham Act. The Lanham Act significantly changed and liberalized the common law to "dispense with mere technical prohibitions," S.Rep. No. 1333, 79th Cong., 2d Sess., 3 (1946), most notably, by permitting trademark registration of descriptive words (say, "U-Build-It" model airplanes) where they had acquired "secondary meaning." See *Abercrombie & Fitch Co.,* 537 F.2d, at 9 (Friendly, J.). The Lanham Act extended protection to descriptive marks by making clear that (with certain explicit exceptions not relevant here), "nothing . . . shall prevent the registration of a mark used by the applicant which has become distinctive of the applicant's goods in commerce." 15 U.S.C. § 1052(f) (1988 ed., Supp. V).

This language permits an ordinary word, normally used for a nontrademark purpose (e.g., description), to act as a trademark where it has gained "secondary meaning." Its logic would appear to apply to color as well. Indeed, in 1985, the Federal Circuit considered the significance of the Lanham Acts changes as they related to color and held that trademark protection for color was consistent with the "jurisprudence under the Lanham Act developed in accordance with the statutory principle that if a mark is capable of being or becoming distinctive of [the] applicant's goods in commerce, then it is capable of serving as a trademark." *Owens-Corning,* 774 F.2d, at 1120.

In 1988 Congress amended the Lanham Act, revising portions of the definitional language, but left unchanged the language here relevant. § 134, 102 Stat. 3946, 15 U.S.C. § 1127. It enacted these amendments against the following background: (1) the Federal Circuit had decided Owens-Corning; (2) the Patent and Trademark Office had adopted a clear policy (which it still maintains) permitting registration of color as a trademark, see PTO Manual § 1202.04(e) (at p. 1200–12 of the January 1986 edition and p. 1202–13 of the May 1993 edition); and (3) the Trademark Commission had written a report, which recommended that "the terms 'symbol, or device'. . . not be deleted or narrowed to preclude registration of such things as a color, shape, smell, sound, or configuration which functions as a mark," The United States Trademark Association Trademark Review Commission Report and Recommendations to USTA President and Board of Directors, 77 T.M.Rep. 375, 421 (1987) (hereinafter Trademark Commission); see also 133 Cong.Rec. 32812 (1987) (statement of Sen. DeConcini) ("The bill I am introducing today is based on the Commission's report and recommendations"). This background strongly suggests that the language "any word, name, symbol, or device," 15 U.S.C. § 1127, had come to include color.

Finally, when Congress re-enacted the terms "word, name, symbol, or device" in 1988, it did so against a legal background in which those terms had come to include color, and its statutory revision embraced that understanding.

Jacobson argues that there is no need to permit color alone to function as a trademark because a firm already may use color as part of a trademark, say, as a colored circle or colored letter or colored word, and may rely upon "trade dress" protection, under § 43(a) of the Lanham Act, if a competitor copies its color and thereby causes consumer confusion regarding the overall appearance of the competing products or their packaging, see 15 U.S.C. § 1125(a) (1988 ed., Supp. V). . . . Trademark law helps the holder of a mark in many ways that "trade dress" protection does not. See 15 U.S.C. § 1124 (ability to prevent importation of confusingly similar goods); § 1072 (constructive notice of ownership); § 1065 (incontestable status); § 1057(b) (prima facie evidence of validity and ownership). Thus, one can easily find reasons why the law might provide trademark protection in addition to trade dress protection.

III. Having determined that a color may sometimes meet the basic legal requirements for use as a trademark and that respondent Jacobson's arguments do not justify a special legal rule preventing color alone from serving as a trademark (and, in light of the District Court's here undisputed findings that Qualitex's use of the green-gold color on its press pads meets the basic trademark requirements), we conclude that the Ninth Circuit erred in barring Qualitex's use of color as a trademark. For these reasons, the judgment of the Ninth Circuit is *reversed.*

Questions

1. Does color alone meet the basic requirements for use as a trademark?

2. Assess the validity of the following statement: "Because of the limited number of basic colors, including red, orange, green, blue, yellow, violet, black and white, most new competitors would be placed at a disadvantage because of the depletion of the supply of usable colors."

3. Review the objectives of trademark law set forth in the decision and the ethical principles set forth on page 190 of this book. Is it ethical for the owners of private label or store brand consumer products to design their private labels with closely similar trade dress or use colors similar to the national brand's trademarks?

Virgil v "Kash N' Karry Service Corporation

61 Md App 23, 484 A2d 652 (1984)

Mrs. Virgil brought a product liability action against the manufacturer and seller of a thermos bottle. The bottle was manufactured by Aladdin and sold by Kash N' Karry. While she was pouring milk into the bottle, it imploded (burst inward), throwing hot coffee and glass into her face and injuring her eye. She alleged liability because of (1) negligence in failing to warn of the dangerous characteristics of the product, (2) breach of implied warranty of merchantability, and (3) strict liability in tort. From a judgment in favor of Kash N' Karry and Aladdin, Virgil and her husband appealed.

BLOOM, J. . . .Mrs. Virgil testified that she purchased the pint-size thermos while shopping at Kash N' Karry two or three months prior to the implosion. Every weekday morning she filled it with coffee and a little milk and took it to work, carrying it either by its handle or in a bag with her shoes. On Saturday mornings, she filled it with coffee and milk and carried it downstairs to the den, where she spent most of the day studying. Although the thermos bottle bore a label, "Easy to Keep Clean," there were no instructions as to how to clean the thermos and no indication that any normal manner of cleaning it might damage it. Mrs. Virgil described how she washed it, filling it at night with a mild solution of baking soda in warm water, then washing it the following morning with a bottle brush. She denied dropping the thermos or misusing, abusing, or damaging it in any way. One morning, after pouring coffee into the thermos, she started to pour milk into it when it imploded, throwing hot coffee and glass into her face and injuring her eye. Appellants [Mrs. Virgil and her husband] presented no expert testimony to give any scientific explanation for the implosion.

To support their claim that appellees [the manufacturer and the seller] breached an implied warranty of merchantability, appellants had to establish that a warranty existed, that the warranty was breached, and that the breach was the proximate cause of the injury. If the seller of goods is a merchant with respect to goods of that kind, a warranty of merchantability is implied in the contract of sale. To be merchantable, the goods must at least be fit for the ordinary purposes for which they are sold and conform to any promises or affirmations of fact made on the container or label.

Strict liability in tort, on the other hand, is described in the Restatement (Second) of Torts § 402 A, as follows:

(1) One who sells any product in a defective condition unreasonably dangerous to the user or consumer or to his property is subject to liability for physical harm thereby caused to the ultimate user or consumer, or to his property, if

    (a) the seller is engaged in the business of selling such a product, and

    (b) it is expected to and does reach the user or consumer without substantial change in the condition in which it is sold.

(2) The rule stated in Subsection (1) applies although

    (a) the seller has exercised all possible care in the preparation and sale of his product,

    (b) the user or consumer has not bought the product from or entered into any contractual relation with the seller.

To recover on either theory—implied warranty or strict liability—the plaintiff in a products liability case must satisfy three basics from an evidentiary standpoint: (1) the existence of a defect, (2) the attribution of the defect to the seller, and (3) a causal relation between the defect and the injury.

We reject the appellees' contention that it was necessary for the appellants to produce expert testimony to establish the existence of a defect. The general rule is well established that expert testimony is only required when the subject of the inference is so particularly related to some science or profession that it is beyond the ken of the average layman. Expert testimony is hardly necessary to establish that a thermos bottle that explodes or implodes when coffee and milk are poured into it is defective. When a product fails to meet the reasonable expectations of the user, "the inference is that there was some sort of a defect, a precise definition of which is unnecessary." . . . An inference of a defect may be drawn from the happening of an accident, where circumstantial evidence tends to eliminate other causes, such as product misuse or alteration. . . .

It would seem to be axiomatic that the defect that caused the implosion either existed at the time Mrs. Virgil bought the thermos or was created thereafter. Mrs. Virgil's testimony, if believed by the trier of fact, tended to eliminate any likelihood that the defect that caused the implosion was created after Mrs. Virgil purchased the thermos. Consequently, her testimony gave rise to a reasonable inference that the thermos was defective when she acquired it. . . .

Products liability law imposes on a manufacturer a duty to warn if the item produced has an inherent and hidden danger that the producer knows or should know could be a substantial factor in causing injury. This duty to warn of latent dangers inherent in the use of the product extends beyond intended uses to include uses that are reasonably foreseeable.

The claim that appellees negligently failed to warn of

the "dangerous propensities of the product" fails simply because there was no evidence that either of the appellees knew or should have known that the thermos bottle presented a danger. Assuming that the thermos had a latent defect that caused it to implode, there is nothing in the evidence to suggest that either the manufacturer or the retailer were or should have been aware of that defect.

Appellants suggest that the thermos label, which recommended that the product not be used by children and advised potential users that the product contained glass, permits an inference that the manufacturer had reason to know that the thermos would be inherently dangerous for a reasonably foreseeable use. Recognizing that a product partially composed of glass is breakable, however, hardly constitutes awareness that the product is defective.

[Judgment affirmed as to directed verdict against negligence counts and reversed and remanded for consideration of implied warranty and strict tort counts]

Questions

1. Why was it important that Mrs. Virgil be able to establish the existence of a defect in the product?
2. Why did the court hold that appellees had not been negligent in failing to warn of the danger of implosion?
3. Is it better for a plaintiff with a product liability claim to sue on a negligence theory, a breach of warranty theory, or a strict liability theory?

How to Find the Law

In order to determine what the law on a particular question or issue is, it may be necessary to examine (1) compilations of constitutions, treaties, statutes, executive orders, proclamations, and administrative regulations; (2) reports of state and federal court decisions; (3) digests of opinions; (4) treatises on the law; and (5) loose-leaf services. These sources can be either researched traditionally or using fee and/or non-fee based computerized legal research accessed through the World Wide Web.

COMPILATIONS

In the consideration of a legal problem in business it is necessary to determine whether the matter is affected or controlled by a constitution, national or state; by a national treaty; by an Act of Congress or a state legislature, or by a city ordinance; by a decree or proclamation of the President of the United States, a governor, or a mayor; or by a regulation of a federal, state, or local administrative agency.

Each body or person that makes laws, regulations, or ordinances usually compiles and publishes at the end of each year or session all of the matter that it has adopted. In addition to the periodical or annual volumes, it is common to compile all the treaties, statutes, regulations, or ordinances in separate volumes. To illustrate, the federal Anti-Injunction Act may be cited as the Act of March 23, 1932, 47 Stat 70, 29 USC Sections 101 et seq. This means that this law was enacted on March 23, 1932, and that it can be found at page 70 in Volume 47 of the reports that contain all of the statutes adopted by the Congress.

The second part of the citation, 29 USC Sections 101 et seq., means that in the collection of all of the federal statutes, which is known as the United States Code, the full text of the statute can be found in the sections of the 29th title beginning with Section 101.

COURT DECISIONS

For complicated or important legal cases or when an appeal is to be taken, a court will generally write an opinion, which explains why the court made the decision. Appellate courts as a rule write opinions. The great majority of these decisions, particularly in the case of the appellate courts, are collected and printed. In order to avoid confusion, the opinions of each court are ordinarily printed in a separate set of reports, either by official reporters or private publishers.

In the reference "Pennoyer v Neff, 95 US 714, 24 LEd 565," the first part states the names of the parties. It does not necessarily tell who was the plaintiff and who was the defendant. When an action is begun in a lower court, the first name is that of the plaintiff and the second name that of the defendant. When the case is appealed, generally the name of the person taking the appeal appears on the records of the higher court as the first one and that of the adverse party as the second. Sometimes, therefore, the original order of the names of the parties is reversed.

The balance of the reference consists of two citations. The first citation, 95 US 714, means that the opinion which the court filed in the case of Pennoyer v Neff may be found on page 714 of the 95th volume of a series of books in which are printed officially the opinions of the United States Supreme Court. Sometimes the same opinion is printed in two different sets of volumes. In the example, 24 LEd 565 means that in the 24th volume of another set of books, called Lawyer's Edition, of the United States Supreme Court Reports, the same opinion begins on page 565.

In opinions by a state court there may also be two citations, as in the case of "Morrow v Corbin, 122 Tex 553, 62 SW2d 641." This means that the opinion in the lawsuit between Morrow and Corbin may be found in the 122d volume of the reports of the highest court of Texas, beginning on page 553; and also in Volume 62 of the Southwestern Reporter, Second Series, at page 641.

The West Publishing Company publishes a set of sectional reporters covering the entire United States. They are called "sectional" because each reporter, instead of being limited to a particular court or a particular state, covers the decisions of the courts of a particular section of the country. Thus the decisions of the courts of Arkansas, Kentucky, Missouri, Tennessee, and Texas are printed by the West Publishing company as a group in a sectional reporter called the Southwestern Reporter.[1] Because of the large number of decisions involved, generally only the opinions of the state appellate courts are printed. A number of states[2] have discontinued publication of the opinions of their courts, and those opinions are now found only in the West reporters.

The reason for the "Second Series" in the Southwestern citation is that when there were 300 volumes in the original series, instead of calling the next volume 301, the publisher called it Volume 1, Second Series. Thus 62 SW2d Series really means the 362d volume of the Southwestern Reporter. Six to eight volumes appear in a year for each geographic section.

In addition to these state reporters, the West Pub-

lishing Company publishes a Federal Supplement, which primarily reports the opinions of the Federal District Courts; the Federal Reporter, which primarily reports the decisions of the United States Courts of Appeals; and the Supreme Court Reporter, which reports the decisions of the United States Supreme Court. The Supreme Court decisions are also reported in a separate set called the Lawyers' Edition, published by the Lawyers Cooperative Publishing Company.

The reports published by the West Publishing Company and Lawyers Cooperative Publishing Company are unofficial reports, while those bearing the name or abbreviation of the United States or of a state, such as "95 US 714" or "122 Tex 553" are official reports. This means that in the case of the latter, the particular court, such as the United States Supreme Court, has officially authorized that its decisions be printed and that by federal statute such official printing is made. In the case of the unofficial reporters, the publisher prints the decisions of a court on its own initiative. Such opinions are part of the public domain and not subject to any copyright or similar restriction.

DIGESTS OF OPINIONS

The reports of court decisions are useful only if one has the citation, that is, the name and volume number of the book and the page number of the opinion one is seeking. For this reason, digests of the decisions have been prepared. These digests organize the entire field of law under major headings, which are then arranged in alphabetical order. Under each heading, such as "Contracts," the subject is divided into the different questions that can arise with respect to that field. A master outline is thus created on the subject. This outline includes short paragraphs describing what each case holds and giving its citation.

TREATISES AND RESTATEMENTS

Very helpful in finding a case or a statute are the treatises on the law. These may be special books, each written by an author on a particular subject, such as Williston on Contracts, Bogert on Trusts, Fletcher on Corporations, or

---

[1] The sectional reporters are: Atlantic—A. (Connecticut, Delaware, District of Columbia, Maine, Maryland, New Hampshire, New Jersey, Pennsylvania, Rhode Island, Vermont); Northeastern—N.W. (Iowa, Michigan, Minnesota, Nebraska, North Dakota, South Dakota, Wisconsin); Pacific—P. (Alaska, Arizona, California, Colorado, Hawaii, Idaho, Kansas, Montana, Nevada, New Mexico, Oklahoma, Oregon, Utah, Washington, Wyoming); Southeastern—S.E. (Georgia, North Carolina, South Carolina, Virginia, West Virginia); Southwestern—S.W. (Arkansas, Kentucky, Missouri, Tennessee, Texas); and Southern—So. (Alabama, Florida, Louisiana, Mississippi). There is also a special New York State reporter known as the New York Supplement and a special California State reporter known as the California Reporter.

[2] See, for example, Alaska, Florida, Iowa, Kentucky, Louisiana, Maine, Mississippi, Missouri, North Dakota, Oklahoma, Texas, and Wyoming.

they may be general encyclopedias, as in the case of American Jurisprudence, American Jurisprudence, Second, and Corpus Juris Secundum.

Another type of treatise is found in the restatements of the law prepared by the American Law Institute. Each restatement consists of one or more volumes devoted to a particular phase of the law, such as the Restatement of the Law of Contracts, Restatement of the Law of Agency, and Restatement of the Law of Property. In each restatement the American Law Institute, acting through special committees of judges, lawyers, and professors of law, has set forth what the law is; and in many areas where there is no law or the present rule is regarded as unsatisfactory, the restatement specifies what the Institute deems to be the desirable rule.

LOOSE-LEAF SERVICES

A number of private publishers, notably Commerce Clearing House and Prentice-Hall, publish loose-leaf books devoted to particular branches of the law. Periodically, the publisher sends to the purchaser a number of pages that set forth any decision, regulation, or statute made or adopted since the prior set of pages was prepared. Such services are unofficial.

COMPUTERIZED LEGAL RESEARCH

National and local computer services are providing constantly widening assistance for legal research. The database in such a system may be opinions, statutes, or administrative regulations stored word for word; or the later history of a particular case giving its full citation and showing whether the case has been followed by other courts; or the text of forms and documents. By means of a terminal connected to the system, the user can retrieve the above information at a great saving of time and with the assurance that it is up-to-date.

There are two leading, fee based systems for computer-aided research. Listed alphabetically, they are LEXIS and WESTLAW.

A specialized service of legal forms for business is provided by Shepard's BUSINESS LAW CASE MANAGEMENT SYSTEM. A monthly fee is required for usage.

Numerous free, private sites offer a lot of legal resources. The federal government offers a variety of case law, regulations, and code enactments, either pending or newly promulgated. To find the most comprehensive source of government-maintained legal information, go to www.law.house.gov/.

Increasingly, some states offer their regulations and codes on-line. As an example, go to the State of California's site, leginfo.ca.gov/, as an example of a government-based legal information provider. For a complete listing of state homepages, go to www.law.house.gov/17.htm.

For sources of all types of law, and legal resources, a new internet site, Hieros Gamos, (www.hg.org) claims that "virtually all on-line and off-line (published) legal information is accessible within three levels." It is important to note, however, that non-fee-based services do not guarantee the integrity of the information provided. Therefore, when accessing free information over the Internet, one should be careful to double check the authority of the provider and the accuracy of the data obtained. This caution extends to sites maintained by federal and state governments as well.

The computer field has expanded to such an extent that there is now a Legal Software Review of over 500 pages prepared by Lawyers Library, 12761 New Hall Ferry, Florissant, MO 63033.

A P P E N D I X 2
The Constitution of the United States

We the people of the United States of America, in order to form a more perfect union, establish justice, insure domestic tranquility, provide for the common defence, promote the general welfare, and secure the blessings of liberty to ourselves and our posterity, do ordain and establish this Constitution for the United States of America.

Article I

Section 1. All legislative powers herein granted shall be vested in a Congress of the United States, which shall consist of a Senate and House of Representatives.

Section 2. I. The House of Representatives shall be composed of members chosen every second year by the people of the several States, and the electors in each State shall have the qualifications requisite for electors of the most numerous branch of the State legislature.

2. No person shall be a representative who shall not have attained to the age of twenty-five years, and been seven years a citizen of the United States, and who shall not, when elected, be an inhabitant of that State in which he shall be chosen.

3. Representatives and direct taxes shall be apportioned among the several States which may be included within this Union, according to their respective numbers, which shall be determined by adding to the whole number of free persons, including those bound to service for a term of years, and excluding Indians not taxed, three fifths of all other persons.[1] The actual enumeration shall be made within three years after the first meeting of the Congress of the United States, and within every subsequent term of ten years, in such manner as they shall by law direct. The number of representatives shall not exceed

one for every thirty thousand, but each State shall have at least one representative; and until such enumeration shall be made, the State of New Hampshire shall be entitled to choose three, Massachusetts eight, Rhode Island and Providence Plantations one, Connecticut five, New York six, New Jersey four, Pennsylvania eight, Delaware one, Maryland six, Virginia ten, North Carolina five, South Carolina five, and Georgia three.

4. When vacancies happen in the representation from any State, the executive authority thereof shall issue writs of election to fill such vacancies.

5. The House of Representatives shall choose their speaker and other officers; and shall have the sole power of impeachment.

Section 3. 1. The Senate of the United States shall be composed of two senators from each State, chosen by the legislature thereof, for six years; and each senator shall have one vote.

2. Immediately after they shall be assembled in consequence of the first election, they shall be divided as equally as may be into three classes. The seats of the senators of the first class shall be vacated at the expiration of the second year, of the second class at the expiration of the fourth year, and of the third class at the expiration of the fourth year, and of the third class at the expiration of the sixth year, so that one third may be chosen every second year; and if vacancies happen by resignation, or otherwise, during the recess of the legislature of any State, the

---

[1] See the 14th Amendment.

executive thereof may make temporary appointments until the next meeting of the legislature, which shall then fill such vacancies.[2]

3. No person shall be a senator who shall not have attained to the age of thirty years, and been nine years a citizen of the United States, and who shall not, when elected, be an inhabitant of that State for which he shall be chosen.

4. The Vice President of the United States shall be President of the Senate, but shall have no vote, unless they be equally divided.

5. The Senate shall choose their other officers, and also a president pro tempore, in the absence of the Vice President, or when he shall exercise the office of the President of the United States.

6. The Senate shall have the sole power to try all impeachments. When sitting for that purpose, they shall be on oath or affirmation. When the President of the United States is tried, the chief justice shall preside: and no person shall be convicted without the concurrence of two thirds of the members present.

7. Judgment in cases of impeachment shall not extend further than to removal from office, and disqualification to hold and enjoy any office of honor, trust or profit under the United States: but the party convicted shall nevertheless be liable and subject to indictment, trial, judgment and punishment, according to law.

Section 4. 1. The times, places, and manner of holding elections for senators and representatives, shall be prescribed in each State by the legislature thereof; but the Congress may at any time by law make or alter such regulations, except as to the places of choosing senators.

2. The Congress shall assemble at least once in every year, and such meeting shall be on the first Monday in December, unless they shall by law appoint a different day.

Section 5. 1. Each House shall be the judge of the elections, returns and qualifications of its own members, and a majority of each shall constitute a quorum to do business; but a smaller number may adjourn from day to day, and may be authorized to compel the attendance of absent members, in such manner, and under such penalties as each House may provide.

2. Each House may determine the rules of its proceedings, punish its members for disorderly behavior, and, with the concurrence of two thirds, expel a member.

3. Each House shall keep a journal of its proceedings, and from time to time publish the same, excepting such parts as may in their judgment require secrecy; and the yeas and nays of the members of either House on any question shall, at the desire of one fifth of those present, be entered on the journal.

4. Neither House, during the session of Congress, shall, without the consent of the other, adjourn for more than three days, nor to any other place than that in which the two Houses shall be sitting.

Section 6. 1. The senators and representatives shall receive a compensation for their services, to be ascertained by law, and paid out of the Treasury of the United States. They shall in all cases, except treason, felony, and breach of the peace, be privileged from arrest during their attendance at the session of their respective Houses, and in going to and returning from the same; and for any speech or debate in either House, they shall not be questioned in any other place.

2. No senator or representative shall, during the time for which he was elected, be appointed to any civil office under the authority of the United States, which shall have been created, or the emoluments whereof shall have been increased during such time; and no person holding any office under the United States shall be a member of either House during his continuance in office.

Section 7. 1. All bills for raising revenue shall originate in the House of Representatives; but the Senate may propose or concur with amendments as on other bills.

2. Every bill which shall have passed the House of Representatives and the Senate, shall, before it becomes a law, be presented to the President of the United States; if he approves he shall sign it, but if not he shall return it, with his objections to that House in which it shall have originated, who shall enter the objections at large on their journal, and proceed to reconsider it. If after such reconsideration two thirds of that House shall agree to pass the bill, it shall be sent, together with the objections, to the other House, by which it shall likewise be reconsidered, and if approved by two thirds of that House, it shall become a law. But in all such cases the votes of both Houses shall be determined by yeas and nays, and the names of the persons voting for and against the bill shall be entered on the journal of each House respectively. If any bill shall not be returned by the President within ten days (Sundays excepted) after it shall have been presented to him, the same shall be a law, in like manner as if he had signed it, unless the Congress by their adjournment prevent its return, in which case it shall not be a law.

3. Every order, resolution, or vote to which the concurrence of the Senate and the House of Representatives may be necessary (except on a question of adjournment) shall be presented to the President of the United States; and before the same shall take effect, shall be approved by him, or being disapproved by him, shall be repassed by two thirds of the Senate and House of Representatives, according to the rules and limitations prescribed in the case of a bill.

Section 8. The Congress shall have the power

1. To lay and collect taxes, duties, imposts, and excises,

---

[2] See the 17th Amendment.

to pay the debts and provide for the common defense and general welfare of the United States; but all duties, imposts, and excises shall be uniform throughout the United States;

2. To borrow money on the credit of the United States;

3. To regulate commerce with foreign nations, and among the several States, and with the Indian tribes;

4. To establish a uniform rule of naturalization, and uniform laws on the subject of bankruptcies throughout the United States;

5. To coin money, regulate the value thereof, and of foreign coin, and fix the standard of weights and measures;

6. To provide for the punishment of counterfeiting the securities and current coin of the United States;

7. To establish post offices and post roads;

8. To promote the progress of science and useful arts, by securing for limited times to authors and inventors the exclusive rights to their respective writings and discoveries;

9. To constitute tribunals inferior to the Supreme Court;

10. To define and punish piracies and felonies committed on the high seas, and offenses against the law of nations;

11. To declare war, grant letters of marque and reprisal, and make rules concerning captures on land and water;

12. To raise and support armies, but no appropriation of money to that use shall be for a longer term than two years;

13. To provide and maintain a navy;

14. To make rules for the government and regulation of the land and naval forces;

15. To provide for calling forth the militia to execute the laws of the Union, suppress insurrections and repel invasions;

16. To provide for organizing, arming, and disciplining the militia, and for governing such part of them as may be employed in the service of the United States, reserving to the States respectively, the appointment of the officers, and the authority of training the militia according to the discipline prescribed by Congress;

17. To exercise exclusive legislation in all cases whatsoever, over such district (not exceeding ten miles square) as may, by cession of particular States, and the acceptance of Congress, become the seat of the government of the United States, and to exercise like authority over all places purchased by the consent of the legislature of the State in which the same shall be, for the erection of forts, magazines, arsenals, dockyards, and other needful buildings; and

18. To make all laws which shall be necessary and proper for carrying into execution the foregoing powers, and all other powers vested by this Constitution in the government of the United States, or in any department or officer thereof.

Section 9. I. The migration or importation of such persons as any of the States now existing shall think proper to admit, shall not be prohibited by the Congress prior to the year one thousand eight hundred and eight, but a tax or duty may be imposed on such importation, not exceeding ten dollars for each person.

2. The privilege of the writ of habeas corpus shall not be suspended, unless when in cases of rebellion or invasion the public safety may require it.

3. No bill of attainder or ex post facto law shall be passed.

4. No capitation, or other direct, tax shall be laid, unless in proportion to the census or enumeration hereinbefore directed to be taken.[3]

5. No tax or duty shall be laid on articles exported from any State.

6. No preference shall be given by any regulation of commerce or revenue to the ports of one State over those of another: nor shall vessels bound to, or from, one State be obliged to enter, clear, or pay duties in another.

7. No money shall be drawn from the treasury, but in consequence of appropriations made by law; and a regular statement and account of the receipts and expenditures of all public money shall be published from time to time.

8. No title of nobility shall be granted by the United States: and no person holding any office of profit or trust under them, shall, without the consent of the Congress, accept of any present, emolument, office, or title, of any kind whatever, from any king, prince, or foreign State.

Section 10. 1. No State shall enter into any treaty, alliance, or confederation; grant letters of marque and reprisal; coin money; emit bills of credit; make anything but gold and silver coin a tender in payment of debts; pass any bill of attainder, ex post facto law, or law impairing the obligation of contracts, or grant any title of nobility.

2. No State shall, without the consent of the Congress, lay any imposts or duties on imports or exports, except what may be absolutely necessary for executing its inspection laws: and the net produce of all duties and imposts laid by any State on imports or exports, shall be for the use of the treasury of the United States; and all such laws shall be subject to the revision and control of the Congress.

3. No State shall, without the consent of the Congress, lay any duty of tonnage, keep troops, or ships of war in time of peace, enter into any agreement or compact with another State, or with a foreign power, or engage in war, unless actually invaded, or in such imminent danger as will not admit of delay.

Article II

Section 1. 1. The executive power shall be vested in a President of the United States of America. He shall hold

---

3 See the 16th Amendment.

his office during the term of four years, and, together with the Vice President, chosen for the same term, be elected as follows:

2. Each State shall appoint, in such manner as the legislature thereof may direct, a number of electors, equal to the whole number of senators and representatives to which the State may be entitled in the Congress: but no senator or representative, or person holding an office of trust or profit under the United States, shall be appointed an elector.

The electors shall meet in their respective States, and vote by ballot for two persons, of whom one at least shall not be an inhabitant of the same State with themselves. And they shall make a list of all the persons voted for, and of the number of votes for each; which list they shall sign and certify, and transmit sealed to the seat of the government of the United States, directed to the president of the Senate. The president of the Senate shall, in the presence of the Senate and House of Representatives, open all the certificates, and the votes shall then be counted. The person having the greatest number of votes shall be the President, if such number be a majority of the whole number of electors appointed; and if there be more than one who have such majority, and have an equal number of votes, then the House of Representatives shall immediately choose by ballot one of them for President; and if no person have a majority, then from the five highest on the list the said House shall in like manner choose the President. But in choosing the President, the votes shall be taken by States, the representation from each State having one vote; a quorum for this purpose shall consist of a member or members from two thirds of the States, and a majority of all the States shall be necessary to a choice. In every case, after the choice of the President, the person having the greatest number of votes of the electors shall be the Vice President. But if there should remain two or more who have equal votes, the Senate shall choose from them by ballot the Vice President.[4]

3. The Congress may determine the time of choosing the electors, and the day on which they shall give their votes; which day shall be the same throughout the United States.

4. No person except a natural born citizen, or a citizen of the United States, at the time of the adoption of this Constitution, shall be eligible to the office of President; neither shall any person be eligible to that office who shall not have attained to the age of thirty-five years, and been fourteen years a resident within the United States.

5. In the case of removal of the President from office, or of his death, resignation, or inability to discharge the powers and duties of the said office, the same shall devolve on the Vice President, and the Congress may by law provide for the case of removal, death, resignation,

___
[4] Superseded by the 12th Amendment.

or inability, both of the President and Vice President, declaring what officer shall then act as President, and such officer shall act accordingly, until the disability be removed, or a President shall be elected.

6. The President shall, at stated times, receive for his services a compensation, which shall neither be increased nor diminished during the period for which he shall have been elected, and he shall not receive within that period any other emolument from the United States, or any of them.

7. Before he enter on the execution of his office, he shall take the following oath or affirmation:—"I do solemnly swear (or affirm) that I will faithfully execute the office of President of the United States, and will to the best of my ability, preserve, protect and defend the Constitution of the United States."

Section 2. 1. The President shall be commander in chief of the army and navy of the United States, and of the militia of the several States, when called into the actual service of the United States; he may require the opinion, in writing, of the principal officer in each of the executive departments, upon any subject relating to the duties of their respective office, and he shall have power to grant reprieves and pardons for offenses against the United States, except in cases of impeachment.

2. He shall have power, by and with the advice and consent of the Senate, to make treaties, provided two thirds of the senators present concur; and he shall nominate, and by and with the advice and consent of the Senate, shall appoint ambassadors, other public ministers and consuls, judges of the Supreme Court, and all other officers of the United States, whose appointments are not herein otherwise provided for, and which shall be established by law: but the Congress may by law vest the appointment of such inferior officers, as they think proper, in the President alone, in the courts of law, or in the heads of departments.

3. The President shall have power to fill up all vacancies that may happen during the recess of the Senate, by granting commissions which shall expire at the end of their next session.

Section 3. He shall from time to time give to the Congress information of the state of the Union, and recommend to their consideration such measures as he shall judge necessary and expedient; he may, on extraordinary occasions, convene both Houses, or either of them, and in case of disagreement between them with respect to the time of adjournment, he may adjourn them to such time as he shall think proper; he shall receive ambassadors and other public ministers; he shall take care that the laws be faithfully executed, and shall commission all the officers of the United States.

Section 4. The President, Vice President, and all civil officers of the United States, shall be removed from office on impeachment for, and conviction of, treason, bribery, or other high crimes and misdemeanors.

Article III

Section 1. The judicial power of the United States shall be vested in one Supreme Court, and in such inferior courts as the Congress may from time to time ordain and establish. The judges, both of the Supreme and inferior courts, shall hold their offices during good behavior, and shall, at stated times, receive for their services, a compensation, which shall not be diminished during their continuance in office.

Section 2. 1. The judicial power shall extend to all cases, in law and equity, arising under this Constitution, the laws of the United States, and treaties made, or which shall be made, under their authority;—to all cases affecting ambassadors, other public ministers and consuls;—to all cases of admiralty and maritime jurisdiction;—to controversies to which the United States shall be a party;—to controversies between two or more States; between a State and citizens of another State;[5]—between citizens of different States;—between citizens of the same State claiming lands under grants of different States, and between a State, or the citizens thereof, and foreign States, citizens or subjects.

2. In all cases affecting ambassadors, other public ministers and consuls, and those in which a State shall be party, the Supreme Court shall have original jurisdiction. In all the other cases before mentioned, the Supreme Court shall have appellate jurisdiction, both as to law and to fact, with such exceptions, and under such regulations as the Congress shall make.

3. The trial of all crimes, except in cases of impeachment, shall be by jury; and such trial shall be held in the State where the said crimes shall have been committed; but when not committed within any State, the trial shall be at such place or places as the Congress may by law have directed.

Section 3. 1. Treason against the United States shall consist only in levying war against them, or in adhering to their enemies, giving them aid and comfort. No person shall be convicted of treason unless on the testimony of two witnesses to the same overt act, or on confession in open court.

2. The Congress shall have power to declare the punishment of treason, but no attainder of treason shall work corruption of blood, or forfeiture except during the life of the person attainted.

Article IV

Section 1. Full faith and credit shall be given in each State to the public acts, records, and judicial proceedings of every other State. And the Congress may by general laws prescribe the manner in which such acts, records and proceedings shall be proved, and the effect thereof.

Section 2. 1. The citizens of each State shall be entitled to all privileges and immunities of citizens in the several States.[6]

2. A person charged in any State with treason, felony, or other crime, who shall flee from justice, and be found in another State, shall on demand of the executive authority of the State from which he fled, be delivered up to be removed to the State having jurisdiction of the crime.

3. No person held to service or labor in one State under the laws thereof, escaping into another, shall in consequence of any law or regulation therein, be discharged from such service or labor, but shall be delivered up on claim of the party to whom such service or labor may be due.[7]

Section 3. 1. New States may be admitted by the Congress into this Union; but no new State shall be formed or erected within the jurisdiction of any other State, nor any State be formed by the junction of two or more States, or parts of States, without the consent of the legislatures of the States concerned as well as of the Congress.

2. The Congress shall have power to dispose of and make all needful rules and regulations respecting the territory or other property belonging to the United States; and nothing in this Constitution shall be so construed as to prejudice any claims of the United States, or of any particular State.

Section 4. The United States shall guarantee to every State in this Union a republican form of government, and shall protect each of them against invasion; and on application of the legislature, or of the executive (when the legislature cannot be convened) against domestic violence.

Article V

The Congress, whenever two thirds of both Houses shall deem it necessary, shall propose amendments to this Constitution, or, on the application of the legislature of two thirds of the several States, shall call a convention for proposing amendments, which in either case, shall be valid to all intents and purposes, as part of this Constitution when ratified by the legislatures of three fourths of the several States, or by conventions in three fourths thereof, as the one or the other mode of ratification may be proposed by the Congress; provided that no amendment which may be made prior to the year one thousand eight hundred and eight shall in any manner affect the first and fourth clauses in the ninth section of the first article; and that no State, without its consent, shall be deprived of its equal suffrage in the Senate.

---

5 See the 11th Amendment.

6 See the 14th Amendment, Sec. 1.

7 See the 13th Amendment.

Article VI

1. All debts contracted and engagements entered into, before the adoption of this Constitution, shall be as valid against the United States under this Constitution, as under the Confederation.[8]

2. This Constitution, and the laws of the United States which shall be made in pursuance thereof; and all treaties made, or which shall be made, under the authority of the United States, shall be the supreme law of the land; and the judges in every State shall be bound thereby, anything in the Constitution or laws of any State to the contrary notwithstanding.

3. The senators and representatives before mentioned, and the members of the several State legislatures, and all executive and judicial officers, both of the United States and of the several States, shall be bound by oath or affirmation to support this Constitution; but no religious test shall ever be required as a qualification to any office or public trust under the United States.

Felony

Article VII

The ratification of the conventions of nine States shall be sufficient for the establishment of this Constitution between the States so ratifying the same.

Done in Convention by the unanimous consent of the States present the seventeenth day of September in the year of our Lord one thousand seven hundred and eighty-seven, and of the independence of the United States of America the twelfth. In witness whereof we have hereunto subscribed our names.

AMENDMENTS

First Ten Amendments passed by Congress Sept. 25, 1789. Ratified by three-fourths of the States December 15, 1791.

Amendment I

Congress shall make no law respecting an establishment of religion, or prohibiting the free exercise thereof; or abridging the freedom of speech, or of the press; or the right of the people peaceably to assemble, and to petition the government for a redress of grievances.

Amendment II

A well regulated militia, being necessary to the security of a free State, the right of the people to keep and bear arms, shall not be infringed.

Amendment III

No soldier shall, in time of peace be quartered in any house, without the consent of the owner, nor in time of war, but in a manner to be prescribed by law.

Amendment IV

The right of the people to be secure in their persons, houses, papers, and effects, against unreasonable searches and seizures, shall not be violated, and no warrants shall issue, but upon probable cause, supported by oath or affirmation, and particularly describing the place to be searched, and the person or things to be seized.

Amendment V

Accusation

No person shall be held to answer for a capital, or otherwise infamous crime, unless on a presentment or indictment of a grand jury, except in cases arising in the land or naval forces, or in the militia, when in actual service in time of war or public danger; nor shall any person be subject for the same offense to be twice put in jeopardy of life or limb; nor shall be compelled in any criminal case to be a witness against himself, nor be deprived of life, liberty, or property, without due process of law; nor shall private property be taken for public use without just compensation.

Amendment VI

In all criminal prosecutions, the accused shall enjoy the right to a speedy and public trial, by an impartial jury of the State and district wherein the crime shall have been committed, which district shall have been previously ascertained by law, and to be informed of the nature and cause of the accusation; to be confronted with the witnesses against him; to have compulsory process for obtaining witnesses in his favor, and to have the assistance of counsel for his defense.

Amendment VII

In suits at common law, where the value in controversy shall exceed twenty dollars, the right of trial by jury shall be preserved, and no fact tried by a jury shall be otherwise reexamined in any court of the United States, then according to the rules of the common law.

Amendment VIII

Excessive bail shall not be required, nor excessive fines imposed, nor cruel and unusual punishments inflicted.

---

[8] See the 14th Amendment, Sec. 4.

Amendment IX

The enumeration in the Constitution of certain rights shall not be construed to deny or disparage others retained by the people.

Amendment X

The powers not delegated to the United States by the Constitution, nor prohibited by it to the States, are reserved to the States respectively, or to the people.

Amendment XI

Passed by Congress March 5, 1794. Ratified January 8, 1798.

The judicial power of the United States shall not be construed to extend to any suit in law or equity, commenced or prosecuted against one of the United States by citizens of another State, or by citizens or subjects of any foreign State.

Amendment XII

Passed by Congress December 12, 1803. Ratified September 25, 1804.

The electors shall meet in their respective States, and vote by ballot for President and Vice President, one of whom, at least, shall not be an inhabitant of the same State with themselves; they shall name in their ballots the person voted for as President, and in distinct ballots, the person voted for as Vice President, and they shall make distinct lists of all persons voted for as President and of all persons voted for as Vice President, and of the number of votes for each, which lists they shall sign and certify, and transmit sealed to the seat of the government of the United States, directed to the President of the Senate;— The President of the Senate shall, in the presence of the Senate and House of Representatives, open all the certificates and the votes shall then be counted;—The person having the greatest number of votes for President, shall be the President, if such number be a majority of the whole number of electors appointed; and if no person have such majority, then from the persons having the highest numbers not exceeding three on the list of those voted for as President, the House of Representatives shall choose immediately, by ballot, the President. But in choosing the President, the votes shall be taken by States, the representation from each State having one vote; a quorum for this purpose shall consist of a member or members from two thirds of the States, and a majority of all the States shall be necessary to a choice. And if the House of Representatives shall not choose a President whenever the right of choice shall devolve upon them, before the fourth day of March next following, then the Vice President shall

act as President, as in the case of the death or other constitutional disability of the President. The person having the greatest number of votes as Vice President shall be the Vice President, if such number be a majority of the whole number of electors appointed, and if no person have a majority, then from the two highest numbers on the list, the Senate shall choose the Vice President; a quorum for the purpose shall consist of two thirds of the whole number of Senators, and a majority of the whole number shall be necessary to a choice. But no person constitutionally ineligible to the office of President shall be eligible to that of Vice President of the United States.

Amendment XIII

Passed by Congress February 1, 1865. Ratified December 18, 1865.

Section 1. Neither slavery nor involuntary servitude, except as punishment for crime whereof the party shall have been duly convicted, shall exist within the United States, or any place subject to their jurisdiction.

Section 2. Congress shall have power to enforce this article by appropriate legislation.

Amendment XIV

Passed by Congress June 16, 1866. Ratified July 23, 1868.

Section 1. All persons born or naturalized in the United States, and subject to the jurisdiction thereof, are citizens of the United States and of the State wherein they reside. No State shall make or enforce any law which shall abridge the privileges or immunities of citizens of the United States; nor shall any State deprive any person of life, liberty, or property, without due process of law; nor deny to any person within its jurisdiction the equal protection of the laws.

Section 2. Representatives shall be apportioned among the several States according to their respective numbers, counting the whole number of persons in each State, excluding Indians not taxed. But when the right to vote at any election for the choice of electors for President and Vice President of the United States, representatives in Congress, the executive and judicial officers of a State, or the members of the legislature thereof, is denied to any of the male inhabitants of such State, being twenty-one years of age, and citizens of the United States, or in any way abridged, except for participation in rebellion, or other crime, the basis of representation therein shall be reduced in the proportion which the number of such male citizens shall bear to the whole number of male citizens twenty-one years of age in such State.

Section 3. No person shall be a senator or representative in Congress, or elector of President and Vice President, or hold any office, civil or military, under the United States, or under any State, who having previously taken an oath, as a member of Congress, or as an officer of the United States, or as a member of any State legislature, or as an executive or judicial officer of any State, to support the Constitution of the United States, shall have engaged in insurrection or rebellion against the same, or given aid or comfort to the enemies thereof. But Congress may by a vote of two thirds of each House, remove such disability.

Section 4. The validity of the public debt of the United States, authorized by law, including debts incurred for payment of pensions and bounties for services in suppressing insurrection or rebellion, shall not be questioned. But neither the United States nor any State shall assume or pay any debt or obligation incurred in aid of insurrection or rebellion against the United States, or any claim for the loss or emancipation of any slave; but all such debts, obligations, and claims shall be held illegal and void.

Section 5. The Congress shall have power to enforce, by appropriate legislation, the provisions of this article.

Amendment XV

Passed by Congress February 27, 1869. Ratified March 30, 1870.

Section 1. The right of citizens of the United States to vote shall not be denied or abridged by the United States or by any State on account of race, color, or previous condition of servitude.

Section 2. The Congress shall have power to enforce this article by appropriate legislation.

Amendment XVI

Passed by Congress July 12, 1909. Ratified February 25, 1913.

The Congress shall have power to lay and collect taxes on incomes, from whatever source derived, without apportionment among the several States, and without regard to any census or enumeration.

Amendment XVII

Passed by Congress May 16, 1912. Ratified May 31, 1913. The Senate of the United States shall be composed of two senators from each State, elected by the people thereof, for six years; and each senator shall have one vote. The electors in each State shall have the qualifications requisite for electors of the most numerous branch of the State legislature.

When vacancies happen in the representation of any State in the Senate, the executive authority of such State shall issue writs of election to fill such vacancies: Provided, That the legislature of any State may empower the executive thereof to make temporary appointments until the people fill the vacancies by election as the legislature may direct.

This amendment shall not be so construed as to affect the election or term of any senator chosen before it becomes valid as part of the Constitution.

Amendment XVIII

Passed by Congress December 17, 1917. Ratified January 29, 1919.

After one year from the ratification of this article, the manufacture, sale, or transportation of intoxicating liquors within, the importation thereof into, or the exportation thereof from the United States and all territory subject to the jurisdiction thereof for beverage purposes is hereby prohibited.

The Congress and the several States shall have concurrent power to enforce this article by appropriate legislation.

This article shall be inoperative unless it shall have been ratified as an amendment to the Constitution by the legislatures of the several States, as provided in the Constitution, within seven years from the date of the submission hereof to the States by Congress.

Amendment XIX

Passed by Congress June 5, 1919. Ratified August 26, 1920. The right of citizens of the United States to vote shall not be denied or abridged by the United States or by any State on account of sex.

The Congress shall have power by appropriate legislation to enforce the provisions of this article.

Amendment XX

Passed by Congress March 3, 1932. Ratified January 23, 1933.

Section 1. The terms of the President and Vice President shall end at noon on the 20th day of January, and the terms of Senators and Representatives at noon on the 3d day of January, of the years in which such terms would have ended if this article had not been ratified; and the terms of their successors shall then begin.

Section 2. The Congress shall assemble at least once in every year, and such meeting shall begin at noon on the 3d day of January, unless they shall by law appoint a different day.

Section 3. If, at the time fixed for the beginning of the term of the President, the President-elect shall have died, the

Vice President-elect shall become President. If a President shall not have been chosen before the time fixed for the beginning of his term, or if the President-elect shall have failed to qualify, then the Vice President-elect shall act as President until a President shall have qualified; and the Congress may by law provide for the case wherein neither a President-elect nor a Vice President-elect shall have qualified, declaring who shall then act as President, or the manner in which one who is to act shall be selected, and such person shall act accordingly until a President or Vice President shall have qualified.

Section 4. The Congress may by law provide for the case of the death of any of the persons from whom the House of Representatives may choose a President whenever the right of choice shall have devolved upon them, and for the case of the death of any of the persons from whom the Senate may choose a Vice President whenever the right of choice shall have devolved upon them.

Section 5. Sections 1 and 2 shall take effect on the 15th day of October following the ratification of this article.

Section 6. This article shall be inoperative unless it shall have been ratified as an amendment to the Constitution by the legislatures of three-fourths of the several States within seven years from the date of its submission.

Amendment XXI

Passed by Congress February 20, 1933. Ratified December 5, 1933.

Section 1. The eighteenth article of amendment to the Constitution of the United States is hereby repealed.

Section 2. The transportation or importation into any State, Territory, or possession of the United States for delivery or use therein of intoxicating liquors in violation of the laws thereof, is hereby prohibited.

Section 3. This article shall be inoperative unless it shall have been ratified as an amendment to the Constitution by conventions in the several States, as provided in the Constitution, within seven years from the date of the submission thereof to the States by the Congress.

Amendment XXII

Passed by Congress March 24, 1947. Ratified February 26, 1951.

Section 1. No person shall be elected to the office of the President more than twice, and no person who has held the office of President, or acted as President, for more than two years of a term to which some other person was elected President shall be elected to the office of the President more than once. But this article shall not apply to any person holding the office of President when this article was proposed by the Congress, and shall not prevent any person who may be holding the office of President, or acting as President, during the term within which this article becomes operative from holding the office of President or acting as President during the remainder of such term.

Section 2. This article shall be inoperative unless it shall have been ratified as an amendment to the Constitution by the legislatures of three-fourths of the several States within seven years from the date of its submission to the States by the Congress.

Amendment XXIII

Passed by Congress June 16, 1960. Ratified April 3, 1961. Section 1. The District constituting the seat of Government of the United States shall appoint in such manner as the Congress may direct:

A number of electors of President and Vice President equal to the whole number of Senators and Representatives in Congress to which the District would be entitled if it were a State, but in no event more than the least populous State; they shall be in addition to those appointed by the States, but they shall be considered, for the purposes of the election of President and Vice President, to be electors appointed by a State; and they shall meet in the District and perform such duties as provided by the twelfth article of amendment.

Section 2. The Congress shall have power to enforce this article by appropriate legislation.

Amendment XXIV

Passed by Congress August 27, 1962. Ratified February 4, 1964.

Section 1. The right of citizens of the United States to vote in any primary or other election for President or Vice President, for electors for President or Vice President, or for Senator or Representative in Congress, shall not be denied or abridged by the United States or any State by reason of failure to pay any poll tax or other tax.

Section 2. The Congress shall have power to enforce this article by appropriate legislation.

Amendment XXV

Passed by Congress July 6, 1965. Ratified February 23, 1967.

Section 1. In case of the removal of the President from office or of his death or resignation, the Vice President shall become President.

Section 2. Whenever there is a vacancy in the office of the Vice President, the President shall nominate a Vice President who shall take office upon confirmation by a majority vote of both Houses of Congress.

Section 3. Whenever the President transmits to the President pro tempore of the Senate and the Speaker of the House of Representatives his written declaration that he is unable to discharge the powers and duties of his office, and until he transmits to them a written declaration to the contrary, such powers and duties shall be discharged by the Vice President as Acting President.

Section 4. Whenever the Vice President and a majority of either the principal officers of the executive departments or of such other body as Congress may by law provide, transmit to the President pro tempore of the Senate and the Speaker of the House of Representatives their written declaration that the President is unable to discharge the powers and duties of his office, the Vice President shall immediately assume the powers and duties of the office as Acting President.

Thereafter, when the President transmits to the President pro tempore of the Senate and the Speaker of the House of Representatives his written declaration that no inability exists, he shall resume the powers and duties of his office unless the Vice President and a majority of either the principal officers of the executive department or of such other body as Congress may by law provide, transmit within four days to the President pro tempore of the Senate and the Speaker of the House of Representatives their written declaration that the President is unable to discharge the powers and duties of his office. Thereupon Congress shall decide the issue, assembling within forty-eight hours for that purpose if not in session. If the Congress, within twenty-one days after receipt of the latter written declaration, or, if Congress is not in session, within twenty-one days after Congress is required to assemble, determines by two-thirds vote of both Houses that the President is unable to discharge the powers and duties of his office, the Vice President shall continue to discharge the same as Acting President; otherwise, the President shall resume the powers and duties of his office.

Amendment XXVI

Passed by Congress March 23, 1971. Ratified July 5, 1971.
Section 1. The right of citizens of the United States, who are eighteen years of age or older, to vote shall not be denied or abridged by the United States or by any State on account of age.

Amendment XXVII

Passed by Congress September 25, 1789. Ratified May 18, 1992.

No law, varying the compensation for the services of the Senators and Representatives, shall take effect, until an election of Representatives shall have intervened.

A P P E N D I X 3
*Uniform Commercial Code**
(Excerpts)

* The Code has been adopted in every state except Louisiana. It has also been adopted for Guam, the Virgin Islands, and the District of Columbia. Louisiana has adopted Articles 1, 3, 4, 7, 8, and 9 of the Code.

In 1972, a group of Amendments to the Code was recommended. These have now been adopted in all states and for Guam. The changes made by the 1972 Amendments to the UCC are confined mainly to Article 9 on secured transactions.

In 1977, Article 8 of the Code, relating to investment securities, was amended. This amended version was adopted by all states except Alabama. The Uniform Law Commissioners have adopted a 1994 Article 8 (Revised), in order to regulate the indirect holding system of securities. The following states have adopted this version: Alabama, Alaska, Arizona, Arkansas, California, Colorado, Idaho, Illinois, Indiana, Iowa, Kansas, Kentucky, Louisiana, Maryland, Massachusetts, Minnesota, Mississippi, Nebraska, New Mexico, Oklahoma, Oregon, Pennsylvania, Texas, Utah, Vermont, Virginia, Washington, West Virginia, and Wyoming.

Article 2A on leases was completed by the Uniform Law Commissioners in 1987 and amended in 1990. The 1987 act has been adopted by Florida and South Dakota. As of November 1994 the 1987 act with 1990 amendments has been adopted by Alabama, Alaska, Arizona, Arkansas, California, Colorado, Delaware, District of Columbia, Georgia, Hawaii, Idaho, Illinois, Indiana, Iowa, Kansas, Kentucky, Maine, Maryland, Massachusetts, Michigan, Minnesota, Mississippi, Missouri, Montana, Nebraska, Nevada, New Hampshire, New Jersey, New Mexico, New York, North Carolina, North Dakota, Ohio, Oklahoma, Oregon, Pennsylvania, Rhode Island, Tennessee, Texas, Utah, Vermont, Virginia, Washington, West Virginia, Wisconsin, and Wyoming.

Article 4A, Funds Transfers, has been adopted in all states, including the District of Columbia, as of February 1996.

The 1988 Article 6, Bulk Sales, Alternative A (repeal) has been adopted in Alabama, Alaska, Arkansas, Colorado, Connecticut, Delaware, Florida, Idaho, Illinois, Iowa, Kansas, Kentucky, Maine, Massachusetts, Minnesota, Mississippi, Montana, Nebraska, Nevada, New Hampshire, New Jersey, New Mexico, North Dakota, Ohio, Oregon, Pennsylvania, South Dakota, Texas, Utah, Vermont, Washington, West Virginia, and Wyoming. Alternative B (revision) has been adopted in Arizona, California, Hawaii, and Oklahoma. Louisiana never adopted Article 6.

The 1990 Article 3, Negotiable Instruments (Revised), and the 1990 Article 4 (Revised), Bank Collections, have been adopted in Alabama, Alaska, Arizona, Arkansas, California, Colorado, Connecticut, Delaware, District of Columbia, Florida, Georgia, Hawaii, Idaho, Illinois, Indiana, Iowa, Kansas, Kentucky, Louisiana, Maine, Michigan, Minnesota, Mississippi, Missouri, Montana, Nebraska, Nevada, New Hampshire, New Jersey, New Mexico, North

Carolina, North Dakota, Ohio, Oklahoma, Oregon, Pennsylvania, South Dakota, Tennessee, Texas, Utah, Vermont, Virginia, Washington, West Virginia, Wisconsin, and Wyoming.

Revised Article 5 (1995) has been adopted by 14 states as of January 1997: Arizona, California, Colorado, Connecticut, Hawaii, Idaho, Illinois, Indiana, Iowa, Kansas, Mississippi, Nebraska, Oklahoma, and West Virginia.

Article 1
GENERAL PROVISIONS

PART 1
Short Title, Construction, Application and Subject Matter of the Act

§ 1—101. Short Title.

This Act shall be known and may be cited as Uniform Commercial Code.

§ 1—102. Purposes; Rules of Construction; Variation by Agreement.

(1) This Act shall be liberally construed and applied to promote its underlying purposes and policies.

(2) Underlying purposes and policies of this Act are
   (a) to simplify, clarify and modernize the law governing commercial transactions;
   (b) to permit the continued expansion of commercial practices through custom, usage and agreement of the parties;
   (c) to make uniform the law among the various jurisdictions.

(3) The effect of provisions of this Act may be varied by agreement, except as otherwise provided in this Act and except that the obligations of good faith, diligence, reasonableness and care prescribed by this Act may not be disclaimed by agreement but the parties may by agreement determine the standards by which the performance of such obligations is to be measured if such standards are not manifestly unreasonable.

(4) The presence in certain provisions of this Act of the words "unless otherwise agreed" or words of similar import does not imply that the effect of other provisions may not be varied by agreement under subsection (3).

(5) In this Act unless the context otherwise requires
   (a) words in the singular number include the plural, and in the plural include the singular;
   (b) words of the masculine gender include the feminine and the neuter, and when the sense so indicates words of the neuter gender may refer to any gender.

§ 1—103. Supplementary General Principles of Law Applicable.

Unless displaced by the particular provisions of this Act, the principles of law and equity, including the law merchant and the law relative to capacity to contract, principal and agent, estoppel, fraud, misrepresentation, duress, coercion, mistake, bankruptcy, or other validating or invalidating cause shall supplement its provisions.

§ 1—106. Remedies to Be Liberally Administered.

(1) The remedies provided by this Act shall be liberally administered to the end that the aggrieved party may be put in as good a position as if the other party had fully performed but neither consequential or special nor penal damages may be had except as specifically provided in this Act or by other rule of law.

(2) Any right or obligation declared by this Act is enforceable by action unless the provision declaring it specifies a different and limited effect.

§ 1—107. Waiver or Renunciation of Claim or Right After Breach.

Any claim or right arising out of an alleged breach can be discharged in whole or in part without consideration by a written waiver or renunciation signed and delivered by the aggrieved party.

PART 2
General Definitions and Principles of Interpretation

§ 1—201. General Definitions.

Subject to additional definitions contained in the subsequent Articles of this Act which are applicable to specific Articles or Parts thereof, and unless the context otherwise requires, in this Act:

(1) "Action" in the sense of a judicial proceeding includes recoupment, counterclaim, set-off, suit in equity and any other proceedings in which rights are determined.

(2) "Aggrieved party" means a party entitled to resort to a remedy.

(3) "Agreement" means the bargain of the parties in fact as found in their language or by implication from other circumstances including course of dealing or usage of trade or course of performance as provided in this Act (Sections 1—205 and 2—208). Whether an agreement has legal consequences is determined by the provisions of this Act, if applicable; otherwise by the law of contracts (Section 1—103). (Compare "Contract.")

(4) "Bank" means any person engaged in the business of banking.

(5) "Bearer" means the person in possession of an instrument, document of title, or certificated security payable to bearer or indorsed in blank.

(6) "Bill of lading" means a document evidencing the receipt of goods for shipment issued by a person engaged in the business of transporting or forwarding goods, and includes an airbill. "Airbill" means a document serving for air transportation as a bill of lading does for marine

or rail transportation, and includes an air consignment note or air waybill.

(7) "Branch" includes a separately incorporated foreign branch of a bank.

(8) "Burden of establishing" a fact means the burden of persuading the triers of fact that the existence of the fact is more probable than its non-existence.

(9) "Buyer in ordinary course of business" means a person who in good faith and without knowledge that the sale to him is in violation of the ownership rights or security interest of a third party in the goods buys in ordinary course from a person in the business of selling goods of that kind but does not include a pawnbroker. All persons who sell minerals or the like (including oil and gas) at wellhead or minehead shall be deemed to be persons in the business of selling goods of that kind. "Buying" may be for cash or by exchange of other property or on secured or unsecured credit and includes receiving goods or documents of title under a pre-existing contract for sale but does not include a transfer in bulk or as security for or in total or partial satisfaction of a money debt.

(10) "Conspicuous": A term or clause is conspicuous when it is so written that a reasonable person against whom it is to operate ought to have noticed it. A printed heading in capitals (as: NON-NEGOTIABLE BILL OF LADING) is conspicuous. Language in the body of a form is "conspicuous" if it is in larger or other contrasting type or color. But in a telegram any stated term is "conspicuous." Whether a term or clause is "conspicuous" or not is for decision by the court.

(11) "Contract" means the total legal obligation which results from the parties' agreement as affected by this Act and any other applicable rules of law. (Compare "Agreement.")

(12) "Creditor" includes a general creditor, a secured creditor, a lien creditor and any representative of creditors, including an assignee for the benefit of creditors, a trustee in bankruptcy, a receiver in equity and an executor or administrator of an insolvent debtor's or assignor's estate.

(13) "Defendant" includes a person in the position of defendant in a cross-action or counterclaim.

(14) "Delivery" with respect to instruments, documents of title, chattel paper, or certificated securities means voluntary transfer of possession.

(15) "Document of title" includes bill of lading, dock warrant, dock receipt, warehouse receipt or order for the delivery of goods, and also any other document which in the regular course of business or financing is treated as adequately evidencing that the person in possession of it is entitled to receive, hold and dispose of the document and the goods it covers. To be a document of title a document must purport to be issued by or addressed to a bailee and purport to cover goods in the bailee's possession which are either identified or are fungible portions of an identified mass.

(16) "Fault" means wrongful act, omission or breach.

(17) "Fungible" with respect to goods or securities means goods or securities of which any unit is, by nature or usage of trade, the equivalent of any other like unit. Goods which are not fungible shall be deemed fungible for the purposes of this Act to the extent that under a particular agreement or document unlike units are treated as equivalents.

(18) "Genuine" means free of forgery or counterfeiting.

(19) "Good faith" means honesty in fact in the conduct or transaction concerned.

(20) "Holder" with respect to a negotiable instrument, means the person in possession if the instrument is payable to bearer or, in the cases of an instrument payable to an identified person, if the identified person is in possession. "Holder" with respect to a document of title means the person in possession if the goods are deliverable to bearer or to the order of the person in possession.

(21) To "honor" is to pay or to accept and pay, or where a credit so engages to purchase or discount a draft complying with the terms of the credit.

(22) "Insolvency proceedings" includes any assignment for the benefit of creditors or other proceedings intended to liquidate or rehabilitate the estate of the person involved.

(23) A person is "insolvent" who either has ceased to pay his debts in the ordinary course of business or cannot pay his debts as they become due or is insolvent within the meaning of the federal bankruptcy law.

(24) "Money" means a medium of exchange authorized or adopted by a domestic or foreign government and includes a monetary unit of account established by an intergovernmental organization or by agreement between two or more nations.

(25) A person has "notice" of a fact when
(a) he has actual knowledge of it; or
(b) he has received a notice or notification of it; or
(c) from all the facts and circumstances known to him at the time in question he has reason to know that it exists.

A person "knows" or has "knowledge" of a fact when he has actual knowledge of it. "Discover" or "learn" or a word or phrase of similar import refers to knowledge rather than to reason to know. The time and circumstances under which a notice or notification may cease to be effective are not determined by this Act.

(26) A person "notifies" or "gives" a notice or notification to another by taking such steps as may be reasonably required to inform the other in ordinary course whether or not such other actually comes to know of it. A person "receives" a notice or notification when
(a) it comes to his attention; or
(b) it is duly delivered at the place of business through which the contract was made or at any other place held out by him as the place for receipt of such communications.

(27) Notice, knowledge or a notice or notification received by an organization is effective for a particular transaction from the time when it is brought to the attention of the

individual conducting that transaction, and in any event from the time when it would have been brought to his attention if the organization had exercised due diligence. An organization exercises due diligence if it maintains reasonable routines for communicating significant information to the person conducting the transaction and there is reasonable compliance with the routines. Due diligence does not require an individual acting for the organization to communicate information unless such communication is part of his regular duties or unless he has reason to know of the transaction and that the transaction would be materially affected by the information.

(28) "Organization" includes a corporation, government or governmental subdivision or agency, business trust, estate, trust, partnership or association, two or more persons having a joint or common interest, or any other legal or commercial entity.

(29) "Party," as distinct from "third party," means a person who has engaged in a transaction or made an agreement within this Act.

(30) "Person" includes an individual or an organization (See Section 1—102).

(31) "Presumption" or "presumed" means that the trier of fact must find the existence of the fact presumed unless and until evidence is introduced which would support a finding of its non-existence.

(32) "Purchase" includes taking by sale, discount, negotiation, mortgage, pledge, lien, issue or re-issue, gift or any other voluntary transaction creating an interest in property.

(33) "Purchaser" means a person who takes by purchase.

(34) "Remedy" means any remedial right to which an aggrieved party is entitled with or without resort to a tribunal.

(35) "Representative" includes an agent, an officer of a corporation or association, and a trustee, executor or administrator of an estate, or any other person empowered to act for another.

(36) "Rights" includes remedies.

(37) "Security interest" means an interest in personal property or fixtures which secures payment or performance of an obligation. The retention or reservation of title by a seller of goods notwithstanding shipment or delivery to the buyer (Section 2—401) is limited in effect to a reservation of a "security interest." The term also includes any interest of a buyer of accounts or chattel paper which is subject to Article 9. The special property interest of a buyer of goods on identification of those goods to a contract for sale under Section 2—401 is not a "security interest," but a buyer may also acquire a "security interest" by complying with Article 9. Unless a consignment is intended as security, reservation of title thereunder is not a "security interest," but a consignment is in any event subject to the provisions on consignment sales (Section 2—326).

Whether a transaction creates a lease or security interest is determined by the facts of each case; however, a transaction creates a security interest if the consideration the lessee is to pay the lessor for the right to possession and use of the goods is an obligation for the term of the lease not subject to termination by the lessee, and

(a) the original term of the lease is equal to or greater than the remaining economic life of the goods,

(b) the lessee is bound to renew the lease for the remaining economic life of the goods or is bound to become the owner of the goods,

(c) the lessee has an option to renew the lease for the remaining economic life of the goods for no additional consideration or nominal additional consideration upon compliance with the lease agreement, or

(d) the lessee has an option to become the owner of the goods for no additional consideration or nominal additional consideration upon compliance with the lease agreement.

A transaction does not create a security interest merely because it provides that

(a) the present value of the consideration the lessee is obligated to pay the lessor for the right to possession and use of the goods is substantially equal to or is greater than the fair market value of the goods at the time the lease is entered into,

(b) the lessee assumes risk of loss of the goods, or agrees to pay taxes, insurance, filing, recording, or registration fees, or service or maintenance costs with respect to the goods,

(c) the lessee has an option to renew the lease or to become the owner of the goods,

(d) the lessee has an option to renew the lease for a fixed rent that is equal to or greater than the reasonably predictable fair market rent for the use of the goods for the term of the renewal at the time the option is to be performed, or

(e) the lessee has an option to become the owner of the goods for a fixed price that is equal to or greater than the reasonably predictable fair market value of the goods at the time the option is to be performed.

For purposes of this subsection (37):

(x) Additional consideration is not nominal if (i) when the option to renew the lease is granted to the lessee the rent is stated to be the fair market rent for the use of the goods for the term of the renewal determined at the time the option is to be performed, or (ii) when the option to become the owner of the goods is granted to the lessee the price is stated to be the fair market value of the goods determined at the time the option is to be performed. Additional consideration is nominal if it is less than the lessee's reasonably predictable cost of performing under the lease agreement if the option is not exercised;

(y) "Reasonably predictable" and "remaining economic life of the goods" are to be determined with reference to the facts and circumstances at the time the transaction is entered into; and

(z) "Present value" means the amount as of a date certain of one or more sums payable in the future, discounted to the date certain. The discount is determined by the interest rate specified by the parties if the rate is not manifestly unreasonable at the time the transaction is entered into; otherwise, the discount is determined by a commercially reasonable rate that takes into account the facts and circumstances of each case at the time the transaction was entered into.

(38) "Send" in connection with any writing or notice means to deposit in the mail or deliver for transmission by any other usual means of communication with postage or cost of transmission provided for and properly addressed and in the case of an instrument to an address specified thereon or otherwise agreed, or if there be none to any address reasonable under the circumstances. The receipt of any writing or notice within the time at which it would have arrived if properly sent has the effect of a proper sending.

(39) "Signed" includes any symbol executed or adopted by a party with present intention to authenticate a writing.

(40) "Surety" includes guarantor.

(41) "Telegram" includes a message transmitted by radio, teletype, cable, any mechanical method of transmission, or the like.

(42) "Term" means that portion of an agreement which relates to a particular matter.

(43) "Unauthorized" signature means one made without actual, implied or apparent authority and includes a forgery.

(44) "Value." Except as otherwise provided with respect to negotiable instruments and bank collections (Sections 3—303, 4—208 and 4—209) a person gives "value" for rights if he acquires them

(a) in return for a binding commitment to extend credit or for the extension of immediately available credit whether or not drawn upon and whether or not a chargeback is provided for in the event of difficulties in collection; or

(b) as security for or in total or partial satisfaction of a preexisting claim; or

(c) by accepting delivery pursuant to a preexisting contract for purchase; or

(d) generally, in return for any consideration sufficient to support a simple contract.

(45) "Warehouse receipt" means a receipt issued by a person engaged in the business of storing goods for hire.

(46) "Written" or "writing" includes printing, typewriting or any other intentional reduction to tangible form.

§ 1—203. Obligation of Good Faith.

Every contract or duty within this Act imposes an obligation of good faith in its performance or enforcement.

§ 1—205. Course of Dealing and Usage of Trade.

(1) A course of dealing is a sequence of previous conduct between the parties to a particular transaction which is fairly to be regarded as establishing a common basis of understanding for interpreting their expressions and other conduct.

(2) A usage of trade is any practice or method of dealing having such regularity of observance in a place, vocation or trade as to justify an expectation that it will be observed with respect to the transaction in question. The existence and scope of such a usage are to be proved as facts. If it is established that such a usage is embodied in a written trade code or similar writing the interpretation of the writing is for the court.

(3) A course of dealing between parties and any usage of trade in the vocation or trade in which they are engaged or of which they are or should be aware give particular meaning to and supplement or qualify terms of an agreement.

(4) The express terms of an agreement and an applicable course of dealing or usage of trade shall be construed wherever reasonable as consistent with each other; but when such construction is unreasonable express terms control both course of dealing and usage of trade and course of dealing controls usage trade.

(5) An applicable usage of trade in the place where any part of performance is to occur shall be used in interpreting the agreement as to that part of the performance.

(6) Evidence of a relevant usage of trade offered by one party is not admissible unless and until he has given the other party such notice as the court finds sufficient to prevent unfair surprise to the latter.

Article 2
SALES

PART 1
Short Title, General Construction and Subject Matter

§ 2—103. Definitions and Index of Definitions.

(1) In this Article unless the context otherwise requires

(a) "Buyer" means a person who buys or contracts to buy goods.

(b) "Good faith" in the case of a merchant means honesty in fact and the observance of reasonable commercial standards of fair dealing in the trade.

(c) "Receipt" of goods means taking physical possession of them.

(d) "Seller" means a person who sells or contracts to sell goods.

(2) Other definitions applying to this Article or to specified Parts thereof, and the sections in which they appear are:

"Acceptance." Section 2—606.
"Banker's credit." Section 2—325.
"Between merchants." Section 2—104.

"Cancellation." Section 2—106(4).
"Commercial unit." Section 2—105.
"Confirmed credit." Section 2—325.
"Conforming to contract." Section 2—106.
"Contract for sale." Section 2—106.
"Cover." Section 2—712.
"Entrusting." Section 2—403.
"Financing agency." Section 2—104.
"Future goods." Section 2—105.
"Goods." Section 2—105.
"Identification." Section 2—501.
"Installment contract." Section 2—612.
"Letter of Credit." Section 2—325.
"Lot." Section 2—105.
"Merchant." Section 2—104.
"Overseas." Section 2—323.
"Person in position of seller." Section 2—707.
"Present sale." Section 2—106.
"Sale." Section 2—106.
"Sale on approval." Section 2—326.
"Sale or return." Section 2—326.
"Termination." Section 2—106.

(3) The following definitions in other Articles apply to this Article:

"Check." Section 3—104.
"Consignee." Section 7—102.
"Consignor." Section 7—102.
"Consumer goods." Section 9—109.
"Dishonor." Section 3—507.
"Draft." Section 3—104.

(4) In addition Article 1 contains general definitions and principles of construction and interpretation applicable throughout this Article.

PART 2
Form, Formation and Readjustment of Contract

§ 2—201. Formal Requirements; Statute of Frauds.

(1) Except as otherwise provided in this section a contract for the sale of goods for the price of $500 or more is not enforceable by way of action or defense unless there is some writing sufficient to indicate that a contract for sale has been made between the parties and signed by the party against whom enforcement is sought or by his authorized agent or broker. A writing is not insufficient because it omits or incorrectly states a term agreed upon but the contract is not enforceable under this paragraph beyond the quantity of goods shown in such writing.

(2) Between merchants if within a reasonable time a writing in confirmation of the contract and sufficient against the sender is received and the party receiving it has reason to know its contents, its satisfies the requirements of subsection (1) against such party unless written notice of objection to its contents is given within ten days after it is received.

(3) A contract which does not satisfy the requirements of subsection (1) but which is valid in other respects is enforceable

(a) if the goods are to be specially manufactured for the buyer and are not suitable for sale to others in the ordinary course of the seller's business and the seller, before notice of repudiation is received and under circumstances which reasonably indicate that the goods are for the buyer, has made either a substantial beginning of their manufacture or commitments for their procurement; or

(b) if the party against whom enforcement is sought admits in his pleading, testimony or otherwise in court that a contract for sale was made, but the contract is not enforceable under this provision beyond the quantity of goods admitted; or

(c) with respect to goods for which payment has been made and accepted or which have been received and accepted (Sec. 2—606).

§ 2—202. Final Written Expression: Parol or Extrinsic Evidence.

Terms with respect to which the confirmatory memoranda of the parties agree or which are otherwise set forth in a writing intended by the parties as a final expression of their agreement with respect to such terms as are included therein may not be contradicted by evidence of any prior agreement or of a contemporaneous oral agreement but may be explained or supplemented

(a) by course of dealing or usage of trade (Section 1—205) or by course of performance (Section 2—208); and

(b) by evidence of consistent additional terms unless the court finds the writing to have been intended also as a complete and exclusive statement of the terms of the agreement.

§ 2—204. Formation in General.

(1) A contract for sale of goods may be made in any manner sufficient to show agreement, including conduct by both parties which recognizes the existence of such a contract.

(2) An agreement sufficient to constitute a contract for sale may be found even though the moment of its making is undetermined.

(3) Even though one or more terms are left open a contract for sale does not fail for indefiniteness if the parties have intended to make a contract and there is a reasonably certain basis for giving an appropriate remedy.

§ 2—205. Firm Offers.

An offer by a merchant to buy or sell goods in a signed writing which by its terms gives assurance that it will be held open is not revocable, for lack of consideration, during the time stated or if no time is stated for a reasonable time, but in no event may such period of irrevocability exceed three months; but any such term of assurance on a form supplied by the offeree must be separately signed by the offeror.

§ 2—206. Offer and Acceptance in Formation of Contract.

(1) Unless other unambiguously indicated by the language or circumstances

(a) an offer to make a contract shall be construed as inviting acceptance in any manner and by any medium reasonable in the circumstances;

(b) an order or other offer to buy goods for prompt or current shipment shall be construed as inviting acceptance either by a prompt promise to ship or by the prompt or current shipment of conforming or non-conforming goods, but such a shipment of non-conforming goods does not constitute an acceptance if the seller seasonably notifies the buyer that the shipment is offered only as an accommodation to the buyer.

(2) Where the beginning of a requested performance is a reasonable mode of acceptance an offeror who is not notified of acceptance within a reasonable time may treat the offer as having lapsed before acceptance.

§ 2—207. Additional Terms in Acceptance or Confirmation.

(1) A definite and seasonable expression of acceptance or a written confirmation which is sent within a reasonable time operates as an acceptance even though it states terms additional to or different from those offered or agreed upon, unless acceptance is expressly made conditional on assent to the additional or different terms.

(2) The additional terms are to be construed as proposals for addition to the contract. Between merchants such terms become part of the contract unless:

(a) the offer expressly limits acceptance to the terms of the offer;

(b) they materially alter it; or

(c) notification of objection to them has already been given or is given within a reasonable time after notice of them is received.

(3) Conduct by both parties which recognizes the existence of a contract is sufficient to establish a contract for sale although the writings of the parties do not otherwise establish a contract. In such case the terms of the particular contract consist of those terms on which the writings of the parties agree, together with any supplementary terms incorporated under any other provisions of this Act.

§ 2—208. Course of Performance or Practical Construction.

(1) Where the contract for sale involves repeated occasions for performance by either party with knowledge of the nature of the performance and opportunity for objection to it by the other, any course of performance accepted or acquiesced in without objection shall be relevant to determine the meaning of the agreement.

(2) The express terms of the agreement and any such course of performance, as well as any course of dealing and usage of trade, shall be construed whenever reasonable as consistent with each other; but when such construction is unreasonable, express terms shall control course of performance and course of performance shall control both course of dealing and usage of trade (Section 1—205).

(3) Subject to the provisions of the next section on modification and waiver, such course of performance shall be relevant to show a waiver or modification of any term inconsistent with such course of performance.

§ 2—209. Modification, Rescission and Waiver.

(1) An agreement modifying a contract within this Article needs no consideration to be binding.

(2) A signed agreement which excludes modification or rescission except by a signed writing cannot be otherwise modified or rescinded, but except as between merchants such a requirement on a form supplied by the merchant must be separately signed by the other party.

(3) The requirements of the statute of frauds section of this Article (Section 2—201) must be satisfied if the contract as modified is within its provisions.

(4) Although an attempt at modification or rescission does not satisfy the requirements of subsection (2) or (3) it can operate as a waiver.

(5) A party who has made a waiver affecting an executory portion of the contract may retract the waiver by reasonable notification received by the other party that strict performance will be required of any term waived, unless the retraction would be unjust in view of a material change of position in reliance on the waiver.

§ 2—210. Delegation of Performance; Assignment of Rights.

(1) A party may perform his duty through a delegate unless otherwise agreed or unless the other party has a substantial interest in having his original promisor perform or control the acts required by the contract. No delegation of performance relieves the party delegating of any duty to perform or any liability for breach.

(2) Unless otherwise agreed all rights of either seller or buyer can be assigned except where the assignment would materially change the duty of the other party, or increase materially the burden or risk imposed on him by his contract, or impair materially his chance of obtaining return performance. A right to damages for breach of the whole contract or a right arising out of the assignor's due performance of his entire obligation can be assigned despite agreement otherwise.

(3) Unless the circumstances indicate the contrary a prohibition of assignment of "the contract" is to be construed as barring only the delegation to the assignee of the assignor's performance.

(4) An assignment of "the contract" or of "all my rights under the contract" or an assignment in similar general terms is an assignment of rights and unless the language

or the circumstances (as in an assignment for security) indicate the contrary, it is a delegation of performance of the duties of the assignor and its acceptance by the assignee constitutes a promise by him to perform those duties. This promise is enforceable by either the assignor or the other party to the original contract.

(5) The other party may treat any assignment which delegates performance as creating reasonable grounds for insecurity and may without prejudice to his rights against the assignor demand assurances from the assignee (Section 2—609).

PART 3
General Obligation and Construction of Contract

§ 2—302. Unconscionable Contract or Clause.

(1) If the court as a matter of law finds the contract or any clause of the contract to have been unconscionable at the time it was made the court may refuse to enforce the contract, or it may enforce the remainder of the contract without the unconscionable clause, or it may so limit the application of any unconscionable clause as to avoid any unconscionable result.

(2) When it is claimed or appears to the court that the contract or any clause thereof may be unconscionable the parties shall be afforded a reasonable opportunity to present evidence as to its commercial setting, purpose and effect to aid the court in making the determination.

§ 2—306. Output, Requirements and Exclusive Dealings.

(1) A term which measures the quantity by the output of the seller or the requirements of the buyer means such actual output or requirements as may occur in good faith, except that no quantity unreasonably disproportionate to any stated estimate or in the absence of a stated estimate to any normal or otherwise comparable prior output or requirements may be tendered or demanded.

(2) A lawful agreement by either the seller or the buyer for exclusive dealing in the kind of goods concerned imposes unless otherwise agreed an obligation by the seller to use best efforts to supply the goods and by the buyer to use best efforts to promote their sale.

§ 2—312. Warranty of Title and Against Infringement; Buyer's Obligation Against Infringement.

(1) Subject to subsection (2) there is in a contract for sale a warranty by the seller that
  (a) the title conveyed shall be good, and its transfer rightful; and
  (b) the goods shall be delivered free from any security interest or other lien or encumbrance of which the buyer at the time of contracting has no knowledge.
(2) A warranty under subsection (1) will be excluded or modified only by specific language or by circumstances which give the buyer reason to know that the person selling does not claim title in himself or that he is purporting to sell only such right or title as he or a third person may have.

(3) Unless otherwise agreed a seller who is a merchant regularly dealing in goods of the kind warrants that the goods shall be delivered free of the rightful claim of any third person by way of infringement or the like but a buyer who furnishes specifications to the seller must hold the seller harmless against any such claim which arises out of compliance with the specifications.

§ 2—313. Express Warranties by Affirmation, Promise, Description, Sample.

(1) Express warranties by the seller are created as follows:
  (a) Any affirmation of fact or promise made by the seller to the buyer which relates to the goods and becomes part of the basis of the bargain creates an express warranty that the goods shall conform to the affirmation or promise.
  (b) Any description of the goods which is made part of the basis of the bargain creates an express warranty that the goods shall conform to the description.
  (c) Any sample or model which is made part of the basis of the bargain creates an express warranty that the whole of the goods shall conform to the sample or model.
(2) It is not necessary to the creation of an express warranty that the seller use formal words such as "warrant" or "guarantee" or that he have a specific intention to make a warranty, but an affirmation merely of the value of the goods or a statement purporting to be merely the seller's opinion or commendation of the goods does not create a warranty.

§ 2—314. Implied Warranty: Merchantability; Usage of Trade.

(1) Unless excluded or modified (Section 2—316), a warranty that the goods shall be merchantable is implied in a contract for their sale if the seller is a merchant with respect to goods of that kind. Under this section the serving for value of food or drink to be consumed either on the premises or elsewhere is a sale.
(2) Goods to be merchantable must be at least such as
  (a) pass without objection in the trade under the contract description; and
  (b) in the case of fungible goods, are of fair average quality within the description; and
  (c) are fit for the ordinary purposes for which such goods are used; and
  (d) run, within the variations permitted by the agreement, of even kind, quality and quantity within each unit and among all units involved; and
  (e) are adequately contained, packaged, and labeled as the agreement may require; and
  (f) conform to the promises or affirmations of fact made on the container or label if any.

(3) Unless excluded or modified (Section 2—316) other implied warranties may arise from course of dealing or usage of trade.

§ 2—315. Implied Warranty: Fitness for Particular Purpose.

Where the seller at the time of contracting has reason to know any particular purpose for which the goods are required and that the buyer is relying on the seller's skill or judgment to select or furnish suitable goods, there is unless excluded or modified under the next section an implied warranty that the goods shall be fit for such purpose.

§ 2—316. Exclusion or Modification of Warranties.

(1) Words or conduct relevant to the creation of an express warranty and words or conduct tending to negate or limit warranty shall be construed wherever reasonable as consistent with each other; but subject to the provisions of this Article on parol or extrinsic evidence (Section 2—202) negation or limitation is inoperative to the extent that such construction is unreasonable.

(2) Subject to subsection (3), to exclude or modify the implied warranty of merchantability or any part of it the language must mention merchantability and in case of a writing must be conspicuous, and to exclude or modify any implied warranty of fitness the exclusion must be by a writing and conspicuous. Language to exclude all implied warranties of fitness is sufficient if it states, for example, that "There are no warranties which extend beyond the description on the face hereof."

(3) Notwithstanding subsection (2)

   (a) unless the circumstances indicate otherwise, all implied warranties are excluded by expressions like "as is," "with all faults" or other language which in common understanding calls the buyer's attention to the exclusion of warranties and makes plain that there is no implied warranty; and

   (b) when the buyer before entering into the contract has examined the goods or the sample or model as fully as he desired or has refused to examine the goods there is no implied warranty with regard to defects which an examination ought in the circumstances to have revealed to him; and

   (c) an implied warranty can also be excluded or modified by course of dealing or course of performance or usage of trade.

(4) Remedies for breach of warranty can be limited in accordance with the provisions of this Article on liquidation or limitation of damages and on contractual modification of remedy (Sections 2—718 and 2—719).

§ 2—317. Cumulation and Conflict of Warranties Express or Implied.

Warranties whether express or implied shall be construed as consistent with each other and as cumulative, but if such construction is unreasonable the intention of the parties shall determine which warranty is dominant. In ascertaining that intention the following rules apply:

   (a) Exact or technical specifications displace an inconsistent sample or model or general language of description.

   (b) A sample from an existing bulk displaces inconsistent general language of description.

   (c) Express warranties displace inconsistent implied warranties other than an implied warranty of fitness for a particular purpose.

§ 2—318. Third Party Beneficiaries of Warranties Express or Implied.

Alternative A

A seller's warranty whether express or implied extends to any natural person who is in the family or household of his buyer or who is a guest in his home if it is reasonable to expect that such person may use, consume or be affected by the goods and who is injured in person by breach of the warranty. A seller may not exclude or limit the operation of this section.

Alternative B

A seller's warranty whether express or implied extends to any natural person who may reasonably be expected to use, consume or be affected by the goods and who is injured in person by breach of the warranty. A seller may not exclude or limit the operation of this section.

Alternative C

A seller's warranty whether express or implied extends to any person who may reasonably be expected to use, consume or be affected by the goods and who is injured by breach of the warranty. A seller may not exclude or limit the operation of this section with respect to injury to the person of an individual to whom the warranty extends. As amended 1966.

§ 2—319. F.O.B. and F.A.S. Terms.

(1) Unless otherwise agreed the term F.O.B. (which means "free on board") at a named place, even though used only in connection with the stated price, is a delivery term under which

   (a) when the term is F.O.B. the place of shipment, the seller must at that place ship the goods in the manner provided in this Article (Section 2—504) and bear the expense and risk of putting them into the possession of the carrier; or

   (b) when the term is F.O.B. the place of destination, the seller must at his own expense and risk transport the goods to that place and there tender delivery of them in the manner provided in this Article (Section 2—503);

   (c) when under either (a) or (b) the term is also F.O.B. vessel, car or other vehicle, the seller must in addition at his own expense and risk load the goods on board. If the term is F.O.B. vessel the buyer must name the vessel and in an appropriate case the seller must comply with the provisions of this Article on the form of bill of lading (Section 2—323).

(2) Unless otherwise agreed the term F.A.S. vessel (which means "free alongside") at a named port, even though used only in connection with the stated price, is a delivery term under which the seller must

(a) at his own expense and risk deliver the goods alongside the vessel in the manner usual in that port or on a dock designated and provided by the buyer; and

(b) obtain and tender a receipt for the goods in exchange for which the carrier is under a duty to issue a bill of lading.

(3) Unless otherwise agreed in any case falling within subsection (1)(a) or (c) or subsection (2) the buyer must seasonably give any needed instructions for making delivery, including when the term is F.A.S. or F.O.B. the loading berth of the vessel and in an appropriate case its name and sailing date. The seller may treat the failure of needed instructions as a failure of cooperation under this Article (Section 2—311). He may also at his option move the goods in any reasonable manner preparatory to delivery or shipment.

(4) Under the term F.O.B. vessel or F.A.S. unless otherwise agreed the buyer must make payment against tender of the required documents and the seller may not tender nor the buyer demand delivery of the goods in substitution for the documents.

§ 2—320. C.I.F. and C. & F. Terms.

(1) The term C.I.F. means that the price includes in a lump sum the cost of the goods and the insurance and freight to the named destination. The term C. & F. or C.F. means that the price so includes cost and freight to the named destination.

(2) Unless otherwise agreed and even though used only in connection with the stated price and destination, the term C.I.F. destination or its equivalent requires the seller at his own expense and risk to

(a) put the goods into the possession of a carrier at the port for shipment and obtain a negotiable bill or bills of lading covering the entire transportation to the named destination; and

(b) load the goods and obtain a receipt from the carrier (which may be contained in the bill of lading) showing that the freight has been paid or provided for; and

(c) obtain a policy or certificate of insurance, including any war risk insurance, of a kind and on terms then current at the port of shipment in the usual amount, in the currency of the contract, shown to cover the same goods covered by the bill of lading and providing for payment of loss to the order of the buyer or for the account of whom it may concern; but the seller may add to the price the amount of the premium for any such war risk insurance; and

(d) prepare an invoice of the goods and procure any other documents required to effect shipment or to com-

ply with the contract; and

(e) forward and tender with commercial promptness all the documents in due form and with any indorsement necessary to perfect the buyer's rights.

(3) Unless otherwise agreed the term C. & F. or its equivalent has the same effect and imposes upon the seller the same obligations and risks as a C.I.F. term except the obligation as to insurance.

(4) Under the term C.I.F. or C. & F. unless otherwise agreed the buyer must make payment against tender of the required documents and the seller may not tender nor the buyer demand delivery of the goods in substitution for the documents.

§ 2—321. C.I.F. or C. & F.: "Net Landed Weights"; "Payment on Arrival"; Warranty of Condition on Arrival.

Under a contract containing a term C.I.F. or C. & F.

(1) Where the price is based on or is to be adjusted according to "net landed weights," "delivered weights," "out turn" quantity or quality or the like, unless otherwise agreed the seller must reasonably estimate the price. The payment due on tender of the documents called for by the contract is the amount so estimated, but after final adjustment of the price a settlement must be made with commercial promptness.

(2) An agreement described in subsection (1) or any warranty of quality or condition of the goods on arrival places upon the seller the risk of ordinary deterioration, shrinkage and the like in transportation but has no effect on the place or time of identification to the contract for sale or delivery or on the passing of the risk of loss.

(3) Unless otherwise agreed where the contract provides for payment on or after arrival of the goods the seller must before payment allow such preliminary inspection as is feasible; but if the goods are lost delivery of the documents and payment are due when the goods should have arrived.

§ 2—323. Form of Bill of Lading Required in Overseas Shipment; "Overseas."

(1) Where the contract contemplates overseas shipment and contains a term C.I.F. or C. & F. or F.O.B. vessel, the seller unless otherwise agreed must obtain a negotiable bill of lading stating that the goods have been loaded on board or, in the case of a term C.I.F. or C. & F., received for shipment.

(2) Where in a case within subsection (1) a bill of lading has been issued in a set of parts, unless otherwise agreed if the documents are not to be sent from abroad the buyer may demand tender of the full set; otherwise only one part of the bill of lading need be tendered. Even if the agreement expressly requires a full set

(a) due tender of a single part is acceptable within the provisions of this Article on cure of improper delivery (subsection (1) of Section 2—508); and

(b) even though the full set is demanded, if the documents are sent from abroad the person tendering an incomplete set may nevertheless require payment upon furnishing an indemnity which the buyer in good faith deems adequate.

(3) A shipment by water or by air or a contract contemplating such shipment is "overseas" insofar as by usage of trade or agreement it is subject to the commercial, financing or shipping practices characteristic of international deep water commerce.

§ 2—326. Sale on Approval and Sale or Return; Consignment Sales and Rights of Creditors.

(1) Unless otherwise agreed, if delivered goods may be returned by the buyer even though they conform to the contract, the transaction is

(a) a "sale on approval" if the goods are delivered primarily for use, and

(b) a "sale or return" if the goods are delivered primarily for resale.

(2) Except as provided in subsection (3), goods held on approval are not subject to the claims of the buyer's creditors until acceptance; goods held on sale or return are subject to such claims while in the buyer's possession.

(3) Where goods are delivered to a person for sale and such person maintains a place of business at which he deals in goods of the kind involved, under a name other than the name of the person making delivery, then with respect to claims of creditors of the person conducting the business the goods are deemed to be on sale or return. The provisions of this subsection are applicable even though an agreement purports to reserve title to the person making delivery until payment or resale or uses such words as "on consignment" or "on memorandum." However, this subsection is not applicable if the person making delivery

(a) complies with an applicable law providing for a consignor's interest or the like to be evidenced by a sign, or

(b) establishes that the person conducting the business is generally known by his creditors to be substantially engaged in selling the goods of others, or

(c) complies with the filing provisions of the Article on Secured Transactions (Article 9).

(4) Any "or return" term of a contract for sale is to be treated as a separate contract for sale within the statute of frauds section of this Article (Section 2—201) and as contradicting the sale aspect of the contract within the provisions of this Article on parol or extrinsic evidence (Section 2—202).

§ 2—327. Special Incidents of Sale on Approval and Sale or Return.

(1) Under a sale on approval unless otherwise agreed

(a) although the goods are identified to the contract the risk of loss and the title do not pass to the buyer until acceptance; and

(b) use of the goods consistent with the purpose of trial is not acceptance but failure seasonably to notify the seller of election to return the goods is acceptance, and if the goods conform to the contract acceptance of any part is acceptance of the whole; and

(c) after due notification of election to return, the return is at the seller's risk and expense but a merchant buyer must follow any reasonable instructions.

(2) Under a sale or return unless otherwise agreed

(a) the option to return extends to the whole or any commercial unit of the goods while in substantially their original condition, but must be exercised seasonably; and

(b) the return is at the buyer's risk and expense.

PART 4
Title, Creditors and Good Faith Purchasers

§ 2—401. Passing of Title; Reservation for Security; Limited Application of This Section.

Each provision of this Article with regard to the rights, obligations and remedies of the seller, the buyer, purchasers or other third parties applies irrespective of title to the goods except where the provision refers to such title. Insofar as situations are not covered by the other provisions of this Article and matters concerning title became material the following rules apply:

(1) Title to goods cannot pass under a contract for sale prior to their identification to the contract (Section 2—501), and unless otherwise explicitly agreed the buyer acquires by their identification a special property as limited by this Act. Any retention or reservation by the seller of the title (property) in goods shipped or delivered to the buyer is limited in effect to a reservation of a security interest. Subject to these provisions and to the provisions of the Article on Secured Transactions (Article 9), title to goods passes from the seller to the buyer in any manner and on any conditions explicitly agreed on by the parties.

(2) Unless otherwise explicitly agreed title passes to the buyer at the time and place at which the seller completes his performance with reference to the physical delivery of the goods, despite any reservation of a security interest and even though a document of title is to be delivered at a different time or place; and in particular and despite any reservation of a security interest by the bill of lading

(a) if the contract requires or authorizes the seller to send the goods to the buyer but does not require him to deliver them at destination, title passes to the buyer at the time and place of shipment; but

(b) if the contract requires delivery at destination, title passes on tender there.

(3) Unless otherwise explicitly agreed where delivery is to be made without moving the goods,

(a) if the seller is to deliver a document of title, title

passes at the time when and the place where he delivers such documents; or

(b) if the goods are at the time of contracting already identified and no documents are to be delivered, title passes at the time and place of contracting.

(4) A rejection or other refusal by the buyer to receive or retain the goods, whether or not justified, or a justified revocation of acceptance revests title to the goods in the seller. Such revesting occurs by operation of law and is not a "sale."

§ 2—403. Power to Transfer; Good Faith Purchase of Goods; "Entrusting."

(1) A purchaser of goods acquires all title which his transferor had or had power to transfer except that a purchaser of a limited interest acquires rights only to the extent of the interest purchased. A person with voidable title has power to transfer a good title to a good faith purchaser for value. When goods have been delivered under a transaction of purchase the purchaser has such power even though

(a) the transferor was deceived as to the identity of the purchaser, or

(b) the delivery was in exchange for a check which is later dishonored, or

(c) it was agreed that the transaction was to be a "cash sale," or

(d) the delivery was procured through fraud punishable as larcenous under the criminal law.

(2) Any entrusting of possession of goods to a merchant who deals in goods of that kind gives him power to transfer all rights of the entruster to a buyer in ordinary course of business.

(3) "Entrusting" includes any delivery and any acquiescence in retention of possession regardless of any condition expressed between the parties to the delivery or acquiescence and regardless of whether the procurement of the entrusting or the possessor's disposition of the goods have been such as to be larcenous under the criminal law.

(4) The rights of other purchasers of goods and of lien creditors are governed by the Articles on Secured Transactions (Article 9), Bulk Transfers (Article 6) and Documents of Title (Article 7).

PART 5
Performance

§ 2—501. Insurable Interest in Goods; Manner of Identification of Goods.

(1) The buyer obtains a special property and an insurable interest in goods by identification of existing goods as goods to which the contract refers even though the goods so identified are non-conforming and he has an option to return or reject them. Such identification can be made at any time and in any manner explicitly agreed to by the parties. In the absence of explicit agreement identification occurs

(a) when the contract is made if it is for the sale of goods already existing and identified;

(b) if the contract is for the sale of future goods other than those described in paragraph (c), when goods are shipped, marked or otherwise designated by the seller as goods to which the contract refers;

(c) when the crops are planted or otherwise become growing crops or the young are conceived if the contract is for the sale of unborn young to be born within twelve months after contracting or for the sale of crops to be harvested within twelve months or the next normal harvest season after contracting whichever is longer.

(2) The seller retains an insurable interest in goods so long as title to or any security interest in the goods remains in him and where the identification is by the seller alone he may until default or insolvency or notification to the buyer that the identification is final substitute other goods for those identified.

(3) Nothing in this section impairs any insurable interest recognized under any other statute or rule of law.

§ 2—509. Risk of Loss in the Absence of Breach.

(1) Where the contract requires or authorizes the seller to ship the goods by carrier

(a) if it does not require him to deliver them at a particular destination, the risk of loss passes to the buyer when the goods are duly delivered to the carrier even though the shipment is under reservation (Section 2—505); but

(b) if it does require him to deliver them at a particular destination and the goods are there duly tendered while in the possession of the carrier, the risk of loss passes to the buyer when the goods are there duly so tendered as to enable the buyer to take delivery.

(2) Where the goods are held by a bailee to be delivered without being moved, the risk of loss passes to the buyer

(a) on his receipt of a negotiable document of title covering the goods; or

(b) on acknowledgment by the bailee of the buyer's right to possession of the goods; or

(c) after his receipt of a non-negotiable document of title or other written direction to deliver, as provided in subsection (4)(b) of Section 2—503.

(3) In any case not within subsection (1) or (2), the risk of loss passes to the buyer on his receipt of the goods if the seller is a merchant; otherwise the risk passes to the buyer on tender of delivery.

(4) The provisions of this section are subject to contrary agreement of the parties and to the provisions of this Article on sale on approval (Section 2—327) and on effect of breach on risk of loss (Section 2—510).

§ 2—510. Effect of Breach on Risk of Loss.

(1) Where a tender or delivery of goods so fails to conform

to the contract as to give a right of rejection the risk of their loss remains on the seller until cure or acceptance.

(2) Where the buyer rightfully revokes acceptance he may to the extent of any deficiency in his effective insurance coverage treat the risk of loss as having rested on the seller from the beginning.

(3) Where the buyer as to conforming goods already identified to the contract for sale repudiates or is otherwise in breach before risk of their loss has passed to him, the seller may to the extent of any deficiency in his effective insurance coverage treat the risk of loss as resting on the buyer for a commercially reasonable time.

PART 6
Breach, Repudiation and Excuse

§ 2—602.   Manner and Effect of Rightful Rejection.

(1) Rejection of goods must be within a reasonable time after their delivery or tender. It is ineffective unless the buyer seasonably notifies the seller.

(2) Subject to the provisions of the two following sections on rejected goods (Sections 2—603 and 2—604),

(a) after rejection any exercise of ownership by the buyer with respect to any commercial unit is wrongful as against the seller; and

(b) if the buyer has before rejection taken physical possession of goods in which he does not have a security interest under the provisions of this Article (subsection (3) of Section 2—711), he is under a duty after rejection to hold them with reasonable care at the seller's disposition for a time sufficient to permit the seller to remove them; but

(c) the buyer has no further obligations with regard to goods rightfully rejected.

(3) The seller's rights with respect to goods wrongfully rejected are governed by the provisions of this Article on Seller's remedies in general (Section 2—703).

§ 2—607.   Effect of Acceptance; Notice of Breach; Burden of Establishing Breach After Acceptance; Notice of Claim or Litigation to Person Answerable Over.

(1) The buyer must pay at the contract rate for any goods accepted.

(2) Acceptance of goods by the buyer precludes rejection of the goods accepted and if made with knowledge of a non-conformity cannot be revoked because of it unless the acceptance was on the reasonable assumption that the non-conformity would be seasonably cured but acceptance does not of itself impair any other remedy provided by this Article for non-conformity.

(3) Where a tender has been accepted

(a) the buyer must within a reasonable time after he discovers or should have discovered any breach notify the seller of breach or be barred from any remedy; and

(b) if the claim is one for infringement or the like (subsection (3) of Section 2—312) and the buyer is sued as a result of such a breach he must so notify the seller within a reasonable time after he receives notice of the litigation or be barred from any remedy over for liability established by the litigation.

(4) The burden is on the buyer to establish any breach with respect to the goods accepted.

(5) Where the buyer is sued for breach of a warranty or other obligation for which his seller is answerable over

(a) he may give his seller written notice of the litigation. If the notice states that the seller may come in and defend and that if the seller does not do so he will be bound in any action against him by his buyer by any determination of fact common to the two litigations, then unless the seller after seasonable receipt of the notice does come in and defend he is so bound.

(b) if the claim is one for infringement or the like (subsection (3) of Section 2—312) the original seller may demand in writing that his buyer turn over to him control of the litigation including settlement or else be barred from any remedy over and if he also agrees to bear all expense and to satisfy any adverse judgment, then unless the buyer after seasonable receipt of the demand does turn over control the buyer is so barred.

(6) The provisions of subsections (3), (4) and (5) apply to any obligation of a buyer to hold the seller harmless against infringement or the like (subsection (3) of Section 2—312).

§ 2—613.   Casualty to Identified Goods.

Where the contract requires for its performance goods identified when the contract is made, and the goods suffer casualty without fault of either party before the risk of loss passes to the buyer, or in a proper case under a "no arrival, no sale" term (Section 2—324) then

(a) if the loss is total the contract is avoided; and

(b) if the loss is partial or the goods have so deteriorated as no longer to conform to the contract the buyer may nevertheless demand inspection and at his option either treat the contract as voided or accept the goods with due allowance from the contract price for the deterioration or the deficiency in quantity but without further right against the seller.

§ 2—615.   Excuse by Failure of Presupposed Conditions.

Except so far as a seller may have assumed a greater obligation and subject to the preceding section on substituted performance:

(a) Delay in delivery or non-delivery in whole or in part by a seller who complies with paragraphs (b) and (c) is not a breach of his duty under a contract for sale if performance as agreed has been made impracticable by the occurrence of a contingency the nonoccurrence of which was a basic assumption on which the contract was made or by compliance in good faith with any applicable foreign or domestic governmental regulation or order whether or not it later proves to be invalid.

(b) Where the causes mentioned in paragraph (a) affect only a part of the seller's capacity to perform, he must allocate production and deliveries among his customers but may at his option include regular customers not then under contract as well as his own requirements for further manufacture. He may so allocate in any manner which is fair and reasonable.

(c) The seller must notify the buyer seasonably that there will be delay or non-delivery and, when allocation is required under paragraph (b), of the estimated quota thus made available for the buyer.

PART 7
Remedies

§ 2—702. Seller's Remedies on Discovery of Buyer's Insolvency.

(1) Where the seller discovers the buyer to be insolvent he may refuse delivery except for cash including payment for all goods theretofore delivered under the contract, and stop delivery under this Article (Section 2—705).

(2) Where the seller discovers that the buyer has received goods on credit while insolvent he may reclaim the goods upon demand made within ten days after the receipt, but if misrepresentation of solvency has been made to the particular seller in writing within three months before delivery the ten day limitation does not apply. Except as provided in this subsection the seller may not base a right to reclaim goods on the buyer's fraudulent or innocent misrepresentation of solvency or of intent to pay.

(3) The seller's right to reclaim under subsection (2) is subject to the rights of a buyer in ordinary course or other good faith purchaser under this Article (Section 2—403). Successful reclamation of goods excludes all other remedies with respect to them.

§ 2—703. Seller's Remedies in General.

Where the buyer wrongfully rejects or revokes acceptance of goods or fails to make a payment due on or before delivery or repudiates with respect to a part or the whole, then with respect to any goods directly affected and, if the breach is of the whole contract (Section 2—612), then also with respect to the whole undelivered balance, the aggrieved seller may

(a) withhold delivery of such goods;

(b) stop delivery by any bailee as hereafter provided (Section 2—705);

(c) proceed under the next section respecting goods still unidentified to the contract;

(d) resell and recover damages as hereafter provided (Section 2—706);

(e) recover damages for non-acceptance (Section 2—708) or in a proper case the price (Section 2—709);

(f) cancel.

§§ 2—705. Seller's Stoppage of Delivery in Transit or Otherwise.

(1) The seller may stop delivery of goods in the possession of a carrier or other bailee when he discovers the buyer to be insolvent (Section 2—702) and may stop delivery of carload, truckload, planeload or larger shipments of express or freight when the buyer repudiates or fails to make a payment due before delivery or if for any other reason the seller has a right to withhold or reclaim the goods.

(2) As against such buyer the seller may stop delivery until

(a) receipt of the goods by the buyer; or

(b) acknowledgment to the buyer by any bailee of the goods except a carrier that the bailee holds the goods for the buyer; or

(c) such acknowledgment to the buyer by a carrier by reshipment or as warehouseman; or

(d) negotiation to the buyer of any negotiable document of title covering the goods.

(3) (a) To stop delivery the seller must so notify as to enable the bailee by reasonable diligence to prevent delivery of the goods.

(b) After such notification the bailee must hold and deliver the goods according to the directions of the seller but the seller is liable to the bailee for any ensuing charges or damages.

(c) If a negotiable document of title has been issued for goods the bailee is not
obliged to obey a notification to stop until surrender of the document.

(d) A carrier who has issued a non-negotiable bill of lading is not obliged to obey a notification to stop received from a person other than the consignor.

§ 2—706. Seller's Resale Including Contract for Resale.

(1) Under the conditions stated in Section 2—703 on seller's remedies, the seller may resell the goods concerned or the undelivered balance thereof. Where the resale is made in good faith and in a commercially reasonable manner the seller may recover the difference between the resale price and the contract price together with any incidental damages allowed under the provisions of this Article (Section 2—710), but less expenses saved in consequence of the buyer's breach.

(2) Except as otherwise provided in subsection (3) or unless otherwise agreed resale may be at public or private sale including sale by way of one or more contracts to sell or of identification to an existing contract of the seller. Sale may be as a unit or in parcels and at any time and place and on any terms but every aspect of the sale including the method, manner, time, place and terms must be commercially reasonable. The resale must be reasonably identified as referring to the broken contract, but it is not necessary that the goods be in existence or that any or all of them

have been identified to the contract before the breach.

(3) Where the resale is at private sale the seller must give the buyer reasonable notification of his intention to resell.

(4) Where the resale is at public sale

    (a) only identified goods can be sold except where there is a recognized market for a public sale of futures in goods of the kind; and

    (b) it must be made at a usual place or market for public sale if one is reasonably available and except in the case of goods which are perishable or threaten to decline in value speedily the seller must give the buyer reasonable notice of the time and place of the resale; and

    (c) if the goods are not to be within the view of those attending the sale the notification of sale must state the place where the goods are located and provide for their reasonable inspection by prospective bidders; and

    (d) the seller may buy.

(5) A purchaser who buys in good faith at a resale takes the goods free of any rights of the original buyer even though the seller fails to comply with one or more of the requirements of this section.

(6) The seller is not accountable to the buyer for any profit made on any resale. A person in the position of a seller (Section 2—707) or a buyer who has rightfully rejected or justifiably revoked acceptance must account for any excess over the amount of his security interest, as hereinafter defined (subsection (3) of Section 2—711).

§ 2—708. Seller's Damages for Non-Acceptance or Repudiation.

(1) Subject to subsection (2) and to the provisions of this Article with respect to proof of market price (Section 2—723), the measure of damages for non-acceptance or repudiation by the buyer is the difference between the market price at the time and place for tender and the unpaid contract price together with any incidental damages provided in this Article (Section 2—710), but less expenses saved in consequence of the buyer's breach.

(2) If the measure of damages provided in subsection (1) is inadequate to put the seller in as good a position as performance would have done then the measure of damages is the profit (including reasonable overhead) which the seller would have made from full performance by the buyer, together with any incidental damages provided in this Article (Section 2—710), due allowance for costs reasonably incurred and due credit for payments or proceeds of resale.

§ 2—709. Action for the Price.

(1) When the buyer fails to pay the price as it becomes due the seller may recover, together with any incidental damages under the next section, the price

    (a) of goods accepted or of conforming goods lost or damaged within a commercially reasonable time after risk of their loss has passed to the buyer; and

    (b) of goods identified to the contract if the seller is unable after reasonable effort to resell them at a reasonable price or the circumstances reasonably indicate that such effort will be unavailing.

(2) Where the seller sues for the price he must hold for the buyer any goods which have been identified to the contract and are still in his control except that if resale becomes possible he may resell them at any time prior to the collection of the judgment. The net proceeds of any such resale must be credited to the buyer and payment of the judgment entitles him to any goods not resold.

(3) After the buyer has wrongfully rejected or revoked acceptance of the goods or has failed to make a payment due or has repudiated (Section 2—610), a seller who is held not entitled to the price under this section shall nevertheless be awarded damages for non-acceptance under the preceding section.

§ 2—710. Seller's Incidental Damages.

Incidental damages to an aggrieved seller include any commercially reasonable charges, expenses or commissions incurred in stopping delivery, in the transportation, care and custody of goods after the buyer's breach, in connection with return or resale of the goods or otherwise resulting from the breach.

§ 2—712. "Cover"; Buyer's Procurement of Substitute Goods.

(1) After a breach within the preceding section the buyer may "cover" by making in good faith and without unreasonable delay any reasonable purchase of or contract to purchase goods in substitution for those due from the seller.

(2) The buyer may recover from the seller as damages the difference between the cost of cover and the contract price together with any incidental or consequential damages as hereinafter defined (Section 2—715), but less expenses saved in consequence of the seller's breach.

(3) Failure of the buyer to effect cover within this section does not bar him from any other remedy.

§ 2—713. Buyer's Damages for Non-Delivery or Repudiation.

(1) Subject to the provisions of this Article with respect to proof of market price (Section 2—723), the measure of damages for non-delivery or repudiation by the seller is the difference between the market price at the time when the buyer learned of the breach and the contract price together with any incidental and consequential damages provided in this Article (Section 2—715), but less expenses saved in consequence of the seller's breach.

(2) Market price is to be determined as of the place for tender or, in cases of rejection after arrival or revocation of acceptance, as of the place of arrival.

§ 2—715. Buyer's Incidental and Consequential Damages.

(1) Incidental damages resulting from the seller's breach

A-30 Appendix 3 Uniform Commercial Code

include expenses reasonably incurred in inspection, receipt, transportation and care and custody of goods rightfully rejected, any commercially reasonable charges, expenses or commissions in connection with effecting cover and any other reasonable expense incident to the delay or other breach.

(2) Consequential damages resulting from the seller's breach include

(a) any loss resulting from general or particular requirements and needs of which the seller at the time of contracting had reason to know and which could not reasonably be prevented by cover or otherwise; and

(b) injury to person or property proximately resulting from any breach of warranty.

§ 2—718. Liquidation or Limitation of Damages; Deposits.

(1) Damages for breach by either party may be liquidated in the agreement but only at an amount which is reasonable in the light of the anticipated or actual harm caused by the breach, the difficulties of proof of loss, and the inconvenience or nonfeasibility of otherwise obtaining an adequate remedy. A term fixing unreasonably large liquidated damages is void as a penalty.

(2) Where the seller justifiably withholds delivery of goods because of the buyer's breach, the buyer is entitled to restitution of any amount by which the sum of his payments exceeds

(a) the amount to which the seller is entitled by virtue of terms liquidating the seller's damages in accordance with subsection (1), or

(b) in the absence of such terms, twenty percent of the value of the total performance for which the buyer is obligated under the contract or $500, whichever is smaller.

(3) The buyer's right to restitution under subsection (2) is subject to offset to the extent that the seller establishes

(a) a right to recover damages under the provisions of this Article other than subsection (1), and

(b) the amount or value of any benefits received by the buyer directly or indirectly by reason of the contract.

(4) Where a seller has received payment in goods their reasonable value or the proceeds of their resale shall be treated as payments for the purposes of subsection (2); but if the seller has notice of the buyer's breach before reselling goods received in part performance, his resale is subject to the conditions laid down in this Article on resale by an aggrieved seller (Section 2—706).

§ 2—719. Contractual Modification or Limitation of Remedy.

(1) Subject to the provisions of subsections (2) and (3) of this section and of the preceding section on liquidation and limitation of damages,

(a) the agreement may provide for remedies in addition to or in substitution for those provided in this Article and may limit or alter the measure of damages recoverable under this Article, as by limiting the buyer's remedies to return of the goods and repayment of the price or to repair and replacement of non-conforming goods or parts; and

(b) resort to a remedy as provided is optional unless the remedy is expressly agreed to be exclusive, in which case it is the sole remedy.

(2) Where circumstances cause an exclusive or limited remedy to fail of its essential purpose, remedy may be had as provided in this Act.

(3) Consequential damages may be limited or excluded unless the limitation or exclusion is unconscionable. Limitation of consequential damages for injury to the person in the case of consumer goods is prima facie unconscionable but limitation of damages where the loss is commercial is not.

§ 2—720. Effect of "Cancellation" or "Rescission" on Claims for Antecedent Breach.

Unless the contrary intention clearly appears, expressions of "cancellation" or "rescission" of the contract or the like shall not be construed as a renunciation or discharge of any claim in damages for an antecedent breach.

§ 2—725. Statute of Limitations in Contracts for Sale.

(1) An action for breach of any contract for sale must be commenced within four years after the cause of action has accrued. By the original agreement the parties may reduce the period of limitation to not less than one year but may not extend it.

(2) A cause of action accrues when the breach occurs, regardless of the aggrieved party's lack of knowledge of the breach. A breach of warranty occurs when tender of delivery is made, except that where a warranty explicitly extends to future performance of the goods and discovery of the breach must await the time of such performance the cause of action accrues when the breach is or should have been discovered.

(3) Where an action commenced within the time limited by subsection (1) is so terminated as to leave available a remedy by another action for the same breach such other action may be commenced after the expiration of the time limited and within six months after the termination of the first action unless the termination resulted from voluntary discontinuance or from dismissal for failure or neglect to prosecute.

(4) This section does not alter the law on tolling of the statute of limitations nor does it apply to causes of action which have accrued before this Act becomes effective.

Article 2A
LEASES

PART 1
General Provisions

§ 2A—103. Definitions and Index of Definitions.

(1) In this Article unless the context otherwise requires:

(a) "Buyer in ordinary course of business" means a person who in good faith and without knowledge that the sale to him [or her] is in violation of the ownership rights or security interest or leasehold interest of a third party in the goods buys in ordinary course from a person in the business of selling goods of that kind but does not include a pawnbroker. "Buying" may be for cash or by exchange of other property or on secured or unsecured credit and includes receiving goods or documents of title under a pre-existing contract for sale but does not include a transfer in bulk or as security for or in total or partial satisfaction of a money debt.

(b) "Cancellation" occurs when either party puts an end to the lease contract for default by the other party.

(c) "Commercial unit" means such a unit of goods as by commercial usage is a single whole for purposes of lease and division of which materially impairs its character or value on the market or in use. A commercial unit may be a single article, as a machine, or a set of articles, as a suite of furniture or a line of machinery, or a quantity, as a gross or carload, or any other unit treated in use or in the relevant market as a single whole.

(d) "Conforming" goods or performance under a lease contract means goods or performance that are in accordance with the obligations under the lease contract.

(e) "Consumer lease" means a lease that a lessor regularly engaged in the business of leasing or selling makes to a lessee who is an individual and who takes under the lease primarily for a personal, family, or household purpose, if the total payments to be made under the lease contract, excluding payments for options to renew or buy, do not exceed $25,000.

(f) "Fault" means wrongful act, omission, breach, or default.

(g) "Finance lease" means a lease with respect in which (i) the lessor does not select, manufacture or supply the goods; (ii) the lessor acquires the goods or the right to possession and use of the goods in connection with the lease; and (iii) either the lessee receives a copy of the contract evidencing the lessor's purchase of the goods on or before signing the lease contract, or the lessee's approval of the contract evidencing the lessor's purchase of the goods is a condition to effectiveness of the lease contract.

(h) "Goods" means all things that are movable at the time of identification to the lease contract, or are fixtures (Section 2A—309), but the term does not include money, documents, instruments, accounts, chattel paper, general intangibles, or minerals or the like, including oil and gas, before extraction. The term also includes the unborn young of animals.

(i) "Installment lease contract" means a lease contract that authorizes or requires the delivery of goods in separate lots to be separately accepted, even though the lease contract contains a clause "each delivery is a separate lease" or its equivalent.

(j) "Lease" means a transfer of the right to possession and use of goods for a term in return for consideration, but a sale, including a sale on approval or a sale or return, or retention or creation of a security interest is not a lease. Unless the context clearly indicates otherwise, the term includes a sublease.

(k) "Lease agreement" means the bargain, with respect to the lease, of the lessor and the lessee in fact as found in their language or by implication from other circumstances including course of dealing or usage of trade or course of performance as provided in this Article. Unless the context clearly indicates otherwise, the term includes a sublease agreement.

(l) "Lease contract" means the total legal obligation that results from the lease agreement as affected by this Article and any other applicable rules of law. Unless the context clearly indicates otherwise, the term includes a sublease contract.

(m) "Leasehold interest" means the interest of the lessor or the lessee under a lease contract.

(n) "Lessee" means a person who acquires the right to possession and use of goods under a lease. Unless the context clearly indicates otherwise, the term includes a sublessee.

(o) "Lessee in ordinary course of business" means a person who in good faith and without knowledge that the lease to him [or her] is in violation of the ownership rights or security interest or leasehold interest of a third party in the goods, leases in ordinary course from a person in the business of selling or leasing goods of that kind but does not include a pawnbroker. "Leasing" may be for cash or by exchange of other property or on secured or unsecured credit and includes receiving goods or documents of title under a pre-existing lease contract but does not include a transfer in bulk or as security for or in total or partial satisfaction of a money debt.

(p) "Lessor" means a person who transfers the right to possession and use of goods under a lease. Unless the context clearly indicates otherwise, the term includes a sublessor.

(q) "Lessor's residual interest" means the lessor's interest in the goods after expiration, termination, or cancellation of the lease contract.

(r) "Lien" means a charge against or interest in goods to secure payment of a debt or performance of an obligation, but the term does not include a security interest.

(s) "Lot" means a parcel or a single article that is the subject matter of a separate lease or delivery, whether or not it is sufficient to perform the lease contract.

(t) "Merchant lessee" means a lessee that is a merchant with respect to goods of the kind subject to the lease.

(u) "Present value" means the amount as of a date certain of one or more sums payable in the future, discounted to the date certain. The discount is determined by the interest rate specified by the parties if the rate was not manifestly unreasonable at the time the transaction was entered into; otherwise, the discount is determined by a commercially reasonable rate that takes into account the facts and circumstances of each case at the time the transaction was entered into.

(v) "Purchase" includes taking by sale, lease, mortgage, security interest, pledge, gift, or any other voluntary transaction creating an interest in goods.

(w) "Sublease" means a lease of goods the right to possession and use of which was acquired by the lessor as a lessee under an existing lease.

(x) "Supplier" means a person from whom a lessor buys or leases goods to be leased under a finance lease.

(y) "Supply contract" means a contract under which a lessor buys or leases goods to be leased.

(z) "Termination" occurs when either party pursuant to a power created by agreement or law puts an end to the lease contract otherwise than for default.

(2) Other definitions applying to this Article and the sections in which they appear are:

"Accessions." Section 2A—310(1).
"Construction mortgage." Section 2A—309(1)(d).
"Encumbrance." Section 2A—309(1)(e).
"Fixtures." Section 2A—309(1)(a).
"Fixture filing." Section 2A—309(1)(b).
"Purchase money lease." Section 2A—309(1)(c).

(3) The following definitions in other Articles apply to this Article:

"Accounts." Section 9—106.
"Between merchants." Section 2—104(3).
"Buyer." Section 2—103(1)(a).
"Chattel paper." Section 9—105(1)(b).
"Consumer goods." Section 9—109(1).
"Documents." Section 9—105(1)(f).
"Entrusting." Section 2—403(3).
"General intangibles." Section 9—106.
"Good faith." Section 2—103(1)(b).
"Instrument." Section 9—105(1)(i).
"Merchant." Section 2—104(1).
"Mortgage." Section 9—105(1)(j).
"Pursuant to commitment." Section 9—105(1)(k).
"Receipt." Section 2—103(1)(c).
"Sale." Section 2—106(1).
"Sale on Approval." Section 2—326.

"Sale or Return." Section 2—326.
"Seller." Section 2—103(1)(d).

(4) In addition Article 1 contains general definitions and principles of construction and interpretation applicable throughout this Article.

PART 2
Formation and Construction of Lease Contract

§ 2A—201. Statute of Frauds.

(1) A lease contract is not enforceable by way of action or defense unless:

(a) the total payments to be made under the lease contract, excluding payments for options to renew or buy, are less than $1,000; or

(b) there is a writing, signed by the party against whom enforcement is sought or by that party's authorized agent, sufficient to indicate that a lease contract has been made between the parties and to describe the goods leased and the lease term.

(2) Any description of leased goods or of the lease term is sufficient and satisfies subsection (1)(b), whether or not it is specific, if it reasonably identifies what is described.

(3) A writing is not insufficient because it omits or incorrectly states a term agreed upon, but the lease contract is not enforceable under subsection (1)(b) beyond the lease term and the quantity of goods shown in this writing.

(4) A lease contract that does not satisfy the requirements of subsection (1), but which is valid in other respects, is enforceable:

(a) if the goods are to be specially manufactured or obtained for the lessee and are not suitable for lease or sale to others in the ordinary course of the lessor's business, and the lessor, before notice of repudiation is received and under circumstances that reasonably indicate that the goods are for the lessee, has made either a substantial beginning of their manufacture or commitments for their procurement;

(b) if the party against whom enforcement is sought admits in that party's pleading, testimony or otherwise in court that a lease contract was made, but the lease contract is not enforceable under this provision beyond the quantity of goods admitted; or

(c) with respect to goods that have been received and accepted by the lessee.

(5) The lease term under a lease contract referred to in subsection (4) is:

(a) if there is a writing signed by the party against whom enforcement is sought or by that party's authorized agent specifying the lease term, the term so specified;

(b) if the party against whom enforcement is sought admits in that party's pleading, testimony, or otherwise in court a lease term, the term so admitted; or

(c) a reasonable lease term.

§ 2A—209. Lessee under Finance Lease as Beneficiary of Supply Contract.

(1) The benefit of the supplier's promises to the lessor under the supply contract and of all warranties, whether express or implied, including those of any third party provided in connection with or as part of the supply contract, extends to the lessee to the extent of the lessee's leasehold interest under a finance lease related to the supply contract, but is subject to the terms warranty and of the supply contract and all defenses or claims arising therefrom.

(2) The extension of the benefit of supplier's promises to the lessee does not: (a) modify the rights and obligations of the parties to the supply contract, whether arising therefrom or otherwise, or (b) impose any duty or liability under the supply contract on the lessee.

(3) Any modification or rescission of the supply contract by the supplier and the lessor is effective against the lessee unless, prior to the modification or rescission, the supplier has received notice that the lessee has entered into a finance lease related to the supply contract. If the supply contract is modified or rescinded after the lessee enters the finance lease, the lessee has a cause of action against the lessor, and against the supplier if the supplier has notice if the lessees's entering the finance lease when the supply contract is modified or rescinded. The lessee's recovery from such action shall put the lessee in as good a position as if the modification or rescission had not occurred.

PART 4
Performance Of Lease Contract: Repudiated, Substituted And Excused

§ 2A—407. Irrevocable Promises: Finance Leases.

(1) In the case of a finance lease that is not a consumer lease the lessee's promises under the lease contract become irrevocable and independent upon the lessee's acceptance of the goods.

(2) A promise that has become irrevocable and independent under subsection (1):

    (a) is effective and enforceable between the parties, and by or against third parties including assignees of the parties, and

    (b) is not subject to cancellation, termination, modification, repudiation, excuse, or substitution without the consent of the party to whom the promise runs.

PART 5
Default

A. In General

§ 2A—501. Default: Procedure.

(1) Whether the lessor or the lessee is in default under a lease contract is determined by the lease agreement and this Article.

(2) If the lessor or the lessee is in default under the lease contract, the party seeking enforcement has rights and remedies as provided in this Article and, except as limited by this Article, as provided in the lease agreement.

(3) If the lessor or the lessee is in default under the lease contract, the party seeking enforcement may reduce the party's claim to judgment, or otherwise enforce the lease contract by self-help or any available judicial procedure or nonjudicial procedure, including administrative proceeding, arbitration, or the like, in accordance with this Article.

(4) Except as otherwise provided in this Article or the lease agreement, the rights and remedies referred to in subsections (2) and (3) are cumulative.

(5) If the lease agreement covers both real property and goods, the party seeking enforcement may proceed under this Part as to the goods, or under other applicable law as to both the real property and the goods in accordance with his [or her] rights and remedies in respect of the real property, in which case this Part does not apply.

§ 2A—503. Modification or Impairment of Rights and Remedies.

(1) Except as otherwise provided in this Article, the lease agreement may include rights and remedies for default in addition to or in substitution for those provided in this Article and may limit or alter the measure of damages recoverable under this Article.

(2) Resort to a remedy provided under this Article or in the lease agreement is optional unless the remedy is expressly agreed to be exclusive. If circumstances cause an exclusive or limited remedy to fail of its essential purpose, or provision for an exclusive remedy is unconscionable, remedy may be had as provided in this Article.

(3) Consequential damages may be liquidated under Section 2A—504, or may otherwise be limited, altered, or excluded unless the limitation, alteration, or exclusion is unconscionable. Limitation, alteration, or exclusion of consequential damages for injury to the person in the case of consumer goods is prima facie unconscionable but limitation, alteration, or exclusion of damages where the loss is commercial is not prima facie unconscionable.

(4) Rights and remedies on default by the lessor or the lessee with respect to any obligation or promise collateral or ancillary to the lease contract are not impaired by this Article.

§ 2A—529. Lessor's Action for the Rent.

(1) After default by the lessee under the lease contract (Section 2A—523(1)) if the lessor complies with subsection (2), the lessor may recover from the lessee as damages:

    (a) for goods accepted by the lessee and for conforming goods lost or damaged within a commercially reasonable time after risk of loss passes to the lessee (Section 2A—219), (i) accrued and unpaid rent as of the date of default, (ii) the present value as of the date of default of the rent for the remaining lease term of the lease agreement, and (iii) any incidental damages allowed under Section 2A—530, less expenses saved in consequence of the lessee's default; and

(b) for goods identified to the lease contract if the lessor is unable after reasonable effort to dispose of them at a reasonable price or the circumstances reasonably indicate that effort will be unavailing, (i) accrued and unpaid rent as of the date of default, (ii) the present value as of the date of default of the rent for the remaining lease term of the lease agreement, and (iii) any incidental damages allowed under Section 2A—530, less expenses saved in consequence of the lessee's default.

(2) Except as provided in subsection (3), the lessor shall hold for the lessee for the remaining lease term of the lease agreement any goods that have been identified to the lease contract and are in the lessor's control.

(3) The lessor may dispose of the goods at any time before collection of the judgment for damages obtained pursuant to subsection (1) and the lessor may proceed against the lessee for damages pursuant to Section 2A—527 or Section 2A—528.

(4) Payment of the judgment for damages obtained pursuant to subsection (1) entitles the lessee to use and possession of the goods not then disposed of for the remaining lease term of the lease agreement.

(5) After a lessee has wrongfully rejected or revoked acceptance of goods, has failed to pay rent then due, or has repudiated (Section 2A—402), a lessor who is held not entitled to rent under this section must nevertheless be awarded damages for non-acceptance under Sections 2A—527 and 2A—528.

Revised Article 3
NEGOTIABLE INSTRUMENTS

PART 1
General Provisions and Definitions

§ 3—103. Definitions.

(a) In this Article:

(1) "Acceptor" means a drawee who has accepted a draft.

(2) "Drawee" means a person ordered in a draft to make payment.

(3) "Drawer" means a person who signs or is identified in a draft as a person ordering payment.

(4) "Good faith" means honesty in fact and the observance of reasonable commercial standards of fair dealing.

(5) "Maker" means a person who signs or is identified in a note as a person undertaking to pay.

(6) "Order" means a written instruction to pay money signed by the person giving the instruction. The instruction may be addressed to any person, including the person giving the instruction, or to one or more persons jointly or in the alternative but not in succession. An authorization to pay is not an order unless the person authorized to pay is also instructed to pay.

(7) "Ordinary care" in the case of a person engaged in business means observance of reasonable commercial standards, prevailing in the area in which the person is located, with respect to the business in which the person is engaged. In the case of a bank that takes an instrument for processing for collection or payment by automated means, reasonable commercial standards do not require the bank to examine the instrument if the failure to examine does not violate the bank's prescribed procedures and the bank's procedures do not vary unreasonably from general banking usage not disapproved by this Article or Article 4.

(8) "Party" means a party to an instrument.

(9) "Promise" means a written undertaking to pay money signed by the person undertaking to pay. An acknowledgment of an obligation by the obligor is not a promise unless the obligor also undertakes to pay the obligation.

(10) "Prove" with respect to a fact means to meet the burden of establishing the fact (Section 1—201(8)).

(11) "Remitter" means a person who purchases an instrument from its issuer if the instrument is payable to an identified person other than the purchaser.

(b);(c) [Other definitions' section references deleted.]

(d) In addition, Article 1 contains general definitions and principles of construction and interpretation applicable throughout this Article.

§ 3—104. Negotiable Instrument.

(a) Except as provided in subsections (c) and (d), "negotiable instrument" means an unconditional promise or order to pay a fixed amount of money, with or without interest or other charges described in the promise or order, if it:

(1) is payable to bearer or to order at the time it is issued or first comes into possession of a holder;

(2) is payable on demand or at a definite time; and

(3) does not state any other undertaking or instruction by the person promising or ordering payment to do any act in addition to the payment of money, but the promise or order may contain (i) an undertaking or power to give, maintain, or protect collateral to secure payment, (ii) an authorization or power to the holder to confess judgment or realize on or dispose of collateral, or (iii) a waiver of the benefit of any law intended for the advantage or protection of an obligor.

(b) "Instrument" means a negotiable instrument.

(c) An order that meets all of the requirements of subsection (a), except paragraph (1), and otherwise falls within the definition of "check" in subsection (f) is a negotiable instrument and a check.

(d) A promise or order other than a check is not an instrument if, at the time it is issued or first comes into possession of a holder, it contains a conspicuous statement, however expressed, to the effect that the promise or order is not negotiable or is not an instrument governed by this Article.

(e) An instrument is a "note" if it is a promise and is a "draft" if it is an order. If an instrument falls within the definition of both "note" and "draft," a person entitled to enforce the instrument may treat it as either.

(f) "Check" means (i) a draft, other than a documentary draft, payable on demand and drawn on a bank or (ii) a cashier's check or teller's check. An instrument may be a check even though it is described on its face by another term, such as "money order."

(g) "Cashier's check" means a draft with respect to which the drawer and drawee are the same bank or branches of the same bank.

(h) "Teller's check" means a draft drawn by a bank (i) on another bank, or (ii) payable at or through a bank.

(i) "Traveler's check" means an instrument that (i) is payable on demand, (ii) is drawn on or payable at or through a bank, (iii) is designated by the term "traveler's check" or by a substantially similar term, and (iv) requires, as a condition to payment, a countersignature by a person whose specimen signature appears on the instrument.

(j) "Certificate of deposit" means an instrument containing an acknowledgment by a bank that a sum of money has been received by the bank and a promise by the bank to repay the sum of money. A certificate of deposit is a note of the bank.

§ 3—106. Unconditional Promise or Order.

(a) Except as provided in this section, for the purposes of Section 3—104(a), a promise or order is unconditional unless it states (i) an express condition to payment, (ii) that the promise or order is subject to or governed by another writing, or (iii) that rights or obligations with respect to the promise or order are stated in another writing. A reference to another writing does not of itself make the promise or order conditional.

(b) A promise or order is not made conditional (i) by a reference to another writing for a statement of rights with respect to collateral, prepayment, or acceleration, or (ii) because payment is limited to resort to a particular fund or source.

(c) If a promise or order requires, as a condition to payment, a countersignature by a person whose specimen signature appears on the promise or order, the condition does not make the promise or order conditional for the purposes of Section 3—104(a). If the person whose specimen signature appears on an instrument fails to countersign the instrument, the failure to countersign is a defense to the obligation of the issuer, but the failure does not prevent a transferee of the instrument from becoming a holder of the instrument.

(d) If a promise or order at the time it is issued or first comes into possession of a holder contains a statement, required by applicable statutory or administrative law, to the effect that the rights of a holder or transferee are subject to claims or defenses that the issuer could assert against the original payee, the promise or order is not thereby made conditional for the purposes of Section 3—104(a); but if the promise or order is an instrument, there cannot be a holder in due course of the instrument.

§ 3—107. Instrument Payable in Foreign Money.

Unless the instrument otherwise provides, an instrument that states the amount payable in foreign money may be paid in the foreign money or in an equivalent amount in dollars calculated by using the current bank-offered spot rate at the place of payment for the purchase of dollars on the day on which the instrument is paid.

§ 3—108. Payable on Demand or at Definite Time.

(a) A promise or order is "payable on demand" if it (i) states that it is payable on demand or at sight, or otherwise indicates that it is payable at the will of the holder, or (ii) does not state any time of payment.

(b) A promise or order is "payable at a definite time" if it is payable on elapse of a definite period of time after sight or acceptance or at a fixed date or dates or at a time or times readily ascertainable at the time the promise or order is issued, subject to rights of (i) prepayment, (ii) acceleration, (iii) extension at the option of the holder, or (iv) extension to a further definite time at the option of the maker or acceptor or automatically upon or after a specified act or event.

(c) If an instrument, payable at a fixed date, is also payable upon demand made before the fixed date, the instrument is payable on demand until the fixed date and, if demand for payment is not made before that date, becomes payable at a definite time on the fixed date.

§ 3—109. Payable to Bearer or to Order.

(a) A promise or order is payable to bearer if it:

(1) states that it is payable to bearer or to the order of bearer or otherwise indicates that the person in possession of the promise or order is entitled to payment;

(2) does not state a payee; or

(3) states that it is payable to or to the order of cash or otherwise indicates that it is not payable to an identified person.

(b) A promise or order that is not payable to bearer is payable to order if it is payable (i) to the order of an identified person or (ii) to an identified person or order. A promise or order that is payable to order is payable to the identified person.

(c) An instrument payable to bearer may become payable to an identified person if it is specially indorsed pursuant to Section

3—205(a). An instrument payable to an identified person may become payable to bearer if it is indorsed in blank pursuant to Section 3—205(b).

§ 3—110. Identification of Person to Whom Instrument Is Payable.

(a) The person to whom an instrument is initially payable is determined by the intent of the person, whether or not authorized, signing as, or in the name or behalf of, the issuer of the instrument. The instrument is payable to the person intended by the signer even if that person is identified in the instrument by a name or other identification that is not that of the intended person. If more than one person signs in the name or behalf of the issuer of an instrument and all the signers do not intend the same person as payee, the instrument is payable to any person intended by one or more of the signers.

(b) If the signature of the issuer of an instrument is made by automated means, such as a check-writing machine, the payee of the instrument is determined by the intent of the person who supplied the name or identification of the payee, whether or not authorized to do so.

(c) A person to whom an instrument is payable may be identified in any way, including by name, identifying number, office, or account number. For the purpose of determining the holder of an instrument, the following rules apply:

(1) If an instrument is payable to an account and the account is identified only by number, the instrument is payable to the person to whom the account is payable. If an instrument is payable to an account identified by number and by the name of a person, the instrument is payable to the named person, whether or not that person is the owner of the account identified by number.

(2) If an instrument is payable to:

(i) a trust, an estate, or a person described as trustee or representative of a trust or estate, the instrument is payable to the trustee, the representative, or a successor of either, whether or not the beneficiary or estate is also named;

(ii) a person described as agent or similar representative of a named or identified person, the instrument is payable to the represented person, the representative, or a successor of the representative;

(iii) a fund or organization that is not a legal entity, the instrument is payable to a representative of the members of the fund or organization; or

(iv) an office or to a person described as holding an office, the instrument is payable to the named person, the incumbent of the office, or a successor to the incumbent.

(d) If an instrument is payable to two or more persons alternatively, it is payable to any of them and may be negotiated, discharged, or enforced by any or all of them in possession of the instrument. If an instrument is payable to two or more persons not alternatively, it is payable to all of them and may be negotiated, discharged, or enforced only by all of them. If an instrument payable to two or more persons is ambiguous as to whether it is payable to the persons alternatively, the instrument is payable to the persons alternatively.

§ 3—112. Interest.

(a) Unless otherwise provided in the instrument, (i) an instrument is not payable with interest, and (ii) interest on an interest-bearing instrument is payable from the date of the instrument.

(b) Interest may be stated in an instrument as a fixed or variable amount of money or it may be expressed as a fixed or variable rate or rates. The amount or rate of interest may be stated or described in the instrument in any manner and may require reference to information not contained in the instrument. If an instrument provides for interest, but the amount of interest payable cannot be ascertained from the description, interest is payable at the judgment rate in effect at the place of payment of the instrument and at the time interest first accrues.

PART 2
Negotiation, Transfer, and Indorsement

§ 3—201. Negotiation.

(a) "Negotiation" means a transfer of possession, whether voluntary or involuntary, of an instrument by a person other than the issuer to a person who thereby becomes its holder.

(b) Except for negotiation by a remitter, if an instrument is payable to an identified person, negotiation requires transfer of possession of the instrument and its indorsement by the holder. If an instrument is payable to bearer, it may be negotiated by transfer of possession alone.

§ 3—203. Transfer of Instrument; Rights Acquired by Transfer.

(a) An instrument is transferred when it is delivered by a person other than its issuer for the purpose of giving to the person receiving delivery the right to enforce the instrument.

(b) Transfer of an instrument, whether or not the transfer is a negotiation, vests in the transferee any right of the transferor to enforce the instrument, including any right as a holder in due course, but the transferee cannot acquire rights of a holder in due course by a transfer, directly or indirectly, from a holder in due course if the transferee engaged in fraud or illegality affecting the instrument.

(c) Unless otherwise agreed, if an instrument is transferred for value and the transferee does not become a holder because of lack of indorsement by the transferor, the transferee has a specifically enforceable right to the unqualified indorsement of the transferor, but negotiation of the instrument does not occur until the indorsement is made.

(d) If a transferor purports to transfer less than the entire instrument, negotiation of the instrument does not occur. The transferee obtains no rights under this Article and has only the rights of a partial assignee.

§ 3—204. Indorsement.

(a) "Indorsement" means a signature, other than that of a signer as maker, drawer, or acceptor, that alone or accompanied by other words is made on an instrument for the purpose of (i) negotiating the instrument, (ii) restricting payment of the instrument, or (iii) incurring indorser's liability on the instrument, but regardless of the intent of the signer, a signature and its accompanying words is an indorsement unless the accompanying words, terms of the instrument, place of the signature, or other circumstances unambiguously indicate that the signature was made for a purpose other than indorsement. For the purpose of determining whether a signature is made on an instrument, a paper affixed to the instrument is a part of the instrument.

(b) "Indorser" means a person who makes an indorsement.

(c) For the purpose of determining whether the transferee of an instrument is a holder, an indorsement that transfers a security interest in the instrument is effective as an unqualified indorsement of the instrument.

(d) If an instrument is payable to a holder under a name that is not the name of the holder, indorsement may be made by the holder in the name stated in the instrument or in the holder's name or both, but signature in both names may be required by a person paying or taking the instrument for value or collection.

§ 3—205. Special Indorsement; Blank Indorsement; Anomalous Indorsement.

(a) If an indorsement is made by the holder of an instrument, whether payable to an identified person or payable to bearer, and the indorsement identifies a person to whom it makes the instrument payable, it is a "special indorsement." When specially indorsed, an instrument becomes payable to the identified person and may be negotiated only by the indorsement of that person. The principles stated in Section 3—110 apply to special indorsements.

(b) If an indorsement is made by the holder of an instrument and it is not a special indorsement, it is a "blank indorsement." When indorsed in blank, an instrument becomes payable to bearer and may be negotiated by transfer of possession alone until specially indorsed.

(c) The holder may convert a blank indorsement that consists only of a signature into a special indorsement by writing, above the signature of the indorser, words identifying the person to whom the instrument is made

payable.

(d) "Anomalous indorsement" means an indorsement made by a person who is not the holder of the instrument. An anomalous indorsement does not affect the manner in which the instrument may be negotiated.

§ 3—206. Restrictive Indorsement.

(a) An indorsement limiting payment to a particular person or otherwise prohibiting further transfer or negotiation of the instrument is not effective to prevent further transfer or negotiation of the instrument.

(b) An indorsement stating a condition to the right of the indorsee to receive payment does not affect the right of the indorsee to enforce the instrument. A person paying the instrument or taking it for value or collection may disregard the condition, and the rights and liabilities of that person are not affected by whether the condition has been fulfilled.

(c) If an instrument bears an indorsement (i) described in Section 4—201(b), or (ii) in blank or to a particular bank using the words "for deposit," "for collection," or other words indicating a purpose of having the instrument collected by a bank for the indorser or for a particular account, the following rules apply:

(1) A person, other than a bank, who purchases the instrument when so indorsed converts the instrument unless the amount paid for the instrument is received by the indorser or applied consistently with the indorsement.

(2) A depositary bank that purchases the instrument or takes it for collection when so indorsed converts the instrument unless the amount paid by the bank with respect to the instrument is received by the indorser or applied consistently with the indorsement.

(3) A payor bank that is also the depositary bank or that takes the instrument for immediate payment over the counter from a person other than a collecting bank converts the instrument unless the proceeds of the instrument are received by the indorser or applied consistently with the indorsement.

(4) Except as otherwise provided in paragraph (3), a payor bank or intermediary bank may disregard the indorsement and is not liable if the proceeds of the instrument are not received by the indorser or applied consistently with the indorsement.

(d) Except for an indorsement covered by subsection (c), if an instrument bears an indorsement using words to the effect that payment is to be made to the indorsee as agent, trustee, or other fiduciary for the benefit of the indorser or another person, the following rules apply:

(1) Unless there is notice of breach of fiduciary duty as provided in Section 3—307, a person who purchases the instrument from the indorsee or takes the instrument from the indorsee for collection or payment may pay the proceeds of payment or the value given for the instrument to the indorsee without regard to whether

the indorsee violates a fiduciary duty to the indorser.

(2) A subsequent transferee of the instrument or person who pays the instrument is neither given notice nor otherwise affected by the restriction in the indorsement unless the transferee or payor knows that the fiduciary dealt with the instrument or its proceeds in breach of fiduciary duty.

(e) The presence on an instrument of an indorsement to which this section applies does not prevent a purchaser of the instrument from becoming a holder in due course of the instrument unless the purchaser is a converter under subsection (c) or has notice or knowledge of breach of fiduciary duty as stated in subsection (d).

(f) In an action to enforce the obligation of a party to pay the instrument, the obligor has a defense if payment would violate an indorsement to which this section applies and the payment is not permitted by this section.

PART 3
Enforcement of Instruments

§ 3—302. Holder in Due Course.

(a) Subject to subsection (c) and Section 3—106(d), "holder in due course" means the holder of an instrument if:

(1) the instrument when issued or negotiated to the holder does not bear such apparent evidence of forgery or alteration or is not otherwise so irregular or incomplete as to call into question its authenticity; and

(2) the holder took the instrument (i) for value, (ii) in good faith, (iii) without notice that the instrument is overdue or has been dishonored or that there is an uncured default with respect to payment of another instrument issued as part of the same series, (iv) without notice that the instrument contains an unauthorized signature or has been altered, (v) without notice of any claim to the instrument described in Section 3—306, and (vi) without notice that any party has a defense or claim in recoupment described in Section 3—305(a).

(b) Notice of discharge of a party, other than discharge in an insolvency proceeding, is not notice of a defense under subsection (a), but discharge is effective against a person who became a holder in due course with notice of the discharge. Public filing or recording of a document does not of itself constitute notice of a defense, claim in recoupment, or claim to the instrument.

(c) Except to the extent a transferor or predecessor in interest has rights as a holder in due course, a person does not acquire rights of a holder in due course of an instrument taken (i) by legal process or by purchase in an execution, bankruptcy, or creditor's sale or similar proceeding, (ii) by purchase as part of a bulk transaction not in ordinary course of business of the transferor, or (iii) as the successor in interest to an estate or other organization.

(d) If, under Section 3—303(a)(1), the promise of performance that is the consideration for an instrument has been partially performed, the holder may assert rights as a holder in due course of the instrument only to the fraction of the amount payable under the instrument equal to the value of the partial performance divided by the value of the promised performance.

(e) If (i) the person entitled to enforce an instrument has only a security interest in the instrument and (ii) the person obliged to pay the instrument has a defense, claim in recoupment, or claim to the instrument that may be asserted against the person who granted the security interest, the person entitled to enforce the instrument may assert rights as a holder in due course only to an amount payable under the instrument which, at the time of enforcement of the instrument, does not exceed the amount of the unpaid obligation secured.

(f) To be effective, notice must be received at a time and in a manner that gives a reasonable opportunity to act on it.

(g) This section is subject to any law limiting status as a holder in due course in particular classes of transactions.

§ 3—304. Overdue Instrument.

(a) An instrument payable on demand becomes overdue at the earliest of the following times:

(1) on the day after the day demand for payment is duly made;

(2) if the instrument is a check, 90 days after its date; or

(3) if the instrument is not a check, when the instrument has been outstanding for a period of time after its date which is unreasonably long under the circumstances of the particular case in light of the nature of the instrument and usage of the trade.

(b) With respect to an instrument payable at a definite time the following rules apply:

(1) If the principal is payable in installments and a due date has not been accelerated, the instrument becomes overdue upon default under the instrument for nonpayment of an installment, and the instrument remains overdue until the default is cured.

(2) If the principal is not payable in installments and the due date has not been accelerated, the instrument becomes overdue on the day after the due date.

(3) If a due date with respect to principal has been accelerated, the instrument becomes overdue on the day after the accelerated due date.

(c) Unless the due date of principal has been accelerated, an instrument does not become overdue if there is default in payment of interest but no default in payment of principal.

§ 3—305. Defenses and Claims in Recoupment.

(a) Except as stated in subsection (b), the right to enforce the obligation of a party to pay an instrument is subject to the following:

(1) a defense of the obligor based on (i) infancy of the

obligor to the extent it is a defense to a simple contract, (ii) duress, lack of legal capacity, or illegality of the transaction which, under other law, nullifies the obligation of the obligor, (iii) fraud that induced the obligor to sign the instrument with neither knowledge nor reasonable opportunity to learn of its character or its essential terms, or (iv) discharge of the obligor in insolvency proceedings;

(2) a defense of the obligor stated in another section of this Article or a defense of the obligor that would be available if the person entitled to enforce the instrument were enforcing a right to payment under a simple contract; and

(3) a claim in recoupment of the obligor against the original payee of the instrument if the claim arose from the transaction that gave rise to the instrument; but the claim of the obligor may be asserted against a transferee of the instrument only to reduce the amount owing on the instrument at the time the action is brought.

(b) The right of a holder in due course to enforce the obligation of a party to pay the instrument is subject to defenses of the obligor stated in subsection (a)(1), but is not subject to defenses of the obligor stated in subsection (a)(2) or claims in recoupment stated in subsection (a)(3) against a person other than the holder.

(c) Except as stated in subsection (d), in an action to enforce the obligation of a party to pay the instrument, the obligor may not assert against the person entitled to enforce the instrument a defense, claim in recoupment, or claim to the instrument (Section 3—306) of another person, but the other person's claim to the instrument may be asserted by the obligor if the other person is joined in the action and personally asserts the claim against the person entitled to enforce the instrument. An obligor is not obliged to pay the instrument if the person seeking enforcement of the instrument does not have rights of a holder in due course and the obligor proves that the instrument is a lost or stolen instrument.

(d) In an action to enforce the obligation of an accommodation party to pay an instrument, the accommodation party may assert against the person entitled to enforce the instrument any defense or claim in recoupment under subsection (a) that the accommodated party could assert against the person entitled to enforce the instrument, except the defenses of discharge in insolvency proceedings, infancy, and lack of legal capacity.

PART 4
Liability of Parties

§ 3—402. Signature by Representative.

(a) If a person acting, or purporting to act, as a representative signs an instrument by signing either the name of the represented person or the name of the signer, the represented person is bound by the signature to the same extent the represented person would be bound if the signature were on a simple contract. If the represented person is bound, the signature of the representative is the "authorized signature of the represented person" and the represented person is liable on the instrument, whether or not identified in the instrument.

(b) If a representative signs the name of the representative to an instrument and the signature is an authorized signature of the represented person, the following rules apply:

(1) If the form of the signature shows unambiguously that the signature is made on behalf of the represented person who is identified in the instrument, the representative is not liable on the instrument.

(2) Subject to subsection (c), if (i) the form of the signature does not show unambiguously that the signature is made in a representative capacity or (ii) the represented person is not identified in the instrument, the representative is liable on the instrument to a holder in due course that took the instrument without notice that the representative was not intended to be liable on the instrument. With respect to any other person, the representative is liable on the instrument unless the representative proves that the original parties did not intend the representative to be liable on the instrument.

(c) If a representative signs the name of the representative as drawer of a check without indication of the representative status and the check is payable from an account of the represented person who is identified on the check, the signer is not liable on the check if the signature is an authorized signature of the represented person.

§ 3—404. Impostors; Fictitious Payees.

(a) If an impostor, by use of the mails or otherwise, induces the issuer of an instrument to issue the instrument to the impostor, or to a person acting in concert with the impostor, by impersonating the payee of the instrument or a person authorized to act for the payee, an indorsement of the instrument by any person in the name of the payee is effective as the indorsement of the payee in favor of a person who, in good faith, pays the instrument or takes it for value or for collection.

(b) If (i) a person whose intent determines to whom an instrument is payable (Section 3—110(a) or (b)) does not intend the person identified as payee to have any interest in the instrument, or (ii) the person identified as payee of an instrument is a fictitious person, the following rules apply until the instrument is negotiated by special indorsement:

(1) Any person in possession of the instrument is its holder.

(2) An indorsement by any person in the name of the payee stated in the instrument is effective as the indorsement of the payee in favor of a person who, in

good faith, pays the instrument or takes it for value or for collection.

(c) Under subsection (a) or (b), an indorsement is made in the name of a payee if (i) it is made in a name substantially similar to that of the payee or (ii) the instrument, whether or not indorsed, is deposited in a depositary bank to an account in a name substantially similar to that of the payee.

(d) With respect to an instrument to which subsection (a) or (b) applies, if a person paying the instrument or taking it for value or for collection fails to exercise ordinary care in paying or taking the instrument and that failure substantially contributes to loss resulting from payment of the instrument, the person bearing the loss may recover from the person failing to exercise ordinary care to the extent the failure to exercise ordinary care contributed to the loss.

§ 3—407. Alteration.

(a) "Alteration" means (i) an unauthorized change in an instrument that purports to modify in any respect the obligation of a party, or (ii) an unauthorized addition of words or numbers or other change to an incomplete instrument relating to the obligation of a party.

(b) Except as provided in subsection (c), an alteration fraudulently made discharges a party whose obligation is affected by the alteration unless that party assents or is precluded from asserting the alteration. No other alteration discharges a party, and the instrument may be enforced according to its original terms.

(c) A payor bank or drawee paying a fraudulently altered instrument or a person taking it for value, in good faith and without notice of the alteration, may enforce rights with respect to the instrument (i) according to its original terms, or (ii) in the case of an incomplete instrument altered by unauthorized completion, according to its terms as completed.

§ 3—409. Acceptance of Draft; Certified Check.

(a) "Acceptance" means the drawee's signed agreement to pay a draft as presented. It must be written on the draft and may consist of the drawee's signature alone. Acceptance may be made at any time and becomes effective when notification pursuant to instructions is given or the accepted draft is delivered for the purpose of giving rights on the acceptance to any person.

(b) A draft may be accepted although it has not been signed by the drawer, is otherwise incomplete, is overdue, or has been dishonored.

(c) If a draft is payable at a fixed period after sight and the acceptor fails to date the acceptance, the holder may complete the acceptance by supplying a date in good faith.

(d) "Certified check" means a check accepted by the bank on which it is drawn. Acceptance may be made as stated in subsection (a) or by a writing on the check which indicates that the check is certified. The drawee of a check has no obligation to certify the check, and refusal to certify is not dishonor of the check.

§ 3—414. Obligation of Drawer.

(a) This section does not apply to cashier's checks or other drafts drawn on the drawer.

(b) If an unaccepted draft is dishonored, the drawer is obliged to pay the draft (i) according to its terms at the time it was issued or, if not issued, at the time it first came into possession of a holder, or (ii) if the drawer signed an incomplete instrument, according to its terms when completed, to the extent stated in Sections 3—115 and 3—407. The obligation is owed to a person entitled to enforce the draft or to an indorser who paid the draft under Section 3—415.

(c) If a draft is accepted by a bank, the drawer is discharged, regardless of when or by whom acceptance was obtained.

(d) If a draft is accepted and the acceptor is not a bank, the obligation of the drawer to pay the draft if the draft is dishonored by the acceptor is the same as the obligation of an indorser under Section 3—415(a) and (c).

(e) If a draft states that it is drawn "without recourse" or otherwise disclaims liability of the drawer to pay the draft, the drawer is not liable under subsection (b) to pay the draft if the draft is not a check. A disclaimer of the liability stated in subsection (b) is not effective if the draft is a check.

(f) If (i) a check is not presented for payment or given to a depositary bank for collection within 30 days after its date, (ii) the drawee suspends payments after expiration of the 30-day period without paying the check, and (iii) because of the suspension of payments, the drawer is deprived of funds maintained with the drawee to cover payment of the check, the drawer to the extent deprived of funds may discharge its obligation to pay the check by assigning to the person entitled to enforce the check the rights of the drawer against the drawee with respect to the funds.

§ 3—415. Obligation of Indorser.

(a) Subject to subsections (b), (c), and (d) and to Section 3—419(d), if an instrument is dishonored, an indorser is obliged to pay the amount due on the instrument (i) according to the terms of the instrument at the time it was indorsed, or (ii) if the indorser indorsed an incomplete instrument, according to its terms when completed, to the extent stated in Sections 3—115 and 3—407. The obligation of the indorser is owed to a person entitled to enforce the instrument or to a subsequent indorser who paid the instrument under this section.

(b) If an indorsement states that it is made "without recourse" or otherwise disclaims liability of the indorser, the indorser is not liable under subsection (a) to pay the instrument.

(c) If notice of dishonor of an instrument is required by Section 3—503 and notice of dishonor complying with that section is not given to an indorser, the liability of the indorser under subsection (a) is discharged.

(d) If a draft is accepted by a bank after an indorsement is made, the liability of the indorser under subsection·(a) is discharged.

(e) If an indorser of a check is liable under subsection (a) and the check is not presented for payment, or given to a depositary bank for collection, within 30 days after the day the indorsement was made, the liability of the indorser under subsection (a) is discharged.

§ 3—416. Transfer Warranties.

(a) A person who transfers an instrument for consideration warrants to the transferee and, if the transfer is by indorsement, to any subsequent transferee that:

    (1) the warrantor is a person entitled to enforce the instrument;

    (2) all signatures on the instrument are authentic and authorized;

    (3) the instrument has not been altered;

    (4) the instrument is not subject to a defense or claim in recoupment of any party which can be asserted against the warrantor; and

    (5) the warrantor has no knowledge of any insolvency proceeding commenced with respect to the maker or acceptor or, in the case of an unaccepted draft, the drawer.

(b) A person to whom the warranties under subsection (a) are made and who took the instrument in good faith may recover from the warrantor as damages for breach of warranty an amount equal to the loss suffered as a result of the breach, but not more than the amount of the instrument plus expenses and loss of interest incurred as a result of the breach.

(c) The warranties stated in subsection (a) cannot be disclaimed with respect to checks. Unless notice of a claim for breach of warranty is given to the warrantor within 30 days after the claimant has reason to know of the breach and the identity of the warrantor, the liability of the warrantor under subsection (b) is discharged to the extent of any loss caused by the delay in giving notice of the claim.

(d) A [cause of action] for breach of warranty under this section accrues when the claimant has reason to know of the breach.

§ 3—417. Presentment Warranties.

(a) If an unaccepted draft is presented to the drawee for payment or acceptance and the drawee pays or accepts the draft, (i) the person obtaining payment or acceptance, at the time of presentment, and (ii) a previous transferor of the draft, at the time of transfer, warrant to the drawee making payment or accepting the draft in good faith that:

    (1) the warrantor is, or was, at the time the warrantor transferred the draft, a person entitled to enforce the draft or authorized to obtain payment or acceptance of the draft on behalf of a person entitled to enforce the draft;

    (2) the draft has not been altered; and

    (3) the warrantor has no knowledge that the signature of the drawer of the draft is unauthorized.

(b) A drawee making payment may recover from any warrantor damages for breach of warranty equal to the amount paid by the drawee less the amount the drawee received or is entitled to receive from the drawer because of the payment. In addition, the drawee is entitled to compensation for expenses and loss of interest resulting from the breach. The right of the drawee to recover damages under this subsection is not affected by any failure of the drawee to exercise ordinary care in making payment. If the drawee accepts the draft, breach of warranty is a defense to the obligation of the acceptor. If the acceptor makes payment with respect to the draft, the acceptor is entitled to recover from any warrantor for breach of warranty the amounts stated in this subsection.

(c) If a drawee asserts a claim for breach of warranty under subsection (a) based on an unauthorized indorsement of the draft or an alteration of the draft, the warrantor may defend by proving that the indorsement is effective under Section 3—404 or 3—405 or the drawer is precluded under Section 3—406 or 4—406 from asserting against the drawee the unauthorized indorsement or alteration.

(d) If (i) a dishonored draft is presented for payment to the drawer or an indorser or (ii) any other instrument is presented for payment to a party obliged to pay the instrument, and (iii) payment is received, the following rules apply:

    (1) The person obtaining payment and a prior transferor of the instrument warrant to the person making payment in good faith that the warrantor is, or was, at the time the warrantor transferred the instrument, a person entitled to enforce the instrument or authorized to obtain payment on behalf of a person entitled to enforce the instrument.

    (2) The person making payment may recover from any warrantor for breach of warranty an amount equal to the amount paid plus expenses and loss of interest resulting from the breach.

(e) The warranties stated in subsections (a) and (d) cannot be disclaimed with respect to checks. Unless notice of a claim for breach of warranty is given to the warrantor within 30 days after the claimant has reason to know of the breach and the identity of the warrantor, the liability of the warrantor under subsection (b) or (d) is discharged to the extent of any loss caused by the delay in giving notice of the claim.

(f) A [cause of action] for breach of warranty under this section accrues when the claimant has reason to know of the breach.

§ 3—419. Instruments Signed for Accommodation.

(a) If an instrument is issued for value given for the benefit of a party to the instrument ("accommodated party") and another party to the instrument ("accommodation party") signs the instrument for the purpose of incurring liability on the instrument without being a direct beneficiary of the value given for the instrument, the instrument is signed by the accommodation party "for accommodation."

(b) An accommodation party may sign the instrument as maker, drawer, acceptor, or indorser and, subject to subsection (d), is obliged to pay the instrument in the capacity in which the accommodation party signs. The obligation of an accommodation party may be enforced notwithstanding any statute of frauds and whether or not the accommodation party receives consideration for the accommodation.

(c) A person signing an instrument is presumed to be an accommodation party and there is notice that the instrument is signed for accommodation if the signature is an anomalous indorsement or is accompanied by words indicating that the signer is acting as surety or guarantor with respect to the obligation of another party to the instrument. Except as provided in Section 3—605, the obligation of an accommodation party to pay the instrument is not affected by the fact that the person enforcing the obligation had notice when the instrument was taken by that person that the accommodation party signed the instrument for accommodation.

(d) If the signature of a party to an instrument is accompanied by words indicating unambiguously that the party is guaranteeing collection rather than payment of the obligation of another party to the instrument, the signer is obliged to pay the amount due on the instrument to a person entitled to enforce the instrument only if (i) execution of judgment against the other party has been returned unsatisfied, (ii) the other party is insolvent or in an insolvency proceeding, (iii) the other party cannot be served with process, or (iv) it is otherwise apparent that payment cannot be obtained from the other party.

(e) An accommodation party who pays the instrument is entitled to reimbursement from the accommodated party and is entitled to enforce the instrument against the accommodated party. An accommodated party who pays the instrument has no right of recourse against, and is not entitled to contribution from, an accommodation party.

PART 5
Dishonor

§ 3—501. Presentment.

(a) "Presentment" means a demand made by or on behalf of a person entitled to enforce an instrument (i) to pay the instrument made to the drawee or a party obliged to pay the instrument or, in the case of a note or accepted draft payable at a bank, to the bank, or (ii) to accept a draft made to the drawee.

(b) The following rules are subject to Article 4, agreement of the parties, and clearing-house rules and the like:

(1) Presentment may be made at the place of payment of the instrument and must be made at the place of payment if the instrument is payable at a bank in the United States; may be made by any commercially reasonable means, including an oral, written, or electronic communication; is effective when the demand for payment or acceptance is received by the person to whom presentment is made; and is effective if made to any one of two or more makers, acceptors, drawees, or other payors.

(2) Upon demand of the person to whom presentment is made, the person making presentment must (i) exhibit the instrument, (ii) give reasonable identification and, if presentment is made on behalf of another person, reasonable evidence of authority to do so, and (. . .) sign a receipt on the instrument for any payment made or surrender the instrument if full payment is made.

(3) Without dishonoring the instrument, the party to whom presentment is made may (i) return the instrument for lack of a necessary indorsement, or (ii) refuse payment or acceptance for failure of the presentment to comply with the terms of the instrument, an agreement of the parties, or other applicable law or rule.

(4) The party to whom presentment is made may treat presentment as occurring on the next business day after the day of presentment if the party to whom presentment is made has established a cut-off hour not earlier than 2 p.m. for the receipt and processing of instruments presented for payment or acceptance and presentment is made after the cut-off hour.

PART 6
Discharge and Payment

§ 3—605. Discharge of Indorsers and Accommodation Parties.

(a) In this section, the term "indorser" includes a drawer having the obligation described in Section 3—414(d).

(b) Discharge, under Section 3—604, of the obligation of a party to pay an instrument does not discharge the obligation of an indorser or accommodation party having a right of recourse against the discharged party.

(c) If a person entitled to enforce an instrument agrees, with or without consideration, to an extension of the due date of the obligation of a party to pay the instrument, the extension discharges an indorser or accommodation party having a right of recourse against the party whose obligation is extended to the extent the indorser or accommodation party proves that the extension caused loss to the indorser or accommodation party with respect to the right of recourse.

(d) If a person entitled to enforce an instrument agrees, with or without consideration, to a material modification of the obligation of a party other than an extension of the due date, the modification discharges the obligation of an indorser or accommodation party having a right of recourse against the person whose obligation is modified to the extent the modification causes loss to the indorser or accommodation party with respect to the right of recourse. The loss suffered by the indorser or accommodation party as a result of the modification is equal to the amount of the right of recourse unless the person enforcing the instrument proves that no loss was caused by the modification or that the loss caused by the modification was an amount less than the amount of the right of recourse.

(e) If the obligation of a party to pay an instrument is secured by an interest in collateral and a person entitled to enforce the instrument impairs the value of the interest in collateral, the obligation of an indorser or accommodation party having a right of recourse against the obligor is discharged to the extent of the impairment. The value of an interest in collateral is impaired to the extent (i) the value of the interest is reduced to an amount less than the amount of the right of recourse of the party asserting discharge, or (ii) the reduction in value of the interest causes an increase in the amount by which the amount of the right of recourse exceeds the value of the interest. The burden of proving impairment is on the party asserting discharge.

(f) If the obligation of a party is secured by an interest in collateral not provided by an accommodation party and a person entitled to enforce the instrument impairs the value of the interest in collateral, the obligation of any party who is jointly and severally liable with respect to the secured obligation is discharged to the extent the impairment causes the party asserting discharge to pay more than that party would have been obliged to pay, taking into account rights of contribution, if impairment had not occurred. If the party asserting discharge is an accommodation party not entitled to discharge under subsection (e), the party is deemed to have a right to contribution based on joint and several liability rather than a right to reimbursement. The burden of proving impairment is on the party asserting discharge.

(g) Under subsection (e) or (f), impairing value of an interest in collateral includes (i) failure to obtain or maintain perfection or recordation of the interest in collateral, (ii) release of collateral without substitution of collateral of equal value, (iii) failure to perform a duty to preserve the value of collateral owed, under Article 9 or other law, to a debtor or surety or other person secondarily liable, or (iv) failure to comply with applicable law in disposing of collateral.

(h) An accommodation party is not discharged under subsection (c), (d), or (e) unless the person entitled to enforce the instrument knows of the accommodation or has notice under Section 3—419(c) that the instrument was signed for accommodation.

(i) A party is not discharged under this section if (i) the party asserting discharge consents to the event or conduct that is the basis of the discharge, or (ii) the instrument or

a separate agreement of the party provides for waiver of discharge under this section either specifically or by general language indicating that parties waive defenses based on suretyship or impairment of collateral.

Revised Article 4
BANK DEPOSITS AND COLLECTIONS

PART 2
Collection of Items: Depositary and Collecting Banks

§ 4—207. Transfer Warranties.

(a) A customer or collecting bank that transfers an item and receives a settlement or other consideration warrants to the transferee and to any subsequent collecting bank that:

(1) the warrantor is a person entitled to enforce the item;

(2) all signatures on the item are authentic and authorized;

(3) the item has not been altered;

(4) the item is not subject to a defense or claim in recoupment (Section 3—305(a)) of any party that can be asserted against the warrantor; and

(5) the warrantor has no knowledge of any insolvency proceeding commenced with respect to the maker or acceptor or, in the case of an unaccepted draft, the drawer.

(b) If an item is dishonored, a customer or collecting bank transferring the item and receiving settlement or other consideration is obliged to pay the amount due on the item (i) according to the terms of the item at the time it was transferred, or (ii) if the transfer was of an incomplete item, according to its terms when completed as stated in Sections 3—115 and 3—407. The obligation of a transferor is owed to the transferee and to any subsequent collecting bank that takes the item in good faith. A transferor cannot disclaim its obligation under this subsection by an indorsement stating that it is made "without recourse" or otherwise disclaiming liability.

(c) A person to whom the warranties under subsection (a) are made and who took the item in good faith may recover from the warrantor as damages for breach of warranty an amount equal to the loss suffered as a result of the breach, but not more than the amount of the item plus expenses and loss of interest incurred as a result of the breach.

(d) The warranties stated in subsection (a) cannot be disclaimed with respect to checks. Unless notice of a claim for breach of warranty is given to the warrantor within 30 days after the claimant has reason to know of the breach and the identity of the warrantor, the warrantor is discharged to the extent of any loss caused by the delay in giving notice of the claim.

(e) A cause of action for breach of warranty under this section accrues when the claimant has reason to know of the breach.

§ 4—208. Presentment Warranties.

(a) If an unaccepted draft is presented to the drawee for payment or acceptance and the drawee pays or accepts the draft, (i) the person obtaining payment or acceptance, at the time of presentment, and (ii) a previous transferor of the draft, at the time of transfer, warrant to the drawee that pays or accepts the draft in good faith that:

(1) the warrantor is, or was, at the time the warrantor transferred the draft, a person entitled to enforce the draft or authorized to obtain payment or acceptance of the draft on behalf of a person entitled to enforce the draft;

(2) the draft has not been altered; and

(3) the warrantor has no knowledge that the signature of the purported drawer of the draft is unauthorized.

(b) A drawee making payment may recover from a warrantor damages for breach of warranty equal to the amount paid by the drawee less the amount the drawee received or is entitled to receive from the drawer because of the payment. In addition, the drawee is entitled to compensation for expenses and loss of interest resulting from the breach. The right of the drawee to recover damages under this subsection is not affected by any failure of the drawee to exercise ordinary care in making payment. If the drawee accepts the draft (i) breach of warranty is a defense to the obligation of the acceptor, and (ii) if the acceptor makes payment with respect to the draft, the acceptor is entitled to recover from a warrantor for breach of warranty the amounts stated in this subsection.

(c) If a drawee asserts a claim for breach of warranty under subsection (a) based on an unauthorized indorsement of the draft or an alteration of the draft, the warrantor may defend by proving that the indorsement is effective under Section 3—404 or 3—405 or the drawer is precluded under Section 3—406 or 4—406 from asserting against the drawee the unauthorized indorsement or alteration.

(d) If (i) a dishonored draft is presented for payment to the drawer or an indorser or (ii) any other item is presented for payment to a party obliged to pay the item, and the item is paid, the person obtaining payment and a prior transferor of the item warrant to the person making payment in good faith that the warrantor is, or was, at the time the warrantor transferred the item, a person entitled to enforce the item or authorized to obtain payment on behalf of a person entitled to enforce the item. The person making payment may recover from any warrantor for breach of warranty an amount equal to the amount paid plus expenses and loss of interest resulting from the breach.

(e) The warranties stated in subsections (a) and (d) cannot be disclaimed with respect to checks. Unless notice of a claim for breach of warranty is given to the warrantor within 30 days after the claimant has reason to know of the breach and the identity of the warrantor, the warrantor is discharged to the extent of any loss caused by the delay in giving notice of the claim.

(f) A cause of action for breach of warranty under this section accrues when the claimant has reason to know of the breach.

§ 4—213. Medium and Time of Settlement by Bank.

(a) With respect to settlement by a bank, the medium and time of settlement may be prescribed by Federal Reserve regulations or circulars, clearing-house rules, and the like, or agreement. In the absence of such prescription:

(1) the medium of settlement is cash or credit to an account in a Federal Reserve bank of or specified by the person to receive settlement; and

(2) the time of settlement is:

(i) with respect to tender of settlement by cash, a cashier's check, or teller's check, when the cash or check is sent or delivered;

(ii) with respect to tender of settlement by credit in an account in a Federal Reserve Bank, when the credit is made;

(iii) with respect to tender of settlement by a credit or debit to an account in a bank, when the credit or debit is made or, in the case of tender of settlement by authority to charge an account, when the authority is sent or delivered; or

(iv) with respect to tender of settlement by a funds transfer, when payment is made pursuant to Section 4A—406(a) to the person receiving settlement.

(b) If the tender of settlement is not by a medium authorized by subsection (a) or the time of settlement is not fixed by subsection (a), no settlement occurs until the tender of settlement is accepted by the person receiving settlement.

(c) If settlement for an item is made by cashier's check or teller's check and the person receiving settlement, before its midnight deadline:

(1) presents or forwards the check for collection, settlement is final when the check is finally paid; or

(2) fails to present or forward the check for collection, settlement is final at the midnight deadline of the person receiving settlement.

(d) If settlement for an item is made by giving authority to charge the account of the bank giving settlement in the bank receiving settlement, settlement is final when the charge is made by the bank receiving settlement if there are funds available in the account for the amount of the item.

PART 4
Relationship between Payor Bank and Its Customer

§ 4—401. When Bank May Charge Customer's Account.

(a) A bank may charge against the account of a customer an item that is properly payable from the account even though the charge creates an overdraft. An item is properly payable if it is authorized by the customer and is in accordance with any agreement between the customer and bank.

(b) A customer is not liable for the amount of an overdraft if the customer neither signed the item nor benefited from the proceeds of the item.

(c) A bank may charge against the account of a customer a check that is otherwise properly payable from the account, even though payment was made before the date of the check, unless the customer has given notice to the bank of the postdating describing the check with reasonable certainty. The notice is effective for the period stated in Section 4—403(b) for stop-payment orders, and must be received at such time and in such manner as to afford the bank a reasonable opportunity to act on it before the bank takes any action with respect to the check described in Section 4—303. If a bank charges against the account of a customer a check before the date stated in the notice of postdating, the bank is liable for damages for the loss resulting from its act. The loss may include damages for dishonor of subsequent items under Section 4—402.

(d) A bank that in good faith makes payment to a holder may charge the indicated account of its customer according to:

(1) the original terms of the altered item; or

(2) the terms of the completed item, even though the bank knows the item has been completed unless the bank has notice that the completion was improper.

§ 4—403. Customer's Right to Stop Payment; Burden of Proof of Loss.

(a) A customer or any person authorized to draw on the account if there is more than one person may stop payment of any item drawn on the customer's account or close the account by an order to the bank describing the item or account with reasonable certainty received at a time and in a manner that affords the bank a reasonable opportunity to act on it before any action by the bank with respect to the item described in Section 4—303. If the signature of more than one person is required to draw on an account, any of these persons may stop payment or close the account.

(b) A stop-payment order is effective for six months, but it lapses after 14 calendar days if the original order was oral and was not confirmed in writing within that period. A stop-payment order may be renewed for additional six-month periods by a writing given to the bank within a period during which the stop-payment order is effective.

(c) The burden of establishing the fact and amount of loss resulting from the payment of an item contrary to a stop-payment order or order to close an account is on the customer. The loss from payment of an item contrary to a stop-payment order may include damages for dishonor of subsequent items under Section 4—402.

§ 4—405. Death or Incompetence of Customer.

(a) A payor or collecting bank's authority to accept, pay, or collect an item or to account for proceeds of its collection, if otherwise effective, is not rendered ineffective by incompetence of a customer of either bank existing at the time the item is issued or its collection is undertaken if the bank does not know of an adjudication of incompetence. Neither death nor incompetence of a customer revokes the authority to accept, pay, collect, or account until the bank knows of the fact of death or of an adjudication of incompetence and has reasonable opportunity to act on it.

(b) Even with knowledge, a bank may for 10 days after the date of death pay or certify checks drawn on or before the date unless ordered to stop payment by a person claiming an interest in the account.

§ 4—406. Customer's Duty to Discover and Report Unauthorized Signature or Alteration.

(a) A bank that sends or makes available to a customer a statement of account showing payment of items for the account shall either return or make available to the customer the items paid or provide information in the statement of account sufficient to allow the customer reasonably to identify the items paid. The statement of account provides sufficient information if the item is described by item number, amount, and date of payment.

(b) If the items are not returned to the customer, the person retaining the items shall either retain the items or, if the items are destroyed, maintain the capacity to furnish legible copies of the items until the expiration of seven years after receipt of the items. A customer may request an item from the bank that paid the item, and that bank must provide in a reasonable time either the item or, if the item has been destroyed or is not otherwise obtainable, a legible copy of the item.

(c) If a bank sends or makes available a statement of account or items pursuant to subsection (a), the customer must exercise reasonable promptness in examining the statement or the items to determine whether any payment was not authorized because of an alteration of an item or because a purported signature by or on behalf of the customer was not authorized. If, based on the statement or items provided, the customer should reasonably have discovered the unauthorized payment, the customer must promptly notify the bank of the relevant facts.

(d) If the bank proves that the customer failed, with respect to an item, to comply with the duties imposed on the customer by subsection (c), the customer is precluded from asserting against the bank:

(1) the customer's unauthorized signature or any alteration on the item, if the bank also proves that it suffered a loss by reason of the failure; and

(2) the customer's unauthorized signature or alteration by the same wrongdoer on any other item paid in good faith by the bank if the payment was made before the bank received notice from the customer of the unauthorized signature or alteration and after the customer had been afforded a reasonable period of time, not exceeding 30 days, in which to examine the item or statement of account and notify the bank.

(e) If subsection (d) applies and the customer proves that the bank failed to exercise ordinary care in paying the item and that the failure substantially contributed to loss, the loss is allocated between the customer precluded and the bank asserting the preclusion according to the extent to which the failure of the customer to comply with subsection (c) and the failure of the bank to exercise ordinary care contributed to the loss. If the customer proves that the bank did not pay the item in good faith, the preclusion under subsection (d) does not apply.

(f) Without regard to care or lack of care of either the customer or the bank, a customer who does not within one year after the statement or items are made available to the customer (subsection (a)) discover and report the customer's unauthorized signature on or any alteration on the item is precluded from asserting against the bank the unauthorized signature or alteration. If there is a preclusion under this subsection, the payor bank may not recover for breach or warranty under Section 4—208 with respect to the unauthorized signature or alteration to which the preclusion applies.

Article 4A
FUNDS TRANSFERS

PART 1
Subject Matter and Definitions

§ 4A—108. Exclusion of Consumer Transactions Governed by Federal Law.

This Article does not apply to a funds transfer any part of which is governed by the Electronic Fund Transfer Act of 1978 (Title XX, Public Law 95—630, 92 Stat. 3728, 15 U.S.C. § 1693 et seq.) as amended from time to time.

PART 2
Issue and Acceptance of Payment Order

§ 4A—201. Security Procedure.

"Security procedure" means a procedure established by agreement of a customer and a receiving bank for the pur-

pose of (i) verifying that a payment order or communication amending or cancelling a payment order is that of the customer, or (ii) detecting error in the transmission or the content of the payment order or communication. A security procedure may require the use of algorithms or other codes, identifying words or numbers, encryption, callback procedures, or similar security devices. Comparison of a signature on a payment order or communication with an authorized specimen signature of the customer is not by itself a security procedure.

PART 4
Payment

§ 4A—406. Payment by Originator to Beneficiary; Discharge of Underlying Obligation.

(a) Subject to Sections 4A—211(e), 4A—405(d), and 4A—405(e), the originator of a funds transfer pays the beneficiary of the originator's payment order (i) at the time a payment order for the benefit of the beneficiary is accepted by the beneficiary's bank in the funds transfer and (ii) in an amount equal to the amount of the order accepted by the beneficiary's bank, but not more than the amount of the originator's order.

(b) If payment under subsection (a) is made to satisfy an obligation, the obligation is discharged to the same extent discharge would result from payment to the beneficiary of the same amount in money, unless (i) the payment under subsection (a) was made by a means prohibited by the contract of the beneficiary with respect to the obligation, (ii) the beneficiary, within a reasonable time after receiving notice of receipt of the order by the beneficiary's bank, notified the originator of the beneficiary's refusal of the payment, (iii) funds with respect to the order were not withdrawn by the beneficiary or applied to a debt of the beneficiary, and (iv) the beneficiary would suffer a loss that could reasonably have been avoided if payment had been made by a means complying with the contract. If payment by the originator does not result in discharge under this section, the originator is subrogated to the rights of the beneficiary to receive payment from the beneficiary's bank under Section 4A—404(a).

(c) For the purpose of determining whether discharge of an obligation occurs under subsection (b), if the beneficiary's bank accepts a payment order in an amount equal to the amount of the originator's payment order less charges of one or more receiving banks in the funds transfer, payment to the beneficiary is deemed to be in the amount of the originator's order unless upon demand by the beneficiary the originator does not pay the beneficiary the amount of the deducted charges.

(d) Rights of the originator or of the beneficiary of a funds transfer under this section may be varied only by agreement of the originator and the beneficiary.

Article 5
LETTERS OF CREDIT

§ 5—103. Definitions.

(1) In this Article unless the context otherwise requires

(a) "Credit" or "letter of credit" means an engagement by a bank or other person made at the request of a customer and of a kind within the scope of this Article (Section 5—102) that the issuer will honor drafts or other demands for payment upon compliance with the conditions specified in the credit. A credit may be either revocable or irrevocable. The engagement may be either an agreement to honor or a statement that the bank or other person is authorized to honor.

(b) A "documentary draft" or a "documentary demand for payment" is one honor of which is conditioned upon the presentation of a document or documents. "Document" means any paper including document of title, security, invoice, certificate, notice of default and the like.

(c) An "issuer" is a bank or other person issuing a credit.

(d) A "beneficiary" of a credit is a person who is entitled under its terms to draw or demand payment.

(e) An "advising bank" is a bank which gives notification of the issuance of a credit by another bank.

(f) A "confirming bank" is a bank which engages either that it will itself honor a credit already issued by another bank or that such a credit will be honored by the issuer or a third bank.

(g) A "customer" is a buyer or other person who causes an issuer to issue a credit. The term also includes a bank which procures issuance or confirmation on behalf of that bank's customer.

(2) Other definitions applying to this Article and the sections in which they appear are:

"Notation of Credit". Section 5—108.

"Presenter". Section 5—112(3).

(3) Definitions in other Articles applying to this Article and the sections in which they appear are:

"Accept" or "Acceptance". Section 3—410.

"Contract for sale". Section 2—106.

"Draft". Section 3—104.

"Holder in due course". Section 3—302.

"Midnight deadline". Section 4—104.

"Security". Section 8—102.

(4) In addition, Article 1 contains general definitions and principles of construction and interpretation applicable throughout this Article.

§ 5—107. Advice of Credit; Confirmation; Error in Statement of Terms.

(1) Unless otherwise specified an advising bank by advising a credit issued by another bank does not assume any obligation to honor drafts drawn or demands for payment made under the credit but it does assume obligation for the accuracy of its own statement.

(2) A confirming bank by confirming a credit becomes directly obligated on the credit to the extent of its confirmation as though it were its issuer and acquires the rights of an issuer.

(3) Even though an advising bank incorrectly advises the terms of a credit it has been authorized to advise the credit is established as against the issuer to the extent of its original terms.

(4) Unless otherwise specified the customer bears as against the issuer all risks of transmission and reasonable translation or interpretation of any message relating to a credit.

Article 7
WAREHOUSE RECEIPTS, BILLS OF LADING AND OTHER DOCUMENTS OF TITLE

PART 1
General

§ 7—102. Definitions and Index of Definitions.

(1) In this Article, unless the context otherwise requires:

(a) "Bailee" means the person who by a warehouse receipt, bill of lading or other document of title acknowledges possession of goods and contracts to deliver them.

(b) "Consignee" means the person named in a bill to whom or to whose order the bill promises delivery.

(c) "Consignor" means the person named in a bill as the person from whom the goods have been received for shipment.

(d) "Delivery order" means a written order to deliver goods directed to a warehouseman, carrier or other person who in the ordinary course of business issues warehouse receipts or bills of lading.

(e) "Document" means document of title as defined in the general definitions in Article 1 (Section 1—201).

(f) "Goods" means all things which are treated as movable for the purposes of a contract of storage or transportation.

(g) "Issuer" means a bailee who issues a document except that in relation to an unaccepted delivery order it means the person who orders the possessor of goods to deliver. Issuer includes any person for whom an agent or employee purports to act in issuing a document if the agent or employee has real or apparent authority to issue documents, notwithstanding that the issuer received no goods or that the goods were misdescribed or that in any other respect the agent or employee violated his instructions.

(h) "Warehouseman" is a person engaged in the business of storing goods for hire.

(2) Other definitions applying to this Article or to specified Parts thereof, and the sections in which they appear are:

"Duly negotiate." Section 7—501.

"Person entitled under the document." Section 7—403(4).

(3) Definitions in other Articles applying to this Article and the sections in which they appear are:

"Contract for sale." Section 2—106.

"Overseas." Section 2—323.

"Receipt" of goods. Section 2—103.

(4) In addition Article 1 contains general definitions and principles of construction and interpretation applicable throughout this Article.
the provisions of this Article are subject thereto.

§ 7—104. Negotiable and Nonnegotiable Warehouse Receipt, Bill of Lading or Other Document of Title.

(1) A warehouse receipt, bill of lading or other document of title is negotiable

(a) if by its terms the goods are to be delivered to bearer or to the order of a named person; or

(b) where recognized in overseas trade, if it runs to a named person or assigns.

(2) Any other document is nonnegotiable. A bill of lading in which it is stated that the goods are consigned to a named person is not made negotiable by a provision that the goods are to be delivered only against a written order signed by the same or another named person.

PART 2
Warehouse Receipts: Special Provisions

§ 7—202. Form of Warehouse Receipt; Essential Terms; Optional Terms.

(1) A warehouse receipt need not be in any particular form.

(2) Unless a warehouse receipt embodies within its written or printed terms each of the following, the warehouseman is liable for damages caused by the omission to a person injured thereby:

(a) the location of the warehouse where the goods are stored;

(b) the date of issue of the receipt;

(c) the consecutive number of the receipt;

(d) a statement whether the goods received will be delivered to the bearer, to a specified person, or to a specified person or his order;

(e) the rate of storage and handling charges, except that where goods are stored under a field warehousing arrangement a statement of that fact is sufficient on a nonnegotiable receipt;

(f) a description of the goods or of the packages containing them;

(g) the signature of the warehouseman, which may be made by his authorized agent;

(h) if the receipt is issued for goods of which the warehouseman is owner, either solely or jointly or in common with others, the fact of such ownership; and

(i) a statement of the amount of advances made and of liabilities incurred for which the warehouseman claims a lien or security interest (Section 7—209). If the precise amount of such advances made or of such liabilities incurred is, at the time of the issue of the receipt, unknown to the warehouseman or to his agent who issues it, a statement of the fact that advances have been made or liabilities incurred and the purpose thereof is sufficient.

(3) A warehouseman may insert in his receipt any other terms which are not contrary to the provisions of this Act and do not impair his obligation of delivery (Section 7—403) or his duty of care (Section 7—204). Any contrary provisions shall be ineffective.

§ 7—204. Duty of Care; Contractual Limitation of Warehouseman's Liability.

(1) A warehouseman is liable for damages for loss of or injury to the goods caused by his failure to exercise such care in regard to them as a reasonably careful man would exercise under like circumstances but unless otherwise agreed he is not liable for damages which could not have been avoided by the exercise of such care.

(2) Damages may be limited by a term in the warehouse receipt or storage agreement limiting the amount of liability in case of loss or damage, and setting forth a specific liability per article or item, or value per unit of weight, beyond which the warehouseman shall not be liable; provided, however, that such liability may on written request of the bailor at the time of signing such storage agreement or within a reasonable time after receipt of the warehouse receipt be increased on part or all of the goods thereunder, in which event increased rates may be charged based on such increased valuation, but that no such increase shall be permitted contrary to a lawful limitation of liability contained in the warehouseman's tariff, if any. No such limitation is effective with respect to the warehouseman's liability for conversion to his own use.

(3) Reasonable provisions as to the time and manner of presenting claims and instituting actions based on the bailment may be included in the warehouse receipt or tariff.

(4) This section does not impair or repeal . . .

PART 3
Bills of Lading: Special Provisions

§ 7—301. Liability for Nonreceipt or Misdescription; "Said to Contain"; "Shipper's Load and Count"; Improper Handling.

(1) A consignee of a nonnegotiable bill who has given value in good faith or a holder to whom a negotiable bill has been duly negotiated relying in either case upon the description therein of the goods, or upon the date therein

shown, may recover from the issuer damages caused by the misdating of the bill or the nonreceipt or misdescription of the goods, except to the extent that the document indicates that the issuer does not know whether any part of all of the goods in fact were received or conform to the description, as where the description is in terms of marks or labels or kind, quantity, or condition or the receipt or description is qualified by "contents or condition of contents of packages unknown", "said to contain", "shipper's weight, load and count" or the like, if such indication be true.

(2) When goods are loaded by an issuer who is a common carrier, the issuer must count the packages of goods if package freight and ascertain the kind and quantity if bulk freight. In such cases "shipper's weight, load and count" or other words indicating that the description was made by the shipper are ineffective except as to freight concealed by packages.

(3) When bulk freight is loaded by a shipper who makes available to the issuer adequate facilities for weighing such freight, an issuer who is a common carrier must ascertain the kind and quantity within a reasonable time after receiving the written request of the shipper to do so. In such cases "shipper's weight" or other words of like purport are ineffective.

(4) The issuer may by inserting in the bill the words "shipper's weight, load and count" or other words of like purport indicate that the goods were loaded by the shipper; and if such statement be true the issuer shall not be liable for damages caused by the improper loading. But their omission does not imply liability for such damages.

(5) The shipper shall be deemed to have guaranteed to the issuer the accuracy at the time of shipment of the description, marks, labels, number, kind, quantity, condition and weight, as furnished by him; and the shipper shall indemnify the issuer against damage caused by inaccuracies in such particulars. The right of the issuer to such indemnity shall in no way limit his responsibility and liability under the contract of carriage to any person other than the shipper.

PART 4
Warehouse Receipts and Bills of Lading: General Obligations

§ 7—401. Irregularities in Issue of Receipt or Bill or Conduct of Issuer.

The obligations imposed by this Article on an issuer apply to a document of title regardless of the fact that

(a) the document may not comply with the requirements of this Article or of any other law or regulation regarding its issue, form or content; or

(b) the issuer may have violated laws regulating the conduct of his business; or

(c) the goods covered by the document were owned by the bailee at the time the document was issued; or

(d) the person issuing the document does not come within the definition of warehouseman if it purports to be a warehouse receipt.

§ 7—402. Duplicate Receipt or Bill; Overissue.

Neither a duplicate nor any other document of title purporting to cover goods already represented by an outstanding document of the same issuer confers any right in the goods, except as provided in the case of bills in a set, overissue of documents for fungible goods and substitutes for lost, stolen or destroyed documents. But the issuer is liable for damages caused by his overissue or failure to identify a duplicate document as such by conspicuous notation on its face.

§ 7—403. Obligation of Warehouseman or Carrier to Deliver; Excuse.

(1) The bailee must deliver the goods to a person entitled under the document who complies with subsections (2) and (3), unless and to the extent that the bailee establishes any of the following:

(a) delivery of the goods to a person whose receipt was rightful as against the claimant;

(b) damage to or delay, loss or destruction of the goods for which the bailee is not liable [, but the burden of establishing negligence in such cases is on the person entitled under the document];

(c) previous sale or other disposition of the goods in lawful enforcement of a lien or on warehouseman's lawful termination of storage;

(d) the exercise by a seller of his right to stop delivery pursuant to the provisions of the Article on Sales (Section 2—705);

(e) a diversion, reconsignment or other disposition pursuant to the provisions of this Article (Section 7—303) or tariff regulating such right;

(f) release, satisfaction or any other fact affording a personal defense against the claimant;

(g) any other lawful excuse.

(2) A person claiming goods covered by a document of title must satisfy the bailee's lien where the bailee so requests or where the bailee is prohibited by law from delivering the goods until the charges are paid.

(3) Unless the person claiming is one against whom the document confers no right under Sec. 7—503(1), he must surrender for cancellation or notation of partial deliveries any outstanding negotiable document covering the goods, and the bailee must cancel the document or conspicuously note the partial delivery thereon or be liable to any person to whom the document is duly negotiated.

(4) "Person entitled under the document" means holder in the case of a negotiable document, or the person to whom delivery is to be made by the terms of or pursuant to written instructions under a nonnegotiable document.

§ 7—404. No Liability for Good Faith Delivery Pursuant to Receipt or Bill.

A bailee who in good faith including observance of

reasonable commercial standards has received goods and delivered or otherwise disposed of them according to the terms of the document of title or pursuant to this Article is not liable therefor. This rule applies even though the person from whom he received the goods had no authority to procure the document or to dispose of the goods and even though the person to whom he delivered the goods had no authority to receive them.

PART 5
Warehouse Receipts and Bills of Lading: Negotiation and Transfer

§ 7—501. Form of Negotiation and Requirements of "Due Negotiation."

(1) A negotiable document of title running to the order of a named person is negotiated by his indorsement and delivery. After his indorsement in blank or to bearer any person can negotiate it by delivery alone.

(2)(a) A negotiable document of title is also negotiated by delivery alone when by its original terms it runs to bearer.

(b) When a document running to the order of a named person is delivered to him the effect is the same as if the document had been negotiated.

(3) Negotiation of a negotiable document of title after it has been indorsed to a specified person requires indorsement by the special indorsee as well as delivery.

(4) A negotiable document of title is "duly negotiated" when it is negotiated in the manner stated in this section to a holder who purchases it in good faith without notice of any defense against or claim to it on the part of any person and for value, unless it is established that the negotiation is not in the regular course of business or financing or involves receiving the document in settlement or payment of a money obligation.

(5) Indorsement of a nonnegotiable document neither makes it negotiable nor adds to the transferee's rights.

(6) The naming in a negotiable bill of a person to be notified of the arrival of the goods does not limit the negotiability of the bill nor constitute notice to a purchaser thereof of any interest of such person in the goods.

§ 7—502. Rights Acquired by Due Negotiation.

(1) Subject to the following section and to the provisions of Section 7—205 on fungible goods, a holder to whom a negotiable document of title has been duly negotiated acquires thereby:

(a) title to the document;

(b) title to the goods;

(c) all rights accruing under the law of agency or estoppel, including rights to goods delivered to the bailee after the document was issued; and

(d) the direct obligation of the issuer to hold or deliver the goods according to the terms of the document free of any defense or claim by him except those arising under the terms of the document or under this Article. In the case of a delivery order the bailee's obligation accrues only upon acceptance and the obligation acquired by the holder is that the issuer and any indorser will procure the acceptance of the bailee.

(2) Subject to the following section, title and rights so acquired are not defeated by any stoppage of the goods represented by the document or by surrender of such goods by the bailee, and are not impaired even though the negotiation or any prior negotiation constituted a breach of duty or even though any person has been deprived of possession of the document by misrepresentation, fraud, accident, mistake, duress, loss, theft or conversion, or even though a previous sale or other transfer of the goods or document has been made to a third person.

§ 7—507. Warranties on Negotiation or Transfer of Receipt or Bill.

Where a person negotiates or transfers a document of title for value otherwise than as a mere intermediary under the next following section, then unless otherwise agreed he warrants to his immediate purchaser only in addition to any warranty made in selling the goods

(a) that the document is genuine; and

(b) that he has no knowledge of any fact which would impair its validity or worth; and

(c) that his negotiation or transfer is rightful and fully effective with respect to the title to the document and the goods it represents.

Article 8
INVESTMENT SECURITIES
PART 1
Short Title and General Matters

§ 8—102. Definitions and Index of Definitions.

(1) In this Article, unless the context otherwise requires:

(a) A "certificated security" is a share, participation, or other interest in property of or an enterprise of the issuer or an obligation of the issuer which is

(i) represented by an instrument issued in bearer or registered form;

(ii) of a type commonly dealt in on securities exchanges or markets or commonly recognized in any area in which it is issued or dealt in as a medium for investment; and

(iii) either one of a class or series or by its terms divisible into a class or series of shares, participations, interests, or obligations.

(b) An "uncertificated security" is a share, participation, or other interest in property or an enterprise of the issuer or an obligation of the issuer which is

(i) not represented by an instrument and the transfer of which is registered upon books maintained for that purpose by or on behalf of the issuer;

(ii) of a type commonly dealt in on securities exchanges or markets; and

(iii) either one of a class or series or by its terms divisible into a class or series of shares, participations, interests, or obligations.

(c) A "security" is either a certificated or an uncertificated security. If a security is certificated, the terms "security" and "certificated security" may mean either the intangible interest, the instrument representing that interest, or both, as the context requires. A writing that is a certificated security is governed by this Article and not by Article 3, even though it also meets the requirements of that Article. This Article does not apply to money. If a certificated security has been retained by or surrendered to the issuer or its transfer agent for reasons other than registration of transfer, other temporary purpose, payment, exchange, or acquisition by the issuer, that security shall be treated as an uncertificated security for purposes of this Article.

(d) A certificated security is in "registered form" if

(i) it specifies a person entitled to the security or the rights it represents; and

(ii) its transfer may be registered upon books maintained for that purpose by or on behalf of the issuer, or the security so states.

(e) A certificated security is in "bearer form" if it runs to bearer according to its terms and not by reason of any indorsement.

(2) A "subsequent purchaser" is a person who takes other than by original issue.

(3) A "clearing corporation" is a corporation registered as a "clearing agency" under the federal securities laws or a corporation:

(a) at least 90 percent of whose capital stock is held by or for one or more organizations, none of which, other than a national securities exchange or association, holds in excess of 20 percent of the capital stock of the corporation, and each of which is

(i) subject to supervision or regulation pursuant to the provisions of federal or state banking laws or state insurance laws,

(ii) a broker or dealer or investment company registered under the federal securities laws, or

(iii) a national securities exchange or association registered under the federal securities laws; and

(b) any remaining capital stock of which is held by individuals who have purchased it at or prior to the time of their taking office as directors of the corporation and who have purchased only so much of the capital stock as is necessary to permit them to qualify as directors.

(4) A "custodian bank" is a bank or trust company that is supervised and examined by state or federal authority having supervision over banks and is acting as custodian for a clearing corporation.

(5) Other definitions applying to this Article or to specified Parts thereof and the sections in which they appear are:

"Adverse claim." Section 8—302.
"Bona fide purchaser." Section 8—302.
"Broker." Section 8—303.
"Debtor." Section 9—105.
"Financial intermediary." Section 8—313.
"Guarantee of the signature." Section 8—402.
"Initial transaction statement." Section 8—408.
"Instruction." Section 8—308.
"Intermediary bank." Section 4—105.
"Issuer." Section 8—201.
"Overissue." Section 8—104.
"Secured Party." Section 9—105.
"Security Agreement." Section 9—105.

(6) In addition, Article 1 contains general definitions and principles of construction and interpretation applicable throughout this Article.
Amended in 1962, 1973 and 1977.

Article 9
SECURED TRANSACTIONS; SALES OF ACCOUNTS AND CHATTEL PAPER
PART 1
Short Title, Applicability and Definitions

§ 9—106. Definitions: "Account"; "General Intangibles."

"Account" means any right to payment for goods sold or leased or for services rendered which is not evidenced by an instrument or chattel paper, whether or not it has been earned by performance. "General intangibles" means any personal property (including things in action) other than goods, accounts, chattel paper, documents, instruments, investment property, rights to proceeds of written letters of credit, and money. All rights to payment earned or unearned under a charter or other contract involving the use or hire of a vessel and all rights incident to the charter or contract are accounts.

§ 9—107. Definitions: "Purchase Money Security Interest."

A security interest is a "purchase money security interest" to the extent that it is

(a) taken or retained by the seller of the collateral to secure all or part of its price; or

(b) taken by a person who by making advances or incurring an obligation gives value to enable the debtor to acquire rights in or the use of collateral if such value is in fact so used.

§ 9—108. When After-Acquired Collateral Not Security for Antecedent Debt.

Where a secured party makes an advance, incurs an obligation, releases a perfected security interest, or otherwise gives new value which is to be secured in whole or in part by after-acquired property his security interest in the after-acquired collateral shall be deemed to be taken for new value and not as security for an antecedent debt if the debtor acquires his rights in such collateral either in the ordinary course of his business or under a contract of purchase made pursuant to the security agreement within a reasonable time after new value is given.

§ 9—109. Classification of Goods; "Consumer Goods"; "Equipment"; "Farm Products"; "Inventory."Goods are

(1) "consumer goods" if they are used or bought for use primarily for personal, family or household purposes;

(2) "equipment" if they are used or bought for use primarily in business (including farming or a profession) or by a debtor who is a non-

profit organization or a governmental subdivision or agency or if the goods are not included in the definitions of inventory, farm products or consumer goods;

(3) "farm products" if they are crops or livestock or supplies used or produced in farming operations or if they are products of crops or livestock in their unmanufactured states (such as ginned cotton, wool-clip, maple syrup, milk and eggs), and if they are in the possession of a debtor engaged in raising, fattening, grazing or other farming operations. If goods are farm products they are neither equipment nor inventory;

(4) "inventory" if they are held by a person who holds them for sale or lease or to be furnished under contracts of service or if he has so furnished them, or if they are raw materials, work in process or materials used or consumed in a business. Inventory of a person is not to be classified as his equipment.

§ 9—110. Sufficiency of Description.

For purposes of this Article any description of personal property or real estate is sufficient whether or not it is specific if it reasonably identifies what is described.

§ 9—112. Where Collateral Is Not Owned by Debtor.

Unless otherwise agreed, when a secured party knows that collateral is owned by a person who is not the debtor, the owner of the collateral is entitled to receive from the secured party any surplus under Section 9—502(2) or under Section 9—504(1), and is not liable for the debt or for any deficiency after resale, and he has the same right as the debtor

(a) to receive statements under Section 9—208;

(b) to receive notice of and to object to a secured party's proposal to retain the collateral in satisfaction of the indebtedness under Section 9—505;

(c) to redeem the collateral under Section 9—506;

(d) to obtain injunctive or other relief under Section 9—507(1); and

(e) to recover losses caused to him under Section 9—208(2).

PART 2
Validity of Security Agreement and Rights of Parties Thereto

§ 9—201. General Validity of Security Agreement.

Except as otherwise provided by this Act a security agreement is effective according to its terms between the parties, against purchasers of the collateral and against creditors. Nothing in this Article validates any charge or practice illegal under any statute or regulation thereunder governing usury, small loans, retail installment sales, or the like, or extends the application of any such statute or regulation to any transaction not otherwise subject thereto.

§ 9—203. Attachment and Enforceability of Security Interest; Proceeds; Formal Requisites.

(1) Subject to the provisions of Section 4—208 on the security interest of a collecting bank, Section 8—321 on security interests in securities and Section 9—113 on a security interest arising under the Article on Sales, a security interest is not enforceable against the debtor or third parties with respect to the collateral and does not attach unless:

(a) the collateral is in the possession of the secured party pursuant to agreement, or the debtor has signed a security agreement which contains a description of the collateral and in addition, when the security interest covers crops growing or to be grown or timber to be cut, a description of the land concerned;

(b) value has been given; and

(c) the debtor has rights in the collateral.

(2) A security interest attaches when it becomes enforceable against the debtor with respect to the collateral. Attachment occurs as soon as all of the events specified in subsection (1) have taken place unless explicit agreement postpones the time of attaching.

(3) Unless otherwise agreed a security agreement gives the secured party the rights to proceeds provided by Section 9—306.

(4) A transaction, although subject to this Article, is also subject to . . . .*, and in the case of conflict between the provisions of this Article and any such statute, the provisions of such statute control. Failure to comply with any applicable statute has only the effect which is specified therein.

§ 9—207. Rights and Duties When Collateral is in Secured Party's Possession

(1) A secured party must use reasonable care in the custody and preservation of collateral in his possession. In the case of an instrument or chattel paper reasonable care includes taking necessary steps to preserve rights against prior parties unless otherwise agreed.

(2) Unless otherwise agreed, when collateral is in the secured party's possession

(a) reasonable expenses (including the cost of any insurance and payment of taxes or other charges) incurred in the custody, preservation, use or operation of the collateral are chargeable to the debtor and are secured by the collateral;

(b) the risk of accidental loss or damage is on the debtor to the extent of any deficiency in any effective insurance coverage;

(c) the secured party may hold as additional security any increase or profits (except money) received from the collateral, but money so received, unless remitted to the debtor, shall be applied in reduction of the secured obligation;

(d) the secured party must keep the collateral identifiable but fungible collateral may be commingled;

(e) the secured party may repledge the collateral upon terms which do not impair the debtor's right to redeem it.

(3) A secured party is liable for any loss caused by his failure to meet any obligation imposed by the preceding subsections but does not lose his security interest.

(4) A secured party may use or operate the collateral for the purpose of preserving the collateral or its value or pursuant to the order of a court of appropriate jurisdiction or, except in the case of consumer goods, in the manner and to the extent provided in the security agreement.

PART 3
Rights of Third Parties; Perfected and Unperfected Security Interests; Rules of Priority

§ 9—302. When Filing Is Required to Perfect Security Interest; Security Interests to Which Filing Provisions of This Article Do Not Apply.

(1) A financing statement must be filed to perfect all security interests except the following:

(a) a security interest in collateral in possession of the secured party under Section 9—305;

(b) a security interest temporarily perfected in instruments, certificated securities, or documents without delivery under Section 9—304 or in proceeds for a 10-day period under Section 9—306;

(c) a security interest created by an assignment of a beneficial interest in a trust or a decedent's estate;

(d) a purchase money security interest in consumer goods; but filing is required for a motor vehicle required to be registered; and fixture filing is required for priority over conflicting interests in fixtures to the extent provided in Section 9—313;

(e) an assignment of accounts which does not alone or in conjunction with other assignments to the same assignee transfer a significant part of the outstanding accounts of the assignor;

(f) a security interest of a collecting bank (Section 4—208) or arising under the Article on Sales (see Section 9—113) or covered in subsection (3) of this section;

(g) an assignment for the benefit of all the creditors of

the transferor, and subsequent transfers by the assignee thereunder.

(2) If a secured party assigns a perfected security interest, no filing under this Article is required in order to continue the perfected status of the security interest against creditors of and transferees from the original debtor.

(3) The filing of a financing statement otherwise required by this Article is not necessary or effective to perfect a security interest in property subject to

(a) a statute or treaty of the United States which provides for a national or international registration or a national or international certificate of title or which specifies a place of filing different from that specified in this Article for filing of the security interest; or

(b) the following statutes of this state; [list any certificate of title statute covering automobiles, trailers, mobile homes, boats, farm tractors, or the like, and any central filing statute.]; but during any period in which collateral is inventory held for sale by a person who is in the business of selling goods of that kind, the filing provisions of this Article (Part 4) apply to a security interest in that collateral created by him as debtor; or

(c) a certificate of title statute of another jurisdiction under the law of which indication of a security interest on the certificate is required as a condition of perfection (subsection (2) of Section 9—103).

(4) Compliance with a statute or treaty described in subsection (3) is equivalent to the filing of a financing statement under this Article, and a security interest in property subject to the statute or treaty can be perfected only by compliance therewith except as provided in Section 9—103 on multiple state transactions. Duration and renewal of perfection of a security interest perfected by compliance with the statute or treaty are governed by the provisions of the statute or treaty; in other respects the security interest is subject to this Article.

Amended in 1972 and 1977.

§ 9—304. Perfection of Security Interest in Instruments, Documents, and Goods Covered by Documents; Perfection by Permissive Filing; Temporary Perfection Without Filing or Transfer of Possession.

(1) A security interest in chattel paper or negotiable documents may be perfected by filing. A security interest in money or instruments (other than certificated securities or instruments which constitute part of chattel paper) can be perfected only by the secured party's taking possession, except as provided in subsections (4) and (5) of this section and subsections (2) and (3) of Section 9—306 on proceeds.

(2) During the period that goods are in the possession of the issuer of a negotiable document therefor, a security interest in the goods is perfected by perfecting a security interest in the document, and any security interest in the goods otherwise perfected during such period is subject thereto.

(3) A security interest in goods in the possession of a bailee other than one who has issued a negotiable document therefor is perfected by issuance of a document in the name of the secured party or by the bailee's receipt of notification of the secured party's interest or by filing as to the goods.

(4) A security interest in instruments, certificated securities, or negotiable documents is perfected without filing or the taking of possession for a period of 21 days from the time it attaches to the extent that it arises for new value given under a written security agreement.

(5) A security interest remains perfected for a period of 21 days without filing where a secured party having a perfected security interest in an instrument a certificated security (other than) a negotiable document or goods in possession of a bailee other than one who has issued a negotiable document therefor

    (a) makes available to the debtor the goods or documents representing the goods for the purpose of ultimate sale or exchange or for the purpose of loading, unloading, storing, shipping, transshipping, manufacturing, processing or otherwise dealing with them in a manner preliminary to their sale or exchange, but priority between conflicting security interests in the goods is subject to subsection (3) of Section 9—312; or

    (b) delivers the instrument or certificated security to the debtor for the purpose of ultimate sale or exchange or of presentation, collection, renewal or registration of transfer.

(6) After the 21-day period in subsections (4) and (5) perfection depends upon compliance with applicable provisions of this Article.

§ 9—305. When Possession by Secured Party Perfects Security Interest Without Filing.

A security interest in letters of credit and advices of credit (subsection (2)(a) of Section 5—116), goods, instruments (other than certificated securities), money, negotiable documents, or chattel paper may be perfected by the secured party's taking possession of the collateral. If such collateral other than goods covered by a negotiable document is held by a bailee, the secured party is deemed to have possession from the time the bailee receives notification of the secured party's interest. A security interest is perfected by possession from the time possession is taken without a relation back and continues only so long as possession is retained, unless otherwise specified in this Article. The security interest may be otherwise perfected as provided in this Article before or after the period of possession by the secured party.

§ 9—310. Priority of Certain Liens Arising by Operation of Law.

When a person in the ordinary course of his business furnishes services or materials with respect to goods subject to a security interest, a lien upon goods in the possession of such person given by statute or rule of law for such materials or services takes priority over a perfected security interest unless the lien is statutory and the statute expressly provides otherwise.

§ 9—312. Priorities Among Conflicting Security Interests in the Same Collateral.

(1) The rules of priority stated in other sections of this Part and in the following sections shall govern when applicable: Section 4—208 with respect to the security interests of collecting banks in items being collected, accompanying documents and proceeds; Section 9—103 on security interests related to other jurisdictions; Section 9—114 on consignments.

(2) A perfected security interest in crops for new value given to enable the debtor to produce the crops during the production season and given not more than three months before the crops become growing crops by planting or otherwise takes priority over an earlier perfected security interest to the extent that such earlier interest secures obligations due more than six months before the crops become growing crops by planting or otherwise, even though the person giving new value had knowledge of the earlier security interest.

(3) A perfected purchase money security interest in inventory has priority over a conflicting security interest in the same inventory and also has priority in identifiable cash proceeds received on or before the delivery of the inventory to a buyer if

    (a) the purchase money security interest is perfected at the time the debtor receives possession of the inventory; and

    (b) the purchase money secured party gives notification in writing to the holder of the conflicting security interest if the holder had filed a financing statement covering the same types of inventory (i) before the date of the filing made by the purchase money secured party, or (ii) before the beginning of the 21-day period where the purchase money security interest is temporarily perfected without filing or possession (subsection (5) of Section 9—304); and

    (c) the holder of the conflicting security interest receives the notification within five years before the debtor receives possession of the inventory; and

    (d) the notification states that the person giving the notice has or expects to acquire a purchase money security interest in inventory of the debtor, describing such inventory by item or type.

(4) A purchase money security interest in collateral other than inventory has priority over a conflicting security interest in the same collateral or its proceeds if the purchase money security interest is perfected at the time the debtor receives possession of the collateral or within ten days thereafter.

(5) In all cases not governed by other rules stated in this section (including cases of purchase money security inter-

ests which do not qualify for the special priorities set forth in subsections (3) and (4) of this section), priority between conflicting security interests in the same collateral shall be determined according to the following rules:

(a) Conflicting security interests rank according to priority in time of filing or perfection. Priority dates from the time a filing is first made covering the collateral or the time the security interest is first perfected, whichever is earlier, provided that there is no period thereafter when there is neither filing nor perfection.

(b) So long as conflicting security interests are unperfected, the first to attach has priority.

(6) For the purposes of subsection (5) a date of filing or perfection as to collateral is also a date of filing or perfection as to proceeds.

(7) If future advances are made while a security interest is perfected by filing, the taking of possession, or under Section 8—321 on securities, the security interest has the same priority for the purposes of subsection (5) with respect to the future advances as it does with respect to the first advance. If a commitment is made before or while the security interest is so perfected, the security interest has the same priority with respect to advances made pursuant thereto. In other cases a perfected security interest has priority from the date the advance is made.

PART 4
Filing

§ 9—401. Place of Filing; Erroneous Filing; Removal of Collateral.

First Alternative Subsection (1)

(1) The proper place to file in order to perfect a security interest is as follows:

(a) when the collateral is timber to be cut or is minerals or the like (including oil and gas) or accounts subject to subsection (5) of Section 9—103, or when the financing statement is filed as a fixture filing (Section 9—313) and the collateral is goods which are or are to become fixtures, then in the office where a mortgage on the real estate would be filed or recorded;

(b) in all other cases, in the office of the [Secretary of State].

Second Alternative Subsection (1)

(1) The proper place to file in order to perfect a security interest is as follows:

(a) when the collateral is equipment used in farming operations, or farm products, or accounts or general intangibles arising from or relating to the sale of farm products by a farmer, or consumer goods, then in the office of the . . . . in the county of the debtor's residence or if the debtor is not a resident of this state then in the office of the . . . . in the county where the goods are kept, and in addition when the collateral is

crops growing or to be grown in the office of the . . . . in the county where the land is located;

(b) when the collateral is timber to be cut or is minerals or the like (including oil and gas) or accounts subject to subsection (5) of Section 9—103, or when the financing statement is filed as a fixture filing (Section 9—313) and the collateral is goods which are or are to become fixtures, then in the office where a mortgage on the real estate would be filed or recorded;

(c) in all other cases, in the office of the [Secretary of State].

Third Alternative Subsection (1)

(1) The proper place to file in order to perfect a security interest is as follows:

(a) when the collateral is equipment used in farming operations, or farm products, or accounts or general intangibles arising from or relating to the sale of farm products by a farmer, or consumer goods, then in the office of the . . . . in the county of the debtor's residence or if the debtor is not a resident of this state then in the office of the . . . . in the county where the goods are kept, and in addition when the collateral is crops growing or to be grown in the office of the . . . . in the county where the land is located;

(b) when the collateral is timber to be cut or is minerals or the like (including oil and gas) or accounts subject to subsection (5) of Section 9—103, or when the financing statement is filed as a fixture filing (Section 9—313) and the collateral is goods which are or are to become fixtures, then in the office where a mortgage on the real estate would be filed or recorded;

(c) in all other cases, in the office of the [Secretary of State] and in addition, if the debtor has a place of business in only one county of this state, also in the office of . . . . of such county, or, if the debtor has no place of business in this state, but resides in the state, also in the office of . . . . of the county in which he resides.

(2) A filing which is made in good faith in an improper place or not in all of the places required by this section is nevertheless effective with regard to any collateral as to which the filing complied with the requirements of this Article and is also effective with regard to collateral covered by the financing statement against any person who has knowledge of the contents of such financing statement.

(3) A filing which is made in the proper place in this state continues effective even though the debtor's residence or place of business or the location of the collateral or its use, whichever controlled the original filing, is thereafter changed.

Alternative Subsection (3)

[(3) A filing which is made in the proper county continues effective for four months after a change to another county of the debtor's residence or place of business or the location of the collateral, whichever controlled the original filing. It becomes ineffective thereafter unless a copy of the financing statement signed by the secured party is filed in the new county within said period. The security interest may also be perfected in the new county after the expiration of the four-month period; in such case perfection dates from the time of perfection in the new county. A change in the use of the collateral does not impair the effectiveness of the original filing.]

(4) The rules stated in Section 9—103 determine whether filing is necessary in this state.

(5) Notwithstanding the preceding subsections, and subject to subsection (3) of Section 9—302, the proper place to file in order to perfect a security interest in collateral, including fixtures, of a transmitting utility is the office of the [Secretary of State]. This filing constitutes a fixture filing (Section 9—313) as to the collateral described therein which is or is to become fixtures.

(6) For the purposes of this section, the residence of an organization is its place of business if it has one or its chief executive office if it has more than one place of business.

§ 9—402. Formal Requisites of Financing Statement; Amendments; Mortgage as Financing Statement.

(1) A financing statement is sufficient if it gives the names of the debtor and the secured party, is signed by the debtor, gives an address of the secured party from which information concerning the security interest may be obtained, gives a mailing address of the debtor and contains a statement indicating the types, or describing the items, of collateral. A financing statement may be filed before a security agreement is made or a security interest otherwise attaches. When the financing statement covers crops growing or to be grown, the statement must also contain a description of the real estate concerned. When the financing statement covers timber to be cut or covers minerals or the like (including oil and gas) or accounts subject to subsection (5) of Section 9—103, or when the financing statement is filed as a fixture filing (Section 9—313) and the collateral is goods which are or are to become fixtures, the statement must also comply with subsection (5). A copy of the security agreement is sufficient as a financing statement if it contains the above information and is signed by the debtor. A carbon, photographic or other reproduction of a security agreement or a financing statement is sufficient as a financing statement if the security agreement so provides or if the original has been filed in this state.

(3) A form substantially as follows is sufficient to comply with subsection (1):

Name of debtor (or assignor) . . . .
Address . . . .
Name of secured party (or assignee) . . . .
Address . . . .
1. This financing statement covers the following types (or items) of property:
(Describe) . . . .

2. (If collateral is crops) The above described crops are growing or are to be grown on:
(Describe Real Estate) . . . .
3. (If applicable) The above goods are to become fixtures on *
*Where appropriate substitute either "The above timber is standing on . . . ." or "The above minerals or the like (including oil and gas) or accounts will be financed at the wellhead or minehead of the well or mine located on . . . ."
(Describe Real Estate) . . . .
and this financing statement is to be filed [for record] in the real estate records. (If the debtor does not have an interest of record) The name of a record owner is . . . .
4. (If products of collateral are claimed) Products of the collateral are also covered.
(use . . . .
whichever . . . . Signature of Debtor
(or Assignor)
is   . . . .
applicable) . . . . Signature of Secured Party
(or Assignee)

(4) A financing statement may be amended by filing a writing signed by both the debtor and the secured party. An amendment does not extend the period of effectiveness of a financing statement. If any amendment adds collateral, it is effective as to the added collateral only from the filing date of the amendment. In this Article, unless the context otherwise requires, the term "financing statement" means the original financing statement and any amendments.

(6) A mortgage is effective as a financing statement filed as a fixture filing from the date of its recording if
(a) the goods are described in the mortgage by item or type; and
(b) the goods are or are to become fixtures related to the real estate described in the mortgage; and
(c) the mortgage complies with the requirements for a financing statement in this section other than a recital that it is to be filed in the real estate records; and
(d) the mortgage is duly recorded.
No fee with reference to the financing statement is required other than the regular recording and satisfaction fees with respect to the mortgage.

(7) A financing statement sufficiently shows the name of the debtor if it gives the individual, partnership or corporate name of the debtor, whether or not it adds other trade names or names of partners. Where the debtor so changes his name or in the case of an organization its name, identity or corporate structure that a filed financing statement becomes seriously misleading, the filing is not effective to perfect a security interest in collateral acquired by the debtor more than four months after the change, unless a new appropriate financing statement is filed before the expiration of that time. A filed financing statement

remains effective with respect to collateral transferred by the debtor even though the secured party knows of or consents to the transfer.

(8) A financing statement substantially complying with the requirements of this section is effective even though it contains minor errors which are not seriously misleading.

§ 9—403. What Constitutes Filing; Duration of Filing; Effect of Lapsed Filing; Duties of Filing Officer.

(1) Presentation for filing of a financing statement and tender of the filing fee or acceptance of the statement by the filing officer constitutes filing under this Article.

(2) Except as provided in subsection (6) a filed financing statement is effective for a period of five years from the date of filing. The effectiveness of a filed financing statement lapses on the expiration of the five year period unless a continuation statement is filed prior to the lapse. If a security interest perfected by filing exists at the time insolvency proceedings are commenced by or against the debtor, the security interest remains perfected until termination of the insolvency proceedings and thereafter for a period of sixty days or until expiration of the five year period, whichever occurs later. Upon lapse the security interest becomes unperfected, unless it is perfected without filing. If the security interest becomes unperfected upon lapse, it is deemed to have been unperfected as against a person who became a purchaser or lien creditor before lapse.

(3) A continuation statement may be filed by the secured party within six months prior to the expiration of the five year period specified in subsection (2). Any such continuation statement must be signed by the secured party, identify the original statement by file number and state that the original statement is still effective. A continuation statement signed by a person other than the secured party of record must be accompanied by a separate written statement of assignment signed by the secured party of record and complying with subsection (2) of Section 9—405, including payment of the required fee. Upon timely filing of the continuation statement, the effectiveness of the original statement is continued for five years after the last date to which the filing was effective whereupon it lapses in the same manner as provided in subsection (2) unless another continuation statement is filed prior to such lapse. Succeeding continuation statements may be filed in the same manner to continue the effectiveness of the original statement. Unless a statute on disposition of public records provides otherwise, the filing officer may remove a lapsed statement from the files and destroy it immediately if he has retained a microfilm or other photographic record, or in other cases after one year after the lapse. The filing officer shall so arrange matters by physical annexation of financing statements to continuation statements or other related filings, or by other means, that if he physically destroys the financing statements of a period more than five years past, those which have been continued by a continuation statement or which are still effective under subsection (6) shall be retained.

(4) Except as provided in subsection (7) a filing officer shall mark each statement with a file number and with the date and hour of filing and shall hold the statement or a microfilm or other photographic copy thereof for public inspection. In addition the filing officer shall index the statement according to the name of the debtor and shall note in the index the file number and the address of the debtor given in the statement.

(7) When a financing statement covers timber to be cut or covers minerals or the like (including oil and gas) or accounts subject to subsection (5) of Section 9—103, or is filed as a fixture filing, [it shall be filed for record and] the filing officer shall index it under the names of the debtor and any owner of record shown on the financing statement in the same fashion as if they were the mortgagors in a mortgage of the real estate described, and, to the extent that the law of this state provides for indexing of mortgages under the name of the mortgagee, under the name of the secured party as if he were the mortgagee thereunder, or where indexing is by description in the same fashion as if the financing statement were a mortgage of the real estate described.

§ 9—404. Termination Statement.

(1) If a financing statement covering consumer goods is filed on or after . . . ., then within one month or within ten days following written demand by the debtor after there is no outstanding secured obligation and no commitment to make advances, incur obligations or otherwise give value, the secured party must file with each filing officer with whom the financing statement was filed, a termination statement to the effect that he no longer claims a security interest under the financing statement, which shall be identified by file number. In other cases whenever there is no outstanding secured obligation and no commitment to make advances, incur obligations or otherwise give value, the secured party must on written demand by the debtor send the debtor, for each filing officer with whom the financing statement was filed, a termination statement to the effect that he no longer claims a security interest under the financing statement, which shall be identified by file number. A termination statement signed by a person other than the secured party of record must be accompanied by a separate written statement of assignment signed by the secured party of record complying with subsection (2) of Section 9—405, including payment of the required fee. If the affected secured party fails to file such a termination statement as required by this subsection, or to send such a termination statement within ten days after proper demand therefor, he shall be liable to the debtor for one hundred dollars, and in addition for any loss caused to the debtor by such failure.

PART 5
Default

§ 9—503. Secured Party's Right to Take Possession After Default.

Unless otherwise agreed a secured party has on default the right to take possession of the collateral. In taking possession a secured party may proceed without judicial process if this can be done without breach of the peace or may proceed by action. If the security agreement so provides the secured party may require the debtor to assemble the collateral and make it available to the secured party at a place to be designated by the secured party which is reasonably convenient to both parties. Without removal a secured party may render equipment unusable, and may dispose of collateral on the debtor's premises under Section 9—504.

§ 9—505. Compulsory Disposition of Collateral; Acceptance of the Collateral as Discharge of Obligation.

(1) If the debtor has paid sixty percent of the cash price in the case of a purchase money security interest in consumer goods or sixty percent of the loan in the case of another security interest in consumer goods, and has not signed after default a statement renouncing or modifying his rights under this Part a secured party who has taken possession of collateral must dispose of it under Section 9—504 and if he fails to do so within ninety days after he takes possession the debtor at his option may recover in conversion or under Section 9—507(1) on secured party's liability.

(2) In any other case involving consumer goods or any other collateral a secured party in possession may, after default, propose to retain the collateral in satisfaction of the obligation. Written notice of such proposal shall be sent to the debtor if he has not signed after default a statement renouncing or modifying his rights under this subsection. In the case of consumer goods no other notice need be given. In other cases notice shall be sent to any other secured party from whom the secured party has received (before sending his notice to the debtor or before the debtor's renunciation of his rights) written notice of a claim of an interest in the collateral. If the secured party receives objection in writing from a person entitled to receive notification within twenty-one days after the notice was sent, the secured party must dispose of the collateral under Section 9—504. In the absence of such written objection the secured party may retain the collateral in satisfaction of the debtor's obligation. Amended in 1972.

§ 9—506. Debtor's Right to Redeem Collateral.

At any time before the secured party has disposed of collateral or entered into a contract for its disposition under Section 9—504 or before the obligation has been discharged under Section 9—505(2) the debtor or any other secured party may unless otherwise agreed in writing after default redeem the collateral by tendering fulfillment of all obligations secured by the collateral as well as the expenses reasonably incurred by the secured party in retaking, holding and preparing the collateral for disposition, in arranging for the sale, and to the extent provided in the agreement and not prohibited by law, his reasonable attorneys' fees and legal expenses.

§ 9—507. Secured Party's Liability for Failure to Comply With This Part.

(1) If it is established that the secured party is not proceeding in accordance with the provisions of this Part disposition may be ordered or restrained on appropriate terms and conditions. If the disposition has occurred the debtor or any person entitled to notification or whose security interest has been made known to the secured party prior to the disposition has a right to recover from the secured party any loss caused by a failure to comply with the provisions of this Part. If the collateral is consumer goods, the debtor has a right to recover in any event an amount not less than the credit service charge plus 10 percent of the principal amount of the debt or the time price differential plus 10 percent of the cash price.

(2) The fact that a better price could have been obtained by a sale at a different time or in a different method from that selected by the secured party is not of itself sufficient to establish that the sale was not made in a commercially reasonable manner. If the secured party either sells the collateral in the usual manner in any recognized market therefor or if he sells at the price current in such market at the time of his sale or if he has otherwise sold in conformity with reasonable commercial practices among dealers in the type of property sold he has sold in a commercially reasonable manner. The principles stated in the two preceding sentences with respect to sales also apply as may be appropriate to other types of disposition. A disposition which has been approved in any judicial proceeding or by any bona fide creditors' committee or representative of creditors shall conclusively be deemed to be commercially reasonable, but this sentence does not indicate that any such approval must be obtained in any case nor does it indicate that any disposition not so approved is not commercially reasonable.

United Nations Convention on Contracts for the International Sale of Goods

(Excerpts)

The States Parties to this Convention,

Bearing in mind the broad objectives in the resolutions adopted by the sixth special session of the General Assembly of the United Nations on the establishment of a New International Economic Order,

Considering that the development of international trade on the basis of equality and mutual benefit is an important element in promoting friendly relations among States,

Being of the opinion that the adoption of uniform rules which govern contracts for the international sale of goods and take into account the different social, economic and legal systems would contribute to the removal of legal barriers in international trade and promote the development of international trade, Have agreed as follows:

PART I. SPHERE OF APPLICATION AND GENERAL PROVISIONS

Chapter I. Sphere of Application

ARTICLE 1

(1) This Convention applies to contracts of sale of goods between parties whose places of business are in different States:

(a) when the States are Contracting States; or

(b) when the rules of private international law lead to the application of the law of a Contracting State.

(2) The fact that the parties have their places of business in different States is to be disregarded whenever this fact does not appear either from the contract or from any dealings between, or from information disclosed by, the parties at any time before or at the conclusion of the contract.

(3) Neither the nationality of the parties nor the civil or commercial character of the parties or of the contract is to be taken into consideration in determining the application of this Convention.

ARTICLE 2

This Convention does not apply to sales:

(a) of goods bought for personal, family or household use, unless the seller, at any time before or at the conclusion of the contract, neither knew nor ought to have known that the goods were bought for any such use;

(b) by auction;

(c) on execution or otherwise by authority of law;

(d) of stocks, shares, investment securities, negotiable instruments or money;

(e) of ships, vessels, hovercraft or aircraft; or

(f) electricity

ARTICLE 3

(1) Contracts for the supply of goods to be manufactured or produced are to be considered sales unless the

party who orders the goods undertakes to supply a substantial part of the materials necessary for such manufacture or production.

(2) This Convention does not apply to contracts in which the preponderant part of the obligations of the party who furnishes the goods consists in the supply of labour or other services.

ARTICLE 4

This Convention governs only the formation of the contract of sale and the rights and obligations of the seller and the buyer arising from such a contract. In particular, except as otherwise expressly provided in this Convention, it is not concerned with:

(a) the validity of the contract or of any of its provisions or of any usage;

(b) the effect which the contract may have on the property in the goods sold.

ARTICLE 5

This Convention does not apply to the liability of the seller for death or personal injury caused by the goods to any person.

ARTICLE 6

The parties may exclude the application of this Convention or, subject to article 12, derogate from or vary the effect of any of its provisions.

Chapter II. General Provisions

ARTICLE 7

(1) In the interpretation of this Convention, regard is to be had to its international character and to the need to promote uniformity in its application and the observance of good faith in international trade.

(2) Questions concerning matters governed by this Convention which are not expressly settled in it are to be settled in conformity with the general principles on which it is based or, in the absence of such principles, in conformity with the law applicable by virtue of the rules of private international law.

ARTICLE 8

(1) For the purposes of this Convention statements made by and other conduct of a party are to be interpreted according to his intent where the other party knew or could not have been unaware what that intent was.

(2) If the preceding paragraph is not applicable, statements made by and other conduct of a party are to be interpreted according to the understanding that a reasonable person of the same kind as the other party would have had in the same circumstances.

(3) In determining the intent of a party or the understanding a reasonable person would have had, due consideration is to be given to all relevant circumstances of the case including the negotiations, any practices which the parties have established between themselves, usages and any subsequent conduct of the parties.

ARTICLE 9

(1) The parties are bound by any usage to which they have agreed and by any practices which they have established between themselves.

(2) The parties are considered, unless otherwise agreed, to have impliedly made applicable to their contract or its formation a usage of which the parties knew or ought to have known and which in international trade is widely known to, and regularly observed by, parties to contracts of the type involved in the particular trade concerned.

ARTICLE 10

For the purposes of this Convention:

(a) if a party has more than one place of business, the place of business is that which has the closest relationship to the contract and its performance, having regard to the circumstances known to or contemplated by the parties at any time before or at the conclusion of the contract;

(b) if a party does not have a place of business, reference is to be made to his habitual residence.

ARTICLE 11

A contract of sale need not be concluded in or evidenced by writing and is not subject to any other requirements as to form. It may be proved by any means, including witnesses.

ARTICLE 12

Any provision of article 11, article 29 or Part II of this Convention that allows a contract of sale or its modification or termination by agreement of any offer, acceptance or other indication of intention to be made in any form other than in writing does not apply where any party has his place of business in a Contracting State which has made a declaration under article 96 of this Convention. The parties may not derogate from or vary the effect of this article.

ARTICLE 13

For the purposes of this Convention "writing" includes telegram and telex.

PART II. FORMATION OF THE CONTRACT

ARTICLE 14

(1) A proposal for concluding a contract addressed to one or more specific persons constitutes an offer if it is suf-

ficiently definite and indicates the intention of the offeror to be bound in case of acceptance. A proposal is sufficiently definite if it indicates the goods and expressly or implicitly fixes or makes provision for determining the quantity and the price.

(2) A proposal other than one addressed to one or more specific persons is to be considered merely as an invitation to make offers, unless the contrary is clearly indicated by the person making the proposal.

ARTICLE 15

(1) An offer becomes effective when it reaches the offeree.

(2) An offer, even if it is irrevocable, may be withdrawn if the withdrawal reaches the offeree before or at the same time as the offer.

ARTICLE 16

(1) Until a contract is concluded an offer may be revoked if the revocation reaches the offeree before he has dispatched an acceptance.

(2) However, an offer cannot be revoked:

(a) if it indicates, whether by stating a fixed time for acceptance or otherwise, that it is irrevocable; or

(b) if it was reasonable for the offeree to rely on the offer as being irrevocable and the offeree has acted in reliance on the offer.

ARTICLE 17

An offer, even if it is irrevocable, is terminated when a rejection reaches the offeror.

ARTICLE 18

(1) A statement made by or other conduct of the offeree indicating assent to an offer is an acceptance. Silence or inactivity does not in itself amount to acceptance.

(2) An acceptance of an offer becomes effective at the moment the indication of assent reaches the offeror. An acceptance is not effective if the indication of assent does not reach the offeror within the time he has fixed or, if no time is fixed, within a reasonable time, due account being taken of the circumstances of the transaction, including the rapidity of the means of communication employed by the offeror. An oral offer must be accepted immediately unless circumstances indicate otherwise.

(3) However, if, by virtue of the offer or as a result of practices which the parties have established between themselves or of usage, the offeree may indicate assent by performing an act, such as one relating to the dispatch of the goods or payment of the price, without notice to the offeror, the acceptance is effective at the moment the act is performed, provided that the act is performed within the period of time laid down in the preceding paragraph.

ARTICLE 19

(1) A reply to an offer which purports to be an accep-

tance but contains additions, limitations or other modifications is a rejection of the offer and constitutes a counter-offer.

(2) However, a reply to an offer which purports to be an acceptance but contains additional or different terms which do not materially alter the terms of the offer constitutes an acceptance, unless the offeror, without undue delay, objects orally to the discrepancy or dispatches a notice to that effect. If he does not so object, the terms of the contract are the terms of the offer with the modifications contained in the acceptance.

(3) Additional or different terms relating, among other things, to the price, payment, quality and quantity of the goods, place and time of delivery, extent of one party's liability to the other or the settlement of disputes are considered to alter the terms of the offer materially.

ARTICLE 20

(1) A period of time for acceptance fixed by the offeror in a telegram or a letter begins to run from the moment the telegram is handed in for dispatch or from the date shown on the letter or, if no such date is shown, from the date shown on the envelope. A period of time for acceptance fixed by the offeror by telephone, telex or other means of instantaneous communication, begins to run from the moment that the offer reaches the offeree.

(2) Official holidays or non-business days occurring during the period for acceptance are included in calculating the period. However, if a notice of acceptance cannot be delivered at the address of the offeror on the last day of the period because that day falls on an official holiday or a non-business day at the place of business of the offeror, the period is extended until the first business day which follows.

ARTICLE 21

(1) A late acceptance is nevertheless effective as an acceptance if without delay the offeror orally so informs the offeree or dispatches a notice to that effect.

(2) If a letter or other writing containing a late acceptance shows that is has been sent in such circumstances that if its transmission had been normal it would have reached the offeror in due time, the late acceptance is effective as an acceptance unless, without delay, the offeror orally informs the offeree that he considers his offer as having lapsed or dispatches a notice to that effect.

ARTICLE 22

An acceptance may be withdrawn if the withdrawal reaches the offeror before or at the same time as the acceptance would have become effective.

ARTICLE 23

A contract is concluded at the moment when an acceptance of an offer becomes effective in accordance with the provisions of this Convention.

ARTICLE 24

For the purposes of this Part of the Convention, an offer, declaration of acceptance or any other indication of intention "reaches" the addressee when it is made orally to him or delivered by any other means to him personally, to his place of business or mailing address or, if he does not have a place of business or mailing address, to his habitual residence.

PART III. SALE OF GOODS

Chapter I. General Provisions

ARTICLE 25

A breach of contract committed by one of the parties is fundamental if it results in such detriment to the other party as substantially to deprive him of what he is entitled to expect under the contract, unless the party in breach did not foresee and a reasonable person of the same kind in the same circumstances would not have foreseen such a result.

ARTICLE 26

A declaration of avoidance of the contract is effective only if made by notice to the other party.

ARTICLE 27

Unless otherwise expressly provided in this Part of the Convention, if any notice, request or other communication is given or made by a party in accordance with this Part and by means appropriate in the circumstances, a delay or error in the transmission of the communication or its failure to arrive does not deprive that party of the right to rely on the communication.

ARTICLE 28

If, in accordance with the provisions of this Convention, one party is entitled to require performance of any obligation by the other party, a court is not bound to enter a judgment for specific performance unless the court would do so under its own law in respect of similar contracts of sale not governed by this Convention.

ARTICLE 29

(1) A contract may be modified or terminated by the mere agreement of the parties.

(2) A contract in writing which contains a provision requiring any modification or termination by agreement to be in writing may not be otherwise modified or terminated by agreement. However, a party may be precluded by his conduct from asserting such a provision to the extent that the other party has relied on that conduct.

Chapter II. Obligations of the Seller

ARTICLE 35

(1) The seller must deliver goods which are of the quantity, quality and description required by the contract and which are contained or packaged in the manner required by the contract.

(2) Except where the parties have agreed otherwise, the goods do not conform with the contract unless they:

(a) are fit for the purposes for which goods of the same description would ordinarily be used;

(b) are fit for any particular purpose expressly or impliedly made known to the seller at the time of the conclusion of the contract, except where the circumstances show that the buyer did not rely, or that it was unreasonable for him to rely, on the seller's skill and judgment;

(c) possess the qualities of goods which the seller has held out to the buyer as a sample or model;

(d) are contained or packaged in the manner usual for such goods or, where there is no such manner, in a manner adequate to preserve and protect the goods.

(3) The seller is not liable under subparagraphs (a) to (d) of the preceding paragraph for any lack of conformity of the goods if at the time of the conclusion of the contract the buyer knew or could not have been unaware of such lack of conformity.

ARTICLE 36

(1) The seller is liable in accordance with the contract and this Convention for any lack of conformity which exists at the time when the risk passes to the buyer, even though the lack of conformity becomes apparent only after that time.

(2) The seller is also liable for any lack of conformity which occurs after the time indicated in the preceding paragraph and which is due to a breach of any of his obligations, including a breach of any guarantee that for a period of time the goods will remain fit for their ordinary purpose or for some particular purpose or will retain specified qualities or characteristics.

ARTICLE 37

If the seller has delivered goods before the date for delivery, he may, up to that date, deliver any missing part or make up any deficiency in the quantity of the goods delivered, or deliver goods in replacement of any non-conforming goods delivered or remedy any lack of conformity in the goods delivered, provided that the exercise of this right does not cause the buyer unreasonable inconvenience or unreasonable expense. However, the buyer retains any right to claim damages as provided for in this Convention.

Chapter III. Obligations of the Buyer
Chapter IV. Passing of Risk

ARTICLE 66

Loss of or damage to the goods after the risk has passed to the buyer does not discharge him from his obligation to pay the price, unless the loss or damage is due to an act or omission of the seller.

ARTICLE 67

(1) If the contract of sale involves carriage of the goods and the seller is not bound to hand them over at a particular place, the risk passes to the buyer when the goods are handed over to the first carrier for transmission to the buyer in accordance with the contract of sale. If the seller is bound to hand the goods over to a carrier at a particular place, the risk does not pass to the buyer until the goods are handed over to the carrier at that place. The fact that the seller is authorized to retain documents controlling the disposition of the goods does not affect the passage of risk.

(2) Nevertheless, the risk does not pass to the buyer until the goods are clearly identified to the contract, whether by markings on the goods, by shipping documents, by notice given to the buyer or otherwise.

ARTICLE 68

The risk in respect of goods sold in transit passes to the buyer from the time of the conclusion of the contract. However, if the circumstances so indicate, the risk is assumed by the buyer from the time the goods were handed over to the carrier who issued the documents embodying the contract of carriage. Nevertheless, if at the time of the conclusion of the contract of sale the seller knew or ought to have known that the goods had been lost or damaged and did not disclose this to the buyer, the loss or damage is at risk of the seller.

ARTICLE 69

(1) In cases not within articles 67 and 68, the risk passes to the buyer when he takes over the goods or, if he does not do so in due time, from the time when the goods are placed at his disposal and he commits a breach of contract by failing to take delivery.

(2) However, if the buyer is bound to take over the goods at a place other than a place of business of the seller, the risk passes when delivery is due and the buyer is aware of the fact that the goods are placed at his disposal at that place.

(3) If the contract relates to goods not then identified, the goods are considered not to be placed at the disposal of the buyer until they are clearly identified to the contract.

ARTICLE 70

If the seller has committed a fundamental breach of contract, articles 67, 68 and 69 do not impair the remedies available to the buyer on account of the breach.

PART IV. FINAL PROVISIONS

ARTICLE 96

A Contracting State whose legislation requires contracts of sale to be concluded in or evidenced by writing may at any time make a declaration in accordance with article 12 that any provision of article 11, article 29, or Part II of this Convention, that allows a contract of sale or its modification or termination by agreement or any offer, acceptance, or other indication of intention to be made in any form other than writing, does not apply where any party has his place of business in that State.

DONE at Vienna, this day of eleventh day of April, one thousand nine hundred and eighty, in a single original, of which the Arabic, Chinese, English, French, Russian and Spanish texts are equally authentic.

IN WITNESS WHEREOF the undersigned plenipotentiaries, being duly authorized by their respective Governments, have signed this Convention.

APPENDIX 5
Uniform Partnership Act

[Adopted by every state including the District of Columbia, Guam, and the Virgin Islands except Louisiana.]

PART I

Preliminary Provisions

§ 1.   Name of Act

This act may be cited as Uniform Partnership Act.

§ 2.   Definition of Terms

In this act, "Court" includes every court and judge having jurisdiction in the case.

   "Business" includes every trade, occupation, or profession.

   "Person" includes individuals, partnerships, corporations, and other associations.

   "Bankrupt" includes bankrupt under the Federal Bankruptcy Act or insolvent under any state insolvent act.

   "Conveyance" includes every assignment, lease, mortgage, or encumbrance.

   "Real property" includes land and any interest or estate inland.

§ 3.   Interpretation of Knowledge and Notice

(1) A person has "knowledge" of a fact within the meaning of this act not only when he has actual knowledge thereof, but also when he has knowledge of such other facts as in the circumstances shows bad faith.

(2) A person has "notice" of a fact within the meaning of this act when the person who claims the benefit of the notice

   (a)   States the fact to such person, or
   (b)   Delivers through the mail, or by other means of communication, a written statement of the fact to such person or to a proper person at his place of business or residence.

§ 4.   Rules of Construction

(1) The rule that statutes in derogation of the common law are to be strictly construed shall have no application to this act.

(2) The law of estoppel shall apply under this act.

(3) The law of agency shall apply under this act.

(4) This act shall be so interpreted and construed as to effect its general purpose to make uniform the law of those states which enact it.

(5) This act shall not be construed so as to impair the obligations of any contract existing when the act goes into effect, nor to affect any action or proceedings begun or right accrued before this act takes effect.

§ 5.   Rules for Cases Not Provided for in this Act

In any case not provided for in this act the rules of law and equity, including the law merchant, shall govern.

PART II

Nature of Partnership

§ 6.   Partnership Defined

(1) A partnership is an association of two or more persons to carry on as co-owners a business for profit.

(2) But any association formed under any other statute of this state, or any statute adopted by authority, other than the authority of this state, is not a partnership under this act, unless such association would have been a partnership in this state prior to the adoption of this act; but this act shall apply to limited partnerships except in so far as the statutes relating to such partnerships are inconsistent herewith.

§ 7.   Rules for Determining the Existence of a Partnership

In determining whether a partnership exists, these rules shall apply:

(1) Except as provided by Section 16 persons who are not partners as to each other are not partners as to third persons.

(2) Joint tenancy, tenancy in common, tenancy by the entireties, joint property, common property, or part ownership does not of itself establish a partnership, whether such co-owners do or do not share any profits made by the use of the property.

(3) The sharing of gross returns does not of itself establish a partnership, whether or not the persons sharing them have a joint or common right or interest in any property from which the returns are derived.

(4) The receipt by a person of a share of the profits of a business is prima facie evidence that he is a partner in the business, but no such inference shall be drawn if such profits were received in payment:

(a) As a debt by installments or otherwise,
(b) As wages of an employee or rent to a landlord,
(c) As an annuity to a widow or representative of a deceased partner,
(d) As interest on a loan, though the amount of payment vary with the profits of the business, and/or
(e) As the consideration for the sale of a goodwill of a business or other property by installments or otherwise.

§ 8.   Partnership Property

(1) All property originally brought into the partnership stock or subsequently acquired by purchase or otherwise, on account of the partnership, is partnership property.

(2) Unless the contrary intention appears, property acquired with partnership funds is partnership property.

(3) Any estate in real property may be acquired in the partnership name. Title so acquired can be conveyed only in the partnership name.

(4) A conveyance to a partnership in the partnership name, though without words of inheritance, passes the entire estate of the grantor unless a contrary intent appears.

PART III

Relations of Partners to Persons Dealing with the Partnership

§ 9.   Partner Agent of Partnership as to Partnership Business

(1) Every partner is an agent of the partnership for the purpose of its business, and the act of every partner, including the execution in the partnership name of any instrument, for apparently carrying on in the usual way the business of the partnership of which he is a member binds the partnership, unless the partner so acting has in fact no authority to act for the partnership in the particular matter, and the person with whom he is dealing has knowledge of the fact that he has no such authority.

(2) An act of a partner which is not apparently for the carrying on of the business of the partnership in the usual way does not bind the partnership unless authorized by the other partners.

(3) Unless authorized by the other partners or unless they have abandoned the business, one or more but less than all the partners have no authority to:

(a) Assign the partnership property in trust for creditors or on the assignee's promise to pay the debts of the partnership,
(b) Dispose of the goodwill of the business,
(c) Do any other act which would make it impossible to carry on the ordinary business of a partnership,
(d) Confess a judgment,
(e) Submit a partnership claim or liability to arbitration or reference.

(4) No act of a partner in contravention of a restriction on authority shall bind the partnership to persons having knowledge of the restriction.

§ 10.   Conveyance of Real Property of the Partnership

(1) Where title to real property is in the partnership name, any partner may convey title to such property by a conveyance executed in the partnership name; but the partnership may recover such property unless the partner's act binds the partnership under the provisions of paragraph (1) of section 9 or unless such property has been conveyed by the grantee or a person claiming through such grantee to a holder for value without knowledge that the partner, in making the conveyance, has exceeded his authority.

(2) Where title to real property is in the name of the part-

nership, a conveyance executed by a partner, in his own name, passes the equitable interest of the partnership, provided the act is one within the authority of the partner under the provisions of paragraph (1) of Section 9.

(3) Where title to real property is in the name of one or more but not all the partners, and the record does not disclose the right of the partnership, the partners in whose name the title stands may convey title to such property, but the partnership may recover such property if the partners' act does not bind the partnership under the provisions of paragraph (1) of section 9, unless the purchaser or his assignee, is a holder for value, without knowledge.

(4) Where the title to real property is in the name of one or more or all the partners, or in a third person in trust for the partnership, a conveyance executed by a partner in the partnership name, or in his own name, passes the equitable interest of the partnership, provided the act is one within the authority of the partner under the provisions of paragraph (1) of section 9.

(5) Where the title to real property is in the names of all the partners a conveyance executed by all the partners passes all their rights in such property.

§ 11. Partnership Bound by Admission of Partner

An admission or representation made by any partner concerning partnership affairs within the scope of his authority as conferred by this act is evidence against the partnership.

§ 12. Partnership Charged with Knowledge of or Notice to Partner

Notice to any partner of any matter relating to partnership affairs, and the knowledge of the partner acting in the particular matter, acquired while a partner or then present to his mind, and the knowledge of any other partner who reasonably could and should have communicated it to the acting partner, operate as notice to or knowledge of the partnership, except in the case of a fraud on the partnership committed by or with the consent of that partner.

§ 13. Partnership Bound by Partner's Wrongful Act

Where, by any wrongful act or omission of any partner acting in the ordinary course of the business of the partnership or with the authority of his co-partners, loss or injury is caused to any person, not being a partner in the partnership, or any penalty is incurred, the partnership is liable therefor to the same extent as the partner so acting or omitting to act.

§ 14. Partnership Bound by Partner's Breach of Trust

The partnership is bound to make good the loss:

    (a) Where one partner acting within the scope of his apparent authority receives money or property of a third person and misapplies it; and

    (b) Where the partnership in the course of its business receives money or property of a third person and the money or property so received is misapplied by any partner while it is in the custody of the partnership.

§ 15. Nature of Partner's Liability

All partners are liable:

    (a) Jointly and severally for everything chargeable to the partnership under sections 13 and 14.

    (b) Jointly for all other debts and obligations of the partnership; but any partner may enter into a separate obligation to perform a partnership contract.

§ 16. Partner by Estoppel

(1) When a person, by words spoken or written or by conduct, represents himself, or consents to another representing him to anyone, as a partner in an existing partnership or with one or more persons not actual partners, he is liable to any such person to whom such representation has been made, who has, on the faith of such representation, given credit to the actual or apparent partnership, and if he has made such representation or consented to its being made in a public manner he is liable to such person, whether the representation has or has not been made or communicated to such person so giving credit by or with the knowledge of the apparent partner making the representation or consenting to its being made.

    (a) When a partnership liability results, he is liable as though he were an actual member of the partnership.

    (b) When no partnership liability results, he is liable jointly with the other persons, if any, so consenting to the contract or representation as to incur liability, otherwise separately.

(2) When a person has been thus represented to be a partner in an existing partnership, or with one or more persons not actual partners, he is an agent of the persons consenting to such representation to bind them to the same extent and in the same manner as though he were a partner in fact, with respect to persons who rely upon the representation. Where all the members of the existing partnership consent to the representation, a partnership act or obligation results; but in all other cases it is the joint act or obligation of the person acting and the persons consenting to the representation.

§ 17. Liability of Incoming Partner

A person admitted as a partner into an existing partnership is liable for all the obligations of the partnership arising before his admission as though he had been a partner when such obligations were incurred, except that this liability shall be satisfied only out of partnership property.

PART IV

Relations of Partners to One Another

§ 18.   Rules Determining Rights and Duties of Partners

The rights and duties of the partners in relation to the partnership shall be determined, subject to any agreement between them, by the following rules:

(a) Each partner shall be repaid his contributions, whether by way of capital or advances to the partnership property and share equally in the profits and surplus remaining after all liabilities, including those to partners, are satisfied; and must contribute toward the losses, whether of capital or otherwise, sustained by the partnership according to his share in the profits.

(b) The partnership must indemnify every partner in respect of payments made and personal liabilities reasonably incurred by him in the ordinary and proper conduct of its business, or for the preservation of its business or property.

(c) A partner, who in aid of the partnership makes any payment or advance beyond the amount of capital which he agreed to contribute, shall be paid interest from the date of the payment or advance.

(d) A partner shall receive interest on the capital contributed by him only from the date when repayment should be made.

(e) All partners have equal rights in the management and conduct of the partnership business.

(f) No partner is entitled to remuneration for acting in the partnership business, except that a surviving partner is entitled to reasonable compensation for his services in winding up the partnership affairs.

(g) No person can become a member of a partnership without the consent of all the partners.

(h) Any difference arising as to ordinary matters connected with the partnership business may be decided by a majority of the partners; but no act in contravention of any agreement between the partners may be done rightfully without the consent of all the partners.

§ 19.   Partnership Books

The partnership books shall be kept, subject to any agreement between the partners, at the principal place of business of the partnership, and every partner shall at all times have access to and may inspect and copy any of them.

§ 20.   Duty of Partners to Render Information

Partners shall render on demand true and full information of all things affecting the partnership to any partner or the legal representative of any deceased partner or partner under legal disability.

§ 21.   Partner Accountable as a Fiduciary

(1) Every partner must account to the partnership for any benefit, and hold as trustee for it any profits derived by him without the consent of the other partners from any transaction connected with the formation, conduct, or liquidation of the partnership or from any use by him of its property.

(2) This section applies also to the representatives of a deceased partner engaged in the liquidation of the affairs of the partnership as the personal representatives of the last surviving partner.

§ 22.   Right to an Account

Any partner shall have the right to a formal account as to partnership affairs:

(a) If he is wrongfully excluded from the partnership business or possession of its property by his co-partners;

(b) If the right exists under the terms of any agreement,

(c) As provided by Section 21; and/or

(d) Whenever other circumstances render it just and reasonable.

§ 23.   Continuation of Partnership Beyond Fixed Term

(1) When a partnership for a fixed term or particular undertaking is continued after the termination of such term or particular undertaking without any express agreement, the rights and duties of the partners remain the same as they were at such termination, so far as is consistent with a partnership at will.

(2) A continuation of the business by the partners or such of them as habitually acted therein during the term, without any settlement or liquidation of the partnership affairs, is prima facie evidence of a continuation of the partnership.

PART V

Property Rights of a Partner

§ 24.   Extent of Property Rights of a Partner

The property rights of a partner are (1) his rights in specific partnership property, (2) his interest in the partnership, and (3) his right to participate in the management.

§ 25.   Nature of a Partner's Right in Specific Partnership Property

(1) A partner is co-owner with his partners of specific partnership property holding as a tenant in partnership.

(2) The incidents of this tenancy are such that:

(a) A partner, subject to the provisions of this act and to any agreement between the partners, has an equal right with his partners to possess specific partnership property for partnership purposes; but he has no right to possess such property, for any other purpose without the consent of his partners.

(b) A partner's right in specific partnership property is not assignable except in connection with the assignment of rights of all the partners in the same property.

(c) A partner's right in specific partnership property is not subject to attachment or execution, except on a claim against the partnership. When partnership property is attached for a partnership debt the partners, or any of them, or the representatives of a deceased partner, cannot claim any right under the homestead or exemption laws.

(d) On the death of a partner his right in specific partnership property vests in the surviving partner or partners, except where the deceased was the last surviving partner or partners, or the legal representative of the last surviving partner, has no right to possess the partnership property for any but a partnership purpose.

(e) A partner's right in specific partnership property is not subject to dower, courtesy, or allowances to widows, heirs, or next of kin.

§ 26.   Nature of Partner's Interest in the Partnership

A partner's interest in the partnership is his share of the profits and surplus, and the same is personal property.

§ 27.   Assignment of Partner's Interest

(1) A conveyance by a partner of his interest in the partnership does not of itself dissolve the partnership, nor, as against the other partners in the absence of agreement, entitle the assignee, during the continuance of the partnership to interfere in the management or administration of the partnership business or affairs, or to require an information or account of partnership transactions, or to inspect the partnership books; but it merely entitles the assignee to receive in accordance with his contract the profits to which the assigning partner would otherwise be entitled.

(2) In case of a dissolution of the partnership, the assignee is entitled to receive his assignor's interest and may require an account from the date only of the last account agreed to by all the partners.

§ 28.   Partner's Interest Subject to Charging Order

(1) On due application to a competent court by any judgment creditor of a partner, the court which entered the judgment, order, or decree, or any other court, may charge the interest of the debtor partner with payment of the unsatisfied amount of such judgment debt with interest thereon; and may then or later appoint a receiver of his share of the profits, and of any other money due or to fall due to him in respect of the partnership, and make all other orders, directions, accounts and inquiries which the debtor partner might have made, or which the circumstances of the case may require.

(2) The interest charged may be redeemed at any time before foreclosure, or in case of a sale being directed by the court may be purchased without thereby causing a dissolution:

(a) With separate property, by any one or more of the partners, or

(b) With partnership property, by any one or more of the partners with the consent of all the partners whose interests are not so charged or sold.

(3) Nothing in this act shall be held to deprive a partner of his right, if any, under the exemption laws, as regards his interest in the partnership.

PART VI
Dissolution and Winding Up

§ 29.   Dissolution Defined

The dissolution of a partnership is the change in the relation of the partners caused by any partner ceasing to be associated in the carrying on as distinguished from the winding up of the business.

§ 30.   Partnership Not Terminated by Dissolution

On dissolution the partnership is not terminated, but continues until the winding up of partnership affairs is completed.

§ 31.   Causes of Dissolution

Dissolution is caused: (1) Without violation of the agreement between the partners,

(a) By the termination of the definite term or particular undertaking specified in the agreement,

(b) By the express will of any partner when no definite term or particular undertaking is specified,

(c) By the express will of all the partners who have not assigned their interests or suffered them to be charged for their separate debts, either before or after the termination of any specified term or particular undertaking; and/or

(d) By the expulsion of any partner from the business bona fide in accordance with such a power conferred by the agreement between the partners;

(2) In contravention of the agreement between the partners, where the circumstances do not permit a dissolution under any other provision of this section, by the express will of any partner at any time;

(3) By any event which makes it unlawful for the business of the partnership to be carried on or for the members to carry it on in partnership;

(4) By the death of any partner;

(5) By the bankruptcy of any partner or the partnership;

(6) By decree of court under Section 32.

§ 32.   Dissolution by Decree of Court

(1) On application by or for a partner the court shall decree a dissolution whenever:

   (a) A partner has been declared a lunatic in any judicial proceeding or is shown to be of unsound mind,

   (b) A partner becomes in any other way incapable of performing his part of the partnership contract,

   (c) A partner has been guilty of such conduct as tends to affect prejudicially the carrying on of the business,

   (d) A partner willfully or persistently commits a breach of the partnership agreement, or otherwise so conducts himself in matters relating to the partnership business that it is not reasonably practicable to carry on the business in partnership with him,

   (e) The business of the partnership can only be carried on at a loss,

   (f) Other circumstances render a dissolution equitable.

(2) On the application of the purchaser of a partner's interest under Sections 27 or 28:

   (a) After the termination of the specified term or particular undertaking,

   (b) At any time if the partnership was a partnership at will when the interest was assigned or when the charging order was issued.

§ 33.   General Effect of Dissolution on Authority of Partner

Except so far as may be necessary to wind up partnership affairs or to complete transactions begun but not then finished, dissolution terminates all authority of any partner to act for the partnership,

(1) With respect to the partners,

   (a) When the dissolution is not by the act, bankruptcy or death of a partner, or

   (b) When the dissolution is by such act, bankruptcy or death of a partner, in cases where Section 34 so requires.

(2) With respect to persons not partners, as declared in Section 35.

§ 34.   Right of Partner to Contribution from Copartners After Dissolution

Where the dissolution is caused by the act, death or bankruptcy of a partner, each partner is liable to his copartners for his share of any liability created by any partner acting for the partnership as if the partnership had not been dissolved unless

   (a) The dissolution being by act of any partner, the partner acting for the partnership had knowledge

of the dissolution, or

   (b) The dissolution being by the death or bankruptcy of a partner, the partner acting for the partnership had knowledge or notice of the death or bankruptcy.

§ 35.   Power of Partner to Bind Partnership to Third Persons After Dissolution

(1) After dissolution a partner can bind the partnership except as provided in Paragraph (3)

   (a) By any act appropriate for winding up partnership affairs or completing transactions unfinished by dissolution;

   (b) By any transaction which would bind the partnership if dissolution had not taken place, provided the other party to the transaction

      (I) Had extended credit to the partnership prior to dissolution and had no knowledge or notice of the dissolution; or

      (II) Though he had not so extended credit, had nevertheless known of the partnership prior to dissolution, and, having no knowledge or notice of dissolution, the fact of dissolution had not been advertised in a newspaper of general circulation in the place (or in each place if more than one) at which the partnership business was regularly carried on.

(2) The liability of a partner under paragraph (1b) shall be satisfied out of partnership assets alone when such partner had been prior to dissolution.

   (a) Unknown as a partner to the person with whom the contract is made; and

   (b) So far unknown and inactive in partnership affairs that the business reputation of the partnership could not be said to have been in any degree due to his connection with it.

(3) The partnership is in no case bound by any act of a partner after dissolution.

   (a) Where the partnership is dissolved because it is unlawful to carry on the business, unless the act is appropriate for winding up partnership affairs; or

   (b) Where the partner has become bankrupt; or

   (c) Where the partner has no authority to wind up partnership affairs; except by a transaction with one who

      (I) Had extended credit to the partnership prior to dissolution and had no knowledge or notice of his want of authority; or

      (II) Had not extended credit to the partnership prior to dissolution, and, having no knowledge or notice of his want of authority, the fact of his want of authority has not been advertised in the manner provided for advertising the fact of dissolution in paragraph (1bII).

(4) Nothing in this section shall affect the liability under section 16 of any person who after dissolution represents himself or consents to another representing him as a partner in a partnership engaged in carrying on business.

§ 36.   Effect of Dissolution on Partner's Existing Liability

(1) The dissolution of the partnership does not of itself discharge the existing liability of any partner.

(2) A partner is discharged from any existing liability upon dissolution of the partnership by an agreement to that effect between himself, the partnership creditor and the person or partnership continuing the business; and such agreement may be inferred from the course of dealing between the creditor having knowledge of the dissolution and the person or partnership continuing the business.

(3) Where a person agrees to assume the existing obligations of a dissolved partnership, the partners whose obligations have been assumed shall be discharged from any liability to any creditor of the partnership who, knowing of the agreement, consents to a material alteration in the nature or time of payment of such obligations.

(4) The individual property of a deceased partner shall be liable for all obligations of the partnership incurred while he was a partner but subject to the prior payment of his separate debts.

§ 37.   Right to Wind Up

Unless otherwise agreed the partners who have not wrongfully dissolved the partnership or the legal representative of the last surviving partner, not bankrupt, has the right to wind up the partnership affairs; provided, however, that any partner, his legal representative or his assignee, upon cause shown, may obtain winding up by the court.

§ 38.   Rights of Partners to Application of Partnership Property

(1) When dissolution is caused in any way, except in contravention of the partnership agreement, each partner as against his co-partners and all persons claiming through them in respect of their interests in the partnership, unless otherwise agreed, may have the partnership property applied to discharge its liabilities, and the surplus applied to pay in cash the net amount owing to the respective partners. But if dissolution is caused by expulsion of a partner, bona fide under the partnership agreement and if the expelled partner is discharged from all partnership liabilities, either by payment or agreement under Section 36(2), he shall receive in cash only the net amount due him from the partnership.

(2) When dissolution is caused in contravention of the partnership agreement the rights of the partners shall be as follows:

(a) Each partner who has not caused dissolution wrongfully shall have,

    (I)   All the rights specified in paragraph (1) of this section, and

    (II)   The right, as against each partner who has caused the dissolution wrongfully, to damages for breach of the agreement.

(b) The partners who have not caused the dissolution wrongfully, if they all desire to continue the business in the same name, either by themselves or jointly with others, may do so, during the agreed term for the partnership and for that purpose may possess the partnership property, provided they secure the payment by bond approved by the court, or pay to any partner who has caused the dissolution wrongfully, the value of his interest in the partnership at the dissolution, less any damages recoverable under clause (2aII) of the section, and in like manner indemnify him against all present or future partnership liabilities.

(c) A partner who has caused the dissolution wrongfully shall have:

    (I)   If the business is not continued under the provisions of paragraph (2b) all the rights of a partner under paragraph (1), subject to clause (2aII), of this section,

    (II)   If the business is continued under paragraph (2b) of this section the right as against his co-partners and all claiming through them in respect of their interests in the partnership, less any damages caused to his copartners by the dissolution, ascertained and paid to him in cash, or the payment secured by bond approved by the court, and to be released from all existing liabilities of the partnership; but in ascertaining the value of the partner's interest the value of the goodwill of the business shall not be considered.

§ 39.   Rights Where Partnership is Dissolved for Fraud or Misrepresentation

Where a partnership contract is rescinded on the ground of the fraud or misrepresentation of one of the parties thereto, the party entitled to rescind is, without prejudice to any other right, entitled,

(a) To a lien on, or right of retention of, the surplus of the partnership property after satisfying the partnership liabilities to third persons for any sum of money paid by him for the purchase of an interest in the partnership and for any capital or advances contributed by him; and

(b) To stand, after all liabilities to third persons have been satisfied, in the place of the creditors of the partnership for any payments made by him in respect of the partnership liabilities; and

(c) To be indemnified by the person guilty, of the

fraud or making the representation against all debts and liabilities of the partnership.

§ 40.   Rules for Distribution

In settling accounts between the partners after dissolution, the following rules shall be observed, subject to any agreement to the contrary:

(a)   The assets of the partnership are:
    (I)   The partnership property,
    (II)   The contributions of the partners necessary for the payment of all the liabilities specified in clause (b) of this paragraph.

(b)   The liabilities of the partnership shall rank in order of payment, as follows:
    (I)   Those owing to creditors other than partners,
    (II)   Those owing to partners other than for capital and profits,
    (III)   Those owing to partners in respect of capital,
    (IV)   Those owing to partners in respect of profits.

(c)   The assets shall be applied in the order of their declaration in clause (a) of this paragraph to the satisfaction of the liabilities.

(d)   The partners shall contribute, as provided by Section 18(a) the amount necessary to satisfy the liabilities; but if any, but not all, of the partners are insolvent, or, not being subject to process, refuse to contribute, the other parties shall contribute their share of the liabilities, and, in the relative proportions in which they share the profits, the additional amount necessary to pay the liabilities.

(e)   An assignee for the benefit of creditors or any person appointed by the court shall have the right to enforce the contributions specified in clause (d) of this paragraph.

(f)   Any partner or his legal representative shall have the right to enforce the contributions specified in clause (d) of this paragraph, to the extent of the amount which he has paid in excess of his share of the liability.

(g)   The individual property of a deceased partner shall be liable for the contributions specified in clause (d) of this paragraph.

(h)   When partnership property and the individual properties of the partners are in possession of a court for distribution, partnership creditors shall have priority on partnership property and separate creditors on individual property, saving the rights of lien or secured creditors as heretofore.

(i)   Where a partner has become bankrupt or his estate is insolvent the claims against his separate property shall rank in the following order:
    (I)   Those owing to separate creditors,
    (II)   Those owing to partnership creditors,
    (III)   Those owing to partners by way of contribution.

§ 41.   Liability of Persons Continuing the Business in Certain Cases

(1) When any new partner is admitted into an existing partnership, or when any partner retires and assigns (or the representative of the deceased partner assigns) his rights in partnership property to two or more of the partners, or to one or more of the partners and one or more third persons, if the business is continued without liquidation of the partnership affairs, creditors of the first or dissolved partnership are also creditors of the partnership so continuing the business.

(2) When all but one partner retire and assign (or the representative of a deceased partner assigns) their rights in partnership property to the remaining partner, who continues the business without liquidation of partnership affairs, either alone or with others, creditors of the dissolved partnership are also creditors of the person or partnership so continuing the business.

(3) When any partner retires or dies and the business of the dissolved partnership is continued as set forth in paragraphs (1) and (2) of this section, with the consent of the retired partners or the representative of the deceased partner, but without any assignment of his right in partnership property, rights of creditors of the dissolved partnership and of the creditors of the person or partnership continuing the business shall be as if such assignment had been made.

(4) When all the partners or their representatives assign their rights in partnership property to one or more third persons who promise to pay the debts and who continue the business of the dissolved partnership, creditors of the dissolved partnership are also creditors of the person or partnership continuing the business.

(5) When any partner wrongfully causes a dissolution and the remaining partners continue the business under the provisions of Section 38(2b), either alone or with others, and without liquidation of the partnership affairs, creditors of the dissolved partnership are also creditors of the person or partnership continuing the business.

(6) When a partner is expelled and the remaining partners continue the business either alone or with others, without liquidation of the partnership affairs, creditors of the dissolved partnership are also creditors of the person or partnership continuing the business.

(7) The liability of a third person becoming a partner in the partnership continuing the business, under this section, to the creditors of the dissolved partnership shall be satisfied out of partnership property only.

(8) When the business of a partnership after dissolution is continued under any conditions set forth in this section the creditors of the dissolved partnership, as against the separate creditors of the retiring or deceased partner or the representative of the deceased partner, have a prior right to any claim of the retired partner or the representa-

tive of the deceased partner against the person or partnership continuing the business, on account of the retired partner or the representative of the deceased partner against the person or partnership continuing the business, on account of the retired or deceased partner's interest in the dissolved partnership or on account of any consideration promised for such interest or for his right in partnership property.

(9) Nothing in this section shall be held to modify any right of creditors to set aside any assignment on the ground of fraud.

(10) The use by the person or partnership continuing the business of the partnership name, or the name of a deceased partner as part thereof, shall not of itself make the individual property of the deceased partner liable for any debts contracted by such person or partnership.

§ 42. Rights of Retiring or Estate of Deceased Partner When the Business Is Continued

When any partner retires or dies, and the business is continued under any of the conditions set forth in Section 41 (1, 2, 3, 5, 6), or Section 38(2b), without any settlement of accounts as between him or his estate and the person or partnership continuing the business, unless otherwise agreed, he or his legal representative as against such persons or partnership may have the value of his interest at the date of dissolution ascertained, and shall receive as an ordinary creditor an amount equal to the value of his interest in the dissolved partnership with interest, or, at his option or at the option of his legal representative, in lieu of interest, the profits attributable to the use of his right in the property of the dissolved partnership as against the separate creditors, or the representative of the retired or deceased partner, shall have priority on any claim arising under this section, as provided by Section 41(8) of this act.

§ 43. Accrual of Actions

The right to an account of his interest shall accrue to any partner, or his legal representative, as against the winding up partners or the surviving partners or the person or partnership continuing the business, at the date of dissolution, in the absence of any agreement to the contrary.

PART VII
Miscellaneous Provisions

§ 44. When Act Takes Effect

This act shall take effect on the day of one thousand nine hundred and

§ 45. Legislation Repealed

All acts or parts of acts inconsistent with this act are hereby repealed.

Revised Model Business Corporation Act

As Amended in 1986 and 1987 (Excerpts)

§ 1.20. FILING REQUIREMENTS

(a) A document must satisfy the requirements of this section, and of any other section that adds to or varies from these requirements, to be entitled to filing by the secretary of state.

(b) This Act must require or permit filing the document in the office of the secretary of state.

(c) The document must contain the information required by this Act. It may contain other information as well.

(d) The document must be typewritten or printed.

(e) The document must be in the English language. A corporate name need not be in English if written in English letters or Arabic or Roman numerals, and the certificate of existence required of foreign corporations need not be in English if accompanied by a reasonably authenticated English translation.

(f) The document must be executed:

    (1) by the chairman of the board of directors of a domestic or foreign corporation, by its president, or by another of its officers;

    (2) if directors have not been selected or the corporation has not been formed, by an incorporator; or

    (3) if the corporation is in the hands of a receiver, trustee, or other court-appointed fiduciary, by that fiduciary.

(g) The person executing the document shall sign it and state beneath or opposite his signature his name and the capacity in which he signs. The document may but need not contain:

    (1) the corporate seal,

    (2) an attestation by the secretary or an assistant secretary,

    (3) an acknowledgment, verification, or proof.

(h) If the secretary of state has prescribed a mandatory form for the document under section 1.21, the document must be in or on the prescribed form.

(i) The document must be delivered to the office of the secretary of state for filing and must be accompanied by one exact or conformed copy (except as provided in sections 5.03 and 15.09), the correct filing fee, and any franchise tax, license fee, or penalty required by this Act or other law.

§ 1.21. FORMS

(a) The secretary of state may prescribe and furnish on request forms for:

    (1) an application for a certificate of existence,

    (2) a foreign corporation's application for a certificate of authority to transact business in this state,

    (3) a foreign corporation's application for a certificate of withdrawal, and

    (4) the annual report. If the secretary of state so requires, use of these forms is mandatory.

(b) The secretary of state may prescribe and furnish on

request forms for other documents required or permitted to be filed by this Act but their use is not mandatory.

§ 1.23. EFFECTIVE TIME AND DATE OF DOCUMENT

(a) Except as provided in subsection (b) and section 1.24(c), a document accepted for filing is effective:

 (1) at the time of filing on the date it is filed, as evidenced by the secretary of state's date and time endorsement on the original document; or

 (2) at the time specified in the document as its effective time on the date it is filed.

(b) A document may specify a delayed effective time and date, and if it does so the document becomes effective at the time and date specified. If a delayed effective date but no time is specified, the document is effective at the close of business on that date. A delayed effective date for a document may not be later than the 90th day after the date it is filed.

§ 1.25. FILING DUTY OF SECRETARY OF STATE

(a) If a document delivered to the office of the secretary of state for filing satisfies the requirements of section 1.20, the secretary of state shall file it.

(b) The secretary of state files a document by stamping or otherwise endorsing "Filed," together with his name and official title and the date and time of receipt, on both the original and the document copy and on the receipt for the filing fee. After filing a document, except as provided in sections 5.03 and 15.10, the secretary of state shall deliver the document copy, with the filing fee receipt (or acknowledgment of receipt if no fee is required) attached, to the domestic or foreign corporation or its representative.

(c) If the secretary of state refuses to file a document, he shall return it to the domestic or foreign corporation or its representative within five days after the document was delivered, together with a brief, written explanation of the reason for his refusal.

(d) The secretary of state's duty to file documents under this section is ministerial. His filing or refusing to file a document does not:

 (1) affect the validity or invalidity of the document in whole or part;

 (2) relate to the correctness or incorrectness of information contained in the document; or

 (3) create a presumption that the document is valid or invalid or that information contained in the document is correct or incorrect.

§ 1.40. ACT DEFINITIONS

In this Act:

(1) "Articles of incorporation" include amended and restated articles of incorporation and the articles of merger.

(2) "Authorized shares" means the shares of all classes a domestic or foreign corporation is authorized to issue.

(3) "Conspicuous" means so written that a reasonable person against whom the writing is to operate should have noticed it. For example, printing in italics or boldface or contrasting color, or typing in capitals or underlined, is conspicuous.

(4) "Corporation" or "domestic corporation" means a corporation for profit, which is not a foreign corporation, incorporated under or subject to the provisions of this Act.

(5) "Deliver" includes mail.

(6) "Distribution" means a direct or indirect transfer of money or other property (except its own shares) or incurrence of indebtedness by a corporation to or for the benefit of its shareholders in respect of any of its shares. A distribution may be in the form of a declaration or payment of a dividend; a purchase, redemption, or other acquisition of shares; a distribution of indebtedness; or otherwise.

(7) "Effective date of notice" is defined in section 1.41.

(8) "Employee" includes an officer but not a director. A director may accept duties that make him also an employee.

(9) "Entity" includes corporation and foreign corporation; not-for-profit corporation; profit and not-for-profit unincorporated association; business trust, estate, partnership, trust, and two or more persons having a joint or common economic interest; and state, United States, and foreign government.

(10) "Foreign corporation" means a corporation for profit incorporated under a law other than the law of this state.

(11) "Governmental subdivision" includes authority, county, district, and municipality.

(12) "Includes" denotes a partial definition.

(13) "Individual" includes the estate of an incompetent or deceased individual.

(14) "Means" denotes an exhaustive definition.

(15) "Notice" is defined in section 1.41.

(16) "Person" includes individual and entity.

(17) "Principal office" means the office (in or out of this state) so designated in the annual report where the principal executive offices of a domestic or foreign corporation are located.

(18) "Proceeding" includes civil suit and criminal, administrative, and investigatory action.

(19) "Record date" means the date established under chapter 6 or 7 on which a corporation determines the identity of its shareholders and their shareholdings for purposes of this Act. The determinations shall be made as of the close of business on the record date unless another time for doing so is specified when the record date is fixed.

(20) "Secretary" means the corporate officer to whom the board of directors has delegated responsibility under section 8.40(c) for custody of the minutes of the meetings of the board of directors and of the shareholders and for authenticating records of the corporation.

(21) "Shares" means the units into which the proprietary interests in a corporation are divided.

(22) "Shareholder" means the person in whose name shares are registered in the records of a corporation or the beneficial owner of shares to the extent of the rights granted by a nominee certificate on file with a corporation.

(23) "State," when referring to a part of the United States, includes a state and commonwealth (and their agencies and governmental subdivisions) and a territory and insular possession (and their agencies and governmental subdivisions) of the United States.

(24) "Subscriber" means a person who subscribes for shares in a corporation, whether before or after incorporation.

(25) "United States" includes district, authority, bureau, commission, department, and any other agency of the United States.

(26) "Voting group" means all shares of one or more classes or series that under the articles of incorporation or this Act are entitled to vote and be counted together collectively on a matter at a meeting of shareholders. All shares entitled by the articles of incorporation of this Act to vote generally on the matter are for that purpose a single voting group.

§ 1.41.   NOTICE

(a) Notice under this Act must be in writing unless oral notice is reasonable under the circumstances.

(b) Notice may be communicated in person; by telephone, telegraph, teletype, or other form of wire or wireless communication; or by mail or private carrier. If these forms of personal notice are impracticable, notice may be communicated by a newspaper of general circulation in the area where published; or by radio, television, or other form of public broadcast communication.

(c) Written notice by a domestic or foreign corporation to its shareholder, if in a comprehensible form, is effective when mailed, if mailed postpaid and correctly addressed to the shareholder's address shown in the corporation's current record of shareholders.

(d) Written notice to a domestic or foreign corporation (authorized to transact business in this state) may be addressed to its registered agent at its registered office or to the corporation or its secretary at its principal office shown in its most recent annual report or, in the case of a foreign corporation that has not yet delivered an annual report, in its application for a certificate of authority.

(e) Except as provided in subsection (c), written notice, if in a comprehensible form, is effective at the earliest of the following:

   (1) when received;

   (2) five days after its deposit in the United States Mail, as evidenced by the postmark, if mailed postpaid and correctly addressed; or

   (3) on the date shown on the return receipt, if sent by registered or certified mail, return receipt requested, and the receipt is signed by or on behalf of the addressee.

(f) Oral notice is effective when communicated if communicated in a comprehensible manner.

(g) If this Act prescribes notice requirements for particular circumstances, those requirements govern. If articles of incorporation or bylaws prescribe notice requirements, not inconsistent with this section or other provisions of this Act, those requirements govern.

§ 1.42.   NUMBER OF SHAREHOLDERS

(a) For purposes of this Act, the following identified as a shareholder in a corporation's current record of shareholders constitutes one shareholder:

   (1) three or fewer co-owners;

   (2) a corporation, partnership, trust, estate, or other entity; and/or

   (3) the trustees, guardians, custodians, or other fiduciaries of a single trust, estate, or account.

(b) For purposes of this Act, shareholdings registered in substantially similar names constitute one shareholder if it is reasonable to believe that the names represent the same person.

§ 2.01.   INCORPORATIONS

One or more persons may act as the incorporator or incorporators of a corporation by delivering articles of incorporation to the secretary of state for filing.

§ 2.02.   ARTICLES OF INCORPORATION

(a) The articles of incorporation must set forth:

   (1) a corporate name for the corporation that satisfies the requirements of section 4.01;

   (2) the number of shares the corporation is authorized to issue;

   (3) the street address of the corporation's initial registered office and the name of its initial registered agent at that office; and

   (4) the name and address of each incorporator.

(b) The articles of incorporation may set forth:

   (1) the names and addresses of the individuals who are to serve as the initial directors;

   (2) provisions not inconsistent with law regarding:

      (i)   the purpose or purposes for which the corporation is organized;

      (ii) managing the business and regulating the affairs of the corporation;

      (iii) defining, limiting, and regulating the powers of the corporation, its board of directors, and shareholders;

      (iv) a par value for authorized shares or classes of shares;

      (v)   the imposition of personal liability on shareholders for the debts of the corporation to a specified extent and upon specified conditions; and

   (3) any provision that under this Act is required or permitted to be set forth in the bylaws.

(c) The articles of incorporation need not set forth any of the corporate powers enumerated in this Act.

§ 2.03. INCORPORATION

(a) Unless a delayed effective date is specified, the corporate existence begins when the articles of incorporation are filed.

(b) The secretary of state's filing of the articles of incorporation is conclusive proof that the incorporators satisfied all conditions precedent to incorporation except in a proceeding by the state to cancel or revoke the incorporation or involuntarily dissolve the corporation.

§ 2.04. LIABILITY FOR PREINCORPORATION TRANSACTIONS

All persons purporting to act as or on behalf of a corporation, knowing there was no incorporation under this Act, are jointly and severally liable for all liabilities created while so acting.

§ 2.05. ORGANIZATION OF CORPORATION

(a) After incorporation:

(1) if initial directors are named in the articles of incorporation, the initial directors shall hold an organizational meeting, at the call of a majority of the directors, to complete the organization of the corporation by appointing officers, adopting bylaws, and carrying on any other business brought before the meeting;

(2) if initial directors are not named in the articles, the incorporator or incorporators shall hold an organizational meeting at the call of a majority of the incorporators:

(i) to elect directors and complete the organization of the corporation; or

(ii) to elect a board of directors who shall complete the organization of the corporation.

(b) Action required or permitted by this Act to be taken by incorporators at an organizational meeting may be taken without a meeting if the action taken is evidenced by one or more written consents describing the action taken and signed by each incorporator.

(c) An organizational meeting may be held in or out of this state.

§ 2.06. BYLAWS

(a) The incorporators or board of directors of a corporation shall adopt initial bylaws for the corporation.

(b) The bylaws of a corporation may contain any provision for managing the business and regulating the affairs of the corporation that is not inconsistent with law or the articles of incorporation.

§ 2.07. EMERGENCY BYLAWS

(a) Unless the articles of incorporation provide otherwise, the board of directors of a corporation may adopt bylaws to be effective only in an emergency defined in subsection (d). The emergency bylaws, which are subject to amendment or repeal by the shareholders, may make all provisions necessary for managing the corporation during the emergency, including:

(1) procedures for calling a meeting of the board of directors;

(2) quorum requirements for the meeting; and

(3) designation of additional or substitute directors.

(b) All provisions of the regular bylaws consistent with the emergency bylaws remain effective during the emergency. The emergency bylaws are not effective after the emergency ends.

(c) Corporate action taken in good faith in accordance with the emergency bylaws:

(1) binds the corporation; and

(2) may not be used to impose liability on a corporate director, officer, employee, or agent.

(d) An emergency exists for purposes of this section if a quorum of the corporation's directors cannot readily be assembled because of some catastrophic event.

§ 3.01. PURPOSES

(a) Every corporation incorporated under this Act has the purpose of engaging in any lawful business unless a more limited purpose is set forth in the articles of incorporation.

(b) A corporation engaging in a business that is subject to regulation under another statute of this state may incorporate under this Act only if permitted by, and subject to all limitations of, the other statute.

§ 3.02. GENERAL POWERS

Unless its articles of incorporation provide otherwise, every corporation has perpetual duration and succession in its corporate name and has the same powers as an individual to do all things necessary or convenient to carry out its business and affairs, including without limitation power:

(1) to sue and be sued, complain and defend in its corporate name;

(2) to have a corporate seal, which may be altered at will, and to use it, or a facsimile of it, by impressing or affixing it or in any other manner reproducing it;

(3) to make and amend bylaws, not inconsistent with its articles of incorporation or with the laws of this state, for managing the business and regulating the affairs of the corporation;

(4) to purchase, receive, lease, or otherwise acquire, and own, hold, improve, use, and otherwise deal with, real or personal property, or any legal or equitable interest in property, wherever located;

(5) to sell, convey, mortgage, pledge, lease, exchange, and otherwise dispose of all or any part of its property;

(6) to purchase, receive, subscribe for, or otherwise acquire; own, hold, vote, use, sell, mortgage, lend, pledge, or otherwise dispose of; and deal in and with shares or

other interests in, or obligations of, any other entity;

(7) to make contracts and guarantees, incur liabilities, borrow money, issue its notes, bonds, and other obligations (which may be convertible into or include the option to purchase other securities of the corporation), and secure any of its obligations by mortgage or pledge of any of its property, franchises, or income;

(8) to lend money, invest and reinvest its funds, and receive and hold real and personal property as security for repayment;

(9) to be a promoter, partner, member, associate, or manager of any partnership, joint venture, trust, or other entity;

(10) to conduct its business, locate offices, and exercise the powers granted by this Act within or without this state;

(11) to elect directors and appoint officers, employees, and agents of the corporation, define their duties, fix their compensation, and lend them money and credit;

(12) to pay pensions and establish pension plans, pension trusts, profit sharing plans, share bonus plans, share option plans, and benefit or incentive plans for any or all of its current or former directors, officers, employees, and agents;

(13) to make donations for the public welfare or for charitable, scientific, or educational purposes;

(14) to transact any lawful business that will aid governmental policy; and

(15) to make payments or donations, or do any other act, not inconsistent with law, that furthers the business and affairs of the corporation.

§ 3.03.   EMERGENCY POWERS

(a) In anticipation of or during an emergency defined in subsection (d), the board of directors of a corporation may:

(1) modify lines of succession to accommodate the incapacity of any director, officer, employee, or agent; and

(2) the principal office, designate alternative principal offices or regional offices, or authorize the officers to do so.

(b) During an emergency defined in subsection (d), unless emergency bylaws provide otherwise:

(1) notice of a meeting of the board of directors need be given only to those directors whom it is practicable to reach and may be given in any practicable manner, including by publication and radio; and

(2) one or more officers of the corporation present at a meeting of the board of directors may be deemed to be directors for the meeting, in order of rank and within the same rank in order of seniority, as necessary to achieve a quorum.

(c) Corporate action taken in good faith during an emergency under this section to further the ordinary business affairs of the corporation:

(1) binds the corporation; and

(2) may not be used to impose liability on a corporate director, officer, employee, or agent.

(d) An emergency exists for purposes of this section if a quorum of the corporation's directors cannot readily be assembled because of some catastrophic event.

§ 3.04.   ULTRA VIRES

(a) Except as provided in subsection (b), the validity of corporate action may not be challenged on the ground that the corporation lacks or lacked power to act.

(b) A corporation's power to act may be challenged:

(1) in a proceeding by a shareholder against the corporation to enjoin the act;

(2) in a proceeding by the corporation, directly, derivatively, or through a receiver, trustee, or other legal representative, against an incumbent or former director, officer, employee, or agent of the corporation; or

(3) in a proceeding by the Attorney General under section 14.30.

(c) In a shareholder's proceeding under subsection (b)(1) to enjoin an unauthorized corporate act, the court may enjoin or set aside the act, if equitable and if all affected persons are parties to the proceeding, and may award damages for loss (other than anticipated profits) suffered by the corporation or another party because of enjoining the unauthorized act.

§ 4.01.   CORPORATE NAME

(a) A corporate name:

(1) must contain the word "corporation," "incorporated," "company," or "limited," or the abbreviation "corp.," "inc.," "co.," or "ltd.," or words or abbreviations of like import in another language; and

(2) may not contain language stating or implying that the corporation is organized for a purpose other than that permitted by section 3.01 and its articles of incorporation.

(b) Except as authorized by subsections (c) and (d), a corporate name must be distinguishable upon the records of the secretary of state from:

(1) the corporate name of a corporation incorporated or authorized to transact business in this state;

(2) a corporate name reserved or registered under section 4.02 or 4.03;

(3) the fictitious name adopted by a foreign corporation authorized to transact business in this state because its real name is unavailable; and

(4) the corporate name of a not-for-profit corporation incorporated or authorized to transact business in this state.

(c) A corporation may apply to the secretary of state for authorization to use a name that is not distinguishable upon his records from one or more of the names described in subsection (b). The secretary of state shall authorize use of the name applied for if:

(1) the other corporation consents to the use in writing and submits an undertaking in form satisfactory to the secretary of state to change its name to a name that is distinguishable upon the records of the secretary of state from the name of the applying corporation; or

(2) the applicant delivers to the secretary of state a certified copy of the final judgment of a court of competent jurisdiction establishing the applicant's right to use the name applied for in this state.

(d) A corporation may use the name (including the fictitious name) of another domestic or foreign corporation that is used in this state if the other corporation is incorporated or authorized to transact business in this state and the proposed user corporation:

(1) has merged with the other corporation;

(2) has been formed by reorganization of the other corporation; or

(3) has acquired all or substantially all of the assets, including the corporate name, of the other corporation.

(e) This Act does not control the use of fictitious names.

§ 5.01. REGISTERED OFFICE AND REGISTERED AGENT

Each corporation must continuously maintain in this state:

(1) a registered office that may be the same as any of its places of business; and

(2) a registered agent, who may be:

(i) an individual who resides in this state and whose business office is identical with the registered office;

(ii) a domestic corporation or not-for-profit domestic corporation whose business office is identical with the registered office; or

(iii) a foreign corporation or not-for-profit foreign corporation authorized to transact business in this state whose business office is identical with the registered office.

§ 6.03. ISSUED AND OUTSTANDING SHARES

(a) A corporation may issue the number of shares of each class or series authorized by the articles of incorporation. Shares that are issued are outstanding shares until they are reacquired, redeemed, converted, or canceled.

(b) The reacquisition, redemption, or conversion of outstanding shares is subject to the limitations of subsection (c) of this section and to section 6.40.

(c) At all times that shares of the corporation are outstanding, one or more shares that together have unlimited voting rights and one or more shares that together are entitled to receive the net assets of the corporation upon dissolution must be outstanding.

§ 6.20. SUBSCRIPTION FOR SHARES BEFORE INCORPORATION

(a) A subscription for shares entered into before incorporation is irrevocable for six months unless the subscription agreement provides a longer or shorter period or all the subscribers agree to revocation.

(b) The board of directors may determine the payment terms of subscriptions for shares that were entered into before incorporation, unless the subscription agreement specifies them. A call for payment by the board of directors must be uniform so far as practicable as to all shares of the same class or series, unless the subscription agreement specifies otherwise.

(c) Shares issued pursuant to subscriptions entered into before incorporation are fully paid and nonassessable when the corporation receives the consideration specified in the subscription agreement.

(d) If a subscriber defaults in payment of money or property under a subscription agreement entered into before incorporation, the corporation may collect the amount owed as any other debt. Alternatively, unless the subscription agreement provides otherwise, the corporation may rescind the agreement and may sell the shares if the debt remains unpaid more than 20 days after the corporation sends written demand for payment to the subscriber.

(e) A subscription agreement entered into after incorporation is a contract between the subscriber and the corporation subject to section 6.21.

§ 6.22. LIABILITY OF SHAREHOLDERS

(a) A purchaser from a corporation of its own shares is not liable to the corporation or its creditors with respect to the shares except to pay the consideration for which the shares were authorized to be issued (section 6.21) or specified in the subscription agreement (section 6.20).

(b) Unless otherwise provided in the articles of incorporation, a shareholder of a corporation is not personally liable for the acts or debts of the corporation except that he may become personally liable by reason of his own acts or conduct.

§ 7.01. ANNUAL MEETING

(a) A corporation shall hold a meeting of shareholders annually at a time stated in or fixed in accordance with the bylaws.

(b) Annual shareholders' meetings may be held in or out of this state at the place stated in or fixed in accordance with the bylaws. If no place is stated in or fixed in accordance with the bylaws, annual meetings shall be held at the corporation's principal office.

(c) The failure to hold an annual meeting at the time stated in or fixed in accordance with a corporation's bylaws does not affect the validity of any corporate action.

§ 7.04.   ACTION WITHOUT MEETING

(a) Action required or permitted by this Act to be taken at a shareholders' meeting may be taken without a meeting if the action is taken by all the shareholders entitled to vote on the action. The action must be evidenced by one or more written consents describing the action taken, signed by all the shareholders entitled to vote on the action, and delivered to the corporation for inclusion in the minutes or filing with the corporate records.

(b) If not otherwise fixed under section 7.03 or 7.07, the record date for determining shareholders entitled to take action without a meeting is the date the first shareholder signs the consent under subsection (a).

(c) A consent signed under this section has the effect of a meeting vote and may be described as such in any document.

(d) If this Act requires that notice of proposed action be given to nonvoting shareholders and the action is to be taken by unanimous consent of the voting shareholders, the corporation must give its nonvoting shareholders written notice of the proposed action at least 10 days before the action is taken. The notice must contain or be accompanied by the same material that, under this Act, would have been required to be sent to nonvoting shareholders in a notice of meeting at which the proposed action would have been submitted to the shareholders for action.

§ 7.05.   NOTICE OF MEETING

(a) A corporation shall notify shareholders of the date, time, and place of each annual and special shareholders' meeting no fewer than 10 nor more than 60 days before the meeting date. Unless this Act or the articles of incorporation require otherwise, the corporation is required to give notice only to shareholders entitled to vote at the meeting.

(b) Unless this Act or the articles of incorporation require otherwise, notice of an annual meeting need not include a description of the purpose or purposes for which the meeting is called.

(c) Notice of a special meeting must include a description of the purpose or purposes for which the meeting is called.

(d) If not otherwise fixed under section 7.03 or 7.07, the record date for determining shareholders entitled to notice of and to vote at an annual or special shareholders' meeting is the day before the first notice is delivered to shareholders.

(e) Unless the bylaws require otherwise, if an annual or special shareholders' meeting is adjourned to a different date, time, or place, notice need not be given of the new date, time, or place if the new date, time, or place is announced at the meeting before adjournment. If a new record date for the adjourned meeting is or must be fixed under section 7.07, however, notice of the adjourned meeting must be given under this section to persons who are shareholders as of the new record date.

§ 7.06.   WAIVER OF NOTICE

(a) A shareholder may waive any notice required by this Act, the articles of incorporation, or bylaws before or after the date and time stated in the notice. The waiver must be in writing, be signed by the shareholder entitled to the notice, and be delivered to the corporation for inclusion in the minutes or filing with the corporate records.

(b) A shareholder's attendance at a meeting:

(1) waives objection to lack of notice or defective notice of the meeting, unless the shareholder at the beginning of the meeting objects to holding the meeting or transacting business at the meeting;

(2) waives objection to consideration of a particular matter at the meeting that is not within the purpose or purposes described in the meeting notice, unless the shareholder objects to considering the matter when it is presented.

§ 7.07.   RECORD DATE

(a) The bylaws may fix or provide the manner of fixing the record date for one or more voting groups in order to determine the shareholders entitled to notice of a shareholders' meeting, to demand a special meeting, to vote, or to take any other action. If the bylaws do not fix or provide for fixing a record date, the board of directors of the corporation may fix a future date as the record date.

(b) A record date fixed under this section may not be more than 70 days before the meeting or action requiring a determination of shareholders.

(c) A determination of shareholders entitled to notice of or to vote at a shareholders' meeting is effective for any adjournment of the meeting unless the board of directors fixes a new record date, which it must do if the meeting is adjourned to a date more than 120 days after the date fixed for the original meeting.

(d) If a court orders a meeting adjourned to a date more than 120 days after the date fixed for the original meeting, it may provide that the original record date continues in effect or it may fix a new record date.

§ 7.21.   VOTING ENTITLEMENT OF SHARES

(a) Except as provided in subsections (b) and (c) or unless the articles of incorporation provide otherwise, each outstanding share, regardless of class, is entitled to one vote on each matter voted on at a shareholders' meeting. Only shares are entitled to vote.

(b) Absent special circumstances, the shares of a corporation are not entitled to vote if they are owned, directly or indirectly, by a second corporation, domestic or foreign, and the first corporation owns, directly or indirectly, a majority of the shares entitled to vote for directors of the second corporation.

(c) Subsection (b) does not limit the power of a corporation to vote any shares, including its own shares, held by it in a fiduciary capacity.

(d) Redeemable shares are not entitled to vote after notice of redemption is mailed to the holders and a sum sufficient to redeem the shares has been deposited with a bank, trust company, or other financial institution under an irrevocable obligation to pay the holders the redemption price on surrender of the shares.

§ 7.22.   PROXIES

(a) A shareholder may vote his shares in person or by proxy.

(b) A shareholder may appoint a proxy to vote or otherwise act for him by signing an appointment form, either personally or by his attorney-in-fact.

(c) An appointment of a proxy is effective when received by the secretary or other officer of agent authorized to tabulate votes. An appointment is valid for 11 months unless a longer period is expressly provided in the appointment form.

(d) An appointment of a proxy is revocable by the shareholder unless the appointment form conspicuously states that it is irrevocable and the appointment is coupled with an interest. Appointments coupled with an interest include the appointment of:

(1) a pledgee;

(2) a person who purchased or agreed to purchase the shares;

(3) a creditor of the corporation who extended it credit under terms requiring the appointment;

(4) an employee of the corporation whose employment contract requires the appointment; or

(5) a party to a voting agreement created under section 7.31.

(e) The death or incapacity of the shareholder appointing a proxy does not affect the right of the corporation to accept the proxy's authority unless notice of the death or incapacity is received by the secretary or other officer or agent authorized to tabulate votes before the proxy exercises his authority under the appointment.

(f) An appointment made irrevocable under subsection (d) is revoked when the interest with which it is coupled is extinguished.

(g) A transferee for value of shares subject to an irrevocable appointment may revoke the appointment if he did not know of its existence when he acquired the shares and the existence of the irrevocable appointment was not noted conspicuously on the certificate representing the shares or on the information statement for shares without certificates.

(h) Subject to section 7.24 and to any express limitation on the proxy's authority appearing on the face of the appointment form, a corporation is entitled to accept the proxy's vote or other action as that of the shareholder making the appointment.

§ 8.01.   REQUIREMENT FOR AND DUTIES OF BOARD OF DIRECTORS

(a) Except as provided in subsection (c), each corporation must have a board of directors.

(b) All corporate powers shall be exercised by or under the authority of, and the business and affairs of the corporation managed under the direction of, its board of directors, subject to any limitation set forth in the articles of incorporation.

(c) A corporation having 50 or fewer shareholders may dispense with or limit the authority of a board of directors by describing in its articles of incorporation who will perform some or all of the duties of a board of directors.

§ 8.03.   NUMBER AND ELECTION OF DIRECTORS

(a) A board of directors must consist of one or more individuals, with the number specified in or fixed in accordance with the articles of incorporation or bylaws.

(b) If a board of directors has power to fix or change the number of directors, the board may increase or decrease by 30 percent or less the number of directors last approved by the shareholders, but only the shareholders may increase or decrease by more than 30 percent the number of directors last approved by the shareholders.

(c) The articles of incorporation or bylaws may establish a variable range for the size of the board of directors by fixing a minimum and maximum number of directors. If a variable range is established, the number of directors may be fixed or changed from time to time, within the minimum and maximum, by the shareholders or the board of directors. After shares are issued, only the shareholders may change the range for the size of the board or change from a fixed to a variable-range size board or vice versa.

(d) Directors are elected at the first annual shareholders' meeting and at each annual meeting thereafter unless their terms are staggered under section 8.06.

§ 8.04.   ELECTION OF DIRECTORS BY CERTAIN CLASSES OF SHAREHOLDERS

If the articles of incorporation authorize dividing the shares into classes, the articles may also authorize the election of all or a specified number of directors by the holders of one or more authorized classes of shares. A class (or classes) of shares entitled to elect one or more directors is a separate voting group for purposes of the election of directors.

§ 8.05.   TERMS OF DIRECTORS GENERALLY

(a) The terms of the initial directors of a corporation expire at the first shareholders' meeting at which directors are elected.

(b) The terms of all other directors expire at the next annual shareholders' meeting following their election unless their terms are staggered under section 8.06.

(c) A decrease in the number of directors does not shorten an incumbent director's term.

(d) The term of a director elected to fill a vacancy expires at the next shareholders' meeting at which directors are elected.

(e) Despite the expiration of a director's term, he continues to serve until his successor is elected and qualifies or until there is a decrease in the number of directors.

§ 8.06.   STAGGERED TERMS FOR DIRECTORS

If there are nine or more directors, the articles of incorporation may provide for staggering their terms by dividing the total number of directors into two or three groups, with each group containing one half or one-third of the total, as near as may be. In that event, the terms of directors in the first group expire at the first annual shareholders' meeting after their election, the terms of the second group expire at the second annual shareholders' meeting after their election, and the terms of the third group, if any, expire at the third annual shareholders' meeting after their election. At each annual shareholders' meeting held thereafter, directors shall be chosen for a term of two years or three years, as the case may be, to succeed those whose terms expire.

§ 8.08.   REMOVAL OF DIRECTORS BY SHARE-HOLDERS

(a) The shareholders may remove one or more directors with or without cause unless the articles of incorporation provide that directors may be removed only for cause.

(b) If a director is elected by a voting group of shareholders, only the shareholders of that voting group may participate in the vote to remove him.

(c) If cumulative voting is authorized, a director may not be removed if the number of votes sufficient to elect him under cumulative voting is voted against his removal. If cumulative voting is not authorized, a director may be removed only if the number of votes cast to remove him exceeds the number of votes cast not to remove him.

(d) A director may be removed by the shareholders only at a meeting called for the purpose of removing him and the meeting notice must state that the purpose, or one of the purposes, of the meeting is removal of the director.

§ 8.20.   MEETINGS

(a) The board of directors may hold regular or special meetings in or out of state.

(b) Unless the articles of incorporation or bylaws provide otherwise, the board of directors may permit any or all directors to participate in a regular or special meeting by, or conduct the meeting through the use of, any means of communication by which all directors participating may simultaneously hear each other during the meeting. A director participating in a meeting by this means is deemed to be present in person at the meeting.

§ 8.30.   GENERAL STANDARDS FOR DIRECTORS

(a) A director shall discharge his duties as a director, including his duties as a member on a committee:

(1) in good faith;

(2) with the care an ordinarily prudent person in a like position would exercise under similar circumstances; and

(3) in a manner he reasonably believes to be in the best interests of the corporation.

(b) In discharging his duties a director is entitled to rely on information, opinions, reports, or statements, including financial statements and other financial data, if prepared or presented by:

(1) one or more officers or employees of the corporation whom the director reasonably believes to be reliable and competent in the matters presented;

(2) legal counsel, public accountants, or other persons as to matters the director reasonably believes are within the person's professional or expert competence; or

(3) a committee of the board of directors of which he is not a member if the director reasonably believes the committee merits confidence.

(c) A director is not acting in good faith if he has knowledge concerning the matter in question that makes reliance otherwise permitted by subsection (b) unwarranted.

(d) A director is not liable for any action taken as a director, or any failure to take any action, if he performed the duties of his office in compliance with this section.

§ 8.31.   DIRECTOR CONFLICT OF INTEREST

(a) A conflict of interest transaction is a transaction with the corporation in which a director of the corporation has a direct or indirect interest. A conflict of interest transaction is not voidable by the corporation solely because of the director's interest in the transaction if any one of the following is true:

(1) the material facts of the transaction and the director's interest were disclosed or known to the board of directors or a committee of the board of directors and the board of directors or committee authorized, approved, or ratified the transaction;

(2) the material facts of the transaction and the director's interest were disclosed or known to the shareholders entitled to vote and they authorized, approved, or ratified the transaction; or

(3) the transaction was fair to the corporation.

(b) For the purposes of this section, a director of the corporation has an indirect interest in a transaction if

(1) another entity in which he has a material financial interest or in which he is a general partner is a party to the transaction or

(2) another entity of which he is a director, officer, or trustee is a party to the transaction and the trans-

action is or should be considered by the board of directions of the corporation.

(c) For purposes of subsection (a)(1), a conflict of interest transaction is authorized, approved, or ratified if it receives the affirmative vote of a majority of the directors on the board of directors (or on the committee) who have no direct or indirect interest in the transaction, but a transaction may not be authorized, approved, or ratified under this section by a single director. If a majority of the directors who have no direct or indirect interest in the transaction vote to authorize, approve, or ratify the transaction, a quorum is present for the purpose of taking action under this section. The presence of, or a vote cast by, a director with a direct or indirect interest in the transaction does not affect the validity of any action taken under subsection (a)(1) if the transaction is otherwise authorized, approved, or ratified as provided in that subsection.

(d) For purposes of subsection (a)(2), a conflict of interest transaction is authorized, approved, or ratified if it receives the vote of a majority of the shares entitled to be counted under this subsection. Shares owned by or voted under the control of a director who has a direct or indirect interest in the transaction, and shares owned by or voted under the control of an entity described in subsection (b)(1), may not be counted in a vote of shareholders to determine whether to authorize, approve, or ratify a conflict of interest transaction under subsection (a)(2). The vote of those shares, however, is counted in determining whether the transaction is approved under other sections of this Act. A majority of the shares, whether or not present, that are entitled to be counted in a vote on the transaction under this subsection constituted a quorum for the purpose of taking action under this section.

§ 8.33.   LIABILITY FOR UNLAWFUL DISTRIBUTIONS

(a) A director who votes for or assents to a distribution made in violation of section 6.40 or the articles of incorporation is personally liable to the corporation for the amount of the distribution that exceeds what could have been distributed without violating section 6.40 or the articles of incorporation if it is established that he did not perform his duties in compliance with section 8.30. In any proceeding commenced under this section, a director has all of the defenses ordinarily available to a director.

(b) A director held liable under subsection (a) for an unlawful distribution is entitled to contribution:

(1) from every other director who could be held liable under subsection (a) for the unlawful distribution; and

(2) from each shareholder for the amount the shareholder accepted knowing the distribution was made in violation of section 6.40 or the articles of incorporation.

(c) A proceeding under this section is barred unless it is commenced within two years after the date on which the effect of the distribution was measured under section 6.40(e) or (g).

§ 8.40.   REQUIRED OFFICERS

(a) A corporation has the officers described in its bylaws or appointed by the board of directors in accordance with the bylaws.

(b) A duly appointed officer may appoint one or more officers or assistant officers if authorized by the bylaws or the board of directors.

(c) The bylaws or the board of directors shall delegate to one of the officers responsibility for preparing minutes of the directors' and shareholders' meetings and for authenticating records of the corporation.

(d) The same individual may simultaneously hold more than one office in a corporation.

§ 8.41.   DUTIES OF OFFICERS

Each officer has the authority and shall perform the duties set forth in the bylaws or, to the extent consistent with the bylaws, the duties prescribed by the board of directors or by direction of an officer authorized by the board of directors to prescribe the duties of other officers.

§ 8.42.   STANDARDS OF CONDUCT FOR OFFICERS

(a) An officer with discretionary authority shall discharge his duties under that authority:

(1) in good faith;

(2) with the care an ordinarily prudent person in a like position would exercise under similar circumstances; and

(3) in a manner he reasonably believes to be in the best interests of the corporation.

(b) In discharging his duties an officer is entitled to rely on information, opinions, reports, or statements, including financial statements and other financial data, if prepared or presented by:

(1) one or more officers or employees of the corporation whom the officer reasonably believes to be reliable and competent in the matters presented; or

(2) legal counsel, public accountants, or other persons as to matters the officer reasonably believes are within the person's professional or expert competence.

(c) An officer is not acting in good faith if he has knowledge concerning the matter in question that makes reliance otherwise permitted by subsection (b) unwarranted.

(d) An officer is not liable for an action taken as an officer, or any failure to take any action, if he performed the duties of his office in compliance with this section.

§ 11.01.   MERGER

(a) One or more corporations may merge into another corporation if the board of directors of each corporation adopts and its shareholders (if required by section 11.03) approve a plan of merger.

(b) The plan of merger must set forth:

(1) the name of each corporation planning to merge and the name of the surviving corporation into which each other corporation plans to merge;

(2) the terms and conditions of the merger; and

(3) the manner and basis of converting the shares of each corporation into shares, obligations, or other securities of the surviving or any other corporation or into cash or other property in whole or part.

(c) The plan of merger may set forth:

(1) amendments to the articles of incorporation of the surviving corporation; and

(2) other provisions relating to the merger.

§ 13.02.   RIGHT TO DISSENT

(a) A shareholder is entitled to dissent from and obtain payment of the fair value of his shares in the event of, any of the following corporate actions:

(1) consummation of a plan of merger to which the corporation is a party (i) if shareholder approval is required for the merger by section 11.03 or the articles of incorporation and the shareholder is entitled to vote on the merger or (ii) if the corporation is a subsidiary that is merged with its parent under section 11.04;

(2) consummation of a plan of share exchange to which the corporation is a party as the corporation whose shares will be acquired, if the shareholder is entitled to vote on the plan;

(3) consummation of a sale or exchange of all, or substantially all, of the property of the corporation other than in the usual and regular course of business, if the shareholder is entitled to vote on the sale or exchange, including a sale in dissolution, but not including a sale pursuant to court order or a sale for cash pursuant to a plan by which all or substantially all of the net proceeds of the sale will be distributed to the shareholders within one year after the date of sale;

(4) an amendment of the articles of incorporation that materially and adversely affects rights in respect of a dissenter's shares because it:

(i) alters or abolishes a preferential right of the shares;

(ii) creates, alters, or abolishes a right in respect of redemption, including a provision respecting a sinking fund for the redemption or repurchase, of the shares;

(iii) alters or abolishes a preemptive right of the holder of the shares to acquire shares or other securities;

(iv) excludes or limits the right of the shares to vote on any matter, or to cumulate votes, other than a limitation by dilution through issuance of shares or other securities with similar voting rights; or

(v) reduces the number of shares owned by the shareholder to a fraction of a share if the fractional share so created is to be acquired for cash under section 6.04; or

(5) any corporate action taken pursuant to a shareholder vote to the extent the articles of incorporation, bylaws, or a resolution of the board of directors provides that voting or nonvoting shareholders are entitled to dissent and obtain payment for their shares.

(b) A shareholder entitled to dissent and obtain payment for his shares under this chapter may not challenge the corporate action creating his entitlement unless the action is unlawful or fraudulent with respect to the shareholder or the corporation.

§ 13.28.   PROCEDURE IF SHAREHOLDER DISSATISFIED WITH PAYMENT OR OFFER

(a) A dissenter may notify the corporation in writing of his own estimate of the fair value of his shares and amount of interest due, and demand payment of his estimate (less any payment under section 13.25), or reject the corporation's offer under section 13.27 and demand payment of the fair value of his shares and interest due, if:

(1) the dissenter believes that the amount paid under section 13.25 or offered under section 13.27 is less than the fair value of his shares or that the interest due is incorrectly calculated;

(2) the corporation fails to make payment under section 13.25 within 60 days after the date set for demanding payment; or

(3) the corporation, having failed to take the proposed action, does not return the deposited certificates or release the transfer restrictions imposed on uncertified shares within 60 days after the date set for demanding payment.

(b) A dissenter waives his right to demand payment under this section unless he notifies the corporation of his demand in writing under subsection (a) within 30 days after the corporation made or offered payment for his shares.

Subchapter C. Judicial Appraisal of Shares

§ 13.30   COURT ACTION

(a) If a demand for payment under section 13.28 remains unsettled, the corporation shall commence a proceeding within 60 days after receiving the payment demand and petition the court to determine the fair value of the shares and accrued interest. If the corporation does not commence the proceeding within the 60-day period, it shall pay each dissenter whose demand remains unsettled the amount demanded.

(b) The corporation shall commence the proceeding in the

[name or describe] court of the county where a corporation's principal office (or, if none in this state, its registered office) is located. If the corporation is a foreign corporation without a registered office in this state, it shall commence the proceeding in the county in this state where the registered office of the domestic corporation merged with or whose shares were acquired by the foreign corporations was located.

(c) The corporation shall make all dissenters (whether or not residents of this state) whose demands remain unsettled parties to the proceeding as in an action against their shares and all parties must be served with a copy of the petition. Nonresidents may be served by registered or certified mail or by publication as provided by law.

(d) The jurisdiction of the court in which the proceeding is commenced under subsection (b) is plenary and exclusive. The court may appoint one or more persons as appraisers to receive evidence and recommended decision on the question of fair value. The appraisers have the powers described in the order appointing them, or in any amendment to it. The dissenters are entitled to the same discovery rights as parties in other civil proceedings.

(e) Each dissenter made a party to the proceeding is entitled to judgment (1) for the amount, if any, by which the court finds the fair value of his shares, plus interest, exceeds the amount paid by the corporation, or (2) for the fair value, plus accrued interest, of his after-acquired shares for which the corporation elected to withhold payment under section 13.27.

§ 13.31   COURT COSTS AND COUNSEL FEES

(a) The court in an appraisal proceeding commenced under section 13.30 shall determine all costs of the proceeding, including the reasonable compensation and expenses of appraisers appointed by the court. The court shall assess the costs against the corporation, except that the court may assess costs against all or some of the dissenters, in amounts the court finds equitable, to the extent the court finds dissenters acted arbitrarily, vexatiously, or not in good faith in demanding payment under section 13.28.

(b) The court may also assess the fees and expenses of counsel and experts for the respective parties, in amounts the court finds equitable:

(1) against the corporation and in favor of any or all dissenters if the court finds the corporation did not substantially comply with the requirements of sections 13.20 through 13.28; or

(2) either the corporation or a dissenter, in favor of any other party, if the court finds that the party against whom the fees and expenses are assessed acted arbitrarily, vexatiously, or not in good faith with respect to the rights provided by this chapter.

(c) If the court finds that the services of counsel for any dissenter were of substantial benefit to other dissenters similarly situated, and that the fees for those services should not be assessed against the corporation, the court may award to these counsel reasonable fees to be paid out of the amounts awarded the dissenters who were benefited.

§ 16.01.   CORPORATE RECORDS

(a) A corporation shall keep as permanent records minutes of all meetings of its shareholders and board of directors, a record of all actions taken by the shareholders or board of directors without a meeting, and a record of all actions taken by a committee of the board of directors in place of the board of directors on behalf of the corporation.

(b) A corporation shall maintain appropriate accounting records.

(c) A corporation or its agent shall maintain a record of its shareholders, in a form that permits preparation of a list of the names and addresses of all shareholders, in alphabetical order by class of shares showing the number and class of shares held by each.

(d) A corporation shall maintain its records in written form or in another form capable of conversion into written form within a reasonable time.

(e) A corporation shall keep a copy of the following records at its principal office:

(1) its articles or restated articles of incorporation and all amendments to them currently in effect;

(2) its bylaws or restated bylaws and all amendments to them currently in effect;

(3) resolutions adopted by its board of directors creating one or more classes or series of shares, and fixing their relative rights, preferences, and limitations, if shares issued pursuant to those resolutions are outstanding;

(4) the minutes of all shareholders' meetings, and records of all action taken by shareholders without a meeting, for the past three years;

(5) all written communications to shareholders generally within the past three years, including the financial statements furnished for the past three years under section 16.20;

(6) a list of the names and business addresses of its current directors and officers; and

(7) its most recent annual report delivered to the secretary of state under section 16.22.

§ 16.02.   INSPECTION OF RECORDS BY SHAREHOLDERS

(a) A shareholder of a corporation is entitled to inspect and copy, during regular business hours at the corporation's principal office, any of the records of the corporation described in section 16.01(e) if he gives the corporation written notice of his demand at least five business days before the date on which he wishes to inspect and copy.

(b) A shareholder of a corporation is entitled to inspect and copy, during regular business hours at a reasonable location specified by the corporation, any of the following records of the corporation if the shareholder meets the requirements of subsection (c) and gives the corporation written notice of his demand at least five business days before the date on which he wishes to inspect and copy:

(1) excerpts from minutes of any meeting of the board of directors, records of any action of a committee of the board of directors while acting in place of the board of directors on behalf of the corporation, minutes of any meeting of the shareholders, and records of action taken by the shareholders or board of directors without a meeting, to the extent not subject to inspection under section 16.02(a);

(2) accounting records of the corporation; and

(3) the record of shareholders.

(c) A shareholder may inspect and copy the records described in subsection (b) only if:

(1) his demand is made in good faith and for a proper purpose;

(2) he describes with reasonable particularity his purpose and the records he desires to inspect; and

(3) the records are directly connected with his purpose.

(d) The right of inspection granted by this section may not be abolished or limited by a corporation's articles of incorporation or bylaws.

(e) This section does not affect:

(1) the right of a shareholder to inspect records under section 7.20 or, if the shareholder is in litigation with the corporation, to the same extent as any other litigant; or

(2) the power of a court, independently of this Act, to compel the production of corporate records for examination.

(f) For purposes of this section, "shareholder" includes a beneficial owner whose shares are held in a voting trust or by a nominee on his behalf.

§ 16.20.   FINANCIAL STATEMENTS FOR SHARE-HOLDERS

(a) a corporation shall furnish its shareholders annual financial statements, which may be consolidated or combined statements of the corporation and one or more of its subsidiaries, as appropriate, that include a balance sheet as of the end of the fiscal year, an income statement for that year, and a statement of changes in shareholders' equity for the year unless that information appears elsewhere in the financial statements. If financial statements are prepared for the corporation on the basis of generally accepted accounting principles, the annual financial statements must also be prepared on that basis.

(b) If the annual financial statements are reported upon by a public accountant, his report must accompany them. If not, the statements must be accompanied by a statement of the president or the person responsible for the corporation's accounting records:

(1) stating his reasonable belief whether the statements were prepared on the basis of generally accepted accounting principles and, if not, describing the basis of preparation; and

(2) describing any respects in which the statements were not prepared on a basis of accounting consistent with the statements prepared for the preceding year.

(c) A corporation shall mail the annual financial statements to each shareholder within 120 days after the close of each fiscal year. Thereafter, on written request from a shareholder who was not mailed the statements, the corporation shall mail him the latest financial statements.

Answers to Odd-numbered AICPA Questions

Chapter 11
Nature and Classes of Contracts

1. (a) The offeror made a promise for an act. When the act was performed, a unilateral contract was created and the offeror is bound to pay. Answer (b) is incorrect because unjust enrichment is generally considered only if there was no contract and the court wishes to provide an "equitable solution." Answer (c) is incorrect because there are no public policy issues involved. Answer (d) is incorrect because a quasi-contract arises only if there was no contract to begin with and the law implies one to prevent an unjust enrichment. Since there was a unilateral contract, there can be no quasi-contract.

Chapter 12
The Agreement

1. (c) If sent by a mode of communication expressly or impliedly authorized by the offeror (e.g., mail or telegram), acceptance of an offer is normally effective on dispatch, even if subsequently delayed or lost. Noll's telegram was an effective acceptance of the offer by Able. The rule applies to any situation in which acceptance is made in a manner expressly or impliedly authorized. This can include telegraph or telephone as well as mail in most circumstances. In this situation the acceptance was effective on dispatch, before Able's attempted revocation.

3. (c) Peters' offer had been revoked. Since revocation notice can be received either directly or indirectly, Mason, in effect, received the revocation notice when he was told the mower had been sold to Bronson; and therefore, Mason's acceptance was ineffective, even though the specified time of the oral contract had not expired. Peters' offer had been revoked prior to Mason's acceptance. There was no obligation on the part of Peters to keep the offer open, since there was no consideration for him to do so.

Chapter 13
Capacity and Genuine Assent

1. (a) Where a mistake is made by only one party (a unilateral mistake), the rule is that the mistaken party is bound by the contract unless the nonmistaken party knew of the mistake or should have known of the mistake. In this question, the nonmistaken party knew of the mistake; thus, the mistaken party is not bound by the contract. Whether the mistake was a result of gross negligence is irrelevant.

Chapter 15
Legality and Public Policy

1. (d) There are two types of licensing statutes. First, there are licensing statutes intended primarily for revenue raising. Second, there are licensing statutes (regulatory) intended primarily to protect the public

against dishonest or incompetent professionals. An individual without a license can collect his total compensation if the primary purpose of the statute was to raise revenue. However, if the purpose was regulatory in nature (intended to protect the public), the individual can collect nothing since the contract is voidable. Thus, an unlicensed individual who enters into a contract to provide regulated services will not be allowed to enforce the contract or recover even the value of the services rendered.

Chapter 16
Form of Contract
1. (d) The contract terms need not appear in a single document so long as the several documents refer to the same transaction. Only the signature of the party against whom enforcement is sought is required. If the performance *could* occur within a one-year period, the contract is not within the statute and need not be written. Only contracts of $500 or more that involve the sale of goods fall under the Statute of Fraud and must be in writing.
3. (c) The parol evidence rule will prevent the admission of evidence concerning the oral agreements regarding who pays the utilities, since the rule excludes evidence of prior or contemporaneous oral agreements, which would vary the written contract. However, the parol evidence rule will *not* prevent the admission of the fraudulent statements by Kemp during the original negotiations. Therefore, answers (a), (b), and (d) are incorrect.

Chapter 18
Third Persons and Contracts
1. (c) An assignment is rebuttably presumed to be an assignment of rights *and* a delegation of duties. Here, assignee Deep Sea Lobster Farms presumably could carry out the lobster delivery duties.
3. (a) Union is a creditor beneficiary under the insurance policy. It is not a donee or incidental beneficiary. Privity of contract is not the issue in this question.

Chapter 19
Discharge of Contracts
1. (b) Glaze will win because he "substantially performed" on the contract. Glaze should receive the contract price less the cost of damages due to minor deviations from the required performance. Glaze can also collect because Parc refused to allow Glaze the opportunity to complete the contract. Glaze can recover for substantial performance of the contract. The breach was a minor breach. Glaze breached the contract by purchasing minor accessories not allowed under the contract. In response, Parc refused to allow Glaze to complete the contract. This is not considered to be anticipatory breach by Parc.

Chapter 20
Breach of Contract and Remedies
1. (b) The statute of limitations in an action for breach of contract begins to toll from the time the contract is breached.
3. (b) The repudiation or renunciation of the contract before performance is due is known as anticipatory breach. Answers (a) and (c) are alternative choices for Foster. Answer (d) is the usual remedy for a breach of contract. Answer (b), which asks for the remedy of specific performance, is not available where the breaching party's performance requires personal services.

Chapter 21
Accountants' Liability and Malpractice
1. (d) A third party need not be an intended beneficiary in order to bring a charge of actual or constructive fraud. However, a third party must be an intended beneficiary, or one whom the accountant knew or should have known would be a user or beneficiary of the work product, before the third party may bring a charge of negligence. Therefore, answer (d) is the correct choice.
3. (a) An accountant's liability to third parties for ordinary negligence normally extends only to those parties who the accountant specifically knew would be users of the work product. Thus, if the accountant did not know that the creditor would use the work product, privity would be a viable defense. Under the *Ultramares* doctrine, accountants owe a duty to all third parties to make their reports without actual or constructive fraud. Gross negligence amounting to a reckless disregard for the truth constitutes constructive fraud. Accountants have a contractual relationship with their clients thus privity would *not* be a defense.

Chapter 22
Personal Property
1. (a) Sklar's inter vivos conveyance to Marsh terminated the joint tenancy with respect to the grantee, Marsh. Therefore, Marsh's interest is that of a tenant in common, a one-third interest with no rights of survivorship. The interest in the building can be transferred without the consent of the other joint tenants.

Chapter 23
Bailments
1. (a) In order for there to be a valid bailment, personal property must be delivered to the intended bailee, who must then retain possession of the property. Although the bailee has a duty to hold the property for the bailor and to follow any of the bailor's reasonable instructions as to the disposition of the property, the bailee's duty is not an absolute one.

Chapter 24

Legal Aspects of Warehousing, Transportation, Factoring, and Hotelkeeping

1. (d)   A common carrier has liability for even slight negligence. A common carrier would thus be liable if the goods were stolen while in the carrier's custody. The carrier would also be liable if the goods were destroyed as a result of its employees' negligence. The carrier would not, however, have any knowledge of or control over how the goods were packed by the bailor or other party.

3. (a)   A negotiable warehouse receipt is a document issued as evidence of the receipt of goods by a person engaged in the business of storing goods for hire. The warehouse receipt is negotiable if the face of the document contains the words of negotiability (order or bearer).

Chapter 25

Nature and Form of Sales

1. (a)   The Statute of Frauds requires that a contract for goods of $500 or more be in writing. UCC 2-207, however, provides that in a contract between merchants, the Statute of Frauds is satisfied if a written confirmation is sent within a reasonable time. The confirmation must be received by the other party who knows or should know the confirmation's contents. If the recipient merchant fails to object to the confirmation's contents within a reasonable time they will be bound to the contract.

3. (b)   An agreement for the sale of goods under $500 need not be in writing to be enforceable. Thus, Bond and Spear had a valid oral contract, and Spear has breached the contract by agreeing to sell the car to a third party. The adequacy of consideration is not a contract issue. The agreement does not need to be in writing because it was under $500. Paying a deposit is not the deciding factor in this case. The key point is that the agreement was for the sale of goods under $500.

Chapter 26

Passage of Title and Risk of Loss: Rights of Parties

1. (a)   Risk of loss passes upon *tender* of delivery when the seller is not a merchant. If the seller was a merchant, risk of loss would pass upon the buyer's receipt of the goods. In this problem, the facts clearly specify that Wool is not a merchant in the goods being sold, so we can determine that risk of loss passed to Bond upon tender of delivery.

3. (d)   Under a sale or return contract, the sale is considered as completed although it is voidable at the buyer's election. As such, risk of loss passes to the buyer, who also has title to the goods until they are returned; therefore, answer (c) is incorrect. Furthermore, the return of the goods is at the buyer's risk and expense; thus, answer (b) is incorrect. Answer (a) is incorrect because, under the definition of a sale or return contract, the buyer is acquiring the goods for resale.

Chapter 27

Obligations of Performance

1. (a)   UCC 1-102(3) imposes an obligation on the parties to contract in good faith. Merchants are frequently treated differently under UCC 2 provisions. UCC 2 covers contracts for goods regardless of the contract price, and the UCC permits the parties to a contract to disclaim many if the UCC's provisions

3. (a)   Answer (a) is correct since the buyer has a reasonable time in which to reject defective goods. Discovering the defect on Monday would be considered within a reasonable time, considering the goods had been delivered on Friday. Answer (d) is incorrect since the specification concerning the linings in the sales contract would be an express warranty which was breached when the linings were found to be inferior to what had been stated. Thus, the merchantable quality of the linings would be irrelevant.

Chapter 28

Warranties and Other Product Liability Theories

1. (c)   Warranty of title may be given as well as disclaimed by merchants or non-merchants, orally or in writing. The disclaimer must be by specific language or circumstances, not simply a phrase such as "AS IS."

3. (b)   An injured plaintiff may sue any seller of a good under strict liability if the plaintiff can show that the good was sold in a defective or unreasonably dangerous condition. The plaintiff need not prove fault or wrongdoing by the defendant; thus, not having an opportunity to inspect or following industry customs are not defenses available to the defendant. Although contributory negligence is a defense available in negligence, it is generally not a defense in strict liability actions.

Chapter 29

Remedies for Breach of Sales Contracts

1. (a)   A seller who discovers that an insolvent buyer has received goods on credit may reclaim the goods by making a demand for their return within ten days after receipt of the goods by the buyer. This ten day limitation, however, does not apply if the buyer made a written misrepresentation of its solvency within three months prior to its receipt of the goods. Anker's fraudulent financials constitute a written misrepresentation of solvency; therefore, Bold may demand

return of the goods even though 14 days have passed. Answer (b) is incorrect because the seller's right to reclaim the goods is subject to the rights of a third party who purchases the goods in good faith from the insolvent buyer. Answer (c) is incorrect because the ten day limitation does not apply when the buyer (Anker) provides the seller (Bold) with a written misrepresentation of solvency (the financial statements) within three months prior to receipt of the goods. Answer (d) is incorrect because Anker may make a demand for the goods rather than sue for damages

Chapter 31

Kinds of Instruments, Parties, and Negotiability

1. (a)   Under the Commercial Paper Article of the UCC, for an instrument to be negotiable, it must be in writing, signed by the drawer or maker, contain an unconditional promise or order to pay a sum certain in money, on demand, or at an ascertainable time, and be payable to order or to bearer. Answers (b), (c), and (d) do not contain requirements for negotiability.

3. (a)   To be negotiable, an instrument must be in writing, signed by the maker or drawer, contain an unconditional promise or order to pay a sum certain in money on demand or at a specific time, and be payable to order or to bearer. Negotiability is not affected by the fact that the instrument recites the transaction which gave rise to the instrument and negotiability is not affected by the fact that it is stated with a specific rate of interest. The note is negotiable from the time it is made on October 2, 1987. It is a note (two-party instrument between maker and bearer-payee) and not a draft (which is a three-party instrument).

Chapter 32

Transfer of Negotiable Instruments

1. (d)   Rex's endorsement did not specify the person to whose order the instrument was then payable; it was, therefore, a blank endorsement. As executed by Hand, the instrument was bearer paper since it was made payable to "Rex or bearer." Ford could, therefore, qualify as a holder without Rex's endorsement. Bearer paper can be converted to order paper by making the last endorsement in the chain of endorsement a special endorsement.

3. (c)   The endorsement is restrictive, since it is " for collection only," and it is not special, since it does not specify the person to whose order the instrument is now payable. A special endorsement on bearer paper converts it to order paper.

Chapter 33

Rights of Holders and Defenses

1. (b)   Under the Commercial Paper Article of the UCC, in order for a person to qualify as a holder in due course of a promissory note, (1) they must qualify as a holder, (2) the note must be negotiable, and (3) they must take the note for value, in good faith, and without notice that it is overdue, dishonored, or there is a defense against it. Answers (a), (c), and (d) do nor contain requirements for becoming a holder in due course.

3. (b)   Under the Commercial Paper Article of the UCC, real (or universal) defenses available against a holder in due course include material alteration of the instrument and discharge of a person with primary or secondary liability in bankruptcy. Breach of contract is a personal defense not available against a holder in due course.

Chapter 34

Checks and Funds Transfers

1. (d)   Certification procured by the holder discharges the drawer and any prior endorsers; the bank becomes primarily liable. An endorser might still be held liable for breach of warranty even if the check is presented late. An endorser would have to cause an instrument to be dishonored for the notice of dishonor to be excused. The insolvency of the maker does not affect the responsibilities of the endorsers.

3. (a)   A bank may charge checks against an account in any order it deems convenient.

Chapter 35

Secured Transactions in Personal Property

1. (c)   Attachment occurs when (1) value is given by the secured party, (2) the debtor attains rights in the collateral, and (3) the debtor and creditor acknowledge the creation of a security interest by a signed security agreement or by collateral in the possession of the secured party. In this situation, attachment occurred on March 10 because the following occurred on or before that date: (1) Easy picked up the car, (2) the car had been identified to the contract, therefore Green had a right in the property, and (3) Green signed a security agreement. Therefore, answers (a), (c), and (d) are incorrect.

3. (b)   Under UCC 9-307, a buyer in the ordinary course of business takes free of a security interest created by his seller even though the security interest is perfected and even though the buyer knows of its existence. Neither Cray nor Zone is subject to the security interest; therefore, answer (a) is incorrect. Answer (d) is incorrect because a security agreement may provide that any or all obligations covered by the agreement are to be additionally secured by property later acquired by the debtor. Answer (c) is incorrect because unless otherwise provided in the security

agreement, the secured party has a continuously perfected security interest in the proceeds that result from the debtor's sale or transfer of the collateral.

Chapter 36

Other Security Devices

1. (d) Marbury Surety, Inc., agreed to act as a guarantor of collection. As such, Marbury is not required to indemnify the obligee, Madison, until the obligee has exhausted collection efforts. Ordinarily, this point is reached when the obligee has exhausted legal remedies and a judgment against the obligor debtor has been returned unsatisfied. In contrast, in a guarantor of payment agreement, the guarantor-surety is primarily liable on the debt with the obligor. No separate demand need be made on the guarantor-surety after the obligor's default. Upon default, both obligor and guarantor of payment are liable. Surety and guaranty agreements are not within the purview of Article 9; thus, there are no filing or recording requirements. Finally, Marbury is not a del credere agent because it is not guaranteeing payment for products sold on credit.

3. (a) A suretyship agreement is a contract which must be supported by consideration. When the suretyship agreement is contemporaneous with the primary contract, there is no need for separate consideration. The surety may exercise any real defenses on the contract which are available to the debtor. Thus, fraud, duress, illegality, forgery, etc., will discharge both surety and debtor. However, the surety may not rely on the debtor's personal defenses (e.g., incapacity, insolvency, or death) to avoid the suretyship obligation. The surety is also discharged from liability if the surety agreement was procured by duress or fraudulent misrepresentation by the *creditor*. Thus, if the creditor fraudulently contracts with the debtor or fraudulently procures the suretyship agreement itself, the agreement is voidable.

Chapter 37

Bankruptcy

1. (d) Voluntary bankruptcy petition is a formal request by the debtor for an order of relief. This voluntary bankruptcy petition may be filed jointly by a husband and a wife. Answer (b) is incorrect because the debtor in a voluntary bankruptcy petition need not be insolvent but needs to state that s/he has debts. Answers (a) and (c) are incorrect because there is no requirement as to the minimum amount of the debtor's liabilities in a voluntary proceeding.

3. (d) Most debtors may file a voluntary bankruptcy petition. Among those that may not are insurance companies, banks, and saving and loan associations.

Answer (a) is incorrect because the number of creditors is not relevant for a voluntary bankruptcy petition. Answer (b) is incorrect because there is no need to show that a Chapter 11 bankruptcy would have been unsuccessful. Answer (c) is incorrect because the inability of the debtor to pay its debts as they become due is not relevant to a voluntary bankruptcy.

5a. (a) When distributing the assets of a debtor's estate, secured creditors have first priority to the property acting as their collateral. Second priority in the distribution is administrative costs which include the trustee fee and the attorneys' fees. All claims of one class are paid in full before the next class receives anything. If the assets are insufficient to pay all claims of a given class, the claimants share pro rata. In this case, the first $5,000 of the remaining assets would be paid to Noll Co. since it is the only secured creditor. Since the remaining $10,000 ($15,000 – $5,000) is insufficient to cover all of the administrative costs of the bankruptcy ($15,000 owed to trustee and $10,000 owed to attorneys), a pro rata share will be distributed to the trustee and attorneys. The trustee will receive 60% of the remaining assets since s/he is owed 60% of the total administrative fees [$15,000/($10,000 + $15,000) = 60%]. Therefore, the trustee will receive 60% of $10,000 or $6,000. Thus, answers (b), (c), and (d) are incorrect.

5b. (b) When distributing the assets of the debtor's estate, the trustee must follow the statutorily prescribed priorities. Thus, in this case, the first $5,000 of the remaining assets would be paid to Noll Co. since it is the only secured creditor. The next $25,000 would be paid to cover bankruptcy administration expenses ($15,000 to trustee + $10,000 to attorneys). Finally, the remaining $11,000 ($41,000 – 5,000 – 25,000) would be distributed to claims arising in the ordinary course of the debtor's business after the involuntary bankruptcy petition is filed but prior to the appointment of a trustee and the issuance of the order for relief. Since Dart Corp. is the only creditor that fits in this category and qualifies as an "involuntary gap" creditor, it will receive the remaining $11,000. Therefore, answers (a), (c), and (d) are incorrect.

Chapter 38

Insurance

1. (a) For an insurable interest to arise, there must exist such an interest between the insured and the risk covered, so that if specified events occur, the insured will suffer some substantial loss or injury. Such an interest includes the possessory interest of a tenant of property and the interests of secured creditors, including mortgages.

3. (c) The formula is:

$$\frac{Face\ Value\ of\ Insurance}{Coinsurance\ Percentage \times \frac{Fair\ Market\ Value\ of\ Property}{}} \times Actual\ Loss$$

Lawfo's insurance recovery will be:

$$\frac{\$200,000}{80\% \times \$300,000} \times \$30,000 = \$25,000$$

Chapter 39

Agency

1. (c) The agent's renunciation of the agency does not automatically terminate by *operation of law*. The other answers listed *do* terminate an agency.

3. (b) It is generally not necessary for an agent to have a written agency agreement. An exception to the general rule exists if the agent's duties will involve the buying and selling of real property, or if the agency agreement is to last more than one year.

5. (a) An agent has a fiduciary duty to be loyal to his principal. The agent cannot compete with his principal without the principal's consent, and the agent cannot deal for his own interests that are adverse to the principal. Answer (c) is incorrect because a principal generally has the *power* to terminate an agency relationship, although he may not have the *right*. In such a case, the agency may be terminated even though he or she could be liable for breach of the agency contract. However, a principal may not revoke an "agency coupled with an interest." This type of agency is created when the agent is given an immediate interest in the subject matter of the agency. An "interest in the subject matter" should not be confused with an agent's contract for compensation. In this instance, Thorp has not received an "interest"; he or she has merely agreed that compensation will be calculated in part as a percentage as sales. Thus, answer (b) is also incorrect because the right of the agent to receive a percentage of proceeds is not sufficient to constitute an agency coupled with an interest. Answer (d) is incorrect because the agency relationship need not be in writing because it can be performed within one year.

Chapter 40

Third Persons in Agency

1. (b) Specific performance is appropriate only when the subject matter is so unique that the aggrieved party cannot be fairly compensated with money damage; therefore, answer (b) is the proper response. The agent of an undisclosed principal binds himself and has the right to sue the third person in his own name; money damages are the appropriate remedy, so answer (a) is not correct. If the principal discloses himself and asserts his rights under the contract, he may also sue the third party as long as the contract does not involve personal services, trust, or confidence; thus, answer (c) is incorrect.

3. (d) As an agent for an undisclosed principal, Datz is solely liable on the contract unless the third party later discovers the identity of the principal, in which case either Datz or Cox may be held liable. Therefore, answers (a) and (b) are incorrect. Answer (c) is incorrect because Cox, as an undisclosed principal, has the right to enforce the contract against the third party as long as it does not involve personal services, trust, or confidence.

Chapter 43

Forms of Business Organization

1. (d) A joint venture resembles a partnership, except that it is formed for only one transaction (or in some cases, a *limited* number of transactions). Answer (a) is incorrect because it is possible to have more than two persons as part of the joint venture. Answer (b) is incorrect because a joint venture is a for-profit undertaking, not a nonprofit undertaking. Answer (c) is incorrect because a joint venture is treated as a partnership and not as a corporate enterprise.

Chapter 44

Creation and Termination of Partnerships

1. (d) A writing is needed in the formation of a partnership only when the partnership would otherwise be in violation of the statute of frauds. For example, any partnership agreement that necessitates the transfer of real property or the continuation of a business for a term in excess of one year must be in writing.

3. (b) Unless otherwise agreed, a partner's interest is freely assignable. The assignee is entitled to receive only profits and capital to which the partner would have been entitled. He or she does not become a partner and is not entitled to exercise control over the partnership. Therefore, answers (a), (c), and (d) are incorrect.

Chapter 45

Partnership, Limited Partnerships, and Limited Liability Companies

1. (c) In a general partnership, any partner may bind the partnership and other partners to all transactions within the apparent scope of the partnership business. Each partner is an agent for the other partners and for the partnership and may bind the partnership based

upon apparent authority, such as what is customary in the business or by previous dealings. Note how there is no apparent authority if the third party is aware of the partner's limitation, *and* there is no apparent authority to transact business outside the normal scope of the business. Answer (c) is correct because a partner would have apparent authority to do normal partnership business, such as order tractors for a farm machinery business. Answers (a) and (b) are incorrect because there can be no implied authority if there is no actual authority. Answer (d) is incorrect because express limitations in a partnership agreement have no bearing on apparent authority unless the third party was aware of the limitation.

3. (c)   It is permissible for a general partner to be a secured creditor of the limited partnership. Answer (a) is incorrect because a limited partner may loan money to and transact other business with a partnership. Answer (b) is incorrect because a general partner may be a limited partner at the same time. Answer (d) is incorrect because only limited partners have limited liability; the general partners are personally liable for the partnership debts.

Chapter 46
Introduction to Corporation Law

1. (a)   Both a limited partnership and a corporation may be created only under a state statute, and each must file a copy of its certificate with the proper state authorities. Further, both a corporation's stock and a limited partnership interest are subject to the federal securities laws registration requirements if they are "securities" under the federal securities laws. Answer (b) is incorrect because general partners in a limited partnership do not have limited liability. Answer (c) is incorrect because partnerships are not recognized for federal income tax purposes as taxable entities. Instead, the income flows through to the partners and is taxed on their individual returns. Answer (d) is incorrect because partnerships do not have perpetual existence. Their existence can be affected by the death of a partner.

3. (d)   Generally, state law requires certain mandatory items to be included in a corporation's articles of incorporation. While the requirements vary from state to state, they usually include the name of the corporation, the incorporators, corporate duration and purpose, location of its initial registered office and the name of its initial registered agent, number of directors, number of authorized shares of stock, and if the shares are to be divided into classes, the designation of each class along with its preferences, limitations, and rights. Therefore, answers (a), (b), and (c) are incorrect.

Chapter 47
Corporate Stocks and Bonds

1. (a)   Corporations are required to keep books and records pertaining to such things as stockholder names and addresses and minutes of corporate-related meetings. Under common law, a stockholder has the right to inspect these books and records, in person or by his or her attorney, agent, or accountant, if there is a proper purpose, such as gathering information to commence a stockholder's derivative suit, to solicit stockholders to vote for a change in the board of directors, or to investigate possible management misconduct. The use of stockholder records for a personal business is not a proper purpose.

3. (a)   A cash dividend on preferred stock becomes a legal debt of the corporation when the dividend is declared, and the preferred shareholder becomes an unsecured creditor of the corporation. However, dividends not paid in any year concerning cumulative preferred stock are not a liability of the corporation until they are declared. Therefore, Universal will be liable to Price as an unsecured creditor for $10,000, which is the amount of the declared dividends. Price has become a general unsecured creditor for the declared dividends and will have the same priority as the bond owners and the unsecured judgment creditors.

Chapter 48
Securities Regulations

1. (c)   Under the Securities Act of 1933, securities are defined broadly as any security that allows an investor to make a profit on an investment through the efforts of others rather than through his or her own efforts. Therefore, a general partnership interest would not likely be considered a security under the 1933 Act since partners in a general partnership have a right to manage and are considered active in the management of the business. Answers (a), (b), and (d) are incorrect because under the 1933 Act, securities are broadly defined to include stock options, warrants, and limited partnership interests.

3. (c)   Under Rule 505, sales can be made to no more than 35 nonaccredited investors and to an unlimited number of accredited investors. Answer (a) is incorrect since an audited balance sheet and other financial statements must be supplied to the nonaccredited investors. Answer (b) is incorrect since no general solicitation is ever allowed under Regulation D. Answer (d) is incorrect since sales to nonaccredited investors cannot exceed 35 in number.

Chapter 49

Management of Corporations

1. (c) A director of a corporation is entitled to rely on information provided by a corporate officer (unless the director had reason to believe that such information was incorrect). Answer (a) is incorrect since it would be a conflict of interest for a director to sit on the boards of competing businesses. Answer (b) is incorrect since a director would breach his/her fiduciary duty by taking advantage of a corporate business opportunity. Answer (d) is incorrect since directors do not act alone, but as a "board." Thus, the director has no actual or apparent authority to individually grant a corporate loan.

3. (d) Generally, a shareholder owes no fiduciary duty to the corporation; his primary concern is his own self-interest. An exception to this rule is the duty of the majority, or controlling, shareholders to the minority shareholders. The courts have held that a group with de facto control of a corporation may not use that control to injure, oppress, or defraud the minority shareholders. Answer (c) is incorrect because a promoter is said to be a fiduciary of the not-yet-formed corporation and has a fiduciary duty to act in good faith and in the corporation's best interest. Answer (a) is incorrect because the director, in addition to his duty of disclosure, has a duty to act with fundamental fairness. If any contract is determined not to be in the corporation's best interest, it may be rescinded, and the breaching director may be liable for any loss resulting to the corporation from the transaction. Answer (b) is incorrect because a director owes a fiduciary duty both to the corporation and to its shareholders.

Chapter 50

Real Property

1. (a) Since a mortgage is considered an interest in real property, it must be in writing and signed by the mortgagor. Recording is necessary to make the mortgage enforceable as against subsequent bona fide parties at interest, but not as between the mortgagor and mortgagee regardless of whether or not it is a purchase money mortgage; thus, answers (b) and (c) are incorrect. Answer (d) is incorrect because, generally, a mortgage must meet the requirements of a deed, including its delivery to the mortgagee.

3. (a) Since both mortgages were recorded, the purchaser (Nunn) of the property is constructively aware of the first mortgage held by Lyn. While Nunn assumed the second mortgage, Nunn purchases the property subject to the first mortgage. If Nunn defaults, proceeds from the sale of the property will go toward paying the first mortgage held by Lyn, and if any money remains, the money will be paid to Jay, the second mortgage holder. Answer (b) is incorrect because a first mortgage is paid in full before a second mortgage receives anything. Answers (c) and (d) are incorrect because Nunn has no personal liability to Lyn since the first mortgage was never assumed.

Chapter 51

Environmental Law and Land Use Controls

1. (a) The federal acts regulating air and water pollution permit citizens or states to enforce the provisions of these acts either by bringing private suits against violators or by suing the Environmental Protection Agency to enforce compliance with the laws.

Chapter 52

Leases

1. (c) The finder of abandoned property obtains an ownership interest in that property. The holder of a lease has only a possessory interest.

3. (d) A tenant has a possessory interest in property according to the lease, and the landlord has a reversionary interest (i.e., once the lease expires, the possession of the property "reverts" to the landlord). If a tenant purchases the building so that the tenant and the landlord are the same party, the lease is terminated since the tenant and landlord are the same. If a lease does not prohibit assigning or subletting, the tenant is free to assign or sublet without the permission of the landlord. The landlord's death does not terminate the lease.

Chapter 53

Decedents' Estates and Trusts

1. (d) For a per capita distribution of an estate, each person takes an equal share of the estate. Since, in this case, there are a total of five issues (two surviving children and three grandchildren of a predeceased child), the estate would be divided into five equal parts. Answer (b) would be correct if the distribution were to be made on a per stirpes basis.

3. (b) A trustee has express powers conferred upon him by the trust instrument and has implied powers which are reasonably necessary to enable the trustee to carry out the purpose of the trust. If not expressly granted, the power to sell trust property (I) and the power to pay trust expenses (III) would be considered reasonably necessary, but implied powers would not extend to mortgaging the trust property or to borrowing money from the trust (II).

GLOSSARY

A

abandon: give up or leave employment; relinquish possession of personal property with intent to disclaim title.

abate: put a stop to a nuisance; reduce or cancel a legacy because the estate of the decedent is insufficient to make payment in full.

ab initio: from the beginning.

abrogate: recall or repeal; make void or inoperative.

absolute guaranty: an agreement that creates the same obligation for the guarantor as a suretyship does for the surety; a guaranty of payment creates an absolute guaranty.

absolute liability: liability for an act that causes harm even though the actor was not at fault.

absolute ownership: a person who has all possible rights in and over a thing.

absolute privilege: protection from liability for slander or libel given under certain circumstances regardless of the fact that the statements are false or maliciously made.

abstract of title: history of the transfers of title to a given piece of land, briefly stating the parties to and the effect of all deeds, wills, and judicial proceedings relating to the land.

acceleration clause: provision in a contract or any legal instrument that upon a certain event the time for the performance of specified obligations shall be advanced; for example, a provision making the balance due upon debtor's default.

acceptance: unqualified assent to the act or proposal of another; as the acceptance of a draft (bill of exchange), of an offer to make a contract, of goods delivered by the seller, or of a gift or deed.

acceptor: a drawee who has accepted the liability of paying the amount of money specified in a draft.

accession: acquisition of title to personal property by virtue of the fact that it has been attached to property already owned or was the offspring of an owned animal.

accident: an event that occurs even though a reasonable person would not have foreseen its occurrence, because of which the law holds no one responsible for the harm caused.

accommodation party: a person who signs a commercial paper to lend credit to another party to the paper.

accord: agreement to a different performance other than what was originally specified in the contract.

accord and satisfaction: an agreement to substitute a different performance for that called for in the contract and the performance of this substitute agreement.

accretion: the acquisition of title to additional land when the owner's land is built up by gradual deposits made by the natural action of water.

acknowledgment: an admission or confirmation, generally of an instrument and usually made before a person authorized to administer oaths, such as a notary public; the purpose being to declare that the instrument was executed by the person making the instrument, or that it was a voluntary act or that that person desires that it be recorded.

action: a proceeding to enforce any right.

action in personam: an action brought to impose liability upon a person, such as a money judgment.

action in rem: an action brought to declare the status of a thing, such as an action to declare the title to property to be forfeited because of its illegal use.

action of assumpsit: a common law action brought to recover damages for breach of a contract.

action of ejectment: a common law action brought to recover the possession of land.

action of mandamus: a common law action brought to compel the performance of a ministerial or clerical act by an officer.

action of quo warranto: a common law action brought to challenge the authority of an officer to act or to hold office.

action of replevin: a common law action brought to recover the possession of personal property.

action of trespass: a common law action brought to recover damages for a tort.

act of God: a natural phenomenon that is not reasonably foreseeable.

act-of-state doctrine: the doctrine whereby every sovereign state is bound to respect the independence of every other sovereign state, and the courts of one country will not sit in judgment of another government's acts done within its own territory.

actual: the physical delivery of an agreement.

adeemed: canceled; as in a specifically bequeathed property being sold or given away by the testator prior to death, thus canceling the bequest.

adjustable rate mortgage (ARM): mortgage with variable financing charges over the life of the loan.

administrative agency: a governmental commission or board given authority to regulate particular matters.

administrative law: the law governing administrative agencies.

administrative regulations: rules made by state and federal administrative agencies.

administrator, administratrix: the person (man, woman) appointed to wind up and settle the estate of a person who has died without a will.

admissibility: the quality of the evidence in a case that allows it to be presented to the jury.

adverse possession: the hostile possession of real estate, which when actual, visible, notorious, exclusive, and continued for the required time, will vest the title to the land in the person in such adverse possession.

advisory opinion: an opinion that may be rendered in a few states when there is no actual controversy before the court and the matter is submitted by private persons, or in some instances by the governor of the state, to obtain the court's opinion.

affidavit: a statement of facts set forth in written form and supported by the oath or affirmation of the person making the statement setting forth that such facts are true on the basis of actual knowledge or on information and belief. The affidavit is executed before a notary public or other person authorized to administer oaths.

affinity: the relationship that exists by virtue of marriage.

affirmative action plan: plan to have a diverse and representative work force.

affirmative covenant: an express undertaking or promise in a contract or deed to do an act.

after-acquired goods: goods acquired after a security interest has attached.

agency: the relationship that exists between a person identified as a principal and another by virtue of which the latter may make contracts with third persons on behalf of the principal. (Parties—principal, agent, third person)

agency coupled with an interest in the authority: an agency in which the agent has given a consideration or has paid for the right to exercise the authority granted.

agency coupled with an interest in the subject matter: an agency in which for a consideration the agent is given an interest in the property to which the agency relates.

agency shop: a union contract provision requiring that nonunion employees pay to the union the equivalent of union dues in order to retain their employment.

agent: one who is authorized by the principal or by operation of law to make contracts with third persons on behalf of the principal.

airbill: a document of title issued to a shipper whose goods are being sent via air.

Aktiengesellschaft: German version of the société anonyme, very similar to the U.S. corporate form of business organization.

allonge: a paper securely fastened to a commercial paper in order to provide additional space for indorsements.

alteration: any material change of the terms of a writing fraudulently made by a party thereto.

alternate payees: those persons to whom a negotiable instrument is made payable, any one of whom may indorse and take delivery of it.

ambiguous: having more than one reasonable interpretation.

ambulatory: not effective and therefore may be changed, as in the case of a will that is not final until its maker has died.

amicable action: an action that all parties agree should be brought and one that is begun by the filing of such an agreement, rather than by serving the adverse parties with process. Although the parties agree to litigate, the dispute is real, and the decision is not an advisory opinion.

amicus curiae: literally, a friend of the court; one who is approved by the court to take part in litigation and to assist the court by furnishing an opinion in the matter.

annexation: attachment of personal property to realty in such a way as to make it become real property and part of the realty.

annuity: a contract by which the insured pays a lump sum to the insurer and later receives fixed annual payments.

anomalous indorser: a person who signs a commercial paper but is not otherwise a party to the instrument.

answer: what a defendant must file to admit or deny facts asserted by the plaintiff.

anticipatory breach: the repudiation by a promisor of the contract prior to the time that performance is required when such repudiation is accepted by the promisee as a breach of the contract.

anticipatory repudiation: the repudiation made in advance of the time for performance of the contract obligations.

anti-injunction acts: statutes prohibiting the use of injunctions in labor disputes except under exceptional circumstances, notably, the federal Norris-La Guardia Act of 1932.

antilapse statutes: statutes providing that the children or heirs of a deceased beneficiary may take the legacy in the place of the deceased beneficiary.

Anti-Pertrillo Act: a federal statute that makes it a crime to compel a radio broadcasting station to hire musicians not needed, to pay for services not performed, or to refrain from broadcasting music of school children or from foreign countries.

antitrust acts: statutes prohibiting combinations and contracts in restraint of trade—notably, the federal Sherman Antitrust Act of 1890—now generally inapplicable to labor union activity.

apparent authority: appearance of authority created by the principal's words or conduct.

appeal: taking a case to a reviewing court to determine whether the judgment of the lower court or administrative agency was correct. (Parties—appellant, appellee)

appellate jurisdiction: the power of a court to hear and decide a given class of cases on appeal from another court or administrative agency.

arbitration: the settlement of disputed questions, whether of law or fact, by one or more arbitrators by whose decision the parties agree to be bound. Increasingly used as a procedure for labor dispute settlement.

arson: willful and malicious burning of another's dwelling.

Article 2: section of Uniform Commercial Code that governs contracts for the sale of goods.

articles of copartnership: *see* "partnership agreement."

articles of incorporation: *see* "certificate of incorporation."

articles of partnership: *see* "partnership agreement."

assault: an act of battery in which the victim apprehends the commission of a battery but is not touched.

assignment: transfer of a right. Generally used in connection with personal property rights, as rights under a contract, commercial paper, an insurance policy, a mortgage, or a lease. (Parties—assignor, assignee)

assumption: the transferee and mortgagor are liable and the property is subject to foreclosure by the mortgagee if payments are not made.

assumption of risk: the common law rule that an employee could not sue the employer for injuries caused by the ordinary risks of employment on the theory that the employee assumed such risks by undertaking the work. The rule has been abolished in those areas governed by workers' compensation laws and most employers' liability statutes.

attachment: creation of a valid security interest.

attempt: criminal activity regardless of failure to commit the intended crime.

attestation: the act of witnessing the execution of a will.

attestation clause: clause that recited that the witness has observed either the execution of the will or the testator's acknowledgment of the writing as the testator's will.

attorney in fact: a private attorney authorized to act for another under a power of attorney.

attorneys: counselors at law who are officers of the court.

attractive nuisance doctrine: a rule imposing liability upon a landowner for injuries sustained by small children playing on the land when the landowner permits a condition to exist or maintains equipment that a reasonable person should realize would attract small children who could not realize the danger. The rule does not apply if an unreasonable burden would be imposed upon the landowner in taking steps to protect the children.

authenticate: make or establish as genuine, official, or final, such as by signing, countersigning, sealing, or performing any other act indicating approval.

authorities: corporations formed by government that perform public service.

automatic perfection: perfection given by statute without specific filing or possession requirements on the part of the creditor.

automatic stay: an order to prevent creditors from taking action such as filing suits or seeking foreclosure against the debtor.

B

bad check laws: laws making it a criminal offense to issue a bad check with intent to defraud.

baggage: such articles of necessity or personal convenience as are usually carried for personal use by passengers of common carriers.

bail: variously used in connection with the release of a person or property from the custody of the law, referring (a) to the act of releasing or bailing, (b) to the persons who assume liability in the event that the released person does not appear or that it is held that the property should not be released, and (c) to the bond or sum of money that is furnished the court or other official as indemnity for nonperformance of the obligation.

bailee: person who accepts possession of a property.

bailee's lien: a specific, possessory lien of the bailee upon the goods for work done to them. Commonly extended by statute to any bailee's claim for compensation and eliminating the necessity of retention of possession.

bailiffs: deputy sheriffs who perform court-appointed duties.

bailment: the relationship that exists when personal property is delivered into the possession of another under an agreement, express or implied, that the identical property will be returned or will be delivered in accordance with the agreement. (Parties—bailor, bailee)

bailment for hire: a contract in which the bailor agrees to pay the bailee.

bailor: the person who turns over the possession of a property.

balance sheet test: comparison of assets to liabilities made to determine solvency.

bankruptcy: a procedure by which one unable to pay debts may surrender to the court for administration and distribution to creditors all assets in excess of any exemption claim, and the debtor is given a discharge that releases from the unpaid balance due on most debts.

bankruptcy courts: court of special jurisdiction to determine bankruptcy issues.

battery: an intentional wrongful, physical contact (without consent) to a person resulting in injury or offensive touching.

battle of the forms: merchants' exchanges of invoices and purchase orders with differing boiler plate terms.

bearer: the person in physical possession of commercial paper payable to bearer, a document of title directing delivery to bearer, or an investment security in bearer form.

bearer paper: instrument with no payee, payable to cash or payable to bearer.

beneficiary: the person to whom the proceeds of a life insurance policy are payable, a person for whose benefit property is held in trust, or a person given property by a will.

beneficiary's bank: the final bank, which carries out the payment order, in the chain of a transfer of funds.

bequest: a gift of personal property by will.

bicameral: a two-house form of the legislative branch of government.

bilateral contract: an agreement under which one promise is given in exchange for another.

bill of exchange (draft): an unconditional order in writing by one person upon another, signed by the person giving it, and ordering the person to whom it is directed to pay upon demand or at a definite time a sum certain in money to order or to bearer.

bill of lading: a document issued by a carrier reciting the receipt of goods and the terms of the contract of transportation. Regulated by the federal Bills of Lading Act or the UCC.

bill of sale: a writing signed by the seller reciting that the personal property therein described has been sold to the buyer.

binder: a memorandum delivered to the insured stating the essential terms of a policy to be executed in the future, when it is agreed that the contract of insurance is to be effective before the written policy is executed.

blackmail: extortion demands made by a nonofficial.

blank indorsement: an indorsement that does not name the person to whom the paper, document of title, or investment security is negotiated.

blocking laws: laws that prohibit the disclosure, copying, inspection, or removal of documents located in the enacting country in compliance with orders from foreign authorities.

blue sky laws: state statutes designed to protect the public from the sale of worthless stocks and bonds.

bona fide: in good faith; without any fraud or deceit.

bond: an obligation or promise in writing and sealed, generally of corporations, personal representatives, and trustees; fidelity bonds.

bond indenture: an agreement setting forth the contractual terms of a particular bond issue.

book value: value found by dividing the value of the corporate assets by the number of shares outstanding.

boycott: a combination of two or more persons to cause harm to another by refraining from patronizing or dealing with such other person in any way or inducing others to so refrain; commonly an incident of labor disputes.

breach: the failure to act or perform in the manner called for in a contract.

breach-of-peace: violation of the law in the repossession of the collateral.

bribery: act of giving something to a person in order to influence his favor of the giver.

bubble concept: method for determining total emissions in one area; all sources are considered in an area.

building: any structure placed on or beneath the surface of the land, without regard to its purpose or use.

bulk sales acts: statutes to protect creditors of a bulk seller. Notice must be given creditors, and the bulk sale buyer is liable to the seller's creditors if the statute is not satisfied. Expanded to bulk transfers under the UCC.

burning to defraud: burning one's own property to collect insurance money.

business ethics: balance the goal of profits with values of individuals and society.

business judgment rule: a rule that allows management immunity from liability for corporate acts where there is a reasonable indication that the acts were made in good faith with due care.

business trust: a form of business organization in which the owners of the property to be devoted to the business transfer the title of the property to trustees with full power to operate the business.

bylaws: the rules and regulations enacted by a corporation to govern the affairs of the corporation and its shareholders, directors, and officers.

C

cancellation: a crossing out of a part of an instrument or a destruction of all legal effect of the instrument, whether by act of party, upon breach by the other party, or pursuant to agreement or decree of court.

capital: net assets.

capital stock: the declared money value of the outstanding stock of the corporation.

cargo insurance: insurance that protects a cargo owner against financial loss if goods being shipped are lost or damaged at sea.

carrier: an individual or organization undertaking the transportation of goods.

case law: law that includes principles that are expressed for the first time in court decisions.

cashier's check: a draft drawn by a bank on itself.

cash surrender value: the sum paid the insured upon the surrender of a policy to the insurer.

cash tender offer: general offer to all shareholders of a target corporation to purchase their shares for cash at a specified price.

cause of action: the right to damages or other judicial relief when a legally protected right of the plaintiff is violated by an unlawful act of the defendant.

caveat emptor: let the buyer beware. This maxim has been nearly abolished by warranty and strict tort liability concepts and consumer protection laws.

cease and desist order: an order issued by a court or administrative agency to stop a practice that it decides is improper.

certificate of deposit (CD): a promise-to-pay instrument issued by a bank.

certificate of incorporation: written approval from the state or national government for a corporation to be formed.

certificate of stock: a document evidencing a shareholder's ownership of stock issued by a corporation.

certiorari: a review by a higher court of the regularity of proceedings before a lower court. Originally granted within the discretion of the reviewing court. The name is derived from the language of the writ, which was in Latin and directed the lower court to certify its record and transfer it to the higher court. In modern practice, the scope of review has often been expanded to include a review of the merits of the case and, also, to review the action of administrative agencies.

cestui que trust: the beneficiary or person for whose benefit the property is held in trust.

challenged for cause: removal of a juror because of a connection with parties in a case.

Chapter 7 bankruptcy: liquidation form of bankruptcy under federal law.

Chapter 11 bankruptcy: reorganization form of bankruptcy under federal law.

Chapter 13 bankruptcy: consumer debt readjustment plan bankruptcy proceeding.

charge: the specific crime a defendant in a criminal case is accused of committing.

charging order: an order by a court after a business partner's personal assets are exhausted and requiring that the partner's share of the profits be paid to a creditor until the debt is discharged.

charter: the grant of authority from a government to exist as a corporation. Generally replaced today by a certificate of incorporation approving the articles of incorporation.

chattels personal: tangible personal property.

chattels real: leases of land and buildings.

check: an order by a depositor on a bank to pay a sum of money to a payee; a bill of exchange drawn on a bank and payable on demand.

choice-of-law clause: a clause in an agreement that specifies which law will govern should a dispute arise.

chose in action: intangible personal property in the nature of claims against another, such as a claim for accounts receivable or wages.

chose in possession: tangible personal property.

C.I.F.: cost, insurance, and freight.

circumstantial evidence: relates to circumstances surrounding the facts in dispute from which the trier of fact may deduce what has happened.

C.I.S.G.: uniform international contract code contracts for international sale of goods.

civil action: in many states a simplified form of action combining all or many of the former common law actions.

civil court: a court with jurisdiction to hear and determine controversies relating to private rights and duties.

claim: a right to payment.

Clean Air Act: a federal legislation that establishes standards for air pollution levels and prevents further deterioration of air quality.

Clean Water Act: a federal legislation that regulates water pollution through a control system.

clerk: a person who enters cases on a court calendar, keeps an accurate record of proceedings, and attests to the record of proceedings.

close connection doctrine: a doctrine that bars holding that a transferee is a holder in due course.

close corporation: a corporation whose shares are held by a single shareholder or a small group of shareholders.

closed shop: a place of employment in which only union members may be employed. Now prohibited.

codicil: a testator's or testatrix's writing executed with all the formality of a will and treated as an addition to or modification of the will.

coinsurance: a clause requiring the insured to maintain insurance on property up to a stated amount and providing that to the extent that this is not done the insured is to be deemed a coinsurer with the insurer, so that the latter is liable only for its proportionate share of the amount of insurance required to be carried.

collateral: property that is subject to the security interest.

collateral note: a note accompanied by collateral security.

collection guaranteed: guarantor agrees to pay only when all remedies against original debtor have been exhausted.

collective bargaining: the process by which the terms of employment are agreed upon through negotiations between the employer or employers within a given industry or industrial area and the union or the bargaining representative of the employees.

collective bargaining unit: the employment area within which employees are by statute authorized to select a bargaining representative, who is then to represent all the employees in bargaining with the employer.

collusion: an agreement between two or more persons to defraud the government or the courts, as by obtaining a divorce by collusion when no grounds for a divorce exist, or to defraud third persons of their rights.

color of title: circumstances that make a person appear to be the owner when in fact he is not the owner, as the existence of a deed appearing to convey the property to a given person gives color of title although the deed is worthless because it is in fact a forgery.

comity: a principle of international and national law that the laws of all nations and states deserve the respect legitimately demanded by equal participants.

commercial lease: any non-consumer lease.

commercially impracticable: when cost of performance rise suddenly and performance of a contract will result in a substantial loss.

commercial paper: a written transferable, signed promise or order to pay a specified sum of money; a negotiable instrument.

commercial unit: the standard of the trade for shipment or packaging of a good.

commission: a consignee's compensation; also called factorage.

commissioner of deeds: *see* "recorder."

commission merchant: a bailee to whom goods are consigned for sale.

common carrier: a carrier that holds out its facilities to serve the general public for compensation without discrimination.

common law: the body of unwritten principles originally based upon the usages and customs of the community that were recognized and enforced by the courts.

common stock: stock that has no right or priority over any other stock of the corporation as to dividends or distribution of assets upon dissolution.

common trust fund: a plan by which the assets of small trust estates are pooled into a common fund, each trust being given certificates representing its proportionate ownership of the fund, and the pooled fund is then invested in investments of large size.

community property: the cotenancy held by husband and wife in property acquired during their marriage under the law of some of the states, principally in the southwestern United States.

comparative negligence: a defense to negligence that allows plaintiff to recover reduced damages based on his level of fault.

compensatory damages: a sum of money that will compensate an injured plaintiff for actual loss.

complaint: the initial pleading filed by the plaintiff in many actions, which in many states may be served as original process to acquire jurisdiction over the defendant.

composition of creditors: an agreement among creditors that each shall accept a partial payment as full payment in consideration of the other creditors doing the same.

Comprehensive Environmental Response, Compensation, and Liability Act (CERCLA): a federal law that authorizes the President to issue funds for the cleanup of areas that were once disposal sites for hazardous wastes.

computer crime: wrongs committed using a computer or with knowledge of computers.

concealment: the failure to volunteer information not requested.

condition: an event that affects the existence of a contract or the obligation of a party to a contract.

conditional estate: an estate that will come into being upon the satisfaction of a condition precedent or that will be terminated upon the satisfaction of a condition subsequent.

conditional sale: a sale that customarily refers to a 'condition precedent' transaction by which title does not vest in the purchaser until payment is made in full.

condition subsequent: an event whose occurrence or lack thereof terminates a contract.

condominium: a combination of co-ownership and individual ownership.

confidential relationship: a relationship in which, because of the legal status of the parties or their respective physical or mental conditions or knowledge, one party places full confidence and trust in the other.

conflict of laws: the body of law that determines the law of which state is to apply when two or more states are involved in the facts of a given case.

confusion of goods: the mixing of goods of different owners that under certain circumstances results in one of the owners becoming the owner of all the goods.

conglomerate: the relationship of a parent corporation to subsidiary corporations engaged in diversified fields of activity unrelated to the field of activity of the parent corporation.

consanguinity: relationship by blood.

consequential damages: damages the buyer experiences as a result of the seller's breach with respect to a third party.

consequential loss: a loss that does not result directly from a party's act but from the consequences of that act.

consideration: the promise or performance that the promisor demands as the price of the promise.

consignee: person to whom goods are shipped.

consignment: a bailment made for the purpose of sale by the bailee. (Parties—consignor, consignee)

consignor: person who delivers goods to the carrier for shipment.

consolidation of corporations: a combining of two or more corporations in which the corporate existence of each one ceases and a new corporation is created.

conspiracy: an agreement between two or more persons to commit an unlawful act.

constables: in county courts not of record, they summon witnesses, take charge of the jury, preserve order in the court, serve writs, carry out judicial sales, and execute judgments.

constitution: a body of principles that establishes the structure of a government and the relationship of the government to the people who are governed.

constitutional law: the branch of law that is based on the constitutions in force in a particular area or territory.

constructive: an adjective employed to indicate that the instrument, described by the noun that is modified by the adjective, does not exist but the law disposes of the matter as though it did, as a constructive bailment or a constructive trust.

constructive delivery: see "symbolic delivery."

constructive eviction: an act or omission of the landlord which substantially deprives the tenant of the use and enjoyment of the premises.

consumer credit: credit for personal, family, and household use.

consumer credit transaction: a transaction referred to by the FTC rule limiting the rights of a holder in due course in this type of transaction to protect consumers of goods or services for personal, family, or household use.

consumer goods: goods used or bought primarily for personal, family, or household use.

consumer lease: lease of goods by a natural person for personal, family, or household use.

contingent beneficiary: the person to whom the proceeds of a life insurance policy are payable in the event that the primary beneficiary dies before the insured.

continuing nuisance: a series of related acts or a continuation of an activity.

contract: a binding agreement based upon the genuine assent of the parties, made for a lawful object, between competent parties, in the form required by law, and generally supported by consideration.

contract bailment: *See "bailment for hire."*

contract carrier: a carrier that transports on the basis of individual contracts that it makes with each shipper.

contracting interference: a tort in which a third party interferes with others' freedom to contract.

contract of adhesion: a contract offered by a dominant party to a party with inferior bargaining power on a take-it-or-leave-it basis.

contract of record: an agreement or obligation that has been recorded by a court.

contract to sell: a contract to make a transfer of title in the future as contrasted with a present transfer.

contracting agent: an agent with the authority to make contracts.

contractual capacity: the ability to understand that a contract is being made and to understand its general meaning.

contract under seal: a contract executed by affixing a seal or making an impression on the paper or on some adhering substance such as wax attached to the document.

contribution: the right of a co-obligor who has paid more than a proportionate share to demand that the other obligor pay the amount of the excess payment made.

contributory negligence: negligence of the plaintiff that contributes to injury and at common law bars from recovery from the defendant although the defendant may have been more negligent than the plaintiff.

conversion: the act of taking personal property by a person not entitled to it and keeping it from its true owner or prior possessor without consent.

convertible shares: shares which entitle the shareholder to exchange owned shares for a different kind of shares or for bonds of the corporation.

conveyance: a transfer of an interest in land, ordinarily by the execution and delivery of a deed.

cooling-off period: a procedure designed to avoid strikes by requiring a specified period of delay before the strike may begin during which negotiations for a settlement must continue.

cooperative: a group of two or more persons or enterprises that acts through a common agent with respect to a common objective, such as buying or selling.

copyright: a grant to an author or artist of an exclusive right to publish and sell the copyrighted work for the life of the author or artist and fifty years thereafter. For a "work made for hire," a grant of an exclusive right to publish and sell the copyrighted work for 100 years from its creation or 75 years from its publication, whichever is shorter.

corporation: an artificial being created by government grant, which for many purposes is treated as a natural person.

corporation by estoppel: a corporation that comes about when parties estop themselves from denying that the corporation exists.

corporation de jure: a corporation with a legal right to exist by virtue of law.

correspondent bank: will honor the letter of credit from the domestic bank of the buyer.

cost plus: a method of determining the purchase price or contract price by providing for the payment of an amount equal to the costs of the seller or contractor to which is added a stated percentage as the profit.

costs: the expenses of suing or being sued, recoverable in some actions by the successful party, and in others, subject to allocation by the court. Ordinarily, costs do not include attorney's fees or compensation for loss of time.

co-sureties: sureties for the same debtor and obligator.

cotenancy: when two or more persons hold concurrent rights and interests in the same property.

Council on Environmental Quality (CEQ): a federal agency that establishes national policies on environmental quality and then recommends legislation to implement these policies.

counterfeiting: manufacturing, with fraudulent intent, of a document or coin that appears genuine.

counteroffer: a proposal by an offeree to the offeror that changes the terms of, and thus rejects, the original offer.

counterclaim: a claim that the defendant in an action may make against the plaintiff.

course of dealing: pattern of performance between two parties to a contract.

court: a tribunal established by government to hear and decide matters properly brought to it.

court criers: assistants to the sheriff with court-appointed duties.

court of record: a court in which the proceedings are preserved in an official record.

court not of record: a court in which the proceedings are not officially recorded.

covenant of quiet enjoyment: a covenant by the grantor of an interest in land that the grantee's possession of the land shall not be disturbed.

covenant of right to convey: guarantee that the grantor of an interest in land, if not the owner, has the right or authority to make the conveyance to a new owner.

covenant of seisin: guarantee that the grantor of an interest in land owns the estate conveyed to a new owner.

covenants: obligations of parties in a lease.

covenants of title: covenants of the grantor in a deed that guarantee such matters as the right to make the conveyance, to ownership of the property, to freedom of the property from encumbrances, or that the grantee will not be disturbed in the quiet enjoyment of the land.

creditor: person (seller or lender) who is owed money; also may be a secured party.

credit transfer: a transaction in which a person making payment, such as a buyer, requests payment be made to the beneficiary's bank.

crime: a violation of the law that is punished as an offense against the state or government.

crimes mala in se: crimes that are inherently vicious or are naturally evil as measured by the standards of a civilized community.

crimes mala prohibita: acts that are only wrong because they are declared wrong by a statute.

criminal court: a court established for the trial of crimes that are regarded as offenses against the public.

cross complaint: a claim that the defendant may make against the plaintiff.

cross-examination: the examination made of a witness by the attorney for the adverse party.

cumulative voting: a system of voting for directors in which each shareholder has as many votes as the number of voting shares owned multiplied by the number of directors to be elected and such votes can be distributed for the various candidates as desired.

customary authority: authority of an agent to do any act that, according to the custom of the community, usually accompanies the transaction for which the agent is authorized to act.

cy pres doctrine: the rule under which a charitable trust will be carried out as nearly as possible in the way the settlor desired, when for any reason it cannot be carried out exactly in the way or for the purposes expressed.

D

damages: a sum of money recovered to redress or make amends for the legal wrong or injury done.

damnum absque injuria: loss or damage without the violation of a legal right, or the mere fact that a person sustains a loss does not mean that legal rights have been violated.

debenture: an unsecured bond of a corporation, with no specific corporate assets pledged as security for payment.

debit transfer: a transaction in which a beneficiary entitled to money requests payment from a bank according to a prior agreement.

debtor: a buyer on credit, i.e., a borrower.

decedent: person whose estate is being administered.

declaratory judgment: a procedure for obtaining the decision of a court on a question before any action has been taken or loss sustained. It differs from an advisory opinion in that there must be an actual, imminent controversy.

dedication: acquisition by the public or a government of title to land when it is given over by its owner to use by the public and such gift is accepted.

deed: an instrument by which the grantor (owner of land) conveys or transfers the title to a grantee.

deed of trust: instrument creating a trust.

de facto: existing in fact as distinguished from as of right, as in the case of an officer or a corporation purporting to act as such without being elected to the office or having been properly incorporated.

defamation: libel, the attacking of someone's reputation.

defeasance clause: clause which states that the mortgage shall cease to have any effect when the obligation is performed.

defendant: party charged with a violation of civil or criminal law in a proceeding.

deficiency judgment: a personal judgment entered against any person liable on the mortgage debt for the amount still remaining due on the mortgage after foreclosure. Statutes generally require the mortgagee to credit the fair value of the property against the balance due when the mortgagee has purchased the property. Also, a similar judgment entered by a creditor against a debtor in a secured transaction under Article 9 of the UCC.

definite time: a time of payment computable from the face of the instrument.

del credere agent: an agent who sells goods for the principal and who guarantees to the principal that the buyer will pay for the goods.

delegated powers: powers expressly granted the national government by the Constitution.

delegation: the transfer to another of the right and power to do an act.

delivery in escrow: transaction in which a deed is delivered to a third person for the purpose of delivery to the grantee upon the happening of some event or contingency.

demand draft: draft that is payable upon presentment.

de minimis non curat lex: a maxim that the law is not concerned with trifles. Not always applied, as in the case of the encroachment of a building over the property line, in which case the law will protect the landowner regardless of the extent of the encroachment.

demonstrative evidence: evidence that consists of visible, physical objects, such as a sample taken from the wheat in controversy or a photograph of the subject matter involved.

demonstrative legacy: a legacy to be paid or distributed from a specified fund or property.

demurrage: a charge made by the carrier for the unreasonable detention of cars by the consignor or consignee.

demurrer: a pleading that may be filed to attack the sufficiency of the adverse party's pleading as not stating a cause of action or a defense.

dependent relative revocation: the doctrine recognized in some states that if a testator revokes or cancels a will in order to replace it with a later will, the earlier will is to be deemed revived if for any reason the later will does not take effect or no later will is executed.

deposition: the testimony of a witness taken out of court before a person authorized to administer oaths.

depositor: person, or bailor, who gives property for storage.

derivative action: a secondary action for damages or breach of contract brought by one or more corporate shareholders against directors, officers, or third persons.

detrimental reliance: *see* reliance and promissory estoppel.

development statement: a statement that sets forth significant details of a real estate or property development as required by the federal Land Sales Act.

devise: a gift of real estate made by will.

devisee: beneficiary of a devise.

directed verdict: a direction by the trial judge to the jury to return a verdict in favor of a specified party to the action.

direct examination: the asking of witnesses about details pertinent to a case.

direct incidental beneficiary: a person who has benefited from the performance of a contract, though not intentionally.

direct loss: a loss that is caused by breach of a contract.

directors: the persons vested with control of the corporation, subject to the elective power of the shareholders.

disability: any incapacity resulting from bodily injury or disease to engage in any occupation for remuneration or profit.

discharge in bankruptcy: an order of the bankruptcy court discharging the debtor from the unpaid balance of most claims.

discharge of contract: termination of a contract by performance, agreement, impossibility, acceptance of breach, or operation of law.

disclosed principal: principal whose identity is made known by the agent as well as the fact that the agent is acting on his behalf.

discovery: procedures for ascertaining facts prior to the time of trial in order to eliminate the element of surprise in litigation.

dishonor by nonacceptance: the refusal of the drawee to accept a draft (bill of exchange).

dishonor by nonpayment: the refusal to pay a commercial paper when properly presented for payment.

disinherited: excluded from sharing in the estate of a decedent.

dismiss: a procedure to terminate an action by moving to dismiss on the ground that the plaintiff has not pleaded a cause of action entitling the plaintiff to relief.

disparagement of goods: the making of malicious, false statements as to the quality of the goods of another.

distress for rent: the common law right of the lessor to enter the premises when the rent has not been paid and to seize all personal property found on the premises. Statutes have modified or abolished this right in many states.

distribution per capita: distribution of equal shares of an estate when all the distributees stand in the same degree of relationship to the decedent.

distribution per stirpes: distribution of an estate made in as many equal parts as there are family lines represented in the nearest generation.

distributive share: the proportionate part of the estate of the decedent that will be distributed to an heir or legatee, and also as devisee in those jurisdictions in which real estate is administered as part of the decedent's estate.

distributor: the entity that takes title to goods and bears the financial and commercial risks for the subsequent sale of the goods.

divestiture order: a court order to dispose of interests that could lead to a monopoly.

divisible contract: an agreement consisting of two or more parts, each calling for corresponding performances of each part by the parties.

document of title: a document treated as evidence that a person is entitled to receive, hold, and dispose of the document and the goods it covers.

domestic bill of exchange: a draft drawn in one state and payable in the same or another state.

domestic corporation: a corporation that has been incorporated by the state in question as opposed to incorporation by another state.

domicile: the home of a person or the state of incorporation, to be distinguished from a place where a person lives but does not regard as home, or a state in which a corporation does business but in which it was not incorporated.

dominant tenement: land that is benefited by an easement.

donee: recipient of a gift.

donor: person making a gift.

dormant partners: partners who take no active part in transacting the business and who remain unknown to the public.

double indemnity: a provision for payment of double the amount specified by the insurance contract if death is caused by an accident and occurs under specified circumstances.

double jeopardy: the principle that a person who has once been placed in jeopardy by being brought to trial at which the proceedings progressed at least as far as having the jury sworn cannot thereafter be tried a second time for the same offense.

draft: *see* "bill of exchange."

draft-varying acceptance: one in which the acceptor's agreement to pay is not exactly in conformity with the order of the instrument.

drawee: person to whom the draft is addressed and who is ordered to pay the amount of money specified in the draft.

drawer: person who writes out and creates a draft or bill of exchange, including a check.

due care: the degree of care that a reasonable person would exercise to prevent the realization of harm, which under all the circumstances was reasonably foreseeable in the event that such care was not taken.

due diligence: the process of checking the environmental history and nature of land prior to purchase.

due process clause: a guarantee of protection from unreasonable procedures and unreasonable laws.

due process of law: the guarantee by the 5th and 14th Amendments to the U.S. Constitution and the guarantee of many state constitutions that no person shall be deprived of life, liberty, or property without due process of law. As currently interpreted, this process prohibits any law, either state or federal, that sets up an unfair procedure or the substance of which is arbitrary or capricious.

dumping: selling goods in another country at less than their fair value.

duress: conduct that deprives the victim of free will and that generally gives the victim the right to set aside any transaction entered into under such circumstances.

E

easement: a permanent right that one has in the land of another, as the right to cross another's land or an easement of way.

easement by implication: an easement not specifically created by deed that arises from the circumstances of the parties and the land location and access.

economic duress: threat of financial loss.

economic strikers: union strikers trying to enforce bargaining demands when an impasse has been reached in the negotiation process for a collective bargaining agreement.

effects doctrine: the doctrine that states U.S. courts will assume jurisdiction and will apply antitrust laws to conduct outside of the United States where the activity of business firms has direct and substantial effect on U.S. commerce.

effluent guidelines: EPA Standards for maximum ranges of discharge into water.

electronic fund transfer (EFTA): any transfer of funds (other than a transaction originated by a check, draft, or similar paper instrument) that is initiated through an electronic terminal, telephone, computer, or magnetic tape so as to authorize a financial institution to debit or credit an account.

eleemosynary corporation: a corporation organized for a charitable or benevolent purpose.

embezzlement: a statutory offense consisting of the unlawful conversion of property entrusted to the wrongdoer.

eminent domain: the power of government and certain kinds of corporations to take private property against the objection of the owner, provided the taking is for a public purpose and just compensation is made therefor.

emissions offset policy: controls whether new factories can be built in a nonattainment area.

employment at will doctrine: doctrine in which the employer has historically been allowed to terminate the employment contract at any time for any reason or for no reason.

encoding warranty: a warranty made by any party who encodes electronic information on an instrument; a warranty of accuracy.

encumbrance: a right held by a third person in or a lien or charge against property, such as a mortgage or judgment lien on land.

Endangered Species Act: federal law that identifies and protects species that are endangered from development or other acts that threaten their existence.

endowment insurance: a policy that pays the face amount of the policy if the insured dies within the policy period.

environmental impact statement (EIS): a formal report prepared under NEPA to document findings on the impact of a federal project on the environment.

equipment: goods used or bought primarily for use in a business.

equitable title: the beneficial interest in a trust.

equity: the body of principles that originally developed because of the inadequacy of the rules then applied by the common law courts of England.

erosion: the loss of land through a gradual washing away by tides or currents, with the owner losing title to the lost land.

escalation clause: provision for the automatic increase of the rent at periodic intervals.

escheat: the transfer to the state of the title to a decedent's property when the owner of the property dies intestate not survived by anyone capable of taking the property as heir.

escrow: a conditional delivery of property or of a deed to a custodian or escrow holder, who in turn makes final delivery to the grantee or transferee when a specified condition has been satisfied.

estate: the extent and nature of one's interest in land; the assets constituting a decedent's property at the time of death; the assets of a debtor in bankruptcy proceedings.

estate in fee simple: the largest estate possible, in which the owner has absolute and entire property in the land.

estate of present possession: a tenant's right to be in possession of the land.

estoppel: the principle by which a person is barred from pursuing a certain course of action or of disputing the truth of certain matters.

European Union (EU): name used to describe the union of the fifteen member countries of Europe who seek to unify their economic, monetary, and political policies.

ethics: branch of philosophy dealing with values, relating to the nature of human conduct.

eviction: depriving a tenant of the possession, use, and enjoyment of premises by the lessor or lessor's agent.

evidence: that which is presented to the trier of fact as the basis upon which the trier is to determine what happened.

exception: an objection, such as an exception to the admission of evidence on the ground that it is hearsay; a clause excluding particular property from the operation of a deed.

ex contractu: a claim or matter that is founded upon or arises out of a contract.

exculpatory clause: a provision in a contract stating that one of the parties shall not be liable for damages in case of breach; also called limitation-of-liability clause.

ex delicto: a claim or matter that is founded upon or arises out of a tort.

execute: to carry out a judgment.

executed contract: an agreement that has been completely performed.

execution: the carrying out of a judgment of a court, generally directing that property owned by the defendant be sold and the proceeds first be used to pay the execution or judgment creditor.

executive branch: the branch of government (e.g., the president) formed to execute the laws.

executor, executrix: man or woman named in a will to administer the estate of the decedent.

executory contract: an agreement by which something remains to be done by one or both parties.

exemplary damages: damages, in excess of the amount needed to compensate for the plaintiff's injury, that are awarded in order to punish the defendant for malicious or wanton conduct; also called punitive damages.

existing goods: goods that physically exist and are owned by the seller at the time of a transaction.

exoneration: an agreement or provision in an agreement that one party shall not be held liable for loss; the right of the surety to demand that those primarily liable pay the claim for which the surety is secondarily liable.

expert witness: one who has acquired special knowledge in a particular field as through practical experience or study, or both, whose opinion is admissible as an aid to the trier of fact.

export sale: a direct sale to customers in a foreign country.

ex post facto law: a law making criminal an act that was lawful when done or that increases the penalty when done. Such laws are generally prohibited by constitutional provisions.

express authority: authority of an agent to perform a certain act.

express contract: an agreement of the parties manifested by their words, whether spoken or written.

express warranty: a statement by the defendant relating to the goods, which statement is part of the basis of the bargain.

ex-ship: the obligation of a seller to deliver or unload goods from a ship that has reached its port of destination.

extortion: an illegal demand by a public officer acting with apparent authority.

extraordinary bailment: a bailment in which the bailee is subject to unusual duties and liabilities, such as a hotel keeper or common carrier.

F

facilitation payments: *see* "grease."

factor: a bailee to whom goods are consigned for sale.

factorage: a consignee's compensation; also called commission.

factors' acts: statutes protecting persons who buy in good faith for value from a factor although the goods had not been delivered to the factor with the consent or authorization of their owner.

fair employment practice acts: statutes designed to eliminate discrimination in employment on the basis of race, religion, national origin, or sex.

Fair Labor Standards Acts: statutes, particularly the federal statute, designed to prevent excessive hours of employment and low pay, the employment of young children, and other unsound practices.

false imprisonment: the intentional, unprivileged detaining of a person without that person's consent.

farm products: goods such as crops, livestock, or supplies used or produced in farming operations.

F.A.S.: free alongside the named vessel.

FCPA: Foreign Corrupt Practices Act; prohibits bribery by U.S.-based companies in their international operations.

featherbedding: the exaction of money for services not performed, which is made an unfair labor practice generally and a criminal offense in connection with radio broadcasting.

Federal District Courts: general trial court of federal system.

Federal Register: a government publication issued five days a week that lists all administrative regulations, all presidential proclamations and executive orders, and other documents and classes of documents that the president or Congress direct to be published.

Federal Securities Act: a statute designed to protect the public from fraudulent securities.

Federal Securities Exchange Act: a statute prohibiting improper practices at and regulating security exchanges.

federal sentencing guidelines: federal standards used by judges to determine mandatory sentencing terms for convicted criminals.

federal supremacy: declared by constitution for use when direct conflict between state and federal statutes exist.

federal system: the system of government in which a central government is given power to administer to national concerns while individual states retain the power to administer to local concerns.

Federal Trade Commission Act: a statute prohibiting unfair methods of competition in interstate commerce.

fee simple defeasibles: a fee simple interest that can b e lost if restrictions on its use are violated.

fee simple estate: highest level of land ownership; full interest of unlimited duration.

fellow-servant rule: a common law defense of the employer that barred an employee from suing an employer for injuries caused by a fellow employee.

felony: a criminal offense that is punishable by confinement in prison or by death, or that is expressly stated by statute to be a felony.

field warehousing: stored goods under the exclusive control of a warehouser but kept on the owner's premises rather than in a warehouse.

Fifth Amendment: constitutional protection against self incrimination which also guarantee due process.

finance lease: three party lease agreement in which there is a lessor and a lessee and also a financier.

financial responsibility laws: statutes that require a driver involved in an automobile accident to prove financial responsibility in order to retain a license, such responsibility may be shown by procuring public liability insurance in a specified minimum amount.

financing factor: one who lends money to manufacturers on the security of goods to be manufactured thereafter.

financing statement: a brief statement that gives sufficient information to alert third persons that a particular creditor may have a security interest in the collateral described.

fire insurance: policy that indemnifies the insured for property destruction or damage caused by fire.

firm offer: an offer stated to be held open for a specified time, which must be so held in some states even in the absence of an option contract, or under the UCC, with respect to merchants.

first-in-time provision: creditor whose interest attached first has priority in the collateral when two creditors have a secured interest.

fixture: personal property that has become so attached to or adapted to real estate that it has lost its character as personal property and is part of the real estate.

floating lien: a claim in a changing or shifting stock of goods of the buyer.

F.O.B.: free on board, indicating a seller is providing for the shipping of goods to the buyer.

F.O.B. place of destination: general commercial language for delivery to the buyer.

F.O.B. place of shipment: a 'ship to' contract.

Food, Drug, and Cosmetic Act: a federal statute prohibiting the interstate shipment of misbranded or adulterated foods, drugs, cosmetics, and therapeutic devices.

forbearance: refraining from doing an act.

forcible entry and detainer: an action by the landlord to have the tenant removed for nonpayment of rent.

foreclosure: procedure for enforcing a mortgage resulting in the public sale of the mortgaged property and, less commonly, in merely barring the right of the mortgagor to redeem the property from the mortgage.

foreign (international) bill of exchange: a bill of exchange made in one nation and payable in another.

foreign corporation: a corporation incorporated under the laws of another state.

forged indorsement: *see* "unauthorized indorsement."

forgery: the fraudulent making or altering of an instrument that apparently creates or alters a legal liability of another.

formal contracts: written contracts or agreements whose formality signifies the parties' intention to abide by the terms.

forum: a court in which any lawsuit should be brought.

four corners rule: rule under which the intention of the parties is concluded from the written instrument as a whole and not from its parts.

Fourth Amendment: constitutional protection against unreasonable searches and seizure.

franchise: (a) a privilege or authorization, generally exclusive, to engage in a particular activity within a particular geographic area, such as a government franchise to operate a taxi company within a specified city, or a private franchise as the grant by a manufacturer of a right to sell products within a particular territory or for a particular number of years; (b) the right to vote.

franchise agreement: sets forth rights of franchisee to use trademarks, etc., of franchisor.

franchisee: person to whom franchise is granted.

franchising: the granting of permission to use a trademark, trade name, or copyright under specified conditions.

franchisor: party granting the franchise.

fraud: the making of a false statement of a past or existing fact, with knowledge of its falsity or with reckless indifference as to its truth, with the intent to cause another to rely thereon, and such person does rely thereon and is harmed thereby.

fraud in the inducement: is fraud in the obtaining of a promise to an instrument, not fraud as to the nature of the instrument itself.

freehold estates: rights of title to real property for an uncertain time.

freight forwarder: one who contracts to have goods transported and, in turn, contracts with carriers for such transportation.

freight insurance: insures that ship owner will receive payment for transportation charges.

fructus industriales: crops that are annually planted and raised.

fructus naturales: fruits from trees, bushes, and grasses growing from perennial roots.

full warranty: the obligation of a seller to fix or replace a defective product within a reasonable time without cost to the buyer.

funds transfer: communication of instructions or requests to pay a specific sum of money to the credit of a specified account or person without an actual physical passing of money.

fungible goods: goods of a homogeneous nature of which any unit is the equivalent of any other unit or is treated as such by mercantile usage.

future advance mortgage: a mortgage given to secure additional loans to be made in the future as well as to secure an original loan.

future goods: goods that exist physically but are not owned by the seller as well as goods that have not yet been produced.

future interest: a land interest that will vest at some time in the future.

G

gambling: making a bet with a chance for profit and similar to a lottery in that there are the three elements of payment, prize, and chance.

garnishment: the name given in some states to attachment proceedings.

general agent: an agent authorized by the principal to transact all affairs in connection with a particular kind of business or trade or to transact all business at a certain place.

general corporation code: a state's code listing certain requirements for creation of a corporation.

general creditor: a creditor who has a claim against a debtor but does not have any lien on any of the debtor's property, whether as security for the debt or by way of a judgment or execution upon a judgment.

general damages: damages that in the ordinary course of events follow naturally and probably from the injury caused by the defendant.

general jurisdiction: the power to hear and decide all controversies involving legal rights and duties.

general legacies: certain sums of money bequeathed to named persons by the testator.

general legacy: a legacy to be paid out of the decedent's assets generally without specifying any particular fund or source from which the payment is to be made.

general partnership: a partnership in which the partners conduct as co-owners a business for profit, and each partner has a right to take part in the management of the business and has unlimited liability.

gift: the title to an owner's personal property voluntarily transferred by a party not receiving anything in exchange.

gift causa mortis: a gift, made by the donor in the belief that death was immediate and impending, that is revoked or is revocable under certain circumstances.

good faith: the absence of knowledge of any defects in or problems.

goods: anything movable at the time it is identified as the subject of a transaction.

grace period: a period generally of 30 or 31 days after the due date of a life insurance premium in which the payment may be made.

grand jury: a jury not exceeding 23 in number that considers evidence of the commission of crime and prepares indictments to bring offenders to trial before a petty jury.

grant: convey real property; an instrument by which such property has been conveyed, particularly in the case of a government.

grantee: new owner of a land conveyance.

grantor: transfers or conveys an interest in land to a new owner.

gratuitous bailment: a bailment in which the bailee does not receive any compensation or advantage.

gray market goods: foreign-made goods with U.S. trademarks brought into the United States without the consent of the trademark owners to compete with these owners.

grease: (facilitation payments) legal payments to speed up or ensure performance of normal government duties.

grievance settlement: the adjustment of disputes relating to the administration or application of existing contracts as compared with disputes over new terms of employment.

guarantor: one who undertakes the obligation of guaranty.

guarantor of collection: the person who is primarily liable to pay a negotiable instrument if collection has failed or is obviously useless.

guarantor of payment: the person who has primary liability for payment of a negotiable instrument.

guaranty: an undertaking to pay the debt of another if the creditor first sues the debtor and is unable to recover the debt from the debtor or principal. (In some instances the liability is primary, in which case it is the same as suretyship.)

guest: a transient who contracts for a room or site at a hotel.

H

hearsay evidence: statements made out of court that are offered in court as proof of the information contained in the statements, and that, subject to many exceptions, are not admissible in evidence.

hedging: the making of simultaneous contracts to purchase and to sell a particular commodity at a future date with the intention that the loss on one transaction will be offset by the gain on the other.

heirs: those persons specified by statute to receive the estate of a decedent not disposed of by will.

"hell or high water" clause: clause in a lease agreement that requires the lessee to continue paying regardless of any problems with the lease.

holder: the person in possession of a commercial paper payable to that person as payee or indorsee, or the person in possession of a commercial paper payable to bearer.

holder in due course: a holder of a commercial paper who is favored and is given an immunity from certain defenses.

holder through a holder in due course: a person who is not a holder in due course but is a holder of the paper after it was held by some prior party who was a holder in due course, and who is generally given the same rights as a holder in due course.

holographic will: an unwitnessed will written by hand.

homeowner's insurance: combination of standard fire insurance and comprehensive personal liability insurance.

horizontal price fixing: a violation of antitrust law whereby competitive businesses—manufacturers, for example—agree on the price they will charge for a good or service.

hotelkeeper: one regularly engaged in the business of offering living accommodations to all transient persons.

hull insurance: insurance that covers physical damage on a freight-moving vessel.

hung jury: a petty jury that has been unable to agree upon a verdict.

I

identified: term applied to particular goods selected by either the buyer or the seller as the goods called for by the sales contract.

identification: point in the transaction when the buyer acquires an interest in the goods subject to the contract.

ignorantia legis neminem excusat: ignorance of the law excuses no one.

illegal lobbying agreement: an agreement to use unlawful means to procure or prevent the adoption of legislation by a lawmaking body.

illusory promise: a promise that in fact does not impose any obligation on the promisor.

IMF International Monetary Fund: a complex lending system for member countries designed to achieve the expansion of international trade.

immunity: not being subject to liability ordinarily imposed by law.

impeach: using prior inconsistent evidence to challenge the credibility of a witness.

implied contract: a contract expressed by conduct or implied or deduced from the facts. Also used to refer to a quasi contract.

implied warranty: a warranty that was not made but is implied by law.

imposter rule: is an exception to the rules on liability for forgery that covers situations such as the embezzling payroll clerk.

imputed: vicariously attributed to or charged to another; for instance, the knowledge of an agent obtained while acting in the scope of authority is imputed to the principal.

incidental authority: authority of an agent that is reasonably necessary to execute express authority.

incidental damages: incurred by the non breaching party as part of the process of trying to cover of sell; includes storage fees, commissions and the like.

income: money earned by the principal, or property in trust, and distributed by the trustee.

incompetent: a person who is morally deficient.

incontestability clause: a provision that after the lapse of a specified time the insurer cannot dispute the policy on the ground of misrepresentation or fraud of the insured or similar wrongful conduct.

incorporation by reference: a contract consisting of both the original or skeleton document and the detailed statement that is incorporated in it.

incorporators: one or more natural persons or corporations who sign and file appropriate incorporation forms with a designated government official.

in custodia legis: in the custody of the law.

indemnity: the right of a person secondarily liable to require that a person primarily liable pay for loss sustained when the secondary party discharges the obligation that the primary party should have discharged; the right of an agent to be paid the amount of any loss or damage sustained without fault because of obedience to the principal's instructions; an undertaking by one person for a consideration to pay another person a sum of money to indemnify that person when a specified loss is incurred.

indemnity contract: an undertaking by one person, for a consideration, to pay another person a sum of money in the event that the other person sustains a specified loss.

indenture trustee: usually a commercial banking institution, to represent the interests of the bondholders and ensure that the terms and covenants of the bond issue are met by the corporation.

independent contractor: a contractor who undertakes to perform a specified task according to the terms of a contract but over whom the other contracting party has no control except as provided for by the contract.

indictment: a grand jury's formal accusation of crime, from which the accused is then tried by a petty or trial jury.

individual proprietorship: a form of business ownership in which one individual owns the business; also called sole proprietorship.

indorsee: party to whom special indorsement is made.

indorsement: signature of the payee on an instrument.

indorser: the holder of a negotiable instrument who writes his signature on the back of the paper.

informal contract: a simple oral or written contract.

infringement: the violation of trademarks, patents, or copyrights by copying or using material without permission.

inheritance: the interest that passes from the decedent to the decedent's heirs.

injunction: an order of a court of equity to refrain from doing (negative injunction) or to do (affirmative or mandatory injunction) a specified act. Its use in labor disputes has been greatly restricted by statute.

inland marine: insurance that covers domestic shipments of goods over land and inland waterways.

in pari delicto: equally guilty; used in reference to a transaction as to which relief will not be granted to either party because both are equally guilty of wrongdoing.

insider: a full-time corporate employee or a director.

insider information: privileged information on company business only known to employees.

insolvency: an excess of debts and liabilities over assets, or inability to pay debts as they mature.

instructions: summary of the law given to jurors by the judge before deliberation begins.

insurable interest: an interest in the nonoccurrence of the risk insured against, generally because such occurrence would cause financial loss, although sometimes merely because of the close relationship between the insured and the beneficiary.

insurance: a plan of security against risks by charging the loss against a fund created by the payments made by policyholders.

insurance agent: agent of an insurance company.

insurance broker: an independent contractor who is not employed by any one insurance company.

insurer: promisor in an insurance contract.

insured: person to whom the promise in an insurance contract is made.

intangible personal property: an interest in an enterprise, such as an interest in a partnership or stock of a corporation, and claims against other persons, whether based upon contract or tort.

intellectual property rights: Trademark, copyright, and patent rights protected by law.

intentional infliction of emotional distress: tort that produces mental anguish caused by conduct that exceeds all bounds of decency.

intentional tort: a civil wrong that results from intentional conduct.

interest in authority: a form of agency in which an agent has been given or paid for the right to exercise authority.

interest in the subject matter: a form of agency in which an agent is given an interest in the property with which that agent is dealing.

interlineation: a writing between the lines or adding to the provisions of a document, the effect thereof depending upon the nature of the document.

interlocutory: an intermediate step or proceeding that does not make a final disposition of the action and from which ordinarily no appeal may be made.

intermediary bank: a bank in between the originator and the beneficiary bank in the transfer of funds.

international bill of exchange: a bill or draft made in one nation and payable in another.

interpleader: a form of action or proceeding by which a person against whom conflicting claims are made may bring the claimants into court to litigate their claims between themselves, as in the case of a bailee when two persons each claim to be the owner of the bailed property, or an insurer when two persons each claim to be the beneficiary.

interrogatories: written questions used as a discovery tool that must be answered under oath.

inter se: among or between themselves, such as the rights of partners inter se or as between themselves.

inter vivos: any transaction which takes place between living persons and creates rights prior to the death of any of them.

inter vivos gift: the ordinary gift that is made between two living persons.

intestate: the condition of dying without a will as to any property.

intestate succession: the distribution, made as directed by statute, of a decedent's property not effectively disposed of by will.

invasion of privacy: tort of intentional intrusion in to the private affairs of another.

inventory: goods held primarily for sale or lease to others; raw materials, work in progress, materials consumed in a business.

investigative consumer report: a report on a person based on personal investigation and interviews.

invitees: persons who enter another's land by invitation.

involuntary bankruptcy: a proceeding in which a creditor or creditors file the petition for relief.

involuntary case: a case in which the creditors of a debtor file a petition with bankruptcy court.

ipso facto: by the very act or fact in itself without any further action by anyone.

irrebuttable presumption: a presumption that cannot be rebutted by proving that the facts are to the contrary; not a true presumption but merely a rule of law described in terms of a presumption.

irreparable injury to property: an injury that would be of such a nature or inflicted upon such an interest that it would not be reasonably possible to compensate the injured party by the payment of money damages because the property in question could not be purchased in the open market with the money damages that the defendant could be required to pay.

issuer: warehouser who prepares a receipt of goods received for storage.

J

joint and several contract: a contract in which two or more persons are jointly and separately obligated or under which they are jointly and separately entitled to recover.

joint contract: a contract in which two or more persons are jointly liable or jointly entitled to performance under the contract.

joint stock company: an association in which the shares of the members are transferable and control is delegated to a group or board.

joint tenancy: the estate held jointly by two or more with the right of survivorship as between them, unless modified by statute.

joint venture: a relationship in which two or more persons combine their labor or property for a single undertaking and share profits and losses equally unless otherwise agreed.

judge: primary officer of the court.

judgment: the final sentence, order, or decision entered into at the conclusion of the action.

judgment lien: a lien by a creditor who has won a verdict against the landowner in court.

judgment note: a promissory note containing a clause authorizing the holder of the note to enter judgment against the maker of the note if it is not paid when due; also called a cognovit note.

judgment n.o.v.: a judgment that may be entered after verdict upon the motion of the losing party on the ground that the verdict is so wrong that a judgment should be entered the opposite of the verdict, or non obstante veredicto (notwithstanding the verdict).

judgment on the pleadings: a judgment that may be entered after all the pleadings are filed when it is clear from the pleadings that a particular party is entitled to win the action without proceeding any further.

judicial branch: the branch of government (courts) formed to interpret the laws.

judicial sale: a sale made under order of court by an officer appointed to make the sale or by an officer having such authority as incident to the office. The sale may have the effect of divesting liens on the property.

jurisdiction: the power of a court to hear and determine a given class of cases; the power to act over a particular defendant.

jurisdictional dispute: a dispute between rival labor unions that may take the form of each claiming that particular work should be assigned to it.

jurisdictional rule of reason: the rule that balances the vital interests, including laws and policies, of the United States with those of a foreign country.

jury: a body of citizens sworn by a court to determine by verdict the issues of fact submitted to them.

jury list: all qualified persons from which a jury may be drawn and whose designation is the first step in forming a jury.

jury panel: persons drawn from a jury list to serve on a trial jury.

justifiable abandonment by employee: the right of an employee to abandon employment because of non-payment of wages, wrongful assault, the demand for the performance of services not contemplated, or injurious working conditions.

justifiable discharge of employee: the right of an employer to discharge an employee for nonperformance of duties, fraud, disobedience, disloyalty, or incompetence.

L

laches: the rule that the enforcement of equitable rights will be denied when the party has delayed so long that rights of third persons have intervened or the death or disappearance of witnesses would prejudice any party through the loss of evidence.

land: earth, including all things embedded in or attached thereto, whether naturally or by the act of man.

last clear chance: the rule that a defendant who had the last clear chance to have avoided injuring the plaintiff is liable even though the plaintiff had also been contributorily negligent. In some states also called the humanitarian doctrine.

law: the order or pattern of rules that society establishes to govern the conduct of individuals and the relationships among them.

law of the case: matters decided in the course of litigation that are binding on the parties in the subsequent phases of litigation.

law of the forum: the law of state in which the court is located.

leading questions: questions that suggest the desired answer to the witness, or assume the existence of a fact that is in dispute.

lease: an agreement between the owner of property and a tenant by which the former agrees to give possession of the property to the latter in consideration of the payment of rent. (Parties—landlord or lessor, tenant or lessee)

leasehold: the estate or interest of a tenant in rented land.

legacy: a gift of personal property made by will.

legal tender: such form of money as the law recognizes as lawful and declares that a tender thereof in the proper amount is a proper tender that the creditor cannot refuse.

legatee: beneficiary who receives a gift of personal property by will.

legislative branch: the branch of government (e.g., Congress) formed to make the laws.

letter of credit: a written agreement by which the issuer of the letter, usually a bank, agrees with the other contracting party, its customer, that the issuer will honor drafts drawn upon it by the person named in the letter as the beneficiary. Domestic letters are regulated by the UCC, Article 5; international letters, by the Customs and Practices for Commercial Documentary Credits. Commercial or payment letter: the customer is the buyer of goods sold by the beneficiary and the letter covers the purchase price of the goods. Standby letter: a letter obtained instead of a suretyship or guaranty contract requiring the issuer to honor drafts drawn by the beneficiary upon the issuer when the customer of the issuer fails to perform a contract between the customer and the beneficiary. Documentary letter: a letter of credit that does not obligate the issuer to honor drafts unless they are accompanied by the documents specified in the letter.

letters of administration: the written authorization given to an administrator of an estate as evidence of appointment and authority.

letters testamentary: the written authorization given to an executor of an estate as evidence of appointment and authority.

levy: a seizure of property by an officer of the court in execution of a judgment of the court, although in many states it is sufficient if the officer is physically in the presence of the property and announces the fact that it is 'seized,' but then allows the property to remain where it was found.

lex loci: the law of the place where the material facts occurred as governing the rights and liabilities of the parties.

lex loci contractus: the law of the place where the contract was made as governing the rights and liabilities of the parties to a contract with respect to certain matters.

lex loci fori: the law of the state in which the action is brought as determining the rules of procedure applicable to the action.

lex loci sitae rei: the law of the place where land is located as determining the validity of acts done relating thereto.

libel: written or visual defamation without legal justification.

license: a personal privilege to do some act or series of acts upon the land of another, as the placing of a sign thereon, not amounting to an easement or a right of possession.

licensee: someone on another's premises with the permission of the occupier, whose duty is to warn the licensee of nonobvious dangers.

licensing: the transfer of technology rights to a product.

lien: a claim or right, against property, existing by virtue of the entry of a judgment against its owner or by the entry of a judgment and a levy thereunder on the property, or because of the relationship of the claimant to the particular property, such as an unpaid seller.

life estate: an estate for the duration of a life.

limitation-of-liability clause: a provision in a contract stating that one of the parties shall not be liable for damages in case of breach; also called exculpatory clause.

limited defenses: a class of defenses that may not be raised against a holder in due course or a holder through a holder in due course claiming under a negotiable instrument.

limited jurisdiction: a court's power to hear and determine cases within certain restricted categories.

limited liability: loss of contributed capital or investment as maximum liability.

limited partnership: a partnership in which at least one partner has a liability limited to the loss of the capital contribution made to the partnership, and such a partner neither takes part in the management of the partnership nor appears to the public to be a general partner.

limited warranty: any warranty that does not provide the complete protection of a full warranty.

lineal descendants: the relationship that exists when one person is a direct descendant of the other.

liquidated damages: a provision stipulating the amount of damages to be paid in the event of default or breach of contract.

liquidation: the process of converting property into money whether of particular items of property or of all the assets of a business or an estate.

liquidation of damages clause: the specification of exact compensation in case of a breach of contract.

lis pendens: the doctrine that certain kinds of pending action are notice to everyone so that if any right is acquired from a party to such action, the transferee takes that right subject to the outcome of the pending action.

living trust: a trust created to take effect within the lifetime of the settlor.

living will: document by which individuals may indicate that if they become unable to express their wishes and are in an irreversible, incurable condition, they do not want life-sustaining medical treatments.

lobbying contract (illegal): a contract by which one party agrees to attempt to influence the action of a legislature or Congress, or any members thereof, by improper means.

lottery: any plan by which a consideration is given for a chance to win a prize.

lucri causa: with the motive of obtaining gain or pecuniary advantage.

M

mailbox rule: timing for acceptance tied to proper acceptance.

majority: of age, as contrasted with being a minor; more than half of any group, as a majority of stockholders.

maker: the party who writes or creates a promissory note.

malice aforethought: determination made beforehand to commit an illegal act without any legal justification.

malice in fact: an intention to injure or cause harm.

malice in law: a presumed intention to injure or cause harm when there is no privilege or right to do the act in question, such presumption cannot be contradicted or rebutted.

maliciously inducing breach of contract: the wrong of inducing the breach of any kind of contract with knowledge of its existence and without justification.

malpractice: when services are not properly rendered in accordance with commonly accepted standards.

malum in se: an offense that is criminal because it is contrary to the fundamental sense of a civilized community, such as murder.

malum prohibitum: an offense that is criminal not because inherently wrong but is prohibited for the convenience of society, such as overtime parking.

marine insurance: policies that cover perils relating to the transportation of goods.

mark: any word, name, symbol, or device used to identify a product or service.

market value: the price at which a share of stock can be voluntarily bought or sold in the open market.

marshaling assets: the distribution of a debtor's assets in such a way as to give the greatest benefit to all creditors.

marshals: in federal courts, they summon witnesses, take charge of the jury, preserve order in the court, serve writs, carry out judicial sales, and execute judgments.

martial law: government exercised by a military commander over property and persons not in the armed forces, as contrasted with military law which governs military personnel.

mask work: the specific form of expression embodied in a chip design, including the stencils used in manufacturing semiconductor chip products.

mass picketing: an illegal tactic of employees massing together in great numbers to effectively shut down entrances of the employer's facility.

maturity date: the date that a corporation is required to repay a loan to a bondholder.

mechanic's lien: protection afforded by statute to various kinds of laborers and persons supplying materials, by giving them a lien on the building and land that has been improved or added to by them.

mens rea: the mental state that must accompany an act to make the act a crime. Sometimes described as the guilty mind, although appreciation of guilt is not required.

merchant: a seller who deals in specific goods classified by the UCC.

merger by judgment: the discharge of a contract through being merged into a judgment that is entered in a suit on the contract.

merger of corporations: a combining of corporations by which one absorbs the other and continues to exist, preserving its original charter and identity while the other corporation ceases to exist.

minitrial: a trial held on portions of the case or certain issues in the case.

minor: at common law anyone under 21 years of age, but now any person under 18 in most states, and 19 in a few.

Miranda warnings: warnings required to prevent self-incrimination in a criminal matter.

misdemeanor: a criminal offense that is neither treason nor a felony.

misrepresentation: a false statement of fact although made innocently without any intent to deceive.

mistrial: a court's declaration that terminates a trial and postpones it to a later date and commonly entered when evidence has been of a highly prejudicial character or when a juror has been guilty of misconduct.

money: a medium of exchange.

money order: draft issued by a bank and a non bank.

moral relativism: takes into account motivation and circumstance to determine whether an act was ethical.

moral standards: rules for conduct dictated by law, society, or religion.

moratorium: a temporary suspension by statute of the enforcement of debts or the foreclosure of mortgages.

mortgage: an interest in land given by the owner to a creditor as security for the payment of the creditor for a debt, the nature of the interest depending upon the law of the state where the land is located. (Parties—mortgagor, mortgagee)

motion for summary judgment: request that the court decide case on basis of law only because there are no material issues disputed by the parties.

motion to dismiss: a pleading that may be filed to attack the sufficiency of the adverse party's pleading as not stating a cause of action or a defense.

multiple insurers: insurers who agree to divide a risk so that each is liable only for a specified portion.

N

National Environmental Policy Act (NEPA): federal law that mandates study of a project's impact on the environment before it can be undertaken by any federal agency.

National Labor Management Relations Act: the federal statute, also known as the Taft-Hartley Act, designed to protect the organizational rights of labor and to prevent unfair labor practices by management or labor.

natural and probable consequences: those ordinary consequences of an act that a reasonable person would foresee.

natural law: a system of principles to guide human conduct independent of, and sometimes contrary to, enacted law and discovered by man's rational intelligence.

necessaries: things indispensable or absolutely necessary for the sustenance of human life.

negative covenant: an undertaking in a deed to refrain from doing an act.

negligence: the failure to exercise due care under the circumstances in consequence of which harm is proximately caused to one to whom the defendant owed a duty to exercise due care.

negligence per se: an action that is regarded as so improper that it is declared by law to be negligent in itself without regard to whether due care was otherwise exercised.

negotiability: quality that affords special rights and standing.

negotiable bill of lading: a document of title that by its terms calls for goods to be delivered 'to the bearer' or 'to the order of' a named person.

negotiable draft: an unconditional order in writing, addressed to one person by another, signed by the person giving it, requiring the person to whom it is addressed to pay on demand or at a definite time, a sum certain in money to order or to bearer; a bill of exchange.

negotiable instruments: drafts, promissory notes, checks, and certificates of deposit in such form that greater rights may be acquired thereunder than by taking an assignment of a contract right; called negotiable commercial paper by the UCC.

negotiable promissory note: an unconditional promise in writing made by one person to another, signed by the maker, engaging to pay on demand or at a definite time a sum certain in money to order or to bearer.

negotiable warehouse receipt: a receipt that states the covered goods will be delivered 'to the bearer' or 'to the order of.'

negotiation: the transfer of a commercial paper by indorsement and delivery by the person to whom then payable in the case of order paper and by physical transfer in the case of bearer paper.

Noise Control Act: federal law that controls noise emissions from low-flying aircraft.

nominal damages: a nominal sum awarded the plaintiff in order to establish that legal rights have been violated although the plaintiff in fact has not sustained any actual loss or damages.

nominal partners: business partners who hold themselves out as partners or permit others to hold them out as such but are not in fact partners.

nonattainment areas: "dirty" areas that do not meet federal standards under the Clean Air Act.

nonconforming use: a use of land that conflicts with a zoning ordinance at the time the ordinance goes into effect.

non-consumer lease: *see* "commercial lease."

nonnegotiable instrument: a contract, note, or draft that does not meet requirements of Article 3.

nonnegotiable warehouse receipt: a receipt that states the covered goods received will be delivered to a specific person.

nontrading partnership: partnership organized for a purpose other than engaging in commerce, such as the practice of law or medicine.

Norris-La Guardia Anti-Injunction Act: a federal statute prohibiting the use of the injunction in labor disputes, except in particular cases.

notice of dishonor: notice given to parties secondarily liable that the primary party to the instrument has refused to accept the instrument or to make payment when it was properly presented for that purpose.

novation: the discharge of a contract between two parties by their agreeing with a third person that such third person shall be substituted for one of the original parties to the contract, who shall thereupon be released.

nudum pactum: a mere promise for which there is not consideration given and which, therefore, is ordinarily not enforceable.

nuisance: any conduct that harms or prejudices another in the use of land or which harms or prejudices the public.

nuisance per se: an activity that is in itself a nuisance regardless of the time and place involved.

nuncupative will: an oral will made and declared to be a will by the testator in the presence of witnesses; generally made during the testator's last illness.

O

obiter dictum: that which is said in the opinion of a court in passing or by the way, but which is not necessary to the determination of the case and is therefore not regarded as authoritative as though it were actually involved in the decision.

objective intent: the intent of parties to an agreement that is manifested outwardly and will be enforced.

obligee: a promisee who can claim the benefit of the obligation.

obligor: a promisor.

obliteration: any erasing, writing upon, or crossing out that makes all or part of a will impossible to read, and which has the effect of revoking such part when done by the maker of the will with the intent of effecting a revocation.

occupation: taking and holding possession of property; a method of acquiring title to personal property after it has been abandoned.

ocean marine: policies that cover transportation of goods in vessels in international and coastal trade.

offer: the expression of an offeror's willingness to enter into a contractual agreement.

offeree: person to whom an offer is made.

offeror: person who makes an offer.

Oil Pollution Act: federal law that assigns cleanup liability for oil spills in U.S. waters.

ombudsman: a government official designated by a statute to examine citizen complaints also used by companies to resolve employee disputes.

open-end mortgage: a mortgage given to secure additional loans to be made in the future as well as to secure the original loan.

opening statements: statements by opposing attorneys that tell the jury what will be proven.

operation of law: the attaching of certain consequences to certain facts because of legal principles that operate automatically, as contrasted with consequences that arise because of the voluntary action of a party designed to create those consequences.

opinion evidence: evidence not of what the witness observed but the conclusion drawn from what the witness has observed; in the case of expert witnesses, what has been observed in tests or experiments or what has been heard in court.

option contract: a contract to hold an offer to make a contract open for a fixed period of time.

option to purchase: a contract in which one party is given the right to buy a property for a consideration to the seller.

order: designates payment to a particular person or entity for their further direction.

order of relief: court finding that creditors have met the standards for bankruptcy petitions.

order paper: instrument payable to the order of a party.

ordinary bailments: all bailments other than extraordinary ones.

ordinary contract defenses: any defense that a party to an ordinary contract may raise, such as a lack of capacity of parties, absence of consideration, fraud, concealment, or mistake.

ordinary holder: *see* "holder in due course."

original jurisdiction: the authority to hear a controversy when it is first brought to court.

originator: is the party who originates the fund transfer.

output contract: the contract of a producer to sell its entire production or output to a given buyer.

outstanding: the name for shares of a company that have been issued to stockholders.

overdraft: negative balance in a drawer's account.

P

paper title: the title of a person evidenced only by deeds or matter appearing of record under the recording statutes.

parens patriae action: a court action based on the theory of the state as the parent of the legally disabled, such as juveniles.

parol evidence rule: the rule that prohibits the introduction in evidence of oral or written statements made prior to or contemporaneously with the execution of a complete written contract, deed, or instrument, in the absence of clear proof of fraud, accident, or mistake causing the omission of the statement in question.

partially disclosed principle: principal whose existence is made known, but whose identity is not.

partnership: the pooling of capital resources and the business or professional talents of two or more individuals with the goal of making a profit.

partnership agreement: document prepared to evidence the contract of the parties. (Parties—partners or general partners)

par value: a specified monetary amount assigned by an issuing corporation for each share of its stock.

passive trust: a trust that is created without imposing any duty to be performed by the trustee and is therefore treated as an absolute transfer of the title to the trust beneficiary.

past consideration: something that has been performed in the past and which, therefore, cannot be consideration for a promise made in the present.

patent: the grant to an inventor of an exclusive right to make and sell an invention for a nonrenewable period of 17 years; a deed to land given by a government to a private person.

pawn: a pledge of tangible personal property rather than of documents representing property rights.

payable to bearer: a term stating that a negotiable instrument, or bearer paper, is payable to the person who possesses it.

payable to order: a term stating that a negotiable instrument is payable to the order of any person described in it or to a person or order.

payee: party to whom payment is to be made.

payment order: a direction given by an originator to his or her bank or by any bank to a subsequent bank to make a specified funds transfer.

pecuniary legacy: a general legacy of a specified amount of money without indicating the source from which payment is to be made.

per autre vie: limitation of an estate. An estate held by A during the lifetime of B is an estate of A per autre vie.

per capita: method of distributing estate assets on an equal-per-person basis.

peremptory challenge: a challenge to a juror that need not be explained, limited number available in each case.

perfected security interest: the security interest of an original creditor that is superior to all such other claims.

permanent nuisance: a single act that causes permanent harm to a plaintiff.

perpetual succession: a phrase describing the continuing life of the corporation unaffected by the death of any stockholder or the transfer by stockholders of their stock.

Perpetuities, Rule against: a rule of law that prohibits the creation of an interest in property that will not become definite or vested until a date further away than 21 years after the death of persons alive at the time the owner of the property attempts to create the interest.

per se: in, through, or by itself.

person: a term that includes both natural persons, or living persons, and artificial persons, such as corporations which are created by act of government.

personal defenses: limited defenses that cannot be asserted by the defendant against a holder in due course. This term is not used in the UCC.

personal property: property that is movable or intangible, or rights in such things.

personal representatives: administrators and executors who represent decedents.

per stirpes: according to the root or by way of representation. Distribution among heirs related to the decedent in different degrees, the property being divided into lines of descent from the descendent and the share of each line then divided within the line by way of representation.

petty jury: the trial jury. Also, petit jury.

physical duress: threat of physical harm to person or property.

picketing: the placing of persons outside of places of employment or distribution so that by words or banners they may inform the public of the existence of a labor dispute or may influence employees or customers.

plaintiff: the party who initiates a law suit.

pleadings: the papers filed by the parties in an action in order to set forth the facts and frame the issues to be tried, although, under some systems, the pleadings merely give notice or a general indication of the nature of the issues.

pledge: a bailment given as security for the payment of a debt or the performance of an obligation owed to the pledgee. (Parties—pledgor, pledgee)

police power: the power to govern; the power to adopt laws for the protection of the public health, welfare, safety, and morals.

policy: the paper evidencing the contract of insurance.

polling the jury: the process of inquiring of each juror individually in open court as to whether the verdict announced in court was agreed to.

positive law: law enacted and codified by governmental authority.

possession: exclusive dominion and control of property.

possessory lien: a right to retain possession of property of another as security for some debt or obligation owed the lienor, such right continues only as long as possession is retained.

possibility of reverter: the nature of the interest held by the grantor after conveying land outright but subject to a condition or provision that may cause the grantee's interest to become forfeited and the interest to revert to the grantor or heirs.

postdate: to insert or place on an instrument a later date than the actual date on which it was executed.

power of appointment: a power given to another, commonly a beneficiary of a trust, to designate or appoint who shall be beneficiary or receive the fund after the death of the grantor.

power of attorney: a written authorization to an agent by the principal.

precatory words: words indicating merely a desire or a wish that another use property for a particular purpose but which in law will not be enforced in the absence of an express declaration that the property shall be used for the specified purpose.

precedent: a decision of a court that stands as the law for a particular problem in the future.

predicate act: a qualifying underlying offense for RICO liability.

preempt: to take precedence over.

preemptive offer of shares: shareholder's right upon the increase of a corporation's capital stock to be allowed to subscribe to such a percentage of the new shares as the shareholder's old shares bore to the former total capital stock.

preferences: transfers of property by a debtor to one or more specific creditors to enable these creditors to obtain payment for debts owed.

preferential: certain transfers of money or security interests in the time frame just prior to bankruptcy that can be set aside if voidable.

preferred creditor: a creditor who by some statute is given the right to be paid first or before other creditors.

preferred stock: stock that has a priority or preference as to payment of dividends or upon liquidation, or both.

preponderance of evidence: the degree or quantum of evidence in favor of the existence of a certain fact when from a review of all the evidence it appears more probable that the fact exists than that it does not. The actual number of witnesses involved is not material nor is the fact that the margin of probability is very slight.

prescription: the acquisition of a right to use the land of another, as an easement, through the making of hostile, visible, and notorious use of the land, continuing for the period specified by the local law.

presentment: formal request for payment on an instrument.

presumption: a rule of proof that permits the existence of a fact to be assumed from the proof that another fact exists when there is a logical relationship between the two or when the means of disproving the assumed fact are more readily within the control or knowledge of the adverse party against whom the presumption operates.

presumption of death: the rebuttable presumption that a person has died when that person has been continuously absent and unheard of for a period of 7 years.

presumption of innocence: the presumption of fact that a person accused of crime is innocent until shown guilty of the offense charged.

presumption of payment: a rebuttable presumption that one performing continuing services that would normally be paid periodically, such as weekly or monthly, has in fact been paid when a number of years have passed without any objection or demand for payment having been made.

presumptive heir: a person who would be the heir if the ancestor should die at that moment.

pretrial conference: a conference, held prior to the trial, at which the court and attorney seek to simplify the issues in controversy and eliminate matters not in dispute.

price: the consideration for sale of goods.

prima facie: evidence that, if believed, is sufficient by itself to lead to a particular conclusion.

primary beneficiary: the person designated as the first one to receive the proceeds of a life insurance policy, as distinguished from a contingent beneficiary who will receive the proceeds only if the primary beneficiary dies before the insured.

primary liability: the liability of a person whose act or omission gave rise to the cause of action and who in all fairness should, therefore, be the one to pay the victim even though others may also be liable for misconduct.

primary parties: parties required to pay the instruments when they are due.

primary picketing: legal presentations in front of a business notifying the public of a labor dispute.

principal: one who employs an agent; the person who, with respect to a surety, is primarily liable to the third person or creditor.

principal debtor: original borrower or debtor.

principal in the first degree: one who actually engages in the commission or perpetration of a crime.

principal in the second degree: one who is actually or constructively present at the commission of the crime and who aids and abets in its commission.

Principal Register: a register maintained for recording trademarks and service marks.

private carrier: a carrier owned by the shipper, such as a company's own fleet of trucks.

private corporation: corporation organized for charitable and benevolent purposes or for purposes of finance, industry, and commerce.

private nuisance: a nuisance that affects only one or a few individuals.

privileged communication: information that the witness may refuse to testify to because of the relationship with the person furnishing the information, such as husband-wife or attorney-client.

privilege from arrest: the immunity from arrest of parties, witnesses, and attorneys while present within the jurisdiction for the purpose of taking part in other litigation.

privity: a succession or chain of relationship to the same thing or right, such as privity of contract, privity of estate, privity of possession.

privity of contract: the relationship between a promisor and the promisee.

privity of contract rule: the rule of law that bars a third person from suing for malpractice.

probate: the procedure for formally establishing or proving that a given writing is the last will and testament of the person who purportedly signed it.

procedural law: the law that must be followed in enforcing rights and liabilities.

proceeds: payments received by a debtor for selling or leasing his or her collateral or insurance payments for damages to the collateral.

process: a writ, notice, summons, or complaint served to a defendant as notice that an action is pending and subjecting the defendant to the power of the court.

product disparagement: false statements made about a product or business.

product liability: liability imposed upon the manufacturer or seller of goods for harm caused by a defect in the goods, comprising liability for (a) negligence, (b) fraud, (c) breach of warranty, and (d) strict tort.

profit: the right to take a part of the soil or produce of another's land, such as timber or water.

promisee: a person to whom a promise is made.

promisor: a person who makes a promise.

promissory estoppel: the doctrine that a promise will be enforced although it is not supported by consideration when the promisor should have reasonably expected that the promise would induce action or forbearance of a definite and substantial character on the part of the promised and injustice can be avoided only by enforcement of the promise.

promissory note: an unconditional promise in writing made by one person to another, signed by the maker engaging to pay on demand, or at a definite time, a sum certain in money to order or to bearer. (Parties—maker, payee)

promissory representation: a representation made by the applicant to the insurer as to what is to occur in the future.

promissory warranty: a representation made by the applicant to the insurer as to what is to occur in the future that the applicant warrants will occur.

promoters: the persons who plan the formation of the corporation and sell or promote the idea to others.

proof: the probative effect of the evidence; the conclusion drawn from the evidence as to the existence of particular facts.

proof of claim: written statement, signed by the creditor or an authorized representative, setting forth any claim made against the debtor and the basis for it.

property: the rights and interests one has in anything subject to ownership.

property report: a condensed version of a property development statement filed with the secretary of HUD and given to a prospective customer no more than 48 hours before the signing of a contract to buy or lease property.

pro rata: proportionately, or divided according to a rate or standard.

prosecutor: party who originates a criminal proceeding.

prospectus: information provided to each potential purchaser of securities, setting forth the key information contained in the registration statement.

protest: the formal certificate by a notary public or other authorized person that proper presentment of a commercial paper was made to the primary party and that such party defaulted, the certificate commonly also including a recital that notice was given to secondary parties.

proximate cause: the act that is the natural and reasonably foreseeable cause of the harm or event that occurs and injures the plaintiff.

proximate damages: damages that in the ordinary course of events are the natural and reasonably foreseeable result of the defendant's violation of the plaintiff's rights.

proxy: a written authorization by a shareholder to another person to vote the stock owned by the shareholder; the person who is the holder of such a written authorization.

public charge: a person who because of personal disability or lack of means of support is dependent upon public charity or relief for sustenance.

public domain: public or government-owned lands.

public easement: a right of way for use by members of the public at large.

public nuisance: a nuisance that affects the community or public at large.

public policy: certain objectives relating to health, morals, and integrity of government that the law seeks to advance by declaring invalid any contract that conflicts with those objectives even though there is no statute expressly declaring such a contract illegal.

public warehousers: entities that serve the public generally without discrimination.

punitive damages: damages, in excess of those required to compensate the plaintiff for the wrong done, that are imposed in order to punish the defendant because of the particularly wanton or willful character of wrongdoing; also called exemplary damages.

pur curiam opinion: an opinion written by the court rather than by a named judge when all the judges of the court are in such agreement on the matter that it is not deemed to merit any discussion and may be simply disposed of.

purchase money mortgage: a mortgage given by the purchaser of land to the seller to secure the seller for the payment of the unpaid balance of the purchase price, which the seller purports to lend the purchaser.

purchase money security interest (PMSI): the security interest in the goods a seller sells on credit.

purchaser in good faith: a person who purchases without any notice or knowledge of any defect of title, misconduct, or defense.

Q

qualified acceptance: An acceptance of a draft that varies the order of the draft in some way.

qualified indorsement: an indorsement that includes words such as 'without recourse' evidencing that the indorser shall not be held liable for the failure of the primary party to pay the instrument.

qualified privilege: media privilege to print inaccurate information with our liability for defamation, so long as a retraction is printed and there was no malice.

quantum meruit: an action brought for the value of the services rendered the defendant when there was no express contract as to the purchase price.

quantum valebant: an action brought for the value of goods sold the defendant when there was no express contract as to the purchase price.

quasi: as if, as though it were, having the characteristics of; a modifier employed to indicate that the subject is to be treated as though it were in fact the noun that follows the word quasi, as in quasi contract, quasi corporation, quasi-public corporation.

quasi contract: a court-imposed obligation to prevent unjust enrichment in the absence of a contract.

quasi-public corporation: a private corporation furnishing services on which the public is particularly dependent, for example, a gas and electric company.

quid pro quo: literally 'what for what.' An early form of the concept of consideration by which an action for debt could not be brought unless the defendant had obtained something in return for the obligation sued upon.

quitclaim deed: a deed by which the grantor purports only to give up whatever right or title the grantor may have in the property without specifying or warranting transfer of any particular interest.

quorum: the minimum number of persons, shares represented, or directors who must be present at a meeting in order that business may be lawfully transacted.

R

ratification by minor: a minor's approval of a contract after the minor attains majority.

ratification of agency: the approval of the unauthorized act of an agent or of a person who is not an agent for any purpose. The approval occurs after the act has been done and has the same effect as though the act had been authorized before it was done.

ratio decidendi: the reason or basis for deciding the case in a particular way.

ratio legis: the reason for a principle or rule of law.

real defenses: certain defenses (universal) that are available against any holder of a commercial paper, although this term is not used by the UCC.

real evidence: tangible objects that are presented in the courtroom for the observation of the trier of fact as proof of the facts in dispute or in support of the theory of a party.

real property: land and all rights in land.

reasonable care: the degree of care that a reasonable person would take under all the circumstances then known.

rebate: a refund, made by the seller or the carrier, of part of the purchase price or freight bill.

rebuttable presumption: a presumption that may be overcome or rebutted by proof that the actual facts were different from those presumed.

receiver: an impartial person appointed by a court to take possession of and manage property for the protection of all concerned.

receiving stolen goods: receiving goods that have been taken with the intent to deprive the owner of them.

recognizance: an obligation entered into before a court to do some act, such as to appear at a later date for a hearing. Also called a contract of record.

recorder: public official in charge of deeds.

recreational use statute: statute providing that a landowner owes to persons using the property, for recreational purposes and without charge, no duty to keep the property safe for entry or use.

recross examination: an examination by the defendant's attorney that follows the redirect examination.

redemption: the buying back of one's property, which has been sold because of a default, upon paying the amount that had been originally due together with interest and costs.

redirect examination: the procedure after the cross-examination, in which the attorney for the plaintiff may ask the same witness other questions to overcome effects of the cross-examination.

referee: an impartial person selected by the parties or appointed by a court to determine facts or decide matters in dispute.

referee in bankruptcy: a referee appointed by a bankruptcy court to hear and determine various matters relating to bankruptcy proceedings.

reformation: a remedy by which a written instrument is corrected when it fails to express the actual intent of both parties because of fraud, accident, or mistake.

registered bonds: bonds held by owners whose names and addresses are registered on the books of the corporation.

registration of titles: a system generally known as the Torrens system of permanent registration of title to all land within the state.

registration requirements: provisions of the Securities Act of 1933 requiring advance disclosure to the public of a new securities issue through filing a statement with the SEC and sending a prospectus to each potential purchaser.

registration statement: a document disclosing specific financial information regarding the security, the issuer, and the underwriter.

reimbursement: the right of one paying money on behalf of another, which such other person should have paid, to recover the amount of the payment from such other person.

release of liens: an agreement or instrument by which the holder of a lien of property such as a mortgage lien, releases the property from the lien although the debt itself is not discharged.

reliance: action taken or not taken by a person in the belief that the facts as stated by another are true or that the promise of another will be performed. Detrimental reliance: a term generally used to refer to reliance of such a degree that the person relying would sustain substantial damages that could not be compensated for by the payment of money; the same concept that underlies part performance as taking an oral contract out of the statute of frauds. In some cases, loosely used when merely reliance was present. See promissory estoppel.

remainder: the land interest that follows a life estate.

remand: decision of appellate court to send a case back to trial court for additional hearings or a new trial.

remedy: the action or procedure that is followed in order to enforce a right or to obtain damages for injury to a right.

remote damages: damages that were in fact caused by the defendant's act but the possibility that such damages should occur seemed so improbable and unlikely to a reasonable person that the law does not impose liability for such damages.

rent-a-judge plan: dispute resolution through private courts with judges paid to be referees for the cases.

renunciation of duty: the repudiation of one's contractual duty in advance of the time for performance.

renunciation of right: the surrender of a right or privilege, such as the right to act as administrator or the right to receive a legacy under the will of a decedent.

reorganization of corporation: procedure devised to restore insolvent corporations to financial stability through readjustment of debt and capital structure either under the supervision of a court of equity or of bankruptcy.

repossession: any taking again of possession although generally used in connection with the act of a secured seller in taking back the property upon the default of the credit buyer.

representations: any statements, whether oral or written, made to give the insurer the information that it needs in writing the insurance, and which if false and relating to a material fact will entitle the insurer to avoid the contract.

representative capacity: action taken by one on behalf of another, as the act of a personal representative on behalf of a decedent's estate, or action taken both on one's behalf and on behalf of others, as a shareholder bringing a representative action.

repudiation: the result of a buyer or seller refusing to perform the contract as stated.

requests for production of documents: discovery tool for uncovering paper evidence in a case.

requirements contract: a contract to buy all requirements of the buyer from the seller.

res inter alios acta: the rule that transactions and declarations between strangers having no connection with the ending action are not admissible in evidence.

res ipsa loquitur: the permissible inference that the defendant was negligent in that the thing speaks for itself when the circumstances are such that ordinarily the plaintiff could not have been injured had the defendant not been at fault.

res judicata: the principle that once a final judgment is entered in an action between the parties, it is binding upon them and the matter cannot be litigated again by bringing a second action.

rescission by agreement: the setting aside of a contract by the action of the parties as though the contract had never been made.

rescission upon breach: the action of one party to a contract to set the contract aside when the other party is guilty of a breach of the contract.

reservation of rights: a stipulation by a party to a contract that even though a tendered performance (e.g., a defective product) is accepted, the right to damages for nonconformity to the contract is reserved.

residuary bequest: a bequest of everything remaining after general and specific legacies.

residuary estate: the balance of the decedent's estate available for distribution after all administrative expenses, exemptions, debts, taxes, and legacies have been paid.

Resource Conservation and Recovery Act (RCRA): federal law that regulates the disposal of potentially harmful substances and encourages resource conservation and recovery.

Resource Recovery Act: early federal solid waste disposal legislation that provided funding for states and local governments with recycling programs.

respondeat superior: the doctrine that the principal or employer is vicariously liable for the unauthorized torts committed by an agent or employee while acting within the scope of the agency or the course of the employment, respectively.

restraints on alienation: limitations on the ability of the owner to convey freely as the owner chooses. Such limitations are generally regarded as invalid.

restricted securities: securities with limits on transfer.

restrictive covenants: covenants in a deed by which the grantee agrees to refrain from doing specified acts.

restrictive indorsement: an indorsement that prohibits the further transfer, constitutes the indorsee the agent of the indorser, vests the title in the indorsee in trust for or to the use of some other person, is conditional, or is for collection or deposit.

resulting trust: a trust that is created by implication of law to carry out the presumed intent of the parties.

retaliatory statute: a statute that provides that when a corporation of another state enters the state it shall be subject to the same taxes and restrictions as would be imposed upon a corporation from the retaliating state if it had entered the other state. Also known as reciprocity statutes.

reverse mortgage: mortgage in which the owners get their equity out of their home over a period of time and return the house to the lender upon their deaths.

reversible error: an error or defect in court proceedings of so serious a nature that on appeal the appellate court will set aside the proceedings of the lower court.

reverse: see "reversible error."

reversionary interest: the interest that a lessor has in property that is subject to an outstanding lease.

revival of judgment: the taking of appropriate action to preserve a judgment, in most instances to continue the lien of the judgment that would otherwise expire after a specified number of years.

revival of will: the restoration, by the writer, of a will that had previously been revoked.

revoke: the testator's act of taking back his or her will and its provisions.

rider: a slip of paper executed by the insurer and intended to be attached to the insurance policy for the purpose of changing it in some respect.

right: legal capacity to require another person to perform or refrain from and action.

right of escheat: the right of the state to take the property that has not been distributed.

right of first refusal: the right of a party to meet the terms of a proposed contract before it is executed, such as a real estate purchase agreement.

right of privacy: the right to be free from unreasonable intrusion by others.

right of redemption: right of the mortgagor to free the property of the mortgage lien after default.

right to cure: the second chance for a seller to make a proper tender of conforming goods.

right to work laws: laws restricting unions and employees from negotiating clauses in their collective bargaining agreements that make union membership compulsory.

riparian rights: the right of a person through whose land runs a natural watercourse to use the water free from unreasonable pollution or diversion by upper riparian owners and blocking by lower riparian owners.

risk: the peril or contingency against which the insured is protected by the contract of insurance.

risk of loss: in contract performance is the cost of damage or injury to the goods contracted for.

Robinson-Patman Act: a federal statute designed to eliminate price discrimination in interstate commerce.

run with the land: the concept that certain covenants in a deed to land are deemed to 'run' or pass with the land so that whoever owns the land is bound by or entitled to the benefit of the covenants.

S

Safe Drinking Water Act: a federal law that establishes national standards for contaminants in drinking water.

sale of goods: a present transfer of title to movable property for a price.

sale on approval: term indicating that no sale takes place until the buyer approves or accepts the goods.

sale or return: a sale in which the title to the property passes to the buyer at the time of the transaction but the buyer is given the option of returning the property and restoring the title to the seller.

scienter: knowledge, referring to those wrongs or crimes that require a knowledge of wrong in order to constitute the offense.

scope of employment: the area within which the employee is authorized to act with the consequence that a tort committed while so acting imposes liability upon the employer.

seal: at common law an impression on wax or other tenacious material attached to the instrument. Under modern law, any mark not ordinarily part of the signature is a seal when so intended, including the letters 'L.S.' and the word 'seal,' or a pictorial representation of a seal, without regard to whether they had been printed or typed on the instrument before its signing.

sealed verdict: a verdict that is rendered when the jury returns to the courtroom during an adjournment of the court, the verdict then being written down and sealed and later affirmed before the court when the court is in session.

search warrant: judicial authorization for a search of property where there is the expectation of privacy.

seasonable: timely.

secondary evidence: copies of original writings or testimony as to the contents of such writings that are admissible when the original cannot be produced and the inability to do so is reasonably explained.

secondary parties: those with conditional liability for payment of a negotiable instrument that may be enforced only if the primary party fails to pay.

secondary picketing: picketing an employer with whom a union has no dispute to persuade the employer to stop doing business with a party to the dispute; generally illegal under the NLRA.

secrecy laws: confidentiality laws applied to home-country banks.

secret partners: partners who take an active part in the management of the firm but who are not known to the public as partners.

secured party: person owed the money, whether as a seller or a lender, in a secured transaction in personal property.

secured transaction: a credit sale of goods or a secured loan that provides special protection for the creditor.

securities: stock and bonds issued by a corporation. Under some investor protection laws, the term includes any interest in an enterprise that provides unearned income to its owner. Investment securities: under the UCC, Article 8, this term also includes any instrument representing an interest in property or an enterprise that is commonly dealt in or recognized as a medium of investment. Uncertificated securities: under the 1977 version of the UCC, rights to securities that are not represented by a certificate but only by a record on a computer of the issuing enterprise.

security agreement: agreement of the creditor and the debtor that the creditor will have a security interest.

security interest: property right that enables the creditor to take possession of the property if the debtor does not pay the amount owed.

self-help: creditors right to repossess the collateral without judicial proceedings.

self-proved wills: wills that eliminate some formalities of proof by being executed in the way set forth by statute.

selling on consignment: entrusting a person with possession of property for the purpose of sale.

semiconductor chip: a product placed on a piece of semiconductor material to perform electronic circuitry functions.

service mark: any word, name, symbol, or device that identifies a service.

servient tenement: land that is subject to an easement.

settlor: one who settles property in trust or creates a trust estate.

severable contract: a contract the terms of which are such that one part may be separated or severed from the other so that a default as to one part is not necessarily a default as to the entire contract.

several contracts: separate or independent contracts made by different persons undertaking to perform the same obligation.

severalty: ownership of property by one person.

severed realty: real property that has been cut off and made movable, as by cutting down a tree, and which thereby loses its character as real property and becomes personal property.

shareholder's action: an action brought by one or more shareholders on behalf of themselves and on behalf of all shareholders generally and of the corporation to enforce a cause of action of the corporation against third persons.

shareholders of record: common shareholders in whose name its stock appears on the books of a corporation.

sheriff: chief executive of a county who maintains peace and order within the territorial limits, summons witnesses, takes charge of the jury, preserves order in the court, serves writs, carries out judicial sales, and executes judgments.

sheriff's deed: the deed executed and delivered by the sheriff to the purchaser at a sale conducted by the sheriff.

Sherman Antitrust Act: a federal statute prohibiting combinations and contracts in restraint of interstate trade, now generally inapplicable to labor union activity.

shopkeeper's privilege: right of a store owner to detain a suspected shoplifter based on reasonable cause and for a reasonable time without resulting liability for false imprisonment.

shop right: the right of an employer to use in business without charge an invention discovered by an employee during working hours and with the employer's material and equipment.

short-swing profit: a profit realized by a corporate insider from selling securities less than six months after purchase.

sight draft: a draft or bill of exchange payable on sight or when presented for payment.

silent partners: partners who, although they may be known to the public as partners, take no active part in the business.

simplification regulations: no license is required unless regulations affirmatively require a license.

sinking fund: fixed amount of money set aside each year by the borrowing corporation toward the ultimate payment of bonds.

sit-down strike: a strike in which the employees remain in the plant and refuse to allow the employer to operate it.

situational ethics: a flexible standard of ethics that permits an examination of circumstances and motivation before attaching the label of right or wrong to conduct.

slander: defamation of character by spoken words or gestures.

slander of title: the malicious making of false statements as to a seller's title.

slowdown: a slowing down of production by employees without actually stopping work.

social responsibility: extension of voluntary conduct beyond legal mandates to business.

social security acts: statutes providing for assistance for the aged, blind, unemployed, and similar classes of persons in need.

société anonyme: European form of business organization.

sogo shosha: provider of comprehensive export services in Japan.

sole proprietorship: a form of business ownership in which one individual owns the business; also called individual proprietorship.

soliciting agent: salesperson.

sovereign compliance doctrine: the doctrine that allows a defendant to raise as an affirmative defense to an antitrust action the fact that the defendant's actions were compelled by a foreign state.

special agent: an agent authorized to transact a specific transaction or to do a specific act.

special damages: damages that do not necessarily result from the injury to the plaintiff but at the same time are not so remote that the defendant should not be held liable therefor provided that the claim for special damages is properly made in the action.

special drawing rights: allows a country to borrow money from other IMF members.

special indorsement: an indorsement that specifies the person to whom the instrument is indorsed.

special jurisdiction: a court with power to hear and determine cases within certain restricted categories.

specific legacies: identified property bequeathed by a testator.

specific lien: the right of a creditor to hold particular property or assert a lien on particular property of the debtor because of the creditor's having done work on or having some other association with the property, as distinguished from having a lien generally against the assets of the debtor merely because the debtor is indebted to the lien holder.

specific performance: an action brought to compel the adverse party to perform a contract on the theory that merely suing for damages for its breach will not be an adequate remedy.

spendthrift trust: a trust that, to varying degrees, provides that creditors of the beneficiary shall not be able to reach the principal or income held by the trustee and that the beneficiary shall not be able to assign any interest in the trust.

spot zoning: allowance of an individual variation in zoning.

stakeholders: owners of a business who have contributed capital.

stale check: a check whose date is longer than six months ago.

standby letter: letter of credit for a contractor ensuring he will complete the project as contracted.

stare decisis: the principle that the decision of a court should serve as a guide or precedent and control the decision of a similar case in the future.

status quo ante: the original positions of the parties.

Statute of Frauds: a statute that, in order to prevent fraud through the use of perjured testimony, requires that certain kinds of transactions be evidenced in writing in order to be binding or enforceable.

statute of limitations: a statute that restricts the period of time within which an action may be brought.

statutory law: legislative acts declaring, commanding, or prohibiting something.

stay of foreclosure: delay of foreclosure obtained by the mortgagor to prevent undue hardship.

stirpes: family lines; distribution per stirpes refers to the manner descendants take property by right of representation.

stirpital distribution: *see* "distribution per stirpes."

stock subscription: a contract or agreement to buy a specific number and kind of shares when they are issued by the corporation.

stop delivery: the right of an unpaid seller under certain conditions to prevent a carrier or a bailee from delivering goods to the buyer.

stop payment: an order by a depositor to the bank to refuse to make payment of a check when presented for payment.

straight (or nonnegotiable) bill of lading: a document of title that consigns transported goods to a named person.

strict tort liability: a product liability theory that imposes liability upon the manufacturer, seller, or distributor of goods for harm caused by defective goods.

subjective intent: a secret intent of a person.

sublease: a transfer of the premises by the lessee to a third person, the sublessee or subtenant, for a period of less than the term of the original lease.

subpoena: a court order directing a person to appear as a witness. In some states it is also the original process that is to be served on the defendant in order to give the court jurisdiction over the defendant.

subpoena duces tecum: a subpoena that requires relevant papers be brought to court.

subrogation: the right of a party secondarily liable to stand in the place of the creditor after making payment to the creditor and to enforce the creditor's right against the party primarily liable in order to obtain indemnity from such primary party.

subsidiary corporation: a corporation that is controlled by another corporation through the ownership by the latter of a controlling amount of the voting stock of the former.

subsidiary term: a provision of a contract that is not fundamental or does not go to the root of the contract.

substantial impairment: material defect in a good.

substantial performance: the equitable doctrine that a contractor substantially performing a contract in good faith is entitled to recover the contract price less damages for noncompletion or defective work.

substantive law: the law that defines rights and liabilities.

substitution: discharge of a contract by substituting another in its place.

subtenant: one who rents the leased premises from the original tenant for a period of time less than the balance of the lease to the original tenant.

sui generis: in a class by itself, or its own kind.

sui juris: legally competent, possessing capacity.

sum certain: amount due under an instrument that can be computed from its face with only reference to interest rates.

summary judgment: a judgment entered by the court when no substantial dispute of fact is present, the court acting on the basis of affidavits or depositions that show that the claim or defense of a party is a sham.

summary jury trial: a mock or dry run trial for parties to get a feel for how their cases will play to a jury.

summation: the address that follows all the evidence presented in court and sums up a case with a recommendation that a particular verdict be returned by the jury.

summons: a writ by which an action was commenced under the common law.

Superfund Amendment and Reauthorization Act: federal law that authorizes the EPA to collect cleanup costs from those responsible for the ownership, leasing, dumping, or security of hazardous waste sites.

Superfund sites: areas designated by the EPA for cleanup of hazardous waste.

supersedeas: a stay of proceedings pending the taking of an appeal or an order entered for the purpose of effecting such a stay.

supervening impracticability: a doctrine that states that a contract can be discharged when subsequent developments prove it to be different than was assumed by the parties.

surety: the obligor of a suretyship; primarily liable for the debt or obligation of the principal debtor.

suretyship: an undertaking to pay the debt or be liable for the default of another.

surrender: the yielding up of the tenant's leasehold estate to the lessor in consequence of which the lease terminates.

survival acts: statutes that provide that causes of action shall not terminate on death but shall survive and may be enforced by or against a decedent's estate.

survivorship: the right by which a surviving joint tenant or tenant by the entireties acquires the interest of the predeceasing tenant automatically upon the death of such tenant.

swindle: the act of a person who, intending to cheat and defraud, obtains money or property by trick, deception, or fraud.

symbolic delivery: the delivery of goods by delivery of the means of control, such as a key or a relevant document of title, such as a negotiable bill of lading.

syndicate: an association of individuals formed to conduct a particular business transaction, generally of a financial nature.

T

tacking: adding together successive periods of adverse possession of persons in privity with each other in order to constitute a sufficient period of continuous adverse possession to vest title thereby.

takeover laws: laws that guard against unfairness in corporate takeover situations.

Taft-Hartley Act: popular name for the Labor Management Relations Act of 1947.

tariff: domestically a government-approved schedule of charges that may be made by a regulated business, such as a common carrier or warehouser. Internationally a tax imposed by a country on goods crossing its borders, without regard to whether the purpose is to raise revenue or to discourage the traffic in the taxed goods.

teller's check: a draft drawn by a bank on another bank in which it has an account.

temporary insider: someone retained by a corporation for professional services on an as-needed basis, such as an attorney, accountant, or investment banker.

temporary nuisance: interference caused by a construction or a method of operation that can be remedied at a reasonable expense.

temporary perfection: state of perfection given for a limited period of time to creditors.

tenancy at sufferance: a lease arrangement in which the tenant occupies the property at the discretion of the landlord.

tenancy at will: the holding of land for an indefinite period that may be terminated at any time by the landlord or by the landlord and tenant acting together.

tenancy by entirety: the transfer of property to both husband and wife.

tenancy by sufferance: a tenant's holding over of the rented land after a lease has expired without the permission of the landlord and prior to the time that the landlord has elected to treat such possessor as a trespasser or a tenant.

tenancy for years: a tenancy for a fixed period of time, even though the time is less than a year.

tenancy from year to year: a tenancy that continues indefinitely from year to year until terminated.

tenancy in common: the relationship that exists when two or more persons own undivided interests in property.

tenancy in partnership: the ownership relationship that exists between partners under the Uniform Partnership Act.

tender: an offer of money as part of a contract.

tender of goods: to present goods for acceptance.

tender of payment: an unconditional offer to pay the exact amount of money due at the time and place specified by the contract.

tender of performance: an unconditional offer to perform at the time and in the manner specified by the contract.

tentative trust: a trust that arises when money is deposited in a bank account in the name of the depositor "in trust for" a named person.

terminable fee: an estate that terminates upon the happening of a contingency without any entry by the grantor or heirs, as a conveyance for 'so long as' the land is used for a specified purpose.

termination statement: a document, which may be requested by a paid-up debtor, stating that a security interest is no longer claimed under the specified financing statement.

term insurance: a policy written for a specified number of years that terminates at the end of that period.

testamentary: designed to take effect at death, as by disposing of property or appointing a personal representative.

testamentary capacity: sufficient mental capacity to understand that a writing being executed is a will and what that entails.

testamentary intent: proper state of mind for making a valid will.

testamentary trust: a trust that becomes effective only when the settlor's will takes effect after death.

testate: the condition of leaving a will upon death.

testate succession: the distribution of an estate in accordance with the will of the decedent.

testator, testatrix: a man, woman who makes a will.

testimonium clause: a concluding paragraph in a deed, contract, or other instrument, reciting that the instrument has been executed on a specified date by the parties.

testimony: the answers of witnesses under oath to questions given at the time of the trial in the presence of the trier of fact.

theory of the case: the rule that, when a case is tried on the basis of one theory, the appellant in taking an appeal cannot argue a different theory to the appellate court.

third party beneficiary: a third person whom the parties to a contract intend to benefit by the making of the contract and to confer upon such person the right to sue for breach of contract.

tie-in sale: the requirement imposed by the seller that the buyer of particular goods or equipment also purchase certain other goods from the seller in order to obtain the original property desired.

time draft: a bill of exchange payable at a stated time after sight or at a definite time.

time-price differential: the difference between the price a seller charges for cash sales and the price the same seller charges for credit or installment sales.

tippee: an individual who receives information about a corporation from an insider or temporary insider.

title insurance: a form of insurance by which the insurer insures the buyer of real property against the risk of loss should the title acquired from the seller be defective in any way.

toll the statute: stop the running of the period of the Statute of Limitations by the doing of some act by the debtor.

Torrens system: *See* "registration of titles."

tort: a civil wrong that interferes with one's property or person.

tortious interference: *see* "contract interference."

Toxic Substances Control Act (TOSCA): first federal law to control the manufacture, use, and disposal of toxic substances.

trade acceptance: a draft or bill of exchange drawn by the seller of goods on the purchase at the time of sale and accepted by the purchaser.

trade dress: a product's total image including its overall packaging look.

trade fixtures: articles of personal property that have been attached to the freehold by a tenant and that are used for or are necessary to the carrying on of the tenant's trade.

trade libel: written defamation about a product or service.

trademark: a name, device, or symbol used by a manufacturer or seller to distinguish goods from those of other persons.

trade name: a name under which a business is carried on and, if fictitious, it must be registered.

trade-secrets: secrets of any character peculiar and important to the business of the employer that have been communicated to the employee in the course of confidential employment.

trading partnership: partnership organized for the purpose of buying and selling, such as a firm engaged in the retail grocery business.

transferee: buyer or vendee.

transferor: seller or vendor.

traveler's check: a check that is payable on demand provided it is countersigned by the person whose specimen signature appears on the check.

treason: an attempt to overthrow or betray the government to which one owes allegiance.

treasury stock: corporate stock that the corporation has reacquired.

treble damages: three times the damages actually sustained.

trespass to the person: any contact with a victim's person for which consent has not been given.

trespass to personal property: an illegal invasion of property rights with respect to property other than land.

trial de novo: a trial required to preserve the constitutional right to a jury trial by allowing an appeal to proceed as though there never had been any prior hearing or decision.

tripartite: three-part division (of government).

trier of fact: in most cases a jury, although it may be the judge alone in certain classes of cases (as in equity) or in any case when jury trial is waived, or when an administrative agency or commission is involved.

trust: a transfer of property by one person to another with the understanding or declaration that such property be held for the benefit of another; the holding of property by the owner in trust for another, upon a declaration of trust, without a transfer to another person. (Parties—settlor, trustee, beneficiary)

trust agreement: *see* "deed of trust."

trust corpus: the fund or property that is transferred to the trustee or held by the settlor as the body or subject matter of the trust.

trust deed: a form of deed that transfers the trust property to the trustee for the purposes therein stated, particularly used when the trustee is to hold the title to the mortgagor's land in trust for the benefit of the mortgage bondholders.

trustee in bankruptcy: an impartial person elected to administer the debtor's estate.

trustor: donor or settlor who is the owner of property and creates a trust in the property.

U

uberrima fides: utmost good faith, a duty to exercise the utmost good faith that arises in certain relationships, such as that between an insurer and the applicant for insurance.

ultra vires: an act or contract that the corporation does not have authority to do or make.

unauthorized indorsement: instrument indorsed by an agent for a principal without authorization or authority.

unconscionable: unreasonable, not guided or restrained by conscience and often referring to a contract grossly unfair to one party because of the superior bargaining powers of the other party.

underwriter: an insurer.

undisclosed principal: a principal on whose behalf an agent acts without disclosing to the third person the fact of agency or the identity of the principal.

undue influence: the influence that is asserted upon another person by one who dominates that person.

unfair competition: the wrong of employing competitive methods that have been declared unfair by statute or an administrative agency.

unfair labor practice acts: statutes that prohibit certain labor practices and declare them to be unfair.

Uniform Probate Code (UPC): a uniform statute on wills and administration of estates.

unilateral contract: a contract under which only one party is obligated to perform.

unincorporated association: a combination of two or more persons for the furtherance of a common non-profit purpose.

uninsured motorist:

union contract: a contract between a labor union and an employer or group of employers prescribing the general terms of employment of workers by the latter.

union shop: under present unfair labor practice statutes, a place of employment where nonunion workers may be employed for a trial period of not more than 30 days after which the nonunion workers must join the union or be discharged.

universal agent: an agent authorized by the principal to do all acts that can lawfully be delegated to a representative.

universal defenses: defenses that may be raised against any plaintiff, regardless of status, claiming under a negotiable instrument.

usage of trade: language and customs of an industry.

usury: the lending of money at greater than the maximum rate of interest allowed by law.

uttering: the crime of issuing or delivering a forged instrument.

V

vacating of judgment: the setting aside of a judgment.

valid: legal.

valid contract: an agreement that is binding an enforceable.

value: consideration or antecedent debt or security given in exchange for the transfer of a negotiable instrument.

variance: permission of a landowner to use the land in a specified manner that is inconsistent with the zoning ordinance.

verdict: the decision of the trial or petty jury.

vertical price fixing: an agreement by a retailer with a producer, for example, not to resell below a stated price, which is a violation of antitrust law.

vicarious liability: imposing liability for the fault of another.

void: of no legal effect and not binding on anyone.

void agreement: an agreement that cannot be enforced is void.

voidable: a transaction that may be set aside by one party thereto because of fraud or similar reason but which is binding on the other party until the injured party elects to avoid.

voidable contract: an agreement that is otherwise binding and enforceable but may be rejected at the option of one of the parties as the result of specific circumstances.

voidable preference: a preference given by the debtor in bankruptcy to a creditor, but which may be set aside by the trustee in bankruptcy.

voidable title: title of goods that carries with it the contingency of an underlying problem.

voir dire examination: the preliminary examination of a juror or a witness to ascertain fitness to act as such.

volenti non fit injuria: the maxim that the defendant's act cannot constitute a tort if the plaintiff has consented thereto.

voluntary bankruptcy: a proceeding in which the debtor files the petition for relief.

voluntary case: a case in which a debtor files a petition with bankruptcy court.

voluntary nonsuit: a means of a plaintiff's stopping a trial at any time by moving for a voluntary nonsuit.

voting by proxy: authorizing someone else to vote the shares owned by the shareholder.

voting trust: the transfer by two or more persons of their shares of stock of a corporation to a trustee who is to vote the shares and act for such shareholders.

W

waiver: the release or relinquishment of a known right or objection.

warehouse receipt: a receipt issued by the warehouser for stored goods. Regulated by the UCC, which clothes the receipt with some degree of negotiability.

warehouser: a person engaged in the business of storing the goods of others for compensation.

warranties: a promise either express or implied about the nature, quality, or performance of the goods.

warranties of indorser of commercial paper: the implied covenants made by an indorser of a commercial paper distinct from any undertaking to pay upon the default of the primary party.

warranties of insured: statements or promises made by the applicant for insurance that, if false, will entitle the insurer to avoid the contract of insurance in many jurisdictions.

warranties of seller of goods: warranties consisting of express warranties that relate to matters forming part of the basis of the bargain; warranties as to title and right to sell; and the implied warranties that the law adds to a sale depending upon the nature of the transaction.

warranty against encumbrances: warranty that there are no liens or other encumbrances to goods except those noted by seller.

warranty deed: a deed by which the grantor conveys a specific estate or interest to the grantee and makes one or more of the covenants of title.

warranty of authority: an implied warranty of an agent of the authority exercised by the agent.

warranty of habitability: an implied warranty that the leased property is fit for dwelling by tenants.

warranty of principal: an implied warranty of an agent that the agent is acting for an existing principal who has capacity to contract.

warranty of title: implied warranty that title to the goods is good and transfer is proper.

wasting assets corporation: corporation designed to exhaust or use up the assets of the corporation, such as by extracting oil, coal, iron, and other ores.

watered stock: stock issued by a corporation as fully paid when in fact it is not.

way of necessity: a grantee's right to use land retained by the grantor for going to and from the conveyed land.

white collar crimes: crimes that do not use nor threaten to use force or violence or do not cause injury to persons or property.

whole life insurance: ordinary life insurance providing lifetime insurance protection.

will: an instrument executed with the formality required by law, by which a person makes a disposition of property to take effect upon death or appoints a personal representative.

willful: intentional, as distinguished from accidental or involuntary. In penal statutes, with evil intent or legal malice, or without reasonable ground for believing one's act to be lawful.

Wool Products Labeling Act: a federal statute prohibiting the misbranding of woolen fabrics.

workers' compensation: a system providing for payments to workers because they have been injured from a risk arising out of the course of their employment while they were employed at their employment or who have contracted an occupational disease in that manner, payment being made without consideration of the negligence or lack of negligence of any party.

World Trade Organization (WTO): agency responsible for administering the objectives of the General Agreement on Tariffs and Trade (GATT).

writ of certiorari: ordered by the U.S. Supreme Court granting a right of review by the court of a lower court decision.

wrongfully dishonored: an error by a bank in refusing to pay a check.

Y

year and a day: the common-law requirement that death result within a year and a day in order to impose criminal liability for homicide.

Z

zoning: restrictions imposed by government on the use of designated land to ensure an orderly physical development of the regulated area.

C A S E   I N D E X

Opinion cases are in boldface type; cited cases are in Roman type.

SUBJECT INDEX